Masters of the Post

DUNCAN CAMPBELL-SMITH

Masters of the Post

The Authorized History of the Royal Mail

ALLEN LANE
an imprint of
PENGUIN BOOKS

To Anne-Catherine

ALLEN LANE

Published by the Penguin Group
Penguin Books Ltd, 80 Strand, London WC2R ORL, England
Penguin Group (USA) Inc., 375 Hudson Street, New York, New York 10014, USA
Penguin Group (Canada), 90 Eglinton Avenue East, Suite 700, Toronto, Ontario, Canada M4P 2Y3
(a division of Pearson Penguin Canada Inc.)
Penguin Ireland, 25 St Stephen's Green, Dublin 2, Ireland (a division of Penguin Books Ltd)
Penguin Group (Australia), 250 Camberwell Road, Camberwell, Victoria 3124, Australia
(a division of Pearson Australia Group Pty Ltd)
Penguin Books India Pvt Ltd, 11 Community Centre,
Panchsheel Park, New Delhi – 110 017, India
Penguin Group (NZ), 67 Apollo Drive, Rosedale, Auckland 0632, New Zealand
(a division of Pearson New Zealand Ltd)
Penguin Books (South Africa) (Pty) Ltd, 24 Sturdee Avenue,
Rosebank, Johannesburg 2196, South Africa

Penguin Books Ltd, Registered Offices: 80 Strand, London WC2R ORL, England

www.penguin.com

First published 2011
1

Copyright © Royal Mail Group Ltd, 2011

The moral right of the author has been asserted

Set in Sabon LT Std 10.2/13.87pt
Typeset by Jouve (UK), Milton Keynes
Printed in Great Britain by Clays Ltd, St Ives plc

ISBN: 978–1–846–14324–3

www.greenpenguin.co.uk

Penguin Books is committed to a sustainable
future for our business, our readers and our
planet. This book is made from paper certified
by the Forest Stewardship Council.

MIX
Paper from
responsible sources
FSC
www.fsc.org   FSC™ C018179

Contents

PART TWO
War and Peace

PART THREE
No Ordinary Business

Illustrations

The illustrations on the front and back endpapers, entitled *A London Loading Platform*, and *Euston Station, Loading the TPO*, are taken from a set of four watercolours by the artist Grace Golden, commissioned by the Post Office in 1948 and displayed as reproductions inside many staff buildings through the post-war era.

Maps

Plates

Acknowledgements

This book was instigated by the late Lord Dearing, Chairman of the Post Office from 1981 to 1987 and chief architect of what became the Royal Mail Group. He remained a passionate champion of the postal service until the very end of his life – he died early in 2009 – and he lobbied former colleagues and their successors for years to have its past captured in a modern and wide-ranging history. I was appointed as the author in June 2008 and am indebted to the Board of the Royal Mail Group, both for entrusting me with the commission and for allowing me to write with complete editorial freedom just as Lord Dearing had always intended. I was fortunate that the project was overseen from the start by Jonathan Evans, initially as the Royal Mail Group's Company Secretary and subsequently, in his retirement, as a Trustee of the British Postal Museum & Archive (BPMA). He organized the commissioning process, in close consultation with Lord Dearing, and carried things forward after the latter's death. I am extremely grateful to him for all his constant support and encouragement, which ran from providing a first response to the initial draft of every chapter to assisting with appendices and the work of late revisions and corrections. In the latter stages of the book's preparation, his role was complemented from within the Royal Mail by his successor, Jon Millidge. I am also indebted to Adam Crozier, who as Group Chief Executive until 2010 gave the project his enthusiastic backing, and to the current Chairman, Donald Brydon, who was quick to endorse it after his arrival in 2009. The latter took a lively interest in the progress of the book, while never wavering in his determination that it should indeed be an independent history.

I would like to express here my sincere thanks to all those who agreed to be interviewed for the book: Michael Allen, Malcolm Argent, Neville Bain, Millie Bannerji, Sir William Barlow, Alex Bell, Bill Bishop, Howard Brabrook, Alan Brown, Colin Browne, Donald Brydon, Ian Cameron, Norman Candy, Danny Carty, Christopher Chataway, Bill Cockburn, Jerry Cope, Adam Crozier, Roger Darlington, the late Lord Dearing, Richard Dykes, Jonathan Evans, Mary Fagan, Lord Freud, Mark Goodridge, Gerry Grimstone, Billy Hayes, Bill Hedley, Lord Heseltine, Daniel

Hodson, Richard Hooper, Alan Huggins, Kate Jenkins, Alan Johnson, Allan Leighton, John Mackay, Michael Mire, Roger Morrison, Sir Bryan Nicholson, Tom Norgate, the late Denis Roberts, John Roberts, David Sibbick, Morag Macdonald Simpson, Brian Thomson, Henry Tilling, Paul Tolhurst, Alan Tuffin, Sam Wainwright, Nigel Walmsley, Derek Walsh, Dave Ward, Sue Whalley, John Woodthorpe and Ken Young. Observations and direct quotations from the interviews, sourced in the notes and generally introduced in the text with a simple 'He recalled . . .', have all been checked with the interviewees to confirm their accuracy. Transcriptions of the interviews were expertly provided by Nicki Brown and her team, to whom I am once again indebted. Several individuals kindly read substantial sections of the book at a draft stage and I am especially grateful to Sir William Barlow, Harry Bush, Danny Carty, Gerry Grimstone, John Mackay, Henry Tilling and Ken Young for their generous help in this way. The full text was also read by some non-postmen whom I should like to thank individually. David Thomas made many helpful suggestions on behalf of the (eagle-eyed) general reader; and Philip Waller suggested many elegant historical asides, just as he used to do at Merton College, Oxford forty years ago when he was my tutor and I was a postmaster (the college's term for a scholar, never satisfactorily explained but sadly nothing to do with the Royal Mail). I am also very grateful to Alan Huggins, Curator of Philatelic Collections at the Royal Philatelic Society London, who enabled me to pull together the stamps shown on the back cover in remarkably short order and advised on the relevant passages of the text. And I must thank Professor Martin Daunton, Master of Trinity Hall, Cambridge, and the author of an earlier study of the Royal Mail since 1840, who gave the book a close reading at a late stage and generously suggested several valuable additions and amendments. The errors that remain are of course entirely mine.

Among the always helpful and considerate guardians of the postal archive at the BPMA, I would like to thank the past and present staff of the reading room who made it such a congenial place to work: Barry Attoe, Jamie Ellul, Claire George, Emily Gresham, Anne-Grethe Jensen, Penny McMahon, Zoe van Well and Claire Woodforde. I owe special thanks to the archivists Louise Todd and Helen Dafter, who together with Jonathan Evans and Claire George painstakingly prepared the data and charts that are included in the appendices. Gavin McGuffie helped with my catalogue inquiries, Barry Attoe kept track of my requests for text illustrations and plates, and Martin Devereux photographed selected contents from the archive for me. Other photographs for the plates I was able to borrow from the Communication Workers Union (CWU), for which I must thank Norman Candy. My thanks, too, to Sian Wynn-Jones for her ready assistance at the BT Archives, and to the friendly staff of the Modern Records Centre at Warwick University for all their help with my work on the archives of the UPW (and its successors). Among fellow inmates of the BPMA Reading Room, Peter Sutton was generous with his knowledge of the modern records while researching for his doctoral thesis on postal mechanization, and Tom Norgate patiently illuminated several aspects of that thorny subject for me. My own research was also made a great deal easier by my having ready access to any number of on-line resources – and for this I must thank Professor Miles Taylor, Director of the Institute of Historical Research at London University, whose award of a Senior Research Fellowship early in 2009 lifted many tiresome subscription barriers. It is also a pleasure to acknowledge here the kindness of Professor Richard Roberts, Director of the Centre for Contemporary British History at King's College London, who was responsible for introducing me to the Royal Mail Group at the outset.

Appendix B sets out a full list of all the political and executive heads of the postal service since *c.* 1512 and of its largest trade union, now the CWU, citing individuals with a full note where appropriate of their titles and honours. These are only sparsely (and a little inconsistently) used in the main text. Many senior figures in the Post Office collected a knighthood before the end of their careers. Keeping track of all the awards would have been tiresome for the reader, but I hope their omission – and the frequent omission of other people's titles, too – will cause no offence.

Turning my completed manuscript into a long book with extensive illustrations and some substantial appendices was a process that drew heavily on many people's time and diligence. In addition to those whom I have already thanked, I would like to acknowledge gratefully the assistance I received from many members of the Royal Mail Group's own staff, including in particular Sue Laban, Shan Lawrence, Peter Restarick, Martin Rush and David Simpson. And it is a pleasure to thank everyone at Penguin who saw the book through to publication. My thanks especially to Shan Vahidy for all her calm and patience, not least in fielding my regular calls for help over several months, but also to Jenny Fry and Natalie Ramm, and to Richard Duguid and his production team along with my copy editor, Mark Handsley. Above all, I owe a huge debt to my editor, Stuart Proffitt, without whose red pen and wise counsel this would be a poorer book indeed. Lucky the author who can turn to such a sympathetic but demanding reader while there yet remains time to pause and think again.

One final acknowledgement is no less sincere for striking a familiar note. This book could never have been written at all without the understanding and forbearance of my wife Anne-Catherine, and it is dedicated to her with my heartfelt thanks for all her constant support.

Foreword

by Donald Brydon CBE, Chairman of the Royal Mail Group

The environment for postal services has been changing so rapidly and so profoundly in recent years that one might be forgiven for supposing that the past has less and less to tell us about the present. Not so. This book makes startlingly clear just how relevant the history of this huge and complex organization is to the issues of today. Royal Mail has played an important role in the economic development of our country, making social mobility practicable, and at the same time, through local post offices, helping maintain social cohesion. Uniquely, Royal Mail stands as a business enterprise with a major social purpose.

Before he began work on this history, the Board of the Royal Mail granted Duncan Campbell-Smith unrestricted access to its archives; it has not, however, sought to influence what he has written, or the opinions he has expressed, in any way. The book is therefore the work of an independent historian, who has written a history which thousands of past and present members of Royal Mail will find fascinating, and which will be of widespread interest to the general reader. He has a remarkable story to tell as he links Royal Mail's evolution to the wider historical context, not least during the two great wars of the twentieth century. Even in this decade Royal Mail has had employees working in Afghanistan, as twenty-first-century conflicts also require effective personal communications.

In recent years Royal Mail has come under pressure from two directions: public policy designed to stimulate competition, and the revolution of the electronic age. The promotion of competition in a declining market within the context of a fixed delivery obligation has set major challenges for Royal Mail. Its future will be determined in large part by how policy-makers and Royal Mail itself respond to them.

The book is also a story of what might have been, and a catalogue of nettles left ungrasped. A recurrent theme is how elusive it has been for generations of managers, politicians and union leaders to find common ground in shaping the future of the enterprise. I hope that, in providing such clarity about the evolution of Royal Mail, this book will better inform all those who have responsibility for its future.

8 February 2011

Introduction

While the bombs were still falling on wartime London in 1944, officials at the Post Office's headquarters near St Paul's Cathedral ordered an overhaul of their Records Department. Sorting through boxes of nineteenth-century correspondence, they came across an exchange of letters involving the Controller of the Money Order Department in 1868, a Mr Jackson, who had written to his superiors explaining that he had a problem with mice nibbling at paid money orders kept in the office for clerical processing. Mousetraps, alas, had proved no solution and Jackson requested permission to buy cats for his department. The official response came back:

> Mr Jackson. Three cats may be allowed on probation. They must undergo a test examination and should, I think, be females. It is important that the cats be not overfed and I cannot allow more than a shilling a week for their support. They must depend on mice for the remainder of their emolument and if the mice be not reduced in number in six months a further portion of the allowance must be stopped. Can any statistics as to mice be furnished from time to time?[1]

This was not written with tongue in cheek. A shilling a week for a cat – or sixpence a week in rural offices – remained the official emolument from 1868; it still applied in 1944. Precedents were always treated in the Post Office as matters of enormous consequence, whatever the context. Once enshrined in the rule book, they could endure for generations. Almost certainly, they would give rise to a stream of numbers like those statistics as to mice. These would be used as a basis of regular reviews, to be drawn upon from time to time for an official report. Today, reviews and reports in their hundreds are neatly filed at the British Postal Museum & Archive (BPMA). In various guises, they account for a good proportion of the nation's postal records, a continuous paper trail that few other individual British archives, public or private, can rival. They fill more than two miles of shelving and stretch back to the days of Charles II and his brother James, Duke of York (and Postmaster General) – during whose reigns the 'Clerks of the Roads' organizing the nightly mails from London were already busily accumulating 'the Custom of the Office', a set of unwritten but comprehensive rules never to be challenged lightly. (The first book of accounts appears to date from 1667 – not coincidentally the year after the Great Fire of London, which incinerated the Restoration Post Office's first headquarters in Threadneedle Street.[2])

From the start, the demands of the postal service necessarily entailed a profound attachment to the importance of routine: this was a working environment in which stability and continuity were all. The conservatism of the Post Office's culture was almost proverbial by the early nineteenth century. It was even more deeply embedded, after the 1840s, by the way in which the constant expansion of a huge, quasi-industrial workforce was handled. In the Victorian Age, discipline was imposed via what an early trade unionist described as 'a snob's inferno' of job grades and pay scales.[3] Their complexity rewarded long and patient service. Since any departure from the rule book could risk having that service cut short, this was a culture that left no room for anyone to wing it on a busy day. Nor was it thought at first to be compatible with any form of trade unionism. Like the early railway companies, the Post Office was initially deeply hostile to any union activity at all. It could never be immune, though, to the wider social and political changes of the day. Trade unions were evolving quickly by 1900, and huge adjustments had to follow. In the first half of the twentieth century, ex-servicemen returning from two world wars filled the postmen's ranks and imbued them with the British Army's traditional respect for a strict demarcation of responsibilities. Ironically, this reinforced the disciplines of the Post Office in many ways, but now they were increasingly to be monitored by the unionized workforce itself, especially after 1945. Most postal workers had no choice but to top up low basic weekly wages with overtime earnings. These were effectively allocated in the second half of the century by local union officials, in line with their own latter-day version of the Custom of the Office. Enforced by weight of precedent rather than legal contract, the overtime regime imposed another hefty bias against experiments of any kind. Modern technology and computers enabled the network (eventually) to cope with an astonishing rate of growth in mail traffic – finally peaking, it would seem, in recent years – but they made far less impact on the culture of the Post Office than had been expected by most outsiders, or at least by those oblivious to its history.

Terms and titles need some explaining. The inaugural 'Master of the Posts', Brian Tuke, took up his duties almost exactly five centuries ago, in the opening years of the reign of Henry VIII. He spent over three decades turning the idea of courier relays at the monarchy's disposal into a system based on local 'posts'.* The first of those five centuries was well past before all mails came to be properly Royal by dint of a monopoly granted by Charles I in 1635. Even then, no one spoke of a Royal Mail, referring rather to the Post or the activities of the Letter Office, or the General Post Office as Cromwell's republicans named it. Only when the words Royal Mail became a familiar sight on the enamelled paintwork of high-speed coaches after 1784 did this become a common term for the Post Office. Thereafter, the two names were often treated as interchangeable – except in Whitehall, where officials invariably stuck to 'Post Office' – and the issue still causes confusion more than two centuries later. In 2001 an attempt was made to reserve 'Post Office', logically enough, for the exclusive use of the nation's post offices. Royal Mail was to be strictly the name of the service delivering letters and parcels. But logic also required a new name for the parent company embracing both entities – and the innocent if ill-advised choice of Consignia brought down such obloquy on the heads of those responsible for it that the old confusion was quickly reinstated. This book is mostly about the mail services – though telephones before the establishment of British Telecom play a part in the story, as do some other non-mail activities like the Post Office Savings Bank – so what follows is a history of the Royal Mail or of the Post Office (and occasionally even the GPO), according to whichever label seems most appropriate in the context. It begins in the period before either name was thought of, and it concludes today just as the two of them may be on the brink of parting company, or at least of acquiring different owners. It is the story of an institution long cherished as part of that hallowed cloth, the national fabric. Its physical presence on our streets, roads and country lanes has been emblematic of British society in all kinds of ways for generations.

An engrained regard for tradition and established practice is one consistent feature of this story, but the counterpoint has been a long and remarkable chronicle of growth and of periodic upheavals that have each been transforming in their day. How to accomplish essential

---

* Courier systems based on relays were a feature of the ancient world. The Roman version was the *cursus publicus*, each station of which was a *positus* – from which 'post' was derived. The word 'mail' came from the French *malle*, meaning a travelling bag. It acquired a postal connotation in fifteenth-century France but seems not to have appeared in common English usage until the middle of the seventeenth century.

changes in the face of an exceedingly low tolerance for risk? That has
been the challenge confronting a good number of the Royal Mail's masters. Those masters have included both those with formal authority over
the service and those with a powerful influence over it, from within or
without. Many have been autocratic civil servants, at the head of a
department of state set apart from Whitehall and functioning as a kind
of civilian shadow of the armed forces. Some have been dynamic businessmen, lured into the service from the commercial world to flex their
management skills in an unfamiliar setting. Others, of great importance
since the end of the nineteenth century, have been leaders of the postal
trade unions, especially the Union of Post Office Workers (evolving
from UPW in 1920 to the Union of Communications Workers in 1981
and the Communications Workers Union in 1995). In Westminster and
Whitehall, there have been ambitious politicians serving as Postmaster
General, or since 1969 as the head of a 'sponsoring' government department with its own officials – shadowed at all times by those grey
eminences Their Lordships of the Treasury, and their modern successors
in Whitehall with less grand titles but no less power. Finally, there have
been the consumer watchdogs and statutory regulators whose impact
since the turn of the millennium is a conspicuous feature of this history's
closing pages.

   For all who ran it, from its first century to its fifth, the glory of the
Post Office lay in the fact that its established routines and close-knit
collegial relationships at every level could be harnessed to pull off astonishing feats of organization. Stable yards and innkeepers all over the
country were somehow coordinated to serve the needs of the Post Roads
network from the days of the travelling post-boy to the mail coach era.
Officials in the magnificent postal headquarters at St Martin's-le-Grand
(opened in 1829) oversaw an exponential growth of the mails in the
wake of tariff reform and the advent of steam trains. Between 1850 and
1914, the service expanded its paid workforce from about 25,000 to
230,000, pioneered the employment of women and reshaped itself
around the railways to lift the annual volume of the nation's mail traffic
from about 500 million items to not far short of 6 billion. In the twentieth century, perhaps its most celebrated triumphs were linked to the
world wars, building the equivalent of whole new postal surburbia in
northern France for the first and providing a giant new communications
infrastructure across southern England for the second. It also managed
its way through thickets of corporate restructuring in the 1930s and
again in the 1980s that would have tested the mettle of most commercial

enterprises. 'Will it work?' asked the 1980s Chairman, Ron Dearing, of a colleague as they teed up a radical reorganization of the Post Office in 1985. 'Chairman,' came the reply, 'this business runs on personal friendships: we can make anything work.'[4]

Not all the masters grappled with change as bravely and successfully as did Ron (later Lord) Dearing. Five centuries of unremitting progress would be unique indeed. Several extended periods of drift and indecision punctuate the history, linked in a couple of cases to individuals mocked by their contemporaries for being notoriously averse to change. The travails of the unreformed Post Office in the post-1815 era and the beleaguered state of the nascent posts-telephone-and-telegraph administration of the 1920s eventually brought the careers of Francis Freeling and Evelyn Murray, both long-serving and in many ways distinguished public servants, to inglorious ends. But fallow years and signs of public disaffection with the posts have historically been the cue for the biggest changes of all. Crises of confidence in the Post Office have several times seen power over its affairs handed to extraordinary outsiders, who arrived with their own vision of how the institution might be galvanized anew – and whose drive, in at least three cases, was the basis of everything that followed. Ralph Allen (1693–1764) built up the rural posts of Georgian England. John Palmer (1742–1818) launched the inter-city coaches of the Royal Mail. Above all, Rowland Hill (1795–1879) imposed uniform penny postage and set the great expansion of the Victorian Age on its way.

Rowland Hill's impact was remarkable, but is often misunderstood. He was adamant that the modern service he did so much to create should be a quasi-commercial business. His legacy was overtaken in the 1860s by an expanded vision of the Post Office that stretched well beyond the mails and grew into a multifaceted public service that constituted, for most of the population, almost the entirety of the state's presence in their daily lives. This broader role presented the late Victorians with a thorny problem, when it came to deciding whether or not the Post Office should take over the nascent telephone industry in the 1880s, as it had done the telegraph business in the 1860s. A consensus was needed on where exactly the line should be drawn between the free market and state-run enterprises. While the philosophers of laissez-faire liberalism (notably John Stuart Mill) were clear on this, however, the politicians allowed the issue to become woefully confused. Not for the last time, their indecision rebounded badly on the Post Office. A takeover was agreed in the end – the telephones were nationalized in

1912 – but only after decades of confusion that ensured the Post Office was hopelessly ill-prepared to run the combination of posts and telephones that emerged after the First World War.

This book is a history of the Royal Mail, not British Telecom. The evolution of the telephone industry from the 1920s onwards is here increasingly relegated to the margins. In one crucial respect, though, telephones remained of central importance. Active lobbying in support of a separation of the telephone arm was a powerful catalyst for periodic reappraisals of the proper status of the postal service, too. This came quite close to prompting a disestablishment of the Post Office as an entity semi-independent of the state at the start of the 1930s – perhaps along the lines of the BBC, with state funding but a governance structure that carefully distanced all executive authority from the government of the day. (Another instance of much the same approach was the London Passenger Transport Board, designed by Herbert Morrison as Labour's Transport Minister in 1931, which set up a public body with an independent board of directors, chosen by five 'appointing trustees'.) Cautious reformers settled instead for a less radical approach. Then, from the mid-1930s until well into the 1950s, considerations of national security precluded any possibility of having either telephones or posts run by anyone other than the state. But the idea of denationalizing the telephone industry was back by the early 1960s, again helping to prompt questions about the Post Office as a whole. The Wilson government's failure – despite the best endeavours of a notably energetic Postmaster General (and hugely entertaining diarist), Tony Benn – to address these questions with the seriousness they deserved was a costly oversight, made worse in the 1970s by some crackpot initiatives foisted on the Post Office by Conservative and Labour administrations alike. The Thatcher Government, after some initial hesitation, broke with years of indecision and finally stripped out the telephone industry as many had urged in the 1920s. Once British Telecom had been successfully privatized in 1984, it was not long before the Post Office itself came to be seen as a candidate for privatization. Here was a proposal that would stir up arguments as passionate as any of those provoked by the postal reforms of the nineteenth century.

The business and financial rationales for transferring post offices or the Royal Mail, or both, to the private sector have now been comprehensively explored for a quarter of a century. Political objections blocked the way in 1987, 1994 and 1998. A fourth aborted sale in 2009 was blamed on market conditions, but was clearly also mired in polit-

ical controversy. The formation of the coalition government in 2010
revived the prospect of privatization and the debate has been rekindled
all over again by the passing of legislation in June 2011 to allow for at
least a partial sale at some future date. Disquiet over the idea throughout this period has hardly been the exclusive preserve of the trade
unions – though their emergence a century ago irreversibly altered the
nature of all political debate over the postal service and their opposition
to privatization has been implacable ever since their firm stand against
the notion of detaching the Post Office from the civil service in 1931–2.
The unions believe they have reasons to fear the potential impact of
private-sector ownership on jobs, but they have also rejected it – none
more passionately than General Secretary Tom Jackson, at the start of
the 1980s – as an assault on an essential feature of British society, fuelled
by doctrinaire politics. It is a view still shared today by many people
with no interest in the unions' plight. It reflects an enduring perception
of the Post Office as the friendly face of the state, and of local post offices
as one of the last bastions of village life in many areas. This legacy of the
Victorian era remains entrenched. The history of the intervening century
perhaps casts as much light on the travails of the privatization policy as
any amount of debate over the strengths and weaknesses of the business
case for a sale. What lingers on is an underlying tension between two
ideological camps with fundamentally different perspectives.

The two camps would probably take conflicting views of an unusual
box sitting in the vaults of the BPMA. When one of the first thousand
copies of James Joyce's *Ulysses* was found in the London post early in
1923, it was impounded in line with instructions from the Home Office
that all copies of the work be treated as obscene material. The book,
Copy No. 895, was deposited in the Royal Mail's archive. It is still there,
in pristine condition.[5] Collectors at London's Unaffordable Arts Fair in
June 2010 were reportedly interested in paying around £95,000 for a
first edition of *Ulysses*. Some want a Post Office business that would
surely dispose of the Joyce in short order and redeploy the profits. Others
want a public service that might (continue to) view the idea of selling
this piece of postal history as distasteful. What line should now be taken
by those who value the traditions of the public service but conclude – as
did Rowland Hill, indeed – that only the rigours of a business can truly
sustain them? The struggle for a persuasive answer to this conundrum
is another of the themes explored in these pages.

Histories of the Post Office, most of them written by former or serving officials, were published fairly regularly prior to the Second World

War. In recent decades there have been more biographies of Anthony Trollope, probably its most famous employee after Rowland Hill, than of the Post Office itself. The two most recent scholarly works – Alan Clinton's *Post Office Workers: A Trade Union and Social History* (1984) and Martin Daunton's *Royal Mail: The Post Office since 1840* (1985) – both opted for a more thematic approach than most of their predecessors. Howard Robinson's *The British Post Office: A History* (1948) took a narrative approach that I have tried to emulate. His elegant work ended with only the briefest sketch of the years after 1914, which is where the weight of this book lies. Like Robinson, I have had to take some liberties with the chronology. Telling one continuous story has involved some unavoidable sequencing of what were actually contemporaneous episodes; it has also meant less attention than they deserve for some aspects of the Post Office that for decades were taken for granted. The social life of the postal workforce or the proud role of the Post Office in the training and education of young people over many generations are only mentioned en passant. The work of the Post Office overseas and its contribution to the spread of postal and cable networks around the world are among several topics only lightly touched upon. In mitigation I can only plead that most features of postal history have already been the subject of excellent specialist studies, some of which can be found in the bibliography. Many subjects even have their own learned societies that have long been producing scholarly studies on a regular basis. Alongside the Postal History Society and the Society of Postal Historians are dozens of others dedicated to promoting research into everything from the local postal histories of British counties to the evolution of postal mechanization. Indeed, tackling a general history at all has sometimes seemed a slightly impertinent undertaking, given the weight of scholarship bearing on so many detailed aspects of postal history. Then there is the whole world of philately. The Royal Philatelic Society London, founded in 1869, has its own library that currently subscribes (astonishingly) to just over 2,200 different periodicals and it has been publishing a continuous journal of its own (*The London Philatelist*) since 1892. Its members over the decades have produced hundreds of erudite books and papers using stamps and other artefacts to trace all facets of postal history – attesting to the fact that any distinction between philately and postal history is really little more than a simple convenience. (Topics covered in the Society's 2010–11 programme of exhibitions included POW mails in East Asia during the Second World War, the pre-1914 postal history of Aden and the postal history of the

Ottoman port of Smyrna.) Postmarks, postage stamps and address systems are the subject of many individual episodes in this history, from the creation of the Penny Black and the nineteenth-century career of Stanley Gibbons to the story of Tony Benn's joust at the Queen's head in the 1960s and the creation of the world's first all-purpose postal code. But although philately is included in these pages, any even vaguely complete philatelic survey would add many chapters, and this is already a sufficiently long book. If *Masters of the Post* provides a useful context for more detailed studies – whether philatelic or social, political or technological – it will have met at least one of its objectives.

The primary goal has been to set down for the general reader a coherent narrative that can help explain the Royal Mail's evolution, especially over the fifth and last of its centuries. At its core over this latter period has been the triangular relationship between the managers of the postal service, the politicians and government officials answerable for it to the electorate, and the union leaders elected to represent the interests of its workforce. For, in reality, the Royal Mail has always had to contend not with one master at a time but a set of them – often at loggerheads, and sometimes locked in open confrontation. It is often said that the core problem for the Royal Mail since Rowland Hill has been its dual nature, as both a public service and a business. This book suggests it might be more precise to say the problem has been its exposure to a long-running contest for control – colourfully manifest before 1800, played out dramatically in the Reform Era of the 1830s and intermittently evident ever since – between those intent on (or resigned to) seeing public service as the priority and those (from Rowland Hill to Allan Leighton) aspiring to run the Royal Mail as far as possible like a business.

Balancing public-service requirements and business objectives has never in itself posed much of an obstacle for economists or lawyers: they have always been able to assess proposed changes to the service/business mix as a relatively simple matter, in theory, of altering rules and regulations. The political difficulties posed by any prospective change have in practice always been much trickier. When the unions in the post-1945 era pressed their dream of a postal service jointly run by managers and workers in unison, ministers and officials baulked at conceding so much power over a service for which they were answerable to the public (and over which officials had wielded power so uncompromisingly until the dawn of the century). When ambitious managers began pressing from the late 1970s for a more businesslike approach under their firm control, ministers baulked again, as did the trade unions – for much the same reason. So long as the wider public seemed likely to hold the politicians accountable for the Royal Mail, it took a bold minister to champion the case for 'commercial' reforms. Yet given rapid changes in the operational environment for all national postal services from the 1980s onwards, bold political leadership was exactly what was needed. A few ministers tried to provide it, but found little support from their colleagues. The result, reflecting little credit on either of the main political parties, was an increasingly dysfunctional clash of political and managerial agendas, which impeded the resolution of many innately sticky issues, from mechanization and productivity bargaining to modern marketing and privatization itself. Once the cumulative damage to the efficiency of the postal service was plain to see, the media moved within a very few years from taking pride in the Royal Mail to routinely ridiculing its inefficiencies. As so often in the past, mawkish praise for the Royal Mail as (in principle) a national treasure was no bar to searing and often unfounded criticism of its perceived shortcomings in practice.

At all points in the story told here, across a great swathe of English and British history, the progress or otherwise of the postal service has held up a mirror to contemporary political life in striking ways. The evolution of this one institution tells us much, for example, about the limitations of eighteenth-century government, the organizational genius of the Victorians and the relations between twentieth-century Whitehall and state-owned industry. As this might suggest, the service has shown in every era an extraordinary capacity to reinvent itself in response to changed circumstances; and observers in the mid-1990s, as in the mid-1890s, could still regard the Royal Mail as the world's pre-eminent Post Office. In how many other industries could the same have been said of a leading British name? The five centuries have ended with a decade of torrid upheaval. Without doubt the postal service is in the throes of yet another reinvention. However it emerges, we can be sure that its history will bear heavily on the outcome.

PART ONE

Arm of the State

I

'A thing above all things', 1512–1659

My lord, when at their home
I did commend your highness' letters to them,
Ere I was risen from the place that showed
My duty kneeling, came there a reeking post,
Stewed in his haste, half breathless, panting forth
From Gonerill his mistress salutations;
Delivered letters, spite of intermission,
Which presently they read . . .

From Shakespeare's *King Lear* (1605–6),
Act II, scene iv

1. PEOPLE'S POSTS AND THE KING'S POSTS

One of the most famous letter-writing families in English history pre-dated the existence of any semblance of a Post Office. The Pastons lived in fifteenth-century Norfolk. Over the course of four generations, they rose from being humble tillers of the land to substantial landlords, acquiring several estates in the vicinity of Norwich, which was then one of the largest and wealthiest places in the country. While impressive, there was nothing especially unusual about their rise, but for one thing: from around 1420 to just after 1500, the Pastons made a habit of hoarding their letters. All those exchanged between members of the family were carefully stored away. So too were drafts of letters to third parties and letters received from them – a wide range of other correspondents, 'bishops or serving men, prisoners or dukes, priests or ribald companions . . .'[1] The result was very unusual indeed. The family accumulated over a thousand private letters. They survive today, most of them in the British Museum,

as one of the earliest collections of its kind in the English language and
certainly one of the most engaging. The Pastons and their correspondents were writing for practical purposes, not posterity, and alluded
constantly to the practicalities of life: the letters amount to a time-capsule
from late-medieval England. And no practicality was more important or
more regularly discussed in the letters than the arrangements made to
ensure their safe delivery.[2]

Central to the family's success was the career of Sir John Paston I
(who named both of his two oldest sons after him, hence John II and
John III). He was a lawyer, born in 1421, who spent much of his adult
life in the City wrangling over the title to various Norfolk estates. His
wife Margaret ran their properties in his absence. She wrote to him
regularly – as did clerks and bailiffs – reporting on business and asking
for instructions. So how were these letters and the replies conveyed
between Norwich and London? The simplest method was to use a family retainer. Most people affluent enough to write letters could afford
servants to deliver them, and the Pastons were no exception. But journeys between London and Norfolk took several days, and were a costly
way to send a single missive. There were essentially two alternatives.
One option was to find someone heading in the right direction on other
business – perhaps ecclesiastical, more often commercial and sometimes
just a friend of the family – who could be employed as a messenger. This
might be hard in the dead of winter, but was common practice at other
times of the year. 'England was still a land of great fairs, to which people
came from far and near. After and during these fairs, the roads were
busy with men going to and fro, and many of these acted as messengers,
and would leave letters at places as they passed.'[3] Many of the Pastons'
letters refer to their services, occasionally using the unavailability of a
reliable person as a reason for not having written sooner: 'if I might
have had a messenger ere this time I had sent it you', as Margaret says
(if we adjust her spelling into modern English) of one letter evidently
despatched with some difficulty.[4] We can be sure letters were never
handed lightly to just any intermediary; those to Sir John were frequently entrusted to individuals who plainly knew where to find him
(even when he was in the Fleet prison, as on three occasions). Margaret
rarely put much of an instruction on the outside of her letters: most of
them seem to have been addressed simply 'John Paston', though he
occasionally provided her with a forwarding address, as in September
1471: 'I pray you send me word hereof by the next messenger and if it
came to Mrs Elisabeth Higgens, at the Black Swan, she shall convey it

to me, for I will not fail to be there at London again within this six days'.[5] His replies were addressed just as sparsely, scarcely ever citing more than 'at Norwyche'. But as various editors have pointed out, it is striking how few references either of them ever made to letters that had gone astray.

The other main option for Sir John and his wife, in deciding how to deliver a letter, was to turn to the services of a 'common carrier'. 'As early as the mid-fifteenth century, extensive systems of overland carriage, by cart, pack-horse and wain were being provided by carriers.'[6] Most treated letters and parcels as a profitable side-line, but for some they were more than that. In most market towns of any importance, there was a carrier licensed by the local worthies to collect letters and deliver them safely along a handful of popular routes. Margaret was chided by her husband on one occasion in 1465 for not pushing the family servants to make better use of this alternative: 'The bearer of this letter is [a] common carrier, and was at Norwich on Saturday, and brought me letters from other men, but your servants inquire not diligently after the coming of carriers or other men'.[7] References to common carriers crop up more often as the fifteenth century wears on, which accords with a general growth of traffic on the main inland trade routes around this time. For letters sent to Calais and well beyond, meanwhile, the Pastons could turn to regular carrier services more reliable and sophisticated than anything to be found within the rest of England. The ties between the City of London and the Low Countries ensured as much.

Fortunes were to be made in the cross-Channel trades centred on the great markets of Antwerp, Bruges and Ghent. Merchants' letters were travelling reliably in both directions by the later fifteenth century, and linked the City via the Low Countries to the more distant markets of the Hanseatic League in the north and the towns of the Rhine and northern Italy to the south. By the first half of the sixteenth century, each side of the Channel had in place its own trusted postal officials. The Continental merchants had a mostly Flemish contingent in London who ran the 'Strangers' Post'. The City had its own 'Merchant Adventurers' Post' with foreign-language speakers stationed on the Continent. Both used the same inns as staging posts for bearers of their mail along the sixty-mile route from London to the Channel ports, travelling overland from the Thames Estuary to Rochester and on through Sittingbourne and Canterbury to Dover, or sometimes Margate or Deal. The surviving correspondence of celebrated merchants like Sir Thomas Gresham – the guiding spirit behind the building in the 1560s of the City's Royal

Exchange, based on Antwerp's Custom House – includes many references to the regularity of these mails by the middle of the Tudor century.[8]

Elsewhere in the country, regularity must have been a rare feature of any delivery service. Several large towns in East Anglia, some of the most prosperous in the country and with vital links to the wool merchants of London, were perhaps exceptions: they set up 'municipal posts' funded out of levies on local innkeepers and requiring them to provide horses for the regular collection of letters from the City. Here Norwich may have scored another notable first in postal history (it was not to be the last): it had a locally regulated service that was first recorded in 1569. In general, however, many ordinary people in the sixteenth century went on relying, much as the Pastons had done, on private messengers and common carriers. The carriers flourished in ever greater numbers, especially after the adoption of long-wheelbase wagons from around the middle of the century. The first public statute aimed at improving the roads, passed in 1555, cited the 'noisome and tedious' conditions resulting from the growth of this carrier traffic.[9] References to the work of the carriers are common enough by the 1580s to show that 'there was an efficient postal service at the time available throughout the country, innkeepers and carriers being ready to arrange for local deliveries'.[10]

At the end of the 1590s, we know of another professional man living most of his time in London while supporting a family and a growing estate in the country, this time Warwickshire rather than Norfolk. If there is one family in all of British history whose correspondence we should most like to have, it would surely be Shakespeare's. It seems entirely plausible that letters of some kind – terse instructions, perhaps, for the management of his growing property portfolio – must have travelled between him and his family in Stratford-upon-Avon, even if (as most suppose) his wife, Anne Hathaway, was herself illiterate, but none have ever been discovered. The exhaustive scrutiny of every archive with even the remotest connection to the Bard has, however, unearthed plenty of details about a man called William Greenway, Stratford's principal common carrier. According to one recent authority on Shakespeare's domestic life, '[Greenway] had been plying the route between his home town and London since 1581, and for the next twenty years played an indispensable role carrying letters, messages, food, goods and gossip back and forth'.[11] We know Greenway brought letters up to London in 1598 for delivery to one Richard Quiney, a Stratford man with the distinction of being the author of the only extant letter ever addressed to Shakespeare. (We still have it because he never sent it.) Greenway hired out horses for the ride between London and Stratford, but also appears to have made the journey many times himself. His will, made out in 1601, has survived and records a sizeable debt owed to him by the keeper of the Bell Inn near St Paul's Cathedral, where it seems he had been dropping off letters for Quiney and other Stratfordians for years.[12]

Greenway's livelihood probably depended on working closely with a network of taverns. Friendly innkeepers were central to the service provided by the carriers, just as they would one day provide the basis of a network for the first stage coaches. Some decades later, in 1637, dozens of London inns were listed in a remarkable publication called *The Carriers Cosmography*. For each inn, it set down the schedules of carriers – hundreds of them, some solitary riders and others running teams of massive horse-drawn wagons – notionally making regular calls each week. All were identified not by their names but by the towns of England to which they travelled. Here were the outlines of a market-driven, or perhaps we should say a fair-driven, postal service for private letters. Sadly for the author of the *Cosmography*, however, his survey appeared in the very year that saw the carriers formally relegated to a subordinate, and eventually moribund, role by a separate postal system altogether – the King's Posts.

The King's Posts were initially devised to provide beleaguered English monarchs as quickly as possible with news from distant places. They were probably first used effectively during the Wars of the Roses. Letters between the royal Court and those on the king's business were nothing new: we know of several, for example, carried from France during the Hundred Years War.[13] But when the battling Yorkist Edward IV gave his support to an invasion of Scotland in 1481–2, while himself remaining at Westminster, he wanted to be sure that regular despatches to and from his kingdom's northern border would travel at the fastest possible speed. Two years later, Richard III had the same compelling need, as he contemplated the possibility of a landing on the Welsh coast by the pretender Henry Tudor. In both cases, arrangements were made for the King's despatches to be relayed like a baton by a long series of 'post-riders'. The latter would travel from one set of stables to another, roughly a dozen miles apart, and be provided at each with a fresh horse and a guide for the next stage of the journey. These 'post stations' were temporary, as after a short time was Richard III himself. But his demise did nothing to discredit the idea, and the English Court could see it being applied successfully by its counterparts in Europe. By the end of the fifteenth century the French kings were keeping couriers on stand-by in scores of towns across the country. Between the far-flung corners of the Holy Roman Empire, post-riders were being efficiently administered by the Count of Thurn and Taxis, whose family had been granted control of the entire imperial postal system.

While the objective was clear, setting up a series of courier relays in practice – even over a distance as short as London to Dover – posed a challenge not easily met in normal times. Henry VII, as the usurper Henry Tudor became, never commanded a reliable 'Dover Road': he had to rely like his forebears on resourceful individuals who could be trusted to make their own way, probably via the inns accustomed to working with the merchants' posts. The story of one such messenger passed into legend. In 1507 the ageing Henry wanted to send an important set of papers to the Emperor Maximilian, then staying with his court in the Low Countries. The King turned to a young Court chaplain whose initiative had been highly recommended. The young man dashed off from the English Court at Richmond-on-Thames, travelled via Gravesend, Dover and Calais to the Emperor's entourage and then dashed back by the same route – all within eighty hours. When Henry emerged from the Royal Bedchamber for early-morning Mass, he found him in the corridor and ticked him off sharply for not having left yet. He was astounded to hear the young man reply that he had been and come back. 'The King being in a great confusion & wonder of his hasty speed, with ready furniture of all his proceedings, dissembled all his imaginations & wonder in that matter ...'[14] But he was mightily impressed – and promptly appointed the winged chaplain Dean of Lincoln. Thus began the worldly career of the future Cardinal Wolsey.

Five years later, as Chancellor to the young Henry VIII and one of the most powerful men in England, it was Wolsey who chose the first man to be given proper responsibility for the running of regular King's Posts. The country was briefly at war with France and Wolsey was anxious to ensure speedy communications between the Court and the coastal towns of the south-east. He assigned the work to Brian Tuke, a court official working in Calais whose seasoned career (he was then forty years old) had included a spell as the King's Bailiff in Sandwich. Tuke seems to have spent much of his two years in Calais since 1510 familiarizing himself with the routines of the Imperial Post and watching the activities of the merchants' posts. He took a lively interest in the organization of the Dover Road from his earliest days in office, and before the end of 1512 was being referred to in papers of the Privy Council as 'Master of the Posts', though this title was not officially endorsed until 1517. There as yet existed no 'Royal Mail'. But Tuke, taking up his role almost exactly five centuries ago, through more than thirty years of diligent administration did much to create a nascent postal service and truly proved himself the first Master.

It is easier to sketch his development of the service in conceptual terms than to chronicle it with precise dates: the surviving records of his work are too patchy for us to be sure of the significance of individual episodes.[15] The broad sequence began with the requirement that all towns in the kingdom be prepared, at their own expense, to make a fresh horse available for any post-rider travelling on the King's commission – meaning two horses in practice since he would need a guide, who could also return with both horses when the post-rider reached the next stage of his journey. Though any reluctance to comply with it might have been unwise, this arrangement unavoidably left much to chance: the townsmen capable of organizing horses might not be at hand when needed, and finding suitable horses might not always be straightforward. In busy places where the demand for horses would be fairly constant, and delays would be especially disruptive, Tuke therefore set up individuals to run a stable and take charge of the necessary tasks in return for a basic wage from the state. These were the posts, briefly known as postmasters and subsequently as deputy postmasters. Installing a series of them in key 'post towns' along a given route was the essence of 'laying a post', as it came to be called. (From the start, the word 'post' was freely commandeered for all purposes, whether as verb, noun or adjective, prefix or suffix.) Exceptional powers were granted to every deputy postmaster. There could never be any excuse for delaying the King's Posts: if the deputy's stables were empty, he had authority to appropriate any suitable horse to hand. As Tuke summarized the position in a famous letter to Thomas Cromwell in 1533: '. . . the King's pleasure is, that posts be better appointed, and laid in all places most expedient; with commandment to all townships in all places, on pain of life, to be in such readiness, and to make such provision of horses, at all times, as no tract or loss of time be had in that behalf'.[16] The heightened dependability of the arrangements decreed for post towns allowed another important step to be taken. The King's Posts – meaning, in effect, all papers and letters sent with the official blessing of the Court, or of someone (however remotely) in attendance on it – could be consigned as 'packets', to be passed along from one post to the next without their needing to be carried by the King's post-riders in person. Some papers would be too important (or their authors too proud) to be handled in this way: these would go on being conveyed by royal messengers as 'through posts', who would expect to be assisted with horses and guides in the usual way. All other packets, though, could travel as 'ordinary posts'. They would be carried not by the deputy postmasters themselves, who would need to mind their 'post station' at all times, but by underlings on their behalf, known as 'post-boys'.

Tuke's legacy was hardly a network of smoothly operating Roads, as is sometimes supposed. There were harsh limits to what could plausibly be ordained from London in the sixteenth century, even by an uncommonly talented and energetic administrator. Most post towns were dots that had yet to be joined. Only on two extended routes were successive post towns from start to finish integrated at all successfully into a reliably working Road with any degree of permanence – the Dover Road and the North Road, which went to Berwick on the Scottish border via Doncaster and Newcastle, straddling twenty-eight stables along the way.[17] Other Roads were much shorter and more local in character, such as those linking London with towns in Essex and Surrey, or were laid from time to time on a more temporary basis. In 1536, for example, special arrangements were made at Henry's command along the route from London to Lincolnshire, in response to the local uprising that prefigured the so-called Pilgrimage of Grace. But once the King's Posts had become the Queen's Posts under Elizabeth I, a state-funded postal network gradually assumed coast-to-coast proportions. To the Dover and North Roads were added three more.

In all three cases, the security of the realm was a compelling incentive for Elizabeth and for Tuke's effective successor as the next great Master of the Posts, Thomas Randolph. The records of the Queen's Privy Council make frequent enough references to postal arrangements – or in many cases, to their absence – to suggest their great importance in the process of imposing the government's authority during Elizabeth's reign. The West Road, stretching via Exeter and Plymouth down into the far reaches of Cornwall and the port of Falmouth, was critical to command of the Queen's navy. Letters from Elizabeth's ministers in London could reach her sea captains in Plymouth within a week or so – though Plymouth was said to be 217 miles from London along the West Road – and the correspondence between them played its part in the defeat of the Spanish Armada. (Letters from Drake and his fellow admirals, including some written at sea, are one of our main documentary sources for charting what happened to the Armada.[18]) The Bristol Road linked London not just to another important port but also to Ireland, via harbours in the south-west tip of Wales. The Chester Road to the north-west of England similarly continued on along the North Wales coast to Holyhead, where 'packet boats' sailed for Dublin with the main bulk of the mail for soldiers and officials of the Crown in Ireland. The layout of all five Tudor Roads paid more heed to the collecting and forwarding of messages for the Court than to linking England's largest towns, many of which were therefore by-passed at a substantial distance; this would have important repercussions later. But in special cases, provision was made for news to be gathered at a distance from the Roads and brought to the post towns. Small parishes along the coast of the West Country, for example, were required in the wake of the Armada to retain 'foot posts' who could be ready at all times to run to their nearest post town with news of anything alarming on the horizon of the sea.

2. A ROYAL MONOPOLY

Many brief accounts of the Royal Mail's origins almost suggest it began as a magical act of creation in the middle of the seventeenth century, and are further spiced with a heavy emphasis on its role as an agency of government censorship. We can be sure the usefulness of the paid deputy postmasters as tools of surveillance was never overlooked – but sure, too, that the Royal Mail was not conjured by the monarchy with a uniquely efficient wave of the royal wand. It emerged, slowly and messily, as the culmination of a process by which the people's posts on the one hand and the Queen's Posts and their successors on the other were gradually merged together. The spur for it had less to do with espionage – though this certainly figured – than with economic necessity.

The postal system devised by Tuke was in theory funded by the state. It might be more accurate to say it was *subsidized* by the state, in a haphazard fashion that left much of the expense effectively falling on local township councils and deputy postmasters. The townships were required to provide horses for the post. A standard payment of one penny per ridden mile was decreed for every horse appropriated, and this would be ostensibly but only intermittently doubled to two pence per mile (and finally back to 'three halfpence') under Elizabeth. In post towns, where stables had to be kept on stand-by at all times, these too had to be funded by the local burghers. The costs must have substantially exceeded the fees payable: the difference amounted, in modern parlance,

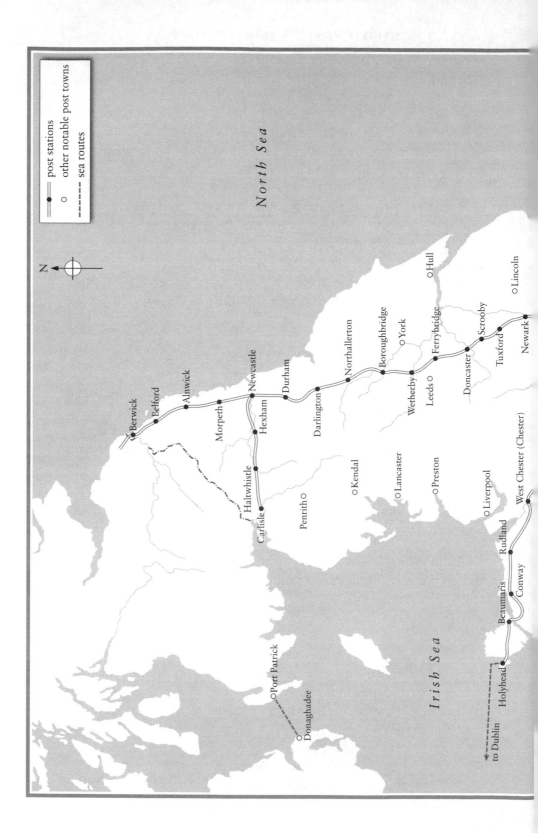

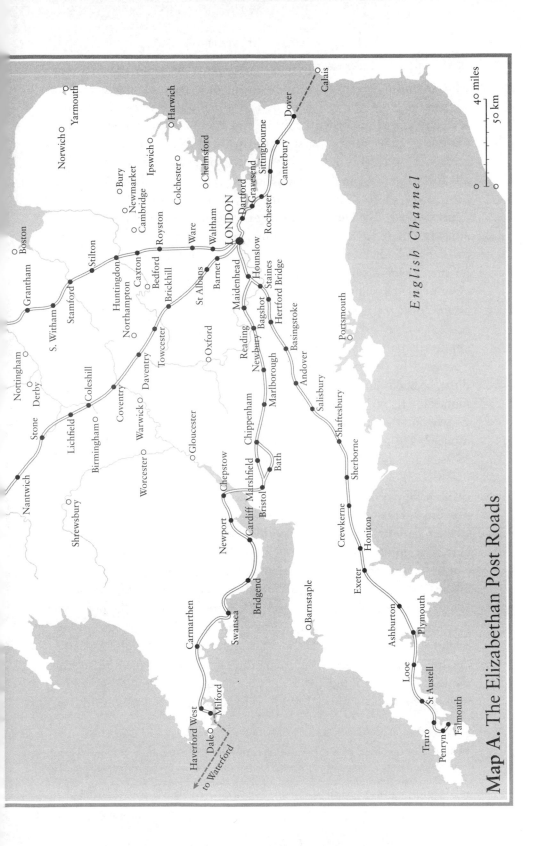

Map A. The Elizabethan Post Roads

to a stealth tax and was often bitterly resented. The deputy postmasters who administered the mails were meanwhile paid a meagre Crown wage – the basic rate was fixed at 12d a day until 1557 – which was scarcely sufficient to provide a livelihood, even when it was paid in reasonable time. We can only assume (on scant evidence) that for many of these local guardians of the King's Post some extra earnings were usually forthcoming from the horse-rental payments – and that running the posts was a sensible side-line for them as innkeepers or ostlers. Even so, many by the end of Henry VIII's reign were heavily out of pocket. Tuke appears to have striven conscientiously to avert serious hardship among the deputies. He himself made a substantial fortune through working for the Crown in various capacities, and we know that he was a beneficiary of the Dissolution of the Monasteries, sharing in the handout of estates formerly owned by Waltham Abbey. He was nonetheless seen by contemporaries as a benign and compassionate man, which is how he appears in more than one portrait painted by his friend Hans Holbein the Younger.* By the time he died in 1545 at the venerable age of seventy-three, he had been regularly topping up the official budget with his own money for years: his executors submitted a postal-expenses claim to the Crown for the equivalent of about half a million pounds in today's money.[19] The postal system he left to his successors was stretched close to its financial limits.

Through the next fifty years, two further strains on the system might easily have wrecked it. On the one hand, unprecedented rates of inflation pushed the operating expenses of the post significantly higher: one modern authority on the horse world of the Tudor era has suggested the cost of grain used as animal feed may almost have quadrupled by the end of the century.[20] And on the other, Elizabeth's penchant for cutting all but the most essential items of government expenditure led to a squeeze on the already deeply unreliable state wages of the deputy postmasters. Their allowance was increased to 20d a day at the start of her reign – which compared with about 8d a day for a highly skilled artisan – but by 1568 the Queen was instructing her newly installed Master of the Posts, Thomas Randolph, to discharge all those deputies unwilling to work for half the official rate.[21] (How far he complied with this is

---

* One of Holbein's images has been made especially familiar by a subsequent copy, clunkingly adorned with a figure of Death in the background and an oversized egg-timer at his right hand. (See *The Burlington Magazine for Connoisseurs*, Vol. 42, No. 242, May 1923. The copy is reproduced in Plate 1.)

unclear, but insufficient resources to foot the wage bill were a regular trial for Randolph, as for Tuke.) In the event, the postal system endured and even prospered in many places – due principally to two fundamental adjustments that had only a murky basis in law, but received the tacit blessing of the Elizabethan authorities. One involved the granting to the deputy postmasters of a de facto monopoly over the often lucrative business of hiring out horses. Private charges could be set at a multiple of the penny-a-mile paid for horses used on official business; and the post-boys themselves could earn a standard fee (a groat, worth 4d) for each hire that they supervised as a guide. Many post towns appear to have embraced this arrangement in exchange for the Government relying wholly on the post stations and more or less abandoning the practice of requisitioning horses from others.[22] The second adjustment was more profound, and was central to the merging of the people's posts and the Queen's Posts. Over the years, Elizabeth's officials gradually came to accept and acknowledge that private letters – or 'by-letters', as they were called – could legitimately be conveyed in the ordinary posts, so ensuring for the deputy postmasters a precious additional source of revenue to supplement their state wages.

It was not a change of stance that was adopted lightly. Elizabeth and her ministers were at first deeply suspicious of the idea that ordinary people might exchange letters via a standing (and government-subsidized) service. In an age fraught with fears of violent insurrection, religious conflict and invasion, the risks involved in any opening up of the Government's privileged postal system to all and sundry were evident. Orders more than once went out from the Privy Council in the 1560s instructing postmasters that there should be 'no passeport for any post horses except the same be for the Queen's Majesty's service'.[23] Private letters could all too easily be the stuff of conspiracy. With or without a helping hand, it might be said, from the Queen's own secret agents under Francis Walsingham. The fate of Mary, Queen of Scots, was sealed in 1586 by a covert plot that tricked her into the despatch of lethally incriminating letters – hidden in kegs of beer that were smuggled in and out of her prison by agents of the Government. (Many contemporary documents attest to Walsingham's power over the posts.) Yet by the 1580s, Elizabethan government had no choice but to confront a steady rise in the number of private letters passing more innocuously along the Post Roads of the nation. Literacy levels were rising, businesses and inland tradesmen were flourishing as never before, and letter writing was spreading far beyond Court circles and the world of City merchants like Thomas Gresham. Ordinary people needing to despatch a letter were turning to the Queen's Posts for a network of message bearers incomparably superior to anything provided by the common carriers. By slipping a modest coin to the postmaster or his post-boy, or both, they could add their letter to the official packet as it passed. This would assure them of a delivery service that was (relatively) predictable, much faster and more secure than any carrier could offer: travelling with the Crown's protection, letters would not be immune to thieves and foot-pads but were far less likely to fall foul of them – tampering with the Queen's Posts was a hanging offence. And for their part, we can imagine postmasters and post-boys were only too happy to eke out an add-itional income by adding the by-letters to their bag in exchange for a fee they could pocket directly.

Here was a terrible dilemma for Elizabethan government. Ignoring the growth of private letters would mean disregarding a potentially dis-astrous proliferation of covert political activity and might even impede the operations of the Queen's Posts themselves; but, equally, laying down explicit rules for the handling of unofficial postal business might be seen as a tacit acceptance of it, only drawing more private letters onto the Roads. The issue was effectively dodged for more than two decades: new rules for the Posts were mostly aimed, in vain, at trying to restrict access for 'uncommissioned' users. Finally, in 1583, an elaborate set of regulations was issued that essentially acknowledged what was happening. These rules confirmed various privileges for the ordinary posts, for example asserting their monopoly over the renting out of horses to post-riders. But their primary significance lies in their unam-biguous nod in the direction of those uncommissioned users:

> *Item.* The post shall receive the sum of three halfpence per mile when riding on her majesty's service, and twopence per mile when otherwise engaged.
> *Item.* Each post shall be bound to keep a fair book well bound, . . . with the number of their horses and date of their commission, as well without as with commission.
> *Item.* No packages save official to be compelled to run with their post.[24]

Penalties were set down for opening private letters, as well as official ones. Post-boys were warned against attending to private letters until they had handed on the official packet – but they were also enjoined to advertise their presence for the benefit of local people: every post-boy was required to carry a horn at all times, '[and] to blow his horn so oft as he meeteth company, or passeth through a town, or at the least thrice a mile'. This was a pivotal moment. The postmasters were still to be left largely to their own devices – using their work for the Posts to cultivate extra business for their inns, keeping account of the pennies from royal messengers on the one hand and by-letters on the other, and doubtless in most cases juggling accounts with local councillors in a constant effort to share the financial burden of their legal obligations to the Crown. But the Government had now crucially accepted that the Posts were being shared with commoners and that they would need in future to be formally supervised with this in mind. Once the Crown had embraced this responsibility, the way was open – in theory – to transform the Posts from a service that officially *excluded* private letters into a service claiming exclusive responsibility *over* them.

How far the subsequent development of the Queen's Posts under Elizabeth should be seen as the start of a public service, truly open to commoners as well as the aristocracy and officers of the Crown, has been one of the more contentious topics in postal history.[25] Perhaps the ambivalence of the Queen herself has clouded the issue, leaving the record full of inconsistencies and apparent contradictions. But it is hard to avoid concluding that the posts were kept ever busier with a substantial and growing volume of private letters by the later years of her reign – just as Randolph, Master of the Posts from 1567 to 1590, found himself kept ever busier providing Walsingham with covert information about them. A state paper endorsed by Randolph in November 1583 noted 'the great charges lying nowadays on the posts more than heretofore hathe been accustomed' – and went on to provide 'the names of such as daily and ordinarily charge the posts with their private Letters . . .'[26] Indeed, letters from Randolph to Walsingham about the running of the posts are themselves a valuable indication of the way they were becoming more generally accessible. Randolph commends one set of suggestions, for example, by telling the Queen's Secretary in April 1584: 'this shall cut off much debate and strife, and further all such as use posting and her Majesty's service'.[27] By contrast, few documentary traces of the first postmasters' labours have survived – but a log-book for 1585, kept by a postmaster on the North Road at Huntingdon, gives us a suggestive glimpse. For the month of August, John Rigges made a special note of five packets received – two to be forwarded to Walsingham and three to other peers of the realm. He also logged handling eighty-nine other packets, eighty-eight 'batches' and forty-four individual letters, with posts coming and going almost daily and often two or three times a day.[28]

The fees earned on the carriage of private letters appear in many towns along the five Roads to have mounted up handsomely. Postmasterships in such places were becoming highly prized appointments, jealously held within families and passed from father to son.* Randolph did everything in his power to consolidate their status, in exchange badgering them constantly to improve the time-keeping of their routines and to ameliorate the worst aspects of the pitted cart tracks that usually had to serve as their local roads. A dependable Post Road from Stratford and Oxford to London, had it existed, might have deprived the carrier William Greenway of a substantial part of his livelihood. But he kept it, because the post towns along his route were not coordinated like those on the principal Roads. Post towns were nonetheless to be encountered in most populated areas of the country, centred on the larger market towns across the country and harbour towns on the coasts. Reflecting their numbers, the activities and terminology of the Posts had clearly passed into common parlance by Shakespeare's day. They were sufficiently familiar to audiences at the Globe for many of his characters to allude to them. Lear, for example, is told by Kent of 'a reeking post / Stewed in his haste, half breathless, panting forth' (II, iv, 29–30). And Cassio tells Othello that the Duke 'requires your haste-post-haste appearance / Even on the instant' (I, ii, 37–8). ('Haste-post-haste', written on the back of many letters, may be self-explanatory; but for the benefit of any post-boy who could not read, the need for urgency was better and more commonly conveyed with an alternative mark – of a hanged man on the gallows.) The role of travelling post-boys as purveyors of local gossip was already familiar, too. The ecclesiastical historian and celebrated Elizabethan preacher John Foxe referred in one sermon to a contemporary proverb: 'posts bare truth in their letters and lyes in their mouthes'.[29]

However much private letters came to be accepted on the Elizabethan Post Roads, there could as yet be no question of the Crown asserting control of the service in practice. The daily business of the Posts – with the labelling of the packets, the accounting for horses and stables and guides, and the despatch of cash wages to deputy postmasters across the length of the country – was already enormously complex; perhaps only

* The best-known son to inherit the office is the postmaster of Scrooby, a Nottinghamshire village just south of Doncaster on the North Road. William Brewster succeeded his father in 1590 and remained the postmaster there until 1607. He owes his fame, however, to what he did next. As a Separatist Puritan, he left Scrooby for Amsterdam in 1608. Twelve years later he sailed to the New World on the *Mayflower* and became one of the founders of the Plymouth Colony. (See entry in *Oxford DNB*.)

the Admiralty and the Treasury faced greater accounting challenges. Only when there were clear benefits for the defence of the realm that coincided with practical possibilities did Elizabeth's officials make a concerted attempt to move towards a de facto monopoly of postal business. With a self-consciously Protestant monarchy in perpetual fear of invasion by Catholic arms from the Continent, and of insurrection fomented on instructions from abroad, any private posts travelling the short Road linking the capital to the Channel were of obvious concern. So the Strangers' Post had had its day: the lingering air of crisis in the post-Armada years was simply incompatible with such an operation. City merchants had their own commercial reasons, too, for wanting to be rid of the Fleming postmasters, who had been accused too often of giving their compatriots at home an unfair advantage by running a subtly 2nd class post for English letters. In 1591, a Royal Proclamation set up a monopoly over foreign courier services and handed it to the rival Merchant Adventurers. One of the oldest and most powerful bodies in the City, based for generations past on a monopoly of the export trade in wool, the Merchant Adventurers were chartered by the Crown and could be relied upon as a proxy for government control over the Dover Road – at least until the anxious years of the 1590s were past. Thereafter the Merchant Adventurers' authority waned, and their courier-service monopoly with it; but a start had been made in the direction of a Royal Mail, solely responsible for all the mails of England.

Taking the idea any further was going to need gifted leadership from the centre, which was not on offer after Randolph's demise. His successor was John Stanhope, a long-serving member of the Elizabethan parliament who was appointed Master of the Posts in 1590. Stanhope extended the North Road from Berwick to Edinburgh but always had to contend with a chronic shortage of funds for the established network. He seems in any case to have been less interested in developing the Posts than in finding creative ways to fleece them. This mostly consisted of extracting various fees from postmasters in exchange for their enjoyment of a Crown salary. His 'royal patent', reaffirmed by James I in 1603 as a grant to him and his son Charles jointly, gave the Stanhopes huge discretion over the finances of the Posts, and they made the most of it. The outcome illustrates why Stuart patents provoked such a deep popular resentment in the years ahead. Little was done to improve the general administration of the Posts, and no further serious thought was given to the underlying tension, which the 1583 regulations had at least begun to address, between the handling of official packets and the carriage of by-letters. Various opaque orders were issued from time to time, which in their ambiguity only confirmed what a muddle now prevailed. An order of 1609, for example, decreed: 'No pacquets or letters shall be sent by the Posts or bind any Post to ride therewith but those on our Special affairs.' But no one can have supposed by this date that by-letters could be abolished. Perhaps the order was merely intended to remind postmasters they were under no legal obligation to accept them. The general upkeep of the Post Roads languished through James's reign, and the upkeep of the postmasters too. In the years after 1617, payment of their state wages became increasingly erratic. This prompted the emergence of what might almost be described as the first postal trade union. A postmaster at Crewkherne, Thomas Hutchins, stepped forward as a tenacious spokesman for many of the stations along the West Road. He organized two petitions to the King's Privy Council, in 1618 and 1619, requesting payment of wages that had fallen seriously into arrears. When Stanhope senior died in 1621, the son promptly treated his succession to the patent as a cue for demanding fresh signing-on fees from the postmasters. This provoked another petition from Hutchins, in 1622, which was referred to a special sub-committee of the Council. The outcome a year later was an official report that made worthwhile concessions to the postmasters – only for Hutchins to find himself consigned to the Marshalsea prison four months later. He was not held there for long, but after his release pursued a series of grievances that left him feuding with the authorities for the next several years. His last petition to the Privy Council about the posts' arrears of wages was filed in 1631, at which date he was back in the Marshalsea. He died in 1633.[30]

More damaging for Stanhope junior than the venality of his family's day-to-day dealings with the postmasters was a losing battle that he triggered over the foreign mail of the country's more prosperous merchants. This was a blatant attempt by the Stanhope family to regain a measure of control over the Dover Road, which by the 1620s had effectively been taken away from them. Stanhope senior had used the patent confirmed in 1603 to take over the Merchant Adventurers' de facto monopoly of both official and private postal business with the Continent – increasingly now described as the 'Foreign Post' – but had subsequently delegated responsibility for it to Mathew De Quester, a Flemish native of Bruges. De Quester had done so well at the job that, much to the Stanhope family's dismay, James had given him his own patent in 1619 to run the Foreign Post independently of the 'Inland' business, cutting back the Stanhopes' patent accordingly. (This was the origin of a split between the Foreign and Inland Posts that was to last until the 1830s.) The Stanhopes and De Quester had squabbled bitterly ever since. In the first year of Charles I's reign, 1626, a legal feud erupted between them which attracted the attention of the King's Principal Secretary of State, John Coke. When this powerful man took a close look at the workings of the Dover Road, he soon drew two momentous conclusions. The first was that only a full statutory monopoly for the King's Posts to and from the Channel could assure the Privy Council of the controlling hand that he thought self-evidently desirable. Otherwise, as he asked rhetorically in a letter of 1627 to one of the Privy Councillors, how could they keep track 'of that which passeth by letters in or out of the land if every man may convey letters under the covers of merchants to whom and what place he pleaseth'?[31] His second conclusion was that the Foreign Post appeared to have been successfully run since 1619 as a business that might profitably be expanded. De Quester accepted private letters for the royal mailbag. But each letter was charged a fee, which instead of being pocketed directly by the recipient – like the fees on inland by-letters – had to be passed back to De Quester's own office in London. On this basis, De Quester had strikingly reduced the net cost of the Foreign Post. Indeed, he had even made a profit. Here was another compelling rationale for establishing a monopoly. By an order in Council of 1628, Coke appointed De Quester as the 'Postmaster of England for Foreign Parts' – and the carriage of all foreign letters, whether official or unofficial, by any other parties was formally prohibited.

Did Coke see lessons to be drawn here for the future management of the Inland Post too? It seems highly likely. The latter had by now been expanded from five Roads to six, with the addition of a laid post from Norwich to London via Colchester. But the whole network was clearly beset with problems. Financially, it was hardly a massive burden to the Crown: within a few years of Charles's accession, it was costing £4,125 a year. (By way of comparison, the cost of escorting a royal bride, Henrietta Maria of France, from Paris to London in 1625 had been £35,986.[32]) Nonetheless, it appears to have grated with officials that it was drawing on the Crown's resources instead of adding to them; it was also an administrative embarrassment, insofar as Stanhope junior on the Crown's behalf evidently lacked the organizational resources to run it. One result was that too many salaries were going astray. The salaried postmasters of England sent in a petition in 1628, describing themselves as 'in number 99 poore men', some of whom 'lye now in prison, and many of the rest daily threatened to bee arrested by reason of their great debts'. Some of them were still petitioning for wage arrears nearly a decade later.[33] Above all, the original rationale for the founding of the Roads had been overtaken by the natural evolution of the service. Post-masters were now poorly paid (if that) for dealing with official letters that were supposedly their priority – and were still to be carried by them at no charge per letter – while private letters that had no official status were probably accounting for most of their income. The same of course was true for the post-boys. It was demanding a saintly forbearance or superhuman attendance to duty to expect that any post-boy would give (unpaid) official packets a priority over (cash-paid) by-letters. How to reform an increasingly anomalous system of remuneration was becom-ing a matter of some urgency.

Various proposals were put forward by enterprising postmasters outside London. One scheme for a self-financing private postal service on the West Road – organized by a City merchant, Samuel Jude – even seems to have won the backing of the King's Privy Council in 1629. Remarkably, the Council outlined the scheme in a long letter to the mayors of Salisbury, Exeter and Plymouth, explaining that its propo-nents had put it forward 'for the better despatch of His Majesty's service and the common good of all others'. The mayors were told that Jude and his associates had the Council's blessing:

> And therefore for their better encouragement and cheerful proceedings in
> the execution of this said undertaking we do heartily entreat the addressees
> not only to permit the posts and their agents to address themselves to the
> execution of this service, but to be assisting them as occasion shall require.[34]

A contemporary reckoned that in 1630 around 25,600 letters were carried in and out of London under this scheme.[35] When Jude tried to expand his customer franchise in the City, however, many postmasters saw a threat to their own by-letter income. They objected to the Coun-cil, and the scheme was reined back. The scope for a radically fresh approach to the King's Posts had nonetheless been graphically illus-trated. What was needed was a solution that could be applied across the whole service. And at this point, just as had happened early in Henry VIII's reign when a fundamental review of the postal concept was needed, it was a man with detailed practical experience of the Contin-ental mails who took up the running. Thomas Witherings came from a well-connected Staffordshire family. We know nothing of his early car-eer, but by the late 1620s he had married well and was ranked prominently enough among City merchants to belong to one of its more exclusive circles, the Worshipful Company of Mercers. More pertinently, he had landed a position at Court as 'harbinger' to the young Queen Henrietta Maria. This required him to sort out accommodation and entertainment in advance, plus various other ancillary arrangements, whenever the Queen travelled. It happens that Henrietta Maria was one of the great letter writers of the age (indeed, her brief courtship with Charles had been conducted entirely by letter, ending with a marriage by proxy in Paris before she ever made that expensive journey across the Channel) so we can assume that assisting the Queen's couriers gave Witherings a good working knowledge of the postal network beyond Calais.[36] At any event, he must have proved his worth in the Queen's service because by the early 1630s he was one of two deputies helping De Quester to run the Foreign Post. In 1632, De Quester retired, after almost three decades in charge, and his patent received from James I was reassigned to his two deputies. Witherings soon bought out his partner, and before the year was out he had handed to Secretary Coke a detailed plan for the reorganization of the Foreign Post, which amounted to an overhaul of the whole operation.

Coke endorsed it, and within a very short time it would lead to a dramatic reduction in the number of days needed to bring letters from Antwerp and other Continental cities via Calais and Dover to London.[37] It must quickly have been apparent to Coke that Witherings was an exceptional individual. He was no aristocrat, and jealous rivals (notably his erstwhile partner) in due course would be quick to denigrate him as a 'homebred shopkeeper without languages', but his drive and regard for detail evidently persuaded Coke to back him as the man to lead a reform of the Posts not just on the Dover Road but across the other five Roads as well.[38] The two men worked closely together over the next few years. Indeed, modern scholars have sometimes been at odds over which of them to acclaim as the 'Father of the Post Office'. Whichever took the lead, the significance of their combined achievement is not in doubt). Coke and Witherings between them built the foundations for everything that followed. The first blueprint for the domestic Post was laid out, by one or the other (it was left unsigned), in 1633. Most historians have attributed it to Witherings.[39] In a fundamental break with the past, it proposed that a fixed scale of charges be set out for all private letters handled on the Post Roads. Letters sent north from London, for example, would be carried for 2d to Yorkshire. The standard rates would apply to 'single' letters consisting of just one sheet of paper. Two sheets, a 'double letter', would cost 4d. Letters to Scotland would cost 8d.[40] Payment would be due from the addressee, though those sending letters would always be free to pay in advance if they wished (and were sufficiently trusting of the service). Above all – this was the critical point – postmasters would no longer pocket the fees paid for private mail, but would be charged with remitting them back to a 'Letter Office' in London. No money would be retained locally, beyond a penny charge for deliveries from post towns to adjacent villages. Some preliminary arithmetic was based on 512 post towns handling fifty private letters a week. At a recommended average 'post rate' of 4d a letter, this would generate £426 a week, which would be enough to pay for all the running costs of the network, even after deducting £1,500 a year to pay directly for the conveyance of the Crown's official packets. It would also (this was left unsaid) leave a tidy sum for those at the head of the Letter Office.

Persuading all postmasters to abandon their income from by-letters, though, would be a prodigious undertaking – not least because they would at the same time be asked to rely on the promise of salaries paid out by the new Letter Office as part of a national administration. It must have been almost as hard to envisage how this might work in the England of the early 1630s as half a century earlier. But none of this deterred Coke and Witherings for long. A couple of years passed while Witherings pinned down the gains – probably in every sense – made through his work with the Foreign Post. Then, in June 1635, there appeared a second remarkable document. It was entitled 'Proposition for settling staffets or packet posts betwixt London and all parts of His Majesties dominions for the carrying and recarrying of His subjects letters'. (The reference to 'staffets' echoes the adoption by Witherings for the Foreign Post of mounted couriers, originally *staffeto* in Italian, who travelled day and night between stations on the Continent.) It elaborated on the unsigned 1633 plan, setting down suggested charges for deliveries along all six main Post Roads and even targeting journey times. Prices would rise commensurately with the distance to be covered, starting at 2d for a single letter up to eighty miles and rising to 8d for delivery to Scotland. All letters would pass through London, and the paper described a basic sorting system for arranging the portmanteau bags – or 'portmantles' as they were usually described – that would be carried away from the capital and back. Bags delivered to post towns could include small bags for nearby county towns, which in turn would have still smaller bags to be taken out to market towns by local foot-posts. Once set in place, as the author rather excitedly suggested, the resulting Post (sic) would be 'a thing above all things observed by all other nations'.[41]

In essence, Witherings – if we can assume him to have been the author once again – was proposing to extend across England the postal practices he had so impressively engineered between London and the Low Countries. The June 1635 paper's objectives were astonishingly ambitious, perhaps unrealistically so, but Coke must once again have voiced his full support. The scheme may to some extent have originated with him. An undated 9½-page draft paper exists in the archive of state papers for 1635, entitled 'Orders for a Letter Office for missives within the Land', which in many respects duplicates the content of the June plan. Its authorship, like that of the other two papers, is open to question and Coke may have written it himself.[42] But whatever his contribution, it was Coke as Principal Secretary of State who must have seen to the final details of a Royal Proclamation of 31 July 1635 which authorized 'the Settling of the Letter-Office of England and Scotland' and the maintenance of six Post Roads. If a day had to be chosen as the founding date of the Royal Mail, this would be it.* Of course, if postmasters were to forgo their entitlement to cash payment on the spot, it followed as night the day that the Royal Mail would have to operate as a monopoly: the state could hardly base its organization of the Post Roads on the collection of standard charges, and then allow others to compete by lower prices. So there would be no room for unofficial rivals: 'his Majesty upon complaint thereof made will cause a severe exemplary punishment to be inflicted upon such delinquents'. As for who should run it, 'his Majesty doth hereby charge and comaund all Justices of Peace Mayors Sheriffs Bayliffs Constables head boroughes and all other his Officers and Ministers whatsoever to be ayding and assisting to the said Thomas Witherings . . .'[43]

3. A GENERAL POST OFFICE

Witherings' appointment cut across the royal patent still held by the younger Stanhope, and it was not until March 1637 that the King received a formal acknowledgement from Stanhope that he had agreed

---

* By what appears to have been a coincidence, Sweden's Royal Postal Agency was established at more or less the same moment. Its official founding date is traditionally given as 1636.

to step aside ('full sore against his will, but in obedience to his Majesty's pleasure').[44] Charles appointed Coke and another of his Secretaries, Sir Francis Windebank, as 'Masters and Comptrollers-General of the Posts'. Five months after Stanhope's retreat, in August 1637, Coke wrote in a letter to his son: 'Your letters come sometimes late. I hope that will, by Mr Witherings' posts, be amended. For we, the Postmasters General, have made him our deputy, that he may the better accommodate his letter office'.[45] Witherings' position appears to have been for life, but English politics in the years before the Civil War were not conducive to the smooth running of life-time appointments. Witherings was a commoner with sole control of a patent of potentially enormous influence and value – and possibly also someone whose Royalist sympathies were by 1640 insufficiently robust in the eyes of the King. His champion, Secretary Coke, fell from power at the age of nearly eighty in February of that year, and six months later Witherings was removed for 'divers abuses and misdemeanors'. His five years in office were rarely less than stormy throughout. In the words of one leading authority on the early Stuarts, his tenure exemplified 'the gap [under Charles I's personal rule] between good intentions and sound execution, that no-man's-land mined with envy, self-interest, factional intrigue and snobbery'.[46] He persevered successfully enough, however, to ensure the seed of a 'General Post Office' was planted before the full onset of the Civil War.

The Letter Office was set up in November 1635, at Witherings' own house in Sherbourne Lane, as a collection point for private letters. Its existence there was advertised, and experimental deliveries were launched on the North Road.* Letters were sent off to Edinburgh – and replies were received back in London within six days. This suggests a rather exceptional effort had been made, for letters from Edinburgh in future would generally take five days or more to reach London. Those from Chester and Plymouth would need about two full days, and those from Bristol a little over one. The distances across the network, in short, were still daunting: riding times had improved very little since Tudor days. Over the next two years, work went ahead to arrange for the weekly despatch (and receipt) of mails on all six main Post roads, with by-posts taking letters on to at least some adjacent county towns. Some of the resulting arrangements can be construed from a document – 'Orders for the

---

* It remained in Sherbourne Lane for two years and was relocated within the City in 1637. It may have moved a few times in the next twenty years, but no clear chronology of dates and addresses has ever been satisfactorily established.

furtherance of our service, as well as to our Pacquets and Letters, as for riding in Post . . .' – which was submitted to the King by Coke and Windebank and signed by him in July 1637.[47] Internally, a strict administration was enforced. Labels had to be attached to packets, for example, noting arrival and despatch times: all letters, in effect, were registered. Every postmaster had to deliver the letters arriving from London 'either at or neere his Stage', in exchange for payment of the postage fee scribbled on them (unless, that is, they were marked as 'Post Paid'). And detailed cash ledgers had to be maintained, noting payments received and sent to London. Such measures allowed for a gradual rise in the volume of mail without the finances being reduced to chaos. Externally, the resentment of those along the Roads who had lost the right to run private mails was gradually overcome; but it has to be wondered how those postmasters living far from the Roads, who had never received much support from a local council and were unlikely ever to do so, adjusted to the new ban on taking letters for a fee. Presumably some turned their back on the King's Post; others went on offering their services surreptitiously; and others again resigned themselves to a largely unpaid role as the local postman, which could be treated as a useful appendage to hiring out horses or running an inn for a living.

The only remaining layer of legal competition for the Post rested by 1637 with those who had been the very first to offer a delivery network of any kind, the common carriers, but once a government-backed national network began to be established, their eclipse was inevitable – whatever the proud claims of *The Carriers Cosmography*. In the year of its publication, postmasters complained bitterly to Witherings about the continuing activities of carriers in competition with the Letter Office, and the result was the beginning of a gradual squeeze on their activities. The carriers' services were not in fact prohibited outright: they would rumble on across the country for another couple of centuries, and in the capital particularly they would flourish as and when the demand for letter deliveries far outran the resources of the Post Office. But the carriers were now burdened with strict rules on the timing of their collections and deliveries. A letter delivered (legally) by common carrier would have to travel, more or less, at cart speed – for a carrier to convey letters separately or in advance of his cart would be illegal. Given the state of England's farm-track roads, no one in 1637 could imagine any wheeled vehicle ever being a threat to deliveries by foot post, never mind a post-boy on horseback. Further legal constraints were added in later years. In Charles II's reign, the carriers were barred from taking

letters unrelated to other goods being carried at the same time, and in
1711 were obliged to give up charging for any letters at all.

Documentary records covering the early growth of the royal monopoly are thin. We have just one extant letter from Witherings, written to
the mayor of Hull in January 1636. Revealingly, it is concerned with a
failure to abandon the use of private mails. Reminding the mayor of the
King's command that a new monopoly Post be run 'day and night
betwixt the Cittie of London and Edenbrough and diverse other by
parts upon this Road as particularly to your Towne of Hull', the letter
is a none-too-gentle warning of trouble ahead unless the town's officials
toe the line. Indignantly, he points out to the mayor that the 1635 Royal
Proclamation has explicitly required the punishment of any 'delinquents' who ignore the new monopoly arrangements:

> ... instead of w[hi]ch punishment I find you that are Magistrats ... hath
> in your owne particulars continually sent and received letters by ordinary
> posts Contrary to his Ma[jes]t[i]es proclamac[i]on and instead of punishing
> the same have supported them as may appear plainely by your own actions
> in receiveing and delivering letters to the said posts w[hi]ich weekly continue
> to goe and come betwixt your towne and the Cittie of London ... a record
> of w[hi]ch I am bound particularly to inform [the Privy Council] ... except
> by this bearer my honoured friend I shall receive a satisfaciall answere not
> by words but in deeds.[48]

We can suppose the letter to be characteristic of those Witherings must
have sent out by the score at this time, and it suggests he was not shy of
exerting his new-found authority. (For a transcript of the entire text, see
Appendix C.)

Few letters have survived at all from the main period of open hostilities
between 1642 and 1648, and fewer still that bear any mark (such as a
postage fee due) to link them overtly to the new Letter Office. Important
individuals on both sides of the fighting unsurprisingly used their own
private messengers (even then, many resorted – as did Queen Henrietta
Maria – to the use of secret codes, so likely was it that their letters would
be intercepted) and we have to presume that sustaining any kind of public
post must have been extremely difficult in many parts of the country.
How, for example, could postmasters have kept horses at the ready, where
the land was being scoured for cavalry reinforcements? Some have argued
that the Post was virtually defunct through most of the 1640s.[49] But this
view is hard to square with the fact that interminable inquiries, lawsuits
and political feuds at Westminster are lavishly documented from 1640 to

Thomas Witherings' letter to the Mayor of Hull, January 1636

1644, and again from 1649 until 1655, showing how various individuals vied for the right to run the Inland Letter Office or the Foreign Post. When Charles in 1644 gave instructions for a rival Royalist post to be set up, based on Oxford and the port of Weymouth, he ordered letters to be taxed 'according to the rules of the Letter Office'.[50] In fact, as this suggests, the Inland Post was still operating under Parliament's control from London – we do not know its precise location – and it was even beginning by this late stage of the war to reassert some semblance of order along key stretches of the network, including the Dover Road. The individual charged by Parliament with running the Post from 1644 was a prominent Parliamentarian, Edmond Prideaux, who replaced many postmasters with supposed Royalist sympathies by new men avowing loyalty to Parliament's cause. By the end of the fighting Prideaux had managed to restore 'weekly services throughout England' and was even rumoured to be turning a handsome profit on them, which would help explain a furious jockeying for control of the Posts from 1649 onwards, and for postmaster positions too.[51] Modern studies have generally concluded that life for the post stations went on, 'disrupted and weakened though not totally destroyed by the Civil War'.[52]

The decade-long conflict brought some respite but little peace for Thomas Witherings. After a two-year investigation by Parliament, and at least one brief imprisonment, he won reinstatement as head of the Foreign Letter Office in 1642, or at least recovered a significant influence over its activities. He seems to have clung on to this through all the vicissitudes of the later 1640s and may even have regained a measure of control over the Inland Office by acting as an adviser to Prideaux. But his spirited championing of the 1635 Proclamation appears to have made him many enemies. He had to defend himself against repeated and increasingly serious charges of sympathizing with Royalists in the last few years of the decade, and the strain evidently took its toll on his health. In June 1651, court charges were brought 'That he is very familiar with delinquents, stands bound for them, conceals their letters, and conveys letters and intelligence to them beyond seas'.[53] He was acquitted in July, but two months later collapsed and died on his way to church at his estate at Hornchurch, Essex. He was buried there, and a memorial tablet inside the church today honours the memory of 'Thomas Witherings Esq. Chiefe Postmaster of Greate Britaine'. But the Civil War had sadly eclipsed his achievement in organizing the first public Post, and deprived him of any great posthumous reputation: Witherings was not deemed worthy by the late Victorians of an entry in their *Dictionary of National Biography*.[54]

In the aftermath of the war, there were isolated attempts to resurrect the idea of private posts in competition with the Inland and Foreign Letter Offices. Prideaux made short work of them on the ground – sometimes resorting to violence in the process – and kept a ruthless eye on the reviving operations of the postmasters' network. As its effective head until 1653, he restored the Road to Ireland via Chester and Holyhead, and arranged posts to various other towns at Parliament's behest.[55] But a succession of parliamentary reviews and committees under the Commonwealth between 1650 and 1653 nonetheless deliberated painstakingly over the future of the Post. Lengthy consideration was even given to legalistic pleas from various individuals who claimed the right to be appointed as its head. The son and widow of Witherings both put in claims, as did various assignees of both Witherings and his old rival Charles Stanhope. Eventually, against Prideaux's wishes and not without an intervention on more than one occasion by Oliver Cromwell himself, Parliament's councils reasserted the monopoly power of the Post and decided to auction control over it to the highest bidder. It was 'farmed out' in 1653 – or, as we might say today, outsourced – to a man called John Manley, who paid a substantial annual sum up front in exchange for the profits he could reap from the Post over a set period of two years.

Unfortunately, Manley was a figure of little weight at Westminster. His contract was soon the target of acrimonious challenges, and he had to appeal to Parliament in January 1654 to help him uphold the monopoly he had been promised. By this point, Cromwell had become Lord Protector – and his Principal Secretary of State, John Thurloe, had begun to rely on regular interception of private letters for intelligence purposes. At Cromwell's direct instigation, the Post's governance was briskly reviewed yet again. As a result, Manley's two-year contract was confirmed, but new and much more detailed regulations were set out by the governing council of the Protectorate for the future administration of the 'General Post Office'. An Executive Ordinance of September 1654 laid down a host of working details, from the geography and administration of the Post Roads to the structure and levels of postal charges. A notable feature of the Ordinance was its confirmation of an earlier suggestion by Parliament in 1652 that all letters sent by MPs should go free of charge – a practice soon known as 'franking'. Every opportunity was also taken to underline the monopoly status of the Posts. The great appeal of this for the Commonwealth was at least as much political as financial: control of the Posts was seen as key to the security of the Protector's realm. Private instructions had been sent out to all postmasters nine months earlier, stressing this point. Nor was their contribution to the safety of the state to be restricted to their handling of the mails. Postmasters were enjoined: 'Have an eye upon the disaffected who live near you: observe their meetings and conversations'.[56] Six months after the 1654 Ordinance, having acknowledged the significance of the Post Office to the Government, the council took the logical step of awarding control over it to Cromwell's Secretary of State: Manley's successor would be John Thurloe himself, 'for such tyme as His Highness [i.e. Cromwell] with the councell's desire shall think fitt'. Two years later, in 1657, a Postage Act was passed by Parliament that formally confirmed all of these arrangements. It was the very first postal statute:

> Whereas it hath been found by experience, That the Erecting and Setling of one General Post-Office, for the speedy Conveying, Carrying, and Re-carrying of Letters by Post, to, and from all Places within England, Scotland, and Ireland, and into several parts beyond the Seas, hath been, and is the best means, not onely to maintain a certain and constant Intercourse of Trade and Commerce betwixt all the said Places, to the great benefit of the People of these Nations, but also to Convey the Publique Dispatches, and to discover and prevent many dangerous, and wicked Designs, which have been, and are daily contrived against the Peace and Welfare of this Commonwealth, the Intelligence whereof cannot well be Communicated, but by Letter of Escript.
>
> There shall be one generall Post Office One Officer stiled Postmaster Generall of England and Comptroller of the Post Office; He shall have the sending of all Letters & Pacquets. [57]

The Act is duly credited as marking the point at which 'the inland and foreign posts had been reunited, reorganized, regulated and placed firmly under government control ...'[58]

The intelligence-gathering mission of the new General Post Office, we can be sure, was actively pursued from the start. Over 200 years later, in the 1890s, a scholar working on private papers from the reign of Charles II discovered a previously unknown account of Secretary Thurloe's intelligence service during the Protectorate. It included a colourful description of a night's work at the Letter Office:

> In the time of the Rump [Parliament], before Cromwell made himselfe Protector, they constantly sent for all the letters to Whitehall, and had every letter opened before them without ceremony; but when Cromwell came to governe he employed one Mr Dorislaus to reside constantly at the [Letter

AN ACT
FOR THE
SETLING
OF THE
POSTAGE
OF
ENGLAND,
SCOTLAND and IRELAND.

Hereas it hath been found by experience, That the Erecting and Setling of one General Post-Office, for the speedy Conveying, Carrying, and Re-carrying of Letters by Post, to, and from all Places within England, Scotland, and Ireland, and into several parts beyond the Seas, hath been, and is the best means, not onely to maintain a certain and constant Intercourse of Trade and Commerce betwixt all the said Places, to the great benefit of the People of these Nations, but also to Convey the Publique Dispatches, and to discover and prevent many dangerous and wicked Designes, which have been, and are daily contrived against the Peace and Welfare of this Common-

A 2   wealth,

Title page of Cromwell's 1657 Act establishing the 'General Post-Office'

Office], who had a private roome allotted him adjoyning to the forreigne
Office, and every post night about 11 a clock he went into that roome
privately, and had all the letter[s] brought and layd before him, to open any
as he should see good, and close them up again, and there he remained in
that room, usually till about 3 or 4 in the morning, which was the usuall
time of shutting up the male, and in processe of time the said Dorislaus had
got such a knowledge of all hands and seals, that scarcely could a letter be
brought him but he knew the hand that wrote it; and when there was
any extraordinary occasion, as when any rising was neare or the like, then
S. Morland [one of Thurloe's secretaries] went from Whitehall between 11
and 12, and was privately conveighed into that roome, and there assisted
Mr Dorislaus, and such letters as they found dangerous he brought back
with him to Whitehall in the morning.[59]

Contemporaries were marvelling by the third year of Thurloe's Post-
mastership at the efficiency of his spy network. Henry Cromwell, the
fourth son of the Protector and de facto ruler of Ireland from 1655,
wrote to his father's Secretary of State: 'Really it is a wonder you can
pick so many locks leading into the hearts of wicked men as you do'.[60]
He might have been less amazed, had he spent a night or two in the
Inland Letter Office watching the letters being opened and re-sealed by
Mr Dorislaus. Here was one consequence of the Post's emergence as a
state-run monopoly. A second and more serious one lay ahead, with the
return of the Stuart monarchy.

2

A network for the nation,
1660–1764

Dear Father and Mother,
... As I may not have opportunity to send again soon, and as
I know you keep my letters, and read them over and over ... and
as it may be some little pleasure to me to read them myself,
when I am come to you, to remind me of what I have gone
through . . .: for all these reasons I will write as I have time, and
as matters happen, send the scribble to you as I have opportunity; and if I do not every time, in form, subscribe as I ought, I am
sure you will always believe that it is not for want of duty ...

I am, &c. [Pamela Andrews]
From Samuel Richardson, *Pamela: or Virtue Rewarded*
(1740), Letter XX

I. POSTAL PLOTS AND CASH FOR THE CROWN

The night life in Cromwell's Letter Office was described for Charles II
in a report with no signature. But there is general agreement today that
the author was a rare maverick called John Wildman. Born in 1623,
Wildman was a shadowy presence close to the centre of English politics
through five decades. His life story, pieced together only half a century ago,
embraced various careers as lawyer, soldier, philosopher, politician –
and Postmaster General.[1] His connection with the Post Office casts
some light on its mixed record, over the next several decades, at grappling with the bold vision of its pre-Civil War founders.

Wildman's real métier from first to last was political skulduggery. He
had the possibly unique distinction in the seventeenth century of being
involved in plots against not just Charles I *and* Cromwell, but Charles II,

James II and William III as well. It was alleged during his lifetime, not
implausibly, that in his twenties Wildman had been one of the two
masked and heavily disguised executioners who greeted Charles I on
the scaffold in 1649 – a good story sadly dismissed by a recent scholar
as 'baseless'.[2] An agitator and prominent republican thereafter, and a
leading figure in the Levellers movement within the army, he played a
notable part in the debates over the future of the Commonwealth and
was more than once an outspoken critic of Cromwell. ('He deserves to
be hanged' was the Great Protector's view afterwards.) He spent sixteen
months in the Tower of London for his complicity in a Leveller plot
against Cromwell unearthed in 1655, but then served as one of Secretary Thurloe's agents in the later 1650s before aligning himself just in
time with the Royalist cause in exile. After the Restoration, Wildman
was quick to present Charles II with his credentials as an authority on
state security. This was his motive for writing the report that looked
back at the Protector's methods. It was called *A brief discourse concerning the businesse of intelligence and how it may be managed to the best
advantage*. Its author was categorical with his advice: '... [a] great
intrigue of Cromwell was carefully to watch the Generall letter Office,
and it very much concerns the publick peace that the same be done
now ...'[3] Suspicious letters on their way in or out of London had been
regularly intercepted at the Post Office, as one of the best ways of keeping track of potential miscreants. Nevertheless Wildman now also
suggested this approach was 'but to shoot at rovers' and he had a better
idea. Common carriers and foot posts in and around the City should be
licensed, he thought, and 'a fit person be chosen to take knowledge' of
their activities on behalf of the Crown. He was at the King's disposal.

Wildman had a ready audience for his views. The Restoration era
was never short of conspiracies, real or imagined. By the middle of the
summer of 1660 Wildman had emerged as a crucial figure in discussions
over the future of the Post Office. He owed his influence in this context
to more than just the lessons he could share of a shady past: he had also
become wealthy from the profits on speculative trading in Royalists'
estates seized during the Interregnum. As soon as it was clear that the
existing structure and governance of the Post Office would be retained
in all essentials – and months before the legislation to this effect
was passed, as the Post Office Act (or 'Charter') of December 1660 –
Wildman set about acquiring control of the whole organization. John
Thurloe had been relieved of his authority even before the return of the
monarchy. Responsibility for the Post Office was being passed from one

unsatisfactory manager to another. Cromwell's Secretary of State, like Manley before him, had paid £10,000 a year for the contractual right to gather in postal revenues as his own. In a fresh auction, Wildman was ready to table a substantially higher figure to acquire this 'farm'. He teamed up with a former soldier called Henry Bishop, an accomplice in more than one hare-brained Royalist plot over the 1650s, who was now living as a respectable member of the Sussex gentry. It was Bishop's name that was put forward as the formal office holder; but it was Wildman who bankrolled all or most of their successful bid, offering to pay £21,500 a year for seven years. The office was granted them within weeks and there is no reason to doubt, in the words of his biographer, that Wildman 'was in fact, if not in name, the first Restoration Postmaster General'.[4] The Charter of December 1660 – drawn up, like other instruments of the Restoration, by the Convention Parliament under the guidance of Edward Hyde, later Earl of Clarendon – largely reaffirmed the arrangements put in place by the (now null and void) 1657 Postage Act. It opened the way for development of the Post Office to continue. There was complete endorsement, for example, of the policy of extending 'constant posts for the carriage of letters to all places, though they lie out of the post roads, as hath been used for the space of three years last past'.[5] Such matters, though, were probably not of much interest to Wildman or his partner. Bishop's name was attached to an important innovation, as we shall see, but it is unlikely he himself spent much time on it. In fact, control of the Post Office had been handed to two men who saw it as a ready source of income and a tool of political surveillance, but who had no very obvious interest in fostering any substantial improvements in the postal service itself.

Things went badly from the start. Bishop reduced the wages of the 300 or so postmasters in the country while demanding side-payments from them in exchange for confirming their jobs. He also brazenly required them to promise 'not to disclose the conditions they make with him' and extracted deposits that would be forfeited if they broke their word.[6] Complaints about his maladministration nonetheless started reaching government ministers before the year was out, and petitions from indignant postmasters continued into 1661. They were targeted not just at Bishop but at also Wildman, 'who puts in and out whom he pleases', as one postmaster observed. Among the clerks working in the General Letter Office, gossip about the wayward handling of the place by their new masters soon turned into reports of something more serious. There was talk of a republican conspiracy against the King involving several members of the Letter Office itself, meeting together regularly at a house in Covent Garden. One clerk in the Office made serious allegations against both men at the top. Bishop might seem innocuous enough, explained this informant in a submission to the Privy Council, but he 'is so absolutely under the dominion of Wildman (as well for purse as conduct) that he cannot be accounted Master [of] himself, much less of his office and that great trust thereby reposed in him . . .' The man plainly had an axe to grind – Bishop had just sacked him for fraud and negligence – and his charges were treated with due caution. But Wildman's personal history was well-known to the King's principal ministers. Clarendon in particular was deeply suspicious as to where his real loyalties lay. By the end of the year, the Government had been persuaded that Wildman was indeed implicated in a plot against the King. He was arrested and sent to the Tower, from where he had the temerity to apply for a writ of habeas corpus. But Clarendon had no intention of putting him on trial. Wildman was consigned in July 1662 to St Mary's Castle prison in the distant Scilly Isles, beyond the remit of any habeas corpus writ, and no term was fixed for his incarceration. In London, Henry Bishop was now on his own. Nine months later, and seemingly out of funds, he sold off the remaining four years of his lease on the Post Office farm and disappeared back to a simpler one in Sussex.[7]

It was an inauspicious renewal of the great General Post Office project. Coke and Witherings had launched the idea of a national monopoly, functioning as a self-standing enterprise that could safely be 'farmed out' to an enterprising administrator. The 1660–63 years did little to recommend this approach from the Office's point of view. On the other hand, the rents paid by Wildman and Bishop had underlined the potential value of the farm only too clearly. There had to be a possibility that a robust postal monopoly might eventually prove to be a lucrative business. By 1663 this had been fully grasped by Charles II and his brother, James, Duke of York, with fundamental consequences for the Post. The Cromwellians had been quick to seize on the monopoly's value as an aid to state security. The Stuarts remained ever mindful of this dimension, too, and Charles took a personal interest in it throughout his reign. (In 1664, for example, he famously gave his royal patronage to the inventor of 'an intelligence machine' that was apparently able to produce a perfect copy of any letter within a few minutes. It was the brainchild of Samuel Morland, the man cited in Wildman's paper as Mr Dorislaus's nocturnal accomplice. Morland was given his own private room at the Letter Office, where secret visitors would occasionally include the King.)

But they also pounced just as eagerly on the prospect of an annual cash windfall. Charles was ever alert to any potential stream of revenues that could help the Crown avoid total reliance on Parliament for its income. Within months of Bishop's departure, he and his brother James had secured control of the Post Office's finances for themselves. By an Act of Parliament in 1663, Charles arranged for all the 'yearly rents, issues and profits' of the Post Office to be assigned henceforth to his brother as private income. James then indulged in some characteristic behind-the-scenes scheming, which was far from transparent even to contemporaries at Court but left the Office under his effective control.* The position of Postmaster General was farmed for ten years in 1667 to the King's Secretary of State, Lord Arlington, for whom it can scarcely have been much of a priority. It was a convenient arrangement, leaving postal matters largely to the oversight of Arlington's brother, Sir John Bennet, and a deputy, Joseph Williamson, who among other duties was head of the Government's spy network. Then, in 1677, James discontinued the farming arrangement and simply made himself Postmaster General.

Financially, the restored Stuart monarchy's embrace of the Post Office was hardly a disaster. The service grew steadily and was impressively administered. The cash accounts for the Letter Office – at least to judge by the records surviving from 1672 onwards – were recorded meticulously. Cash paid on all inland and foreign letters was carefully tracked, whether collected at the Letter Office or remitted there by postmasters delivering letters all over the country; clerks and postmasters were paid their quarterly salaries on time; ships' masters handing in letters at the ports – under arrangements in place since the Ordinance of 1654 – were promptly paid by local postmasters, who were then reimbursed for forwarding the 'ship letters' to London. The earliest documents in the postal archives – aside from that letter sent to Hull by Thomas Witherings in 1636 – are testimony to these elaborate finances. They start with a record of postmasters' salaries, probably from the year after the Great Fire of

---

* Bishop sold his farm contract to an Irish Protestant called Daniel O'Neale, a soldier-adventurer who had commanded Prince Rupert's foot regiments at the Battle of Marston Moor. It happens that O'Neale had just a few months earlier become the third husband of the Countess of Chesterfield. She was a confidante of the royal family and a close companion to the Duke of York's wife. How far this may have assisted O'Neale's emergence as Postmaster General, we can only surmise. But when he died less than a year later, his widow succeeded him and retained the farm for three years in her own name. The Countess was a formidable presence in Court circles – she was said to have turned down an offer of marriage in the 1630s from Van Dyck, the great Dutch painter and favourite of Charles I – but there is no evidence that she ever had much interest in the affairs of the Post Office.

miles	Stages	Postma[r] Names	Old Sallarys	Sallary accor[ding] to Derby[s]
16 single	Charinge crosse	Andrew Snape —	40: 00: 00	16: 00: 0
16 and 16	Stanes —	Humphry Gladyon	60: 00: 00	32: 00: 0
9: and 16	Hartford bridge	William Gowers —	40: 00: 00	25: 00: 0
10: and 24	Alton —	Mary Sibley —	70: 00: 00	78: 00: 0
— — —	Wm̃foster —	Richard Alcod —	— — —	— — —
14 and 10	East meane	Honory Bury —	100: 00: 00	52: 00: 00
14 and 14	Chicfoster —			
14 single	Portfmouth —	Robert Vyman —	30: 00: 00	14: 00: 00
— — —	Southampton	John Spooringe —	20: 00: 00	— — —
— — —	Jslewigh∫ —	George Newland	60: 00: 00	60: 00: 00
18: and 9	Bafingftoke	Richard Spittle —	40: 00: 00	27: 00: 00
16 and 19	Andouer —	John Hatzbano —	40: 00: 00	34: 00: 00
19 and 16	Salfbury —	Roger Bodbury —	40: 00: 00	35: 00: 00
16 and 19	Shafton —	Hugh fry — —⅛	96: 3: 7	
19: and 16	Crowkorne	John Ronciuill —	43: 00: 00	35: 00: 00
13: and 16	Showborno	John Hall — —	184: 00: 00	139: 00: 00
15: an: 19	Huniton & Chard			
20 and 15	Exotor — —	Geo: Brownonigo	160: 00: 00	99: 00: 0
24 and: 20	Afburton — —	William ford —	100: 00: 00	100: 00: 0
— — —	Cottnofs —	Mary Crueman —	10: 00: 00	— — —
— — —	Dartmouth —	John Lindfey —	20: 00: 00	— — —
— — —	Plymouth —	John Clarke —	270: 00: 00	12: 7: 0
			1423: 3: 7	894: 00: 0

Opening double-page of 'Roades, Salarys, Stages &c', 1667(?), listing the post towns on the Western Road to Plymouth and their incumbent postmasters, with a note of their former salaries and of those to be paid to them in the future

Sallary accordingr to Judgment		ſmrs
30: 00: 00	Viz 24ˡⁱ for ridingo and 6ˡⁱ ſ..m for Sendingo ſ..s horse oart po..t ma..ⁱ to the ſtird	30: 00: 00
50: 00: 00	Viz 48ˡⁱ for ridingo & 2ˡⁱ for bringingo the Malē quite thorough to the oſtir	50: 00: 00
37: 10: 00		37: 10: 00
70: 00: 00	to gaue downos oſt Hartford bridge to carry the Malē to Alton	70: 00: 00
————		
78: 00: 00		78: 00: 00
30: 00: 00	Viz for ridingo 21ˡⁱ and 9ˡⁱ for servicuomigo and vehiding the ſottvrſ	30: 00: 00
10: 00: 00		10: 00: 00
60: 00: 00		60: 00: 00
40: 00: 00		40: 00: 00
40: 00: 00		40: 00: 00
40: 00: 00		40: 00: 00
96: 3: 7	to continue at ..g on all ſettˡⁱ too & from Shaſton	100: 00: 00
43: 00: 00		43: 00: 00
184: 00: 00		100: 00: 00
60: 00: 00	Viz for ridingo 148ˡⁱ and 12ˡⁱ for ..g tˡⁱ..arrgo oſ his oſtir	60: 00: 00
100: 00: 00		100: 00: 00
5: 00: 00		5: 00: 00
20: 00: 00		20: 00: 00
70: 00: 00	Viz for ridingo 192ˡⁱ and 78 ſam allowed for the trargo	100: 00: 00
67: 13: 8	oſ his oſtir Viz a rlav ir, 3 ſett rarry and ſmiſelf	270
		1113: 10: 00

Opening page of Colonel Whitley's 'Book of Annual Payments', 1672, identifying the sums due not just to the Duke of York and various senior officials but also associates of the King, most notably his mistress, the Duchess of Cleveland

1666, entitled 'Roades, Salarys, Stages &c'. After that, the accounts for the years 1672–7 survive in ten volumes that comprise cash books, quarterly accounts, monthly records of charges against postmasters and 'The Book of Annual Payments', listing the Post Office's principal revenues and outgoings.[8]

Cash books were compiled annually thereafter. But Charles II and his brother left another, more problematic legacy. They set the institution on its way to being treated unambiguously as a ward of the Treasury, and a standing source of tax revenues. The process unfolded gradually across four reigns. Starting in the mid-1660s, it was at first just a matter of channelling net income from the Post Office into the royal coffers. But the sums at stake climbed quickly. The Book of Annual Payments was recording a yearly total by 1672 of £37,250, out of which £12,250 went to Arlington and other senior figures at the Post Office, leaving just under £20,000 a year for the Duke of York and just over £5,000 for the King – of which £4,700 went directly to his mistress, the Duchess of Cleveland. (The payments to Arlington were due to him as the owner of the farm, which made him in effect the sub-contractor in charge of the business.) By the 1680s, James was drawing on the Post's revenues for institutionalized annual handouts to family members and ministers alike: known as 'pensions', these had nothing to do with old age and everything to do with securing a cadre of close supporters at Court. After his accession in 1685, James passed the Postmaster General's office to the First Lord of the Treasury, the Earl of Rochester, and had the Post Office's income consigned to the Crown as part of its hereditary revenues. From then on, weekly financial statements had to be submitted to the Treasury, and any non-standard expenditure required formal authorization. James, meanwhile, went on disbursing royal pensions out of the profits, just as before. The late King's mistress went on receiving hers, for example, until her death in 1709.* By then, pensions drawn on the Post Office had multiplied alarmingly and were probably accounting for almost a quarter of its annual revenues: Queen Anne's consort husband, Prince George of Denmark, received £29,250 in 1703–4 alone.[9] That same year, the Treasury introduced accounting and auditing regulations for the Post Office known as 'Lord Godolphin's Instructions', in deference to Sidney Godolphin, the most powerful influence over the Government's finances then as for many years past, and a man 'who possessed an impeccable Tory ancestry and the conservative instincts of an accountant'.[10] All that remained was for the Treasury to make the final leap and assert the logic of a fiscal claim on postal revenues. The heavy cost of the War of the Spanish Succession provided the cue. Higher postage payments offered scope for a new tax that would be spectacularly easy to collect. Under the Post Office Act of 1711, letter rates were raised and the Post Office received a swingeing

* The Duchess of Cleveland's pension was inherited by the Duke of Grafton, her illegitimate son by Charles II. His heirs then went on collecting it out of Post Office profits until 1856, when it was commuted for the princely sum of £91,000 – equivalent to more than £6m today (see Howard Robinson, *The British Post Office: A History*, Princeton University Press, 1948, p. 79).

tax return. Henceforth, it would have to remit £700 a week to the Treasury, payable every Tuesday. The Government's handling of the Post Office thus exemplified, albeit on a tiny scale, that growing sophistication of public administration – and of fiscal arrangements in particular – which in the early eighteenth century was starting to underpin Britain's role as a leading military power in Europe.[11]

2. LOYAL SERVANTS, BOLD RIVALS AND A PENNY POST

The Stuart monarchy's inclination to think about the Post Office primarily as a source of cash or secret intelligence posed a challenge for those in charge of its day-to-day operations who were primarily intent on improving the postal service. They were the first to rue the disappearance of surplus earnings into the Treasury which they might have preferred to see invested in the service (a perennial regret in later centuries) The diversion of postal profits might have made a more serious dent in morale, but for a remarkable *esprit de corps* already evident among the fewer than sixty staff of the Letter Office. Many of them had already worked there for some years by 1660, and their expertise underpinned a continuing development of the Post Office which over the course of twenty years or so consolidated the separate operations of the Inland and Foreign departments and of the six Post Roads in impressive fashion. Nothing illustrates this achievement better than the career of James Hickes, who rose to a senior level and left behind a voluminous correspondence, full of wit and character. He first appears in the historical record in 1642, being abducted by five Roundhead troopers as he made his way into London carrying the Chester Road's post. He was briefly imprisoned until set free on the grounds that, as a Post Clerk, he was a servant of the House of Commons. He next surfaces a year later, organizing postal deliveries for Charles I, who sent him off to Weymouth to coordinate packet boats to France. He was appointed a Clerk in the reorganized Inland Letter Office in 1651 and would later claim to have settled the postal arrangements on the West Road to Bristol and from York to the North Road. After the Restoration, it was Hickes who was given responsibility for a review of the in situ postmasters and of the myriad demands for reinstatement by men claiming to have been dispossessed since 1642 by the King's enemies. Ever conscientious, he concluded that many were impostors, which resulted in far less upheaval to the network than contemporaries had feared. Like many of his colleagues, Hickes took a house very close to the Office – which by now was located at the heart of the City, in Threadneedle Street – in order to accommodate some unsociable working hours.[12] (More junior employees were given beds within the building.) He was soon confirmed as a Clerk, one of six who watched over the six Post Roads. His was once again the Chester Road, rated the most important – and busier even than the Dover Road – partly by virtue of carrying the Dublin mails; and in due course he had responsibility for the work of all the Clerks.

The system worked out by Hickes and his colleagues was to stay in place for more than a hundred years. Incoming mails arrived in the City on Mondays, Wednesdays and Fridays of each week. Starting around 5 a.m., all letters needed stamping with the amount due to the Post Office: it was the recipient, not the sender, who paid for postage. Stamped and sorted, they went to an 'alphabet man' who knew his ABC and could deal quickly and efficiently with those who called at the Office to collect their letters and pay for them. On Tuesdays, Thursdays and Saturdays it was the turn of the outgoing mails to be sorted. 'Window men' took in letters delivered to the Office or brought in by thirty or so 'letter carriers', who had collected them from eight stations run by 'receivers' and dotted at points west of the City via the Inns of Court to Covent Garden and Westminster. In a clever innovation introduced almost from the start of Charles II's reign, all letters were stamped with the date of their despatch day: this was the first recorded use anywhere of 'postage stamps' – or postmarks, as we would now call them.* Then Hickes and his fellow clerks reviewed all of the outward-bound letters individually, calculating the postage on them according to officially decreed rates tied to the distance of the address from London and the length of the letter (two-sheet letters paid a double rate, and additional charges could be levied by weight on anything heavier). Rates appear to have stayed at the levels introduced by the 1657 Act, at 2d on a single sheet for journeys up to eighty miles, 3d for longer distances and 4d to or from Scotland. The sums due were entered into a 'Road Book' and marked against the name of the country postmaster whose job it would be to collect the money from the recipient and return it to the Office in London. This work lasted from 6 p.m. in the evening until midnight. Then

---

* These first stamps were in fact known as Bishop marks, in deference to Henry Bishop, and would go on being used until 1787. 'Stamp collecting' was assured of a future from 19 April 1661, when the first letter appeared with a Bishop mark.

the doors of the Office were closed and the sorting of letters into mail-bags and 'portmantles' could begin. All bags were given their own labels – these would be completed by the postmasters with 'in' and 'out' times as the bags made their way along the Roads – and were finally handed to the post-riders for their journey to start. Generally all were seen off by about 2 a.m., which Hickes described as his usual time for going to bed. He and his colleagues, though, were often required by late-arriving mails from the Court and Whitehall to stay up an hour or two beyond that, arranging express riders to take the late packets on to the Roads in pursuit of the departed mails.

Such, in brief, was the daily business of the Office – always accompanied, we should not forget, by the activities of Dorislaus, Morland and their, opening and closing dozens of letters each night in their secret rooms. Hickes was of course a party to their work. Indeed, contemporaries referred to him as Joseph Williamson's agent inside the Post Office, and letters between the two of them – a principal source for our knowledge of the Office routines – make up much of Hickes's correspondence through the 1660s.[13] It was Williamson who instigated the Post Office's long relationship with the newspaper business, by having copies of the Government's official news sheet, the *London Gazette*, sent free of charge to postmasters, who could sell them for a penny. Selected postmasters also received confidential summaries of the juiciest bits of government news, collected and summarized by Hickes before being laboriously copied out and circulated. The Chester Road Clerk was plainly a remarkable man – and a brave one, too, to judge by the passages in his correspondence relating to the traumatic events of 1665 and 1666. First came the Great Plague, in the hot summer of 1665. There were fears that the contents of the mail might somehow be spreading the epidemic, so elaborate procedures were set up for letters to be sprinkled with vinegar in the Office and warmed over coal fires. Hickes memorably observed of his colleagues that the 'Post Office is so fumed morning and night that they can hardly see each other', wryly concluding: 'Had the contagion been catching by letters they had been dead long ago'. As it was, between twenty and thirty of his colleagues had died by the end of the outbreak – more than half of the Inland Office's complement. Then came the Great Fire of London in September 1666. Hickes monitored the progress of the flames from the Office in Threadneedle Street, remaining with his wife and children inside the building for as long as he dared and rescuing what papers he could. He penned a celebrated note to Williamson after escaping, explaining how he and his family had fled at 1 a.m., 'fearing lest they should be quite stopped up'.[14] Samuel Morland's intelligence machine had to be abandoned, never to be reconstructed – and whatever paper records had been accumulated since the 1630s must have burned with it. The Office was completely destroyed. Forwarding some salvaged state letters to Arlington's secretary, Hickes appended a forlorn note of his own: 'How we shall dispose of our business, only the wise God knows'.[15]

After Arlington took on the Postmaster Generalship in 1667, Hickes and his colleagues set up the Letter Office anew at a house in Bishopsgate. It was not to be a happy time for the Chester Road Clerk, who developed a cordial dislike of the man to whom Arlington delegated the running of the place, Sir John Bennet – a man of such consuming self-importance, as Hickes reported to Williamson, that when he entered the Bishopsgate premises, 'it is with such deportment and carriage that no King can exceed'.[16] In his letters to Williamson, Hickes kept up a lively commentary on his differences with Bennet, who seems to have regarded the entire clerical staff as easily replaceable:

> [Sir John] said he could have 40 [army] officers who wanted employment. Told him that blades with swords at their sides, and velvet jackets, would not do the business, as some had proved very rogues and cheats and were rooted out . . . Told him there was not a man in the office who did not deserve continuance and encouragement instead of reduction of salary, and that such severity would ruin the office.

After three years, Hickes apparently decided he had had enough and resigned his post – though not before leaving behind a memorable third-person picture of his last days in the Letter Office:

> Is hardly dealt with, as whatever care and pains he takes, it contributes not a candle, nor a cup of beer as formerly granted; and the taking away of these poor petty things is the present reward for the most considerable and advantageous service done. Writes all this to him [Williamson], as being the only person to whom he can unbosom himself . . . [H]is service is so severe that he has not two hours' rest between the post going out and coming in, and seldom has half an hour's sleep, by which means he is becoming decrepid and dropsical . . . [However] he will wait with patience; and if he die without consideration, it will be a comfort to know that he has discharged his duty faithfully in all hazards and hardships.

Hickes was far from the only distinguished servant of the Post in the twenty years or so after the Restoration. Colonel Roger Whitley, who

was a former private secretary to Charles II and ran the Office as Arlington's deputy in place of Bennet from 1672 to 1677, was briefly a Master
of the Posts in all but name. In addition to the Book of Annual Payments
and the cash accounts that have already been noted, Whitley took personal responsibility for the supervision by letter of all the postmasters in
the service. His surviving correspondence runs to six extraordinary volumes, transcribed into six volumes of typescript papers by the Post
Office a century ago.[17] On an almost daily basis, Whitley was busy chiding
(or berating) his deputies, often with a warmth and humour that suggests he was another engaging character. Thus on 12 August 1673, an
entirely typical day, we find him despatching twenty-two letters, some
to a standard format but most of them personal and quite lengthy.[18] The
recipients are based in Boston, Newcastle, Monmouth, Shaston, Daventry, Nantwich, Stone and Beckles. Many have incurred the Colonel's
displeasure:

> [To Boston:] 'To be plaine with you I doe not like your proceedings . . .'
> [To Shaston:] 'I will be noe longer disappointed by you, but will apply my
> selfe to other meanes, to recover my money . . .'
> [To Daventry:] 'I see the more civill I desire to be to you, the more you
> impose upon mee . . .'

The Letter Books throughout display a fine balance between Whitley's
decency towards postmasters struggling with their work and his powerful sense of duty, well illustrated in this one to a Mr Watts, on 12
November 1672:

> I am troubled you are not well, nor will I presse you to Come Up, to ye
> prejudice of your health, if I can passe this businesse over without further
> Examinacion; It is my duty to see his Ma[jes]ties Service well and diligently
> performed; and I will Imploy None that shall Neglect it; however I am not
> for Severity, when there is unavoydable accident in ye case. But your Boy
> hath an ill Character; & therefore you are too blame, to Imploy him; let
> him be punisht when he deserves it; As I believe he does (highly) in this
> businesse, and be sure there be noe more Miscarriages of this Nature, soe
> far as I can, I will excuse you, and Remaine
>
>   Your very loveing Freind[19]

   Whitley was sustained through his five years in charge by a total conviction that the public would come to see the monopoly granted to the
Post Office as more than justified by its performance. Users of the mails
would see 'the usefullnesse of this office to their commerce and how wee

worke and travaile night and day for them . . . and how cheape and easy their correspondence is to them'.[20] He noted in a letter of April 1677 that the Duke of York 'decides to take the management of the Post Office into his own hands and appoints me to manage [the] office' – but

Colonel Whitley's letter to Postmaster Watts, November 1672

six months after this formal end to the farm arrangement, and apparently entirely at his own request, Whitley decided to retire.[21] He was succeeded by Philip Frowde, who reported directly to the Treasury. Frowde had worked alongside Hickes in the 1660s – he too had had to flee the burning Letter Office on that fateful night in September 1666 – and he would remain as 'Governor of the Post Office', until the 1688 Revolution. Frowde presided over the relocation of the Letter Office from Bishopsgate to a grand building in Lombard Street in 1678. This was the former City home of Sir Robert Viner, Lord Mayor of London in 1674 and a prominent banker who at one time had had the dubious privilege of being Charles II's 'largest single individual creditor', losing a fortune in the process.[22] The size and elegance of the Lombard Street building gave the Post Office a new headquarters suited to its rising status. Its workforce by now consisted of around seventy-five London clerks and porters, with 182 deputy postmasters working in often quite remote places across the country; in Ireland, there were eighteen in the

Dublin office and forty-five country postmasters.[23] For all of these employees, the Post Office commanded a special kind of loyalty. Every local official enjoyed a certain cachet within his township and was part of something far larger and more important than being a mere carrier or innkeeper. They were part of a Crown service – though without incurring any of the hostility with which local officers of His Majesty's Customs and Excise were generally regarded. Many post stations were still handed on as family concerns, their postmasters proudly inheriting their positions as William Brewster had done a century earlier.

It was as yet a Crown service, however, with some glaring inadequacies. One was the surprisingly thin provision it had made to date for the citizens of London – already a teeming city that accounted for around a tenth of England's population. Another was the sparseness of the network between the Post Roads and so many of the kingdom's largest towns. (Here was the result of mapping out the Roads primarily with a view to conveying official messages to Scotland, Ireland and the Channel ports as quickly as possible.) Moves to redress this latter problem were core to the Post's growth in the 1670s, and were dependent to a great extent on the postmasters acting semi-independently of the centre. They were actively encouraged to lay down 'by-posts', providing for letters to be carried regularly by their post-boys to and from the Post Roads. (The term by-post also applied to letters carried between two points on the same Road, without passing through London. 'Crossposts' carried letters between one Road and another. 'Country letters' were all those that reached their destination via London.) Towns along the Roads were in this way increasingly linked via branch services to their most populous neighbours – some of them towns like Derby, Leeds and Sheffield that were expanding rapidly. Where postmasters acted in a private capacity, the Office was content to let them earn a living on the side by coordinating by-posts for which there was evident demand and by charging their own fees. Where the volume of mail warranted it, official rates would apply and the by-roads had to be accounted for as part of the national network. It was inevitably a rather haphazard arrangement, with supervision from the centre greatly hindered by the scale of the network and the lack of good maps; the first printed surveys of the Roads began to appear only in 1675. Nevertheless, the work patiently undertaken in the aftermath of the Great Fire began a gradual transformation, 'tending to make the ill-shaped wheel of the main post roads into a web of routes that would in time gossamer the whole land'.[24]

In the absence of any statistics for these years, one of the surest indicators of the rapid rise in the volume of the mails is the frequency with which Post Office Notices were being issued – by local postmasters as well as Lombard Street – to alert the general public and postal employees alike to new routes.[25] Some were set up to serve the King's Court on its travels (to Newmarket, Windsor and Bath); some linked the Letter Office in Lombard Street with the activities of the King's fleet (in Portsmouth, Southampton and other south-coast ports); but the great majority of them across the country were simply services newly established in a locality, where the postmaster's name and the regular postal schedules needed advertising to a public increasingly enthusiastic about the joys and usefulness of written correspondence. One contemporary in 1677 marvelled at the results: 'The number of letters missive is now prodigiously great . . . Every twenty-four hours the post goes 120 miles and in five days an anser may be had from a place 300 miles distant'.[26] Inside the Letter Office a few years later, Frowde made the same observation in recommending higher salaries for his clerks: 'The number of letters in the post office is very much of late increased'.[27] And a senior official, Thomas Gardiner, was tasked with making a comprehensive survey of how the emerging posts were actually working. Gardiner completed the work in two instalments, in 1677 and 1682, which together provided a first complete guide to the layout of the network and the names of the postmasters running it (they still included a Mr Watts in 1682, at 'Basing Stoke'). The surveys recorded the six main routes as 'tree-charts', with a trunk listing the post towns with horse stations on the Great Roads from London; and all six trunks sported impressive branches, along which by-posts carried the mails to dozens of places well beyond the post towns themselves.[28]

Neat charts on paper, though, were not necessarily a reliable guide to what was happening on the ground – and without doubt the embryonic service was often struggling to cope with a rising demand for postal deliveries. Studies by local postal historians tend to record a catalogue of contemporary complaints from the 1670s and 1680s, and are a useful corrective to any overly romantic image of the earliest mails. They note the bags lost in transit, the wagons abandoned on impassable roads, the attacks on defenceless post-boys – and, above all, the frequent wretchedness of the horses at hand:

> Between 1672 and 1677 the postmasters of Deal, Canterbury, Rochester and Dartford were admonished by letter for providing inadequate horses.

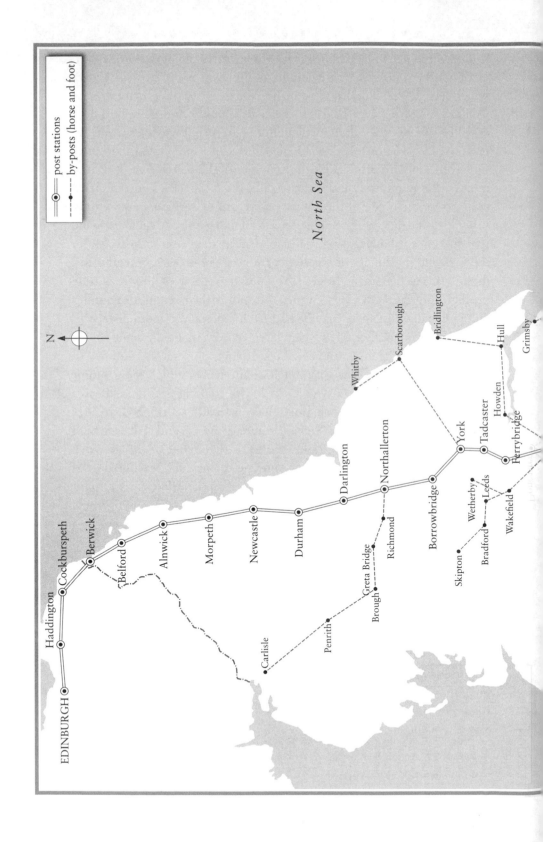

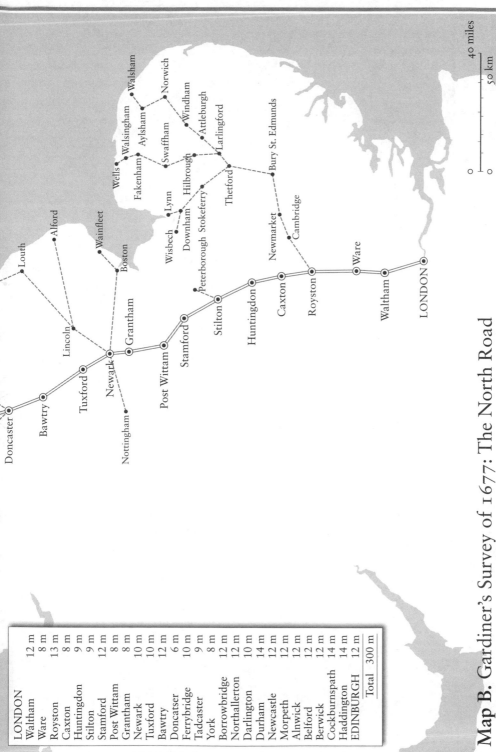

LONDON	
Waltham	12 m
Ware	8 m
Royston	13 m
Caxton	8 m
Huntingdon	9 m
Stilton	9 m
Stamford	12 m
Post Wittam	8 m
Grantham	8 m
Newark	10 m
Tuxford	10 m
Bawtry	12 m
Doncatser	6 m
Ferrybridge	10 m
Tadcaster	9 m
York	8 m
Borrowbridge	12 m
Northallerton	12 m
Darlington	10 m
Durham	14 m
Newcastle	12 m
Morpeth	12 m
Alnwick	12 m
Belford	12 m
Berwick	12 m
Cockburnspath	14 m
Haddington	14 m
EDINBURGH	12 m
Total	300 m

Map B. Gardiner's Survey of 1677: The North Road

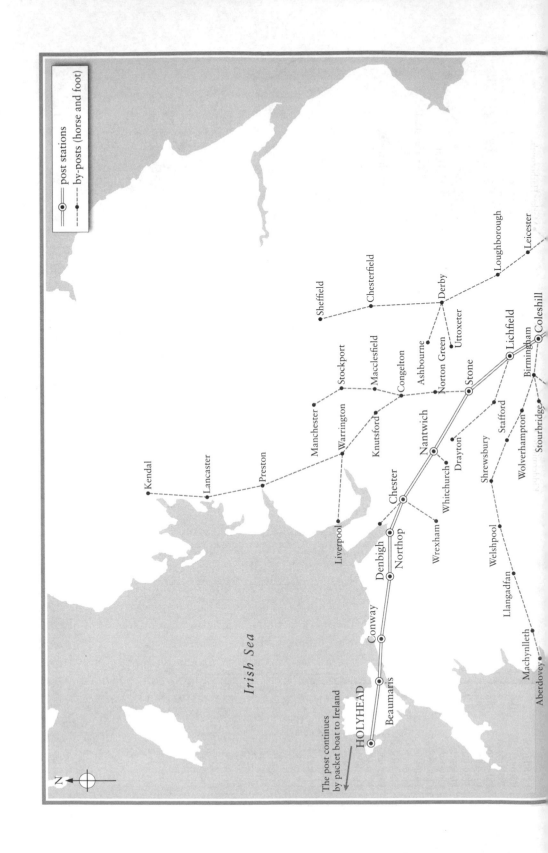

N

Irish Sea

The post continues
by packet boat to Ireland

HOLYHEAD
Beaumaris
Conway
Denbigh
Northop
Chester
Liverpool
Wrexham
Whitchurch
Nantwich
Drayton
Shrewsbury
Welshpool
Llangadfan
Machynlleth
Aberdovey
Stourbridge
Wolverhampton
Stafford
Birmingham
Coleshill
Lichfield
Stone
Norton Green
Uttoxeter
Ashbourne
Congelton
Macclesfield
Stockport
Knutsford
Warrington
Manchester
Preston
Lancaster
Kendal
Sheffield
Chesterfield
Derby
Loughborough
Leicester

post stations
by-posts (horse and foot)

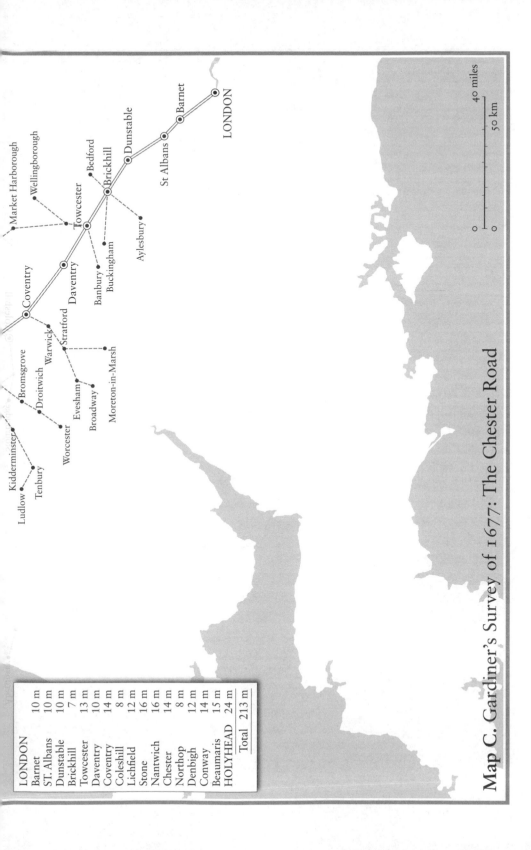

Map C. Gardiner's Survey of 1677: The Chester Road

LONDON	
Barnet	10 m
ST. Albans	10 m
Dunstable	10 m
Brickhill	7 m
Towcester	13 m
Daventry	10 m
Coventry	14 m
Coleshill	8 m
Lichfield	12 m
Stone	16 m
Nantwich	16 m
Chester	14 m
Northop	8 m
Denbigh	12 m
Conway	14 m
Beaumaris	15 m
HOLYHEAD	24 m
Total	213 m

40 miles

50 km

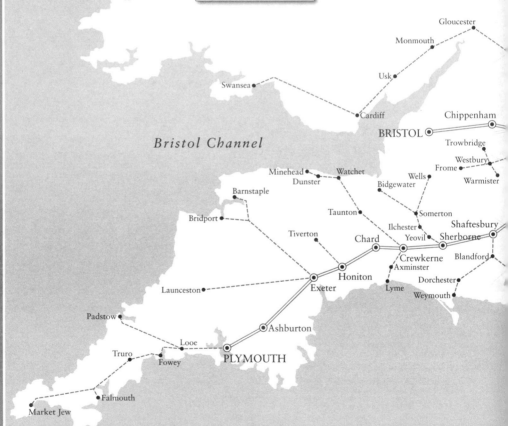

WESTERN ROAD
LONDON

Staines	16 m
Hartford Bridge	16 m
Basingstoke	9 m
Andover	13 m
Salisbury	10 m
Shaftesbury	19 m
Sherborne	15 m
Crewkerne	13 m
Chard	19 m
Honiton	7 m
Exeter	15 m
Ashburton	20 m
PLYMOUTH	24 m
Total	201 m

BRISTOL ROAD
LONDON

Hounslow	10 m
Maidenhead	16 m
Reading	22 m
Newbury	16 m
Marlborough	15 m
Chippenham	15 m
BRISTOL	20 m
Total	104 m

DOVER ROAD
LONDON

Dartford	14 m
Rochester	14 m
Sittingbourne	12 m
Canterbury	15 m
DOVER	15 m
Total	104 m

YARMOUTH ROAD
LONDON

Romford	16 m
Brentwood	7 m
Ingerstone	18 m
Chelmsford	7 m
Witham	8 m
Kelvedon	12 m
Colchester	9 m
Ipswich	15 m
Saxmundham	16 m
Beccles	16 m
YARMOUTH	10 m
Total	104 m

Map D. Gardiner's Survey of 1677:
The Western, Bristol, Dover and Yarmouth Roads

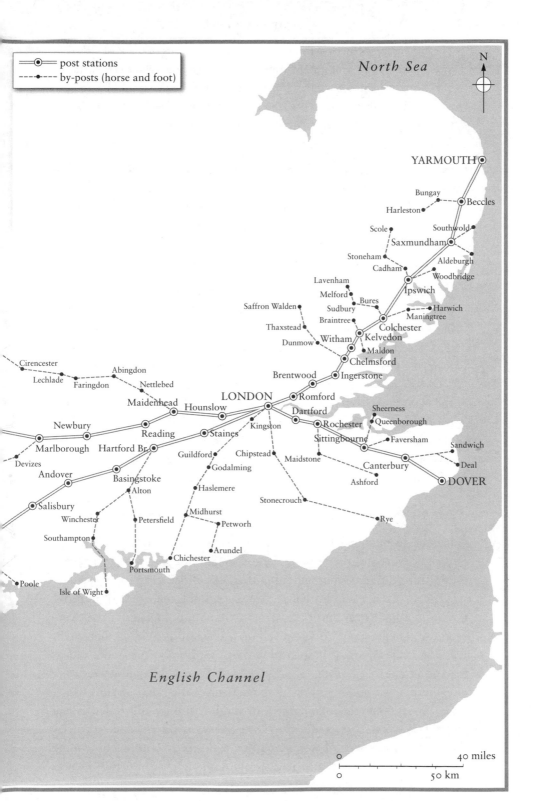

post stations
by-posts (horse and foot)

North Sea

N

YARMOUTH

Bungay
Harleston
Beccles
Scole
Southwold
Saxmundham
Stoneham
Aldeburgh
Cadham
Woodbridge
Lavenham
Melford
Bures
Ipswich
Saffron Walden
Sudbury
Harwich
Braintree
Maningtree
Thaxstead
Witham
Colchester
Dunmow
Kelvedon
Maldon
Chelmsford
Brentwood
Ingerstone
Cirencester
Abingdon
Nettlebed
Lechlade
Faringdon
Maidenhead
LONDON
Romford
Hounslow
Dartford
Sheerness
Newbury
Kingston
Rochester
Queenborough
Reading
Staines
Sittingbourne
Faversham
Marlborough
Hartford Br.
Guildford
Chipstead
Maidstone
Sandwich
Devizes
Andover
Basingstoke
Godalming
Canterbury
Deal
Alton
Haslemere
Ashford
DOVER
Salisbury
Winchester
Petersfield
Midhurst
Stonecrouch
Southampton
Petworh
Rye
Chichester
Arundel
Poole
Portsmouth
Isle of Wight

English Channel

0   40 miles
0   50 km

The hire of horses to travellers was put before the needs of the Post Office. The Canterbury postmasters in September 1677 had only three horses 'and not one of them fitt for service', while the Dartford postmaster in June 1674 hired his best horses to travellers and provided a mount which the post-boy found so weak that he was obliged to walk. The horse died before reaching Rochester.[29]

Gardiner's main grievance was the weakness of the financial controls at the disposal of Lombard Street. Given also its reliance on postmasters in the field to lead the process of expanding the network, the Post Office was everywhere vulnerable to excessive moonlighting by its own employees, as he bemoaned in a 'Memorandum concerning By Letters' that appeared with his second of his two instalments:

> [By Letters], having therefore no check upon them, were wholly swallowed up by the Postmasters or [their] Servants. And although wee have found out a method . . . in some measure to prevent that fraud, and to draw in to the Office 2 or 300 pounds per annum, yet it seems not perfectly effectuall to oppose their confederacy, especially in places where there is a great intercourse of letters, and no stage or good cheque between. For this consideration, and many more of consequence, it would be good work done, to send a fit person through all the Roads, to ride with the Maile from end to end, examining the furniture of the severall Postmasters and conveniences for his office; to observe the generall riding through the stages, and what expedition they are capeable of performing; and chiefly what number of [By] Letters are received in every stage, both going and returning. This would give the best light into the mistery, and direction how to govern it.

Gardiner recommended that these fit persons be known as 'Ryding Surveighors' – and they duly emerged as an elite corps of inspectors, establishing a regime that existed in the Post Office until the 1930s.

While Gardiner and his colleagues were doing their best to improve the basic administration of the service, though, bolder initiatives were required. The Duke of York showed no interest in providing them. This was not a case of Stuart indolence: James's cardinal virtues were 'industry and intense seriousness of purpose'.[30] But his principal interests lay elsewhere, most notably in the management of the navy, and his insistence on retaining personal control of the Post Office precluded giving effective leadership of its affairs to someone more interested in them. By the start of the 1680s, it was struggling to keep up with a burgeoning enthusiasm for letters that it had surely done much to nurture. A new mode of travel was becoming increasingly popular: the stage coach, drawn by six horses and covering forty or fifty miles a day on some routes. Many were as keen to carry letters as passengers, and posed an obvious threat to the Post Office. Though it commanded a *de jure* monopoly over the sending of letters, it was far from clear how it could enforce the monopoly if private operators found ways of providing an effective competing service. This they now did, both within the capital and far beyond it.

Private carriers of letters were still commonplace in Restoration London. In his diaries for 1660–69, Samuel Pepys refers to using them at several points. As a senior government official, Pepys could also afford to pay to have his letters sent by express courier whenever the need arose: 'the charge of express is not considerable to the King', as he noted at a time of crisis in 1667, when Dutch warships were setting fire to the King's fleet at Chatham docks.[31] For most of his humbler contemporaries, and especially the merchants of the City, the absence of a Post Office service in the capital was more irksome. It came to seem increasingly anomalous in the 1670s, as the expanding network of the General Post Office became more familiar. Why could letters be sent reliably to Bristol or Dublin, yet not from one side of London to the other? Even letters to and from the rest of the country via the Inland Office could be bothersome. Delivering a letter to the Office meant the inconvenience of a short journey for most people, or the cost of a paid servant; and all incoming letters likewise needed to be collected. The business opportunity was obvious, and it was taken up early in 1680 by an official called William Dockwra working in the Customs House.

Dockwra launched a Penny Post in London at a time of acute political sensitivity in the capital. Those opposed to the future accession of James, as an avowed Catholic with a Italian Catholic wife, were bent on blocking it through legislation. Events in Westminster were played out against the backdrop of a frenzy of conspiracy theories, sparking what was known as the Exclusion Crisis (because it centred on battles over 'Exclusion Bills' in Parliament designed to exclude James from the throne). Its intensity gave rise directly to the birth of English party politics and was reflected in a surge of newspaper publishing: dozens of new titles appeared in London between 1679 and 1682. In this wider context, the appearance of Dockwra's self-styled 'New and Useful Invention' added to a general sense that profound changes were under way. It was a postal service without precedent. Scores of receiving stations were set up across a metropolitan area seven miles wide, from Poplar and Blackwall in the east to Westminster and Lambeth in the west. Letters were collected from them hourly. Those intended for the Post Office were carried straight there (where they could be forwarded, with postal charges to be paid by the end-recipient in the normal way). Those with London addresses were taken to not one but five Penny Post stations for sorting – the largest of them at Dockwra's own house in Lyme Street, Camden Town. They were then hand-delivered within a few hours, to the house of the recipient where possible, by regular deliveries – as many as a dozen a day around the business areas and flourishing coffee houses of the City. All this was provided at a charge, to be prepaid by the sender, of just a penny per item – regardless of the length of the letter. (An extra penny was charged for 'country letters' delivered beyond the defined districts of the city.) The 'Penny Well Bestowed', as Dockwra's advertising had it, compared with a minimum official rate for a single-sheet letter that was still 2d for any journey up to eighty miles and 3d beyond that, with higher rates for letters to Scotland and Ireland; and multiple-sheet letters were still charged double. Dockwra's penny was even better value than this suggested, because his rate included insurance cover – and excluded interception by nimble-fingered sleuths at the Inland Office.

The business took off immediately. It was soon an indispensable part of the commercial life of the post-Fire city, now evolving into a metropolis that was beginning to resemble the outline shape of modern London. Unable to outlaw it so long as the Exclusion Crisis was in full flood, and impressed by its evident profitability, James hesitated over the most appropriate response. But not for long. Once his political opponents had been swept aside, as they were in 1682, he crushed the Penny Post under a welter of legal suits that forced its closure. Its owner was given a hefty fine by the courts for infringing the Crown's postal monopoly. Then, just four days later, the Duke announced plans for a 'London District Post'. Within a few weeks, Dockwra's operation was back on the streets as a separate subdivision of the General Post Office, still known to all as the Penny Post and with its penny rate intact, still to be prepaid unlike other inland letters. In later years, its efficiency would be one of the glories of the capital. (Daniel Defoe in 1727 thought it had introduced 'so exquisite a Management, that nothing can be more exact, and 'tis with the utmost Safety and Dispatch, that Letters are delivered at the remotest Corners of the Town . . .'[32]) Shamefully, its architect was left without redress and had to wait until after James's removal from the throne in 1688 before he could even petition for a pension.* Dockwra's defeat extinguished any lingering notion that the Crown might be prepared to share its legal ownership of the postal service. It would defend its monopoly in the courts, even if it was in no position yet to assert it in the marketplace. Dockwra's challenge was not the last of its kind: another, in 1709, saw the launch of a halfpenny post in London, but its backer, Charles Povey, was prosecuted within a matter of months and a similar fate seemed sure to befall any other maverick service.† The Dockwra episode made it abundantly clear that the Post Office was now aligned with the status quo against external proponents of reform. It was the first instance of a pattern that would recur many times in the future.

3. BY-POSTS, CROSS-POSTS, FARMS AND BLACK MARKETS

Openly advertised private posts were forbidden, but hidden ad hoc services were making a dramatic return. This was all but inevitable given the proliferation of by-posts around the country, with independent operators as well as the postmasters themselves responding to local demand. The volume of mails carried by the stage coaches grew especially quickly in the towns nearest to London. Neither legal penalties nor price competition could deter their drivers and guards from running a letter service on the side. The one real constraint on deliveries into London had hitherto been the inability of non-Londoners to find their way around, or to pick out individuals' houses. (Street names and house numbers were introduced by law only in 1767.) The newly assimilated Penny Post made a lasting impact in this respect after 1682. Letters carried illicitly from outside London could now be delivered to the London District Post's receiving stations. A prepaid missive from the countryside – handed over with the penny needed for its delivery in

---

* Dockwra got his pension in 1689 – paid out of the Penny Post's revenues, naturally – and even ran the Penny Post again on the Post Office's behalf from 1696 to 1700, but made little further contribution to the Post's development in England. He acquired land in the American colonies, in East Jersey, and in the 1690s may have befriended there a Scotsman called Andrew Hamilton who went on to launch a number of postal routes across the colonies of the North Atlantic seaboard, from Boston to Philadelphia.

† Povey's halfpenny post had one long-lasting legacy: it employed letter collectors who announced their arrival in each street by ringing a bell. The Post Office took up the idea, and 'Bellmen' walked the streets until the 1840s.

the capital – could reach its destination much more quickly than the official mail, and still be cheaper as well as far more convenient. By the time James had succeeded his brother on the throne in 1685, the trend was plain to all. 'No stage-coach entered London without the driver's pockets being stuffed with letters and packets, and he was moderate indeed if he had not a bagful besides.'[33]

The post was growing of its own accord into a network that the Post Office itself had no idea how to control. It was a conundrum worthy of a brave reappraisal by someone with real influence over policy – instead of which James only confirmed again the primary role of the Treasury. Even the most humdrum departure from normal practice needed letters to be laboriously exchanged between the Letter Office in Lombard Street and 'The Right Honourable The Lords Commissioners of His Majesty's Treasury', with copies made for a 'Treasury Letter Book'. This would run eventually to 1,185 volumes, covering every year from 1686 to 1977. It would be a boon for future historians – but it did nothing to inspire a spirit of enterprise under Governor Frowde or his successors. Rather, it entrenched a deeply cautious approach which proved immune even to James's departure. The Glorious Revolution of 1688 brought a fresh start for many institutions in English life. Some, like the East India Company, were legally reconstituted; others were created from scratch to enshrine audacious new ideas, like the Bank of England. In due course, the changed political climate of the 1690s would have a notable impact on the Post Office, too: changes to the law on news-paper licensing would trigger a boom in newspaper publishing around the turn of the century, adding substantially to the volume of mails leav-ing the capital every day.* More immediately, though, the Revolution brought only a slightly bizarre return to the earliest days of the Restor-ation era – featuring, remarkably, the reappearance of the man who had briefly led the Post Office all those years ago.

Now aged sixty-five, John Wildman had been released from prison in the aftermath of Clarendon's fall from power in 1667 and had clawed

* The first two non-official newspapers successfully established in London, in the 1690s, were both linked directly to their mode of delivery: they were called *Post Boy* and *Post Man*. Another newspaper in 1712 looked back on an extraordinary boom in demand for news over the previous fifteen years or so: 'Hence sprang that inundation of *Postmen, Postboys, Evening Posts, Supplements, Daily Courants* and *Protestant Post Boys*, amounting to twenty-one every week, besides many more which have not survived to this time, and besides the *Gazette* which has the sanction of public authority'. (Quoted in G. A. Cranfield, *The Development of the Provincial Newspaper, 1700–60*, OUP, 1962, pp. 9–10.)

his way back to the fringes of power as a close associate of Clarendon's main political enemies. He had even served, briefly, as a Member of Parliament at the time of the Exclusion Crisis. At a time of vicious scheming and conspiracies on all sides, Wildman was as obsessed as ever with political machinations but had somehow managed to avoid paying the ultimate penalty. (It was a close-run thing. He was mixed up in both the principal plots against the Crown in the 1680s – the Rye House Plot and the Duke of Monmouth's rebellion – and he had been several times imprisoned in the Tower of London.) In 1686, he had fled to Holland, where his assistance to the Protestant opponents of James II in exile at the Dutch Court assured him of a place at the centre of events after James was overthrown: in the turmoil of the 1688 Revolution, he was appointed to no fewer than sixty-four committees. William of Orange, once safely installed as James's successor, acceded to Wildman's request to return to the Post Office. He walked into the Letter Office on Lombard Street to be greeted as its new head on 11 April 1689, the day of William and Mary's coronation. Like Frowde, he reported to the Treasury and was to be formally known as the Governor of the Post Office, rather than 'Postmaster General'.[34] But whatever his title, Wildman was back in his element. Within weeks of his reappointment, he was reporting to the Government on the interception of letters on the North Road to Scotland and on the packet boats to France and offering the Post Office's assistance in the struggle against scheming Jacobites at home and abroad. This kept Wildman extremely busy for almost two years; but when he was dismissed in 1691, the cause seems to have been less to do with any clandestine matters than 'his failure to provide an efficient and regular postal service, particularly with Scotland and Holland'.[35] It was also widely rumoured that he had been caught conspiring with Dutch republicans against William III, though such rumours did not deter William from making him Deputy Lieutenant of Middlesex – with a knighthood – in 1692. The following year, still a wealthy man at the age of seventy, John Wildman died in his bed.

In succession to Wildman, the Governorship was divided between two joint holders, to be known as Postmasters General, reporting to the Treasury. The doubling up may have been politically convenient – it allowed the post to be shared by the two principal parties in the Commons – but was perhaps also an acknowledgement of the rising volume of paperwork now entailed in running the Post Office. If so, it went nowhere near far enough to tackle the problem. The first holders of the joint office, Robert Cotton and Thomas Frankland, simply lacked

the necessary resources to tackle improvements on the scale that was
now required; and they struggled, as did several of their successors, to
leave behind any mark at all of their tenure.[36] Their staffs at Lombard
Street were kept at full stretch, just running the Inland and Foreign
Offices and the six Post Roads. No other administrative machinery
existed to further the affairs of the network as a whole or to devise
future reforms: the Joint Postmasters started out with a solitary clerk to
copy their letters and it was three years before they could add to their
own office by employing a 'Secretary to the Post Office' – whose tasks
included getting up in the small hours to authorize express despatches.[37]
Even the smallest decisions were referred to the Treasury, where any
additional expenses were shunned and investments for a future return
were rarely considered at all. What became known around this time as
'the Custom of the Office' was a potent mix of inherited routines and
Treasury control, less geared to what we might regard as an embryonic
public service than to the dictates of early eighteenth-century record-
keeping.

This stance was especially unfortunate, given the fast-rising demands
on the postal network. By-posts were being set up in ever greater numbers, but the Treasury's parsimony made it virtually impossible for the
Post Office to extend any meaningful control over them, and rural postmasters could easily agree among themselves to pocket the postage fees
with little fear of detection by their superiors. How many by-way letters
were slipping through the Post Office net, unseen from the Inland Office,
no one could know; but contemporaries treated the implicit fraud as a
commonplace. The same applied to illicit posts criss-crossing the Roads.
The Treasury insisted that all letters despatched on one Post Road to an
address on another had to go on being delivered via the Inland Office in
London. Whatever its advantages for the spymasters, this edict no
longer made sense for the public. It could entail a letter from some
remote market town having to travel all the way to the Office and then
back again (as a 'country letter'), to reach an address perhaps fifty or
sixty miles from its starting point. Not only did the letter take days
longer to arrive, but postage had to be paid on both halves of the journey, at the standard rate. In many cases this more than doubled the
putative cost of the disallowed 'cross-post'. The result was that, by the
middle of the decade, private by-posts and cross-posts became, in effect,
a thriving black market. And because the law still allowed private
servants to carry letters as a personal errand for their masters, there yet
remained plenty of grey markets, too.

Cotton and Frankland were conscious of the revenues being lost to the Post Office, but were in no position themselves to apply a direct remedy. Instead, they resorted again to outsourcing via the old farming principle. Modest 'by-post farms' had been contracted out for some years: Whitley had offered farm contracts in the 1670s to postmasters whose accounts he thought suspiciously lightweight (though few appear to have taken up his offer).[38] Much larger concessions were now agreed with several individuals who between them took on the management of postal services across broad areas of the Midlands, northern England and the West Country.[39] Some of those with the largest contracts – like the brothers Richard and Stephen Bigg, whose mails ranged from Hertfordshire to Westmorland – had a huge impact on the coherence of the postal network. They even managed to get around the Treasury's veto on direct mails between different Roads, establishing some much-needed cross-posts. The first of these was set up in 1696 by the postmaster of Exeter, a notable pioneer called Joseph Quash, who settled a postal route north to Bristol and extended it over the next twelve years to Bath, then Chester and Oxford. (Thus, for example, letters from Exeter to Bristol were carried for 2d each instead of the 6d needed for the scenic route via Lombard Street.) To many contemporaries, this process of connecting up the Post Roads laterally was a self-evidently sensible next step for the Post Office itself. The problem, no less true now than in the reign of Charles II, was that the finances of a far-flung chain of postal stations seemed all but impossible to coordinate effectively. This was borne out by the business failure of many of the farmers. In 1701, Stephen Bigg had to abandon a contract covering the north-west, including the growth towns of Liverpool and Manchester. By 1708, Joseph Quash was also in trouble, having taken on additional responsibilities as a tax collector in Devon and underestimated the challenge of running posts as far as Oxford.

The 1711 Post Office Act might have been helpful to the concept of farming out posts, insofar as it raised the legal barriers against the private carriage of letters. As part of a comprehensive restatement of the Post Office's monopoly, which would provide its basis in law well into the nineteenth century, the Act forbade carriers from accepting letters unless they related directly to goods in their charge, and barred stage coaches from taking on mail. But the primary purpose of the Act, as noted earlier, was to increase the value of the Post Office as a source of revenue. Postage rates were generally increased – the basic 2d rate, for example, went up to 3d – and this placed an unmanageable strain on the farming model. The principles behind it were far less familiar in Britain than in, say, contemporary France, and there existed much less scope for a ruthless pursuit of targeted revenues. Higher rents seemed warranted, but no one could agree on what these should be. The Treasury cancelled all but one of the farm contracts, and the surviving farmers were instead taken on as salaried managers. The one farmer who had his contract renewed, for reasons that are unclear, was Joseph Quash – and it did him no good at all. He was declared bankrupt in 1713.

By then, though, Quash had done his Post Office masters a greater service than he or they were yet in a position to appreciate.[40] As Exeter's postmaster, he had been responsible for overseeing the accounts of stations all along the Cornish Post Road to Truro. Some time in 1706 or 1707 he got to know a fourteen-year-old youth who was helping his grandmother to serve as a temporary postmaster for the station at St Columb. The boy's name was Ralph Allen, and Quash saw immediately that he was a remarkably talented individual. When the grandmother had to step down in December 1707, Quash gave him a job in Exeter assisting with the management of the cross-post to Bath and Bristol. He trained and coached him in the complexities of cross-post administration before assigning him less than three years later, in 1710, to Bath, with responsibility for the cross-post's extension via that city to Oxford. For two years, the young Allen hobnobbed with postmasters all across the Cotswolds and built a name for himself with many of the leading citizens of Bath, including its Member of Parliament and various other dignitaries; there were probably also demands on him to deal with officials sent from the Inland Office in London to talk to Quash about his rapidly deteriorating finances. Then, in 1712, the postmaster's position in Bath suddenly fell vacant. Presumably greatly impressed by his knowledge of the area and his growing reputation, the Post Office turned to Ralph Allen. He was just eighteen years old.

4. RALPH ALLEN'S BUSINESS RUN FROM BATH

Allen's appointment as Bath's postmaster at eighteen was extraordinary enough, but he soon built on this stellar start to his career. When Quash's cross-posts empire collapsed the following year, Allen was one of several postmasters who were given a second – and tellingly rather larger – salary from Lombard Street to keep the cross-posts going. The young man's rapid rise to provincial prominence was consolidated in 1715, when rumours swept through the West Country of a Jacobite rising against the new king, George I. Troops were encamped in Bath, watching for signs of trouble. In a shrewd move that John Wildman would no doubt have applauded, Allen passed on local intelligence to their commander, Major-General (later Field Marshal) George Wade, and the two men struck up a rapport. This did not extend, as some accounts would have it, to Allen's marrying the general's daughter, but it seems likely that Wade was sufficiently impressed by Allen to make known in London his respect for the young man's flair.*

Allen worked hard on his ideas for postal reform over the next four years. He had no desire for promotion within the Post Office itself, but appears to have grown steadily more convinced that, properly monitored, the by- and cross-posts could be made the basis of a profitable separate business. Undeterred by the fact that farm contracts had been abandoned eight years earlier, Allen in 1719 sent a proposal to the Post-masters General that he be granted a farm over all the by- and cross-posts of an extensive stretch of the West Country (quite how the geographical franchise was defined is unclear). This, from a provincial employee aged twenty-five, must have caused some astonishment in Lombard Street – at which point Wade's support may have made a critical difference.

If so, Wade's voice would have been one among several raised on Allen's behalf. There was also a strong endorsement of Allen's potential from the newly established Department of Travelling Surveyors, which had been set up in 1715 to police the postal network, insofar as this was possible. In a private memoir some four decades later, which he wrote in the third person and entitled *Ralph Allen's Own Narrative*, Allen attributed this internal backing to the support of a Surveyor sent to Bath to check on his finances. The man had been greatly impressed to find the young postmaster 'had faithfully accounted to the Government for the Postage of all the Bye & way Letters which had been committed to his care: And this truth that Surveyor was even forced [by the young Allen himself?] to report to the Board'.[41] The same memoir also recalled the firm views Allen had already formed by 1719 on many conspicuous abuses of the existing postal system. Post-boys, for example, were taking

---

* He married a London merchant's daughter, Elizabeth Buckeridge, in 1721. Her family's money may have helped Allen build his career, but he made clear in later life that his early success was based 'on his own personal Character alone'. His friendship with the Field Marshal deepened in the 1720s, after Wade became the MP for Bath. (See entry by Brenda J. Buchanan, *Oxford DNB*.)

payment from the senders of letters instead of the recipients, which
resulted in many letters disappearing without trace:

> It was the constant practice to demand and receive the Postage of all such
> letters before they were put into any of the Country Post Offices. Hence
> (from the general temptation of destroying these Letters for the sake of the
> Postage) the joynt mischiefs of Embezling the [Post Office's] Revenue and
> interrupting and obstructing the Commerce fell naturely in, to support and
> inflame one another.[42]

In his proposal to the Postmasters General, Allen drew on his ample
experience of running the cross-posts laid by Quash to devise a new
administrative system that he believed could eliminate the ubiquitous
cheating. He was privately dismissive of the possibility of the Travelling
Surveyors having much impact and would later sniff at their efforts:
'with all their Vollumes of Reports, [they] had made the matter appear
still more desperate than they found it'. But the Surveyors must have
helped him secure an audience in London. Here, according to Allen, the
Postmasters General demanded that he give a detailed explanation of
how he intended to proceed. They must have thought him very naïve.
Allen declined to elaborate on his scheme – 'with good reason', as he
noted in his memoir – instead asking how much the Post Office currently earned on the mails under discussion. He was told £4,000, which
was a highly optimistic estimate as he must have known – and Allen
promptly offered to pay the Post Office a rent of £6,000 a year. This was
almost twice what the Post Office had any realistic expectation of earning unaided, and promised the Postmasters General a chance to shuffle
off an increasingly awkward burden. It was an offer they might easily
have refused, given Allen's youth. But, on the contrary, they decided to
give him a contract to run from 1720 for seven years.[43]

Over the next forty-four years, that contract would be renewed six
times. After the expiry of the second (or perhaps the third) seven-year
term, the Post Office suggested that a higher rental payment than £6,000
would be appropriate, in view of the substantial profits that Allen was
evidently making. Allen concurred with this, but shrewdly offered the
Postmasters General a choice. Either they could ask for a larger annual
rent in cash – or they could allow him to extend his franchise, at his
own cost, over additional areas of the country, ensuring that the Post
Office thereby received substantially more income each year through a
growth of the London and country letters as a consequence of more and
better by- and cross-posts. The first option, suggested Allen, would be

'without any advantage to Publick Commerce'; but the second would be 'a project that wou'd be of infinite advantage to Commerce'.[44] Their Lordships chose the second, allowing Allen in due course to expand his network of cross-posts and by-posts until it stretched across most of England and Wales. In effect, he was allowed to build a second monopoly in parallel with the one run by the Post Office along the six Great Roads. Allen set down in his memoir the essence of his success:

> He so contrived, that every Postmaster on the same Road, and in all the Branches in the same Road, shou'd check and be checked, by every other: Nay further, this Security against frauds was extended even to operate reciprocally between the Postmasters on different Roads and on the different Branches of different Roads, by means of certain regulations which he kept in places where these different Roads are intersected by Cross road Branches; and which, for this reason, he chose to call Key Towns.[45]

It took several years to construct this perpetual monitoring machine and to prove its worth. His memoir skips quickly over 'the incredible pains and Labour he underwent before he cou'd subdue that System of fraud & peculation which had spread thro-out the whole Country, by this combination of corrupt Deputys' – and Allen refused even in old age to provide further details to Lombard Street, agreeing only to have his methods fully disclosed at his death.[46] But they certainly involved a daunting amount of travel, by horseback and stage coach, along often appalling roads. (Traffic had grown enormously, but effective road construction and repair techniques were still some way off.) 'He visited countless places,' notes his modern biographer, 'met the deputies, studied roads and distances, observed actual practice, and acquired the groundwork of his later uncanny familiarity with the geographical and personal intricacies of the whole system.'[47]

Important innovations included the use of town stamps: all letters had to be stamped at the point of departure, or at least – if posted at a remote stage between towns – had to have their place of origin scribbled on the back. Provincial town stamps had been used years before by Joseph Quash, then largely abandoned. Allen took them up again as one of many safeguards against illicit mail. It has been suggested that their reappearance may be evidence that Quash joined Allen in some capacity from 1720. Previously unknown Allen family papers unearthed in the Cornish Records Office only at the end of the 1960s suggest that Quash was still seen as a close and trusted friend by his former protégé in 1731. If he was indeed involved in supporting Allen's operations, at least through the 1720s, this would help explain how Allen was able to master a task that had proved beyond the powers of the Post Office itself.[48] With or without his mentor's help – and after a long struggle against all those 'corrupt Deputys' (at the end of 1723, his business was still showing a loss) – Allen established a regime that would eventually prove astonishingly effective. Detailed instruction books were sent to all postmasters. 'Post bills' (or 'vouchers') had to be remitted each quarter to Bath, showing the postage due on despatched letters. These were then matched by Allen's clerks against postmasters' accounts recording their cash receipts. (Uncollected, or 'dead', letters could be handed in for reimbursement – always provided they were stamped.) How much cash was remitted, and how much was paid out in wages, was subject to constant review. And the network as a whole was open at all times to random inspections by the Travelling Surveyors. These remained formally answerable to Lombard Street – the Post Office Act of 1711 barred anyone but the Postmasters General from appointing employees to the postal system, much to Allen's frustration – but it was agreed he would pay their wages and in practice the Surveyors served as his enforcers.

Not that Allen wielded his authority in a heavy-handed way: he was famously courteous and considerate in his business dealings. This was true even during the early years of his farm, when many postmasters – in an echo of their forebears' reaction to the first imposition of postal rates back before the Civil War – expressed resentment at the curtailment of their free-wheeling ways. Indeed, attempts were made to subvert Allen's whole approach by alerting the Treasury to the potential losses that might result from a drop in the number of country letters passing through London. The Treasury, intensely sceptical about the viability of Allen's first contract, demanded that he provide some assurance of compensation were this to happen. Allen, rightly convinced that efficient cross-posts would in due course draw by-posts away from illegal carriers and lift mail volumes in every direction, placated the Postmasters General with some generous guarantees. Sure enough, by the end of his second contract, it came as 'a very great, as well as agreeable surprize to them to find . . . [country letters] to be considerably Augmented'.[49]

The growth in the mails made Ralph Allen a huge personal fortune. Exactly how much he earned each year was and remains a mystery. One later estimate reckoned he had made an annual profit (on average) roughly twice his £6,000 farm rental – the equivalent of approximately £2m today – but this was perhaps a reference to the profits he made on his original franchise alone; the spread of his work across England must surely have lifted his annual earnings even higher.[50] Whatever the true scale of his wealth, contemporaries joined in universal admiration of the man. Allen had a genius for friendship, which is recorded more extensively than is usual for a businessman, however successful, because among his friends were two of the greatest writers of his day. The novelist Henry Fielding included an affectionate portrait of Allen in *Tom Jones*, where he was the inspiration for the aptly named Squire Allworthy. And from the poet Alexander Pope, Allen received many letters over more than a decade and at least one memorable couplet:

> Let humble Allen, with an awkward shame,
> Do good by stealth and blush to find it fame.*

He spent all of his adult life in Bath, and was a model of the city father once common enough in England but more familiar in modern times in American life. Allen helped transform the face of the city, both as a businessman and as a philanthropist. He developed huge local quarries that provided much of the Bath stone for the city's extensive reconstruction from the 1720s. He took a leading role – initially as the personal representative of General Wade – in a project making the River Avon navigable between Bath and the Bristol seaport. And he donated enormous sums to many local charities, in particular the city's general hospital, as well as to hospitals in the West Country and London. As befitted his station, he had a stately home built for himself and his wife Elizabeth on a hillside above the city, where 800 tons of stone blocks from his quarries were needed just for the foundations.[51] With plenty of advice from Pope, among others, Prior Park was laid out to include magnificently landscaped gardens – and ample offices to house some of the senior clerks working at the centre of Allen's postal network. When he died in 1764, the *Annual Register* – a yearly review of politics and literature, launched a few years earlier and written by Edmund Burke – was elegant in its praise for 'a gentleman not more remarkable for the

---

* Pope was an intimate friend for many years and often stayed with Allen in Bath. A mutual friend described the bond between the businessman and the poet: 'They are extremely happy in each other; the one feeling great Joy in the good Heart, and Strong Sense of his truly generous Host, while the other, with the most pleasing Attention, drinks in Rivers of Knowledge continually flowing from the Lipps of his delightful Stranger.' The observer was a Dr Oliver, inventor of the Bath Oliver biscuit, who described their friendship in a letter to his cousin, the Cornish antiquarian and geologist William Borlase (1696–1772). (This extract from the Borlase Correspondence is taken from Benjamin Boyce, *The Benevolent Man: A Life of Ralph Allen of Bath*, Harvard University Press, 1967, p. 86.)

ingenuity and industry with which he made a very great fortune, than the charity, generosity, and politeness with which he spent it'.[52]

The impact of Allen's network on eighteenth-century England had a historic importance that far transcended its contribution to the wealth and beauty of Bath. Most obviously, it consolidated the physical presence of the Post Office itself. Allen added dozens of post offices to the network: one survey of the Great Roads and principal cross-roads in 1756 recorded post offices in 200 towns across England.[53] This increased coverage of the country and the increasingly reliable by-posts probably did at least as much as the 1711 Act to discourage illegal mails. Without Allen, the official postal service might have surrendered much of the growing postal traffic, letting it be run as a sideline by postmasters and enterprising local tradesmen. As it was, the Royal Mail retained at least a nominal monopoly, even if a sizeable slice of it was effectively run from Bath. (Staff numbers in Lombard Street remained more or less steady, at around eighty employees, during his lifetime.) The financial benefits to the Post Office of his work were assessed by Allen himself in 1761 with a wonderfully modern-looking exercise in creative accounting. In an appendix to his memoir, he added together the Office's cash receipts from his own farm payments (oddly at £2,300 a year rather than £6,000), the elimination of losses on country letters, the putative value of the incremental volume of London and country letters over the past forty years, the cost savings made for the Post Office by his shouldering of the salaries for Surveyors and other Post Office personnel, *and* the future profits and cost savings on by- and cross-letters as well as country letters to accrue to the Post Office for thirty years after his own death. The total came to precisely £1,516,870. The benefits to date, meanwhile, were certainly reflected in the aggregate finances of the Post Office. Its gross annual revenues climbed from around £180,000 in the 1720s to about £230,000 at the time of Allen's death, and its net annual income was held more or less steady around £100,000 despite a substantial rise in its expenses, especially during the Seven Years War of 1756–63.[54] Within ten years of his death, both gross revenues and net profits had jumped about 40 per cent (to £313,000 and £164,000 respectively, in 1774), which is probably a better guide to the value of his work – and may also be a reflection of how much profit, unseen from Lombard Street, had been ending up in Bath during Allen's own lifetime.

How far the Post Office's expansion led to the growth of general correspondence is impossible to quantify, but a rising awareness of the postal service was a striking feature of Georgian England. One scholar,

Susan Whyman, suggests the role of the Post Office as a catalyst has
been overlooked. 'At the opening and close of letters, all classes stated
that they needed the Royal Mail for practical and emotional reasons. . . .
Because most writers' comments are deleted in printed collections, historians have under-estimated the significance of the Post Office. Yet [its
services] must have seemed astonishing to people whose parents had
lived without it.'[55] Contemporaries were certainly conscious that personal letters had assumed a new and greater prominence. Two of the
earliest and most influential novels in English literature were published
in this period, Richardson's *Pamela: or, Virtue Rewarded* (1740) and
Clarissa. Or, The History of a Young Lady (1747–8); the narrative of
both was supplied by a series of private letters. The idea was put to
Richardson originally by two astute London publishers, who predicted
a lively demand from budding letter writers keen to pick up tips on
correspondence. Their instincts were right: *Pamela* was reprinted three
times within six months of its first publication.

   A second aspect of the growth of correspondence was its novel
importance to business. Those engaged in trade and commerce, provincial banking, land management and the first industrial ventures could
rely on letters as never before. The ability to turn out a page of elegant
copperplate handwriting became an essential skill for any young man
aspiring to a career in commerce, and would soon become a hallmark
of British business methods around the world. Whyman's researches
into more than sixty collections of private letters from the eighteenth
century have pointed to a level of literacy among ordinary people, and
a rapidly growing dependence on both social and commercial correspondence, that has surely been underestimated. 'By 1800, all ranks of
society were participating in a vibrant culture of letters.'[56] And the
importance of letters was rooted in the existence of a comprehensive
postal service across the land. Allen was in this sense one of the innova-
tors who helped prepare the way for Britain's Industrial Revolution.
Modern scholars have devoted much attention to the emergence in
eighteenth-century Britain of a consumer society, studying the activities
of those who led the way in marketing, advertising and the creation of
popular fashions, where earlier generations of historians chronicled the
achievements of men like Thomas Newcomen or Abraham Darby with
their steam engines and iron-making. This reappraisal might have been
expected to leave Ralph Allen looking a rather more significant figure,
yet his achievements have still generally gone unremarked.[57] Did Pope
perhaps have this mind, as much as Allen's charitable donations, when

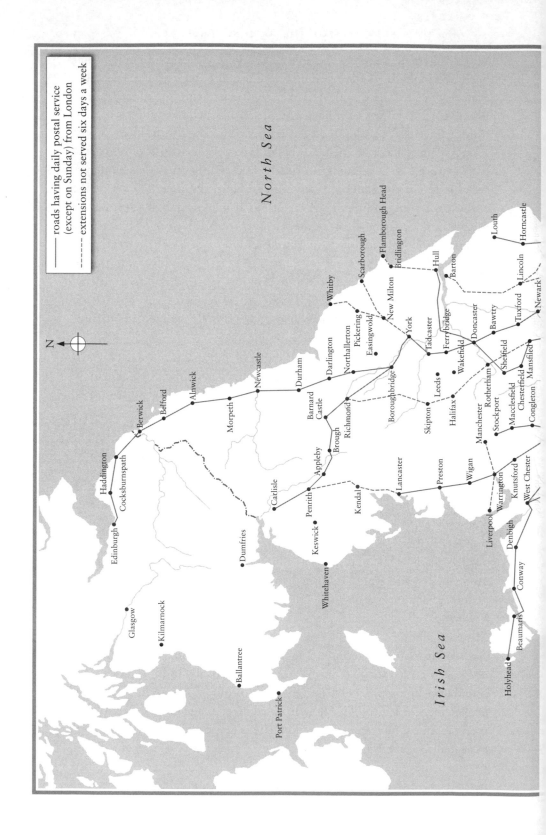

roads having daily postal service
(except on Sunday) from London
extensions not served six days a week

North Sea

Irish Sea

N

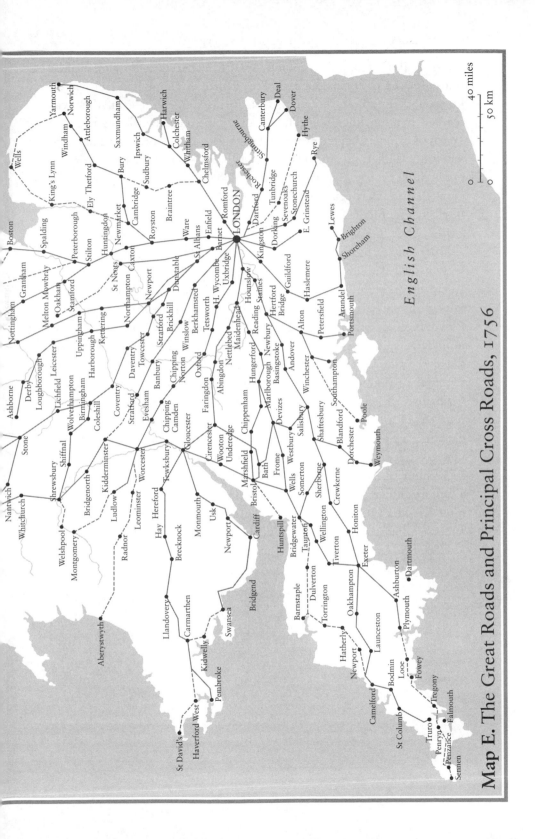

Map E. The Great Roads and Principal Cross Roads, 1756

he wrote about him doing 'good by stealth'? There was no such explicit praise for the provincial General Post Office as Defoe had lavished on London's Penny Post, though its transformation in Allen's lifetime was scarcely less startling. In effect, he had completed the task begun in the 1630s of bringing haphazard postal services into a coordinated national network. Witherings and his successors had marshalled the London mails along the six great Post Roads; Allen did the same for most of the mails that ran between them. No doubt it would have amazed his forebears that he fulfilled this role at such arm's length from the staff of the Letter Office in London.

After his death, as had been agreed, his Post Office papers with all the secrets of his success were bequeathed to the Inland Office in London. Allen's nephew Philip and other members of his office moved with them, taking up newly created positions in Lombard Street and enabling the Post Office to assimilate the practices of Prior Park. Assimilating the innovative spirit that had conjured them up was a different matter. By the 1760s, the Post Office's officials had become hardly less conservative in their outlook than their Treasury masters, and both parties saw themselves as responsible for providing the careful book-keeping required of a national postal network. Improving the efficiency of the network was seen, if at all, as a strictly incremental affair – though where others came up with bold and manifestly successful new ideas, they might be co-opted just as Dockwra's Penny Post had been, almost a century before. The absorption of the network created by Ralph Allen must have looked for many years like a triumphant vindication of this approach. But it had its drawbacks, as would shortly become apparent.

3
Coaches and communications, 1764–1829

'The Post Office is a wonderful establishment!' said she. 'The regularity and despatch of it! If one thinks of all that it has to do, and all that it does so well, it is really astonishing!'

'It is certainly very well regulated.'

'So seldom that any negligence or blunder appears! So seldom that a letter, among the thousands that are constantly passing about the kingdom, is ever carried wrong – and not one in a million, I suppose, actually lost! And when one considers the variety of hands, and of bad hands too, that are to be deciphered, it increases the wonder.'

'The clerks grow expert from habit. They must begin with some quickness of sight and hand, and exercise improves them. If you want any further explanation, . . . they are paid for it. That is the key to a great deal of capacity. The public pays and must be served well.'

Jane Fairfax and John Knightley in conversation,
from Jane Austen's *Emma* (1815)

1. CUSTOM AND CORRUPTION

The Post Office headquarters to which Ralph Allen's young nephew relocated in October 1764 resembled a cross between a miniature Oxbridge college and a regimental barracks. It occupied the former home of a wealthy banker, ruined by lending to Charles II, on the south side of Lombard Street at the heart of the City of London. Over the decades it had been gradually expanded to include most of the buildings between Abchurch Lane to the east and Sherborne Lane to the west.*

---

* The lanes are still there, though the latter is now a post-Blitz alley called Post Office Court where it runs along the former site. A stone plaque commemorates the spot, long since

The main entrance was an imposing gateway, which opened into a courtyard 'paved from end to end for the merchants to walk in while waiting to receive their letters'.[1] Adjacent to the entrance was the sorting room for the Inland Office, with steps leading down to a basement. Here the humble letter carriers came and went with their bags and bells. On the ground floor at the one end of the courtyard was the Foreign Office for overseas mail (not to be confused with Whitehall's Foreign Office, which did not appear until a hundred years later). At the other end was the formal residence of the Postmasters General – still resident in 1764, though they were to move out the following year. On the higher floors above the courtyard, and in a warren of smaller buildings all around it, were the lodgings of the Post Office staff. These included some lavish apartments for the most senior officials, a few of them furnished at considerable, and occasionally much-criticized, expense.[2] But they also comprised many modest garrets for single clerks and crowded dormitories for the lowest ranks. These included perhaps a couple of hundred 'outdoor staff' like the letter carriers, messengers and porters. Accommodation also had to be provided for a body of domestic servants who, among other duties, manned a dozen or so kitchens.

Housing its staff on the premises was the only practical way for the Post Office to conduct its business, given the long night hours involved in the daily routine of the mails. But the all-embracing way of life also helped engender among the staff a strong sense of loyalty to the Custom of the Office. This set great store by careful routines, conscientiously followed from day to day. An innovative turn of mind was not required. Each week's basic timetable remained very much as laid down by James Hickes and his colleagues a whole century earlier. Inward mails arrived from around the country on Mondays, Wednesdays and Fridays, to be priced and sorted for the alphabet men to hold against collection, or for letter carriers to deliver within the boundaries of the London District Post; and outward mails received directly by the window men or brought in by the 'outdoors men' of the District Post would be priced, stamped and sorted for despatch each Tuesday, Thursday and Saturday. Additions to the staff establishment were not a common occurrence. A 'Supplier of Newspapers' had been added in 1737: the purchase of London papers for resale (free of any postage) to country postmasters had become an essential part of the clerks' livelihoods, and they were granted

surrendered – like other head office sites within the City in later centuries – back to the bankers.

an organizer to coordinate (and keep an official eye on) their busy retail side-line. And a 'Resident Surveyor' had been appointed since 1743, to manage the Travelling Surveyors inaugurated in 1715 and to take general charge of the inland network. Otherwise, the arrival of Philip Allen himself as 'Comptroller of the By and Cross Road Letter Office' in October 1764 was the first innovation of its kind for many years. It added a fourth department to the Inland and Foreign Offices in Lombard Street and the District Penny Post, based nearby in an alley off Threadneedle Street. The new man's appointment was a highly unusual departure, which officials began planning with some care well ahead of the death of his famous uncle. But it was true to the spirit of the Office in one notable respect: Philip Allen was there largely by dint of being Ralph Allen's nephew. Family connections and patronage were the recruiting sergeants for both the clerical staff in Lombard Street and the deputy postmasters across the country.

The Post Office was still headed jointly by two Postmasters General. Ten had served since 1720, including the Earls of Leicester, Bessborough and Egmont as well as a handful of financiers and diplomats approaching the end of their careers. None had come to the Post Office with much of a political reputation, and none left it with their reputation greatly enhanced. As one confided to another in 1765, the office was 'a very good bed for old couriers to rest in'.[3] They exerted their authority through 'the Board', to which a small group of officials reported, all with their own deputies and clerks to handle much of the day-to-day paperwork and sometimes more. These officials included a Receiver General to look after the cash flow, an Accountant General to balance the books (after a fashion) and a Solicitor to advise the Board and the Postmasters General – not least on all their dealings with the Lords Commissioners of the Treasury. The most senior figure by 1764 was the Secretary. Hardly more than glorified clerks in the 1690s, the holders of this office had steadily accumulated authority for half a century.

The man who by the autumn of 1764 was just approaching the end of his second year as Secretary was a consummate office politician by the name of Anthony Todd. The son of a Weardale farming family, he had joined the Post Office at the age of fifteen in 1732 on the strength of some chance connections. Todd had spent his entire career in the Foreign Office, and had been at its head since 1752. As 'Foreign Secretary' he had had very little to do with the workings of the inland postal network at all. Easily his biggest concern had been the management of the Secret Office, where all foreign letters were monitored, and many opened, in response to warrants from Treasury ministers, or sometimes just at the discretion of its staff.[4] (Inland letters were still intercepted separately and opened on all sorts of pretexts, preferably in the Private Office of the Secretary but also in Dublin, Edinburgh and even country post offices where the need arose. The Post Office was under a legal obligation after 1711 to give a close inspection to all inland letters specified to it by Secretaries of State. The lists of these letters grew steadily longer under the Hanoverians.) Situated next to the Foreign Office within Lombard Street, the Secret Office had a staff of eight by the 1760s, three rooms with their own fires and an abundant supply of candles at all times, and their own private entrance off the street. It also took over the duties of a 'Deciphering Department' within the Post Office around this same time. Todd's role as Foreign Secretary put him at the helm, in effect, of England's foreign intelligence service. It was a busy operation, with a network of spies operating as Post Office agents in the ports and capital cities of the Continent: one agent ran a spy ring in Spain, France and the Netherlands from 1748 to 1770. It was able to rely on constant usage of the Post Office by foreign governments, who trusted it remarkably heavily in their dealings with diplomats and bankers in London – in marked contrast to at least the better-informed politicians of Westminster, who generally relied on private messengers and trusted coach drivers, committing nothing to the post that could not be 'read at Charing Cross'. Most letters sent to and from other countries' ambassadors in London were still opened as a matter of routine, just as in Secretary Thurloe's day. ('Neither time nor trouble were spared, three hours being regularly spent on the King of Prussia's despatches [to London] in mid-century.'[5]) Indeed, a general warrant from the Treasury in 1765 ordered the copying of *all* embassy letters passing through London. This extraordinary state of affairs put the Post Office's Foreign Secretary into a highly select company. 'Probably not more than thirty [people] in Britain knew, and only partly in some cases, what diplomatic correspondence was being read at any one time.'[6] Todd made the most of his contacts during the 1750s, patiently staking his claim to the Post Office Secretaryship in every way he could, including dynastic ties. In 1758, he married the niece of a former Secretary, whose wealthy father was the Resident Surveyor.*

* Always determined to found a dynasty of his own, Todd was tireless thereafter in promoting the marital prospects of three daughters. He succeeded with the second, who married into the Scottish aristocracy and lived until 1856. Her two sons died unmarried, but a

Realizing his ambition in 1762, Todd took over the day-to-day administration in Lombard Street of an institution with few memorable accomplishments to its name in half a century. The most notable was the invention of the letter box, at a date that no one recorded. On the debit side, the arteries of the Post Office had been slowly furring up as any student of monopolies would expect. Senior officials' salaries, for instance, had come to pale by comparison with the fees and side-payments to which the Custom of the Office entitled them. A widespread reliance on handsome perks rather than fixed and regulated salaries was a commonplace of eighteenth-century institutions, inviting rampant corruption. Well-placed individuals could go on scratching each other's backs through long careers, without concerning themselves unduly over plans to improve efficiency or promote faster growth. As ever, the Post Office held a mirror to the age. What remained to be seen in the late 1760s was how far it might yet prove capable of accommodating more dynamic outsiders, as it had adjusted itself to Ralph Allen's ambitions. Left to its own devices, the institution in Lombard Street looked as much of an obstacle to change as any part of the Georgian state, with its governance structure creaking and its finances under heavy strain.

While Anthony Todd had been cultivating the smooth manners of a deferential spymaster, the Post Office had managed to hold net earnings more or less steady but no more. They jumped appreciably higher following the end of the Seven Years War – but a rapidly changing environment sapped the finances thereafter and exposed the inadequacies of the cautious bureaucracy in Lombard Street as never before. With the exception of a brief interval in 1765–8 – when he was forced to step aside for a rival, who later dropped dead in a hackney carriage – Todd was Secretary over the next quarter-century, while also retaining the position of Foreign Secretary throughout. This put the Post Office under the control of one individual in an unprecedented manner. Todd, in fact, was the first Secretary to entrench his position to the point where his tenure was effectively immune to changes of government. He was thus one of the very first Whitehall officials whose role equated with that of a modern Permanent Secretary.[7] He paid for this distinction, however, by having to preside single-handedly over a series of protracted disasters.

Four proved especially damaging to the Post Office, and they almost

daughter married a James Balfour – and their grandson was Arthur James Balfour, the Conservative Prime Minister in 1902–5.

fatally loosened its grip on the mails monopoly that Ralph Allen and others had worked so hard to cement. The first was a spiralling use of postage-free, or 'franked', letters. In Ireland, for reasons now obscure, these had carried a 'FREE' stamp since the start of the century; elsewhere, the signature of the sender or even just a distinguished addressee was enough to confirm their status. (Envelopes had yet to appear: letters were folded in half before sealing, so that the address and any additional information could be written on the back, left blank for the purpose.) The privilege of using the Post Office without charge had been granted to members of both Houses of Parliament since the days of Cromwell. But while the notional value of 'franks' had accounted for just over 15 per cent of all postal revenues in 1715, this was up to almost 50 per cent by 1764.[8] Letters went free of postage for Whitehall officials and anyone connected with the army or navy, as well as to Lords and MPs at Westminster. All were now guilty of distributing 'franked stationery' – often no more than a sheet of paper, bearing an eligible signature – to their family, friends and business associates in ever more outrageous quantities. For all those in positions of power, franks were regarded as a perk of the job (much like parliamentary expenses, one might say, prior to 2009). No one could see the harm in them, and anyone with access to franks abused them shamelessly. When Dr Johnson wrote to his friend Mrs Thrale, he often addressed the letters to her husband: he was an MP, so they went as franked mail – as did her replies, courtesy of her husband's signature on the back, which she was adept at counterfeiting.[9] (This was riskier. Forging someone's handwriting for the sake of a frank was technically punishable after 1764 by transportation to the colonies for seven years.) The correspondence of Horace Walpole, the writer and antiquarian who was an MP from 1741 to 1768, is littered with references to letters that have been sent to him by friends so that he could sign them on the outside and forward them free of charge.

The notional value of franked mail trebled between 1765 and 1783. Over this same period, the damage done to the Post Office's finances was compounded by the futile if well-meant efforts of the Government to tackle the issue. A Franking Act was passed in 1764, with the unintended consequence that MPs were empowered to make bulk purchases of newspapers for free despatch in the post, rather than buying and franking newspapers individually as they had previously done. These despatches had accounted for about a quarter of all the papers sent through the Post Office in the early 1760s, but by 1782 were covering

60 per cent of posted papers. This was a huge boost to the supply of fresh news from the capital to the rest of the country, greatly assisting trade and commerce in a myriad of ways – but it was a calamity for the Clerks of the Roads in Lombard Street and many of their subordinate colleagues: all of them had been financially dependent on their newspaper sales for many years. Some of them were facing personal ruin by the mid-1780s: it was widely noted in 1786 that the Clerk of the Chester Road had died insolvent.[10] Neither Todd as Secretary nor the Board seemed able to remedy a problem that by then was threatening to bankrupt a large proportion of the Inland Office's staff.

A second fundamental challenge to the Post Office struck directly at the livelihood of those working in the country's 440 post towns. The problem here went back to the topography of the Post Roads' network and the Inland Office's decision, in the time of Charles II, to let postmasters charge private fees for distributing letters beyond the vicinity of the Post Road itself. In most market towns along or near the Roads, and the cross-roads built by Allen, letters had usually been delivered free of charge to the recipient's door if it lay close to the main thoroughfare. Others had carried a penny or halfpenny charge on top of the normal postage fee due to the Post Office. (Nowhere outside London was there yet a penny post like the capital's, though legislation in 1765, the year after the Franking Act, gave the Postmasters General the power to authorize them in future.) In towns that were further afield, these 'extra' delivery charges were commonplace. In many such towns – including places later to become famous for their explosive growth, like Manchester and Leeds – the population first began to rise significantly in the 1760s. The early stages of industrialization were drawing together previously isolated villages into communities with shared trade and manufacturing activities. Postal deliveries to such areas could be onerous, even after cross-roads had linked them to the national network. Postmasters now increasingly began to charge accordingly, and to extend their additional charges to cover long-standing routes as well. It caused widespread resentment – especially after 1765, when national postage rates were themselves marginally reduced. In dozens of towns, traditional arrangements for free delivery actually began to be withdrawn altogether, which caused particular anger. It culminated, in 1772, in an appeal to the High Court. The good townspeople of Sandwich, ten miles from the Dover Road on the south coast in Kent, argued that free delivery was their long-established legal right – and the judge agreed with them. Other towns rushed to take up the cause, including some that had actually not

enjoyed free deliveries within living memory. This so alarmed the Postmasters General that they arranged for a test case to be heard in 1774,
on behalf of the Berkshire market town of Hungerford. The judgment
this time was even more emphatic. Within the vicinity of the town's post
office, ruled the court, citizens were entitled to the free delivery of their
letters. Here was the seed of a compelling notion – that addressees
everywhere might expect free delivery, placing on the Post Office what
would eventually be labelled its 'universal service obligation'. It was not
a seed that postmasters on the whole cared to nourish. Unable to charge
for delivery beyond their immediate vicinity, many simply withdrew
their services or heavily curtailed them. Additional carriers were not
recruited in any significant numbers, as universal service would have
required. Lawyers questioned the court ruling, pointing out that the
1711 Act had in fact made no specific reference to the idea at all. The
result was a curious stand-off between the Post Office, which saw any
universal obligation as a recipe for disaster, and the Attorney General,
who made clear his own belief that free delivery was exactly what Parliament had intended in the Act of 1711. By the 1780s, the Postmasters
in General were congratulating themselves that they had managed to
avoid any mass appointment of new letter carriers across the network.
But it was an impasse that could not last for long.

Neither the crisis over franked newspapers nor defeats in the High
Court struck many of Anthony Todd's contemporaries outside the Post
Office as much of a drama. The third great setback over these years was
a more obvious embarrassment, albeit part of a national calamity. The
loss of the American colonies in the War of Independence left the Post
Office with a modest offshoot in Canada but deprived it of a wider network down the Atlantic seaboard. This American Post Office had taken
a long time to nurture into profitability. A monopoly for the colonies
had originally been awarded in 1691 to an official of the London Mint,
Thomas Neale. As his man on the ground in the New World, Neale had
employed a Scottish merchant called Andrew Hamilton, who in the 1690s
had set up – possibly, as we noted, with William Dockwra's assistance –
the first American posts. Hamilton acted with considerable autonomy,
but the Post Office Act of 1711 reined the colonial system into closer
harness. A station in New York was established as Lombard Street's
counterpart, under two joint Deputy Postmasters General. There then
followed a long struggle to ensure that the network based on New York
was financially self-sustaining. Only after 1753 did this objective seem
even remotely attainable, with the promotion to the top job of an excep-

tional man. He had already served for fifteen years in Philadelphia, where he had launched a penny post, and he became an energetic Controller of the whole network. This was Benjamin Franklin – printer, inventor, diplomat, statesmen, polymath *extraordinaire* and luminary of the Post Office.

Franklin's introduction of additional regular posts, especially between Philadelphia and New York, enabled a profit to be remitted to Lombard Street for the first time in 1761, and modest annual surpluses were recorded from that year onwards.[11] Especially helpful was an expansion of the packet-boat services between Falmouth in Cornwall and the colonies from 1765, serving the West Indies, Charleston and New York. But the passage that same year of the Stamp Act – imposing a tax on all printed matter, from newspapers to playing cards – angered many colonists. The Act was repealed within months, but a serious movement in favour of independence from the British Crown had begun, and opposition to the Post Office was a lively part of it. In London, a Parliamentary Committee was set up to review future postal policy in the colonies. The Board in Lombard Street thereafter trailed along in the Government's wake through a succession of humiliations. Benjamin Franklin was dismissed by ministers in 1774, on the back of a messy scandal involving an interception of private letters (almost certainly by the Secret Office) from Crown officials in Massachusetts. A year later, Franklin was appointed the first Postmaster General for the rebellious United Colonies in Philadelphia. By Christmas Day 1775, the Post Office's own officials in New York were having to announce the cessation of all their inland services in the colonies. Within weeks of the Declaration of Independence in July 1776, Franklin was organizing post-riders from Maine to Georgia and giving the patriot militias a significant communications advantage in their war with the Redcoats.*

The Post Office, meanwhile, was left struggling to come to terms with the implications of the war for its packet boats. The Postmasters General applied to the Treasury in February 1776 for the costs of arming nine of them on the Atlantic run. But there was little of the urgency in Lombard Street that the crisis demanded, and no concerted attempt to work together with the King's soldiers and sailors in the colonies. While the paperwork went to and fro, no extra guns appeared on the packet ships, nor were their captains issued with any new standing orders to prepare for wartime contingencies. Once naval hostilities began

---

* Franklin was the first of several famous postmasters in US history – including two men who reached the White House, Abraham Lincoln and Harry Truman. Another was the novelist William Faulkner.

in earnest, the Post Office's losses were dire. Of fourteen packets owned by the Office itself on the North American routes in 1777, fully ten were captured and two more damaged in action by the end of hostilities in 1782.

GENERAL POST-OFFICE,

M A Y the 22d, 1784.

NOTICE was given by an Advertifement from this Office of the 18th of November laft, that the Packet Poftage of one Shilling for a fingle Letter, and fo in Proportion, between LONDON and NEW-YORK, might or not be paid before-hand; but Difficulties having arifen in the Collection of the Packet Poftage in NORTH-AMERICA, it now becomes neceffary to inform the Public, that both the Inland and Packet Poftage on all Letters from any Part of GREAT-BRITAIN or IRELAND for NORTH-AMERICA, which are forwarded from this Office on the firft Wednefday of every Month, muft abfolutely be paid quite to NEW-YORK, and alfo to HALIFAX, without which they muft be opened, and returned to the Writers.

By Command of the Poftmafter-General,

ANTHONY TODD, Sec.

Notice that pre-payment is required for letters to New York, May 1784

Another twenty-seven boats on contract to the Office were captured, needing the owners to be compensated at the Office's expense. Regular packet services were resumed in the wake of the war, but it took more than two years to reach agreement with the ex-colonies on how postal affairs should be managed. Officials in Lombard Street had to announce on more than one occasion that letters bound for New York would only be accepted if the postage was prepaid by the sender.

The historian who looks up that February 1776 application for help in arming the packet boats in the Post Office's copy book of Treasury correspondence will find that it follows a six-line note from Anthony Todd to the Prime Minister's secretary. Dated two months earlier, Todd's note informs Lord North of a £7 10s increase in the weekly salary of the deputy postmaster for the small Scottish town of Perth, 'to Forty-five pounds a year, which there is no doubt will be quite satisfactory to him, being fully sufficient for the duty of that Office'.[12] Even allowing for the rigorous demands of the Treasury bureaucracy, this was a curious note for the Secretary of the Post Office to be sending to the country's Prime Minister, in the midst of a major war. There might have been more time to attend to the needs of the packet boats, and a plethora of broader policy issues, had the administrators of Lombard Street been less immersed in the minutiae of day-to-day operations.

Complaints about the dysfunctional governance of the Post Office sparked the fourth and most telling crisis of all: the Office was increasingly regarded by the 1780s as a service that fell far short of the speed, reliability and regularity that were needed by the public. On the Post Roads, and many lesser highways, stage coaches and smaller post-chaises – carriages originally so-called because they could be hired from post stations – were now a common sight, and these travelled appreciably faster than the solitary post-boys on their horses. The condition of many roads was still appalling, but the 1760s and 1770s were at least marked by a jump in the number of turnpike acts, setting up local trusts with the wherewithal to pay for road improvements. None of this had any impact on the post-boys. A complaint to the Postmasters General from a body representing the royal boroughs of Scotland was widely quoted: the first thing that most travellers passed on the Great North Road, as they made their way south from the border, was the King's mail *from Edinburgh*.[13] As for security, the introduction of capital punishment for mail robbery in 1767 did nothing to stop highwaymen divesting the unarmed post-boys of their mailbags on a regular basis. This had been a problem since the 1720s. The Post Office put a notice about every mail robbery in the *London Gazette*: notices appeared frequently, but showed no discernible trend. Some years saw just a dozen or so reported, other years three or four times that number.[14] Society's growing dependence on the mails, though, probably meant richer pickings for the highwaymen. All the Post Office could suggest as a remedy, in

1782, was that correspondents should send banknotes one half at a time, in separate mails. Only the rightful recipient, matching the two halves together, would be able to make the due claim for cash on the issuing bank.* (It was not unknown for robberies thereafter to happen two at a time, on consecutive mails.) On both counts, of speed and safety, people were turning ever more conspicuously to the privately run stage coaches, which could legitimately accept parcels and were none too fussy about sorting parcels from letters. Even newspapers, though posted free of charge by the Clerks, were starting to be sent from London by coach rather than post-boy, for a speedier delivery. The Post Office's income ('Net Product') had stopped growing: in the ten years to 1782 it averaged £151,563, little different from the £150,312 average achieved in the ten years to 1772. And as business stagnated, so the structure of the Post Office was beginning to fall apart – literally so, in the case of its offices in both Edinburgh and Dublin. Todd received a cheeky letter in November 1776 from John Lees, who had been the Secretary in Ireland since 1774, about the need for a new Dublin office. Over the prior summer, wrote Lees, 'an accurate survey was made of the present Building, and by the Report of the most competent people that could be resorted to, it appears that the Roof has fallen in . . .'[15]

It would be wrong to suggest universal disaffection with the Post Office. No doubt many regular correspondents all over the country were delighted at the relative ease with which letters could now be sent and received, as compared with earlier times. The post-boy was a familiar sight – and a familiar sound, too, blowing his horn at regular intervals as he rode through country villages. The poet William Cowper penned a memorable portrait of the post-boy in 1785, floating a theme many others would echo in the centuries to come:

> Hark! 'tis the twanging horn o'er yonder bridge . . .
> He comes, the herald of a noisy world,
> With spatter'd boots, strapp'd waist and frozen locks;
> News from all nations lumbering at his back.
> True to his charge, the close-pack'd load behind,
> Yet careless what he brings, his one concern
> Is to conduct it to the destin'd inn:
> And, having dropp'd th' expected bag, pass on.

---

* This is the origin of the practice, still observed today, of printing the serial number on every British banknote twice – once at each end.

He whistles as he goes, light-hearted wretch,
Cold and yet cheerful: messenger of grief
Perhaps to thousands, and of joy to some;
To him indiff'rent whether grief or joy.
Houses in ashes, and the fall of stocks,
Births, deaths, and marriages, epistles wet
With tears, that trickled down the writer's cheeks
Fast as the periods from his fluent quill,
Or charg'd with am'rous sighs of absent swains,
Or nymphs responsive, equally affect
His horse and him, unconscious of them all.[16]

In the famously detailed country diaries that he kept from 1776 to 1803, Parson James Woodforde made no criticism at all of his local post office in Norwich. Living in a small village some ten miles from the city – much like the Paston family of the fifteenth century – he made his own arrangements for collecting his letters, and presented the Norwich postmaster with a Christmas box each year. Woodforde, a Somerset man, wrote regularly to relatives he had left behind in the West Country and was seemingly content that a letter from them would usually take several days to reach Norwich, though it was on the Yarmouth Road.[17] But for men of a more urgent turn of mind than the parson, the unchanging timetables of the post-boys were by 1780 becoming a serious irritant. No one was more affronted by them than a hard-driving businessman from Ralph Allen's home city of Bath. A frequent traveller to and from London by stage coach, John Palmer thought it unconscionable that the mail should still take the best part of two days to cover a distance he customarily travelled overnight. There is no evidence that he ever met Ralph Allen. But we can be sure that, as mindful of Allen's story as anyone else in Bath – he was twenty-two when Allen died – he looked at the Post Office with a keen entrepreneurial eye. And the thought occurred to him that *another* fortune was there to be made, by anyone who could by-pass the Office's antiquated ways and put the mails into fast-moving coaches of their own.

2. AN IMPRESARIO'S DICTATORSHIP

Palmer decided that he would take on the challenge. His background suited him for the task in several ways. To start with, he was a genuine entrepreneur, endowed with volcanic energy and determination. Now a striking-looking man his late thirties, he had followed in his father's foot-steps as a theatrical impresario. He ran the two finest theatres in the country outside London, in Bath and Bristol, and managed both with a toughness that was not to be crossed lightly. On one occasion, the casts of both his theatres went on strike, to protest against a stage manager they regarded as over-zealous. Palmer instantly took to his horse, spent a fort-night riding around the West Country to find replacements, then fired all the strikers and reopened his theatres with fresh casts a few days later.[18] If this story gives a measure of the man's ruthlessness, it also reflects the fact that he knew his way around the country. He was very familiar with the roads across large parts of the south of England. Better than most, he also sensed the potential benefits from better roads and faster carriages, both highly topical issues by the early 1780s. The General Turnpike Act of 1773 was aimed at the promotion and easier regulation of turnpike trusts, which were spreading rapidly as townships struggled to address the generally dreadful state of their local roads. Better-built and better-organized stage coaches, celebrated by contemporaries as 'flying machines', were already reducing the time needed to travel many popular routes, in some cases dramatically so.[19] (A genuine revolution in road-making techniques, though, would take a little longer to materialize: only after 1816 was the Scottish engineer J. L. McAdam able to propagate successfully his building technique, based on the use of small stones that could be compacted into a durable and reasonably weather-proof surface.) And judged by any pro-vincial standards, at least, Palmer was extremely well-connected. He had been a young man of twenty-six in 1768 when his father had sent him to London to organize a petition to Parliament for their playhouse in Bath to be licensed as a Theatre Royal.* Palmer had succeeded at this, making many influential friends and contacts in the process. (Bath's Theatre Royal is still there today, one of the oldest continuously operating theatres in Britain.) More than ten years after this mission, he could count among his friends not only leading figures of the theatre like Garrick and Sheridan but many politicians and influential peers, too.

   With plenty of money behind him, Palmer put his theatre career to one side and sat down to pen a detailed set of recommendations for presentation to the Treasury. The result was always referred to then and

---

* The Theatre Licensing Act of 1737 had prohibited the performance of plays without the approval of the authorities, which a theatre licensed by the King would have less problem obtaining. The title 'Theatre Royal' would later come to be a popular but meaningless appendage.

since as his Plan. Ranging across the gamut of postal operations, it even included a proposal for higher postage rates and a squeeze on franking practices.[20] The core of the Plan was its remedy for the notorious slowness of the post. On all Post Roads (now meaning the main cross-roads as well as the principal Roads from London) and a good proportion of other routes, too, he proposed replacing the post-boys – and slow-moving, horse-drawn 'mail-carts' that had begun to appear in rising numbers – with specially designed Royal Mail coaches. Most contemporary stage coaches, as large passenger vehicles, had six-horse teams. Mail coaches would focus primarily on the post: they would be smaller, lighter and more manoeuvrable with teams of four, to be renewed with fresh horses at even shorter intervals than the 10–15 miles that typically applied to the flying machines. They would travel through the night as well as by day, and would be exempt from stopping at turnpikes for the payment of tolls. Just as people had been able to 'ride post' by hiring horses from postmasters in past generations, the Royal Mail would provide a facility for passengers, too – but they would be a secondary consideration, with just four allowed to travel inside the coach. (Extra seats would in time be allowed, on a bench behind the coachman.) Everything would revolve around the safe and punctual delivery of the sacred mail, which would travel at the back of the coach in a locked box under the feet of a guard packing two pistols and a blunderbuss. Just as important, each guard would also carry a specially locked timepiece to help him monitor progress against the clock. Arrival and departure times would have to be strictly observed and marked down on a 'time bill' – and only supervisors at the beginning and end of the route would have a key to the clock, preventing convenient adjustments to the hands en route.* Departure times would be waived for no man, not even messengers from Whitehall with delayed official papers. As for the optimal schedules, Palmer suggested (with a characteristic dig at the officials in Lombard Street) that 'committees[s] of gentlemen merchants etc might perhaps suggest a better method of regulating the post for their own district than persons always employed in an office in London . . .'[21]

---

* Passengers were unlikely to be coach-lagged, but local time varied on the longer journeys: Plymouth, for example, was twenty minutes behind London. Not until the 1850s would all clocks in Britain move together – on 'railway time' – as a necessary side-product of train timetables. '[C]locks were regulated to gain or lose so many minutes in twenty-four hours, according to the direction in which the coach travelled, in order that local time might be kept.' (Charles G. Harper, *Stage Coach and Mail in Days of Yore*, 2 vols., Chapman & Hall, 1903, Vol. 1, p. 260.)

Palmer had no interest whatever in being employed in that office himself. He envisaged spending much of his time on the road, monitoring routes and ensuring the efficiency of the coaching inns where horse teams would be changed. In fact he had no intention of actually joining the Post Office at all. He would work from outside it, pressing his ideas for a better service on the Office's masters at the Treasury. He would keep his distance from the bureaucracy in Lombard Street, citing Allen's approach as a precedent. This evocation of the past suited Palmer: by temperament an autocrat with a scarcely hidden disdain for committees, office manners and paperwork, he was almost the antithesis of the Lombard Street archetype as personified by Todd. But it was also a slightly disingenuous interpretation of Allen's career. As Palmer must have known, his predecessor had been steeped in the ways of the Post Office before striking out on his own, and carefully complied with its rule book throughout his career – never questioning, for instance, that the Surveyors had to remain formally answerable to Lombard Street, much though he would have preferred otherwise. Palmer ignored such subtleties, just as he would later do his best to ignore any Post Office procedures of his own day that he found inconvenient. He established many of his early coaching routes, in 1785, entirely at his own expense. Planning a surcharge on remote routes through the Scottish Highlands in 1791, he would brush aside calls for the policy to be cleared first with the Treasury – and would force it through by threatening to cancel some principal Lowland routes unless his wishes were allowed to prevail.[22] No doubt such behaviour helped him accomplish a huge amount in a relatively short time; it also led eventually to a clash of personalities quite as dramatic as anything ever staged in one of his own theatres.

His rise to power was a melodrama in itself. Palmer's political friends won him a meeting in 1782 with William Pitt, just appointed – at the tender age of twenty-three – as Chancellor of the Exchequer. Pitt took no time to grasp that Palmer's Plan was at the very least worth putting to the test. He was also, it must be said, a Chancellor in urgent need of extra funds who must have been impressed by the reference in the Plan to higher rates. Whatever his mix of motives, Pitt pushed for a trial run of a 'mail coach' as soon as possible. His own fall from office delayed matters until 1784; in the interval, the Plan was sent off to the Post Office for its comments. These came back at almost comical length, in the summer of 1783, and ran to three thick volumes of objections. One included the memorable observation, re the many stations of the Post Office, that 'the constant eye that has long been kept towards their improvement in all situations and under all circumstances have [sic] made them now as perfect as can be without exhausting the revenue arising therefrom'.[23] Palmer put down written responses, item by item, while acerbically noting how alarmed he was 'to find the habits of office seem to create a sort of confirm'd opinion of [the Post Office's] perfection and resistance to all improvement'.[24] This was indeed the nub of the matter: Lombard Street's introverted culture, as Palmer rightly protested, would probably have reacted with hostility to almost any reform ideas floated by an outsider. The implications of Palmer's Plan – upending the finances of the Post Office and comprehensively rejigging many of its basic routines and timetables – were so breathtakingly ambitious as to guarantee a fierce rebuttal. The Post Office's officials had no doubt it would end in disaster. Only Pitt himself, back in power in 1784 at the head of his own ministry, could resolve the ensuing stand-off. Both sides were summoned to the Treasury in June 1784. It was a famous meeting, brought to an abrupt close by Pitt. He stood up, announced to the Post Office officials that he was overruling their advice and declared to their dismay that Palmer's Plan should be trialled on the Bristol–London Road at the beginning of August. Then he strode out of the room, reportedly leaving a stunned silence in his wake. Palmer departed for Bath immediately to start making arrangements for the trial. And Anthony Todd went back to Lombard Street to start planning its disruption: 'With natural zest, great influence, experience and obstructive capacity, he determined to ruin Palmer.'[25]

What followed was a bizarre struggle for control of the postal network. There exists a school of thought among historians that the Georgian state, however sclerotic it might sometimes appear to us, was nonetheless adept at providing an administrative framework flexible enough to encourage the local innovations that fuelled the start of the Industrial Revolution. Perhaps so, but there was little conspicuous flexibility in the Post Office's response to Palmer. His coaches notched up exactly the speeds he had projected for them – the Bristol coach set off at 4 p.m. and arrived in London at 9 a.m. the next morning, a whole day and a half quicker than the post-boys – and they were extended over the next two years, at Palmer's own expense, to cover a dozen or more additional routes. (The idea spread to the new United States, too, where mail coaches began running in 1785.) New and faster modes of transport were much in vogue – the first hot-air balloons were causing a sensation in these same years – and the public's enthusiasm for Palmer's innovation was obvious.[26] Todd and his senior colleagues, however,

suppressed the new coaching schedules wherever possible, issuing directions to the country's postmasters that cut clean across Palmer's own
instructions and generally trying, as Palmer despairingly complained to
Pitt, 'to do the plan all possible mischief'.[27] They even prepared a report
backing the horse-drawn cart as the Post's best next step.* By the spring
of 1786, the feud had brought the network to the brink of chaos. Then,
quite suddenly, Pitt prevailed on Todd to abandon the struggle. Almost
overnight, Lombard Street's opposition to mail coaches dropped away.
A celebratory reception was held at the Inland Office to mark the truce.
(Privately, Palmer confessed his amazement that the Treasury had not
simply dismissed Todd from office. But then, Palmer seems to have had
no inkling of the Secretary's role as the head of the Secret Office.) For
the time being, at least, Todd's influence in Lombard Street was much
diminished. The Treasury Lords in August 1786 instructed the Postmasters General to vest Palmer 'with full and sufficient authority over all
Surveyors, Comptrollers, Postmasters, Contractors, Deputies, Clerks,
Sorters, Window Men, Letter Receivers, Letter Carriers, Messengers
and other Officers and servants employed in the sorting, conveying and
delivery of Letters . . .'[28] Against all the odds, Palmer had triumphed. He
had Pitt's support not just to implement his Plan but to carry through a
radical overhaul of the whole Post Office.

Travelling thousands of miles over the next five years, Palmer rescued
the fortunes of the Post Office by laying the foundations of the Royal
Mail coaching network. This required a daunting set of tasks to be
accomplished more or less together. New patents were arranged on a
custom-built carriage, designed by one John Besant, and an exclusive
contract for the supply and maintenance of all mail coaches was granted
to Besant in partnership with a man called Finch Vidler, who ran a large
coach workshop on London's Millbank. (Vidler and his successors in the
business would retain the contract until 1836.) Independent coach operators were taken on, persuaded to lease the new coaches from Vidler and
tied into timetable commitments set by Palmer. It was their responsibility
to coordinate the movement and stabling of horses, which in turn relied
on the work of hundreds of sub-contracted ostlers and coaching inns in
a rapidly expanding list of towns. The logistics of this business made it a

* One model was to be entirely built of iron, which officials hoped would make it robber-
proof – though recent experience with a prototype on the North Road suggested otherwise.
'This cart had not long begun to run before it was stopped by highwaymen and rifled of
all its contents.' (Herbert Joyce, The History of the Post Office, Richard Bentley & Sons,
1893, p. 290.)

forerunner of the kind of commercial venture that would face the architects of the Empire Air Mail scheme in another century. Four-horse coaches, like four-engined aeroplanes, were expensive capital items in their day, needing lavish maintenance. But it was providing an infrastructure for their services that posed the real challenge. Horses, properly watered and fed, needed to be standing in place at every scheduled halt, at exactly the right time around the clock to relieve the tired team on an arriving coach; and the latter in their turn would need attentive stabling in preparation for their next run. The travelling passengers needed to be fed, too, and operators had to coordinate their schedules with innkeepers across the country to ensure that hot meals would always be available with the minimum of delay. (The larger coach operators grew into being among the most sophisticated businesses of their time, and some would one day adapt their skills to the running of the railways.[29])

By October 1785, the *London Gazette* was carrying departure times for coaches to twenty-five destinations all over the country, leaving from half a dozen of London's leading coaching inns – including names like the Swan with Two Necks in Lad Lane (off Gresham Street), the Bell and Crown in Holborn and the Bull and Mouth off St Martin's-le-Grand.[30] The published journey times left many contemporaries incredulous – especially the sixty hours advertised for the journey from Edinburgh back to London, hitherto needing at least five days. One early passenger, the Chief Justice of England, wrote of his experience:

> I was to perform [the journey] by a mailcoach, which had been recently established and was supposed to travel with marvellous celerity, taking only three days and two nights for the whole distance. But this speed was thought to be highly dangerous to the head, independently of the perils of an overturn, and stories were told of men and women who, having reached London with such celerity, died suddenly of an affection [sic] of the brain. My family and friends were seriously alarmed for me, and advised me at all events to stay a day in York to recruit myself . . . [but] I boldly took my place all the way through to London.[31]

The timetables put the mails ahead of even the fastest express riders, and at the same time coordinated the Royal Mail coaches with the running of the by-posts and cross-posts, generally still carried by post-boys. The latter had to go on contending with thieving highwaymen – but attacks on the Royal Mail, while far from unknown, were to be rare events. Palmer's armed guards deterred all but the most foolhardy highwaymen. Meanwhile, employees and customers of the new network alike needed reconciling to its unfamiliar demands. Many postmasters now had to rise twice nightly, to see the 'up' and 'down' coaches on their way with local letters and fresh horses. In London, bankers and merchants had to be persuaded to accept that all posts bound for the country would leave at 8 p.m., requiring letters to be handed in, not by midnight, but by 7 p.m. at the latest. Neither group took instantly to the new way of things. To help him push through these and a myriad other changes, Palmer appointed his own team of gifted lieutenants and restructured the Post Office hierarchy, setting up six districts across England. Each had its own Riding Surveyor, while a seventh, unattached Surveyor – an impressive young man promoted from Bristol's post office, called Francis Freeling – acted as his personal assistant with a roving brief.

By 1791, the man referred to by one Postmaster General as 'our Dictator' had begun, in effect, to rebuild the organization in his own image as a highly profitable business enterprise.[32] (In anticipation of his success, the Treasury had from the outset increased its weekly tax bill from £700 to £2,300 – still payable every Tuesday.) Palmer's timing, in some ways, could hardly have been better. The outdated ways and introverted culture of the Georgian institution – 'a rotten old Post Office', as Palmer himself referred to it – had become so apparent as to be an embarrassment even to its friends. It was epitomized by an unedifying squabble between two serving Postmasters General, Lord Tankerville and Lord Carteret, between 1784 and 1786. Their bickering stretched even Todd's courtier skills and caused William Pitt intense irritation. (He summarily sacked Tankerville in August 1786, much to the latter's astonishment.) And it was amply documented by a Parliamentary Commission in 1788, which professed to be shocked at the convoluted nature of the Post Office's finances – not least those of Todd himself, whose official salary of £200 for 1787 had been transmuted into a total payment for that year of £1,738, not including free coal and candles, and complimentary tea from the East India Company.[33] The 1788 Commissioners added their explicit support for Palmer to the weighty backing that he received from the Prime Minister. Dismissing the objections raised by his opponents, they happily acknowledged the way that the mails were now travelling at unprecedented speeds, '[and] with a degree of punctuality never experienced before'.[34] The door was wide open for whatever reforms he wanted to propose.

Palmer rode his luck, finding his refurbished Royal Mail even more popular and lucrative than he had expected. The volume of illicit mails dropped sharply. The newspaper business grew rapidly in the 1780s, with a proliferation of new titles – including *The Times* in 1785. The rising shipments via the mail coaches, taken together with a boost to their salaries from Pitt, rescued the Clerks' finances. Best of all, as the Treasury certainly noted, the volume of letters showed no sign of dipping in response to a hike in postage rates in 1784. The cheapest letter, a single sheet over one stage, was lifted from 1d to 2d. Letters going more than two stages went from 3d to 4d for up to eighty miles, 4d to 5d for up to 150 miles and 4d to 6d for any destination beyond 150 miles. A single letter from London to Edinburgh now cost 7d, up from 6d. Contrary to most expectations, the revenue shot up: by 1791, it had risen nearly 50 per cent in eight years – from just over £393,000 to £575,000 – and net income, thanks to a lower than projected outlay on mail coaches, had trebled since 1782, reaching £356,000.[35] Palmer was richly rewarded. The contract he signed in August 1786 confirmed him as 'Surveyor and Comptroller General' on a salary of £1,500. He was also entitled to an annual bonus linked to the growth of revenues, which earned him an additional £6,900 in 1791.* No wonder that Palmer was by then beginning to think about expanding his business plans. Next on his agenda was a reorganization of the Penny Post, which he actually offered to run on a lease contract like the farms of old. It must have looked to Palmer as though he really did have an opportunity to emulate his predecessor from Bath, and to make another huge fortune. But Palmer wholly lacked Ralph Allen's remarkable skills as a diplomat, and was less blessed with his timing. His disdain for the traditional ways of the Post Office was matched by a contempt for its governance that he made little effort to conceal. As he would eventually set down in a letter to Pitt, Palmer believed his own appointment had left the Postmasters General looking surplus to requirements. He thought their positiôns, as also that of the Secretary, were virtually sinecures and should all be abolished.[36] Such an antipathy towards these top officials would eventually have brought Palmer into a head-on collision with the culture of Lombard Street, under any circumstances; in the event, a severe clash was made inevitable by the arrival as a Postmaster General in 1787 of Thomas De Grey, and Baron Walsingham.

By the late 1780s, faced with the irresistible – not to say abrasive –

---

* His contract specified an annual bonus equivalent to 2.5 per cent of any revenues for the year in excess of £300,000. The details are set down in the first of ten Appendices to 'Palmer's Memorial', a documentary record of his career with the Post Office that was printed in 1797 (Post 10/200). His total earnings in 1791 were equivalent to approximately £1m in today's money.

Palmer, most of the Post Office's senior employees had decided either to keep their heads down (like the ageing Todd) or to take a lofty view of proceedings (like Carteret, who opined that 'it was no part of a Postmaster General's duty to check accounts').[37] Walsingham took a different line. He saw himself as the unmoveable rock upon which the probity of the Post Office could be rebuilt. Appointed to strengthen its defences against an attack by the Parliamentary Commissioners that everyone knew was coming, he was an obsessional stickler for detail. He loved nothing better than crawling over the minutiae of public accounts, noting omissions, errors and discrepancies in a stream of marginalia – and reprimanding offenders, whatever their station. In many ways he was the ideal antidote to the venal cheating that riddled the Post Office of the 1780s, especially its packet-boat services.[38] But, to the modern eye, much of Walsingham's behaviour looks odd, if not downright bloody-minded. His scrutiny of every paper that crossed his desk – and his tireless pursuit of many that did not – suggests a man utterly incapable of distinguishing between the essential and the trivial. And to Palmer, his constant interference in the operations of the Post Office was anathema. No doubt there was fault on both sides. But Walsingham struck the impresario of the Royal Mail coaches as a pedant and a menace.

Palmer flaunted this view, regularly ignoring letters, minutes and invitations to attend Board meetings at Lombard Street. (He often sent along a letter carrier to represent him. This caused huge offence, as intended, but was also Palmer's way of promoting a humble letter carrier called Edward Johnson, whom he considered worthy of higher office.) His impatience with the culture of the Inland Office as a whole can be gauged from the fact that, needing a deputy to run the place when he was out of London, Palmer chose to appoint not an existing official in Lombard Street but one of his more successful actor friends. Charles Bonnor had appeared on stage in Covent Garden as recently as 1783 and was a well-known man of the theatre; but he was no accountant or budding Clerk of the Road. When financial irregularities in Bonnor's affairs surfaced at the Office within weeks of Walsingham's arrival, a series of quarrels began that grew steadily nastier over the next three years. Walsingham took every opportunity to try to assert more control. Palmer pressed on as though the Postmasters General ('those Two coxcombly Lords') were almost figures of fun – and he dashed off letters to Bonnor about them that were extraordinarily indiscreet, even by the standards of theatre gossip. Their flavour can be judged from an early letter, in which Palmer suggested ways to embarrass Walsingham over the very first clash of wills between them:

> The matter should be quietly to throw this Load upon his Lordship; let him be bullied, perplexed and frightened, and made apprehensive that his foolish Interference may even occasion a rising of the Mail Prices . . . The fun would be to get Wilson [one of the two biggest mail-coach operators and renowned as a tough customer] to a Board, and let him bamboozle his Lordship with his Slouch and his Slang, and his Blackguard. Wilson must be well lessoned . . .[39]

Disaster struck in 1792. Palmer and Walsingham were by this time in open confrontation, and Bonnor's financial affairs – both personal and professional – were in deep trouble. Having stood by his deputy through a succession of awkward episodes, Palmer finally lost patience with Bonnor and dismissed him. With his usual eagle eye for the small print, Walsingham pointed out that the terms of Palmer's appointment gave him the authority to hire Post Office staff, but not to remove them. The Board encouraged Bonnor to return to his Lombard Street office. In equally characteristic style, Palmer refused him entry, pocketed the key to his office and warned Bonnor he would be arrested if he turned up in Lombard Street again. All this was reported back to the Board by Bonnor – at which point, the Board suspended Palmer and actually tried to appoint the wretched Bonnor in his place. Palmer stood his ground – and in May 1792, not for the first time, the warring parties within the Post Office turned to Pitt to sort out their mess. A first audience for Walsingham with the Prime Minister did not augur well for the Postmasters General: Pitt had a better understanding than they did of Palmer's importance and gave the case against him a cool response. A few days later, their Lordships received a package from Charles Bonnor. Inside it, with all the timing and venom of a real-life Iago, the ex-actor enclosed six of the most inflammatory letters he had received from Palmer in 1788–90 – and Walsingham, as Herbert Joyce put it, 'in an evil moment accepted them'. Their colourful, not to say scandalous, contents made it impossible for Pitt to insist on Palmer's reinstatement.[40] So ended, after eight years, the career of one of the half-dozen most important individuals in the history of the Post Office. The man dismissed for 'contumely and insubordination' – as Walsingham relished informing the House of Lords in 1807 – was showered with civic honours over the next two decades.* He was eventually granted a huge financial settlement from the Treasury, although it was not finally approved by Parliament until 1813. By then, the lasting impact of his years as 'Comptroller-General' was clear to all. Not least, he had advanced the careers of two men who by 1792 already seemed capable of consolidating the work he had begun. One was Thomas Hasker, who would preside over the operations of the mail coaches until 1817. The other was Francis Freeling, who would emerge after a brief interval as Palmer's successor at the head of the Post Office.

Hasker has received surprisingly little credit from historians for his quarter-century in charge of the mail coaches, though he left behind a better documentary record than the memo-shy Palmer.[41] His was a vital contribution to the new era. For all of Palmer's brilliance, the coaching network by the early 1790s was showing the defects of an organization cobbled together in great haste, with too little capital invested and too many deals struck on the fly without formal legal contracts. It was left to Hasker 'to manage a great sprawling organization run at desperately cut prices by outsiders whom he could never wholly trust ... [with a] staff of clerks and deputies [that] was miserably small, overworked and underpaid' – and in the process to build a service robust enough to answer to the needs of a society in the throes of the Industrial Revolution.[42] The explosive growth of manufacturing, an unprecedented phenomenon in human history, required that letters could be exchanged swiftly and reliably between a mass of new businesses, their suppliers and their customers – and, in some instances, between proprietors and the men they employed to manage their businesses on the spot. (One of the most celebrated correspondences of this kind, the Dowlais Iron Company letters, linked the owners of a leading iron works – who spent much of their time in London – to their managers in South Wales: it stretches from 1782 to 1860, and the successful development of one of the largest industrial concerns in the world was heavily dependent by 1800 on the reliability of the Royal Mail in bearing a constant stream

---

* Palmer was given the freedom of no fewer than eighteen cities. He was twice elected Mayor of Bath and sat as its Member of Parliament from 1801 to 1808. He died aged seventy-six in 1818 and was buried in Bath Abbey. Walsingham died in that same year, having left the Post Office in 1794 to serve for many years as Chairman of Committees in the House of Lords. Charles Bonnor was retired from the Post Office in 1795, endured a spell in the King's Bench prison for debt and then devoted himself to producing a stream of recriminatory pamphlets. These, according to Herbert Joyce, 'proved nothing more than that the writer was a poltroon as well as a traitor' (*History of the Post Office*, p. 280). But he went on receiving his Post Office pension until his death in 1831.

of directives from the capital to the staff of Dowlais in and around Merthyr Tydfil.[43]) Entrepreneurs also needed ready access to the bankers and bill-brokers of London, who could put at their disposal the evolving sophistication of the City's money markets and the indispensable documentary tools for conducting trade with overseas customers. And while commercial and financial transactions were boosting the volume of the mails, so too were the social consequences of a massive upheaval in the distribution of the population. The gathering migration of workers from the rural hinterlands of industrial settlements saw Lancashire's population, for example, grow by 23 per cent in the first decade of the nineteenth century, and the largest towns within Lancashire were soon absorbing huge numbers: Liverpool and Manchester grew by 46 per cent and 40 per cent respectively in 1821–31.[44] Behind such demographic statistics were countless families split apart, for some of whom letters (though none too cheap) offered at least the chance of a lingering contact.

In consolidating a Royal Mail capable of responding to these rising needs, Hasker accomplished what was without question the second great advance in the evolution of Britain's postal system. Over the course of 150 years, the Post Office had laid down the Post Roads and all the by-roads and cross-roads that put Lombard Street at the centre of a remarkable national network. Its expansion over recent generations had turned a putative monopoly into something close to the real thing. Now mail coaches took this whole process to the next level. Exploiting the monopoly and the benefits of improving technology – notably in road-building techniques, thanks to the Scotsmen Thomas Telford and John McAdam, but in the breeding of horses, too – mail coaches altered the very nature of communications.[45] Under Hasker's management, they provided for the first time a delivery service that was far more frequent, far more punctual and much faster than anyone had thought possible. (And of course much safer: Hasker regularly enjoined his guards to have their pistols 'clean, well loaded and hung handy', as one of his directives put it in 1793.) Letters posted in London to almost any city in England south of York on a Sunday evening, for example, could see a reply back by the close of business on Wednesday. And the same service was available every night of the week. Edinburgh and Dublin were at most three days away. Between many large towns and cities, the business classes could talk of exchanging commercial correspondence 'by return of post' – meaning a letter by Royal Mail could fetch a reply within two days. At the same time, the transformation wrought by the coaches went well beyond the business community, and beyond even the conveyance of letters. The Royal Mail linked together the cities, towns and villages of Britain with a sense of proximity that

General Post-Office,

March 25th, 1793.

S I R,

I HAVE the Honor of the Postmaster General's Commands, to direct you to be very attentive to your Arms, that they are clean, well loaded, and hung handy.

And further, that you do not suffer on any Account whatever, any Person except Superior Officers of this Department of the Post-Office, to ride on your Mail Box, which Mail Box you must never leave unlocked, when the Mail is therein.

If you are ever seen Sleeping while on Duty, you will be dismissed, as you will be for disobeying any Part of these Orders.

THOMAS HASKER.

N.B. The above Orders have been all given before; but I have now the particular Commands of the Postmaster General to repeat them, and to desire you will read over your Instructions.

Thomas Hasker's directive to the Royal Mail guards, March 1793

marked a profound break with the past. More than just a source of up-to-date correspondence and the latest newspapers, its coaches were a daily reminder of the wider world that they and their passengers had just come from – bringing word, now and then, of sensational events. Printed government hand-bills were sometimes sent out from Lombard Street and distributed via the postmasters when accurate details were thought to be important.[46] The process on other occasions was more spontaneous. In 1815, it was famously the Royal Mail coach that broke the news of Wellington's victory at Waterloo to huge crowds in Birmingham, just by arriving along the London road into the city 'covered with waving boughs of laurel'.[47]

Indeed, the mail coaches were themselves revered for a discipline and efficiency that was more usually associated with the dash and glory of the military world. This was shrewdly encouraged from the earliest days of the service, with the 'enlisting' of more than 250 guards who were then required to take an oath of fidelity before donning their bright scarlet tunics, replete with blue lapels and gold braiding. The drivers were employees of the coaching contractors, not the Post Office, but they too were given smart Royal Mail uniforms. It is only slightly fanciful to see the whole organization as a kind of miniature version of the King's navy, with its own Admiralty in Lombard Street and the time-bills from every mail coach – recording arrival and departure times along the Roads – winging back like the log-books of the fleet. Certainly, the image of the Royal Mail in the popular imagination shared some familiar features of the senior service. Both pitted tough, hard-drinking men against the elements, requiring them to keep going in all weathers and over long, lonely distances. The guard perched high on his rear seat, called the 'dicky', in the pitch darkness and driving sleet of a winter's night, travelling 100–150 miles at a time, seemed no less heroic than the sailor in the crow's nest – though he could also be feared as a social menace quite as threatening as any drunken sailor in a port. As a contemporary wrote in 1792: 'These guards shoot at dogs, hogs, sheep, and poultry as they pass [along] the road, and even in towns to the great terror and danger of the inhabitants.'[48] During the French wars, they were allowed to shoot at anyone they suspected of being an escaped French prisoner of war, and were paid £5 for each one killed or wounded – a craziness that well reflected the paranoia of the times, and had eventually to be reined back with an Act of Parliament in 1811 prohibiting the use of the guard's blunderbuss except in self-defence.

Scarcely less than fighting ships and the sea, mail coaches came very quickly to occupy a lasting place in the idyll of English life as peddled by popular writers and artists – who went on embellishing the romance of the Royal Mail coaches long after the railways had consigned them to history. Commercial Christmas cards, gathering momentum from the middle of the nineteenth century, latched on to mail coaches in the snow as one of their favourite themes from the start. Until the arrival of the motor car, Victorian and Edwardian authors could rely on the reading public's appetite for their tales of the coachmen on the open road, with any number of anecdotes to keep them going. None better, perhaps, than the story of the Exeter mail coach in 1816. As it rumbled through the night across Salisbury Plain, its guard was amazed to see it being shadowed by what he took in the darkness to be a large calf. It was in fact a lion – or rather, a lioness – that had escaped from a travelling

JUST  ARRIVED,

And to be SEEN in a COMMODIOUS BOOTH,

During the Fair,

BALLARD's

GRAND COLLECTION OF

Wild Beasts,

Among which are, THE NOBLE

LIONESS,

FROM AFRICA,

Which attacked the Horse

In the Mail Coach, at Wintersloo Hut, near Salisbury, in October last,

But was diverted from its Prey, by a large

MASTIFF DOG.

These Three Animals may now be seen together,
IN PERFECT AMITY!

For this unprecedented Accident, the Proprietor paid Mr. WEEKS the Value of the Horse; and Surveyors also were appointed to examine his Carriages, who pronounced them perfectly secure; nor would it ever been possible for the Animal to have broken out, but by the daring Attempt of some Person to plunder, who thereby loosened the Den.

THE ROYAL

Bengal Tiger

An Animal next in size and strength to the Lion, with whom it frequently contends, and the most savage and blood-thirsty of the brute Creation. When grown to maturity, it is able to run at full speed with a Buffalo or Horse on its back; and so daring, that it will attack, when hungry, the Camp itself. It was one of these Animals that seized the unfortunate Captain MUNRO, and bore him away in his Mouth, in the Face of his Companions, whilst out with a shooting Party, a few Years ago, in the Neighbourhood of Bengal.

THE REAL SENEGAL

LEOPARD,

The Beauty of which surpasses all Description.—The

Laughing Hyæna,

The same Kind of Animal that is described by BRUCE, in his Travels through the Deserts of Abyssinia, and are said to be so Untameable, that they dwell in Caves, and Caverns of the Earth, and so Blood-thirsty that they frequently take up the Bodies of the Dead; but this will prove the contrary of such Representation, it being perfectly Tame.

Also one of these scarce Animals, the

PORCUPINE,

A Native of the Interior of Africa, but now so extremely Rare, that it is even there seldom to be met with, and is the ONLY REAL PORCUPINE that has been exhibited for nearly Twenty Years. It has variegated Quills on its Back, 18 Inches long, and when provoked or attacked, it erects them so formidable in its Defence, as to form a complete Bulwark against all its Enemies, so that Nothing can injure them, as every Quill forms a Spine to its Possessor, which are as Sharp as the Point of a Needle—THE

OURANG OUTANG,

One of the most beautiful in Symmetry, and placid in temper ever yet exhibited.—It stands Six Feet high, and its Limbs are astonishingly powerful. This Animal does any thing but speak.

The Black Bear,

OR POLAR MONSTER, JUST IMPORTED.

THE

Coatimondi, or Ant Eater,

From EGYPT, a very curious and interesting Animal, with a remarkable long Nose:

The JACKALL, or Lion's Provider;

This curious Animal provides Food for the Lion.

ALSO ONE OF THOSE SCARCE ANIMALS, CALLED THE

NEGRO FOLLOWERS,

FROM THE INTERIOR OF AFRICA.

It is customary for these Creatures to go in Droves, where they have an Opportunity to plunder the Natives of their Food,

THE INDIAN APE,

Who lost his Arm in an Engagement at Sea, in a British Ship.

With a Variety of other curious Animals, too numerous to insert.

Admittance, Ladies and Gentlemen, 1s.　　　Children and others, 6d.

BILLS of the largest Description, at an HOUR's Notice, by W. GLINDON, 48, Rupert Street, Haymarket, London.

The return of the lion that attacked the Royal Mail, 1816

menagerie. The coach soon pulled up at an inn, the Winterslow Hut, where the lion leapt out of the shadows and mauled one of the horses.[49] The incident can hardly have been witnessed by more than a handful of people at the time, but would soon be familiar to generations of travellers as one of the most frequently illustrated of all nineteenth-century coaching scenes.*

Palmer's other important heir, Francis Freeling, was a young man of twenty-eight in 1792, but in seven years at Palmer's side had shown himself such a gifted administrator as to be widely seen already as his natural successor. Over the next few years he gradually assumed effective control over the whole organization. Charles Bonnor, whose treachery towards a friend and colleague had been almost as alien to the Custom of the Office as Palmer's disrespect for the Postmasters General, received promotion for the sake of appearances, but was quickly pensioned off. Anthony Todd, now into his late seventies, managed to salvage his position as Secretary and insisted on receiving his full salary, though he made little pretence of doing any real work. This scandalized a parliamentary inquiry in 1797; yet a public rebuke from this quarter failed to dislodge the old man. Freeling was made Joint Secretary, while Todd clung on to the bitter end.[50] He died, aged eighty, in June 1798, at last leaving the reins to Freeling – who would grip them just as tenaciously until his own death in office a full thirty-eight years later.

3. FRANCIS FREELING'S
REVENUE MACHINE

Where Hasker may be thought to have fully lived up to Palmer's expectations of him, one can only wonder what Palmer in old age must have made of Freeling's impact on the Post Office. He ran it from his first days with all of Palmer's determination to maximize its net income, but little of his mentor's boldness and imagination. The young Freeling had

---

* To complete the tale: a bull mastiff was released from the inn, which the lion promptly tore to pieces while all but one of the terrified passengers fled inside. A straggler was left in the open, to be brushed aside by the lion as it ran for cover in a barn. The poor man was traumatized by the incident, literally frightened out of his wits, and spent the rest of his life in an asylum. But the menagerie keeper seems to have retrieved his animal safely. A poster appeared a few months later, advertising a 'Commodious Booth' in which spectators could behold not just 'the noble lioness, from Africa' but the horse and the miraculously recovered mastiff, too. 'These Three Animals may now be seen together, in Perfect Amity!'

helped establish the mail coaches – he had supervised the first cross-post coach, from Bristol to Portsmouth – and in 1790 had set up a range of new mail services in Scotland. (Walsingham had promptly suspended them all, over a breach of etiquette in not first reporting the project to the Postmasters General.) But he had been working, then, to Palmer's radical agenda. Left to his own devices, Freeling exerted a different kind of leadership. He was content for the Post Office to be judged, ultimately, by its success in contributing to the Government's finances. Where Allen had developed the Post Office as a highly lucrative 'farm' operation and Palmer had run it with a constant eye to the Royal Mail's potential as a commercial business, Freeling in effect cemented its status as a government department. Its record through his tenure as an engine of taxation was certainly impressive. Here was the full realization of the fiscal role assigned to the Post Office in 1711 for the War of the Spanish Succession, and Freeling was plainly as proud of it as the Treasury was grateful. The interminable years of war against Napoleon – which would surely have brought an early end to any schemes that Palmer might have advanced for private ownership of the postal service – left the wartime Exchequer needing all the financial support it could find, and Freeling did his best to oblige. He implemented a series of increases to the postage rates – in 1797, 1801, 1805 and 1812 – with meticulous care. Their scale can be seen from the rising cost of a letter from London to Edinburgh: it rose from 7d to 8d in 1797, one shilling in 1801, 1s 1d in 1805 and 1s 2d in 1812. Annual net income climbed from an average of £375,481 in 1790–94 to £1,125,787 for the years 1805–9 and £1,531,280 over the four post-war years 1815–19.[51] A huge haul of his personal papers survives in the Royal Mail archive, attesting to a workrate and appetite for administration that understandably awed his contemporaries. But Freeling's devotion to the bottom line could sometimes be less than inspiring. When peace was finally declared in 1815 and hundreds of letters trapped in Paris since 1803 were at last posted on to the City, Freeling sniffed at suggestions they be delivered free of charge. Anything less than the full going rate, he said, would be a breach of the law.[52]

By this time, Freeling was in his early fifties, governing the Post Office as a deeply conservative autocrat scarcely checked by any kind of peer pressure. Not a single meeting of the Board had been held between 1797 and 1817 – though it was supposed to meet weekly – and the Postmasters General had made little or no real contribution for years. Lombard Street itself he ruled almost as a personal fiefdom. Indeed, he had two sons on the payroll, one of whom had been appointed Assistant Secretary in 1810 and was living in the Secretary's official residence. (Freeling had his own houses in the West End and the country.) This and many other instances of high-handed behaviour would come eventually to be seen as abuses of the system, bringing down a torrent of criticism on his head. What really damaged the Post Office under Freeling's direction, though, was not a lack of integrity but a failure to keep moving ahead. As the years passed, its Secretary's mastery of detail was gradually eclipsed by his failure to grasp how profoundly the times were changing.

This is not to say these were years of abject failure: occasional setbacks betrayed the deeper shortcomings, but the expansion of the mails was no mean achievement. Its response to a proliferation of local posts, for example, showed the Post Office in a positive light in many ways. As noted earlier, legislation in 1765 had given all towns the right to launch their own penny post, subject always to Lombard Street's consent that the proposed service would be 'necessary and convenient'. The London District Post in the first years of the nineteenth century was a source of wonder to many visitors, and rightly so: it had been impressively overhauled in 1792, by none other than Edward Johnson, Palmer's humble letter bearer. Since then several deliveries a day had made cross-town letters a familiar part of daily life in the metropolis. (After John Keats had sat down just after dawn one October morning in 1816 and written out his great sonnet 'On First Looking into Chapman's Homer', he put a clean copy into the post in Southwark and it reached the recipient's breakfast table in Clerkenwell by ten o'clock the same morning.[53]) Many places were keen to emulate London's example and other encouraging precedents that had been set by Dublin and Edinburgh.[54] Penny posts had been running in both these cities since 1773 and had more than proven their worth.* By the end of 1793, penny posts had also been launched in Manchester, Bristol and Birmingham. A slew of smaller towns and cities followed in their wake after 1800 and their numbers went on growing steadily. By 1820, self-standing penny posts were

* Edinburgh's penny post was run as a business by an extraordinary individual called Peter Williamson, who had been kidnapped as a young boy on the Aberdeenshire coast and sold into slavery in the American colonies, where he was captured by Indians before escaping back to Scotland. From a coffee shop called Indian Peter's, he operated a private network of letter carriers who were known around Edinburgh as Williamson's 'caddies' – popularizing the term adopted by golfers half a century later. His post was taken over by the General Post Office in 1793 rather as Dockwra's had been in 1682, although Indian Peter was properly compensated.

running in 155 English post towns – helping to coordinate the growth of commercial activities in and around places like Sheffield and Derby at the heart of Britain's Industrial Revolution.[55] Post Office officials busied themselves diligently with all the paperwork needed to authorize these newcomers, and to link their operations into the postal network as effectively as possible.

This effort might have seemed more forward-looking if Freeling had not tried to coerce many of the penny posts into raising their rates. Several, including the London Penny Post, were turned into twopenny or even threepenny posts. Nor did Freeling and his colleagues make much of an effort to find in the widespread growth of local posts any lasting resolution to those two great headaches of the pre-Palmer era: excessive franking and the impasse over local delivery obligations. It might have been supposed, given his dedication to the enhancement of postal revenues, that Freeling would have been the man to tackle the franking problem, and perhaps he tried: several Acts of Parliament were passed in his day to try curbing it. But little headway could be made. Wartime conditions through the long struggle against Napoleon resulted in even more people being granted special dispensation for cheap or free postage. (The rank and file of the army and navy were allowed to send cheap letters for a prepaid penny.) The rising cost of standard letters meanwhile made franking rights ever more valuable to those in office of any kind. The Post Office felt compelled to protect the privilege, and indeed the insistence of the Postmasters General on this point effectively stymied a short-lived burst of private posts in small towns and villages that briefly offered a possible way out of the local delivery conundrum.* The private posts fell away, and many towns without their own penny posts were left, as before, in the legal limbo where postmasters were technically supposed to be delivering local letters but had no carriers to do the job. In the 1820s, hundreds of towns still remained without a local service.[56] As Freeling would later explain: 'We have never established penny posts, unless we find it [sic] was much sought for, and also that it would produce a revenue'.[57]

There were many other areas where the same resolutely bean-counting approach was adopted. Some of the results were positive. Freeling insisted,

---

* The private posts were authorized in a statute of 1801. Its fifth clause allowed towns and villages to run their own appendage to the official mails, provided these 'Fifth Clause Posts' were self-financing. They largely disappeared after 1807, once obliged to deal with franks which brought them plenty of letters but no revenues.

for example, on channelling postal business – and certainly 'express' letters needing to be given priority – wherever possible through post offices, rather than the inns which had served the service so well for generations. (Postmasters were generally more amenable than innkeepers to financial instructions and supervision from London.) By the 1820s, most of the network could rely on dedicated post offices. Other consequences were less encouraging. The Royal Mail coach services were steadily cut back in the years after 1812, in response to a fierce controversy over turnpike tolls. Turnpike trusts all over the country resented the exemption from tolls that had been granted to all mail coaches since 1782. Legislation to abolish the exemption was only just averted in 1812, and the Post Office subsequently needed to find constructive ways of contributing to the cost of new roads as the McAdam revolution gathered pace. Instead, it simply set its face resolutely against the turnpikes – and where it encountered angry local trustees equally uninterested in compromise, it cut back its services. By the early 1830s, and before the arrival of the railways, the number of mail coaches in regular schedules across England and Wales had fallen from around 220 to 130 or so. It was much the same story over the management of the packet-boat fleet, where another revolution in transport technology challenged the status quo. For a while after 1815, the Post Office enjoyed some reflected glory from the heroic exploits of several packet-ship captains who had fought famous actions against the French at sea. But awkward questions soon resurfaced. How, for example, was the Post Office to deal with the thorny matter of privately carried ship letters? (Was it really fair to charge postage on a letter that would be carried overseas on a ship unrelated to the Post Office in any way? And how could such a system be effectively imposed?)[58] Above all, the Post Office had to respond to the advent of steam-powered vessels, which within five years had fatally undermined the finances of the old packet ships. The latter had been run for the Post Office since the end of the 1780s by independent operators, who counted on additional income from passengers. When steam ships lured their passengers away, notably on the crossings to Ireland, the fleet needed to be fundamentally reconfigured. Freeling decided the Post Office should resume direct ownership of its ships, and invested heavily in new steam vessels and dock facilities. But too few changes were made to the culture and organization of the packet fleet, and its hugely inflated costs only exacerbated the public's growing disquiet over its services. It came as a blow to the prestige of the Post Office, but hardly a surprise to contemporaries, when the running of all packet ships out of Falmouth was taken over in 1823 by the Admiralty, a measure that the embattled Secretary had long opposed. The other dozen or so packet stations – including Harwich, Dover, Milford and

EXPRESSES.

To all Postmasters.

GENERAL POST-OFFICE,
2/ᵗ December, 1825.

IT having recently appeared that the Post-Boys charged with Post-Office Expresses, are in the habit of delivering them at the *Inns*, in the different Towns on the Road, instead of at the *Post-Offices*, which is both irregular and improper ;—You will, therefore, give immediate Orders to the Party who conveys Expresses from your Office, in all cases to deliver them to the *Postmaster at the end of his Stage*, no other Person being authorised to date the Time Bill, or give a Receipt for the Express.

By Command,

FRANCIS FREELING.

Add this to your Instructions No. 8, on Expresses.

Printed by J Hartnell, Wine Office Court, Fleet Street, for His Majesty's Stationery Office.

Freeling's ban on the delivery of express letters to inns, December 1825

Holyhead – remained under the Post Office's charge but came in for plenty of harsh criticism. The Secretary's elder son, George F. Freeling, had charge of them. Some years later, he would ruefully admit to a parliamentary inquiry that no one in Lombard Street had a clue how to run a dockyard.[59]

The biggest challenge to the Post Office by the 1820s was scarcely acknowledged by Freeling and his colleagues at all. This was what to do about the mind-boggling complexity of postal rates. There was scarcely a town in the nation where the local postmaster, if asked the price of post-age to any other town, would have been able to give a definitive answer. The accumulated jumble of penny posts and general posts, free deliveries and double charges, distance tables and weight allowances, incremental pennies here and halfpennies there, had complicated the steadily rising basic cost of sending a letter to the point where even the clerks of Lombard Street had trouble keeping track of the system. Had any of them conceived a way of simplifying it, however, there would have been little point in speaking up after 1823. For this was the year that a Parliamentary Commission of Inquiry into the state's finances began its work by turning to the books of the Post Office. It laboured for six long years, during which time not a single initiative of any significance was taken forward by Lombard Street or its masters in the Treasury – with just one exception. After twenty years of deliberation, the task of relocating to a new head office had finally been waved ahead in 1815.

A site covering two acres had been cleared by 1818 – just to the north of St Paul's Cathedral and less than half a mile from Lombard Street – and an architect had been chosen, too. This was Robert Smirke, who was busy at the same time on plans for a British Museum. His neoclassical lines appealed to the Treasury; they also met the call in Parliament for a public building that would look suitably august, without resembling a prison or a hospital. Smirke's General Post Office encased a cavernous central hall, two storeys high, running from a portico at its front entrance through to the rear of the building. Begun in 1824, it came complete, like the museum, with Ionic columns and a Portland stone façade on the outside and gas pipelines on the inside, for the very latest in indoor lighting. (The first gas lights had begun replacing oil lamps in 1821.) The exterior was lit up at night by a thousand gas burners. Its address was St Martin's-le-Grand – almost directly opposite the Bull and Mouth coaching inn and a stone's throw from the Swan with Two Necks – and it would be home to the Foreign Office and the London District Post as well as the Inland Office, the Secretary's Office and the principal administrative offices.[60] Their thousand or so employees moved in during September 1829. Generations of clerks would follow them into 'the Grand', until its (shameful) demolition in 1912–13.

For the 1st Baronet Sir Francis Freeling (as he had become in 1828), the occupation of the new headquarters was the peak of an extraordinary career. Had he retired at this point, Freeling could have departed with plaudits on all sides while neatly leaving to others the job of coping with the outcome of the Parliamentary Commission. He chose instead to soldier on – partly, perhaps, for financial reasons. His pension was geared to a basic salary of £500 a year, while he was actually pocketing nearly ten times that amount from a range of lavish perks and privileges.* The result was something of a personal tragedy for Freeling. The first and second of the Commissioners' reports on the Post Office were published before the end of 1829. Inevitably, they devoted most of their attention to identifying shortcomings of the postal service – related, inter alia, to its rates, its delivery times, its local services in the countryside, its employment practices and its accounting – and they produced a long list of grievances. But the reports went much further. They began a process, continued in the three volumes that soon followed, of stripping away much of the mystery surrounding the postal service. Here was something new: 'men were beginning to wonder, not, as in the past, at the things which the Post Office was able to do, but how it was that these things were not done better'.[61] Conceivably a much younger man might have turned the Commission's findings to his own advantage, launching a fresh chapter to coincide with the new start at St Martin's-le-Grand. Freeling simply ploughed on as though nothing had really changed. The consequences would ensure an acrimonious end to his regime and leave Freeling a broken man.

---

* These included £3,000 p.a. as compensation for no longer being able to send newspapers overseas as franked items; £700 p.a. for being Resident Surveyor, the post he had given up on becoming Secretary in 1797 and which had then been abolished; and £700 in lieu of free accommodation in the Secretary's apartment at Lombard Street, which he had handed over to his son. Freeling's finances were fully in line with past practice at the Post Office, and shed light again on Palmer's dismissive attitude towards it.

4
Rowland Hill and postal reform, 1830–64

As for the iron pillar boxes which had been erected of late years for the receipt of letters, one of which – a most hateful thing to her – stood almost close to her own hall door, [Miss Jemima Stanbury] had not the faintest belief that any letter put into one of them would ever reach its destination. She could not understand why people should not walk with their letters to a respectable post office instead of chucking them into an iron stump – as she called it – out in the middle of the street with nobody to look after it. Positive orders had been given that no letters from her house should ever be put into the iron post.

From *He Knew He was Right* (1869) by Anthony Trollope, describing a postal innovation for which he himself was responsible in 1851

1. CAPITALISM AND THE CLAMOUR FOR CHEAP MAILS

The size and glamour of St Martin's-le-Grand attracted many distinguished visitors in the 1830s. Government ministers and royalty from half the nations of Europe included a trip to St Paul's and St Martin's on their list of sights, to include on a tour of London. They came especially in the evenings, when a procession of twenty-eight Royal Mail coaches – all freshly cleaned and greased at Vidler's in Millbank – assembled on the broad forecourt of the General Post Office, having picked up their paying passengers at a number of coaching inns around the City (or just across the road, for those boarding at the Bull and Mouth). The coaches began collecting their mails at 8 p.m. sharp before setting off for their various Roads from the capital, while officials of the Post Office reeled off for their admiring guests the names of all the distant towns and cities to be reached within just a day or two – and the exact times at which these very coaches would arrive there. Then the dignitaries would be treated to a walking tour of the headquarters building. We know that the queen of one of the German states was taken around it, for example, because a junior clerk accompanied her – 'walking backwards, as I conceived to be proper, and often in great peril as I did so, up and down the stairs' – and he described the episode forty years later in his autobiography. The young Anthony Trollope was mortified when the queen's German retainers slipped him half a crown as a tip. 'That also was a bad moment.'[1]

Ten years after its official opening ceremony, almost to the day, St Martin's had to lay on a special reception for a rather less welcome guest – so unwelcome, in fact, that he had been refused permission for a private visit in the past.[2] Less than three years earlier, no one there had ever heard of Mr Rowland Hill. Now, on 16 September 1839, he was entering the Grand in style. By his side was the Chancellor of the Exchequer, Francis Baring, and the two of them were being given a formal tour of the building. Hill had been appointed as an adviser to the Treasury. It was his first day, but his mission was no secret. He had been taken on by the Government to watch over the execution of a plan for the improvement of the postal service by the introduction of a 'uniform penny postage' – a plan which its senior officials, to a man, regarded as a reckless throw of the dice by an ill-informed and over-zealous amateur. It had been slighted in the House of Lords a year and a half earlier by the Postmaster General himself, Lord Lichfield, in memorable terms: 'of all the wild and visionary schemes which he have ever heard or read of, it was the most extraordinary'.[3] Post Office officials had been unremittingly hostile towards it from the outset, castigating it to a Select Committee as 'a most preposterous plan, utterly unsupported by facts . . .'[4] They had counted on the greatest defenders of the realm to see it off – 'no experiment could be more fatal', opined the Duke of Wellington, heeding the officials' predictions of a haemorrhage in postal revenues – but they had seen caution thrown to the winds. The Government had chosen to back Hill as yet another outsider like Allen and Palmer with a vision to revitalize the Post Office. He had been given a two-year contract by a fully supportive Treasury, where he was installed with his own office: ministers knew that nothing would induce officials at St Martin's to take him in as a colleague. It was all a far cry from the days of 1829, and the penny-pinching but inviolable autocracy of Sir Francis Freeling. How had such a sea change come about, over the intervening decade?

The answer has to start by seeing the Post Office's story within the broader narrative of British politics over the period. The first twin-tracked commercial railway opened for business in 1830, and if the engine of the state in that pre-Victorian era was a train of few carriages, the Post Office was definitely one of them.[5] With a switch in government from the long-dominant Tory party to a Whig party bent on electoral reform, the train was sent off down a different line, and the Post Office was inevitably pulled along behind it. The change that swept across political life after 1830 saw the power of the old and reactionary landed aristocracy being contested by a new generation of reformers – some of them leading members of aristocratic families themselves, like the 2nd Earl Grey and Lord John Russell, and others drawn from the ranks of the middle classes imbued with Evangelicalism on the one hand and Utilitarianism on the other. The result was not just a febrile two years culminating in the Great Reform Act of 1832, but a stream of radical reforms that went far beyond an extension of the electoral franchise. In this altered political climate, there was little or no chance of the Parliamentary Commissioners' Reports of 1829–30 on the Post Office being left to gather dust on the shelf, alongside the forgotten tomes of 1788 and 1797. Secretary Freeling and his colleagues initially seemed to assume that this was exactly what would happen; but once the Whig government under Lord Grey had been installed in November 1830, they were swiftly disabused.

Within a few weeks, a new Postmaster General was appointed. The practice of splitting this office between two joint holders had been abandoned on cost-saving grounds in 1823; but the traditional fondness for aristocratic nonentities had since been upheld as robustly as ever. The appointment of Charles, Duke of Richmond, was a notable departure. He took a keen interest in Post Office affairs and worked harder than any predecessor since Walsingham. Even more of a novelty than a conscientious Postmaster General was a Chancellor of the Exchequer determined to push through reforms for the benefit of the Post Office's customers. John Spencer, better known as Viscount Althorp (and later the 3rd Earl Spencer), was a long-standing champion of parliamentary reform and a leading force in Grey's Cabinet. He and Richmond together were soon bearing down on the reforms recommended by the Commissioners. The first target was the structure of postage rates in London. In theory, these were graded roughly according to a series of concentric bands rather in the same way as ticket prices on today's London Underground: the longer the distance, the higher the price. In practice, various District postage rates cut across each other and were mixed up with free delivery routes of the General Post Office in a chaotic fashion. Althorp took his cue from the Commission and proposed that all inward letters arriving in the capital, having been paid for as far as St Martin's, should then be delivered free of charge anywhere within a three-mile radius of the building. In a rare case of a government department rebuking the Treasury for profligacy, Freeling declined to have anything to do with an idea that he thought disproportionately costly. Althorp went ahead anyway, and imposed the new delivery rules within four months of taking office.

That set the tone. Some other recommendations by the Commissioners were similarly pushed through, with a pointed disregard for objections voiced by Freeling. His policy towards the packet-boat services, for example, was smartly reversed. In modernizing the packet fleet to take account of the impact of steam-powered vessels, Freeling had spurned commercial companies that offered to provide new steam technology on a contract basis. The mails, he said, were too important to be entrusted to private hands. The Post Office had itself taken charge of commissioning no fewer than twenty-six new steamships, including six for a new Irish service out of Liverpool. But too much had been spent, on less than exemplary designs. Running costs had soared and heavy losses had been made in every year since 1822.[6] Althorp, like the Parliamentary Commissioners, took a dim view of the whole business and wasted no time before inviting commercial tenders for carrying the mails to Holland and Germany. The first contract – with the General Steam Navigation Company – was awarded in 1831. Althorp and Richmond also moved with impressive speed to address the parlous state of the Irish Post Office, another scandal exposed by the 1829–30 Reports. The Government was anxious to set to rights much that had gone wrong in Ireland, building upon the Catholic Emancipation granted in 1829. Leaving Dublin to govern its own postal affairs, as it had been doing since 1784, now looked out of the question. Its Secretary was Edward Lees, son of the John Lees whose sometimes unsavoury influence was already paramount in the 1770s. Father and son had held sway in Dublin for not far short of sixty years; and it was said that Edward outdid his father in every way. A statute reuniting the Irish and General Post Offices was passed in August 1831. Lees Junior was packed off to Edinburgh – despite endless tales of his venality in Dublin – to run the Scottish Post Office. Richmond then pushed for the dismissal of all those on the payroll of the Dublin Office who had never actually set foot in the place. This alone cut its staff establishment by half.

Under pressure from the Government, officials within the Post Office had also to contend with a groundswell of criticism on a much wider front. Support for the principle of free trade had for some years been nurturing a deep hostility to the old chartered monopolies of the eighteenth century, exemplified by the East India Company with its stranglehold on the trade routes to the East. 'John Company' had been stripped of its monopoly on trade with India in 1813 and was now under intense pressure to surrender its grip on trade with China, and in particular the import of Chinese tea. What incensed critics was the way in which a monopoly could be used to sustain high prices – an argument by the early 1830s that seemed at least as applicable to the Post Office and the price of postage as to the East India Company and the price of tea. Both were an affront to the increasingly vocal advocates of a market economy unfettered by the distorting effect of monopolies or of constraints on free trade like the Corn Laws. There were other grievances against the Post Office, too. The expense of posting letters was also singled out for attack by proponents of another radical cause, the promotion of education. The standard inland rates of the day, for a single letter, started at 4d for a distance not exceeding fifteen miles, climbing steadily to 9d for up to 120 miles (London to Birmingham, say) and 12d (one shilling) for up to 300 miles with an extra penny for every additional 100 miles: the rate for London to Edinburgh was 13½d. And postage prices were looking increasingly questionable to anyone in public life who stopped to notice how high a proportion of the country's letters were evading the Royal Mail net: 'smuggled' letters were as obvious to contemporaries by the early 1830s as they had been in the early 1780s. Leaving aside those illicitly franked, enormous numbers were once again passing via private posts, parcel posts and couriers. Richard Cobden, the radical free trader making a name for himself in Manchester, told a parliamentary select committee in 1837 that five sixths of the letters that were sent to London from Manchester did not pass through the Post Office.[7] So much for the Royal Mail's monopoly. After the triumph of the Great Reform Bill, and with the momentum for radical causes building inexorably, the case for postal reform was impossible to ignore.

A vociferous new Scottish MP in the first reformed House of Commons was determined to speed it on its way. Robert Wallace came from a Glasgow merchant family and represented the freshly enfranchised manufacturing and trading classes of Greenock, on the banks of the Clyde. Wallace attacked the Post Office so hard and so often that he came close to attracting ridicule from those less obsessed with the cause – which meant almost everyone else. But his constant demands in the House for another commission did at least force Parliament to send Freeling a series of formal inquiries. In relation to one item after another from among the 1829–30 recommendations, it asked the same questions: had the Post Office complied? And if not, why not? As the ostrich tendency within St Martin's emerged more clearly with each exchange, Wallace and his supporters adopted an ever more adversarial stance, drawing responses that upset the whole House. MPs were irked by the disclosure of a series of errors and ineptitudes. They professed shock at the overall financial performance of the Post Office: its net income of £1,532,000 for 1833 was actually marginally lower than the £1,598,000 recorded for 1815, despite the rapid expansion of the British economy over the period.[8] They were angered to discover that, despite years of pressure on the Post Office to accede to the courts' ruling in favour of free delivery in all post towns, no fewer than eighty-nine large towns in England were still without it.

Given the one-man rule he had exerted for so long, Freeling by 1834 was inevitably the target of much personal criticism. He was hardly, at seventy years old, a figure of biblical antiquity, and Robert Wallace was only eight years his junior. But the Secretary was pilloried as an old man, out of touch and left over from an earlier century – or as one of his gentler antagonists in the House of Lords put it, a man who 'had not adapted his notions to the altered circumstances of the times'.[9] He was blamed for neglecting the 1829–30 proposals and for failing to keep up with postal practices in France and other Continental countries – where prices now varied with weight, not distance. He was pilloried by Wallace and others for his authoritarian ways, and was openly criticized for raking in excessive emoluments to supplement his official income. There were few ready to speak up for him. Nor was there a Postmaster General with any credibility at his side. Richmond was intent on pushing him to make reforms; and after Richmond's departure, in July 1834, three new Postmasters General came and went in less than a year as short-lived ministries followed each other in quick succession. A fourth, Lord Lichfield, was made of sturdier stuff. Indeed, he vilified Wallace in the House of Lords, in terms that almost prompted a duel at dawn between them. But by the early summer of 1835, Freeling was on the ropes. Then, to the Secretary's dismay, the Government gave in to Wallace and ordered yet another Treasury Commission 'to inquire into the Management of the Post Office Department'. (It would sit for two and a half years, producing no fewer than ten substantial reports between

June 1835 and January 1838.) Within months, more reform recommendations were being tabled. Some required immediate attention, to a
deadline that was scarcely practical. It was decreed within a couple of
months, for example, that Finch Vidler's fifty-year-old monopoly on the
supply of mail coaches was no longer acceptable. The Commissioners
demanded that his whole fleet be replaced by the start of 1836. No
sooner had his contract been torn up, than it became embarrassingly
obvious that the logistical problems had been seriously underestimated.
The Royal Mail's services were growing less frequent, but its routes in
1835 still represented a formidable network. Vidler was asked to go on
providing his services for a further six months, a request that met with
a ferocious sneer. Greatly to his credit, Freeling pulled off an exceptional feat of organization in enabling the Royal Mail to move from
Vidler's regime to a new supplier in January 1836 without a hitch. But
the effort involved almost killed him.

By now, he was a deeply disillusioned man. Even he could see that,
behind the individual items on the reform agenda, there lurked a potent
vision of the Post Office that was profoundly different from his own. He
was proud of belonging to the tradition that stretched back through
several generations to James, Duke of York, and saw the Post Office as
predominantly a source of revenues for the state. This dictated a set of
priorities that had seemed all the more pressing, in his own day, given
the cost of the wars against Napoleon's French Empire. Whatever the
original rationale for its monopoly status, Freeling never doubted this
was the bedrock of the Royal Mail's existence – and no one had been
more diligent in the pursuit of illicit mails through the courts. What he
found opposing him by the mid-1830s, unsurprisingly given the tec-
tonic shifts underway in a rapidly industrializing society, was a strikingly
more commercial approach. His critics talked of *managing* the Post
Office, as though it was a business rather than a government department. Freeling was totally perplexed, but it was an approach with which
the outsiders in the Post Office's history to date, not only John Palmer
and Ralph Allen but lesser mortals like Dockwra and Indian Peter as
well, would have had much sympathy. Indeed, when one of the keenest
reformers in the House of Lords gave evidence to the Commission in
1835, he spoke of '[looking to] England as being in a great degree the
post office of the world if facilities were offered' – a viewpoint that
faintly echoed the commercial sentiments of John Witherings from the
very earliest days of the Post Office.

These past champions of progress had seen business disciplines as a

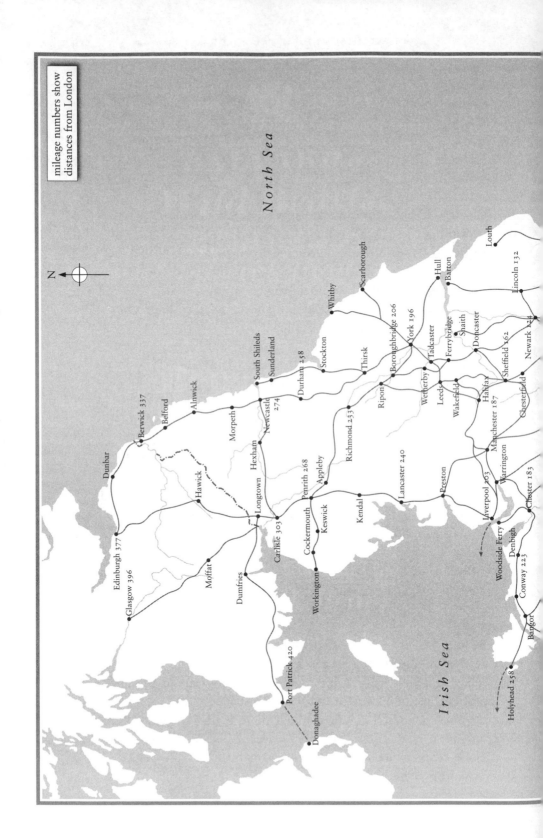

mileage numbers show
distances from London

N

North Sea

Irish Sea

Louth

Scarborough

Whitby

Hull

Barton

Lincoln 132

Boroughbridge 206

York 196

Tadcaster

Ferrybridge

Snaith

Doncaster

Newark 124

South Shields

Sunderland

Durham 258

Stockton

Thirsk

Ripon

Wetherby

Leeds

Wakefield

Sheffield 162

Chesterfield

Richmond 233

Halifax

Manchester 187

Berwick 337

Belford

Alnwick

Morpeth

Newcastle 274

Hexham

Lancaster 240

Preston

Warrington

Chester 183

Dunbar

Hawick

Longtown

Penrith 268

Appleby

Kendal

Liverpool 203

Woodside Ferry

Denbigh

Conway 223

Bangor

Edinburgh 377

Moffat

Dumfries

Carlisle 303

Cockermouth

Keswick

Workington

Glasgow 396

Port Patrick 420

Donaghadee

Holyhead 258

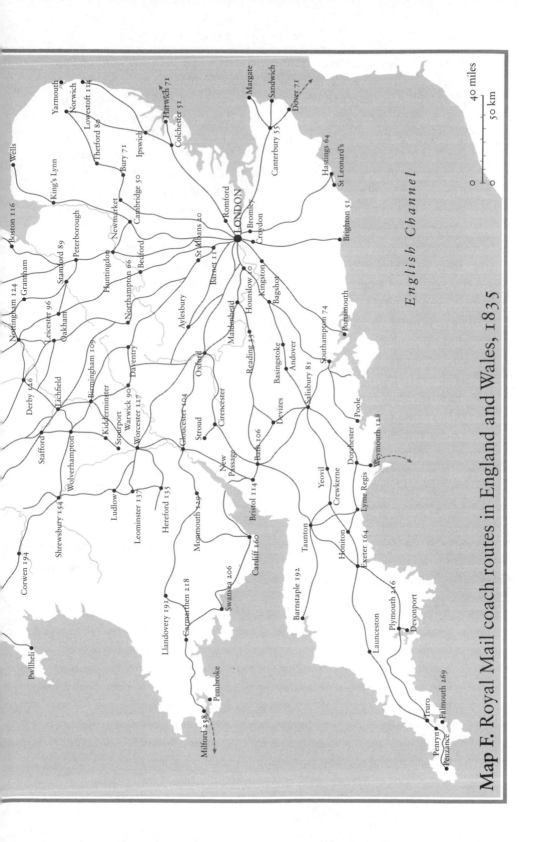

Map F. Royal Mail coach routes in England and Wales, 1835

English Channel

40 miles
50 km

Wells
Boston 116
Grantham
Nottingham 124
Leicester 96
Oakham
Derby 126
Lichfield
Stafford
Wolverhampton
Shrewsbury 154
Corwen 194
Pwllheli
Ludlow
Kidderminster
Stourport
Birmingham 109
Warwick 90
Worcester 117
Leominster 137
Hereford 135
Llandovery 191
Carmarthen 218
Pembroke
Milford 258
Swansea 206
Cardiff 160
Monmouth 129
New Passage
Gloucester 104
Stroud
Bristol 114
Barnstaple 192
Bath 106
Cirencester
Devizes
Taunton
Crewkerne
Yeovil
Honiton
Exeter 164
Launceston
Plymouth 216
Devonport
Truro
Penryn
Falmouth 269
Penzance
Lyme Regis
Dorchester
Weymouth 128
Poole
Salisbury 81
Andover
Basingstoke
Reading 33
Oxford
Daventry
Warwick 90
Banbury
Aylesbury
Maidenhead
Hounslow 10
Kingston
Bagshot
Southampton 74
Portsmouth
Brighton 51
St Leonard's
Hastings 64
Canterbury 55
Dover 71
Sandwich
Margate
Harwich 71
Colchester 51
Ipswich
Bury 71
Thetford 80
Lowestoft 114
Norwich
Yarmouth
King's Lynn
Peterborough
Stamford 89
Huntingdon
Bedford
Northampton 66
Newmarket
Cambridge 50
St Albans 20
Barnet 11
Romford
LONDON
Bromley
Croydon

Pontefract

release for the Post Office from the constraining habits of officialdom. Freeling's adversaries had a similar attitude, albeit from a much more philosophical viewpoint. They were not intent on making a private fortune in the process, like Palmer or Allen. They were driven instead by an ideology. As advocates of the new liberal capitalism, they wanted to see the Post Office a commercially vibrant institution and a bastion, insofar as was possible, of free trade economics. Of course, the Post Office itself could hardly be a straightforward case of *laissez-faire* in practice. But if it had to be allowed a monopoly, this was a necessary evil. As the 1835–8 Commissioners would cagily put it, in the last of their ten reports, the post was 'a particular service, which it has been found expedient to have executed under the control and supervision of the Government', but this did not belie the market principles they wished to see underpinning it.[10] Robert Wallace wanted the Post Office to be run by men 'bred up to business'.[11] And as was becoming increasingly clear, these commercially minded souls were intent above all on reducing the cost of letters. Wallace made plain his own preferred approach, in giving evidence to the 1835–8 Commissioners: 'I am convinced of two things – that the cheapening of postage rates would increase the revenue . . . and the expense ought not with good management to be increased at all'.[12] Lower prices, higher volumes – it was a recurring idea in the Commission's early reports.

It was all too much for Freeling. The Victorian Herbert Joyce painted a lugubrious but not implausible tableau of the embattled Secretary, seated alone in his office at St Martin's. 'There he brooded over the past and contrasted it with the present. Notes jotted down haphazard on official papers that chanced to be on his table reveal the inner workings of his mind. We know few sadder records.'[13] On one paper, alluding to the possibility that cheaper postage rates might be of benefit to all, was scrawled a *cri de coeur* for posterity:

Cheap postage! What is this men are talking about? Can it be that all my life I have been in error? If I, then others – others whose behests I have been bound to obey. To make the Post Office revenue as productive as possible was long ago impressed upon me by successive ministers as a duty which I was under a solemn obligation to discharge. And not only long ago. Is it not within the last six months that the present Chancellor of the Exchequer has charged me not to let the revenue go down? What! You, Freeling, brought up and educated as you have been, are you going to lend yourself to these extravagant schemes? You, with your four-horse mail-coaches, too.

Where else in the world does the merchant or manufacturer have the materials of his trade carried for him gratuitously or at so low a rate as to leave no margin of profit?

A fortnight later, in June 1836, Freeling was dead. He was succeeded by a man whose background and temperament seemed in many ways hardly less redolent of a bygone age than his own: Lt. Col. William Leader Maberly was an absentee Irish landlord who had joined the army before Waterloo and been on half-pay since 1832.* But Freeling's passing had added to a sense at Westminster that a fresh start could finally be made – and that the whole impact of the reforms under way should amount to more than the sum of their parts. What was still missing was any articulation of a comprehensive policy to pull them together. In particular, there was no coherent proposal on how to turn widespread support for lower rates into a clear policy objective. It was a nettle that the 1835–8 Commissioners seemed most reluctant to grasp. They felt much more comfortable just detailing the operational flaws in the Post Office – their brief, after all, was to review the management of the Department, not its policies – and reviewing the clauses of an 1837 statute to codify all previous postal legislation. (The running of the packet-boat services was the next target, which would lead in 1837 to its being handed over to the Admiralty.) To mobilize public support over an innately complex subject, a campaign would need to be launched both within Parliament and beyond it. And the key to building a successful platform would be finding a simple slogan.

2. HILL'S UNIFORM PENNY POSTAGE

Rowland Hill was forty-one years old in 1836, and a man burning with ambition to make his mark on public life. He belonged to an unusual (not to say very strange) family, and was the third-born of six sons and two daughters. His father, Thomas, was of Birmingham artisan stock and had worked for a while in the 1790s as the manager of a Wolverhampton brass foundry. He must have had a lively mind. He was active in local politics and a friend of the internationally renowned chemist

---

* How Maberly came to be appointed is unclear. Trollope used him as the model for Sir Boreas Bodkin, the Post Office Secretary in his novel *Marion Fay*, described as 'a violent and imperious martinet, but not in the main ill-natured'. (See R. H. Super, *The Chronicler of Barsetshire: A Life of Anthony Trollope*, University of Michigan Press, 1988.)

and educationalist Joseph ('Inflammable Gas') Priestley, who helped
him to carve out a living as a teacher. Thomas and his formidable wife
Sarah instilled in all their children an unassailable sense of their own
destiny. As young men, Rowland and his brothers were co-opted by
their father to work as teachers in a progressive school that he established, first in Birmingham and then in North London. By the mid-1830s,
the five surviving brothers (one had died in 1830) were ready to embark
on separate careers, but determined also to remain in league with each
other in a most unusual fashion. They had resolved since 1832 to pool
a significant portion of their incomes into a 'Family Fund', to provide
mutual support for each other, and had agreed to submit all their
important career decisions to a family council. Contemplating his next
objective, Rowland by 1836 could take pride in some lasting accomplishments in the educational field. He and his eldest brother Matthew
had published in 1822 a widely remarked book, *Public Education*,
drawing on their practical experience to suggest a blueprint for other
enlightened schools, in contrast to the brutish philistinism of most
private establishments at that time.[14] The two of them had also been
founder members in 1826 of the Society for the Diffusion of Useful
Knowledge, a Utilitarian-minded venture – supported by, among others,
James Mill – that reflected their interests in science and social reform as
well as education.

Nevertheless, ten years later, Rowland Hill was a deeply frustrated
man. By his own high expectations, life had so far brought a string of
disappointments. He had lacked the financial means to study at Cambridge, to his lasting regret. He had failed to find any kind of position in
public life, despite privately publishing a paper in 1832 grandly titled
*Home Colonies: A Plan for the Gradual Extinction (by Education) of
Pauperism and the Dimunition of Crime*. He had dabbled with the
communitarian ideas of Robert Owen without finding them sufficiently
compelling to join forces with him, though offered the chance to do so.
Several promising science projects and inventions had come to naught,
including an ingenious design for a rotary printing press: the prototype
worked well enough, but to be commercially viable for the newspaper
industry it relied on the Treasury cancelling the need for pages to be
printed and stamped separately; this the Treasury refused to do. In
short, here was someone convinced that a vocation lay in wait for him,
but who had not yet found it. He was a passionate champion-in-waiting,
without a cause. As he had confided to his diary many years before, he
saw himself, not unreasonably, as part of an extraordinary family, that

needed to be fired with a mission: 'we only want full scope for our powers to operate, to convince the world of our superiority'.[15] This fierce
self-belief was undimmed as Hill entered his forties. But at a time in his
life when he had aspired to be cutting a figure in the world – like, say, his
contemporary George Stephenson, busily fathering the railway age – Hill
was still employed as an impecunious headmaster in the school established by his family in North London.

He finally threw up teaching in 1835, accepting a post he had first
been offered two years earlier as secretary to a body promoting the colo-
nization of South Australia. But by 1836 he was also taking a serious
interest in a subject that he had merely flirted with on various occasions
in the past, the fast-growing movement for postal reform. After consulting in the usual way with his father and brothers, he made up his mind.
While helping to plan the future of Kangaroo Island by day, he immersed
himself by night in the details of the Post Office's business and the public
finances. He had no problem digging up research material. The Commissioners appointed in 1835 – aided by the contemporary obsession
with investigations and the new science of statistics – saw to it that parliamentary papers were made available as 'Blue Books', official annual
publications now on sale to the public for the first time. Hill also made a
direct approach to George Wallace, who unhesitatingly filled a carriage
with paperwork and sent it straight over to his new-found collaborator.
Hill did not disappoint him. At the beginning of January 1837, a draft
was shown to Wallace, and to a select few others, of a paper he had
written (with some help from his brothers) entitled *Post Office Reform:
Its Importance and Practicability*.* Hill had found his vocation – and
the postal reform movement was about to find its slogan.

Hill proposed a comprehensive demolition of the Post Office's historical approach to the pricing of letters. In a pamphlet of just over a hundred
pages – printed in a first public edition (usually referred to as the *second*
edition) the following month, and incorporating various changes since
the first draft – he put forward three new ways of handling letters so as to
revitalize an institution 'rendered feeble and inefficient by erroneous

---

* By a curious coincidence, it was actually history's second pamphlet on the subject by a Mr
Hill. The first, simply entitled *A Penny Post*, was written by John Hill and published in
London in 1659. Its author ran a private postal network between York and London during
the Protectorate. His seven-page booklet argued for the right of every Englishman to run his
own postal business 'against restraint of Farmers of such Employments'. Apparently Rowland Hill only learned much later of its existence. (See Howard Robinson, *The British Post
Office: A History*, Princeton University Press, 1948, p. 43.)

financial arrangements'. The practice of 'candling' letters – opening their wax seal to discover any additional sheets wrapped inside the outer page – was still necessitated by postal rates that decreed a double price for a double-sheeted letter, but had seemed anomalous and intrusive for decades. In future, rates should vary not by the number of sheets per letter but by their weight. As for the variation in price according to the distance to be covered by a letter, this should simply be abolished. All letters between post towns should be subject to one uniform charge, regardless of the distance between them.* The interminable business of 'taxing' every letter individually, with clerks poring over the mileage charts to remind themselves of distances and to take account of endless anomalies in the structure of the postage rates, would all be a thing of the past. And finally, moving from the price to the payment method, all letters should be paid for not by the recipient but by the sender. Payment on delivery had once made sense: how else to ensure the post-boys actually delivered their letters rather than dumping them in a ditch? But no self-respecting modern carrier ever lost his mail. The Post Office by the 1830s had developed a service ethic that was now well appreciated by the general public: surely few indeed would object to making a pre-payment. And if letters could simply be handed over by carriers, or even dropped through a slit in the recipient's door, with no need to collect a charge – as applied in the case of so many existing penny post systems – the savings in time and security for the Post Office would be an immeasurable gain.

As for what the uniform charge should be, Hill buried his bombshell in the middle of the pamphlet. Where others had been talking vaguely for years about the merits of a cheaper post, Hill put down a goal of breathtaking simplicity. 'A uniform rate of one penny would, I conceive, be sufficiently low to neutralise all pecuniary objection to its being invariably paid in advance . . .'[16] Hill could point to many quasi-precedents. He cited the assurance given him by a Birmingham manufacturer that

---

* The 'secondary' distribution of letters in rural areas beyond the post towns was a different matter, and would still need an incremental rate. This rather important qualification to the principle of uniform rates is often overlooked, but remained in place until almost the end of the century. Only in 1897, under the so-called 'Jubilee Concession', did the Post Office agree to guarantee delivery at standard postage rates to every house in the kingdom. 'Oddly, this [Jubilee] concession did not specify the frequency of delivery but it was assumed to mean a minimum of one delivery weekly.' (See W. K. Mackenzie, 'Postal Circulation', *Bulletin of the Postal History Society*, No. 197, 1976, p. 16.) It was estimated that the Jubilee Concession added about 60 million letters to the annual mailbag – far more than the Post Office had itself anticipated in agreeing to the concession – increasing it by about 2 per cent. (See *Encyclopaedia Britannica*, 11th edn, 1911, p. 182.)

illegal letters were profitably carried for a penny each to towns all round the city, and in quantities that far exceeded the volume of the Royal Mail. He also referred to the house paper of the Society for the Diffusion of Useful Knowledge, the *Penny Magazine*, which was widely circulated at that price with no loss to the organization. And most people were familiar with the local penny posts to be found in several of the larger cities. But Hill can have been in no doubt about the shock he was meting out to his readers. Everyone knew 4d was now the price of the very cheapest letter. Those with any detailed knowledge of the Post Office would be aware that a penny was the *incremental fee* just to carry a letter over *each* of the new Menai and Conway bridges on the Post Road from London to Dublin. When the private draft of January proposed a penny for letters up to one ounce in weight, even Hill's confidants were taken aback by his boldness. His supporters at Westminster counselled a more cautious approach. The Chancellor of the Exchequer suggested that Hill settle instead for a penny per half-ounce, with an extra penny for each additional half-ounce. Hill followed this advice in his second edition of the pamphlet. And he had already had second thoughts on another matter, too: his initially intended title had been 'uniform penny postage'. No doubt he decided that this might alarm too many wavering politicians, and understandably so. But we can be sure that Hill, a consummate propagandist, was alive to the power of uniform penny postage as a rallying cry for postal reform, and it was taken up from the day the first public edition appeared.

There was one other difference between the January and February editions, and it was to prove momentous. How were post offices and receiving houses to make provision for a more general resort to the prepayment of letters? (It was not at this stage envisaged as being compulsory.) In his private draft, Hill explained that letters would be handed over at a counter, weighed and postmarked with a 'tell-tale stamp' not so different from the postage marks in use since the days of Charles II. But by February, he had had a better idea. Pre-stamped materials could be stored in bulk at post offices. These could be stamped sheets of paper, to be folded as letters in the normal way. There would be no more nonsense in future about single and double letters, so wrappers and covers (or 'envelopes') could also be pre-stamped in this way. Prior to posting, the 'frank-stamp' would be cancelled by having a postage mark (or in many cases just a postmaster's scribble) impressed on top of it. Here was a much quicker and more convenient way for prepaid letters to be despatched – unless, of course, the person bringing a finished but unstamped letter to the post office happened to be illiterate, in which case adding an address to a wrapper or cover would be an embarrassing problem. Almost as an afterthought, Hill suggested his solution. 'Perhaps this difficulty might be obviated by using a bit of paper just large enough to bear the stamp, and covered at the back with a glutinous wash, which the bringer might, by applying a little moisture, attach to the back of the letter . . .'[17] Thus was born the adhesive postage stamp.*

Hill's pamphlet was a sensation with the general public: it was re-issued with minor amendments in another three editions before the end of the year.[18] (He also pushed its recommendations forward very effect-ively over the next few months by presenting his thinking on prepaid postage to the 1835–8 Commissioners: they backed his ideas in their 9th Report, which looked at the workings of the London District Post.) In Whitehall, the pamphlet meanwhile prompted a searching review of his figures. For Hill argued his case with some prodigious number-crunching, a financial analysis (of sorts) showing the likely impact of the plan on the performance of the Post Office. He was careful not to provide specific figures that might be hostages to fortune, but he needed to illustrate the practicability of his proposals. It was central to his cri-tique that the Post Office should be regenerated through an application of the strictest rules of liberal capitalism, or what he came to refer to as 'economical reform'. The Treasury estimated the current average letter price at 6d. To retain the present revenue base of the 1837 Post Office, therefore, a cut in the postage rate to 1d would have to be balanced by a roughly sixfold increase (later revised on occasions to a fivefold increase) in the number of paid letters. A simultaneous end to franked mail would provide an additional counterweight. Hill was confident a sixfold jump would be achieved, and quite possibly surpassed: 'it will be difficult to fix a limit to the amount of correspondence that may be looked for' from the 'rising spirit of adventure' that his plan would do so much to stimulate. While a dip in the revenues could be expected in

---

* Hill indicated that the idea had come to him by contemplating a proposal put forward for stamped covers to be put on newspapers. Stamped marks of one kind or another had been used for generations on important documents and on patent medicines, so his inspiration might have come from elsewhere too. Inevitably, others claimed to have provided it. The family of James Chalmers from Dundee gave their relative a tombstone as 'Originator of the adhesive postage stamp' and kept his claim going for well over a century. Willcocks, writing in the 1970s, noted that a fierce battle between the descendants of Hill and of Chalmers 'still raged up to 1950 or thereabouts . . . and the author well remembers that meetings of the Postal History Society had an uncomfortable atmosphere if both factions attended' (R. M. Willcocks, *England's Postal History to 1840*, privately publ., 1975, p. 133).

the immediate aftermath of introducing penny postage, this would represent only a brief transitional phase. Thereafter, rising volumes would mean not just restored revenues but higher net income: Hill projected little or no increase in the fixed costs of the Post Office, implying a sharp drop in the handling costs per letter.

Over the next two and a half years, scarcely anyone was persuaded to back penny postage on the basis of this analysis. The professionals of the Post Office under Colonel Maberly, once they had recovered their composure, poured scorn on them. The growth in the volume of the mails would in their view come nowhere near compensating for the loss of revenues: a steep deficit, they predicted, would be a sure and lasting outcome. This was endorsed by some of the most notable economists of the day.[19] Few of the plan's supporters – not even an influential Select Committee chaired in 1837–8 by George Wallace himself – felt enough confidence in Hill's numbers to back them publicly.[20] The Government eyed them nervously and remained non-committal to the end. Had it needed to rely solely on its merits as a business plan, in fact, Hill's pamphlet would have been a non-starter. The better informed its critics, the more sceptical seemed to be their view of its financial viability. Given all that had passed since 1830, however, it was not the analysis in the paper that counted but its vision. Quite simply, Hill's arguments reinforced the moral, philosophical and broader commercial case for a penny postage with such brilliance that his plan finally turned the reform of the Post Office into a powerful *political* cause. Once it became apparent to him – as it did within a matter of months – that the Government was not prepared to act on his proposals of its own volition, Hill threw all his energies into supporting a widespread campaign on behalf of that cause, uniform penny postage. And he was greatly assisted by a remarkable young civil servant and like-minded Utilitarian, Henry Cole, who was given leave by his own department, the Records Commission, to work at Hill's side. (Cole was later to prove himself almost as formidable a campaigner and administrator as Hill himself, and was one of the principal organizers behind the Great Exhibition of 1851.)

To write of a campaign today suggests a public-relations exercise, coordinated from the top. Instead, this was a mass movement, far beyond the control of Hill or any other individual, which equalled anything seen on behalf of the abolition of slavery or even the reform of the parliamentary franchise. Pamphlets, lectures, public rallies and fierce parliamentary speeches railed against the iniquities of the unreformed Post. The cause was promoted all across the country (with one advertisement stitched into the back of an episode of the new novel from Charles Dickens, *Nicholas Nickleby*). Hundreds of thousands of signatures were gathered for mass petitions to Parliament. After Victoria's accession to the throne in the summer of 1837, the young queen's (fictitious) support for the cause was quite unscrupulously paraded in cartoons. The leading newspapers were overwhelmingly in favour of reform, with *The Times* thundering in an editorial that uniform penny postage 'may well be termed the cause of the whole people against the small coterie of place holders in St. Martin's-le-Grand and its dependencies'.[21] The place holders were hopelessly outgunned. Officials' attempts to explain their point of view were undone by splenetic, and disastrously counterproductive, outbursts against Hill, and their wobbly grasp of the relevant statistics on existing operations did nothing to inspire much confidence among neutrals. There was, too, always the unfortunate historical precedent, much trumpeted by its adversaries, of the Post Office's initial hostility to Palmer and his mail coaches. If Hill could stir such bitter opposition in St Martin's, it struck many neutrals that his plan must have some merit.

By the time that Parliament came to settle the issue with a vote in the summer of 1839, the contest was effectively over. More than 2,000 petitions in support of penny postage had been presented since the start of the year – nothing like it had ever been seen before. Public meetings had attracted huge crowds, not least in the City of London, where there was enthusiastic support for penny postage. With the public budget already under severe strain, the ministers in the Whig government had grave doubts. These could hardly be voiced in the face of the public's enthusiasm, but the nervousness was evident. A lobbying group on behalf of City interests, the Mercantile Committee, responded by putting forward an option with (to modern ears) a familiar ring about it. One of its members suggested that the Government, if apprehensive about the Post Office's ability to realize the potential inherent in penny postage, might think of letting private interests take over the running of the mails: 'there would be no difficulty in finding a body of high mercantile character to carry out the plan proposed and secure to the government the full amount of the revenue which is now obtained from the Post Office'.[22] Ignoring this kind offer, the Cabinet under Lord Melbourne pressed ahead with a Penny Postage Bill. It authorized the Treasury, in due course, to adopt Hill's uniform penny rate, while in the meantime arranging for the printing of 'adhesive stamps' and stamped stationery – and scrapping, at long last, the use of franked mail.

The Bill was introduced in July 1839 and given the royal assent barely four weeks later. This triumph, however, did not mark any great vote of confidence in Hill's financial predictions. He and other reformers had grown more sanguine about them as the months had passed. But many others, especially in Tory circles, had contrariwise become

UNIFORM PENNY POSTAGE.

A Public Meeting
Of the Bankers, Merchants, & Traders, of the City of London,
WILL BE HELD AT THE

EGYPTIAN HALL OF THE MANSION HOUSE,
ON
Wednesday Next, July 10,
To Petition Parliament for the Adoption of Mr. ROWLAND HILL'S *Plan of a* UNIFORM PENNY POSTAGE,
AS RECOMMENDED BY THE SELECT
Committee of the House of Commons.

THE RIGHT HON. THE LORD MAYOR,
Will take the Chair at TWO o'Clock precisely.

The Metropolitan Members are expected to attend.

PRINTED BY T. BRETTELL, RUPERT STREET, HAYMARKET.

Notice of a City of London rally for uniform penny postage, July 1839

more convinced of their implausibility. The Government's opponents withdrew their opposition – 'though with great reluctance and pain', as the Duke of Wellington wearily observed – because they recognized, in effect, that the campaign over postal reform since 1837 had lifted debate over the Post Office's affairs to another level where disagreements over the cost of uniform penny postage were of only secondary importance. Just as Freeling's pursuit of higher postage rates had been overtaken earlier in the 1830s by a concern that the Post Office should be run on more imaginative commercial lines, so talk of the Post Office as a business had now begun to evolve into something grander by far. As one of the leading advocates of reform, Henry Warburton, candidly acknowledged in the

Commons that summer, the general public had come to see the Post
Office as an institution whose 'primary object was to contribute to their
convenience'.[23] Indeed, the 1837–9 campaign had planted the seed of a
new idea about the Post Office's role in society that, within a generation
or so, would come to overshadow Rowland Hill's own radical but 'economical' vision of the future. But that is to jump ahead. For the moment,
Hill's vision was quite challenging enough and, backed by the 1839 Act,
had left the Post Office with a startlingly bold agenda. No one outside
the Post Office could by now imagine there was anyone better qualified
to monitor its progress than Rowland Hill himself. He was quickly persuaded – after a brief altercation over his salary – to exchange his secure
position at the South Australia Commission for a two-year assignment
as adviser to the Treasury, charged with preparing the Post Office for his
plan's implementation. Hence that first visit, in September 1839.

A few months after Hill's first-day tour of St Martin's with the Chancellor, the Post Office duly launched a first trial arrangement for the
uniform tariff, limiting the cost of all domestic letters to 4d. It was a
cautious approach, and it evoked such a hostile response from the public that the Government was forced to announce an abrupt change of
plan.[24] Without further ado, the uniform *penny* post was launched
across the postal network on 10 January 1840. But as every dedicated
stamp-collector has known from that day to this, the rush to enact it left
the penny post with a problem: no stamps. Work on the first 'bit of
paper with a glutinous wash' was still underway, so temporary prepayment alternatives had urgently to be made while preparations for the
manufacture of adhesive stamps were completed.

The biggest challenge had been to find a suitably august design that
would make life impossibly difficult for aspiring forgers. A competition
had been launched by the Treasury the previous August, inviting the
public to send in their ideas. About 2,600 entries were submitted, but
none was thought exactly right. Four competitors were awarded a consolation prize of £100; it was one of them, Benjamin Cheverton, who
suggested that a beautiful woman's profile would be the best deterrent
to forgery: the human eye, he said, would be far more alert to any flaw
in a face than it would be to some errant line in 'any mere mechanical
or ornamental device'. The Treasury concurred, and fortuitously could
turn to an engraving of the eighteen-year-old Queen Victoria which had
been struck for a commemorative medal two years earlier by the chief
engraver of the Royal Mint, William Wyon. Immense pains were taken
to transfer this portrait with suitably hard-to-forge embellishments

onto two steel dies, to produce a 'Penny Black' for standard letters and a 'Twopenny Blue' for the slightly heavier category. The Queen herself was so delighted with the result that British stamp designers were obliged to continue using the same portrait until her death over sixty years later.

Responsibility for supervising the printing and storage of sheets of 'postage stamps' was naturally taken on by the Stamp Office, based in London's Somerset Place (now Somerset House) off the Strand. Established in 1694, it had spent its first century and a half stamping official marks on a wide range of goods, from property-title deeds to playing cards and newspapers, as evidence that the appropriate taxes (or 'stamp duties') had been properly paid on them. Now it would be expanded and would preside over the distribution of postage stamps in exchange for reimbursement by the Post Office, a role it would retain until 1922.[25] The first man to head the new operation, as 'Superintendant', was none other than Rowland Hill's brother Edwin. He was to remain there for the next thirty-two years; and, in the finest traditions of the Hill family, he would in due course be joined by his son, Ormond Hill. It was Edwin who procured the services early in 1840 of an independent printer, Messrs Perkins, Bacon & Petch, for the postal project. Supplies of the 'Penny Black', the world's first postage stamp, were coming off their presses by mid-April. Maberly was then required to swallow his long-aired objections and to send out an appropriate notice to all postmasters ('It has been decided that Postage Stamps are to be brought into use forthwith . . .'), instructing them on the use of stamps and the mixing of a red ink with which to 'efface' them on all letters about to be despatched. The first Penny Blacks were released for sale to the public on 1 May, for use on letters posted on or after 6 May.* The first Twopenny Blues followed shortly afterwards.

Nine letters out of ten were bearing a stamp by the middle of the

---

* A few individuals in London tried to jump the gun by sending off letters with a stamp on them before 6 May. Postmasters humoured them but charged them a postage fee as well, scribbled on the envelope. Only one postmaster appears to have sent his own illicit letter. This was the Postmaster of Bath, Thomas Musgrave, who put a 2 May 1840 postmark on a letter bearing a Penny Black and sent it off to an address in Peckham. The stamp was untouched, but was scored with other London postmarks two days later. The stamp and postmarks survived and have been in private collections ever since: the scrap of paper bearing them was auctioned for more than £50,000 in 1990. As no doubt he intended, Musgrave's misdemeanour afforded Bath (and the owners of a modern postal museum in the city) another claim to postal history – as the first place to despatch a stamped letter – to set beside the achievements of those other Bath men, Allen and Palmer.

TO ALL POSTMASTERS
AND
SUB-POSTMASTERS.

GENERAL POST OFFICE,
25th April, 1840.

IT has been decided that Postage Stamps are to be brought into use forthwith, and as it will be necessary that every such Stamp should be cancelled at the Post Office or Sub-Post Office where the Letter bearing the same may be posted, I herewith forward, for your use, an *Obliterating Stamp*, with which you will efface the Postage Stamp upon every Letter despatched from your Office. *Red Composition* must be used for this purpose, and I annex directions for making it, with an Impression of the Stamp.

As the Stamps will come into operation by the *6th of May*, I must desire you will not fail to provide yourself with the necessary supply of Red Composition by that time.

Directions for Preparing the Red Stamping Composition.

1 lb. Printer's Red Ink.
1 Pint Linseed Oil.
Half-pint of the Droppings of Sweet Oil.
To be well mixed.

By Command,

W. L. MABERLY,
SECRETARY.

Maberly's instructions for the cancelling of stamps, April 1840

year, and by the end of 1840 a good many were starting to be posted in envelopes, which until then had been relatively rare.* (Envelopes grew in popularity through the 1840s, but only really took off after a way was invented of automatically folding them and applying a splash of glutinous wash to the back of the flap. At the Great Exhibition of 1851 a machine went on show that could do this, on the stand of the printers De La Rue, and ever more envelopes were sold thereafter. Some letters continued to be sent with a simple seal until the early 1860s, but in ever dwindling numbers.) Meanwhile, problems soon arose over the red ink used for cancelling: its composition made it easy to remove with chemicals, allowing the cancelled stamp to be used again. By September 1840, postmasters were being instructed on how to use a black ink instead. This was much harder to remove, but could be difficult to discern on a black stamp. Hence the replacement of the Penny Black by the Penny Red from February 1841. By then, the Post Office had issued just over 68 million Penny Blacks, of which perhaps six million (counting new and used stamps together) have survived. Any one of them, found in perfect mint condition today, might fetch up to several thousand pounds at auction – or a good deal more, in the case of those few improperly posted between 1 May and 6 May 1840.[26] And collectors have been in pursuit of them almost from the very start. As early as 1842, *Punch* magazine was reporting 'a new mania' that had sprung up among 'the industriously idle ladies of England' and the stamp-collecting hobby was off to a flying start.

3. THE COLOURFUL CAREER OF STANLEY GIBBONS

The first collectors were actually more interested in quantity than quality: they wanted to accumulate enough stamps, say, to paper the wall of a study or to line the dado of a sitting room. But once other countries

---

* Hill and his associates had tried to launch their own version of a pre-stamped envelope, but this had proved rather less successful than the Penny Black. In fact it was a disaster. They commissioned a Royal Academician, William Mulready, to produce an elegant design for the front of the envelope – but his creation, which also first appeared on 6 May 1840, was so overwrought that it provoked an unofficial competition in cruel parodies. Within a few months it had to be ignominiously withdrawn. Hill had expected 'the Mulreadies' to be more popular than adhesive stamps, and huge stocks of the printed envelopes had to be destroyed.

began to issue their own postage stamps – starting with Brazil in 1843 and three of Switzerland's cantons in 1844–5 – the peculiar fascination of collecting individual designs for their own sake soon took hold. Within twenty years, collecting had become a serious business, ably promoted by a small group of entrepreneurs – including one individual whose name would become almost synonymous with the world of stamps and valuations. In the very same year the Penny Black was born, a Plymouth pharmacist and his wife, William and Elizabeth Gibbons, had a fifth child, whom they christened Edward Stanley. As a schoolboy, the young Stanley developed an obsession with Hill's bits of paper with a glutinous wash. The British Post Office had put out only a handful of designs, but by the mid-1850s about fifty other countries were producing issues of their own. (The first British colony to release a stamp was Mauritius in 1847, resulting in one of the rarest stamps of all.*) Starting work in his parents' pharmacy in 1856, Gibbons showed such an impressive knowledge of stamps from all over the globe that his father soon gave him his own counter to serve customers more interested in stamps than pills and potions. And so it came about, some seven years later, that a couple of sailors called at the shop. They had just returned from Cape Town with a kitbag bulging with thousands of stamps they had won there in a raffle. Might the young Stanley be interested in buying them? Most were 'Cape Triangulars', an attractive blue triangular stamp in 1d and 4d denominations recently issued by the Cape colony and already much coveted by collectors in England. Gibbons bought the lot for £5. He later reckoned to have sold them for perhaps £500.

No doubt this helped focus his thinking, and young Gibbons now began to apply his obvious marketing talents single-mindedly to the promotion of 'philately' (a word, based on a Greek derivation, which seems to have first emerged as a name for stamp-collecting in Paris in 1861). In 1864 he published his first 'Descriptive Price List and

---

* The printing of a 1d Red and 2d Blue was commissioned to a half-blind watchmaker on the island, or so it is said, who engraved his first copper plate incorrectly, using the words 'Post Office' instead of 'Postage Paid'. The error was soon corrected, but not until a thousand stamps had been printed for the Governor's wife, who wanted to use them immediately on invitations to a ball to mark her husband's inauguration. The stamps were duly posted and most promptly disappeared – but not quite all. Modern collectors have traced twenty-six specimens of the 'Post Office Mauritius' and each has its own recorded 'biography', as do all rare stamps. Any reader fancying the presence of a twenty-seventh in a long-neglected family album should contact a good auctioneer. A 2d Blue went under the hammer in London on 28 June 2011 for just over a million pounds. (See L. N. and M. Williams, *Stamps of Fame*, Blandford Press, 1949, pp. 22–44.)

Catalogue of British, Colonial and Foreign Postage Stamps', detailing a thousand stamps from a hundred countries. Stamps were spreading fast. The next year's edition of the list included an advertisement for stamp albums, which Gibbons at first purchased from a Belgian supplier called Moens. Before long he was developing his own line in albums, and early in the 1870s he produced the artfully titled 'V.R.'. Heavily illustrated and annotated, this album purported to provide a little space for every stamp ever issued. The timing was perfect. The defeat of the US Confederacy in 1865, and the recent unification first of Italy and then of Germany, had brought an end to many regional postal administrations. Their stamps were still around but supplies were rapidly dwindling. Elsewhere in the world, new colonies with new stamps were springing up across the emerging empires of the European powers. The demand for Gibbons' products and his skills as a dealer were providing him with a handsome income. He was still listed in the 1871 census as a 'chemist and dealer in foreign stamps'.[27] But his father had died in 1867 and Gibbons sold the chemist's shop in 1872, moving two years later to London.

The public's enthusiasm for stamp-collecting showed no sign of being a passing fad – the Philatelic Society London had been founded in the capital in 1869 – and a monthly magazine, the *Philatelic Record*, went on sale in 1878 to help sustain the momentum. To make up for the fact that there were relatively few British stamp designs in circulation, Victorian collectors by the early 1860s were scrutinizing every detail of the printing, colouring, watermarks and perforation of individual specimens. (Perforation had been introduced in 1854.) Expert advice was in constant demand, and Gibbons provided it. Generally ducking face-to-face contact with his customers if it could possibly be avoided, he worked gruelling hours in a small office near the British Museum on what was effectively a mail order business on the buy-side and sell-side alike. He wrote continuously to postmasters around the world, in his quest for unusual issues. (Some of the replies were memorable. 'A West Indian postmaster returned his money-order, stating that the stamp he had ordered did not exist, but the letter was prepaid with a copy of the stamp in question.'[28]) He also had a brother, Alfred, who was an officer in the Royal Navy, for whom every port of call was a potential source of new supplies for the business. In 1861, the total number of stamp designs in existence had scarcely exceeded 500. By the end of the 1870s, as an article in the London press marvelled, 'an album to be complete would have to contain about 3,200 different sorts'.[29] The days of aspiring to a collection that boasted every stamp in the world would soon be over.* By the 1880s, Gibbons' Descriptive Price List had given way to an annually revised Catalogue, stretching to more than a hundred pages. (Stamps in Britain now existed for thirteen different values, running up to a '£5 Orange' issued in 1883 – which remained the most expensive of Britain's stamps until 1969.) And at this point Gibbons had another brilliant idea: catalogue numbers from various sources were being widely used for the stamps of every country, but he reserved the spaces in his albums for the numbers specifically listed in his own catalogue.[30] Here was a lure that no conscientious collector could resist, and sales boomed anew. Seldom can any entrepreneur have demonstrated the power of what the business textbooks call 'first-mover advantage' to such effect. The catalogue-number albums gave the business an unassailable position in the stamp-collecting world and Stanley Gibbons was soon a household name, as it remains to this day.

The man himself now had a yen to visit some of those exotic locations so exquisitely depicted on the stamps he had pored over for more than forty years. In 1890, having successfully launched his own *Monthly Journal* the previous year, he sold the business to a part-time dealer in Birmingham, Charles Phillips, for £25,000 (equivalent to a little over £2m today). While he accepted the position of chairman – and Alfred joined the board of directors – Gibbons left the business strictly to his successors and devoted himself to a life of pleasure. Taking his accumulated dealing profits together with the proceeds of his sale to Phillips, he was a wealthy man and intended to enjoy his fortune. He took to foreign travel with a passion, twice circling the globe among many other extended trips. A scrapbook survives of his globe-trotting, complete with snaps of himself braving the noonday sun, posing on spectacular hotel verandas and donning various national costumes in the photographer's studio.[31] He bought a large suburban villa near the Thames in Twickenham, where (as a journalist interviewing him for the company magazine put it in 1893) 'with Mrs Gibbons, he gives himself up to the rollicksome entertainment of his numerous friends'. Indeed, he worked

---

* One of the very last 'complete' collections, and the only one to survive, was assembled by a businessman called Thomas Tapling. At the end of the 1880s, he could still claim to have one copy of every stamp ever issued. His only rival was an Austrian aristocrat living in Paris, Philipp von Ferrary, who went on amassing a priceless collection until the First World War. But Ferrary died before the war ended, and the French government seized his collection and sold it off piecemeal to help fund Austrian war reparations. Tapling died at the age of 35 in 1891, bequeathing his collection to the British Library – where it has remained ever since, as the Holy Grail of philately's first half-century.

his way through one Mrs Gibbons after another. A short man, with tough features and a conspicuously bulbous nose, Gibbons was no Adonis but he collected young wives as his customers had once collected Cape Triangulars. None bore him any children and they had a tragic propensity for dying before reaching middle age. Two passed away in England, in 1877 and 1899. Two expired in the tropics, in 1904 (or thereabouts) and 1908. A fifth wife was forty when he married her in 1909, but separated from him within three years. His early career as a chemist and a marital track record to rival Bluebeard's have prompted suspicions of a darker tale. No such allegations surfaced in his lifetime, though plenty of rumours surrounded his death. He left most of his (much depleted) fortune to a close lady friend who was perhaps expecting to become wife number six. It was said that he had died suddenly in the arms of another woman at the Savoy Hotel, and that his body had been hurriedly removed to a nephew's house near Baker Street to avoid a scandal. If true, it seems a pity they did not arrange for him to have died across the road in the shop and company office of Stanley Gibbons Ltd, opened in 1890 at 391 Strand. A plaque could then have marked the spot in modern times, just a few doors away from The World's Largest Stamp Shop at 399 Strand to which the business moved in 1981.

4. TRAINS, TROLLOPE AND TRANSFORMATION

The immediate impact of cheap postage seemed to vindicate Rowland Hill's vision and to confirm the worst fears of his critics in about equal measure. Uniform penny postage proved an overnight sensation, in terms of its popularity with people at all levels of society. Our contemporary excitement over e-mails and websites perhaps offers a modern parallel with what contemporaries certainly felt to be an utterly transforming development. London's affluent middle classes quickly got down to chopping holes in their front doors and fixing 'letter boxes' to the inside of them. To working-class families for whom the expense of a letter's arrival in past times might easily have matched the cost of a precious loaf of bread, the new access to use of the Royal Mail was a wonder indeed. Contemporary writers and poets hailed the outcome as a social revolution, for better or worse. (Much worse, was William Wordsworth's view: 'the reduction of postage to a trifle' had hugely aggravated the inconvenience of time-wasting letters from strangers.[32])

The abuse of franked mail was ended – even the new young Queen voluntarily gave up her franking privileges – and penny postage all but eliminated the illegal mails that had challenged the monopoly before 1840.* On every count, the volume of letters in the post rose impressively. It was very soon apparent, however, that the rise would be nothing like the huge jump envisaged in Hill's calculations. Over the whole of 1840, the number of letters merely doubled, from 82.5 million to 168.8 million. Gross revenues at the same time slumped from £2.4m to £1.3m. The Post Office's costs, meanwhile, went up 13 per cent – which was puzzling to many, given the greatly reduced labour involved in sorting and delivering prepaid and uniformly charged letters. Net income dropped to £500,789, less than a third of 1839's £1.6m.

Ministers in the Whig government were naturally dismayed. They stood by penny postage – no politician could now contemplate abandoning it – but it wrecked all their budget calculations. It also dealt Hill's own credibility a heavy blow. Net income for 1841 staged only a very slight recovery, as costs went on climbing and volume growth slowed alarmingly. Those inside St Martin's-le-Grand, who since 1837 had had to suffer Hill's stern censure for the Post Office's 'erroneous financial arrangements' of the past, were swift to take their revenge. Even before the fall of the Whig government in September 1841, with its finances in disarray, Hill found himself cold-shouldered by officials at the Grand and losing authority in the Treasury. He noted in his diary a warning he had received from the outgoing Chancellor, Baring, 'that from the very highest to the lowest [in the Post Office] they were hostile to me and my plan'. He nonetheless had his contract extended for one year by Baring, which was almost the latter's very last act in office. Nine months later, in July 1842, Hill was informed by Baring's Tory successor that his further assistance on postal reform could 'safely be dispensed with'.[33] Hill's bitter protestations over the Tories' failure to reappoint

---

* Minor infringements of the monopoly occurred after 1840, but are no more than historical curiosities. One such was the use of college servants to run private mails in Oxford and Cambridge between 1871 and 1885. Having indulged the colleges at first, the Post Office had second thoughts once the colleges began to issue stamps and started collecting from letter boxes available to the public. The Secretary appealed formally to the colleges in 1885 to comply with the Post Office's legal monopoly. All agreed to do so – except the Oxford Union, which fought a protracted legal action and was eventually allowed in 1887 to retain a reduced messenger service that lasted well into the next century. (See R. H. Coase, 'The Postal Monopoly in Great Britain: An Historical Survey', in J. K. Eastham (ed.), *Economic Essays in Commemoration of the Dundee School of Economics, 1931–55*, privately publ. 1955, pp. 33–6.)

him filled his last three months, and were brought to a close only by a firm letter from the Prime Minister, Robert Peel. Other letters, from allies in the postal reform movement like Richard Cobden, were more encouraging and pledged Hill their support in a campaign to have him reinstated. One note, received in May 1843, came from the poet and humorist Thomas Hood. Given the Government's folly and ingratitude, wrote Hood, 'it would never surprise me to hear of the railway people some day, finding their trains running on so well, proposing to discharge the engines'.[34]

The railway metaphor was probably more timely than Hood realized, for Hill had just accepted a directorship with one of the railway companies now sprouting up all over the country. He would serve on the Board of the London and Brighton Railway for the next three years. Even as a stop-gap position, this appointment was not without its irony. Casting round for an explanation as to why the financial impact of penny postage had deviated so alarmingly from the forecast in his plan, Hill had hit upon two obvious answers. Predictably, one was the bloody-minded obstructionism (as he saw it) of the officials in St Martin's-le-Grand. The other was the spiralling cost of conveying letters – thanks to the arrival of the railways. Freeling, so often maligned for his old-fashioned ways, had seen the potential of the railways in an instant. The Post Office had begun transporting mails via the railways within a few months of the opening of the very first commercial line, the Liverpool and Manchester, in 1830. (The first step involved loading the whole mail coach and its guard onto the back of the train, but it was soon deemed a better idea to load just the mailbags onto the train. The guard was still required to travel with the bags, of course, and was even obliged to fill out time-bills for a while, noting the arrival times at each station along the line.) In the third year of penny postage, mails were being conveyed along about 1,400 miles of track by some forty different railway companies. Hill had no quarrel with the efficiency of the railways: steam trains, after all, were by now sustaining a steady 20 mph, which compared with an average of just over 8 mph for all mail coaches in 1836.[35] But where coaches in the mid-1830s had been costing the Post Office around £150,000 a year, expenditure on train services was already perhaps twice that sum by the early 1840s (and would rise to more than £400,000 by the early 1850s). Hill purported to see this as 'an untoward coincidence' that had wrecked his sums. Penny postage might have prospered much as projected, he claimed, had the railways never been invented. It is not easy to see how Hill or anyone else – and there were others – could have reconciled this analysis with what happened to the volume of the letter mails. Without the railways, the Post Office might have held costs lower for a matter of months – but would very soon have been overwhelmed. The mail coaches had already been heavily overloaded for years by 1840; and the Post Office steadfastly refused to resort to sending mails via ordinary stage coaches. Once mail volumes had doubled in 1840, the era of the mail coach was effectively over. (Services between many other cities survived into the 1850s, but the very last London evening mail departed from the forecourt of the Grand on 6 January 1846.) Indeed, it seems obvious to us with hindsight that the astonishing spread of the railways in the 1840s was integral to the success of penny postage. To the extent that Hill failed to anticipate this at the start of the decade, and even bemoaned the coming of the railways, we can only conclude that he was luckier with his timing than he realized.

The dramatic events unfolding at the top of the Post Office should not be allowed totally to overshadow the progress being made at the grassroots through these years. The steep rise in letter traffic may have disappointed some expectations, but it still necessitated a rapid expansion in the network of provincial post offices and the workforce behind them. Someone else who moved out of the Grand around this time was the junior clerk Anthony Trollope, who had only just survived the tedium of seven years in a tiny office with five others – one of whom, John Tilley, had married Trollope's sister before leaving for a position in the North Country. Trollope volunteered in 1841 to work as a field officer in Ireland. He spent the next ten years there as a Surveyor's Clerk, travelling round the country post offices of central and southern Ireland – 'a big young man on a big horse' – to inspect their accounting, tighten up their procedures and generally improve on the efficiency of their pre-railway rural deliveries.[36] The Irish had their own distinctive practices – a mail business set up by an Italian immigrant, Charles Bianconi, ran a network of four-wheeled carriages called 'Bians' that were the backbone of the country's transport system by the 1840s. Trollope's agenda there was nonetheless the kind of work with which teams of diligent Post Office Surveyors and their assistants, through the 1840s and 1850s, were constantly upgrading the machinery of the postal service all across the nation. He was especially concerned with devising additional routes for rural letter carriers, which after 1846 entailed frequent excursions across Irish countryside disfigured by the terrible consequences of the potato famine, and the typhus and cholera epidemics that accompanied it. His dedication to the work won him promotion back to England and he was given responsibility for organizing the 'walks' of letter carriers across the West Country and the Channel Islands.[37] It was a job that one contemporary in Cornwall described as

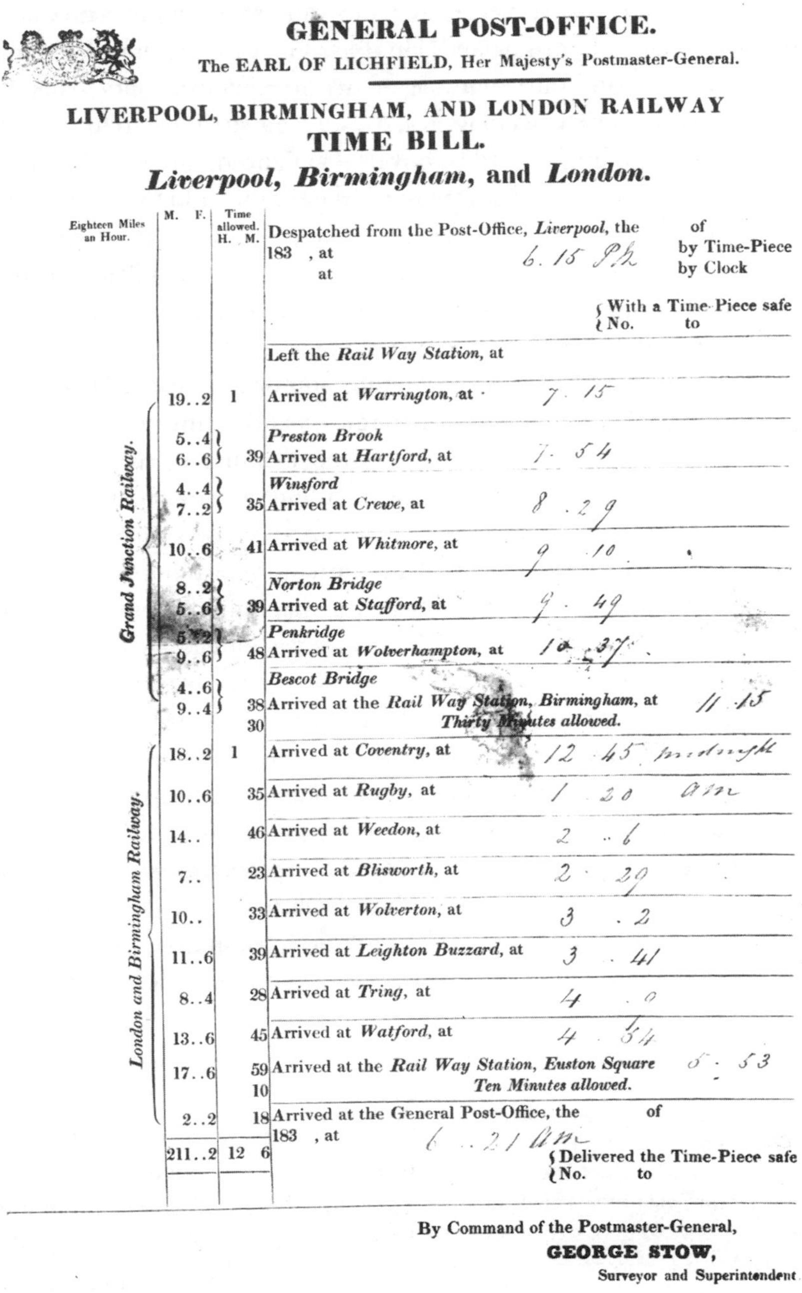

GENERAL POST-OFFICE.

The EARL OF LICHFIELD, Her Majesty's Postmaster-General.

LIVERPOOL, BIRMINGHAM, AND LONDON RAILWAY
TIME BILL.
Liverpool, Birmingham, and *London.*

Eighteen Miles an Hour.	M. F.	Time allowed. H. M.		
			Despatched from the Post-Office, *Liverpool,* the of	
			183 , at *6. 15 P.M.*	by Time-Piece
			at	by Clock
				{ With a Time-Piece safe
				{ No. to
			Left the *Rail Way Station,* at	
	19..2	1	Arrived at *Warrington,* at · *7 . 15*	
	5..4 ⎱ 6..6 ⎰	39	*Preston Brook* Arrived at *Hartford,* at *7 . 54*	
	4..4 ⎱ 7..2 ⎰	35	*Winsford* Arrived at *Crewe,* at *8 . 29*	
	10..6	41	Arrived at *Whitmore,* at *9 10*	.
	8..2 ⎱ 5..6 ⎰	39	*Norton Bridge* Arrived at *Stafford,* at *9 . 49*	
	5..2 ⎱ 9..6 ⎰	48	*Penkridge* Arrived at *Wolverhampton,* at *10 . 37* ·	
	4..6 ⎱ 9..4 ⎰	38	*Bescot Bridge* Arrived at the *Rail Way Station,* Birmingham, at *11 . 15*	
		30	Thirty Minutes allowed.	
	18..2	1	Arrived at *Coventry,* at *12 . 45 midnight*	
	10..6	35	Arrived at *Rugby,* at *1 . 20 a.m.*	
	14..	46	Arrived at *Weedon,* at *2 .. 6*	
	7..	23	Arrived at *Blisworth,* at *2 . 29*	
	10..	33	Arrived at *Wolverton,* at *3 . 2*	
	11..6	39	Arrived at *Leighton Buzzard,* at *3 . 41*	
	8..4	28	Arrived at *Tring,* at *4 . 0*	
	13..6	45	Arrived at *Watford,* at *4 . 54*	
	17..6	59	Arrived at the *Rail Way Station, Euston Square* *5 . 53*	
		10	Ten Minutes allowed.	
	2..2	18	Arrived at the General Post-Office, the of	
			183 , at *6 .. 21 a.m.*	
211..2	12 6		{ Delivered the Time-Piece safe	
			{ No. to	

(Left margin labels: *Grand Junction Railway.* — *London and Birmingham Railway.*)

By Command of the Postmaster-General,
GEORGE STOW,
Surveyor and Superintendent.

A Time Bill completed for a railway Travelling Post Office, *c.*1840, retaining precisely the format used on the Royal Mail coaches for half a century and noting the exact times of arrival at each station along the route.

being 'about as easy for a stranger in those days as to lay out a post road on the Upper Congo'.[38] But Trollope loved it, riding forty miles every day and conceiving the story of *The Warden* (1855), the first of *The Barsetshire Chronicles*, in the process. Then his career progressed again, with appointments to Surveyor positions in Belfast, Dublin and finally the 'Eastern District' of England. He retired in 1867, by which time he was earning a handsome multiple of his Post Office salary from his books.[39] He left a rich postal legacy, including a stream of references to the Post Office in his forty-seven novels – and, above all, the pillar box, an idea that he heard was being pioneered in France and that he success-fully championed in the Channel Islands in 1851. Trollope amused his readers by having one of his own characters dismiss the pillar box as 'a most hateful thing' but it quickly became a cherished part of the postal service, and indeed of the British urban landscape in general.*

But there is no escaping the paramount importance to the Post Office story, through the middle third of the nineteenth century, of Rowland Hill and his relatives. The pressure on the Treasury to reappoint him after 1842 was unrelenting, not least from Hill himself: invited to give evidence to yet another Select Committee in 1843, he provided enough material to fill 130 pages of the Committee's final report. The public acclaim for his penny post was so overwhelming that its long-term financial viability seemed assured, whatever the immediate difficulties – and new applications for cheap postage were still emerging. (During 1843, Hill's brilliant accomplice in their 1837–9 campaign, Henry Cole, conceived the idea of encouraging people to send greetings cards to each other for Christmas. Cole himself commissioned the design of the first 'Christmas card', which went on sale to the public that year.) The repu-tation of the Post Office that had opposed cheap postage was meanwhile exposed to public scorn on yet another matter. It was discovered in 1844 that letters to and from an Italian nationalist in exile, Joseph Maz-zini, had been intercepted on instructions from the Home Secretary of

---

* Its popularity endures, with about 115,000 red pillar boxes still in use, but it has suffered some indignities over the years. After the accession of Queen Elizabeth II in February 1952, the Post Office incorporated the new royal cypher 'EIIR' into its corporate livery. This provoked angry protests in Scotland, where the new monarch was not the second but the first of her name to reign as queen (Elizabeth I's reign having preceded the 1707 Act of Union). A campaign ensued of intermittent vandalism against postal property north of the border, and especially new pillar boxes adorned with the offending cypher. Several were blown up. The Post Office defeated a civil action brought against it in the courts by the Rector of Glasgow University ('MacCormick vs Lord Advocate'), but nonetheless opted in 1953 to adopt a fresh livery in Scotland, with 'EIIR' replaced by a Scottish crown.

the day. Mazzini's case was taken up in Parliament, where Thomas Duncombe MP stirred up a public furore over the issue and forced Peel's government into appointing a Secret Committee of Inquiry. Its subsequent report to the Commons, in August 1844, was accompanied by a long and detailed history of the Government's use of interception, revealing that some 372 warrants had been issued by ministers since 1798. A mighty row erupted when it then emerged that Duncombe's own private correspondence had been intercepted by the Post Office two years earlier. (A series of acrimonious Commons debates had no impact on the legal position, but appear to have resulted in a very much more circumspect use of the Government's interception powers through the rest of the century.)[40] The collapse of Peel's Tory government in 1846 restored to power Hill's radical Whig friends, who were quite prepared to overlook the immediate financial consequences of the penny post – or, like him, to blame them on the hierarchy inside St Martin's-le-Grand. With a sublime disregard for the lessons of the Palmer era, he was given a newly created role as 'Secretary to the Postmaster General'. The resident Secretary, three years younger than Hill, was understandably mortified. 'Maberly is in a sad way at the disgrace and dishonour (he will call it) which he considers we inflict upon him by appointing Rowland Hill,' wrote the Postmaster General to the Prime Minister. '. . . Nothing but a baronetcy, it seems, will heal his wounded spirit . . . There is no doubt Rowland Hill's appointment is a sad blow to him and will affect his credit in the country.'[41]

Maberly was right to be so put out. Hill was no longer prepared to acquiesce in another outsider's role. Bursting with new ideas and enough energy for ten men, he (like Palmer before him) wanted to run the whole show. Predictably, he and Maberly sparred from the outset, each vying for the upper hand. Hill was relentless in his criticism of the old guard and schemed unashamedly to have his rival removed. Yet the standoff between them lasted, incredibly, for eight long years. We have a colourful, if less than impeccable, account of it that was penned years later by a clerk called Edmund Yates. He had himself only joined the Post Office in 1847 as a lad of fifteen, so was hardly in a position to have spent much time watching Maberly and Hill at first hand. But Yates grew up to be a novelist and a pioneer of gossip journalism, retiring from the Post Office aged forty in 1872. In an autobiography published in 1884 he left a characteristically juicy account of life inside the Grand in the middle years of the century.[42] He remembered Maberly as 'a clear-headed man of business; old-fashioned, inclined to let matters run in their ordinary groove, detesting all projects of reform, and having an abiding horror of Rowland Hill'. The colonel, as he was always known, 'was exceedingly jealous of the new arrival, and hated "that man from Birmingham", as he always called him, with a holy hatred'.[43] But Hill persevered, 'in the face of unbelievable opposition and obstruction in every quarter'.[44] As he struggled to assert his primacy, he was undoubtedly more sinned against than sinning, and he finally prevailed, at the age of fifty-eight, in 1854. Maberly was shunted off to another branch of the civil service altogether – he was put in charge of the Audit Office – and Hill then served as Secretary to the Post Office until 1864. During his eighteen years at the Grand, he brought aboard his brother Frederic as Assistant Secretary and employed so many other younger relatives (including his son Pearson) that he was said by a contemporary wit to have resembled the sun, 'because he touches the little Hills with gold'.[45] The extended family involvement was not a symptom of financial impropriety on Rowland Hill's part. But it was a fair reflection of the way in which this outsider came in the end to dominate every aspect of the Post Office's activities, with the freedom to shape the institution in line with the vision he had set down in the 1830s.

The list of advances made under Hill's leadership is a long and remarkable one. He oversaw a steady growth in the number of post offices and sub-offices around the country (to 920 and 9,578 respectively, by 1855), so laying the basis of an organization and workforce that within a generation would be the largest of any kind in Britain. By 1864, almost 95 per cent of letters were being 'delivered free' to their postal address – with no special fee, that is to say, beyond the postage stamp, torn from a perforated sheet after 1854 and almost universally adopted thereafter. The charging of additional pennies by rural postmasters for the final leg of a letter's delivery, that vexatious issue for the Post Office over so many decades, was at last all but eliminated. Within the capital, which accounted for roughly a quarter of the Post Office's business, the old distinctions between the Inland, Foreign and District Posts were finally scrapped. All three were subsumed within a new Circulation Office, headed by a Controller of the London Postal Service, whose territory was organized round ten new districts. This ended (not before time) the need for St Martin's-le-Grand to be treated as a central clearing house for letters posted within the capital to a London address.*

---

* The General Post Office in St Martin's nonetheless retained its hold on the popular imagination as the centre of the postal world. Nothing exemplified this better than a large painting of the interior of its portico by the artist George Elgar Hicks. Entitled *The General*

The districts were named in relation to their compass bearings from St Martin's – thus, the Westminster area at the heart of the capital was South-West, the City of London on the doorstep of St Martin's was East Central, and so on – and were instantly known to all by their initials. The resulting letters (SW, EC, E, N, NW, W, WC and SE – plus NE and S, which were soon amalgamated into their neighbours) remain the basis of London's postcodes to this day. All inland mails outside the capital, meanwhile, were put under an Inspector-General of the Mails, assigned to the Secretary's Office, whose responsibilities encompassed the Post Office's activities on the railways. Special carriages in which men could sort letters had first been added to trains as early as 1838, and 'Travelling Post Offices' (TPOs) had since then transformed the handling of mail across the country. It was Hill himself who conceived the clever idea of putting inward mails to London from the home counties onto night trains headed *away* from the capital: they could travel to, say, Birmingham and then back again, allowing time for them to be sorted en route and still distributed to the London postal districts early the next morning.

While not everything achieved in these years should be attributed directly to Hill, all projects fell within his orbit, and his personal role was unquestionably critical to many of them. They included an expansion of the 'Money Order Department', founded in 1792, which provided working families with a means of sending small payments safely through the postal system. And it was Hill the former teacher who persuaded the Government, in 1848, to accept that a 'Book Post' should be allowed for the encouragement of self-education, though parcels remained outside the Royal Mail monopoly then and for some years to come. As for his approach to the general management of the Post Office, Hill spent his career battling procedural niceties that had clogged up the running of the service since the previous century. He greatly improved its day-to-day efficiency, even while presiding over a data-gathering machine that continued to amass information on every aspect of operations in often astonishing detail. Statistical returns over many years, for instance, included a tally of how many postmen had been bitten by dogs – and it would be no great surprise to see a file emerge, one day, that records the

---

Post Office: One Minute to Six, it presented a social panorama of people from all classes of London society, hastening to catch the last evening post. First exhibited at the 1860 Royal Academy Summer Exhibition, it attracted huge numbers of visitors, prompting a critic in *Punch* to suggest: 'The crush represented in Mr Hicks's picture gives only a faint idea of the crowd around it'.

number of dogs bitten by postmen. Hill led the way in the Post Office's adoption of the so-called Northcote–Trevelyan reforms of the civil service, unveiled in 1854, which would gradually phase out patronage in favour of entrance exams and promotion according to merit (though an exception, naturally, might have to be made for future little Hills).* That same year, he also oversaw a fundamental change to the administration of the Post Office's finances: revenues had in future to be kept entirely separate from any spending and handed over directly to the Exchequer, while each year's expenditure would be authorized by annual votes of Parliament and channelled through the Treasury. (Parliament's 'Annual Estimates', setting out the authorized expenditure and anticipated revenues for the financial year ahead, were first published in 1856.) And in 1855 Hill initiated, apparently at his brother Frederic's suggestion, the sending of an annual Postmaster General's Report to the Treasury, the first three of which set down valuable summaries of the Post Office's development to date.[46] The 1857 summary, reviewing developments in Ireland, was written by Trollope.

Hill did not always get his way. He was defeated in his attempts to foreclose the option of sending unpaid letters through the post: it continued to be possible – as indeed it still is, today – to post a letter with no stamp, leaving it to the Post Office to collect payment, as in the past, from the recipient (though letters with no stamp did incur a surcharge after 1853, the precursor of a heavy charge in the modern day). More importantly, he also failed to overturn constraints on Sunday services that were a legacy of the Cromwellian era. Attitudes towards postal work on the Sabbath varied from place to place before the 1840s. Hill tried to standardize a more businesslike approach, starting with a plan in

---

* Trollope, still working as a Surveyor in Ireland, was vehemently opposed to the North-cote–Trevelyan reforms. Having himself won a position at the Post Office through the patronage of a family friend, he could see no rationale for awarding positions on the basis of a competitive examination that could not possibly be a meaningful guide, in his view, to a young man's aptitude for a career in the civil service. He considered the whole idea hopelessly Utopian – and wrote a long article explaining why, published in October 1855 in the *Dublin University Magazine*. 'It has for some years been apparent to us, that if a real Utopia could be peopled with emigrants from Great Britain, Sir Charles Trevelyan would be the only man to whom could be confided the chief magistracy of the colony. Sir Stafford North-cote, who rode worthily into fame on the cupola of the London Exhibition, is a fitting associate for so great an administrator' (quoted in R. H. Super, *Trollope in the Post Office*, University of Michigan Press, 1981, p. 31). Trollope caricatured the two reformers as Sir Gregory Hardlines and Sir Warwick Westend in his novel *The Three Clerks* (1858) – in which his employer appears thinly disguised as the Inland Navigation Office, described by the author as being much like the Post Office, but 'not so decidedly plebeian'.

1849 to introduce Sunday deliveries (hitherto virtually non-existent) in London and to facilitate the sorting of mail for Sunday evening trains. This move backfired, provoking a campaign by the Lord's Day Observance Society against sorting and delivery work across the whole country. Feelings ran so high over the issue that the Government had to back away from supporting Hill, and an Act of 1850 outlawed all collections or deliveries on Sundays. But this triggered a second backlash, this time from the angry representatives of all those in the provinces with businesses and rural livelihoods that had come to depend upon Sunday mails. The Government back-tracked a second time. A parliamentary motion allowed postal services to resume, subject to various conditions that in practice were applied or ignored according to local circumstances. But the capital went back to being post-free on Sundays, and the rest of the country became a patchwork of inconsistencies, cross-hatched with a few new legal peculiarities – an individual householder, for example, could opt to exclude his address from the local postman's Sunday walk. This would remain the position for the rest of the century.

Like Palmer, Hill reckoned his impact had made the politicians superfluous. He was twice thwarted in his efforts to have himself appointed as the Executive Chairman of a Post Office Board, dispensing altogether with the need for a political head of the Department, a radical reform which had to wait until 1969. But in the Victorian public's perception, and his own, Hill by the 1860s had anyway come to embody the Post Office as no man before him. And the dramatic growth of the mails had finally vindicated the boldness of his Penny Post plan in spectacular fashion. The 1840 traffic of almost 169 million paid-for letters had quadrupled to 679 million by 1864, roughly equating to the whole population sending not three letters a year per capita but twenty. A cheap and reliable postal system has been a commonplace of British society ever since, so the profound implications of the Penny Post are perhaps easily overlooked. Its impact transformed many lives – especially among the poor, as G. M. Trevelyan noted in his classic survey of English social history a century after its introduction. 'Prior to this great change, the poor who moved in search of work either inside the island [i.e. the British Isles] or by emigration overseas, could seldom exchange news with the parents and friends they had left behind, owing to the charge made for the receipt of letters. Rowland Hill's plan … enabled the poor, for the first time in the history of man, to communicate with the loved ones from whom they were separated.'[47]

As for the financial state of the Department – for those to whom it still mattered – the 'reformed Post Office' had rebuilt its gross revenues to their 1839 level (around £2.3m) by 1852. Its net income took longer to restore. This had run at just over £1.6m for each of the three years prior to 1840. On a roughly comparable basis, net income was back to £1.8m by 1862 and rose steadily thereafter. (The reported figures are slightly more complicated. The transfer of packet services back from the Admiralty to the Post Office in 1861 added about £1m to total costs, thus cutting back the 1862 net income to £0.8m. On the basis of this changed cost structure, the pre-1840 net income figure was not exceeded until 1874 – see Appendix A, Chart 1.) Maberly had prophesied to Wallace's Select Committee back in 1838 that 'the revenue would not recover itself for forty or fifty years', but his dire warning had been confounded.[48] Above all, by the 1860s, Hill had won for the Victorian Post Office a priceless asset: immense popular esteem. It was universally seen as unique, not just as a flourishing business enterprise run by the state but as an organization of unparalleled efficiency and trustworthiness. Indeed, for most people in Britain over the next half-century, the Post Office would now be increasingly seen as *the* public face of the state. Their exposure to other state institutions was usually minimal. The daily rounds of the Royal Mail, and the services provided at the counter of local post offices, would become easily the most familiar manifestation of the state in ordinary daily life.

Ironically, Hill was in many ways lucky to keep his job into the 1860s. His relations with ministers were generally uneasy at best. He was never prepared to kow-tow to Postmasters General with uppity notions about their own role in the Department. He behaved as though his reporting line went directly into the Treasury, which in effect it did: he called there once a week for his own private briefing. Even before he attained the Secretary's post, this attitude was almost his undoing. A new Postmaster General appointed in 1852, the 4th Earl of Hardwicke, was a gruff and overbearing rear admiral who quickly made clear that Hill's feud with Maberly would be treated as mutinous if it continued. (Yates would later recall some bizarre exchanges with 'the Bosun', as he was nicknamed in the Grand: 'his general idea was that late attendance, or any other shortcomings on the part of the clerks, should be punished by Keel-hauling or the cat'.[49]) Fortunately, Hardwicke soon hove to and his successors over the next seven years were generally content to let Hill usurp their constitutional position.

Not so Lord Stanley of Alderley, who arrived at the Post Office in

1860. By then, 'Hill's sense of self-importance had grown almost as rapidly as the Post Office'.[50] Stanley, like Walsingham seventy years earlier, thought the time had come to reassert some political clout over the executive. A series of altercations ensued. By now Hill was in his mid-sixties, plagued by ill-health – almost certainly stress-related – and not averse to reminding the world, whenever necessary, of his own past achievements. A seemingly decisive clash with Stanley occurred in June 1861 – after a row over staff appointments – and Hill threatened to resign, but he was sufficiently mollified by a private audience with the Prime Minister, Lord Palmerston, to change his mind. He noted in his *Journal* after their hour-long meeting on 9 June:

> I don't think Lord Palmerston is fully impressed with the difficulties of my position – [he] asked for explanations on this point which did not appear to convince him. Will, I fear, do nothing more than attempt to patch up the case, in the hope (though I distinctly told him there was none), that I shall consent to go on with Lord Stanley.[51]

By this stage, to use a modern expression, Hill was a public servant requiring very high maintenance indeed from his political masters. By the summer of 1863 they were tired of it. Renewed difficulties between him and Stanley brought Hill back for a second meeting with the Prime Minister. This time Palmerston was in no mood to be lectured on the needs of the Post Office. He lost his temper with Hill, and brought the discussion to a rapid close. '[He] spoke rather crossly of the right of the head of a Department to have his own way', as Hill noted afterwards, '. . . though it is right to add that he appeared, after some very plain speaking on both sides, to recover his temper'.[52] Palmerston subsequently wrote a letter to Gladstone, the Chancellor of the Exchequer, about their exchange. Given the encomiums to Hill later dished out on all sides, not least by Palmerston himself, the letter is illuminating:

> I clearly perceived from what he [Hill] said to me that he entirely misunderstood the relative positions of a Secretary and the head of the department. He appeared to imagine that he ought to be Viceroy over his chief, and the substance of his complaint was that Stanley acted upon his own opinions instead of being invariably governed by his. I told Sir Rowland Hill that I consider Stanley quite right in the matter . . . Rowland Hill had no doubt the merit of suggesting penny postage, but he seemed to me to be the spoilt child of the Post Office, and he ought to make up his mind to be what he really is, a subordinate officer, or retire from a post which his own notions

of his personal importance make it unpleasant for him to hold. As to leave of absence, if I was Stanley, I would give it to him *sine die*.[53]

Hill took the leave, on grounds of ill-health. At the end of February 1864, seeing no prospect of Stanley being removed, he formally tendered his resignation. Generously, and expensively as it turned out, the Treasury awarded him a full-salary pension for the rest of his life. Parliament in addition made him a personal grant of £20,000. With Hill now safely out of the way, Palmerston took the occasion of its announcement, in June 1864, to laud the retired Secretary in the House of Lords as 'a man of great genius, of great sagacity, of great perseverance and

PUNCH, OR THE LONDON CHARIVARI.—MARCH 19, 1864.

POST OFFICE
SAVINGS BANK

SIR ROWLAND LE GRAND.

Cartoon of 'Sir Rowland Le Grand' in *Punch*, 1864

industry [who] has rendered great services . . .'[54] There was no denying the public's adulation. A Tenniel cartoon in *Punch* presented him on his retirement as Sir Rowland Le Grand – he had been knighted in 1860 – entitled to laurels on every count. He was duly showered with them. The cartoon's caption suggested he was at least as deserving of a statue as Oliver Cromwell, whose suitability for a public memorial had been mooted but remained a matter of controversy. 'For one is celebrated for cutting off the head of a bad King, and the other for sticking on the head of a good Queen.' Hill died in 1879 and was buried, in accordance with his own long-held aspiration, in Westminster Abbey. Three years later, a statue was indeed unveiled to him, in front of the Royal Exchange building at the heart of the City, paid for out of public subscriptions.* It was subsequently moved and stands today in King Edward Street, just off St Martin's-le-Grand. No doubt to *Punch*'s satisfaction, Cromwell had to wait another seventeen years before his statue was erected in front of the Commons in 1899.

5. HILL'S LEGACY: THE LIMITS OF 'ECONOMICAL REFORM'

Reaching a balanced view of Hill's peculiar genius is not easy. He and his family had begun very effectively to transmute his career into an institutional myth long before his death. The two-volume autobiography that appeared the next year – with a lengthy third-person account of his early life, largely written by a nephew – used a rich feast of stories and correspondence to enshrine Hill's iconic status as the Father of the Post Office. Others, publishing their memoirs within a few years of his, added their own pinch of salt. Edmund Yates remarked that Hill had a distinctive 'way of saying a caustic and unpleasant thing' and was never remotely prepared to acknowledge the importance of any idea not envisaged in his own plan.[55] Without doubt, he was a difficult man who made many enemies. And reading the monumental diary that he kept

---

* The public appeal that paid for the statue, and for a bust of Hill in Westminster Abbey, was so oversubscribed that a Rowland Hill Benevolent Fund was set up a few months later to make use of the remaining money. It was one of the first official Post Office bodies to admit representatives of the postal trade unions onto its governing board, which it did in 1910. It still flourishes today, dispensing grants to Post Office employees and their dependants in financial distress. The fund is topped up by voluntary contributions out of staff salaries and wages.

for 1839–55 and 1861–69, it is not hard to see why. His *Post Office Journal*, comprising eighteen manuscript volumes, was seen almost from the start by Hill as a way of storing up facts and commentaries that might one day be used as ammunition against his adversaries. It provided the source material for much of his autobiography, and was published in full by the Royal Philatelic Society London in 2000. Many entries through the early 1860s, full of bile and recriminations, make painful reading. There seems scarcely a page that does not convey two overwhelming impressions. Its author laboured like Hercules on the fulfilment of his vision; but he clung to that vision with a passion that bordered on paranoia when dealing with anyone he suspected of dissenting. Confronted with obstructive individuals, Hill was never slow to spot a conspiracy (or a 'cabal', as he was inclined to say) against his plan. Faced with awkward facts, he was a master at seeing the world not as it was, but as he intended it to be. A common enough trait, perhaps, among history's great reformers.

One lasting consequence, ironically, was that the champion of change ended up entrenching a key feature of the *un*reformed Post Office. Though he tried in some respects to encourage more independence of mind among the clerical staff – pressing them, for example, to prepare their own minutes on policy questions requiring a decision – Hill was never prepared to delegate too much real authority, at least not to anyone outside his own extended family. There is a celebrated anecdote, again recounted by Yates, about Col. Maberly waving aside a long list of papers after they had been read aloud to him over a mid-morning breakfast. (Working hours at the Grand remained less than onerous until well after 1840.) When a clerk had the temerity to suggest some might perhaps be of importance, the Colonel rounded on him. 'Yes, yes, my good fellow; no doubt *you* think they're important: *I* call them damned twopenny-ha'penny!'[56] The story has been retold many times to illustrate Maberly's idleness. In his soldierly impatience with the deluge of trivia that daily landed on the Secretary's desk, though, the Colonel may just have had a more instinctive feel than those who came before or after him for the burden being imposed by excessive centralization. Like Freeling, Hill ruled as a workaholic autocrat – and the highly centralized culture that he left behind would remain a defining and indelible feature of Post Office administration for generations to come.

His legacy in this respect was mixed. While Hill's uncompromising temperament was undoubtedly essential to his many extraordinary achievements as an innovator, it was less attuned to the needs of the Post Office as these evolved through the 1850s. This was not much noted outside the organization. The distinction between building a large business and running one may be familiar enough to readers of modern books on management – but was scarcely a commonplace in Hill's day. The general public made little distinction between Hill the Great Reformer and Hill as the man who managed the Royal Mail. No less a figure than Gladstone saw his impact as an administrative triumph and the world at large agreed.[57] Nevertheless, those who knew and worked with Hill always had their reservations. He was not generally liked by his subordinates. Three apparently serious threats of assassination were received by him in the 1850s.[58] Anthony Trollope had dealings with him on many occasions and the two men plainly loathed each other. Trollope wrote Hill a generous letter in March 1864 to express 'my thorough admiration for the great work of your life'. But in his posthumously published *Autobiography*, published four years after Hill's death, the novelist famously observed that he 'was always an anti-Hillite, acknowledging, indeed, the great thing which Sir Rowland Hill had done for the country, but believing him to be entirely unfit to manage men or arrange labour'.* There is no reason to doubt this was Trollope's firm conviction. As he added mischievously: 'I never came across anyone who so little understood the ways of men – unless it was his brother Frederic'.[59]

Modern historians have been torn between acknowledging Hill's accomplishments and distancing themselves from the Hill family's iconography. The editors of his *Journal* understandably acclaimed Hill's career, reminding readers that the enactment of his reforms 'might have been delayed for decades', had it not been for Hill's obsessive personality and single-mindedness.[60] Many, like Howard Robinson, have been

---

* Of course, much the same could have been said of Trollope himself. But, in most other ways, the two men could hardly have been more different – as Yates enjoyed recalling. 'One small, pale, and, with the exception of a small scrap of whisker, closely shaven; the other big, broad, fresh-coloured, and bushy-bearded: one calm and freezing, the other bluff and boisterous; one cautious and calculating, weighing well every word before utterance, and then only choosing phrases which would convey his opinion, but would give no warmth to its expression; the other scarcely giving himself time to think, but spluttering and roaring out an instantly formed opinion couched in the very strongest of terms' (Edmund Yates, *Recollections and Experiences*, 2 vols., Richard Bentley & Sons, 1884, Vol. 2, p. 228). It greatly riled Hill in the 1860s that Trollope was prepared to speak in public about being a writer, 'as though literature were his "profession"'. He was also scornfully dismissive of some of Trollope's views on the workings of the Post Office – 'and as T. is undoubtedly clever, it follows in my opinion that he is dishonest' (*Journal, 1839–1869*, 6 and 16 September 1862).

more ambivalent, taking their cue from the *Encyclopaedia Britannica* of
1885, which noted the peaks of an illustrious career but frankly opined
that Hill was lacking in 'suavity of manner, tact in dealing with large
bodies of inferiors, and reverence for the good things of past times'. Of
course, a personally abrasive style has never disqualified anyone from
making a mark on history, as was bluntly noted by C. P. Snow, a Trollope biographer and shrewd observer of the cross-currents between
public and private life in his own day: '[Hill] might not know a man
from a bull's foot, but he did know how to shape the world's postal
service'.[61] But the case against Hill is not that he was simply a difficult
man, but that his approach was increasingly ill-suited to the running of
a complex organization. As the historian Martin Daunton put it in
1984, 'Hill created twenty years of acrimony and tension within the
Post Office which probably hindered rather than helped the successful
development of the Penny Post'.[62] Daunton perhaps took a slightly
ungenerous view of Hill's early contribution to the triumph of uniform
penny postage ('an enthusiastic amateur expounding the fashionable
theories of the day') and may have played down his later achievements
a little severely. But his broad view, that Hill's fierce pursuit of the
abstractions of his 1837 pamphlet too often militated against the kind
of pragmatic management needed by the Post Office, is persuasive.

The managerial challenge was not just a consequence of the Post
Office's rapid expansion. It sprang also from a subtle evolution of the
role that outsiders – and a growing number of insiders, too – thought
appropriate for the Post Office, but which posed a dilemma for the die-
hard proponents of 'economical reform'. It was a fundamental issue
brought most sharply into focus by the Post Office's adjustment to the
impact of trains and, even more critically, steamships. In its dealings
with the railway companies, it had been given the right in 1838 to com-
mandeer carriages or whole trains where necessary. But the relevant
statute had failed to lay down a clear basis for the pricing of rail-mail
contracts, simply asserting that arbitrators on behalf of the two sides
should agree on 'reasonable remuneration'. Bitter wrangling over this
filled the two decades, as payments to the railway companies rose to 20
per cent or so of the Post Office's total expenditure. Hill wanted all costs
of conveyance to be covered by the revenue from the mail being carried.
This put a premium on using as few routes as possible, which could be
accounted for more easily, though the result would be less convenient to
the public. In the end he had to bow to popular pressure for a much
heavier and more costly use of the trains, but he hugely resented it. 'The

"convenience of the public" could not, in Hill's view, be considered apart from "the commercial nature of the transaction", for he insisted that they were identical.'[63] A similar tale unfolded with the shipping companies and overseas mails. Here again Hill was adamant that all payments should ideally be covered by revenues earned on the respective shipments, and it was a policy objective that prompted sharp disagreements. But these were played out on a grander stage than the quarrels over railway contracts, for the efficiency of the Royal Mail overseas touched on Britain's place in the world and the strategic requirements of her empire.

Through most of Hill's time, the foreign mails had been only indirectly managed by the Post Office. Those questions raised about its packet-ship activities by the Parliamentary Commissioners' Reports of 1829–30 had been followed by even more searching inquiries in 1836, uncovering yet more serious losses since 1832. This time, the remedy was not just a move towards putting a few individual routes out for commercial tender but the assignment in 1837 of responsibility for all ship-mail activities to the Admiralty. The Post Office and the Treasury would in future submit jointly their requirements and recommendations, but the Admiralty would be in charge – directly or indirectly – of all operations. It retained some existing Post Office packet ships, but contracted out most of their erstwhile duties to private operators. The beneficiaries of this policy were those commercial enterprises at the forefront of the great switch from wooden sailing ships to steam-powered ocean liners built entirely of iron. Among the three most important of these new 'shipping lines' was the Royal Mail Steam Packet Company, a privately owned venture founded by City investors in 1839 to run the mails to the West Indies and the North and South Atlantic seaports of the Americas.* Though independently chartered by the Queen and run by its own Court of Directors, its fleet was invariably referred to as the Royal Mail and its existence was wholly bound up with its work for the Post Office. More problematic for officials in St Martin's-le-Grand – because their commercial terms were always far more keenly contested – were the contracts granted by the Admiralty to

---

* Operating out of Southampton, its inaugural fourteen vessels were all built of wood and sheathed in copper, but had cast iron steam engines to drive their paddles. Its first iron ship, the *Atrato*, was launched in 1853. Not until 1871 did the fleet's last wooden ship pass out of commission, and the Royal Mail Line went on commissioning paddle ships until 1865 (see T. A. Bushell, *Royal Mail: A Centenary History of the Royal Mail Line, 1839–1939*, London, 1939, pp. 98 and 110.)

two other, larger companies which came to acquire virtual monopolies over their respective routes: the Cunard Line on the North Atlantic, and the Peninsular & Oriental Steam Navigation Co. (P&O) linking Britain first to the Peninsula (meaning principally Lisbon and Gibraltar at first, later superseded by the ports of the Mediterranean) and beyond it to the Orient (meaning above all India and Australia). Over the two decades following the award of contracts to them by the Admiralty in 1837–40, these three companies and half a dozen much smaller enterprises succeeded in laying down mail routes across the globe that contemporaries came to see as being almost as emblematic of the age as the Penny Post and the railways. Naturally linking all three to the splendours of free trade, the *Economist* enthused in 1851:

> Arrangements have been made on the grandest scale for regular postal communications, by steam, with all the chief countries of the world – with India, China, North America, the West Indies, South America, the Cape of Good Hope (and we hope we may soon include Australia), not to mention every port of Europe from the Baltic to the Levant; and they are now all combined with this country by steam postal communication with as much regularity as Edinburgh and London could boast of twelve years ago.[64]

Especially intriguing for many contemporaries was the development of the route to India and the East. While most cargoes bound in this direction faced a voyage of more than 12,000 miles via the Cape, mails and passengers with personal baggage had increasingly switched since the 1830s to 'the Overland Route' across Egypt. Packet ships sailed via Gibraltar and Malta to Alexandria. The journey then continued via the Nile to Cairo and thence east via an eighty-mile coach ride across the desert to the port of Suez on the Red Sea.* The East India Company

---

* An express service for letters and parcels across Egypt was set up in 1835 by Thomas Waghorn, whose agency then established amenities for P&O mails and travellers on the Overland Route in the 1840s. (Letters stamped 'Care of Mr Waghorn' are much prized by philatelists.) It took passengers eighty-eight occasionally uncomfortable hours to complete the journey; and mails went rather more quickly, reaching Suez from Alexandria in sixty-four hours. Of course, the opening of the Suez Canal in 1869 transformed P&O's operations – but the handling of the mails took some time to change, mostly because the Post Office regarded the risk of blockages in the Canal as unacceptable and preferred to stick to the pre-Canal arrangements. 'The insistence of the Post Office on the mails going overland was at last reduced to farce by the P&O dropping the mails at Alexandria, steaming through the Canal and then picking up the same mails at the other end. This continued until 1874, when a revised contract allowed the mails to be carried through – but only on the company accepting an ill-afforded reduction on the contract of £20,000 a year' (Boyd Cable, *A Hundred Year History of the P&O, 1837–1937*, London, 1937, p. 166).

began a steam-ship connection between Suez and Bombay in 1830, which went on carrying some mails on this leg until 1854; but the P&O, already contracted by the Admiralty to take mails across the Mediterranean, began contracted services from Suez in 1842 which eventually provided a more fully commercial 6,000 mile 'sea and desert route' from Southampton to India. (The mails to Alexandria took additional short cuts by travelling overland from Calais to the Mediterranean, mostly by rail via Paris to Marseilles. When the Franco-Prussian War of 1870–71 interrupted this service through Paris, the Post Office took advantage of much improved Italian railways – and a new tunnel under the Alps – to send the mails further south to Brindisi. This was retained as the principal route after the opening of the Suez Canal. By 1880, Brindisi was the only European port used by P&O for mails to and from points east of Suez, and it remained pivotal to the Eastern posts for many years thereafter.)[65]

But the pioneering of steam-ship routes in this way was expensive, requiring a huge investment in harbours and coaling stations as well as new ships. The Admiralty acknowledged this by obliging the Post Office to pay what was effectively a subsidy on behalf of the Government: the postal freight fees paid to the shipping lines substantially exceeded the postal income earned on the mails they carried. The net deficit for 1852, according to parliamentary papers for 1852–3, came to almost £342,800.[66] This was a standing affront to the principles underlying Hill's 'economical reform' and the sums involved also prompted bitter complaints from unsubsidized shipowners. The packet-ship contracts were the subject of a parliamentary review in 1853, under a committee chaired by the Postmaster General, Charles Canning. Its broad conclusion, warmly welcomed by Hill, was that whereas generous subsidies had been warranted to help set up new routes, they could not be allowed to feather-bed monopoly operators of established businesses. More competition was the prescribed remedy. But attempts to apply it over the next few years went badly awry, not least because of clashes over the policy between the Admiralty, the Treasury and the Post Office. (These were shrewdly exploited by Samuel Cunard, who managed to secure a handsome new contract for his Atlantic line in 1858.) In search of a more coherent approach, the Government in 1860 handed complete responsibility for packet ships and the sea mails back to the Post Office. Hill and his brother Frederic, who assumed direct charge of the packet fleet, immediately committed themselves to eliminating the deficits on the business. All services provided by the Post Office should float commercially in their own watertight compartments, and this would certainly now apply to sea mails. As the opportunities arose, the Hills would reassert the primacy of strictly self-financing contracts. The underlying debate, however, was far from resolved. Many in White-hall – and some senior figures in the Post Office, too – felt more keenly than ever the importance of secure postal communications to the East after the trauma of the Indian Mutiny in 1857. Britain's links with the Empire were now to be a hugely sensitive issue. The potential import-ance of the shipping companies as a future source of armed cruisers and troopships for the Royal Navy added to the rationale for covert subsi-dies via the sea-mail contracts. As one Treasury official put it to yet another parliamentary inquiry into sea mail contracts, in 1860, 'I do not regard the Post Office revenue as merely a question of revenue . . . The primary object, is to have the service very efficiently performed'.[67] There could hardly have been a clearer statement than that of the way atti-tudes to the Post Office were shifting – nor was the change restricted to the context of the sea mails.

By the late 1850s, that seed sown in 1837–9 – the notion of a Post Office built round serving the public *as a primary goal* – was coming to fruition. The Post Office remained, with the Inland Revenue and the Customs & Excise departments, one of the three great revenue depart-ments of the state; but its gross revenues were 60 per cent offset by its costs. Judged as a tax-gathering mechanism, it was hopelessly ineffi-cient. A growing number of politicians, perhaps most, were now choosing instead to see it as a public service. When the finances of the revenue departments (or their 'Estimates', in parliamentary language) were openly debated in the Commons for the first time, in 1856, there was sniping at individual postal expenses – such as the cost of employ-ing postmasters in the Caribbean or Hong Kong – but no one challenged the principle of a high-spending Post Office. On the contrary, as the Chancellor of the day pointed out, the Government had to contend with a chorus of demands 'not to diminish [postal] expenditure but to increase it . . .'[68] The demand for expanded postal services was unmis-takable, and the political classes were none too interested in arcane disputes at St Martin's over the philosophical acceptability of cross-subsidies. As one MP declared in 1859, the Post Office's own convenience now had to be seen as 'quite secondary to the interests of the public; in fact, the Post Office was made for the public, not the public for the Post Office'.[69]

Neither Hill nor his brother Frederic were ready to accept the ideo-logical implications of this, or indeed the financial implications: they rejected any suggestion that short-term financial losses should be accepted in the hope of longer-term gains or in the interests of 'public convenience'.* There were other senior officials at St Martin's, however, who felt entirely at ease with it. Two of them, Frank Scudamore and George Chetwynd, proved as much in 1860–61 with their pursuit of an idea promoted by the Chancellor, Gladstone, who proposed that the Post Office launch a network of Savings Banks to promote thrift among the working classes. This extension of its role beyond the conveyance of the Royal Mail was almost as radical in some ways as had been the idea of cheap postage thirty years earlier. But Scudamore and Chetwynd accomplished it, with no misgivings about stretching the finances to accommodate the needs of the public – or, indeed, about having the Post Office expand into a wholly new activity. To the two Hill brothers, it was all deeply disquieting. They saw the Savings Bank as a distraction, and they had profound reservations about using the Post Office to pro-vide a prop for the public finances. (The 'POSB' paid its depositors a fixed rate and then channelled their money directly into redeeming the National Debt, purchasing government securities with a marginally higher rate of return. The heavily state-regulated trustee savings banks, against which the POSB would be competing, in effect arranged for the payment of a fixed rate by the Government to depositors, which left the Government out of pocket.) Between themselves, the Hills took to describing their younger colleagues in the Grand as 'the zealots', with as little sense of irony as usual. The most senior of these zealots was Trol-lope's former brother-in-law, John Tilley. (His wife, Trollope's sister, had died in 1849.) It was Stanley's move to put Tilley at the head of the Sav-ings Bank department that triggered Rowland Hill's threat to resign in 1861. Hill then did his best, over the following two years, to spoil Tilley's chances of taking over from him as Secretary: his brother Fred-eric was the only credible in-house successor, as Hill several times reminded Gladstone, confiding to his *Journal* on 5 June 1861 that Tilley was 'quite incapable of the duties'.

---

* How Rowland Hill would have coped in 1839 with a crystal ball, revealing how long would be needed for the penny post to pay its way, is a moot point. But then, as Daunton has noted fairly, 'Hill was not a systematic thinker . . .' (Martin Daunton, *Royal Mail: The Post Office since 1840*, The Athlone Press, 1985, p. 37).

Tilley's appointment to the Secretaryship in 1864 was seen within Whitehall as a deliberate break with the past. It opened the way for the next generation of officials within the Grand, with their far more expansive views on the proper role of the Post Office in society. As with the passing of Freeling in 1836, it took a few years for the full significance of this to become apparent to contemporaries. The process was aided by the emergence of Gladstone – champion of the Savings Bank and never averse to considering worthwhile extensions of the Post Office's role – at the head of his first Liberal administration in 1868. But it was a crisis within the Post Office itself, arising from that long-running feud over sea-mail contracts, that crystallized the true significance of Hill's departure. His brother Frederic, still in charge of the overseas business, gave Cunard and the P&O notice in 1867 that their contracts were to be terminated. In his determination to cut the cost of mails on the Atlantic and India sea routes, Frederic displayed a willingness to endanger the continuity of services that Tilley and Scudamore saw as simply reckless. When the two companies refused to comply with fresh tendering arrangements, the Post Office reached a nasty impasse, and Frederic's authority was destroyed at the Grand. Tilley first steered a pragmatic course by striking a compromise with Cunard. In the process, he asserted that Frederic, 'having taken up the idea that every branch of the Service must be made to pay its own expenses . . . has suffered it to run away with him and has failed to see that it might lead to disaster'.[70] The outcome of the P&O story was even more brutal. In the Commons, Frederic was bitterly criticized by one MP as 'a most dangerous man if you make him your master instead of adviser'. Tilley backed a solution that effectively put the Post Office into a partnership with the P&O – with a long-term contract providing a fixed price, but also a profit-share provision and a facility for additional subsidies in the event of the company's profits rising above or below some agreed parameters – and he left Frank Scudamore to negotiate its financial terms. Scudamore's recommendation was bracing:

> The question cannot be dealt with on commercial principles because the conditions of the Postal service compel the contractors to disregard commercial principles . . . For the sake of keeping up such a communication with the East as the Nation requires, [the Post Office] must set commercial principles at defiance, and, cost what it may, the Nation must either pay [P&O] what they lose [on handling mail services] or forego the communication.[71]

1. Four who built the postal network. *Top left*: Brian Tuke (d. 1545), first referred to as Henry VIII's Master of the Posts by Cardinal Wolsey in 1512 and holder of the post until his death; (*top right*)Ralph Allen (1693–1764), who procured a contract to farm the by- and cross-posts of the West Country in 1720 and built a highly lucrative postal business across the country over the next forty-four years; (*below left*) John Palmer (1742–1818), theatrical impresario and entrepreneur, who launched the Royal Mail coaching network in 1784–92; and (*below right*) Francis Freeling (1764–1836), whose mastery of detail gave him total command of the Post Office for almost forty years from 1798.

2. Two postal palaces. *Above*: The inner courtyard of the General Post Office in a former banker's grand villa in the City of London's Lombard Street, where junior clerks slept in dormitories and sorted letters for the nation's Post Roads from 1678 until 1829. *Below*: The stately home built at Prior Park outside Bath by Ralph Allen between 1737 and 1741, drawing on Alexander Pope for planning advice and on local quarries for vast quantities of Cotswold stone.

THE POSTMAN.

3. From post-boys to postmen. *Top left*: A post-boy such as might have been encountered in the lanes and villages of England at almost any date from the start of the Elizabethan Age until the late Georgian era; (*top right*) a postman in Newcastle, from a print dated 1821, though many still spoke of 'letter carriers' until well into the Victorian era; (*below left*) a rural postman at Windsor in the late 1850s beside one of the earliest examples of the iron pillar box championed by Anthony Trollope; (*below right*) a Victorian postman near the end of the century, in quasi-military uniform and bearing four of the 'good conduct stripes' used as a reward for exemplary service between 1872 and 1914.

THE GENERAL POST-OFFICE—(BY AUTHORITY.)

THE LETTER CARRIERS' OFFICE.

4. At the centre of the network. *Above*: The Inland Letter Office at Lombard Street in 1809, where clerks had to assess the correct pricing of every item according to distance and the number of sheets being despatched, before marking each letter with the postage to be collected from the recipient. *Below*: Inside the new St Martin's-le-Grand GPO opened in 1829 with innovative gaslighting. The Letter Carriers' Office, one of several halls, sorted the newspapers that would leave the capital with each evening's mails.

5. Stage coaches of the Royal Mail. *Above*: In many places along principal routes like the Bath–London run, the mail coach merely slowed to a trot for the collection of pouches from the local postmistress (a routine later adapted by the railways, with trains collecting mailbags from an overhead apparatus by the line). *Below*: Some operators, on routes usurped by the railways, tried to accommodate the steam age by loading their coaches onto the back of the trains, an arrangement abandoned for the Louth–London Mail after a last run in December 1845.

6. Labour-intensive distribution. *Above*: The proud team of this late-Victorian travelling post office comprised eleven men – and all were so well accoutred for their group portrait that it is hard now to distinguish the supervisors from the Manipulative-grade sorters. *Below*: Mails bound for India after 1870, having travelled across Europe and down through Italy by rail, were loaded aboard a steam ship at Brindisi for the passage to Egypt. It was a route already in use for express mails before the opening of the Suez Canal in 1869, and thereafter became virtually the only route for mails to the East.

7. The great reformer and a celebrated Postmaster General. *Above*: The fearsome Rowland Hill (1795–1879) was appointed as an adviser to the Treasury in September 1839 to oversee the introduction of the reforms he had promoted since 1837. Dismissed in 1842, he returned in 1846 and served as Post Office Secretary in 1854–64 – but never attained the executive chairmanship he wanted. *Below*: Henry Fawcett (1833–84), the blind Postmaster General of 1880–84, whose visit to the GPO building in St Martin's once reduced the sorting hall to an awed silence. His labour reforms and support for women in the workplace characterized a progressive era that many at the time saw as a Golden Age.

8. St Martin's-le-Grand. *Above*: The newly opened General Post Office on a moonlit winter's evening in 1830, as the Royal Mail coaches set off for the country. Passengers had already embarked at inns around the City and West End before the coaches lined up at St Martin's, where their guards were entrusted with the mails and the locked clocks for use in filling out time-bills. *Below*: The recently closed GPO in 1911, viewed from the St Paul's end of the street, awaiting the demolition crews that would clear the site during 1912–13.

This was a far cry from the *laissez-faire* principles that had infused Hill's *Post Office Reform* in the 1830s.[72] Economical reform, as a guiding star, had set. And if the Post Office was freed in the public interest from needing ever again to aspire to a strictly commercial return on sea mails, what other applications of this same liberated philosophy might lie over the horizon?

5

In a league of its own,
1864–1914

Those young [City] novices had a hectic time on mail days,
when the clerk deputed to post the Bank's despatches to the
East usually had to race the clock. Those who arrived early in
the great central hall of the General Post Office used to form a
passage-way for those coming in at the last minute. The late-
comers, dashing up the steps at the entrance and seeing that the
great clock was about to strike the hour for closing the mail,
would often fling their packages of letters across the hall at the
postman who was waiting to shut the window at the reception
counter, and an accurate shot used to draw applause from the
lookers-on. . . . [For] to miss the post was a serious matter [in
the 1860s] when there was no telegraph to facilitate remittances
or communicate instructions of vital urgency and importance to
the Bank's branches and agencies in the East.

> From Compton Mackenzie, *Realms of Silver:*
> *One Hundred Years of Banking in the East* (1953)

I. A POSTAL KINGDOM OF RAILWAYS

Two weeks after Rowland Hill's retirement, a senior official of the Post
Office called William Lewins finished the preface to a book he had written in his spare time about its history and operations. It was intended by
the publisher to be the first of a series, 'to do for the great *Governmental*
industries' (sic) what Samuel Smiles had done for private enterprise,
self-help and the engineers. As Lewins pointed out, few authors before
had ever tackled a whole history of the Post Office.[1] He began his story,
like a good Victorian, with the letter-writing Israelites of the Old Testa-
ment. But the most striking aspect of *Her Majesty's Mails* is the attention
he gave to an aspect of the Post Office that simply had not existed at all

just a quarter of a century earlier. For, as Lewins happily acknowledged, 'The railway-mail service has now assumed quite gigantic proportions'.[2] It would hardly have been tactful to say so, but here lay the most import- ant single factor behind the astounding recent growth of the mails. Had there been trains but no penny postage, it is not hard to imagine some less radical reduction in postage rates prompting a dramatic growth in the business, but without the railways penny postage might have floun- dered.

By the mid-1860s, the organization of the Post Office had come to revolve around the operations of the rail network to a truly remarkable extent. The railways accounted for 15–20 per cent of the Post Office's total annual spending on the mails, via contracts with around thirty dif- ferent companies. (It was estimated in 1859 that carrying a single letter from Land's End to John O'Groats required contracts with twenty-one separate railways.[3]) But the financial outlay by the Post Office is less revealing than even a brief glance at its daily routine. As each evening's deluge of letters and newspapers for despatch from the capital poured into the central hall of St Martin's-le-Grand, the first stage of the sorting process began by assigning each item to one of twenty-eight divisions (four rows of seven compartments being the optimal arrangement for a single sorter). A majority of these accorded with divisions of the nation's rail network, adopting the topography of Britain that had been deter- mined by the likes of the London & North-Western, the Great Western, the Great Northern and all the other companies, big and small, of the railway revolution. The second stage of sorting saw the contents of each of these divisions split again into twenty-eight compartments. Each of these in turn represented a line of destinations that was still known as a Road, but related now to a sequence of railway stations. The mails bound for some Roads needed to be skimmed off for a further round or two of sorting. But there were many others that could be consigned at this interim stage to mailbags, and despatched in carts straight to one or other of the capital's main railway terminals. For there, awaiting them on the trains, were not just freight wagons but a sufficient number of travelling post offices (TPOs) to comprise in effect a giant mobile annex to the whole sorting process, covering almost every major railway line in the country.

Each TPO had its own clerks and sorters, typically working five- to six-hour shifts – often through the night, but not exclusively so – along journeys of 170 miles or thereabouts. Though Lewins considered them 'warm and cheerful' places by contrast with the often cold and ill-lit stations they sped through, he had to acknowledge their frugal fittings. Windowless and stuffy with neither seating nor proper sanitation, the TPOs must often have been acutely uncomfortable places to work. One wall of the standard carriage was covered with sorting boxes, the other with upright pegs on which hung dozens of canvas mailbags. On each of these was painted the name of its destination town. And there were many of them, for the Post Office had invented an ingenious device in 1852 which enabled each TPO to function as a sorting office for addresses all along the line. A 'mail-bag apparatus' was bolted to the side of a carriage coupled to the TPO. Sorted bags of mail pushed out of the carriage into this contraption would be caught by a mechanism beside the track as the train raced through a no-stopping station; and full pouches of mail left hanging there would be hooked aboard the train in much the same way. (It was a mechanical version of the arrangement adopted throughout the mail coach era, by which rural postmasters or their assistants at remote inns held the mailbags out from a balcony for the passing guards of the Royal Mail to snatch as their coaches rumbled by.) This device, never given a satisfactory name, added hugely to the spread of addresses covered by each TPO: more than a hundred stations already had the apparatus in place by 1865. As a result, it was not just the larger cities boasting railway terminals that could mesh a postal service with the arrivals and departures of trains. A sizeable proportion of the 900 or so post offices in the country reporting directly into London, Edinburgh or Dublin on their operations had a direct link to the trunk routes of the rail network. Beyond them, too, lay thousands of smaller post offices, many serviced by their own tiny country trains. Really quite remote towns and villages were in this way linked to the daily flood of mail to and from London. The resulting integration of the postal and railway networks had produced a communications system of exquisite precision that left even its architects marvelling at the outcome.

It was all lovingly portrayed by Lewins. He pictured the sealed bags of the Royal Mail sitting on platforms all over the nation each evening, in readiness for their return journey to the capital. Here was more than just a miracle of logistics. He quoted a lyrical (but unidentified) contemporary's description of their contents: 'the thoughts of rogues, lovers, bankers, lawyers, clergymen, and shopkeepers; the loves and griefs, the weal and woes, of the town and country lie side by side, and for a few hours at least will enjoy the most complete and secret companionship'.[4] They are lines that instantly bring to mind W. H. Auden's 'Night Mail', which seventy years later would be the perfect embodiment of the poetry that Lewins saw in the system. It would have surprised the Victorian not a jot that the most celebrated poem about the Post Office would one day take the movement of letters by rail as its inspiration.

More prosaically, the railways over the half-century from 1864 to 1914 enabled the Post Office to handle an exponential growth of its basic business. Moore's Law has associated 'exponential' in our computer age with a doubling every two years (which was the pace of growth in the number of transistors on an integrated circuit through the five decades after 1958). The nineteenth-century postal version was less frenzied, but had this much in common: the number of letters carried annually in the post roughly doubled every twenty years. It rose from 564 million in 1860 to 1.2 billion in 1880 and 2.3 billion in 1900 – and was well on track for 3.5 billion in 1914. Postcards grew even faster. They were cheaper than letters, and offered those away from home a novel way of sending a brief message – the Victorian equivalent, perhaps, of our twenty-first-century texting. After their introduction in 1870, with 75 million posted in that first year, they settled to a growth rate that saw volumes more or less double every *ten* years, from 123 million in 1880 to 871 million by 1910. (Postcards were for many years only available as pre-stamped stationery from the Post Office. But in 1894 the use was permitted of 'private cards', to which the sender could affix a stamp in the usual way. This quickly led to the retailing of picture postcards, especially in seaside towns where the tourist business was expanding fast – their volumes climbed again, to 927m in the year to March 1914.) The total volume of all mail traffic by the end of the fifty-year period was fast approaching 6 billion items a year, representing almost a tenfold increase since 1860. Every large city in Britain by then had four postal deliveries each day – except London, which had five. (The fifth began at 7 p.m. each evening, so that a business in the capital could receive a local letter, reply to it in the early afternoon and get a response the same evening.) The network of post offices that handled this traffic grew commensurately. The organizational unit that covered all aspects of Post Office business in any main locality – sorting and delivering the mails, handling all administrative matters and overseeing the management of counter operations – was the Head Post Office (HPO). The counters were run either as 'Crown offices' (or 'Branches') manned by Post Office employees, or as 'sub-offices' run by self-employed business people, usually shopkeepers, on a commission basis. The latter was based on a kind of piece-work arrangement known as 'scale payments' that attached a certain number of units to each postal task and then paid the sub-postmaster according to the tally of units he submitted. If he hired assistants to work behind a counter, their wages were his responsibility; but for regular postal work like sorting and delivering the local mail, full-time Post Office workers had to be employed – postmen with uniforms and all the usual benefits of belonging to the establishment – and the postmaster would receive an annual payment for supervising them. The number of sub-offices jumped in this era from fewer than 10,000 to more than 23,000. Crown offices grew more modestly, from just over 900 in 1864 to almost 1,100 in 1914, but many were hugely expanded and often relocated – as part of an HPO's site – into altogether grander premises. Where cities and large towns in France had their *hôtels de ville*, many of their counterparts in Britain by the 1890s had Post Offices that were no less grand.* And the businesses they housed were, even by then, great oaks compared with the acorns of the 1860s.

This was graphically illustrated by another official-turned-author from St Martin's, a former Inspector of Mails called F. E. Baines, who on his retirement in 1893 penned a lively account of the changes he had seen in a career stretching back more than forty years. In a list comprising a dozen of the biggest cities in Britain – plus Barnet in Hertfordshire, for the endearingly simple reason that he had lived there most of his life – Baines compared the annual cost of their post offices in the early 1860s with the cost at the time of writing. Leaving aside Barnet, the average cost had risen from £1,189 a year to £62,148. In Liverpool and Manchester, most strikingly, the cost had risen roughly a hundredfold.[5] Behind such figures lay a startling rise in the size of the postal workforce. The expansion was proudly acknowledged by Henry Cecil Raikes, a Tory Postmaster General who presided over a string of fiftieth-birthday celebrations for the Penny Post in 1890. Addressing a London banquet in January that year, attended not just by senior officials but hundreds of postmasters as well, Raikes noted that as head of the Post Office he

---

* The architects behind them went largely unsung. From the 1860s onwards, the design and construction of post offices was the responsibility of the Office of Works, renamed the Ministry of Works in the 1950s. Many distinguished architects worked there as more or less anonymous civil servants, with the Post Office as their most important client. Perhaps the most distinguished was Sir Henry Tanner, Chief Architect from 1884 to 1913, who designed two additional headquarters buildings in St Martin's-le-Grand, GPO North and King Edward Building, as well as more than a dozen imposing Crown post offices in city centres across the country. For a detailed and lavishly illustrated survey of the Post Office's architectural history, see Julian Osley, *Built for Service*, BPMA Publications, 2010.

commanded a bigger army than Her Majesty's Secretary for War.[6] This may not have come as a surprise to his audience; but it might have astounded them, and Raikes too, had anyone that evening predicted a doubling of the 113,000 workforce over the coming quarter-century. Yet that is what happened. (See Appendix A, Chart 3.) The total of full- and part-time workers in the Post Office, which stood at around 25,000 in 1850, had grown by the beginning of 1914 to more than 225,000 – a force comfortably larger than the British army and the total manpower of the Royal Navy and its shipyards all combined.

2. AN INDUSTRIAL LABOUR FORCE AND A FIRST BUREAUCRACY

Military codes of discipline enabled the armed forces to keep their ranks in order. But how did the Post Office manage it, faced with at least as great a need to rely on the very strictest of routines? How, for example, were letter carriers in the reformed Post Office to be prevented from taking gratuities in the street in exchange for their services (or for 'working the walk' as it was known)? More basically, how could punctual attendance at work be enforced and heavy drinking be kept in check? Its employees were civil servants and there was a limit to how far they could be treated like enlisted men. Admittedly, the limit could be stretched. Letter carriers could be put into uniforms – as many more were, in the 1850s and 1860s, with martial designs in line with the scarlet jackets worn in London since 1793 – and could even be rewarded with 'Good Conduct Stripes', introduced in 1872 and discontinued only after the outbreak of the First World War. Uniformed telegram boys late in the nineteenth century were even given basic military training. ('The [boy] messengers were to be drilled when they came on duty [sic], and were to learn how to march and salute. Carbines were borrowed from the War Office, corporals were appointed and prizes awarded to the best offices.')[7] But there was no martial law in the Post Office and harsh punishments for misbehaviour, extending all the way to capital punishment for stealing a letter, had been scrapped in the Reform Era.* Nor,

* The last man executed for a postal crime was a London sorter, John Barrett, who was hanged at Newgate in February 1832 for smuggling a letter out of the Inland Office. He was shown no leniency for pleading guilty. 'He was stated to have been most respectably connected, and was intended for the medical profession, which was not to his liking' (Note by J. G. Hendy, 22 March 1895, Post 30/27). In a chilling illustration of how the Post Office,

after the 1850s, was it possible to lean on patronage and personal networks as a means of governing the behaviour of employees. There were simply too many of them – and besides, the whole civil service was moving, in these years, away from its old patronage culture and into a world of open competition, with recruitment subject to examination even for the humblest jobs. So a fresh approach was needed. Acknowledging that it was now building a service of industrial proportions (tasked with many physical duties that were tantamount to industrial labour), the Post Office looked for instruction to the employment practices of that other fast-growing service sector with a strong flavour of heavy industry, the Victorian railways. On display there by the 1850s were several companies with proudly uniformed labour forces, organized along military lines and sub-divided into multiple grades that could be used as promotion ladders rewarding loyalty and long service.[8] Starting with a formal *Report upon the Post Office* in 1854, and beginning with an elaboration of its traditional organization, the Post Office set out to shape its own early industrial workforce into one of the first civilian bureaucracies of the modern world.

All manual workers, occupying what the Post Office called 'Manipulative Grades', were assigned carefully defined ranks within a complex hierarchy. It began at the bottom with 'outdoor' workers (messenger boys and rural, town and metropolitan letter carriers) and progressed up through the various 'indoor' workers (sorting clerks, sorters and counter clerks), via a pecking order that split every job category into several grades – and each grade carried its own separate pay-scale, rising incrementally with length of service. The resulting grid was then made multi-dimensional. Town scales differed from rural scales, and London's differed from all the others. When certain jobs were designated for women – who by the end of the 1870s were accounting for half of the counter clerk jobs in London – here again a separate (and sharply lower) set of scales would apply. Within many grades of this teeming hierarchy, moving from the bottom of the pay scale to the top could take an individual from parity with an unskilled labourer to the level of a qualified craftsman. The transition would take many years and require an unblemished record of diligence and loyalty. For those (mostly men) who could meet the challenge, though, the Post Office offered far more

---

like the Royal Navy, could be both paternalistic and devoted to a by-the-book culture, Freeling's officials spent a small fortune making sure of the conviction, then made secret contributions to a fund set up for the dead man's widow.

than just a secure job. It offered a career, in which the rewards did not start tailing off – as with most other working-class livelihoods – as soon as a man was past his physical prime. And those rewards went significantly beyond a living wage. Free medical facilities were made available for employees in 1855 – or, at least, for the sorters, letter carriers and messengers: better-paid clerks had to go on fending for themselves – and non-contributory pensions were introduced in 1859. Annual paid holidays were introduced from 1883.

In short, to belong to the Post Office establishment in late-Victorian Britain was to enjoy a range of privileges scarcely available to the working man anywhere else in the economy. But there was the rub, for many employees. A fundamental distinction was made between those *on the establishment* and those – including all boys and 'auxiliary workers', all sub-postmasters and sub-postmistresses working on a commission basis in the sub-post offices (though not their full-time postal staff, who were usually establishment workers) and the great majority of its female employees – who were designated as 'non-establishment'. The former were entitled to receive the special benefits of Post Office employment, the latter were not, and from the 1870s non-establishment workers comprised 40 per cent or more of the total. This high proportion flowed from the nature of postal work, with sorting activities peaking early in the morning and late in the evening. Restricting the workforce to full-time employees would have entailed asking many of them to work on two separate shifts in the same day ('split duties'), always deeply resented, and would have saddled the Post Office with total numbers far in excess of its needs for many hours a day. So as mail volumes went on climbing steeply, the Post Office had little option but to turn instead to employing auxiliaries who generally had other jobs but could be available to work through one or other of the daily peak periods. (One analysis of the part-time staff found they 'held a wide range of occupations outside the Post Office, and in London in 1887 included 345 shoemakers, 106 gardeners, 55 porters and 51 tailors . . .'[9]) They were paid at lower rates and were steadfastly refused any entitlement to the pension and holiday benefits of being on the establishment. This lowered the Post Office's costs even while greatly increasing the flexibility of the aggregate labour force. Tensions between the auxiliaries and their better-off full-time colleagues were a constant feature of the workplace. Far from being a problem, though, this usually played to the Post Office's advantage, at least until the closing years of the century. The aspirations of non-established workers to join the establishment simply

NOTICE.

1788

MEDICAL DEPARTMENT.

REGULATIONS.

CLERKS whose Salaries exceed £150 per Annum are not to receive either Advice or Medicine from the Medical Officer of the Post Office, except in the case of Epidemic Sickness, when all Officers of the Department may have both Advice and Medicine.

Clerks whose Salaries do not exceed £150 per Annum may receive Advice, but not Medicine.

Sorters, Letter Carriers, Messengers, &c., may receive both Advice and Medicine on producing an Order for Attendance signed by the Chief of their Department.

Applicants should attend between the hours of 11 and 1, if possible ; but the Dispenser will be in attendance throughout the day.

After the first visit to the Medical Officer, Patients should bring the Prescription previously written for them. In all cases the Empty Bottles should be returned to the Dispensary.

GENERAL POST OFFICE,
14th Dec., 1855.

H. & G. 250 12|55

Notice of Medical Department regulations, December 1855

underpinned again the system of incentives and long-term rewards at the heart of the management process. How the Post Office used it to marshall a mass labour force was a critical feature of the half-century to 1914. Martin Daunton has deemed it 'in many ways more significant and impressive than the invention of the postage stamp'.[10] It was the perfect complement to the transformation wrought by the railways.

Not the least remarkable aspect of its successful marshalling of an industrial labour force was the way it enabled the Post Office to reconcile tumultuous growth with a sense of unbroken traditions. This applied to many of its administrative routines. 'The overwhelming impression one receives from departmental records [for the fifty years or so up to 1910] is that of continuity in the mechanics of decision-making.'[11] The same went for lesser aspects of life at the Grand. There was still an Inland Office in the 1890s, just as the London District mails had gone on being called the 'Twopenny Post' until well into the 1860s. Indeed, the Post Office's expansion seems in many ways to have strengthened the conservative instincts of officialdom: slightly unnerved by the sheer speed of the post's transformation, those in charge of all procedures seem to have clung to the rule books ever more tenaciously; any unauthorized activity might now unleash disruption on a scale too ghastly to contemplate. No Departmental business, however seemingly trivial, could pass untouched by the need for scrutiny and compliance – in ways that sometimes smacked of self-parody long before the twentieth century. No doubt the continuity of the Post Office culture also owed much to the fact that, into the 1890s and sometimes beyond them, an extraordinary number of senior positions in the Post Office were held for decades by the same individuals. Reminiscing in 1893–4, Baines could fondly recall a long line of his peers in this category. They included a head of the Post Office in Scotland, A. M. Cunynghame, who had been appointed in 1866 and retired just as Baines was publishing his memoir. The Solicitor in the Edinburgh office, retiring in 1892, had been in his post since 1855. In London, the Surveyors Department was still being run in 1890 by someone appointed in the early 1840s. His name was William Godby and his background was another reminder of how ubiquitous were family dynasties within the Post Office: his father had been the Secretary in Dublin and his son was the city postmaster of Gloucester. The man in charge of the Returned Letter Office in the 1890s, G. R. Smith, had similarly been there since the first days of the Penny Post, witnessing a rise in the number of letters forwarded each year from 3 million to 17 million by Baines's day. (He could remember coping with a letter addressed to 'Mr Owl o Neill', which turned out to be for Rowland Hill.)[12] The Post Office Solicitor, Robert Hunter, had been appointed in 1882 and would remain in office until his death in 1913. (Having already established himself as a leading authority on land law by the time he arrived at St Martin's, Hunter was also one of the co-founders in 1893 of the National Trust.) Given all those grades and climbing pay-scales, long-service records at every level were only to be expected.* More surprising is the fact that so many formidable individuals were appointed, in the mid-Victorian era, as departmental heads at a relatively young age – and then managed to remain in office, as the institution ballooned beneath them. It certainly added to an air of stability and continuity at the top.

Behind this apparent serenity, however, politicians and permanent officials were adjusting to a profound shift in the role of the Post Office and the public's expectations of it. After Rowland Hill's departure and the emergence of Tilley's zealots, policy debates continued over the proper balance between the need for a commercial return and the desire to provide a convenience for the public. These could still trigger an occasional clash of deeply held convictions, as happened most strikingly over Frederic Hill's stand on the handling of ship mails. In general, though, debates came down to striking a sensible compromise with the Treasury. The cost of heavy letters was cut in half, for example, to allow for small packages – such as a tradesman might use for a sample – to be sent by letter post without exorbitant expense: a full ounce weight could be sent after 1871 for 1s 4d instead of 2s 8d. The commission payable on money orders for less than £2 was reduced in that same year, which meant a loss for the Post Office on this category of business but was deemed to be worthwhile given the importance of low-value orders to

---

* Long-serving letter carriers were also part of Departmental folklore. F. E. Baines knew of one individual, appointed in 1846, who had walked sixteen miles a day between Basingstoke and North Waltham for twenty-four years – and the Post Office had only appointed him when he was already fifty-five years old. As a young man of eighteen, James Smith had enlisted in the British army in 1809, served in India and been one of the soldiers detailed to guard Napoleon on St Helena. He took up his Post Office job after working for a quarter of a century as a navvie on the roads of Hampshire. He retired in 1870 on a tiny Post Office pension, and Baines seems to have taken a hand in helping him wring a military pension out of the War Office. The first army payment finally arrived in 1893, by which time Smith was 102. He cherished it for two days, then died – or as Baines put it with a gloriously Pythonesque flourish, 'grounded the arms of life and departed for the barracks of Light and Eternity' (F. E. Baines, *Forty Years at the Post Office: A Personal Narrative*, 2 vols., London, 1895, pp. 266–7).

working people, most of whom had no other means of cash remittance. (The concept of the cheap 'postal order' was first mooted in the early 1870s, too, but would take some years to win the Treasury's approval.) Incremental measures of this kind – modest in themselves but weighty in their implications for the Post Office – combined with the helter-skelter growth of the mails to turn the Department into a 'Governmental industry', to use Lewins' phrase, in a league of its own. Just as Palmer's work had given the Royal Mail coaches an importance that far transcended the bare conveyance of letters, so now the Post Office found itself assigned – and set out to champion – a role that stretched even further beyond the traditional postal service. And more significant policy departures arose from time to time, making plain the way that the expanding institution was taking on a broader role in the economy. One such had been the launch of the Post Office Savings Bank in 1861. But the Government had seen the POSB as a long-term alternative that might eventually displace the trustee savings banks, not as an encroachment on the private sector. What happened next was another matter. A fresh assignment arose for the Post Office in the second half of the 1860s that was to entail an even more drastic break with the past.

3. FRANK SCUDAMORE AND THE TELEGRAPH SCANDAL

This transformation came along, indirectly, as another profound consequence of the railways. After Volta's invention of the prototype modern battery in 1800, various entrepreneurs and pioneers of electricity had spent the first forty years or so of the nineteenth century turning the signals-and-telescopes telegraphy of the Napoleonic era into the magic of electro-magnetic telegraphy. By the late 1830s, Morse in America and the partnership of Cooke and Wheatstone in England had separately devised workable telegraph systems. Both used electrical impulses down a wire to move an armature and so convey a written signal. But neither Congress in Washington nor the Admiralty in London had been easy to persuade of the new idea's value. It was the railways, in both countries, that gave telegraphy its opportunity. The 'wayleave' agreements struck for the laying of train tracks could be exploited to lay telegraph wires, too. Telegraphy could be used to alert stations to the position of distant trains on the line. And it was urgent messages sent between railway stations – especially those allowing the interception of villains, who had escaped on trains thinking nothing could overtake them – that ignited the first sparks of popular enthusiasm for telegraphy.*

The first two properly capitalized companies to promote national telegraph systems were finally set up in 1845: the Electric Telegraph Company in Britain and the Magnetic Telegraph Company in America (backed by Samuel Morse, whose code was eventually adopted for use on the fledgling British network). By 1865, 'The Electric' had put down about 10,000 miles of network line, sending almost 3 million 'telegrams' that year. It had also consolidated its position at the head of a cartel of five companies, which since 1861 had fixed a uniform shilling rate for twenty words (including the address) across much of their combined network.[13] This cartel approach initially served the public better, probably, than a system dominated by the state (as in France) or by a single acquisitive monopoly (as in the US, where Western Union soon snapped up all its competitors). But gestures of public appreciation for the cartel members had been less conspicuous since the mid-1850s than a rising swell of dissatisfaction. The complaints had much in common with those levelled at the unreformed Post Office in the 1830s: the companies were attacked for overly complicated rate tables, inflated prices, inadequate services and a generally unsympathetic approach to the long-term interests of the public. The answer in the 1830s had been brutal reform. But the victim then had belonged to the state; the telegraph companies belonged to private shareholders. Herein lay an awkward dilemma.

We have long been accustomed to associating nationalization in Britain exclusively with the Labour governments of the middle of the twentieth century. The two belong together in any pastiche of British economic history, just as do the Victorians and *laissez-faire*. On both counts, the resort to nationalization in the 1860s jars with a simplistic narrative of the rise of state ownership but was in fact entirely in keeping with the classical economists' prescription for a liberal economic policy: commercial monopolies that threatened to militate against the public interest were to be as rigorously opposed as the old charter

---

* The pursuit of fugitive murderers was not the only application to catch the London public's eye. The Duke of Wellington caused a stir in August 1844 by using a telegraphed message to rescue himself from a right royal embarrassment. He had taken a train from London to Windsor for a celebratory banquet in honour of the birth of Queen Victoria's second son, only to discover on arrival that he had left behind his dress suit. Orders went back down the freshly installed wire to Paddington for its immediate despatch. Sure enough, the Duke was able to appear at the banquet, suitably attired, a few hours later. (See Tom Standage, *The Victorian Internet*, Phoenix, 1999, p. 51.)

monopolies of the pre-Reform era. (Gladstone, after all, had suggested in the 1840s that it might one day be necessary to nationalize the railways; and Manchester, the home of free trade liberalism, had benefited from a publicly owned gas utility since the 1820s.[14]) Nationalization of the telegraph industry was accordingly embraced as the only practical way of bending it to the needs of the nation. Nonetheless it was a slightly shocking innovation. It would be romantic, but wrong, to attribute it to the inspired thinking of a youthful F. E. Baines. He did indeed start his forty years, sitting in a cupboard-size office at the Grand as a 24-year-old clerk in 1855, by dreaming up the idea of replacing the telegraph industry with a new department inside the Post Office that could parallel the postal service. But his detailed written submission to the Treasury two years later fell on stony ground: the idea that the state should actually buy out the businesses of five bona fide joint-stock companies and consolidate them within a revenue department of the civil service was just too bold.[15] Several more years' dissatisfaction were required to make Whitehall and the public more receptive. Progress in this direction relied, first, on acknowledgement of a deep and widespread public disaffection with the companies themselves. This was effectively cemented in the summer of 1865, when the five of them unwisely decided to abandon their uniform rate in favour of higher prices. The Postmaster General of the day, Hill's nemesis Lord Stanley, decided just a few weeks later – in one of the most important personal initiatives taken by anyone in his position in the nineteenth century – to authorize a formal in-house report on the feasibility of setting up an Electric Telegraph Service run by the Post Office.[16] The second prerequisite for any serious consideration of nationalization depended on the Post Office being generally perceived as up to the job. By handing responsibility for the telegraph brief to Frank Ives Scudamore, Stanley usefully reminded the world at large of the high reputation now enjoyed by some of the Department's leading officials.

Scudamore, in particular, was one of the most extraordinary men ever to work for the Post Office. Another of its officials with literary gifts, he had been a regular contributor to *Punch* and several other magazines for years. A collection of his articles about rural France was published as a book in 1875, entitled *The Day Dreams of a Sleepless Man*. Anyone chancing on it today, with no knowledge of its author, would find in it no clue as to his profession. From its erudition and scholarship, he could easily be supposed a professor (in Oxford or Paris) of the classics, of history or literature, or even of natural history. Edmund

Yates was a close friend and rather in awe of him; as he wrote in his memoirs: 'of all the men I have known in my long experience, there was scarcely one to beat him'.[17] What Yates perhaps most admired was Scudamore's versatility, for he was also a brilliant organizer. His obvious business skills led to his appointment as Tilley's deputy in 1864 and he was widely admired – not least by Gladstone – as the architect behind the undoubted success since 1861 of the POSB.* Scudamore had set about expanding the POSB network with a competitive flair that rather belied the modesty of the Government's original objectives for it. He and his colleagues were soon aspiring to compete against financial services companies in the private sector with undisguised relish, adding life insurance and annuities to the products on sale through post offices. In the long term, the outcome would be nothing short of spectacular. (By the turn of the century, with 14,000 branches, the POSB had not just eclipsed the trustee savings banks but established itself as the largest banking system in the country. Its life insurance operation fared less well, though. Like many other public-sector entities in the twentieth century to come, the POSB failed to grasp how much salesmanship would always be involved – as 'the man from the Prudential' would attest – in finding willing customers for insurance and annuities products.) In the short term, Scudamore's dynamism inspired huge confidence in his abilities. As the *Spectator* put it in November 1867, 'we have noticed for some years past that whenever Government intends to construct anything, ... Mr Scudamore is engaged in the matter, and the ultimate scheme comes out large, simple, and efficient'.[18] The Post Office by then really was emerging as a unique branch of the civil service that could be trusted to run new businesses.

But ought it to be allowed to do so? The advocates of a nationalized telegraph had one further hurdle to surmount, and it was the toughest. As just noted, there was no theoretical obstacle to a government department intervening in the private sector, if this was clearly seen to be conducive to the functioning of a free economy. Yet there was still no

---

* Trollope was senior to Scudamore in the pecking order of the Post Office, having joined six years earlier, and took great offence at thus being passed over for the Assistant Secretary position. Their superiors had to choose between, on the one hand, a man who hunted three days a week in winter, enjoyed a reputation as one of the best-known novelists in England and was not renowned for his patience with committees, and, on the other, one of the ablest men of his generation in the civil service. Trollope harrumphed for a few months, then quietened down. But the episode encouraged thoughts of resigning, which he finally did three years later. (See C. P. Snow, *Trollope*, Macmillan, 1975, pp. 129–36.)

real precedent for such a move in practice, and there remained a deep prejudice against the idea among most Victorian politicians. To win parliamentary support, the Post Office needed to mount a campaign – much as Rowland Hill and the reformers had done in the 1830s. In fact, there were several curious parallels between that era and the story that now unfolded. Scudamore delivered a report on the Telegraph business which presented a compelling case for nationalization, as Hill had done for the Penny Post. The Assistant Secretary then abandoned the usual reserve expected of a civil servant and threw himself, as Hill had done, into leading an impassioned public campaign. He teamed up with the leading social reformer of the day, Edwin Chadwick, and their arguments drew powerful support from trade lobbies on the one hand – notably Edinburgh's Chamber of Commerce – and the press on the other. (The calibre of the available telegraph services was of acute concern to provincial newspapers, which had lost faith in the ability of the five companies to deliver the instant news that readers now expected.[19]) Their campaign went ahead against the backcloth of another debate over the electoral franchise, this time centred on the Reform Bill of 1867. And no less than the erstwhile champions of the Penny Post, Scudamore and his allies had their critics. Indeed, there was a spirited attack by the pot on the kettle in 1869, when the Hills accused Scudamore of being so obsessed with his cause that he had taken a cavalier approach to its financial consequences.[20] But the opponents were swept aside. It was a good measure of how far popular attitudes to the Post Office (and to the economy more generally) had changed in thirty years. With the Treasury lending tacit support from the sidelines, the nationalization campaign persuaded consecutive Conservative and Liberal governments in 1868 and 1869 to endorse an act of state intervention – and to treat it not as some bizarre exception to the rules of classical liberalism, but as a wholly proper catalyst for the smoother working of the capitalist economy. In this spirit, the Telegraph Act of 1869 provided for an indefinite state monopoly, which Scudamore had actually never sought; yet even the free market *Economist* concurred with the logic of the award. The Post Office was voted £7m – in line with Scudamore's latest calculations, though ominously close to three times his initial estimate of the cost, back in 1866 – to cover the costs of acquiring the private companies and launching the new department at the beginning of 1870. 'We have not the slightest doubt', pronounced a leader in *The Times*, 'that, even at the price paid, the country will find it has made a good bargain.'[21]

Unfortunately, there was to be one further parallel with the introduction of the Penny Post: an unwelcome financial surprise. Hill's Penny Post caused dismay in its first few years, and had then clawed its way back to financial respectability. Scudamore's Telegraph Department went in the opposite direction.[22] The net revenue for its first year broadly matched expectations. Many feted this as a triumph, since at the same time a uniform, and much lower, rate (with addresses sent free) had been reintroduced for all telegrams – and almost 2,000 additional telegraph offices had been opened in post offices across the country by the end of 1870. The pre-nationalization network had been almost doubled. Nearly 10 million telegrams were sent in 1870–71, over 50 per cent more than in the previous year. Scudamore, the hero of the hour, revelled in the new department's apparent success as a vindication not just of his telegraph plan but of his wider concept of the Post Office. (The hugely successful launch of halfpenny postcards by the Post Office in these same months was also widely accredited to Scudamore.) The Post Office would be the advance guard of a 'cooperative society'. Scudamore's was a bold vision: 'a network of public institutions planned and directed by technocrats such as himself so well that social harmony and economic prosperity would inevitably result'.[23] In its pursuit, he drove ahead with his new stations for the telegraph almost as frenetically as John Palmer had once spread inn stations for the mail coach. '[Scudamore] and his devoted band of followers . . . sat up night after night, denying themselves rest, comfort, almost food, in order that the compact with the Government might be duly executed.'[24] But Scudamore shared some of Palmer's other traits, too, including an impatience with procedure and a readiness to cut corners that was startling in someone who had worked at the Post Office since 1840. He kept none of his senior colleagues properly informed about the finances of his project. By 1871, in defence of his increasingly conspicuous neglect of normal Treasury approvals, he was writing to Gladstone with a breathtaking insouciance: 'you might as well expect a canary to hatch a setting of ostrich eggs, as expect the Treasury to dry nurse the telegraph system'.[25]

Scudamore was that rare creature in the history of the Post Office – a genuine insider with the radical instincts of an outsider. But he had picked a bad time to make free with his private thoughts on the Treasury. By June 1871, he was returning cap in hand to Gladstone's Chancellor, Robert Lowe, for a top-up to the initial telegraph grant. Nine months later, he was back again for more. The sad truth was that, financially speaking,

Scudamore's plan was rapidly unravelling. He had purchased the stock of the five private companies at hopelessly inflated prices that left too little in the till for subsequent development work. The Hills had been right about that; but this was only the start of Scudamore's problems. He had also agreed contracts with the railways and the newspapers which, however beneficial in other ways, proved horribly over-generous as their usage of the telegraph soared.[26] Operationally, there were problems with the workforce (which we shall return to later) that prompted excessive wage awards. Most culpably of all, perhaps, the Post Office found it impossible to prevent a runaway expansion of this workforce: within eight months of its launch, the Telegraph Department was employing twice as many people as had worked for the five companies. Under intense pressure to meet rapidly rising public expectations, and scrambling desperately to hold the finances together, Scudamore resorted to a desperate and fatal remedy. He channelled £812,000 from the POSB and other Departmental accounts into the Telegraph business. When this was unearthed early in 1873 during an investigation by Parliament's Public Accounts Committee, a mighty row ensued. MPs pored over the details in endless debates that Gladstone described as 'truly mortifying'. It was spoken of as the greatest administrative scandal since the Crimean War, two decades earlier.

It may seem to us disproportionate that Scudamore's zeal on the public's behalf should have been compared with logistical calamities in the army costing the lives of tens of thousands of soldiers, but both Parliament and the Treasury had taken a great deal on trust since the Act of 1869 and now felt badly let down. And Scudamore had transgressed in the worst possible way: no priority ranked higher for Gladstone and his Liberal government colleagues than the redemption of the National Debt, to which all POSB deposits were strictly committed. In a move that redrew the boundaries of ministerial responsibility for Departmental affairs, the Postmaster General of the day, William Monsell, was forced to resign. Gladstone nobly spoke out in defence of Scudamore, which probably explains why he was allowed to keep his job. But he was given a torrid time in the press. As his son would one day bitterly recount, articles in The Times 'almost conveyed to the public the impression that Mr Scudamore had gone down to Brighton ... with a million of this country's money in a small black bag'.[27] He was publicly censored by the House of Commons – even while being awarded a grant of £20,000 in appreciation of what he had achieved. As this suggests, views on his misconduct were sharply divided. What seems clear is that his attitude to money had always been distinctly casual.* Scudamore attached little importance to book-keeping details, being preoccupied with accomplishing the great mission he had set for the Post Office. Sadly for him, many others took a different line. His next two years in the Grand were miserable. He oversaw a significant development of the national telegraph network, including the opening of a new Central Telegraph Office (also known as GPO West) in a grand building, under construction since 1870, facing the General Post Office on the other side of the street, but he never recovered the authority he had enjoyed before the scandal. He resigned in the summer of 1875, taking up an invitation from the Turkish government to reorganize the postal system of the Ottoman Empire. Having decamped to Istanbul with his wife, ten children, a governess, several English servants and a boatload of furniture, he arrived just in time to witness Turkey's declaration of bankruptcy in October. Thereafter even Scudamore's organizational skills were no match for Ottoman corruption and procrastination.[28] Nothing ever came of the projects he proposed. He died in 1884, leaving behind him a career that offered later generations of Post Office men a salutary reminder of the great virtues of risk-aversion.

The funding scandal prompted no second thoughts in the public's mind about the wisdom of the nationalization. As one London newspaper would put it in 1876, 'Cheap telegrams have become a necessity of modern existence; and be they irksome or not, profits or no profits, the public must have them'.[29] Nor was any serious attempt made to prune back the service in a quest to make it profitable. Sixpenny telegrams were introduced in 1885, a move which proved as hugely popular as it was financially calamitous. But regular net losses over the next three and a half decades would do nothing to shake the Post Office's conviction that telegrams were an indispensable public service.† It

---

* As if to prove the point, his son years later told a curious story about how he had accompanied his father from St Martin's to the Bank of England, to cash the Treasury Bill for £20,000 granted by Parliament. His father took the money in notes from the cashier, then father and son set off back together to the Post Office. 'There was some jostling in Cheapside, and when we got back to St Martin's-le-Grand the first words . . . my father's private secretary said were, "Good God, sir, what has happened to your clothes?" He found then that his light overcoat and frock coat had been sliced as though with a razor, and that his pocket-book, watch and chain, and sovereign purse had disappeared. But he had thrust the notes loosely into his trouser pockets, and they were intact' (Frank Scudamore, *A Sheaf of Memories*, T. Fisher Unwin, 1925, p. 17).

† The service soon acquired a romance of its own, too, especially after the completion of the Central Telegraph Office in 1874. Not the least glamorous of its activities was the network

resisted pressure from Whitehall to have unprofitable parts of the network closed down, even as the size and cost of the workforce went on rising alarmingly. Telegraphy, it turned out, enjoyed nothing like the same economies of scale as the letter post. By the Edwardian era, the network was delivering 80–90 million telegrams a year – and net losses, after interest costs, soared to £1m and more from 1905–6. None of this would have dismayed Scudamore, but it led to a profound change in the Treasury's attitude towards the Post Office. That crucial relationship, after the 1870s, had been changed for ever.

4. THE GOLDEN AGE OF BLIND POSTMASTER FAWCETT

Largely informal links between the Post Office and the Treasury had suited the latter well enough when it could regard the Secretary as a close ally, as in Rowland Hill's time and for much of the Freeling era. But unwritten rules seemed less satisfactory by the start of Gladstone's first administration, in 1868. Robert Lowe was a famously adversarial Chancellor, and his attempts to impose more formal controls had cast a chill over this traditionally amicable relationship. (Secretary Tilley wrote to his Postmaster General in 1872, complaining that 'these rude scolding letters from the Treasury are a little too bad. We attempt to make improvements and we are told we are idiots and don't know our business'.[30]) For all of the ill-will engendered, the Treasury had made little real headway with its demands for more formal supervisory procedures by 1873. Then came the telegraph scandal, which triggered an acrimonious battle between the two departments that lasted almost two years, as Treasury officials seized their chance. They had no illusions about being able to return the Post Office to its narrower pre-1860s remit. There was no denying the popular support for what *The Times* would in 1876 call the Post Office's 'immense invasion of spheres which were once believed to be proper for private enterprise alone'. The public had seen what might be done with the huge network of Crown and sub-offices around the country, and there was no question of seeking to

---

of pneumatic tubes that was built to connect the CTO with post offices in central London and important locations like the Stock Exchange and the Houses of Parliament. Almost sixty separate lines carried telegraph forms into the CTO for onward despatch. The network incorporated more than forty miles of tubing by 1914 and remained in constant use right up to the Second World War.

narrow the Post Office's day-to-day operations; but they would henceforth be monitored much more rigorously. Indeed, quarterly financial
reports and internal-audit arrangements were introduced to this effect
before the end of 1873. More significantly, Tilley and his colleagues in
1874 had to accept the appointment within the Grand of a senior Treasury official as 'Financial Secretary', whose watchdog brief was only too
obvious. In sum, future heirs to the Scudamore vision would need to be
unusually resourceful individuals – with clearly defined objectives and
strong political support – if they were to have any chance at all of pursuing further public-service goals.

By a nice irony, just such an individual was already at hand – none
other than the first man to be seconded from the Treasury as Financial
Secretary. His name was Stevenson Arthur Blackwood. Apart from the
striking good looks that accounted for his Whitehall nickname, 'Beauty'
Blackwood was known outside the Treasury for his religious convictions.
He had experienced a moment of epiphany while serving on the army
commissariat with cholera-stricken troops in the Crimea in 1855, and in
recent years had become a writer of popular Evangelical tracts. (His latest
collection, published a year before his arrival at the Post Office and happily anticipating his new position, was entitled *Heavenly Places: Addresses
on the Book of Joshua*.) Now Blackwood underwent a second conversion
of sorts. John Tilley played a shrewd part in this, by co-opting him onto
the staff of his central Secretariat. Once immersed in its work, and in a
political environment dominated by Disraeli's great reforming administration of 1874–80, the ex-Treasury man warmed to the notion of seeing
his Department as a public service. 'In less than two years . . . Blackwood
had adopted the prevailing Post Office ethic that expenditure proposals
should not be judged solely on their impact on revenue . . . and by 1880,
he had emerged as a forthright advocate of expansion into new fields.'[31]

No doubt, in rebuilding their credibility, it helped the officials in the
Grand that the Post Office's annual contribution to the Exchequer was
now rising rapidly: from telegraph and postal operations together, it
jumped from £1.4m to £3.1m between 1869–70 and 1879–80. (This
helped to make possible a radical reduction by Disraeli's government in
the standard rate of income tax.) But Blackwood's presence there,
hugely resented at the outset, also played its part. He would become,
over time, one of the most eloquent advocates for the Post Office's
unique mix of fiscal and social objectives. On several occasions in the
1880s, it was Blackwood who would spell out for Westminster the
limits to the commercial rigour that the Post Office now thought appro-

priate to its conduct of business. (As he told a select committee in 1888, 'It cannot close a post office because it is unproductive, or discontinue a part of the business to which the public has been accustomed, because it thinks it is not remunerated'.[32]) Blackwood's administrative skills marked him out no less than the breadth of his vision. When Tilley retired as Secretary, just days after the April 1880 election which brought down Disraeli's government, Blackwood was appointed as his successor. This had two immediate implications. It meant, first, that the Treasury's supposed control over the Post Office was not necessarily going to lead, after all, to the stranglehold that some casual observers had assumed. And second, it opened up the possibility that the Post Office might seek a broader franchise again sooner than anyone had expected. The odds on this happening shortened appreciably the very next week, when Gladstone formed his second administration, for the start of Blackwood's tenure coincided with the arrival in the Postmaster General's office of Henry Fawcett. For the first (and almost only) time in the nineteenth century, the Post Office had a political head deserving at least as much attention as its Secretary.

Fawcett was by far the most distinguished Postmaster General of the pre-modern era. Almost forty-seven at the time of his appointment, he had been Professor of Political Economy at Cambridge since 1863. His *Manual of Political Economy* was a popular treatise on economics and (while not without its critics) had run through several editions by 1880. A Liberal MP since 1865 – and known mockingly at Westminster as the Member for India, because of his close interest in the administration of the Empire and the welfare of the subcontinent's indigenous population – he appeared a leading contender for one of the highest offices in the new government. Gladstone's failure to offer him a seat in the Cabinet was generally attributed at the time to the singular fact that Fawcett was blind. He had lost his sight in both eyes as the result of a shooting accident when he was just twenty-five (shot, even more tragically, by his own father). Privately, there was much speculation about Gladstone's real motive. Always an awkwardly independent spirit, Fawcett had attacked the GOM's 1868–74 administration on many occasions and had been a harsh critic of Gladstone personally. The two men had since then found themselves more happily aligned in opposition to Disraeli's government, and especially its foreign policy.* It was nonetheless widely

---

* Along with Gladstone, Fawcett was at the forefront of a national campaign alerting the public in 1876 to the so-called Bulgarian Atrocities, committed by Turkish troops in what

supposed that sending Fawcett to the Post Office in 1880 was Gladstone's way of keeping his old adversary in line, without having to
accommodate his Radical views at the very highest level.

Modern scholars have been less interested in Fawcett's work as Postmaster General than his influence as an economist and a Radical
dissident at Westminster: 'There is something odd in the image of
Fawcett – all moral fervour and righteous indignation – shackled to a
desk in the Post Office.'[33] But his close friend Leslie Stephen, the father
of Virginia Woolf, took a different view. In an affecting and deeply
affectionate biography of Fawcett the year after his early death, Stephen
wrote that Fawcett took to it 'as though the administration of the Post
Office had been less a duty than the passion of a lifetime'. In many
respects, Fawcett shared the inclinations of his newly appointed Secretary. Like Blackwood by this time, he 'regarded the Post Office as an
engine for diffusing knowledge, expanding trade, increasing prosperity,
encouraging family correspondence, and facilitating thrift . . . [and was]
convinced that an energetic development of the business would do
much to increase the public welfare'.[34] Within a fortnight of arriving at
St Martin's, by his own account a few years later, he had set out a list of
five things to be done. The Treasury bridled at many points along the
way; but he and Blackwood together achieved all five and much else
besides. Stephen recorded in his *Life* the letter from Fawcett to his father
in which he looked back on his agenda three years later:

> Curiously enough, before I had been a fortnight at the Post Office I felt that
> there were five things to be done – (1) The parcel post; (2) the issue of postal
> orders; (3) the receipt of small savings in stamps and the allowing small
> sums to be invested in the funds; (4) increasing the facilities for life insur-
> ance and annuities; (5) reducing the price of telegrams.[35]

So these were the years in which the Post Office, after several false
starts in the past, finally launched a parcel post in conjunction with the
railway companies. (The latter had for many years offered a poor service, burdened with the difficulties of straddling the separate railway
franchises; but they went on competing with the Post Office, even while
conveying the Royal Mail's parcels.) It also installed pillar boxes at rail-

---

was then a rebellious province of the Ottoman Empire. Fawcett vilified Disraeli's government for its supposed acquiescence in the consequences of 'Turkish corruption . . . Turkish
savagery and Turkish lust'. (See Lawrence Goldman (ed.), *The Blind Victorian: Henry
Fawcett and British Liberalism*, CUP, 1989, p. 31.) One has to wonder what Frank Scudamore made of it all, reading *The Times* in his villa by the Bosphorus.

way stations, and put letter boxes on the side of TPO wagons. It improved on the convenience of the long-established money order by introducing postal orders in 1881, easily purchased and cashable at most post offices – a valuable amenity indeed for the great majority of the population who still had no banking facilities open to them. Inland money orders retained a significant presence in the remittance services offered by the Post Office, but it was postal orders that now attracted all of the growth in this area and their numbers rose dramatically: from just under 8 million (worth £3.5m) in 1882–3, they rose to 85.7 million (worth £30.1m) in 1900–1901 and 159.2 million (worth £57.2m) in 1913–14.[36] Here once again was a service of sometimes questionable financial value to the Post Office itself, but of enormous benefit to the general public – not least the many thousands of migrant workers in the Victorian economy. Fawcett's Post Office expanded the staff and the operations of the POSB, with a new headquarters building, occupied in 1880 and known as GPO South, a short walk away from the Grand in Queen Victoria Street. It set up a savings scheme, by which twelve penny stamps could be accumulated on a 'stamp slip' for deposits of a shilling with any POSB branch. Life assurance and annuity packages were made more generally flexible, and the cost of telegraphy was cut (as we have noted). Many positions in the workforce were opened up to women for the first time and postmistresses who married were freed from the ancient obligation to re-register their premises in the name of their husband.

Fawcett's instigation lay behind these and many other innovations, and it was his determination that brought them to fruition. Cheaper telegrams, for example, needed him to force a parliamentary division in which his own government had to be outvoted (and was). The public soon came to appreciate his importance. *Punch* celebrated the start of the parcel post with a cartoon of him as 'The Man for the Post', dressed as a postman and standing bent with the burden of his round, a caged duck and a cat box in one arm, children's toys and a hat box in the other. It was his loathing of what he called 'officialism' that fortified the staff at the Grand against regular objections to this or that measure from the Treasury. (When the Treasury – ruled over by Gladstone as both Prime Minister and Chancellor of the Exchequer at this time – demanded precise revenue forecasts for the parcel post, Fawcett brushed aside the request as 'a rather futile formality'.[37]) And it was his ardent feminism that lay behind the new policies on women employees. Others might endorse jobs for women from time to time because they would accept lower pay and go without a pension. Fawcett, with his wife's spirited backing, had a principled objection to the barriers placed in front of them in the workplace.* And there was one other policy area, too, in which he intervened to great effect. The story of industrial relations in the Post Office really begins with Fawcett.

As an academic economist, he had long been preoccupied with the problem of how an industrial society ought to respond to the desire of working men to organize themselves in pursuit of their own interests. His first book, in 1865, had been entitled *The Economic Position of the British Labourer*. By the time he arrived at the Grand in May 1880, he had come to a firm view that was summarized succinctly by his biographer. He acknowledged the important influence of supply and demand on fixing the rate of wages. 'But he did not admit that the rate should be the lowest which would attract any class of physically capable persons. The end should be to have such a rate of wages as would secure really efficient service by obviating discontent.'[38] Rowland Hill had encountered thoughts of this kind in his day, and had dismissed them out of hand: in his view, supply and demand, gauged within a local market context, could be the only acceptable determinant of wages. Any alternative would leave the employer, he warned, 'subject to some undefined, and, indeed, utterly incomprehensible duty to pay some higher price . . .'[39] Since Hill's departure, both Scudamore and Tilley had suggested in private to Gladstone and the Treasury that a more pragmatic approach was required. This had only led the Treasury to float the idea of linking pay to the performance of units within the Department – a notion sternly rejected by Arthur Blackwood by the end of the 1870s, during which decade the Post Office had moved to national pay-scales. As of 1880, official policy towards labour unrest was therefore unchanged, and as uncompromising as ever. Dissident workers would be summarily dismissed, as had happened twice

* Today's Fawcett Society, a UK charity in aid of women's rights, dates back to the feminist movement of the nineteenth century. It took its name, in 1953, not from Fawcett himself but from his wife Millicent, whom he married in 1867 when she was just twenty. (He had been turned down by her sister, Elizabeth Garrett, who went on to become Britain's first woman doctor.) Millicent was co-founder, in 1871, of Newnham College, Cambridge and was later president of the National Union of Women's Suffrage Societies from 1897 to 1919. She also chaired the Fawcett Commission, a formidable group of ladies who conducted an official investigation into conditions in the British concentration camps of the Boer War in 1901, and which she led with 'a professionalism that made Kitchener look like a bungling amateur' (Thomas Pakenham, *The Boer War*, Weidenfeld & Nicolson, 1979, pp. 515–17). It was largely Millicent's constant attendance that allowed her husband to surmount the handicap of his blindness, deeply impressing their contemporaries.

in the late 1860s and again, more notably, in 1871. Telegraphy workers newly transferred from the private sector to the Post Office had gone on strike in Manchester, Liverpool and Glasgow when action was taken to

THE MAN FOR THE POST.

Cartoon of Henry Fawcett in *Punch*, 1882

block their plans for a representative committee to forward their interests. When they picked up only limited support elsewhere, the strike collapsed and over 200 men were dismissed – though many were later reinstated. Unsurprisingly, local working men's committees had since then remained, as before, largely clandestine organizations. As word spread in 1880 that the new Postmaster General might be prepared to engage with them, committee leaders stepped one by one into the open.

Contacts were made between committees across the country, and in January 1881 a first national conference was attended by representatives from all the main offices, including the Grand. Fawcett was not short of advisers at this point, most of them urging a sharp crack of the whip. Instead, driven by his own liberal instincts and his conviction that better than minimal wages would reap rewards from improved morale and higher productivity, he threw himself into a strenuous review of working conditions, studying a list of grievances – over poor wages, compulsory (unpaid) extra hours, capricious supervisors and arbitrary dismissals – that had been circulating for three years. The rise of organized labour among postal workers was the subject, twenty years later, of one of the classic texts of trade union literature, H. G. Swift's *A History of Postal Agitation*. Its author tells the story of how, at this point, Fawcett left his study one evening and turned up unannounced at the Grand, requesting a guided tour of the sorting operations. 'He was conducted to a position on the gallery overlooking the busy, crowded Letter Branch . . . [His] form and features were not familiar to the majority; but presently the whisper went round that the tall, silent man seeming to stare down upon them through the big black spectacles which hid his closed eyes, was the Postmaster General himself. For a few moments strict discipline was forgotten in curiosity . . .'[40] The image of hundreds of postal workers turning to look upwards at this revered figure, who perhaps heard their pausing but could not see it, is a memorable one. And the experience, if Swift is to be believed, made a forceful impression on the visitor:

> It chanced – or it may have been that Mr Fawcett himself preferred it – that a young junior sorter was deputed to take him over the building. The young man acting as guide succeeded in so interesting him by his manner of describing all that the blind eyes could not see, that at last Professor Fawcett asked him his position in the service, and further questioned him as to his pay and prospects. Presumably, from what he gathered on that occasion, he learnt much that set him thinking.

Fawcett agreed a short while later to meet with a workers' delegation – and in June 1881 he produced a series of detailed labour reforms ever afterwards known as Fawcett's Scheme. Pay-scales and overtime arrangements for London's telegraphy workers and letter sorters were significantly improved. The awards did not apply to outdoor sections of the workforce, but at least all 'postmen' – as the letter carriers were to be officially re-designated, from October 1883 – shared in a general extension to employees of a modest annual entitlement to paid holidays. 'Instead of attempting to suppress discontent in the same fashion as his predecessor, he gave to postal servants their first charter of liberty . . . and honour was due to its author for his rare courage.'[41]

Blackwood and many of his colleagues were privately appalled at the initiative, which in their view threatened to open a Pandora's box of calamities. The establishment, the very next month, of the first permanent postal union, the Postal and Telegraph Clerks' Association (PTCA), seemed to them to confirm as much. Like the Treasury, though, they gave way with good grace. Perhaps Fawcett's prestige in the country was such that they had little choice; but it is nonetheless striking from the private papers of the time how genuinely devoted to Fawcett were Blackwood and the other permanent officials. And he returned their praises: Fawcett said of the Post Office Solicitor whom he appointed in 1882, for example, 'that nothing in his official career had given him greater pleasure than the securing of a man of Hunter's character and ability for the country's service'.[42] Despite his physical disability – or perhaps, in part, because of it – Fawcett managed to rise above more than one important policy difference and to command the respect of the whole Department. He gave a bold lead, while at the same time being quite unusually solicitous of his officials. This helped engender a palpable air of shared purpose and achievement that mark out these years. The Post Office exuded the confidence and self-belief of so many Victorian institutions. Operationally, it ran what were generally acknowledged to be the best mail and telegraph systems in the world. Financially, its performance had been improving for twenty years. In terms of its net income as a percentage of each year's expenditure – the Department's own measure – profitability had risen from less than 20 per cent to just over 60 per cent in the early 1880s, a level that suggested the Treasury might be persuaded to allow some exploration of wider service aspirations in the future. (No one could have guessed it, but under pressure from rising labour costs this profit margin was to fall below 40 per cent by the turn of the century and well into single figures by the 1920s.[43]) Politically, Fawcett and Blackwood enjoyed a level of trust in Whitehall that had seemed, several years earlier, unlikely to be attained again. The practical constraints of the pre-railway age lay in the past; the harsher realities of managing a vast labour force within a democracy based on universal suffrage lay ahead. And the public image of the Post Office, as a unique organization to be cherished and revered, was hugely embellished by the popular reputation of its Blind Postmaster General – a man who collected heartfelt compliments and praise like no man in its history since Ralph Allen.

Then, early in November 1884, the Fawcett era slipped suddenly into the past. He caught a heavy cold that developed into pleurisy. A week later, he died of cardiac failure. Among many tributes cited by Leslie Stephen in his much admired biography published the next year was a touching appreciation by Blackwood. There were humbler tributes, too.* One was 'a letter from a post office clerk sent with a wreath to be laid upon Fawcett's coffin'. That Stephen chose to quote from the clerk's letter suggests that it was a fair measure of the sadness felt across the whole institution at Fawcett's death:

> The humblest servant within the dominion of his authority was not left uncared for. During his history as Postmaster General, a greatly improved state of feeling has been introduced among the officers in their general tone towards each other and towards those beneath them, and the whole service in all respects has been greatly and wonderfully improved.[44]

5. THE GREAT TELEPHONE IMBROGLIO

There was, however, one legacy of Fawcett's tenure that was deeply unfortunate. Though his political instincts had dictated a compromise over wage levels, in general he was always strongly averse to anything that smacked of a constraint on the principle of *laissez-faire* in the economy. In the 1870s, he had been opposed to any further restrictions on the hours of labour worked in factories, or to restrictions on the activities of the drink trade (which must have vexed Blackwood, a long-serving president of the Post Office Total Abstinence Society). Indeed, Fawcett in this respect had less in common with Blackwood than with Rowland Hill and the Utilitarian reformers of the 1830s. He was deeply distrustful of any scheme that might encourage a greater dependence on the state.

---

* Another indication of the popular affection that Fawcett inspired can be found inside the parish church of Aldeburgh on the Suffolk coast. A fine bust of him sits above a memorial plaque, noting it was paid for by the inhabitants of the town. Fawcett's wife Millicent and her sister Elizabeth came from a well-known family in Aldeburgh, and Fawcett stayed with their parents each year as 'part of his regular programme for the annual holiday' (Leslie Stephen, *Life of Henry Fawcett*, Smith, Elder & Co., 1885, p. 416).

If this applied to social reforms impinging on individual responsibilities, it was doubly applicable to any interference with the business world. 'The corollary of Fawcett's principled aversion to privilege was an almost wilfully serene faith in the virtues of free competition.'[45] This did not pose a problem for the launch of the parcel post, since there was never any question of the latter being granted a monopoly; nor did it preclude improving the services of the Post Office as an aid to thrift among the working classes. In a different context, however, it was to prove extremely awkward. Just a few years prior to Fawcett's appointment, in 1876, the émigré Scotsman Alexander Graham Bell had made the world's first telephone call in America. Travelling from his home in Boston, Massachusetts, to London in 1877, Bell had proposed to Post Office officials that he give them a private demonstration of his new invention – an offer that the Engineer-in-Chief, William Preece, in an ominous augury of future attitudes, saw fit to decline. Its potential value, Preece thought, was so nugatory as scarcely to merit the time that a demonstration would require. A handful of private companies in England had since then launched competing telephone businesses. But they were contravening the monopoly given to the Post Office by the 1869 Telegraph Act – as the courts confirmed late in 1880 – and a critical choice had to be made. Should the Post Office push the merits of a state-owned telephone system? License entrepreneurs to exploit the invention? Or seek a compromise accommodating both state and private interests?

Cautiously at first, then with steadily more desperation, Blackwood proposed a bold approach that would do for telephones what Scudamore had done for the telegraph. Given the timing, and the popular appeal of the idea, there was undoubtedly an opportunity here for the Post Office to consolidate its earlier expansion in some style. Predictably, though, the once-bitten Treasury was now twice shy: its officials soon made clear their opposition to his plan. To have any chance of prevailing over them – and some dissenting views within St Martin's, too – the Secretary and his supporters looked to their Postmaster General for robust support. Instead, to Blackwood's ill-concealed dismay, Fawcett's analysis of the situation moved ever further in the opposite direction. With the full backing of the Treasury, he insisted finally on liberalizing the telephone-licence system to facilitate as much competition as possible among private operators, with minimal constraints even within a single locality. Legislation to this effect went through in mid-1884. Licences were issued to private operators with a 1911 expiry date.

The sorry saga of the resulting private industry extended over the next thirty years. At no point did telephones assume the importance of telegraphy: almost everyone was agreed that telegrams were a necessity, telephones a luxury. (Or not even that: Preece thought they had no future at all.) Nonetheless, every failure to match public expectations prompted a chorus of complaints much like those levelled against the telegraph companies in the 1860s. And where the Post Office had then represented an appealing solution, it was now seen as part of the problem. Whether as licensor, regulator, statutorily decreed partner or occasional competitor in its own right, the Post Office was willy-nilly a party to every contortion of the nascent industry that followed, and suffered a share of the blame accordingly. The competitive pageant envisaged by Fawcett soon faded. It left behind one business, the National Telephone Company (NTC), with what was virtually a private monopoly by the end of the 1880s. Those few officials within St Martin's espousing a state monopoly watched the process in despair, none more anguished than a senior official in the Secretary's office called J. C. Lamb. He went so far as to argue that the Post Office was acting outside its statutory powers in giving away the monopoly to private interests. Nothing he could say or do, though, dented the Treasury's implacable opposition to a GPO telephone service. As one official wrote to the Post Office in 1890: 'My Lords are not prepared to embark upon another enterprise gigantic in itself, while the developments it might lead to are beyond their powers of prediction'[46] An anonymous Post Office hand scribbled a cheeky observation in the margin: 'My Lords' powers of prediction are evidently very limited. They cannot see beyond their noses at present.'[47] Even when events compelled the Treasury to give the Post Office a bigger role, the 'restrictionists' still prevailed over the 'expansionists'. New legislation in 1892 eventually allowed the Post Office to take over the principal ('trunk') routes of an emerging national network, which the Treasury promoted as a sensible compromise. In the event, it trapped the Post Office into a second round of half-baked competition, this time made even more bewildering by the determination of several leading municipal councils in the 1890s to build their own local networks.

Not until 1901 were officials at St Martin's able to regain the initiative in discussions over the telephone industry's future. By then Britain was already looking like a late beginner – with one telephone to every 433 people in London, by one estimate around this time, compared with 82 in Berlin – and the Treasury accepted the need for a fresh approach. In effect, the Post Office decided there was little option but for it to strike up a partnership with NTC, entailing a purchase of NTC's London-based assets. The deal would be completed in 1911, just prior to the expiry of its licence, and telephone services would be delivered jointly for the capital in the meantime. The terms left NTC responsible for most of the rest of Britain, though – and it was clear within a few years that the company lacked anything like the necessary resources for the job. Under a second deal struck in 1905, the Post Office therefore agreed to take over the whole of NTC's operations at the start of 1912. The mind-boggling complexity of the previous two decades was aptly reflected in the process of agreeing a price. Talks lasted three years, from 1908 to 1911, and at one point engaged more than 600 participants.[48] Even then, arbitration was required. The businessmen wanted £18.4m; the Post Office offered £9.4m. The courts settled on £12.5m. Thus came about the second nationalization of a British industry.

In spirit, this was a very different kind of nationalization from Scuda-more's. The telegraph companies had been taken over in a bravura display of confidence and ambition. Arthur Blackwood had carried the torch forward, strongly supported in 1890 by Henry Cecil Raikes, the Postmaster General who spoke up so proudly for the Post Office at the celebrations of the Penny Post's fiftieth birthday. After Raikes and Blackwood had died – in 1891 and 1893 respectively, both of them dying in office, exhausted men – Lamb had been left struggling almost single-handedly against repeated rebuffs from a deeply sceptical Treasury, always nervous that St Martin's might have overreached itself. As one Treasury mandarin put it at the start of the 1890s, the Post Office's expansion had arguably produced 'an empire over which they rule but do not govern'.[49] (It was a sentiment that would still reverberate within the Treasury a century later.) Another senior official, George Murray, harked back to 1875 in a memo to St Martin's in 1896: 'The greatest administrative blunder of the last generation was the price paid for the telegraphs. Let us, if we can, save the present generation from making another like it'.[50] Three years later, this same man moved from the Board of Inland Revenue to become the Post Office's Secretary himself. Murray was a hugely influential figure in Whitehall. An aristocrat who came close to inheriting a dukedom, he was the elder son of an Oxford academic.* The combination of blue blood and a sharp brain marked

---

* Murray's great-grandfather, a bishop of St Davids, was the second son of the 3rd Duke of Atholl (1729–74). The 3rd Duke's own father, a fifth son who never held the title, was General Murray, who commanded the Jacobite army under Bonnie Prince Charlie at Culloden

him out from the earliest years of his career. Having served with distinction as the secretary to a string of royal commissions in the 1880s, he had been Private Secretary to Gladstone in his final premiership and to his successor in Downing Street, Lord Rosebery. Murray's analytical mind soon grasped the case for telephone nationalization – and it was his painstaking study of the options that drove forward the resolution of the whole imbroglio between 1901 and 1905. But Murray embraced his protracted nationalization scheme only reluctantly, as an unavoidable way of honouring the Post Office's monopoly obligations and escaping an arrangement with NTC that was plainly not working. His was no clarion call for another great advance by the Department.

6. HENNIKER HEATON AND IMPERIAL PENNY POSTAGE

In this respect, Murray's stance on telephones was in keeping with a new and notably less bullish mood evident at the Post Office by the turn of the century. Other potentially significant policy innovations were rejected or grudgingly accommodated with a conspicuous lack of zeal. In the 1890s it had been suggested by one of its own clerks that the rigidly separated services of the Postal Order Department and the POSB might be linked, so that depositors in the Savings Bank could write postal orders in favour of third parties – creating, in effect, a modern chequebook service. Other European countries had successfully pioneered this so-called 'Giro' system in the 1880s. The Post Office turned it down. When the opportunity arose a decade later, in 1911, for a dual-nationality Giro system allowing payments between Britain and Germany, the Post Office anguished over its response for two years before spurning the German Post Office's offer. (An internal memo noted snootily that it was quite understandable why the Germans would want a Giro, given their inferior banking system, 'but it is not seen why the Post Office should embark on a new service of this kind for the benefit of the German public'.[51])

Again, other changes in the financial world had prompted many to ask whether it was not high time to reappraise the thrift institutions

Moor. While still a sixteen-year-old at Harrow, George Murray the future Whitehall mandarin became the heir presumptive to the dukedom, a status he enjoyed for six years until the birth of the future 8th Duke (1871–1942).

launched by Scudamore four decades earlier – but the Post Office seemed to lack the will for any proper reassessment. The POSB, burdened with a fixed deposit rate to savers while depending itself on sharply lower yields in the money markets, had recorded its first annual deficit in 1896. The annuities and life insurance business had never really taken off, given a consistent refusal by the Post Office to contemplate the kind of positive selling always required, as it belatedly came to appreciate, for products of this kind. On neither front were there any signs of the enterprising approach adopted a generation earlier. On the contrary, policy reviews at the Grand were, as often as not, interchangeable now with those emerging from the Treasury. As, indeed, were the officials themselves: George Murray left the Grand in 1903 to return to the Treasury as its Permanent Secretary (a post he held until 1911). Just as he remained the driving force behind the Post Office policy on telephones, so his line on financial services went on being voiced by his successor at St Martin's. The general principle, said Henry Babington Smith in 1906, should be that 'it is undesirable for the State to compete with private enterprise in any sphere where a public need is adequately supplied by private enterprise under competitive conditions'.[52] Losses at the POSB soared.

Contemporaries remarked the Post Office's apparent loss of nerve. It was especially conspicuous in the context of the international mail business. Here St Martin's seemed to be consistently on the back foot as had not happened since the 1830s. It was confronted, as then, with a populist champion of cheaper rates. Rowland Hill had arrived on the scene as a planning officer for South Australia; John Henniker Heaton came to it as a prominent figure in Australian journalism. Having emigrated from Kent as a sixteen-year-old, Heaton had returned to England in his mid-thirties in 1883 as a successful New South Wales newspaper editor. As a young man, he had spent a few years farming on the great sheep stations of the outback. He knew the value of a letter from far-off friends and family – and saw cheap mails between Britain and its colonies as a mainstay of the Empire. Setting out in politics in the mid-1880s, he soon embraced postal reform as his great mission in life. He became MP for Canterbury in 1885 and a year later moved a resolution in the Commons urging the Government to begin negotiating a uniform rate of one penny for letters to anywhere in the world. For the next quarter of a century, Heaton obsessively pilloried and pestered the Post Office not just to adopt his policy of 'universal penny postage' but to act on a long list of other reform proposals. (On his sixty-second birthday, in

1910, he sent the Postmaster General sixty-two recommendations. Some had already been implemented but most were yet to be tackled.) In his almost manic persistence, and the ridicule it often earned him, Heaton more closely resembled the Glasgow MP Robert Wallace than Hill himself – but his relentless questioning of Post Office policy and practices throughout the 1890s prompted no great reform initiative as Wallace's had done sixty years earlier. There was to be no latter-day Rowland Hill. Heaton's philosophy, admittedly, went far beyond anything espoused in the Reform Era and posed an even bigger financial conundrum than the Penny Post. He argued for the Post Office to be seen as a servant of the state and Empire, no less than the police or the armed services; and if this role entailed deficit financing, as in the case of sea mails, he thought it simply inappropriate to look for policies that might yield a profit. Neither the Post Office nor the Treasury accepted this view of the world; yet they failed to counter it with a robust alternative. As a result, they were left addressing an international agenda largely set by others.

The danger of this happening had been apparent since the 1860s, when efforts to establish an international postal regime had been mooted, a little surprisingly, not from London but from Berlin and Washington. Then in 1874, while the repercussions of the Scudamore affair were still ricocheting round Whitehall, a conference of nations in 1874 to agree the regime's details was hosted not by the world's leading Post Office but by the Swiss government, in Berne. The resulting General Postal Union was later expanded and rechristened in 1878 to become the Union Postale Universelle (UPU). It created a single postal territory of twenty-two (mostly, but not exclusively, European) countries. Letter rates between them were fixed at the equivalent of 2½d, and all the member countries agreed, in essence, to forward mails without charge that had been posted within the union's territory. (A central UPU organization was set up in Berne for sharing information between the members and standardizing key aspects of their postal services, including the basic format of national stamps. But it was sensibly decided to let international revenues fall wherever the prepaid letters were posted, without even attempting a complex clearing mechanism.) What outraged Heaton, over a decade later, was that the Post Office was still charging more than the standard UPU postage on mails to much of the Empire. Most of the colonies had joined the Union, but Britain had taken advantage of incremental 'transit charges' allowed under the rules for long sea journeys. Other countries in Europe had not. The outcome was bizarre in many ways: letters to India, for instance, cost twice as much to post from London as from Paris or Berlin.

Heaton launched a campaign in 1887 to fight not just for the abolition of the transit charges but for 'imperial penny postage' as a stepping stone to his universal goal. For ten years he battled on without success. But in 1897 he won the support of Joseph Chamberlain, the Colonial Secretary and champion of imperialist causes within the Cabinet. This put the Post Office in a difficult predicament. Its losses on sea mails were bad enough already. (Such was the legacy of those non-commercial contracts with the shipping companies, agreed back in the 1860s. In 1896, the Post Office's packet-service costs equated to roughly 70 per cent of its railway costs – even though mails sent by rail were *forty* times the volume of mails sent by sea.) It opposed imperial penny postage accordingly. When a Conference on Empire Postage was convened by Chamberlain in 1898, officials at the Grand went on resisting the idea of sea letters at 1d ... until confronted by radical delegates from the colonies, arguing in its favour. Then they capitulated. The imperial penny post was rolled out over the next few years. It proved just as financially non-viable as predicted, but this did not deter Heaton and his allies from launching a league for universal penny postage in 1905. In the event, though he kept up a series of campaigns until his death in 1914, Heaton met with limited further success: only postage rates to the US were cut back into line, in 1908, with the imperial (and hence Canadian) post. This might look to us like a modest victory for the Post Office. What struck Edwardian contemporaries was that, in this arena as in telephones and financial services, the Post Office seemed a beleaguered institution, far more often reacting to outside pressure than pursuing its own initiatives.

This was evidence, for some, of a decline in its morale. Others saw a pragmatic adjustment by the Post Office to its de facto role as a ubiquitous public service that had become hugely more difficult to manage. Both perceptions identified a profound shift of outlook within St Martin's after Blackwood's death in 1893. The offices of the Postmaster General, the Secretary and the headquarters administrative staff were moved in 1895 from Smirke's General Post Office to a new building on the other side of the street at its north end. This was 'GPO North', later to be known generally as Headquarters, its foundation stone laid by Henry Cecil Raikes in 1890 as yet another commemoration of the Penny Post anniversary.* And it was almost as though this physical relocation had somehow inaugurated a new era. Senior positions were now starting to pass to university graduates with just a decade or so of service behind them, rather than the lifetime's climb up a long ladder exemplified by Trollope's career. A similar change had taken place at the very top. For generations, the Secretary and his immediate colleagues had been life-long Post Office men, wholly identifying with the interests of the service and imbued with its culture. Though Blackwood himself had come to St Martin's as a Treasury man, he had fitted himself to the traditional mould (as, in a sense, had that other initially spurned Treasury interloper, Rowland Hill). From 1893 to 1914, there followed a succession of five Secretaries – in itself a telling change, reducing the average tenure to just over four years rather than almost fourteen since the death of Francis Freeling – and all but one of the five were career civil servants with extensive prior experience outside the Post Office.† Three of them left it, like George Murray, to pursue careers elsewhere. None served long enough to command the same authority as their predecessors. This relative inexperience at the top of the hierarchy was evident in various ways. There was a greater willingness to toe the line of their Treasury masters on most policy issues, and a reluctance to speak up boldly for the new technologies being applied in telephony and (soon to be wire-less) telegraphy, an attitude some construed as wilful neglect. Above all, there was a distinct lack of enthusiasm for any confrontation with the forces of organized labour – now emerging as a power base for a whole new set of aspiring masters.

---

* The stone can still be seen, on the corner of St Martin's and Angel Street. Now a bank, the building also bears a blue plaque in remembrance of the Bull and Mouth Inn, which was knocked down in 1888 to make way for GPO North.
† The odd man out was Alexander King, a career official who joined the Post Office via the competitive entry system in 1873, aged twenty-two. He worked his way steadily up the lad-der, reaching the Second Secretary rung in 1907. But in 1909 he welcomed the external appointment of the next Secretary, a colonial administrator called Matthew Nathan, by writing to him with unusual candour. 'I shall be glad to see you in charge here . . . because I don't care for the chief post. I have no ambition and am naturally lazy; at any rate mentally.' He got the job anyway when Nathan moved on to chair the Inland Revenue in 1911 and served for exactly three years, until August 1914, under a single Postmaster General, Her-bert Samuel, who managed to include an entire chapter on the Post Office in his memoirs without mentioning King at all (Herbert Samuel, *Memoirs*, Cresset Press, 1945).

7. POSTAL UNIONS AND NON-STOP INQUIRIES

Within a few years of Fawcett's death, the workforce set out to win further concessions. There was a widespread frustration that the promise of the Fawcett Scheme had not been fulfilled. Discontent among the provincial postal clerks led to the formation of a second permanent union, the United Kingdom Postal Clerks' Association (UKPCA). The London sorters in February 1890 formed a third, which they christened the Fawcett Association as a reminder of the Scheme they thought had been betrayed. More fundamentally, there was a gathering resentment among many employees against the underlying philosophy of the Post Office's bureaucracy. They saw its web of pay-scales and grade classifications not as an inducement to work harder but as a disingenuous regime designed at every turn to reduce labour costs. Officials might present it as a hierarchy offering endless hopes of promotion; to many in the workforce, it looked more like 'a labyrinth of sub-groups with a complex set of relationships between the slightly superior and the slightly inferior', in the words of the postal unions' modern historian, Alan Clinton.[53] One of the leaders of the Fawcett Association, W. E. Clery, memorably described the outcome as a 'snobs' inferno'. Rivalries and jealousies between one group and another – usually over the status of jobs reserved for established rather than non-established individuals – plagued the whole organization. Nor could anyone fail to see that groups excluded from the Post Office establishment were set at a perennial disadvantage. The plight of London's young telegram boys, for example, was keenly debated in 1890. A widespread concern was the injustice of employing them at the start of their teens when they ought instead to have been learning a trade, then dumping most of them back into the labour market at the age of sixteen. (The discovery in 1889 of a male brothel in London's Cleveland Street, employing Post Office boys and supposedly frequented by members of the royal family, was a reminder of other ills that had long attended the employment of boy messengers.) There were many in the workforce who by 1890 saw trade unions – or associations, as they were called within the civil service until after the First World War – as their only effective response.

Arthur Blackwood at the start of the 1890s was still as vigorously opposed to the whole idea as he had been during Fawcett's lifetime.

Along with most of his immediate colleagues and their counterparts at the Treasury, he regarded the notion of postal unions as irreconcilable with the Post Office's status as a public service. This entitled postal workers to privileged terms of employment; but by the same token, in Blackwood's view, it required them to forfeit the right, then being pressed hard in parts of the private sector, to strike or to belong to trade unions. (Much the same rationale had been deployed by the leading railway companies, where a similarly paternalistic approach to the workforce had been coupled with a fierce resistance to the emergence of organized unions.) The progress of a successful strike by a nascent dockers' union in London in 1889 had been watched with acute anxiety by officials at the Grand, who were well aware of how alienated many in their own workforce had become.* A series of minor incidents followed through the next several months, some involving the Scottish labour leader James Keir Hardie and men from the dockyards. Events took on a more serious complexion in July 1890. Street marches and rallies by postmen in London led to threats of a strike at Mount Pleasant, a vast sorting office in Islington, soon to be universally known as just 'The Mount', opened just the previous year. (It had once been the site of a gigantic rubbish dump, hence its name, but had most recently been occupied for almost a hundred years by a large gaol, Cold Bath Prison.) The Postmaster General since 1886, Henry Raikes, had shown a readiness to meet workers' leaders – indeed, a propensity for involving himself generally in the details of administration – that had frequently grated with his officials. But Raikes and Blackwood were now agreed that a stand needed to be taken. Auxiliary postmen were brought into Mount Pleasant to replace any strikers. Scuffles erupted inside the building, prompting a hasty exit by the auxiliaries ('without their hats', one

---

* Official celebrations for the fiftieth birthday of the Penny Post ran foul of the disaffection in the ranks, as a contemporary noted in his biography of one of Blackwood's three Postmasters General. At a huge banquet in South Kensington Museum in July 1890, thousands of guests watched as the Duchess of Edinburgh, representing the Queen, touched a telegraph transmitter to send a telegram to offices all over Britain. Provincial postmasters had been instructed to treat the day as a holiday, but to gather their teams together in readiness for the receipt of the signal from Kensington. At 6 p.m., as agreed, 'a message was despatched from the Museum to the provincial offices inviting the men there assembled to join in simultaneous cheers for the Queen. The signal met with a hearty response, save in a few districts where the men, by a curious perversion of reasoning, had determined to reply with groans, in order to draw attention to the fact that certain grievances, then under consideration at headquarters, had not been redressed' (Henry St John Raikes, *The Life and Letters of Henry Cecil Raikes*, Macmillan & Co., 1898, p. 327).

observer noted). Early the next morning, Blackwood himself appeared with a group of senior officials to take pre-emptive action. What was afterwards often called 'The London Postmen's Strike' actually never happened. No sooner had the morning shift arrived than Blackwood stood up on a sorting table and announced the dismissal of almost a hundred postmen suspected of planning action for later that day. Both he and they then beat a path to the Grand, half a mile away. The Islington men were met by a large force of police, while the Secretary disappeared inside the building to address the postmen preparing for their morning rounds in the City. Had they walked out in sympathy with their dismissed colleagues from The Mount, the Post Office might have found itself confronting the kind of sustained crisis that had swept through the London docks the previous year. In the event, the postmen took up their bags and braved the crowds outside. The strike threat collapsed and hundreds of employees were dismissed.

Blackwood believed his stance had been vindicated. Though he was personally genuinely distressed by the need to punish individual workers and their families – he wrote to a friend that they were 'Christian men – lots of them. They've just been led wrong' – he took every opportunity in the aftermath to remind government ministers that allowing professional trade unionists to represent the workforce would be disastrous (or, as he put it more than once, tantamount to inviting the Goths into Imperial Rome: 'We know the result').[53] It was soon clear, however, that the averted strike of 1890 had in fact marked an important step forward for the unions' cause. A subsequent inquiry in 1891 led to significant improvements in existing contracts. There was a de facto recognition of the right of employees to communicate through organized channels. And there was a realization among the labour leaders themselves that their efforts to date had been ill-prepared and indecisive, weaknesses they set about remedying partly through the formation in 1891 of a fourth major union, the Postmen's Federation (PF). A decision was also taken to set about promoting the interests of the workforce by lobbying MPs for more public scrutiny of conditions in the postal service.

Step by step over the next dozen years or so, the four nascent postal unions squeezed their way into a formally acknowledged role as representatives of the workforce. All restrictions on union meetings were lifted in 1893. Union deputations were first officially received by the Secretary's office in 1900. The Postmaster General in 1906, Sydney Buxton, recognized the right of postal workers to be represented by union officials who might not even be employees of the Department. (This latter concession would no doubt have been compared by Blackwood to the final indignities of the fallen Roman Empire.) But as a member of the great reforming Liberal government that had won a landslide victory at the start of the year, Buxton had little choice: the Trades Disputes Act, passed in the autumn of 1906, utterly changed the legal status of all unions and granted them virtual immunity from prosecution. The postal unions, like their counterparts in other leading industries, went on expanding from year to year: by 1912, they represented 87 per cent of the established postmen and 82 per cent of the London sorters. And as they grew in size, a dilemma faced by the Government since the aftermath of the 1890 crisis became steadily more acute. Postal communication in Britain was an industry, but one managed by civil servants and owned by the state. Its role as the state's agent in handling the payment of old age pensions, after their introduction in 1908, only underscored the state's ownership of the Post Office. So would not wages have to be settled, in the end, via an inevitably political dialogue between elected representatives of the labour force on the one hand – and elected representatives of the state, government ministers, on the other? The logic was hard to avoid, but such an approach would leave civil servants and managers caught uncomfortably in the middle. All nationalized industries in the British economy would pose the same question over the next eighty years. It was first confronted at the Post Office, and ministers took many years to come to terms with it.

The learning process was reflected in the changing nature of a sequence of official inquiries into the Post Office. These were set up partly in response to the lobbying strategy adopted by the unions themselves. The Government's principal motive was to use an 'independent' and fair-minded inquiry to settle grievances in a more convincing fashion than seemed possible so long as the Grand's officials had complete charge of the process, subject only to rubber-stamping at the Treasury. Blackwood's death in 1893 made it easier to contemplate a break with this latter tradition. At one level, the inquiries could simply be seen as wage tribunals; but they were far more than that, doubling up as comprehensive reviews of pay and working conditions in the Post Office. The first was set up in 1895 and chaired by Lord Tweedmouth, a Liberal peer and member of the Cabinet during Rosebery's short-lived government of 1894–5. It deliberated for almost two years, and one of the conclusions in its final report carried an ominous note for the future of Smirke's building in St Martin's-le-Grand:

At an early stage in our proceedings we visited and closely inspected the whole of the Post Office buildings at St. Martin's-le-Grand. The new buildings opened in 1895 and the Central Telegraph Office left little to be desired, but the General Post Office East, where the postal work is carried on, appeared to us incommodious, insanitary, and overcrowded.[55]

In the process of gathering information from several officers of the newly founded unions, Tweedmouth's committee took evidence from Charles Garland, an officer of the London branch of the PTCA who had joined the Post Office as a telegraphy clerk at the age of fifteen in 1882. He was a remarkable man and had made himself something of an expert on the link between rarely cleaned postal premises full of dusty mailbags and a remarkably high incidence of tuberculosis among its clerks and sorters. An airborne bacterial disease, TB was accounting for a half of all deaths in service. Garland addressed Tweedmouth's committee at his own request and attracted useful press attention to his cause.[56] This angered some Post Office medical staff: one officer wrote to Garland and accused him of 'meddling in subjects which you have publicly demonstrated to be beyond your grasp . . . You must be totally incapable of formulating opinions of any value'. But Garland persevered and used his 1895 appearance as the basis of a campaign that eventually won the Post Office's full support.*

Other committees followed Tweedmouth's in due course, with further mixed reactions from the Post Office itself. Industrialists and others with a special interest in the conditions of the working class were appointed to the Bradford Committee of 1903–4 (without any representation for the Post Office, though Blackwood's successor, Spencer Walpole, had sat on the Tweedmouth Committee). Its report was notably

---

* Garland proposed a mutual insurance scheme for the workforce which could be used to fund a sanatorium for TB victims. His plan was backed by the PTCA's annual conference in 1903, and a committee of union representatives joined forces with an existing TB charity to form the Post Office Sanatorium Society in 1905. More than 30,000 postal workers subscribed to 'The Society' in its first year and a sanatorium was built at Benenden in the fresh countryside of the Kentish Weald, taking its first patients in 1907. The Post Office inaugurated annual medical inspections of all its premises two years later. Opening a new wing of the sanatorium in 1910, Postmaster General Herbert Samuel suggested medical officers in the Post Office should encourage all employees to join The Society. It extended its membership to the whole of the civil service in 1923, and the sanatorium survives today as a private hospital for workers in the public sector. Garland subsequently worked as an official in the Ministry of Health and helped launch the National Playing Fields Association. He was awarded the OBE in 1939 and died in 1955. (Sarah Smelik, *Caring for Generations: The Benenden Story 1905–2005*, Benenden Healthcare Society, 2005.)

sympathetic to the unions and duly caused consternation among officials. George Murray, now back at the Treasury, wrote to the Chancellor of the Exchequer, Austen Chamberlain: 'This is an amazing document; and will, I fear, give us a great deal of trouble in the future'.[57] Most of its findings were shelved. The Government turned next to MPs, with two parliamentary select committees: the Hobhouse Committee of 1906–7, which included two new trade union MPs among its members, and the Holt Committee of 1912–13. Both were charged with inquiring into the wages, conditions and employment prospects of the postal workforce – and both produced massive reports that overwhelmed the Commons. The most conspicuous feature of their work was the mind-numbing scale of it, and they were duly abused for their pains. The second was reckoned so incomprehensible that another committee was appointed to look into it. Under the chairmanship of a railway boss, the Gibb Committee convened early in the summer of 1914. On it was a Treasury official called Roland Wilkins. In a much-circulated memo, he spelt out what many saw as the only sensible conclusion to be drawn from watching the select committees' labours: the settlement of wages in the Post Office was now an irreversibly politicized struggle between the unions and Parliament, in which there was little if any room for Treasury adjudication. Wilkins also noted that two members of the Gibb Committee sat on it specifically as representatives of the unions. 'For the first time in the history of English public life the staff take a hand in administrative questions', he commented drily. 'This they have long coveted in vain.'[58]

In fact, all four inquiries left the unions feeling frustrated and often more than a little cheated. Either the subsequent reports dashed their inflated expectations or (even worse) they delivered unexpectedly favourable findings that were then rejected by the Government. It only added to the anger of the unions that the Post Office appeared in these years to be as financially strong as it had ever been: although the profitability margin was shrinking, the volume growth of the business seemed unstoppable. Net annual income was heading for about £5m by the end of 1913, even after taking account of the mounting losses on telegraphy, which by then were running at around £1m a year. (See again Appendix A, Chart 1.) Against this backcloth, many labour leaders reacted to the inquiry reports with undisguised hostility. The publication of the fourth, in 1913, drew an ominous observation in the labour movement's trade journal, *The Post*. Its one achievement, wrote the leader of the Fawcett Association, C. G. Ammon, would be 'to hasten the uniting of all Postal

Associations – and the at one time wild improbability of an all-grade Postal Strike has been brought into the realm of probability'. A National Joint Committee had existed since 1903, to try to coordinate the work of the different postal unions. Little progress had so far been made with the idea of union mergers. Now this changed, and the UKPCA and the PTCA merged as the Postal and Telegraph Clerks' Association early in 1914.

The Post Office's perception of the inquiries grew more positive over the years. While relieving it of the need to handle thorny pay negotiations, they usefully documented many operational difficulties and pulled no punches in diagnosing deeper structural problems. Enforcing significant reform, however, was not their brief and fell to a series of parallel committees. Some of these achieved significant changes, notably in response to an important edict from the Government in 1897 that half of all new vacancies in the minor grades of the Post Office establishment should be reserved for ex-soldiers. This instantly set back the prospects for all those auxiliaries working for low pay rates in the hope, one day, of gaining a position on the establishment. But a redefinition of many auxiliaries as 'assistant postmen' opened the way to a compromise, allowing them to share in many establishment benefits. Attaching a new priority to the recruitment of ex-servicemen had another serious consequence. It threatened to exacerbate the callous treatment of telegram boys, even more of whom would now face being dismissed after two years as sixteen-year-old 'boy-labourers' with few skills of any relevance outside the Post Office. The impact of the 1897 ruling was delayed by the Boer War of 1899–1902, but was plainly visible by 1909. The issue came to a head in 1909–10 when four fifths of that year's sixteen-year-old cohort were dismissed. With the progressive Liberal government of the day intent on social reforms to curb unskilled casual labour and promote apprenticeships, it was scarcely acceptable for the Post Office to be moving in the opposite direction – as was scathingly observed by a Royal Commission looking at poverty and unemployment. The Post Office mended its ways: all boys in the service had been reclassified as apprentices by 1914, with a guaranteed claim to future employment on the establishment. (The expansion of the workforce meant plenty of ex-servicemen could be taken on, all the same. By 1913 the Post Office was providing a position for three out of every four ex-servicemen employed by the state.)

Other committees fared less well. After the 1907 Hobhouse Report had urged a strong case for decentralization of the postal service, internal committees were devoted to this agenda from 1908 to 1910 under two successive Secretaries. Both acknowledged a need for some urgency, if changes were to be made successfully ahead of taking on 19,000 additional employees with the nationalization of the telephone industry in 1912. Besides, as George Murray commented in 1909 from his eyrie at the Treasury, 'the highly centralized system under which Post Office administration has hitherto been carried on has been slowly breaking down for some years; and things cannot go on as they are much longer'.[59] Unhappily, they did. The second committee, under Matthew Nathan, produced a report sharply critical of its predecessor and the Postmaster General of the day, Herbert Samuel, shrank from choosing between them. Samuel blocked any significant restructuring of the Post Office. Justifying instead only the delegation of a few minor duties to postmasters, his best advice to colleagues at the beginning of 1912 seemed to be that they should cross their fingers and hope for the best. No other single episode in the post-Blackwood era was quite so starkly suggestive of an institution now grown so big and complicated as to leave its minders feeling more than occasionally overwhelmed.

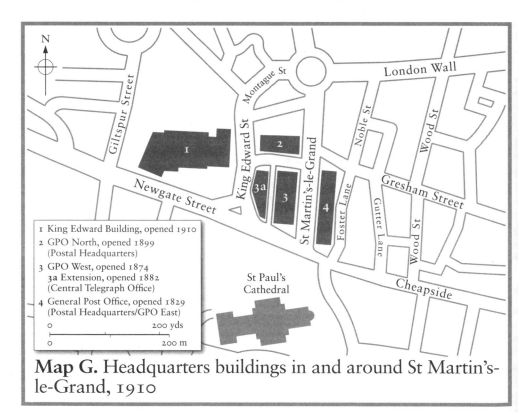

1 King Edward Building, opened 1910
2 GPO North, opened 1899
   (Postal Headquarters)
3 GPO West, opened 1874
   3a Extension, opened 1882
   (Central Telegraph Office)
4 General Post Office, opened 1829
   (Postal Headquarters/GPO East)

0   200 yds
0   200 m

Map G. Headquarters buildings in and around St Martin's-le-Grand, 1910

The extraordinary range of its activities was annually on show in the Postmaster General's report to Parliament. For the year ending on 31 March 1914, Samuel noted a list of new advances that would have amazed the mid-Victorians. Building on the popular adoption since 1900 of bicycles for all rural postmen – as opposed to earlier and more exotic versions of pedalled cycles – there were plans to purchase a first consignment of 'Motor Cycles with Side Cars' and to add to the first 200 'Motor Vans' that had been successfully trialled. Experiments were to begin with a mechanical sorting device for letters and the Post Office had started preparing facilities at Mount Pleasant to take over the manufacturing of stamps from the Stamp Office. Plans were well-advanced for work to start on a new 'GPO East' building to replace Sir Robert Smirke's great edifice in St Martin's: in the wake of severe criticism from the Tweedmouth Committee and other, subsequent inspections, but much to the disgust of many contemporary architectural pundits, the old GPO had been demolished over the winter of 1912–13.* The City and Foreign operations, along with the executive of the London Controller's office, had been relocated in 1910 to a new 'Chief Post Office' called King Edward Building. 'KEB' had taken five years to construct, on land across the street from the west side of the GPO North headquarters. KEB filled a historic five-acre site, encompassing a Christopher Wren church, between King Edward Street and Newgate Street, and was given a fairly grand frontage of its own. This did not stop critics of GPO East's destruction complaining that a temple had been replaced by a factory.[60] But it did ensure that St Martin's-le-Grand remained a location wholly identified with the Post Office. (Indeed, when London Underground opened a station between St Martin's and St Paul's Cathedral in 1900, it was christened 'Post Office' – which it remained until becoming St Paul's Station in 1937.) Arrangements were under way for the construction of an underground postal railway in London, extending from Paddington to Whitechapel, and wireless technology was being harnessed with ever more confidence. 'Radiotelegrams' had been made

---

* Work on the new GPO East building never got further than the drawing board. The site of the old Smirke building was finally sold off in 1923. (Today, it is mostly occupied by a modern office block that bears no reminder of the past and even presents itself as '2 Gresham Street'.) Attempts to find a new London home for the magnificent portico of the Smirke building similarly came to naught, though many institutions were approached late in 1912 with salvage proposals. A series of hostile questions on the Asquith government's intentions had to be handled in the House of Commons by the Liberal Member for St George's-in-the-East, William Wedgwood Benn, the future 1st Viscount Stansgate and father of Tony Benn (Post 30/2385B).

available for ship-to-shore messages since 1910 – hence the celebrated arrest that year of Dr Crippen, caught on a transatlantic liner after an exchange of messages between the ship's captain and Scotland Yard – and a 'wireless telegraph chain' was being proposed that would stretch across the Empire from London to Australasia. More prosaically, meanwhile, the next stage of an underground telegraph line was to be built between the capital and the coast of East Anglia, to connect with two submarine cables landing there from the Netherlands and Germany.

All of these schemes, and more, were detailed in the 1913–14 Annual Report that went off to the printers early that summer. Alas, the introduction needed altering at proof stage before proceeding to publication. 'A large portion of this Report', ran the revised text, 'was in print before the outbreak of war and several of the schemes described as in progress or under consideration, have necessarily been suspended.' How long a suspension would be needed, nobody could say. In case the war should soon be over, thousands of establishment men had rushed to enlist before the end of August. They were promised the continuation of their normal wages, less their army pay, for the duration of their service. As far as anyone could tell, this arrangement might need to last for many months.

PART TWO

War and Peace

6

'Men to trenches, women to benches', 1914–21

'Letter writing had become practically a lost art until the yearning of the men in the trenches for the precious letters from home revived it ... In all probability some of the letters that are now passing to and from the trenches will make the poignant history of these – our own times – live far more thrillingly and truly than all the memoirs of the Joffres, and the Hindenburgs, and the Grand Dukes that will come out after the titanic struggle is ended.'

Editorial in The Sphere newspaper, November 1915[1]

1. POSTMEN SOLDIERS AND SOLDIERS' POSTMEN

At the beginning of August 1914, as every summer since 1908, a thousand or so of the younger men working for the General Post Office in London headed off for the best two weeks of their year. They belonged to the British Army's volunteer reserves, transformed seven years earlier into the Territorial Force. It consisted of fourteen divisions and one of them, the 1st London, had a City of London Regiment, made up of twenty-eight battalions (you can see them listed today on a memorial that stands in front of the Bank of England). The GPO enthusiasts manned the 8th of these, and were known to all as the Post Office Rifles (POR). Its members enjoyed activities blissfully unrelated to their daily postal duties. In addition to a full calendar of social events, they came together in the evenings and at weekends for sporting fixtures and a series of training programmes run by the regular Army, which culminated in a summer camp, held each year at a different location in the Home Counties. Eastbourne had been chosen for the 1914 camp, assembling on 3 August, Bank Holiday Monday. That morning, the men set off to the south coast on two special trains from Victoria station, but they did not get far. At East Croydon and at Three Bridges, the two trains were halted by police and sent back to London.[2]

All over Europe, from the Urals to the Pyrenees, millions of other soldiers were travelling by train that day to unfamiliar destinations – all part of the cataclysmic mobilization of armies that had begun in the wake of Austria's declaration of war against Serbia on 28 July. The POR trains had been called back by officials at the War Office, clearing the diary of peacetime commitments. Whether Britain would remain neutral or join the wider war that now looked certain was still officially undecided, but it seems unlikely the postmen soldiers had much doubt of the outcome by the time they were back in the capital that Bank Holiday evening. (A bank clerk returning the same day from a trip to the Chilterns found the city 'in a state of hysteria. A vast procession jammed the road from side to side, everyone waving flags and singing patriotic songs'.[3]) From Victoria station, three of the battalion's eight companies were sent to camp down for the night in the basement of the Chief Post Office in King Edward Building, where they made themselves as comfortable as they could on hundreds of empty mailbags. The remaining five companies had to find floor space in smaller post offices across the City. Twenty-four hours later, all eight were in situ as military guards. War was declared on Germany at 11 p.m. on the Tuesday night.

The first duty of the Post Office Rifles was to protect the GPO premises against any lurking German spies or saboteurs. London, like Berlin, swirled with rumours of enemy spies on the loose. There was a heightened need of general security, too: the Government had plans for postal orders held in stock to be declared as legal tender, replacing gold coins that were to be withdrawn from circulation. (It would take a few months to print enough £1 and 10/- notes to substitute fully for the coins.)[4] But as there was no evidence of any immediate assault on the post offices, the men had plenty of time over the next few days to enlist for overseas action – it was never a legal requirement of service with the Territorials – and all but a very few did so. They were soon being marched off to Kent, to begin training of an altogether more serious nature which would last for most of the next seven months.[5]

The public's anxiety over spies and saboteurs, frenzied in these first days of the war, had been growing steadily for years, egged on by scaremongering bestsellers and scurrilous campaigns in the press about the possibilities of a German invasion. This had already had important consequences for the Post Office. A counter-espionage 'Secret Service', the forerunner of MI5, had been set up in Whitehall in 1909. Its initial stalking expeditions had met with little or no success, not least because the officials at St Martin's had shown a great reluctance to be drawn into any supporting role. The Mazzini scandal of 1844 had left behind it a long-lasting aversion at the Post Office to tampering with the mails. Even the Metropolitan Police Special Branch (formed 1883) had always had to present a separate Home Office Warrant for every individual letter that it wanted to see intercepted. But the Post Office's reservations had been swept aside by Winston Churchill when he arrived at the Home Office in 1910. Churchill introduced a new 'general warrant', allowing the Secret Service to ask for the interception of all letters to and from individuals cited on a constantly updated list. Between 1911 and 1914, the Post Office had to handle a constant stream of requests for suspects' letters to be identified, set aside in the sorting office and forwarded to the Secret Service's bureau. A few suspects were even discovered through the vigilance of the Post Office itself, though exactly how suspicious letters were spotted is hard to say. Not all aspiring spies were as obliging as a Royal Navy deserter in 1912, who wrote out his own job specification as a spy and then posted it with his personal contact details to 'Head, Intelligence Department, War Office, Germany'.[6]

For the most part, it was a matter of keeping track of the correspondence of individuals already under surveillance. By far the most important of these were some German nationals who were employed as 'postmen' by the intelligence service of the German Admiralty; the Post Office intercepted letters between these men and their Berlin controller at a rate of more than one a day for three years.[7] The resulting intelligence allowed the Secret Service to monitor the activities of more than twenty spies, all of whom were promptly arrested or forced to make a hurried exit during the first two weeks of the war. This remarkable coup must have played its part in ensuring that no news of the British Expeditionary Force reached Germany during the first days of the war. The first contingents of the BEF began crossing to France on 9 August in complete secrecy, and the Post Office was instructed to do everything possible to stifle news of them for at least a week longer. The first postmen to follow the BEF, setting off on 11 August, were thus tasked not with delivering soldiers' letters but with making sure none of them got through. Only on 18 August were initial deliveries made to England, of mail amassed over several days from the troops marching towards Mons.

The unit dedicated to postal duties with the Army bore as its formal title the 'Royal Engineers Special Reserve (Postal Section)' – known to everyone by its abbreviated acronym, REPS – which had been established in February 1913 as part of a well-timed reappraisal by the War Office of the lessons learned to date about handling soldiers' letters. Until Francis Freeling introduced a special penny rate for men in the ranks, in 1795, there was scarcely a problem to be addressed. During the Peninsular Wars, Wellington took a personal interest in his army's intermittent postal links with Lisbon but relied mostly on the Portuguese civil post to manage them. Half a century later, during the Crimean War of 1854–6, officials at St Martin's tried to offer more assistance and sent out some brave officials to help organize an 'Army Post Office' under a clerk of the Inland Letter Office called Edward Smith. His position, though, was awkward at best: 'he was neither in the Army, nor was he independent of it'.[8] Smith and his few civilian colleagues were answerable to both the Postmaster General in London and the local Commander-in-Chief, Lord Raglan, with predictably unhappy consequences. Some clear understanding was needed of the demarcation lines between civil and military responsibilities. This was reached, in principle, by a government committee of 1877 which aspired to provide for soldiers serving overseas a mail service worthy of a society hugely proud of its penny postage. To deliver it, a hybrid civil/military organization would draw on the Post Office for its personnel and technical expertise, and on the Army for its structure and discipline. This body would be a part-time reserve unit in peacetime, made up of GPO men with some lightweight military training. In the event of war, it would then be completely subsumed into the Army, when its men would be assigned to Army, corps, divisional and brigade headquarters – running both stationary offices and mobile 'Field Post Offices' – while all reporting to an Army Postmaster under orders from the Chief of Staff.

This arrangement was first put into practice five years later. In the brief interval, a keen ex-army officer on the Post Office payroll called John Du Plat Taylor persuaded the War Office to let a thousand GPO men come together as the '48th Middlesex Rifle Volunteers' battalion. (They had originally been enrolled by City of London aldermen in 1867, as special constables charged with protecting Post Office premises against Irish republican bombers.) Here was a 'reserve unit' ideally suited to the 1877 concept, which was no coincidence since the committee findings had been pushed hard by Du Plat Taylor himself. It was decided – with firm sponsorship from Henry Fawcett and that veteran of the Crimea,

Arthur Blackwood – that an army bound for Egypt in 1882 should be accompanied by a new 'Army Post Office Corps' consisting of forty-three men from the Middlesex Volunteers. Demand for places was so strong that names had to be drawn from a ballot. The lucky few did well. The whole expedition lasted less than three months, but the sorters and post-men won high praise from the Commander-in-Chief, Sir Garnet Wolseley, who hoped 'a similar corps may be employed on any future occasion on which it may be necessary to despatch an Expeditionary Force from this country'.[9] This encouraged the War Office to build on the original idea: Du Plat Taylor was asked in 1884 to raise volunteers for a 'Field Tele-graph Corps' as part of his unit. The limited scale of operations in Egypt, though, was hardly extensive enough to provide a real test of the hybrid approach. This was to come three years after Du Plat Taylor's retirement, with the outbreak of the Boer War in 1899. When the normal postal ser-vice beyond Cape Town to the rest of South Africa was soon effectively suspended, the Post Office turned its mind to providing a service for the Empire's fighting men.

The war in South Africa marked a new era: both the men in the field and their families at home genuinely expected, as never before in his-tory, to be able to stay in close contact via regular mails. The Army Post Office Corps rolled out the model envisaged twenty years before, and the GPO produced the men via the mobilization of an entire company of what was now known as the 24th Middlesex. Over the whole cam-paign, about 630 of them served in the Army. They were led at first by a Captain Treble, assisted by Lieutenants Price and McClintock, and from April 1900 by the head of London's North District Office, a Lieutenant Colonel Greer. Given the novelty of the assignment, their achievements were impressive. The British and Empire forces in the field rose to 180,000 men, for whom the soldiers' postmen over most of the war delivered around half a million letters and newspapers every week. Accounts of their experiences were published in the *St Martin's-le-Grand* magazine, where colleagues at home must have marvelled at the mix of familiar routines and *Boy's Own Paper* stuff. (One writer, at the beginning of 1900, described a fiercely hot day on the veldt when 'within three hours, we sold 1,600 letter cards, 1,300 embossed envelopes and nearly 2,000 penny stamps from an open truck. I shall never forget the scene, the men hustling and pushing to buy the cards, the envelopes and stamps in order to write home ... On the night of the Battle of Modder River [a few days later] we slept at the ford among the dying and the dead.'[10])

POSTAL COMMUNICATION

WITH

TRANSVAAL,

ORANGE FREE STATE,

AND OTHER PARTS OF

SOUTH AFRICA.

THE POSTMASTER GENERAL can at present only secure as far as Cape Town the transmission of letters, parcels, &c., intended for delivery in the Transvaal (South African Republic) and Orange Free State. The Postal Authorities of the Cape Colony may or may not be in a position to effect delivery to the addressees, many of whom are no doubt at Cape Town or in other places in communication with Cape Town.

Letters, parcels, &c., for Rhodesia and other parts of British South Africa with which communication has been or may be cut off are also being forwarded to Cape Town or Durban, for transmission to destination by the first available means. What means, if any, may be available at the present juncture the Postmaster General is not in a position to say; but he has reason to think that all possible measures for the maintenance of postal communication in British South Africa will be adopted.

Money Order business with the Transvaal and the Orange Free State is suspended.

By Command of the Postmaster General.

GENERAL POST OFFICE,
    31 October 1899.

[255]   Printed for H.M. Stationery Office by W. P. GRIFFITH & SONS, LIMITED, Prujean Square, Old Bailey, London, E.C.   10/99

Notice of interrupted services to South Africa's Boer republics, 1899

South Africa stretched the concept of the Army Post Office close to breaking point, especially in the early months. Inevitably, theory took a while to be translated into practice – not least because the War Office repeatedly underestimated how many men were needed in the field – and there were bitter complaints from both putative partners along the way. (As Lieutenant William Price caustically observed later, 'If I may be allowed to say so, the Army postal critic is very much like the civil critic, only more so'.[11]) But there was a bigger problem. Fighting the Boers was far removed from any campaign envisaged by the authors of the 1877 blueprint. Base post offices in Cape Town and Durban were two to three weeks' shipping distance from England and over a thousand miles from the forward positions of troops in the Transvaal. The fluidity of the war – with early incursions south by the Boers, followed by fast-moving British offensives from February to August 1900 – posed huge difficulties for some forty or so Field Post Offices. Decent intelligence on unit locations was practically impossible thereafter for large numbers of men deployed in about 120 mobile columns, tracking down Boer guerrilla forces across a vast area. This was not a style of warfare conducive to postal efficiency, but the verdict at the end of hostilities in far-off South Africa was nevertheless that the Army Post Office Corps had more than proved its mettle. Given a combat zone with clearer front lines and shorter lines of communication, the capacity of the Post Office and the War Office together to bring mails to the brink of the battlefield could hardly now be doubted.

The partnership arrangement was restructured in the years that followed. A fundamental reorganization of the army in the years after 1906 ('the Haldane reforms') included the setting up of a Territorial 'Army Postal Service'. After some years of confusion, this emerged as REPS.* Responsibility for REPS was handed to a Territorial officer, tasked with organizing a mobilization plan: the postmen reserves, in Royal Engineer uniforms and subject to full military discipline, would need assigning to all divisions of the regular army in the event of war. (The 24th Middlesex was meanwhile transformed into the Post Office Rifles, which remained quite separate.) The man appointed as the first 'Director of Army Postal Services' was William Price, who was given a full establishment of 300 officers and men – enough, it was reckoned in

---

* It was paralleled by an RE Signal Service, which picked out telegraphers and engineers from all directions and grew into a large regular unit, the precursor of the Royal Corps of Signals.

1913, for the six divisions of any Expeditionary Force likely to be sent
overseas. Price himself would be attached to the Army's Inspector-General
of Communications and would report to the Quartermaster General.
Here at last was a structure that looked equal to the demands of the
hybrid concept. By the time those first REPS men set off with the BEF
in August 1914, confidence in its effectiveness was high.[12]

Two nasty shocks followed, much as they had done in South Africa –
and identical in nature. The scale of the action had been badly
underestimated, quickly leaving Price with far too few men. This problem, though, was soon redressed: several hundred more were recruited
in haste from the ranks of the POR battalion (a return, ironically, to the
model left behind with the 24th Middlesex), so trebling the size of the
REPS force in France. The second early crisis sprang from the speed of
the enemy's advance in the opening weeks of the war. The Germans'
push for Paris engulfed several of the first postal facilities, established in
and around Amiens; no sooner had others been set up than they had to
be hurriedly abandoned, and thousands of bags of mail were hastily
shuttled back from the front lines by train, lorry and rented boats ever
further to the west, ending in near chaos at the port of Nantes on
France's west coast.[13]

Once the Germans' Schlieffen Plan had failed to win an abrupt
victory, a very different prospect opened up. The static warfare of the
trenches – whatever its horrors in every other respect – posed the kind
of logistical challenges that were meat and drink to the men from the
Post Office. The BEF's layout, while embracing ever more army divisions, could in effect be treated as stationary from the Channel to the
front line. Of course, individual units were still shuttled regularly
between different locations, but most of those locations themselves
remained as fixed as London suburbs. After some initial months of trial
and error, REPS built a delivery system to match. By the onset of the
winter in 1914, it had raised its force from 900 to 1,500 to cope with a
huge increase in the mails for Christmas. The result, amid the grimness
of the Western Front, often verged on the bizarre. Letters were usually
reaching addressees in the trenches on the second day after being posted,
and London newspapers (also sent over in great numbers) were being
widely distributed within a day or two of their publication. As one
officer confided to his diary on 30 December 1914: 'I got three letters
posted in Ireland on the 26th and in England on the 28th, this afternoon, so letters are reaching us as quickly as if there were no war. It's
really rather wonderful.'[14]

2. POSTAL SUBURBIA
ON THE WESTERN FRONT

To say that postal services on the Western Front marked the high-water mark of the Victorian Post Office might be stretching a point – but not by much. The REPS contingents working with the BEF, though they grew steadily through 1914–15, never numbered in total more than a few thousand men. (The numbers recruited into the Signals Service, and later the Royal Flying Corps, were much greater from the start: telephones on the Western Front relied on the work of some 19,000 men from the GPO.[15]) Yet this modest postal force was able to impose order on a vast network of interwoven roads and railways that linked London and the Channel ports with up to five army groups, each of them roughly representing the needs of a provincial city the size of Southampton. Losses of mail due to accidents or enemy action were extremely rare.[16] Of course, the task demanded courage and initiative in the ranks far beyond anything normally expected of peacetime sorters and postmen. But it was also achieved on the back of traditional strengths that made the GPO a natural partner for the Army – harnessing the meticulous attention to detail, the strong internal disciplines and the by-the-book culture that were all so central to the Victorian postal legacy.

Plainly, outward mail could not be sent directly to a serving soldier or sailor using any normal address. The Post Office issued a series of notices advising the public on how to address letters to men at the front. Only the details of the addressee's fighting unit could be used, and all letters for the British Expeditionary Force were then diverted by the Post Office to a clearing centre where they could be sorted for onward despatch. This was 'Home Depot', an operation that came eventually to employ 2,500 staff. It also handled inward mail from serving men and trained around 5,500 recruits, who went off to join the swelling ranks of REPS men serving in France and other overseas postings. The Depot was under the nominal command of the Army and employed many uniformed men, but it was controlled by the GPO: it was run by the pre-war postmaster of the capital's WC district, now installed with the pay and allowances of a REPS captain.[17] It began life scattered among different buildings, but by the end of 1915 had been pulled together in a vast hut erected across five acres of Regent's Park, reputedly the largest wooden edifice in the world.[18] A fleet of 220 three-ton army lorries was eventually kept busy ferrying mailbags to and from the trains which

linked London to Folkestone and Southampton. Several steamers a day
left these ports for 'Base Post Offices' in Boulogne/Calais and Le Havre
respectively, where formal responsibility for the mails passed from the
GPO to the British army. Most outward bags were loaded onto trains
that plied back and forth across Picardy under cover of darkness, some
of them to be dropped at stationary 'Army Post Offices' along the way,
linked to the Lines of Communication, or at large troop placements
(such as labour battalions or artillery placements) that were a semi-
permanent fixture. The remainder went on as far as the railheads that
serviced 'supply trains' to individual divisions; every railhead eventually
had its own post office, running a branch network between the railhead
and the trenches. The mails usually left the railhead in special REPS
lorries, which took them to the spots designated for the collection of all
divisional supplies, known as 'refilling points'. Here they were taken up
by the Brigade HQs. The final stage of their journey was described in an
article in the *St Martin's-le-Grand Magazine* of July 1915 by 'F.H.W.' –
the newly appointed head of REPS on the Home Front, Frederic
Williamson, just back from an initial tour of the lines to see for himself
how things worked:

> At some pre-arranged point, the regimental post orderlies drive down [to
> meet the motor lorries from their Brigade HQ] to receive their mails. The
> mails are stacked and sorted by the roadside; the long line of carts comes
> up, each in turn to receive its quota of the mails from home; and each
> orderly then clatters off with his letters and parcels, which he carries to his
> comrades right up to the firing line.[19]

It was normal practice in the trenches for each day's post to be
handed out with the evening meal by ration parties. These would also
collect the men's letters and postcards for home, which – unlike in the
Boer War – could be posted without charge. They were generally first
collected together at 'Field Post Offices' – large black steel boxes, usually sporting a pole with a distinctive red and white striped flag, which
were relocated from time to time as the need arose. Most FPOs had all
the kit to provide a good range of the usual counter services available
from a village post office in England, from the sending of registered
letters to the buying and cashing of postal orders; after the summer of
1915, they even sold war savings certificates and war loans. Letters
were stamped with a field postmark, from January 1915, showing the
date and an APO or FPO number (and making rich pickings for collectors in decades to come). Then the postmarked letters were sent up the

line via the Divisional Railhead Post Office and Base Post Office for the return journey to Home Depot.[20]

Four years after the war was over, the British Army made a thorough study of the Field Postal Service that had been used by the Kaiser's army. It had been substantially bigger, and had delivered about four times as many bags of mail each month. The resulting 200-page report nonetheless compared it unfavourably with REPS on many counts. It concluded without any reservation at all that there was 'little of value to learn from the German experience'.[21] For all their prowess in many dimensions of military planning, and despite their experience of three nineteenth-century wars of their own, the Germans seemed to the authors of the report to have spent the second half of the war constantly reorganizing their posts and scrambling to copy a British model that had endured to the end and proved significantly more efficient. It was a proud boast – but not an empty one. Of course, the division of responsibilities between REPS and the Post Office did evolve over time, and developed in some ways that were not remotely foreseen at the outbreak of the war. The Postmaster General, for example, agreed to answer in Parliament for the whole operation. This had not been anticipated, but seemed sensible given that the GPO not only provided many of its personnel but also made all of the transport arrangements as far as overseas Base Post Offices.[22] In general, though, the structure laid down by the end of 1915 needed few substantial changes. And through the remainder of the war on the Western Front – leaving aside the temporary crises precipitated by the Germans' spring offensive in 1918 and the final Allied counter-attack – it expanded steadily without serious mishap.

The critical importance of letters to the morale of the troops was acknowledged from the outset: as everyone agreed, letters came close behind food, leave and suitable clothes, and the press wasted no opportunity to remind readers of this truth. At an early stage in the war, one of the London papers published a letter from a soldier in the trenches saying he was lonely and would appreciate a letter. In the ensuing weeks, he reportedly received 3,000 letters, ninety-eight large parcels and three mailbags of smaller ones.[23] But even the Post Office was taken aback by the vertiginous growth of the three main categories of outward-bound post to the Western Front.[24] (See Appendix A, Chart 4.) The Christmas peaks were scarcely less impressive than the growth from one year to the next: not far short of 5 million parcels went to France in the month before Christmas, 1916. Supplies of tobacco and cigarettes – given duty-free status by the French from the start – remained a staple item at

all times of the year. (Matches to light them with were a more complicated matter. Faced with a dire shortage of them in the trenches, the War
Office in October 1914 prevailed on postal officials to lift a ban on
matches that had been in place since 1884. But it was waived against
the better judgement of the Post Office, which specified elaborate rules
on how safety matches (only) were to be packed for postage. Several
serious fires in mail depots in 1915 were nonetheless blamed on the
ignition of matches, and the ban was reimposed in May 1916. It was
diligently enforced, too: the Post Office brought 178 prosecutions against
offenders before the end of the war.[25]) Outbound parcels soared to just
over a million a week by the spring of 1917, though food shortages at
home, compulsory rationing after December 1917 and, eventually,
much improved field canteens at the front saw this number contract
steadily (except at Christmas) through the rest of the war. Sending cash
was a much better option, and accounted for a high volume of registered letters in the last two years of the war. Outbound letters peaked at
more than 12 million a week early in the first quarter of 1918. (In the
last year before the war, by way of comparison, about 66 million letters
and 2.5 million parcels were posted in Britain during an average week.)
Behind these bare numbers were mountainous piles of mail that needed
shifting at each stage of the journey from Home Depot – entailing, at
many stationary Army Post Offices, the arrival of 400–500 mailbags
every single day.

While the Western Front accounted for more than 90 per cent of the
numbers, it was far from the only theatre served by Home Depot. By the
time the War Office was ready to launch another Expeditionary Force,
early in 1915, sending any significant number of troops into action
without an Army Postal Service unit in attendance was out of the question. Wherever combat forces were to be engaged, REPS men would
have to follow – and usually not far behind, as a post-war collection of
operational reviews recounted.[26] These were never published, but offer
a useful commentary on many of the campaigns beyond Flanders. In the
Dardanelles, REPS men sorted mail in trenches along the beach within
range of Turkish snipers. Through that disastrous campaign, the
unopened letters coming back down the line were almost as numerous
as those going up it, so heavy were the casualties.* By the time five shat-

* A Royal Commission of Enquiry was held into the Dardanelles Campaign in 1916–17.
Williamson noted in a memorandum to colleagues in January 1917 that one of the Commissioners had had a son in Gallipoli who had apparently 'suffered severely from the

4713

SENDING OF MATCHES BY POST.

THE despatch of matches by post has resulted in numerous fires which have destroyed a large quantity of mails. It has consequently been necessary to withdraw the concession which permitted the despatch of safety matches to the Expeditionary Force in France. The despatch of any kind of matches, no matter how carefully packed, by post to any destination at home or abroad is now, as formerly, prohibited altogether. Persons contravening this regulation render themselves liable to prosecution.

By Command of the Postmaster General.

GENERAL POST OFFICE,
9th May, 1916.

[55] 27,500   Printed for H.M. Stationery Office by W. P. Griffith & Sons Limited, Prujean Square, Old Bailey, London, E.C.   5/16 s

Prohibition against sending matches in the mail, 1916

tered divisions from Gallipoli were evacuated to Salonika that autumn, two hundred or so peacetime postmen were running a Base Post Office and five FPOs in the still sweltering heat – and most of them remained in the Balkans for the rest of the war, as the post-war review put it, 'buoyed up by their sense of duty as soldiers and their loyalty to the Post Office'. Other units of the defunct Mediterranean Expeditionary Force went east via Sinai to Syria and west to Italy. The REPS network in Italy covered a range of 1,000 miles from Tarranto to the Alps and reckoned to deliver all letters from GHQ to the front within twenty-four hours. ('This, it may be remarked, was considerably quicker than the Italian Civil Post and infinitely more reliable.') Perhaps most remarkable of all was the assignment of a REPS detachment to Murmansk and Archangel in the autumn of 1918. Its men had to contend not just with the Arctic winter but also with inter-service squabbles at home, where the Sea Lords of the Admiralty 'were instructing the GPO when to send out mails for the Navy in North Russia but ignoring the existence of the Army . . .' In the process of servicing the Allied troops sent to intervene in the Russian Civil War, these hardy souls found themselves handling around 2,000 letters a day for the White forces. By the summer of 1919, the head of the unit in Murmansk was writing home to William Price in optimistic vein. 'Should . . . the Bolsheviks [be] cleared out of Petrograd, the question of sending mails for North Russia via the Baltic to Petrograd will have to be considered.'

With these far-flung operations to track as well as the progress of individual units on the Western Front, successful sorting in Home Depot needed all of the GPO's peacetime expertise – and absolute trust between its staff and the military authorities. The sorters in London had to juggle with around 8,000 units at the height of the war. In preparing the mails and forwarding outward bags via the Base Post Offices, they relied completely on a daily provision by GHQ of information on the

---

deficiencies of the Postal Service'. He warned that the Commission was therefore likely to take a close interest in the activities of the APS. So it proved – but Williamson in his own evidence the next month blamed criticism of the APS on the failures of the Military Forwarding Office, which some troops (especially in the New Zealand contingent) had unwisely used in preference to the APS's parcel post. He also asked the Commissioners to keep any complaints in perspective. As he recalled afterwards, 'I explained that we were dispatching about 1,000,000 letters and 80,000 or 90,000 parcels a week to the Dardanelles so that even if . . . the aggregate number [of complaints] would seem considerable in itself . . . by comparison it was relatively trifling' (Post 33/58A). The level of casualties had also posed appalling difficulties. By the end of September 1915, the APS had had 58,000 names on its list of hospitalized men and was needing to make 8,000 amendments to the list every week.

latest deployments. The process was subject to all kinds of safeguards. Loading teams on the Channel coast, for instance, were only given details of train destinations at the last possible moment each evening. But if it wanted the mails to be delivered promptly, GHQ still had no real option but to entrust top-secret information to REPS.

A parallel arrangement applied in the case of mails for those serving in the Royal Navy, which remained the responsibility of the civil Post Office throughout the war. Letters addressed to a name, rank and ship could simply be posted 'c/o GPO, London'. They were sorted in Home Depot and forwarded in sealed bags to the appropriate port – of which there were 265 around Britain's coastline – where the nearest Admiralty Mail Officer would take charge of their offshore distribution; home-bound letters travelled by the same route in reverse. The authorities were hypersensitive in the early months of the war to possible breaches of security, especially in the post offices that served the main naval bases. Lerwick's post office in the Shetlands, for example, handled all bags to and from Scapa Flow, where the British Grand Fleet was based. When it was alleged that someone in the Lerwick office had tampered with naval correspondence, the entire forty-strong staff were summoned to the post office on a Sunday morning and marched off to the town prison by Royal Navy Reservists with bayonets fixed. (They had to spend six days in the cells, detained under the Defence of the Realm Act, while it was established by the Admiralty and the Post Office in London that someone had blundered. No evidence of tampering was ever found, and the staff were all awarded compensation a few months later.)[27] Such scares were rare after the end of 1914 – perhaps surprisingly so. The system relied on daily communication by the Admiralty to the Post Office of all changes in ship locations – obviously a highly sensitive matter, affecting the security of every vessel from the largest Dreadnought battleship to the smallest tramp steamer under government contract. Some 17,000 names came and went on lists that stretched to about thirty pages each morning. Daily despatches gave way to bi-weekly ones in October 1915, but in most respects the system remained remarkably constant. True, the Admiralty had had plenty of time to refine it before hostilities began, but this in no way diminished the pride that many took in it. As the Naval Correspondent for the *Liverpool Daily Post* wrote on 22 August 1914: 'One of the most encouraging things about the part this country is playing in the great war [sic] is the businesslike way in which we have faced the situation. ... [Just address a letter to any sailor by name, rank and ship] and the Post Office will do the

rest. . . . What a marvellous thing it is that the fleet engaged in killing
Germany's commerce and waiting for its chance to smash the upstart
Teuton navy should get its letters from home as usual!'[28]

Many other aspects of the GPO's war-work similarly called for close
attention to government schedules and absolute secrecy. Official communications between Whitehall and the generals in the field were the
business of an Express Service that ran parallel to the ordinary post, but
could deliver papers to GHQ in France within twelve hours of their
despatch. Cross-posts were developed on the Western Front from
November 1914 onwards to provide a motorized 'internal' postal system for the Army, so that letters from one part of the front to another
did not have to travel far up the railway line and back again. From
August 1915, the top brass ditched many of their own courier services
and asked REPS to take on most of the post between GHQ and other
headquarters depots, too. (Communications directly affecting operations in the field went on being handled by the Despatch Riders run by
the Signals Service, and there was inevitably some overlap.)[29] Cross-
posts eventually carried about 5 million letters a week.* At home, the
main departments of state hugely expanded their use of both privately
installed telephone lines and the public exchanges. While accommodating their demands, Post Office engineers also had to maintain what was
virtually a parallel telephone organization to service the needs of home
defence, including the coordination of warnings to the public about air
raids by Zeppelin airships and, later, heavy bombers. One German bomber
scored a direct hit on the Central Telegraph Office in St Martin's-le-Grand
during a daylight raid in July 1917. There were no postal casualties –
due in large part to a timely warning of the raid – but damage to the
CTO's roof brought the country's entire telegraph network to a halt for
a few hours. Government telegrams by 1917 were running not far short
of a million a month, so the impact was felt immediately. This was one
of two especially damaging bombs that fell in the last eighteen months
of the war: the other completely destroyed one of the Base Post Offices
on the Channel coast, at Calais, in January 1918.

Other demands on the GPO included the organization of inbound
mails for German prisoners of war and outbound mails for British prisoners in Germany, both of which passed through intermediary agencies

---

* As every schoolboy used to know, the Army also employed some 22,000 carrier pigeons
on the Western Front to help with its cross-posts, but the birds had their own assigned
fanciers within each unit and were not the specific responsibility of REPS or the GPO.

in neutral Holland. Of course, they also passed through the hands of the Postal and Cable Censors of the War Office, and the logistics of transferring POW correspondence and large amounts of other mail on a daily basis to and from the censors was another responsibility of the GPO.[30] The actual business of opening and censoring letters, however, was now left to the professionals of the intelligence community, just as checking soldiers' mail home was left to the Army.[31] And then there was the terrible business of dealing with the carnage of the war. Card indices were kept on the movements of wounded men, whose whereabouts after hospitalization were frequently unknown to their fighting units. (Hospitals were given Redirection Cards to send to the Base Post Offices, but the system never worked very well.) Dead men's personal effects had to be returned to the Base Post Offices, sorted and forwarded to relatives; officers' effects were sent directly to an army agency in Charing Cross. A Returned Letters Office at Home Depot was staffed by twenty-five women who dealt with letters sent back from the front, directly or indirectly, marked 'Killed' or 'Missing', but the organization of the Post Office telegrams to next of kin ('OHMS War Office Lon . . . Deeply regret to inform you . . . army council express their sympathy . . .') was administered by the War Office, not the GPO, though of course it was still the telegram boys who had to deliver the dreaded envelopes. All returned letters were scrupulously checked between the two departments, to confirm the wording on them and to ensure that none was returned to sender in advance of the official telegram. During every big battle from the summer of 1916 onwards, these unopened letters from the Western Front 'were received at the rate of 30,000 per day, and the staff at Home Depot were aware of the extent of the [battle] losses before the press could glean this information from official sources'.[32]

After the fighting was over, the extraordinary contribution that REPS and the Post Office had made to the war effort went largely unsung. No one could have accused senior postal officials of seeking to inflate their role. The Secretary – Evelyn Murray, son of the distinguished George Murray, who had been appointed just a few weeks into the war – asked his senior colleagues in 1919 to pull together a series of reports on the wartime record, telling them he proposed to publish a summary in place of the Postmaster General's Annual Reports that had been suspended since 1916. Of the twenty or so reports that were submitted, thirteen described the exploits of REPS – but all of them sat at the bottom of Murray's in-tray, until being quietly archived in August 1921 as 'useful records of what was done' in the war.[33] Again, invited by the Imperial

War Museum in 1919 to suggest an exhibit honouring the achievements of REPS, postal officials scratched their heads and eventually decided there was nothing worth putting on show.[34] And years later, when General Sir James Edmonds approached the Secretary's office just before Christmas 1928 for help in writing a section on REPS for his Official Military History of the war, he seems to have come away with a meagre haul of papers that kept him busy for scarcely a few weeks. Even so, when they saw the outcome early in the New Year, those who had been closely involved with the Army Postal Service were clearly dismayed. The most senior of them, Colonel Lidbury, declined to comment on the author's draft at all, given that 'General Edmonds apparently wishes to deal with the APS in the barest outline', as his assistant explained in passing the chore to a junior officer.[35] When the finished volume appeared in 1932, REPS was dealt with in under five pages – one fewer than Edmonds devoted to the contribution of Auxiliary Social Services like the YMCA and the Concert & Theatrical Parties unit. Only in connection with the novel skills of the telephone engineers was it noted that 'the General Post Office rendered great and unstinted assistance'.

Perhaps ubiquitous postal services had been so familiar in peacetime, for so long, that the achievements during the war were simply taken for granted. It is easy to imagine, too, that officials in St Martin's-le-Grand might have wished to err on the side of modesty, given the scale of the nation's sufferings. Those relatively (very) few men of the Post Office who had managed to enlist with REPS, after all, were the lucky ones. Many thousands of their colleagues were less fortunate – especially those who had marched off to training camp with the Post Office Rifles back in 1914.

3. THE POST OFFICE RIFLES

The POR was not technically one of Kitchener's 'Pals' battalions. When it embarked for France in the middle of March 1915, 'Pals' battalions were just being newly formed, each drawing on the civic pride of a single town or city for local recruits, and they would only start arriving at the front nine months later. Nonetheless, the POR shared much of the Pals spirit and represented, like them, a concentration of young men from one close-knit community – in its case, the London Postal Service. Unfortunately for the POR, the comparison goes further. For like the Pals battalions, it was also heavily engaged in many of the most harrowing episodes of the war and suffered accordingly. Indeed, there was scarcely a single major battle on the Western Front after May 1915 that did not leave the POR with heavy, sometimes devastating, losses. The last wartime head of the battalion was Lt. Col. A. D. Derviche-Jones (nicknamed 'Kill-Boche Jones' after the enthusiasm of his pre-battle pep-talks), who took command in July 1918 and wrote a private history in the immediate aftermath of the war that was published early in 1919. Of the twelve senior officers arriving with the battalion four years earlier, only one had survived; and forty-six second lieutenants had been killed. But Derviche-Jones, a small dapper man with a keen sense of posterity, evidently drew on the recollections of many men from the ranks as well as surviving officers, and made extensive use of army reports. He penned the POR's story in unrelenting detail.[36]

Legend has it that the battalion spent its last night in England, in March 1915, at the Chief Post Office in King Edward Street. If true, even KEB's cavernous public-counters hall must have struggled to billet a thousand soldiers with all their embarkation kit. The gaps left by men switching to REPS in the early months of the war had long been filled. In fact, a second thousand-strong battalion had already begun training in England. The first POR men over the Channel were therefore listed as the '1/8th', a battalion of four companies. Their initiation into the grim attrition of trench fighting came at Festubert, eight kilometres east of Béthune, in May 1915. More than half of all those who had prepared themselves through ten long months of training were killed or wounded in the space of just a few days.[37] (This was one of the disastrous failed offensives that triggered a political furore over the British Army's dire shortage of shells.) One can sense the shock felt in St Martin's-le-Grand by scanning the Roll of Honour notices published at the front of the Post Office Circular, the weekly update on administrative business sent to all postmasters. A short list of employees killed in action with other units had appeared every week since 24 November 1914. So far, those named had come from every part of the country. On 15 June, in the fourth Circular to appear since the Festubert action, a special item appeared: 'The Postmaster General is sure that the staff generally will be interested to hear that the Post Office Rifles were in action on the 22nd ultimo and following days, when, after hard fighting, they were successful in capturing one of the enemy's trenches. Unfortunately they sustained severe losses . . .' The POR's dead entered the lists over the next three weeks – fifty-three names, all but four of them from the London Postal Service. Hundreds more were wounded or still unaccounted

POST OFFICE CIRCULAR.

TUESDAY, 15 JUNE, 1915.
No. 2231.

The Postmaster General is sure that the staff generally will be interested to hear that the Post Office Rifles were in action on the 22nd ultimo and following days, when, after hard fighting, they were successful in capturing one of the enemy's trenches.

Unfortunately they sustained severe losses, 4 officers and 44 men being killed, and some 300 men wounded.

The names of the men who were killed will be inserted in due course in the Roll of Honour.

POST OFFICE ROLL OF HONOUR.

The Postmaster General has learnt with deep regret that the following Officers of the Post Office have lost their lives in the Service of their Country while serving with the Naval or Military Forces of His Majesty.

Name	Post Office Rank	Office	Regiment or Ship
Allaway, W. E.	Postman	L.P.S., W.C.D.O.	8th London (Post Office Rifles).
Ansell, F.	Labourer	Engrg. Dept., S. Midland Dist.	1st Herts.
Backhouse, A. D.	Cleaner	L.P.S., Leytonstone, E.	East Yorks.
Barclay, F. J. J.	Labourer	Engrg. Dept., London District	3rd City of London.
Boswell, T.	Postman	Darwen	East Lancashire (Territorial Force).
Botting, A. C.	Postman	Brighton	8th London (Post Office Rifles).
Brooks, G.	Telephone Hand and Wirer	Stores Department, Birmingham	5th Royal Warwick.
Bruce, E. V.	Postman	Woking	Hood Battalion, 2nd R.N. Brigade.
Butters, W. E. M.	Sorting Clerk & Telegraphist	Lyndhurst, Lymington	Royal Engineers, 2nd Signal Company.
Carr, T. A.	Part-time Night Operator	Scarborough	Royal Field Artillery, North Riding Battery.
Carroll, J. A.	Unestablished Night Telephonist and Call Office Attendant	Manchester	Royal Lancaster.

PRINTED BY W. P. GRIFFITH & SONS LTD., PRUJEAN SQUARE, OLD BAILEY, E.C., PRINTERS TO H.M. STATIONERY OFFICE.

Post Office Circular of 15 June 1915, reporting Festubert losses

for. The Post Office Rifles Cemetery, to be found today just outside the village of Festubert, contains the graves of only twenty-six identified POR men but has over ten times as many unnamed tombstones dedicated simply to 'A Soldier of the Great War'.

Twelve months later, at Vimy Ridge, the battalion was somehow able again to field four companies, three of which 'were practically wiped out'. Replacements must have been found in great haste – and a third battalion of POR reserves had been in training since mid-1915 – because the Rifles were engaged again in the fighting on the Somme in the autumn of 1916. The battalion lost a third of its men at Mametz Wood in September. The following month at Butte de Warlencourt, two companies went forward under fire – more than 400 men, of whom just seven returned.[38] By this stage, the POR dead in the Post Office Circular's Roll of Honour were individuals from post offices all over Britain, and Ireland too: of those listed in October 1916, only a third came from the London Postal Service. From that October to June 1917, what was left of the battalion was pulled out of the line to be rested, heavily reinforced and provided with new officers from other battalions. Then, from July 1917, it was asked to hold one of the most notorious stretches of the Ypres Salient, losing a fifth of its men in three months.

Meanwhile the second battalion, the 2/8th, had come to the front in January 1917. It had fought in the Arras sector of the line in the spring, and had joined the 1/8th on the Ypres Salient since September, losing a hundred men from artillery bombardments and gas attacks in its first four days. The battalion was then heavily engaged in what was later to be known as the Third Battle of Ypres. Though it distinguished itself in the early weeks – with the award of a Victoria Cross to one of its NCOs, Sergeant A. J. Knight – it later found itself ruthlessly sacrificed in the grim fighting around Passchendaele. On the evening of 29 October, it got 'a sudden order' to go over the top at first light in support of a major offensive by Canadian units that were struggling to capture the Passchendaele Ridge. Like most of his officer contemporaries, Derviche-Jones brought a blithe understatement to many of his descriptions of encounters with the enemy, but even his hearty bravado failed him in recounting what happened next:

> The ground [to be assaulted] was almost unknown, and there was practically no time for reconnaissances. . . . From aeroplane photos the ground to be traversed seemed like a vast morass of mud and slime, as indeed it turned out to be. But little progress could be made. Men sank to their armpits in

mud, and provided easy targets for the enemy. No support was forthcoming on the right. In spite of that, progress was made in the course of the day to about 500 yards, and outposts established, which, however, were ordered to be evacuated at night ... The casualties were very severe: five officers killed ... and five wounded ...; and of other ranks, 34 killed, 173 missing (all believed to have been killed or drowned), and 42 wounded. To illustrate the state of the ground, four men tried for two hours with ropes to extricate a comrade, and failed. Though no objectives of this Battalion were taken, the main purpose of the attack was achieved, in that this lone Battalion, struggling against an even more implacable enemy than the Boches, drew so much artillery and machine-gun fire as to materially relieve the main attack on the Passchendaele Ridge.[39]

This was no less than the truth, as the Divisional Commander openly admitted a few days later. Addressing the POR survivors, he told them not to feel too badly about falling short of their objectives: the High Command had never supposed them attainable. It is hard to imagine this provided any solace, given the atrocious fighting conditions and the number of men lost. Many of them are buried in the huge Tyne Cot military cemetery laid out below the modern village of Passchendaele, and the names of 103 officers and men of the POR can be found on the walls there which, like the Menin Gate in Ypres, commemorate the dead with no known graves.

By the end of the year, the 1/8th had taken more heavy losses, this time at the Battle of Cambrai, and in January 1918 its remnants were transferred to other units or reassigned to the depleted 2/8th – so the POR once again consisted solely of the 8th Battalion. It was the only unit in its division to be out of the line when the Germans launched their spring offensive in March; but it was quickly thrown back into the intense fighting around Saint-Quentin and Amiens, and remained there over the next several weeks. The casualty figures were shocking on many days, never more so than in late April when a single gas shell wiped out ninety men at the battalion headquarters. By August, as Derviche-Jones recorded, 'a large number of [the battalion] consisted of youngsters hurriedly sent out as reinforcements to make good the gaps ... These lads were seen to show their mettle, even without the advantage of training ...' Not yet nineteen years old, several hundred of them fell in the Allied counter-attacks that began in August. Derviche-Jones himself was wounded that month, though he managed to return to his command in time to see the POR through a desperate last few weeks of fighting across the Scheldt river and the canals of Belgium.

It comes as something of a surprise, in the face of this terrible chronicle, to discover that any of the early volunteers for the POR survived at all – but many brave men did. They can be spotted in group photographs taken at the war's end, wearing '1915 Stars' on their tunics. Company Sgt Major 'Darkie' Richardson, for example, endured life on the front from the very first month of the POR's engagement to the last. He died in 1979, an honoured member of the Post Office Rifles Association, which held reunions every March until 1957.* In all, the two POR battalions with a nominal fighting strength at any point of a couple of thousand men had seen 12,000 men through their ranks. Of this total, 1,800 were killed and 4,500 wounded – with just over a third of all these casualties suffered in the last nine months of the war. Casualty rates among the 36,000 or so other postal workers who enlisted with local regiments around the country were less shocking, but still heavy enough. In total, 75,000 Post Office men enlisted, including the 8,000 in REPS and the 19,000 in the Signals Section of the Royal Engineers as well as the men of the POR battalions. A toll of 8,858 men killed therefore represents almost 12 per cent of the total. An internal report of May 1920 reported 5,502 deaths among postmen (including a tiny minority of porters) and 1,039 among sorters and counter clerks.[40]

Of all those who enlisted, a majority did so before national conscription was declared in January 1916. No doubt many were keen to serve. On the other hand, there cannot be much doubt that the Government had few recruiting sergeants more formidable than the Post Office. The first wave of enthusiasm, prompting 11,000 to join up in August 1914, initially caused officials some alarm. They appear to have been particularly concerned about losing qualified operators from the Central Telegraph Office: the War Office had to step in at one point to persuade the Post Office to release fifty-two CTO volunteers, much to the chagrin of the newly installed Secretary; this concern to retain qualified telegraph men at home was to persist throughout the war, but Evelyn Murray and his senior colleagues soon rallied – emulating the men's union leaders, who had abandoned all talk of the international brotherhood

---

* The last survivors died out in the late 1970s and early 1980s. They and all their colleagues are commemorated in a Book of Remembrance in St Botolph's, 'the Postman's Church', in St Martin's-le-Grand. Their reminiscences were the basis of *Terriers in the Trenches*, a history of the POR by Charles Messenger, commissioned by the POR Association and published in 1982. In addition to the memorials in the war cemeteries of France, church plaques commemorating the POR can be found in the villages of Abbots Langley and Uckfield, where the men trained before leaving for the Western Front.

of workers at the outbreak of hostilities.[41] Then, with the return of Herbert Samuel as Postmaster General for a second time – as a minister in the coalition government formed by Asquith in May 1915, though outside the Cabinet – efforts to put the Post Office workforce fully at the disposal of Kitchener's new army moved into gear. Samuel was certain where the Post Office's priorities lay. Within a fortnight of taking office, he was off on a tour of REPS facilities in France.[42] At the end of June, a Secretary's Circular went out to all postmasters reminding them that 'voluntary' enlistment was a relative term: 'temporary staff who are eligible for military service may be dispensed with as opportunity offers . . . Any man of military age who represents himself to be physically unfit for military service should be required to produce a medical certificate in support of his statement, unless his unfitness is obvious'.[43] Through October and November, the Postmaster General then arranged for a personal letter from himself to go to every nineteen- to 41-year-old male employee – with the exception of skilled telegraphy operators and trainee telegraphists – urging them to sign up. But, as his first letter noted, there were no more places left in REPS, so men would have to take whatever posting Fate had in store for them. 'Recruits are most needed in the Infantry Regiments.'

While officialdom moved from caution to virtual coercion, many postal workers seemed to be having second thoughts. In the first months after August 1914 another 24,000 men enlisted. The fervour of that early rush to the Colours cooled appreciably once the attrition rates on the Western Front became apparent – a process that we can easily imagine might have been quickened within the Post Office by news of the POR's losses at Festubert. By May 1915, senior POR officers were already appealing urgently to their colleagues at home for more recruits, and the Secretary and his staff responded in kind. The Dublin and Edinburgh offices were urged by the Secretary in March 1915 to come up with 1,400 volunteers so that the 2/8th could be brought to 'full strength'. Plans were set in train for an appeal in thirty provincial towns of Ireland, as well as in Dublin itself, with a view to raising an entire company of Irish postmen.[44] But the situation of the Post Office in Ireland, a country that had been on the brink of civil war in August 1914, was more complicated than this acknowledged – as events there would shortly prove (and as we shall see in Chapter 7).

In the meantime, by early December 1915 some 29,475 replies had been received to Herbert Samuel's personal letters. Fewer than half of the respondents offered themselves for enlistment. Some 8,500 had expressed a willingness to serve as telegraph operators, an ambiguous gesture in view of the Post Office's reluctance to part with trained men from this group. Remarkably, there were 1,302 letters actually declining to serve. And some supervisors, far from being pressed by men eager to go, seemed to be looking for ways to help them stay. The Chief Engineer, W. Sligo, was plainly incensed at the failure of supervisors in his department to send out the Postmaster General's letters as instructed. The results were 'very disconcerting', as he complained in a letter to them all in November: 'I have scrutinized the lists [of volunteers] which have been submitted direct to the Secretary and am staggered at their general tenour'. Sligo had expected to see around 30 per cent of the 'workmen and labourers' in the department signing up; but the numbers seemed unlikely to reach anywhere near that level. The slow progress with indoor workers seemed equally lamentable. 'In many cases 3rd Class Clerks and Clerical Assistants who are not ex-Telegraphists and Draughtsmen have been scheduled as irreplaceable. This again is untenable.'[45] Meanwhile the Secretary, Evelyn Murray, was writing to postmasters to point out that any vacancies with REPS – obviously highly sought after – were now being reserved, in effect, for married men over forty.

The days of voluntary enlistment, anyway, were almost over. By Christmas 1915, Murray was writing again to his postmasters, this time with the proposed arrangements for conscription. A massive call-up of men was planned for 20 January 1916. The local recruiting authorities would soon be contacting the postmasters about the men under their charge. They were to reply saying 'the Postmaster General offers no objection'. Call-up papers would then be issued to the men themselves, who would be told that all arrangements had already been made for their release. This etiquette was duly observed, and the number of postal workers called up for active service had jumped by March 1916 to 54,000. It would go on climbing until the end, and entailed the recruitment, over four years, of virtually *all* the Post Office's able-bodied eighteen- to 41-year-old men. Sustaining the mails in their absence soon began to look impossible. Faced with just one obvious remedy, officials seemed to linger in a state of denial for the first nine months or so. However, the staffing gaps by the early summer of 1915 left no option but to turn elsewhere, as the Secretary announced in a circular to postmasters at the end of June: 'You are accordingly authorized to employ women at your discretion on both indoor and outdoor duties which can reasonably be allotted to them . . .'[46] Or as the new approach soon came to be tagged, 'Men to trenches, women to benches'.

4. COURTESY AND CONDESCENSION

Wartime deprivations weighed heavily on the Post Office's domestic operations. There were fewer daily deliveries, shorter opening hours and tighter constraints in general on the operations of the sub-offices network. Since these constrictions were in many respects never reversed, the levels of service seen in 1914 were left behind for ever. Gone were the days when 'the City businessman who wished to inform his wife that he would be late for dinner could . . . send a letter'.[47] Shortages of petrol and tyres curtailed the early experiments with motor vehicles, and a steep rise in the cost of fodder for horses led to the suspension of a broader trend towards using more road transport of any kind. Only on the critical urban routes linking main sorting offices with their local railway stations were road vehicles to be given precedence. At the same time, the railways themselves were under steadily more duress. There was 'a practically continuous modification of particular train arrangements for one reason or another throughout the period of the War' and scarcely one mail train in ten managed to run to anything resembling its pre-war schedule.[48] The daily routines of every counter clerk, meanwhile, were regularly stretched to embrace a long list of new government-related services. These included the payment of 'Separation Allowances' to the wives of men on active service, the sale of various tax stamps and the administration, eventually, of rationing. One official estimate of counter services on behalf of government departments valued them at £3.4m in 1917–18, compared with a little over £700,000 in 1913–14.[49] Few aspects of the Post Office escaped bracing changes – even the penny post had to surrender to the exigencies of war. As in the Napoleonic era, and in the Spanish Wars a century before that, the revenue needs of the Treasury forced postage rates higher. The Penny Red paid for only the lightest of letters after November 1915, and – much to the dismay of the old guard at St Martin's – gave way altogether to a 1½d stamp in June 1918. (*Punch* ran a cartoon of the Post Office as 'another war profiteer'.) The cost of telephone calls was broadly doubled. But of all the changes that swept through the postal service in these four dark years, none changed the day-to-day life of the Department more dramatically than the hugely expanded role of women in its workforce.

The Post Office is often described as a pioneer of women's employment. This might have raised a hollow laugh among women's labour leaders in 1914, but is a fair accolade for the lead it provided over the last quarter of the nineteenth century. When Anthony Trollope retired in 1867, he and his contemporaries had been accustomed to dealing with women in charge of small rural post offices – but the Department's clerical workforce had still been exclusively male. By the close of the Victorian era, thousands of women clerks were working for the Post Office. When F. E. Baines took the reader of his memoirs on a tour 'Behind the Scenes' less than thirty years after Trollope's retirement, he found nothing especially noteworthy about discovering, stationed inside the Central Telegraph Office, '1,897 telegraphists (young men) and 751 *telegraphistes* (young women)'. Nowhere else in his text did Baines actually comment on the presence of women, but this was entirely in keeping with the usual attitude among senior officials of his day that women employees were in fact invisible.[50] We can still see them, though, staring back at us in long rows from behind their work desks, all dressed alike in their white blouses, posing for the Victorian or Edwardian photographer. These were indeed the elite troops of what scholars have nicely named the White Blouse Revolution. By 1914, however, a deep disaffection had set in – which to our way of thinking is easily under-standable. The constraints on Post Office women in the years immediately preceding the Great War smacked less of 'glass ceilings' than of solid Victorian ironwork. Their pay rates were still typically 30–50 per cent lower than the rates paid to men for identical jobs. Female clerical teams worked in strictly segregated areas and had only just, in 1911, been granted permission to leave the office at lunchtime. They had also since 1876 been barred from further employment if they got married. (Post-mistresses and sub-postmistresses had been long exempt from this bar, but it was extended to cover them in January 1914.)[51] The White Blouse, for many, had come to feel more like a Hair Shirt. To take a proper measure of the war's impact, we need to see first why the legacy of the previous forty years was so ambiguous.

The pioneering days began with what was, in effect, a mutually con-venient social contract. One party to it, the Post Office, was an employer with a huge bureaucracy that was awkwardly flawed in a crucial respect. Relatively few employees grew more productive as they grew older: most went on performing essentially the same tasks until the day came for them to collect their pension. Yet the more years an employee worked for the Post Office, in general, the higher their pay. This arrangement, inspired by the need to build a disciplined culture, was proving lethally expensive by the 1860s as the Department mushroomed in size. The other party to the social contract was a demographically disadvantaged group of jobseekers – young, educated and conscientious women from lower middle- and middle-class backgrounds – for whom even a niggardly wage packet would represent a novel sense of independence in the years before marriage. The prospect of working in a well-ordered and professional workplace, with none of the socially undesirable encounters with the artisan classes all too likely in teaching or nursing, offered many such women an immensely appealing escape from the suffocating constraints of the parental home and late-Victorian gentility.[52]

The two parties were introduced to each other courtesy of the Post Office's acquisition in 1869 of the telegraph companies. The latter had already hired and trained forty-five women operators in a skill that was in desperately short supply. The Post Office had no choice but to retain them. It then took a hard look at its future organization. It was the farsighted Frank Scudamore who spelt out for his colleagues, in a famous deposition to an internal review body in 1871, how women could be the perfect answer to their cost predicament. Here was a cohort of young workers who would have the right aptitude, be amenable to low wages, and be generally inclined to leave before climbing too far up the pay ladder while expecting no pension. And in addition to all of this, as Scudamore pointed out:

> [existing telegraphy wages] which will draw male operators from but an inferior class of the community, will draw female operators from a superior class . . . [who] will, as a rule, write better than the male clerks, and spell more correctly; and, where the staff is mixed, the female clerks will raise the tone of the whole staff.[53]

His argument was accepted, and advertisements appeared for a first twelve female counter clerks in 1872. The Civil Service Commission was swamped with applications. In addition to the Telegraph Office, women comprised within a few years the majority of the staff in clerical departments like the Returned Letter Office (in 1873) and the Savings Bank (in 1875). Before the decade was over, thousands of women had been taken on. Officials at the Grand did especially well to hire, as the first head of the women's section in the Savings Bank, a formidable 23-year-old daughter of an Oxford don called Maria Constance Smith. '"Efficiency" was her watchword, and the force of her dominant purpose and magnetic personality was brought to bear to ensure that the women under her control should become efficient.'[54]

The new recruits proved capable of handling any tasks assigned to them. Indeed, there was plenty to suggest that these young women –

typically far better educated than their male counterparts and from more advantaged social backgrounds – might actually be better than men at many postal jobs. This was occasionally put to the test in the early years. 'In 1876, in the Central Telegraph Station, the men raced the women [at] sending out the Queen's opening speech to Parliament. The detailed results are not known, but in the aggregate the women significantly out-scored the men'.[55] Such tests soon came to be discouraged. As this might suggest, male chauvinism could only retreat so far. Attitudes to the employment of women remained deeply ambivalent, both in the work-place and in the evolution of departmental policies. A young man working in the Cannon Street office of the telegraph services in 1888 recorded in a memoir, decades later, that the recruitment of women teleg-raphists was still causing huge resentment among the older men, twenty years after the arrival of the first female operators. (Those in their early twenties often reacted quite differently: there was much flirting over the wires, with illicit messages finding their way onto the end of customers' telegrams. Clerks caught sending them were fined at the rate of 6d for every twelve words.[56]) At the most senior levels, there was a determin-ation to ensure that, while women's numbers were rising steadily, their influence on the culture of the Post Office would be carefully restrained. The import of the marriage bar was craftily reinforced, for example: single women were offered the prospect of a dowry on leaving to get married. It would be payable after six years, but it would only grow in size until the twelfth year of employment.* And every opportunity was taken to tag the work of selected activities, invariably the most mundane, as a natural occupation for women, implicitly confirming their unsuit-ability for other, more senior roles. Here technology lent a hand. For no sooner had it been suggested that women might in fact make exemplary clerical workers, thanks to their nimble fingers and their customary saintly patience, than along came an invention in the early 1880s that suited these paragons to perfection: the typewriter. A special functional expertise was the ideal complement to the desirability, for propriety's sake, of segregating women in their own rooms. Thus was born the typ-ing pool, a triumphant confirmation of the social contract launched in the 1870s. In 1894, forty vacancies for typists attracted 740 candidates.

---

* On the basis of statistics collected in 1919, the median length of women's careers in the pre-war era appears to have been 13.2 years, suggesting that the dowry arrangement had indeed had a perceptible impact on women clerks' marriage plans (Samuel Cohn, *The Pro-cess of Occupational Sex-Typing: The Feminization of Clerical Labour in Great Britain*, Temple University Press, 1985, pp. 108–9).

Towards the end of the 1890s, an awkward squad among the women began to question how far the contract really served their interests. The Post Office had successfully replaced men in many lower echelons by the end of the 1880s, lifting women in the process to about 25 per cent of the total workforce. Now it seemed intent on blocking any further incursions, but the growing disquiet had much less to do with the Post Office's stance on hiring additional women than with its treatment of those already on board. With supply looking so robust, the Post Office had apparently decided that it could legitimately demand more from its female employees. It had started in 1891 by increasing the working day for women from six to seven hours. In 1897, it cut their starting salary from £65 to £55 a year. Later the same year, it resorted to the time-honoured practice of adding more rungs to the bureaucratic ladder: a new grade of 'Girl Clerk' for sixteen- to eighteen-year-old recruits allowed aggregate labour costs to be shaved again. The women clerks of the day 'gained the firm impression that they had been swindled'. The re-slicing of the hierarchy was simply too blatant: it was 'a bureaucratic ruse of creating a grade which in every way except pay and age of recruitment was indistinguishable from the one above it'.[57] The women responded much as the male workforce had done before them, setting up their own trade union: the Association of Post Office Women Clerks was founded in September 1901. But their leaders made little headway against the entrenched conviction of officialdom – and, of course, most male contemporaries – that to pay single women the same rates as men would be a travesty, demeaning the status of every breadwinner with a family to support. When the Government announced a higher scale of wages for Post Office men in 1909, women's rates were left unchanged. Officials defended their decision as a way of discouraging 'the exploit-ation of female labour' and actually argued that 'to compel a girl to earn 13s. 6d. [as her male counterpart now would] savours of benevolent despotism'.[58]

This was the frame of mind that was still holding back any further gains for the White Blouse Revolution after 1909, even as the campaign for women's suffrage moved ahead with increasing urgency in the back-ground.* Decades of low-cost, high-quality labour had failed to persuade

---

* Nor was there any sign at all of the Post Office being prepared to think again about the marriage bar, which it consistently defended as a part of the natural order of things. As a Departmental committee report back in 1892 had put it, one of the bar's great merits was that it removed any incentive for young married women to put off child-bearing in the interests of remaining at work: 'It may be urged that [family planning] is a matter for

officials that any fundamental reappraisal was called for – though the Post Office could have paid women higher rates and still cut its labour costs substantially by allowing them into more areas of the service. With no financial alibi for their deeper patriarchal instincts, officials placed limits on the growth of the female workforce with arguments that can look grotesque a century later. Once they stopped attributing the inadmissibility of extra women workers to a shortage of female toilets, the notion of a 'scientific frontier' gained some currency. Jobs for men fell on one side of it, jobs for women on the other. It was a biological divide, which as it happened left most of the more junior and monotonous tasks to the women. For as Sir Matthew Nathan generously put it during his brief stint as Secretary in 1910, women had a 'natural resisting power to the dulling effect of monotony on the sharpness of attention'. No doubt greater powers of self-effacement belonged on the same side of the divide, which must have helped the Secretary and his immediate entourage to understand why there were no women in the higher reaches of the Post Office hierarchy. Even those who did command widespread respect within the organization were afforded scant public recognition. When the Savings Bank reached its fiftieth anniversary in 1911, a jubilee celebration was held at London's Guildhall. Its Lady Superintendent was still Miss Maria Constance Smith, now in her thirty-sixth year in charge of all the female clerks in the Bank. Her long service failed to count when she arrived at the event. 'No seat on the platform had been allotted to the woman who had done so much to build up the Savings Bank, and only at the last moment was she remembered and sought out and asked to fill an inconspicuous place.'[59]

A women's deputation to the Postmaster General that same year rebuked officials for their 'trivial and vexatious' arguments against better pay and conditions: 'the so-called "scientific frontier" proves to be no frontier at all, by the ease with which the landmarks are moved to different positions to suit the special end in view'. This was a newly confident and assertive voice, determined to launch a different era after all the setbacks since the late 1890s. There was bitter resentment against discriminatory practices such as the proliferation of 'special duties' for women clerks, a transparent device to pile extra demands on those in

---

Husband and Wife to arrange between themselves, and that the Post Office has no further concern than to see that its work is done. To this view we venture to demur'. (Meta Zimmeck, 'Jobs for the Girls: The Expansion of Clerical Work for Women, 1850–1914', in Angela V. John (eds.), *Unequal Opportunities: Women's Employment in England 1800–1918*, Basil Blackwell, 1986 p. 162.)

the second-class grade without having to pay them first-class rates. Women now wanted better wages, access to more-interesting work and the prospect of promotion to higher grades where their work merited it. (All three were already features of some private-sector workplaces, especially in banking and commerce, which for a decade past had been setting the pace in the employment of female office workers.) The Association of Post Office Women Clerks threw in its lot with a new Federation of Women Civil Servants in 1913. In evidence given to the Holt Committee some months later, one of the founders of the first women's trade union asserted their outlook in a memorable exchange:

> Chairman: In other words . . . so far as the clerical staff of the Post Office is concerned, there should be no distinction of sex at all?
> Miss Cale: Exactly.
> Chairman: You contemplate a Lady Secretary to the Post Office?
> Miss Cale: Yes, certainly; and a Lady Postmaster General eventually.
> (Laughter)
> Chairman: That really is your claim?
> Miss Cale: Yes, that is our ambition.[60]

On the eve of the war, the Postmaster General's Annual Report for 1913–14 recorded 60,659 women in the workforce – close to a quarter of the total, as in the late 1880s.[61] Non-established women – that is, those with either full-time or part-time positions that carried no entitlement to a pension – made up the majority of these, at 37,173, not least due to the assimilation of thousands of telephone operators after the takeover of the National Telephone Company in 1912. (The first operators had been teenage boys, but they were soon replaced in what quickly came to be seen as quintessentially women's work. A London training school set up for women operators in 1899 was the first of its kind anywhere in the world.[62]) This still left 23,486 women on the establishment payroll – split very roughly between Savings Bank staff on the one hand and counter/telegraphy clerks on the other, but also including about 3,500 first-grade clerks who represented no less than 40 per cent of the Post Office's entire clerical staff at this level. It must have seemed a decent platform from which to make bold predictions of the future – but the war, of course, was to open up new horizons in a way that even the bold Miss Cale could never have envisaged.

The last Annual Report to be signed off during the hostilities, for 1915–16, appeared nine months after the end of the financial year. It described a Post Office only just about managing to hold things together.

The lack of manpower was graphically illustrated: a storm in March 1916, reportedly the worst experienced in Britain since the founding of the telegraph service, had blown down 40,000 telegraph poles across the country. Repairs depended on an engineering staff that had been reduced by 50 per cent since 1914. Yet while resources had been severely cut back, the workload had gone on growing. Postmaster General Joseph Pease noted in his commentary for the 1915–16 report that the Department 'has been required to undertake new work on an extensive scale and to cope with phenomenal development in certain branches of its business'. He then recounted in matter-of-fact fashion the inevitable outcome. Under a deal struck between the Government and the country's trade unions in March 1915, the so-called Treasury Agreement, it had been decreed that skilled-job vacancies could be opened up to unskilled workers – which of course included women. Gender barriers inside the Post Office that had been treated as insuperable for years were suddenly set aside. Women were taken on as temporary workers in huge numbers: 2,000 of them by March 1915, then 22,000 by March 1916, rising to 35,000 by November. In the later stages of the war, the cumulative figure peaked at more than 53,000.[63] The number of male temporaries remained around 21,000 from start to finish.

Whether any of the new women employees were put to work re-planting telegraph poles is unclear – but they certainly took on a wider range of jobs than any official since Scudamore could have imagined possible. By November 1918, 20,700 were working as full-time or part-time postmen; another 17,700 were employed as Inland sorters, sorting clerks or non-qualified clerks in the telegraphy section.[64] All of these had been strictly men-only occupations in the pre-war world. (Women sorters had their own enclave in the Savings Bank, which was a different matter. They even had their own union, led by a lady called Miss Rose Smith-Rose.) There were 7,000 Girl Messengers under eighteen years old, hired 'purely as a war measure'; and hundreds more young women in their twenties worked on transporting mails between head offices and the railway stations. The new workforce made a big impression on the public and gave the newspapers a welcome source of light relief from the grim news elsewhere. As an editorial in the *Dundee Advertiser* exclaimed in August 1917, 'We like to see some slip of a girl, very official in her Post Office uniform, with white-topped cap jammed down over her eyes, sitting perched up on the high seat of a red mail van'.[65]

For women's leaders in the Post Office, the cardinal question was how far such banter reflected an essentially unchanged attitude towards the role of women in the service. So long as the fighting continued, no one could be confident of the answer. In quantitative terms, the war's impact on the Post Office had obviously been seismic. The recruitment of another 53,000 women, albeit in temporary roles, left the numbers of men and women in the Post Office by 1918 very close to parity, at around 114,000 of each.* This was not quite so sweeping as the shift within the civil service as a whole – where women went from 21 to 56 per cent of the total in four years, broadly in line with the rise in their importance to commercial occupations all across the economy – but appears even more startling, given the extent of manual labour in the postal service.[66] But the drastic overhaul of the workforce was far from certain to bring subtler changes of a *qualitative* kind in its wake. Contemplating an expanded role for women in the future, the Report of the 1912–14 MacDonnell Commission on the Civil Service had been in no doubt that any change 'should be quantitative rather than qualitative, [entailing] an increase in women's numbers but not in their penetration of the hierarchy'.[67] If the war were simply to fulfil this prediction in extreme form, the progress made by women might yet prove illusory.

Within the workplace, women continued to be treated with an extraordinary mixture of courtesy and condescension that to a modern eye looks infinitely closer to Victorian sensibilities than our own. They were eventually deemed capable of replacing men in labour-intensive activities like sorting. But more intellectually demanding positions, such as clerical posts in the Chief Engineer's Department, remained firmly closed to them. We might turn to the files of the Returned Letter Office, largely dependent on women, expecting to find some acknowledgement of the stressful place it must have been, as the casualties mounted appallingly. Instead, we discover male officials fretting endlessly over the risk of women 'Opening Officers' being exposed to obscene photographs in the mail. The rules insisted that letters and packages should only be opened by women who were married – the marriage bar having been suspended – and who were being supervised by men at very close quarters. As a hand-wringing minute noted in December 1915: 'The supervision should be as close as possible to ensure the transfer of objectionable articles etc to men as soon as the packets have been opened'.[68]

---

* Precise workforce numbers for the Post Office need always to be treated with caution. Figures drawn from different sources, primary as well as secondary, are rarely exactly aligned. Many grades (especially among part-time workers) are defined inconsistently, even within the same statistical series, compounding the innate complexity of the postal bureaucracy.

And it was always official policy that men who volunteered to fight were guaranteed their jobs when they returned. So, the question remained: would contemporary manners and government edicts between them leave enough space to satisfy at least some of those women's aspirations of 1914? Now a leading suffragist, Millicent Fawcett, the seventy-year-old widow of the blind Postmaster General, told the *War Illustrated* magazine in 1917 that '[women] have gained in dignity and self-reliance, and the country has found in their labour an asset which will not be neglected in the future as it has been in the past'.[69] The ink was scarcely dry on the Armistice papers before this brave prediction came to seem rather wide of the mark.

5. OLD SOLDIERS, NEW UNIONS

The Government asked the Post Office to begin planning for the return of demobilized men in the spring of 1918. It was estimated that perhaps 50,000–60,000 employees on active service, many of them now seriously disabled, would eventually want to return to their old workplace. And as one of the principal employers within the public sector, the Post Office would have to set a strong example in re-assimilating its own ex-servicemen and where possible taking on others with no previous experience. It was quickly apparent that the process was likely to be brutal, involving a swift ejection of the women temporaries taken on since 1915. Evelyn Murray and his senior colleagues in the Department had reasons of their own to feel torn over this 'substitution' policy, as it was soon dubbed. Women had in general proved themselves to be both dependable and significantly cheaper to employ. There was nothing new in that; but officials in their private post-war correspondence were also ready to acknowledge, as they had rarely been before 1914, that many women now depended on their Post Office earnings for their livelihood. Some came from families left almost destitute by the death or injury of male relations. And if they were dismissed from jobs they had done successfully for two or three years, it would take more than a measure of blind patriotism (as officials knew from experience) to suppose that ex-servicemen in their place would perform as well. It was going to be a desperate business.

The stark reality was that no one – least of all, officials in the public sector – could question the general sense of a crushing obligation to the ex-servicemen returning home. The assumption that women should step back to make way for them was practically universal. It was largely a matter of society's debt to those who had waged the war to end all wars. It was also, in part, a reassertion of basic attitudes: 'men's conception of women often remained precisely the same as it had been before the war ... Women themselves may have gained much from the experience of war work, but men's attitudes to them were another matter.'[70] Within months of the Armistice, substitution had swept hundreds of thousands of women out of the workforce. A government body, the Joint Substitution Board, led the way, resolutely backed up by a host of vigilant leagues and associations on behalf of the ex-serviceman. Those women reluctant to step aside found themselves bitterly attacked – 'degraded in the public press to the position of ruthless self-seekers depriving men and their dependants of a livelihood'.[71] With a shocking suddenness, the female 'saviours of the nation' were now liable to find themselves re-cast as 'bread snatchers' and 'bloodsuckers'. In these circumstances, there was scant room for Post Office officials to equivocate; nor were they minded to do so. Some postmasters around the country tried hard to cling on to their women staff, and certainly officials did what they could on the margin to lessen the anguish for women made redundant with just a week's notice. But the Secretary's Office drew up binding substitution arrangements with its customary thoroughness. Women working in segregated areas, or in buildings with no available space for new men's lavatories – a consideration, plainly, that cut both ways – were in general ruled to be irreplaceable. A few dozen others were deemed to be (just) eligible for competitive entry onto the established staff. But most of the rest, including virtually all of the temporary workers hired since 1915, would eventually fall foul of substitution. And where there might have been a case for weighing their claims to stay on, all debate was cut short by the standard pre-1914 creed – that wide swathes of postal work, from the walks to the sorting office, were ordained by nature as 'proper to men'.

Few demobbed servicemen actually reached England until well into 1919, but those presenting themselves to the Post Office were not kept waiting. The total number of temporary workers, of both genders, had already been cut from 74,000 to 47,000 by June 1919.[72] By the end of March 1920, the figure was down to 25,000: the workforce of temporary women had been reduced from 53,000 to just 14,000.[73] The number of temporary men had fallen from 21,000 to 11,000, of whom 7,600 were ex-servicemen. Confirming these latter totals in a memorandum towards the end of 1920, one of Murray's officials noted that the Post

Office had already hired almost 30,000 ex-servicemen since July 1919.[74] The pressure on St Martin's to do more was relentless. The National Ex-Servicemen's Union of Civil Servants wrote to the Postmaster General in December 1920, asking if all the ex-servicemen hired as temporary staff for the Christmas rush could be retained in the New Year at the expense of 'civilian' temporary workers, 'in view of the setting up of substitution machinery in your Department'.[75] The PMG demurred, but explained that other measures were forthcoming. Within the service, there was some impatience to get the job completed. 'It is true that we have been making a special effort to clear out our full time women and I have good hopes that by the end of this month there will not be many of them left', wrote the head of the London Postal Service to the Secretary's Office in January 1921, adding that civilian male post-men and porters would also have to go. 'That being so, why not make a present virtue of an impending necessity and tell us to give them all notice to quit?'[76] By March 1921, there were fewer than 2,500 tempor-ary women left. In August 1921, at the request of the Prime Minister, Lloyd George, a memorandum was prepared to summarize the impact of substitution on the Post Office to date. It recorded that 38,000 ex-servicemen had so far been taken aboard, no less than half of them disabled, lifting the total of ex-servicemen on the payroll to 90,000, 'which represents' more than half of the total male staff'.[77]

The long-term consequences for the Post Office included an un-mistakeable deterioration in the quality of its workforce, regularly remarked upon during the interwar years. Too many ex-servicemen – with or without post-traumatic stress disorder, itself as yet scarcely acknowledged – found it dispiritingly hard to adjust to the routines of civilian postal work. For women's leaders in the Post Office with aspira-tions to upgrade the status of the female workforce, the substitution policy was a disaster. By 1925, women were essentially back where they had started in 1914. They once again represented well short of 25 per cent of the postal workforce. Preparations for any future major war would start from a gender balance much the same as the one that had prevailed at the outset of the last one. Those women's jobs that remained were invariably to be found in the lowest strata of the workforce pyra-mid, and equal pay was still as remote a prospect as ever. Yet 'equal pay for equal work' had been adopted as a formal policy by the then twenty-year-old Trades Union Congress (TUC) in 1888. So where had the Post Office's trade union organizations been while the tumult of the post-war substitution was under way?

Looking hard in the opposite direction, one might say. The leaders of the postal unions were embarrassed (like the Labour Party) by the harsher aspects of substitution. The largest of the men's associations, to the credit of their leaders, had made an effort to distance themselves from the open – and invariably futile – hostility towards women workers that had been a prevalent feature of trade unionism in the pre-war era.* The Postmen's Federation (PF), led by the single most impressive officer among all the postal union staffs, George Stuart-Bunning, had taken the lead in opening up its membership to women. The PF had consistently objected to the way in which bonus awards had always been structured to yield smaller increments for women. In March 1918, the Federation even submitted a claim for temporary postwomen, as well as postmen, to receive the same pay as permanent male colleagues. (It was flatly rejected.) This enlightened approach had plenty of logic to recommend it. If the partial feminization of the postal workforce had been useful to the Treasury as a foil for organized (male) labour in the pre-war era, after all – as no one doubted was the case – it was a threat to the male unions only so long as women represented a source of cheap labour. In the wake of the Armistice, however, the cause of gender equality quickly slipped by the board.

Nor could there be any disguising the fact that, in the workplace, a return to the traditional demarcation lines between the sexes was going to be welcomed by many men. The main association journals had bristled with 'Intemperate Articles' (the name of the file in which officials collected them), voicing a keen animosity towards working women that appears to have been quite widely shared. It nettled establishment staff to hear the 'temps' – seven out of ten of them women – praised for their rapid mastery of tasks supposedly needing a long apprenticeship. Work genuinely requiring years of experience had in some instances been demystified to suit the newcomers. (In 1917, for example, London's postal sub-districts had been assigned numbers – as in 'SW6' for Fulham or 'E2' for Bethnal Green – so that uninitiated women sorters could more reliably allocate their mails to the correct districts.) In other cases, 'skilled' jobs had simply been refined as 'unskilled', in a process of 'dilution' that was much resented. 'It seems as if we are back again in the

---

* The associations thought of trying to block feminization, but lacked the power to do so. When it was announced in 1890 that all future Savings Bank vacancies would be reserved for women, the remaining male clerks went on strike. Their action collapsed within days and 240 of them were suspended from duty. Protest strikes after that were very rare, but the resentment lingered on. (Cohn, *Process of Occupational Sex-Typing*, pp. 155–6.)

Black Ages of Postal History', ran a January 1916 commentary in *The Post*, the house paper of the sorters' Fawcett Association. 'We are continually told that there is a war on, if representations are made to the "powers that be". But war or no war, the continual pin-pricks and annoyances of which the established staff are the victims cannot be justified.' The correspondence columns of *The Post*, in particular, printed a regular stream of complaining letters, some of them less than courteous in their descriptions of the offending party. One, signed by 'A Mere Man', prompted this indignant, and also poignant, reply:

> Is it chivalry and a striving to attain this ideal [of brotherhood] which prompts men to criticise unmercifully those who have come forward to take men's places in the sorting office? We girls do not pretend to fill those places, but we are at least fired with the longing to 'do our bit' and surely 'mere man' might be less hasty in his judgment of us. Is it the smiling faces of 'the little bits of fluff' to which he objects?
>
> Signed, ONE OF THE LITTLE BITS OF FLUFF[78]

It would be unfair, though, to portray the labour leaders' stance after the Armistice as simply pandering to the more benighted elements of the male workforce. They made more than a token effort to ameliorate the plight of the women: for example, urging that widows with children 'be treated in the same way as male civilian temporary staff'.[79] If the process of substitution was of relatively little concern to them, this reflected a degree of realism about what could be done – and the fact, above all, that the labour organizations were preoccupied with making a fresh start of their own. And they had other pressing issues to pursue – not least their opposition to the continued use by the Post Office of auxiliary workers as a primary means of coping with the peaks and troughs of the daily sorting cycle. Part-time jobs outside the service were hard to find in the post-war economy, and most auxiliaries had now to depend far more heavily on their postal earnings. The unions pressed for all to be taken onto the establishment, which the Post Office refused to do. (It would remain a bitterly contentious issue into the 1930s, and only after 1935 was it agreed in principle that sorting routines should be revised to allow eventually for the adoption of an entirely full-time staff.)

There were still almost as many separate federations and associations for the postal workforce in 1918 as there were infantry regiments in the British Army (sixty-three compared with seventy-four, respectively). There had been intermittent attempts throughout the war to negotiate amalgamations, and so bring postal workers into line with the single unions adopted by workers in other industries. (The railwaymen, for example, had merged many of their unions in 1913.) This had added another dimension to the politics of the National Joint Committee (NJC), led throughout the war by Stuart-Bunning of the Postmen's Federation. These were complicated enough already, as it struggled with its role as the main coordinating body in negotiations with the Secretary and his officials. Top of the NJC's agenda from the start had been a desperate need to protect the workforce from the ravages of inflation, which had ripped ahead since the very first months of the war. By its end, retail prices had more than doubled. Labour leaders at the Post Office never resorted to wartime strikes – though they threatened to do so on many occasions – and agreed to the award of (notionally temporary) bonuses rather than permanent wage rises. Six bonuses had been awarded between May 1915 and November 1918. They had trailed some way behind the cost of living at every point, resulting in a significant drop in real wages and an increasingly militant atmosphere within the Post Office through the second half of the war. On the other hand, some critical precedents had been established in the workforce's favour. The tortuous business of parliamentary inquiries was consigned to history: it was accepted from the outset that bonus details would be determined via direct negotiations between the workers' representatives and the Government. Even better, the War Cabinet decided at the end of 1916 to switch the Government's brief away from the Treasury to a new 'Conciliation and Arbitration Board' – where decisions that had been taking several months to extract were magically available within hours. Again, starting with the initial claim lodged by the NJC in 1915, it was tacitly agreed for the very first time that changes in the cost of living should be the primary benchmark heeded by both sides. And once the Arbitration Board started conferring back to labour leaders on the progress of their claims, wage bargaining had arrived in all but name.

This was not the only precursor of a profoundly changed approach to industrial relations in general. A government proposal had arisen in mid-1917 for serious unrest in the mines and factories of Britain to be addressed by Joint Industrial Councils, which would bring together representatives of management and the workforce with a more or less open agenda to discuss any issues dividing them. The civil service unions, seeing the councils as potentially beefed-up appeal boards, asked to be included in the scheme. This was flatly rejected by the Treasury. Stuart-Bunning then turned directly to the Liberal MP behind the idea, a Yorkshireman called J. H. Whitley, and recruited his support. By the end of the year, the Government was faced with little choice but to include the public sector in the experiment. Final approval for the 'Whitley Councils' was granted by the War Cabinet in July 1918 – and the Post Office, not for the last time in its history, found itself in the van of a bold stab at 'industrial democracy'.

The Whitley Councils involved having forums for discussion at local, regional and national levels. As soon as peace had been declared, the unions began the work of setting up committees and appointing chairmen. The Government, no longer quite so desperate to appease labour leaders, made a vain attempt to rein back on the whole project: an official report in March 1919 proposed that Whitley Councils should function in a strictly consultative role. But it was too late. Consultation was far short of what the unions had in mind and a rumpus ensued. At a celebrated meeting in London's Caxton Hall, in April 1919, a conference of union representatives succeeded in coercing the Chancellor of the Exchequer, Austen Chamberlain, into commissioning a second report. The committee charged with writing it was chaired by a Treasury mandarin, Sir John Ramsey, with the PF's Stuart-Bunning as his deputy. Two months later, the committee's report proposed setting up a National Council, with Departmental Councils and District Committees beneath it. Crucially, it recommended that decisions signed off by the National Council 'shall be reported to the Cabinet, and thereupon shall become operative'. The implications seemed ominous, not to say wholly unrealistic. The Cabinet and the Treasury, however, accepted Ramsey's advice that turning down his report was not an option. Rejection would leave the state, as he had put it rather alarmingly, 'embarked upon a sea of troubles far more stormy than we have had to navigate and we shall be in great danger and disaster'.[80]

Officials and staff representatives of the Post Office first sat down together under the auspices of their National Council on 2 September 1919. No fewer than 109 staff delegates (nine of them women, including Miss Rose Smith-Rose) turned up to represent the interests of the workforce. Facing them were just twenty of the most senior officials, led by the Secretary, Evelyn Murray, and the Postmaster General, Albert Illingworth. The conference began with a few blunt words from Illingworth, another Yorkshireman like Whitley and a businessman who had been elected as a Liberal MP in 1915. It was, he said, 'a very big experiment' – and if he could offer some advice for the future, it would be that they should begin with the small potatoes and edge their way gradually over time towards 'the higher, the more complicated and more important affairs'. The main item on the agenda for that day, a formal resolution for the establishment of their own Departmental Whitley Council, seemed straightforward enough. What followed, though, was a heated and often acrimonious three-hour debate that left even the ultra-cautious Illingworth sounding like a half-crazed visionary. The transcript of the occasion ran to forty-four pages.[81] We might paraphrase the early exchanges, to catch the flavour of many conferences to come:

> The SECRETARY: All we need now is a formal proposal for our Whitley Council.
> Mr POSTMAN: My association is pleased to propose one.
> Mr ENGINEER: My members belong to a technical industry that needs its own Council.
> Mr HEAD POSTMASTER: Impossible. If we agree to more than one, where might it end?
> Mr IRISH CLERK: Yes, indeed, we need our own separate Council for Ireland, too.
> The POSTMASTER GENERAL: I call on Mr Postman to withdraw his resolution.
> Mr POSTMAN: Unfortunately I have been given no power by my members to withdraw it.
> Mr ENGINEERING CLERK: We would not want to be any part of an Engineers' Council.
> The SECRETARY: Voting would be very awkward. The staff must speak with one voice.
> Mr ENGINEERING INSPECTOR: We are proud of our separateness and must stand alone.
> The POSTMASTER GENERAL: It seems there is no alternative but to have two Councils.
> Mr ENGINEERING CLERK: But my members would be left stranded between them!
> The POSTMASTER GENERAL: I am afraid this is not leading to harmony [sic].
> Mr ENGINEERING CLERK: I propose that my members should belong to both Councils.
> [*Conference briefly suspended for staff representatives' discussions.*]
> Mr POSTMAN: We have decided to accept the need for there to be two Councils.
> The POSTMASTER GENERAL: Thank you. So now we can proceed to the main business.

Mr ENGINEER: On behalf of my Federation, I think I ought . . . (Cries of 'No')

Mr IRISH CLERK: Shouldn't the next agenda item be our need for an Irish Council?

The SECRETARY: That must be for another occasion. And it looks an unlikely idea.

The POSTMASTER GENERAL: We must draft the constitution of the Main Council.

Mr POSTMAN: My members wish to be better represented on the drafting body . . .

[*A lengthy discussion follows, on the make-up of the drafting body for the constitution.*]

Somehow agreement was reached on a constitution by the end of 1919. Not surprisingly, it enshrined an ambiguity over the extent of the Councils' executive power. Would it be subject to government veto, or not? In paragraph 19 of the transcript, it was noted that decisions 'shall be arrived at by agreement between the two sides . . . and thereupon shall become operative'. But immediately preceding this bold assertion is the caveat that all decisions 'shall be without prejudice to . . . the overriding authority of Parliament and the responsibility of the Postmaster General . . .'[82]

Confident at first in their interpretation of the relevant wording, labour leaders were elated at the apparent prospect of joint control over the Post Office for its employees. In parallel with the drafting of the Council's constitution, the leading associations had in the meantime succeeded at last in pulling off a grand amalgamation: the Union of Post Office Workers (UPW) had come into being that September. At its core were the three largest unions – the Fawcett Association, the Postmen's Federation, and the Postal and Telegraph Clerks' Association. An assortment of smaller, London-based unions soon joined, and the process of amalgamation drew in other narrowly defined national associations behind them.* The outcome stopped well short of accounting for all of the sixty or so representative bodies in the Post Office. Several went their own way as the Post Office Engineering Union (POEU); more than twenty-five associations retained their independence – many of them on behalf of supervisory grades – and a scattering of other names

---

* The London unions included the London Postal Porters' Association, the Central London Postmen's Association, the Tube Staff Association and the London Postal Bagmen's Association.

held out for a separate existence, only to see their membership dwindle away over the next few years. But with 107,000 members in its inaugural year, the UPW immediately accounted for almost half the total workforce. Joint control of the Department was immediately listed as one of the new union's formal aims.[83] The first edition of the UPW's house newspaper, *The Post*, appeared on 3 January 1920 and carried a slightly breathless account of recent events from the union's first General Secretary. 'We have had a Postal Revolution', wrote J. W. Bowen, a member of the PF's executive council since 1906 and a former postman from Swansea. 'Its history will not be reported in the Annual Report of the Postmaster General, but we have had our bloodless revolution . . . and instead of jostling one another we are now better able to march forward in proper formation with the fullness of comradeship swelling in the breast.'[84]

Comradeship had been a little thin on the ground in recent months, with the eclipse of the National Joint Committee. It had been widely assumed for years that its leader, Stuart-Bunning, would in due course become General Secretary of any combined postal union to emerge. In 1918–19 he had been President of the TUC and one of the moving spirits behind the formation of the UPW. Yet a series of private quarrels with other union leaders over the summer of 1919 led Stuart-Bunning to resign all his positions, leaving the way open to Bowen.* Stuart-Bunning's exit seemed to do morale within the UPW no lasting harm, however, and by mid-January – when the NJC was finally disbanded – Bowen and his colleagues were leading the union in its first ever wage negotiation with the Government. A general claim had to be dealt with by the Treasury, while the Department's Whitley Council tackled the details of another cost-of-living bonus. Among Whitehall officials, alarm at the prospect of growing militancy in the workplace was all too evident. The union's leaders, by the same token, had to struggle to contain an ebullient mood among the rank and file: if ever there was a time for the workforce to take the upper hand, as many thought, this was it. Certainly the UPW had limited room to compromise, as a mass rally of

* These murky events prompted an unusual valedictory speech from Stuart-Bunning at the conference approving the UPW's constitution. He reminded delegates of an old Italian custom 'of inviting a man to dinner and poisoning him or stabbing him to get rid of him by some convenient means'. Then a glorious monument would be put up in his honour. 'Your vote of thanks reminds me of that custom'. The conference broke up in painful silence. (Quoted in Alan Clinton, *Post Office Workers: A Trade Union and Social History*, Allen & Unwin, 1984, p. 266.)

postal workers reminded the negotiators at the Albert Hall in April 1920. 'The size, militancy and enthusiasm of this assembly was remembered for more than a generation . . .', according to the union's historian.[85] The outcome, taking the general claim and the bonus together, was an increase in Post Office wages for most grades that was large enough to recoup their decline in real earnings over the war years.

The direct involvement of the Treasury was a first indication for many union activists that the initial euphoria over the Whitley Councils might have been misplaced. As the number of the Post Office's local Councils multiplied through the rest of 1920, so too did the activists' misgivings. These were compounded during the winter of 1920–21, as unemployment rose sharply and the Government showed a renewed determination to take a stand against union militancy. The possibility of a miners' strike, supported by the rail and transport unions of the so-called Triple Alliance, was faced down in April 1921. Meanwhile, officials within the Post Office had a new and compelling reason to take a stand of their own against the recent tide of events. In the formal accounts for 1919–20, signed off in February 1921, the annual wage bill had jumped by almost 40 per cent. The profit margin on traditional postal operations had dropped sharply, pulling net income down to £3.5m from £8.2m the previous year. At the same time, aggregate net losses in the Telegraph and Telephone departments had soared from £4.6m to £8.4m. For the first time in almost three centuries, the Post Office as a whole was deeply in deficit.

7

From *ancien régime* to modern age, 1921–39

This is the Night Mail crossing the border,
Bringing the cheque and the postal order,
Letters for the rich, letters for the poor,
The shop at the corner and the girl next door . . .
. . . Letters of thanks, letters from banks,
Letters of joy from girl and boy,
Receipted bills and invitations
To inspect new stock or visit relations,
And applications for situations, and timid lovers' declarations,
And gossip, gossip from all the nations . . .

From W. H. Auden, 'Night Mail' (1936)

I. THE BREAK WITH IRELAND

The most compelling impetus for change in the 1920s sprang at first less from any sense of financial emergency than from the imperatives of resolving a protracted political crisis. Albert Illingworth, just into his fifth year as an unusually long-serving Postmaster General, put his signature in January 1921 to an important letter to His Majesty's Chief Secretary in Dublin. The Home Rule Act, passed in 1920, had finally determined that there were to be two future governments for Ireland. The Postmaster General's letter set out the essential framework to govern a separation of 'Irish Services' from the British Post Office, and the transfer of responsibility for them – and for 17,000 post offices – to the new regimes in Dublin and Belfast. Since large areas in the far south of the country were now under martial law, with clashes between Republican forces and the Black and Tans of the paramilitary police growing more violent by the month, envisaging a smooth transition of any kind required at this point a certain detachment from reality. But then, the same had applied to many aspects of Post Office administration in Ireland since the surreal Monday morning in 1916 when the GPO headquarters in Dublin had become the centre of the Easter Rising.

The GPO building itself, halfway along Dublin's Sackville (now O'Connell) Street, was not unlike the Smirke building in St Martin's-le-Grand that had been demolished a few years earlier. Opened for business eleven years before St Martin's, in 1818, it was smaller but had its own majestic portico in Portland stone adorned with six giant pillars and three fine rooftop statues. Its grandeur made it a symbol of British rule in Ireland second only to Dublin Castle itself. This was appropriate, given the way in which the Irish Post Office had been largely administered (and heavily subsidized) by its British parent ever since the end of its brief era of independence in 1784–1831. The Secretary in 1916 was a forthright and well-respected 57-year-old veteran of the service called Arthur Norway, who had been in Dublin since 1912. When James Connolly, Patrick Pearse and their small force of armed Irish Volunteers stormed the recently renovated GPO that Easter Monday, Norway had left minutes earlier for the Castle and an appointment with the most senior civil servant resident in Ireland. This was Sir Matthew Nathan, the former Post Office Secretary with pronounced views on the status of women in the workplace. The two men did not get along – and the extraordinary events of the next seven days cast them in very different lights. The crisis left Nathan floundering; Norway responded to it with a clear-headed decisiveness that probably saved many lives.

The ground floor and public areas of the GPO building were quickly occupied, ransacked and made the backdrop for Pearse's immediate and historic proclamation of a republic. Curiously, the Volunteers failed to take instant control of the Telegraph Office upstairs: it was an hour or so before the last civilian staffers were courteously shepherded downstairs to the street and out of harm's way.[1] This suggests that the GPO was targeted more for its symbolic value than for its practical importance. Disastrously for the leaders of the Rising, they similarly made no attempt on that first day to capture or destroy the Post Office's wider communications network. A surrogate telegraph office was up and running by nightfall in a nearby railway station, and the Central Telephone Exchange remained in government hands. Able to coordinate their response, the military authorities arranged for a speedy despatch of soldiers into the city, after which the outcome was never in doubt. From the start of the Rising on 24 April until its final collapse on Sunday, 30

April, Dublin was a confused and dangerous place, with intermittently
heavy fighting that left hundreds dead in the streets. Norway presided
over the Post Office's response from his family's apartment in the
Royal Hibernian Hotel. (They had moved there the previous year, probably to leave behind a family home haunted by memories of Norway's
nineteen-year-old son, recently killed on the Western Front.) At several
key locations, postal employees were effectively besieged in their offices,
unable to come or go in safety, and with scant food or drink. Norway
sent round constant messages to keep up their morale. He also worked
hard to ensure that telephone and telegraph links were kept open for
the Army's use. Realizing the vulnerability of the Central Telephone
Exchange, he prevailed on Nathan to have the CTE building put under
a stronger armed guard. Meanwhile Nathan himself, desperate to play
down the gravity of what was happening, went on summoning Norway
from his hotel for a series of fatuous meetings at the Castle. As the latter
recalled in a vivid account of the week – written some ten years later but
amply corroborated by contemporaneous papers – this entailed 'some
personal risk, and much interruption, without any reason of real advantage'.[2] Nathan's primary concern, shared by many in government, seems
to have been to persuade the Post Office to resume its mail deliveries
immediately around the streets of the city, and Norway was repeatedly
pressed to issue orders accordingly. His categorical response to this left
no doubt as to his opinion of his former superior:

> The fact that the rebels were firing on any one who wore uniform, even the
> Fire Brigade, and that the postmen would certainly have been shot, was
> either unknown to [the Government], or treated as of no importance. To
> me it was the governing consideration. . . . I then wrote at once a short
> report to the effect that . . . my own observation led me to the conclusion
> that no such steps were practicable at the time, and that the lives of postmen
> would be in great danger if they appeared upon the streets. I therefore
> declined respectfully to order them to go out. I took this [report] myself to
> Sir Matthew Nathan, who received it ungraciously, not concealing his opin-
> ion that my attitude was obstructive. I had not, however, nor have I now,
> the least doubt that I was right.[3]

Norway showed the same strength of character and good judgement
in the immediate aftermath of the Rising. The general in command of
the British Army demanded the names of all those Post Office employees who had been swept up in the wholesale arrests made in the streets
during Easter Week and kept in detention. Reluctantly, Norway handed

over several lists that had been collated. He also stressed that, in all probability, many of those detained had had no association whatever with the Rising. He was assured no action would be taken without further consultation, but this quickly proved an empty promise:

> The next morning the lists were returned to me, marked in the General's own hand 'Dismiss', opposite some scores of names, or more, but without any indication of evidence justifying the sentences. I did not see my way to dismiss men and women without evidence. . . . The General was absent from Dublin, and the officers I saw could only say that in his absence nothing more could be done. 'You mean', I said, 'that I must at once dismiss these men?' 'Since military law is declared, you must indeed', was the reply. 'Well, gentlemen,' I said, 'the Post Office does not dismiss men without evidence that it is acting justly. I shall suspend these instructions. But I will go to London tonight, lay the matter before the Postmaster General, whose authority is supreme in his Department, and take his instructions.' . . . [The Postmaster General and Evelyn Murray the next day] approved what I had done and as the result of somewhat protracted negotiations, a small committee was sent to Dublin . . . and assumed the responsibility of indicating who were to be dismissed, – a number, I may add, considerably less than had been indicated by the General.[4]

In the meantime, once he was confident that employees were no longer at risk, Norway supervised the resumption of normal services. He was generous afterwards with his praise for the courage and resilience of many of his staff. He himself was also warmly complimented by the Army – notwithstanding the fracas over those lists of suspected Republicans – for his handling of postal operations in the days after the Rising. (Typical of his resourcefulness had been the commandeering of an armoured car for the distribution around Dublin's post offices of money to pay out Separation Allowances to the families of serving soldiers.) Many of Norway's superiors fared less well. Like the Irish Chief Secretary in London, Augustine Birrell, Nathan was asked to resign the following month and served out the rest of his career in backwater posts. Norway returned to St Martin's in 1917 and might have expected to serve at the highest levels for several more years had not increasing deafness forced him into early retirement.*

---

* Norway was also a part-time author, whose books included a history of the Post Office's packet service during the Napoleonic Wars, published in 1895 and recently reprinted, and a volume on Devon and Cornwall in the *Highways and Byways* series, published in 1898 and many times reprinted. His second son abandoned the family surname but inherited his father's literary bent, writing many best-selling novels under the nom de plume of Nevil Shute.

Another consequence of the Rising was the gutting of the GPO by British shellfire. But the front wall and portico survived, and it was decided to reconstruct the building – a process finally completed in 1929. Nor was any great damage done to the country's postal records, since most of them were stored at the main offices of the civil service in a building called the Custom House. If this was a lucky reprieve, the luck soon ran out once violence returned to the streets of Dublin in the crisis that engulfed Ireland after the war. In May 1921, as fighting between Republicans and British soldiers continued to escalate, the IRA burned down the Custom House and most of the early records of Irish postal history were lost. Those that survived were transferred to the Irish Public Records Office in the Four Courts building at the centre of the city. Sure enough, the IRA took possession of the Four Courts in 1922, triggering a bombardment by the Provisional Government which effectively marked the start of the Irish Civil War of 1922–3. At the end of June 1922, fires sparked a huge explosion in the Records Office, which had been used by the Republicans as an ammunition dump. This completed the destruction of the remaining postal records.

Or, at least, of those records held in Dublin. The Post Office archives in St Martin's, meanwhile, could still boast over 200 enormous volumes – all recording, in neat half-page columns of copperplate entries, the 140,650 minutes written in the Secretary's Office since 1831 in relation to papers from the Irish Post Office. The giant books, and over a hundred boxes of filed papers to which the minutes relate, still sit today in the archives of the BPMA in London, many of their leather spines flaking with age.[5] To scan the yards of shelving that bear these volumes – orphaned, as it were, by history – is to catch a sense of how shocking the break with Ireland must have seemed to many officials in 1921–2. Perhaps the idea of full Irish independence seemed a little unworldly, even after Illingworth's January 1921 letter. But the so-called Partition Treaty of December 1921 set a seal on the implementation of the Home Rule Act: the Irish Free State (and the six counties of Northern Ireland) would come fully into being a year later, on 6 December 1922. In the meantime, the 'Irish Provisional Government' had a Postmaster General of its own – one J. J. Walsh – but it possessed no forms, no postal stationery and, above all, no postage stamps. There was no option but for the nascent republic to turn to the GPO for help.

Initially it seemed likely that the GPO would run the Irish postal service for a further year, on an agency basis. But this raised an awkward question: would the GPO's senior man in Dublin report to London or to the contractor, Mr Walsh? For the Secretary, Evelyn Murray, the latter was simply unconscionable. Indeed, the whole notion of casting off the Irish Office seems to have taken him a while to grasp. When Walsh suggested within the first few weeks of taking office that the British should hand over new stamps overprinted with the words 'Irish Provisional Government' – and in Gaelic, too! – Murray wrote to a senior colleague expressing his dismay. The mere idea of overprinting British stamps as Walsh proposed showed how detached the Irish were from reality: '. . . the Irish Provisional Government or their representatives are apparently under the impression that they are actually in control of the Post Office at the present time'.[6] But Murray had to climb down four days later, on 8 February, when Walsh and an official Irish delegation visited London for talks. Under the guidance of the Colonial Office, the Secretary had to accept the overprinting proposal and the first 'Irish stamps' were issued on 17 February.*

Feelings between the British and Irish parties at these talks were less than fraternal. The Irish did not endear themselves by lodging a formal lawsuit against Westminster for a million pounds in damages as compensation for the destruction of the Dublin GPO in 1916. As bickering continued over the exact status of any British officials still in Dublin for the duration of 1922, the idea of the Post Office acting in an agency role until December was quietly abandoned. British control of the Irish department was brought to an end at midnight on 31 March. By then, Walsh had issued the first of Dublin's own weekly Postal Circulars, akin to the traditional bulletin from St Martin's. 'In its dealings with the Staff', declared the first issue, 'the administration will be guided solely by the interest of the service, and the extraneous considerations which have in the past been allowed to influence service decisions will no longer operate.' What exactly this meant was unclear. If it was implying happy days ahead for the lower ranks of the Irish bureaucracy, it was misleading: Walsh had just ordered a 5 per cent reduction in all wages, and by September would be grappling with a national postal strike over pay. If it was intended as a mild rebuke to the departing British officials, it was hubristic. As the foremost authority on the transition process has

---

* As this implies, British stamps had already been used in the provisional Free State for ten weeks since the Partition Treaty in December 1921, and they remained in use around Ireland for some weeks longer – giving rise to a category of postal anomalies much prized by modern collectors. Another such category relates back to the APO and FPO postmarks used by REPS sections stationed in Ireland from mid-1920, by which time there were 50,000 British troops based in the country – and precluded from using the Irish post.

written, Walsh and his colleagues were in no position to run an independent post office: 'for some time to come, for years in some cases, the British Post Office exercised a considerable influence on the Irish Post Office. In some instances, this virtually amounted to directing the policy of the Irish Post Office'.[7]

Superficially, the break was made quite cleanly. A financial settlement was reached between the two sides over outstanding balances in May 1922, and arrangements were quickly made for the introduction of Gaelic terms (starting with the replacement of 'Royal Mail' by 'An Post'). In time, all red pillar boxes and mail vans would be repainted green. Behind the scenes, it was a different matter – especially after fighting between the pro-Treaty Nationalists and the anti-Treaty Republicans lurched into open civil war. Attacks on rural post offices, in a country overwhelmingly dependent on money orders and postal orders for the transmission of cash, played havoc with the clearing systems. By May 1923, no fewer than 322 post offices had been attacked by Republican gunmen and almost a third of the Free State's post offices had had to suspend their money order services. To sustain the day-to-day administration of postal services, Dublin again had little choice but to call upon a continuing supply of printing materials, technical advice and even seconded personnel from London. It was an ironic outcome, given the target status of the GPO in 1916, but at least it ensured a practical approach to the reorganization of the Irish service required by the emergence of the Irish Free State.

2. STRUGGLING WITH A POOR CONNECTION

Other prospective reorganizations of the British Post Office were being examined with rather less urgency. As the upheavals of the world war subsided, some preoccupations of the pre-war Post Office gradually reasserted themselves. One unresolved issue stood out above all others: how best to manage the country's telephone service? In 1919–20, it had incurred a net loss of £4.7m which more than matched the profits of the postal service itself, plunging the whole of the Post Office deeply into the red. The introduction of higher telephone tariffs and a return to pre-war growth rates soon began to stem the losses. While this allayed the immediate financial crisis more quickly than many had expected, the prospect of faster growth led keen advocates of telephony's importance – including leading figures in the Federation of British Industry – to press their case harder: they wanted brilliant engineers and marketing men to be given their head to go for a speculative expansion of the national network. Officials within the Secretariat in St Martin's were far more wary. Indeed, alarmed at the cost of trying to meet even existing levels of demand, they insisted on proceeding like men caught in a minefield. It was a clash of attitudes that led inexorably to a debate over the size and structure of the Post Office itself – and eventually to another personalized battle over the Department's future, comparable in many ways with the historic feuds over the start of the penny post.

The gestation of the telephone service's nationalization, we should recall, had been a long and unhappy one. The state had curbed the earliest entrepreneurs where it should have encouraged them. It had then done everything possible to encourage competition when it should have been steering the industry smoothly towards a national monopoly; once the logic of a monopoly had become impossible to ignore, it had dithered for years over how best to arrange for it. Seldom in business history can there have been a starker illustration of the adage that some changes, like chasms, are best traversed with a single leap. Unsurprisingly, the industry finally embraced by the Post Office in 1912 was saddled with the consequences of years of under-investment.* In the immediate wake of nationalization, though, it was not the hardware but the intangibles of organization, personnel and accounting that needed the most urgent attention. An internal committee bravely questioned whether the traditional ways of the postal service were well-suited to the technology-driven needs of its new sister business. A radical notion that telephones might even be run as a completely separate function within the GPO – an approach which had actually been proposed by a House of Commons Select Committee as early as 1898 – was briefly explored by the committee. But faced with implacable objections from the Treasury, it was quickly ditched.[8] The implicit duplication of plant and personnel looked too burdensome. Instead, the committee endorsed a long-considered plan to give the Post Office's District Surveyors complete control over the branch managers of the old NTC. The Surveyors soon warmed to

---

* The National Telephone Company had failed, for example, to exploit a breakthrough pioneered in the US twenty years earlier by a former undertaker from Kansas City called Almon B. Strowger. He had invented a device that allowed calls to be connected automatically without the intermediation of a call operator. NTC employees – now re-badged as 'GPO engineers' – scurried to order the first 'Strowgers' in the months after the 1912 takeover.

the task of extending the postal bureaucracy in some challenging directions. As Glasgow's Surveyor reported back, a firmly hands-on approach was needed, given that 'many of the senior officers in the telephone service show a lack of experience of official methods and are inclined to be satisfied with a lower standard'.[9] By the summer of 1914, little had been achieved in terms of replacing obsolete plant, but a strong start had been made at bringing the managers of the Telephone business into line. Whether this was really what the fledgling business needed, very few senior officials stopped to ponder.

The world war accelerated some technologies, but left others by the wayside. Radio technology, like aeronautics, raced ahead. The telephone was neglected. While half the engineers in the Post Office were scooped up by the Army, investment in the domestic telephone network was effectively halted. Thus was the stage set for a tense post-war tussle between the frustrated expansionists in the industry, the pragmatists of St Martin's and the nay-sayers of the Treasury. Public anger over the poor management of the service was soon apparent. In the City and among the leading business associations, dismay over the telephone network's slow development prompted many to question whether nationalization had after all been such a sensible idea. Late in the day, the entrepreneurial limitations of a giant bureaucracy were now openly challenged. Meanwhile, officials privately rehearsed the reasoning for a cautious, not to say leisurely, approach. There was no proven evidence that a larger network would attract more subscribers. There was no possibility of extracting additional funds from the Treasury, where plans were being laid for steep cuts in public spending. And as for the notion of suddenly upgrading the status of engineers, that would risk destabilizing the whole elaborate edifice of employee grades on which the Post Office rested. It was a classic manifestation of what an American sociologist would describe, decades later, as the 'trained incapacity' of officials in large bureaucracies to adjust to altered circumstances.[10]

At least all could agree the priority had to be a rescue of the telephone service's finances. The Postmaster General ordered an internal reappraisal of tariff charges, which reported in June 1920. The Government then decided to ask a Select Committee under Sir Edward Coates to review the findings – and this opened the gates to a torrent of critical submissions from the public. A 'Special Correspondent' in *The Times* led the way with a series of articles in July 1920, based on '40 years' experience of telegraph and telephone work in many countries'. All were fiercely critical of the Post Office, and drew an official reply that autumn regaling readers with a host of technical reasons to set the Post Office on a par with the much admired American Bell Telephone System. This provoked a sequel to the July articles, under the headline 'Our Archaic Telephones: Post Office to Blame – A Policy of Drift and Muddle':

> The Post Office apologists would have us believe that they are going to do all sorts of things towards modernizing their plant and system after the war, when all construction is immensely more difficult, which they neglected to do before the war, when supplies and facilities were unlimited and the public demand for improved service was insistent. I say they cannot do it ... Under Post Office methods of administration the lost ground will never be made up; the Post Office will always be ... years behind the general industrial and social development of the country. Bureaucratic management can by no possibility make the progress that commercial management could make ...
>
> The Post Office telephone system has not a friend from Land's End to John O' Groats. ... [because] the Post Office has failed in its capacity of telephone authority, and no telephone user in the country has any other opinion. There are many square miles of houses in every big English city where a telephone, or perhaps two or more telephones, could be placed in every house. But nobody has been to those houses to tell the occupants how useful the telephone is; or advertised to them the advantages of the telephone service and its low cost or sent them pamphlets illustrating and describing the varied uses of the telephone ... [and] it never seems to occur to the Post Office that if A, G and H have each obtained a telephone, B, C, D, E and F occupying similar houses or running similar businesses, might be induced to become telephone customers also.[11]

The Coates Committee's report that followed, perhaps not surprisingly against this background chorus in the press, went well beyond its brief, to comment stringently on what it had heard:

> Your Committee consider, from the evidence which came before them, that in many instances there is undoubted ground for complaint. Considerable sections of the public are convinced that Government ownership [of the telephone service] of itself produces a sort of inertia fatal to any service which is dependent for its success on initiative and enterprise ... It is the view of your Committee that development on commercial lines, combined with economy and increased efficiency, may produce more favourable financial results ...[12]

The message was underlined by the resignation in 1921 of the telephone service's top official: A. J. O'Meara, the Engineer-in-Chief, walked out in protest at an organizational structure that treated technical experts like tradesmen. (It did not even allow O'Meara himself to report directly to the Secretary.) With attitudes hardening on both sides, the Government asked a second Select Committee to look more generally at the state of the service.

The Cecil Committee published its report in 1922, almost a year after starting work. It had plainly taken some time for the Committee members to come to terms with 'a marked practical divergence between the official views of the General Post Office on the one hand and the opinions of the public and the business community on the other . . .' What they heard from officials was that, on the whole, the existing organization of the telephone service within the GPO worked pretty well. But they sided in the end with those who thought otherwise. The conclusion was couched as courteously as possible, with deference shown to the skills of the Post Office hierarchy in all sorts of ways – and yet:

> Yet there is something wanting. No one acquainted with the evidence before your Committee can fail to be struck with the almost universal antagonism – often, it may be, unreasonable – manifested so widely and persistently against British telephone administration. . . . [In Scandinavia, Switzerland and the US, the public seemed well-disposed towards their telephone regimes and keen to be partners in a constant process of modernization.] In the British Isles this disposition is conspicuously absent. The public have little mind to help the Post Office, which we think unfortunate; the Post Office, on the other hand, have given some ground for saying that it appears to believe that the public was made for the Post Office, and not the Post Office for the public. It tends too much to a cast-iron application of regulations in an improper way . . .[13]

Here was an old refrain – we heard it in Parliament in 1859, for example – taken up in a new cause. The Cecil Committee's conclusion was bracing. The telephone and telegraph services should be merged and then decoupled from the Post Office altogether. At a local level, there seemed no point in preserving any role for the Surveyors who monitored the workings of the postal service: their position in regard to the district telephone managers appeared 'to be often that of a fifth wheel to the coach'. At Headquarters, meanwhile, the total lack of any telephony expertise (or indeed technical qualifications of any kind) within the

Secretariat suggested there was nothing to be gained from integration with the postal service. The newly separated department should report in parallel to the Postmaster General, 'who might be called the Minister of Communications, if preferred'. And the Committee only just stopped short of another, even more arresting recommendation. Though '[it] is not within our reference to consider the restoration of the telephone service to private enterprise, for which practically all US authorities claim advantages', it urged that the new Telephone Department be split into several distinct districts with their own accounts, so that comparisons could be made in due course of their relative performances.[14] A return to the private sector, it was clearly implied, might be a logical next step.

The response from the Post Office stopped a long way short of that. Two new directorships were set up, for the postal service on the one hand and for telephones and telegraphs on the other. (The first Director of Postal Services was Frederick Williamson, whom we encountered as the wartime head of REPS on the Home Front.) Both men reported to the Secretary, though, and their operations in the field remained closely intertwined within a single organization. The creation of the directorships at Headquarters meanwhile had the unintended consequence that they worsened a trend towards ever greater centralization, which was growing more difficult to manage with each passing year. The strain was telling at every level.

At Headquarters, staff numbers in the 1920s rose to 10,000 and beyond (excluding the head offices of the mail, telegraph and telephone operations for London). All-powerful were the eight administrative divisions of the Secretariat. The Postal Services, Inland Telegraphs, Overseas Telegraphs (including wireless services) and Telephones divisions were the four principal 'operational branches'. Alongside them were the support divisions. Three of these comprised what might today be grouped together as Human Resources: 'Establishments' managed the 'Manipulative' grades that made up most of the workforce; the 'Chief Clerk's Branch' handled the clerical ranks; and the 'Staff' branch was broadly responsible for administrative personnel. This left 'Buildings and Supplies', which had to work closely with other Whitehall departments, above all the Office of Works. The Secretariat also included an Investigative Branch which kept track (or tried to) of all theft and fraud. Below these eight administrative divisions were a dozen or so supporting departments. These included Traffic Inspection units, advising on the efficiency of the principal services, and relatively self-contained operations such as the Savings Bank and the Money Order Department. Also among them were the two hugely important departments that hostile critics thought worthy of a much higher billing in the overall scheme of things. One was the Engineer-in-Chief's Department. The other was the Accountant General's department, controlling all financial and accounting matters – or, at least, all those not retained by the Treasury. And the single most striking feature of this whole monumental head office, in all of its various divisions, was that its officials had to cope daily not just with policy issues but with executive decisions reaching down to the tiniest details. The prevailing culture remained, in essence, that of Rowland Hill's day, when an omniscient St Martin's coordinated a workforce swelling towards 40,000 people. Now the Post Office employed 230,000 – and the clerical routines remained largely unchanged. The only additional resources were carbon-copying and the typewriter. These quickened the flow of papers, but only added to their volume.

Nor was the state of the Post Office any happier away from the centre. The world of the traditional Surveyors was creaking badly. The august Surveyors still held sway over every aspect of the postal service outside London: at least in theory, they continued to audit and challenge everything from mail statistics and staffing requirements to transport logistics and the maintenance of postal properties. But in practice they were finding themselves increasingly deferring to expert advice from others. Or as two of them later expressed it, in a jointly authored history of the service, 'the routine of the [Surveyor's] household was governed more and more by prescribed procedure and periodical planning'.[15] Put more bluntly, the Surveyors were being squeezed from above and below. The growing technical demands on the service, the ubiquitous influence of the staff associations, the heightened scrutiny of its operations by the national press – all were curtailing, from above, the semi-autonomous status long enjoyed by the Surveyors within their own domains. The growth of the telephone network, meanwhile, was corroding their power from below. There were twenty-one of them in all, twelve in charge of large provincial districts and nine, known as Postmaster-Surveyors, in metropolitan areas based on the largest nine cities, excluding London. (The capital had its own structure, with separate functional hierarchies for mails, telephones and the telegraph.) Local telephone operations were run from day to day by twenty-eight 'District Managers', whose geographical distribution did not coincide with the Surveyors' districts, and who were not entirely comfortable being subordinated to colleagues with no technical training whatever. Many District Managers worked in close conjunction with the 490 Head Postmasters around the country, leaving the Surveyors to preside uneasily over their joint decisions. An added complication for the Surveyors – and for the District Managers, too – was that anything defined as 'engineering work' had to be handled by local staff who reported directly to the Engineer-in-Chief's Department in London. This led to endless complications: for example, over the installation of new or replacement equipment for telephone exchanges.

It was not just the demands of the telephone that were causing Surveyors a collective headache. The 'District Establishment' in the middle of the 1920s was losing much of its former straightforwardness. For a start, the network of HPOs – that is, head offices with their own sorting depots and usually a Crown office attached with counters – was gradually being consolidated. There had been more than 900 in the 1890s, but their numbers had declined to around 770 at the start of the First World War and had then dropped by a third to just over 500 by the early 1920s. (This included the loss of about seventy offices to the Post Office of the new Irish Free State.)[16] Many were downgraded to reduce costs, becoming 'salaried sub-offices', still with postal employees but losing their administrative responsibilities; some gave up their sorting activities and continued as counters-only branches; and about twenty were actually turned directly into 'scale payment' sub-offices. All this had to be watched over by the Surveyors. Meanwhile there were pressures in the other direction, to upgrade some of the 23,000 or so sub-offices run by self-employed sub-postmasters (or sub-postmistresses – many were run by women) under 'scale-payment' contracts that tied their remuneration to the volume of completed transactions, measured for the purpose as defined 'GPO units' of work. A few thousand of them were now important enough to have not just counters but their own sorting operations for local deliveries, too. The pre-war Hobhouse and Holt Committees had recommended that most sub-postmasters be converted to salaried employees, and the growth of larger sub-offices encouraged the unions to press harder for this to happen. The Post Office was understandably anxious about the cost implications: scale-payment contracts were not intended to mirror employee contracts, but to provide payments for postal business transacted, typically alongside other retail activities in a small shop. The conversion programme was stalled in many places, creating a sensitive backdrop for operational decisions over the routing of mails, the deployment of full-time staff, investment in new or leased premises and so on. Here again, Surveyors had no choice but to turn increasingly to Headquarters for guidance.

The need for a thoroughgoing scheme of reform was evident to many within the Post Office by the mid-1920s. Some scholars of the period have confessed surprise that none was forthcoming: '. . . the fact that the Post Office remained relatively immune from the assault [of critics] until the beginning of the 1930s is puzzling'.[17] In truth, there is no real mystery involved. In part, it must be attributed to a volatile political backdrop – with the arrival and departure of the first Labour government in 1924 – which saw Postmasters General come and go even more rapidly than usual: Illingworth finally moved on within weeks of the Cecil Committee's launch and was followed by six others in less than four years. But above all, one explanation seems inescapable. Even the largest organization takes its cue from those at the top. The Post Office owed its relative immutability in these years to the nature of its leadership, as personified by George Evelyn Pemberton Murray.

3. THE AUTOCRATIC RULE OF EVELYN MURRAY

Appointed Secretary in 1914 at the remarkably early age of thirty-four, Evelyn Murray had led the service through its wartime upheavals with a cool authority that belied his relative inexperience. A knighthood in 1919 confirmed the general image of him as his father's son – a patrician, destined for the highest honours in Whitehall, and in all likelihood another Permanent Secretary of the Treasury in the making. He installed a like-minded colleague, Edward Raven, as his deputy after the war and was not averse to a sensible delegation of tasks to his immediate associates. But Murray was an autocrat by nature, and the scope for a permanent official to wield enormous personal power within the Post Office was as evident now as in the Victorian era. Senior officials in St Martin's had never enjoyed the social kudos bestowed on their colleagues in the leading departments of Whitehall. Their great consolation was that, largely unhampered by politicians for whom postal affairs were usually a bore, they could run their own show. So the most senior men had potentially far more power than their grander Whitehall counterparts – over an organization that remained, as in the nineteenth century, one of the biggest in the country. As was occasionally noted by shrewd insiders, this made the Secretaryship of the Post Office arguably 'the most powerful position in the whole of the civil service'.[18] Even before the post-war growth of the telephone business, many had argued that the centralized and hierarchical institution of the Post Office made the scope of the Secretary's responsibilities simply too broad for one man, but this was not a view Murray himself shared. It was his own father who had commented in 1909 that 'things cannot go on as they are' – but Murray seemed determined to prove his father wrong. Many things would go on, in fact, *exactly* as they were. He had no more interest in decentralizing the Post Office than in heeding vulgar demands for a more commercial approach – as exemplified by the pleading of the telephone industry's salesmen.

He presided over the Department rather in the manner of the India Office running the affairs of the subcontinent – wholly undaunted by the size and complexity of his empire, and seemingly as remote from it. He almost never visited a post office or telephone exchange building, and generally went out of his way to avoid meeting staff in their workplace. An exception was made for GPO cable ships out at sea, which he liked to visit (in fair weather) for a few days each summer. The principal provincial officers of the service he met on just two occasions a year, when obliged to chair their six-monthly conferences. He was scarcely less aloof even within the confines of Headquarters at GPO North. Like his father, he set great store by the meticulous drafting of papers (Murray *père* in 1908 had famously refused to set aside paperwork in favour of oral briefings, as requested by a new Chancellor, David Lloyd George) but he was no respecter of office conventions. He would rarely turn up in the morning much before midday and preferred to work on important papers at home, which he did most nights until well into the small hours. He was more inclined to deal with others via a waspish minute than in face-to-face meetings, and rarely met with more than one other official at a time. If he disliked meetings, he loathed committees and had a dread of anything to do with external scrutiny – or, indeed, public relations of any kind. All discussions with the Treasury he dealt with single-handedly. A future senior official, Dudley Lumley, worked as his private secretary for five years from 1922, and penned in retirement an account of life in the Secretary's office. He admired Murray in many ways, but had to concede that working for him had often been an ordeal, especially at the start: '[It] could be a nerve-racking experience. He said very little as a rule, his instructions were laconic and he disliked going into explanations or answering any but the most essential questions.'[19]

Murray had no time for meddlesome outsiders, especially those wanting to revise the basic shape and standard practices of his Department – or of the telephone service within it. No doubt his attitude was largely a matter of his conservative temperament. We should also remember, though, that he had responsibility for a vast and complicated organization that had been shaken to the core by its wartime upheavals: restoring its equilibrium was Murray's priority. He believed the Post Office, like a giant clock, needed stability above all, coupled with expert attention to any loose workings. Another round of clumsy changes, coming on top of the massive shifts in the workforce since 1915, might disrupt its intricate rhythms beyond repair. Murray was supremely confident of his own administrative abilities – and justly so, in the view of most of those who worked closely beside him. Looking back from the vantage point of the late 1940s, Lumley thought the Post Office kept chaos at bay in the 1920s 'solely because of the immense administrative ability and experience which Murray brought to its management', with 'an almost uncanny gift for sifting the essential from the unimportant . . .'[20]

He was lucky, too, insofar as general price movements in the economy greatly strengthened his position. A return to profitability was achieved in 1922–3, largely as a result of higher telephone and telegraph tariffs and of a hike in the basic letter rate from $1\frac{1}{2}$d to 2d in 1920. The Royal Mail's letter deliveries were still the bedrock of the Department's finances, accounting for about 90 per cent of all revenues. When prices in the economy began falling sharply in 1922, the Treasury was quick to enforce a cut in the postal workers' cost-of-living bonus but sheltered Murray from pressure for a full return to penny postage. The compromise was a restoration of the $1\frac{1}{2}$d basic rate, which was enough to ensure a steady rise in profits through the next several years. (It was a replay, in effect, of the penny post's profitability in the second half of the nineteenth century, when long years of deflation made the basic letter rate increasingly lucrative.) Murray's Postmaster General from 1924 to 1929 was an amiable Tory placeman, Sir William Mitchell-Thomson, for whom the job represented the acme of a largely uneventful twenty-six years in the Commons. In practice, once he had presided over the recovery in the postal finances, Murray's authority within the Post Office was unassailable, and the initials 'GEM' on a document reigned much as had 'FF' a century earlier.

And just like Freeling, Murray was capable of steering through important projects with supreme efficiency. Bringing to bear those administrative gifts acknowledged by Lumley, for example, Murray oversaw a fundamental revision of the Post Office's circulation methods – a dimension of postal operations that caught the imagination of very few people outside the Department (or inside it, either, for that matter) but which made a huge difference to the daily working of the mails. Until the early 1920s, the Post Office had almost prided itself on not obliging the public to adopt any formal system of addressing mail at all. An Alphabetical Circulation Book of England in 1885 cited 1,300 destinations with their own postal services, most of them identifiable as the former stopping places of the Royal Mail's coaches, and these comprised the basic network. W. K. Mackenzie, a retired senior official who wrote a short history of postal circulation in 1972, thought the natural growth of the network and the addition of place-names in Scotland, Wales and Ireland might have lifted the total number of destinations nearer to 5,000 by the end of the century. The proliferation of minor destinations on the railway network by then ensured that many of these were far smaller than the post towns of the mail coach era. The complexity of the sorters' task was further compounded by the fact that many addresses omitted to mention anywhere cited in the Circulation Book at all: the last line of the address might comprise a small market town or even a village. 'Sorters had therefore to be able to identify addresses (often pretty vague) with place names in the Circulation Book and so sort the letters to the prescribed Office of Service. . . . It is difficult to imagine how sorters coped with unsystematic addressing . . . during the first decade of the twentieth century as business burgeoned due in part, at least, to the Jubilee concession of 1897 which gave [i.e. guaranteed] a delivery of letters to every house in the UK.'[21]

By the 1920s, this non-system was no longer sustainable. Murray presided over the transition to a new regime, based on a division of Britain – and, notwithstanding its independence, of Ireland too – into counties. By clustering together various smaller counties, a total was devised of forty-six county units. This was the magic number for the manual sorting of the mail: a sorter, standing at a specially designed horizontal wooden frame with forty-six bags suspended from it, could reach across to all forty-six without needing to leave his station. The frame – known as a 'drop-bag fitting', or DBF – was used for sorting parcels and letters already tied into 'county' bundles. (The letters would be sorted into

counties on the traditional vertical frame with forty-eight pigeon holes.)
Every county unit was assigned a county distributing office, which could
act as a clearing station for mails. The need for this system was succinctly explained by Murray himself in 1927, though he modestly gave
no hint there of just how novel it was:

> As every post office may have letters for every other post office, of which
> there are many thousands, it is obvious that a system relying entirely upon
> direct communication would be unworkable. Between large towns the
> correspondence can be, and usually is, transmitted in direct mails, but letters
> passing to and from the rural areas and smaller towns must be forwarded
> to some intermediate office which performs the functions of a clearing
> house. . . . For each county or group of counties, one or more central distrib-
> uting offices are selected which have a direct postal connection with all
> other offices in the same county or group. Letters from the smaller offices
> are dispatched from the office of posting to the most convenient county
> distributing centre and are then sorted and included in the mails dispatched
> by that office.[22]

This was the manual system that would be honed to something like perfection over the next thirty years. The county distributing offices were
backed up by seventeen 'general forwarding offices' – most of them
placed strategically at the biggest rail intersections like Crewe, Bristol
and York – and by smaller 'local forwarding offices', all of which played
their part by aggregating the small quantities of mail for one destination
from many posting places into a volume large enough to warrant at
least a daily delivery. The resulting network coordinated more than 500
Head Post Offices, sixty of them handling outward mail volumes in
excess of 100,000 items a day and those in each of several large provincial cities managing ten times that amount. The HPOs were
complemented by the TPOs, which acted in effect as mobile distributing offices. They were also backed up by the salaried sub-offices (and a
small number of scale-payment offices) with sorting operations under
postmasters who reported to a Head Postmaster. And maintaining the
clockwork reliability of this whole infrastructure were the 'Mail Standards'. These laid down the volume criteria to be used by every individual
post office in the direction of outward mail – specifying, for example,
how many letters were needed to justify according to any destination a
'Direct Bag' in the sorting process, as opposed to dropping them into a
'Residue Bag' that would go to a distributing office. On every Head
Postmaster's staff was a Mails Clerk, responsible for upholding the

Standards. Typically tweed-jacketed and pipe-smoking, with a row of pens along an inside pocket, individuals in this position were not renowned for their tolerance of ambiguity. Rules were rules, and the road to postal chaos was seen as paved with exceptions.

It would be facile to suggest that Murray used his ascendancy to stymie other, more conspicuous kinds of modernization; and it was hardly in his power to do so. The Army's use of motorized transport for the wartime mails was now emulated with a steady expansion in the use of Royal Mail vans, motorcycle combinations and motorbikes: there were hardly more than sixty being used in 1920, but over a thousand vans and more than 200 motorcycles were in operation by 1926.[23] A new telegram-transmission device was introduced in 1922, the 'teleprinter', which could at last replace the dot-dash transmitters of the Morse code era. (As well as removing the need for highly trained operators, it almost doubled the transmission rate, from 35 words to 65 words a minute.) And for its international business, the Post Office took up civil aviation for overseas mails and laid bold new plans for international communications via telephone and radio networks to supplement existing submarine cables. Murray himself played a critical role at many points. The choice of which hardware to buy in rolling out an automated-exchange telephone network across London determined the future of equipment manufacturing in Britain for decades to come: and it was the Secretary, in 1922, who effectively sealed the decision.[24]

Nevertheless, the hallmark of his Department's general approach remained a deep attachment to established routines. Where others clamoured for technical innovations to be adopted enthusiastically, Murray's inclination was always to seek a cautious accommodation. Thus, he watched over the expansion of motorized operations, but rejected any fundamental review of the Post Office's reliance on the railways for its parcel post. The proportion of parcels carried by road (at well under 10 per cent) stayed roughly the same into the 1930s, despite the potential of motorized vans and the onerous terms imposed by the rail companies. Teleprinters were adopted at a glacial pace: only 130 of them had been installed across the post offices network by 1927.[25] Murray acknowledged a future for airmail services, but pulled the Post Office back from making any long-term financial commitment to the sector. He had good reason to be cautious, as we shall see later, but this did not stop one leading proponent of civil aviation from publicly describing the GPO in 1930 as 'the blackest reactionary in all matters concerned with the air'.[26] Faced in 1923 with a political decision that the Post

Office should set up a publicity department, Murray responded in characteristic fashion. A first 'Intelligence Officer', one Bertie Chapman, was appointed. Murray ruled that Chapman could issue absolutely nothing to the press without his prior approval and then proceeded to ignore him. Chapman struggled on for three years, then to be replaced by a (not very senior) GPO clerk. Union officials of the UPW pressed the Secretary in July 1926 to say what further plans were in store for publicity: 'the Staff Side were not satisfied that the Department was doing sufficient to advertise its services or to defend itself against the various attacks made on it in the Press and elsewhere'.[27] (The use of 'Staff Side' and 'Official Side' for the workforce and the executive had passed into common usage throughout the Post Office since 1919.) Cornered on the topic again at the 1926 annual meeting of the main Whitley Council in December, Murray simply announced that he had nothing further to say on the matter.

He probably saw the unions' persistence as an impertinence. For the most part, he was more than content to leave relations with the trade unions to his deputy, Raven, who had worked at St Martin's since 1897, and who brought to bear the requisite mix of firmness and procrastination. The Whitley Councils were steadily reduced to talking shops after 1923 and achieved very little. When an official history of Whitleyism came to be written in the 1970s, one interviewee gave its author an account of Murray's behaviour:

> 'You can't really separate what happened [in the 1920s] from the attitude
> of the then Secretary of the Post Office, Sir Evelyn Murray, who was very . . .
> starchy, and, I think, regarded Whitley Councils as nonsense . . . There was
> a man who came from Stornoway or somewhere, . . . a representative of
> some Post Office union, who used to come down to the Whitley Council,
> spending a day and a half getting down and a day and a half getting back.
> And Evelyn Murray used to arrange that the Whitley Council never lasted
> more than thirty-five minutes. And there's a wicked story that he [once]
> came out of the meeting which he had . . . bulldozed through . . . and he
> turned to his secretary and said, "Was the man from Stornoway there this
> morning?"'[28]

Again, a reorganization of the administrative and clerical classes, supposedly accepted in 1920 and aimed at promoting more mobility within the Department, produced a new set of titles – including an 'Executive' class between the 'Administrative' and 'Clerical' grades – but no substantive change to the age-old pecking order. Official policy on the position of women in the Department remained much as it had been before 1914: that is to say, a gradually expanding role for women workers was encouraged on cost-saving grounds, while being kept within carefully demarcated lines to preserve their subordinate position. The marriage bar had been restored in 1919, with scarcely a second thought and certainly no objection from the UPW (which voted in favour of the bar in 1921). A Whitley sub-committee wrangled from 1923 to 1926 over a possible extension of jobs for women, only to issue a report declaring its view 'that the respective points of view of the Official and Staff sides of the Sub-Committee are irreconcilable and that there is no purpose to be served by prolonging the discussion'.[29] The male unions had demanded a pay-off, which Raven refused to concede. (Not until the mid-1930s were altered staffing arrangements finally pushed through on the Whitley committees.) Women were of course now welcome to apply to work in the administrative grades – but of 490 posts awarded via open competition between 1925 and 1939, only thirty-nine went to women.[30] As a prescient contributor to one of the in-house papers had bitterly warned her fellow women readers in 1921:

> You are square pegs, and all the holes are spherical;
> ... There are no posts for you but Lower Clerical ...[31]

For the Treasury, at least, the fruits of Murray's conservatism seemed entirely satisfactory. Having restored its profitability in 1922–3, the Post Office pushed its net income steadily higher through the rest of the decade: profits of £4.4m had more than doubled to £9.4m by 1929–30. (Telegraph and telephone losses, included in this net figure, varied within a range of about £1m to £1.5m each year.) Nor did the Government see any cause to doubt that the largest employer in the public sector, after all the disruptions of 1918–21, was restored to its former dependability. In the crisis over industrial wage levels in 1926, the Post Office (like the BBC) stood fast at the Government's side. As the General Strike loomed that spring, local Whitley Councils gave postal workforces an outlet for their feelings, but no real platform for action. Officials drew up a set of 'secret instructions' to deal with any militancy; union officers wrung their hands and anguished over what to do. In the event, given a promise that they would not be asked to blackleg any striking workers, the unions decided 'the best service our own members can render [to the TUC General Council] is by sticking to their job'.[32] (The officials' instructions remained a secret – except those that successfully laid on a fleet of charabancs in London to bring the Department's women into work from the rail-struck suburbs.)* The Postmaster General, Mitchell-Thomson, was confident enough of his department's reliability to accept an appointment by the Government as 'Chief Civil Commissioner' during the strike. It was a nominal post, but might have entailed serious responsibilities if civil order had broken down. The aftermath of the strike was a disaster for the unions' cause: the Trade Disputes and Trade Union Act of 1927 precluded unions in the civil service from having any link with the TUC, or indeed any political party.

Within a few months of the General Strike, Murray was happily absorbed in writing a short book, *The Post Office*, to set beside those of his Victorian predecessors.[33] Published in April 1927, his history and profile of the Department was elegantly balanced, beautifully written – and magisterial in its dismissal of the criticisms levelled by outsiders. Some might carp that it 'should be, but is not, organized on "business lines"'; or cavil over 'a far more centralised organisation than would be tolerated by a commercial company'; or even have the temerity to suggest 'some particular service, it may be telegraphs or telephones or wireless, should be divorced from the Post Office machine and administered by a wholly or partially distinct organisation'. But readers could be assured that all was for the best in the best of all postal departments, run by a Secretary 'who virtually holds a position equivalent, both in its administrative and executive aspects, to that of a general manager in a large commercial undertaking'.[34]

This was all a bit rich for those who had seen the recommendations of the Coates and Cecil Committees languish since 1922, and for whom the Post Office's handling of the telephone industry had been a constant source of frustration. Their complaints, until now usually quite broad-brush, began to focus specifically on the alleged shortcomings of the Post Office's management. Murray devoted a chapter of his book to the telephone industry, listing its achievements since 1919 with evident pride. Some later accounts of the industry's interwar era credited the

---

* An official memorandum on the GPO's experience of the General Strike described some of the problems encountered by these charabancs. 'Miss Pike, Telephonist, City Exchange, stated that about 6pm, while passing through the Bricklayers Arms neighbourhood (Old Kent Road), a mob endeavoured to rush the charabanc and turn the passengers out. They were prevented from doing so by the Police and the charabanc was diverted to another route. The charabanc following [next] … was pelted by a crowd of women with refuse (rotten fruit, tomato, potato). Miss Hume, Telephonist, City, was hit in the face with a piece of raw potato.' (Post 65/192.) While the subject of the memorandum was unusual, its flat tone, attention to staff positions and complete disregard for any distinction between the big picture and tiny details nicely caught a flavour of Post Office reports through the centuries.

Post Office with a skilful handling of its protectionist relationship with British telephone manufacturers.[35] But Murray's critics in business and the City bemoaned a timid approach, rejecting the argument that speculative investment would land the Post Office with idle plant, earning no income. (The Federation of British Industry wrote to the Secretary more than once, dismissing his fears. A month after publication of *The Post Office*, it sent another letter, copied to the Chancellor of the Exchequer, Winston Churchill: 'The Federation desires to make a further suggestion, that in order to stimulate demand, the General Post Office should adopt the ordinary commercial practice of advertising the advantages of the [telephone] service'.[36]) Both sides, though, were agreed that the subscription rate for new telephones across the country was disappointing. As Murray himself had to acknowledge in his book, 'Compared with Northern America, and even with the Scandinavian countries, telephonic development in Great Britain at present makes a poor show'.

The question was: how best to remedy this? The industry in 1924 had formed its own 'Telephone Development Association', devoted to beating every bush in sight for new customers. By the end of 1927, according to one eulogistic account of the Association's activities, the Post Office 'was being subjected to so much hustle and bustle, it was being so prodded and slapped and bumped that each morning in St Martin's-le-Grand they looked at their papers in terror to see what awful bomb the TDA had let off that day'.[37] Murray took a different line. Americans had gone for more telephones just as they had gone for more motor cars. It was partly a matter of national temperament, and partly a reflection of their higher income levels. There was little to be done on either count. Nor was there any point in the Post Office adopting optimistic projections of future growth, now being pushed forward by outsiders with little understanding of the Department's customary disciplines. Did Murray ever reflect on the way the arguments were echoing those distant battles over the prospective impact of uniform penny postage, at the end of the 1830s? The great debate over Rowland Hill's proposal was accorded a solitary paragraph in his book. Murray was growing increasingly exasperated, just like the irascible Colonel Maberly before him, with the critics of his day-to-day management who seemed intent on pursuing their own agenda for sweeping reforms of the Post Office. Certainly, it was not a parallel lost on some of his detractors, and one in particular would soon come to relish re-playing the role of That Man From Birmingham.

4. WOLMER AND THE RENEWAL OF
POSTAL REFORM

This would-be instigator of another watershed era for the Post Office
seems to have taken officials by surprise. Roundell Cecil Palmer – Viscount
Wolmer since 1895, when he was eight years old, and known to his
friends as 'Top' – was a Tory MP. He was just seven years younger than
Murray, and hailed from the same privileged background of the English aristocracy. Indeed, his pedigree was even loftier: his mother was a
daughter of Lord Salisbury, who had occupied 10 Downing Street
through most of Wolmer's childhood and adolescence. In January 1928,
he made a speech in a small village hall in his Aldershot constituency,
attacking the evils of socialism. Wolmer had had a reputation as a bit of
a political firebrand since his undergraduate days at Oxford. On this
snowy mid-January evening, he was moved to include in his category of
evils the state's ownership of the Post Office. 'I see the working of the
postal system as pure Socialism ... There is great difficulty in a State-
run department in finding the right man to control a great business
organization.' On several counts, he suggested, the service would be
better off in the private sector. This, given the Victorians' long debate
over the Department's encroachment on the business world, was not in
itself such a shocking observation. What made the speech especially
newsworthy – and worth Wolmer's drawing it to the advance attention
of the *Daily Express*, which ran it on their front page the next day – was
the fact that the speaker was the Assistant Postmaster General, a post he
had held since 1924.*

It was not an especially demanding role, with the rank of a Parliamentary Under Secretary, and for much of the time involved managing
business in the Commons. Until 1924, all but three recent PMGs had
coped without an Assistant. In fact, just prior to Wolmer's appointment,
Murray was asked whether he thought a deputy was really worth having. He suggested not, adding in a characteristic aside: 'I have been
constantly impressed with the difficulty of finding [each past Assistant

---

* In later years, Wolmer would brush aside his speech as a 'platitudinous utterance', but it
prompted a furore at Westminster and in the press. The Prime Minister, Stanley Baldwin,
was challenged in the Commons to repudiate Wolmer's remarks. He declined to do so, only
caustically observing of his younger colleague: 'It struck me that when he has attained years
of discretion, he will speak with that caution which characterizes every one of our utter-
ances' (*The Times*, 15 February 1928). Wolmer kept his job.

PMG] sufficient work to occupy him . . .'[38] No doubt one reason for this was that Murray drafted all parliamentary materials himself, with fastidious care – 'and it must be set down', as Lumley recalled, 'that he didn't at all relish it if the Minister made any alteration to his drafts . . .'[39] Explicit references to the relationship between Murray and Wolmer are hard to find in the postal records of their day – eloquent, perhaps, in itself – and they seem never to have corresponded directly with each other. But we can be sure relations were strained between them by the time Wolmer fired off his 1928 speech. He clearly intended it to be a shot over the Secretary's bow. The *Express* – always on the alert for a popular campaigning cause – obliged the next morning, with a feisty leader to accompany the front page story:

> Why is it that a Government Department can never make a success of a commercial enterprise? There are a dozen main reasons at least, but at the top of them we should put the fact that a Government office . . . has always to be thinking of politics and Parliament and questions in the House of Commons. How can an undertaking be successfully run . . . when initiative is frowned upon by the superior officials and playing for safety becomes the golden rule, when no one dares take any responsibility for fear of getting into trouble, and when decisions that in a private firm would be settled on the spot require weeks of correspondence and yards of red tape before they can finally be determined? That is a picture of the Post Office . . . and it explains the hash they make of every business they attempt.[40]

It was an extraordinary attack on a Department making record profits for the Treasury, and so far only the butt (in public, at least) of carefully modulated official strictures. The author of *The Post Office* sailed ahead; but, from this time on, the basic question posed by the Coates and Cecil Committees, over the extent of the Post Office's franchise, was back on the public agenda. Business lobbying groups, led by the Telephone Development Association, grew bolder by the month with their complaints that the Treasury's parsimony was strangling the growth of a potentially spectacular new industry – and leaving the Post Office with an impossible mission.[41]

A third parliamentary select committee report added its weight to their campaigning in March 1928. The Hardman Lever Committee, comprising three eminent industrialists, had spent its time looking not at the telephone service but the Inland Telegraph Office. It was not inspired by what it saw. The introduction of the sixpenny telegram in 1885 (via a private member's bill in the Commons and 'against the advice of the Government') had consigned the Office to thirty years of chronic insolvency. The basic charge had been doubled in 1920 to a shilling for a twelve-word telegram, plus a penny per extra word. This had halved the level of annual losses, but done nothing to alter the long-term outlook. Since the war, the spreading use of telephones had gone far to supersede the use of short-distance telegrams. Income earned on services for the press had also slipped away, with newspapers increasingly turning to their own private-line networks. It was generally assumed that annual deficits – running at around £1.5m in recent years – would continue indefinitely. The morale of those working in the Telegraph Office had slumped: the Hardman Lever Report noted an 'atmosphere of inertia'.[42] It refused to accept that telegrams were a lost cause. And while the Report had specific remedies to suggest – better marketing, tighter cost controls, more flexible staffing practices – it was the general premise underlying its recommendations that gave it a brief celebrity.

Any resurrection of the Inland Telegraph as a truly sustainable business, it suggested, would need to end the Telegraph's existence as a civil service department. The press seized on a paragraph indicating that staff costs might be cut by as much as 30 per cent 'on the assumption of a free hand as in a commercial enterprise'. What equally appalled the leaders of the unions, though, was an observation elsewhere that the lifetime job security of the civil service might be inappropriate for telegraph staff. 'It is generally admitted . . . that, by the time [a telegraphist] has reached 35, the monotony of the work, the mechanical nature of operating and the lack of incentive tend to produce slackness.' This remark coincided by chance with the retirement of the cohort of workers who had joined the Inland Telegraph at the age of twenty in the inaugural year of the sixpenny telegram; the implication that telegraphists might one day enjoy roughly the same career span as footballers was not well received. (The UPW declared, with its customary reserve, that 'a more outrageous document was never produced'.[43]) Perhaps to defray some of the predictable reaction, the Report stopped short of openly advocating a return of the Telegraph to the private sector. Instead, the Committee members contented themselves with noting that 'the complete fusion of the Telegraph, Cable, Wireless and Telephone Services might with advantage be explored'.

Explorers duly set off, both to Continental European countries and to North America, in search of edifying lessons for the future. A heavyweight Post Office delegation would tour the US for six weeks that autumn, under a future Director of Telegraphs and Telephones at the

Post Office, Leon Simon. It discovered, among other things, that neither of the two leading US telegraph companies allowed employees to belong to trade unions. This afforded them, noted the Simon group's report wistfully, 'the advantage of a considerable degree of elasticity in the handling of their staffs'.[44] In the meantime, rising public support for a return to penny postage prompted more comment than the shape of the Post Office. The Postmaster General, Mitchell-Thomson, tried to make light of the Hardman Lever Report when he spoke in July 1928 on the annual Post Office vote in the Commons, confirming its authorized spending levels. ('He had noticed during recent months an ever increasing tendency in the Press . . . to level attacks against members of the Post Office staff . . . [which] was both unjust and improper'.)[45] His most senior official, though, was making no such concessions to the prevailing mood. Murray roundly attributed the breakdown of the Whitley Councils around this time to the behaviour of the UPW's leaders. They responded with a fierce attack on the Secretary in an August edition of *The Post*. This earned a rebuke from *The Times*, which deplored their breach of the convention that permanent officials were beyond public criticism: 'it is a quite impossible deviation from the theory', proclaimed the paper's Civil Service correspondent with more passion than style, 'that a distinction should be made where, in the view of the critic, the permanent official is a headstrong person driving a weak and gentle-spirited Minister. This simply will not do'.[46]

Wolmer, meanwhile, kept his head down, amassing useful data on the performance of the Post Office for later reference.* There was not much a humble Assistant Postmaster General could do directly to reshape the future of the Department. Any worthwhile reform would require, he believed, an explicit mandate from the public, via a general election. But he could plan for the debate and find ways to promote it. As an election loomed in 1929, Wolmer wrote a private memorandum setting out his case for reform, and he sent copies of it to both the Postmaster General and the Prime Minister.[47] Neither of them offered him the faintest encouragement – and when campaigning began for the election of May 1929, it was not Baldwin's Conservatives but Lloyd George's Liberals who rallied to the cause. The Liberal manifesto was harshly critical of

---

* There was no shortage of data, with officials collecting postal statistics as avidly as ever. One survey, produced around this time, gave a breakdown of the Post Office's annual traffic. It comprised approximately 3 billion letters, 1.75 billion 'book packages', 450 million postcards, 165 million newspapers, 160 million parcels and 60 million registered packages. (*Posts and Postal Services*, by Frederick Williamson, Post 72/211.)

the Post Office, citing the now familiar charge that a civil service department was incompatible with the commercial needs of the Telephone
business. But arguments over the Post Office were a sideshow for an
electorate fearful of rapidly rising unemployment and still embittered
by the General Strike three years earlier. After the installation in June of
Ramsay MacDonald's second Labour government, Wolmer retreated to
his extensive family estate in Surrey to consider his next move.

At some point during the summer, Wolmer showed his reform memorandum to Geoffrey Dawson, the influential editor of *The Times*. It so
happened that, in joining the civil service after graduating from Oxford
in 1898, Dawson had spent a year employed in the Post Office. (He won
election to a fellowship at All Souls College while working at St Martin's, which probably hastened him on his way to the Colonial Office.)
Its future genuinely interested him, and Dawson agreed to throw his
newspaper's weight behind a campaign in favour of postal reform. The
outcome, in September 1929, was a series of three outspoken articles
'by Lord Wolmer MP' in consecutive editions of the paper.[48] The first set
down the case against the Post Office for mismanaging the telephone
system, leaving Britain ranked twelfth in the world in terms of telephones per 1,000 of the population and London ranked twenty-seventh
among cities. The second alleged various egregious examples of waste-
ful spending by the Post Office. Wolmer took the Post Office to task, for
example, for its management of the 'Mail Rail', a small-bore underground railway between the Eastern District Office in Whitechapel and
Paddington Station via six intermediary stops that had been completed
towards the end of 1927. It had cost almost twice as much as budgeted
at the time of its authorization in 1913, and was due to incur a loss of
more than £100,000 a year where an annual profit of £50,000 had been
forecast.* And the third of the three articles identified what Wolmer saw
as the root cause of the problem – namely, 'that the Post Office still
retains, roughly speaking, the organization it assumed about the year

---

* It was not until 1925, alleged Wolmer, that the Post Office had thought to consult anyone
from London Underground about the project. When independent experts were at last
engaged, in the final stages of construction, their findings were less than reassuring. 'The
tube was too small . . . ; the curves were too sharp, the stations were not designed for efficient mechanical handling, the wagons were obsolete and inefficient . . . and there was no
margin for [future] expansion'. Otherwise, it looked perfect – except that its failure to link
with more than two main railway terminals greatly reduced its lasting impact. (It was an
overly harsh assessment: the Mail Rail would run efficiently if expensively until 2003, as
part of the Post Office's London operations.)

1855'. It was a message driven home in a powerful leading article by Dawson himself that appeared on the first of the three mornings:

> [The staff of the Post Office], like their political chiefs for the time being, are the victims rather than the villains of a system that is still, as it were, emblazoned with the young Queen's head, with 'V.R.' and a date in the fifties, and survives into our own day as a ponderous and costly anachronism . . . The question provoked by the cost of the post, the exasperations of the telephone, and the decay of the telegraphs is not 'Is this Socialism?' but 'Is this the best that seventy years of industrial experience can do for our communications?' . . . The [later] nineteenth century [Post Office] was cheap and progressive and Rowland Hill's reforms had simplified the handling of mails. But as science more and more diversified the means of communication, . . . the machine began to labour and to declare its limitations . . . [Today] the failure of the Post Office is no more and no less than the failure of a Government Department to do work which, while it remains a Department, it cannot be organized to do with success.

Wolmer's signed articles, and their endorsement by *The Times*, at a stroke changed the nature of the debate over the Post Office. Through the 1920s, it had been about the compatibility of the Department and the telephone industry. Now it was about the constitution and culture of the Post Office as a whole. The Department's slow response over telephones had become the pretext for a general assault. The Labour government distanced itself from Wolmer's allegations within a week. They amounted to 'a bundle of half-truths, inaccuracies and political rancour', said the new Postmaster General, Hastings Lees-Smith (who combined being an MP and government minister with the post of Reader in Public Administration at the London School of Economics). Wolmer hit back fiercely in a letter to *The Times*: 'It is pathetic to see a new Postmaster General gaily don his blinkers and, without pausing to answer or investigate criticisms, conceive it to be his duty to repudiate with warmth the suggestion that an organization that was good enough for the time of Rowland Hill is not adequate for the 20th century'.[49] He acknowledged that a careful study would be needed into how best to replace the present Department. But there were 'a dozen different ways' to set about that task. The immediate priority was for all sides to agree on the nature of the challenge. 'Such a subject ought not to be a matter of party politics at all. The whole matter is essentially a business question, and should be considered purely as such.'

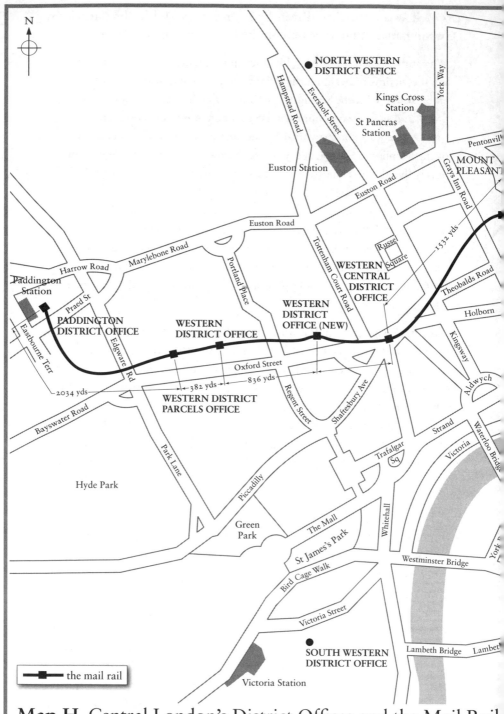

Map H. Central London's District Offices and the Mail Rail completed in 1927

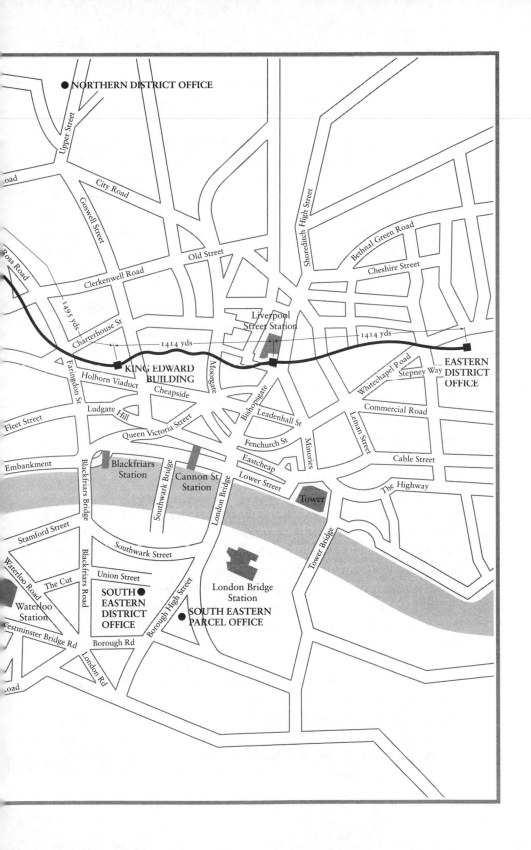

● NORTHERN DISTRICT OFFICE

Upper Street

City Road

Goswell Street

...oad

...oss Road

Clerkenwell Road

Old Street

Shoreditch High Street

Bethnal Green Road

Cheshire Street

Liverpool
Street Station

1495 yds

Charterhouse St

1414 yds

1414 yds

KING EDWARD
BUILDING

Moorgate

EASTERN
DISTRICT
OFFICE

Faringdon St

Holborn Viaduct

Cheapside

Bishopsgate

Whitechapel Road

Stepney Way

Fleet Street

Ludgate Hill

Leadenhall St

Commercial Road

Queen Victoria Street

Fenchurch St

Minories

Leman Street

Embankment

Blackfriars
Station

Southwark Bridge

Cannon St
Station

Eastcheap

Lower Street

Cable Street

The Highway

Blackfriars Bridge

London Bridge

Tower

Stamford Street

Southwark Street

London Bridge
Station

Tower Bridge

Waterloo Road

The Cut

Union Street

SOUTH ●
EASTERN
DISTRICT
OFFICE

Borough High Street

SOUTH EASTERN
PARCEL OFFICE ●

Waterloo
Station

Blackfriars Road

Westminster Bridge Rd

Borough Rd

London Rd

...oad

5. UNION OPPOSITION AND
COALITION POLITICS

Wolmer's stance was not unreasonable, but overlooked one of the most salient aspects of the organization's growth since Hill's day. It now had an enormous and comprehensively unionized workforce. Its largest union had sponsored six successful candidates for Parliament in the 1929 election, including the UPW's own Secretary Bill Bowen and his deputy, Walter Baker. Given the close alignment of the unions with the Labour government – and their dedication to goals that were antipathetic to a purely commercial approach – Wolmer's attitude was heroically optimistic. His articles helped prompt a debate in the House of Commons in February 1930 'as to whether it would be for the public advantage that all or any of [its] services should be transferred from the Post Office to an *ad hoc* public corporation and under what conditions'. The motion was swept aside by a heavy majority. With a Labour government in power, Post Office reform was a highly politicized subject, as Wolmer now came to accept. As he would later complain, '[under Labour] there was no hope of ever getting any reform of the Post Office, because the mere fact that it was a "nationalised industry" made it immaculate in the eyes of the average Labour MP ...'[50] While the Labour government had no interest in tackling Post Office reform *per se*, however, it had a radical agenda that soon impinged on the sheltered world of Murray and his colleagues. In October 1929, it appointed a Royal Commission under a distinguished judge, Lord Tomlin, to look into the structure and organization of the civil service. Murray and Edward Raven were invited to appear before it over two days in December. The impact of their oral and written evidence was to be far-reaching.

The December sessions began with some cool exchanges between the Secretary and the Commission members, notably a tough Labour MP, John Bromley, who had left school at the age of twelve in 1888 and had led one of the biggest railway trade unions, ASLEF, since 1914.[51] Bromley was incensed to discover that the Post Office was paying a scarcely subsistence-level wage to its lowest-paid employees and in particular its lowest-paid women, while officials' salaries were in a different league altogether. (Basic wages for those in the Manipulative grades generally equated to salaries of between £80 and £180 a year while male clerks in the Registry department of Headquarters earned £60 to £250 in 1929, with five women clerks there paid £60 to £180. Only a dozen or so

ANTHONY TROLLOPE
(From a drawing by Samuel Lawrence in the possession of Mrs. Anthony Trollope)

9. Four eminent Victorians. *Top left*: Anthony Trollope (1815–82), who joined as a clerk in 1834 and rose through the ranks as a Travelling Surveyor in Ireland, England and the Channel Islands to become an Assistant Secretary before resigning in 1867 to devote himself to his writing; (*top right*) Stanley Gibbons (1840–1913), whose stamp-trading business helped to establish a lively market for the bits of paper with a glutinous wash that no one had foreseen prior to 1840; (*below left*) Frank Scudamore (1823–84), who bent the rules in pursuit of his bold vision for a posts and telegraphy service, ending his days in a villa on the Bosphorus; (*below right*) Stevenson Arthur ('Beauty') Blackwood (1832–93), who embraced the notion of the Post Office as an institution with social as well as financial obligations, but saw professional trade unionists as Goths at the gates of Rome.

10. Three rural post offices of Edwardian East Anglia. *Top*: Aldeburgh, whose citizens twenty years earlier had subscribed funds for a bust of Henry Fawcett to be placed in their parish church. *Middle*: Wangford, a typical sub-office with a self-employed sub-postmaster receiving 'scale payments' for work done, and being paid a fee for his supervision of postmen who were fully employees of the Post Office. *Bottom*: The Crown Office at Woodbridge on George V's Coronation Day in 1911, with just the one horse but a proud force of cycling postmen, each covering up to twenty-six miles in a day. Bicycles had been introduced in 1900.

11. Postal life in London. *Above*: King Edward Building postmen setting out on their morning walks, *c.*1896, to deliver post around the EC district. As a badge of their distinctive status, London postmen would go on using bags thrown over their shoulders long after the rest of the country's postmen switched to the far more practical 'pouch'. *Below*: The indoor staff of London's South-East District Office, c.1900, comprising both clerical staff and postmen working at the primary sorting desks at the far end of the room.

12. Pre-1914 women's work. *Above*: The Post Office assimilated many thousands of female telephone operators who until 1912 had been employed by the National Telephone Company, boosting the total proportion of women in the workforce to around a quarter by 1914. *Below*: Women were also employed in large numbers – and as part of the Establishment workforce – as PO Savings Bank clerks. On the left is the main supervisor: as in the telephone exchanges, men filled most of the senior supervisory grades.

13. Inside the Home Depot. *Above*: The Christmas post of 1916 threatened to overwhelm the central sorting depot for the armed forces, specially assembled in Regent's Park a year earlier. Generally credited as the largest building ever made entirely of wood, it employed around 2,500 staff, including many soldiers tasked with shifting mountains of mail along half-lit passageways. *Below*: The Depot on Armistice Day 1918 (a banner in the distance on the right reads 'God Save the King') with sorting sections for Aden and Mesopotamia.

14. Breaking taboos on the Home Front. *Above*: Nowhere in the country allowed for the possibility of women postmen before 1914, but more than 20,000 were employed by the end of the First World War – with many towns, like Barnet, taking pride in their bicycling postwomen. *Below*: As the proportion of women in the postal workforce rose to a half, sights such as women drivers for horse-drawn post vans became familiar, attracting plenty of boisterous comment in the contemporary press.

15. Bringing comfort on the Western Front. *Above*: Letters being collected at a Field Post Office, the start of a journey by road back to a Divisional Railhead and thence by train to a Base Post Office near the Channel. *Below*: Letters from home ranked with food, leave and reliable clothing as the least dispensable features of the soldier's life. Handed a letter and an evening meal, it was said, no infantryman in the trenches ever ate before reading the letter.

16. From cockpit cargoes to lifeblood of the Empire. *Above*: Airmails to Europe in 1919–20 being loaded aboard an RAF De Havilland DH9 aircraft, almost certainly destined for Cologne and the British Army of Occupation in Germany. This was the precursor of the first commercial airmail service to Paris, launched in the autumn of 1919. *Below*: An airmail service to Australia being inaugurated by Postmaster General Kingsley Wood at a ceremony in 1934. He is standing in front of *Hengist*, one of the huge four-engine biplanes devoted to this and other long-distance airmail routes by Imperial Airways.

officials had a basic annual salary of £1,000; but many in senior positions received bonuses of several hundred a year, so Bromley's summary
of the pay disparities was broadly right.) He pressed Murray to agree
that, as a state employer, the Department ought to be setting a better
example. This Murray flatly refused to concede.* But the real business
lay elsewhere. The Commission's members responded with ill-concealed
bemusement to much of what they heard. They were evidently startled
to discover the total exclusion not just of women from the Administrative ranks of the Department, but of engineers and technical experts
too. A profound suspicion of all professional and technical qualifications had just been fingered as a critical weakness of Britain's ruling
elites, and a threat to economic progress, in the 1929 report of the Balfour Committee on Industry and Trade, which had been conducting its
investigations since 1924. There could scarcely have been a more vivid
illustration of the problem. The complexity of the pay structures, the
failure to see the supposed reorganization of 1920 through to a proper
implementation, the glacial progress in converting sub-postmasters into
salaried staff, the continuing separation of women's promotional opportunities from men's, the lack of respect for technical officers – the list of
topics that troubled the Commissioners was a long one. The Post Office,
delivering almost 6 billion letters a year, indeed seemed in too many
ways to be recognizably the institution left behind by Rowland Hill in
the 1860s, when deliveries had been running at around 600 million a
year. The evidence from the sessions was published in 1930, and attracted
widespread comment. The Secretary emerged looking more than ever a
figure from the past. Even Lumley concluded in his later memoir that
Murray 'was essentially of another era' – and the parallel between Murray and Freeling, apt for the 1920s, seems even more applicable in the
early 1930s. Public criticism of the Post Office began to depict it as a body
ill-suited to any technological innovation at all – an accusation hardly

---

* Bromley: 'Have you had perfect contentment, having regard to the exceeding steepness
with which the wages, salaries and bonus go up when you get beyond the rank and file?'
Murray: 'I have never found any case of perfect contentment with wages in the Post Office,
or elsewhere. I am not aware that the discontent in the Post Office is greater than elsewhere'. Bromley went on to accuse the Post Office of paying its lowest earners 'such wages
that they feel they cannot live in decency ... [and] are practically forced by financial difficulties into straying from the strict path of honesty ...' Would not better rates of pay, he
asked, allow the same volume of work to be done by a smaller but more productive and
enthusiastic workforce? 'I think that is highly improbable' was Murray's curt reply. (Minutes of evidence given by Murray and Raven to the Tomlin Commission, 12 December
1929, paras. 3669–99, Post 33/4451.)

warranted, but now credible to most observers. The conclusions drawn by the Tomlin Commission comprised only a short chapter of its Final Report on the civil service as a whole, published in July 1931. They were almost teasingly understated. But they set an official imprimatur on the campaigning by Wolmer and his allies since 1928 and left Post Office reform looking inevitable. Murray had spoken of a gradual delegation of responsibilities away from St Martin's, which he considered a marked feature of the decade just closing. The Commissioners took a contrary view, noting: 'we should expect to find a greater degree of decentralization than appears to exist at present . . .' Their report concluded that the time had come to review the Department's organization 'and whether the wide differences in its functions are sufficiently taken into account . . .'[52]

Publication of the Tomlin Report coincided with the mounting economic and political crisis that marked the summer of 1931. Four weeks later, Ramsay MacDonald resigned as Prime Minister, returning at the helm of a National Government coalition in September. There was no real prospect of a junior post for Wolmer, but the mood at Westminster was certainly receptive to the suggestion of a full-blooded Post Office review. After the election of October 1931 had reduced the Labour Party to just fifty-two MPs – sweeping away in the process all five MPs sponsored by the postal unions (Walter Baker having died in 1930) – the pace of events began to quicken. In his new role as head of the coalition, MacDonald largely ceded effective control of domestic politics to Stanley Baldwin and Neville Chamberlain. Appointed as Tory Party Chairman in 1930, Chamberlain had been attending closely for many months to the grassroots organization of the National Union of Conservative and Unionist Associations, working alongside the MP who had been his diligent parliamentary secretary throughout the 1924–9 government. This was Sir Kingsley Wood, a prominent City solicitor – he had written the textbook on the law of National Health Insurance – who had entered the Commons in 1918. Wood's most distinctive contribution to national politics to date had been his successful orchestration of proposals for a Ministry of Health after the war, for which he had been awarded his knighthood. But Chamberlain had formed a high regard for his political skills and grasp of what made organizations tick. Looking for a suitable promotion for him after the October 1931 election, he had Wood appointed Postmaster General.

The new head of the Post Office 'was a far from imposing personality: short, plump, and bespectacled. One experienced observer described him as an "appalling speaker" . . . [But] he was respected because he was efficient, and was generally liked because he was genial'.[53] Not all of his contemporaries were so generous: the fast political footwork that impressed friends often struck others as a devious pursuit of private ambition. 'He was more party-minded than any of his predecessors; both ears to the ground', as one of them put it.[54] Kingsley Wood turned out, though, to be the most influential politician at the Post Office since Henry Fawcett in the 1880s.* Energetic and hard-working, he lost no time getting to grips with the reform arguments – nor was Wolmer slow to reassert them. An abbreviated version of his confidential 1929 memorandum was published, in the *Lloyds Bank Monthly Review*, in the week of Wood's appointment. By the end of the month, Wolmer had drawn up a lengthy memorandum to the Prime Minister, petitioning for 'a thorough and impartial examination' of the Post Office in line with the Royal Commission's suggestion. He had also succeeded in getting fully 320 MPs in the newly elected House to sign it. The officials within St Martin's must have awaited Wood's reaction with trepidation. Characteristically, he looked first for a way to defuse any sense of confrontation. Curiously, perhaps, no one had yet shown Wolmer's 1929 memorandum to the Post Office's Secretary. Wood set this to rights early in December – no doubt as part of many briefing sessions – and Murray immediately assigned a working party to put the campaigner's arguments under the microscope. By Christmas, a forensic 64-page report was ready for the Postmaster General.[55] It must have been a challenge, finding so many ways to say 'wrong', but the authors rose to it. Having identified a list of forty key quotations, they examined each in turn with a less than festive spirit. They started with a mild reproof, accusing Wolmer of 'a peculiarly disingenuous attempt to compare [apples and oranges]'. Thereafter, the verdicts were unrelenting: '. . . pure prejudice . . . pure nonsense . . . quite incorrect . . . a mare's nest . . . inevitably fallacious . . . obviously nonsensical . . . entirely a misconception . . . very wide of the mark . . .' and so on to the end.

After years of mounting public concern over the Post Office, Wood was conscious of the urgency of finding some kind of resolution. In the event, he was to make the first half of 1932 a pivotal moment in the Department's history. His immediate reaction to the hatchet job by his officials was to look for some way of slowing down the reform bandwagon at

---

* As it happens, Wood married the daughter of another Henry Fawcett, an artist of some distinction.

Westminster before it could build up a dangerous momentum. In an unusual move for a government minister, he wrote an anonymous letter to *The Times*, signed 'OUTIS' (the Greek word for 'Nobody' that Odysseus adopted with the Cyclops), at the beginning of January, flagging eight tough questions 'to which any Committee of Enquiry would have to furnish answers'.[56] How was the Treasury to be persuaded, for example, to part with 'eight or nine millions of rather easily earned revenues'? How would Parliament be talked into surrendering control of 'a service which has so many points of contact with our everyday life'? If a new Post Office was to be run on commercial lines, what would happen to its non-profitable activities? And what would happen to the existing staff, with their present civil service perks?

This last question had already been exercising the staff associations for several weeks. Nine of their leaders, including the UPW's John Bowen and the long-serving Rose Smith-Rose for the Sorting Assistants, now led a deputation to Wood's office and handed him a bound copy of a booklet, *The Post Office: Control and Organisation*.[57] It was no less robust for being entirely predictable in its opposition to an inquiry, let alone any radical reorganization of the Department. Wolmer's memorandum had made no reference to the possibility of private ownership, never mind a sale to foreign interests, but the staff associations took a swing at both ideas anyway. 'We believe that the transfer of State services to direct or indirect foreign control, implied in the proposal, would be prejudicial to the national interests, and we regard this as a wrong approach to the problem of Post Office control and organisation.' The statement acknowledged that various Select Committees on the telephone service had expressed support for structural changes – 'usually quite outside their terms of reference' – but the public was being misled. All that was needed for the future success of the service, and of the Post Office in general, was a much heavier investment in advertising and public relations. Plus, of course, a continued appreciation of the loyalty and hard work of the staff, both so conveniently documented only a few years earlier in the Secretary's own book. The vilification of Murray in the summer of 1928 was forgotten, as the union leaders vied with each other to condone the autocratic ways of the Secretary as a practical necessity. Unions and officials were now at one in praise of the status quo at a great and inviolable institution, as Wolmer himself wryly remarked a couple of months later. The self-congratulatory tendency among union leaders, he thought, 'bears a family likeness to an attitude that has been noticed in other circles at St Martin's-le-Grand, and affords the industrial psychologist with an interesting example of a great idea penetrating a whole service from top to bottom'.[58]

Wood did not take long to make up his mind that the opposition to structural reform, among unions and officials alike, would land him in the middle of a bloody political battle if he adopted Wolmer's head-on approach. He was also persuaded that the Telegraph Office could not feasibly be detached from the postal service – both relied, in all rural offices, on the same counter staff – and that trying to separate the cable-sharing Telephone and Telegraph businesses would make no sense. (The industry itself had no problem with cable-sharing, but saw no reason why a separate telephone and telegraph business could not be run in parallel with the postal workforce. Telephone revenues were rising steadily, and it was not inconceivable that they might one day equal or even surpass the revenues of the postal service itself – see Appendix A, Chart 5.) Whatever else was required for the Post Office, Wood reckoned, there was no need of a Great Reform programme. While appeasing the defenders of the status quo, however, he had nonetheless decided that the endless criticism of the Post Office's culture was amply justified. Radical surgery might be too risky, but there was an irrefutable case for a severe change of lifestyle. This would still involve tackling fundamental aspects of the Department's operations, while offering a more practical way forward. Keen to pursue it, Wood turned his back on the debate over a change in the constitutional status of the Post Office, which he clearly feared might prove a huge distraction.

By the beginning of February 1932 he was ready to proceed. First, as expected, he announced a Committee of Enquiry. He gave it an ostensibly wide brief to investigate 'whether any change in the constitution, status or system of organization of the Post Office would be in the public interest'. Then he took great care in picking the chairman. The man he recommended was not someone he knew personally, but was a former Conservative Home Secretary and close friend of Baldwin's, William (now Lord) Bridgeman. He was also, as Wood must have been aware, a man much respected by Wolmer: the two of them had been active together in Church of England affairs for many years.* Bridgeman's

* Home Secretary in the 1922–4 Tory governments, Bridgeman had been First Lord of the Admiralty in Baldwin's 1924–9 Cabinet. He had retired from the Commons in 1929, but remained an influential figure at Westminster: his personal intervention in March 1931 was thought to have persuaded Baldwin to withdraw his resignation as the Conservative Party leader. After his death in 1935, Bridgeman's widow received a letter from Wolmer, saying that her husband had been 'all my political life the inspiration and example of the Christian

two colleagues would be Lord Plender, one of the City's leading accountants, and Sir John Cadman, a former university professor and now
Chairman of the Anglo-Persian Oil Company. This cast of players went
down badly with the Prime Minister. MacDonald regarded Bridgeman
as a 'stiff-necked die-hard' and sensed trouble ahead: '[he] feared that
the proposed membership might result in a recommendation to hand
the Post Office over to private control'. This would be 'a considerable
setback for the Government', stamping it as 'thoroughly reactionary' –
and in Cabinet it 'might give even more trouble than tariffs'.[59] Eventually
MacDonald's objections were overcome, and with hindsight we can see
he need not have worried. Bridgeman and his colleagues were hardly
supine individuals accustomed to taking orders, but Wood used all his
political wiles to find a way of squaring their independence with the
outcome he had in mind. Shortly before they began their work, he wrote
to the Committee members offering them a little guidance – or as he
amiably put it, 'I think it convenient that I should submit what I hope
may be regarded as certain relevant preliminary observations'.[60] In a
long private memorandum to the three men, he then proceeded to
anticipate the outcome of the Enquiry in a quite remarkable fashion.

   Practical and political considerations, Wood suggested, effectively
ruled out breaking up or reconstituting the Post Office:

> I am satisfied that any change under which the Post Office staff ceased to
> be Civil Servants and direct employees of the Government would be vigor-
> ously opposed by the Unions . . . Even if their opposition was ignored, . . .
> any board of Governors might well hesitate to assume control of a staff of
> 230,000 who were hostile to the transfer.

Assuming it was agreed that 'the problem to be dealt with must be
[assessed] in relation to the position as we find it', he was confident the
Enquiry would find plenty to keep it busy. It could look at improving
the internal organization of the Post Office, as Tomlin had urged. It
might consider ways to lighten the Treasury's grip on its budget, and it
could even think about diluting Parliament's supervisory role, by
strengthening the existing Advisory Committee (first set up by Illingworth's successor as Postmaster General, Frederick Kellaway, in 1921).
Any role for outsiders, though, would need to be very carefully defined,
or else – and here, at least, Wood gave a firm nod to the reformers – 'the

---

gentleman in politics' (Philip Williamson (ed.), *The Modernisation of Conservative Politics:
The Diaries and Letters of William Bridgeman 1904–35*, The Historians' Press, 1989, p. 9).

machine would be equipped with an additional brake, which it does not require, instead of an accelerator, which it does'.

6. THE BRIDGEMAN REPORT AND A QUIET COUP

Bridgeman and his colleagues took oral and written evidence between March and July 1932.[61] Their Enquiry started with separate appearances by Wolmer and Murray, who contradicted each other on virtually every point that was put to them. It was encouraged to be bold by the technical and engineering unions, and was warned against madcap reorganization schemes by virtually all the other staff associations. It was presented with a stream of alarming presentations by business lobbies, 'efficiency experts' and market research consultants – even Cuba's Havana, it learned, had a higher telephone density than London, as did every large city in Germany – and it was reassured by the officials of St Martin's that, in any comparison with other departments of the state, the Post Office was a paragon of good housekeeping. Meeting a remarkably short timetable it then delivered a report in August 1932 that, on all the critical issues, landed more or less exactly on the spot marked out by the Postmaster General in February. It even helped to minimize any risk of a confrontation with the staff, too, by heaping praise on many aspects of the Department, especially the postal service. Unsurprisingly 'much gratified', Wood declared 'few comparable organisations today . . . would wish for a more favourable verdict'.[62]

In reaching this favourable verdict, the Committee rejected some of the most interesting submissions it received. These focused, as expected, on various ways of distancing the Post Office from day-to-day political oversight of its executive activities. The front-runner since 1929 had been the idea of converting the Department – or rather, its post and telecommunication services – into a 'public utility corporation', much like a commercial company but with the Government as sole shareholder. In a powerful submission to the Enquiry in its first month, a former Labour Postmaster General argued for a different approach. Clement Attlee had held the post for six months, from March to September 1931. He had had some frustrating battles of his own with Parliament and the Treasury, but was nonetheless opposed to the idea of a public corporation. He thought the ideal solution might be an 'administrative agency', run by a semi-autonomous manager on a fixed term of office in place of a political minister (answerable, Attlee suggested, to the Ministry of Transport). If the Committee decided to retain the post of Postmaster General, the key would be to ensure that he presided over the Department as Chairman of a fully professional board, free of day-to-day interference from Whitehall. At all costs, the future relationship between the Post Office and politicians should preclude the need for any future Postmaster General 'to master the intricacies of the postal service at Little Pedlington or the reasons why his sixteen immediate predecessors have turned down Mr Smith's claim to a pension'.[63]

Attlee's views were broadly endorsed by another luminary whose link to the Post Office was still in place. This was the fearsome John Reith, Director General of the British Broadcasting Corporation, established in 1927. Originally formed five years earlier as a company, the BBC enjoyed a monopoly on broadcasting by courtesy of the Post Office, which in 1922 decided that it would be impractical to license transmissions by competing broadcasters. (All wireless transmissions needed a licence from the Post Office, under an Act of Parliament passed in 1904.) As the regulatory authority for wireless telegraphy, the Post Office had to ensure that Whitehall's allocation of wavelength bands always made sufficient provision for the BBC's needs; but its regulatory role extended little further than that. After the inauguration of the BBC as a corporation with a royal charter, however, the Postmaster General was given the task of answering for it in Parliament. This could entail his being called upon, one day, to account for aspects of broadcasting policy – a possibility that Reith, while nominally reporting to the PMG, was always determined to ensure remained strictly theoretical. Thus, while the Post Office regarded its tie to the BBC as a source of some prestige by 1932, it was openly resented by Reith himself. He was acutely sensitive to any suggestion of government interference – and this had prompted him occasionally to speak publicly about the governance of public services. Making a presentation to the Bridgeman Committee, Reith referred back to a paper he had given at a conference in January 1930 insisting on the critical importance, for any public service, of ensuring it was removed from (and protected against) political control. He parted company with Attlee in suggesting that the BBC's own status as a 'statutory corporation' did in fact offer a sensible role model for the Post Office: 'I consider a body, constituted much as the Broadcasting Corporation, to be suitable for the conduct of public services such as posts, telegraphs, pensions and insurance, power, transport and mines'.[64]

Inevitably, Wolmer was the stoutest advocate of a constitutional realignment for the Post Office. In a 22-page memorandum to the Enquiry in April, entitled *Constructive Proposals*, he wanted the postal, telegraph and telephone services to be reconstituted together in a 'new Post Office', leaving the administrative services (pensions, savings, licences and so on) to be run by the Treasury. They might even go further: 'It is perhaps just worth mentioning that the entire German Post Office, including the mails, were transferred to a non-political independent authority (the Deutsche Reichspost) in 1921 with, I believe, very good results'. He proposed that his born-again Post Office should at least resemble a public utility or the BBC in being able to stand apart from Whitehall. It would also have a share structure allowing it to turn to the public for additional equity capital one day, as well as providing for a profit-sharing scheme for all employees.[65] Wolmer attached great importance to profit-sharing, as he told the Bridgeman Committee in person when he appeared before them in July. (He was their final witness, as he had been their first.) Six weeks later, all his arguments appeared together in a substantial book, *Post Office Reform: Its Importance and Practicability*. In adopting Rowland Hill's 1837 title, Wolmer set out to show (at much greater length than the original) how his own proposals amounted to no less than a completion of the great Victorian's project. He believed Hill's business principles had lain neglected for sixty years. Separating the Post Office from the forces of Whitehall officialdom would allow it to resume the development of postal services launched by 'a commercial genius and a leader'.

The Bridgeman Committee Report appeared four days after the publication of Wolmer's book. As no doubt Kingsley Wood had intended, it was a document leaving him scope for very different interpretations. Its rejection of calls for a transfer of any services away from the Department and its gradualist approach to suggested innovations came as a bitter disappointment to many reformers. By the same token, these aspects of the Report seemed to encourage Murray and his senior colleagues – along with many union leaders – to think that Bridgeman's proposals would fade away as so many pious resolutions. (Murray's confidence on this score seemed apparent even before the end of the hearings. By the time of his own final evidence, at the end of June, he had risen above the fray and was dryly making fun of his adversaries. 'His main complaint about the Office of Works was that they were over-centralized . . .'[66]) But not all of the Report's objectives were couched in vague terms. Essentially endorsing all of Tomlin's observations about the excessive centralization of the Department and its failure to separate policy and executive decisions, it recommended nothing less than the abolition of the Secretary and his Secretariat. It suggested replacing them with a Board of senior men (including engineers) charged with the oversight of policy, while delegating the implementation of that policy to local officials, working under Regional Directors in place of the hallowed Surveyors. It urged a proper recognition of technical skills and an end to the existence of administration, finance and engineering functions across the country that seemed to be run in parallel, 'coordinated and focussed only at the top in the person of the Secretary and his Secretariat officers'. And it proposed a new relationship with the Treasury that might at least allow the Post Office a semblance of commercial independence.

Here was a programme that, with the right support behind it, could prove far-reaching. All would depend, as several lobby spokesmen pointed out, on whether the Postmaster General was ready to pursue the Report's proposals in the spirit with which they had been put forward. Wolmer, writing to *The Times* with his response at the end of August 1932, noted wryly that fulsome praise for the Post Office was 'perhaps a little difficult to reconcile with the drastic reforms recommended'. But he was determined to make the best of it. Bridgeman's proposals, if enacted, might go a long way towards meeting the reformers' objectives. The thrust of all the recommendations was thoroughly practical, but their implementation might nonetheless help to prepare the way, one day, for a new statutory authority. In the meantime – and the sting was kept for last – it was 'of vital importance that [Bridgeman's principles] should be applied by men who are whole-hearted supporters of the proposals, and not by those who are wedded to the *ancien régime*. On this we can, I feel sure, look to the present Postmaster-General to give us a square deal.'[67]

The Bridgeman Committee had stopped some way short of identifying the subservience of St Martin's to the Treasury as the source of all evil; in fact, there was 'no reason to assume that the ordinary departmental control exercised by the Treasury is unduly vexatious'. Nevertheless, its Report acknowledged that the Post Office's status as a revenue department opened the way to Parliament's questioning of any and all postal activities. It was 'the liability to such questioning [that] breeds a tendency to require documentary authority for every action taken' – and this in turn dictated the need for a heavily centralized culture. It was therefore proposed to give the Post Office a (tiny) measure of financial autonomy. Instead of handing over all net income to the

Treasury, it should in future make a fixed annual payment: this was initially assessed at £11.5m, which was setting the bar very high from the outset. Half of any surplus over this amount would be retained by St Martin's, in a 'Post Office Fund', to be spent (almost) at its own discretion. Wood took the proposal to the Cabinet in September. It was approved in principle, and a committee was set up to pursue the details. Reporting on its deliberations in May 1933, the Strohmenger Committee endorsed the plan, but made it subject to an amendment that would one day come to haunt the Post Office.* The Treasury and the Postmaster General, said the Report, 'have agreed to substitute for the Bridgeman formula an arrangement by which the Exchequer gives up its 50% interest [in the surplus] ... in return for the taking over by the Post Office of entire responsibility for the future growth in pension charges'.[68] It probably seemed a good idea at the time.

Since Murray and his Accountant General, Sir Henry Bunbury, were drafted onto this committee, the Postmaster General's intentions towards his most senior officials may not at first have appeared quite 'the square deal' that Wolmer had had in mind. This changed once the depth of Murray's opposition became clear. Over the next twelve months, the Secretary and his deputy mounted a rearguard action against the Bridgeman proposals that infuriated Wood. As conscientious officials, they prepared a series of reorganization plans at his request; but they also did everything possible to discourage and disparage the idea of regional directorates. Setting these up, as Raven put it privately to Murray in March 1933, would entail 'a hazardous experiment involving a large measure of dislocation and an immense amount of hardship to individuals'.[69] The Secretary had already revealed his attitude, in his inimitable way. Forwarding the reorganization options to Wood, he suggested 'the third [plan] probably approximates most clearly to what the Bridgeman Committee must be presumed to have had at the back of their minds. But prima facie, apart from the general upheaval, it looks as if it would add materially to our overhead charges and what quid pro quo it is to offer is not self-evident'.[70]

There was much more in the same vein throughout the first half of 1933. The decentralization of engineering responsibilities, in particular, the two men regarded as a recipe for disaster. Eventually Wood invited

---

* In view of the fact that current annual income was running a little under £11m, it was decided to reduce the fixed payment to £10.75m. But in the event of a year's income falling short of this, any accumulated surpluses were to be drawn upon, to make up the deficit.

the officials to submit their counter-proposals. This they did, with Murray confiding to his deputy that he was deeply sceptical about the whole business.[71] Had their objections been more widely aired, the two officials' views might ironically have strengthened the lobby calling for a complete separation of the postal and telephone services. As Murray told Raven, he had concluded that 'we are attempting an impossibility, and that the Bridgeman recommendations are based on incomplete knowledge and a misconception of the position . . . In general, my feeling is that the existing organization has justified itself on the whole by results and that it would be safer to mend it than to scrap it'. Forwarding their counter-proposals to Wood, Murray almost casually asserted that there was nothing fundamentally amiss, other than 'a certain lack of coordination between the Administrative and Engineering Staffs in the Provinces'. He and Raven were therefore in favour of a modest revision of current procedures, rather than any radical restructuring. They would retain the Surveyors and give them their own Boards (though 'any difference of opinion [on these Boards] would be referred to Headquarters by means of an agreed minute, setting forth both points of view . . .'). Murray seems genuinely to have expected that his edict would prevail, as it had done for nearly twenty years. 'In my opinion the main outlines of this scheme are a great improvement on the Bridgeman organization . . .'[72]

Wood did not agree. More than that, he decided the time had come for Sir Evelyn to be found a well-earned promotion. As Postmaster General, he was determined to rebuild the credibility of the Post Office – and to restore, if he could, some of the popular affection for it that had seeped away since the end of the war. Other initiatives were under way, and he could not afford to spend more time wrangling with his Secretary over Bridgeman's principles. Nor could he risk provoking a renewed campaign by the reformers, who were watching closely for any sign of a capitulation to those privately wedded (as Wolmer had put it) to the *ancien régime*. By November, Wood was announcing in public his intention to establish a new Post Office Board, and his readiness to act on Bridgeman's support for 'a radical change in the existing methods of staffing the more important administrative posts'.[73] In December, strong Westminster backing for his leadership of the Department was confirmed with his promotion to the Cabinet. Then, on 18 January 1934, it was announced in *The Times* that Sir Evelyn Murray had been appointed to the chairmanship of the Board of Customs and Excise, so returning to the department where he had served as a commissioner in 1912–14;

the same announcement confirmed that Edward Raven would be retiring in March. The two men were given a shared farewell dinner, but their exits were conspicuously low-key. On the day the news broke of their departure, a commentary on changes at the Post Office in *The Times* scarcely mentioned them at all.*

Far more interesting to outsiders than the demise of Murray and Raven was the confirmation of the first Director General. Bridgeman had heaped praise on the Post Office Savings Bank for its 'very high degree of enterprise' and the man who had been its Controller since 1930 (and its Deputy-Controller since 1924) was now given the top job. Donald Banks had joined the Post Office as a clerk in 1914 and had served with distinction on the Western Front for three years. The first Deputy-Director General was to be an Irishman, Thomas Gardiner, the son of an Irish Post Office Surveyor and the Controller of the London Postal Service since 1926. Their appointments, wrote the Civil Service Correspondent of *The Times*, 'are expected to have a great influence on the future administration of the Department ... [and] are fully in keeping with the forward policy which has been pursued by Sir Kingsley Wood since he became responsible for the Post Office'. Wood chaired the first meeting of the new, eleven-man Post Office Board on 17 April 1934. The tumbrels had rolled, and it was time to prepare for decisive action in the wake of the Bridgeman recommendations. A Committee on Metropolitan and Regional Organization was set up to adjudicate on the various plans prepared under Murray and Raven. The chairmanship was given to Gardiner, whose valuable understanding of provincial postal administration went back to his own early career as an Assistant Surveyor before the Great War. By the end of 1934, plans were approved for the setting up of regions that would be significantly larger than the existing Surveyors' districts. Each would have its own officials covering the full range of Departmental functions, and would assume as many as possible of the executive powers previously wielded by the centre. In

---

* The Customs and Excise chairmanship was to be Murray's last position. He died, aged sixty-seven, in 1947. Kingsley Wood's redirection of the Post Office also brought an effective end to Wolmer's involvement with its affairs, but the leader of the postal reform camp went on to a long and distinguished political career. A friend of Churchill's, he remained on the backbenches throughout the 1930s and joined the wartime coalition government in 1940. From 1942 to 1945 he was Minister of Economic Warfare, a convenient title for the political head of the Special Operations Executive charged by Churchill with fostering subversive activities in occupied Europe. Wolmer succeeded to his family title as the 3rd Earl of Selborne in 1942, took a prominent part in the politics of the Church of England after the war and died in 1971.

effect, this amounted to creating 'a number of Secretariats in miniature in the provinces', which was exactly what Murray had rejected in his August 1933 note.

Now that the time had come to plan them in detail, some officials must have wondered ruefully whether the old autocrat might not have been right all along: the complexity of the transformation was daunting. The Post Office by now was employing around 280,000 people and was once again the largest employer in the country. Its services were expanding, thanks to the telephone phenomenon, more rapidly than ever before. Never prone to reckless experiments, it responded to the challenge in time-honoured fashion by launching a thousand committees. Or, more precisely, it launched a Devolution Committee, which then spawned a host of sub-committees and working parties, and an entire Reorganization Branch – under Colonel Lidbury, another REPS veteran – to investigate every aspect of the project in minute detail. The resulting reports tumbled from desk to desk throughout 1935 and early 1936.[74] At last, in March 1936, the first two regions were inaugurated: Regional Directors in Edinburgh and Leeds took over all responsibility for Scotland and for the north-east of England respectively. Two years later, a London Postal Region emerged with Lidbury himself as its first Director, and a London Telecommunications Region alongside it. It would take two more years – and the onset of another world war – to hasten the regionalization process through to its conclusion, finally consigning the much revered Surveyors to history and rounding off the transformation instigated by Wood in 1931.

7. STEPHEN TALLENTS, PR AND THE GPO FILM UNIT

Fortunately for Wood and the Post Office alike, not all of his initiatives between 1931 and 1935 took so long to consummate. In weaning the Department away from Murray's loathing of public relations, in particular, Wood set it on a new trajectory that was to transform the popular perception of the Post Office within a surprisingly short time. The constant barracking from industry lobbyists was already beginning to coax officials into a less timid – and far more effective – approach to marketing telephones by the start of the decade. The change of heart in the years that followed went much further. It arrived just in time, reversing a strange state of affairs at the time of Wood's appointment. The

Post Office had been made highly profitable. It had embraced new technologies across the board, from motor vans and teleprinters to wireless radio and automated exchanges for local telephone networks. (Long-distance networks posed a bigger problem, the solution to which had notable consequences, as we shall see.) Yet as the crisis over the reform campaign showed, its achievements were little appreciated by the public at large. Despite all the praise heaped on the Department during the Great War, it seemed to have left far behind it the glory days of the late-Victorian era. And a low standing with customers left the Post Office open to critics, well-intentioned or otherwise, who could seriously embarrass the Government. Low morale among the workforce, meanwhile, incurred a future risk of industrial disruption, once the immediate fear of unemployment abated. After spending much of his first eighteen months coming to terms with the realities of the Post Office, Wood turned in 1933 to restoring its public image.

It would be misleading to suggest he did this in the manner of a modern, hyperactive minister keen to make his mark. Once he had confidence in his officials, he soon stepped back from the details. (Many years later, Donald Banks would give one of Wood's successors a colourful account of his boss's leisurely style: '[He] would come into the Office about twice a week when Parliament was sitting, for a glass of port at noon. All the minutes for him to sign would then be laid around a long table in his office and he would walk round and sign them one after the other, have another glass of port and then disappear'.[75]) This put a high premium, once he had decided to relaunch the long-derided Public Relations Department, on finding someone capable of leading it with real authority. Wood was looking for a suitable candidate when he heard that the Empire Marketing Board (EMB) was to be scrapped. Set up in 1926 to bolster closer ties, and thereby trading links, between all the bits of the globe still coloured in red, the EMB was no longer needed (said the Treasury) by 1933: the protectionism of the Great Depression was ushering in 'imperial preference' tariffs, which left the EMB surplus to requirements. But it had been an innovative body, led by a highly unusual civil servant, Sir Stephen Tallents.* Sometimes given credit as

---

* Severely wounded on the Western Front in 1915, Tallents had recovered to spend 1916–18 effectively in charge of food rationing under William Beveridge. He had worked as a British commissioner in the Baltic region for twenty-one months after the Armistice, lending Whitehall's support to the struggling new governments of the region. From 1921 to 1926, first in Dublin and then in Belfast, he had been working as a civil servant in Ireland – where he was 'perhaps in a career backwater' (*DNB*).

the man who coined the phrase 'public relations', he had been knighted in 1932 for tackling the promotion of the EMB with a missionary zeal almost worthy of John Reith at the BBC. Tallents was known to Wood because he had been put on to the Post Office Advisory Committee by Clement Attlee in 1931. Wood offered him the job of Public Relations Officer, starting in September 1933.

Picking up on some initiatives already mooted and instigating many of his own, Tallents masterminded a campaign aimed, as he put it himself a couple of years later, at 'creating in the public mind an interest in [the Department's] work, a conviction that it is actively trying to serve the public, a belief that it is more likely to be right than to be wrong, and a desire on the part of the public to cooperate with it . . .'[76] The influence he wielded within St Martin's, after Murray's departure, was extraordinary and went far beyond matters of simple presentation. It soon became second nature for the Board to take account of the publicity angle, in matters big and small. The decision to restore the sixpenny telegram in 1935, for example, owed much to a confident prediction that the telegraph service would benefit hugely from an association with the celebrations for George V's Silver Jubilee.* When the Board received a slightly quixotic proposal early in 1935 to provide roller skates for the staff handling priority telegrams on the third floor of the cavernous CTO building, it was earnestly noted that 'such a step might prove a stimulus to the staff and provide good publicity . . .'[77]

No doubt some of the most effective work done by Tallents, largely unremarked, went into softening the public face of the postal bureaucracy. Signs and symbols were updated, post office interiors were redesigned, stationery was redrafted. There was more than a semantic difference between, say, the terse, impersonal GPO letter of old to confirm a lost letter ('I have to inform you that the [letter] for which you enquire cannot, it is regretted, be found in this office') and the more polite, updated version introduced in 1935 ('With reference to your enquiry of the [date] I am sorry the [letter] cannot at present be traced').[78] A glossy new *Post Office Magazine* was launched for the staff and by May 1935 it had built a circulation of 172,000 copies. Popular brochures and guides were introduced for the customers, and at least one

---

* It paid off, with anniversary telegrams enjoying a huge popularity over the next five years. Forecasters had warned that the 1934 telegram traffic, of 35 million, would halve within seven years. Instead, it rose to 50 million by 1939 – lifting morale, though scarcely denting the telegraph deficit.

book was written for children. A trade publisher was found in 1934 for a sponsored title, *Peter in the Post Office* – a charmingly illustrated story about a young boy being given a tour on the back of a dolphin round the postal services of central London ('At Mount Pleasant Peter saw what looked like an ocean of parcels . . .').[79] Meanwhile, at the other end of the publishing spectrum, a series of 'Green Papers' was instigated, to describe the Department's latest progress in a more academic vein. The first, appearing in November 1933, provided an overview by Frederick Williamson, now the Director of Postal Services, of the growth of airmail services. But it was Tallents' work with luminaries of the arts world that most intrigued his contemporaries and left the Post Office with a lasting reputation for its publicity. To produce a series of eye-catching posters, Tallents not only assembled a team of distinguished young artists, but subjected their output to regular review by a group of advisers that included the art historian Kenneth Clark and the painter Clive Bell.

Above all, there was the work of the GPO Film Unit. Two years into his stint at the EMB, in 1928, Tallents had been persuaded by a gifted and uncompromising Scotsman, John Grierson, to set up a film-making unit. Grierson was fired with an ambition to turn out 'documentary' features about the working lives of ordinary people. Their relevance to the EMB's mission was not always obvious. Grierson's own most famous feature, *Drifters*, was a 1929 film about the harsh life of England's herring fishermen. Grierson's real passion, it might be argued, was to introduce the British upper and middle classes to the working class they hardly ever encountered outside the armed services. But Tallents had allowed, even encouraged, Grierson to take on appealing commissions wherever he could find them, as a way of financing the overall costs of the operation. Indeed, Tallents had used his influence within St Martin's, prior to his recruitment, to persuade the Post Office to commission a series of films from the EMB about telephones. Wood and Tallents were agreed in 1933 on the importance of keeping the film-makers together. Why not bring them to the Post Office? They came, and the EMB Film Unit became the GPO Film Unit.

The Unit was in the midst of making two feature films at the time of its transition: *Song of Ceylon*, for the Ceylon Tea Propaganda Board (which explains how the Post Office came to issue a film about Sri Lankan tea plantations) and *BBC: The Voice of Britain*, for John Reith's BBC. Tallents adopted the same policy as had applied at the EMB, and GPO films were made in later years about, for example, the mining industry (*Coal Face*, 1935) and the life of East Coast fishermen (*North Sea*, 1938). Still, even when its work was focused on Post Office subjects, there remains something slightly improbable about Grierson and his team. In its grubby offices in Soho and a studio in Blackheath, Grierson gathered around him a group of highly talented young contemporaries for whom the Unit served, in effect, as a singularly privileged film school. In the immediate wake of the first sound films, they pioneered the art of documentary film with innovative techniques that won them a niche in the history of the cinema. As the novelist J. B. Priestley put it, after working with them on the commentary of a film (*We Live in Two Worlds*, 1937): 'I liked the enthusiasm of these rather solemn young men in their high-necked sweaters. Most of them worked like demons for a few pounds a week, far less than some imported film stars were spending on their hair and finger nails . . . [But] if you wanted to see what sound and camera really could do, you had to see some little film sponsored by the Post Office'.[80] They flourished in the teeth of indifference or outright hostility from the commercial industry, in thrall to Hollywood. Distributors had little interest in their output, which stretched to more than thirty feature films between 1933 and 1939. 'In the vast majority of cases, outside of exhibitions, professional groups, film societies and schools, GPO films merely provided cheap padding for programmes built round the latest offerings from Gracie Fields or George Formby.'[81] There were more mundane obstacles nearer to home, too. Politicians suspicious of the film-makers' generally left-wing convictions had them trailed by the Special Branch, and a perplexed Treasury baulked at any spending on films unrelated to the Post Office – the Accountant General's office in St Martin's was ever hovering in the background, to check that (always tight) budgets were met on time. But given robust protection from Tallents, and Wood behind him, these obstacles and a constant stream of technical difficulties were overcome with impressive ingenuity and the occasional flash of genius.

It never flashed to better effect than in 1935–6, when Grierson set one of his directors, Harry Watt, to make a film about the backbone of the Post Office's national rail network – the Travelling Post Offices known as the 'Up and Down Specials' running nightly between London Euston and Aberdeen, via Birmingham, Crewe and Glasgow. The result was *Night Mail*, a 24-minute feature tracking the progress of one of the TPO trains heading northwards, via Crewe station, where mails from all over the country were collected and redirected in a nightly miracle of precision timing. After a typically chaotic schedule of filming and editing, Grierson was shown the first rough assembly of the film. 'There's something missing', he told his anxious younger colleagues. 'What we haven't got here is anything about the people who're going to get the letters. We've only had the machinery of getting letters from one point to the other. What about the people who write them and the people who get them?'[82] For some months, the Unit had had on its staff a young crew member already building a reputation as an accomplished poet. Grierson and Watt (whose arm needed twisting) turned to W. H. Auden and asked him to write some verse for the closing section of the film. One of the editors recalled Auden's work space:

> ... at the back, running parallel to the theatre at 21 Soho Square, there was a narrow passage, and we were provided by the Post Office at that time with Post Office messenger boys. They used to wear little pillbox hats, and they were fourteen-, fifteen-year-old Cockney kids, wild as hell, and they made their tea and whistled and played cards up at one end. The only place we could find for Auden was at the other end of this passage – say, twenty yards from them. There, on that old Post Office table, he wrote the most beautiful verse.[83]

The finished text of *Night Mail* was to become one of the most popular poems written in the twentieth century. Auden provided the perfect narrative commentary for the train's arrival north of the border, while at the same time putting Grierson's 'people who're going to get the letters' at the centre of the story – and speaking of their lives in a voice far removed from the bland assertions of any marketing department:

> Asleep in working Glasgow, asleep in well-set Edinburgh,
> Asleep in granite Aberdeen,
> They continue their dreams;
> And shall wake soon and long for letters,
> And none will hear the postman's knock
> Without a quickening of the heart,
> For who can bear to feel himself forgotten?

After it had been set to music by another of Grierson's young protégés – the 23-year-old Benjamin Britten, brought onto the payroll at the same time as Auden – the poem helped ensure the film a celebrity that has far outshone that of most of the Unit's other titles.*

---

* For many film buffs, the celebrity of *Night Mail* has attached to the GPO Film Unit as a whole. But even its keenest admirers tend to rate the Unit's historical significance a little

By the mid-thirties, the impact of the fresh approach to publicity was already apparent. It was as though, having seen off the restructuring ideas of the reform camp, the Post Office was intent on demonstrating that a state-owned business could, after all, deliver what the public wanted, and indeed more than it expected. In large measure, it succeeded. Nor was its revival just a matter of a much enhanced public image: the finances were improving, too. Telephone profits went from roughly breakeven in 1929–30 to £2.1m in 1934–5, and annual telegram losses were running at well under a million by the middle of the decade. Total net income was running at about £12m a year. Before the end of its second year, the new Post Office Board was having to contend with an unanticipated but very welcome problem. As the minutes of its January 1936 meeting recorded, it 'considered the position created by the continued growth of the Post Office Fund, which if not checked might prove embarrassing both politically and in connection with wage negotiations . . .' Board members agreed that 'the tendency of the Fund to become excessive must be watched . . .'[84] In contrast with the burden that it had too often seemed to be in the 1920s, by the later 1930s the fast-expanding telephone service was a source of considerable pride. Underground cables had comprised only a quarter of the 'trunk circuit' telephone network in 1914, the rest depending on overhead wires that crossed some urban landscapes in huge profusion. By 1936, 85 per cent of the network was underground, with about 2.8m miles of single wire safely laid in cables.[85] Now, though, telephony was only one of many impressive services. Such was its progress in the thirties that people talked of a 'new Post Office'. As early as December 1934, the Parliamentary Correspondent of *The Times* was congratulating the Post Office on 'the orderly development of a great State department on bold and progressive lines to meet the needs of our time'. No department enjoyed a higher reputation with the public, he believed, 'and the reason is not far to seek in the considerable transformation of its outlook and methods'.[86] The plaudits piled up over the next few years, in stark contrast with so much of the public commentary that had preceded Wood's arrival. As another national newspaper put it in 1938: 'The praise of the

---

ahead of the watchability, today, of most of its films. Ironically, Auden himself expressed severe reservations, after quitting rather abruptly as soon as the work on *Night Mail* was completed: '[The documentary school's] puritanical attitude to reality and entertainment has resulted in films which have many excellent qualities, but to the ordinary film-goer were finally and fatally dull' (quoted in Scott Anthony, *Night Mail*, British Film Institute, 2007, p. 67).

Post Office is nowadays in everybody's mouth; its efficiency, its enterprise, its alertness and responsiveness, its courtesy and humanity'.[87]

There was certainly an openness to new ideas, evident in some
surprising ways. Architects at the Office of Works, for example, were
emboldened to chance their arm with one or two modernist designs that
abandoned the neo-Georgian style ('Post Office Georgian' as it was
known in the profession) otherwise almost invariably adopted for new
post offices since 1919. A flat-roofed, round-cornered two-storey building appeared first in 1936, at Penarth in South Wales, opening the way
for an approach more in tune with Continental trends and the modern-
ism of Le Corbusier.[88] (The war would put this initiative on hold for
twenty years, but the modernists – for better or worse – would prevail
in the end.) When Cambridge University Press decided in 1938 to commission a series of books on 'English Institutions', it seemed natural that
it should turn for its first subject to the Post Office. (The general editor
of the series was a prominent economist and government adviser, Lord
Stamp.) The outcome was yet another glowing profile of the Post Office
by a serving official: *GPO*, written by the head of its Public Relations
Department since 1935, E. T. Crutchley.[89] Naturally, he dedicated the
book to his boss, the Director General.

By that time, the cast of characters at the top of the hierarchy had seen
many changes. Grierson had left in 1937, voicing frustration over the
constraints that he felt were crippling the Film Unit's work. This was in
part a measure of his expanding horizons, after the two best years in the
Unit's short history; but Grierson had also been worn down by the carp-
ing of the accountants, having lost the protection of both his main patrons.
Following Ramsay MacDonald's replacement as Prime Minister by Stanley Baldwin in June 1935, Wood was promoted in the subsequent Cabinet
reshuffle to become Minister of Health. His successor at the Post Office
was a man ten years older than Wood and far less ambitious, George
Tryon, whose feet were scarcely under the desk before he was suggesting
to his officials that the whole PR programme be reined back: there was a
danger of the Post Office's own staff 'becoming a little surfeited with the
good things that are spread before them ... [and] the time has arrived to
slow things up and consolidate'.[90] Within weeks of Wood's departure, it
was announced that Tallents, too, was on his way. If this came as little
surprise to insiders, his destination could hardly have been predicted. For
he had accepted an appointment as Controller of Public Relations at the
BBC, reporting directly to John Reith – whose contempt for the just
departed Postmaster General was an open secret in Whitehall.

March 1914

N

Leeds
Hull
Liverpool
Sheffield
Birmingham
Stony Stratford
LONDON
Swansea
Cardiff
Guildford
Canterbury

0   80 miles
0   100 km

March 1922

N

0   80 miles
0   100 km

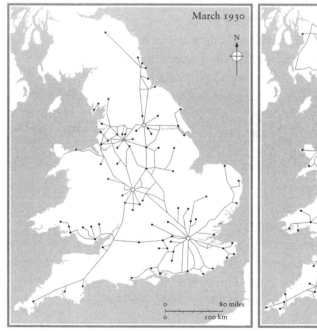

March 1930

N

0   80 miles
0   100 km

March 1938

N

0   80 miles
0   100 km

Map J. Underground cables in the long-distance telephone network, 1914–38

The Post Office's relations with the BBC had remained fractious throughout Wood's tenure, not helped by his brittle personal relationship with Reith. By temperament the two men could hardly have been more different. Forthright to the point of being abrasive, Reith abhorred the kind of political calculation at which the rising Tory minister was so adept. He saw Wood as a threat from their very first meeting. Reith's diaries, published posthumously in 1975, are littered with insulting references. But while he could sniffily dismiss Wood as 'a feeble little creature' in 1932, Reith soon learned that he was not a politician to be crossed lightly: by the last days of the MacDonald government in 1935, Reith was noting angrily that it was 'utterly damnable that the BBC should be made the political catspaw of a little bounder like Kingsley Wood'.[91] For his part, Wood disclaimed any intention of meddling with the BBC. As he told the Commons in February 1933, 'I don't mind handing round the hat, but I won't turn the handle'.[92] This did not avert further acrimonious squabbles; nor were relations improved by the appointment in March 1935 of Bridgeman as the BBC's chairman. A month into his tenure, Bridgeman and Reith were invited to the House of Commons by Wood for a discussion about plans for a committee on broadcasting in the event of another war. Reith's own characteristically clipped account of the meeting in his autobiography is of interest, given Wood's apparent influence over the Bridgeman Enquiry three years earlier.[93] 'An unpleasant meeting. Bridgeman told me afterwards that it was the first time he had ever been called "Willie" by Kingsley Wood; he did not like it.' (It was to be his last meeting with Wood: Bridgeman died a few months later.)

Wood presided over the establishment of two critically important committees to pronounce on the future of the Corporation. The first, chaired by his predecessor at the Post Office, Mitchell-Thomson, now Lord Selsdon, and reporting early in 1935, made the BBC the operating authority for Britain's television service (launched the next year). The second, the Ullswater Committee, was set up shortly afterwards to review the future of the BBC after the expiry of its ten-year charter, awarded in 1926. Wood had left the Post Office by the time the Ullswater Committee recommended a fresh ten-year charter, in March 1936. But his influence over the Department lingered on, much to Reith's dismay. The Cabinet set up its own committee to approve (or otherwise) the charter's renewal – and made Wood the chairman. A tense few months ensued, with Reith trying in vain to have the Post Office's role restricted to technical oversight, before the charter was authorized. They were marked by considerable hostility towards the BBC within Baldwin's Cabinet, which Reith blamed directly on the former Postmaster General. As he later recalled, Tryon did his best to iron out the difficulties, but 'we all knew he was only a ghost'.[94] When yet another committee was set up in 1937 to look at the idea of the BBC broadcasting in foreign languages, it was once again Wood who was appointed to the chair. At this point, the story of the strange and strained relationship between the BBC's founding spirit and the Post Office's new deliverer might have ceased to be of much consequence to postal history – but there was to be one more extraordinary twist to the tale. It would round off, too, the interwar history of the airmail service which itself signally contributed to the rising reputation of the Department in the 1930s.

8. KINGSLEY WOOD AND THE EMPIRE AIR MAIL SCHEME

The first recorded airmail service in Britain was arranged in September 1911, to commemorate the coronation of King George V. It ran for fifteen days, carrying 120,000 or so letters between an 'Aerodrome' at Hendon and a landing strip twenty minutes away, close to Windsor Castle. It was organized by a few brave entrepreneurs, while the Post Office offered a cautious helping hand from the sidelines.* This, it turned out, was to be the policy template for many years to come. The wartime acceleration of aviation technology seemed at first to presage a dramatic take-off for this intriguing new dimension to the mails. The RAF and REPS together ran a courier service to Versailles for the peace talks in 1918–19, and flew mails from Folkestone to Cologne for the occupation forces in Germany. But the first commercial air companies that followed in the RAF's wake looked to the Post Office for support and

---

* The Post Office drew up *Instructions for Pilot Aviators Carrying Aerial Mails* and handed a copy to each of the four pioneering pilots. It tried to cover all eventualities: 'In the event of your being obliged to alight before you have proceeded five miles . . . telephone the Aerodrome so that a car may be sent to bring back the mails . . . or if you are **very close** [sic] when you have to alight and can get a conveyance, take the mails in yourself after putting someone in charge of the aeroplane . . .' Alas, the first Pilot Aviator having to alight prematurely had crashed just after take-off and broken both his legs. But his three colleagues completed the scheduled service, raising enough cash to put £500 aside for the injured man. The remaining surplus of £937 went into a charity, under the trusteeship of His Serene Highness the Duke of Teck. (Francis J. Field and N. C. Baldwin, *The Coronation Aerial Post, 1911*, published privately in 1934.)

were disappointed. Unnerved by its own mounting financial problems, the Department set its face against any kind of subsidies. It was happy to dispense sticky blue 'By Air Mail' labels over post office counters, and it set up a sorting channel to bring the labelled letters to Croydon aerodrome for collection. But it restricted its direct involvement with the air companies to helping them clear the legal niceties, as they flew to and fro across the Channel. None managed to make a sustainable profit, competing with highly efficient rail and ferry services. To attract any substantial business, it was soon realized, airmails would need to offer a drastic reduction in delivery times. This implied long routes, which the entrepreneurs were not yet ready to tackle. The RAF again led the way, launching a service in 1921 between two quite distant British-controlled cities – Cairo and Baghdad. It was the first route in a network that was then pioneered by the RAF, extending its reach both eastwards via the Gulf into Asia (reaching Australia in 1934) and southwards down the continent of Africa (reaching Cape Town in 1932). A modest government subsidy meanwhile bailed out the struggling cross-Channel businesses, in exchange for their agreeing to merge in April 1924 as Imperial Airways.

Over the next several years, Imperial Airways gradually took over and consolidated the RAF's far-flung operations. It took over the Cairo–Baghdad service from the RAF in December 1926, flying its first mails from Croydon airport in a Handley Page biplane called *City of Baghdad*. It launched the first mails to India ('Saturdays only') via Iraq and Persia in 1929. Aerodrome by aerodrome, a skeletal infrastructure was laid in place. As of the end of the 1920s, however, the Post Office's stance on the finances remained unchanged. Imperial Airways tried in 1927 to persuade postal officials to accept what was called an 'All-Up' policy: it wanted letters to be carried by airmail at no extra charge, wherever this offered a reliable prospect of quicker delivery. Rejecting the idea, the Post Office conceded that mails in Europe might one (far-off) day use aeroplanes and trains interchangeably, but insisted that mails beyond Europe would always need to belong to a 'superpost' with higher rates of their own. This, as Martin Daunton has observed, 'was a rational analysis of the economics of air mail' and in the end it prevailed – but it was filed away, to be forgotten in the 1930s.[95] For the time being, the Post Office was adamant that its own costs could not be allowed to exceed its anticipated revenues. All airmails from the UK accordingly would go on bearing a significant surcharge over and above the 1½d imperial letter rate or the 2½d foreign-country rate applicable

NOTICE.

AERIAL POST.

By Sanction of His Majesty's Postmaster-General.

IN COMMEMORATION OF THE CORONATION OF THEIR MAJESTIES THE KING AND QUEEN.

THE NET PROFITS DERIVED WILL BE DEVOTED TO A PUBLIC CHARITY TO BE APPROVED BY THE POSTMASTER-GENERAL.

An Aerial Post between London and Windsor will be in operation daily, for a limited period only, commencing Saturday, the 9th September, 1911, and will be available for use by the public under the regulations of the General Post Office in connection with the ordinary Inland and Foreign Mail Services.

Only the special pictorial Post Cards and Envelopes issued by the Honorary Organising Committee, with the sanction of the Postmaster-General, will be conveyed by the Aerial Service, and they must be posted only in the *special boxes* placed in the following establishments in London, [where the Post Cards and Envelopes are on sale] on and from Friday, September 8th, 1911:—

ARDING & HOBBS, Ltd., Clapham Junction, S.W.
JOHN BARKER & CO., Ltd., Kensington High Street, W.
JOHN BARNES & CO., Ltd., 191-217, Finchley Road, N.W.
BENETFINK & CO., Ltd., 107, Cheapside, E.C.
D. H. EVANS & CO., Ltd., Oxford Street, W.
A. W. GAMAGE & CO., Ltd., Holborn, E.C.
HARRODS, Ltd., Brompton Road, S.W.
SELFRIDGE & CO., Ltd., Oxford Street, W.
WILLIAM WHITELEY, Ltd., Westbourne Grove, W.
LONDON AERODROME, Hendon, N.W.
OFFICES OF THE AERIAL POST, General Buildings, Aldwych, W.C.

The Post Cards and Envelopes which bear a copyright design of Windsor Castle, printed in brown, green or red, are issued stamped.
   Postcards, stamped for Inland.   Postage, price 6½d. each.
   Envelopes,   do.   do.   do   price 1s. 1d. each.
A sheet of Notepaper with Special Heading is supplied with each envelope.
Adhesive stamps must be affixed to make up the fee required for postage abroad.

Post Cards and Letters conveyed by Aerial Post will bear over the ordinary postage stamp a special post-mark, "FIRST UNITED KINGDOM AERIAL POST," and the date. They will be collected from the special boxes referred to above, and conveyed to a central Post Office, and then be taken to the London Aerodrome for conveyance by aeroplane from London to Windsor, and thence will be despatched in the ordinary course to their destination in any part of the world to which they are addressed.

NO RESPONSIBILITY in respect of loss, damage, or delay will be undertaken by the Postmaster-General, or by the Honorary Organising Committee.

CAUTION.

Letters by Aerial Post cannot be registered. They must not contain coins or other valuables.

If the special Post Cards or Envelopes be posted in any other than the *Special Boxes* referred to in this notice, they will not be carried by the Aerial Service.

DONATIONS TO THE CHARITY.

LLOYDS BANK, Limited, St. James' Street, London, S.W., has consented to receive, on behalf of the Honorary Organising Committee, donations in sums of One Shilling and upwards which will be acknowledged by the Committee by Aerial Post Cards.

Persons resident in the country and abroad will thereby be enabled to secure an Aerial postal souvenir of unique interest and, at the same time, benefit the Charity to which the net profits will be devoted.

Remittances must be made by cheque or postal order made payable to the "Coronation Aerial Post," crossed "Lloyd's Bank, Ltd." *Stamps cannot be accepted.*

Subscribers when sending their remittances should give the names and addresses to which the Aerial Post Card receipts are to be sent.

ORDERS BY POST.

Orders for small quantities of the Post Cards and Envelopes may be sent to the Secretary, Aerial Post, General Buildings, Aldwych, London, W.C. The cost of postage, at the rate of 1d. for each dozen or less ordered, must be included in remittance.

WHOLESALE ORDERS.

Messrs. P. C. BURTON & Co., LTD., General Buildings, Aldwych, London, W.C., have been appointed Sole Agents for the sale of the Post Cards and Envelopes.

August, 1911.

Issued by authority of the Honorary Organising Committee, Contractors to H.M.'s Postmaster-General for the Coronation Aerial Post, General Buildings, Aldwych, London, W.C.

Notice announcing the Aerial Post to mark George V's Coronation, 1911

to normal delivery. The complex table of surcharges resembled nothing so much as the tariff of inland postal rates in the mail coach era, with the capital cities of the world substituted for England's county towns. It

TO	DEP.	POST AT G.P.O.
INDIA **IRAQ** **PERSIA**	**SAT.** ONLY	**FRIDAY MIDNIGHT**
EGYPT **PALESTINE** **ITALY** **GREECE**	**WED.** & **SAT.**	**TUESDAY** & **FRIDAY MIDNIGHT**
PARIS AND ALL PARTS OF THE **CONTINENT**	EVERY WEEK DAY	**6** A.M. EACH DAY (**9 A.M. FOR PARIS** ONLY)

IMPERIAL AIRWAYS
AIR-MAIL
LATEST TIMES FOR POSTING

DETAILS AND RATES FROM ANY POST-OFFICE

POST AT ANY POST-OFFICE

Notice of the first Air Mail to India, 1929

was easy for the opponents of this policy, by no means all of them working within the civil aviation world, to see it as yet another wretched manifestation of the *ancien régime* in St Martin's. There were howls of complaint in 1930 when Murray and his Labour Postmaster General turned down flat an appeal from the London Chamber of Commerce for the Post Office to organize new airmail services across Europe. The whole idea, said officials, was based on a misconception of the

Department's role. Wolmer, of course, poured scorn on this reply when he turned to the subject of airmails in his 1932 book: 'The Department joyfully shovels off responsibility on to any other authority it can find, and sits with folded hands whilst Air Mails are to grow by themselves'.[96] It was a service needing enterprise and initiative, he told the Bridgeman Enquiry in his *Constructive Proposals*, and was 'being stifled in infancy by the Post Office'.[97]

The truth was more complicated. The great pioneering aviators of the 1920s who opened up the globe, straddling oceans, jungles and deserts, had fired the public's imagination. By stuffing a few letters into the side of the cockpit, most of them could even claim to have 'launched' an airmail route. But building such routes in practice was going to require a heavy investment in the local infrastructure at many points overseas. Postal services were based on dependability, not derring-do. Even on routes where the boldest pilots had cut flight times remarkably, what mattered was not the fastest possible speed but the availability of flights operating with a clockwork regularity. The US Post Office had undertaken to pay whatever it took, to ensure a continent-wide airmail service – and this policy was reportedly costing it $20m a year by the early thirties. The prospective cost of a comparable network across the globe, even on a minimal basis, was daunting to say the least. It reminded the Post Office only too well of the costs incurred in building the great shipping lanes of the nineteenth century – similarly dependent on heavy investment in physical facilities overseas – when the oceanic steamship companies had absorbed massive subsidies from the Post Office even though conveying the mails had been an almost incidental part of their business. For aeroplanes with just a handful of passengers, the putative contribution from hidden subsidies on their mail business was going to be far more important. No wonder the alarm bells were ringing in Murray's Secretariat.

Nor did its senior officials need to be qualified engineers to see that aviation technology was still developing in scarily unpredictable ways. A more 'imaginative' approach to airmails might well have seen the Department committing large sums to the services offered by airships, keenly heralded by many in the 1920s as the future of intercontinental travel. The crash of the R101 in October 1930 – killing forty-eight passengers, including the Secretary of State for Air, Lord Thomson, and the Director of Civil Aviation, Sir Sefton Brancker – finished off the airship industry overnight. There was one other factor that weighed on the official mind, too. Giving a lecture on the airmail service a month after the

R101 disaster – it was to be the text of the first Post Office Green Paper – Frederick Williamson acknowledged the enthusiasm of those who claimed that lower airmail letter rates would prompt soaring volumes. They were fond, he said, of citing Rowland Hill's Penny Post in support of their vision. But Hill's reform had been slow to vindicate itself, landing the Department's finances in a deep hole for decades. 'With such an example before it, the Post Office can hardly avoid looking with a certain amount of scepticism at the claim that lower [airmail] postage rates are, or soon will be, gold mines.'[98]

The Post Office had nonetheless been inching forwards towards more practical goals, and felt it was making progress. Important legal groundwork for international mail routes had been laid in the late 1920s – culminating in an Air Agreement annex to the Postal Union Convention, agreed at an international conference in London in 1929 – and the volume of airmail letters began to creep upwards quite encouragingly. The Department was now providing a lot more than sticky labels. Blue 'Air Mail' pillar boxes appeared around the country in 1930. The letters they collected were sorted into bags by the Air Mail Division (according to global routes designated in time-honoured fashion as 'Roads') and taken in special blue 'Royal Air Mail Service' vans to Croydon airport, where the enormous four-engine biplanes of Imperial Airways – with names like *Hercules*, *Horatius* and *Hengist* – bore them off to distant lands, flying by night as well as day. There was plenty here to help the new Publicity Committee sell the excitement of airmails, once Kingsley Wood as Postmaster General had swept aside all the old inhibitions over marketing.

Notwithstanding their glamour, airmails in Wood's second year of tenure were still accounting for less than 5 per cent of all the letters 'susceptible to acceleration', as the analysts of St Martin's put it.[99] Clearly, more initiatives were required. Nowhere was the need for them felt more urgently than in the boardroom of Imperial Airways. By 1933, the company's government subsidy was dwindling towards its expiry date. Hoping desperately to extract more revenues from the Post Office, its managers were inclined to take a much more optimistic view than Williamson of the volume benefits of lower pricing. With the support of the Air Ministry, the company pressed to be paid for airmails in advance, at a freight rate based on poundage. This was eventually agreed, along with the adoption in 1934 of a greatly simplified set of postage charges. Sure enough, the volume of airmails jumped the following year from just over 120 million tons to just short of 190 million tons.[100] But to promote the fastest possible growth, an Assistant General Manager of Imperial Airways had proposed that they take a Hill-type hatchet to the postal surcharges and abolish them altogether for the whole of the Empire.[101] Heartened by the recent surge in volume, Wood gave the idea his support. In May 1935, he announced plans for an 'Empire Air Mail Scheme'. In line with the 'All-Up Scheme' mooted in 1927, *all* standard letters would henceforth go by airmail. The total charge would be 1½d for a half-ounce letter addressed to anywhere in the Empire (with the exception of Canada, since no transatlantic mail service was yet possible), which compared with only 1½d for a full ounce letter going by sea. The Scheme was introduced in three stages over the course of 1937–8.

The impact on the volume of mails was spectacular, and might have gratified Rowland Hill himself. (See Appendix A, Chart 6.) By a curious chance, another doubling sequence recurred. Penny Post volumes had doubled every twenty years from 1860 to the Great War. Now, the minimal flat rate of 1½d resulted in the number of airmail letters more or less doubling *annually* – taking them steadily from 10.8 million in 1935–6 to 91.2 million in 1938–9.[102] This totally confounded the remaining sceptics inside the Post Office. Unfortunately, it also left behind even the most sanguine projections within Imperial Airways. It soon transpired that the company's commercial plans had disastrously underestimated the resulting demand for space. As the mailbags piled up at the aerodromes, so the capacity available for lucrative passengers and freight had to be cut back. This fatally compromised the airline's business model. To save the company from insolvency, the Post Office soon had no choice but to accept a renegotiation of the tonnage payments that had been agreed at the outset. If these had originally included merely a 'hidden subsidy', the Post Office now found itself propping up the company only too obviously. Nor was this the first time that Imperial Airways had been a source of embarrassment to both the Post Office and the Government. A couple of years earlier, in 1935, the poor reputation of the company's European services had caused a stir when it failed to deliver on promises by the Government that all Continental destinations were to enjoy the 'All-Up' mail service. The impasse that had followed that setback had been resolved by the formation of a new public company, British Airways, which since 1935 had taken over much of its rival's European business. The question by 1938 was how best to finesse a looming crisis over the funding of Imperial Airways and by extension the whole airmail service.

It was at this point that the career paths of Kingsley Wood and John Reith crossed again. As the Minister of Health since 1935, Wood had confirmed the promise he had shown as Postmaster General, as 'a capable minister ... [who] could be relied on to represent the government effectively in the Commons'.[103] He had also been elected by the Conservative Party a few months earlier as Grand Master of the Primrose League – a society founded in the Victorian era for propagating Tory values, with many features redolent of Freemasonry – in succession to Stanley Baldwin, a sure sign of his popularity within Tory ranks. His friend and long-time patron, Neville Chamberlain, was now Prime Minister – and in May 1938, Chamberlain promoted Wood as Secretary of State for Air.* Easily the biggest issue confronting the new minister was a mounting crisis over the failure to build additional fighter aircraft to counter the threat of Hitler's air force. But Wood was also quick to turn to the difficulties being encountered by the Post Office with Imperial Airways. Within weeks of taking up his new job, he paid a surprise call on Reith at the BBC. The combative Director General's readiness to consider a move from the Corporation had been common knowledge in Whitehall for a long time. Their discussion, recorded later by Reith with his usual candour and brusqueness, closed on a curious note:

> At the end he asked me if I were any busier. No. Terrible, he said; something must be done about it. I said I did not think anything would be done; politicians did not like me because I had kept the BBC constitutionally clear and politically impartial. He disliked me himself, I added; and for that reason. He denied it in a flustered way; said I was a 'genius'; must certainly be properly employed.[104]

Days later, Wood invited Reith to take over the chairmanship of Imperial Airways. His appointment was announced, to widespread amazement, in the middle of June 1938. Five months later, Reith emerged at the head of a new statutory corporation, combining Imperial Airways and British Airways into a single publicly funded entity named – at Reith's instigation – the British Overseas Airways Corporation.

The fifteen-year contract signed by the Post Office with BOAC's precursor in June 1937 remained essentially unchanged, helping to underpin

---

* Coincidentally, the move allowed Wood to renew his working partnership with Donald Banks, the first Director General at the Post Office, who had moved to the Air Ministry in 1936. Wood had actually tried to take Banks with him to the Ministry of Health in 1935, a transfer that had been blocked by the head of the civil service, Warren Fisher. (John Reith, *Into the Wind*, Hodder & Stoughton, 1949, p. 223.)

the finances of a British airmail organization that soon stretched across the globe. The first regular transatlantic mails were launched in the summer of 1939: Pan American Airways of the US actually led the way in June, but BOAC inaugurated its own service in August. It was a glamorous addition to a network with some sombre ulterior objectives, now increasingly to the fore. The ocean mail contracts of the nineteenth century had provided, in various 'Admiralty' clauses, for the needs of national defence to be given priority in the event of war. Now, in precisely the same way, the worldwide postal arrangements for BOAC's huge Empire flying boats were subject at any time to suspension 'in time of emergency'. The service to North America survived intact for just four weeks before the Government needed to activate this provision, following the outbreak of war with Germany.

8

Pillar of the nation, 1939–49

> Are there really such things as nations? Are we not 46 million individuals, all different? And the diversity of it, the chaos! ... But talk to foreigners, read foreign books or newspapers, and you are brought back to the same thought. Yes, there *is* something distinctive and recognisable in English civilisation. It is a culture as individual as that of Spain. It is somehow bound up with solid breakfasts and gloomy Sundays, smoky towns and winding roads, green fields and red pillar boxes. ... The suet puddings and the red pillar boxes have entered into your soul.
>
> George Orwell, *The Lion and the Unicorn: Socialism and the English Genius* (1941)

I. CONFRONTING ARMAGEDDON

'Air Attacks Renewed' ran a headline in *The Times* in August 1928. 'Fighting Over London. A 50-Mile Chase. Bombs on Air Ministry.' Squadrons of heavy bombers, spotted crossing the Channel late in the evening, had succeeded in reaching the capital despite continuous attacks by fighter formations ordered up from airfields across Kent.[1] Though reported by the newspaper with an alarming plausibility, it was of course an exercise laid on by the Air Ministry – just the first of several dummy battles over the capital through the following years, which were intended to sharpen the RAF's skills and to show the public that (notwithstanding those 'Bombs on Air Ministry') any future air bombardment of London would encounter well-prepared defences. Few were persuaded. Reports in the later 1930s of devastating German and Japanese air raids against civilian centres in Spain and China only exacerbated a widespread conviction that any future war would unleash Armageddon from the skies.

Accounts of the Post Office's war by its senior officials leave no doubt that the demands of defensive and offensive aerial warfare were always their foremost concern.[2] In particular, the widespread conviction that 'the bomber will always get through' posed problems for the Post Office – with its 24,000 individual post offices – that ranged from the merely nightmarish to the totally insuperable. The proximity of its central operations to the Channel, such a convenience in the Great War, was now a crippling weakness. The creeping decentralization since the Bridgeman Report would bring significant benefits after the outbreak of war, insofar as regional management teams had been formed that were capable of responding to local crises far better than the centralized, pre-1935 Post Office might have done. But decentralization had done nothing to alter the fact that sorting operations, TPO routes and telephone trunk networks were still effectively spider webs that extended outwards from inner London. In fact the physical infrastructure was more than ever concentrated on the capital by the closing years of the decade, after a consolidation of the telegraph network aimed at reducing the number of major exchanges to a minimum: in 1939 fully a quarter of the nation's telegrams passed through the Central Telegraph Office in St Martin's. Other sources of vulnerability included the design of many post offices and sorting halls, which had been given as many large windows as possible; most telephone exchanges had positioned their operators on the top floor, to take advantage of skylight windows. The layout of telephone and telegraph cables was even more problematic, with most laid just a few feet into the ground, for ease of access. Again, the main Post Office buildings in almost every city had been grouped together in clusters, with no one sparing a thought for the possible impact of bombing. How could they have done? Most of the Department's physical assets had been set in place before anyone conceived of men flying at all, let alone dropping bombs from the air.

The delicate business of preparing the Post Office for a war that might not come was begun well before it finally arrived. 'In the two or three years preceding the war ... steps were taken deliberately to utilise any possibility of improving the defence aspect of new work [on the network]'.[3] Bold leadership was provided by Thomas Gardiner, who took over as Director General in 1936. An imposing figure with a forceful down-to-earth style of management, expressed in a rich Ulster brogue – he was born in Cork, but educated in Armagh and Edinburgh – Gardiner had joined the Secretariat staff in 1910, aged twenty-seven. Soon identified as an unusually able administrator, he had served as Private Secretary to Murray during the First World War. (Some saw in him more than a touch of Murray's autocratic manner, but Gardiner had an Irish charm altogether beyond his forebear.) He assumed from the outset that another war would reduce the Department to chaos, unless preparations could be completed in time. Ten years later, in his retirement, Gardiner wrote a private memoir strewn with references to the work accomplished before the fighting began – and confessing, indeed, that '[t]he experience, fortunately, proved less formidable than the expectation'.[4] By May 1938 the steady expansion of the country's civil telephone network was being significantly held back by 'the work of meeting the telephone requirements of the Defence Services', and this work grew more intense through the summer of 1938 as the crisis worsened over Hitler's true intentions towards Czechoslovakia.[5] At the height of the crisis that September – with posters and leaflets on Air Raid Precautions (ARP) being displayed near every postal counter – 'Emergency Arrangements' were put in place 'to provide communication services for the military and civil defence departments', as we know from a secret Board paper prepared for the Committee of Imperial Defence the following month, to review how well the arrangements had worked in practice.[6] Gardiner may also have been referring to this when he noted in his post-war memoir that '[a] code of emergency instructions had been prepared [before the war] and issued under seal to Head Postmasters and others'. There is no evidence that Post Office planning for the war was relaxed after Neville Chamberlain's return at the end of September from the Munich Conference, holding out the hope of 'Peace in Our Time'. Gardiner himself was called away by the Government to join a small team led by Sir John Anderson (he of the corrugated steel 'Anderson' air shelter, soon to be a garden feature across the land) and charged with coordinating Whitehall's civil defence measures. The Post Office in his absence pursued an intense schedule of preparations for war, given an added urgency after March 1939 by Hitler's betrayal of the Munich Agreement and the German occupation of Czechoslovakia.

Like other Whitehall departments, the Post Office had to equip an alternative Headquarters far from London, with plans to staff it at short notice if the need arose.* But the contingency arrangements at the Post Office went much, much further. Sorting offices had their windows

---

* The Post Office workforce in April 1939 comprised 283,000 employees, made up of postmen (24 per cent), indoor postal and telegraph staff and telephonists (22 per cent), industrial staff (18 per cent), other full-time and part-time permanent staff (33 per cent), and non-establishment temporary staff (3 per cent) (see BP 27(40), Post 69/12, and BP 13(41), Post 69/13).

bricked up and basements converted into bunk dormitories. Central facilities in London and other large cities were replicated with shadow facilities in remote suburban locations. Intense effort went into designing contingency railway schedules, against a day when trains would no longer be able to whisk TPOs nightly in and out of London. The telephone network, relatively insignificant in 1914 and now providing a basic service for about 4 million subscribers, was equipped with duplicate switching stations in the most unlikely places. Instructions went out for the stockpiling of all essential engineering supplies. Several miles of deep tunnels were dug in central London for duplicate cables into critical exchanges; other cables were diverted into the London Underground network and the Post Office's own Mail Rail.[7] Emergency trunk systems were built and earmarked for immediate diversion to the defence services in the event of war. TIM the 'Speaking Clock', set up in London in 1936, was given a back-up delivery system based in Liverpool: launched as a PR gimmick, it had become an enormously popular service, too valuable to be left exposed to any bombing of London. (Establishing the back-up did not involve a Liverpudlian version of the celebrated Miss Jane Cain, however, and hers remained the inimitable voice of TIM until 1963.*) And steps were taken to safeguard the security of the Post Office's less glamorous businesses, too – especially its Savings Bank. The POSB held savings for about a third of the population by 1939: its deposits amounted to just over £1bn in cash, savings certificates and government stock. Many vital records were now copied and squirrelled away for safe keeping far from London. There remained, though, around 11 million ledger cards and 200 million counterfoils that it was just too risky to remove. These were relocated to specially reinforced premises in the capital, while emergency plans were drawn up for how the POSB might be kept going in the event that they were nonetheless incinerated. As Britain prepared for the least unexpected war in its history, the Post Office more than played its part.

---

* Cain was a London telephone operator who had won a competition to become the voice of TIM. The success of the service since 1936 had amazed the Post Office. It cost about £8,000 annually, and brought in £64,000 in 1938. Cain was chosen by a panel of judges that included John Masefield and Sybil Thorndike, but her tones were not to everyone's liking. The Engineer-in-Chief, Sir George Lee, pressed the Board to find a substitute in 1938, complaining to his colleagues that Cain's voice 'was not constant in volume and unsatisfactory in its pronunciation of the word "six" ...'. He played them other voice recordings, presumably with more six-appeal, but to no avail. (Post Office Board Minutes, 14 June 1938.) The name of the service itself was shortened from 'Time' and could be dialled with the three digits 8, 4 and 6 which corresponded with TUV, GHI and MN on the dial.

While the war itself may have come as no surprise, its early course proved to be very surprising indeed. The dreaded waves of bombers failed to appear. Within weeks of war being declared on 3 September, as the newly appointed Engineer-in-Chief, Stanley Angwin, recorded in his diary, the Post Office was back to its routines:

> The order given in the early days for staff to remain at home was not altogether popular with the personnel. After one or two days at home practically the whole of the staff found excuses to resume duty, prior to the general recall. The general feeling of the apparent triviality of the normal daily job, as compared with the larger issue of war, which was evident in the early days, has now passed and the staff has again settled down to their normal work.[8]

Yet it was hardly back to business as usual. The process of devolving administration to newly formed regions had been hurriedly brought forward in the final few weeks of peace, and the remaining four – the Home Counties, the Midlands, the South-West, and Wales and the Borders – were now launched on the back of some desperate last-minute improvisation. (The Midlands Region was inaugurated on the morning of 4 September with three small rooms in the centre of Birmingham, and its first Regional Director arrived from Edinburgh that day. He had to borrow furniture and typists from the city's Postmaster-Surveyor.) The mainstream postal business was reconfigured by the declaration of war in dozens of ways. The TPOs ceased operations from the outset. The cancellation of the football season meant a suspension of the pools business, which by 1939 accounted, astonishingly, for no less than 7 per cent of all mail and 45 per cent of all postal orders.[9] (It was extremely profitable, too, accounting for about 20 per cent of the Surplus pot in 1938.) Service levels in the telephone network, with its 4 million subscribers, were abruptly downgraded, as almost a quarter of the long-distance 'trunk' capacity was switched over to government departments. Home Defence facilities clamoured for additional connections, and the Post Office's monitoring of the ARP took on a new urgency. Millions of letters needed redirecting through the autumn, as evacuees poured from the cities into the countryside – some 660,000 of them from London alone, and more than a million from other big towns and cities – and as freshly enlisted servicemen joined their units. (Before the war was over, the Post Office would register no fewer than 39 million changes of address.) Above all, the staffing of the Department itself was depleted overnight. About 20,000 of the 270,000 workforce were reservists, all of whom disappeared to training camps 'under a pre-arranged plan' in the week after Chamberlain's radio broadcast to the nation: 4,000 went into service with the Royal Engineers Postal Service (REPS), while the rest, mostly engineering staff, joined the Royal Signals Corp.[10] Thousands more from various London operations, notably the Savings Bank and other clerical departments, began relocating to temporary homes in Harrogate and Morecambe.

Despite all these upheavals, a creeping return to normality was evident by the end of the year. Stanley Angwin's diary caught the mood again: 'Events have not occurred as anticipated, and many of the department's normal activities, which had languished in the early days of the war, shew signs of recovery'.[11] Mail trains went back to running more or less on schedule (though not the TPOs). Football matches were resumed and a truncated, albeit much less lucrative, pools system was back in action by February 1940. Some evacuees were by then returning to London and complaining crossly about the difficulties of arranging to have their telephones reconnected. For those with a working line, cheap-rate calls on the telephone network, suspended in September, were restored in March. Airmail deliveries for Europe were back to peacetime levels; there was even talk of restoring the suspended transatlantic service. Papers submitted to the monthly Post Office Board – and temporarily organized from March by an Acting Secretary with the slightly unfortunate name of R. E. German – began alluding to the war as though it was a vexing and mysteriously prolonged bout of stormy weather. Certainly it was not judged serious enough to disrupt plans for a joint exhibition with the Royal Philatelic Society London at Lancaster House, to run from 6 to 14 May, in commemoration of the centenary of the Penny Post. The French government seized on the occasion to propose the joint issue of a Franco-British stamp. The idea was at first rejected in St Martin's, where officials felt their own planned issue of a set of commemorative stamps – each bearing the heads of both Victoria and George VI – was quite enough for one year. But the idea had to be hurriedly revisited when given the nod by the King himself. A working party was set up, and a draft design was received from the Ministry of Posts in Paris 'which after some discussion was accepted as a working basis by the British representatives'.[12]

The British 1840 commemoratives, including a double-headed Penny Red, appeared on the opening day of the centenary exhibition; the Franco-British design was overtaken by events. In the eight days between the opening of the exhibition and its close, Hitler's armies overran the Low Countries and launched their Blitzkrieg offensive through the Ardennes into northern France. The shocking events that followed over the next several weeks – culminating in the retreat from Dunkirk, the fall of Paris and the Franco-German Armistice of 16 June 1940 – confronted the Post Office, like every other arm of the British state, with a potential catastrophe that was utterly unforeseen. Its officials had grafted tirelessly to anticipate the horrors of an aerial bombardment. Now they faced the scarcely believable prospect of invasion, and of seeing Hitler's Wehrmacht fighting its way across East Anglia and the Home Counties. The minutes of the Board held on 4 July 1940 give us a glimpse of this extraordinary moment, with no parallel in almost four centuries of history. For anyone around the table still inclined to doubt the reality of the crisis, a verbal account was given of what had just happened in the Channel Islands:

> The higher Post Office staff had been evacuated in consultation with the local civil Government and a number of other Post Office staff had also been withdrawn. Some of the staff elected to remain. Two members of the engineering staff at the last moment had to remain and had been unable to get away. Full communication with the Islands had been maintained until the afternoon of 30th June (Sunday). On that day first of all four German planes landed on Guernsey and ... communication ceased between 7.30 and 8 a.m. on the 1st July. The [telephone] circuits were kept under observation and on Tuesday morning a German spoke on a circuit asking if the speaker at this end was London. The reply was given in German that 'this was not London'. The cable had now been cut near the mainland.[13]

If this episode had had a faintly comic close, there was nothing remotely entertaining about the prospect of a similar debacle following shortly in Southend or Tunbridge Wells. The Board had been secretly informed in June about the probable need for a compulsory evacuation of up to 60 per cent of the population out of the coastal area from The Wash to Hastings. Now it was warned by one director that this might rise to around 90 per cent, not least in view of 'the fact that voluntary evacuation had already reached the proportion of 60 per cent in some areas and was approaching it in others'. There was a lengthy discussion of the Department's plans for its own offices and staff. Sub-offices were already being closed where their business had dried up. 'Arrangements were in hand for the disposal of establishment records and stocks of value, which were already being kept as low as possible. ... [In addition] numbers of vehicles had already been withdrawn and only those retained which were essential for the [remaining postal] services.' Head and branch offices, meanwhile, would be kept going until the last moment. Once the civilian population had gone, mail vans would be provided as transport for postal staff, along roads which by then would be closed to civilian vehicles: 'It was contemplated that all evacuation should be completed in advance of an actual landing, and the programme envisaged one day's notice and two days' execution'. Telephone operations posed a trickier problem, for their services could not be abandoned altogether: 'but if the traffic does not justify the retention of all the staff, [exchange] personnel would be transferred after making a generous provision for military requirements and contingencies. . . . A margin of staff must be retained after civil evacuation to meet military requirements'. One other immediate concern was how best to provide for the mails of army units pitched in to battle against the invaders. Almost all units stationed within Britain had been using the civilian Post since September 1939, with letters openly addressed to individuals c/o the Post Office nearest to their billet. The Board heard that the forces would continue to rely on civil channels 'as long as these were open, but that when actual operations commenced or the civil Post Office ceased to operate in any area, the Army Postal Service should take over . . .'

The individual picked to sort out the arrangements for the Army Postal Service (APS) was William Roberts, one of the few remaining Surveyors still in office in September 1939. At the age of fifty-one, he had been among the 4,000 or so Post Office reservists who – like their forebears in 1914 – had enlisted with REPS immediately upon the outbreak of war. Roberts took up his REPS duties as Assistant Director of the APS at the beginning of July 1940. Based at St Martin's, he immediately set about implementing a two-stage approach for the handling of army mail, devised by Headquarters colleagues over the preceding weeks. Phase I described the status quo, whereby 'open addresses' were being used by most units of the Army. Phase II (already employed for most Headquarters units) would involve a move to 'closed addresses', providing only the name and unit of the recipient. This 'Home Forces' mail would be strictly excluded from civil channels. It would be handled by six 'Army Distribution Offices' (ADOs). These would be run by REPS personnel and provided by the War Office with a Top Secret daily list of unit locations, allowing distribution to the frontline troops by the APS. Or that, at least, was the intention. But as the Board was warned in a paper for its 4 July meeting, the reality might prove less straightforward. 'Should serious fighting take place in this country, the Army Mail Service may have to be restricted to letters not exceeding 2 oz in weight, the acceptance and delivery of parcels, packets or registered letters being suspended for as long as circumstances demand.'[14] Roberts spent much of his time through the tense days of July visiting Head Postmasters and APS units around the south-east, coordinating what was now, as he himself described it, an 'Army-cum-Civil postal service'.* He was laying the groundwork for a rapid transition to Phase II, which, as he noted in his diary, 'would come into effect when circumstances become such that the civil Post Office could no longer operate owing to enemy action'.[15] At the beginning of August, he sent a memorandum to commanding officers, the ADOs and all serving REPS postal units with the Army, to put them at the ready: 'The time has now come when . . . the Army Postal Services must be prepared for the introduction of Phase II at short notice'. In fact, though he could not know it, Hitler's plans for an invasion had been put on hold a fortnight earlier, pending the promised destruction of the RAF by Herman Goering's Luftwaffe.

And so arrived, rather later than expected, the aerial offensive for which the Post Office had done its level best to prepare. There had also been, since the start of the summer, a frenetic acceleration of work on the defence services' needs. 'With invasion of our own country now a definite possibility, fresh aerodromes, battery sites, searchlights and Radar stations were needed everywhere', as the author of an official Post Office booklet on the war years, Ian Hay, recalled in 1946, 'and every one of them had to be linked up in a fresh network of intercommunications, all to be provided and installed by the Post Office.'[16] A special unit, manned by the Post Office's engineers and known as Defence Telecommunications Control, had responsibility for switching emergency telephone circuits in and out of play to ensure that contact was never lost between the service commanders and their front line forces. The demands made of the whole network were at their most intense through the weeks from mid-July to mid-September 1940, when the Battle of Britain hung in the balance. One of the prerequisites for victory was that the communications web linking the airfields of south-east England to the headquarters of Fighter Command near Stanmore

* One sensitive issue that Roberts had to address was the unhappiness of the UPW about any involvement of REPS personnel in the sorting work of civilian post offices. Roberts decreed that Head Postmasters should feel free to draw on the Army's assistance wherever they needed it. He held them responsible 'for arranging such consultation as is necessary' with the staff representatives on their local Whitley Committee; but he was adamant that discussions should go no further, as he made clear to a conference at St Martin's the following month. 'In no circumstances whatever should REPS officers have any personal contact with the UPW'. (Minutes of Conferences at GPO Headquarters, 20 August 1940, Post 47/409.)

in North London should fulfil all the fearsome demands made of it –
which it did. But the Post Office's infrastructure was then subjected to
the Blitz that followed, through the next eight months. This proved, if
not a sterner test, an ordeal for the entire Department.

Returning from Whitehall to the Director General's office in October
1940, Thomas Gardiner was satisfied that every realistic effort had been
made to persuade the British public to lower its customary expectations
of the Post. The public had taken no notice whatsoever. The total number of letters scarcely dipped at all, and people went on posting them at
the last possible moment, just as they always had. When London's night
trains were replaced by afternoon trains, to reduce the impact of bombing on the terminal stations, wagons went off half-empty – and the
evening bags piled up as usual, for night sorters struggling with the
black-out if they were lucky, or much worse if they were not. Telephone
and telegraph traffic, meanwhile, had been climbing remorselessly since
the early summer. Never, perhaps, had so many people had so much to
say to friends and family at such little cost. And always in the background, unseen by most of the public, there were the constantly
upgraded requirements of the Government and armed forces. Given all
of these demands, the burdens on the Post Office once the bombing
began in earnest were simply immense. Contemporaries generally marvelled at the way they were shouldered, and were all the more impressed
where they were ignorant of the pre-war planning. Insiders knew better:
the Deputy Engineer-in-Chief, A. J. Gill, looking back in a memorandum of November 1944, concluded in a matter-of-fact fashion that
pre-emptive action had saved the day on countless occasions. (Had the
preparations made in advance paid off? 'In most cases the answer is definitely in the affirmative.')[17] It was a truth borne out by the regularity
with which utter devastation was followed by the provision of stand-by
services in amazingly short order. When thousands of bombs fell directly on the City of London on Sunday, 29 December 1940 – the night
that came to be known as the 'Second Great Fire of London', captured
for ever in the photographs of the dome of St Paul's rising above the
flames – the nearby buildings of St Martin's-le-Grand and its surrounding streets did not share the miraculous luck that spared the cathedral.
The Central Telegraph Office (CTO) and the country's largest telephone
exchange in nearby Wood Street were both gutted. But emergency
circuits for the defence services were operating from the reinforced
basements of King Edward Building within hours, and alternative networks were up and running for most public subscribers within ten days.

(About 3,000 staff were employed in the CTO, but warnings of the raid appear to have averted serious casualties.) While many of the wrecked buildings were abandoned, the CTO was rebuilt in 1941 – only to be heavily bombed a second time in March 1942.

Inevitably, London was hit worst: in just the first few weeks of the Blitz, some 234 of the capital's post offices were damaged, including both Mount Pleasant and KEB as well as seven of the ten District Head Offices.[18] (The South-Eastern District Office was to be hit five times before the end of the war. It kept going throughout, without a single break.) But the trail of devastation soon engulfed Post Office premises from Birmingham and Belfast to Swansea, Southampton and a score of other cities. Everywhere the story was essentially the same. 'Men and women died, post offices and telephone exchanges were destroyed or damaged, but somehow the mails were delivered and emergency switch-boards set working, usually within a few hours.'[19] Behind all this resilience lay more than just the practical benefits of pre-war planning. The pride and professionalism of the Post Office prompted thousands of ordinary men and women in its ranks to respond to the horrors of the Blitz with extraordinary courage. When the 'imminent danger' sirens went at night, many worked on regardless: postal workers, like ARP staff and fire-fighters, were classified as 'essential personnel', given exemption from the normal air-raid drills. While the fires still raged, Post Office engineers (especially 'cable-jointers') were often to be found perched inside fresh craters, tackling repairs even before the sound of enemy aircraft had faded from the sky. And in the morning, among the rubble and despair, the sight of the local postman – sporting a steel helmet, after November 1940 – could usually be relied on to bring at least a semblance of routine back to the neighbourhood. (All played their part in nurturing that 'spirit of the Blitz', captured by the Department's own GPO Film Unit in a short documentary, London Can Take It!, filmed within the first five weeks.*)

* Most of those gathered together by Grierson were now working as the Crown Film Unit, under the Ministry of Information. The nine-minute documentary on the Blitz was one of a series of wartime propaganda films made by Night Mail's director, Harry Watt, with Humphrey Jennings, who was to become the most distinguished of all the original Unit's film-makers. Other wartime titles included The First Days in 1939, Dover: The Front Line in 1940, Target for Tonight in 1941 and one full-length feature film, Fires were Started in 1943. The voice-over for London Can Take It! was provided by an American journalist, Quentin Reynolds, who hurried to Washington with a print of the film and reportedly arranged for President Roosevelt to see it within forty-eight hours of its completion. (Elizabeth Sussex, The Rise and Fall of British Documentary, 1975, University of California Press, p. 128.)

In adjusting to the daily emergencies of 1940–41, the Post Office showed
a pragmatism that would have been unthinkable a decade earlier. The
regionalization launched by the Gardiner Committee back in 1935 made
it possible for Regional Directors five years later to direct their own War
Rooms. While coordinated by a Central War Room, all responded to the
bombing with a flexibility and a knowledge of the locally available
resources that made a critical difference.

By the middle of June 1941, there was a sense that the worst of the
bombing might perhaps have passed. After a lull of three weeks or so in
the nightly air raids, it was far from certain that the Blitz was over (we
now know it was) but there were signs of a return to relatively dependable operations. Post offices set up 'poste restante' counters where
people whose houses had been destroyed could collect mail that was no
longer deliverable, and businesses forced to relocate their premises were
given 'redirection cards' to assist the Post Office with changes of address
and telephone number. Mail trains to Scotland were running more or
less on schedule again, for the first time in many months. Several hundred tons of mail still needed carrying in and out of central London in
van convoys each day, to meet trains at suburban stations instead of
relying on the central railway terminals. But the national network was
broadly back to normal. Again, while contingency plans for a German
invasion went on being refined in considerable detail, the prospect of an
imminent assault on the coast had steadily faded since the Battle of Britain.[20] Then came the astonishing news, on 22 June, that Hitler's armies
had invaded the Soviet Union. Britain had an immensely powerful ally,
and the war at once entered a new phase. The country had survived
potential Armageddon. Now it could turn to the business of replacing a
last-ditch defensive strategy with longer-term plans that might, ultimately, help to reverse the defeats of 1939–41. The contribution of the
Post Office to what lay ahead can be summed up in four words: money,
men, technology and morale.

2. REVENUES, RECRUITS AND ALMOST A WOMEN'S CORP

The Second World War, like every major war since the start of the eighteenth century, boosted the importance of the Post Office as a source of
additional revenue. We last glanced at the finances of the Department in
1936, when Board members were expressing concern at the possibility

of making too much money. They need not have worried. The Post Office Fund, set up in 1934 to receive any surpluses over a fixed annual payment to the Treasury, peaked at £3m in the spring of 1938 before a general downturn in the economy slowed the growth of revenues. Spending on the Empire Air Mail Scheme, the motor vehicle fleet – boasting 17,500 vans by 1939 – and the ever-expanding telephone network also rose much faster than expected. The result was a net profit for 1938–9 of £10.2m, far smaller than expected and less than the £10.75m promised to the Treasury under the deal blessed by the Strohmenger Committee in May 1933. As some had feared when the deal was struck, the Post Office had struggled ever since to earn anything substantially in excess of the guaranteed payment to the Treasury. (See Appendix A, Chart 7.) The Post Office had accumulated only a very meagre Surplus Fund, and now it was required to dip into it to make good the 1938–9 shortfall. This almost halved the Fund – and by March 1939 the Comptroller was forecasting worse to come. A shortfall of perhaps £3.85m for 1939–40 would consume the £1.6m left in the Fund and leave it more than £2m in deficit. A radical contraction of postal services – possibly including cuts, according to one official paper, 'which in some cases would be likely to lead to strong public protest' – was under active consideration when the war intervened.[21]

The Comptroller's 1939–40 forecast proved remarkably accurate, in the circumstances, with postal revenues declining much as expected. The early months of the war saw a lively jump in telephone and telegraph revenues, which suggested they might soon be more than just marginally profitable – but, by April 1940, the Post Office was no longer the dependable milch-cow that the Treasury needed. The net profit for 1939–40 was just £7m. The decision was taken to raise the basic letter rate from 1½d to 2½d as of 1 May (much to the chagrin of those organizing the Penny Post Centenary Exhibition, opening five days later). Higher parcel, telephone and telegraph tariff rates followed on 1 July. By then, part of the rationale for higher charges was that ordinary subscribers to the network needed to be discouraged, to make way for steeply rising demands from the government sector. As we have seen already, this objective was comprehensively foiled. The public's usage of telephones rose sharply over the summer of 1940 and went on climbing. Even on the shrunken and much-maligned telegraph service, traffic levels rose by 45 per cent over the duration of the war. Letter post deliveries fell by almost 50 per cent within Inner London during the early months of the Blitz, but rose across most of the rest of the country. Contrary to officials' expectations, the

post then went on expanding every year, though not quite as prodigiously as the volume of telephone calls. The result of all this was a 27
per cent rise in total Post Office revenues for 1940–41 and a 10–12 per
cent rate of annual growth over the next four years. Total annual revenues by 1944–5, at £179m, were double those in the last years of peace.
And along the way, starting in 1942–3, telegraph and telephone revenues
came to exceed the postal revenue for the first time. Once the war was
won, a new era for the Post Office beckoned.

Total profits, meanwhile, almost quadrupled: postal profits leapt up
in 1940–41, then slipped back marginally under the growing weight of
wartime wage bonuses. The telegraph network more or less broke even
throughout the war, but the telephone business soared. (See Appendix
A, Chart 8.) Having annually notched up only a million pounds or so,
on average, through the ten years before the war – with a peak of £2.1m
in 1934–5 – telephone profits produced a spectacular wartime rise: in
the last year of the war, they were more than a third higher than profits
on the postal service (£23.2m, compared with £16.9m). This was of
course in large part a reflection of the critical role of telecommunications in the war, and the provision of private facilities for the Government
boosted revenues in some of the most profitable parts of the business.
Immediately after the end of all hostilities, the accountants at St Martin's drew up an adjusted series of 'Surplus figures' – now standing for
net projects and leaving behind the old Strohmenger 'surplus' – which
eliminated the special income earned on engineering services for the
Government.[22] They also excluded the impact of the 1940 tariff increases
and the cost of war bonuses. This produced a more sober-looking record
of wartime Surpluses but it left telephone profits in the ascendancy by
1944–5, just the same. The adjusted postal profits slipped from a pre-
war £10.8m to a low of £5.5m in 1940–41, then clawed their way back
to £10.6m in the last year of the war; adjusted telephone profits, hardly
significant before the war, rose steadily from early 1941 and reached
£13.3m in 1944–5.

Once the Post Office Fund had been suspended in 1940, all of these
profits flowed directly to the Treasury. However welcome the Department's unexpected profitability, however, it scarcely compared in
importance with the Post Office's contribution to the manning of the
war effort. While there were some obvious parallels with the experience
of the First World War, there was no rush of postmen and sorters to the
Colours as Post Office Riflemen. The brave POR had disappeared,
merged in 1921 into another battalion of the London Regiment, which

had since become an anti-aircraft unit of the Royal Artillery. Of the 25,000 reservists called up in September 1939, about 4,000 went into REPS and another 16,000 joined the Royal Signals Corp. The rest were variously assigned, under the provisions of the conscription statute passed immediately after the outbreak of the war. (There was no early reliance upon voluntary enlistment, as there had been in 1914–16.) Thereafter, the Ministry of Labour and National Service watched over the rules of eligibility for enlistment, while a special committee under the Home Secretary, Herbert Morrison, applied them in the specific circum-stance of individual industries. There were regular appeals to the Post Office for drafts of additional men, especially of those with technical skills. It was noted early in 1941 that the Post Office still had about 8,000 people on its staff with a Morse code qualification, effectively obsolete in civilian life by 1939 but still much prized in the armed forces. Towards the end of 1942, with not far short of 70,000 postal workers already enlisted – including over a third of the Engineering Department's 43,000 pre-war staff – Morrison asked Post Office officials to explore the pos-sibility of releasing another 20,000–25,000 men as a matter of urgency. This prompted misgivings among the Department's officials, and a deep intake of breath by the staff associations' leaders. The Postmaster General, a Scottish Tory called W. S. Morrison who had been one of Chamber-lain's last ministerial appointments in 1940, wrote back to his namesake at the year's end:

> You did not say in your letter whether you wished us to take the Staff Unions into consultation. It would have been contrary to Post Office practice – and in my opinion wrong – not to have done so. The outlines of your enquiry have been conveyed to the Unions and they are brooding over the matter. They protest, and it seems to me with reason, that a question of this magni-tude cannot be dealt with in the space of a few days . . . No doubt it is right that we should strain every nerve to keep clerical complements in general at as low a level as possible. This may involve taking what you describe as 'administrative risks'. . . . Other considerations, however, apply in the case of the work of the manipulative staff of the Post Office. The country cannot do without communications any more than it can do without supply.[23]

The unions voiced their unhappiness on many occasions over the Department's reluctance to push back harder against government requests for more men.[24] Perhaps their strictures had some influence in the end, for the 20,000–25,000 draft was never implemented and the total number of enlisted men from the Post office workforce rose by only another 10 per cent or so through the rest of the war, topping out at about 78,000 by April 1945 – almost exactly the same number as had signed up in 1914–18, and more than a quarter of the 1939 workforce. While the Phoney War lasted, the Department was able to cope without fully replacing the men gradually lost to the forces: as staff numbers declined, those left behind adjusted to working a 54-hour week (or more) and sidelining non-essential tasks. From June 1940, however, this decline had to be reversed: so great were the demands on the Post Office, from both the public and the Government, that it needed not only to replace the growing cadre of absent men but actually to begin augmenting what was described as the 'effective staff'.

Perhaps surprisingly, given the 1914–18 precedent, it took a little while for officials and union leaders alike to grasp one of the inevitable consequences. At a Board discussion early that June, a few days after the BEF's exodus from Dunkirk, it was agreed that the range of women-friendly tasks in the Post Office had diminished since the last war: 'the field for [their] useful employment was somewhat narrow . . . [but the possibility that] they could be usefully employed was borne in mind'.[25] There was little reason to suppose that the unions' general attitude towards the employment of women had changed much since the years before the war, which had witnessed endless wrangling – and occasionally some distinctly unsavoury episodes – over the issue.[26] The UPW had always connived with officials to exclude women altogether from writing duties, and it was never slow to discern new threats to male dominance elsewhere. There had been a bizarre altercation in 1933, over rumours that women telegraphists were about to be employed in, of all places, the grandstand at Newmarket Races, contrary to a tradition that male telegraphists handled such business. The UPW had fired off a letter to Evelyn Murray expressing 'the strongest objection to such an innovation as being dangerous and undesirable in every respect'. This did not deter officials from backing up local Head Postmasters who decided to employ postwomen at a growing list of 'Special Events' over the rest of the 1930s. The UPW went on resisting the policy with whatever arguments it could muster. An objection was made to the use of women at Ascot and Henley post offices in 1934 'in view of the travelling involved to and from the Station . . . [along a road] frequented by undesirable persons . . .' Other racecourses were similarly deemed quite unsuitable by the union, typically on account of 'arrangements for the female operator [that] are described as "primitive"'. This had Head Postmasters, rather ludicrously, sending clerks off to grandstands around the country to check on the existence of ladies' cloakrooms. But from Ascot and Newmarket to Henley and Cowes, a growing number of postwomen volunteered to work at Special Events and the Post Office deemed it 'only fair' to let them do so – a trend, as the Assistant Secretary of the UPW warned the Director General in 1936, 'which re-acts very badly on the male staff . . .'[27]

Confronted with the ultimate Special Event, the male staff seemed readier to make concessions. Given the pressing need in May and June 1940 for more night-time telephone operators, the UPW (according to D. J. Lidbury, now the Assistant Director General responsible for personnel matters) was 'quite reconciled to the employment of women, at any rate up to 9.30pm'.[28] But the outlook for women changed decisively that October. This was partly due to the courage many displayed in the terrifying circumstances of the Blitz. Women operators ready to brave the Luftwaffe's bombs needed no protecting from undesirables on their way home. It was also a consequence of the return to St Martin's of the redoubtable Thomas Gardiner, always a strong proponent of giving women an expanded role in the workplace. When thousands of women were taken on to help with the Christmas post two months later, Lidbury asked if he could keep many of them on afterwards '[as] it would be a tragedy if the best of this staff could not be retained without further formality'.[29] Gardiner urged him to do so.

By the start of spring 1941, the proportion of women on the staff had jumped from a quarter to a third. From the sorting halls to the motor-fleet garages, sacred gender barriers soon began to tumble. By the summer, women were even being allowed to drive post vans, so long as the unions could be satisfied that none of them was to be a full-time driver. The reality of the situation was then borne home forcibly on everyone by a dramatic proposal from the Army that a uniformed Post Office Women's Corp should be created. The War Office had calculated that, in the event of a German invasion, the Army would need at least 12,000 telephone operators on military duty. The Post Office had over 30,000 telephonists, and it was thought that uniforms and badges would ensure they stayed at their posts when the civilian population fled.[30] The Army was persuaded to drop the idea – and the implication that only a uniform would persuade telephonists to stick to their posts was much resented – but the implications were plain. They were given more urgency by an announcement in October that over 800,000 men would be called up in 1942. The Post Office would be losing all of its male administrative and executive personnel under the age of thirty.

From November 1941, 'Woman Power' was a regular item on the Board agenda. All constraints on the recruitment of women were waived aside. Indeed, it was noted that the Ministry of Labour wanted the Post Office to take the lead in the employment of part-time female labour on the Home Front. The Postmaster General, a cautious lawyer, thought it would be better to move in tandem with the rest of the civil service: he was worried, too, that hiring many more women part-timers 'would be very unpopular with the Post Office staff'. But Gardiner had no such reservations and pressed his colleagues to keep the percentage of women in the workforce moving briskly ahead. Starting early in 1942, the Post Office took on an additional 25,000 part-timers, almost all of them women. By the end of the war, it had also hired a total of 53,000 additional full-time women (as well as 19,000 full-time men ineligible for service) to fill the gaps left by enlistment. The Director General, looking back in his retirement, took pride in the fact that the net total of full-time hires fell short of the absentees' total by 6,000, despite the increase in the Post Office's workload; and he heaped praise on the female recruits in particular: 'It is impossible to speak too highly of the work done by these temporary employees, especially on the postal side, where most of the women were housewives and no longer young, and on the engineering side where the work on which they were employed was of a kind not normally regarded as suitable for women'.[31]

In the Post Office, the 'temporary' label simply meant 'not entitled to a pension', and was a category that included both full-timers and part-timers. There had been few temporaries in 1939. We know the proportion of women in the wartime workforce rose steadily from 23 to 47 per cent – with their absolute numbers rising from 64,000 to 142,000 by April 1945 – and it can be safely assumed that all but a very few of the extra 78,000 were hired as 'temps'. Many could be categorized as 'non-directable women' – which is to say, they were above or below the ages of recruitment into the armed services. All were volunteers, for a job with very few perks. But how many of them aspired to establishment status? Gardiner's reference to the importance of women engineers is significant. Many women received extensive training, especially in the Engineering Department, and were thought unlikely to give up their jobs after the war quite as readily as their mothers' generation had done in 1919–20. The staff associations were assured early in 1942 that this would be the legal requirement, as before.[32] But as the search for more women grew increasingly desperate over the next three years, officials clearly moved into new territory. To compete against other employers, the Post Office by 1943 had to offer 'jobs for life', not just war jobs like any old munitions factory. It needed to campaign especially hard for more temporary women in the summer of 1944, when the demands made by the Normandy landings in June – exacerbated by the impact on London of the flying bombs that began arriving the same month – prompted the last great staffing crisis of the war.* Asked at the October 1944 Board meeting whether establishment jobs had been promised to newcomers, Lidbury confirmed as much and it was agreed 'the adoption of this course had been very helpful'.[33] How long the new female recruits to the establishment would be content to forgo the principle of equal pay – largely conceded by this date in the industrial sector – was not immediately addressed. But as Gardiner more than once pointed out to his Board colleagues, it looked certain to be an important question for the future.

3. COMPUTERS FOR BLETCHLEY, AIRGRAPHS FOR THE TROOPS

Beyond blood and treasure, the Post Office brought to bear all the benefits of its burgeoning technology. If the postal story in the First World War had marked the apogee of the Victorian institution, the story in the Second World War was more a portent of the Post Office's future, and of the telecommunications world to come. As Ian Hay observed in 1946, the conflict was in many ways 'an Electricians' war'. We have already noted the monumental tasks of first retrenching the country's civil communications network against aerial attack and then enhancing its capacity to serve the needs of the armed forces. The latter aspect of the electricians' war remained a priority for the Post Office from the first days to the last. It began the war with 6 million miles of 'single wire' underground cabling – laid over a period of twenty-five years – and ended it with 10 million miles underground. Individual episodes in

---

* The flying bombs, dropping at random hours of the day or night, were in some ways more frightening than the Blitz. Damage was done to around 15 per cent of all postal buildings in the capital and absenteeism rates rose over 30 per cent among London regional staff. As the Director of the London Telecoms Region explained: 'The staff were nervous in particular about glass and not without reason . . . the blast effect from glass caused by the bombs used in earlier raids being much less serious than with Flying Bombs'. By contrast, they caused the engineering staff little concern, because they lacked the penetration to cause much harm to underground cables. (POBM 7 July 1944, Post 69/23.)

the war prompted intense bursts of activity. Busloads of PO engineers
were sent to Scotland in the spring of 1940 to support the ill-fated
Allied campaign in Norway; and many more were assigned to Ulster in
1940–41, to upgrade the rather threadbare infrastructure of the Province in support of the allied campaign in the Battle of the Atlantic. Their
work involved a doubling of Ulster's telephone links to mainland Britain. Again, as fleets of US aircraft began arriving in support of the RAF
from 1942, and there was talk of Britain becoming one giant aircraft
carrier for the assault on occupied Europe, the bombers' bases across
Eastern England needed to be linked with their command centres. Telephone networks were adopted for 'wire broadcasting' to the air bases,
in ways much discussed in the late 1930s as an alternative to wireless
broadcasting by the BBC, but shelved with the onset of war.[34] Meshing
British and American practices – in labour relations as well as technical
matters – was not entirely without incident, but was accomplished without serious difficulty.[35]

As preparations went ahead for a Second Front, the country was
fortunate in the pre-war choice of Stanley Angwin as the Post Office's
Engineer-in-Chief. Having joined the Department in 1908, he had commanded a divisional signals company throughout the First World War
'and subsequently retained a close association with army signals for
many years'.[36] Angwin instinctively understood the military's needs and
worked closely with the Combined Staffs to ensure that London and the
whole of the south coast of England were wired efficiently in support of
the D-Day communications programme. Gardiner listed some of the
spectacular results in his memoir after the war. Where the entire civil
telegraph system in 1938 had employed 3,300 teleprinters, the Post
Office linked 10,000 into a network now built for the services; the trunk
telephone network specially installed for the invasion preparations had
a greater capacity than the whole of Britain's public trunk network of
1939. No wonder the Supreme Commander felt it appropriate, in the
aftermath of the Normandy landings, to pen a letter to the Postmaster
General (Morrison's successor since January 1943 and himself a man
with a distinguished Great War record) expressing his gratitude:

Dear Captain Crookshank,

The build-up of the necessary forces for the current operations has
involved the construction of a vast network of communications radiating
from key centres of vital importance in the United Kingdom. The greater

part of this work has been undertaken by the Engineers and Staff of the General Post Office.

It is my great pleasure, on behalf of the Allied Expeditionary Force, to ask you to pass on to them my sincere appreciation for this contribution and for the long hours they have worked and for the excellent cooperation they have given toward our success.

Sincerely,

Dwight D. Eisenhower[37]

For one other critical application of technology by its engineers, the Post Office received no such official acknowledgement – or, indeed, any public recognition at all. While most attention was focused in 1942–4 on its expansion of the country's cable (and wireless) infrastructure, few were allowed to know about the activities of the Post Office's Research Station. It was generally known as Dollis Hill, after the name of its sub-urban home in north-west London. (The building is still there, now converted into a block of residential flats, Chartwell Court.) Originally founded in 1921 and greatly expanded by Kingsley Wood in 1933, it had already achieved a string of significant technical advances by 1939. Its laboratories were thereafter devoted almost exclusively to solving war-related problems.* A. J. Gill's survey of the Engineering Department's record noted the importance of Dollis Hill's work on navigational aids, battlefield telephone reception, radar and radio, 'and many other subjects too numerous to mention'.[38] Or too secret. Most sensitive of all was the Station's involvement with Bletchley Park, the country estate in Buckinghamshire that was the wartime headquarters of all the Government's codebreaking activities. A post-war generation of postal managers only knew of Bletchley as the location for many years of one of the Post Office's main staff-training centres. For almost thirty years after 1945 no mention was made of another and far more momentous link. This was forged in the earliest days of the war, with the relaying by the Post Office of intercepted German radio signals to Bletchley. Until 1941, these consisted entirely of Morse signals. But after the interception that year of some highly intriguing non-Morse German radio traffic, the Post Office became far more than a relay medium.[39] What followed,

---

* Dollis Hill also had an important wartime role unconnected with its laboratories: from June 1941, it provided the location for the Post Office's Defence Telecommunications Control, previously based (all through the Blitz) at HQ and KEB in the City.

according to many accounts of an extraordinary story, may have helped turn the course of the war.

The Germans' Morse traffic had been deciphered increasingly effectively, thanks to the codebreakers' grasp of the enciphering process used by the now celebrated Enigma machine. The non-Morse material, first picked up on a regular basis from mid-1941, posed a new and in many ways far tougher challenge. It consisted of high-speed teleprinter messages, nicknamed 'Fish' at Bletchley; and as the network of transmitter stations was gradually identified, it became apparent that Fish in various versions comprised the main channel of personal communication between Hitler and his most senior commanders. (Enigma was principally used at less elevated levels, between individual units of the military.) Intense trouble was accordingly taken, through 1941, to deduce the workings of the cipher equipment – which the Germans called their *Geheimschreiber*, or 'Secret Writer' – used by this top-secret teleprinter network. Various kinds of Fish were identified. It was decided at an early stage to focus on the German army's version, which was codenamed Tunny. By the start of 1942 and without so much as a blurred photograph of the physical original – only in the last days of the war did the Allies finally succeed in capturing one – a handful of brilliant individuals at Bletchley had managed to deduce the workings of Tunny's *Geheimschreiber* and had then, in April 1942, turned to Dollis Hill to build a replica of it. This was accomplished with the absolute minimum of documentation, and the first of several 'Tunny machines' was handed over two months later. It used electrical switches to simulate the essentially mechanical operations of the German original. The codebreakers were delighted, and struck by the ingenuity of the Post Office engineers who had made it, led by the head of Dollis Hill's teleprinter section, Frank Morrell. 'It was certainly not a machine in the normal sense', as one veteran of Bletchley would recall, 'but was made from a variety of the components used in the automatic and manual telephone exchanges of that time.'[40] It was a singular achievement, but Dollis Hill's biggest contribution was yet to come.

The replica Tunny machine contained many preliminary settings. It could only decipher any given Fish message after these had been fine-tuned to match exactly those used for the original transmission of the message. The settings were constantly being changed, often on a daily basis, which was one reason why the Germans believed their Fish cipher to be impregnable. Once again, though, Bletchley proved them wrong. A logical process for determining any current setting was devised before the end of 1942. Unfortunately, it involved a tortuous statistical analysis of the signals carrying the message, and this could be immensely time-consuming – which left commensurately less time to apply the settings before they were next altered. Relatively few intercepts were successfully deciphered as a result – and the proportion dwindled alarmingly in 1943, as the Germans took further steps to make the settings even harder to analyse successfully. Then a new recruit to Bletchley, a 45-year-old Cambridge mathematician called Max Newman, showed his colleagues how the essential statistics could in theory be collated at high speed by a machine. To help them build it, they appealed once again to Dollis Hill's engineers. The head of the Research Station's telephone switching department was Tommy Flowers, the son of an East End bricklayer who had joined the Post Office as a 21-year-old telephone engineer in 1926. He had worked at Dollis Hill since 1930. Flowers was not at first involved in the Fish project; but he had already been to Bletchley several times, in connection with work on an earlier and rather simpler machine that assisted the teams busy breaking the Enigma code. (He and the head of Dollis Hill, Gordon Radley, were the first men in the Research Station to be admitted to the highly exclusive company of those outside Bletchley informed of the Enigma secret.) Flowers had met and impressed the mathematician Alan Turing, one of the moving spirits behind the whole Bletchley endeavour. Turing personally urged that Flowers be closely involved again. The result was a daring and totally unexpected proposal. Flowers had made his name inside the Post Office as a brilliant electrical engineer through his work with electronic valves: in particular, just before the war, he had invented a way of using them on telephone trunk networks in order to direct long-distance calls via automatic exchanges. Flowers suggested to the Fish team at Bletchley that Newman's putative calculating machine could effectively be based *entirely* on electronic valves – and made more robust in the process.

This idea was received with some incredulity, not to say hostility. A more traditional machine, nicknamed the 'Robinson' (after the ramshackle machines drawn by the cartoonist Heath Robinson) and largely based on electro-mechanical circuits, was already being constructed for Newman by Morrell's Post Office team that had built the Tunny machine. Electronic valves were generally regarded as a scarce resource in short supply, so the project put forward by Flowers – which he suggested might require 1,500 valves compared with the 150 used by the Robinson – was seen by some as unforgivably profligate as well as misconceived: it was argued that so many valves would render his machine fragile and deeply unreliable. (One of his stauncher opponents at Bletch-ley, reviewing the position in an official report a few months later, saw no room for compromise: 'He [Radley] might have informed us [at Bletchley Park] of the acute shortage of valves instead of encouraging Flowers to squander them. ... The influence of Dr Radley and Mr Flowers must be completely removed'.[41]) But Flowers had spent years before the war studying the properties of valves and understood their potential better than anyone else. As he recounted in later life: 'By 1939, I felt able to prove what up to then I could only suspect: that an elec-tronic equivalent could be made of any electro-mechanical switch or data-processing machine'.[42] He was confident not only that his machine would identify a given setting for Fish transmissions significantly faster than the Robinson – allowing perhaps seven times as many settings to be resolved in a typical day – but also that it would go on working round the clock more reliably than any electro-mechanical device. A stand-off ensued. It did not help Flowers' cause that his previous deal-ings with one or two of Bletchley's directors had ended in some rancour. The Dollis Hill man recalled the outcome in an interview that he gave to the Imperial War Museum, shortly before his death aged ninety-two in 1998:

> I told them it would take a year to build the first [valves-only] machine. They said 'in that time the war could be over and be lost', so they decided to go on with the Robinsons. That was what really put them against it, the idea of the electronic machine, the time it would take to build. They didn't commission me. They said, 'if you feel like it, that's up to you'. So we said, we'll do it.[43]

And they did. Flowers was backed by Radley and his deputy, who together took the decision to divert many extremely scarce resources to the venture, including scores of engineers and technicians – fully half of the research station's total staff.[44] Considering the demands being made of research staff at this time, it was a brave gamble. With their support, Flowers assembled a small team of colleagues, including Sidney Broad-hurst, Bill Chandler and Allan Coombs, all leading figures at Dollis Hill.[45] What they built between February and December 1943 – partly at their own personal expense – was 'Colossus', the world's first pro-grammable electronic computer. It was assembled at Dollis Hill, with many of its components sourced from one of the Post Office's own 'factories' in Birmingham. (These had been centres for the repair and renovation of telephone equipment in peacetime, but had since taken on a significant level of primary production work.) Flowers himself described the achievement as 'a feat made possible by the absolute priority [we] were given to command materials and services, and the prodigious efforts of the laboratory staff, many of whom did nothing but work, eat and sleep for weeks and months on end . . .'[46] Colossus well deserved its name: it stood two metres high and was big enough to fill a large room. Transporting it to Bletchley strained a few nerves, but in January 1944 it was installed and ready to run. Its impact was imme-diate, surpassing all expectations. It completely eclipsed the relatively modest achievements of the Robinson and proved remarkably robust. In March, Flowers was asked to produce three more machines, the first for commissioning on 1 June. A Mark 2 version of the original was built on site at Bletchley, to meet what at first appeared an impossible dead-line. It processed data five times faster than the first Colossus, facilitating a stream of Tunny decodes over the five days and nights before D-Day and the weeks that followed. The intelligence derived from these mes-sages is now widely seen as having made a critical contribution to the success of the Normandy landings.[47]

The secrets of Dollis Hill were invisible to all but a handful of contemporaries (and remained so for many years thereafter).* But the essence of the wartime postal service, in most other respects, was to go on being 'the Government's shop' as visibly as possible – delivering people's letters, taking in their savings, handing out their ration books, and paying their pensions and allowances across the counter with the minimum of disruption. Officials at every level of the Department fully appreciated that a 'normal' Post Office was critical to the country's morale. The point was regularly reinforced by MPs, who were quick to complain to the Postmaster General about any closures in the network.

---

* Ten models of Colossus were eventually built, of which eight were destroyed immediately after the war, along with related documents and blueprints. The other two were kept by the Government and scrapped in 1959–60. While the story of Enigma emerged in some detail in 1974, Colossus went undisclosed until 1976 and was little noted outside the computer scientists' world for another quarter of a century. Flowers retired from the Post Office in 1964, better known for his work on the STD telephone system than for anything he had done in the war. But his extraordinary achievements in 1943–5 were eventually recognized and he was the first recipient, in 1980, of the Post Office's Martlesham medal for distin-guished research. The Government released a 500-page technical report on Colossus to the Public Record Office in 2000. In 2007, a team of retired PO telephone engineers led by Tony Sale completed a reconstruction of the Mark 2, which remains on display at Bletchley Park today. (For a summary of the 1976 paper that revealed the significance of Colossus, see *New Scientist*, 10 February 1977.) Sale died in August 2011.

Rural sub-offices were to be especially treasured, as the Regional Directors were reminded by the PMG at their annual conference in March 1944. The public held them in great affection. All possible remedies should therefore be sought, wherever staff shortages threatened to leave any village without its own post office.[48] (A series of elegiac essays about a late-Victorian country childhood, published in 1939, had proved a surprising success for its publisher – and a first sequel published in 1941 had featured, as it happened, the life of the local village post office. A second sequel in 1943 embraced the author's happy memories of life as a rural postwoman in 1890s Oxfordshire and Buckinghamshire. The complete trilogy was reprinted in 1945 as *Lark Rise to Candleford*, by Flora Thompson, and has remained in print ever since.) For the most part – and leaving aside the dent to its services in central London at the height of the Blitz – the Post Office more than lived up to the public's (scarcely adjusted) expectations. As *The Times* portentously observed in a congratulatory leader of 8 April 1942, 'Routine has triumphed over the cataclysm of circumstance ...'

The real test in wartime lay not on the Home Front but in the effectiveness with which the Post Office and the Army Postal Service, working together, linked those at home to the men and women on the front line. That the front line was little different from the Home Front, after the disasters of 1940, was undoubtedly a blow to the influence and authority of the REPS men charged with organizing the APS: there was no obvious role for them. Once the threat of invasion began to recede, the forceful direction of the service by William Roberts and his colleagues seemed less appropriate, and Roberts himself was moved to other duties in November 1940. Under his 'Phase I', most of the mail for the Army continued to be carried by the Post Office, through normal civilian channels. Every unit received at least one delivery a day. So why not leave everything to the civilian service? Many senior regimental officers, stationed in their camps around the country, appear to have decided by the end of the year that a separate APS was indeed surplus to their needs. The Divisional Postal Officers from REPS could put forward plenty of reasons why their special expertise should be retained; 'but, at times, they seemed to lack that conviction which could only finally be provided when the Army Postal Service was operating overseas and was the sole provider of service'.[49] The result, when serious military exercises were begun in England from the autumn of 1941, was often an uphill struggle for the 'posties'. For the first major operation, involving 450,000 British and Canadian troops across the south of England, about 350 soldiers of the APS were engaged. They struggled to cope. The objective, one day, would be to ensure that mail arrived at the front line as reliably as it had reached the trenches of Flanders, via Base and Field Post Offices. Given the enhanced mobility of the modern army, though, it was plain from the start that – when the day did eventually come for Allied forces to return to Continental Europe – getting letters to the front was going to pose a challenge more akin to the experiences of the Boer War than the Great War.

In the meantime, the real front line created by the Italian army's invasion of the British protectorate of Egypt in September 1940 had been throwing up special problems of its own. Airmails to the Middle East had been suspended since the collapse of the Empire Air Mail Scheme at the start of the war. (The flying boats of Reith's BOAC had been commandeered by the Air Ministry and the airline itself had become part of the Royal Air Force Transport Command.) Surface mails via the Mediterranean had been a fair substitute – but Italy's entry into the war finished off that option, too. The beleaguered troops in Cairo were left to rely on sea mails via Cape Town, steaming around what came to be known as the Horseshoe Route. Since the best cruisers of the civilian shipping lines had been appropriated by the Admiralty – and in several cases subsequently torpedoed by the Germans – the Cairo mails were travelling by slow boats in convoys whose usual journey time from Southampton was eleven weeks. The Post Office and APS put forward the only feasible alternative. They proposed that room should be found for mails on the cargo aircraft that the RAF soon began flying over a 6,000-mile route from West Africa, via the Upper Niger and Khartoum. Pressure on the space was intense, however, and the APS lacked sufficient clout to win more than a nominal share of it. The minimum postal charge was fixed at an exorbitant 1s 3d – which some newspapers attacked as scandalous – but the APS was nonetheless overwhelmed with letters. The result was an acrimonious battle over cargo space, waged against a backcloth of bitter complaints from the public about the inadequacy of the Middle East service.

An ingenious solution was found in the 'airgraph'. This was a message form available from post offices for a prepaid charge of 3d, which could be photographed by the Post Office and conveyed as part of a microfilmed batch. The concept had been developed some years earlier by the Eastman Kodak company of Rochester, New York. Its microphotography process had been used by the Post Office, as by several leading City banks, for the efficient storage of paper records. Kodak had even formed a company called Airgraphs Ltd for the application of microphotography to airmails, but had stopped short of marketing it. Late in 1940, the idea was picked up again by the coalition government's Minister of Transport, John Moore-Brabazon, who fortuitously was also a director of Kodak's UK subsidiary. Within a few months, the technical apparatus had been finalized and the postal arrangements set in place. The first consignment was sent by Kodak from Cairo to London, arriving in May 1941.[50] It comprised 50,000 letters, photographed on 16mm film at a rate of 1,700 to every 100 feet of film. On arrival, the process was simply reversed: the reels were enlarged, for copies of the letters to be printed off, folded and despatched in 'window' envelopes. The initial load of film, weighing 13 lb, accounted for letters that would have weighed 1,600 lb – which by that date represented the total poundage of Army airmail crossing Africa in a typical week. Airgraphs in the opposite direction were begun three months later, and were inaugurated by the Queen with a message ('on behalf of all the women at home') from Buckingham Palace to General Auchinleck, the Commander-in-Chief of the Middle East forces.

The Post Office was proud of its innovation, which was quickly adopted by all of the Allied countries (including the US, where it was known as 'V-mail'). Confident that it would prove popular with the British public, the Department estimated that up to 3 million airgraphs might be carried in a year. A fee per airgraph was agreed on this basis, so as to cover Kodak's fixed costs. Alas, this soon left Post Office officials facing serious embarrassment. By December 1941, 8 million airgraphs had been carried on the London–Cairo route. In 1942, the service was opened up to purely civilian mail, Kodak stations were established across the Empire – and the number of airgraph deliveries shot up to 61 million. The following year, the total rose to 135 million, with 1.5 million despatched from London in a single week of March 1943.[51] Well before that, it was clear someone had blundered: Kodak was entitled to huge payments under the terms of its 1941 contract. The company generously volunteered a substantial refund in 1942 and in each of the two following years, paying back the Post Office some £660,000 in all. By 1945, no doubt to the relief of officials at St Martin's, airgraph volumes were in decline. Allied airpower was supreme everywhere and cargo space was plentiful. The Post Office had introduced a pre-stamped, wafer-thin blue 'air letter' that had proved to be even more popular. It was sealed, and could take twice as many words. By the closing months

Sender's Address:

1 Buckingham Palace

Date. AUGUST. 1941.

My dear General Auchinleck

In this first message by the new Airgraph
Service to the Middle East, I wish to tell you, on behalf of all the
women at home how constantly our thoughts turn to all those
under your Command.

I know how grievous is the separation which parts wife from
husband, and mother from son, but I would assure those
whose achievements have already filled us all with pride
that their example is an inspiration, and I do not doubt
that even greater accomplishment lies before them.

Many of them come from homes in our Dominions,
and to them I send a special message of greeting.
Their valour has been the admiration of the world,
and to one and all I wish a speedy victory, and a
safe return to their homes and those they love.

I am, Yours very sincerely   Elizabeth R

The address
should be
written as
large as
possible in
BLOCK letters
wholly within
this panel ⟫⟫⟫

GENERAL SIR CLAUD AUCHINLECK, G.C.I.E.,
ETC.

COMMANDER-IN-CHIEF.

MIDDLE EAST FORCE.

The address
should be the
same as is
appropriate
in the case of
an ordinary
letter, that is,
the full and
correct postal
address
should be
used — see
paragraph 4
overleaf.

The first airgraph, from Queen Elizabeth to Auchinleck in Cairo, 1941

of the war, up to 70,000 lb of airmail cargoes a week were crossing
Africa to the Middle East. The airgraph was obsolete, and in the summer of 1945 was finally discontinued.

The blue air letter was first unveiled early in October 1942. It was
only made a practical proposition by an increase in the number of mail-
carrying aircraft from West Africa to Cairo – which in turn was only
secured by the intervention of a forceful commander, newly arrived in
Egypt and deservedly known for identifying strongly with the interests
of his rank-and-file soldiers. Montgomery was a passionate believer in
the importance of regular letters to an army's morale. His attitude was
not universally shared in the upper echelons of the country's top brass,
though there were probably very few prepared to endorse the extreme
approach adopted by the Germans at their most ruthless: after the
Wehrmacht had launched its Russian offensive in 1941, the soldiers and
their families at home were told to forget about the possibilities of mail
because no transport capacity could be spared for it. But there were
undoubtedly many senior British staff officers who thought early mails
would be an unthinkable luxury for any invasion armies fighting their
way into Europe. At the early 'Operation Overlord' planning conferences in the second half of 1942, it was broadly agreed that no mails
would be sent to the attacking force for at least the first fortnight. Dedicated Postal Units would not accompany their respective formations
but would be shipped out later, as required. As for letters home from the
troops, these would have to await the establishment of a safe port on
the Channel coast.[52] It was an approach broadly in keeping with the
rather dismissive view of the APS so noticeable since the last months of
1940.

In the interim, the civilian Post Office had kept up its deliveries for
most of the Army stationed at home. Its Foreign Section at King Edward
Building in St Martin's had accommodated the Wrens who sorted the
mails for all vessels on the daily Admiralty List reporting their location.
Civilian premises and assistance had also been provided, in Manchester
and Birmingham respectively, for the postal arrangements of the Canadian and US forces, arriving in ever greater numbers after 1942. This
left the APS to run only the six Army Distribution Offices, catering for
High Security personnel within Britain, and the Army Post Office based
on the 'Home Postal Centre' at Nottingham, the equivalent of the Home
Depot built in Regent's Park in 1915. Nottingham on this basis managed mails for the overseas forces of the Army and the RAF, and for

prisoners of war.* But its involvement in the planning of Operation Overlord was still looking decidedly peripheral as late as mid-1943. Two developments changed this situation dramatically.

The first was the return of William Roberts in August 1943, accompanied by two other powerful Post Office figures, Norris Drew and C. R. Smith. Roberts, known to all REPS personnel as 'the Chief', had the gravitas of the elder statesman; Drew, sporting a magnificent handlebar moustache, had a famously explosive temper; Smith, universally known as 'The Smudger', was a clever, abrasive individual who cheered up his subordinates ahead of the first cross-Channel invasion for almost three centuries with a memo announcing: 'Napoleon funked it and so did Hitler, both under more favourable conditions than face us'.[53] What especially distinguished the three men in 1943 was the fact that they could all have passed for career army officers: they dealt easily and effectively with the military and commanded respect among the staff officers. They quickly assumed the leadership of the APS – 'form[ing] a triumvirate which ... dominated and inspired the postal planning for Overlord' – and by the end of the year they had succeeded in transforming the way the APS in general was regarded.[54] Even so, they were still battling, by the end of 1943, to win acceptance for the idea that mail services for the invasion troops should move in step with the invasion itself. Their proposal that airlifts be used for ordinary letter mail in both directions as early as possible had met with a blanket rejection. At this point, the second critical influence came to bear: Montgomery himself, who arrived in England at the start of 1944 to take up command of all Allied ground forces committed to the invasion. Roberts and Drew found themselves summoned by the new Commander-in-Chief, who made it clear in his customary fashion that regular mails to and from

* Red Cross parcels and 'next-of-kin' letters and packages to Germany were sent via Lisbon, where they were exchanged with the Germans who flew in mails for their own POWs in Britain and North America. (After the liberation of France, mails were exchanged via Switzerland.) Some 26 million parcels were despatched between March 1941 and May 1945. The APO did its best for POWs held by the Japanese, too, and designed a card complying with the Japanese government's strict limitation of fifty words (later cut to twenty-five) per message. The Post Office sold the cards in large numbers – and many thousands of them were discovered in 1945, lying in unopened mailbags inside Japanese POW camps. The bitterness this helped engender can be judged from remarks included in the official 1946 history of the wartime Post Office, whose author observed that 'the conduct of the Japanese in the matter of postal facilities was callous and inhuman to the degree only to be expected of that subhuman race' (Ian Hay, *The Post Office Went to War*, HMSO, 1946, p. 44).

the troops would be given priority from the outset. In particular, aircraft dedicated exclusively to the mails were to operate from France just as soon as the first landing strips could be laid. This uncompromising edict opened the way for some ambitious planning by Roberts and his colleagues.

Among all the many published and unpublished studies of the background to the D-Day landings, there can be few to compare in depth of detail to an account of the mail services by one of the senior REPS officers engaged behind the front lines in 1944–5, Kenneth Holmes.* His slim volume *Operation Overlord*, written for the Postal History Society and published in 1984, provides a record of postal activities that, coming from a lesser source, might be thought more than a little exaggerated in the telling – for it documents a remarkable tale. When considering how to distribute mail in the vicinity of the beaches after the landings, the APS's C. R. Smith saw an obvious problem. There would be approximately 4,000 army units ashore, far more than could be assigned their own individual Field Post Offices (FPOs). A dozen or so stationary Army Post Offices would be quickly established and there would be numerous FPOs attached to divisional and corps formations. But the majority of units, if left to follow the customary practice, would have no choice but to contact their nearest FPO when the first opportunity arose, requesting that details of their position be signalled down the line to the Home Postal Centre at Nottingham so that their mail could then be forwarded to them. It might take three or four days to arrive – by which time, of course, the units might have moved to new positions. To avert the all too likely prospect of postal chaos, Smith proposed what he called his 'pre-location scheme'. All units would be given sealed instructions in England telling them where to go, through the first seventeen days or so after the landings, to find FPOs that would be receiving mails for them from the outset. Obviously the pre-designated FPOs would need to be in direct proximity to the pre-assigned positions of the units, on the right days – so the Post Office would need to have full access to the British forces' battle plan weeks ahead of the invasion. This singular request was approved by Montgomery's commanders and

---

* After the war, Holmes would rise to become Director of Postal Services, 1956–65, and Director of London Postal Region from 1965 until his retirement in 1970. He also took on the part-time role of Director of Army Postal Services, which carried the rank of Brigadier. One of the luminary figures of the post-war service, Holmes was thereafter referred to as 'the Brigadier' – and not infrequently as 'Our Briggo' – until the day he departed.

the pre-location scheme was adopted – so successfully as to be almost surreal:

> the great majority of pre-locations proved to be accurate and the result of this was that the mail for most units went to the right [postal station] as from the word GO. . . . Divisional, Corps and other formations arriving in the theatre found their mail awaiting them there. Non-formational units, of whom there were hundreds, not only found that the [post office] to which they had been told to go while still in the UK was in fact the right one but, when they called at [it], they also found their mail awaiting them. From comments made at the time it was clear that not a few units regarded this as something in the nature of a minor miracle.[55]

Minor miracles went on being worked by the Army Postal Service from the D-Day landings to VE-Day (and beyond). Thanks to Montgomery's insistence, it was decided in the months before June 1944 that there were to be virtually no delays between the start of the Normandy campaign and the instigation of a postal service – providing mails back from the beaches as well as letters from home. 'All this required that Field Post Offices on the far shore should be supplied and kept supplied with adequate stocks of cash, postage stamps, postal orders, forms, and all other requisite items of postal equipment as from the word "go".' We might suppose the posties who accompanied the first troops into battle would have been excused the need to carry the contents of a postal counter. On the contrary: even those who dropped by parachute in the early hours of D-Day, ahead of the assaulting ground troops, had their supplies tucked under their tunic. 'Men of the [6th] Airborne Divisional Postal unit took their stock of stamps with them – on the person, strapped to the chest'.[56]

The first 500 bags of mail from Nottingham were shipped out via Southampton – now addressed not to 'APO England' as before the invasion, but to 'BLA' for British Liberation Army, at Churchill's own request – and they landed (a day later than planned) on D-Day +2. Along with letters for the troops came the London newspapers, to be distributed free; within weeks, the army authorities were buying 96,000 newspapers a day for despatch to France. A Base Army Post Office was established at the beachhead, and by early July the first airlifts of mail were being carried in Dakota aircraft to makeshift landing sites beyond the beaches. The numbers of postal staff grew rapidly, from 200 men by D-Day +6 to 800 or so by the end of August. They assisted the work of the FPOs accompanying field units and manned a line of stationary

Army Post Offices that crept into France as the Allied armies pushed forward – from Caen (set up on 5 August) and Falaise (22 August) to Arras (18 September), and thence south to Paris (3 October) and east into Belgium and the Netherlands. Early in September, a second Base APO was established at Antwerp, in a 50,000 sq. ft warehouse owned by the Société de Congo; and in the days that followed two regular air services were begun, bringing mails daily into Amiens and Brussels. Once Hitler's defences in northern France had been overcome, the east-ward advance accelerated and the British forces stretching from the 'Rear Maintenance Area' in Normandy to the Netherlands confronted the Army Postal Service with a challenge even greater than it had faced in 1914–18: the logistics equated to delivering the daily post to a popu-lation the size of Birmingham's – in transit between London and Newcastle. The officers of REPS drew on many lessons learned in those army exercises across the south of England and built a postal system their Great War counterparts would surely have admired. Postal trucks ran convoys across northern France and the Low Countries with clock-work regularity. There was even an 'Up Special' (from Rouen, the main sorting depot linking the Channel coast and most inland APOs, to Ant-werp) and a 'Down Special' (from Brussels airfield to Rouen). As the mails grew steadily in volume, German POWs were employed in shift-ing bags and many civilians were recruited to help with sorting. This was one dimension of relations between the Allied armies and the citizens of liberated Europe; another was the rampant black market in consumer goods, especially cigarettes, which many soldiers sold for sums that were well worth remitting to their families in England. The result was a huge demand for postal orders at the FPOs. 'Vast quantities were purchased ... before the higher authorities realized what was going on. It was barely possible to keep pace with demand.'[57] Only in December 1944, after 21 Army Group Headquarters had placed severe restrictions on their purchase, was the postal-order-remittance business brought firmly under control.

That month saw the Germans' offensive in the Ardennes, which in combination with a long spell of bad weather led to a serious disruption of the pre-Christmas posts. (The catch-up operation involved a flight of eight Dakota aircraft into Ostend with 150,000 bags of mail on 23 December, all delivered – or so Holmes recalled – by Christmas Day.) There were other setbacks. The first V1 flying bombs, hitting London in June 1944, had caused serious delays to the passage of mails through the capital. Now the Antwerp warehouse depot was completely destroyed, in March 1945, by a flying bomb. When the first Base APO was established in occupied Germany immediately after the end of the fighting, at Herford in North Rhine-Westphalia, it came as a shock for REPS officers to discover that locals recruited for postal work were in many cases simply too close to starvation to last through the day. 'Two army lorries were in fact kept on standby throughout the 24 hours to act as ambulances.'[58] (Mid-shift meals were soon introduced on site.) Within a few months, Home Postal Depot in Nottingham had been closed and all mails for the troops from Britain were being sent direct to Herford, addressed not to BLA but to BAOR, for the British Army of the Rhine.* In his retrospective account, Holmes encapsulated the Army Postal Service's achievements with the story of a sample of 50,000 letters received from England by frontline soldiers at their FPOs in September 1944. The average time per letter, from posting to delivery, came to 2.5 days. As a proud author wryly concluded: 'Not bad going, really'.

4. COUNCILS AND CONCESSIONS

When the news broke of Germany's surrender on 8 May 1945, the Union of Post Office Workers was enjoying the second day of its Annual Conference in Blackpool. Delegates had already heard a fiery opening address by their Chairman, Archie Wood, promising them that 'in peace we shall find war – an industrial war, between the common people and those who live on interest and profit . . .'[59] There was no mistaking conference's support for a radical break with the past. The British public had taken for granted a superb service, but it had been delivered by postal workers, or so Wood suggested, 'at the expense of their social and family life'. Night work, early-morning 'attendances' (the postal jargon for agreed duty hours), 'split' duties requiring attendances two or even three times a day – when there were sorting duties to be done, as he might almost have put it, the postman's lot was not a happy one. Special sacrifices had been made during the war, and rightly so. But now a new world beckoned and by the afternoon of the 8th, delegates were lining up to proclaim their appetite for a general election that would change the old order for ever.† At this point the proceedings were abruptly

---

* The BAOR postal system set up by REPS gave way to the worldwide British Forces Post Office (BFPO) service in 1957.

† This did not result in any enthusiasm for giving money to the Labour Party's General

interrupted to make way for a radio broadcast by Mr Churchill. A respectful silence descended as delegates strained to catch every word of his announcement of victory in Europe, relayed over loudspeakers in the hall. Then delegates got down to debating the details of a government White Paper on temporary staffing in the civil service.

The UPW, like Britain's other leading unions, felt its members had made a contribution to the war effort that now warranted a substantial political realignment. First, though, it had to address a more specific issue. Keen to play its part in shaping this realignment, the UPW had first to reclaim its right, as a union within the civil service, to participate in any formal political activity at all. It turned quickly in the months after VE-Day to campaigning angrily against the shackles placed on it by the 1927 Trade Disputes Act. It had in fact challenged the Act during the war, announcing plans to apply for membership of the TUC in 1943. Churchill had not been amused, and Attlee had warned the union that Labour ministers in the coalition would stand by the Act, even though he 'realised that this might lead to a break-up of the whole show'.[60] The Treasury had issued a formal statement pointing out that all UPW members were in danger of losing their jobs and their pensions if the application was pursued, a dire threat that was fortunately never put to the test: the union backed down. Its post-war campaign met with a different response, and the Act was repealed in 1946 as the Attlee government's very first legislative measure. The UPW affiliated with the TUC immediately, the only civil service union to do so. In the meantime, it had already assumed a new importance on the reactivated National Whitley Council. All the postal unions had been treated as little more than bystanders on the Council before 1939: other unions in the civil service had in particular seen the UPW's formal classification as a 'non-industrial' union as a charade, and had kept their distance. Now attitudes had changed. While the National Council had only met on a single occasion during the war, the Post Office's Whitley Council and its various sub-committees had been adopted as the forum for meetings that had brought the Official and Staff Sides together in a way that had never remotely happened in the Department before. Far from consigning the Whitley formula to history as a virtually moribund template, the war had invested it with real substance. The UPW came to the

---

Election Fund. Where the railwaymen gave £10,000 and the miners gave £23,506, the UPW chipped in £110. (Martin Harrison, *Trade Unions and the Labour Party since 1945*, Allen & Unwin, 1960, p. 67.)

National Council with its status enhanced accordingly – and other unions welcomed the muscular lead it could provide in negotiations with the Treasury, which had centralized the handling of civil service pay deals under its own direction.*

The wartime achievements of the Post Office Whitley Council had another, far more important consequence. It had been an explicit objective of the UPW since 1920 to organize itself into 'a comprehensive Industrial Union with a view to the [Postal] Service being ultimately conducted and managed as a Guild'. Its Annual Conference in 1942 had adopted a detailed plan for the establishment of workers' control over the Post Office through a 'Post Office Administrative Council'. Union officers and senior officials would have equal power on a series of executive boards, whose responsibility it would be 'to hold the balance between justice to the staff, consistent with the right conception of the Post Office as a national service, and obligations due to the community as a whole'.[61] The Whitley Council's work allowed the UPW to make significant progress towards this eventual goal. Key to this signal development was the leadership of Charles Geddes, who became the UPW's General Secretary in 1944. 'He did not suffer fools gladly, still less so his opponents', according to the UPW's historian; and he was not a man to be overly troubled by pocket revolutionaries among the rank and file. 'By sheer force of personality he probably dominated all aspects of the Union to a greater extent than any other holder of the office.'[62] A tough union boss rather in the mould of Ernest Bevin – with whom, however, he did not get along – Geddes put his authority squarely behind the Whitley machinery and used it to transform the status of his union. As he himself recalled in an interview almost thirty years later: 'You got to the stage [in the war] . . . where men no longer were discussing things from that and this side of the table. They were really a body co-operating together to try and find a solution to so many of the wartime problems . . . [It] was the commencement of a dialogue . . .'[63]

Geddes set about taking this dialogue forward into the peace. He saw Board representation for his union as a logical development in pursuing the interests of the workforce. The Whitley Council had been a useful

* Representing postmen, sorters, telephonists, telegraphists and some clerk grades, the UPW had 156,076 members. The second largest union, the Post Office Engineering Union, had 46,134 members; and 30,906 staff belonged to the next four biggest unions in the Department. The total of 233,116 accounted for almost exactly half of the 473,000 union members in the whole of the civil service in 1945. (R. W. Rawlings, *The Civil Service and the People*, London, 1945, p. 159.)

learning process, but for thirty years it had left the Staff Side on the periphery of policy initiatives until officials chose to involve them. He believed the time had come to allow the workforce a real influence over new policy at the formative stage. The idea was warmly endorsed by others in the UPW hierarchy and prompted plenty of fire-and-brimstone motions about Workers' Control of the Post Office in the immediate post-war Annual Conferences, while the leaders set about trying – in vain – to persuade their engineering peers in the POEU to accept a merger as the basis of a single postal union. The radical implications of advancing well beyond 'Whitleyism' set the UPW down a path that was taken by no other large industrial union in the country. Most leading figures on the Left of British politics could agree in principle that the time had come for organized labour to take a far more active role in the management of the economy, but they took a different line on what this meant in practice. Within Attlee's Cabinet and on the council of the TUC, it was held that individual union leaders, like retired generals and former Whitehall mandarins, ought to be recruited into boardrooms on merit, taking their seats as weighty figures in their own right. The only logical alternative was that union leaders should sit on boards as representatives of their members, fully answerable to their unions – with 'reference back', as the jargon had it – for all of their decisions. This latter approach was rejected as dangerously tantamount to syndicalism by the Labour establishment at Westminster (and was also scorned by those union bosses, like Will Lawther of the National Union of Mineworkers, who saw their role solely in terms of championing their members' interests and wanted nothing to do with the running of their industries). Geddes embraced it, and under his leadership from the UPW headquarters at Crescent Lane in Clapham the Union pursued a joint role with officials of the Department whenever the opportunity arose.* The consequences for the Post Office were to be far-reaching.

Insofar as it promoted a continuation of the wartime spirit of engagement and cooperation between the Official and Staff Sides, the approach taken by Geddes was warmly welcomed by the Post Office. Its benefits were exemplified by the success, in 1945, of a fundamental reorganization for the indoor postal and telegraphy workforce. As the end of the war loomed, there were nineteen grades between the Inner London

---

* The headquarters had been moved to Crescent Lane, from South Kensington's Cromwell Road, in 1937.

Counter Clerks and Telegraphists (maximum wage: 138s a week) at the top and Class III provincial postmen (maximum wage: 92s 6d) at the bottom.[64] Each grade had its own unique pay terms and conditions. In the first significant attempt to roll back the salami-style classification of employees pursued so ruthlessly in the nineteenth century, the Post Office proposed replacing the whole lot with just three job categories, defined by functions. 'Counter and writing duties' would be handled by a new cadre of 'Postal & Telegraph Officers', or P&TOs. Most specialized sorting work would fall to a second new grouping of 'Postmen Higher Grade', or PHGs, though postmen and even P&TOs would be able to handle sorting duties wherever appropriate. Telegraph work would mostly be assigned to the third group, comprising 'Telegraphists' (almost all of them women). Behind the introduction of these superficially innocuous titles lay a vision of the future – first suggested by the Tweedmouth Committee in 1897 and wrestled over for fifty years – in which postmen and sorters would be ready to share work between themselves, in defiance of an elaborate demarcation that had prevailed almost everywhere (outside London) since the day that the first letter carriers set off down the road officially designated as 'postmen' in 1883. Securing the agreement of all the trade unions and reordering the workforce accordingly – in a process that came to be known as the Reallocation – was not a job for the faint-hearted.

The proposals were first published in February 1945. Intensive discussions followed under the auspices of the Whitley Council in the spring. Then, from June until October, Geddes and ten Staff colleagues sat down regularly with a team of fourteen officials led by D. J. Lidbury, now the Personnel Director, to grind out the details, including the scale of the generous upward adjustments to wages (10 per cent in many cases) that would inevitably have to sugar the pill.* A Special Reorganization Conference was held in Blackpool by the UPW at the end of November. Presenting the final recommendations of the joint working party, Geddes justifiably described them as 'probably the most important thing that any conference of the Union, since it was formed in 1920,

---

* When Lidbury retired in March 1947, the Postmaster General bade him farewell in glowing terms at his last Board meeting: 'More was owed to him than to almost any other senior official who had left the Department since the beginning of the war. It was primarily due to him that relationships with the staff had been so amicable during the difficult transition from war to peace, which included the whole Reallocation Scheme itself' (POBM 7 March 1947, Post 69/33).

has had to deal with'.[65] The outcome was a success: final agreements were signed in April 1946 and Reallocation was implemented on 1 June. (A parallel reshuffling of the engineering grades followed two months later.) What stands out from the November conference papers is the speech in which Geddes spelt out the choice before delegates. The scheme was theirs to accept or reject – but they should harbour no illusions that it could be further improved by negotiation or arbitration: 'we have reached practically finality on wages ... and on structure ...', as he put it to them. '[The sum total] is not all that the Executive Council wants ... but you have never had in the last 25 years so great an upgrading of offices as is included in this scheme.' Geddes was in effect speaking on behalf of the entire Reallocation project, with a degree of bipartisan authority that, coming from the Staff Side, struck a new note in the history of the Post Office.

He believed the next few years – given the post-war mood of the country, a Labour government and the difficulties confronted by the Post Office on every side – would present the Union with a historic opportunity to transform the relationship between Headquarters and the Staff Side, without resorting to the dubious rhetoric of Workers' Control. This proved a shrewd calculation. Returning most operations to (relative) normality after the seismic disruptions of the war would take the Post Office about four years. Only by early 1949 would postal traffic fully return to pre-war levels and telephone services to the Continent be properly restored. (Airmails were relaunched within Europe and beyond in July 1948 and April 1949 respectively.) The Post Office Savings Bank would have to weather a torrid few years in which the massively inflated deposits of the war would be largely withdrawn. Officials would gradually resume responsibility for the remaining workload of the Army Postal Service from January 1948 onwards. Over the whole of this period, and against the backcloth from 1947 onwards of a severe downturn in the British economy, the Board's directors would struggle to surmount managerial problems on a scale confronting few if any organizations in the private sector. So long as they were assured a level of cooperation from the Staff Side that averted open clashes or blatant disruption to the postal service, they – and their masters in the Labour government – were prepared to make enormous concessions. Indeed, they had little real choice in the matter, given the dire shortage of the two resources the Post Office needed most: labour and capital.

To start with, it took longer than expected for demobilization to return all of the Department's enlisted men. By the end of 1945, when

Thomas Gardiner retired and was succeeded as Director General by his deputy, Raymond Birchall, only 20,000 or so had been reinstated. There remained almost 55,000 classified absentees, about 15 per cent of the nominal staff total. This did not include the 3,800 employees killed in action and the 400 or so killed on civilian duty. Thereafter, men returned at the rate of about 1,000 a week until October 1946. It was to be another couple of years before the final 15,000 returned from peacetime army duties or work with other government departments.[66] Unfortunately, as the demobbed men returned, married women and female temporary workers departed in more or less equal numbers: there were 142,000 women on the books on V-E Day, and their numbers had stabilized at around 105,000 by October 1947. This was not the consequence of a substitution policy, as after the Great War. These women were leaving of their own volition, often for easier and better-paid jobs elsewhere. But the Post Office desperately needed to expand its workforce: it was faced with a boom in demand for virtually all its services from the moment peace in Europe was declared. An 'effective' workforce of 320,000 by the end of 1945 was lifted to 350,000 a year later, but still trailed far behind its needs. Directors with any personal experience of the labour market knew wages at the Post Office were too often below the going rate.[67]

There were other problems, too. It was restricted by law from recruiting other than ex-servicemen for most establishment positions until the end of 1946; the raising of the school-leaving age to fifteen in 1944 had greatly reduced the supply of boy messengers; and the staff associations objected fiercely to the hiring of any additional temporary workers. The marriage bar, observed since 1875 with a temporary break for the First World War, was at last lifted in October 1946 as the result of legislation to abolish it across the whole of the civil service. But married women were still being deterred from joining the Post Office in the following years by the six-day week it demanded, and by the written tests for P&TO positions, which many women seemed to find unaccountably difficult.[68] The effect of these many constraints together was severe. Officials grappled with crippling shortages of labour that posed almost a monthly crisis – as was sometimes apparent in surprising ways, with German and Italian prisoners of war digging cable ducts for the telephone engineers, and troops in uniform assisting with the Christmas post at many of the largest offices for two years running. (The soldiers worked unpaid alongside schoolboys who were making a decent casual wage, which predictably was not an arrangement that recommended itself for the future. For decades to come, the Post Office would offer good rates to attract hordes of students as temporary postmen to cope with the seasonal peak. A Christmas vacation job at their local post office became almost a rite of passage for two generations of young people.)

Then in January 1947, as the country struggled with the impact of the worst winter in living memory and anxiety mounted over the bleak outlook for Britain's economy, the Labour government ordered a freeze on manpower levels across the whole civil service, including the Post Office. Requests soon followed from Whitehall for the headcount to be reduced, so that more men might be released for jobs in heavy industry. Officials responded by discharging several thousand non-establishment part-timers. This left many individual families in desperate straits, and a 'Committee on behalf of Temporaries' tried in vain to persuade the Post Office to offer more of them jobs as full-time postmen. The Board decided to stick to the immediate post-war policy of hiring ex-servicemen, largely at the union's behest: as a Board paper from Lidbury's successor as Personnel Director, J. Scholes, made clear: 'The UPW have expressed the view very strongly that our present arrangements should not be disturbed'.[69] (A deputation of worried Labour MPs visited St Martin's around this time to submit a complaint to the Postmaster General 'over the discharge of temporary staff problem', but was flummoxed to find the Board and the UPW at one on the issue.[70]) More use of part-time workers in general might have reduced wage costs for the Post Office, and encouraged more flexibility in working practices, but all the postal unions objected fiercely to the introduction of part-timers as a matter of principle. Meanwhile, the veto on any further additions to the (over-whelmingly full-time) establishment workforce gravely exacerbated a crisis of morale in many sections of the Department. The clerical staff of the Savings Bank, still largely exiled in Harrogate and Morecambe, where they had lost their wartime billets and were lodged in dismal hostels, struggled with a volume of withdrawals that had soared since the war. The peak had passed in 1946, with almost 75 million with-drawals compared to fewer than 17 million in 1938, but business levels in 1947 were scarcely less overwhelming. Transactions across the counter were taking ten days or more just to be recorded in the ledger accounts, so buried in paperwork were the Bank's unhappy clerks.[71] The telephone business was another source of chronic concern to the Board. In the first nine months of 1947, staff resignations in London equated to two thirds of the total number of new recruits. Among those who remained, especially young women operators on £4 a week – far below the range of wages affected by Reallocation – morale was perilously low. The head of the London Telecoms Region told his Board colleagues in October that there was 'a general feeling of discontentment, or even grievance' among his female telephonists, and he warned that 'there might be a real breakdown in the service in London – local, toll and trunk'.[72] By the spring of 1948, the Director General was at a loss to know how to reply to a request from the Ministerial Manpower Committee for more restraints on staffing. He believed the Post Office really needed another 9,000 heads – which 'might give the Committee a nasty shock' – and confessed to the Board that 'services were already cut to the bone on the postal side'. In the event, workforce numbers hovered around 350,000 through the next eighteen months (more than 5 per cent of them registered as disabled), with female staff fairly steady at just under 30 per cent of the total. Discussions of the staffing predicament only began to fade from the minutes of the Post Office Board from the early months of 1949.

The Department's shortage of capital prompted less sense of crisis, at least in the first year or so of peace, perhaps disguised by its robust financial performance. The published 'Commercial Accounts' of the Post Office certainly presented an impressive picture. As we have already noted, postal and telephone revenues had risen dramatically through the war years. Having peaked at just over £40m in 1944–5, the Surplus naturally dropped away as profitable wartime services to the Government were discontinued; but the decline was obligingly gradual – from £36m (1945–6), £24m (1946–7) and £20m (1947–8) to £15m (1948–9). The Accountant General, George Ismay, delivered a remarkable forecast in the summer of 1945: he correctly picked out 1948–9 as the year that would see business volumes returning to pre-war levels, and (again correctly) saw £15.3m as a likely figure for that year's Surplus.[73] But, rather oddly, Ismay expected to see telephone and telegraph profits returning more or less to pre-war levels (i.e. zero, with telephone profits cancelling out a telegraph deficit) and postal profits rising steadily. The actual outcome – with telephone profits proving much more resilient and postal profits flattening out – suggested that the Post Office could enjoy a sustainable level of profits markedly higher than he thought possible, if only the losses on the telegraph network could be reined back. (The reintroduction in 1949 of greetings telegrams, suspended since 1943, was confidently expected to do the trick, but didn't.)

This happy prospect, while encouraging enough in itself, was only a notional guide to the Department's financial situation. In the first place, the Commercial Accounts were exactly that – notional. They were based on the pretence that services to the Government would be paid for, whereas in reality no government departments were even being invoiced for the Post Office's services through these years, let alone charged. The accounts were intended to provide as close an approximation as possible of how Post Office financial statements might appear were it a commercial business. Prior to the war, the discrepancy between the Commercial Surplus and the 'Post Office Net Receipt' – the actual excess of cash revenues over the cash spending authorized each year by Parliament – had been quite modest. As a result of the war, as Ismay was at pains to explain to his Board colleagues in November 1945, the position was 'very different'.[74] Indeed, the greatly expanded Surplus was positively awkward, as was more than once admitted in Board meetings over this period. Surprisingly, as some thought, there was no call from the public for lower postage rates. But there surely had to be a limit to the size of the Surplus, beyond which it would trigger a popular reaction – unless, perhaps, some effort was made to explain the curious nature of the Commercial Accounts. Ismay made it quite clear in February 1947 that he thought elaborate explanations would be a bad idea and might invite closer scrutiny of the Post Office's actual rising costs.[75] So the Surpluses went on being reported, as boldly as ever. No doubt this encouraged many to see postal profits as a pocket worth picking whenever possible – and not just on the wages front. Late in 1946, as one of their last combined initiatives as private businesses, the big railway companies successfully pressed the Treasury to grant them higher conveyance rates for Post Office parcels. And early in 1949, the Civil Aviation Ministry similarly managed to extract higher airmail rates from the Postmaster General on behalf of BOAC. As the minutes of a subsequent Board discussion recorded: 'It seemed clear that, taking Post Office postal finance as a whole, the Department was not in a strong position to drive too hard a bargain with the Corporation'.[76]

Nonetheless, and however much of a boon they proved for some third parties, the Surpluses brought the Post Office itself no joy at all when it came to the sourcing of capital funds. No effort was made to relaunch the Post Office Fund, abandoned at the start of the war: all postal profits, however defined by the accountants, flowed straight back to the Exchequer (like any other form of indirect taxation). Cap in hand, officials had to turn to the Treasury each year with fresh capital-spending plans – and the response in the post-war years went from cool

to very chilly indeed. The result was a dire shortage of the capital investment fondly envisaged by the Post Office in the immediate aftermath of
the war. Additional plant for a telephone industry besieged with eager
customers (subscribing at twice the peak pre-war rate); new and bigger
buildings for many large provincial towns, where postal workers were
still toiling in cramped conditions that dismayed more than one newly
installed Postmaster General; spending on innovative services, such as a
much-discussed use of helicopters for inland airmails – all were squeezed
back ruthlessly, as the Treasury struggled with the country's mounting
balance-of-payments crisis.[77] Some categories of discretionary spending,
though, were less easily curtailed. The pension provision was running in
1947 at almost 19 per cent of all current pay to pensionable staff, up
from about 11.5 per cent in 1939–40 – and even this sobering jump, as
Ismay warned his colleagues late in the year, 'was probably not adequate
on a strict actuarial basis. It was a big burden for the [Estimates] account
to carry'.[78] A substantially larger pension fund was necessitated by pay
awards that were bringing in more generous wage scales, implying
substantially higher earnings for many employees in future years.

Success with its wage claims was the first test of the UPW's negotiating skills under Geddes, and it passed with flying colours. Following the
consolidation of the war bonuses in 1945 and the payment of the Reallocation 'adjustments' in 1946, Geddes in 1947 secured the biggest
award in the history of the union. The rise in the cost-of-living index
since 1938 was matched, and comfortably exceeded for many in the
workforce. By 1948 he was personally inclined to support a plea from
the Labour government for a freeze on all wage claims: he believed that
he and his colleagues had a duty to stand by a Labour government in
crisis. But Geddes found himself more or less obliged by the Annual
Conference to push for yet another claim. This included a demand that
incremental pay scales linked to age should offer maximum rates to
workers aged twenty-five – several years earlier than currently applied
in most cases – which was tersely characterized for the Board by Scholes
as 'completely fantastic, and out of touch with what seemed to him the
realities of the situation'.[79] It also sought a 12½ per cent overall increase
at the top end of the wage scale. This too was rejected and went to the
Civil Service Arbitration Panel. But the UPW emerged after a two-day
hearing in May 1949 with a 4–6 per cent award which was accepted
without demur. Geddes could fairly claim by the summer of 1949 to
have consolidated a seminal improvement in the position of the postal
workforce.

The progress made on equal pay for women was much less clear – but then the same was true of the UPW's fundamental stance on this whole issue. Like the Post Office itself, all of the male-dominated postal unions remained profoundly ambivalent on 'Equal Pay'. The UPW had formally adopted a policy supporting it in 1920, but only as a negotiating stance. Not to favour Equal Pay, in theory, might weaken Union arguments against the use of cheaper women employees for men's jobs. In practice, Equal Pay was stealthily resisted at every turn. The union steadfastly opposed women working on night shifts, for example. But because they therefore did not do any night work, their overall responsibilities were not equal to men's and thus Equal Pay did not apply. Officials were consistently happy to connive at this kind of nonsense. A Royal Commission on Equal Pay from 1944 to 1946 had made little headway, but had at least exposed some of the doublethink on both sides. The UPW kept careful notes on the public proceedings of the Commission, and they were referred to in a debate on the union's Executive Council in June 1945 over whether or not the union should give evidence. It was noted that the Director General during his appearance 'was asked if women would work at night if given equal pay, and [he had] replied you must not ask me for information about the attitude of the staff'. Geddes bluntly asserted to his Council that the union's policy had always been equal pay for equal work, *not* equal pay for men and women. One of his deputies challenged him, asking what would happen if the Commissioners ever asked him outright if he believed women *ought* to do night duty: '[The deputy] did not think the Royal Commission would allow the General Secretary to skate about in his reply to this question'. This drew an indignant response: 'Mr Geddes said he had no need to skate about on the question'. Then he set off across the ice: 'If the Royal Commission asked did women do the same work as men, the answer would be yes; but if they asked did they do the same attendance, he would have to say no ... The only issue was[:] did the fact that they did different attendances impose another feature against equal pay for equal work?'[80] Fortunately for the union, perhaps, the Government rendered the debate academic by asserting in 1947 that the country simply could not afford to pay women equal wages. As the Chancellor, Hugh Dalton, told the House of Commons in June, the Government could accept equal pay 'as a broad affirmation of a general principle' but could not at present contemplate taking on the additional costs it would involve for the public sector. 'Some limit must be set to the rate at which new projects, involving fresh expenditure, can be undertaken. ... This question should be further examined at a later date, in the light of the development of social policy and of the economic and financial circumstances of the country.'[81]

The impact of the UPW on industrial relations at the Post Office in 1945–9 went far beyond the success of its strategy on wage negotiations. The Union also helped to foster a profound shift in the consensus view of what the Department could reasonably expect to demand of its Manipulative workers. Of course, broader social changes in post-war Britain played their part here, but an uncompromising stand by the UPW undoubtedly made a big contribution to a material improvement in the quality of life for many lower-paid postal workers. Officials made elaborate plans through 1944 and early 1945 for a virtual restoration of the Post Office's pre-war services. The programme was to unfold in two stages: 'Interim Services' for a first year or so, followed by the introduction of 'Final Services'. This timing was actually achieved – with implementation of the two stages in October 1945 and June–October 1946 (January 1947 in London), respectively – and it was generally felt at Board level that the Director of Postal Services, Alexander Little, had handled the whole process in some style. But the details revealed a subtler process at work. That speech by Archie Wood at the 1945 Blackpool Conference, about the disrupted social and family lives of postal workers, had struck a rich chord of disaffection. 'Even the authorities themselves had to admit that 53 per cent of provincial postmen [in 1938] still had two attendances [a day] and 6 per cent had three'.[82] The 'split' rota hours, the early-morning compulsory attendances, the sustained pressure of late-evening collections – these were service terms, as the UPW insisted from the earliest post-war days, that were not merited by the wage scales on offer. The union made its objectives clear before the launch of the Interim Services: it wanted no duties before 6 a.m., no delivery walks that lasted more than two hours and no collections later than 8 p.m., with final deliveries beginning at 4.30 p.m. rather than 7 p.m. Little reported back to his colleagues that these proposals had been pitched 'in a reasonable spirit'. He anticipated plenty of resistance to the argument that the public would find the resulting curbs on pre-war services unacceptable, but 'was inclined to think that, if need be, he would be able to convince them'.[83]

He never did. On the contrary, gradual concessions led to further demands. By October 1946, it had been agreed that the last mail collection of the day would be at 6 p.m. across almost the whole country. By March 1947, the union was pressing for the last collection to be made at 5.30 p.m. Compromises had in many instances to be imposed by executive action, against the union's opposition. At King Edward Building, where sorting operations for the City had employed 500 postmen at 5 a.m. before the war, proposals for a 150-man shift at 5 a.m. were rejected by the UPW and all the other staff associations involved. Whether their implementation in January 1947 caused any trouble is unclear – the general crisis prompted by the severe winter weather and a transport strike in London that month helped finesse the problem. Indeed, the same may have applied, in a sense, at a national level. At regular intervals through 1947–9, the Board had to contemplate service cutbacks that one director or another would habitually warn 'might lead to a public outcry'. Yet the outcry never came. A sense of crisis over Britain's faltering economy left the public unfazed by incremental curbs to the daily postal services – and people seemed broadly sympathetic, too, to the idea of better terms and conditions for the postmen. A new Postmaster General, Wilfred Paling, expressed private astonishment in May 1947 at the meagre wages paid to rural postmen – and Paling, a coal miner in his youth, was no stranger to the wages paid for manual labour.* That same month, more service restrictions were announced. Paling asked the Board what he should say in the Commons if anyone pointed out that there were 5,000 more postmen on the books than in 1939, yet fewer services. Wasn't the Post Office costing more and delivering less? Birchall advised a stoical response. 'The Director General suggested that this was a phenomenon to be observed in almost every aspect of life nowadays . . . [Besides,] the staff simply would not put up with pre-war conditions, eg attendances'.[84]

Whatever the general public's reaction, the decline in postal services certainly grieved many long-serving officials, especially those whose careers in the Post Office had begun before the Great War. It seemed a painful irony to them that the Commercial Accounts went on reporting huge Surpluses, prompting some to ask if the 2½d standard letter rate (introduced in 1940) should not be reduced. Raymond Birchall scoffed at the very idea: 'the present standard of postal service was far worse than pre-war . . . [and] no reduction in tariffs should be considered until the standard of service had been improved'.[85] It was no longer possible,

---

* Born in 1883, Paling had been a Labour MP since 1922, bar a two-year interval after Labour's collapse in 1931. He had enjoyed the distinction of winning the largest majority in the House of Commons at the election of 1945, for the Yorkshire constituency of Wentworth. He was Minister of Pensions in 1945–7 and served as PMG, his last post in government, from 1947 to 1950.

as of October 1948, even to guarantee a same-day delivery for any letter headed outside its own postal district! The cancellation of the pre-war last delivery, accounting for about 15 per cent of the daily post, meant some letters mailed on Day A would not arrive until Day C – unless postmen could be persuaded to resume second daily deliveries in the afternoon, which it seemed was impossible. Whether talk of better future services was realistic, many doubted. Little's successor as Director of Postal Services (Little and Ismay had moved up to become Birchall's deputies), J. E. Yates responded bleakly that the Department 'would be lucky if it could hold the present standard of postal services for more than twelve or eighteen months' as the pressure was continuing to mount for a reduction in the standard working week. The UPW had first pressed for a forty-hour week in 1933. After a 44-hour week had been conceded to the engineers in 1947, it began pressing much harder for agreement in principle to a five-day week that would pose a serious threat to traditional Saturday services. Nor was the Post Office's heavy reliance on self-employed postmasters and postmistresses working in small post offices for a commission – in 'scale-payment sub-offices' – free from attack. In May 1949, as a review of rural offices gathered pace, the UPW 'contended that the Sub-Office system was based on sweated labour, and [that it] could make out a strong case for abolishing Sub-Offices, or at least a considerable number [of them]'.[86]

There was one other aspect of the relationship between the Post Office and its workforce in the post-war years to which Geddes paid special heed. He was determined that the UPW should be recognized as the sole negotiator on behalf of all Manipulative grades in the Department. Such an assertive approach wrecked his relationship with the first post-war politician appointed to St Martin's. This was the 5th Earl of Listowel, who sounded like a throwback to the days when possession of a title was virtually *de rigueur* for any holder of the office. Listowel, though, was a most unusual aristocrat. Preferring to be known in his youth as Billy Hare, he had been a socialist since his school days at Eton in the 1920s, much to the 4th Earl's consternation. After studying at Cambridge and the Sorbonne, and writing a respectable textbook on aesthetics, he had been one of a tiny group of hereditary Labour peers in the House of Lords through the 1930s and had served as a junior minister in the wartime coalition government. Outwardly genial and self-effacing, Listowel had a steely core and was not afraid to stand his ground on matters of principle. He felt one such matter of principle to be that any trade union with a substantial following had a right to be formally recognized. He rejected a concerted attempt by the UPW in the autumn of 1946 to change his mind, merely conceding that a proper review of the issue might be timely. Having conducted his own review, he then announced a theoretical underpinning for the policy upheld by his predecessors. (The 'Listowel formula' set a threshold for any aspiring union: it had to have a membership equal to 40 per cent of the relevant workforce.) Geddes reacted badly to this and there was a briefly colourful spat.* But Listowel moved on in April 1947 – to take charge of the legislation for India's future independence – and his successors proved more amenable. By the end of 1949, after an interminable correspondence between the two sides, Paling and his officials effectively agreed to ditch Listowel's stance. Geddes was assured in December that – while existing unions like the National Guild of Telephonists (a particular UPW bugbear) would not be cold-shouldered – any future applications for union recognition would take account of 'wider questions, such as the effect of a change in representation on the general working relationships in the Post Office'.[87] The UPW, in this respect at least, would not be crossed again.

The progress made by Geddes and his colleagues over these four years – whether in terms of pay, working conditions or the political clout of their union – had finally separated the Post Office altogether from that already remote debate of the early 1930s over the Department's optimal constitutional status. The top-heavy unwieldiness of its traditional structure had been replaced by 1940. The public's perception of its efficiency had been transformed by Kingsley Wood, and vindicated by its emergence during the war as a pillar of the nation. Now its workforce had achieved a say in the direction of its affairs that effectively precluded any further discussion of Wolmer-style reforms. If Wood had found the prospect of union opposition too daunting to contemplate in 1931–2, how much more unthinkable must it have seemed

---

* The letter containing Listowel's conclusions was unfortunately released to the press before it reached the UPW. Geddes was tracked down by a reporter for the Press Association, who read him the key passages. His reward was a quote from the General Secretary, to the effect that Listowel's snub was 'the most disgraceful and discourteous act of any Postmaster General', a remark that featured prominently in several newspapers over the following days. Angry letters were exchanged between the two sides, with Geddes rehearsing the history of union recognition with his usual stamina and reminding Listowel of the Holt Committee's findings in 1913 that a 'multiplication of Associations within the same class' should be discouraged. 'It would appear that your Lordship's decision is even more reactionary than the views expressed 33 years ago' (UPW Executive Council Minutes 1946–47, pp. 759–64, UCW/2/1/30).

to his post-war successors that structural reform, still less privatization, could be broached against the wishes of the unions. Wolmer and his supporters had sought to present the period from the 1860s to the 1920s as a kind of aberration in Post Office history, when its business instincts had been subordinated to the broader political agenda of the state. There was little doubt by the end of the 1940s that it was Wolmer and the proponents of a fully commercial postal business that were themselves cast as the aberration. The great wave of post-war nationalizations by the Labour government ensured plenty of public debate over the efficacy or otherwise of public corporations. Scarcely anyone, however, thought it worth mentioning the Post Office. A series of articles on 'The Public Corporation' in *The Times*, that erstwhile champion of postal reform, referred to it in passing, but only to rule the Post Office out of the discussion.[88] There were obvious, if unstated, reasons for doing so. As the Cold War descended, the Department's contribution to national defence would have ruled out any talk of increasing its autonomy. (As late as 1952, the Postmaster General was still reminding Parliament that a third of the Post Office's capital expenditure was defence-related.[89]) And the Labour government was set on pulling industries closer to Whitehall, not the other way round – under a Prime Minister, and former Postmaster General, who had told the Bridgeman Enquiry in 1932 that he was 'entirely opposed to turning the Post Office into a public utility corporation'.[90] Nevertheless, the silence in these years over the constitutional position of the Post Office is striking.

Attlee had told Bridgeman all those years ago that, in his opinion, 'union leaders have shown much practical statesmanship and reasonableness in dealing with very complicated questions'. It was a view shared by many senior officials by 1949. By the time Wilfred Paling was giving way to the UPW over union recognition, Birchall had given way in October 1949 to a new Director General: Alexander Little. He and Geddes enjoyed a strong relationship and had long been running the Department's Whitley Council together. In the months before his promotion, in response to an appeal from the Chancellor for every business to pursue higher productivity as an urgent national goal, Little had taken up a novel scheme to draw the unions further into the management of the Department. He had instigated a 'Joint Productivity Council', which would function in parallel with the Whitley Council. (It was soon being referred to on all sides as the 'Joint Production Council' – Joint Production Councils had existed across much of the engineering industry during the war.) The JPC would have separate panels for Clerical, Postal and

Telecoms Operations, and Internal Publicity. Days after stepping up as Director General, Little sent a notice out to all his Regional Directors and Head Postmasters, alerting them to the importance of this innovation: 'It is not too much to say that the introduction of Joint Production [sic] machinery marks a new departure in the relationship of the two Sides in the Post Office'.[91] Years later, Geddes would recall the inaugural meeting of the JPC:

> In the normal way [with Whitley meetings] . . . the Staff Side were always in their place first, and then the Official Side filed in, in order to show their superiority. In this case, we were all in, and Little said . . . 'Come over here, Geddes, you sit next to me. There's no "both sides of the table" here. Take your seats!' And the Official Side just went to the nearest seat they could and sat beside a member of the Staff Side.[92]

Expectations were running high on all sides.

PART THREE

No Ordinary Business

9
Bright hopes blighted,
1949–64

'Were there postmen then, too?'

'With sprinkling eyes and wind-cherried noses, on spread, frozen feet they crunched up to the doors and mittened on them manfully. But all that the children could hear was a ringing of bells.'

'You mean that the postmen went rat-a-tat-tat and the doors rang?'

'I mean that the bells the children could hear were inside them . . . They were just ordinary postmen, fond of walking and dogs and Christmas and the snow. They knocked on the door with blue knuckles . . .'

'Ours has got a black knocker . . .'

'And then they stood on the white Welcome mat in the little, drifted porches and huffed and puffed, making ghosts with their breath, and jogged from foot to foot like small boys wanting to go out.'

From Dylan Thomas's *A Child's Christmas in Wales* (1954)

I. DREAMING OF PARTNERSHIP

Early in December 1949, the General Secretary of the UPW was approached by the Post Office Board with an intriguing invitation.[1] The Director General had been asked if the Post Office would like to send a working party to the US on a six-week fact-finding mission in the spring. Would the union care to participate? The trip would be organized under the auspices of a recently established Anglo-American Council on Productivity and all expenses incurred in the US would be paid by the Government in Washington out of funds provided by the Marshall Plan.

Alexander Little had immediately seized on it as an opportunity to give his new Joint Production Council real substance: seven of the sixteen places available in the party were to be reserved for Staff Side representatives. Charles Geddes moved almost immediately to begin discussing appropriate arrangements. Some days later, he chaired the first meeting of the Staff delegates assigned to the JPC. (They were all union figures: the UPW had refused to have any truck with the idea of non-union representatives on the JPC.) But when Geddes announced the US invitation to the JPC, suggesting '[such a trip] would be extremely valuable', he seems to have met with a stony silence. At a special meeting in the New Year, held to discuss the invitation, he was then bitterly disappointed to hear it being derided by one colleague after another as a capitalist joy ride that would be of no benefit to the Department whatever. Was there really anything that the Post Office could learn from the Americans? And were not all US companies run by 'Private Enterprise'? There followed a round of pejorative comments about all things American, of a kind that Geddes had heard too often before.[2] It was even suggested that the consequences of participating in the visit 'might be dangerous in view of past history'. (This was a reference to the aftermath of Leon Simon's visit to the US in 1927, which had brought back such unfavourable comparisons of British and US labour relations.) By a vote of 14–5, the meeting opted to defer any decision until all constituent staff associations of the JPC had had a chance to reflect on the idea. When Geddes turned to the Executive Council itself, it promptly voted to give the visit a cold shoulder.

The rebuff was especially embarrassing for Geddes insofar as cooperation with the Marshall Plan since 1947, while thought intrinsically desirable, was also seen as part of a broader campaign by leading figures in the TUC to counter Communist influence in the union movement. The Plan – embraced by unions in Western Europe, rejected by unions in Soviet Russia and Eastern Europe – had taken on an obvious political significance. Any union openly opposing it might risk being seen as complacent, in the face of Communist activity in the workplace. Negligible before the war, it had grown significantly in the wake of Soviet Russia becoming an ally against Hitler in 1941. The unions had backed the war effort, and Communists had worked within many unions to further the interests of country and Party together. The Party's membership had always been tiny – only two Communist MPs were elected in 1945 – but Communists had set out to capture union posts that might afford them real power in the post-war labour movement, and had been successful enough to prompt genuine alarm among TUC leaders once the Cold War began in earnest in 1947.* The Post Office Engineering Union had been hugely disrupted by a Communist bid for the leadership in 1947: half its Executive had backed a Communist candidate for the Presidency, Bill Hurst, and his eventual defeat by a wider vote of POEU conference delegates – and the subsequent expulsion from the union of a Communist chairman of its Glasgow branch, Jimmy Kirkwood – had been a bitter struggle involving battles in the High Court.[3] If the Communist Party had by contrast made little headway among UPW officials, this was partly down to the stand taken by Geddes himself: he displayed a fierce personal animosity towards anyone he suspected of Communist sympathies. (When the Government in 1948 proposed excluding Party members from most positions in the civil service, Geddes strongly endorsed the policy to his Executive Council – and it must have taken some courage for one of the few avowed Communists at a senior level in the union, a Council member called Fathers, to object that '[he] thought the Executive Council were becoming imperialistically minded. If the job of Trade Union leaders was to bolster up capitalist states going to war then he was wasting his time on the EC . . .'[4]) To have his union's stand on this issue impugned by the rejection of the US invitation in 1949 was plainly mortifying for the General Secretary.

For seven weeks, he scurried to retrieve the situation, while fending off the protestations of other union leaders that 'the adverse reaction of the Americans [to] a refusal to participate could not be overemphasized'. He sent a list of his colleagues' objections into the Post Office – all of them tediously bureaucratic and not overtly political at all – and relayed to the Staff Side the painstaking, item-by-item responses he received back from officials who 'urged with very great sincerity that . . . it would be a grave mistake if it had to be reported that the Post Office had declined to cooperate in the venture because of staff opposition'. In a letter to the Executive Council in mid-February, he implored his colleagues to think again. There was, he said, 'a real danger here of creating a completely false impression in the mind of the Americans on the question of nationalized industry versus private enterprise'. The Council met

---

* The Electrical Trades Union, the Foundry Workers' Union and the Fire Brigades Union were all Communist-controlled by 1947, as were the Welsh and Scottish constituent unions of the National Union of Mineworkers, which had a Communist General Secretary, Arthur Horner, from 1946. Communist members comprised almost a quarter of the Transport & General Workers' Union's executive council, and many unions had to contend with strong Communist influence at a local level, especially in London.

on 21 March – and when a motion by Geddes to rescind the earlier decision produced a tied vote, the Buggins figure in the chair cast his deciding vote against it.[5] That effectively closed the door to participation in the Marshall Plan for the UPW. Another invitation was received from Washington a year later, prompting one last appeal by Geddes to the Executive Council. His motion that invitations to participate in future visits of this kind to the US should be considered on their merits was heavily defeated.[6]

The Marshall Plan episode showed just how difficult it could be to choreograph UPW politics, even at the Executive Council level. There was a limit to how far the Council, with its entirely elective membership, could be truly distanced from an often unpredictable workforce and a network of district councils and branch committees that included many prickly characters – some of them keen to bring on the socialist revolution sooner rather than later. Not everyone in the union hierarchy shared their General Secretary's basic belief in the efficacy of constructive engagement with the Official Side. If Geddes by the late 1940s generally enjoyed an unprecedented degree of control over the UPW's affairs, his authority relied at all times on an indefatigable attention to detail and constant attendance at an astonishing number of meetings – from those of the Executive Council and its many sub-committees, convened weekly, to those held under the aegis of the UPW Annual Conference at a seaside resort each May. Sometimes he found himself wrong-footed, as in 1949. For the most part, however, the General Secretary managed to carry the union with him. And he dedicated himself above all to leading it into an unprecedented bond of active partnership with the Official Side in the management of the Post Office.

Board seats were not on offer at the start of the 1950s, but the JPC appeared a big step in the right direction. Geddes accordingly committed the UPW to full support of Little's initiative. The union provided eight representatives, who joined eleven other union representatives on the Staff Side. An equal number from the Official Side made up the rest of the JPC's thirty-eight members. Within six months, no fewer than 500 JPC sub-committees had been set up across the country, reinforcing the activities of Whitley and UPW local bodies and giving representatives of the workforce a powerful say over how things were to be done from day to day. There were fewer constraints on this development than in any other industrial setting in Britain. Postal work involved no heavy machinery, dangerous chemicals or the like – nor indeed, for many thousands of postal workers in the big cities, any direct contact at all

with the customer. It required only basic skills and no extensive training, and relied on experience more than anything else. If the men in the
workplace insisted they understood their job better than any supervisor,
it was usually hard to say they were wrong. Union control of that workplace began to seem a natural consequence of the JPC experiment.

The arrival of a third Labour Postmaster General in March 1950
only confirmed the apparent direction of events. Ness Edwards, a close
associate of Aneurin Bevan, was a Welsh trade unionist who had been
working as Parliamentary Private Secretary at the Ministry of Labour
since the end of the war, and was predictably delighted with what he
found going on at the Post Office. It was particularly pleasing, Edwards
told the union members of the JPC in April 1950, 'to see how you have
faced up to this problem of becoming, shall I say, partners in this very
great service'.[7] The JPC sub-committees were inundated with workplace suggestions for ways to crank up productivity in the postal service.
True, the immediate results were often hard to quantify, but then had
not postal operations been steadily improving for years? 'The statistics
of achievement might not seem very spectacular', as Geddes admitted in
a speech to the next full JPC meeting in November 1950, 'but they
were, in all, astonishing in relation to the high standard of efficiency
which had always obtained in the Post Office.'[8]

It came as a disappointment to the Staff Side in the summer of 1951
when Edwards refused to take the next step towards full Board representation, a joint UPW and POEU proposal from 1949 for a 'Joint
Advisory Council' as a forum for debating major policy issues. It was
envisaged that this Joint Advisory Council would have the Postmaster
General as chairman, with a vice-chairman elected by the workforce,
and would 'be entrusted with the task of advising the Post Office Board
on all matters relating to the policy and administration of the various
Post Office services'.[9] Since this would have been a shadow Board in all
but name, even Edwards had to draw back at this point: the Advisory
Council would have entailed extensive disclosure of confidential papers
to its members 'and I consider that no Minister could properly accept
such a position'.[10] But the Postmaster General was so anxious to
reassure the trade union councils of his best intentions that, as a UPW
official put it in a private memo, he seemed 'to concede informally the
discussion on policy matters which he feels unable to concede formally'.
Edwards himself was confident no harm had been done. He told the
Board in June that 'he had had a lot of experience with the socialized
industries and he knew of no public institution with better staff relations

than those that existed in the Post Office. He thought the Post Office could teach other organizations a lesson in this respect.'[11]

Labour's defeat in the General Election of October 1951 effectively ended the dream of UPW representation on the Board. It was quickly apparent, however, that Geddes would still have ample scope to pursue a less formal parity of status between the Staff and Official Sides. The new Conservative Postmaster General was the Earl De La Warr, who seemed almost to regard the UPW and POEU as de facto partners from the outset.* When the new government's Chancellor of the Exchequer, Rab Butler, asked the Post Office early in 1952 to curtail its services and cut back its workforce, De La Warr told the Board there was no question of simply acquiescing in such demands 'and that he would need to discuss with the Staff Side all the proposals'.[12] Geddes and his colleagues in the UPW worked tirelessly to confirm the PMG's understanding. Every remotely contentious policy decision was taken up by them as a suitable pretext for forming a joint committee of Official and Staff Side representatives. The detailed minutes of the UPW's Executive Council for the next few years record the work of a succession of such committees, which began to parallel at the centre what was already happening around the country. Had the time come to reconsider upper age limits for recruitment to the Manipulative grades? Should Saturday services be reduced? Was there a case for raising the basic age of retirement for postal workers beyond sixty? How might employee terms and conditions be adjusted to take account of working with new mechanical aids? Again and again, the first response from Headquarters was to put the question to a working party including half a dozen or so representatives of the UPW, as often as not led by Geddes in person.[13] Not infrequently, the union's delegation outnumbered the officials around the table.

The subsequent discussions did not always lead to agreement, but the extent of the bipartite approach to the management of the Post Office through the first half of the 1950s was nonetheless remarkable. One immediate outcome was the elevation of Geddes himself to a prominence scarcely contemplated by any of his predecessors. There survive many circulars written by the General Secretary, addressing issues of general concern to the Department, which could almost have been penned by the head of one directorate or another. Take, for example, his response to the problem of soaring sickness rates. The Personnel

---

* De La Warr's parliamentary private secretary was the Earl of Selkirk, so the Post Office had a brace of earls to its name for the first time since the eighteenth century.

Director in 1953, F. T. Dixon, undertook a careful review of finalized statistics for the calendar year of 1951. They showed that, on average, each man in the Post Office had taken 14.9 days of sick leave. (Among postmen over eighteen the figure was 17.6 days.) The average woman had taken 18.6 days. These rates represented almost exactly a doubling since 1938, when the rates had stood at 7.6 and 9.3 days respectively. The total of man-years forgone in 1951 equated to a financial loss for the Post Office of £2.25m (not far short of half the commercial profit shown for 1951–2). Dixon was alarmed over what had been a steady upward trend since 1948, but was at a loss to know how best to respond.* He appealed to Geddes and the UPW's executive for assistance, and it was agreed that a joint committee of the Whitley Council would be set up to investigate the problem. There is no evidence that its deliberations ever came to much – but the General Secretary made a rallying call to the whole of his membership in the late summer of 1953, over '[an issue that] must be a matter of great concern to us all, both as Post Office people and as citizens'. Geddes said the Post Office was doing everything it could to tackle the problem – but he appealed to all the district committees of the union 'to consider whether anything further can be done to encourage the sort of team spirit which reduces sick absence to a healthy minimum'.[14]

While the senior officers of the union edged ever closer to policy-making and the overall management of the Post Office, the UPW's own hierarchy – extending down through regional councils to district councils, and branch and sub-branch committees – went on increasing its de facto control over operations at a local level. And the UPW's officers naturally brought to their expanding role all of the meticulous regard for the rule book that had originally been inculcated into the workplace by the Post Office itself. Thus were the disciplines of the Victorian era now reborn as the labour rigidities of the post-war world. It was hardly a phenomenon unique to the Post Office – economists and business historians debating the causes of Britain's poor post-war productivity have

---

* There was no ignoring that the launch of the NHS in 1948 had deprived the Post Office of its own medical service, which for almost a century had maintained savvy medical officers at all the main sorting sites. There were new routines for the issuance of medical certificates, and taking sick leave had never been easier. It was also the case that those on sick leave received full pay, while being relieved of the need to pay national health insurance: they actually earned more by staying at home than by going to work. As the Board noted in July 1950, 'it seemed to be rather straining the honesty of an ordinary man to expect him to return to work earlier than he need and lose money for doing so' (POBM 4 July 1950, Post 69/49).

long identified the legacy of earlier labour systems as a prime culprit. But in few other contexts were the ramifications of the problem drawn out quite so comprehensively. The detailed routines of the postal service were laid down in the voluminous *Head Postmaster's Manual* – covering everything from attendance hours, disciplinary and sick leave procedures to overtime duties, vehicle maintenance and dress codes – and the slightest local deviation from its text was increasingly subject to interminable negotiation. These were the years in which the convention was gradually adopted that all communications with the workforce directly should be left to union officers. Management's voice was effectively banished from the workplace. Even the staffing of new offices, like all other local recruitment and redundancy planning, was made effectively subject to union veto.

Upward pressure from the union membership also determined a wide range of policies adopted by the Post Office nationally. Thus, by 1955, the UPW dictated how often cash balances were totted up at all office counters (daily); when a Postman Higher Grade could be required to do outdoors work (ever more rarely); where postmen could be allowed to use bicycles (not at all, within Inner London); or when pools literature could be included in the day's first delivery (never). It was effectively the union that chose which traditional taboos should be dropped (like the blanket ban on smoking while on duty) and which should be retained (like the veto on women or part-timers being allowed to work as postmen). Fortunately, perhaps, there was one staffing issue on which the union was ignored. The 1953 Annual Conference voted in favour of a motion – proposed by a single woman from the Edinburgh Female Telegraphs Branch – asking the Executive Council to see the restoration of the marriage bar. (Married women with no eligibility for the retirement dowry were blocking the way, it was argued, for single women who would like to have gained promotion before then accepting the dowry.) Union delegates put the same motion to the National Staff Side of the Whitley Council in September 1953, where it was heavily defeated, but not before the UPW had attracted plenty of obloquy from all sides. Geddes appears to have been embarrassed by this episode, and insisted on a motion at the Annual Conference in 1954 distancing the union from what had happened.* Meanwhile, whatever the union's policy on this or

* It went mostly unnoticed by the outside world that Geddes nonetheless insisted on retaining a marriage bar in place within the union itself: official positions, as he argued in a report to the Executive Council in December 1954, simply involved too much work to be shoul-

that specific issue, a culture was being steadily entrenched that revolved around a strict job demarcation – a staple feature of life in the army that huge numbers of postmen had experienced at first hand. The attendant 'restrictive practices', curbing management's ability to allocate labour except as permitted by the staff associations, now defined the postal workplace almost as much as the incremental grading of every job. And with almost 160,000 members out of the Post Office's total of around 330,000 employees, it was more often than not the UPW that determined the outcome of day-to-day decisions in the workplace.

Presiding over all this, Alexander Little and his Board colleagues were generally inclined to see the unions' much greater involvement in the running of the Post Office as a notable achievement, the culmination of a long historical process. They were impressed but not surprised by the responsible lead taken by Geddes and other union leaders – whose personal integrity and loyalty to the Department had been amply demonstrated during the war – and they regularly expressed their satisfaction with the new sense of partnership. In a candid November 1953 Board paper, Dudley Lumley (now risen to the post of Deputy Director General) looked back on the hunt for cost savings since 1951 and thought it 'clear that the latter could hardly have produced such striking results, had there not been a substantial fund of goodwill in many parts of the country flowing from the personal efforts of leaders on both sides at all levels . . .'[15] Every Postmaster General through the period felt moved to comment on the singularly helpful attitude adopted by the staff associations. Charles Hill, the erstwhile leader of Britain's doctors at the creation of the NHS who was appointed Postmaster General in Anthony Eden's government in 1955, was amazed to see his new Department pull off a drastic contraction of the telegraph service, cutting its workforce by a fifth, with no disruption in the workplace at all:

---

dered by married women. It was no good taking 'an emotional approach to a principle'. The UPW had only nine full-time officers. It would be unfair on the union to saddle it with a women officer with her own domestic responsibilities. (UCW/2/1/38, pp. 255–6.) Geddes stopped short of suggesting that single women, too, might not have the stomach for working at the highest levels of the union – but his audience must have been aware that this was a sensitive issue. The Executive Council at the time had only one woman, Miss Whitehead, and twenty-six men. Miss Jenny Duncan, a former Council chairman and leading champion of women's rights through the war, had retired at the end of 1953, absenting herself from her last few meetings 'due to domestic circumstances'. Miss Winifred Rowe, another prominent wartime figure, had been allowed to retire in April 1954 after a second nervous breakdown in three years; Miss C. Taylor had been absent on long-term sick leave for most of 1954. (UCW/2/1/37, pp. 168 and 355.)

The Postmaster General noted [at the May 1955 Board meeting] that only remarkably good relations with the staff associations could have made it possible to carry through such a difficult exercise with so little friction . . . The help given by the Staff Side was, in his view, a salutary result of the productivity movement, which had engendered a new spirit of cooperation throughout the Post Office as a whole. This was not only his view, but had also been expressed by the [UPW General Secretary] . . .[16]

Misgivings were occasionally voiced in the early days, about the price perhaps being paid for this new spirit – but they seem rarely to have excited much debate. One of the few Board-level discussions about the Post Office's relationship with the unions cropped up early in 1951. The Personnel and Administration Director, S. D. Sargent, offered his colleagues a shrewd analysis. There were, he suggested, four degrees of commitment between the two sides. The first was straightforward, comprising negotiations over wages and hours. The second concerned welfare issues such as training, medical facilities, recruitment and so on (discussions of which, in Sargent's view, had in recent years come close to being formal negotiations). The third comprised consultations over the efficiency of the Department, which was the ground covered by the Whitley Councils and the new Joint Production Council. What beckoned in 1951 was a fourth and final stage – the sharing of responsibilities for policy formulation. This, said Sargent, had been the union's real objective in proposing the Joint Advisory Council rejected by Ness Edwards. In endorsing its rejection by the PMG, Sargent agreed that accepting it would have taken the Post Office into uncharted territory.[17] The Assistant Postmaster General of the day, C. R. Hobson, concurred, declaring it 'fraught with danger to the Post Office'. But over the next few years, the union went on pushing in exactly this direction. By 1954, many within the UPW had moved on from Joint Production or even Joint Advisory blueprints: now, just as Sargent had foreseen, they wanted to see a Joint *Administrative* Council. A proposal to this effect was put before the National Staff Side of the Whitley Council. 'After thirty-three years' experience of consultation and negotiation, the Union believes that the staff associations have the knowledge and ability to make a more direct contribution . . . [so] what is being advocated in the Union's policy is an advance from consultative to administrative status.'[18] The proposal was shelved, for lack of support from the other civil service unions.

Meanwhile, the Post Office Board itself was spending an ever diminishing proportion of its time on postal matters. There were so many pressing telecom issues to be addressed – from telephone tariffs and technologies to international submarine cables and the future of broadcasting – that the postal service scarcely featured on many of the Board's regular agendas. This was acclaimed as a sign of the service's maturity. As the Director General himself put it in May 1953: 'the brevity of the postal report [submitted to the Board] confirmed that the postal services had now been stabilized, after a somewhat chequered career in the immediate post-war years. His general conclusion was that the public were satisfied with the postal services which they now received.' But the scant attention paid to them at Board level did not mean policy questions had ceased to arise. Rather, they were being settled in a pragmatic fashion by whichever directors were responsible for them – and pragmatism, in the absence of any firm directive otherwise, often entailed taking the line least likely to prompt a confrontation with the staff. Looking back across the scarred industrial-relations landscape of the 1960s and 1970s, it is hard to share the optimism of those at St Martin's in the early 1950s who saw this development in a positive light. But their optimism was real enough at the time. In a paper written about a year after his Four Degrees analysis for the Board, Sargent assessed the impact to date of the JPC initiative, then a little over two years old: 'there has been a noticeably more accommodating attitude among many local Staff Sides towards ordinary routine staff revisions involving economies. There is no doubt that, by bringing a new spirit to the mutual relations in the Post Office of leaders and led, and by giving the rank and file in the vast Post Office machine a feeling of partnership, the productivity movement is bringing ... very great benefits to the Post Office.'[19]

And besides, what choice did the officials of St Martin's really have? The Post Office was already struggling to find enough commission-based sub-postmasters for its network of village post offices in many rural areas, and to recruit enough postmen in the big cities. With both main political parties now committed to the maintenance of full employment – and with the relative advantages of postal work over other working-class occupations now fading fast in the welfare state – this was no time for the Post Office to acquire a reputation as a confrontational employer. Nor would Churchill's Conservative government have allowed it. With his cordial approach, De La Warr was perfectly attuned in 1951–5 to the outlook of Churchill's Minister of Labour, Walter Monckton. Not for nothing was Monckton known in Whitehall as 'The Oilcan'. His brief from Churchill was to preserve industrial peace at almost any price, and he kowtowed before the TUC and its leading members accordingly. The UPW was the ninth-largest of them. The Post Office could not have taken a contradictory line. In the event, its stance exemplified the Government's approach.

Some historians have construed the outcome, for the British economy, as a period of blissful equilibrium between management, unions and the state. Keith Middlemas, in a much cited work, even characterizes the 1951–6 years as a 'brief golden age'.[20] The conscientious public servants of St Martin's seemed occasionally to suggest as much themselves: Little reviewed the 1954 finances and thought them 'most satisfactory because they reflected not only the present prosperity of the country, but also good administration within the Post Office'.[21] If he and his fellow directors had one serious concern, it was the fear that too much was being demanded of the UPW's leadership. More than 3,000 jobs had been eliminated since 1951 in the quest for higher productivity. Many officials were in fact acutely conscious that Geddes and those around him were often the targets of bitter criticism from the rank and file for not extracting more concessions in exchange. For the 'golden age' was viewed differently by some in the workplace. Especially critical were the postal workers of London, who had begun to take on the mantle of disaffected militancy hitherto more usually identified with the workforce in northern cities like Manchester and Liverpool and had broken with precedent in resorting to an unofficial strike in 1951. An angry protest meeting in Westminster's Central Hall in May that year attracted more than 7,000 postmen, several hundred of whom had to stand outside in the street for lack of room. When Geddes rose to speak from the platform, he had to wait twenty minutes to make himself heard. The London District Council's Secretary was unable to speak at all.[22] Geddes himself warned the JPC from the start that a combined approach to productivity would be fatally undermined if the workforce ever decided that advantage was being taken of it: 'the [productivity] movement might dry up unless it could be shown to the staff that something had been attained. It would be a tragedy if this happened.'[23] Those with most knowledge of the workplace, like Sargent and Lumley, issued several warnings to the same effect. To make the point as graphically as he could, Lumley gave his November 1953 Board paper on productivity and staff morale a colourful title: 'The Turn of the Screw'. He thought that 'oft repeated appeals *pro bono publico* have spent their force' and listed half a dozen instances over the course of 1953 of concessions being wrung from the UPW leadership, only for them to be rejected by the rank and file in subsequent conference votes. 'If the screw was given another turn', he told the Board, 'the atmosphere could not fail to be more disagreeable – it might become dangerous.'[24]

These were prescient words. While officials worried over the pressure it was putting on the UPW, there was one other – and, to us at least, rather more obvious – flaw in the productivity movement that effectively negated its impact. The relatively meagre gains it made in output were being dwarfed by the incremental costs of a soaring wage bill. The unions accepted a de facto wage freeze at the behest of the Labour government in 1949. Even before the election of its Conservative successor in 1951, though, they had taken up a far more implacable stance. Over the years that followed, pay negotiations came to adhere to an annual cycle, and each year brought another significant rise for large sections of the workforce. The UPW secured claims of roughly 7 per cent in 1951, 10 per cent in 1952, and 6 per cent in each of the three years 1953–5. The whole productivity movement was in fact predicated on the willingness of the Post Office – or, more often, of the Treasury and the Arbitration Court that ruled over many of the pay claims – to concede a series of demands that even the UPW's leaders often considered a bit of a stretch.[25] Since its staff costs in 1951 equated to 72 per cent of total spending by the postal service – the parallel figure in the Telephone Department was only 31 per cent – the outcome was never really in doubt. Higher expenditure on wages would not just preclude gains in productivity but would also, sooner or later, blow away the profitability of the postal service altogether. The hopelessly excessive level of wage awards was noted in a four-year forecast of the Commercial Accounts in May 1952: 'Only a complete change in the economic climate could remove the fear that . . . [wage] increases far beyond the measure of the modest surpluses shown in the forecast will eventuate.'[26] In other words, unless a severe recession and a sharp rise in unemployment forced the unions into retreat, higher wages would overwhelm the Post Office. The predictions of 'modest surpluses' for the years up to 1954–5 proved, by dint of some exceptionally adroit administration, to be remarkably accurate. Postal profits were kept pegged within the £3m–5m range, down from £11m in 1948–9, even though expenditure levels climbed steadily. But by the middle of the decade wages paid to the postal workforce were half as high again as in 1949, up from £60m to just over £90m in 1954–5. And in 1955–6, just as predicted, an under-budgeted wage concession finally forced the postal service into the red: a loss of £1.5m for that financial year was the first ever deficit in its history.*

The loss presaged a premature end for the Post Office to its very own Never-Had-It-So-Good era. The departures of De La Warr in April 1955 and of Little in October were accompanied by several other changes in the upper echelons of the Department. The revised top team had to take stock of a new challenge. For several years, running the Post Office had essentially been about sustaining a sense of equilibrium – between officials and unions, between staffing levels and traffic volumes, between breaking even and avoiding profits that might cause embarrassment. (De La Warr had remarked in 1952 that he thought the Post Office would be 'vulnerable to criticism' if its aggregate commercial surplus rose above £10m. George Ismay and Kenneth Anderson, as Comptroller & Accountant General and Finance Director respectively, saw less than half that as the optimal profit figure.) Management attitudes in every department since the end of the 1940s had returned to their customary pre-war emphasis on reacting to the postal environment, not changing it. It is only a slight exaggeration to say that the most truly enterprising officials had been those who coped best with the Christmas mails, or with the impact of a strike on the railways or chaos at the docks. From early 1956, the mood changed. The 1955–6 deficit was no great calamity in itself, but given that the recent sharp rise in wages could never be reversed, the Post Office had to confront the fact that it could not indefinitely continue to handle rising mail volumes by its time-honoured, heavily labour-intensive systems. The number of letters and packets had risen by more than 20 per cent since 1949. Assuming their continued growth, the mails would somehow have to be handled in a more labour-efficient manner in the future, to put the Departmental finances once again on a secure footing.

2. THE BRAVE NEW WORLD OF THE RATTLER

A postman, counter clerk or sorter from the 1890s, magically transplanted to the middle of the 1950s, could have turned up for work almost

* The Post Office deficits from 1919–20 to 1921–2 were the result of postal profits being overwhelmed by the post-war telegraph and telephone losses. By the same token, the postal loss in 1955–6 was concealed in the aggregate Post Office accounts for that year by a £4.9m profit on the telephone service.

anywhere in the country and found himself in utterly familiar surround-ings. In the sorting halls, men in much the same uniforms were preparing the mails with similar, and in some cases actually the very same, office fittings. There was recognizably the same graded, acronym-laden hier-archy in place, albeit in a simplified version after the Reallocation of 1945–6. Mailbags were tied, and open coal fires were set, just as they had been for generations, often in the very same buildings, and the discipline and quasi-military atmosphere were as pervasive as ever – all the more so, since 1945. Among the returning soldiers were many who had worked for the Post Office before the war. Denis Roberts, who would later rise to the top of the service, had joined his local post office in Barnsley in 1933 as a sixteen-year-old sorting clerk and telegraphist. After an eventful and distinguished war with the Royal Signals and a couple of years managing telephone exchanges in Yorkshire, he was promoted to Headquarters as an Assistant Inspector of Postal Services. For five years, from 1949 to 1954, Roberts travelled around England, visiting Head Post Offices in every region to check on their procedures and performance. The single feature of the whole organization that struck him most forcibly was its apparent immutability: 'it was still the Post Office I knew from the 1930s: everything was the same'.[27]

This is not to suggest that the Post Office had remained precisely the same for a century or more, but the absence of any transformational change since the young Roberts had signed on in Barnsley was real enough, and for one very good reason.[28] The traditional manual tasks of postal work had only twice been significantly altered to take advantage of mechanization, and both episodes had been effectively completed by the mid-1930s. The first saw the stage coach replaced by the railways. The initial switch from one to the other happened with shocking speed, as we have seen, with the first use of a train in 1830 leading to the end of the London mail coaches just sixteen years later. Incremental improve-ments had then followed over several decades, but the sophistication of the Royal Mail's usage of the rail network by the 1930s could hardly be taken any further, and never was. The speed and reliability of steam trains matched the geography of the country and the overnight requirements of the mails to perfection: this above all else explained why the Post Office, with its national next-day delivery, could legitimately claim to be the world's best mail service – indeed, a unique mail service. The very unflat-tering international comparisons made from time to time between the telephone service and its foreign counterparts found no echo on the pos-tal side. What struck pre-war observers was the remarkable efficiency of the mails. To stand on a platform at Crewe station for three hours around midnight, watching the arrival and departure of no fewer than twenty-six TPOs, each shedding and collecting hundreds of mailbags as quickly as men could shift them, was to witness as fine a demonstration of practical logistics as a pre-computer economy could offer.

The second great mechanization saw the horse and cart replaced on short journeys by motor vehicles. This, too, was a relatively speedy transition, completed by the 1930s.[29] A small horse-drawn fleet was retained in central London until after the Second World War – the last of its carts left King Edward Building in 1949, 103 years after the departure of the last mail coach from St Martin's in 1846 – but it was a quaint survival. Most short-haul postal transports were motorized over the decade and a half before the First World War, using a variety of new-fangled machines from motorcycles with wicker-basket trailers to motor tricycles, three-wheeled 'tricars', motor vans and heavyweight parcel lorries. Horse-drawn services plodded on in some rural areas for many years, but those surviving as late as the early 1930s attracted comment as the very last of their kind. Along with the takeover by the internal-combustion engine came a parallel shift in the ownership of the motor fleet. Initially run entirely by contractors on the Post Office's behalf, it was gradually brought in-house through the inter-war years: the last external contracts were wound up in May 1950.[30] The pivotal year was probably 1932, when the Motor Transport (MT) Branch was established, and the Post Office took delivery of its first Morris Minor 'bullnose' van, built to the Department's own design. This was the van, painted red and inscribed with the Royal Mail insignia, that soon became a familiar sight in every town street and country lane of pre-war Britain. By the end of the thirties, the motor fleet had dramatically altered the 'circulation' methods of the Victorian Post Office. Its impact was eloquently summarized by one of the last Assistant Surveyors, W. K. Mackenzie, in a paper on postal circulation that he wrote after his retirement in 1972:

> Motorisation usually involved the complete replacement of relatively simple main and branch foot and cycle posts by all-embracing motor posts, without a distance limit, working out of a central point i.e. a Crown or a large sub-office. As a consequence, the number of staff out-stationed at small sub-offices was greatly reduced. . . . These developments swept away the last old time rural postman who was a welcome feature of the rural scene as late as fifty years ago. Few now remember the country postman with his

walking stick and his dog, whistling or ringing a bell to let people know that he was passing by and would 'collect' their letters. Delivering (and gossiping) from 6am to 9am, off-duty at his official 'shelter hut' from 9am to 3pm (when he could usually be found . . . unless he was helping the local farmer), walking back with his collection from 3pm to 6pm – six days a week, come hell or high water.[31]

We should bear in mind Mackenzie's sketch as a corrective to the idea that in the early 1950s little had changed for a century. Nonetheless, there was undoubtedly a perception that traditional practices were perhaps stifling further progress. For those intent on proving otherwise, there was one obvious goal. The railway and motor revolutions had taken the transportation of the mails to and from post offices up to a wholly new level. But there had been no such upheaval in the handling of the mails inside those offices. Yet out of every hundred staff, around a third were employed either as full-time sorters or as postmen with sorting duties as a part of their daily round.[32] So might the sorting process now be amenable to mechanization as well?

This was a question that had been urgently asked in the opening months of the First World War. Releasing large numbers of men from sorting duties had been a critical objective for the recruiting sergeants. The Post Office had come up with a successful near-term solution – the employment of women – but no one had ever produced a better idea for normal times. One of the officials most frustrated over this failure was the wartime head of the Army Postal Service, Frederic Williamson. Four years after the war's end, he was appointed Director of Postal Services. It was in that capacity, in 1927, that Williamson attended a conference of the UPU in The Hague where all the delegates were invited by a Dutch company to attend an intriguing sales presentation. What the company unveiled in nearby Delft was a mechanical sorting machine, of a kind that Williamson had dreamed about for years. It was the postal world's first glimpse of the 'Transorma'. Its inventors – one of them a veteran of the Dutch Post Office called J. J. L. M. Marchand – were hoping for some instant orders, perhaps including one from Britain. They were initially disappointed. Williamson instead came home determined that the Post Office should steal a march on its Dutch friends by sponsoring the development of a rival machine by a British manufacturer. Only after this had proved a wild-goose chase did he turn back to the creators of the Transorma, in 1931. By then a working model had been installed in the Rotterdam Post Office, but the Dutch were still struggling to generate international orders. Williamson's renewed interest was warmly received, and work was soon begun to amend the original design in line with requests from the Post Office. Under Williamson's chairmanship, a Departmental committee was set up to oversee the project – it was soon known as the MAC, the Mechanical Aids Committee – and the first two British machines were installed in the Head Post Office at Brighton in October 1935.

The concept behind the Transorma was quite simple. In place of the traditional sorting frame that typically would only allow for any batch of mail to be broken down into forty-eight pigeonholes at a time – necessitating a 'primary' sort and then one or more 'secondary sorts' of each pigeonhole for all outward-bound items, and a similar (but simpler) process in reverse for inward items – the Transorma enabled a continuous stream of mail to be segregated according to hundreds of separate destinations at one fell swoop. Letters could therefore be collected from the mechanized process and despatched, in most cases with no further sorting at all. This represented a potentially enormous boost to productivity, especially given the faster sorting speeds supposedly achievable by Transorma operators compared with manual sorters. The physical embodiment of the concept was more complicated. It consisted principally of a massive oblong box, almost the size of a telephone exchange and weighing more than ten tons. Around the top of it ran a kind of balcony, with work stations for a row of keyboard operators. (Their number could be varied to suit the customer, but the standard model had a team of five.) In front of each of them was a 'supply-trough', the shape of an elongated shoe-box, into which fresh mail was periodically loaded by hand with all addresses facing the operator. A spring kept the letters pressed up to the operator, so that he could take them out one by one, read their addresses and pop them into a slot in front of him. As he did this with one hand, the operator had to type a numerical code onto a small keyboard with his other. The keys were attached to a highly ingenious series of levers, push-rods, conveyor belts, flaps and buckets that clattered around inside the body of the machine like the workings of some giant fairground attraction. The combination of keys chosen for each letter determined the path it would follow and the destination bin it would eventually reach. It follows that each operator had to have memorized a few hundred numerical codes which were unique to each location: perhaps a third of the numbers would typically relate to nearby destinations, while the rest had to cover everywhere else with whatever set of priorities best suited the average contents of the local mail.

It so happened, in 1935, that the MP for Brighton was George Tryon, who arrived in St Martin's as the new Postmaster General just four months before the Transormas landed in his constituency. This ensured plenty of interest in the new experiment, though the choice of Brighton genuinely had nothing to do with Tryon's appointment. (It had been made by Williamson in 1933, for reasons now lost.) Nor did the choice of Brighton have anything to do with there being an especially receptive local branch of the UPW in the town. The union refused to countenance the possibility of women telegraphists or typists being employed as operators, though their skills were plainly better suited to the task than were those of the average clerk or postman. Instead, the Post Office had to find twenty-seven men from the (substantially higher paid) Sorting Clerk & Telegraphist grade. Some volunteered, but not that many – and all of them needed every minute of their eight weeks' training. The machines were fully operative by the time that Williamson retired from the Post Office in 1937. For the more dedicated stalwarts of the phila- telic community, they spawned a welcome new set of collectible items even more recherché than mobile army unit postmarks: the Transorma left identification marks on envelopes identifying individual keyboards, a special feature designed to allow supervisors to keep track of the proficiency of their operators.

Predictably, perhaps, the machines were rather less warmly embraced by the workforce. It is not hard to see why. The operators who were perched on top of them found their positions uncomfortably hot in the summer, and tiresomely noisy all the year round: the Transorma was known to its co-workers as 'The Rattler'. It functioned efficiently enough, but its effect on the workplace was profoundly alienating. A promotional book written by Marchand and published in English just after the end of the war did nothing to promote its cause: the training for its operators, the Dutchman recommended, should consist of '(a) practice on the keyboard; (b) chorus singing; and (c) card-reversing'. The choral sessions were intended to assist the process of memorizing codes, which were to be written on small cards for subsequent tests. 'The instructor should keep himself fully informed about the progress made by his pupils, each of whom should be tested at least once a week.' Marchand claimed the machines were 'practically noiseless' – and even advocated their adoption as a remedy for the noise problem in traditional sorting offices 'caused by the accumulation of a large number of employees, who are occasionally obliged to speak to one another'.[33] This was not an approach ever likely to be endorsed by the UPW, or indeed anyone else in the Post Office.* Even before the outbreak of the Second World War, the financial benefit of the Transormas at Brighton was also perceived to be marginal at best, not least due to the inflexibility of the staffing arrangements. While those machines already installed would be kept going, the decision was taken at Headquarters to purchase no more of them.

By the time the Mechanical Aids Committee reconvened in 1946, under Alexander Little's chairmanship, its title had become a little outdated. Huge advances had been made in electronics, not least with the technology of photo-electric cells. Dollis Hill had played a distinguished part in this, and an overview of the Research Department's work by the Engineer-in-Chief in March 1946 drew the inevitable conclusion. 'It has now been realized that many of the problems of Postal Mechanisation require the application of scientific principles not hitherto applied.'[34] The future surely belonged not to mechanical devices, or even to their electro-mechanical cousins except on a transitional basis, but to the world of electrical and computer systems that had been pioneered by Colossus. Fresh from their wartime work for Bletchley Park, the scientists of Dollis Hill did not take long to identify the critical components of a fully automated letter-sorting system. These were brilliantly spelt out in a couple of short papers written by two of the Department's most distinguished engineers, W. T. Gemmell and R. O. Carter, and submitted to the MAC in late 1946. Using the Transorma system as its point of departure, the first paper proposed that the operators' role could one day be entirely separated from the mechanical sorting process. Instead of each keyboard being linked directly to an ironmongery of levers and ram-rods, it would be used to type a code onto the surface of each passing letter. This code would embody instructions that could then be read by a sorting machine located at some distance from the operators and translated into electronic signals that would drive a much-enhanced version of the mechanical sorting process used in the Transorma.[35] The

---

* Marchand's book sang the glories of his invention. In addition to its postal functions and displacement of overly talkative workers, he saw the Transorma as a cure for flat feet and body odour. 'The tiring movements necessitated by hand-sorting also cause much accretion of sweat in the armpits. The necessity of constantly raising the right arm during the process of sorting by hand spreads this unpleasant odour in every direction' (J. J. M. L. Marchand, *Modernization of Postal Services*, De Boekerij of The Netherlands, 1946, p. 125).

second paper focused on the nature of the coding system. Electronics would make it possible for letters to be coded in one building and sorted in another. So why not use a code in, say, Southampton that could be used in, say, Glasgow? If it was accepted that the principle of divorcing coding from sorting was sensible, then it had to follow 'simply and directly' that a *universal* coding system – in place, that is, of codes dependent on the operator's location – would be a logical requirement. 'It is envisaged that every street, or possibly even every address, would have its individual code, which would be noted or remembered with the name and address of a correspondent in the same way as are telephone numbers at the present time.'[36]

Had the outcome of a world war depended upon it, all this might have been brought to fruition within a few years. Even without a war, officials took a bullish view of the prospects. In a paper of October 1946 confirming the MAC's renewed objectives, Little himself suggested 'there is reason to expect that in due course in the largest offices electrical devices will cover the complete sorting office sequence, leaving only for human operation the actual decipherment of the address and the tying up of the bag for despatch'.[37] Gemmell and Carter, as practical engineers, were more wary of encouraging unrealistic timescales: in their view, it was 'likely to be a ten-year project'. A coding system had to be devised, which they thought would be not too difficult. But devising a way to record the code on each letter would be *very* difficult – and designing a scanner that could read them reliably at high speed would be harder still. As for persuading the public to add a code to traditional addresses, Carter confessed '[he] mentioned [it] merely with the object of showing that the scheme, as a long-term plan, is not entirely fantastic'. When the two papers were circulated to the members of the MAC working party on letter-sorting, the engineers' caution prompted some indignation. The chairman, J. E. Yates, announced at a meeting in January 1947 that he had to say 'he felt appalled' at the mooted ten-year horizon.[38]

Yates might have been struck dumb, had he and his colleagues been told that the realization of the Gemmell–Carter vision would actually stretch more than thirty years into the future. The Transorma machines at Brighton kept rattling on into the 1960s, and when the time eventually came to decommission them in 1964, as a potential health hazard, the MAC's members had to make a striking confession: 'If the machines were withdrawn, there would be nothing with which to replace them ...'[39] That is to say, eighteen years after Gemmell and Carter submitted their papers, the Post Office had still not settled on *any* mechanized sorting process that it felt ready to install across the service.* Planning for the adoption of mechanized letter-sorting turned out to mean preparing the postal service for a complete overhaul of its core activity, which would one day necessitate a physical rearrangement (if not rebuilding) of every post office and a conceptual redesigning of every postal address. In the late 1940s, the high noon of mechanization was still many years away, and even a sense of what it would entail was going to take a long time to dawn in St Martin's-le-Grand.

3 . PURSUING THE UNIVERSAL POSTCODE

An awkward discovery awaited the keenest prophets of the new era. The paramount importance of engineering came as no surprise in itself: plainly, no amount of electronic wizardry at the front end of any sorting machine could displace the need for a basic mechanical process at its heart. Streams of letters had to be sped down slipways, caressed round corners and plucked apart at high speeds that would allow not the slightest margin for mechanical error. It made no difference whether a future machine got its instructions directly from an operator – as in the case of the Transorma – or indirectly from an electronic gadget that could somehow decipher addresses, as was envisaged by the clever scientists of Dollis Hill by 1947. Sorting would in either case depend ultimately on rude mechanics. In the quest to take a giant step beyond the Transorma as quickly as possible, it was therefore decided – ironically, as things turned out – not to wait upon the outcome of the more advanced research programmes. The MAC resolved to develop a machine that would link the operators' keyboards to the sorting process via some trusty electro-mechanical devices. It would be a half-way house, and so was soon known as the Interim Machine.

The prototype parts of a machine for six operators – each handling fifty letters a minute – were ready for viewing by the end of 1948, and

---

* In the event, no announcement was made about the proposed decommissioning at Brighton until 1965. It was opposed by the UPW, since it entailed the cancellation of the special bonuses paid to the Transormas' operators, and negotiations over it lasted three years. Postman Ron Simms recalled the final end in July 1968. 'One day we just stopped and the following week the breakers came in, broke it up and took it away. The bits were just thrown away as scrap' (quoted in *The Transorma at Brighton* by Douglas Muir, Postal Mechanisation Study Circle, Monograph No. 1, privately published in 2006, p. 39).

stirred much excitement among the MAC officials. They looked forward to an export version, 'not only as a dollar earner but as something superior to the Transorma machine which is now being pushed by the Dutch to the limit'.[40] Then came the awkward discovery that perfecting the mechanics, though never seen as an easy task, would prove immeasurably harder than anyone had expected. It was more than three years before the Post Office felt able to launch Interim into its first trials. Then the verdict in October 1952 recorded gloomily: 'While no major breakdown occurred during the trial, there was a considerable number of lesser machine faults ... [and] the standard of efficiency of the machine ... fell far short of operational requirements'.[41] The outlook never really brightened: the Interim was almost as ill-conceived as those first attempts by Williamson to rival the Transorma more than twenty years earlier. 'The machine is very complex and its maintenance would present a serious problem in the field', noted a private MAC memorandum in March 1953.[42] Trials were finally abandoned in 1955. Dutch export sales of the Transorma, such as they were, fizzled out at the same time.

But the slow demise of the Interim had stalled other research work, too. Given the intractable problems encountered over the mechanics of dealing with 300 letters a minute, the prospect of coping successfully with 1,000 or more per minute – as envisaged by the champions of 'automatic' sorting – seemed very remote indeed. Sorting speeds much higher than the Interim's were integral to the concept of using machines that could take instructions from codes printed onto letters. The research into coding at Dollis Hill therefore struck many members of the MAC as a waste of time and resources. An added complication was the fact that difficulties had arisen over the use of a fluorescent dye for the printing of the codes, which had been successfully demonstrated in 1948, when Lever Brothers, the supplier of the fluorescent material, decided to take out a patent on it. By 1952, the Post Office's chemists with the help of consultants from ICI had produced an alternative, phosphorescent solution – but the Interim's travails nonetheless led to the effective mothballing of the whole coding project.

The Interim's stuttering progress had also impeded another post-Transorma concept launched in the early 1950s. This was a smaller, three-ton machine designed, like the Interim, to apply electro-mechanical devices to the sorting process, but for a single operator rather than a team. It improved on the Transorma in many ways. Letters were carried on a miniature conveyor belt rather than handled by the operator, leaving him free to use two hands on the keyboard as he watched addresses passing through a window in front of him. This made it critically important for letters to be faced in the correct position, and a separate machine – based on a photo-electric recognition of lines implanted in stamps – was being developed in parallel for this task. It was called ALF (for Automatic Letter Facer) and a valiant attempt was made to christen the new sorting machine ELSIE (for Electronic Letter Sorting Indicating Equipment). Sadly the lady's name never stuck and the Post Office was saddled with SPLSM (for Single Position Letter Sorting Machine), which was pronounced to rhyme with 'spasm'. Despite this unfortunate title, it was a promising newcomer. The SPLSM's operator would be able to sort 110 letters per minute into 144 selections, sitting at a machine small enough (17 ft long × 7 ft high × 3 ft wide) to be adopted in a wide range of offices. Ready for trialling by 1953, the SPLSM, like the phosphorus code, was sidelined while engineers struggled with the Interim.

The arrival as Director General in October 1955 of the wartime head of Dollis Hill – the first ever engineer in the role – gave the mechanization movement a much-needed fillip. Gordon Radley's appointment coincided with a heightened awareness in government circles by the middle of the decade that some way had to be found to improve the efficiency of the basic postal service. Radley and his engineering colleagues had their doubts that mechanization would bring the service any significant financial benefits in the short term, given the rebuilding implications; but they valued the possibility of reducing the burden on staff of the most tedious manual operations. They also had an instinctive faith in the potential of good research to deliver the unexpected. Radley reconstituted the MAC 'into a small high-powered body charged with the task of progressing a number of mechanisation projects as soon as possible'.[43] A distinguished engineer himself, he made no attempt to disguise his view that mechanization to date had been impeded by too much bureaucracy: the reformed MAC had to 'get things done rather than produce papers ...' Their first decisive action was to back the SPLSM, after it had (at last) emerged successfully from some initial prototype trials in Bath. Four years after serious work on it had begun, orders were placed early in 1956 for twenty machines, while more prototype trials continued at Southampton. At this point, too, it was decided that demonstrating the true value of mechanization would need the Post Office to focus on the maximum possible application of all new technology in one location. This was the cue for the market town of the fifteenth-century Pastons to make another appearance in postal history. A new sorting office was due to open in Norwich later in 1956, and was chosen by the MAC as its primary testing ground.[44]

Radley also set up, in October 1956, a Mechanization and Buildings Department (MBD), a coupling which reflected a shrewder understanding by this stage of the scale of the challenge that faced the Post Office. The first head of MBD was Kenneth Holmes, who oversaw work on a prodigious number of innovatory working tools, from chain conveyors and fork-lift trucks to photocopiers and ball-point pens, as well as producing a regular survey of mechanization with the latest news on prospective machines for a bewildering array of basic postal tasks. These included parcel-sorting, bag-folding, bundle-tying and packet-stamping – in addition to counter machines for the dispensing of stamps, labels and postal orders. The quest continued, meanwhile, for a modernized sorting process, but progress here was constantly frustrated by trial setbacks in Southampton and delays to the manufacturing process. Not until the autumn of 1958 were the first production models of the SPLSM delivered by the Thrissell Engineering Company of Bristol and finally installed. At least this allowed more time for the development of the hardware needed as appendages to the sorting machinery itself – in addition to ALF, for example, the Post Office finalized the production of a 'Segregator', the first machine of its type in the world, which could separate parcels and packets from letters. By the start of 1959, although the logbook on live SPLSM operations had scarcely yet been opened, officials were generally confident that they had finally cracked the devilish business of channelling letters through machines.

Conceivably, the Post Office might at this point have declared itself the proud owner of an effective successor to the Transorma: after serving an apprenticeship in Norwich, the SPLSM might have been purchased in large numbers and installed at many points of the postal network. Instead, in replacing the Interim, the SPLSM soon found itself cast as another interim solution. After more than a decade of jam tomorrow in the mechanization story, the limitations of the basic SPLSM were still evident: it was essentially an electro-mechanical device that marked no conceptual advance on the pre-war technology. It still required the use of locally memorized codes; it was limited to 144 selections; and attempts to combine several machines together into a 'multi-position' LSM had been turning engineers grey for several years. But there was another, much more positive reason to treat the SPLSM as just a precursor of things to come. The MAC meeting which had

confirmed the go-ahead for the order of twenty production SPLSMs, in
April 1956, had also turned its attention once again to the idea of marking codes onto letters. This, it was generally agreed, was 'likely to be one
of the most useful things in the future of postal mechanisation'.[45] Given
the putative resolution of the mechanical issues, the Post Office had
quietly revived the original vision of Gemmell and Carter. Perhaps, after
all, ways might now be found to plant a code on letters so that they
could be 'automatically' sorted. The die was cast at the ninth meeting of
Radley's MAC in January 1957.[46] 'It was agreed that maximum research
effort should be concentrated on development of a coding/sorting
machine . . . [It must be ensured that] maximum effort by [the] chemist
staff at Dollis Hill is put into the problems of devising suitable coding
media, and to assess the possibility of a solution to the coding problem
being available in two years' time . . .' This objective was strongly
endorsed a couple of months later by a firm of management consultants, Harold Whitehead & Partners (though its views on the future
scheduling of the project struck officials as utopian).[47] Holmes, himself
an analytical chemist by training, soon agreed, declaring in January
1958: 'It seems to me that coding is much the most significant of all the
developments on which we are working'.[48] By the time the SPLSMs
arrived at Norwich ten months later, the new 'coding/sorting' agenda
had already rendered them half-obsolete. Progress on coding/sorting
had (for a change) exceeded expectations, and officials were intent on
pursuing it.

What this would involve was spelt out in a comprehensive paper by
two of the Post Office's leading engineers, G. P. Copping and H. J. Langton. It was written for engineers, but the two of them used it as the basis
of an acclaimed presentation to postal officials in London and five other
cities in the early months of 1959. Having operators code letters, rather
than tap out instructions for the machines that would sort them, was 'of
course an obvious approach' and the time had come at last for the introduction 'of the long awaited code letter system'.[49] It needed to leave
behind the local codes on which all machines had so far depended –
codes adapted for specific locations, which could be memorized by
sorters in those locations but would necessarily be of no use elsewhere.
Thus, Bristol would have one set of codes; Newcastle would have
another. Both would share a number of important national destinations
like London, but Bristol would also devote many codes to local places
which would not warrant codes of their own for use in Newcastle, and
vice versa. ('CHE' might be code for letters to Chepstow in the one, for

example, and letters to Chester-le-Street in the other.) A 'universal' code, by contrast, would enable a treated letter to be scanned anywhere along its journey: it would be equally applicable, as it were, in both Bristol and Newcastle. It would also provide sufficient information for both outward and inward sorting (handling letters, that is to say, through their postal journey 'outward' after a collection, and 'inward' prior to final delivery). This would incidentally have the great merit of putting the Post Office back at the forefront of international developments, because most other postal services around the world were limiting themselves to an outward code only. This was important to the MAC, as its members readily acknowledged at their April 1959 meeting: 'There was a risk that the tremendous effort now being put into postal mechanisation by the USA, Germany, Holland and other countries might result in our being overtaken. Germany and Holland were giving much thought to public coding schemes and we must press forward at all speed to be first in the field with public coding'.[50]

Two alternative methodologies were available and by 1959 had already been the subject of extensive studies for at least three years. An 'extraction code', as its name suggested, required the operator to scan an address and to extract key letters according to a specified formula, which he would type into his keyboard. A formula had been identified already that was plainly workable, for both outward and inward sorting. The boffins had trawled through all 1,700 post-town names and found that only around 5 per cent of all possible addresses would share the same code. Mis-sorting of these awkward places could be avoided by grouping them as a selection for subsequent manual sorting. (Thus, BRIghtON and BRIdlingtON both produced BRION as the first half of their extraction code, and mails to both would be given special treatment accordingly.[51]) Above all, extraction coding asked nothing of the public: in adopting it, most of the risks would be readily quantifiable. Not all of them, however: the code required ten letters, which implied a burden for the operator on which the medical and psychology professions – not to mention, for the moment, the trade unions – had yet to take a view.

Copping and Langton made no secret of their preference for the alternative approach, known as 'public coding': it was 'of course by far the most attractive system . . .'[52] The Research Department had devised a clever format – again, for both outward and inward sorting – that could capture any address within five to eight digits, using both letters and numbers. Devised as a two-part code, the first part would provide for outward sorting by specifying which of about 125 post towns best represented the destination; the second part would facilitate inward sorting by identifying a delivery post office and an actual location within its range. This was intellectually gratifying to the scientists, who regarded ten-digit codes as prolix, and pleased officials by offering an opportunity to underline the superiority of the Royal Mail; it also placed much less onus on the operator. The coding was 'public' because it would be written on the envelope as part of the original address. Operators would sit in front of a moving stream of letters, copying the address of each into their keyboard, to activate the imprinting onto the envelope of the code as a series of phosphorescent dots. These would then be read by a 'translator' unit which would pass the code electronically to the automatic sorting equipment. No one supposed that public coding would be embraced by the public overnight, but the mathematicians of Dollis Hill had the answer: where an address omitted the new item, the operator would be able to fall back on extraction coding. The code-translating unit would have an electronic memory pre-configured to recognize an extraction code and assign the corresponding public code automatically. With so much brilliant homework already accomplished, the decision was taken by the early summer of 1958 to press ahead with public coding. It only remained for the Post Office – or rather, the Head Postmaster of Norwich, a widely respected official already past his retirement age, John Fryer – to complete two additional tasks. He and his staff were asked to demonstrate how the theoretical coding format could be applied to postmen's walks in practice; and Norwich was invited to show how the public, once apprised of the new addressing system, could be cajoled into actually using it.

Redefining the nation's standard address format was not an exercise that had been regularly undertaken over the preceding three centuries. In fact it had been done only once before, as we have seen, back in the early 1920s. Over the settled and coherent world of the County Sorting Scheme, continuously refined over the intervening decades, the Post Office's itinerant young Assistant Postal Controllers journeyed five days a week, mostly by bus and train, and just occasionally by taxi. The APCII grade was the first rung on the management ladder – usually leading to the APCI rung after seven years or so – and was the entry point for most management trainees in the 1950s. (Only a few joined Headquarters as Assistant Principals.) Appointed to East Anglia in May 1958 were two new APCIIs, Ian Cameron and Peter Milne, whose careers in the Post Office could hardly have got off to a luckier start.

They found themselves assigned to spend at least a day a week with the Head Postmaster's staff in Norwich, drawing up the first ever postcode map of a British city. The basic format was handed to them; but which streets should share which digits, how many addresses should fit together as one code, what volume thresholds should be adopted for the assignment of unique numbers – these and a long tail of other postcode riddles fell to be answered by a group of young men scarcely out of university.

It was an intricate and time-consuming business, and it lasted into the early summer of 1959. At some point the decision was made to take one of Norwich's new electro-mechanical SPLSMs and convert its keyboard for use with the emerging technology of translators and phosphorescent dot codes.[53] This was successfully accomplished. The minutes of the June 1959 Board meeting have a proud Ken Holmes affirming: 'It was the first time that the process of impressing "live" letters with a pattern of phosphorescent spots [sic] had ever been undertaken; the British Post Office would be about a year ahead of the Americans in the field'.[54] The Postmaster General of the day, Ernest Marples, ever alert to any PR opportunity and skilled at exploiting them, saw a chance for his Department to unveil another in its long line of postal world-firsts stretching back to the Penny Black. As soon as the postal map of Norwich had been completed, the converted SPLSM was rigged up for a demonstration of automated inward sorting and representatives of many overseas postal ministries and the London correspondents of the world's press were invited to Norwich to see it; they would hear from Marples in person what it portended for the future of the British Post Office. The great day arrived, on 28 July 1959, and Head Postmaster Fryer readied his staff to receive their guests. Then, with Marples half-way to Norwich on the train from London, Fryer received a telephone call in his office from the engineers in the sorting hall. One of the conveyor belts linking the SPLSM's keyboard/printer and translator unit to the basic sorting machinery had jammed and was, alas, irreparably broken. Should they call off the demonstration? Impossible, said Fryer, and minds turned to a devious solution. There was just time to run a hundred letters through the keyboard and dot-printer unit, and pick them out of the machine. The area behind the SPLSM was thoroughly screened off, to conceal a couple of postmen, one of them clutching the pre-dotted mail. When all the guests had arrived and the time came for the demonstration, the conveyor in front of the operator worked perfectly. Letters were printed and disappeared

into the machine – where one postman fished them out before they hit
the dud conveyor, while the other dropped his pre-dotted letters into the
working sorter. When letters began emerging into the destination boxes
visible to the guests, it was naturally assumed that they were the *same*
letters they had seen being dotted by the operator. The surprising quiet-
ness of the machinery between the two ends was credited to the
sophistication of the latest postal engineering. The event was a huge
success. 'Every householder and firm in Norwich is to have a postal
code by October', announced *The Times* the next morning. The city
would lead the way, according to Mr Marples, with 'an experiment in
automation which would be in advance of anything else in the world'.[55]

Unfortunately, the last-minute hitch at Norwich was to prove only too
typical of the practical problems now encountered with the automation
project. Converting it from an experiment into a tested process ready for
the application of standardized coding machines turned out to be an
arduous business and entailed, according to one of the project leaders,
Stanley Scott, 'a vast amount of work at Headquarters, in the Regional
office and at Norwich'.[56] There was no option but to use converted
SPLSMs in trialling automated postal operations and they were prone to
constant breakdowns. Equally frustrating was the public's reluctance to
embrace the new universal postcode. A carefully targeted campaign was
begun in October 1959, but in February 1961 more than half of all letters
posted locally for local destinations in the target area were still omitting
the added ingredient from their addresses. The records of these years
read a little like those of the early 1950s, when anguished officials had
begun to wring their hands over the Interim. The story this time was
more complicated – sometimes bewilderingly so. Norwich pioneered
the postcode, but experiments on the best use of phosphorescent-dot
coding were carried out at the Head Post Office in Luton, and work on
the conversion of operator-controlled SPLSMs into trial coding/sorting
machines was mostly centred on Southampton. The result was a mechanization programme that could sometimes look horribly disjointed. Luton
had the dots but no public codes: its operators always had to employ
extraction coding. Norwich had the public codes but no dots: keyboards
and code-translating devices were fitted to its SPLSMs for inward sorting only in 1961, two years after the start of the Norwich project.

While these difficulties prompted endless delays, however, there was
never any question but that an automated coding-machine design would
be settled in the end, given a huge commitment to the task by the engineers and scientists of Dollis Hill. They had distractions of their own:

planning was underway through 1963 for the closure of Dollis Hill and the relocation of the Post Office Research Centre to Martlesham, a small village set in the midst of a heathland between Ipswich and the Suffolk coast. Most people regarded this as the main news out of Dollis Hill when the move was announced the following year. But 1964 was a landmark date for the mechanization saga, too. Five years after the slightly hubristic declaration of world leadership by Ernest Marples, orders were at last placed with Thrissell Engineering for prototype versions of a new coding machine intended for use in sorting offices all across the country. This decision was seen as a potential catalyst for unprecedented changes in the basic working routines of the Post Office. At a meeting of the MAC's senior members in September that year, an Assistant Secretary, Dennis Wesil, scanned the horizon:

> If the trials with these machines proved successful – and there was every reason to expect they would be – then by the end of 1966 orders would be placed for large numbers of coding desks, sorting machines etc and this would be the beginning of a flow of many million pounds' worth of equipment. The first batch would be delivered in early 1969 when probably two or three large offices would be equipped. Thereafter all the larger provincial offices and the Head District Offices in London, some seventy-five offices in all, handling 75 per cent of the letter mail of the country, would be mechanized.[57]

Wesil was not inviting his colleagues to engage in self-congratulation. His purpose was to jolt them into acknowledging that critical decisions were imminent – and that without a resolve to push on, the timetable he was laying out would go the same way as every other timetable since 1947. For as he and they must have been well aware, if there was 'every reason' to be optimistic about the potential impact of the prototypes, there were even more compelling grounds to fear further delays. The zip of Radley's early years had diminished badly since 1960. Radley himself had been succeeded in June 1960 by Ronald German – last encountered as the young secretary to the Post Office Board in 1940 – to whom mechanization seems to have looked a bit of a side-show. German had been away from St Martin's for nine years until 1959, serving very successfully as head of a regional posts and telecommunications authority in East Africa.* Where Radley had arrived five years earlier impatient to

* This was the East African Posts & Telecommunications Administration, which issued stamps, familiar to generations of British schoolboys, on behalf of Kenya, Uganda and

get mechanization rolling, German reminded his very first Board meeting 'that mechanization on the postal side could not provide the whole answer [to the service's financial problems] as inevitably it was limited in its scope'.[58]

The MAC that Radley had enjoined 'to get things done rather than produce papers' had by 1964 churned out well over a hundred reports – many resembling scholarly dissertations on topics, such the standardization of envelopes, that had absorbed countless months of work to no avail.[59] The less than dynamic progress at converting preparations into solid achievements was a consequence not of poor engineering but of a managerial environment that had often left officials cowed by the broader demands of postal mechanization. After a fact-finding mission to Paris late in 1963, the head of the (now self-standing) Postal Mechanization Branch, R. O. Bonnet, made a wry note of a conversation he had had with the deputy head of the French Posts. Their officials were never required to demonstrate the financial viability of new machinery, wrote Bonnet. 'It is accepted that mechanization is the only possible philosophy in this day and age.' As for relations with the workforce, the French way was primitive indeed. 'The drill was to tell the staff but not to consult them.'[60] On both counts, life at home could hardly have been more different.

4. A SPREADING DISAFFECTION

Whether sufficient funding would be available for a continued R&D programme – never mind the implementation of any successful outcome – had always been uncertain, not least because of the shifting context of postal finances. Before 1939, the financial legacy of the Bridgeman reforms had left the Post Office enjoying more or less a free hand with its capital spending, with Parliament and the Treasury restricted to keeping an eye on the revenue and spending of the Department via the

---

Tanganyika. The three countries first formed a customs and postal union in 1927, and cooperated as the East African High Commission from 1948 to 1961 – through most of which period Ronald German was a member of its legislative assembly, answerable for the affairs of the P&TA. He made a big contribution to the development of telephone services in the region. German was obviously fond of life in Africa: he had spent the last three years of the war as Assistant Director of Posts & Telegraphs in the Sudan. His years as a neo-colonial administrator evidently furthered his career in the Post Office very effectively, as he returned to St Martin's as a Deputy Director General in 1959.

Annual Estimates procedure. Since 1945, however, the Treasury had retained its wartime control over the Post Office's capital spending as well – and the often parlous state of Britain's finances cast a pall over all the mechanization planning. The national economic crisis of 1948–9 limited most new government investment to export-oriented activities, a category from which the postal service was excluded. Even after economic growth had been restored in the early 1950s, the straitjacket on the service was scarcely loosened. Charlie Geddes, reviewing the prospects of mechanization for his UPW Executive Council in April 1953, suggested his colleagues bear in mind 'that in the present economic circumstances, it is somewhat doubtful whether the Post Office will embark upon a general [and] costly mechanization scheme'.[61]

Geddes did not know it, but De La Warr and his officials were by then exerting pressure in Whitehall for a return to the pre-war financial regime so that the Department might at least regain some scope for spending at its own discretion. They appeared to have won a notable victory in 1955, when the Government agreed to let the Post Office run its own books in exchange for handing the Treasury a fixed dividend (in lieu of tax) of £5m a year. This was welcomed at St Martin's as 'a new concordat with the Treasury, reintroducing all the essential features of the Bridgeman scheme'.[62] It was a fair-weather concession, however, and the return of stormy skies in 1957 scuppered it: the dividend remained payable, but a government freeze on all capital spending in the public sector for two years effectively reasserted the Treasury's right to veto Post Office investment plans. The reneging on the 1955 agreement caused much resentment and set in train a fresh attempt by the Post Office to alter its rules of engagement with the Treasury. The result was in some ways a repeat of the 1955–7 experience, on a grander scale. Two White Papers in 1960 and the resulting Post Office Act of 1961 ceded nominal control over various financial activities to Department officials.[63] This was presented as a fundamental change of status for the Post Office – but since capital spending was one of the activities specifically excluded from the handover of responsibilities in April 1961, the change was hardly more than cosmetic. Once fresh capital-spending restrictions were imposed on the public sector in 1962–3, the Treasury moved brusquely to reassert its authority over all important decisions.

The Treasury's continuing dominance made life more difficult for the advocates of mechanized sorting. They knew bland French-style assurances about the demands of the modern world would impress no one in Great George Street. Worse, they often doubted their own ability to

present a compelling financial case. Prospective returns on mechanization had never much excited the accountants. Taking on the MAC
chairmanship in 1955, Radley told its first meeting 'they would have to
satisfy themselves that the things that were technically possible would
pay, although he thought the Post Office should take a broad view of
this because of the imponderables in the equation'.[64] This was a sensibly
pragmatic view, but underestimated the difficulties ahead. Most cost/
benefit analyses had a bewilderingly short shelf-life. Many innovative
gadgets – like the 'translator' charged with reading phosphorescent dots
and turning them into sorting instructions – soared in price when the
time came to negotiate production contracts. For imponderables such
as better working conditions and an improved flow of work which
might result from mechanization, there was little real enthusiasm even
within the Post Office hierarchy. Asked by the MAC to survey opportunities around the regions in 1956, W. K. Mackenzie (then Deputy
Director of the Midlands Region) reported back that 'there was no
scope for any dramatic increase in the mechanical aids in existing
offices'. He found Head Postmasters, perhaps unsurprisingly, were
really interested only in hearing about aids that promised instant cash
savings.[65] The Treasury's attitude to mechanization was not much different, and seemed unlikely to change unless an overwhelming case
could be made that a long-term expansion of the Post Office depended
on it.

Such a case could be made, and was, for telephones. Here was another
grievous disadvantage for the postal service. In the 1920s, the telephone
industry had complained bitterly about being deprived of capital by an
imperious postal service. Now the old order had been reversed. Once
the immediate post-war years had passed, the disparate needs of the
two businesses inevitably provoked renewed calls – especially from the
telephone engineers – for them to be allowed to go their separate ways,
perhaps even as distinct public entities. As Postmaster General from
1957 to 1959, Ernest Marples made no secret of his view that in an
ideal world, though not perhaps in a pragmatic Tory Britain, telephones
would be a separate business. Any real prospect of its happening in the
fifties was in any case thwarted at the outset by a review of the Post
Office's organizational structure, completed in 1951 by a committee
under the chairmanship of Dudley Lumley, whose primary purpose was
to check that Bridgeman's recipe for regional divisions had worked out
well in practice.[66] In giving it high marks, the Lumley Report concluded
that Regional Directors, Head Postmasters and Telephone Managers

were generally working together in happy harmony. Posts and telephones, concluded Lumley like so many before him, were effectively
inseparable. Many officials on the telephones side of the Post Office
were angered by this verdict, insisting their work was often impeded by
their postal colleagues.[67] But the continued co-existence of posts and
telephones under one roof posed a bigger problem for those postal colleagues, at least when it came to capital spending. Huge sums were needed
through the mid-fifties to ready the telephone network for subscriber
trunk dialling (STD) – an automated system allowing long-distance calls
to be made without the assistance of an operator – which was to be
launched by the Queen in December 1958 and left little in the coffers
for the plain old Post Office. At the first Board meeting of 1956, a newly
appointed Assistant Postmaster General, C. J. M. Alport, confessed 'he
had the impression that research and development on postal matters
was very small compared with the effort devoted to the telephone side,
and the Postmaster General agreed'.[68] The Engineer-in-Chief had presented a paper to the Board on all the development work currently
under way. Out of thirty-eight substantial paragraphs, just three were
devoted to the postal service – and two of those looked at conveyor
belts and labelling machines.[69]

By the time that STD was inaugurated, in December 1958, the profitability of the telephone network was rising quickly. Having fallen away
in the post-war years from the peak of £23.1m in 1944–5, almost disappearing completely in 1956–7, telephone profits in 1959–60 jumped to
a level that had not been achieved in the postal service since the immediate post-war years. They leapt higher again in the early 1960s, reaching
almost £40m in 1963–4, which was far beyond anything ever earned in
one year by the postal service. The profit figures for telephones on the
one hand and the post on the other – as interpreted for the Commercial
Accounts – were ever afterwards in different leagues. (See again Appendix A, Chart 8.) The postal service's unprecedented deficit of 1955–6
was followed by two more loss-making years despite a rise in the basic
letter rate from the 2½d of 1940 to 3d in October 1957. The Post Office
was forced into raising many of its prices across the board over the next
three years – though not the basic letter rate, which remained at 3d until
1965 – but this staunched the mails' losses only briefly. By the end of
1963–4, the cumulative deficit over nine years came to £3.3m; and as
one generous pay award succeeded another with no substantial change
in the output of the workforce, losses of a quite different magnitude
were looming. In the summer of 1964 the Finance Department began

forecasting some alarming deficits, and Kenneth Anderson would warn
the Board a few months later to expect a cumulative loss of £123m over
the next five years.[70] This was the bleak future (or an even bleaker version of it) that officials in the mid-fifties had hoped mechanization might
help avert.

By 1964 the Post Office had been gravely weakened in one other
important respect, too. The putative productivity gains from mechanization had yet to materialize – yet doubts had already appeared over the
ability of the Department to translate them, one day, into higher profit
margins. The UPW thought its members were entitled to a substantial
share of the fruits – and it was determined to use them as a justification
for higher wages and shorter hours even before the gains had been
made. In adopting this more combative stance, the union was responding to an unmistakable hardening of attitudes within the workforce
since the mid-fifties. Indeed, for the UPW as for the Board itself, the
mid-fifties had marked a watershed. The lofty rhetoric of the joint councils and fine words on both sides about shared goals and cooperation had
led in the end to a sense of mounting disenchantment in the workplace –
with grave consequences, much as officials like Sargent and Lumley had
warned might happen. The most conspicuous single factor behind the
change of mood was a seething resentment over the results of a Royal
Commission on civil service pay. The Priestley Commission began its
investigations in 1953 and reported in November 1955. The central
issue for the postal workforce was how far Priestley was prepared to
amend the so-called Tomlin formula, which since 1931 had provided a
theoretical basis for paying wage rates broadly in line with comparable
wages in the rest of the economy.* This had left no room for any notion
of the state as an exemplary employer, no support for the idea that civil
service employees might be regarded as special in any way and no real
basis for offering exceptional awards to acknowledge improved productivity. Since 1950, as we have seen, actual awards to the UPW had
seen postmen's wages rising quickly, and they had certainly outpaced

* The key passage of the 1931 Tomlin Report lay in its para. 308: 'We are satisfied . . . that
broad general comparisons between classes in the Service and outside occupations are possible and should be made. In effecting such comparisons the State should take a long view.
Civil Service remuneration should reflect what may be described as the long term trend,
both in wage levels and in the economic condition of the country. We regard it as undesirable that the conditions of service of civil servants when under review should be related too
closely to factors of a temporary or passing character' (Tomlin Commission Report on the
Civil Service; P.P. 1930–31 Cmd 3909 x 517).

those of comparable groups in the economy. The union, in effect, was now seeking a change in the theoretical basis for postmen's pay that might allow more scope for similarly superior awards in the future. Its executive officers, like the officials at St Martin's, put a huge effort into their evidence for the Commission. The eventual findings came as a genuine shock to the union, which reacted with 'a combination of hostility and bewilderment'.[71] The Priestley Report broadly urged retention of the Tomlin formula, with a more rigorous approach to establishing parities with the private sector. In recommending immediate awards, it excluded the postal unions from increases paid to the rest of the civil service – and it made clear that, while other civil servants could move to shorter working weeks, the postal workforce would be required to stay with a six-day, 46-hour week for the foreseeable future. The union, observing correctly enough that this regime had been in place since 1897, had sought a five-day week – with a 44-hour rota that might eventually be reduced to forty hours.

In January 1956, returning to his full-time position after a year serving as Chairman of the TUC, Geddes threw himself into negotiations over the idea of a fact-finding body on pay parities. This would emerge in due course as the Civil Service Pay Research Unit (CSPRU), with half a dozen members from each side of the National Whitley Council. Geddes believed it was as fair a way of proceeding as could reasonably be devised, and put all his weight behind it in a report on Priestley that he prepared for the 1956 Annual Conference. Persuading his Executive Council to go along with it exposed him to some bitter criticism. At the crucial meeting in March 1956, a recently elected 31-year-old delegate from the Leeds branch 'gave notice that he reserved his right to speak against the [Geddes] Report at Annual Conference' – though what the young Tom Jackson said went unreported, because the General Secretary insisted that the conference session in May be held in camera. Geddes could afford to brush aside his critics. The 1956 conference was to be his last as General Secretary: he would turn sixty before the next one – and retire in a state of exhaustion that caused his colleagues some concern towards the end. His elected successor was Ron Smith, the 41-year-old son of an East End postman who had been an active UPW official since joining the Post Office as a messenger boy in 1929. (His election made him the youngest member of the TUC's General Council.) It fell to Smith to cope with the first formal report of the CSPRU, which did not arrive until October 1958. It looked at the relative position of the Post Office's cleaners, a group that by then had already been at the centre of several acrimonious disputes in recent years. Both the UPW and the Department were taken aback to be told that the comparative data warranted a *reduction* in the cleaners' pay. Officials manfully insisted 'they had never accepted that fair comparisons could only be used to produce increases' while hastily burying the report in the Whitley Council's in-tray.[72] The union rejected the findings out of hand – and went on to challenge the methodology of all subsequent CSPRU reports that fell short (as most did) of backing their demands.

Lumley had warned in 1953 about the reaction to another 'turn of the screw'. The Priestley Report provided it. For those heavily engaged in local union activities who had dreamed of setting postal workers in the vanguard of a socialist state, the Report confirmed that fewer concessions had been extracted in the early 1950s than met the eye. One study written in 1980, and strongly sympathetic to this view, accused officials in the Post Office of preaching the benefits of cooperation and then resorting in practice to 'unilateral decision-making and ... excessively bureaucratic procedures as a means of achieving conflict resolution'.[73] There is no reason to doubt that many in the workforce felt this way – though we might question the validity of the sentiment, given the extraordinary extent to which union representatives had actually succeeded in imposing Staff Side decisions and procedures on the Post Office by the mid-fifties. The outcome, anyway, was a spreading disaffection in the workplace through the post-Priestley years that went much deeper than disappointment over a solitary Royal Commission. Among the minor and Manipulative grades, in particular, there arose a palpable insecurity about the prospects for postal workers in general.* They had lost many of the perks – like in-house medical services, swept aside by the arrival of the National Health Service in 1948 – that had historically set their jobs at a premium to other working-class occupations. Their job-for-life status, pensions and paid holidays were effectively enjoyed now by a growing number of workers in the private sector,

---

* Probably not many postmen in 1957 were readers of the *Economist*, but an August edition of the paper carried a piece almost calculated to inflame their worst fears. It asked its readers rhetorically '[w]hether there should not be some retreat, however regrettable, from what may be called the Victorian luxury element in the basic service of letter delivery. . . . It would be a nuisance to have to fetch one's letter from a roadside box, from several storeys down or from a distant Post Office (but so it is to do one's own washing up). Americans and others accept these nuisances; they are, like the nuisances arising from the disappearance of errand-boys, domestic help, caddies and the like, a feature of a high-wage economy. The postman at the front door is, in fact, a delightful anachronism' (*The Economist*, 17 August 1957).

many of whom had also begun to earn higher wages. And the Manipulative grades could not even feel secure about their standing within the Post Office: promotion to head postmasterships, for example, seemed increasingly to be the preserve of clerical and executive staff.[74] This was itself a reflection of other changes in the make-up of the workforce. Turnover in the Manipulative grades was typically low in rural areas, but dramatically higher in London and other big cities. In 1951, the head of the London Postal Region had told the Board that a force of 18,000 postmen in London had seen a turnover of one third in each of the two prior years; anecdotal evidence suggests the churn rate remained almost as high for years thereafter.[75] As the proportion of new entrants rose, so the strength of the military ethos that had prevailed into the early 1950s declined. It survived a lot longer on the Official Side, with colonels and brigadiers sporting their army titles for many years yet to come. But in the sorting halls and canteens, the discipline and camaraderie of the ex-servicemen's world faded more quickly, as new recruits came into the workforce with little or no army background. (The retention of National Service until 1960 appeared to make little difference.) Nor was this the only shift in the background of new entrants. Before the war, there had been many school-leavers aged fourteen – like young Denis Roberts in Barnsley – for whom entry into the Post Office was one of the few available avenues to a professional career. The Post Office provided evening classes twice a week for them in many large cities. The 1944 Education Act created new opportunities for these able youngsters, and many now remained at school who might previously have joined the Post Office. The post-war scrapping of the boy messengers, too, had closed off a valuable stream of adult recruits already imbued with traditional Post Office habits of mind (though the messenger grade remained in place for sixteen- to eighteen-year-olds, who went on delivering telegrams – and being photographed regularly for Post Office publicity purposes, lined up on their BSA Bantam motorcycles – until the end of the 1970s).

As had been the case earlier in the decade, relations between the Official and Staff Sides of the Post Office largely reflected the national picture. The emollient approach of the Churchill years had given way since 1955 to the less accommodating stance of the Eden and Macmillan years, which were increasingly preoccupied with the great conundrum of how to avert inflationary wage settlements in an era of full employment. As politicians and union leaders wrestled over the answer, 'a sort of hardening of the arteries of communication set in during the late

1950s'.[76] While a more adversarial atmosphere at the Post Office may in this respect have been just a product of the times, the implications for the Department were singularly damaging. So much had been conceded to the postal unions, and in particular the UPW, earlier in the decade that a gradual leakage of goodwill between the two sides could scarcely be afforded. The postal service resembled a high-performance engine that was running dangerously low on lubricants.

Starting in the late fifties, ominous grinding sounds began to emerge across the postal network of the capital and several other cities. There was no discernible pattern – it was usually local issues that prompted trouble, individually quite trivial – but they led to unofficial stoppages on a scale that was wholly new to the Post Office and their net effect was an unfortunate drain on the effectiveness and morale of the Department. An episode in Newcastle in 1958 was not untypical.[77] Early in the year, a Tyneside soap-powder manufacturer, Thomas Hedley Ltd, arranged 'a very large posting' of samples through the mail. The city's Head Post Office offered the company some space on its premises to prepare the posting. The Newcastle branch of the UPW took great exception to this – objecting to the presence of non-union personnel without prior consultation – and agreed to it only after the intervention of officials from Headquarters in London. The union then took up the principle of the matter at Headquarters level. When officials insisted that similar arrangements with private firms might be required else-where in the future, it was agreed that a new instruction would have to be added to the *Head Postmasters' Manual*. Many weeks of negotiation resulted in a final draft that went to the union's Executive Council. This allowed for accommodation to be offered to third parties '[provided] its use for the work in question will not be detrimental to the normal day-to-day work of the office'. The Council insisted that the words 'or the welfare of the staff' be added – which in practice would give branch representatives at least theoretical grounds to oppose any future invita-tions. It was agreed by the Council that, if this amendment were to be refused, 'we should advise Branches of their right to raise with Union Headquarters any point of difficulty or disagreement' about the pro-posed instruction. No doubt wisely in the circumstances, the Department gave way.*

---

* This was not quite the end of the story for Hedley's: two months later, the UPW's Council returned to the Department with angry representations from 'a number of branches to the effect that recent postings of samples of soap powder by [Hedley's] were a source of embar-

In time, some regularly contentious issues became clearer. Most of them impinged in one way or another on the increasingly elaborate – not to say impenetrable – world of local overtime agreements. Attempts by Regional Directors or Headquarters to override 'standing agreements' struck by branches of the union in their own areas were fiercely opposed. This represented a basic challenge to the role of the travelling APCs, but in effect the point was often conceded. Equal pay for women remained a lively issue, even though a landmark agreement in 1956 conceded it to those agreeing to work the same rota as men. (Only about a quarter of women opted to do so, given onerous evening hours, but of the remainder many were now able to achieve rates much closer to parity than ever before.) But as the decade wore on, there was no doubt about the biggest issue of all: the potentially transforming impact of mechanization on the working week inevitably sent it to the top of the agenda. The UPW was by no means opposed to mechanized sorting. In the immediate post-war years, some on the Executive Council had urged the union to set its face against all experimentation, but Geddes had outmanoeuvred them. 'He could sympathise to some extent with the fears which were still existent about mechanical aids,' as the minutes of a November 1947 meeting recorded, 'but as reasonable people the Council should have got beyond the stage of believing that all mechanical aids were bad from a worker's point of view. Rather they should endeavour to exploit the machine in the interests of the workers and not allow the worker to be exploited by the machine . . .'[78] A broad consensus backed Geddes' approach by the mid-fifties. Invited by Radley to join the MAC in November 1955, Geddes was personally too stretched already to accept – and was approaching retirement – but he encouraged the UPW's Executive to accept membership, which it did a few days later.[79] Still, it remained to be seen what 'exploiting the machine' might entail in practice. At its Annual Conference in 1956, the Union resolved to link the benefits of mechanization into a campaign to win – at last – the battle for a 44-hour week. This had been rejected in 1919 and again in 1947 on the basis that no prospect existed of recouping the cost through higher productivity. Mechanization had opened up that prospect.

Through 1956–7, officials and their Union counterparts circled each

---

rassment to staff . . .' It was alleged that 'owing to the poor quality of the container, the contents were released and this caused serious irritation to the hands and other exposed parts of the body'. More inquiries had to follow.

other warily. The workforce's contribution to the mechanization programme elicited regular praise in public from ministers and departmental
heads alike, but this looked a blatant attempt to mitigate the ill-effects
of the Union's covert hostility. The UPW laid down some tortuous
ground rules for the use of SPLSMs – only Postmen Higher Grade to be
employed, no redundancies to result from introduction of the machines,
'surplus' staff to be redeployed only 'against vacancies, absences and
pressure' – and it policed them vigilantly. As the Union was well aware,
the putative adoption of a universal code would also be of concern to
postal sorters. As the UPW's man on the Mechanical Aids Committee
pointed out, 'the implications of eliminating the need for local geographical knowledge on the part of the coder/sorter raised many issues
of vital interest to the staff associations'.[80] Tensions rose as the ultimate
aim of mechanization – fewer staff and higher productivity – grew steadily less amenable to a fudge. Both sides resorted to talking about 'human
problems', as shorthand for the implications of new technology for current manning levels. Officials had in mind the advantages of shedding
labour; the UPW was intent on the backlash that would flow from any
dishing of their members' expectations. At its 1958 conference, the
UPW decided it could wait no longer for the benefits of mechanization
to appear: it wanted to see the shorter week with immediate effect – in
anticipation, as was wryly observed by the official charged with handling the demand, of the benefits to come.[81] This was the comment of a
young Director (the son of a telephone manager) who had first attracted
attention at Headquarters as Private Secretary to De La Warr and had
since risen quickly up the ladder. Now head of the Establishments and
Organization Directorate (EOD), William Ryland took a tough line: his
letters to the union struck a note very different from those of his counterparts earlier in the decade. His first detailed rebuttal of the
shorter-week claim, in April 1959, was terse to the point of being dismissive. When the two sides met six weeks later, Ron Smith started the
proceedings by saying 'he felt bound to point out that the letter was perhaps the most disappointing the Union had ever received'.[82] There were
to be many more in the same vein. One of Smith's UPW colleagues at
that same May 1959 meeting summed up the union's reaction as soon as
Ryland's stance became clear: 'If union members had known earlier what
was the present position [on the shorter week], the Post Office would not
have had the cooperation in the past that had in fact been freely given'.
    Five months later, in October 1959, the political context for any
discussions with the unions was transformed: the Conservatives won a

much increased majority in the general election and Marples was succeeded as Postmaster General by Reginald Bevins. The two politicians
had followed curiously similar career paths. Both came from humble
social backgrounds; both had served with the Royal Artillery during the
war and then found parliamentary seats on Merseyside (in Toxteth and
Wallasey respectively); and both had made their mark at the Ministry of
Housing before coming to the Post Office. But Bevins – who had been a
Labour councillor on the Liverpool City Council before the war – was
a far grittier and more combative character than Marples. A working-
class Thatcherite before his (or her) time, he would later recount, in an
autobiography that he produced in 1965, how he scorned his predecessor's advice to 'keep sweet with the two Smiths' – that is, the POEU's
General Secretary Charles Smith as well as his namesake at the UPW –
and cast a cold eye on what he saw as the Department's appeasement of
the unions. 'I soon discovered what I had rather suspected, notably, that
the unions had been more or less running the Post Office for a long
time. . . . [By then] I was tired of the dictatorial attitude of the unions in
general, not only towards employers but to the Government and the
public.'[83] If the Government were to decide that a hard line needed
taking with the unions – which seemed ever more likely after the 1959
election – Bevins was more than ready to have the Post Office lead the
way.

The Department thus began the 1960s beset by an increasingly
embittered workforce on the one hand, and a Postmaster General on the
other itching to make his mark as a politician ready to stand up to the
trade unions. It was an inflammatory environment – and it prompted
the adoption, for the avoidance of sparks, of a most remarkable entente
between two individuals equally committed in their different ways to
sustaining the welfare and stability of the Post Office. One was the Director General, Ronald German, and the other was his counterpart at the
UPW, Ron Smith. Exactly how and when the rapport between them
developed is hard to say, though it was plain to insiders in the early sixties that the two men were close. What only emerged much later was
that they struck a secret deal together over the conduct of pay negotiations.* German would privately tell Smith the absolute maximum that
the Post Office was prepared to concede. A public offer would then be
made at about half that level, allowing Smith to respond with enough

---

* Even Alan Clinton, writing his voluminous history of the UPW published in 1984, seems
not to have known of it.

anger and indignation to satisfy the militants in his union ranks. A lively negotiation could ensue, satisfying honour on both sides and ending with agreement to abide by the number that German had first thought of. Neither Bevins nor successive Assistant Postmaster Generals had any inkling of it, though German made a clean breast of the arrangement to their successors after the 1964 election. The first Assistant Postmaster General in the Labour government, a former miner called Joe Slater, reportedly commented on hearing of the still extant pact 'that if Ron Smith's executive knew what was happening, they'd murder him'.[84]

This was a singular variation on the partnership theme pioneered by Geddes and Little; but the fact that the Post Office and its largest union could be run by wholly compatible personalities, quite happy with this kind of understanding, says much about both institutions. Like a surprising number of his senior colleagues, German came from a working-class background in the West Country: his father was a builder's foreman, and he had trained as a shipwright's apprentice in Devonport before joining the Post Office. A Deputy DG, William Wolverson, was a boilermaker's son; he, too, had done an apprenticeship in shipbuilding as a young man. These were able men, who had risen to the top of a department of state that was conspicuously more socially accessible and meritocratic in many ways than others. (At a time when it was still rare to hear voices in the corridors of Whitehall that did not echo the Queen's English as spoken by the BBC, there were several individuals at the top of St Martin's with pronounced regional accents.[85]) As Director General, German presided over an intensely hierarchical organization – the top five ranks of which were regularly sprinkled with decorations from CBEs up to full knighthoods – but he had no inclination whatever to regard union bosses as his social inferiors. German befriended Smith, just as many other officials generally enjoyed close personal relations with the union officers they dealt with on a regular basis. There was also a keen awareness in the Department that the union executives had a huge and demanding organization of their own to manage. Indeed, since the union hierarchies were both less disciplined and far more decentralized – and since Executive Council members were dependent for their power on democratic election by the rank and file – the managerial challenge for the union leaders was in some ways even more formidable. German appreciated this, and did what he could to lighten Smith's difficulties in the broader interests of the Post Office.

Smith was not the man to let slip such precious help. Like Geddes, he was diligent and extremely hard-working. He also followed his predecessor in bringing a formidable physical presence to bear. He was well over six feet tall, and with his heavily rimmed glasses and thick black hair brushed back from his forehead, Smith bears an unfortunate resemblance in many photographs to the Kray twins of London gangland fame. It is not hard to imagine him laying down the law with his colleagues. His entry in the *Oxford DNB* describes him as a man of 'mild manners, a gentle character and a reflective outlook', but he could be a bruiser behind the scenes.[86] Colder and more calculating than Geddes, he was at best a mediocre speaker and was rarely seen on the party circuit at conference time. Doing little to court personal popularity, he relied on his skills as a negotiator: the back room was his milieu, not the big stage.* But all pay negotiations unavoidably entailed plenty of theatricals. Smith had no qualms about stage-managing them, once he was reasonably sure of the script in advance. After his first four years in office, he could point to his record with some pride. A wide-ranging improvement in pay and conditions in 1957 was subsequently hailed by the 1958 Conference chairman as even more important than the benefits of Reallocation at the end of the war. Retail prices since 1950 had risen about 50 per cent and national wage rates for manual workers had climbed by roughly 70 per cent. Postal workers had more than kept abreast of these increases, with wages rising by 70 per cent for London postmen (at the maximum end of the scale), by 83 per cent for P&TOs, by 130 per cent for female clerks working on equal pay with men after 1956, and by 114 per cent for female telephonists.[87]

In his New Year message in *The Post* of January 1961, Smith talked of 'ten tremendous years' for the workforce. As he was well aware, however, some within the union were fiercely critical of his failure to make faster progress towards a shorter week. At a mass rally in November 1959 organized by the union's London District Council (LDC), almost 3,000 members had publicized a scathing contempt for their General Secretary and his moderate approach. 'Has the UPW been taken over

---

* When he went to the US as a guest of the National Association of Letter Carriers' national conference in August 1958, Smith found himself marching through the streets of San Francisco to the convention hall behind a band and a baton-whirling Drum Majorette. As he noted in his report to the Executive Council, 'we marched down the centre aisle with the whole Convention standing and applauding! Although more than bewildered, I managed to talk for about forty minutes to an extremely attentive audience.' He gave them a blow-by-blow account of the amalgamation of the UPW's constituent unions since 1918. (UPW Executive Council papers, June–September 1958, UCW/2/4/1, pp. 887–98.) When all the delegates of the NALC took to the streets of San Francisco that night, the parade was five miles long.

by a Little Mouse?' ran the banners, when he had declined to address
the rally. Open calls had been made for strikes to be considered.[88] Since
then, a rancorous discontent with the union's leadership had spread
among many branch and sub-branch committees, especially in London –
where, as Geddes had always feared might happen, members of the British
Communist Party had risen to prominent positions in the local UPW
hierarchy. They included J. R. (Dickie) Lawlor and Willie Failes, both of
whom Geddes had publicly rebuked more than once during his tenure.[89]
Smith was almost as passionately anti-Communist as Geddes, but his
ability to hold the moderate line was greatly weakened after the union's
Annual Conference in 1961. This was as volatile as any in its history,
voting to turn its back once and for all on the Priestley Report and to
use the union's industrial muscle to go after the biggest wage increases
it thought achievable. The workforce still had a quasi-military air about
it in many ways, turning up for 'duty' each day and taking holidays as
'leave', but its deference towards the higher ranks was rapidly slipping
into the past.

   An unprecedented national 'work-to-rule' action in January 1962
involved a ban on voluntary overtime and an officious regard for the rule
book which badly disrupted the mails. Despite the shock of this action
and a blunt insistence by Bevins that the Post Office would stand by the
dictates of a pay pause for all civil servants imposed some months earlier,
Smith managed – with the covert assistance of his ally in Headquarters –
to avert further serious disruption through 1962–3. The importance of
the UPW leader's role was acknowledged by the Government. He was
invited – slightly to the Postmaster General's dismay – to join other TUC
leaders taking seats on the National Economic Development Council,
one of the various initiatives launched around this time to seek a resolution to the problems of an inflation-threatened economy. But Smith's
evident readiness to play the role of an enlightened intermediary went
down much less well with many of his own members, whose readiness to
go on negotiating for pay like patient white-collar civil servants was all
but exhausted.[90] The consequence for the UPW hierarchy was an acrimonious feud that almost tore it apart in 1963–5, entailing court actions
and bitter confrontations. For the Post Office, the more immediate result
was that Smith had little choice by 1964 but to lead the union into its
first ever national strike, in support of a pay claim far beyond the 4 per
cent limit set by the Government as a 'guide' to acceptable awards (and
surely *not* pre-agreed with German). The UPW was egged on by the
TUC and the leading industrial trade unions; and its officers were con-

fronted in person by the Chancellor of the Exchequer, Reginald Maudling. Thus a trade union representing members of a government department was thrust anomalously into the front line of a gathering political battle in Britain over employee relations within heavy industry. The crisis came to a head in July 1964, after a one-day stoppage. It was resolved only on the eve of a national strike by all postmen and PHGs, to run from 25 July 'until further notice'.

The final settlement was a disaster for Bevins himself. At the outset of the negotiations in January, he had urged his government colleagues to accept a 5 per cent award at the outset, which he always claimed later would have been accepted. His advice was firmly rejected, in favour of a 'non-negotiable' ceiling of 4 per cent. The Government capitulated in the end, daunted by the prospect of what might happen if the mails ceased to run altogether, and agreed a 6½ per cent award. Bevins – who had managed neither the media nor his colleagues' expectations with much aplomb – was held to blame for the damage done to the Cabinet's putative incomes policy. 'If any man "carried the can" for others,' as he recalled bitterly in his autobiography, 'I did, and politically it put me out.'[91] He lost his Liverpool seat at the 1964 election – after a passionate local campaign against him by the city's postal workers – and abandoned his political career. For Ronald German and his senior colleagues, meanwhile, an abrasive confrontation with the workforce was yet another blow to morale at the end of a dispiriting five years. Letter volumes had fallen in 1957–8 for the first time since the year of the General Strike. Nothing had happened since then to lift the Department's gloomy assessment – first conveyed to the Whitley Council's Staff Side in May 1959 – that postal traffic had probably peaked and was now destined for a long, slow decline.[92] The 1961 Post Office Act – described by Bevins as 'a landmark in the history of the Post Office' – had proved to be nothing of the kind, merely a modest milestone at best on the seemingly interminable road to real independence from the Treasury.[93] Its aftermath was a wretched anticlimax, adding to the sense of drift under a Postmaster General who thought the postal service 'a pretty mundane business' and spent most of his tenure embroiled in a struggle to launch commercial television in Britain. For the four years after November 1960, regular meetings of the Post Office Board were abandoned altogether. Added to all of these many slights and disappointments were the repercussions of one further setback, a humiliation for the Department that began on a remote stretch of railway line in Buckinghamshire in the early hours of an August morning in 1963.

5. INSPECTOR OSMOND AND THE
GREAT TRAIN ROBBERY

Outsiders rarely tried to rob the mails in the nineteenth century. The fearsome reputation of the Royal Mail's armed guards lingered on well beyond the heyday of the stage coach – and mail theft remained punishable by death until 1837, and by transportation until the second half of the century. A snatch of mailbags from a Post Office branch in London's Hatton Garden in 1881 successfully netted a haul of diamonds worth a spectacular £80,000 (equivalent to more than £6m today), but the 'Great Diamond Robbery' was a rare event and had no lasting influence on postal procedures.[94] 'Security' in the Victorian Post Office was mostly a matter of cracking down on light-fingered postal workers and was handled by the Missing Letter Branch, renamed the Confidential Inquiry Branch in 1883. Perhaps the popularity of the Sherlock Holmes stories in Edwardian England encouraged another change of name in 1908, when it became the Investigations Branch – 'the IB'.

The criminal classes started taking a more concerted interest in the Royal Mail's conveyance of cash consignments, especially around the City of London, in the 1920s. A series of mail van robberies in the last years of that decade prompted the introduction in 1929 of a set of new security measures. Cash and other valuables would henceforth be carried as 'High Value Packets' (HVPs), with attendant special precautions to deal with 'the bandit problem', as Department papers often quaintly referred to it. The HVP system kept the bandits at bay for many years. When the IB issued its first annual report, in 1947, it surveyed the work of more than 200 officers around the country – including sixty-four police sergeants – but was mostly restricted to accounting for the dismissal of a few hundred employees per year since 1945, most of them temporary staff.[95] So it came as a shock to the Post Office, in May 1952, when a Royal Mail van containing almost £300,000 in used banknotes – worth, as it happens, about the same in contemporary money as the Hatton Garden haul of 1881 – was ambushed in the West End. ('Used' was the term generally applied to banknotes already in circulation, rather than those just emerging hot from the printers. In practice, used banknotes meant either batches being transferred between the branches and headquarters of the big banks or else consignments from one or more of the banks to the Chief Cashier's office at the Bank of

England, to be sent for incineration.) The 'Eastcastle Street raid' was easily the biggest robbery in Britain since the war and caused a sensation.[96] Seven men in two cars sandwiched the mail van in the road, overpowered its driver and two attendants – leaving them injured on the pavement – and drove off with its load intact. The money vanished, and so did the villains. No one was ever prosecuted for the robbery, though in later years it was often confidently alleged to have been the work of a gang that was well-known to the Metropolitan police. It included, by his own account, at least one subsequent associate of a young London gangster called Bruce Reynolds.[97]

The Post Office (naturally) set up a committee to take stock of its security rules.[98] Its findings, discussed at a Board meeting within a few weeks of the robbery, were happily reassuring. Various third-party proposals were rejected. It had been suggested, for example, that used banknotes headed for burning should be defaced before being loaded into trains or vans for their last journey. This idea had been exhaustively researched in 1930 and found to be impractical on numerous grounds. Some had urged that truncheons or even firearms be handed out to those in charge of HVP loads; but the staff associations made it clear that this would not be acceptable. The PMG, De La Warr, wondered whether a special force of Post Office guards might be considered. He was told that those driving HVP vans within the London Postal Region were already selected quite carefully – and they 'were mainly of the active type, who might be expected to give a good account of themselves if attacked'. As for the threat posed to the Department's own finances, there was virtually no liability for the hundreds of millions of pounds conveyed in cash each year on behalf of the banks. The Post Office paid compensation of just £5 on each HVP packet that went missing. Given that so few had done so, over the years, Director General Little was anxious on that June morning of 1952 to avoid any over-reaction. Letters would be sent out to all the Region Offices specifying some sensible additional measures, but the DG 'felt that the Department must preserve its sense of proportion and perspective in this matter, because . . . it might well be ten years or more before any further big losses were suffered'.[99]

In the years that followed, the DG's judgement was vindicated. There were no copy-cat versions of the Eastcastle Street attack, which many had feared. The statistics of postal crime, as the IB happily reported in 1956, had been on a steady downward trend since the early 1950s.[100]

Close cooperation with the police had helped the Branch to smash several gangs specializing in Post Office burglaries.* Intermittent discussions were now held between the Post Office and the Railways Executive about the possibility that HVP mailbags on trains might be put beyond the reach of corridors open to the public. Perhaps the bags might even be stored, one day, within security cages. But schedules for any action were generally measured in years. There was no external pressure for change from the banks themselves, or even from the police: a Scotland Yard report for the Chief Constables' Annual Conference in 1955 'gave a clean bill of health to Post Office security arrangements', as the Board proudly noted.[101] Internally, the unions were a little more exercised about the crime threat. The National Federation of Sub-Postmasters, for example, sought improved compensation arrangements for any losses they might incur in raids on scale-payment offices. The Establishments and Organization Department retorted in 1958 that it had looked into the robbery statistics, 'but the numbers were so small that it was difficult to draw accurate conclusions'.[102] The IB's 1957–8 Annual Report noted that total losses from crime during the year had amounted to only about £250,000. Rash expenditure on anti-crime devices could easily exceed this amount, so it was 'important to be selective in our precautions'. This ruled out a blanket distribution of 'bandit alarms', although Headquarters was willing to support any Regional Director who thought he had particularly unsavoury neighbourhoods to consider.

The early months of 1959 unaccountably brought a spate of mail van robberies, which prompted the media to take a fresh interest in Post Office security. The *Today* programme on BBC Radio's Home Service had a regular 'Crime Comment' slot. One of its presenters with a fondness for hyperbole suggested in March that the Queen's mail had 'become one of the favourite objectives of the commando-type gangster'.[103] Just a fortnight later, three men on the Caledonian Express passenger train from Euston to Scotland managed to break into a carriage containing mailbags. They spent three hours rifling the contents before jumping off at a slow points-crossing outside Preston. Their

---

* They included an especially audacious outfit known as the Flame-Cutting Gang, because they used oxyacetylene equipment to burn their way into Post Office safes. They used various ruses to smuggle the tools of their trade into position: 'in one case, for example, the cylinders of oxygen were taken to the Post Office precincts in broad daylight and left inside Post Office premises marked "GPO, Do Not Touch" ... which enabled them to arrive under cover of darkness with all the necessary equipment near at hand'. (BP 49(56), 'The Investigation Branch', 23 June 1956, p. 6, Post 69/60.)

takings amounted to an unprincely £100, but media commentators – including a bevy of retired Scotland Yard detectives, writing for the tabloids – were quick to see danger signals here for the Royal Mail's use of the railways. One of them, an ex-Detective Superintendent Webb writing in the *Evening News*, accused the Post Office of a careless disregard for security on the trains.[104] This prompted an internal reappraisal and a subsequent briefing for the PMG. It was true, he was told, that attempted thefts had risen sharply in 1958–9. But the figures were still a fraction of those recorded a decade earlier. The Post Office daily carried about a million bags of mail by road and rail, and its losses in recent years equated to about one bag a day. Of the 300 or so attempted robberies each year, the great majority were recorded at non-Crown sub-offices; a bare handful targeted the Department's 14,500 mail vans, which motored unmolested for 200 million miles a year. As for the conveyance of mails by rail, several hundred wire cages had been installed on trains in recent years (the impudent ex-Detective Superintendent Webb had shown 'a lamentable lack of knowledge of Post Office procedures . . .'). There was general agreement at the last Board meeting of 1959 that crime levels might now have peaked. Occasional small losses were to be expected at the hands of amateurs like the gang plaguing the Caledonian Express, who carried out a string of further attacks in the months ahead, none apparently more profitable than the first, but anything more serious seemed very unlikely. 'Perhaps Post Office precautions were now so adequate', as the minutes noted, 'that professional criminals were concluding that the game was not worth the candle'.[105]

A new Inspector of the IB, C. G. Osmond, took over in January. He had been in the job less than nine months when he had to send an urgent note to the Postal Services Director on 21 September 1960. Thieves had tampered with the signals on the London to Brighton line during the night, halting a train and enabling them to break into it. 'It is alleged that the thieves left the train after attacking the guard and escaped by car, which was waiting for them at a predetermined spot.'[106] The estimated loss was set at only about £9,000 – the train had been a passenger service with no TPO carriages, just a pile of mailbags in the guard's van. Nonetheless, it was a crime with profound implications, as Inspector Osmond was quick to grasp. For if a passenger train could be halted at night in this way, why not a TPO? Here was a game that professionals might think well worth the candle. For the price of a platform ticket, anyone could stroll the length of terminal stations like Euston, Glasgow or Bristol of an evening and watch TPO carriages being loaded with hundreds of mailbags, a large number of them helpfully tagged with a small red HVP label. It was widely known among postal and railway workers that these in many cases denoted bags containing used banknotes. Huge sums were being shipped in this way every week, though of course no outsiders could ever be sure of the exact quantities or timing. (It would emerge much later that the total figure ran to a staggering £4,000m a year.[107]) And once on board the TPOs, the HVP bags were steadily separated from the rest and passed to an easily identifiable HVP carriage at the head of the train for the remainder of their journey. As for the timing of that journey, TPOs ran to schedules no less regular than those of passenger trains. All this was information, as the new head of the IB appreciated, that skilled criminals might find it appallingly easy to come by. At the last of the regular Board meetings which he chaired as Postmaster General before allowing them to lapse, even Bevins had to acknowledge that their earlier assessment might have been too complacent. 'The Postmaster General concluded by expressing his concern at the problem of train robberies and robberies at sub-post offices, and said he would like a thorough examination of the whole question.'[108]

In fact officials had already held a meeting in October 1960 at King Edward Building to review the vulnerability of TPOs, 'particularly when a train is brought to a halt (genuine or otherwise) outside a station'.[109] On one side of the table were the two departments most anxious to see changes made: Osmond's IB and the Personnel Department (PD). On the other were officials from the London Postal Region (LPR) who had direct responsibility for all TPO operations and who at first had their doubts about the level of danger posed for a stationary HVP carriage, sceptical that any assailant would be able to break into it from track level. The boys from the IB knew better. A professional gang would make sure they had the time to crash their way in, they insisted. 'The PD/IB representatives pointed out that if a raid on the scale envisaged were to take place, it would doubtless be planned to the last detail in a spot where the chance of police interruption would be very slight.' To their minds, the solution was obvious. 'In such circumstances the release of a very noisy bandit alarm would be the most effective method of scaring the attackers and attracting early aid.' A few years earlier, hundreds of Crown post offices had had their safes fitted with a special burglar alarm designed by the IB, and it had proved a very effective deterrent.[110] The IB put down a formal request 'to see alarms fitted to all postal vehicles on TPOs liable to carry HVPs'. There were fifty-one

TPOs in all, most of which combined passenger and sorting carriages. Priority would need to be given to the trains that were dedicated exclusively to sorting, the 'Great West' on the West Country line between Penzance and Paddington – and the 'Specials' between Aberdeen/Glasgow and Euston, on the line made so famous by Auden's poem.

This was accepted by the meeting – after which the implementation of the idea moved forward at a pace which might have been deliberately calculated to ensure that, if there were any plans afoot in the criminal underworld to take out a TPO, those organizing them would not be inconvenienced by any sudden change of Royal Mail procedures. Part of the problem was that the Post Office needed to coordinate the fitting of the alarms with the one other giant organization in Britain that could rival it in the thoroughness of its clerical procedures – the Railways division of the British Transport Commission. Nine months of 1961 had passed before it was even officially confirmed between the two of them that the initiative should rest with the Post Office.[111] Difficulties were also encountered with the manufacture of a bandit alarm that would be up to the job. The IB was adamant that it should produce a sound 'which could be heard over a distance of several miles'. Attacked in a remote spot of countryside, any TPO should be able to let off a noise that would ensure (thinking of Auden's marvellous image) that in the farms passed all would be woken, and by rather more than the gentle shaking of a jug. When a specially designed gas-operated 'siren alarm' was tested at a railway siding in February 1962, however, officials from the IB thought the noise carried for only about 150 yards, and sounded too much like a passing diesel engine. In a detailed memo shortly afterwards, the IB confessed its doubts. Perhaps they should resort instead to having every TPO fitted with 'a large bell'? But it clung to the basic concept of an alarm. 'A strongly mounted attack pressed home with determination would probably succeed in penetrating a TPO, but would take some time and would be likely to meet stiff opposition from the TPO staff . . .'[112] All that would be needed, at this critical juncture, was an effective way to alert the neighbourhood.

Meanwhile, late in January, the Post Office had been given another bad scare. Days prior to the alarm test, thieves were thought to have targeted the main TPO bringing mail from East Anglia to the capital. Fourteen detonators had been planted along the track to bring it to an emergency halt on a remote stretch of track in Essex. Luckily for the TPO, a delayed goods train had gone ahead of it at the last moment. The detonators had gone off, leaving a puzzled train crew to speculate with investigators about what might have been intended. ('Great Train Robbery foiled' ran a headline story in the *Daily Express*.[113]) This prompted a flurry of anxious correspondence within the Department and a further report from the IB in April 1962, with additional recommendations – such as iron bars and steel-mesh grilles for window openings – to back up the adoption of alarms. But four more months slipped by, with little sign of any real progress being made by the LPR. Under pressure from the IB, one of the top men in the Postal Services Department chivvied the LPR's Director in November to knock a few heads together. 'I must confess that I should feel much happier if I knew that all possible precautions against attacks had in fact been taken. My worry stems from the fact that criminal gangs seem to be turning more to attacks on points where fairly obvious concentrations of cash occur . . .'[114]

Within a few weeks, the decision was at last made – more than two years after that formal request from the IB in October 1960 – to push ahead with the installation of mechanical alarm-bells on all TPO carriages used for moving HVPs. Fitting would start at the beginning of February 1963, which it transpired was not a moment too soon. Just as the work was commencing, Osmond and his colleagues in the IB received a tip-off – from a source they did not disclose – that thieves were planning two attacks on the Post Office, one of them targeted at the South-West TPO (running between Paddington and Bristol/Penzance). The most senior officials involved in Post Office security hurriedly convened a meeting to take stock of the situation:

> 1. The Chairman said he had called the meeting to consider what action might be taken to meet threatened attacks on the SWTPO and on a van conveying diamonds in London.
> SWTPO
> 2. Nature of attack. Mr Osmond explained that it was not yet known whether the attack would be made on the TPO itself or, for example, at a loading or unloading point in a station. If it was to be made in a station, the IB would probably get to know beforehand.
> 3. Present protection. It was confirmed that the recommendations made by PD/IB as a result of their recent review of TPOs and Sorting Carriages had been implemented as far as the SWTPO was concerned . . .
> At an unauthorized stop the standard instructions forbade the opening of doors but allowed discretion to open a window if necessary to find out the cause of the stop.

From observations made by travelling Divisional staff it was confidently thought that the TPO security drill was automatically and regularly performed. . . .

6. Mechanical Bells. It was agreed the [London Postal Region] should make sure that a mechanical bell was always fitted in the carriage containing the HVP cupboard in the SWTPO . . . and that it should be tested by a supervising officer each night.

It was agreed that LPR should ensure that mechanical bells were fitted in all TPO carriages containing HVP cupboards, or if no cupboard, in the carriage used for the conveyance of HVPs.[115]

While there is no record of any further steps taken on the SWTPO specifically, or of any further information about the possibility of an attack on it, the work of installing the alarms certainly went ahead. Even once it had begun, however, it took several months; and for the rest of the year, HVP carriages without bandit alarms would have to remain on stand-by, just in case mechanical faults should cripple any of the newly equipped carriages and leave the railways short of rolling stock. It would probably be late in the year before all HVP carriages had received alarms. One other novel idea was put forward by the IB in these early weeks of 1963. Why not install a VHF radio in every carriage with a valuable cargo? Contact in an emergency could then be made with local radio stations. 'It is also possible', suggested the IB to Postal Services, 'that County Police Authorities might be prepared to accept in [an] emergency a TPO "SOS" signal on the Police radio communications system frequency.'[116] It was urged that the Radio Services Branch should be asked to look into the details 'as a matter of urgency'. Alas, the whole idea looked far too expensive to Postal Services. The proposal was returned to the IB in the first week of August, with a note 'indicating that the idea [was] not being proceeded with on grounds of cost'.[117] In the meantime, a staff booklet had been prepared, entitled *Postal Security*, and all 'Officers-in-Charge' were reminded by the Chief Superintendent of Postal Services to pay special heed to TPO regulations: 'The possibility of an attempt to secure possession of the mails from a TPO, especially at a lonely station during the small hours of the night, or following an irregular stop of the train, can no more be discounted now than when [modern TPO rules were first drawn up].'[118] There was a Whitley Committee dedicated to the interests of TPO staff, and at the end of July it distributed copies of the booklet with a special message ('remember . . . how carelessness can help a thief . . .') to all sorters working on the TPOs, urging extra-special vigilance for security on the railways.[119]

The four sorters and their supervisor working in the HVP carriage of the 'Up Special' from Aberdeen to London on the night of 7–8 August 1963 were probably not thinking much about vigilance by the time their TPO had passed its last scheduled stop at Rugby. Just over an hour remained of the journey south to Euston, where they were due in at 4 a.m. It had been a particularly tiring run. The volume of mail being sorted by seventy or so colleagues in the ten carriages behind them was not much out of line with the average, but they had picked up a much heavier than usual load of HVP mail in Glasgow. The previous Monday, 5 August, had been a Bank Holiday, and many Scottish banks had spent Tuesday and Wednesday collecting and packaging English bank-notes spent north of the border over the long weekend. Despatched to the Post Office on the Wednesday afternoon, the banks' consignments explained the presence in the HVP now of 128 mailbags. All had their little red tags and their destination labels, mostly addressed to bank branches across the City of London and postmarked 'Glasgow, 7 VIII 1963'. The fact that the bags together contained millions of pounds in used notes is unlikely to have prompted any special concern among the Post Office crew. Theirs was a well-worn routine. Even when the train pulled up in the darkness of the Buckinghamshire countryside just south of Leighton Buzzard, there would have been no cause for concern. Brief halts close to engineering works were quite common.

Then something strange happened. The train moved off again, and a loud bang alerted the sorters to the fact that a steam pipe between their carriage and the one behind it had been pulled apart. Over the next few moments – the time required to shunt the engine half a mile further along the track – it dawned upon the five men that their carriage (and one other, full of parcels, between them and the engine) had been disconnected from the rest of the train. We can only imagine their dismay as they turned to locate the new alarm as a way of telling the driver and the abandoned carriages that something was amiss, for they were travelling that night in one of the 'old' HVP carriages that had yet to be refitted. There was no alarm at hand of any kind. Suddenly those 'Standard Instructions' for staff encountering 'an unauthorized stop' were of no help at all. The supervisor, Frank Dewhurst, could only pull the communication cord. When this had no effect, the men were reduced to opening the (as yet still unbarred) windows and shouting for attention. For all we know, they were still shouting when the train came to a halt again. Then a masked man brandishing a broad-blade axe smashed his way through one of the windows and jumped down into the carriage. Other masked men followed him. After a brief gesture of defiance from the postmen, one of their attackers shouted to someone down on the trackside: 'They're putting the bolts on. Fetch the guns!' There seemed to the terrified postmen no doubting that they would be dealt with violently if they attempted to resist. (They did not know it, but the driver of the train, 58-year-old Jack Mills, had already been badly coshed over the head for trying to stop the robbers climbing into his cab when the train had first halted. Luckily for the robbers, he had recovered just enough to be able to restart the train, when threatened with another coshing, and had managed to move it forwards as they directed to its second stopping place.) Within moments, all the postmen had been bundled into a corner of the HVP carriage, where they lay trussed and tied as its contents were swung, bag by bag, over their heads and out into the night.

The duty officer in charge of Headquarters – known for centuries as the Clerk-in-Waiting – received a call around 5.30 a.m. from a senior TPO division official at the LPR. The news of the attack, and the unimaginable loss of 120 mailbags containing 636 HVPs, had left him in a state of shock, and all he could say at first was 'They've done the Up Special'.[120] The Director of Postal Services was contacted at once – and by 7 a.m. the press calls had begun. By the end of the morning, the enormity of what had happened was becoming horribly apparent: the thieves had disappeared with a mail load weighing well over two tons, containing used banknotes valued at substantially more than a million pounds. (Only a day or two later was the exact value confirmed as £2.6m – equivalent to more than £40m today.) A press conference, held jointly by the Post Office and the Buckinghamshire Constabulary in Aylesbury that afternoon, attracted more coverage around the world than any other event in the Department's history. ('History's Greatest Robbery – There'll Always be an England', ran a headline in the *New York Herald Tribune*, capturing immediately a sense of the misplaced romanticism that would colour accounts of the robbery for years to come.) The Postmaster General, on holiday in Spain, flew back to London and gave an interview in his private office to *The Times* that evening. His remarks prompted a headline next day: '"INSIDE JOB" CANNOT BE RULED OUT, SAYS MR BEVINS'.

The story of the Great Train Robbers – and of the ways in which they were hunted down, leaving twelve of the fifteen-man gang tried and

BANK LOSES £500,000 IN MAIL TRAIN RAID

TWO REWARDS TOTALLING £35,000 OFFERED

G.P.O. CHIEFS DISCUSS WAYS TO TIGHTEN UP SECURITY

Suggestions for tightening up Post Office security were discussed by Mr. Bevins, the Postmaster General, yesterday after the overnight Scotland to London Post Office express had been ambushed in Buckinghamshire. The raiders' haul is likely to amount to over £1m.

The National Provincial Bank stated last night that they had lost "in excess of £500,000". The British Linen Bank in Scotland (a subsidiary of Barclays Bank) put its loss at about £55,000. Nearly all the money is in notes. On behalf of the two banks a London firm of loss adjusters has offered a reward of £25,000. Mr. Bevins, the Postmaster General, has authorized a reward of £10,000 for information leading to the conviction of those responsible.

Mr. Bevins was kept informed of the progress of inquiries at his home in Liverpool, but yesterday he decided to interrupt his holiday and fly to London for consultations with Post Office

officials. Buckinghamshire constabulary, Scotland Yard, railway police and Post Office investigators are cooperating in the search for the gang, estimated to number between eight and 15.

Mr. Bevins on his arrival at London Airport last night said that he wanted to find out " why the precautions taken were not adequate ". He had authorized the offer of £10,000 because, with the large number of persons involved, there was a substantial chance of a reward bringing in information.

Mr. Bevins was asked if Post Office security needed to be tightened. "That depends on the facts ", he said. "But we shall certainly see how far we can go to cut out the possibility of it ever happening again." He left the airport saying he was " determined it should not happen again ".

Later he met senior Post Office officials to consider suggestions for tightening up security.

Before the two banks announced their losses, the Post Office stated that the loss " is likely to be very heavy indeed and may well run into seven figures ". About 120 sacks of mail, mostly registered packets, were stolen, but the precise amount of the loss will not be known until checks have been made.

FAKED SIGNALS

For audacity and skilful planning the Post Office and British Railways cannot recall a parallel to what is widely believed to be the biggest train robbery in the country's history.

Briefly, the pattern of the raid was as follows: the train was halted by faked signals, driver and co-driver were attacked and handcuffed, the engine and first two carriages were uncoupled and driven to a bridge over a country road, the registered mail carriage was forced open and Post Office employees overpowered, and finally the mail bags were tossed over the bridge to be loaded into a waiting lorry.

The Post Office say it is the first successful robbery of a travelling Post

Office train since the trains were instituted 125 years ago. The train carries no passengers, but has a staff of up to 75 postmen, who sort mail en route.

Known as the Up Special, the train left Glasgow at 6.50 p.m. on Wednesday and was due at Euston at 3.56 a.m. yesterday. It consisted of nine carriages, and stopped at Crewe and Rugby. Mail was picked up and set down as usual while the train was in motion, the postmen sorting the letters as they came aboard. Access to the registered mail coach could be gained only by those inside unlocking the door in answer to a signal in code.

DRIVERS HANDCUFFED

As the train approached Cheddington it slowed for an amber signal and then ground to a halt at a red at 3.15 a.m. Both signals had been tampered with. The green light was obscured and batteries were used to illuminate the red after the cables had been cut.

The co-driver, Mr. D. Whitby, aged 26, of Crewe, went to use the telephone at the signal, but found the wires had been cut (later the police discovered that other telephone wires in the district had also been cut).

" I went back to tell the driver and saw a man looking out from between the second and third coaches ", Mr. Whitby said. " He walked across the line and said: ' Come here. He pushed me down the bank and another man grabbed me, put his hand over my mouth and said: ' If you shout, I will kill you.' They took me back to the engine and I found they had cushed my driver."

Mr. Whitby and the driver, Mr. J Mills, aged 58, who had handcuffs snapped on their wrists and were forced by the gang—who by this time had uncoupled the engine and first two coaches—to drive on for about a mile to Bridego bridge, where the line crosses a road leading to a village near by. When they arrived the two drivers were handcuffed together and told to lie at the side of the track.

MEN UNAWARE

The gang—all masked and carrying wooden or iron coshes—then broke into the registered mail carriage with axes, overpowered the four Post Office men inside and unloaded the sacks. When they had finished, the two drivers were bundled inside the carriage with the postmen and told to wait for half an hour.

Meanwhile, postmen in the uncoupled portion of the train went on working, unaware of the robbery. " It was dark and they would be very busy sorting the mail ", the Post Office said later. " It is not unusual for the train to stop at a signal, and they would have no way of telling that the train had been uncoupled."

It was not until the guard walked along the track and discovered that part of his train was missing that the alarm was raised—but he had to run on to Cheddington station before he could find a telephone in working order. Both drivers were taken, still handcuffed, to hospital at Aylesbury, where Mr. Mills was detained last night with head injuries.

Detective-superintendent Ward, of the Railway Transport Police, announced that investigation headquarters were being set up at Cheddington. " We will stay here as long as necessary ", he said.

Detective-superintendent M. Fewtrell, head of Buckinghamshire C.I.D., said last night: " The amount stolen is clearly well over £1m. The handcuffs used were of the very latest type.

" This was obviously a brilliantly planned operation. The train is always dead on schedule. It always carries a lot of money but this time there was a much higher sum aboard than usual." The fact that it was immediately after a Bank holiday might have been the reason for the large amount of money.

Detectives at Cheddington, Buckinghamshire, examining the couplings of a coach of the Glasgow-Euston postal train.

"INSIDE JOB" CANNOT BE RULED OUT, SAYS MR. BEVINS

Mr. Bevins spent about 80 minutes last night closeted with senior Post Office officials, including Mr. W. A. Wolverson, deputy Director-General of the Post Office; Brigadier Kenneth Holmes, Director of Postal Services; Mr. G. A. Downes, Director of the London Postal Region, who is responsible for travelling post offices; and Mr. C. Osmond, head of the Investigation Branch. In his private office afterwards Mr. Bevins said he might make a detailed statement today after he had fairly considered some of the suggestions made to tighten up security.

He had been concerned that things should be tightened up. "About half-a-dozen suggestions have been under consideration during the day and this evening for tightening them up."

Asked about security arrangements on the train, he said there were normal security arrangements covering travelling Post Offices. " You have to bear in mind we have about 40 T.P.O.'s running throughout the night between various parts of the country and London ", he said. " I feel as uncomfortable as anyone in my position would, to the extent that when a successful robbery like this is perpetrated then clearly our security arrangements have not been satisfactory in the circumstances."

NOTES NOT RECORDED

Mr. Bevins agreed that the banknotes carried on the train were not recorded in any way. Numbers were known of new notes carried by the Post Office and railways from head offices of banks to provincial branches, but in a case such as those involved in the train robbery they would not be known.

Banks on the train's route, particularly in Scotland, had note surpluses and wanted to return them to their head offices. Some of the notes were on their way to be destroyed. The recording of banknotes, or some means of making

them no longer negotiable, would have to be considered, he said, particularly when banknotes were not to be used again.

Mr. Bevins said he did not think it could be ruled out altogether that the raid was an inside job.

Asked whether there was any alarm system between the engine and carriages, he said he would rather not answer, adding: " It would help these people." He agreed there was a system warning people on travelling Post Offices of any irregularities, but it was not invariable.

LIMITED COMPENSATION

Replying to questions earlier on his arrival at London Airport, Mr. Bevins said: " People will be compensated to a limited extent, because £20 is the maximum compensation paid for the loss of a registered package. In the case of diamonds the people concerned will probably have made, as they invariably do, their own insurance arrangements which would cover diamonds while they are travelling."

M.P. TO RAISE MATTER IN THE COMMONS

Mr. D. Jones, Labour M.P. for Burnley, who tried to introduce a Bill in the Commons in April, 1961, to force railway authorities to give greater protection for carrying mail, said yesterday that he would raise the question of this latest robbery in the House.

" I think that robbery of these mails can be made near enough impossible ", Mr. Jones added. A Stockport firm had shown him a truck in May, 1961, he said. " They could have held up the driver for a month of Sundays but they would never have got the loot."

British Railways were interested in the truck, he continued, and he told the Postmaster General about it " but it looks as if nothing has been done ".

Coverage of the Great Train Robbery in *The Times* of 9 August 1963

convicted within ten months, and the other three on the run until the last member of the gang, Bruce Reynolds, was caught in 1968 – has been recounted many times.[121] (One of them, Ronnie Biggs, escaped from gaol in 1965 and fled to a new life in Brazil, which refreshed the story with an additional angle for years to come.) The Post Office played a substantial role in bringing them to the dock, as was afterwards acknowledged by the police in generous terms. 'Without your help, we should have got nowhere', wrote the Buckinghamshire Chief Constable to the Department in May 1964.[122] Its activities were coordinated by the IB. An early suggestion that 'an outside expert' might be invited into the Department to lead the work was rebuffed in an icily pointed letter from the IB's long-frustrated head to his superiors twelve days after the raid:

> In making available to the outside expert the history of the TPO train robbery, it would not, I think, be possible to keep within the Post Office, as it is at the moment, the fact that several security warnings about the risk of possible attacks on TPOs were given by the IB over the past three years or that IB recommendations were made in detail as early as April 1962 . . . which might have prevented the recent robbery if they had been fully and speedily implemented and in force in the Up Special TPO on 8 August 1963.[123]

Osmond's point was taken and the suggestion went no further. Meanwhile, the speed with which the IB's long-standing recommendations were now implemented would have been comical but for the gravity of the provocation. At a meeting on 9 August, the day after the robbery, instructions were issued for an alarm to be fitted to the Up Special TPO 'in time for tonight's run'. All Up and Down Special carriages were to be so equipped by the start of the following week. High-level talks on the installation of VHF radio sets were scheduled for 12 August. A blizzard of memoranda followed through the next two months, as action was taken to ensure that the first serious attack on a TPO in 125 years would also be the last.

What caused all senior Post Office officials the deepest concern was the unpalatable possibility mentioned by Bevins with his usual candour on the evening of the robbery. The press took a while to learn the truth, but there were in fact strong grounds to suspect an 'inside job'. The Up Special's HVP carriage on the night of the attack ought never to have been on the train at all. It had been consigned to the sidings, awaiting an overhaul and its premature recall had been a curious business. Not just one but three recently refitted HVP carriages (complete with alarms) had been withdrawn, one by one, with mechanical faults in the days preceding the raid. If any one of the three had been present on the train that night, as officials were acutely aware, it was hard to imagine how the robbery could have been pulled off at all. Breaking into the carriage would have been significantly more difficult – and the gang would have had to contend with a bandit alarm and the arrival, presumably, of dozens of postmen from the abandoned carriages of the TPO down the track. With the last-minute substitution of the 'old' carriage with no alarm, the robbers appeared to have been very lucky indeed. They themselves seem to have had no inkling of this. By one account, written in 1978, their only foray into the marshalling yards of North London to examine the insides of an HVP carriage had been made early in the year. They had been amazed at the lack of any anti-theft devices.[124] But could such a critical aspect of the raid really have been given no more thought? Many doubted it.* For months after the arrest of the gang members (and various accomplices) arraigned for trial in January 1964, three main questions hung in the air. The press and public speculated endlessly about the existence of an unidentified mastermind behind the crime and the whereabouts of the money, most of which had completely disappeared (and it was never recovered). But it was the third question that haunted the Post Office. Had someone on the inside connived at ensuring the unavailability on 7 August of the three refitted carriages?

The Department poured resources into its in-house investigations with all of its customary thoroughness. It was discovered that three of the postmen on that night's Up Special had criminal records. It was also seen as a cause for anxiety that sixteen of the others were Irishmen. All had their backgrounds exhaustively researched. A report completed by a senior official of the TPO division, R. F. Yates, in May 1964 noted that thirty-five individuals in all had been carefully checked as possible insiders – and 'no evidence has come to light that any detailed inside information or any general knowledge of the movement of HVP money

---

* The possibility that the planning of the raid had in fact simply overlooked the impact of an alarm in the carriage began to seem more credible in time, as the amateurish behaviour of the robbers in the aftermath of the raid came to light. They spent days hiding in a nearby farmhouse, leaving fingerprints on every conceivable surface, and then failed to burn it down as had apparently been intended. After its discovery by the police, the arrest of most of the gang followed inexorably. But for some unlucky slips, the police might even have caught them at the farmhouse. Some of the HVP bags found there, and subsequently produced as courtroom exhibits for the Crown, can be found in the BPMA archives, at Post 120/148.

has been passed on'. Nor had the inquiry found any evidence of sabotage to the three withdrawn HVPs. Nonetheless, the report's author
was not prepared to rule it out. He concluded that there were aspects of
the story 'which in my view must raise suspicion that some sabotage
occurred. . . . [but] it might never be proved'.[125] (Much the same conclusion was reached later by a *Guardian* journalist steeped in the story as
it unfolded, Peta Fordham, whose book appeared in 1965.[126]) A reward
of £10,000 was offered to anyone coming forward with important
information, but drew no takers. Undeterred, however, the IB went
on searching for more clues. Postal workers living anywhere near the
former homes of the convicted men, for example, were kept under surveillance for months. A postman living in the East End a few streets
away from the family home of one of the gang leaders was watched
through much of July and August 1964 'for any sign of undue affluence'; the hapless Mr Bish was even trailed for some time after
mid-November, when he had retired from the Post Office on grounds of
ill-health – and as short of undue affluence as ever. Long reports on
potential insiders were still being filed two years later. Osmond went on
pressing his IB colleagues to keep up the hunt, as though it might somehow be possible one day to prove that no collusion had existed. Nothing
less, it seemed, could redeem the blow struck to the pride of the Post
Office by the Great Train Robbery.

10

Getting out of the civil service, 1964–9

> In place of the cosy complacency of the past 13 years, we shall
> seek to evoke an active and searching frame of mind in which all
> of us, individuals, enterprises and trade unions are ready to re-
> examine our methods of work, to innovate and to modernise.
> Here, too, the Government can give a lead by subjecting to con-
> tinuing and probing review the practices of its own Departments
> of State ...
>
> From the Labour Party's General Election Manifesto, 1964

I. THE VERY MODEL OF A MODERN POSTMASTER GENERAL

When Harold Wilson turned in the summer of 1964 to finalizing the
allotment of posts in his first government, in readiness for a Labour victory in the approaching election, a job had certainly to be found for
Anthony Wedgwood Benn. One of a small coterie of young advisers and
speech-writers on whom Wilson had relied heavily since becoming
leader of the party in January 1963, he was still only thirty-nine. But he
had first entered the Commons in 1950, as its youngest MP, and had
already been on the party's National Executive for almost five years.
Though he had narrowly missed being elected to the Shadow Cabinet in
1963, he had since become Chairman of the Fabian Society, fairly reflecting his status as one of the leading figures of the Left. A man totally
committed to a career in politics from his earliest youth, he had run
into a serious problem in 1960 when the death of his father had saddled
him with a peerage and barred him from the Commons.* A successful

---

* Benn belonged to a remarkable political dynasty. His paternal grandfather was a progressive Liberal MP. His father William – who had to cope in the Commons with the hostile

two-year battle to win a change in the law allowing him to renounce the peerage and resume his Commons career had made 'Wedgie' – or just plain 'Tony' Benn, as he himself later came to prefer – a household name.

More importantly, Benn had established himself through Labour's thirteen long years of opposition as a brilliant public speaker and one of the party's rising stars. His energy matched his ambition, and a decidedly radical turn of mind inclined him to impatience with all the conventions of a society that he believed to be in steep decline. Anything that smacked of privileged traditions, mindless rituals or unmerited hierarchies was part of the Britain that all good socialists must confront. Surveying the decrepit institutions all around him, Benn was a young bull in a street full of china shops. One of the first to catch his eye, according to the diaries that he kept on a more or less daily basis from 1963, was the Post Office.[1] He wrote a paper on its future, 'incorporating a lot of ideas which have been buzzing round in my mind for many years', and sent it to Wilson in October 1963. 'Here is a science-based industry, already in public ownership', he confided to his diary, 'which could be made to serve the more sophisticated needs of a modern community and make a profit.'[2] (The need to show that socialism and economic efficiency were fully compatible was one of his constant preoccupations.) Benn began writing a weekly column for the *Guardian* newspaper shortly after-wards, and devoted a column in June 1964 to 'The Future of the Post Office', suggesting ten ways in which it could extend its services.[3] The next month, Wilson told its author to prepare for the role of Postmaster General in the event of victory at the polls. He would not have a seat in the Cabinet, but would be the only newcomer to the Front Bench with his own department, as well as the youngest member of the Govern-ment. On 19 October, after Labour had been returned with a majority of four, Benn was duly summoned to Downing Street and appointed as the new PMG. He was pleased to be following in the footsteps of Attlee, whose ministerial career had begun the same way, but his impact on the

questions about the destruction of Smirke's GPO building in 1912–13 – was elected as a Liberal MP in 1906 and later defected to Labour, serving as a Cabinet Minister in the 1929–31 Labour government. In 1942, faced with a shortage of Labour peers in his war-time coalition government, Churchill elevated William Wedgwood Benn to the House of Lords as the 1st Viscount Stansgate. The death of his older brother on active service in 1944 left Benn heir to the title. The Peerage Act of 1963 enabled him to relinquish it. (It also allowed Alec Douglas Home to follow suit and to return to the Commons as Macmillan's successor as Prime Minister, an appointment that was confirmed just six days before Benn's own return to the House.)

Post Office was easily to eclipse Attlee's – or that of any other PMG in the Department's history.

On the afternoon of his appointment, a car from St Martin's drew up outside his Holland Park house to take him to his office for the first time. Sitting in the back seat awaiting him was an official of about Benn's own age. Henry Tilling had been in the Post Office since 1947 – he had been the Clerk-in-Waiting on the night of the Great Train Robbery – and he had been appointed Private Secretary to the PMG in the last months of Bevins' tenure. He was in many ways an archetypal Post Office man, imbued with all the best traditions of the Department. It was a matter of pride to Tilling that his father had been in the service, joining it in 1914 and rising to become a Head Postmaster in North Wales. He himself had entered the administrative class of the Post Office as an Assistant Principal (AP), after passing through the 'country house' recruitment system set up by the civil service in 1946 to provide opportunities for those (including many demobbed soldiers) whose higher education had been interrupted by the war. On average, the Post Office took in just a couple of APs each year. Few of them had volunteered for the Department – most APs simply went wherever they were assigned – but Tilling was one of four between 1947 and 1967 who, in doing so, followed in the footsteps of a parent. He had proved himself a consummate committee secretary at an early stage: he had at one point served simultaneously on the Joint Production Council's postal panel, the Lumley Committee on regionalization *and* the committee of inquiry set up after the Eastcastle Street robbery. Thereafter he had worked through a succession of jobs in the time-honoured fashion, and had married a colleague in the Assistant Principal ranks. As he and Benn were driven back across town, the new Minister asked him what his main interests were, outside the office. Heraldry, replied Tilling, and orders and medals. As Benn dryly recorded later, it was 'not the best start'.

The new Minister's political inclinations were hardly a secret, but Tilling thought a straight question deserved a straight answer. (The two of them actually went on to have a good working relationship, though it surprised the official that he was never addressed as anything other than 'Mr Tilling'.[4]) But the gulf between Benn's world view and the cloistered ways of the Post Office was wide enough to ensure plenty more comical moments in the weeks ahead. Out went the Minister's Georgian porcelain tea-set, to make way for a pint mug. (His ability to drain it of tea several times a day would soon become one of Benn's most celebrated characteristics.) Out went the red coats and top hats of the Headquarters doormen, replaced with cheerless grey uniforms. Out *almost* went the chauffeured Austin Princess, in favour of a London taxi – though this was one fresh start that officials managed to talk their way round. The customary drinks reception for an incoming PMG to meet the senior officers of the trade unions had to be ditched in favour of discussions over tea and biscuits with this (teetotal) PMG, providing a chance for his guests to hear about the sunny uplands that lay ahead. 'I gave them all a copy of our manifesto, *The New Britain*,' noted Benn afterwards. 'I told them I have presented each director in the Post Office with it as well, and the meeting almost broke up with astonishment and suppressed laughter.'[5] The Minister's hospitality extended to many Headquarters staff whose forebears had rarely, if ever, crossed the threshold of the PMG's office in three centuries. Benn reciprocated by visiting parts of the Department scarcely visited by his own senior officials, let alone his predecessors. He took to using the staff luncheon club, too – the first PMG ever to do so. In their usual professional way, his civil servants gradually came to terms with this most unusual of politicians – but Benn managed to go on surprising them from time to time, as he did at the end of November. 'After lunch I got out my camp bed and went soundly asleep for forty minutes behind my desk, having arranged to be woken with a cup of tea. It was the first time I had tried it and it worked like a dream. I suspect that Tilling and Co think I am completely nuts.'[6]

Both parties had ample grounds for complaint over the next few months. Benn was predictably driven to distraction by what he saw as the antediluvian practices of the Department. He saw indolent routines, class-ridden attitudes and a general aversion to modernity wherever he looked: the Post Office was almost a caricature, to his mind, of so much that had gone wrong in contemporary Britain. Splenetic asides litter his diary over this period. His private office was 'utterly decayed and does practically nothing'. The whole Department lumbered on, 'using the techniques and filing systems of the twenties'. Unquestionably, morale at Headquarters was at a low ebb. Benn saw this not as a consequence of the troubled events of recent years – the financial losses, the clashes with the unions and the setbacks to postal mechanization – but as confirmation of a general lack of oomph. Managers whom he invited to his office for beer and sandwiches sat glumly round his table 'like a lot of middle-aged bankers on a church outing'. When he asked a Regional Director what he would like the PMG to do, he was told: 'Frankly, Minister, sit quiet'. Nor did his senior officials fill Benn with much confidence:

the Comptroller and Accountant General, for example, was 'in fact neither an accountant nor an economist . . .' As for the Director General and his deputies, Benn had sized them up as 'rather limited, ageing and unimaginative' even before he set foot in Headquarters.[7] Once there, he was intensely suspicious of their motives at every turn. Like many others in the Wilson government, he was quick to perceive a conspiracy among the mandarins to forestall Labour policies. He noted in his diary how the Director General, when he handed him a copy of Labour's manifesto, 'picked it up with a look of infinite disgust and carried it out of the office with two fingers'. It particularly irked Benn to find his officials treating him as though his tenure as PMG was merely a fleeting interlude in the long history of the Department – which is precisely what both sides knew it to be. It would have surprised Ronald German and his colleagues not a jot to know that Wilson, in appointing him, had privately promised Benn promotion and a seat in the Cabinet after eighteen months or so.[8]

The officials found much of Benn's general approach as exasperating as he clearly found them. The Post Office was not just a government department but a huge business placing enormous managerial demands on those who ran it. Notwithstanding his obvious enthusiasm and exceptional gifts as a publicist, Benn had never had even the remotest experience of running any organization, let alone a heavily unionized body with almost 400,000 employees. Yet he presumed, in defiance of the entire history of the Post Office, to set himself up as its fully executive head. It had been German's intention that the formal Post Office Board, effectively made defunct in the Bevins era, should be replaced after Bevins' departure by a new and much smaller management board. Benn embraced the idea – then took the chair himself and made clear that he would be hard at work in St Martin's almost as regularly as any of his officials. By the start of 1965, he felt ready to start challenging the Director General on his choice of the right people to promote as Regional Directors. (German 'was rather shaken'.[9]) As he noted to himself after his very first day in St Martin's, 'in American terms I am PMG, chairman of the Federal Communications Commission, president of the largest bank and president of the Bell Telephone Company all rolled into one. It is quite a job . . .'[10]

In reality, he was a man fired with creativity and imagination, but was no executive. He had a dozen ideas before breakfast on an average day, and the resulting lists that descended on German and his team soon came to be dreaded. Some were substantial proposals. Benn was

especially keen on the idea of using postmen and post offices for additional non-postal services: he wondered why post office counters had
not been used, for example, as the basis of a money remittance system
along the lines of the Giro banking networks familiar in many European countries. Always fascinated by new technology, he suggested post
offices might run computer facilities which could be rented out by the
hour to small businesses. And perhaps some post offices could be used
to house mini art galleries. The Solicitor's Department initially baulked
at the whole idea of straying beyond the traditional activities of the Post
Office, but eventually retreated. Benn was confident of his ground by
July 1965 and happy to tease the lawyers: 'I even said I thought that if
we caught fish from our cable ships and sold them in post offices there
could be no objections'.[11] He stopped short of this, but regularly pushed
the notion that postmen might work in harness with the social services:
each postman might be equipped, he thought, 'with a guide to local
social services which he would be able to use if asked for advice by the
people whose homes he served and who might need help'.[12] Nothing
came of it in the end. Allowing mail vans to provide local transport in
remote areas of the country was another of his proposals, and fell on
more fertile ground.* Most notes for the attention of his officials,
though, were more interrogatory. In his first twelve months, Benn sent
the Director General more than a hundred minutes – many of them
aimed at the 'continuing and probing review' of the Department's work
that had been foreshadowed in Labour's election manifesto. Detailed
questions and requests for information rained down on the staff at
every level, while the PMG himself scurried from one initiative to
another at a pace that his officials could only try to view with a wry
detachment. (As one of them, Tilling's successor in the private office,
would recall twenty-five years later: 'Sir Ronald German would come in
after an ample lunch, sink into an armchair ... and say, "What has that
young man been up to today?"'[13]) Some of Benn's innovations caused
serious disquiet. He insisted on his right to hold discussions on Post
Office business with whomever he liked, with no officials in attendance;
these included meetings with senior trade union figures, which the
Department considered extremely naïve. Indeed, he disregarded all
advice about union relations from the outset, even appointing one of

---

* He made a diary note on 19 April 1966 about a scheme to deliver the mail in minibuses
that could be used to offer lifts to local people. The initial trials were launched in rural
Wales, but it was in the Scottish Highlands that the idea really took off (see Chapter 13).

the three UPW-sponsored MPs, Charles Morris, as his parliamentary private secretary. When German urged him 'not to hobnob with the unions', Benn tartly suggested that no one had told his Tory predecessors to steer clear of social contacts with big businessmen in the telecoms supply industry.[14] (It was not until April 1965 that German felt able to apprise Benn of the special understanding he himself had developed with Ron Smith over the years.)

And yet, after a difficult first few months, the Post Office and its new Minister grew to respect each other's strengths. The officials appreciated Benn's robust championing of their Department – especially at Westminster, through a difficult time when the dire financial position of the postal service had to be confronted. It had reported a deficit of £11m in 1963–4, overhauling a £9m profit on telephones and telegraphy, to leave a £2m loss for the Post Office as a whole. Benn brought at least a temporary halt to the worrying deterioration in industrial relations by in effect conceding in March 1965 all of the UPW's wage demands and backdating a 19 per cent pay rise (including July's 6½ per cent award) to January 1964. The basic letter rate had then to be lifted from 3d to 4d, as part of a widely derided campaign to fund the wage bill and to avert another serious worsening of the postal finances. 'Hunting the Post Office, with which is associated the subsidiary sport of bullying Mr Benn, has become one of the leading Tory exercises in the Commons', noted a political commentator on the *Guardian* in July 1965.[15] Their Minister bravely boxed his corner with some skill, and within St Martin's was given credit for doing so.* His novel regard for commercial opportunities – selling surplus computer capacity, perhaps, or using the Post Office's eight telephone-equipment factories to manufacture products for the general market, such as deaf-aids – went on causing some unease: even German himself worried it might sap the strength of the Post Office as a public service.[16] But his drive was irresistible. Benn's diaries suggest that his perception of the Post Office mellowed over time – and anyway need reading with caution. Impatient to make his mark, he ended many days with an evident need to vent his frustration over the hard slog at the office ('trying to resuscitate a dying

---

* It pleased officials, too, when he rejected vexatious complaints out of hand. In November 1964 the Board had to review its policy of collecting children's letters to Santa Claus over the Christmas season and sending back replies postmarked 'Toyland'. 'There had been protests from Lord Arran on behalf of the Anglo-Danish Holidays Scheme.' Benn ignored them and announced his decision to continue with the children's letters scheme, linking it to a charity appeal for UNICEF. (POBM 25 November 1964, Post 69/73.)

elephant', as he put it in December 1964). But looking back on his ten-ure in later years, he himself offered a corrective to the diaries' harsher tone. 'Of all the departments I ever worked in, the one I liked most was the Post Office', as he told a biographer in 1990. 'I liked the people, the inspiration, its history. It reflected all that was best and all that was worst in British society.'[17]

The outcome was a creative tension between the PMG and his offi-cials that helped to make St Martin's in 1964–6 a more lively and stimulating place than it had been for many years, notwithstanding a deep ambivalence on both sides.[18] A formal event in May 1965 caught all this rather nicely. Benn was invited to address a dinner to mark the 250th anniversary of the founding of the Post Office Surveyors and their successors. Having sat through an earlier speech by the longest-serving Postal Controller, Philip de Grouchy, protesting only half in jest at the gadgetry of automatic telephones that needed no operator, he stood up and bluntly regaled his hosts with some less than glorious slices of postal history – starting with the rejection of Palmer's mail coach plan in 1784 and including the Engineer-in-Chief's notorious dis-missal of the telephone in 1879. Then he floated the notion, for the first time in public, that postal deliveries might need to be restricted to one per day in order to restore the economic viability of the mails. We can easily suppose all this might have prompted a tense silence, or worse. In the event, an octogenarian survivor of the pre-1935 cadre of Surveyors rose to his feet and deftly averted any ill-feeling by wittily restating the case against the wicked Mr Palmer and his evil mail coaches – much to Benn's great delight. 'He was a wonderful old man, upright, with a stern sense of duty [and] a good sense of humour . . . He couldn't have done it better', as he recorded later. The evening was rounded off in high spirits. Benn was quick to relish a rare institutional culture that had room for such exchanges. But he was also pleased to have aired an unpalatable message successfully, and the speeches 'did bring to a head the conflict between innovation and conservatism which has been rumbling along inside the department since I've been there'.[19]

Two issues in particular exemplified this conflict. One was a debate over how best to tackle a root-and-branch reform of the Post Office – to which we shall return. The other was much less fundamental but carried a high rumble rating, as Benn was well aware. Indeed, looking for a potential *cause célèbre* with which to sound the socialist trumpet after the 1964 election, it was he who raised it in the first place, even before being appointed as Postmaster General. Speaking at the Oxford University

Labour Club in May 1963, Benn had listed for his young audience a few 'mood changing measures' that he thought might announce the arrival of a Labour government in appropriate style. The biggest cheer went up for postage stamps without the Queen's head on them.[20]

2. TONY BENN AND THE QUEEN'S HEAD

Few aspects of the Post Office in 1964 were more encumbered by tradition than the issuance of new stamps. A profound aversion to novelty had been instilled by Queen Victoria's stand, until the day she died, against any revision by the designers of her portrait as a young woman made in 1840. (A set of stamps to mark her 1887 Jubilee – the first British stamps to employ two colours – carried the same image as the Penny Black.) King George V, a celebrated philatelist in his own right, had railed against the vulgarity of stamps put out by other, less regal post offices around the world – though this did nothing to discourage his passion for collecting them. ('For seventeen years he did nothing at all but kill animals and stick in stamps' was his official biographer's private verdict on his married life before he acceded to the throne in 1910.[21]) He served for fourteen years before his accession as president of the Philatelic Society London, prevailing on his father in 1906 to allow it to become the *Royal* Philatelic Society London. He himself awarded a royal warrant to the country's best-known stamp-dealing company, Stanley Gibbons, in 1914 and by the time he died his own personal collection ran to no fewer than 328 red leather albums.[22] From 1934 onwards, a Stamp Advisory Committee presided over the approval process for all new issues, under the chairmanship for thirty years of the art historian Sir Kenneth Clark – who had himself been cautioned by George V in person never to let any British stamp design omit the sovereign's head. Clark had promised to defend the cause.[23]

'Commemorative' stamps, as opposed to plain 'definitive' stamps with no specific date, were shunned by the Post Office long after most European countries had begun to issue them. Admittedly, some George V definitives carried highly ornate designs – notably a series based on a vision of three seahorses riding the waves alongside a trident-wielding Britannia – but it was not until 1924 that the King deigned to allow a first commemorative stamp. The whole idea was for many years regarded as slightly cheap. One prominent designer of the interwar years confided to the Post Office that, in his view, 'to use a pictorial subject is simply to pander to sentimentality and the appetite of collectors . . .'[24] Only three such issues appeared in the entire reign of George V (commemorating the British Empire Exhibition of 1924–5, the UPU Congress of 1929 and the King's own Silver Jubilee in 1935). A fresh approach to stamp design seemed in prospect in 1936 under his successor – and a strikingly new image was adopted for the new monarch's first definitive issue – but Edward VIII's rapid departure soon restored the status quo. Only in the 1950s were slightly more liberal guidelines at last adopted. It was decided in 1956 to put out one new commemorative issue every year, and a project team in 1957 recommended setting up a special department to coordinate more frequent issues, which it was thought might prove highly profitable for the Post Office.[25] This led eventually – though not without some misgivings at Board level – to the opening in 1963 of the 'Philatelic Bureau' to oversee sales to the philatelic community, and thereafter commemorative issues started to become a much more familiar event. A splendid set of five stamps was issued, for example, to mark Shakespeare's quatercentenary in April 1964. The rising frequency of pictorial designs would have caused the old king apoplexy – but all bore the Queen's head and were still deeply conservative by international standards. Members of the Advisory Committee, confronted from time to time with more colourful specimens from abroad, would mutter disdainfully about stamps that looked like cigarette cards. Benn's officials had done nothing to challenge this attitude, though in private many of them were far from condoning it.[26] It was generally thought to reflect the wishes of the Queen, whose personal approval was still required for every new issue.

So a quiet declaration by the Postmaster General in November 1964 that he was in favour of pictorial stamps *without* the Queen's head on them was regarded by many within St Martin's as faintly akin to high treason. It was also very irritating: most of Benn's officials were dismayed at the prospect of chasing after yet another idea that none thought remotely likely to prove politically acceptable – or practical either. Even if it were somehow approved in principle, it would pose an awkward problem. The sovereign's head was a unique emblem that allowed the British Post Office to ignore the UPU edict that all stamps must designate their country of origin. Without it, would not British stamps have to carry the names of all the constituent countries of the United Kingdom (not to mention the Isle of Man and the Channel Islands)? This admittedly remote prospect was enough to help persuade the Board, after the 1956 change of policy on commemoratives, to turn down a paper proposing the establishment of a special philatelic section of the Postal Services Directorate: one liberalizing measure might lead to another, provoking all kinds of wild demands from the uninitiated.[27] But no senior official at St Martin's in 1964 really expected the issue to surface on their watch. Any notion of removing the Queen's head would surely be scuppered first on political grounds. The initial reaction of Joe Slater, the Assistant Postmaster General, seemed to confirm as much. A sixty-year-old former Durham miner, Slater was appalled at the idea.[28]

Benn resolved to press on. To his diary, he confided that an overtly republican stance might soon be needed. ('It's no good pretending one is a monarchist and then have difficulties with ideas of this kind.') In public, he opted for a more oblique approach. He talked of encouraging philately and of using stamps to extend public support for the arts. Meeting the Stamp Advisory Committee in January, he merely suggested that designers might be given more room to pursue their ideas 'independently of the Queen's head' – a formulation that surprisingly slipped by without much ado.[29] Then a great stroke of luck came his way. Announcing to Parliament just before Christmas that a new approach to stamp design was in the offing, Benn invited suggestions from the public. Out of the blue in the middle of February came a letter from a well-known and greatly respected designer, David Gentleman. He proposed – off his own bat – that British stamps should be allowed to drop the Queen's head altogether and that the liberated space should be exploited by tackling a much wider range of subjects. Benn saw immediately that this would allow him, if he could publicize Gentleman's letter, '[to] open up a controversy about the Queen's head at exactly the right level – design-wise rather than politically'.[30] Gentleman was rather startled, a couple of weeks later, to receive a telephone call from the Postmaster General; within days, he found himself eating cornflakes at the kitchen table in Benn's Holland Park home.[31] Over breakfast on 15 February the two men struck up an instant (and lasting) rapport. The designer went through some of his latest work. Benn was much impressed – and not just by the quality of the artwork. Gentleman was adamant that the name of the country could be integrated into a good design without spoiling it. They agreed there and then that he would present 'no-head' versions of his future designs.* So now Benn could

---

* Within hours of their breakfast, Gentleman produced revised versions of a design he had just finished working on (with two associates) for an issue to commemorate the life of Churchill, who had died a few weeks earlier. To Benn's dismay, the revisions mysteriously

advance his plans for a radical initiative on design grounds alone. He was quite ready to turn a blind eye to any political complications.

The Queen herself could hardly be expected to do so. Benn had an audience with her scheduled for 10 March and settled on a tactical approach. He would propose only that the Queen consent to let designers submit work either with or without the head, after which she would be free to exercise her discretion in the usual way. But he would also arrange for any rejected designs – including those rejected for having no head – to be published, as he explained to Brigadier Holmes on the day of his breakfast with Gentleman, 'so people could judge for themselves . . .'[32] In this way the official procedure for the submission of prospective designs might allow a steady trickle of no-head stamps to be seen by the public – which might eventually make a blanket rejection of the no-head approach difficult if not impossible. On the morning of his visit to the Palace, Benn arranged another breakfast with Gentleman. This proved fortuitous. The designer turned up with display cards showing a set of beautiful new stamps commemorating the twenty-fifth anniversary of the Battle of Britain, all but one of which carried the words 'Great Britain' in place of the Queen's head. (The Advisory Committee had reviewed them the previous day. It had made no recorded comment on what were the first submissions of their kind since 1840, but chose three of the designs 'as second choice and [decided] that they should be returned to [Gentleman] for inclusion of The Queen's head'. The Committee's first choice was a design based on a painting by Paul Nash.[33]) Benn swept the cards up into his case and took them with him to the Palace three hours later.

His own account of the ensuing audience with the Queen is classic. He began by mentioning plans for a new definitive ('which would have a more beautiful picture of the Queen on them') and went on to explain the potential for new commemoratives ('a most exciting field that had never been explored') before venturing to suggest that this opened up the whole issue of the use of the monarch's head on stamps ('the Queen frowned and smiled'). Then he elaborated a little on the awkwardness that had been encountered over the need always to include the head in new designs, which many stamp designers saw as 'restrictive and embarrassing'.

> I said that the real difficulty was that, up to now, it had been understood in the Office that by the Queen's personal command stamps that did not

---

went missing on their way to a meeting of the Stamp Advisory Committee the next day. Gentleman's earlier designs, complete with head, were later approved by the Queen.

embody the head could not even be submitted for consideration. I said this had led to a most unfortunate situation in which designers were full of new ideas but these were not allowed to be transmitted because it was generally thought that the Queen herself had refused to consider them. I said I didn't know whether this was true or not but it seemed to me the straightforward thing to do was to come along and ask whether this was as a result of a personal command of this kind. The Queen was clearly embarrassed and indicated that she had no personal feeling about it at all. I said I knew she wouldn't and that I knew this was all a misunderstanding but that it was rather ridiculous that there should be these lovely stamps available which she wasn't even allowed to see. . . .

I said that I foresaw a controversy developing about the heads on stamps which I thought would be most undesirable [sic] . . . In these circumstances it seemed to me that the right thing to do was for us to establish that design-ers could put in any designs they liked, that they could all be submitted to the Queen for approval, and that I should be able to say in answer to a ques-tion in the House of Commons that the Queen had approved a procedure under which all stamps of all kinds were submitted to her for consideration. This seemed to me to be the best way of tackling it and I hoped she agreed.[34]

The Queen listened politely. There were certainly cases, she acknow-ledged, of British stamps being reissued without the head in some Commonwealth countries. She then remarked that she had never seen any stamps without the head – at which point she was in for a surprise.

I said, 'Well, I've got some in my bag' (having brought David Gentleman's collection as provided this morning). The Queen wanted me to leave the new designs with her but I explained the difficulties and she agreed to see them on the spot. This was exactly what I had hoped would happen so I unlocked my bag and spread out on the floor twelve huge design models of the stamps . . . I then knelt on the floor and one after the other passed up to the Queen the Battle of Britain stamps bearing the words 'Great Brit-ain' and no royal head on them. It was a most hilarious scene because I had my papers all over the place and she was peering at something that had obviously never been shown to her or even thought about at the Palace before. At the end I packed up and said I would take them away but that I was delighted to hear that she approved of a scheme under which we could submit things to her for her consideration.

Even by Benn's own account, the Queen had approved of no such thing. As he made his way out of the Palace, he remarked to her secretary,

Sir Michael Adeane, how pleased he was 'that now we could submit all sorts of designs . . . [and] we could see where and when it [i.e. the use of the monarch's head] was appropriate'. Unsurprisingly, Adeane 'looked extremely uncomfortable'. Benn clearly thought the audience a triumph, enthusing about it later in the day to German and the Director of Postal Services. ('They were a bit astonished that I had gone straight to the Queen . . .') Over the next few months, having persuaded himself that the Queen had given it the nod, he ploughed on with his new policy while Palace officials, his own Post Office officials and the members of the Stamp Advisory Committee all did their best to stall him. At the start of July the Queen approved a set of Gentleman's Battle of Britain stamps *with* the head – but not before Benn had succeeded in by-passing the Stamp Advisory Committee, to place the alternative no-head versions before her. This prompted its chairman to resign. For three decades, Clark had presided quietly and effectively over periodic discussions about new stamp designs between artists and photographers, civil servants and Palace officials. Since he had always adhered to the belief that stamp design policy should draw as little attention to itself as possible, it was perhaps fitting that his departure passed without much comment at the time. (Some years later, he explained that he had been out of sympathy with the way events were unfolding – 'I was afraid that the admission of pictorial stamps would lead to complete banality, and I have been proved right' – but Gentleman took a different view: 'Clark's judgement was that of a distinguished aesthetic autocrat who had been bypassed and sidelined. . . . [We broke with] the essentially traditional, reverential and boring policy to which Clark had loyally committed himself'.[35])

The Battle of Britain issue helped to bring months of acrimonious wrangling between the PMG and his officials to, well, a head. At the press conference to launch the issue, Benn insisted on having a small exhibition of all the Gentleman designs, including those that had been rejected. It was the first time the Post Office had ever displayed any stamps without the head. The press took not much notice: it was also the first time that a swastika had ever appeared on a British stamp – albeit on a German plane sinking into the Channel – and there were heated objections from the Board of Deputies of British Jews which attracted far more attention. Inside the Palace, however, it was decided that the saga had lasted long enough. When the Prime Minister went to stay at Balmoral early in October 1965, the opportunity was taken to make it unambiguously clear that stamps without the head were not acceptable to Her Majesty. As Wilson's private secretary, Derek Mitchell, put it in a letter afterwards to Benn's office:

> Adeane said [to me] the fact was, that the Queen had pretty strong views on this ... [and] it may be that a number of her subjects will have equally strong feelings. In other words there may be a political aspect to this to which the Postmaster General and other ministers will wish to give some thought ... [the Prime Minister, after hearing of Adeane's remarks] takes the view that the Postmaster General should not even go so far as to commission experimental designs without The Queen's head.[36]

Benn was enraged both by the content of the letter and by the roundabout tactics that had apparently been adopted to defeat his plans. He angrily noted in his diary that 'it was an astonishing letter for any civil servant to have written' but he had to acknowledge what it meant: 'it looks as if my new stamp policy has been torpedoed'.[37] He was right, though it took a while to sink and he clung to hopes of salvaging something from it until the end of his tenure as PMG. He had been rebuffed, and it came as little consolation to hear six months later from the Earl of Listowel that as the new PMG in 1945 he too had tried and failed in much the same way. None of Benn's officials had mentioned this precedent, and perhaps it had been forgotten. But it would have confirmed what the officials had known instinctively from the outset: it was a battle that could not be won.

So had Benn indeed been wasting his time and theirs? It turned out that while he may have lost a battle, Benn was about to win the wider war. Back in March, flushed with his apparently successful foray at the Palace, he had asked Gentleman to prepare a portfolio of the kind of designs that might flow from a more liberal stamp policy. Six days after hearing of the veto from Balmoral, Benn met Gentleman and his wife to see what the two of them had produced. They showed him a range of work that was effectively to change the history of British stamp design. By the end of October, Gentleman was able to hand over a collection of stamp sets aligned to seventeen different themes in all – from trains, which captivated the Prime Minister (a railway history scholar in his youth), to fine art works depicting famous race horses, which delighted the Queen. Best of all, he had come up with a perfect compromise on the problem of the head. A portrait of the Queen had been prepared in 1952 by an artist called Mary Gillick for the coinage of the new reign. Gentleman had taken the 'Gillick head' as his model for a portrait that could be printed as a silhouette, and reproduced at a size much smaller than the traditional head. Wilson applauded this solution, and the Queen approved it. Two days later, Benn was at a private dinner in Downing Street when the Prime Minister returned from one of his regular audiences with the Queen. As he recorded:

> [Harold] told me that he had been there for an hour and a quarter. 'We spent ten minutes on Rhodesia, and an hour and five minutes on stamps', he said. I'm sure this reflects the proportion of the Queen's mind which is devoted to Rhodesia as compared with stamps. He told me that she was perfectly happy to accept a silhouette, and to accept the rulers of Britain [series], including Cromwell and Edward VIII, but that her head had to appear on everything and the press was not to see any stamps without her head.[38]

An insouciant Benn wrote to his officials, suggesting the Palace had changed its mind: 'it has become plain that the Queen does now wish her head to appear on stamps, though she is content for this to be represented by silhouette'.[39] But securing full acceptance of the Gillick silhouette still required all of his relentless drive. The Stamp Advisory Committee learned of Gentleman's work for the first time only in January 1966 and was quick to reject it. The Royal Mint remonstrated in February over the fact that its 1952 copyright had been infringed. The Queen, though generally supportive, worried that the cameo was a little *too* small. A corner was finally turned in March 1966 when a set of landscape designs appeared as a new issue: it was the first to be adorned by the silhouette (and the first special issue, as the purists groaned, that had no commemorative pretext). In April, the completed album of Gentleman's stamps was formally presented to the Queen, who was said by the Palace to have looked at them 'with the greatest interest'.[40] Benn then arranged for a public seminar on stamp design to be held in June, under his chairmanship, at which the Gentleman album could be exhibited alongside the work of several other leading designers. The occasion passed off successfully, despite much hostile harrumphing from the more conservative corners of the philatelic world in the months leading up to it. A glamorous feature on British stamps in the colour magazine of the *Sunday Times* endorsed the impression that stamp design had captured the public's imagination, as Benn had hoped would happen. Meanwhile, he had also pushed through the establishment of a National Postal Museum, based on an inaugural collection of early Victorian stamps that had been bequeathed to the Post Office by an elderly collector called Reginald Phillips in 1965. The Museum was established in the King Edward Building, but earlier notions of somehow combining it with the Philatelic Bureau were forgotten – and the Bureau was in fact relocated to Edinburgh, later in 1966.

It was clear that postage stamps, for better or worse, would never be quite the same again. 'Everything to do with them had changed – reasons for issue, the number of issues, subject matter and their design.'[41] The old Stamp Advisory Committee had been discontinued, to be replaced in February 1966 by a new body appointed by the Post Office itself – though it kept the same name, and most members of the relaunched 'SAC' were drawn as before from the wider world of design and philately. The Gentleman Album shaped much of its thinking. When a new, specially commissioned portrait was finalized in 1967 for all definitive stamps – the so-called Machin Icon – its designer was asked to produce a cameo version akin to Gillick's; it then proved a simple matter for Gentleman to substitute the new silhouette for the old.* Individual designs in the Album thus remained available for new issues, and many more were indeed adopted. The Album 'introduced a new size of stamp, and themes and designs which were to influence stamp issues for almost 20 years'.[42]

At the end of the Stamp Seminar on 23 June, Benn held a press conference. He was asked directly whether he intended to remove the Queen's head from British stamps, and he fudged the answer. 'I felt I was marginally betraying my cause', as he noted for his diary, 'but things have to change slowly.' It was an uncharacteristically downbeat reflection – and totally contradictory to his determination, since 1964, to tackle the second great issue of the day at Full Steam Ahead: nothing less than the break-up of the Post Office.

---

* The first set of definitive stamps of the Queen's reign was based on a 1952 photograph by Dorothy Wilding – also used for many commemorative stamps, starting with a celebrated design by Edmund Dulac for the Queen's coronation in June 1953. For an updated portrait, the Stamp Advisory Committee turned in August 1965 to Arnold Machin, a sculptor and designer who had just produced a new effigy of the Queen for the first decimal coins (introduced into circulation in 1968, three years ahead of the changeover to decimal coinage in 1971). Machin worked from a clay model of his earlier effigy, producing a stamp from his coin design rather as the original Penny Black was derived from Wyon's medal of 1837. Whereas the Penny Black had passed from concept to sale in just four months, Machin's design took almost two years to appear as a stamp for the first time, in June 1967. (A large £1 'Machin definitive' issued two years later echoed the original of 1840 by appearing in black.) For connoisseurs of stamp design, both stories are comprehensively chronicled in Douglas N. Muir, *Postal Reform & the Penny Black: A New Appreciation*, National Postal Museum, 1990, and the same author's *A Timeless Classic: The Evolution of Machin's Icon*, BPMA Publications, 2007.

3. THE 'BREAK' AND THE 'SPLIT'

Forewarned by a few months of his likely appointment as Postmaster General, Benn read everything he could find on the Post Office. The fact that Victorian and Edwardian histories easily outnumbered anything published since 1918 confirmed his impression that he was not joining 'an up-to-date, go-ahead organisation'.[43] But he photocopied and read piles of reports of more recent vintage, so arrived at the Department well-versed in the arguments of those in the early 1920s and early 1930s who pressed the case for detaching it from the Crown service. (This option was often conveniently referred to as a departure from the civil service – though this was technically incorrect and took no account of the fact that a huge slice of the Post Office, namely its network of sub-post offices, was already run by small shopkeepers and tradesmen who were no part of the civil service. It was, and long remained, a feature of the Post Office that opponents of reform often found it convenient to ignore.) Benn needed less than two months to reach a none-too-tentative conclusion of his own: '. . . it is becoming increasingly clear to me', as he noted on 18 December 1964, 'that a Civil Service department cannot generate the impetus to make a growth industry grow and expand at the necessary rate.' If the Post Office was to prosper, the Government would have no choice but sooner or later to break it away from the civil service. Thereafter, his conviction on this score never wavered. Nor did he stop at envisaging the possibility of changing the Post Office's status as a government department. In addition to a break from the civil service, he was also ready by December 1964 to contemplate a split, divorcing telephones and telegrams from the postal service: 'Unless we break up the monolithic structure that now exists and encourage some younger leadership, there will never be the great leap forward that is required,'[44] he recorded with a dash of Maoist fervour. By the New Year, Benn was floating the concept of a Ministry of Communications, with not two but three separate businesses under its wing – posts, telecommunications and a Girobank. (A fourth might even be possible, if a national data-processing service could be spun out of the Telecoms business.) He mentioned the idea in January 1965 at the first of what was intended to be a series of informal meetings with a committee including the leaders of the POEU and the UPW. The engineers' leader, Charles Smith, welcomed it wholeheartedly; Ron Smith objected a little startlingly that the Split would see the mails 'shrivel away'. This ominous difference of opinion had no perceptible impact on Benn's enthusiasm for his twofold objective. It now became 'my major scheme' for turning the Post Office into the equivalent of a nationalized industry.

He set down his intentions in a minute to the Prime Minister at the beginning of March 1965. The Post Office was 'a novel hybrid organism half-way between the normal Government department and the normal public corporation', he told Wilson, a compromise that was no longer workable. He listed some of the old, historically familiar problems consequent upon Crown service status, and drew attention also to the opportunity costs of not being able to attract private capital. 'I can think of many fields in which the Post Office could diversify itself easily and profitably if it were able to move into joint ownership with private industry in the fields of telecoms equipment and other comparable enterprises.' There was 'a strong case' for both the Break *and* the Split. But there were broad questions over accountability and Whitehall positioning that would require a lot of work. The unions' views would also need plenty of consideration. (He was sure of the POEU's support for a change of status, 'whether for the Post Office as a whole or for telecoms separately', but acknowledged that others might take a different stance: the UPW 'would no doubt be less enthusiastic, but I believe I might carry them with me'.) So would the Prime Minister support him in a bid to develop detailed organizational and legislative plans and to 'prepare the way psychologically'?[45]

The level of support for the Break forthcoming within St Martin's itself must have come as a pleasant surprise to Benn, given his gloom over the civil service in general. Six days after his minute to Downing Street, he travelled to Norwich with Brigadier Holmes, the Director of Postal Services, to review the latest progress there on mechanized sorting, another topic that interested him greatly. He was delighted to hear Holmes confess that he strongly favoured turning the Department into a nationalized industry, and would welcome a separate future for the Posts as well, 'in order to restore their morale and give them a chance'. Benn may have thought the Brigadier was being a touch obsequious. ('I think Holmes is a good chap', ran that night's diary entry, 'though he is a bit too anxious to please . . .'[46]) In fact, at German's behest, many senior officials had been giving serious thought for a couple of years or more to the notion of 'disestablishing' the Post Office, as the Director General put it. The outcome of the 1961 Act had been deeply disappointing to them, as we have seen. Since then, a fact-finding mission to the US in May 1963 (William Ryland had led a small party on a month-long visit to several of the American Bell companies) had left many senior managers on the telecoms side convinced of the need to reconstitute the telephone service as a nationalized industry as soon as possible. According to an astonishingly detailed report that resulted from the trip, the British service urgently needed 'freedom from hierarchical and other restrictions and conformist attitudes, particularly in the personnel field, that are inseparable from civil service practices'.[47] In the summer of 1964, German had asked Sir John Ricks, Solicitor to the Post Office and long-serving head of its well-staffed Legal Department, to explore the legal ramifications of a change of status. His advice, sent back to German that July, was prescient:

> You suggested that we ought to do some preliminary thinking about the possibility of legislation to put some or all of the Post Office's functions under the management of a Board instead of a Minister . . . Generally I have been assuming [in my findings] that there would be only one Board – not eg a Posts Board and a Telecoms Board. Splitting the functions between two or more Boards would add excessively to the legislative and administrative complications. With one Board, I should expect that there would be no ground for turning down the plan at the outset on the score of insuperable legal difficulties, but we must recognize that the legislation would be very long and complicated, and would take very much time and labour to prepare.[48]

This certainly struck a chord with German, reinforcing his own conviction – shared by most, though not all, of his senior colleagues on the postal side – that the Split was a distraction and that only by focusing ruthlessly on the Break could they really hope to achieve it. Genuine independence from the civil service would be a great prize. But it was not just legal and administrative obstacles that would need surmounting. Within the Post Office, it would almost certainly be opposed by the UPW and probably by a sizeable minority of managers, too. Within Whitehall, there would almost certainly be an attempt by the Treasury to ensnare it. The Post Office would have to avoid at all costs complicating the Break by linking it to other goals, which might simply become hostages to fortune. Hence Benn's determination to lead the way was, to German, a mixed blessing. His forceful agitation for the Break was welcome. His enthusiasm for the Split, and perhaps more than one Split, was slightly alarming.

It did not take long for the Treasury to begin setting the traps, under a Chancellor whose own career as a trade unionist in the civil service had encompassed a cordial rapport with the UPW.[49] Shown a copy of Benn's minute, James Callaghan was careful to avoid being confrontational. 'I think there is a good deal to be said for this idea and I would certainly be ready to examine it sympathetically.' But naturally there would be many daunting problems. Callaghan proposed that a working party be set up under the Treasury's chairmanship, ostensibly to identify these problems and how to tackle them.[50] Once this course had been agreed in Downing Street, the Treasury proceeded to ignore the fact that the Postmaster General had committed himself to the Break in principle: every opportunity was taken to question Benn's declared goal. The Post Office officials on the committee ruefully noted the tactic, and responded by submitting a cogent paper in May 1965 entitled 'The Case for Change'. Its author, Eric Shepherd, was the Finance and Accounts Director at St Martin's who had been one of Ryland's companions on the Bell trip two years earlier. His essential point was that the 1961 Act, for all of its financial tinkering, had made little impact. 'Many of the potential advantages of financial independence have not been realised because the restrictions which fall on the Post Office and derive from its status as a department of the Crown have continued.' In fact, even the financial independence had been largely neutered: the Government had continued to treat Post Office finances 'as though they were an inseparable part of the Exchequer'. (Shepherd was even bold enough here to point a finger at the Chancellor himself, for referring in the recent Budget Debate to the effect on public expenditure of increased postal charges.) The net result was that the management of the Post Office remained as heavily encumbered as ever by its current status. With parliamentary questions about the Office running at the rate of about 1,000 a year, the time wasted on trivial political inquiries alone represented a huge burden on the Department.[51]

The working party's deliberations lasted three months, until the end of July 1965. Over this period, the Post Office's future status again became a topic of lively public debate, as it had been in 1927–32. The press was generally sympathetic to the idea of a reorganization of some kind: Ernest Marples was one of those invited to write articles in favour of the Split. At the same time, the opposition of the UPW to change of any fundamental nature surfaced with some venom. Its leader used a speech in Ireland at the beginning of June to rebuke the Postmaster General for mentioning even the possibility of a one-per-day delivery service at the Controllers' Dinner. (Benn managed to reassure himself in his diary that this was no surprise: 'Ron Smith made a violent attack on me . . . He said that I was out to "smash" the postal service and one or two other things just as bad. This is the explosion I expected . . .'[52]) More encouraging was a debate in the Commons on postal services, which left Benn confident that MPs were not going to baulk at the idea of Parliament losing control over the Post Office. 'I am firmly convinced in my own mind that this is the right thing to do and believe that the opportunity lies within our grasp in the next twelve months. In this respect, I shall have the department working wholeheartedly for me and I may as well take advantage of their enthusiasm.'[53]

Winning the Treasury's approval remained the biggest challenge – and here progress was less forthcoming. Some of the objections put to the working party by the Treasury struck Shepherd and his colleagues as ridiculous. One moment it was argued that postal employees would be unaffected by the Break, rendering it more or less superfluous; the next, that employees' prospective terms and conditions would be so out of line with those of the civil service as to be contrary to government policy. Above all, the Treasury was much exercised by the risk that an independent corporation might abuse the postal monopoly. Its formal submission to the working party in mid-June was predictably negative but no less depressing for that. 'The Treasury paper raises so many bogies that its effect . . . is excessively discouraging', wrote Shepherd in an internal note. 'Any idea that the Post Office can pay fancy rates of pay to corner the labour market and then charge fancy prices to its customers is so unrealistic as hardly to need a serious answer!'[54] The committee's Final Report, when it appeared late in July, went close to damning the whole idea with the kind of faint praise customary in such circumstances: true, there were numerous potential advantages, 'but the weight to be given to them and the extent to which a change in status would bring a real benefit is not always easy to quantify'.[55] Four days later, Callaghan moved to shelve Benn's great project with the briefest of minutes to the Prime Minister, copied to St Martin's: 'At this stage I have not discussed [the Report] with Treasury officials, but on a quick reading, I am inclined to doubt whether there is much profit in pursuing the matter just now.'[56]

For almost any minister in the long line of Postmasters General since Henry Fawcett, a setback of this kind would have been a cue to give up the fight. Not so Benn: he had seen Callaghan's put-down coming, and had been laying his plans for many weeks to ensure that the momentum behind his scheme was not lost. He had not turned the future status of the Post Office into a popular talking point for the first time in thirty years only to back away now. His determination to pull off both the Break and the Split had grown stronger since the start of the year. As he noted early in July, 'I can see little point in doing what every other Postmaster General seems to have done – fume with frustration while in office and then write a strong pamphlet or book or article when he leaves office saying what ought to be done'.* That diary entry came at the end of a weekend during which Benn began drafting another detailed paper for the Prime Minister on his reorganization proposals. Attached to it would be an appendix, 'Post Office Reform: A Hundred Years of Argument for Reform, 1864–1965', into which Benn had gathered a compelling list of quotations from every notable advocate of the Break since the nineteenth century. The departmental heads at St Martin's were all invited to comment on the first draft over the rest of July, and many of them did so. In the final version, which went off as a minute to the Prime Minister on 9 August, Benn nailed his colours to the mast:

> The Post Office . . . is gravely handicapped by its status as a Government Department, run on civil service lines, and it is really too big and its functions too diverse to be run as one organisation. It should therefore be divided into three independent public corporations, covering Telecommunications, Mails and Banking . . . It would of course be open to us to make the change in two parts: first, transforming the Post Office into a single nationalised industry and later, reorganising the industry into independent public corporations as suggested . . . But [this approach] would prolong the disturbance and, on balance, I am against taking it in two stages and in favour of a division as part of the major change. . . . [While legislative plans are being laid] I shall continue my own plans for internal re-organisation which will be necessary whether or not the major operation takes place.[57]

By the time Wilson saw this, a strong personal plea for the Break had also been made by the Director General, at a meeting of permanent secre-

---

* This entry, for 11 July 1965, was partly a dig at Reginald Bevins, whose autobiography, *The Greasy Pole*, had just appeared. Benn's predecessor made free with his criticism of the Post Office for having 'a form of organisation which I believe does not fit its functions' – but he had done little to remedy this in five years at the job. Benn was informed in December 1965 by his private secretary, Donald Wratten – Tilling's successor – that Bevins had never even been shown a copy of the Ryland Report of May 1963 with its explicit support for the Split. Benn thought this 'the most astonishing revelation about the way in which the Office treats its Ministers'. Six months later, he was furious to discover that he himself had been kept in the dark in just the same way, about a report on telecoms procurement policies written by an official in 1965. It was 'little short of scandalous . . .' (Tony Benn, *Out of the Wilderness: Diaries 1963–67*, Arrow Books, 1988, pp. 356 and 416.)

taries on 28 July. Supported by his counterpart from the Ministry of Labour, German had managed to extract from them an agreement in principle to the Break, though emphatically not to the Split (not least because they thought the UPW 'most unlikely' to accept it). During August, Benn was able to talk privately to Wilson about his plans. The latter remained only 'lukewarm' about them, and ruled out any hope of legislation before 1967 – but he did at least agree to chair a further discussion among the key ministers on 14 September. Callaghan used this occasion to sniff at Benn's latest paper: 'Jim spoke and pooh-poohed it . . . he thought the difficulties – especially on the staff side – were too great to risk'.[58] But Wilson, listening once again to Benn's impassioned argument, gave ground. So out of the meeting came yet another working party, tasked with reaching 'preliminary views' on how to proceed. These were to be finalized before February 1966, when a review was to be begun of the Post Office by the Parliamentary Select Committee on Nationalised Industries. (Since the Post Office was not a nationalized industry, the Committee had been given special leave to embark on what would be the first such formal inquiry since the Bridgeman Committee in 1932.)

At this point, events took a curious turn. Almost seven months earlier, at the end of February 1965, the Director General had hired some management consultants from the small London office of a US firm called McKinsey, as yet little known in Britain. They had been recommended by Sir Leslie Rowan, a former Treasury official (and one of Churchill's wartime private secretaries), who had left Whitehall in 1962 to become managing director of Vickers, then the largest industrial conglomerate in Britain. The Vickers Board, said Rowan, had been greatly impressed by the help McKinsey had given them with a series of structural reforms.[59] This settled the matter for German, who had been pondering since the autumn of 1964 how best to set about reviewing the Post Office's operations in search of substantial cost savings, an agenda he had assumed would be given priority by any new Postmaster General. Hearing of McKinsey's appointment, Benn had urged German to make sure they had a wide brief. He himself met them on only a couple of occasions, in April and May.* Behind a closed door with no officials present, Benn had left them in no doubt about his assessment of the Post Office; but he

---

* Many at the time wrongly attributed McKinsey's appointment to Benn's influence. In fact his initial involvement was mostly restricted to fending off the bitter complaints of various British management consultants that the Post Office had turned to a US rival – after ten of them had worked for the Department since the early 1950s.

seems not to have expected much of a return on this. Indeed, after a brief discussion in August with German and McKinsey's team leader – a tall, gravelly-voiced Midwesterner called Roger Morrison – Benn had not been much impressed: 'Morrison . . . concentrated on the very points to which I had drawn his attention. In fact he said practically nothing that I hadn't said, but we are paying him many thousands of pounds a month to say it with greater authority.'[60] Morrison used this meeting to hand over a written report, the first substantial outcome of his team's work since February. After he had read it – and scribbled 'It is extremely interesting' on the cover note from German – Benn appears to have formed an altogether more generous view of the men from McKinsey. And, over the months that followed, the rising champion of the Left in Britain formed an intriguing de facto alliance with the praetorian guards of management efficiency from corporate America.

Aged thirty-seven, Morrison had been working in London since 1962. It so happened that his very first job, while still at high school, had been as a part-time postman in Hutchinson, Minnesota (population: 5,000), so he knew what to expect when walking into a sorting office. But he brought a lot more to the job than that. McKinsey was a consultancy, founded in Chicago during the years of the Great Depression, which had carved out an enviable reputation since the war for helping to improve the efficiency of some of the best-run firms in the US, which is to say in the world. (Since graduating from Harvard Business School in 1953, Morrison himself had worked his way up the ranks via studies for illustrious corporate names such as Chrysler and Texaco.) Having established an outpost in London in 1959, it had already worked for a handful of the largest companies in Britain – but the Post Office was its first foray into the UK public sector, and it meant to make its mark. Two British colleagues in the London office joined Morrison's small team. Their mandate from German was primarily about finding ways to cut costs, but was much more open-ended than this might suggest. McKinsey had the scope, in its own words, 'to highlight, and to some extent quantify, any significant disadvantages to the postal services of the GPO's civil service status, thus providing a background for further discussion of this basic issue'.[61]

The firm's *modus operandi* was an iterative process of hypotheses, investigations, recommendations and more hypotheses. Once unleashed, it could roll forward remorselessly. Interim reports would provide updates from time to time, and it was the first of these that landed in August 1965. Since February, Morrison and his colleagues had been working ferociously hard. Now they presented a withering summary of those 'significant disadvantages' of civil service status, spelt out with a disarming simplicity. Too few rewards for innovation, too little regard for productivity in pay procedures, too much interference by Parliament and too little consultation with staff . . . the problem faced by the Post Office was multifaceted, but could be summed up as a dysfunctional environment. Or as the clipped prose of the McKinsey verdict put it: 'THE PROBLEM. Environment inhibits postal management from pursuing profit improvement opportunities with the drive typical of successful commercial organizations . . . Problem is compounded by use of Civil Service organization and management methods in parallel with commercial objectives and status'.[62] The consultants treated it as almost axiomatic that the Post Office should be removed from the civil service, but in order to alter the whole environment and instill what Morrison liked to call a sense of 'constructive dissatisfaction' – meaning an appetite for constant improvement, which he thought was glaringly absent – it was just as important to chase a programme of internal reforms. 'A transition to nationalized [industry] status, even if practicable, would only be one step in this programme.' Others could be pursued more immediately. They included cost-cutting projects on the one hand and a reorganization of District Office procedures on the other. The Director General and his colleagues bravely waved them all ahead – and other, more far-reaching studies quickly followed. In particular, McKinsey turned to the overall organization of the Post Office.

For Benn, this was rather like David Gentleman turning up unexpectedly with his designer's objections to the Queen's head on stamps. In McKinsey he had another authoritative outsider, voicing precisely his own criticisms of the Post Office – and backing them up with hard evidence that Benn could employ to sweep away sentimental and ill-considered opposition; so just as earlier in the year over stamps, he felt encouraged to push ahead with a radical idea that he might otherwise have had to abandon. The 'Queen's head' objective, in the context of reorganizing the Department, was the Split. It was plain by September that the Treasury and most of his own officials were against it. But McKinsey took a different line, and Benn embraced them as a way of keeping the option alive.

The consultants approached this issue a little gingerly: their client, after all, was the Director General and his objections to the Split were never in doubt. Nonetheless, in the consultants' view, the case for divorcing the postal and telecoms operations was absolutely compelling.

McKinsey had built its post-war reputation in the US on helping large corporations to decentralize their operations, putting separate businesses under the control of virtually autonomous divisions. Its enormous influence had been one of the key reasons why 'the multidivisional structure had become the dominant organisational form among American industrial companies . . .'[63] The rationale for just this same approach at the Post Office could hardly be ignored. The Telephone business, which until 1959 had spent ten years earning well under £5m a year, was now reliably producing profits of almost £40m a year. McKinsey's analysis of the Post Office's predicament was disarmingly matter-of-fact, and its findings echoed many of those arguments put forward for a separation of posts and telephones in the 1920s. Posts and telecoms shared the characteristic of being natural monopolies at the level of local delivery, but in most other key respects they amounted to a chalk-and-cheese combination. The postal service was wary of innovation and heavily labour-intensive. It was centred upon the orderly management of routines and mass logistics (though all the evidence so far suggested this orderly approach was hardly promoting greater efficiency). Above all, it was geared to *meeting* public demand, not stimulating it. The Telephone business, said McKinsey, was in many respects exactly the opposite. Its engineers had to keep abreast of the latest telecom technology. Its managers had to invest enormous sums, to pay not for people but for new plant and equipment. Their market was growing at a breakneck pace – and it demanded marketing skills that were wholly alien to the postal culture. Morrison and his colleagues were well aware by the summer of 1965 that an uncompromising call for the Split would almost certainly fall on deaf ears. Instead, they proposed that the Post Office opt for what we might term (though McKinsey never did) the 'Semi-Split'. That is to say, they urged a division of the management structure from top to bottom, splitting Posts from Telecoms in almost all essentials, but not actually splitting the Post Office itself, which would remain a single entity under one chief executive.

This implied a far-reaching set of changes for the Department, which McKinsey believed should be pursued whether the Break went ahead or not, and they summarized them for German at the end of October 1965.[64] A start had in fact just been made. Prior to that autumn, there were two senior officials with the title of Deputy Director General. (The same status attached to two other positions which had their own titles, the Comptroller and Accountant General and the Engineer-in-Chief.) Each DDG had a portfolio of clear responsibilities, but these cut across the Post Office's postal and Telecoms businesses: neither DDG had overall charge of the one business or the other. McKinsey had urged that the two jobs should be unequivocally aligned with the businesses. One of the DDGs, William Wolverson, had retired in September, and McKinsey's idea was now adopted. The appointments were announced of a DDG for Posts, Alan Wolstencroft, and a DDG for Telecoms, William Ryland. The consultants wanted the process to go much further, with separate Regional Directors across the country for the two businesses. All common service departments at Headquarters – including, crucially, the jealously guarded fiefdom of the Engineer-in-Chief – would also need to lose their executive powers and be realigned as advisers to the two line-management hierarchies. It was the blueprint for an even bigger upheaval than had followed the Bridgeman Enquiry in 1932 – which had taken seven years to implement. Four months later, Morrison handed over another report elaborating on the Semi-Split's implications, and suggesting that the existing Post Office Board could either be restructured with some non-executive directors – to 'follow the general industry practice' – or be scrapped altogether.[65]

German and his DDG for Posts were privately dismayed.[66] But Benn could not have wished for a stronger endorsement of his ideas, and he took up the Semi-Split concept immediately. He found other allies, however, hard to come by. When he made his first public reference to the Semi-Split, in an October speech that must have slightly puzzled the staff of the Head Post Office in Aberdeen, there was a predictably fierce reaction from the UPW. Its General Secretary was as opposed to the Semi-Split now as he had been to the Split in January. In a front-page editorial of *The Post*, Ron Smith declared darkly that 'sometimes, ideas can run away with the men who propound them'. The Postmaster General needed to think again. 'If he listens to us, he will discover his error in imagining the Communications Industry to be two giants . . . for these are but two ways of providing the one service.'[67] Nor did Benn find much support for the Semi-Split at the Regional Directors' Annual Conference at the start of November 1965. Its reaction was overwhelmingly hostile: attempting such a massive change at the same time as the Break, said one speaker after another, would strain the Post Office to breaking point.[68] But Benn was undeterred. Indeed, he seems still to have had his sights set firmly on a full-blown Split eventually. Getting his officials and the Treasury to accept the Semi-Split – like getting the Queen to agree that new stamp designs could be submitted without her head on them – would be a tactically useful half-way house. After a formal adoption of the Break as government policy, he would then be able to push through the Split as a practical and none-too-difficult next step. By late November he was ready to begin the campaign. A good start, he thought, would be the promotion of both Wolstencroft and Ryland to Director General status. This was put to German one morning as a firm instruction: 'I told the DG that I really did insist upon [it] . . . [and] I said that I wanted him to prepare a scheme as quickly as he could. The DG went out at about 12.15, having had a double whisky and appearing to accept what had been decided.'[69]

German, though, had certainly not accepted it. What followed was a stand-off at the top of the Post Office, as colourful as some of the more celebrated feuds from the distant past. Starting at the beginning of November, Benn and German exchanged increasingly bitter letters and minutes for the next several months.[70] In what he characterized as 'an extremely obstinate clash of wills', Benn went on demanding that the management changes be launched – and German went on blocking them. The Director General was not instinctively opposed to radical change, as Benn more than once complained. Indeed, he was hard at work through these months on a complicated project to divide the Home Counties Region into two new regions, acknowledging the extraordinary growth of the counties around London since the post-war years. (Letter postings in the region had gone from 655 million in 1945 to 1,646 million in 1965; use of the region's telephone system had trebled over the same period, with the number of 'working exchange connections' rising from 298,000 to 960,000.[71]) But he gave local action of this kind a higher priority than reform of St Martin's. Above all, the mood in Whitehall was now turning encouragingly positive on the Break. The working party set up by Wilson broadly endorsed its adoption by January 1966. As German saw things, it would be madness to risk losing this historically elusive prize by making additional demands that he knew would be unacceptable to the Treasury (as headless stamps had been to the Palace). Benn saw the situation in a different historical light. He swept aside the restructuring of the Home Counties Region as an irritating distraction 'at this time when far more fundamental changes are under consideration'.[72] Opportunities to split the Post Office had been rare, and neglecting them had cost the Post Office dearly. He would stick to the task. An official visit to Japan at the start of the New Year strengthened his resolve. By splitting their Post Office and allowing telecoms to flourish under the management of an independent publicly owned corporation (NTT), the Japanese had given their telephone industry a massive boost. It was true their postal service remained in a sorry state – but this was entirely attributable to the fact that it had been left to vegetate as a government department.[73] Only the defeatism of the British postal service, egged on (as Benn thought) by the UPW, could blind it to the obvious lessons to be drawn.

In the teeth of firm resistance from his Director General – and the barely suppressed fury of the Comptroller and Accountant General, Sir Kenneth Anderson – Benn finally despatched a memo to the Treasury early in March 1966, outlining some of the Semi-Split changes he wanted to make.[74] Wilson had just called a general election for 31 March. He and Labour's Deputy Leader, George Brown, had by now come round to accepting the case for the Break – and Wilson suggested that 'a major reorganisation of the Post Office' should be mentioned in the Labour manifesto. To the leadership's surprise, Benn demurred.* He seems to have feared that a premature declaration on the Break would pre-empt any progress on the Split. His approach to the Treasury followed a couple of days later. In seeking approval for his changes to be made in the wake of the election, he was a little disingenuous: the recommended changes, he suggested, 'have no direct connection with the question of Post Office status ... and do not prejudice the main status question either way'. This fooled no one at the Treasury, and its response was brutal, as German had repeatedly warned would be the case. It insisted that the Break, if implemented, would be conditional on having one Board – and there was no question of 'an interim [re]organisation which might appear to prejudice the question [of what structure to adopt below the Board]'.[75] Benn shrugged off the rebuff and threw himself into electioneering. German and his colleagues sat back to await the fondly expected post-election news of Benn's promotion to another ministry.

Summoned to Number Ten in the usual way after Labour's victory, Benn certainly went along expecting to be promoted. It came as a shock when Wilson told him 'you have a big job of industrial reorganisation with the Post Office' and he wanted him to remain there. Other jobs were available, said the Prime Minister, but he could only move him sideways. Benn agreed to stay put, and returned immediately to St Martin's.

---

* The 1966 Labour Manifesto contained no explicit reference to the Post Office – though Benn's membership of the drafting committee can perhaps be discerned in the final text: 'Throughout our national life there was a stubborn refusal [under Tory governments] to root out obsolete ideas and modernise obsolescent institutions. Instead of setting an example to the timid and old-fashioned in industry and commerce, Tory governments funked the radical reorganisation of the whole machinery of the state ... which was so desperately required.'

'I had the DG in and I told him that I'd been offered another job but had decided to stay on', Benn gleefully recorded that night. 'He was shaken to the core.'[76] Hostilities were quickly resumed. In mid-May, Benn invited Ron Smith to St Martin's for a private lunch. The UPW leader, as ever relishing the opportunity for a little horse-trading behind the scenes, suggested he might after all be able to win his members' acquiescence in the Break, 'so long as there was no division into three corporations'.[77] It strengthened Benn's now gathering conviction that the full Split was not, after all, going to be achievable – but this only bolstered his determination to consolidate planning for the Semi-Split instead. Neither the Director General nor the Permanent Secretary of the Treasury, Sir Lawrence Helsby, could persuade him to drop his campaign for a division of the regions, and by the start of June he had prepared a draft announcement to this effect.

German fought desperately to avert it. It would be 'most unwise', he warned Benn on 3 June, 'mainly because everyone in the postal service would see this as relegating that service to second place. There could not fail to be [a] serious lowering of morale of middle management.' Back in February, German had responded to McKinsey's last memo on the topic by asking them to set out in detail the arguments for and against the regional division. (Perhaps the Director General had hoped Benn would be gone before the analysis came back.) Now he played the McKinsey card back to the Postmaster General. 'I hope ... that you will agree that before we decide on any change, we should discuss the whole question with Mr Morrison to consider whether his views would be of help to us.'[78] Alas for German, the indefatigable Mr Morrison was almost ready with his answers, and they were none too helpful. In a report simply entitled 'Regional Organization', his team had investigated each of seven specific problems identified by postal managers in the field. Some of them, like the fact that posts and telecoms shared premises and staff in many locations, had been trotted out as killer objections to the Split since the Coates Committee hearings of 1920. None was thought by McKinsey to pose more than transitional difficulties.[79] Benn snapped up this conclusion for his next presentation to the Treasury. On 14 June, the ever unpredictable Callaghan confided that he had decided to swing his support behind the Semi-Split after all, and Benn seemed on the brink of victory. Then Helsby took his objections straight to the Prime Minister and yet more altercations threatened. To cut through the impasse, Benn told German he would announce the division of the regions along with the Break on 20 July, together with the publication of the Annual Report.

What happened next left a lasting memory for Henry Tilling, who had been with Benn on his very first day. Now an Assistant Secretary, Tilling was on holiday with his family in Cornwall at the start of that July. 'I was sitting on a harbour wall, when I saw in the far distance a familiar figure striding purposefully towards me. It soon became a familiar face from the Office – and as soon as it was within earshot, it shouted, "He's gone."' Tilling knew immediately what this meant.[80] Benn had been moved to another ministry. And so indeed he had. A sudden resignation in the Government had opened up an opportunity at last for Wilson to give him a meaningful promotion: he was to be Minister of Technology. Benn's tenure at the Post Office thus ended as abruptly as it had begun. He called at St Martin's the next day, 4 July, to pick up his ashtray and blue china tea mug and to say goodbye to his private secretary. 'Wratten was punch-drunk', he noted later, 'and said that he felt everything would stop now.'[81] At a small farewell party arranged for the departing Postmaster General at the end of the week, Wratten took him aside and told him 'the DG was almost delirious with excitement at my departure ...'[82] Sure enough, Benn's announcement set for 20 July had been cancelled and his Semi-Split restructuring of the Directorate had apparently been shelved. It was another battle lost. Word went out from St Martin's within days that a stormy interlude had passed: the Treasury was assured of the Post Office's determination to remain a single body, and the Palace was at the same time assured that no stamps would ever appear without the sovereign's head.* British stamp design had nonetheless been set on a new course – and so had the Post Office. As the next twelve months would show, Benn's persistent advocacy of the Semi-Split had given it a powerful momentum.

4. 'A UNIQUELY SUITABLE OPPORTUNITY'

Benn's successor as Postmaster General on 4 July was Edward Short, a schoolmaster in his youth who had spent his life in the political trenches

* After Benn had been to the Palace on 5 July to be sworn into his new position, alongside one or two other new appointments, he recorded a revealing exchange with the Queen. 'Afterwards, she made a few remarks to us and as I shook hands with her she said, "I'm sure you'll miss your stamps." I replied, "Yes indeed I shall. But I shall never forget your kindness and encouragement in helping me to tackle them." She gave me a rather puzzled smile and I bowed and went out backwards' (Benn, *Out of the Wilderness*, '5 July 1966', p. 446).

as a local councillor and MP for Newcastle before serving as the Labour government's Chief Whip since 1964. He had accepted Wilson's offer of the Post Office, as he frankly admitted in his political memoirs, 'not without some misgivings about taking over a highly technical department'.[83] Once in office, though, he was not afraid to move quickly where he could see decisive action was needed. (When England won the Football World Cup at the end of July, he authorized an immediate reissue of two of the commemorative stamps produced earlier in the year, with a new design by David Gentleman adding the words 'England Winners' to the original. They went on sale on 18 August.) Anxious to avoid a summer of press speculation about his intentions, and with no inclination to reverse a policy he knew had been exhaustively debated in Whitehall for months, Short pressed his ministerial colleagues for a speedy decision on the Break. It was approved by Wilson's Cabinet just three weeks after Benn's departure, and the decision to reconstitute the Post Office as a public corporation was duly announced in Parliament on 3 August 1966. The new body, Short told the Commons, would be infinitely better suited than a Crown service department to the running of 'a complex of vast business enterprises'. Wolmer, now the 79-year-old 3rd Earl of Selborne and still tending his Surrey estate, must have enjoyed that – as must Benn, too, though he made no reference to it at all in his diary, which scarcely mentioned the Post Office again. A White Paper followed in March 1967. It broadly modelled the future corporation along the lines of existing nationalized industries, while acknowledging 'the special role of the Corporation's services in the social fabric of Britain . . .' In all important respects – including, on the postal side, the retention of its monopoly, a continuing obligation to deliver a universal service and 'a high degree of security of tenure' for all staff – the Post Office would go on exactly as before.[84] It would keep the same name, too – though plenty of possible alternatives were drawn up inside St Martin's, most of them utterly improbable, from 'Postelo' and 'General Telpo' to the positively Trollopian 'Conveyance and Ways Board'.[85] This was still emphatically an organization with no formal marketing department.

Despite the continuities between Department and Corporation, drafting the subsequent bill and making the statutory preparations for the transfer proved a monumental task. A fresh Directorate was established, with the task of coordinating the work. It went far beyond the structuring of the new entity and the defining of its relations with the rest of Whitehall. While the Post Office was going to continue running the 'Royal Mail', it was to lose its 'Crown exemption' – its status, that is, as an entity exempt from taxation; and this created dozens of potential snags for the future Corporation, all of which needed to be carefully pre-empted.* The legislative process was arduous in itself: hundreds of postal statutes stretching back to 1711 (and a mass of telegraph legislation passed since 1870, too) all had to be revised, removing every reference to the Postmaster General and reassigning his responsibilities. The bill took over a year to complete. When it was published at the end of October 1968, it ran to 224 pages, containing 142 Sections and 11 Schedules; more than a hundred clauses provided for the amendment of 500 existing Acts of Parliament. This level of technical detail helped ensure a protracted series of debates in both the Commons and the Lords, even though the Conservative Opposition was in favour of incorporation. And there was a further complication when a fresh-faced young Conservative backbencher, Kenneth Baker, intervened at one point to speak out in favour of selling off the telecoms side of the future Corporation to the private sector. The Opposition Front Bench appeared to dither before disowning this old chestnut, which left a residue of distrust between the main parties. (Fifteen years later, Baker, as Minister for Information Technology, would oversee the privatization of British Telecom during the Thatcher era.) Eventually, in July 1969, the bill was passed and the Post Office was finally cleared to make the historic exit from the Crown service that so many had advocated over the preceding half-century. It emerged ten weeks later, on 1 October, as easily the single largest business in the UK, employing 425,000 people – almost 2 per cent of the country's working population.

While this legislative process was under way, decisions over the Split (or the Semi-Split) remained to be resolved. A consensus had emerged by the middle of 1966, as even Benn had had to acknowledge, that trying to establish two independent corporations was likely to be counter-productive, especially given the antagonism of the UPW. But the Semi-Split would still mark a historic milestone, if it could be achieved. And while its political champion had moved on, its most formidable proponent within the Department remained in place: McKinsey.

---

* The existing rules on stamp duty, to take just one tiny instance, meant that every postal order would in future have to carry a 2d stamp duty, making a nonsense of the low-value postal orders that were used in great numbers; and every order for £2 or more would attract a second 2d stamp duty when payment was acknowledged. To avert a wipe-out for the Postal Order service, its long-standing exemption from stamp duty – as a Crown department – had to be preserved in the incorporation statute.

In espousing a top-to-bottom division of the management tree, in defiance of the senior officials' reluctance to consider it, the consultants came close to sawing through the branch they were sitting on. German dropped a note to Roger Morrison in March 1966, just to put on record that the firm's work would essentially be finished by June.[86] The DDG-Posts, Alan Wolstencroft, made no secret of his desire to see McKinsey gone. Two weeks after Benn's departure in July 1966, and seeing the firm still in situ, he wrote a candid recommendation for the incoming Minister, Ted Short. McKinsey, he pointed out, was an expensive firm. 'Although we have learned a lot by employing them, it seems increasingly doubtful if we should get value for money by retaining them much longer ... They may well propose to you that they should undertake further detailed studies on [their proposal to split posts from telecoms] or other aspects of Post Office organization. Studies are needed, but I think we should undertake them ourselves.'[87] The ever-cautious Short decided to make up his own mind about this, and spent some time in his first few weeks looking carefully at McKinsey's output. The new Postmaster General was no connoisseur of business practices, but he was shrewd enough to see that McKinsey's presence at the Post Office marked, at the very least, a highly unusual chapter in its recent history. The use of costly consultants within the public sector was not yet the highly controversial issue that it would become a generation later, and Short felt under no outside pressure to heed Wolstencroft's advice. He thought McKinsey should continue its work – and even appeared to welcome the notion that the Department might be starting to appraise itself as a commercial operation.

Progress in this direction was still painfully slow. Few substantial changes of any kind had yet been made to the daily routines of the Department; nor had the civil service culture of the organization across the country – and the forceful presence at every turn of local union representatives – undergone any noticeable shift over the past eighteen months. Nevertheless, the intensity of McKinsey's work had unmistakably launched the Post Office on a course that seemed, by the middle of 1966, capable over time of transforming the nature of the postal service. The cost reduction projects instigated the previous summer had triggered a frenzy of data collection, analysis and discussion without precedent in the twentieth century.[88] Roger Morrison and his team identified the issues needing to be clarified, but most of the endless fetching and gathering was left to teams manned by the Post Office itself. Staff at all levels, from the Postal Services Directorate to the Regional Offices and below them the Head Postmasters, were swept up in the work. Not that it was resented: most of the work was applauded at a local level. As the in-house magazine of the Association of Head Postmasters put it, McKinsey's studies were 'refreshingly different from those used by consultants previously commissioned by the Post Office ... How much more desirable it is, ... to have the surgeon in attendance during these investigations than for him to leave his opinion with the registrar.'[89]

There was nothing new about the idea of collecting more data: if the accumulation of numbers was all that mattered, then McKinsey had more than met its match. Postal traffic data had been documented to the nth degree since the days of Rowland Hill. (The postal archives were, and remained, a monument to centuries of meticulous record-keeping.*) The crippling weakness of the Department, in the consultants' view, was its failure to ask searching questions of the data in a bid to improve the status quo. So long as the wheels were kept turning, there was little or no interest in finding ways to make them turn more efficiently. Officials appeared honestly to believe that after years, decades, of incremental improvement and horse-trading with the unions, the returns on further innovation had usually diminished to the point of being scarcely worth considering. McKinsey took the opposite approach. It collected numbers in order to validate or disprove starting hypotheses that simple, basic jobs could be done better. In the space of just nine months, it oversaw efficiency studies for the Crown offices' counter services, all writing rooms and the standard sorting office; it analysed the administration of Head Post Offices and the operational procedures of the North-West and South-East District Offices of the London Region; and it started laying the groundwork for a Long Term Plan for Postal Services, establishing the Department's first Planning Branch. The results were persuasive. Compiling a report for the benefit of the Commons Select Committee on Nationalised Industries as early as February 1966, the Post Office confirmed its belief that future savings of about £3m a

---

* Benn thought the archives deserved more recognition. 'I went to have a look at the Post Office archives and was appalled by the Dickensian atmosphere in the sub-basement [of Headquarters] where these poor people try to gather some sort of historical records. All the vehicles, equipment, stamps, uniforms and papers will need to be coordinated into an effective Post Office museum and historical library' (Benn, *Out of the Wilderness*, '19 September 1965', p. 322). This was apparently his intention when the National Postal Museum was set up, but the archives remained separate. They were only moved in 1992, to their present location in the refurbished boiler rooms beneath the Mount Pleasant sorting office in Islington. This is less Dickensian than it sounds – but still some way short of Benn's vision of a combined museum and historical library.

year were eventually going to result from all this. (Saving the same amount via workforce reductions would have involved shedding up to 12,000 jobs a year over the next five years, the report suggested – 'an impossible task whether measured by the past results of the GPO or general industry experience'.[90])

If he was impressed by the scale of McKinsey's ambitions for the Post Office, Short was also acutely conscious of his political need to offer a vision of what incorporation would mean. Four days after announcing the Government's commitment to the Break on 3 August, Short chaired a meeting with Morrison and his colleagues and asked them to under-take a fresh study. Its dual purpose would be to identify the ideal structure for the reconstituted Post Office, and to suggest what steps needed to be taken while it yet remained within the civil service. By the time McKinsey returned in the middle of September 1966 with a refined version of the brief, it was clear that the Semi-Split was back at the top of the agenda. What would be the most appropriate field organization for posts and telecoms? How should the Headquarters be organized around the two of them? How should they share common services like engineering and finance?[91] Short's commissioning of this new work, envisaged to last six months, gave McKinsey a fresh authority. The retirement of Ronald German in the autumn, and his replacement by a businessman, John Wall – previously Managing Director of EMI, the recording company, and the first outsider appointed to the top executive position since 1910 – seemed to confirm as much. In November, Wall wrote to the head of the Director of Reorganization, Maurice Tinnis-wood: 'I believe McKinsey's can be of great value to us in putting down forthright views about the role and constitution of the new Board and about the functions and proposed location of the central Departments. It could well be that it is here that they will do their most valuable work.' Tinniswood agreed, telling Wall in reply that he had told McKin-sey 'that in my view their recommendations should be uncompromising and should be aimed at the ultimate position they think we should strive for . . .'[92]

Here, then, was a golden opportunity, for no one was in any doubt about the strength of what Tinniswood referred to as McKinsey's 'bias towards splitting'. Now that an irrevocable commitment had been made to the Break, it was surely time to separate the two sides of the Post Office into distinct businesses. This was the conclusion that had been reached by most senior men in the Post Office beyond the confines of St Martin's. In a conspicuous reversal of their earlier views, the Regional

Directors now decided to make clear that their past opposition to the Semi-Split – as voiced at their November 1965 Annual Conference – had been mistaken. They prepared a presentation for McKinsey, which was delivered at their November 1966 Annual Conference. While their backing for the Semi-Split was wholehearted, it was also uncompromising: the RDs had no interest in seeing posts and telecoms divorced in the field but run from the centre by a still undivided Headquarters. A detailed note was kept of the 1966 Conference:

> The [Regional] Directors were satisfied that the time had come to split the two services and they accordingly welcomed the proposal that the split should take place. They wished, however, to emphasize that the split should be complete [sic]. In saying this they had in mind suggestions which had received some currency that it was only the operational elements of the services which needed to be separated, there being a body of ancillary services which could be organized territorially in units common to both the operational services. The Directors regarded this suggestion as misconceived and revealing a lack of understanding of the integral relationship of an operational service and its ancillary parts and of the necessity, therefore, for its parts to be managed together.[93]

There followed a review of the implications for every aspect of the postal service, from staff and buildings to finance, engineering and computers. Much the same refrain applied in every case. The RDs wanted to be part of a self-standing postal business, with as many powers devolved as possible to their own offices in the regions.* McKinsey responded by setting down a plan of action with its usual conciseness. In all essentials this was ready by December 1966, when a preliminary report was completed. The year-old recommendation that the regions be split was restated, but it was now accompanied by a clear prescription for the Headquarters organization too: 'Main conclusion is that it is desirable and feasible to split almost all significant headquarters departments between posts and telecommunications.'[94] Only a few

* It is striking that German, in his contretemps with Benn a year earlier, had taken a similar line in response to Benn's evolving ideas about reorganization: 'If such a split of the organisation is to be contemplated [i.e. dividing posts from telecommunications in the field] then I hold strongly to the view that it should be complete . . . Neither can I accept that it will be a satisfactory permanent solution to split the Posts and Telecoms functions on the one hand, and, on the other, to try to continue to serve them with the same common service departments' (German to Benn, 16 November 1965, Post 122/12107). But since German had gone on to oppose any meddling with those same service departments, his 'all-or-nothing' stance had been swept aside by Benn as a pretext for taking no action at all.

residual functions like the Legal Department and Public Relations would continue to be shared at the centre. In effect, the postal and telecommunications services would have their own 'support activities' and be free at last to go their own way. A final report, 'Organizing for Corporation Status', was handed over in March 1967.

Yet the opportunity was lost. Over the thirty months that elapsed between March 1967 and 'Vesting Day' for the Post Office Corporation – the date on which it was legally inaugurated, 1 October 1969 – the Semi-Split was badly diluted just as the Regional Directors had feared might happen. Enormous effort went into reshaping the regional offices after October 1967. Two separate businesses were at last established, each under its own Regional Director. Many long-standing managerial anomalies – such as the requirement that Head Postmasters and Telephone Managers should share the responsibility for telephonists in their local area – were resolved. At the centre, however, the process stalled. The two DDGs were retitled in March 1967 as the Managing Directors for Posts and for Telecommunications – and that was that. Alas, the White Paper that same month effectively ducked the issue. The Paper talked about the need to manage posts and telecoms entirely separately, with a structure that 'should provide for this at all levels – national, regional and local'; but it hedged its commitment to this goal by noting in the previous paragraph that posts and telecoms were complementary and interdependent businesses, so that there were 'real advantages in the continued overall direction of their affairs by a single body'.[95] The traditional fiefdoms of finance, personnel, engineering and procurement duly remained in place. The Government produced a booklet in August 1967 entitled *The Post Office: Preparing for Corporation Status*, which was a highly selective rehash of McKinsey's work. The coming change of status, it said, represented 'a uniquely suitable opportunity to do what is necessary'. By then, however, McKinsey's services had been dispensed with; and much they had deemed necessary was in the event left undone. The shift towards seeing the Post Office as a business was stymied. Detailed plans for the division of Headquarters were set aside.[96] The postal service that was left to emerge as an integrated part of a public corporation in 1969 was still to be essentially run like a department of the civil service, rather than the commercial business that to some had looked attainable by 1967.

Why did this happen? Three explanations stand out. In the first place, too many of the senior officials at St Martin's – especially those in service functions like finance, engineering and personnel whose status would inevitably have been downgraded in any wholehearted adoption of the Split – vindicated some of Benn's less flattering observations of the past by circling the wagons round Headquarters. There were fine civil service traditions to be preserved, and career-long relationships too. There was much talk about upholding the morale of the Office, which scarcely disguised an atavistic aversion to change. At their November 1966 conference, the Regional Directors had openly acknowledged their own fears on this score. As the note of their discussions recorded, they 'were much concerned at what seemed to be an unhealthy resistance to change in, and departure from, [Headquarters] doctrine on the part of those responsible for it'.[97] Wolstencroft and his Director of Postal Services, George Downes, were openly opposed to McKinsey's prescription for the central services. As for the division of the regions into two businesses, Wolstencroft wrote to Ryland in November 1966 that he thought it 'inevitable that a split of our regions will have to be done piecemeal over a period of years, although no doubt we should make as good progress as we can before vesting day'.[98] He also appears to have grown increasingly uncomfortable over the early months of 1967 with the challenge posed for the centre by McKinsey's efficiency initiatives at a local level. The cost-saving studies had eventually led to a programme known as Ripple, which was intended to replicate the gains made in London at Head Post Offices across the country. This plan was running into some concerted opposition from the UPW – which nominated a fiery new General Secretary, Tom Jackson, in February – and there were calls for urgent help to be provided from the centre.[99] It is hard to avoid the conclusion that, faced with doubts at the centre and protests in the field, the new Director General and those around him lost courage. Wolstencroft, long since opposed to retaining McKinsey, made light of Morrison's final report on organizational priorities when it landed in March.[100] Within a couple of months he had persuaded Wall that the firm was surplus to requirements, and the two of them thereafter blocked McKinsey's attempts to hold further meetings with the Postmaster General. When Morrison offered a few thoughts for Short on an early draft of the Government's August booklet, Wall forwarded them along with 'a draft notional reply' that was petulant in the context of what the firm had done for the Post Office since 1965. 'I call it notional', he told the PMG, 'since we all feel that further correspondence with McKinsey on these questions would be undesirable. We are under no obligation to defend our decisions to our consultants!'[101]

The sudden anti-climactic outcome to the 1965–7 years must also be ascribed, secondly, to a failure of political leadership. Short had been quite prepared to renew McKinsey's mandate in the summer of 1966 when he was feeling insecure about his new ministerial brief. But he saw the Post Office simply in terms of the political problem posed for him by the Break. Once this policy had been broadly accepted at Westminster, by the middle of 1967, Short had little interest in delving any deeper into its implications. His attitude, not Benn's, was the more accurate reflection of the political establishment's general view of the Post Office: when it came to assessing the potential of an organization with such a long past, there was a collective failure of imagination. This did not apply to McKinsey's consultants, with their international background. (One of them, Michael Allen, went on to become head of strategy for the giant General Electric in the US through most of the 1970s.) But Short never formed the slightest rapport with Morrison and his colleagues, and was content to see the back of them when told by his officials that their job was done. He then remained as PMG until April 1968. His successor, Roy Mason, lasted only three months. Neither had any interest in fostering a new spirit of commercial enterprise at the Post Office. As for the very last Postmaster General – the ineffable John Stonehouse from July 1968 – he also had other priorities, which included, as we now know, a unique responsibility for intelligence matters. Stonehouse was of course far from being the only Postmaster General to engage in espionage activities, but we can be fairly certain he was the only one to do so for the other side. He had been recruited by the Czech secret service in the late 1950s.* This apart, he had his hands full with the management of the Post Office Bill on the one hand and the daily business of St Martin's on the other. Scarcely three months after his appointment as PMG in July, John Wall brought an end to an

---

* A Czech defector gave him away to US intelligence officers in 1969, but the case against him was flimsy and Stonehouse managed to assert his innocence, remaining in Wilson's government until its fall in 1970. Only ten years later, in 1980, was hard evidence of his past supplied by a second Czech defector. The Thatcher government decided against prosecuting him, since the new evidence could not be used in court, but it was confirmed a quarter of a century later, and long after Stonehouse's death in 1988, when the freshly opened files of the Czech service in Prague showed that he had dealt with it for many years under the code-name 'KOLON'. (Soviet intelligence apparently often preferred using the Czech service rather than the KGB to approach British politicians and trade unionists.) 'Had that information [disclosed in 1980] been available in 1969, Wilson would have been faced with an intelligence scandal worse than the Profumo affair.' (Christopher Andrew, *The Defence of the Realm: The Authorized History of MI5*, 2009, pp. 541 and 707–8.)

uncomfortable couple of years at the helm (as 'Deputy Chairman' of the Board) and headed back to the private sector as Chairman of the computer company ICL. It was announced in November 1968 that Stonehouse had decided to take on the combined roles of chairman and chief executive of the putative Corporation's Board, pending the appointment of a permanent chairman. In his new role, Stonehouse was actually very effective at steering the Bill to a successful conclusion in Parliament – but he gave little or no thought to McKinsey's prescriptions for the postal service. 'A new age has begun this year for Britain's Post Office', was his proud claim in the Foreword to a short book, published in September 1969 to help celebrate its rebirth as a public corporation.[102] In truth, the legal repositioning of the Post Office would turn out to be more a matter of form than substance.

Meanwhile, there had been one other issue on Stonehouse's agenda. In the very last years of its long existence as a government department, the Post Office contrived an episode that exemplified to perfection its professional expertise on the one hand and a disarming commercial ineptitude on the other. This was its launch of a two-tier post, introducing 1st and 2nd class mails for all letters. The outcome directly set back any progress on a more fundamental reorganization of the postal service, for the simple reason that it necessitated major changes of its own that cut clean across the work on McKinsey's productivity schemes. In dealing a heavy blow to the self-confidence of the Post Office at a crucial point, it also made a stronger impression on most postal workers than anything else that happened in the run-up to the 1969 change of status.

5. THE LAUNCH OF THE TWO-TIER POST

For decades past, there had existed two streams of post. Ever since being confronted with the rapid volume growth of the early 1920s – and the growing opposition of the UPW to the use of auxiliaries – the Post Office had begun discreetly prioritizing the mails each evening and dealing first with the fully paid letters. Printed papers and samples, both carrying the lowest postage rates and typically about 40 per cent of the total, were identified as a second stream to be dealt with at the end of the evening, or even 'deferred' – that is, set aside for sorting the next day. Given the public's seemingly incorrigible determination always to post about 80 per cent of each day's mail in the late afternoon or early evening, there was little choice but to adopt this approach. A blanket delivery of all items the next day ('Day B' in the postal jargon) would have seriously exacerbated the problems over using part-timers – an option effectively ruled out by the unions – or would have entailed an absurdly bloated permanent workforce. So substantial numbers of printed papers were deferred and landed on the doorstep two days after posting – on Day C. This de facto arrangement had largely replaced the dependence on auxiliaries since the late 1930s and had met little or no resistance from the public for forty years.

By the mid-1960s, postal volumes were almost twice those of 1922. The strain on the service had been growing steadily more acute for years. Around 60 per cent of each day's mail comprised fully paid letters, sent on the assumption of next-day delivery. (This was still a letter service, we might note in passing, unparalleled among the world's postal services for its speed and reliability.) Many sorting offices were now stretched to the limit, even after the deferral of *all* printed papers and the like. The question this posed was urgent: how could more capacity be built into the system on profitable terms? Had the Post Office been a commercial enterprise, it is not hard to imagine how it might have responded – a quota of fully paid letters would have been quietly added to the deferred post. As and when the consequent (marginal) decline in average delivery times led to demands in the marketplace for a more assured next-day delivery, it would have proposed a greater price differential across the postbag and charged substantially more for the fully paid letter – or sufficiently more, anyway, to finance faster sorting systems.

The Post Office had already asked itself the same question – how to build in more capacity? – several times: annual conferences had been addressed on the topic, and no fewer than five committees had pondered it, the most recent of them sitting in 1957–8 and 1964. Neither a surreptitious use of additional deferred sorting nor demand-led pricing was seen as properly admissible for a government department, so all five committees had come up with variants of another, rather different answer.[103] It would consist of launching a cheaper service for a sizeable proportion of the hitherto fully paid letters, which would be transparently deferred for Day C delivery. This had an appealing logic. If speed of delivery was what the customer valued – as surveys confirmed – surely a choice of speeds at different prices would be a happy embellishment of the postal service? Crucially, it would enable the Post Office to iron out the more egregious peaks and troughs in the daily workload, a rich prize by any calculation. But a 'two-tier' post, as it was christened, would offer the public a proposition that few businessmen would ever have contemplated: namely, a cut-price product none too easily distinguishable from the top-of-the-range version. Launching the two of them in parallel would have posed a scary challenge for the Post Office's marketing department – if it had had one.

In its absence, the Post Office had focused almost exclusively since the late 1950s on the operational aspects of the two-tier post, which were themselves more than a little disconcerting (and all of which needed to be considered against the background of the Department's ambitions for a more mechanized future too). All sorts of overdue improvements could be made to the structure of the mails. The complex system of postal tariffs built up through the nineteenth century could be simplified as two streams, fast and slow.* But nothing could be done to escape the central conundrum: no one could be certain how the general public would respond to being given an explicit choice between fast and slow posts at different prices. If they stuck with the dearer service out of distrust for the newer alternative, the burden of next-day deliveries would be no lighter. It might even grow much heavier, as items previously deferred at the Post Office's discretion found their way into the fast post. Conversely, if the public turned overwhelmingly to the cheaper service, the resulting shortfall in revenues might pose a threat to the stability of the whole postal system. By the mid-sixties, there was a growing consensus among officials that some radical step would need to be taken, if the staffing and financial pressures on the Post Office were to be relieved. But the more they discussed the concept of the two-tier post, the more daunted they felt by two inescapable conclusions: it would involve a reshaping of the basic postal service more fundamental than anything attempted since the days of Rowland Hill; and just like Hill's Penny Post, it would be a leap in the dark.

It was only a matter of time before the idea occurred to Tony Benn. In October 1965, he summoned to his office the Director of the Postal

* The five main categories of the post comprised fully paid letters (from 1840), printed papers (from 1848), samples (from 1863), newspapers (from 1870) and postcards (also from 1870). In 1965, a total postal traffic of approximately 11,000 million items consisted of 6,200 million letters, 4,000 million printed papers, which included many newspapers, 400 million samples and equivalent items, 100 million 'other' newspapers and 300 million postcards. Of the printed papers, about 1,600 million were deferred. The letter post made a net profit of about £17m. The other postal categories lost money, to the tune of about £5m on printed papers and samples, and £1m each on postcards and on other newspapers.

Service, George Downes, and put the idea of a two-speed mail to him 'as a serious and immediate possibility'.[104] The Director then responded with well-practised deliberation ('Downes was much struck by this and said he would think about it'). In fact there had already been lengthy debates about the idea at the Postal Controllers' Conference in May and the Regional Directors' Conference in June.[105] In their wake, German and his colleagues had been left still agonizing over what might represent the optimal combination of higher postal tariffs, a two-speed mail and curtailed delivery schedules – the latter now being widely aired as a package labelled 'a feasible service'. Benn cut through all this over the next couple of months with his usual zeal. He chaired a Board-level seminar in Birmingham that December ('I can see a very, very great deal in this', as the minutes had him saying) and by February 1966 he had produced his own detailed two-tier scheme. Unless it was adopted, he warned officials, he was not prepared to sanction any further increase in postal tariffs. This was a potent ultimatum: latest forecasts suggested that, without higher tariffs, a modest profit on the postal services in 1966–7 was going to give way to a sizeable loss the following year. By the time the Postal Controllers were together again for their 1966 Annual Conference, it was said that Benn was preparing to announce the reform as early as July.

But the whirlwind had passed on by then, and for some months thereafter the exact intentions of the next Postmaster General were unclear. So Benn's departure was the cue for another long and impassioned debate. Even leaving aside the dangers of an unforeseen shift in traffic patterns, there were several bones of contention. How would returned cheap-rate letters be handled (since they could hardly be destroyed, as by custom were most of the deferred printed papers that came back)? Again, how would fast and slow letters be segregated, and how far would this basic task nullify hopes of cutting back on peak-period staffing? The Regional Directors were so anxious about the prospects that they sent a joint letter to Alan Wolstencroft in February 1967. It warned him that 'there are such grave operational risks and financial uncertainties associated with a move into two-tier as must make its introduction a very hazardous and risky operation'.[106] The Managing Director of Posts (as he was about to become) weighed these words carefully. Wolstencroft had chaired the 1957–8 inquiry into two-tier posts and was not the man to belittle any of the technical problems.[107] Together with Downes, he led a painstaking review of all the preparations, involving teams of people all across the organization. (It was this effort, and the realization that duty patterns were going to have to be changed significantly after September 1968, that sidelined much of McKinsey's work.)[108]

The response in many ways showed the Post Office at its best. Prospective traffic flows were comprehensively analysed; new sorting procedures and staffing requirements were resolved down to the finest detail; operational amendments were endlessly discussed and incorporated as appropriate. (It was agreed, for example, that the slow-stream post would be redefined as 'deferr*able*' instead of 'deferred' – the critical difference being that local offices would be empowered in many instances to defer or not, at their own discretion.) All this homework left a few hostile voices unconvinced: one was that former scourge of indecisiveness in the mechanization arena, Dennis Wesil – now the Regional Postal Director for the North-East – who stuck to the position he had set out in an eloquent paper on the two-tier post for his peers in March 1967: 'I am in no doubt that we should be against its introduction. ... There may be something in two-tier politically, although I doubt whether there is much, but commercially, there is everything against it. Must we wait until corporation status before we can act commercially and sensibly?'[109] This was seen as a rather intemperate attack. A public commitment to the plan was made in September 1967, and over the next twelve months, until its inauguration in September 1968, most of the internal critics were won round.

Only in the final few months of this whole process – which stretched back, in effect, to 1958 – did the Post Office give any thought to active marketing of its bold new proposition. 'Marketing' was mostly construed as a listening activity. This was congenial enough, since occasional surveys of public opinion were generally favourable to the principle of a two-tier post; there was also a chorus of support from the PO Users' Council, the Select Committee on Nationalised Industries and the Prices and Incomes Board. But any real analysis of the customer's perception of the mooted changes went no further than a perusal of all the ticks in those crude pollsters' categories ('fairly good', 'good', 'very good'), and as an explanatory activity marketing hardly existed. This was especially unfortunate, given three decisions that were to have a calamitous impact on the public's actual reaction. The blame for these can be shared out quite equitably. The politicians, from Benn onwards, obliged the Post Office to combine the launch with a hike in the cost of postage: the 4d stamp for fully paid letters was to be replaced by a 5d stamp for next-day delivery and 4d for the slower service. Then there was the little matter of labelling the new approach. Wolstencroft and his colleagues considered all the possible names for the two future postal streams, ignored earlier recommendations that they be called 'Ordinary' and 'Deferred' and plumped for the terms most explicitly derided by the Regional Directors, and by quite a few officials within Headquarters too: 1st and 2nd class.[110] Thirdly, the UPW stood firm against any suggestion that 2nd class letters to local addresses should wherever possible be given next-day delivery. The unions were sceptical throughout 1965–8 that the benefits of the two-tier idea would outweigh the risks. But if there were to be new rules, with some promised attendance benefits, those rules could not be bent.[111]

As the launch date approached, the full enormity of the risks was increasingly apparent to those responsible for publicity and advertising, and some fierce squabbles broke out. The agency that had advised the Post Office since 1954, Charles Higham, tried early in 1968 to persuade its client that the price changes would need to be prominently flagged. This was blocked by John Wall, in favour of a low-key campaign fronted by posters bearing cheery letters from the Post Office signed off 'Yours faithfully'. A creative agency sub-contracted by Charles Higham took their own line: they suggested putting the new postage rates at the centre of the campaign and they provided some more colourful copy (if that is a fair description of slogans such as 'Don't spend a penny unless you have to'). When they were fired, they leaked their views on the Charles Higham campaign to *The Times* ('a complete waste of the public's money') and went public about the mounting disarray within St Martin's. Having arrived at the Post Office only on 1 July, Stonehouse found himself presiding over a desperate scramble to regain the initiative. The press coverage was unhelpful. 'The Post Office constantly denies that there will be any deliberate delay of 4d. letters,' carped the *Daily Mail*. 'But this is not the way the postmen see it. A sorter at Mount Pleasant said: "You can take it as definite that 4d. letters will be delayed all down the line".'[112] The admen from Charles Higham turned up at a crisis meeting early in September, bearing ominous news. Polls suggested that reactions to the campaign had been 'very unfavourable'.

When the day finally arrived for the inauguration of the two-tier post, torrential rains swept the south and east of England, flooding many roads and seriously delaying the mails. But this was nothing as compared with the deluge of criticism that fell upon the Post Office. The launch proved a PR disaster. It was widely seen as a ruse, foisting higher postal charges on the public for a bogus upgrade of the system. The next-day delivery service was no different from before, but cost a penny more. Given its 1st class tag, any letter with a 5d. stamp *not* receiving a next-day delivery (about ten per cent of the total) was now liable to attract bitter complaints. News of awkward anomalies in the 2nd class post soon surfaced even more damagingly. A 4d stamp in August had taken a letter overnight from Land's End to John O'Groats! Now it meant a letter from Upper Piddlington at one end of the road could take two, perhaps even three, days to reach Lower Piddlington at the other. At Stone in Staffordshire – where the Post Office happened to have its largest staff-training college – a postman told a reporter from *The Times* that letters posted locally for delivery within the village were being sent for sorting in Stafford, eight miles away. This, he thoughtfully added, was 'really a safety valve to make sure four-penny mail does not get five-penny treatment'. In the High Street in Yeovil, a hawk-eyed local alderman spotted a hapless postman sorting through the collection from a pillar box – and then putting all the letters with a 4d stamp back into the box. Reported by the *Western Daily Press*, it became a national story the next day. After a truly wretched week for the Post Office, a Gallup Poll in the *Daily Telegraph* reported a thumbs-down for the new service from 80 per cent of its interviewees. Of those asked about their future use of the 1st class post, fewer than 10 per cent said they intended to use it for all or most of their correspondence.

In fact, once the new service had settled into place, the proportion of the total post sent via 1st class turned out to be around a third, which was almost exactly as the Post Office had ended up predicting. Wolsten-croft and his officials had correctly forecast the traffic outcome, in broad terms, and the elaborate staffing rearrangements they had made for it quickly proved their worth. This, though, was rather less than half the story. The Post Office had once again shown an unfortunate propensity for getting the numbers right while missing the bigger picture (just as had happened in 1840). Once the public post-mortem on the two-tier post began, there was little interest in hearing about its positive aspects. The first debate in Parliament over the episode was scheduled in the Lords for mid-October. Draft notes prepared for the Post Office's spokes-man, Lord Bowles, described two-tier as 'the biggest change in postal working for over a hundred years'. His Lordship scrubbed the reference, which he told officials 'will only provoke laughter in the House . . .'[113] A fortnight later came the Commons debate on the Queen's Speech – looking forward, inter alia, to the passage of the Post Office Bill. This gave Tory MPs a handy opportunity to demand that the Postmaster

General make it his priority 'to rebuild the shattered reputation of the Post Office...' So sustained had been the outcry over the September launch that the Opposition chose to make the two-tier post the subject of an all-day debate on 4 November. Stonehouse was duly pilloried for 'a classic example of incompetence and of bungling'. He did his best to explain the rationale behind the innovation; but it was hardly possible to defend the way it had been introduced, given the casualty rate among those responsible. The Charles Higham agency had been summarily sacked. John Wall had left on 27 September. The future of Wolstencroft was the subject of intense speculation at Headquarters – not least because he had elected to go on holiday just prior to the launch. Nor had Stonehouse himself emerged with much credit, though he had only inherited the plans at a very late stage. His efforts to distance himself from the debacle dismayed his senior officials, for many of whom the seemingly universal condemnation of the two-tier post – after all their careful preparations – had been traumatic. Very few emerged with their reputations enhanced.

But one man did. After Stonehouse had promised the Commons that a full internal review of the 'New Inland Letter Service' would be completed and published within six months, there was an obvious candidate to chair it: Dennis Wesil. The North-East Director, whose 1967 critique of the reform now looked wise indeed, made a thorough job of it. His paper, published on time in April 1969, offered a comprehensive survey of the current state of the mails. By making clear the substantial gains already evident from the use of two postal streams, and pointing to the realistic prospect of bigger gains to come, Wesil sounded a welcome note of optimism and put the misadventures of 1968 into a saner perspective. As he usefully reminded the world:

> Internal planning was thorough and very largely successful – only someone well acquainted with the scope and complexities of the postal system can appreciate how great the hazards and possibilities of disaster were, in moving the whole of the country's letter services into such unknown territory.

Nevertheless, acknowledgement had to be made of the public's extraordinary hostility towards the launch. Wesil blamed it on a serious misunderstanding of the background – but he was forthright in identifying the ultimate responsibility:

> The reasons for this turn of events are, I think, essentially to be found, not in the nature of the new services, or in the way they are performed, but in

a failure by the Post Office to act with sufficient insight into customer needs and responses and in inadequate attention to the customer relations side of the exercise when preparations for the change were being made. . . . More consideration and greater awareness of potential . . . customers' reactions might have led to a better appreciation of possible risks and so to a different and perhaps more successful strategy. . . . In business terms, the introduction of the new service could be described as a major marketing operation carried out with inadequate marketing skill and preparation. What is required in modern conditions is for the postal service to become market orientated and rather less process orientated.[114]

It would have been easy for the fastidious Wesil to say '*more* market orientated' in that last sentence, but he did not. He was aware of the fact that – notwithstanding all the effort expended by Tony Benn, McKinsey and thousands of its own hard-pressed staff and officials – the Post Office had as yet scarcely begun its metamorphosis into a commercial business. Wesil's report was endlessly dissected at postal conferences over the summer. There was general agreement that it offered a shrewd summary of the problems being bequeathed to the new Post Office Corporation in October. By the summer, though, the future Corporation had already begun to store up new problems of its own.

11

A dismal decade,
1969–79

The sky is white as clay, with no sun.
Work has to be done.
Postmen like doctors go from house to house.

Philip Larkin, Aubade (1977)

1. THE CHAIRMAN WHO NEVER WAS

A mischievous whisper went round Whitehall in the summer of 1969. It was well known along the corridors that finding an outsider to be the first chairman of the reconstituted Post Office had been a protracted affair. When in May an industrialist called Hall had been mentioned to the Postmaster General by Harold Wilson, or so it was said, there had been a disastrous mix-up between two men of that name – and Stonehouse had gone off and hired the wrong one. (Could Wilson conceivably have been referring to Sir Arnold Hall, a distinguished company chairman in the aerospace industry who had begun accepting board positions in the City in 1965 and would later serve on the boards of Rolls-Royce and ICI?) Whatever the truth, it was an appointment that certainly came as a big surprise, not least in Whitehall. Responding to the initial proposal two months earlier, the head of the Home Civil Service, Sir William Armstrong, had written to Stonehouse to pass on a vigorous thumbs-down from a City grandee who knew the Minister's candidate well. ('Don't give it another thought – nice fellow, but a lightweight – could not run anything'.[1]) Beyond Whitehall, many had hoped to see a chairman who might rank in stature with some of the impressive individuals running other public corporations – men like Lord Robens at the National Coal Board, or Lord Melchett at the British Steel Corporation, founded just a couple of years earlier. (Ron Smith had left the Post Office and the UPW late in 1966 to become Melchett's first

Director of Personnel and Social Policy.) Some press commentators had fancied the job might go to Lord Beeching, late of British Rail. Instead, Stonehouse had plucked from obscurity the son of a Welsh Labour Party stalwart, George Hall, who had served in the wartime coalition and been rewarded with an hereditary peerage by Attlee in 1946. Leonard Hall had inherited his father's title, Viscount Hall of Cynon Valley, in 1965 but had yet to make his own mark in public life. He was a 56-year-old businessman, currently employed by one of the World Bank's subsidiaries and running investment portfolios in Africa, Asia and the Middle East.*

The tale of mistaken identities was an especially juicy rumour because it seemed, for a few weeks, all too plausible. Announced as Chairman in May, Hall readily confessed to the media that he knew nothing whatever about the Post Office. His professional background was medicine: he was a qualified GP and had been a surgeon with the Royal Naval Volunteer Reserve in the war. Apart from having had an uncle who served as a postman for thirty years, as *The Times* dryly noted, '[Hall] is basically a complete stranger in his new field'.[2] Stonehouse introduced him at a press reception as 'an outstanding team leader', though it was not clear what, if anything, he had ever led in the past. For many, the appointment confirmed the doubts they had long harboured about the Postmaster General. (Ministers in those days made no use of headhunters.) Bemusement turned to disbelief within the Post Office in July, when a City tax accountant, Geoffrey Vieler, was announced as the new head of the postal service. It was rumoured that Vieler should have been offered the job of Finance Director and had been invited to become Managing Director by mistake. The appointment was made personally by Hall, and the fact that Vieler was thought to have worked in the past as the Chairman's own tax adviser did not improve matters. Alan Wolstencroft, whom Vieler replaced, had for years been seen as a future head of the Posts: a dry and scholarly Mancunian with a Double First from Cambridge, he had been one of the Department's youngest ever directors. But Wolstencroft, not helped by his ill-timed holiday, had

---

* There was certainly a mix-up over his family lineage. The first Lord Hall's political career had culminated in five years as First Lord of the Admiralty, from 1946 to 1951. This prompted a widespread belief that Leonard Hall was related to Admiral Sir Reginald ('Blinker') Hall, Britain's Director of Naval Intelligence through the First World War. George Hall was working at the coalface down a pit in South Wales in the 1890s while Blinker Hall was rising through the ranks at sea. Whether either one of the admiral's two sons was included on the Stonehouse shortlist in 1969 has gone unrecorded.

been made the scapegoat for the mishaps of the two-tier post's launch and was appointed 'Special Adviser to the Chairman'. For the senior officials at St Martin's, the new appointments must have seemed grotesquely inappropriate. The reverberations had hardly settled by the time that Vesting Day came round, on 1 October. An advertisement in *The Times* that day carried a slightly quirky message from the new Chairman. ('The Post Office is big. It is getting bigger every year. . . . There is room for everyone worth his salt.')[3] Hall then showed his inexperience with some inaugural interviews that cannot have endeared him to his future colleagues. 'Letters are on the way out', he told one journalist, blithely disregarding his new status as head of an organization handling 40 million letters every working day. Then he took a swipe at the Post Office – just a few days into his job there – for having 'its tail . . . embedded in the treacle of tradition'.[4]

The last time the Post Office had been relaunched with a fresh constitution, it had been handed over to two chancers who scarcely lasted a couple of years. If Hall and Vieler were to serve longer than their Restoration forebears Wildman and Bishop, they were going to need the support of a strong-minded and loyally supportive Board. Alas, the line-up of members approved by Stonehouse failed dismally on both counts. The new Corporation's first Board was a disaster. It included three other outsiders. Whitney Straight, a Deputy Chairman of Rolls-Royce, was an American with a dashing past – he had been a pre-war racing car champion and a wartime fighter pilot – but he seemed loath to engage with any serious Board discussion at all. Stonehouse had originally offered him the chairmanship, which Straight had declined because of the pressure of his other commitments while agreeing to a half-time role as Deputy Chairman.[5] Equally reluctant to commit himself over any strategic decisions was Tony Ashton, a mild-mannered former Finance Director of Esso Petroleum. The third arrival from the business world was a tougher character by far: Ned Fennessy was a feisty, no-nonsense engineer of great distinction – his pioneering work on radar defences had been critical to the defeat of Hitler's Luftwaffe – and he came to the Post Office straight from chairing the telecoms research arm of Plessey Electronics. But as the new Managing Director of Telecoms, Fennessy had taken on a business that had been run since 1961 by just one, increasingly dominant individual. This was Bill Ryland, the man whose rise through the Post Office hierarchy in the late 1950s had chimed with the adoption of a less conciliatory stand towards the unions. Ryland was not a man to let go of executive power lightly, and had released the telecoms reins only in exchange for being appointed to the new position of Post Office Chief Executive (and Joint Deputy Chairman with Whitney Straight). In any tussle for power in the boardroom, there was never much doubt that Fennessy's loyalties would go to Ryland, not Hall. The same applied to the two other engineers on the Board, F. J. M. Laver and J. H. H. (Jim) Merriman, both of whom had joined the Post Office in 1935–6. As for the remaining director, in charge of Personnel – how poor Dick (now Sir Richard) Hayward would juggle his loyalties, after a lifetime serving the UPW and the Staff Side of the National Whitley Council, was anyone's guess.

Taking the Post Office out of the civil service was one thing; taking the civil service out of the Post Office would be quite another. Ministers had talked confidently about the rejuvenating virtues of a change of status. If turning it into a public corporation was really to mark a historic milestone, however, all would depend on robust leadership from the top. The terms of the 1969 Act in themselves imposed only modest alterations to the structure of the Post Office. There was now a corporate headquarters – at 23 Howland Street, W1 – some distance away from the hallowed turf around St Martin's-le-Grand. In place of a Postmaster General there was a Chairman answerable, in ways that were none too clear, to a Minister of Posts and Telecommunications set in a fledgling ministry on the South Bank next to Waterloo Bridge. Some responsibilities were hived off to other Whitehall departments, notably the Post Office's erstwhile role as the licensing authority for the broadcasting industry, and the Post Office Savings Bank, which were taken aboard by the Home Office and the Exchequer respectively. But it was left to those in charge, building on all the internal reforms since 1964, to determine how far they could reform the culture of the place. The question in 1969 was how far might Hall the former surgeon yet surprise his critics and take a knife to the old Department.

His task was made no easier by the rapid discovery that his postal Managing Director was a less than ruthless cost-cutter. Sent around the Regional Directors in September 1969 to set out the priorities for immediate spending reductions, Vieler returned to pass on to the Board a message from the RDs 'that they saw little scope in practice for improvements beyond those planned earlier ... and that a substantial improvement in productivity was difficult to achieve when so much of the work (of collection and delivery) was not suitable for detailed control'. Vieler's credentials for suggesting otherwise may not have been strengthened by a report, instantly disseminated by incredulous officials at Headquarters, that he had approved a supply contract for a million pounds' worth of elastic bands. Hall invited him to go back and remind the RDs of 'the possibilities that seemed to exist by improving management and [of] the guidance given to them by the Chairman, that . . . they were expected to take the initiative to the Staff sides in proposing modifications to suit local circumstances'.⁶ The cigar-chomping Chairman made a slightly more forceful impression on his hosts, as he toured the regions himself over the next few months, with a glamorous American wife at his side and few expenses spared. He asked plenty of questions – some of them admittedly a little eccentric (Why could large offices not exist as profit centres?) but others sensible enough and an echo of issues raised by McKinsey after its first acquaintance with the Post Office five years earlier. Why were there so few management accountants, or indeed accountants of any feather? Why were there no proper marketing activities? Why was all decision-making so heavily centralized? One outcome was a decision to try prising open the Post Office to more external influence. Hall instigated the formation of Regional Boards, starting in the North-West, Scotland and North-East regions, which local businessmen and public-sector figures were to be invited to join. A parallel innovation at the centre saw the formation of a think-tank, whose members included the novelist and mandarin C. P. Snow and the Tory politician and bisexual roué Robert Boothby – a shockingly quixotic innovation by the standards of St Martin's.

Many of the Board papers from 1970 suggest a period of thoughtful and energetic stock-taking, consistent with the notion of a fresh start intended by the 1969 Act. A Special Board was convened on the first anniversary of the Corporation's existence. The minutes looked back on 'a vast amount of work' and set down a careful review of umpteen reform possibilities for the year to come.⁷ But the formal papers tell much less than half the story. They were still being prepared, after all, by officials whose fine drafting skills could make a silk purse out of any rambling pig's ear of a meeting. When Hall wanted to argue for a more confrontational stance towards the Government, for example, the case against Whitehall for taking an improper interest in postal matters was set out with an eloquent pen by Maurice Tinniswood, now the Secretary to the Board. A candid paper, circulated in March 1970, identified 'signs that the Government is using its influence in a way that goes beyond Parliament's intention', notably to interfere on tariff rates and staff pay.⁸ 'If this analysis is accepted', Tinniswood boldly concluded, 'the position must be challenged and attitudes changed before they become accepted as the new pattern . . .'* The challenge that Hall actually posed to the status quo seems in reality to have been more pedestrian, not to say embarrassingly clumsy. He found it difficult to sustain a coherent line in any of the many complex discussions that filled the Board's agenda, and neither he nor Vieler managed to win the intellectual respect of the senior officials. Without it, their chances of pulling off a palace revolution (where even Tony Benn had struggled) were soon scuppered. They spoke and behaved like interlopers.

Worse, Hall flaunted his private wealth in front of junior staff and appalled colleagues with oddball observations on routine matters. Suddenly the old jokes about his appointment did not seem quite so funny. Red carpets were demanded for regional visits, and official cars had to be laid on in duplicate (in case one broke down). The senior men of the Post Office began to whisper their dissent. After Hall had insisted on his wife accompanying him, complaints must have circulated in high places, for they prompted a discussion at the Board in February 1970. It was minuted, rather absurdly, 'that it was in the interests of the Post Office that . . . he should be accompanied by Lady Hall as this would enable more attention to be given to welfare, catering and matters relating to female staff than would otherwise be the case'.[9] When Hall licensed two young private assistants in his personal office to roam the organization, challenging their superiors on existing policies wherever they thought appropriate, it was deeply resented. This, after all, was an established hierarchy where the unwritten rules about who could write to whom were still perfectly clear. The first report submitted by C. P. Snow's think-tank drew howls of complaint from directors.[10] As for various grandly titled reports commissioned by the Chairman and presented by his Managing Director of Posts, such as 'The Long Term Size, Shape and Scope of Postal Services', these were received as hopelessly innocent.[11] No one could fairly doubt the effort expended by Hall and Vieler; but it was construed as a rush to draw ill-informed conclusions where the wiser grey-beards of the old Department feared to tread, knowing better how infinitely complex was the running of the mails.

Above all, there was embarrassment over Hall's handling of relations with the Government. The financial case for an increase in postal rates

---

* Perhaps he felt free to speak his mind, since he knew by this date that he would be leaving the Post Office, to become the Director of Personnel at the BBC. Candidates with Post Office experience seem to have enjoyed a special cachet with other organizations when it came to appointing personnel directors.

during Hall's first year was compelling. The new Board inherited a postal service heading for an even bigger deficit than the £19.6m recorded in 1964–5 that had prompted Benn to raise the basic letter rate from 3d to 4d. Postal rates had lagged behind inflation for years: at 5d compared with 2½d in 1950, the price of a 1st class stamp had risen 100 per cent, where the prices of most other daily staples had risen far more steeply.[12] Adjusted for inflation, the real cost of posting a half-ounce letter had never been lower (and was substantially below the relative cost of the penny post in the nineteenth century – see Appendix A, Chart 9). It was plain by May 1970 that significant losses had been made in the Corporation's first six months to March. (The detailed accounts, published six months later, would report a £15.4m deficit on the postal services.) What was also plain to anyone with a sliver of political nous, was that with a general election in the offing Stonehouse had no prospect of gaining the Cabinet's approval for higher postal rates. If an increase in rates were to prompt an outcry from the public, it was the Government that would pay the price. Whatever the small print of the 1969 Act, the Post Office was now a nationalized industry and its pricing policies, like those of the state-owned utilities, were going to have to be determined via a delicate compromise between commercial and political realities. Hall disregarded all this and naïvely put his trust in the legal niceties of the Post Office's independence. The result was a nine-month-long battle of wills between the Chairman and his Minister. Hall proposed that 1st class stamps should rise from 5d to 7d and 2nd class from 4d to 6d. The imminent launch of the decimal coinage, in February 1971, would turn 7d into 3 new pence and 6d into 2½ new pence, so at least four new sets of stamps were required. Stonehouse and his Permanent Secretary, a supremely urbane Frank Wood, endlessly prevaricated while Hall and his Board sent over a stream of letters that culminated in May 1970 with a virtual ultimatum. Orders were going to be placed with the stamp printers, in anticipation of an announcement of higher rates after the June election.[13] The career officials of St Martin's had never seen anything like it.

Of all those who watched and anguished, we can be sure that none felt more aggrieved than Bill Ryland. Though appointed Chief Executive at the outset, it was Hall's job that Ryland really wanted – and he very soon set out to get it. Having joined the Post Office in 1933 – his father was a telephone manager and he himself had begun his career as a 'cord boy', replenishing the worn cords behind the connecting plugs on telephone switchboards – Ryland had worked his way up the ladder rung by rung, and seemed never to have forgotten anything he had learned along the way. Known as Elephant Bill in deference to his memory as much as his huge physical presence, he had an encyclopedic knowledge of the workings of the Post Office. His command of detail no less than his often brusque manner thoroughly intimidated most of those around him and left Ryland easily the dominant personality in the boardroom by 1970 – a legacy he was not prepared to compromise by playing second fiddle to some fresh-faced puppet Chairman. As the months went by, civil servants at the Ministry grew accustomed to seeing Ryland flitting in and out on solo visits. As relations between Hall and Stonehouse nose-dived, Ryland set about courting support in Whitehall – just in case a Conservative victory at the polls in June should offer an opportunity, as Sir Humphrey might have put it, to take stock.

The Posts and Telecommunications brief in Edward Heath's government, elected in June 1970, went to Christopher Chataway, a man as famously charming and self-effacing as Stonehouse had been vain and bombastic. He and Hall had a first meeting late in June, after which Hall was disappointed to hear that no firm decision on higher postage rates would be forthcoming any time soon. Undeterred, the Board pressed ahead with its announcement of the long-shelved plan for higher rates from January 1971. In the Commons, Chataway distanced the Government from commitment to the plan, but at least acknowledged that postal deficits looked a serious problem. (His predecessor brazenly disputed this and predictably laid into the Government for going along with 'swingeing increases' – a line supported in the House by Tony Benn, as though Benn's own experience with the deficits of 1963–5 had never happened.)[14] By August, Chataway had concluded there was little choice but to treat the Post Office plan as a *fait accompli* – though he wanted some concession over the timetable that he thought would help sell it to the public. This entailed a difficult series of negotiations, involving at one point a rare 'Letter of General Direction' from the Minister, forcing the Post Office Board to comply with his wishes. The tariff increase was eventually settled, but other discussions over future strategy had in the meantime gone even less well. In fact, Chataway and his Permanent Secretary together decided by the late autumn that Hall had to be replaced. Wood had compiled a confidential inventory of his more glaring transgressions, which made for sad reading. 'It is indeed difficult to think of anything with which the Ministry has been concerned in its relations with the Post Office, and in which Lord Hall has taken a hand, where his performance has been even satisfactory', concluded the Permanent Secretary grimly.[15] No doubt Chataway was also made well aware of feelings within the Post Office itself. In the last week of November, Hall was summoned to a meeting at Waterloo Bridge House and relieved of his position. He returned straight to Howland Street, where a special meeting of the Board was hastily convened. Hall withdrew and Ryland read out a statement informing the directors of his own appointment as the Acting Chairman. Hall then emptied his desk and left the building for the last time. Chataway, meanwhile, had gone to the annual lunch of one of the television industry's trade associations, where he was the guest of honour – and found himself sitting for a deeply uncomfortable hour and a half next to an understandably distressed Lady Hall.[16]

Neither the long-running feud over postal tariffs nor the levels of discord on the Post Office Board had been much aired in public. Hall's dismissal therefore came as a shock to outsiders. The minutes of the special meeting included a courteous tribute to Hall, but the idea of a public statement to the same effect was given short shrift by his successor.[17] The press made a stab at various explanations for what had happened, most of which were wide of the mark. Chataway could only insist there had been no clash over policy, which was correct, and he stuck in gentlemanly fashion to a bland mantra about 'the best interests of the Post Office and the public'. This was ill-received in the Commons, where his announcement of the decision on 25 November drew fire from no fewer than three of his Labour predecessors – Stonehouse, Short and Benn. But when the Opposition moved a motion of censure against him, Chataway saw off his critics with some aplomb and was given a glowing press. Hall himself was devastated. He briefly and ill-advisedly toyed with the idea of challenging the legal basis for his dismissal and told the press it amounted to 'a monstrous rape' of the Corporation. He thus ended his tenure as he had begun it, with some injudicious language which confirmed for the mandarins that his had been an odd appointment from the start. Once the waters had closed over him, the whole story of Hall's chairmanship was effectively erased from the Post Office's corporate memory as a false start, never to be referred to again.

Across the organization, the curious goings-on at Headquarters confirmed a general assumption among officials – or the 'managers', as they had now become – that the Post Office would remain the old Department in all but name, still essentially subservient to the government of the day. This was the message received in the workplace, too, and it went down badly. Unofficial strikes broke out in offices and telephone exchanges across the country over the next few days – a rare case of the postal workforce's tribal loyalties being displayed on behalf of a Chairman. The unrest probably reflected a lively distrust of the new Conservative government's intentions rather than any genuine regard for Hall, but was a fair measure of the disquiet felt by the unions over the way he had been treated. His dismissal also fuelled a belief that Hall had been removed out of a fear, after a notably generous wage award in 1970, that he would be a soft touch for the unions. Actually, the Board under Hall had been making contingency arrangements for several months against the possibility of a serious clash over pay. This now seemed imminent, following the submission of an ambitious claim by the UPW in October. None could doubt that a trial of strength was just a matter of time, between the Union and an Acting Chairman eager to prove his mettle.

2. THE 1971 STRIKE AND ITS AFTERMATH

The UPW that confronted the new Corporation was a much more aggressive organization than the Union over which Ron Smith had presided in the 1950s. As noted already, Smith found it increasingly difficult from about 1961 to retain his authority in the face of a growing number of local activists hostile to his generally cautious stance. Chief among these were the leaders of the London District Council (LDC), which consisted of three sections – for telephones, counters and posts. The postal section, known as LDC3, was headed by a committee that saw itself as a kind of workers' soviet. It held enormous power over the entire postal service, controlling as it did all of London's sorting offices and mainline station facilities, and it was not averse to flexing this power with or without the approval of the Union's national headquarters in Clapham. The LDC, and especially LDC3, had for years resisted any attempt to interfere in its affairs by Clapham's Executive Council. It also, in the final years of Macmillan's Conservative government, deeply distrusted the reluctance shown by Smith and his colleagues to resort to industrial action. The stand-off between Smith and the London activists came to a head in 1964–5. The Executive Council in September 1964 suddenly, and to general amazement, expelled from the Union the seven senior officers of LDC3, including its Communist leader, Dickie Lawlor – and were promptly, and just as amazingly, obliged by the

intervention of a High Court judge to reinstate them. A tense truce prevailed thereafter, but only just. At a Special Conference in May 1965,
Smith laid into his LDC enemies with an uncharacteristic passion that
would find an echo in many other outbursts against union militancy in
years to come:

> I have seen enough of crowds on the lawns of UPW House shouting for
> 'him' to be brought out – as if the fact that people pay 3d. or 4d. a year
> towards my salary entitled them to a lynching party. I dislike, particularly,
> sawdust Caesars ranting through UPW House followed by their minions
> trying to intimidate people who have been entrusted by this Conference
> with the carrying out of a task on their behalf . . .[18]

In the wake of Smith's departure to British Steel in 1966, his 'sawdust
Caesars' extended their influence. Three of the expelled LDC3 men
actually became national officers of the Union. (Dickie Lawlor himself
was elected in 1969 to a new post as Assistant to the General Secretary
and his deputy.) These were tough, uncompromising characters and
their promotion worried many observers. Even the UPW's own historian, writing just over a decade later, saw the election of the London men
as a fair measure of the growing belligerency in the ranks. 'There can be
no doubt . . . that the Union itself changed in a profound way in the
mid-1960s. . . . The new militant style and spirit in the leadership
reflected a membership that had become at the same time less deferential and less content.'[19] Fuelling support for a more radical stance was a
spreading dissatisfaction across the wider trade union movement in the
face of the Wilson government's attempt to reform industrial relations
as part of its drive to install a prices and incomes policy. Many union
leaders – notably Hugh Scanlon of the Amalgamated Engineering Union
and Jack Jones of the Transport and General Workers' Union respectively, from 1968 – were vehement critics of the government (it was
Scanlon whom Wilson famously ordered to 'take your tanks off my
lawn'). Their willingness to confront Labour ministers in public helped
create a climate in which hard-liners like the leaders of the London postal workers had no trouble extending their influence behind the scenes.
   Smith's successor as General Secretary, however, was very far from
being a hard man of the Left – and he came not from London but Yorkshire. Brought up with three siblings by a widowed mother in one of the
poorest neighbourhoods of Leeds, Tom Jackson had left school in 1939
at the age of fourteen to become a telegraph messenger boy. After
wartime service in the Royal Navy, he had returned to Leeds as a post-

man. He took up union politics with the same energy and lively intelligence that he brought to a wide range of other interests – including, in later life, a love of antiquarian books – and won election to the UPW's Executive Council in 1955. If his rise to the top of the Union thereafter seemed inevitable, this was attributable not to his standing with the sawdust Caesars but to his own rare leadership skills and the dedication he brought to his work on the Council. He was also hugely popular at all levels of the Union. Where Smith was a rather cold man who kept his distance – Benn had memorably described their first encounter in 1964 as like 'rubbing against granite' – Jackson was an engaging extrovert of real charm.[20] It was rare to see Smith at any of the Annual Conference parties, but Jackson was always happy to drink with fellow delegates – and to entertain them with an excellent reper-toire of folk songs and a good strong voice – into the early hours. He continued to do so well after 1967, when at the age of forty-two he became the youngest ever General Secretary. He sported a splendid black handlebar moustache like some latter-day RAF fighter pilot and would joke that he had grown it to add an air of gravitas to his youthful appearance. In fact his shrewdness and natural authority required no props. In discussions with the Official Side over mechanization and over the Ripple programme put forward by McKinsey, he was in command of his brief from the start.[21] The whiskers did assure him, though, of constant attention from Fleet Street's cartoonists – and the travails of the Wilson government in its dealings with the trade union movement guaranteed that such an articulate and readily recognizable union leader as Jackson would have a national audience. He played to it with gusto, pushing the UPW to the fore of the TUC's campaign against Labour's efforts to hold back inflationary wage agreements.

Jackson's outspoken opposition to any constraints on collective bar-gaining did away with the last vestiges of the UPW as a staff association of the civil service and marked its full emergence as a trade union rep-resenting a large and vociferous industrial labour force. His prominence in the media and on the political stage undoubtedly helped him to avoid the vicious squabbles with the hard Left in his own ranks that had beset his predecessor – and also entailed a much more combative stance by the UPW on pay negotiations, which almost led in May 1968 to a national strike by postal counter clerks. Above all, though, it cemented Jackson's hold over the rank and file, which in his early years was rem-iniscent of the power of Charlie Geddes in his heyday. It was therefore fortunate for the Post Office that Jackson acknowledged the logic of the

Break and backed its implementation. The reaction of many in the postal workforce to Tony Benn's original proposal of the Break in 1965 had been instinctively hostile. Ron Smith had traded his support in exchange for Benn's agreement, back at their private lunch in May 1966, not to persist with the Split. Even then, however, general acquiescence had seemed unlikely – but Jackson's personal standing after 1967 persuaded the Union to accept it. It was his endorsement of the Break that induced postal workers to give up their precious status as peers of the clerical and professional staffs of the government sector (still valued, whatever the UPW's changed image), to part company with the Pay Research Unit and to relinquish their Whitley Councils. It would be exaggerating to say the 1969 change of status was ever embraced with the kind of expectations that the post-war workforce had invested in the Joint Councils of the Geddes era. But after Jackson had thrown his support behind the public corporation, speaking enthusiastically (prior to Hall's exit) of a future free at last from government interference, there was a palpable optimism in the Union that leaving the civil service might after all bring fundamental benefits for postal workers.

Jackson himself appears to have miscalculated the extent to which its change of status would allow the Post Office more scope for concessions to the workforce. He certainly pursued these vigorously from the start. Within days of the new Corporation's launch, he was faced with serious unofficial strikes by his members in the telegraph service. He took up their case, organized widespread stoppages in January 1970 and forced through an agreement that amounted to a total capitulation by Stonehouse, now the Minister of Posts: he conceded a pay rise backdated to the previous August, and the Labour government was left looking wrong-footed. An annual pay claim lodged back in 1969 was settled shortly afterwards on conspicuously generous terms – having rejected an offer of 10 per cent, the Union won an award not too far short of 15 per cent – but with inflation now running just over 8 per cent, and the wages index rising much faster, the UPW was intent on winning an even bigger claim in 1971. No schemes had been put forward to replace the Tomlin formula. Under constant pressure from his membership, Jackson and his negotiating team pressed ahead with objectives that were broadly in line with awards being made elsewhere in the public sector – a 'fair comparison' of the kind that had been valid under the Tomlin approach before 1969. The UPW put in a claim in October 1970 for a basic increase of 15 per cent across all pay scales. Ryland's Board replied early in January 1971 with a 7 per cent offer, revised within a few days to 8 per cent but still just below the rate of inflation. This was not the kind of response that the membership of the UPW had been led to expect of the new Corporation. The Post Office cited its own finances as the critical determinant of what could be paid. This was a 'non-Tomlin' benchmark that had never been cited before in annual pay negotiations. There was genuine disappointment in the workplace, and anger that such a radical change of approach had been sprung on them with little if any prior explanation. It left Jackson with no room to manoeuvre – which was unfortunate, because the Union had badly overplayed its hand. If conceded, its claim would not only strain the postal service's finances but also leave a massive dent in the new Conservative government's nascent incomes policy. Chataway and his officials were bound to oppose it. Ryland, meanwhile, was only too keen by January 1971 to demonstrate his grip on the Post Office and his support for plans by the Heath government to change the whole climate of industrial relations in Britain. True to a commitment made in their 1970 general election manifesto, the Conservatives had already intro-duced an Industrial Relations Bill that went far beyond anything mooted by Wilson's Cabinet. (It proposed, inter alia, a National Industrial Rela-tions Court with the power to award injunctions against threatened strikes.) The TUC organized a 'Kill the Bill' rally at the Albert Hall on 12 January, which was addressed by Harold Wilson before hearing from the TUC General Secretary, Vic Feather, that opposition to the Bill would mark 'the biggest campaign ever mounted by trade unions'.[22]

Three days later, Jackson and his Executive Council met to weigh their options. Reports of Feather's defiant speech had done nothing to cool the membership's evident support for a strike, and Jackson had no doubt that the Council's credibility with the rank and file was at stake. 'This . . . is a struggle to the end and it may well be a fight which we cannot win. On the other hand it is a fight which we cannot run away from, for unless we take industrial action the credibility of the [Execu-tive Council] – and indeed the Union – would be destroyed in the eyes of many of its members.'[23] The threat of an all-out strike, after just a one-day stoppage, had used successfully in July 1964. The Labour government had caved in after a token stoppage in support of the telegraphists in January 1970. Perhaps they could hope for another last-minute capitulation by the Government? But none came, and at midnight on 19/20 January – almost fifty years, as it happened, since the Union's decision in 1921 to abolish its strike fund and turn its back on industrial action – the UPW withdrew its labour. Counters were manned on a voluntary basis for the payment of pensions and other benefits, but the nation's sorting offices fell silent.

Unfortunately for the Union, the silence extended to very few telephone exchanges. Half of the 50,000 telephone operators belonged to the UPW, but a mere handful chose to join the strike as they were asked to do. Many quit the union altogether.[24] The POEU offered sympathy and a significant cash contribution, but brought no pressure to bear on its members to join the strike (prompting an estrangement from which the relationship between the two Post Office unions never really recovered). And much the same applied to the union movement in general: the TUC offered moral support in abundance, but no secondary industrial action and little money. Most dismaying of all for the UPW, the country was plainly capable of struggling on without its post. It was brutally clear within a week or two that mail deliveries were simply not an essential service, as were the coalmines or the utilities – or, indeed, as the Royal Mail itself had been in the world before 1914. Buoyed by illusions that the opposite was true, postal workers took up their cause with plenty of courage and imagination from the very first day. There were weekly rallies in Hyde Park (many in the pouring rain), regular demonstrations across the country and endless stories of good-humoured postmen making light of desperately straitened family circumstances. As the action dragged on through a cold February, those on the streets refused to contemplate the possibility of defeat. Pickets surrounded all the largest post offices and huddled through the night around street braziers, providing the media with a daily diet of the sort of images that would come to embody the 1970s before the decade was done. And the General Secretary seemed to be everywhere at once, praising the resilience of his members and lifting their spirits where he could with limitless bravado: 'They laughed at us in the beginning', he told a rally in Cardiff on 9 February. 'Well, we are the Brigade of Guards now.'[25]

Away from the cameras, it was a different story. Jackson probably knew before the end of January that the strike was a lost cause. By the middle of February, 35,000 members were drawing on the Union's Hardship Fund at a cost of about £100,000 a week. Total debts already stood at just over £300,000. Jackson's recommendation was that the Union should regard £600,000 as the very most it could afford to borrow, though many unions were prepared to offer cheap loans. 'We are therefore faced with a dilemma', as the General Secretary put it in a paper to his Executive Council on 24 February.[26] There was no sign whatever of the Government or Ryland's Board moving an inch towards them. Jackson suggested there were only two possible outcomes. Either the Council would bring the strike to a close, or there would be a drift back to work as the hardship funds dried up. Recommending the first option, Jackson then made the unpleasant discovery that his hold over the Council was less secure than he had supposed. At a meeting in the Union's Crescent Lane headquarters, Jackson asked his colleagues for their authorization to seek a way out. Many of them, particularly those from Scotland and the North-East, were taken aback. Jackson's proposal was overruled and the Council, to his consternation, voted to press on. 'I think it hit him very hard, that he couldn't persuade the Executive', recalled one of his Assistant Secretaries (and his eventual successor), Alan Tuffin. 'The realization came to him and those close around him that the membership had changed.'[27]

Jackson had no choice but to go on leading the rallies and the razzamatazz, while exhorting the Executive Council behind the scenes to let him cut short the Union's agony. It put him under intolerable strain over the weeks that followed. On at least two occasions he met privately with Chataway, who formed a high regard for him personally but could offer him no compromise to take back to Clapham.[28] Eventually, at the beginning of March, Jackson persuaded his Council to accept a face-saving ploy that all knew would be tantamount to abject surrender. He publicly proposed a Committee of Enquiry as 'the best way out of a bad situation', as he put it to the press: both sides would give evidence before the Committee and be bound by its findings. This was accepted by ministers on 4 March – on terms that would allow the Government, in effect, to dictate those findings – and after forty-seven days the strike was over. It had been the longest stoppage of its kind since the National Strike of 1926. A three-man Committee was appointed, chaired by a former Whitehall Permanent Secretary, Henry Hardman. The Post Office put forward a prominent industrialist, Thomas Carlile, the head of Babcock and Willcox. The UPW nominated the Vice-Principal of Ruskin College, John Hughes. Hearings lasted through most of April and their report was published on 5 May. Eleven of its fifty-six pages comprised a minority report from Hughes, dissociating himself from its bottom line: 'The only, and unavoidable, conclusion is that postal pay rates were "well below" those in other industries by 1969, [were again so] by late 1970, and will be even more so as 1971 progresses'.[29] This made Hughes a hero of the UPW, but was little consolation to the Union when it saw the Enquiry's majority recommendation – a 9 per cent

award, backdated to January. It was generally seen as a crushing humiliation.

The defeat gave rise to much bitterness in the workplace: individual
postmen who had failed to support the strike were subjected to fierce
recriminations, and relations between the workforce and management
remained prickly in many parts of the country long after the delivery of
Hardman's Report.* Within the Union itself, paradoxically, the consequences of the strike over the next few years were in a sense to be quite
benign. Jackson pulled off a masterly presentation of the defeat as the
UPW's Dunkirk moment, revealing the plucky spirit of the Union as
never before. Had there only been more treasure in the coffers, their
cause must unquestionably have triumphed in the end. While this line
was adopted as balm to the wounded morale of his members, it did not
stop Jackson drawing a more salutary lesson to the attention of his local
and regional union officers. Militant tactics were bound to be self-
defeating, unless the Union had the cash resources to back up industrial
action, which it did not. It took until 1976–7 to pay off all its debts.
Over these five years, Jackson towered over the Union's activities. He
was also an influential proponent of moderate policies on the national
stage – he had been a member of the TUC's General Council since
1967 – and he did his best to counter the uncompromising tactics of
left-wing leaders in the TUC like Jack Jones and Hugh Scanlon. Mindful of the failures of the 1966–70 Labour government, Jackson was now
determined that the UPW should take what might be described as a
robustly pragmatic line on pay bargaining. While devoted to lifting the
living standards of the postal workforce, he was adamant that the union
movement had to play its part in the achievement of a wage-settlement
system compatible with a sensible management of the economy, whatever the government of the day. This approach led to more bitter clashes
between the UPW's leadership and its left-wing activists, invariably led

---

* A new graduate recruit in 1974, Jonathan Evans, experienced this at first hand in making
regular visits to Peterborough Head Post Office, where the Head Postmaster still attributed a
general stickiness in his dealings with staff to the strike that had ended more than three years
earlier. This had a faintly comical consequence later that year. It happened that Peterborough
could boast an unusually celebrated baker, who for some years had prepared a Christmas
cake for the Queen. When the time came for her 1974 cake to be delivered to London with its
own personal courier, the Union refused to cooperate and no one in the sorting office would
agree to take on the job. So Evans found his graduate training course included being presented
with two seat tickets for the train from Peterborough to London – one for himself and one for
the royal cake, which he duly handed to a uniformed Palace official waiting for him at King's
Cross. (Jonathan Evans, interview with author, 17 May 2010.)

by the leaders of LDC3. Jackson had the temerity in December 1973 – in the midst of a miners' strike, no less – to suggest in a television interview that any unions breaking Stage Three of the Heath government's incomes policy 'would have a lot to answer for'. At the UPW Annual Conference five months later, he was censured in a motion carried by the LDC3 men for having 'brought the Union into disrepute and lent aid to the enemies of the Trade Union movement generally . . .' Even setting this clash aside, Jackson could never take the support of the Annual Conference for granted. His pleas for realism on the pay front were often rejected. At the same May 1974 Conference, he told delegates it was 'vitally important' that they should reject a motion demanding a reduction in the working week, if only to signal their awareness that both of the Post Office's two main businesses were awash with red ink. The motion was carried just the same.[30] Despite many such setbacks, however, the calculation that Jackson had presented to Council on 15 January 1971 essentially held good for several years. The national leadership, thanks largely to the force of Jackson's personality, managed to salvage its credibility.

Where did the outcome of the 1971 strike leave the Post Office itself? If the UPW had been beaten but allowed to regroup in defeat, the Post Office had prevailed but found itself mired in criticism. The Hardman Report represented the first independent scrutiny of what had been happening there since the summer of 1969. It did not paint a flattering picture. In particular, its verdict on the decision to retain one combined corporation for the postal and Telecoms businesses was unequivocally negative: 'the problems and development of the postal services require the undivided attention of a separate management'.[31] So much for all those who had rejected the Split. The Committee had looked for evidence of any improvement in management practices as a result of the change of status, and found none. It was especially scathing in its analysis of the still glacial pace of measures aimed at boosting productivity. 'We think that what is wanted on both sides is a change in attitudes . . . We suggest that, at least until recently, the two parties have opted for a cosy life and been anxious to avoid pursuing measures which would disturb traditional work patterns and relationships.'[32] The Report could hardly say so, but at least the strike had broken with this past more effectively than Hall's brief hour upon the stage – albeit at a heavy cost. (The financial impact of the prolonged stoppage made a serious dent in the steady upward trend in real Post Office revenues that had been evident since the start of the 1950s: see Appendix A, Chart 10.)

In truth, the boardroom since the start of 1971 had been anything but cosy, with an emergency executive sitting virtually seven days a week as a sub-committee of the main Board. The pressure had been too great for some. It had reduced Vieler to a sorry figure, sitting slumped at the table through many meetings with his head in his hands.[33] Within three weeks of the strike, and once his chairmanship had been confirmed, Ryland had shunted Vieler aside to make way for Ken Holmes as Managing Director of Posts. Vieler departed a few months later. Sadder still had been the plight of Dick Hayward. The former UPW man had been put in an impossible position as Director of Personnel – and his 1969 knighthood had been of little consolation to him in the aftermath of the strike when the Union had stripped him of his honorary membership. When the call had come for him to present evidence to the Enquiry on behalf of the employers, Hayward had had a nervous breakdown. This was glossed over with typical ebullience by Ryland, who appeared in Hayward's place, but Hardman and his colleagues perceived the bigger problem. 'The Post Office did not accept that there was a lack of experience in industrial relations at Board level', noted their Report with the merest hint of incredulity. But industrial relations had been made a great deal more complicated by the move to corporate status. 'That this problem has not been tackled before is unfortunate, but both parties now seem to accept that action is needed . . .'[34] At Hardman's behest, the Board and the UPW agreed to the setting up of a Joint Working Group on industrial relations. Little of substance would happen, though, until a permanent replacement for Hayward had been found. It was obviously going to be a critical appointment.

By chance, the postal strike had coincided almost exactly with a strike of clerical staff at the Post Office's principal supplier of telecommunications equipment, GEC. Ministers had fretted over the possibility that a settlement by GEC's management might embarrass the Post Office. A mandarin at the Department of Employment had accordingly taken some trouble to establish a rapport with the company, telephoning the head of its Personnel Department every few days to compare notes on the progress of the two strikes. The GEC man on the other end of the line was Ken Young, an executive with a plausible claim to being one of the most respected industrial relations professionals in British industry. Though still only forty, he had played a key role in organizing the integration of the AEI, English Electric and GEC workforces in the 1967–8 mergers that had transformed Britain's electrical power industry, under the watchful eye of Arnold Weinstock.* The newly expanded GEC was one of only two companies in the country with workforces broadly of the same size as that of the postal service. (The other was British Leyland.) When the shortlist for Hayward's job at the Post Office was compiled in the early summer of 1971, the mandarin ensured that Young's name was on it. What happened next was as serendipitous as the Board appointments of 1969 had been calamitous. Ryland was firmly opposed to the appointment of another outsider, but he and the Permanent Secretary from the Ministry were joined on the interview panel by the Minister himself. Notwithstanding his clash with Hall, Chataway was keen to inject more new blood into the Post Office – and knew before the interview started that Young was the man he wanted. The two of them had met a few years earlier. Chataway had been a television journalist as well as a famous athlete; and during an enforced absence from the Commons after losing his seat in 1966, he had presented a BBC television series on management in British industry. Young had appeared on one of the programmes, wearing his GEC hat, and had made a big impression on the production team: he was taken on as an adviser to the rest of the series. Now Chataway ensured that he was taken on again, this time as the Post Office's 'Board Member for Personnel and Industrial Relations' (a title that very quickly ensured he was known to all as 'The Bumper').

Shortly before joining in January 1972, Young was given an opportunity to meet a handful of the postal trade unions' leaders. Only at this meeting did he discover he would be joining the Board at the same time as Derek Gladwin, a 42-year-old regional official of the General and Municipal Workers' Union who had been appointed a Non-Executive Member.[35] The surprise was mutual – but the two men represented a powerful addition to Ryland's team, and would enjoy a strong working relationship for the next twenty years. (Gladwin was two years later given one of the most influential jobs in the Labour Party, and sat as chairman from 1974 until 1990 of its Annual Conference Arrangements

---

* Young was technically only the Deputy Director of Personnel, but since he reported to Jack Scamp, who had spent most of his time since 1964 trouble-shooting in the car industry, the Glasgow shipyards and a dozen other hot spots on behalf of the Wilson government, Young was effectively left in charge. The credit for the amalgamation of the electrical industry workforces is solely and misleadingly attributed to Scamp in the latter's entry in the *Oxford DNB*, where it is incorrectly implied that the AEI and EE mergers with GEC occurred in 1962-4.

Committee. This acknowledged his prowess as a backroom fixer and facilitator. He brought the same skills to bear in the Post Office board-room, as well as his practical experience of trade union affairs, and was to offer the Board sage advice on many fraught occasions in the future.) Other surprises followed for Young as soon as he took up his post in the New Year. He found the Industrial Relations Joint Working Group had been mothballed for months, awaiting his official start in the job: its only action so far had been the recruitment, with the Board's blessing, of an 'independent member' proposed by the UPW – and this was Will Paynter, the retired Communist General Secretary of the National Union of Mineworkers. Having grown up in a small Welsh mining village, where his father ran the books for the local pit, Young struck up an easy rapport with the former leader of the Welsh miners; but Paynter did not stay long, once the new director had begun to impose himself on the Joint Group. It was a culture far removed from GEC, and indeed from the commercial world in general, and Young had to surmount consider-able scepticism within the Post Office that he would stay the course. He did so with great patience and a painstaking attention to detail that soon became his hallmark.

Young's next shock was to discover that he would have to deal with no fewer than seventeen different unions, each of them requiring sepa-rate pay negotiations. Half demanded an annual pay round in January (dominated by the UPW), and the rest expected the same in July (dom-inated by the POEU). Just coping with every year's round of negotiations would be enough to fill his desk diary from one New Year to the next. One reason for the past proliferation of unions was that they were not restricted to wage-rate workers: to Young's amazement, there were sev-eral management associations representing salaried staff, from sorting office supervisors to Head Postmasters. And just as managers were happy to think of themselves as workers, so were the workers keen to see themselves as quasi-managers. Young had never encountered any-thing like the UPW's Annual Conference, where 1,500 or more delegates assembled to deliberate over not just pay and conditions but a host of operational matters. Each year's agenda ran to hundreds of pages, packed with the minutiae of motions and 'composite amendments' sub-mitted by branch committees over many months. Each year's debates constituted the policy-making forum of the Union, and decisions taken by a majority vote of the May Conference were binding on all its offi-cers, including those of the Executive Council. This meant they were effectively binding on the Post Office, too, given the comprehensive nature of local and regional consultation processes between management and the UPW. Young and other senior managers attended many conference proceedings as observers, and were not there simply out of courtesy. Without this participation by the Union in day-to-day management at a local level, most postal operations (which depended heavily on overtime arrangements dictated by UPW officers) would have ground to a halt. Every large sorting centre had its 'Book Room' where each man's entitlement was scrupulously monitored according to the Union's own rules. Here were allocated the staff hours for which management had budgeted, though how closely those hours related to actual time spent on allotted tasks did not repay too close a scrutiny. (There were 'Overtime Kings' in London who worked a miraculous 24-hour day, seven days a week.) The Post Office's overtime culture was the key to many workplace attitudes. It explained the Union's fierce opposition to the introduction of part-timers, and the bias against women who might demand flexible hours needing a more literal reading of work schedules.

Nor was it just the workforce that sustained a parallel universe of rules and conventions beyond the reach of any formal manual. Young found that the managers, too, had their own unwritten codes. All name and career details were recorded in what was universally known as the 'Stud Book'. Managers were entered in order of their longevity, which was seen as precisely synonymous with seniority – and therefore with eligibility for promotion. The resulting list was avidly studied by all managers (and their wives), as it had been for generations. Any appointment that cut across the existing order was liable to prompt great resentment among those who had been passed over. The significance of the Stud Book was twofold. Most obviously, it was a monument to Buggin's Turn. It also reflected a strong supposition in the Post Office that no job would be held by the same individual for too long: for all officials, and at regular intervals, there would be 'a time to move on', often to a wholly different department. This bias in favour of generalists rather than specialists was no doubt part of what made lifetime careers in the Post Office so attractive to many good men, but it also helped explain why the operating businesses were strikingly bereft of specialists. They contained not one single qualified accountant in 1972. It also lay behind the fact that Young was the first and only executive with detailed knowledge of personnel matters to have been externally recruited, at any level.

His appointment was duly contentious and prompted gossip for months. Yet of all the recommendations in the Hardman Report, it was probably the single easiest measure to enact. Others included an over-haul of the systemically excessive overtime regime and a reappraisal of incremental pay-scales. As part of the settlement of the 1971 strike, it was naturally supposed that both the Board and the UPW had signed up to this heroic agenda. But its scope, as Young was quick to acknow-ledge, transcended the mechanics of any single department and posed a challenge for the Post Office as a whole. Implementing it might have tested the management skills of Young's old boss at GEC, Arnold Wein-stock, and a hundred of his henchmen. While Young grappled with the novelties of non-stop pay negotiations, the former civil servants of the Post Office set out to do their best under the indomitable Bill Ryland.

3 . IMPOSSIBLE ODDS

Ryland was almost displaced at the outset. The Government tried very hard to attract more than one senior figure from the business world into the chairmanship left vacant in November 1970.[36] All turned it down. Hall's defenestration and the evident ambiguity of the Post Office's rela-tionship with Whitehall had made it a difficult pitch. By March 1971, Ryland's image as the tough guy in Howland Street had entrenched his position – and he was taking every opportunity to set out his own mani-festo for the job. Giving a lecture at the Institution of Electrical Engineers on the very day that the postal strike was brought to an end, he laid out the Post Office's elaborate corporate-planning 'system' as the blueprint for its emergence as a business. Even the 1969 Act, he said, had not resolved the dilemma over how best to reconcile parliamentary control with commercial independence. The Post Office was nonetheless ready to match the performance of any public corporation in the land. He and his colleagues had embraced a commercial approach tantamount to 'a philosophy of management – a willingness to anticipate needs, respond to them, be adaptable and create both responsibility in those dealing with problems and dynamism and drive throughout the organisation'.[37] Brave words – and Ryland backed them up with a working knowledge of the Post Office that no rival could possibly offer. He was confirmed as Chairman before the end of April 1971.

It was probably only Ryland's unique background and authority that made an executive chairmanship of the Corporation viable at all. Con-fronted with copious reasons for believing that no single entity could any longer be expected to run both posts and telecoms, Harold Wilson's ministers had nevertheless ducked the issue and supposed the Post Office would somehow muddle through. Between 1971 and 1977, this assumption was tested to destruction. The 1,200 staff at Howland Street ran a Central Headquarters (CHQ) that presided over two vast businesses, with their own central management structures at the head of elaborate local and regional office networks. (Other relatively tiny businesses also reporting to Howland Street included a Data Processing subsidiary offering computer services to third parties, notably a company handling cargo services at Heathrow Airport.) Conceivably, as a disciplined holding company, CHQ might just have served a sensible purpose at the apex of what was, once again, by far the largest business in Britain. But CHQ's role went well beyond that of a holding company. The failure properly to complete the Semi-Split in the late 1960s left it with direct responsibility for many activities, from financial planning and personnel to procurement services and public relations, on which both main operating businesses were heavily dependent. And given the way that the Post Office had worked for three centuries, it followed inexorably that most key decisions would revert to CHQ.

Perhaps a less assertive Chairman might have struggled harder against the centralizing tendencies of the postal culture. Ryland, by contrast, effectively aligned himself with the lineage from Francis Freeling to Evelyn Murray via Rowland Hill, donning the mantle of the all-controlling Secretary and leaving a succession of ministers to hover in the distance like the largely absent Postmasters General of old. Chataway and his successor, Sir John Eden, had little time or inclination to steep themselves in Post Office matters once the UPW had been defeated, and after April 1974 the Ministry of Posts and Telecommunications was subsumed into the Department of Industry. A confirmed workaholic, Ryland burrowed through enough paperwork in a typical week to keep three ordinary men busy – a good part of it he completed over his weekend, and delivered back to Headquarters in two bulging black leather pouches early each Monday morning. A torrent of fresh papers deluged his office on most days – all of them needing to be carefully processed and then passed to the Chairman himself. Ryland always had a gargantuan appetite for detail, and he employed a handful of bright young men to help ensure his mastery of every brief. These lieutenants included Malcolm Argent, as his office director from the beginning of 1975, and private assistants like John Roberts (1969–71 and 1976–7) and Bill Cockburn (1971–3), all of them men whose cards were marked for higher things after their survival at the centre. For Howland Street was no place for the faint-hearted. ('Two and a half years of hell' was how Argent would recall it.[38]) The pace was unrelenting, and Ryland a fearsome taskmaster. While seeking to control ever more activities down the line, he also held sway over all Board meetings. This extended to control of the minutes: he vetted them meticulously, often rewriting them in a tiny, spidery handwriting that drove his private office to despair. Protests from time to time about overly blatant distortions of the record were probably the nearest that his fellow directors ever came to challenging him in the open.*

No man could have done more than Ryland to sustain the Post Office as the Department it had once been – but this, unhappily, was now an increasingly mixed blessing. Even his greatest admirers did not see the Chairman as a visionary man of business. His instincts were those of a remarkable civil servant. *Pace* the speeches about dynamism and drive, he had little intuitive understanding of how to transform the Post Office into the commercial entity it was now supposedly to become. His closest colleagues remained former civil servants to a man (and Alan Wolstencroft was restored to court, within months of Ryland's taking over, as Secretary to the Board – meaning the familiar corporate position, of course, which was a very different matter from the role played historically by the Secretary to the Post Office). Five Year Plans and Ten Year Plans piled up remorselessly. Key decisions were subject to endless second-guessing about their political ramifications. Bureaucratic procedures

---

* Only one covert challenge can be documented, and it was a strange affair indeed. Ken Young was astonished, soon after the return of the Labour government in March 1974, to receive a telephone call from Tom Jackson saying he had been offered the chairmanship by Whitney Straight. The Deputy Chairman had apparently assured him that any reappointment of Ryland, on the expiry of his contract in April, would be met by a Board rebellion. The idea was perhaps not completely absurd: Jackson had been a Governor of the BBC since 1967 and had recently been appointed to the Press Council. (He would later accept a seat on the Board of BP, offered to him by the Labour government in 1975.) But it was a bold move, to say the least, and bizarre that Straight should have taken the initiative single-handedly as though the chairmanship was in his gift. Jackson told Young he had flatly rejected the approach. Young, with his permission, arranged a private meeting with the new Minister, Tony Benn. 'I told Benn it was a cock-and-bull story from Whitney Straight. And I asked him to accept that as far as the Board was concerned, there was an expectation that Ryland would be reappointed – and there would certainly be no revolution if he was.' (Young, interview with author, 23 February 2010.) Ryland was reappointed for two years. Straight, apparently unscathed by the episode, retired from the Board at the end of the year. Benn only noted in his diary that he had pressed Ryland to think about a new series of stamps that might celebrate the country's trade unions (Tony Benn, *Against the Tide: Diaries 1973–76*, Hutchinson, 1989, p. 140).

were endlessly cross-checked with Whitehall. But when it came to responding pragmatically and imaginatively to the dictates of the marketplace, Ryland and his managers often seemed scarcely attentive. Budding prospects in need of skilful marketing were woefully neglected.

None of the new Corporation's activities were more blighted in this way than its 'Giro and Remittance Services', which had been launched in 1968 after a less than auspicious gestation. The historical background itself was none too encouraging. Having sniffily rejected the idea of a joint Giro system with Germany in 1913, the Treasury had spent decades ignoring the possibility that well over 20,000 Crown post offices and sub-offices might be harnessed as a network for low-cost money transmissions between accounts owned by Post Office customers.* The potential benefits for those with no bank account were so obvious – and so evident in many countries of Continental Europe – that creating a Giro system had resurfaced as a popular idea in the post-war trade union movement. It also intrigued Post Office officials, who worked out the details of a possible scheme in the late 1950s. Progress was again blocked by the Government, however, supposedly under pressure this time from clearing bankers apprehensive about the competition it might pose. This at least was Tony Benn's understanding when he arrived at the Post Office, and nothing could have been better calculated to stir his enthusiasm for it.[39] As we have already seen, Benn championed the concept – the press hailed it as 'Benn's Bank' – as part of his dream of turning the Post Office into three separate nationalized industries. He won the Cabinet's approval in 1965 for a move that turned out to require no fresh legislation, but a lot of tortuous preparation. Leading figures like the Comptroller and Accountant General, Kenneth Anderson, were keen on the notion of using a Giro system as the basis of a widely diversified enterprise. As Benn noted with delight in November 1965, '[Anderson] has put in a powerful paper on the future organization of the Post Office saying that the Giro, Savings Bank and [customer] investment accounts ought to be organised together under a banking corporation with dynamic and aggressive business practice'.[40] Enough

---

* The notion of a Post Office bank of some kind surfaced intermittently between the wars. Commenting on a recently published official report on the banking sector, for example, *The Times* of 24 January 1928 made this suggestion: 'Much could be done ... to make the Trustee and the Post Office Savings Banks more efficient, not only in attracting deposits from the small investor, but also in servicing local needs by closer cooperation with the National Savings Committees, a proportion of whose funds may be invested in local undertakings'.

momentum had been established by the summer of 1966 to ensure that even Benn's departure did not derail an innovation with potentially far-reaching social consequences.

Following its launch in 1968, however, the Giro proved a huge disappointment. Some initial effort was made to attract useful publicity, but fundamental marketing considerations went by the board.* Its name, for a start, was unfortunate: unemployment benefits were posted out from government offices via green 'Giro' cheques, to be cashed at post offices. ('Getting the Giro' was almost the equivalent of an earlier generation's 'going on the dole'.) The Post Office's Giro was consequently seen by many as no more than a conduit for state hand-outs. More fundamentally, it suffered from falling disastrously short of being a full-range service: it was prevented from offering deposit accounts or indeed any other retail banking products. Having quickly amassed about half a million customers in its first few years – many of them Post Office employees – its activities on behalf of individual customers had atrophied by the mid-1970s, despite the best efforts of the UPW to interest the Labour government in reviving it.[41] Its core business by then consisted of handling the cash and cheque takings of large retail chains such as Sainsbury and Marks & Spencer, and providing cash-management facilities to other businesses reliant on front-line workers with money in their pockets, like Unigate's local milkmen. This generated vital income, kept 4,000 staff busy at its computer centre in Bootle and was a boon for the cash logistics of the Post Office – but it was a far cry indeed from the original concept of Benn's Bank.

Ironically, given Ryland's career history, the Telecoms business enjoyed far more independence from Howland Street than the Post. Based in Gresham Street, a few hundred yards from St Martin's-le-Grand, telecoms had a Managing Director with long experience of the business world, whom Ryland greatly respected and allowed considerable autonomy. Too many decisions were still channelled through CHQ, but they were rarely overruled. Ned Fennessy was happy to keep his distance

---

* This gave rise to a curious story. As the Postmaster General in the launch year, Stonehouse regularly arranged to have himself photographed by the press withdrawing money from his own Giro account at a Post Office counter. It was good PR for the new service – and handy for Stonehouse, since he never had more than a few pence in his account. He made a habit of asking for £50, which could hardly be refused under the glare of the cameras but which he never returned, despite repeated reminders from Giro staff. Reports of this behaviour were known to very few before 1974; but they began to circulate more widely in the Post Office after Stonehouse faked his suicide late that year and ended up in the dock on embezzlement charges, for which he eventually served a three-year sentence.

insofar as was possible – his relationship with Ryland was often strained – and he had charge of one of the fastest-growing businesses in the country. It was under enormous pressure: public criticism of the quality of telephone services in these years was a by-word for public-sector inefficiency. But at least industrial relations posed no problem: the POEU had been bought off with a remarkably generous 'productiv-ity' agreement that simply linked wages, in effect, to the revenues of the entire Telecoms business. Indeed, wages climbed from just over 43 per cent of revenues in 1970 to more than 50 per cent in 1974–5 – over a five-year period in which telecom revenues themselves jumped by 80 per cent to almost £1.4bn. (Young was appalled when he discovered the agreement's details and the lack of any personalized incentives for POEU members. It surprised him that the UPW made so little effort to exploit the POEU's good fortune.[42]) This left Fennessy and his senior team to concentrate on a massive expansion of the telephone network and the early stages of a development programme aimed at the next generation of switching technology, already known as System X. Find-ing the money for its capital investment programmes was no more difficult than sorting out the POEU: spending more than doubled from £372m in 1969–70 to £787m in 1974–5.

Investment in the postal business, meanwhile, fluctuated on either side of £30m a year – a fair reflection, as many thought, of its relative status as an operation in the throes of a managed decline. The net out-put of the postal business in constant 1970 pounds was marginally lower by the middle of the 1970s than it had been in 1960–61.[43] (That of telecoms over the period had almost quadrupled.) CHQ's impact on this ailing business seemed to exacerbate all of its weaknesses. The retirement in June 1972 of the Brigadier, Ken Holmes, removed a Post Office luminary who had always been one of those closest to Ryland.* His successor was not a businessman but another civil servant. Alex Currall came to the Post Office from the Treasury, where he had been in charge of the National Savings Bank. Planning and reporting activities multiplied alarmingly, while new marketing initiatives made little or no impact at all. A nascent 'marketing department', established in 1971, struggled with a tiny staff while the general administrative headcount

---

* Their long careers in the Post Office had had much in common, stretching back to war-time service with REPS. Clandestine meetings between them outside the office had been a feature of the dark days in the aftermath of Hall's dismissal. They had met for afternoon walks on Hampstead Heath when the going got especially bad. (Howard Brabrook, inter-view with author, 15 February 2010.)

soared. The postal HQ remained in the old headquarters building of St Martin's, the former GPO North. Between 1968 and 1975, staff numbers employed there and across the regional head offices of the business rose by more than 40 per cent.[44] This kept the paperwork churning, but whether it did much to enhance the quality of the postal management may be doubted.

One insider's doubts filled an entire book in 1979. The author, Michael Corby, was a former executive who had left in 1976 after seven years with the Post Office to become Director of the Mail Users' Association, an independent group lobbying on behalf of large business customers. In *The Postal Business, 1969–79*, Corby had many peppery things to say about the lack of drive in Ryland's Post Office – which he attributed partly to a dearth of good recruits at the centre in the immediate post-war years, and a neglect of traditional promotion opportunities in the field. (A severe retrenchment of the country's Head Post Office network had reduced it from 432 HPOs in 1964 to only 195 by 1972.) The result, Corby believed, was a general torpor from top to bottom:

> progress [after the 1969 Act] in setting up an internal-reporting system which would enable more responsibility to be devolved to Head Postmasters was desultory. There was a lack of pull from Head Postmasters combined with a lack of push from headquarters. The system whereby local managers could blame failures on their want of authority, and central administrators [could blame it] on the lack of effective monitoring and control systems was quite cosy: it well suited the mediocre to have authority diffused.[45]

But Corby also identified in blunt fashion an even more fundamental problem, reflecting a critical weakness of government policy towards the Post Office before and after the 1969 Act that would eventually be widely acknowledged, but that few others yet cared to mention. Incorporation had left the Post Office, he observed, almost exclusively in the hands of career civil servants with no aptitude for running a business, as though merely changing its legal status might somehow be sufficient to transform it into the great new public enterprise hailed by the politicians. Those tasked with the challenge were simply not equipped to handle it:

> The failings of those promoted beyond their ceilings were to prove a costly legacy to the corporation. Nearly every problem with which Posts is now faced can be traced back, at least in part, to the period between the mid-1960s and mid-1970s when it had to bear the incubus of too many

inadequates in senior and central positions. Most of these worked hard and were loyal but the difficulty was, like First World War generals, that although they were good men after their own lights, their lights were rather dim.[46]

Corby's book was unremittingly negative, and its harsh criticisms were predictably resented by the 'generals'. But no account of the 1970s could fail to note signs of the malaise he described with the detailed knowledge of an observant insider, and there were many young managers who shared Corby's frustration: 'A lot of people of my vintage who joined in the 1960s – and got to the highest positions in the 1980s – felt in the 1970s that many of our seniors had lost the will [to manage]. They co-managed, but never did anything without taking the Union with them'.[47] Nowhere was the lack of drive more conspicuous than in the melancholy plight of postal mechanization (every aspect of which, noted Corby in characteristic style, was pervaded by a 'miasma of ineptitude').[48]

We left the automated-coding saga in 1964, just as orders had been placed with a manufacturer for prototype models of a first fully automated machine designed for the job. The first two were installed in Norwich in 1966. After some fine-tuning of the phosphorescent dot patterns to be adopted in the coding stage, a batch of the 'first-generation coding desks' went into Norwich and London's EC sorting office in 1968-9. Plans had been approved in the meantime for more than seventy offices to receive them, including all of Inner London's District Offices and the HPOs of all the big cities. During the course of 1969, it was belatedly decided that simply adding a layer of mechanization on top of the existing circulation system, which still bore essentially the shape of its late-Victorian forebear despite the adoption of county addresses in the 1920s, would make little sense. Some 200 main sorting depots and 1,000 other, smaller offices handled the mail on its way through the night – via 1,400 railway stations and about 3,000 road links – to 1,600 destinations, where postmen would begin their day by sorting it into the 'walks' that would go into their shoulder pouches. ('Pouches' were used everywhere except Inner London, where postmen still insisted on walking the streets with a sack of mail over their shoulder – which was far less practical but another badge of the London workforce's special status.) Retaining this circulation system would leave perhaps 45 per cent of the mail untouched by mechanization. And many of the offices blessed with coding desks would be running them at well below the capacity rates needed to ensure a decent financial return on the capital invested.

It was not until after the launch of the Post Office Corporation that the solution was formally proposed – in a paper written and presented to the Board by Geoffrey Vieler.[49] This led to a momentous decision to concentrate all sorting of the mails into a smaller number of larger offices. Under the 'Letter Post Plan' that was adopted, 120 Mechanized Letter Offices (MLOs) would take in everything collected from 1,600 post offices and deliver it back again. (A parallel arrangement under a 'Parcel Post Plan' would similarly draw on thirty Parcel Concentration Offices.) The new system was to be in place by 1976.

Hardly had the implementation of this plan begun than it was overwhelmed by second thoughts at Board level. Two main problems were encountered. Both were genuinely formidable obstacles, made all but insurmountable when things went wobbly in Howland Street. The first was the financial viability (or otherwise) of the project: mechanization looked in danger of falling flat on its face. This was a sobering conclusion to reach, after almost a quarter of a century of endeavour by the engineers, but the numbers were stark. Vieler's original paper laid out cashflow projections to 1990–91. To determine the real worth of the project, these flows had to be discounted back to 1970, to take account of the cost of money in the meantime; the resulting gross total had then to be reduced by the amount of the initial capital expenditure that was required. The resulting 'net present value' (NPV) of the 120 MLOs in the Letter Post Plan came to . . . almost exactly zero. (An investment of £130m yielded an NPV of £8,000.) The case for pressing ahead in 1969 had hardly been advanced in stirring terms – '. . . there is good reason to believe that the proposals will be very worthwhile . . .'[50] By 1972, it was apparent that the postal business would have no reserves to cushion itself against any cost overruns on the project. Against this background, mechanization posed some awkward questions. The correct and courageous decision, some now argued, would be to can it.

The financial outlook was not improved by the UPW's decision in 1972 to withdraw all cooperation on the project. This second major obstacle appears to have taken the Post Office by surprise, though it is hard to see why. True, the engineers were predictably not much interested in the politics of the workplace. Introducing an international conference on mechanization in May 1970, the Post Office's director responsible for it N. C. C. de Jong, noted *en passant* that switching manual tasks over to machines 'depends wholly on its acceptance by the personnel involved and their acquisition of new skills'. The index to the voluminous conference papers made no reference at all to industrial relations and de Jong simply implied to delegates that matters were in hand: 'Discussions have begun with our progressive trade unions on the form of the Letter Post Plan'.[51] But genuine disquiet among postal sorters stretched back to the days of the Rattler. As trials with the converted SPLSMs had inched ahead through the years up to 1964, Head Postmasters had had to step through ever more hoops placed in their way by the UPW. After the strike of 1971, slipping the production models of the first-generation coding desks into place without a showdown would have required a miracle, and the UPW did not do miracles. In the event, the Union's 1972 Conference voted to boycott 'piecemeal mechanisation proposals' and to withdraw all cooperation until management could offer a perfect solution, covering every aspect of the topic. Jackson spoke out bravely against this approach, making an eloquent appeal for common sense. 'You are operating your service today in almost exactly the same way as you were operating it in 1840', he told the delegates. 'And I say ... [this]: if you insist on penny-post systems, you'll get penny-post wages.'[52] But he and his Council colleagues were easily outvoted. Thereafter, talks with the UPW descended into a tortuous wrangle. New pay demands from the Union were linked to grievances over weekend working and the imminent adjustment to equal pay for women – resisted to the end by the Union, but now to be forced upon it by the Equal Pay Act of 1970. (The postman grade would be finally opened up to women applicants in 1975.) The outcome, not agreed until 1975, conceded a pay-off for machine operators that blew an ugly hole in Vieler's financial forecasts: the payments to be made as the price of mechanization represented about half of the expected gross yield on the investment. Worse, the concessionary payments – like the productivity awards of the late 1950s – had to be paid in advance of any benefits actually accruing to the Post Office.

The Board pulled back in the face of all this gloom, but refused to abandon hope entirely. Critics accused it of an obstinate determination to mechanize at any price. There was some justice in this, as was tacitly acknowledged in a monumental review of the topic overseen by Currall and concluded in September 1973. But the review noted that the putative costs and savings of the MLO programme (now reduced from 120 to eighty-one large offices) were small beer when set beside the totality of Post Office funding. It therefore made sense to persevere, even if only to avoid a massively disruptive change of plan. But what were the positive arguments for pressing on? Two stood out. First, encouraging progress was being made on an improved version of the coding desk.

A revised design would put letters on a conveyor belt moving in front of the operator's keyboard from right to left, instead of dropping them vertically into a window above the keyboard. The so-called 'Easy View Coding Desk' promised faster speeds, better ergonomics for staff and more reliable systems. (It did not disappoint after its first introduction in 1975, at Redhill in Surrey, and large numbers of this second-generation model were installed over the following eleven years. The last of them remained in service until 2003.) A second consideration was the international standing of the Post Office. Currall did not hide the importance to the organization, in his view, of keeping up with its foreign peers. The emerging hope for the future was the technology of 'optical character recognition' (OCR) – scanning devices that would obviate the need for manned keyboards – on which other countries seemed much readier to spend money without expecting a quick return. Still new to its culture, Currall thought too many of his colleagues regarded world leadership for Britain's Post Office as the natural order of things, and gently challenged that assumption. 'If we are overtaken in the near future by other countries it will be due to their much more expensive and optimistic development efforts, along with much greater capital investment in buildings and equipment.' Even more important was the unthinkable implication of abandoning automatic coding. 'Any proposal to abandon the system now would produce much unfavourable publicity, probably demands for compensation [from companies that had adopted postal codes] and marked resistance in the future to any attempt to introduce any alternative system. OCR development assumes the reading of postcodes, so that a change of direction in longer term planning would also be required.'[53] No one drew the analogy at the time, but it was essentially the rationale advanced in the early 1840s, after its ruinous costs had been exposed, for persevering with uniform penny postage. This way lay the future of the postal service, whatever the financial complications of the day.

With hindsight, we know Currall's stance was vindicated by the march of technology, much as he asserted it would be. Those who argued for an end to mechanization were left in the end looking like Luddites. Nevertheless, there were many aspects of the project in the first half of the 1970s that deserved some of the harsh criticism they received. The lack of progress was a good measure of the Post Office's dire lack of marketing skills. Postcodes had been promoted with all of the finesse exhibited when the two-tier post had been sold to the public in 1968 – which is to say, the campaign behind them was in serious trouble by 1976. A national system of postcodes had been laid out between 1966 and 1973. (It was based on a slightly revised version of the first codes devised for Norwich, so the distinction of sporting the first codes is sometimes claimed by Croydon's Head Post Office, which began applying them in 1966 and pioneered the national network in 1969.) Persuading the public to use the codes was another matter entirely. The take-up of codes had flattened out at just under 50 per cent since the start of the decade and looked ominously poised for a slow decline. And no wonder – by 1976, scarcely more than a dozen of the planned eighty-one MLOs, which were central to the new coding system, were in place. The Post Office's apparent lack of commitment was spreading confusion among the general public. Among philatelists and other connoisseurs of all things collectible in the postal service, it was spreading alarm: a 'Postal Mechanization Study Circle' was formed, partly with a view to lobbying the Post Office for some more forthright declaration of its intentions. (The Study Circle kicked off with a monthly newsletter in December 1976, followed a year or so later by the first quarterly edition of a bulletin called *Ident*. Both are still going strong.)

Mechanization's travails also exposed the general failure in the Ryland years to register any improvement in productivity. The industrial-relations record was not wholly discouraging. Ken Young forged a close and generally constructive relationship with his union counterparts, especially Jackson, whom he came to admire as a brave and resourceful leader. Significant advances were made in the workplace. The total number of recognized unions was reduced to five. (Even the National Guild of Telephonists, bane of UPW officials' lives for half a century, was frozen out, though not without a legal battle that went to the House of Lords in 1974.) An agreement was reached with the UPW in 1976 for the operation of a closed shop, on strict conditions that in Young's view made it a wholly welcome development. These included a promise by the Union not to victimize individuals who had conscientious objections to joining it, and not to try spreading their membership to include employees in the supervisory and management grades.* Above all, a 'Facilities Agreement' was struck with the unions. It defined and pre-scribed the only representational arrangements that managers would

---

* It was a deal opposed by Ryland and the rest of the top management team. Ken Young pushed it through by appealing, in unprecedented fashion, over their heads to the main Board of the Post Office. 'That didn't go down too well. Ryland didn't like it at all.' (Ken Young, interview with author, 23 February 2010.)

henceforth be allowed to acknowledge at local and regional levels everywhere. It was aimed at a curtailment of the almost anarchic conditions prevailing in some branches, where union officers spent most of their time creating local difficulties with no effective oversight by their own union hierarchy, never mind the management. No one imagined that the Post Office, with one Promethean bound, could suddenly spring free of its intractable labour problems – but here at least was a sizeable jump in the right direction, towards a more disciplined workplace where it might at least be worth trying to negotiate future deals on higher productivity. The harsh reality since 1972 was that productivity, having slumped badly in the first year of the Corporation, had only briefly rebounded and was slipping lower again: using the volume of mail handled by each postal worker in 1965–6 as a base index of 100, productivity had fallen from 101 in 1969–70 to 92 in 1970–71, and was down to 89 for 1975–6.[54] Until after his arrival at the Post Office, Young had had no inkling of the extent to which every move on pay had to be checked and orchestrated with ministers. Clerical assistants and officers in the civil service shared grades that were still identical to those in the Post Office: this gave postal pay and conditions a parochial as well as a national importance for the politicians and their Whitehall advisers. Young found his every move monitored even more consistently by Government than were Jackson's activities by local activists of the UPW. It was not an environment conducive to the kind of productivity deals that might have begun to eliminate deeply entrenched restrictive staffing practices. Faltering mail volumes (down from 11.4 billion letters and small packets to fewer than 11.0 billion in 1974–5) had no impact whatever on manning levels in the sorting offices. And where mechanization deals were agreed, extraordinary concessions were made, including an edict that the older and more senior postmen – those of the PHG grade – would be given exclusive access to the keyboard jobs on the new coding desks. It would have made no less sense had young women at the same time been given the exclusive right to shift heavy mailbags in and out of TPO carriages.

The story was much the same in many other areas. Few attempts were being made to package new services for the public. Pricing policies generally remained subject to the traditional Post Office ruling that all services should bear 'fully allocated costs', as the accountants described a notionally fair share (estimated without regard to revenues) of underlying fixed costs; this effectively precluded the addition of services that might in theory be seen as involving a portion of those costs but which in practice could be bolted onto the status quo at little or no extra cost. Cut-price deals to attract direct-mail advertisers could have been seen as highly profitable if assessed on this 'marginal-cost pricing' basis. Instead, any 'cut' price made viable by marginal-cost pricing was usually construed, and rejected, as a hidden cross-subsidy by the standard mails. Prospective new business fell by the wayside, and some long-standing customers continued to drift away. (The football pools operators had accounted in 1969–70 for revenues of £7m, equivalent to a fortnight's wages for all postal workers, but had switched more than half their business to in-house agents running private collection and delivery services by 1975.[55]) In short, the Post Office Corporation was proving no more commercial than the old Department. To blame this outcome solely on Ryland and his colleagues would be unfair. No doubt they should have picked up the postal business and sprinted with it into a new era. Unfortunately, the political context in which the Board had to function through the Ryland years was so intensely hostile that its members were reduced to running flat out just to keep the Post Office in the same place. Any lack of drive was scarcely of significance compared with a desperate lack of time. Indeed, ministers could hardly have made a better job of it had they set out deliberately in the 1970s to render the new Corporation dysfunctional.

4. CRISIS AND THE CARTER COMMITTEE

As in all trials by ordeal, the Post Office in the 1970s was subjected to three severe tests. The first exposed it to the risk of financial disaster. Letter and parcel volumes from the start of the decade generally struggled even to match the levels of the previous year. By a cruel irony, the letter volume in the Corporation's debut year (11.4 billion) began to look as though it might prove to have been the historical high-water mark. Meanwhile, the outgoings of the postal business – largely driven by labour costs, now accounting for almost 80 per cent of the total – rose broadly in line with inflationary trends which were causing alarm all across the British economy. The Post Office had no option but repeatedly to plead the case for higher prices. Edward Heath's Conservative government, battling inflation on the one hand and the trade unions on the other, felt equally impelled to plead for restraint. The result was a stand-off. A postal deficit of £73m for 1970–71 was easily blamed on that year's strike, but also reflected a £30m cost to the Post Office of postponing the new stamps championed by the ill-fated Hall. Covert ministerial pressure was applied in 1971–2 through various intermediaries, including the CBI and the public's statutory postal watchdog, the Post Office Users' National Council (POUNC). The postal business notched up a third annual deficit, albeit this time a relatively modest loss of £13m. The 1969 Act had charged the business with delivering an annual profit margin of 2 per cent on total revenues. It had been awash with red ink ever since, and the notion of any profit at all was looking academic by mid-1972. (The Government duly dropped the target.)

Thereafter, as the annual rate of inflation quickened from around 8 per cent to 12 per cent in 1973, and then doubled to 24 per cent over the next two years, ministers resorted to desperate steps that made a mockery of the Post Office's supposed independence. In exchange for the Board abandoning any attempt to break even with economic pricing, the Government handed over a cheque at the end of the financial year as 'compensation' for the resulting deficit. The arrangement covered the Telecoms business, too: even here, forgone price rises were ensuring net losses, starting in 1972–3. The aggregate losses for the Corporation as a whole mounted steadily, as did the compensatory cheques. The process culminated, in the financial year following the fall of the Heath government in March 1974, with a grotesque and record-breaking corporate loss for 1974–5 of £308m (of which £109m was attributable to the posts). The Tories' compensation scheme was honoured by the new Labour government – but as Ryland had noted in his Chairman's Statement for 1973–4, 'although helpful, [it] does not deal with the basic issue of under-pricing'. It had in fact left the Post Office's finances ever more detached from reality.

The losses were made worse by another aspect of the financial landscape that Alice might have encountered in Wonderland. This was the Post Office pension fund. Prior to 1969, staff pensions had been funded by the Exchequer on Whitehall's normal pay-as-you-go basis. The Corporation had then been required to set up a funded scheme, to which staff contributions would be made as in the private sector. But its staff at that point had already accumulated pension rights as civil servants, which would one day need to be honoured by the fund. The Government had therefore agreed to make what was in effect a bequest to the fund that would match its inherited liability. That, at least, was the theory. What had happened in practice was rather different, and had given rise to a ghastly problem. The Government, not foreseeing future levels of inflation, had badly underestimated the liability; it had chosen to fund its obligation to the Post Office with government securities (or 'consols') that proved to be singularly ill-suited to the task; and it had tied up the arrangement in a financial package that even the actuaries found hard to explain by the middle of the 1970s. The unprecedented inflation rates of the seventies were not the cause of the problem – though the Post Office generously and diplomatically pretended that they were, in its public statements on the issue – but they had greatly compounded the difficulty.[56] The net result, anyway, was that inflation had boosted the pension fund's liabilities, since the staff pensions were all index-linked, while reducing the value of the capital sum made available by the Government to fund them. This opened up a yawning deficit which the Post Office itself had to fill with annual payments out of its profit-and-loss account. These 'deficiency contributions', made separately by both posts and telecoms, climbed steeply through the decade and accounted for over £41m of the postal business's bumper loss in 1974–5. They rose to around £70m annually in each of the next three years. Only towards the end of the decade was a settlement apparently reached, allowing the Post Office to plug the deficit with annual contributions drawn from its balance sheet reserves rather than its income statement.

Another oddity of the financial pressure on the postal business in the Ryland years was that the Post Office and the Government parted ways not just over pricing but over wages as well. Despite the UPW's best endeavours – and an ever more creative approach to overtime arrangements by all the unions – there was little doubt by 1973 that postal workers' take-home earnings were trailing behind the rate of inflation, and of wage settlements elsewhere in the economy. Ryland's Board deplored this not just out of a genuine concern for the morale of the workforce, but out of a need to address a serious shortage of postmen. Across the country, vacancies amounted to about 10 per cent of the workforce. It caused a public furore over the Christmas period in 1972, when millions of cards were left undelivered into the New Year. The Heath government shortly afterwards set up a 'Pay Board', in the latest reworking of its counter-inflation strategy, and work began on a report into 'anomalies' in the pay landscape that might be deemed worthy of correction. There was general anger inside the Post Office when these anomalies were meticulously defined so as to cover civil servants but not those postal workers who would have been automatically included prior to 1969.

The 1973 Anomalies Report prompted Ken Young and Tom Jackson to work together on making representations to the Government, setting out the case for 'catch-up' pay increases for the UPW. The two of them even presented the case jointly in Whitehall in the early months of 1974. It was a time of extraordinary happenings, as the Heath Cabinet's Three-Day Week brought its long-running battle against Arthur Scargill's National Union of Mineworkers to a climax. (From New Year's Day 1974, commercial users of electricity were restricted to working no more than three consecutive days each week, in a bid to conserve coal supplies at the power stations.) But there were few more curious twists in the 1970–74 story of Heath and the unions than this rapprochement, which saw the two sides to the bitter postal strike of 1971 turning to the Government as joint supplicants in search of a 'Special Award'. They got nowhere before the general election at the end of February 1974; nor was the subsequent second Wilson government much inclined at first to make an exception for the postal workers. The defeated Conservative government's statutory incomes policy was to be retained until July, and Labour ministers were anxious to hold the line against any potential surge of public-sector pay rises. But the Board opted to persevere with its joint approach, withholding details from the Department of Industry until it was ready to present them in league with Jackson's UPW.[57] Several meetings were eventually held with Michael Foot, the Employment Secretary, and they led in July to a 'Special Pay Supplement' for the postmen, awarding them a rise of 11 per cent, which was roughly in line with inflation. (Similar concessions were made for the state's teachers and nurses.)

Having secured re-election in October and the backing of the TUC for its 'Social Contract' approach to the settlement of wage claims, the Wilson government decided the time had come for a gradual restoration of 'economic pricing' to the public sector. The Post Office had considerable leeway to make up, after the 1972–4 restraints, and was still faced with the prospect of a soaring wage bill. Ryland and his colleagues applied for tariff increases on an unprecedented scale. No sooner had they been approved and implemented, in March 1975, than the Board sought another round of increases, in July 1975, which were waved ahead that autumn. It was an uncompromising counter-attack against the chronic unprofitability foisted on the Corporation since its earliest days, but its boldness triggered passionate debate, both within the Post Office and far beyond it. Nervous commentators suggested that the public's use of the posts would collapse. Angry opponents pointed out that, by the end of 1975, there had been six tariff increases in ten years – which compared with a single one between 1940 and 1960, and just two in the preceding century back to 1840. Ryland brushed all this aside, merely noting in his statement for the 1975–6 Annual Report that the Post Office's own concern 'was matched not unreasonably by a good deal of public criticism'. All that mattered to him by then was that the strategy had worked. 'The bare statistics of this Report are enough to show that the price increases did not take the Post Office to the point of diminishing returns as some predicted.' On the contrary, they had brought the postal business to the point of returning a profit. A marginal loss of £9m in 1975–6 was converted, once the new tariffs were in place for a full financial year, to a profit of £24m in 1976–7, its first profit in nine years. Ryland's statement in the latter year's Annual Report was understandably triumphant. 'The postal service remains unquestionably one of the best in the world; regrettably this is more widely and readily accepted abroad than it is at home. . . . It is one of the few postal services in the developed world now to be operating in the black.'

Financial survival was just one of the three tests to be endured in the 1970s. The second followed immediately in its wake – and exposed the Post Office to the danger of being smothered by investigation. The very measures adopted by the Ryland Board to help it escape from financial disaster led directly to a series of official inquiries that swamped all senior levels of the Post Office with a staggering load of paperwork over the next two years, from about April 1975. The scale of the tariff increases early in 1975 – lifting 1st and 2nd class postage costs across the board by more than 55 per cent – put the public on its guard against the Post Office and drew a hostile response from POUNC. This in turn prompted Parliament's Select Committee on Nationalised Industries (SCNI) to make another foray into the postal world, picking up in April 1975 where it had left off in 1965–6. The Committee had just finished taking evidence, in July, when its members were mightily put out to hear that the Post Office had filed for that year's second round of price increases. Complaints poured in to MPs, and the Committee indignantly recalled Alex Currall and his new Senior Director, Denis Roberts, to appear before it again.[58] With unfortunate timing, the Post Office then had to disclose that it was looking into the possibility of substantial curtailments to the postal service. POUNC had been upset by a withdrawal in 1972 of the daily third delivery in London districts. Now it was further incensed by plans that included killing off Sunday collections and closing all counters on Saturday afternoons. Suddenly the public's evident irritation with the Post Office turned to virulent and politically toxic exasperation. The Government felt it had no choice but to approve the July pricing proposals and to authorize the service cuts – Sunday collections would disappear in May 1976 – but it needed to duck any charges of being soft on the perpetrator. It gave way to growing pressure for a full-blown review of the Post Office.

The Chairman of POUNC, Lord Peddie, put the case for this robustly in September 1975: 'It is five years since the Corporation was established, and the traumatic experience of the Post Office during that period justifies some examination of the framework in which it is required to operate'.[59] The Board itself seems at first to have argued against yet another inquiry: it was already having to contend with a government-sponsored study of nationalized industries' performances and scrutiny of its pricing policies, as well as meetings with POUNC and public appearances before the Select Committee. (The latter sniffily dismissed this objection, reporting later that the directors 'appear . . . to have failed to appreciate the widespread criticism and concern with which the general public viewed the disclosure of huge and unexpected deficits . . .'[60]) But it quickly dawned on Ryland and his colleagues that a full-blown official review was one test they could turn to their own advantage in historic fashion. For there was by now a growing conviction on the Board that not splitting the Post Office in 1969 had indeed been a grievous mistake.

Leading the way, as ever, were those in charge of the telecoms business. Ryland himself had been an early advocate of setting it free from the civil service: he had argued for this back in 1963, in the report on the executive team tour of the American Bell companies.* Now much grander ambitions beckoned. Equipment manufacturers in the private sector were not delivering the level of support that Ned Fennessy thought essential, and significant improvements were 'unlikely to be achieved by persuasion and consultation'. The former Plessey man wanted the Post Office to take over the entire British equipment-supply

---

* By coincidence, comparisons between the Post Office and the Bell system were once again on the agenda at around this time. McKinsey had been commissioned to make a comparative study of the Post Office and the New York Bell Telephone company – which ran a similarly sized operation with exactly half as many employees. One of Roger Morrison's partners, John Woodthorpe, led a presentation of the resulting report to the Board on 20 October 1975. Whatever its impact on the British business over the ensuing years, the report was impressive enough to ensure McKinsey an advisory role to the Telecoms business that it retained through the rest of the 1970s. (John Woodthorpe, interview with author, 20 October 2009.)

industry, or at least to develop a substantial telecom manufacturing capacity of its own. Months earlier, in May 1975, the Board had endorsed this remarkably bold objective but had had to acknowledge that an even bigger Post Office might well be impossible to manage. It had therefore been agreed 'in principle, [that] a decision to proceed with acquiring control of a manufacturing capacity should be accompanied by a decision to divide the Post Office'.[61] Unfortunately, the Prime Minister was known to have no interest at all in pursuing this division. He had proclaimed as much at the UPW's 1974 Conference, cheered to the echo by delegates still as opposed as ever to the Split.[62] Board members by the autumn of 1975 were reluctantly coming to the conclusion that an even more gigantic Corporation might have to be contemplated as the price of their telecoms strategy – until along came the proposal for an official review. What better way to finesse Downing Street's resistance to a fundamental reorganization?

The Government was nervously aware of the ambush possibilities inherent in a review. It sought to exclude any specific mention of the Split issue from its terms of reference, and proposed giving the chairmanship to a former Whitehall Permanent Secretary. Ryland could see what was afoot here, and moved quickly to pre-empt it. After a horse-trading session early in October with the new Industry Secretary, Eric Varley, a compromise was reached. The chairmanship went to an eminent academic economist, Charles Carter, who was Vice-Chancellor of Lancaster University and had served on a string of professional and advisory committees since the 1960s, including a seat on the new North-West Regional Board set up by Hall in 1970 – so he was no stranger to the Post Office.[63] But the terms of reference for his committee would be defined rather vaguely: there would be no explicit invitation to side for or against the Split, merely a requirement 'to consider whether any changes would better enable it to perform its functions under the Post Office Act 1969 . . .'[64]

Ryland reported back to his Board members that 'the decisive influences [on the outcome of the Split issue] would be the determination on the part of the Post Office – and possibly others – that the question be given full public debate, and the attitude of the Government'.[65] He then led by example, openly calling for the Split in a speech at Bath ten days later, and preparing a formal paper for the Board over the Christmas break which was debated and approved at the end of January 1976.[66] The decision to shelve the Split in 1969, it was noted, 'had been substantially influenced by UPW opposition' but had produced a situation in which directors of the Post Office now shouldered 'a workload . . . that only their personal dedication to the Post Office made tolerable'. The notion of a Semi-Split, with the Board fulfilling the role of a holding company, was impracticable given the persistent demands made on the Board by the Government. The result was a Corporation that it would be 'wrong and unfair' to suggest had failed to meet the past and present demands of it – but which would in future be hopelessly ill-suited to the 'critical and complex problems' looming for posts and telecoms alike. It was agreed that an end to the unitary Board concept would be recommended to the Review in due course.[67] Four months later, in a widely noted public lecture, Ryland spelt out a 'personal' view that he would go on reiterating for the next year. 'To manage these [two businesses] under the same roof sometimes seems like bringing harmony to Gog and Magog – and trying to make them believe in God at the same time. It is not very easy . . . The need for separate corporations is becoming more insistent and imperative . . . [and] the sooner it happens the better.'[68]

Meanwhile, the Carter Review itself had been launched on a flood of background papers – starting with the report of the Select Committee, published in December 1975, which unambiguously urged that 'the separation of posts and telecommunications should be examined by the review committee'.[69] There was never any danger of Carter and his seven colleagues overlooking it.* They conducted a review that was comprehensive even by the encyclopedic standards of past inquiries into the Post Office. Witnesses were cross-examined and written reports were pored over from January 1976 into the early weeks of 1977. The Committee members then set out their findings, in July 1977, in a report that was at least as searching as any of its predecessors, and a great deal more lucid than most. An Appendix in November 1977, with passages extracted from evidence submitted to the Committee, ran to 545 pages – a quarter of them representing a sample of the massive volume of material submitted by the Post Office itself. This was one measure of the Post Office's burden. The other was the devastating picture that emerged, of a postal service overwhelmed by its shortcomings when assessed as a commercial business.

The Report courteously acknowledged that, by focusing on what needed fixing, it might have been 'unfair to the real achievements and

---

* The other members of the Carter Committee comprised one trade unionist (L. W. Buck), two businessmen (B. S. Kellett and D. Sainsbury), a Ministry of Defence scientist (George Macfarlane), a City accountant (E. R. Nicholson) and two representatives of the consumer sector (R. McRobert and M. Waddilove). Its secretary was a civil servant and former official of the P&T Ministry, David Sibbick.

17. Sixty years of Post Office motoring. The first motor vehicles supplied either to the Post Office or (more often, in the pre-1914 era) to independent contractors working for it came from a variety of manufacturers, including (*top left*) Daimler in 1899 and (*top right*) the Maudslay Motor Co. of Coventry in 1907. When the Post Office began building its own in-house motor fleet in the 1920s, it ran into opposition for buying foreign-made vehicles, even those (*middle left*) from Ford, and eventually decided to rely almost wholly on Morris Motors. Models like (*middle right*) the Morris Minor van and (*bottom left*) the 'Z' type Morris van would eventually become integral to the public image of the postal service. The fleet's transition to diesel vehicles was led by (*bottom right*) a Morris commercial van, introduced in 1958.

18. Railways and the post in the 1930s. *Above*: More than fifty separate routes made up the TPO network, an essential part of the postal service from the 1840s until the start of the twenty-first century. Apart from the introduction of electric light, TPO interiors changed very little across the decades and remained much the same into the 1960s. *Below*: Postmen loading London's Mail Rail in 1935. Launched in 1927, the small-bore underground railway ran between Paddington and Whitechapel's Eastern District Office via six intermediary stops and remained in service until 2003.

19. Four who shaped the interwar years. *Top left*: the autocratic Evelyn Murray (1880–1947), Secretary from 1914 to 1934 and deeply sceptical of all reorganization proposals; (*top right*) Viscount Wolmer (1887–1971), in a portrait of 1919, whose 1928–32 campaign for a break-up of the Post Office attracted support from 320 MPs; (*below left*) former City solicitor Kingsley Wood (1881–1943), Postmaster General in the 1931–5 National Government, who used his tenure to instigate a radical reorganization of the Post Office and a successful rejuvenation of its public image; (*below right*) Stephen Tallents (1884–1958), sometimes described as the founder of corporate public relations, whose many clever publicity initiatives included his championing of the GPO Film Unit.

20. Nightwork in the 1930s. *Above*: Postmen in their distinctive 'shako' caps (phased out after 1932) emptying bags of mail down chutes to a conveyor belt at Birmingham Head Post Office. The figure to the right in spats and a trilby hat is the Unloading Bay supervisor, one of many ranks between management and the Manipulative grades. *Below*: Inside Mount Pleasant sorting office, the largest depot of its kind in the country (and generally known as just The Mount). Opened in 1889, it handled all inland mails posted in London as well as a substantial proportion of the inland mails passing through London or to addresses in the capital.

21. Spirit of the Blitz. *Above*: The sight of the morning post being delivered in the aftermath of night-time bombing was much prized by the authorities to help in sustaining morale. Steel helmets were issued to all postmen and postwomen from November 1940. *Below*: Many telephone exchanges had been designed with their switchboards on the top floor to take advantage of skylights, which added to the tension for switchboard operators who stayed at their posts (as many did) after warnings of an air raid.

22. Under the bombs. *Left*: The Central Telegraph Office in St Martin's-le-Grand was destroyed in the raid of 29–30 December 1940. *Right*: The narrow lane to the back of the CTO revealed the true extent of the damage to the building, which retained its frontage but had to be gutted and rebuilt. *Below*: The Royal Mail lost 77,000 parcels when a single bomb devastated Mount Pleasant's parcel-sorting section on 18–19 June 1943. Many of the country's largest Head Post Offices – including those of Birmingham, Liverpool, Manchester and Glasgow – suffered direct hits at some point during the war, and more than 400 postal workers were killed in the workplace by enemy raids.

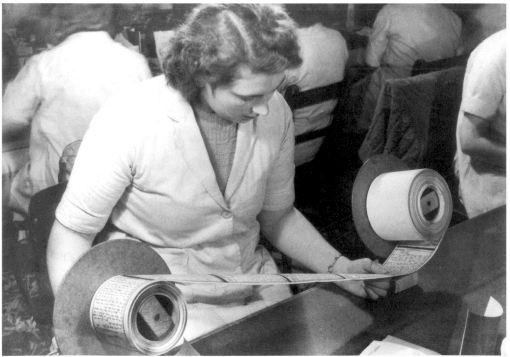

23. Adjusting to the needs of war. *Above*: Special wartime stationery included cards designed for POWs and for their relatives in Britain. A postal service to and from POW camps in Germany relied on intermediaries in Lisbon, and later Switzerland. *Below*: An airgraphs technician reviews an enlarged print-out of microfilmed letters, processed using a system developed by Eastman Kodak. It could record 1,700 letters on 100 feet of 16mm film.

COLOSSUS

COUNTERS

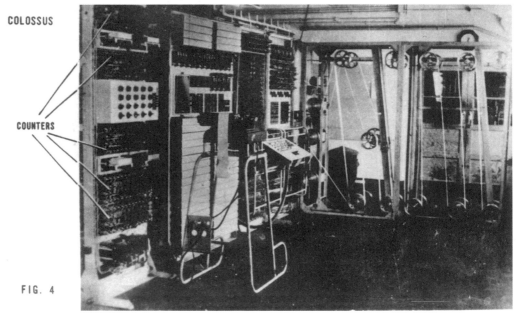

FIG. 4

24. Giants of the Second World War. *Left*: Thomas Gardener (1883–1964), Director General 1936-46, who combined a powerful personality with an unrivalled knowledge of the Post Office gained in a thirty-year career with the Department before his appointment to the top job. *Right*: Tommy Flowers (1905–98), clutching a handful of wartime valves in one hand and their 1990 equivalent in the other. His remarkable insight into the potential of electronic valves led him to propose and build the first programmable and wholly electronic computer. *Below*: The result, captured in a rare post-war picture for a Post Office manual, was Colossus, delivered by Flowers and his team to the codebreakers of Bletchley Park in January 1944. Ten were eventually built, of which eight were destroyed in 1945 and two scrapped in 1959–60.

good qualities of the Post Office'. But the list of grievances was nonetheless daunting. Some had a familiar ring: management was far too centralized and autocratic. ('The style of management . . . retains bad habits as well as good from the Civil Service tradition. The bad habits include a tendency to defend established positions with the utmost tenacity, sometimes long after they have ceased to be defensible. This conveys . . . an irritating impression that the management is so sure that it is always right that it feels no need to conceive of the possibility of being mistaken . . .'[70]) There were overly elaborate reporting lines and poor internal communications; there was too little respect for professional qualifications and a generally inadequate appreciation of engineering and research. But many other observations were a reflection of how far the performance bar had now been raised. The Post Office had no coherent pricing strategy or any real grasp of marketing at all; it had insufficient basic accounting data and it lacked the management-information systems required to tackle higher productivity objectives, or indeed any long-term financial planning. The essential drift of the Carter Report from start to finish was that the Corporation had so far covered little or no ground on its journey from being a government department to being an efficient and quasi-commercial operation. Its recommendations stretched over several pages, and even included a putative solution to the pension fund mess. (This had been a 'confused and sorry story', said the Report, putting forward urgent relief measures without which 'the burden will inescapably be greatly and excessively increased'.[71]) Most of its proposals were aimed specifically at the individual businesses, but these took second billing to the findings on general management principles and the structure of the Corporation – and there was one overriding conclusion that stood out above all others. The Report urged that the existing Post Office be divided into two separate authorities – one for the Posts and Giro, and the other for Telecoms and Data Processing – and that the present Board should begin to prepare for this without further delay. Its verdict on the Split could hardly have been more emphatic:

> The case [for separation] is reinforced by the general impression from the evidence given to us that the present combined management has led to over-centralisation, poor delegation and slow decision-taking. The overloading of the present single Board has, in our view, inhibited sound strategic thinking. The Post Office Board has not been an effective policy-making body producing a coordinated strategy . . .[72]

This prompted much disappointment and resentment within the UPW, rather as had the Priestley Commission twenty years earlier. But for Ryland and his colleagues, it meant that seven years of seemingly interminable interrogation had finally led to an outcome they could genuinely welcome. Talks about the Split were begun with officials at the Department of Industry even while Carter and his committee colleagues were still awash with early drafts of their text.

The Government appeared to have accepted the inevitable by March 1977 – and thoughts turned immediately to hiring a successor to Ryland, someone capable of serving as chairman and chief executive to a company with 430,000 employees while at the same time masterminding the Split's implementation. Ryland himself agreed to a further extension of his contract, already extended a year earlier, but it was understood that he would make way as soon as the new man was ready to start.* Eric Varley's Permanent Secretary, Peter Carey, set out to find him. The British economy at this point in the 1970s was beset with ailing national champions, from Clydeside shipbuilders and British Leyland to Rolls-Royce and British Airways. The Government had its own Industrial Development Advisory Board to help it sort out the lame ducks from the dead ducks, and one of the several heavyweight figures on this body was an industrialist called William Barlow. Carey approached him, presenting the Post Office job from the outset as fundamentally a task of corporate deconstruction and a unique opportunity. It was fifteen years since Barlow had returned from a four-year stint in North America, running a large business in Canada, but he had retained a certain detachment from the wretched performance of the UK economy in the meantime. He was disturbed by the falling standards of service and efficiency that he saw everywhere in 1970s Britain. It was easy to see the Post Office as a microcosm of the bigger picture, and he was soon persuaded by Carey that the chairmanship was a chance for him to make his own significant contribution to arresting the country's dismal decline. Barlow agreed to take it on, accepting in the process a huge drop in his salary.

Days after Barlow had resigned from his other main executive positions, but before his contract was finalized, news of his impending appointment leaked to the press.[73] But no immediate confirmation fol-

---

* But not a moment sooner. 'Ryland desperately didn't want to retire. In his final week, I said to him: "I assume you're not coming in on Friday?" His successor was due to start on the following Monday. He said "Why not?" and worked through on his last day until five o'clock' (John Roberts, interview with author, 16 October 2008).

lowed. Instead, Barlow was invited to Whitehall for a private meeting with the Minister. He was about to hear news of the third test posed for the Post Office in the 1970s – the obligation shortly to be placed on it by the Government to invite union representatives to take up seats in the boardroom. Barlow recalled:

> Varley asked me if I knew about the work being done on Industrial Democracy. I said yes, I'd followed it quite carefully. He said: 'It's a bit awkward, but I've got to tell you that the government has decided to go ahead with an experiment and we've chosen the Post Office. If you want to withdraw from the job, I'll quite understand.' I told him it was all very well talking about withdrawing, but I'd just withdrawn from all my other main roles![74]

In the course of a short discussion about the Government's objectives, Barlow learned that preparations for the experiment had gone a great deal further in private than he had realized. But he saw no reason to be deterred at the thought of working with the postal unions: they were hardly in the vanguard of union militancy, or so he thought. He would go ahead with the assignment, Industrial Democracy and all. His appointment was confirmed on the last day of May 1977 and he would start at the beginning of November.

5. INDUSTRIAL DEMOCRACY VERSUS A CAPTAIN OF INDUSTRY

The notion of workers' control had been cherished by the UPW since its earliest days. It was a legacy of the Guild Socialism that had been a potent influence on the leaders of the pre-UPW unions before the First World War. The closest the Union had ever come to fleshing out the idea was in 1954, with its vain attempt that year to win support for a Joint Administrative Council at the helm of the Post Office, on which union representatives and managers could enjoy equal status. Most other unions were at best ambivalent, and the TUC opposed it for years thereafter. But in 1966 Labour's National Executive set up a working party on 'Industrial Democracy' (as joint control by workers and managers had by now been christened), and it was chaired by Jack Jones, then still Assistant General Secretary of the T&GWU. The idea began to attract renewed interest, as part of the tumultuous debate over how best to reconcile free collective bargaining and the first Wilson government's fight against inflation. A year later, worker-directors were being appointed to regional boards at British Steel, under the direction of one Ron Smith.[75] By the early 1970s, when Jones was one of a small group of trade unionists wielding king-maker power in the country, the idea was receiving active support from the TUC. It was soon back on Labour's agenda as a valuable ingredient in its emerging pact with the unions. One of its keenest champions after Labour's return to power in March 1974 was the new Industry Secretary, Tony Benn. He saw Industrial Democracy as a 'one of the key components in the social contract for bringing Britain through the present crisis', as he would later put it to a meeting of the Institute for Workers' Control on the (far) fringe of the 1974 Labour Party Conference.[76] Benn at this time was full of ideas for extending the public ownership of British industry. The cumulative impact of what the press took to ridiculing as 'Bennery' was fast turning him into the Bogeyman of the political establishment. The Department of Industry took over Posts and Telecoms in April 1974. Within a few weeks, Benn had asked Ryland to let him have the Board's thinking on what might be done with Industrial Democracy at the Post Office.

Led from the front by Ryland, the Board had no doubt it was a bad idea. A reply went off to Benn in October 1974, explaining that 'the concept of a supervisory board with "worker directors" was unnecessary and undesirable in the Post Office, firstly because it would extend an already elongated decision-taking process, and secondly because of the conflict of interest that would inevitably result'.[77] Benn was of course no stranger to pained notes from postal officials, carefully explaining why this or that could not be done. Taking the reply with more than a pinch of salt, just as he might have done ten years earlier, he asked the two main unions for their views. These followed several months later, suggesting that the unions had a natural right to participate in decision-making rather than just consultative processes (in language that might well have been lifted wholesale from the early 1950s). When the directors took stock of the unions' proposals in October 1975, Ken Young was far from dismissive of the unions' proposals – strengthening a concern among some colleagues that he was becoming too close to the unions. But even Young thought they 'appeared to owe more to TUC dogma than to an attempt to develop solutions particular to Post Office problems'.[78] Given the steam building up behind them, the Board was going to have to tread warily. Jackson and his POEU counterpart, Bryan Stanley, stoked up the pressure in March 1976. Both told Eric Varley, now Industry Secretary in the wake of Benn's move to the Department of Energy in mid-1975, that ugly scenes might follow at their Annual Conferences in the spring unless progress was made – 'and that the Post Office had been placing too many obstacles in the way'. Varley duly asked the Board to cooperate in a tripartite study of the way forward, along with the unions and a posse of officials from the Department of Industry under the Deputy Secretary responsible for the Post Office, Ron Dearing. The Board had no real choice but to back down, conceding that 'one or two worker directors' might in fact have something to offer.[79]

Young and his staff had to devote an enormous amount of their time to these talks over the next six months. He himself believed a set of hard-nosed productivity deals was what the postal service really needed, but there was little opportunity to think about that, given the Government's preoccupation with its Industrial Democracy goals. (These were being pursued in the private sector, too, with an official inquiry under the historian (and biographer of Ernie Bevin) Alan Bullock, sitting between December 1975 and January 1977.) Still, Industrial Democracy at the Post Office did have some logic to it: the two main unions were solely concerned with the postal industry; their leaders were on close terms with Board directors; there was the long tradition of consultation between Official and Staff Sides that surpassed anything seen in the private sector; and union representatives at the grass roots enjoyed de facto control over much of what actually happened to the nation's mails each day. If union participation in Board management was to prove viable anywhere, it would surely have to be at the Post Office. Young himself was intrigued by the possibility. His Board colleagues, whatever their reservations, accepted his lead. A formal paper on Industrial Democracy arrangements was adopted in September 1976, in effect accepting the unions' long-standing demand for a 50/50 representation on the Board – though with more scope for guidance by the executive members and with more stringent conditions than had been developed, or even advocated, elsewhere.[80] Arriving at a joint recommendation to the Government still took several more months, but an agreement was finally hammered out in May 1977. Ryland appears to have been unhappy at the outcome, and certainly it was one of the more curious final acts of his chairmanship. But Gerald Kaufman, as Minister of State for Industry, congratulated him on 'a splendid final achievement' and the scene was set for Barlow's entry.[81]

Trained as an electrical engineer during the war – when he had served on minesweepers in the North Sea and the Mediterranean ('my finishing school') – Barlow was a 52-year-old Mancunian who had made his

mark as a top-notch manager with English Electric, one of the few
major British industrial companies with a genuine claim to world leadership in the post-war years. He was a man who knew his own mind, as
he had demonstrated by resigning in 1968. He had been with the company for twenty-one years, rising to become the youngest director on its
main Board – but had strongly objected to his colleagues' decision to
approve a merger between English Electric and Arnold Weinstock's
GEC. (This was the merger Ken Young did so much to bring to effect.)
Barlow quit the day the deal was signed.* Through most of the 1970s
he chaired a group, Ransom, Hoffman & Pollard, pulled together by the
Government's own Industrial Reconstruction Corporation to consolidate the country's ball-bearings industry. He led it effectively enough to
make it a world-class competitor, for which he was awarded a knighthood early in 1977. To Carey and the officials of the Department of
Industry, his past achievements by then as a troubleshooter, and his
extensive experience of business mergers, seemed to fit him ideally for
the task of seeing through the huge impending agenda for the Post
Office. For Barlow, engineering the Split would be a challenging prelude
to the real prize: he had his eye fixed from the start on emerging in the
end as head of an independent (and privatized) giant of the world telecoms industry. Naturally this private agenda was never openly flaunted
at the Post Office, but Barlow never made any effort to conceal his
enthusiasm for the future of the Telecoms business from his colleagues,
and his ultimate ambition was certainly understood in Whitehall ('there
was never any doubt about it'). His appointment thus marked an
important milestone. John Wall in 1966 and Leonard Hall in 1969 had
been token businessmen by comparison, given little if any scope to run
things any differently from their predecessors. Barlow was the real
McCoy, a captain of industry hired with an explicit brief to reconfigure
the Post Office.

   Though unfailingly courteous in his dealings with others, Barlow was
a no-frills professional manager, a down-to-earth and plain-speaking
character. Within a week or two of arriving at Howland Street, he

* His principal objection was to Weinstock's leadership. 'If the idea was good, he was the
wrong man to run it. I told the main board, "that man counts the cash on Monday morning
and counts it again on the next Monday morning – and if he's got more of it, then he thinks
he's made a profit. Well, this is a whole world of research, development and technology that
we have in strength at English Electric, and that he doesn't have at GEC. If he's going to run
it, I'm out!" It was a terrible blow to me.' (Sir William Barlow, interview with author, 21
September 2009.)

summoned the top 250 managers of the Corporation to a conference centre near St Martin's and addressed them with typical candour. He had heard plenty of stories about the Post Office over the years – not least from Gordon Radley, the former Director General, who had been his Chairman at English Electric – so Barlow was well aware of the impact his words would have, there in the hall and in their subsequent retelling across the organization. After a brief review of his own career, he set out a portrait of himself that in many ways presented a negative print of the image ever more associated with Post Officer managers by an increasingly hostile public since 1969:

> I like to start everything on time and as I try not to be late myself I therefore expect others to be punctual as well. I do not like long meetings and, in fact, I am not very keen on meetings at all . . . I do not like to be swamped with unnecessary detail . . . I do not like delay in decision-making and this is one thing that I shall be watching for from the start. I urge managers to make their own minds up, sometimes take a risk, but get on with it. I do not like bureaucracy and its stultifying effects. I do not like flannel or any of the other less complimentary expressions which mean the same thing . . .[82]

What followed was no ordinary pep talk. Barlow had warm words for the best traditions of the Post Office, 'this enormous collection of ability, knowledge and goodwill' as he put it. But he then proceeded, with a slightly clipped Lancashire delivery not yet familiar to his audience, to itemize a long list of operational weaknesses that he warned them would have to change. These included a poor use of statistics, a woeful neglect of marketing and public relations, a slack approach to management accounting and financial forecasting, and a lack of self-criticism and self-analysis in general. While setting out to remedy these flaws, said Barlow, he would be seeking every opportunity to pursue higher productivity in the workforce and a decentralization of responsibilities within the ranks of management, at every level.[83] He fully acknowledged the break that this decentralization would represent with the years under Ryland's leadership. Towards the end of a longish speech, Barlow then spelt out his view of the Corporation's relations with central government – which presaged an even sharper contrast between himself and not just Ryland but all his civil servant forebears:

> I feel that we have been ill-served by politicians in general since the war, because so often they have dealt with matters on a short-term basis that should be long-term issues and we have had too much stop-start, changes

of policy, interference with the running of business, interference with prices and interference with capital investment because of political pressure. I shall, therefore, insist that the Post Office business is given every chance to run its own show . . .

Unhappily for the new Chairman, he was about to get his own first taste of stop-start. The Carter Report's recommendation of the Split had galvanized its opponents at the UPW, who remained as opposed to it as ever. The Union assumed that all of its members in a separated telecoms business would abandon it, leaving a post-Split UPW much reduced in size and influence. There was also a strong ideological opposition to the move, which Jackson had already warned his 1977 Annual Conference 'will be the first and logical step towards hiving off sections of the profitable telecoms business to private industry'.[84] While Barlow had been preparing his remarks for the assembled managers, the UPW's General Secretary had been leaning heavily on the former Whitehall trade union official now in 10 Downing Street – and Callaghan gave way. Barlow, dismayed that Jackson had easy access to the Prime Minister where he had none, found himself before Christmas 1977 being asked to make no further public references to the Split and to abandon work on it: 'I got instructions to drop it'.[85] The mission for which he had quite expressly been hired was to be postponed indefinitely. The Labour government also made clear around this time that it had no interest in pursuing the idea of a grand advisory council, mediating between the Secretary of State and the Post Office. This had been the Carter Committee's second big idea. To complete its dismissal of the hapless committee's painstaking work, the Labour government then reaffirmed its commitment to the one radical innovation that the Carter Report had gone out of its way to reject: Industrial Democracy. 'Had we been consulted [about it] . . . we would have recommended Government to be cautious in encouraging developments in the superstructure of worker representation before the foundations had been laid . . . [The Government] would have been wiser to consider the implications . . . more deeply.'[86] Enabling legislation was nodded through, and Barlow was left no option but to press ahead on welding the superstructure into place.

By the time that Barlow appeared, the agreed blueprint for Industrial Democracy at the Post Office was probably already unworkable. The Government had forced two changes on the one agreed by Young. The first was an expansion of the Board's size. The Liberal Party in the Commons had refused to vote for the enabling legislation – which would have blocked its passage, given Labour's lack of an overall majority in the House – unless two 'consumer representatives' were included. As a result, whereas the original intention had been to have sixteen directors at most, there were now to be seven drawn from the management, seven from the trade unions and five independent members. Ryland had insisted in vain that this was an unmanageable number. Barlow concurred, but put a brave face on it and pressed ahead with eighteen directors, leaving one of the management seats empty.* It was mutually agreed that only individuals with no negotiating duties could be trade union directors. This allowed the experiment to go forward on the basis that, at least in theory, all its Members sat on the Board to further the interests of the Corporation as a whole, with no sectional interests. It also posed the obvious danger, though, that the union Members would be second-tier figures, always looking in practice to the leaders behind them, but such flaws in the initial structure were not at first seen as fatal. A two-year trial was launched in January 1978, with a fanfare in the media and plenty of genuine optimism around the Post Office. 'For a start, it has a long, strong history of worker–management cooperation based on a highly developed consultative and negotiating system', proclaimed the main internal newspaper, *The Courier*, in its February issue. 'The new scheme can therefore be seen as a natural progression, building on very firm foundations.' Parallel arrangements were set up at local and regional levels in the months that followed.

Those tiny flaws were soon great fissures. The trade union directors applied themselves conscientiously, but constantly found themselves torn between their loyalties to the Board and to their own Executives. (Were they there as Board members in their own right, or as representatives of their unions? It was a reprise of the debate inside the Labour movement of the late 1940s, when Geddes had taken up places for the UPW on Alexander Little's Joint Production Council.) The management

---

* The management directors were Barlow himself, Young, Peter Benton (Telecoms), Denis Roberts (Posts), Sam Wainwright (Giro and Remittance Services) and Frederick Waterhouse (Finance). The original union directors (some of whom gave way to others in the course of the experiment) were Fred Moss (UPW), Ivan Rowley (UPW), Peter Shaw (POEU), Arthur Simper (POEU), Nina Williams (CPSA), Robert Thomas (NFSP) and Ron Barrett (POMSA). The five independents were George Macfarlane (fresh from sitting on the Carter Committee), Derek Gladwin (a leading figure on the TUC who had already been on the Post Office Board since 1972), Peter Walters (Managing Director of BP), Michael Winstanley (a journalist and Liberal politician) and Janice Walsh (the manager of a consumer advice bureau in Islington, who was chosen from more than 1,000 applicants to represent the voice of the general consumer).

directors steadily retreated into their shells, leaving issues of any real sensitivity to be settled outside the boardroom – and leaving their Chairman to struggle with the conduct of a hopelessly overextended Board. Its table was so large that microphones had to be installed so that members at one end could hear those at the other. In public, each side stoutly praised the other and acclaimed the steady progress being made. Behind the scenes, there was rarely any rancour or animosity but nor was it all sweetness and light. Keen to have an unvarnished record of proceedings for his own personal use, Barlow asked the Company Secretary, Malcolm Argent, to prepare a set of confidential notes about each meeting in addition to the official Board Minutes.[87] Argent's reports, each fastidiously entitled 'Impressions of the Board Meeting' and typically running to several typescript pages, reveal – in entertaining if occasionally acerbic detail – how excruciatingly tiresome many of the Board discussions must have been, especially for a Chairman who was initially intent on keeping to a brisk timetable:

> Mr Barrett is proving to be an increasingly disruptive element in the Boardroom; Mr Willett continues to be repetitive; Mr Shaw continues to improve his technique; Miss Williams' contributions consist largely of criticisms of management in those areas in which the CPSA has a particular interest (although research and development seems also to have become a favourite subject of hers). Although her criticisms sometimes have some substance, they often fail through lack of coherence. Messrs Moss and Rowley seem to have re-established themselves after a bad patch. They have the ability to stand back from the 'constituencies' and take a more broad view of their responsibilities. The 'consumer' members and Mr Walters seem to be fading more and more into the background, making little if any contribution.[88]

After a generally good-humoured first few months, a row erupted in April 1978 over Union claims that too little information was being made available to Members. The Chairman duly arranged for the distribution of papers originally written for circulation below Board level – but a rising volume of paperwork did nothing for the effectiveness of the meetings. Argent commented of the July Board that it had been 'perhaps as depressing for some of the participants as for those who observe and take note'. Some of the union directors, notably the two UPW officers, proved to be extremely able and made many useful contributions as they gained in confidence. Others found adjusting to their unfamiliar environment (why were there no votes?) much more difficult, as the unofficial minutes recorded. One customarily gave 'his normal impression of a rumbling volcano'; another was prone to long monologues, many of them 'reasonably clear and almost audible'; a third specialized in the verbatim repetition of his colleagues' earlier remarks. By the summer of 1978, Barlow was reporting back to Kaufman that it was very heavy going.[89] The autumn brought the first big test over the conflict of interests posed for the UPW Members by a contentious pay negotiation. In November, Barlow heard from Young that the two UPW men had been instructed by their Executive to walk out of the Board and resign, rather than go along with discussions unfavourable to the Union.[90] Barlow's exasperation over the whole experiment reached a new high the next month, when Varley overrode his objections to the appointment of a new Member whose own Union Executive had been only too keen (or so it was reliably reported) to get rid of him.[91] Barlow told his Secretary of State that the size and composition of the Board meant its affairs were taking up an insanely disproportionate amount of his time.

The burden was doubly irksome considering the progress that was meanwhile being made on other fronts. For Barlow had been delivering on his promise to delegate and decentralize from Howland Street wherever he could – and had been helped by the successful outcome of a general changing of the guard. Fennessy had retired in June 1977 and been succeeded as Managing Director for Telecoms by a former McKinsey consultant, Peter Benton; work on the System X project was accelerating encouragingly, and plans were being made for a national network of fibre optic cables. In Posts, Currall had given way to Denis Roberts, who, though sixty-three years old, was determined to prove himself more than a stop-gap. Once he had recovered from the shock of being told by his new Chairman that the postal workforce was going to have to shed 30,000 posts, Roberts applied his long experience with a vigour that belied a famously cautious temperament. By mid-1978, he had already achieved a break-even performance in parcels, described in the Carter Report as a business 'in deep trouble'.[92] Other Board changes included the departures of the Technology Director, the Finance Director and the head of the Giro and Remittance Services. In fact, the Personnel and Industrial Relations Director was almost the only survivor in the boardroom. (Young probably enjoyed being described by Jackson as 'the last little Indian' in the latter's monthly column in *The Post*.[93]) This sweeping change of faces could hardly fail to suggest the start of a new era – and the state of the underlying businesses obligingly took a turn for the better, too. Revenues taken at Post Office counters were slowly rising after years of decline. Even the outlook for traffic volumes, on which Carter and his colleagues were consistently pessimistic, offered some slight grounds for optimism: the volume of overseas letters had jumped by 10 per cent in 1977–8, with a significant shift from surface mails to airmails. In a Five Year Plan for the postal business, Roberts saw the number of overseas letters growing by a third by 1983. He was also confident that the recent sharp fall in inland letters – down almost 20 per cent from 10.8 billion in 1974–5 to 8.8 billion in 1976–7 – could be halted, though like everyone else he doubted there was much that could be done to reverse a downward trend in the longer term: he forecast that letter volumes might be falling by about 2.5 per cent a year by 1983.[94] Meanwhile, the Giro – which had been languishing for years – had been handed over to a former City banker, Sam Wainwright, who had moved immediately to revitalize its business model. All three main businesses at the Post Office would report decent profits for the year to March 1978 – though of course 'telecom' profits had by now swollen to cuckoo-in-the-nest proportions. (See again Appendix A, Chart 8.) The numbers eventually emerged at £40m for Posts, £327m for Telecoms and just under £2m for the Giro – which prompted an upbeat feature in the *Financial Times* in May talking of a honeymoon period for the recently installed Chairman.[95]

Nor was it just at the very top that new appointments were beginning to work some much needed magic. Barlow buzzed around the country visiting local offices from his very first month. He encountered everywhere an airy disdain for the most basic marketing principles: 'the reactions I got just typified the complete ignorance [among our staff] about what they were supposed to be doing, [for] service to the customer. . . . I couldn't believe how totally uncommercial they were . . .'[96] He was soon taking a close look at the postal business's ailing Marketing Department in St Martin's. Its first director, George White, had striven valiantly for years against a prevailing culture that too often saw marketing as an avoidable frippery. (Carter had been scathing about this: 'Sometimes its customers get the feeling that they are being graciously permitted to use the [postal] systems'.[97]) White's successor, Nigel Walmsley, had been appointed in May 1977 after a year at Manchester Business School. Having joined the Post Office straight from university as a civil service graduate trainee in 1964, Walmsley was still only thirty-five, which in the old days would have glued him fast to a point somewhere half-way up the career tree. Barlow insisted, with ready support from Denis Roberts, that Walmsley be given additional resources and active encouragement to break with the past. This went much deeper than simply allowing Walmsley the extra budget to rent a first car fleet for his sales force (though that happened, too), as he recalled:

> If I developed a plan or a proposal, I found that I was being able to access larger resources than anyone else could do. What we did seemed revolutionary at the time, but was nothing especially clever. I just wanted to import the language and vocabulary of marketing – words like 'segmenting the market', 'pricing along the demand curve', 'targeting market sectors' and so on. These started to become a natural part of the daily dialogue. And the more the activities were clothed with the right labels, the more they became a part of the way that people around the organization began to think.[98]

Another 35-year-old picked out for special promotion was Bill Cockburn. Since leaving Ryland's office in 1973, he had worked for a couple of years in the Post Office Treasury at Howland Street and then as Assistant Finance Director in Postal HQ. These were years in which the Post Office was a frequent borrower on the international capital markets, issuing a spate of (mostly) dollar-denominated Eurobonds. (Heavy capital spending on new plant and equipment for the Telephone business far exceeded the annual cash proceeds of the Corporation, so loans from either the Treasury or the markets had to make up the difference.) All its bonds were government-guaranteed and involved Cockburn in constant dealings with the Bank of England. The Post Office was one of a coterie of guaranteed public-sector borrowers – another was British Gas – whose access to the international bond market provided some relief for a hard-pressed Treasury during the Chancellorship of Denis Healey.* Cockburn's obvious commercial instincts attracted Barlow's attention and he found himself in 1978 appointed as Howland Street's Director of Corporate Planning. To make up for his own lack of a Post Office background, meanwhile, Barlow turned to a couple of talented executives recommended to him by Ryland. One was Malcolm Argent, who had finally escaped the centre for a job as Regional Director in East Anglia: Barlow pulled him back as Company Secretary. Another was

---

* Indeed, Post Office funds seem to have attracted the Treasury's attention as a welcome source of ready cash on more than one occasion in the crisis years before and after Britain's 1976 loan from the IMF. 'I remember we got a message one night from the Chancellor's office saying we had to provide £200m and get it over to the Treasury in cash, in double-quick time. We had to sell off a lot of telephone exchanges and lease them back.' (Malcolm Argent, interview with author, 16 October 2009.)

John Roberts, who had been working in the Chairman's office (for the second time) since 1976 and who now became Barlow's right-hand man as he set about a root-and-branch assault on the old Post Office culture.

This had its lighter moments. One of Barlow's pleasanter surprises on arriving at Howland Street was to find that he had a personal steward, complete with pinstriped trousers and a cream jacket. The post had been a typical piece of extravagance by Lord Hall, but the incumbent had made himself so useful since 1969 that he was still there. Bob Young introduced himself to the Chairman with characteristic bluntness. 'I'd just like to say to you, sir, that we should have a month's trial period. Then if you don't like me, I'll go back to being a postman; and if I don't like you, well I'll still ask to go back to being a postman.'[99] Flummoxed by this, Barlow agreed to the terms. The two men soon discovered that they had both served on minesweepers during the war, and there was no looking back. The new Chairman learned much about the Post Office from his steward. It intrigued him that references were constantly made in the early days to 'The Manual'. Young presented him one morning with a whistle, assuring him that a quick blast at any time would bring his steward running. When Barlow raised an eyebrow at this, he was told the Chairman had to have his whistle – it was in 'The Manual'. Such references continued for weeks. Each time Barlow asked to see a copy of 'The Manual', some distraction always prevented it. Eventually, he demanded that his steward fetch it for him to see. 'I can't do that', said Young, and Barlow was led downstairs to a big room in the basement. There sat 'The Manual', along more than thirteen feet of shelving. It was the *Head Postmaster's Manual*, accumulated over many generations and still being kept up to date with regular amendments. Barlow stopped it immediately. The Manual Department was abolished and no more editions were ever issued. The Treasury Letter Books, maintained since 1686, fell in the same culling of outdated traditions.

There was one tradition that Barlow found almost impossibly difficult to combat through his first year. He was disconcerted from the outset to discover that, for all of Ken Young's strenuous efforts to overhaul relations with the unions, almost any initiative sought by senior managers, however trivial, was still subject to extensive prior discussion with union representatives in the workplace. His disquiet turned to dismay after his own first few personal encounters with some of the representatives in the larger city post offices. Barlow was no stranger to tough industrial relations. As an English Electric manager in Liverpool in the mid-1950s, he had brought an end to a climate of constant strikes there by dismissing from his payroll the local head of the Electrical Trades Union on Merseyside, a Communist Party member called Leslie Cannon.* What he found at the Post Office seemed to him far more disruptive. Yet there was never any question of purging its union problems by taking punitive action against the union leaders, as Ken Young wasted no time explaining. The UPW and POEU hierarchies were more sensibly approached as allies in the struggle to channel all workplace disagreements through the Facilities Agreements, achieved by Young earlier in the 1970s. Unfortunately, this provided no quick fix for debilitating problems in many regions, especially in London, which included an increasingly regular resort to unofficial strikes. Nor did it offer a solution to the constant problem posed by the disparate priorities of the postal and Telecoms businesses. Generous pay awards to the engineers made sense for the Telecoms business – but the same awards would apply to their engineer counterparts in the postal business, and were always liable to be used there as a basis for awards to the manual grades. Like many other dilemmas that Barlow faced, it led him back to the urgent case for splitting the Post Office apart.

Callaghan's veto on the Split was confirmed in a White Paper of July 1978 spelling out the Government's objections. Its scepticism about the practicalities of effecting the Split was exceeded only by its faith in the catalytic properties of Industrial Democracy, the success of which at the Post Office would 'show how technical change and improvements in performance can better be managed with the participation of employees at all levels'. By contrast, legislation for a Split would be complex, 'and its preparation and implementation would divert scarce managerial and administrative skills at some cost, at least in the short term, to the management priority that the Government considers should be given to promoting efficiency and containing costs . . .'[100] In a backhanded compliment to Barlow's impact, it was suggested that less would be achieved by a Split than by the measures he was taking to decentralize the organization. Barlow himself thought this was nonsense. It was also a blatant betrayal of the understanding he had reached with the Department before his appointment. He was ready for a political battle; but with a general election looming in the autumn, it seemed prudent to wait and see how events might unfold at Westminster. This strategy paid

---

* Years later, with greatly modified views, Cannon would rise to become his union's General President and one of the most widely respected figures in the trade union movement. He was awarded a knighthood in 1970, but died before the honour was published.

off handsomely, once Callaghan had passed on the election opportunity and been engulfed by the electorate's reaction to a climactic winter of strikes all across the public sector. By March 1979, the prospect of a thumping defeat for Labour in the approaching election was motivation enough for Barlow at last to prepare for action against the Split veto. By this time, his patience with Industrial Democracy was all but exhausted, too. He began to prepare for a Conservative government, on which he was relying to sweep aside both obstacles.

He wrote his own paper for the Board, reminding it of the conclusion reached by Ryland and his colleagues in January 1976. The Semi-Split, he acknowledged, was well advanced (though he did not use that term). The two main businesses nonetheless remained closely integrated at the centre, in a Corporation that was now too big to be managed effectively from one Board. There was a gulf between the businesses, and it was getting wider every year. He had done what he could to allow senior managers more freedom of action. 'But in my experience, decentralisation and devolution of decision-making cannot in themselves provide a satisfactory solution to the fundamental issues. . .'[101] The paper was debated by the Board on 24 April 1979, along with a paper from Ken Young that made clear, in effect, that coordinating the industrial relations of the two main businesses, and the National Giro as well, had begun to involve damaging compromises.[102] Barlow told the Board he 'was finding it increasingly embarrassing that he was not able to give the views of the present Board on this important issue'. It was vital that he should be able to approach the next Industry Secretary, regardless of the election's outcome, with a straightforward recommendation. The discussion lasted almost two hours. It provided plenty of material for another of the Impressions recorded privately for Barlow.* The result, though, was never really in doubt. The two UPW men had objected to

---

* 'Mr Barrett [of the Post Office Management Staffs Association] then volunteered his contribution. He started off by saying that he had looked into the background of this subject and had noted that, of those bodies not directly involved with the Post Office who had given evidence to the Carter Committee, only four had positively favoured a split of the Corporation. . . . He also commented that the Carter Report itself did not recommend a total split. The Chairman, obviously fearing that Mr Barrett's contribution was going to develop into a major dissertation, attempted to stem his flow by asking for his own views; Mr Barrett replied that he was opposed. But he then went on to quote from a table of figures . . . [and] to indicate that in real terms the Corporation had not grown all that much over the last thirty years and, therefore, what was good enough then was good enough now . . . [an argument] that did not seem to cut very much ice with anybody . . .' (Impressions of the Board Meeting, 24 April 1979, Barlow papers, WB2).

the issue being raised at all prior to the election: they thought no view could be taken until the autumn of 1979 at the earliest, and two other union Members broadly concurred. All the executive directors lined up with Barlow. The official minutes noted that, with the exception of the four union Members, the Board 'was firmly of the view that the present Post Office Corporation should be split at the earliest possible opportunity'.[103]

Very soon after the election of the Thatcher government in May, Barlow was invited to a meeting at the Department of Industry with its new Secretary of State, Sir Keith Joseph. He arrived alone, expecting a private discussion. He found Joseph flanked at the table by Peter Carey and a dozen other civil servants. By his own account, it was a bad start: Barlow felt ambushed and refused to continue the meeting on such unequal terms. He was eventually placated by a promise that he would be allowed to see the minutes of the meeting. Joseph then opened the discussion by explaining that he was just calling in all the chairmen of the nationalized industries for a preliminary talk to lay down the ground rules that the Conservative government had in mind for their dealings with Whitehall. Barlow recalled his response very clearly:

> I said: 'As a matter of fact, I was just going to give you a ring, Sir Keith, to ask if I could come and see you. I've been in this job for eighteen months. I'm sick to death of the Government's interference and the fact that the Split still isn't being done – and I'm just about ready to say I'm off, to do something else. So we've got a chasm between us, Sir Keith, and I suggest that you and I need to have a chat on our own.'[104]

The chat followed the next day. Over a glass of whisky, it was agreed that the Split would go ahead. The two men struck up an immediate understanding, which was also the start of a warm friendship. At long last, the general outlook for the Post Office – and for his own ambition to run a world-beating telecoms company – looked to its Chairman to be a good deal brighter. There seemed no doubting that British politics was on the brink of a fundamental transformation. It was hard for Joseph to go into the Government's plans in any detail, of course. Much remained unclear – and as Joseph himself was quick to point out, he was merely the Industry Secretary. It was the lady in Downing Street who would be making the crucial decisions.

12

Once more unique,
1979–87

Satchel on hip
the postman goes
from doorstep to doorstep
and stooping sows

each letterbox
with seed. His right
hand all the morning makes,
the same half circle. White

seed he scatters,
a fistful of
featureless letters
pregnant with ruin or love . . .

Jon Stallworthy, 'The Postman' (1980)

I. THE SPLIT WITH TELECOMS, AND WITH WILLIAM BARLOW

No one was talking about 'privatization' in the immediate aftermath of Margaret Thatcher's May 1979 election victory, but the Tories' manifesto had committed them to a speedy reversal of the main nationalization measures since 1974, notably the state's takeover of the aerospace and shipbuilding industries in 1977. Anxious about a growing Public Sector Borrowing Requirement and urgently seeking ways to finance it that would not add to an already worrying surge in the rate of inflation, ministers were very soon under obvious pressure to go further by coming up with 'special asset sales' that might generate a quick return for the Treasury. Perhaps William Barlow's hour had come at last. He was

keen to win clearance for the eventual sale of a very special asset indeed –
a flotation on the stock market of the Post Office's Telecoms business.

There was another speedy reversal in prospect that suited Barlow,
too: the new administration was determined to confront head-on the
power of the trade unions, particularly in the public sector, and the
UPW was one of the most obvious targets. It was exclusive to the Post
Office, whose monopoly of the country's postal service allowed the
Union – or so the new Government believed – to push its demands with
no regard for their impact on financial performance or quality of service. The Industry Secretary, Keith Joseph, was the politician whom
Thatcher had charged a few years earlier with the task of formulating a
fresh economic and social agenda for the Conservatives: his leadership
had provided much of the intellectual driving force behind what became
Thatcherism. Within months of the election, Joseph was talking about a
possible abolition of the postal monopoly as a price that might be worth
paying, if it could help transform the productivity of the postal workforce. (This led to a referral to the Monopolies and Mergers Commission
(MMC) in September, asking it to look at the functioning of the Post
Office in Inner London to see whether it 'operates, or may be expected
to operate, against the public interest'.[1])

Barlow did not take threats of an end to the postal monopoly too
seriously, but he did welcome the apparent new willingness to square up
to the unions. It happened that a serious strike by computer operators
in Post Office Telecommunications was badly disrupting the issuing of
bills through that summer, with potentially damaging consequences for
the Treasury as well as for the Post Office's own cashflow. Barlow asked
the new Chancellor, Geoffrey Howe, if he and the Prime Minister were
sure they had the stomach for what might be a long dispute. The answer
was a resounding yes, as he recalled: 'Howe said: "Yes, I'm definitely
with you" and then "I'd better check it out with the Prime Minister";
and of course she said: "Yes, we're right behind you."'[2] Against this
background, it can be no surprise at all that by the end of the year the
Thatcher government had washed away the last objections to the Split
and had thrown out Industrial Democracy. Yet when they then began to
make arrangements for working with Barlow on future plans for the
Post Office, ministers found they had unintentionally disposed of his
services.

By the time the government changed in May 1979, the Chairman's
disenchantment with life at the helm of a nationalized industry was well
advanced, as he had several times hinted to the senior civil servant

responsible for Post Office affairs at the Department of Industry, Ron Dearing.[3] Barlow was never comfortable dealing with the media, as he frequently had to do; nor was he much interested in navigating his way smoothly through Whitehall. The constant interference of politicians in his domain irked him, and as a new set of ministers now turned their attention to privatization and industrial relations he was disappointed to find his situation hardly less frustrating than before. Of course, it was gratifying that Callaghan's veto was past and that the Split could be endorsed as a government objective, especially when Joseph announced a legislative timetable for it in September. But when it came to building on the Split as he intended, Barlow struggled to make any progress beyond broad agreement that he would head the Telecoms business while another executive chairman would be found for the postal service. Among his other formidable characteristics, Barlow was renowned for his directness, and in July, when he met with Joseph and Dearing at a private dinner at Lockett's restaurant in Westminster, he perhaps rather rashly laid down a market flotation of the Telecoms business as one of his conditions for staying at the Post Office.[4] But careful inquiries in the City had persuaded Thatcher that investor support for a privatization of the Telecommunications business would not be forthcoming, and she personally vetoed it.

Barlow continued to think otherwise. He also believed that direct access to the capital markets, free of Treasury constraints, would be essential for the telecoms business if it was to grow as he envisaged. He was bitterly disappointed by Thatcher's reaction but decided to persevere in the hope of winning her over. His efforts culminated in a dinner with the Prime Minister and her advisers, hosted in the autumn of 1979 by the Governor of the Bank of England, Gordon Richardson.[5] It did not go well. The officials at the dinner insisted that, whatever the legal status of the business, the markets would always infer a tacit Treasury guarantee for any loans that 'British Telecom' – as it was soon to be rechristened – might raise in the open market, and Thatcher was not about to grant anyone a licence to add to the Government's borrowing levels. This scotched Barlow's principal argument in favour of a sale. The political rationale for wider share ownership of the telecoms business seems not to have been broached at all: the appeal of privatization as the fulfilment of a compelling ideology had yet to emerge, and Barlow found himself facing a Prime Minister weighing her options with a pragmatism he had not expected. Around the same time, 'cash limits' were announced for the Post Office and other nationalized industries, setting a ceiling on the extent to which they could borrow money to top up their internal funding for capital expenditure. Cash limits were to be an integral part of the Thatcher government's campaign to reduce public spending, but for Barlow they confirmed that running British Telecom as a state-owned company would be a fool's errand.

This, by the middle of 1979, was also more or less how Barlow regarded the mission he had been assigned in November 1977 with the launch of Industrial Democracy. Over the summer, he and his fellow 'Full-Time Members' had handed a long written appraisal to Joseph, cataloguing the defects of the hybrid Industrial Democracy Board in often colourful detail.[6] It seemed by September that it only remained for the last rites to be administered, in order for the experiment to be interred at the end of its two-year trial, or earlier. But this took no account of wider political calculations. The Minister responsible for the decision was James Prior, the Employment Secretary, whose main priority was the drafting of an Employment Bill aimed at a wide-ranging reform of trade union law. Prior was anxious to avoid upsetting the TUC, which he hoped might yet be won over to reform without a bruising confrontation. This approach did him no good at all in the long run (for it was starkly at odds with his Prime Minister's instincts), but it led to a word in Barlow's ear, warning him that he might have to abandon hopes of an early end to Industrial Democracy as one snub too many to the TUC.[7]

This drew an angry response at the end of October 1979. Barlow wrote to the Industry Department, itemizing the main objectives of the experiment in six paragraphs. Under each was written in capital letters, 'THIS HAS NOT HAPPENED'. He urged that Industrial Democracy 'should be dropped now'.[8] But this did not happen, either. On the contrary, Barlow was alarmed to find arguments for an extension of the trial gathering momentum. Suddenly the outcome of the debate looked uncertain. Reactions to an inch-thick report on the experiment from academics at the University of Warwick perfectly encapsulated its failure: the Board could not agree even on their interpretation of the report, let alone how best to respond to it.[9] The Secretary dryly recorded that its findings were 'essentially anthropological'. When the moment finally arrived to take stock of the Board's position, eight Members were against continuing the experiment – but ten were for it, or at least thought it too early to reach a decision. They included Ken Young, who indicated a readiness to continue if the Board could be made smaller. This was not acceptable to Barlow.

The showdown came one evening early in December, in Jim Prior's office. By Barlow's own account, the Minister put it to him that turfing the union Members off the Board at this point would be awkward, given the Department's wider agenda. The presence at the meeting of Keith Joseph and Nigel Lawson, the Financial Secretary to the Treasury, reflected the importance attached by the Government to this advice. The Chairman's characteristic response was nonetheless unequivocal: 'I said, "That's got nothing to do with me. Tomorrow morning, I'm going to Canada for Christmas. If I don't get a message from my assistant that you've agreed to stop it, I shall take a good, long holiday with my family over there and I won't be coming back in January." Then I got up and walked out.'[10] Days later, on 12 December, Joseph announced in the Commons that the Post Office's trial of Industrial Democracy was over.

So Barlow came home in the New Year. The Government's capitulation, however, had restored his appetite for the public sector only fleetingly. Altogether, he had had enough. He presented a formal paper to the Board on the transitional structure that he had devised for the run-up to the Split.[11] Days later, he set off on a trip to the US. Accompanied as usual by John Roberts, he visited AT&T and Bell Laboratories in New Jersey, then IBM and ITT. Everywhere the two Post Office men heard senior executives of the US telecoms industry confidently spelling out their plans for the future – and how they would finance them. The contrast with his own situation at the Post Office was more than Barlow could bear. Soon after his return, late in January 1980, he told Roberts he had made up his mind to return to the private sector.[12] He dropped a resignation note on Keith Joseph's desk at the start of February. The Industry Secretary was astounded, and deeply disappointed, as were Barlow's colleagues in the boardroom.

His decision landed officials in the Department of Industry with a delicate timing problem. The future British Telecom had lost its putative first chairman before it had even got going. Meanwhile the search for a chairman of the reconfigured Post Office, under way for a few months, had worked its way through dozens of candidates without result.[13] It was unthinkable that news of Barlow's departure could be released without having a new transitional chairman for the Post Office or anyone to name as head of either of the two separated businesses. Months earlier, Barlow himself had had no hesitation in pushing his choice as the best man for the postal job – the Department of Industry's own Ron

Dearing, with whom he had been working closely on the details of the Split. Dearing had been offered the job but had turned it down, saying that he lacked the qualifications. After Barlow's resignation, such laudable modesty fell on deaf ears and Dearing was persuaded to change his mind. His appointment, announced in April 1980, left many feeling distinctly underwhelmed. A full decade had passed since the Post Office had been extricated from the civil service (not to mention the fiasco over its first chairman) – and now the Government was putting a civil servant back in charge. It seemed only too likely that Whitehall had stuck to the letter of the 1969 Act, while laying its spirit to rest. Few supposed a mandarin with no public profile would really be capable of continuing the transformation of the Corporation that had at last begun to gain momentum.

At least Barlow undertook to remain in the chair until September 1980, to complete the Split agenda he had launched within weeks of the 1979 election. He led this work himself, with two executive assistants and a war-room at Howland Street but no outside consultants. Neither at the time nor subsequently was he given due credit for this in the outside world. Of course, much of the separation had already occurred: those employed within posts and telecoms were coexisting as virtually discrete tribes even before Barlow's arrival in 1977, and at the level of local and regional operations they almost everywhere occupied different locations. In Birmingham, for example, the Midlands Postal Board sat at one end of the city's Lionel Street while Midland Telecoms sat in a tower at the other; the two regional head offices had scarcely anything to do with each other.[14] Across the country, the divergence had gone well beyond a physical division of premises and budgets: the management cultures of the two businesses were palpably different. This was largely attributable to the greater importance to telecoms of technology and innovation, but also reflected the latter's more progressive policies on recruitment, training and promotion. And at the policy level it had been a bugbear since the start of the Ryland era that the chiefs met only once a month, at Board meetings where each side sat in uncomprehending silence through discussions about the other's affairs. Nevertheless, this unsatisfactory Semi-Split had relied upon an extensive sharing of the financial, administrative and logistical corporate services which underpinned a business employing about 450,000 people. Barlow recalled that 'a vast amount of the resources were all pooled'. Assigning them to separate legal entities was a formidable undertaking.[15]

Only in two areas did the Chairman meet with any real equivocation.* One came as no surprise at all, the other as a shock. The Post Office Solicitor did not take kindly to the idea of dividing his department and its team of fifty lawyers. In the end, with all the courtesy he could muster, the Chairman simply took a cleaver to the Department and chopped it down the middle. The shock was the reaction of many of his senior colleagues in the Post Office, when Barlow offered them all a choice between two careers. He himself had no doubt where the future lay and assumed others would make the same calculation, opting to join British Telecom. 'I thought there was going to be a mass migration', as he recalled. 'But there wasn't. Strangely to me, [some of the best] people on the postal side seemed to want to stay there.'[16] Those choosing to remain in the future Post Office included Ken Young as well as John Roberts, Nigel Walmsley and Bill Cockburn. Iain Vallance, the son of a former Chairman of the Post Office in Scotland and like Roberts a former Personal Assistant to Bill Ryland, tried at first to stay with his postal peers but was chivvied by Barlow into joining British Telecom – where he would later rise to become Chief Executive and eventually the Chairman.

From April to September 1980, Barlow soldiered on while the telecoms chairmanship passed to a new appointment, Sir George Jefferson, and the postal chairmanship to Dearing. Both would serve as designated chairmen until the Split actually happened in October 1981, respectively heading their own telecom and post boards that reported to the main Board. At Barlow's last appearance on the Board in September 1980 – to be succeeded as 'transitional' chairman by a distinguished engineer from the academic world, Sir Henry Chilver – it was Dearing who spoke for all in praising his role since 1977: 'his generous delegation of responsibility, coupled with encouragement to show initiative, had stimulated not only his Board colleagues but all levels in the Corporation'.[17]

Finding the right words on important occasions came naturally to Dearing, who brought with him to the Post Office a set of fine mandarin skills. He was soon in need of them, when he and Jefferson were plunged by the Treasury into tortuous negotiations over the future of the Post

---

* Actually, the Split encountered one other delicate issue. Buckingham Palace insisted that its switchboard should remain under the control of the state-owned Post Office rather than a telecommunications company that looked likely to end up in private ownership before long. The Post Office graciously accepted this royal appointment, which it retained until 2007.

Office pension fund. Dearing scored a coup in persuading the Treasury that the whole of the existing actuarial deficit on the fund – around 45 per cent of which was attributable to postal workers – should pass to British Telecom, whose employees were to have their own separate pension fund. The Post Office Board had decided during the 1970s to charge the costs arising from the deficit to the telecoms side of the business, given its far superior earning power, and the Treasury agreed with Dearing that the outcome to date should, in effect, be made permanent. The logic remained as before: British Telecom in 1979–80 had generated profits of £236m, almost five times the £49m earned by the postal service.

The decision added, however, to mounting disquiet among Jefferson's colleagues at the Telephone business through the early months of 1981. Much as predicted by Barlow, Treasury cash limits forced British Telecom into a series of unpopular price increases and the postponement of several critical investment projects. This triggered a crisis over the future of the business, and Keith Joseph would belatedly accept the thrust of Barlow's case less than ten months after the latter's departure, authorizing his Department in July 1981 to begin confidential work on legislation for a sale of British Telecom – 'an important moment in the history of British privatisation'.[18] The Government announced its intended flotation of the company in July 1982, and a majority stake in the business was sold off in November 1984. It was the first privatization of a leading British utility and in addition to attracting strong demand from the institutional investors of the City, it proved far more popular with the wider public than most Whitehall officials had thought possible a few years earlier. Barlow had by then resumed a successful career in the private sector – where he subsequently took up directorships with two leading names in the international telecoms industry, Ericsson and Vodafone – but his judgement had been vindicated in the end.

Meanwhile, in the first nine months after his appointment in May 1980, Dearing had to contend with an even bigger test of his mandarin skills than the pensions imbroglio. He was appalled to find himself presented shortly after his arrival as Chairman-designate in May 1980 with an all but unavoidable proposal for a steep rise in the price of 1st and 2nd class stamps. Having had the misfortune to lose one chairman rather suddenly, the Post Office now came carelessly close to losing a second in short order. The request for approval of a 2p rise in the price of both 1st and 2nd class stamps went off to Downing Street for approval – and met with a blast of indignation that echoed round

Whitehall. 'I heard that Margaret Thatcher asked how quickly she could discontinue my appointment', as Dearing himself recalled.[19] The timing of the request could not have been worse. All public bodies in 1980 were under intense pressure from the Government to rein back wages and postpone price increases: no exception could be made for the Post Office, and its effrontery in supposing otherwise seems to have incensed the Prime Minister. It strengthened her suspicion that too many of its senior managers were semi-detached from reality. She was already contemplating some radical remedies; the pricing proposal suggested these might have to include replacing the hapless former Deputy Secretary. More fundamentally, the question of the postal monopoly's viability – first raised by Joseph rather airily in the summer of 1979 – was now squarely on the table. So too was privatization, not just for telecoms but for the Post as well.

Joseph had warned as much in a letter to the Board just ahead of Dearing's arrival. The Split-enabling bill would be drafted, said the Minister, to include powers for the Government to tamper with the letter monopoly. As the Board noted, these powers 'might then be used both in relation to categories of mail and to circumstances when industrial action or other internal causes seriously affected mail services in either the whole country or part of it . . . The aim of the Government was to put pressure on the workforce in major black spots in the [postal] system . . .'[20] In the subsequent Board discussion, it was acknowledged that postal competition was a real possibility. The Post Office would not oppose it *per se*, but had serious reservations about the process: 'the Post Office would certainly wish to avoid the odium of being the licensing authority for its own competitors . . .' No sooner had Dearing moved from Whitehall to the Post Office's boardroom than he was pitched into an unexpected crisis over the very future of its franchise. In July he was confirming with his old Department the names of those to be appointed as members of his Board; and by the autumn it was being noted in the Main Board's minutes that the same members had decided to set aside 'the serious but fundamentally unconstructive possibility of resignation'.[21]

Nor was it just the sanctity of the letter monopoly that was under review. The Department of Industry gave formal notification in September 1980 that ministers 'wished to take general powers in relation to the formation of [Post Office] subsidiaries and privatising them, possibly leading to the "privatisation" of public office counters'. This dramatic proposal was casually and rather slightingly conveyed in a letter to the Board with none of the security which would usually be accorded to such a communication – and someone in St Martin's passed a copy of it to Tom Jackson. This might have led to a spectacular public row which would have done nothing for the Post Office's relations with its unions. Fortunately, the General Secretary of the UPW saw nothing to be gained from this and contacted Dearing directly about the leak. A private meeting was hurriedly arranged, at which Dearing and Ken Young assured an angry Jackson that the Post Office, while wholly supportive of the Split, was entirely opposed to curtailing the monopoly or selling off parts of the business to the private sector. The three men agreed it was critical 'to handle the issue at least initially outside the public domain, to gain time and the right conditions for the Corporation to argue to Government in their view the clear merits of maintaining PO control of counters'.[22]

Dearing and his Board colleagues duly argued their corner against the Government for the next three months. They did not succeed in persuading it to drop the idea of reconstituting the Post Office into legally distinct subsidiaries: this remained part of the British Telecom Bill, when it was published in November. (In 1967–8, Labour ministers had stopped short of the Split that was needed; now it seemed Conservative ministers might be about to err in the opposite direction.) But the Board did eventually manage to talk the Government out of adopting what Dearing called a 'Big Bang' approach to the Post Office, actually breaking it up into separate parts. The alarm this idea prompted can be seen from a note of the policy discussion that ensued on the day Dearing's Board heard about the leak to Jackson of the Government's intentions. There was acute concern over the threat to Counters, but also to the Post Office more generally: 'the singling out of Counters for possible special treatment was a particular threat which in the view of some could ultimately lead to a dismembering of the present Post Office in a way not envisaged in the separation proposals [for the Split]'.[23] As the year came to a close, Dearing was still busy orchestrating a rearguard action against a Prime Minister whose zeal for reform seemed to be growing rather than abating as the months went by. He suggested to his colleagues that they should all press their views individually on Joseph, though 'it would be wrong to underestimate the pressures on the Secretary of State against moderation of present policies towards liberalisation and privatisation . . .'[24]

In fact, Dearing had by then made the decisive move that may well have blocked a dismemberment of the Post Office going well beyond the splitting away of British Telecom. In October, the former Deputy Secretary had drawn upon all his drafting skills to pen a long letter explaining why the Big Bang should be shelved in favour of letting the Post Office put its own house in order. Addressed to Joseph in October but clearly intended also for the Prime Minister's eyes, it had amounted to a promise of action in exchange for a lifting of the privatization threat. As the Board minutes had it:

> Mr Dearing had written to the Secretary of State summarizing Posts' case, its considerable recent achievements and economies (of which the Government was possibly unaware), of the risks and effect of any loss of credibility that could arise if Government was to dictate unrealistic terms, including the possible threat to moderate trade union leadership which had joined management in securing changes leading to greater efficiency, and stressing the Board's determination to act toughly in difficult times.[25]

The Prime Minister relented, a compromise was reached over the request for a 2p price rise on stamps and Dearing's protestations won the Post Office a chance to prove that it could reform itself. (As one of his former colleagues, a Permanent Secretary, remarked to Dearing by way of a compliment: 'We do know how to pen a good letter, don't we!'[26]) Even in the short term, the threat to the postal monopoly was not entirely vanquished. The British Telecom Bill kept its clauses allowing small bites to be taken out of the postal monopoly, at the discretion of ministers.* In the longer term, it was clear that falling short of performance targets in the future might prompt severe retribution. But for the moment, thoughts of privatization were set aside. The Post Office had won a temporary reprieve. Dearing had secured it a breathing space and an opportunity – urged on by Downing Street – to embark, in 1981, on a genuine break with the past.

---

* A walk round the City of London could confirm the existence already of private operators on the margin of the law. Solicitors' firms had run their own 'Document Exchanges' ever since the crisis weeks of the 1971 postal strike, to pass important papers between themselves that needed same-day delivery without fail. Meanwhile, motorcycle couriers were providing an essential service for many in the City and were revving up their lobbyists in Westminster to make a broader case for private mails. Both these niche activities were effectively legalized after the Telecom Bill was enacted. The Prime Minister arranged in 1982 for the postal monopoly on packages costing more than £1 to be 'temporarily' suspended for a period of twenty-five years – a questionable use of secondary legislation powers for which she was roundly criticized by a Standing Committee of the House of Commons.

2. MAN IN THE MIDDLE

Developments within the UPW, meanwhile, had ensured that for the Union, too, 1979 had proved an eventful year. Certainly the election of the Thatcher government had played its part in this, helping to trigger a crisis between the Union's leadership and local activists whose dealings with each other had soured badly since the mid-1970s. Tom Jackson, so dominant in the aftermath of the 1971 strike, had found it increasingly difficult to persuade his membership that the state of the Post Office – and of the wider national economy – required them to adopt moderate policies far removed from the brash demands of the 1960s. As national politics polarized in the winter of 1978–9 and in the wake of Thatcher's election, Jackson found himself stranded in the middle of an often belligerent membership on the one hand and a steadily less cautious government with radical instincts on the other. But the predicament of the Union and its leader went deeper than a clash of views over the implications of the 1979 election – indeed, it was one of Jackson's most bitter complaints that his opponents seemed scarcely to have noticed the outside world changing around them. Acute tensions within the UPW were largely a consequence of the evolution of the postal work-place. Whitleyism had morphed between the 1950s and the later 1970s into a world in which few management proposals, however trivial, could pass without interminable negotiation, not just with senior offic-ers of the various unions but with their representatives – and those of the UPW in particular – at local branch level. 'Consultation' by the end of the 1970s was virtually continuous, and synonymous in many instances – and in all main postal locations – with ad hoc negotiation.*
In the larger city offices, where the workforce could run to many thou-sands of men, close-knit communities revolved around elaborate hierarchies, with senior managers responsible for the superintendents who watched over the inspectors who supervised the postmen. These hierarchies had to function, if the daily clearing of the posts was to

---

* In addition to London (and its principal depots at Mount Pleasant, South-East District Office and East-Central Office), the Post Office ranked the cities of Britain by size. Class A comprised just four: Birmingham, Glasgow, Liverpool and Manchester. Class B included Belfast, Edinburgh, and Cardiff and several others like Bristol, Leeds and Leicester. Class C were smaller cities like Oxford and Dundee – and so on. The gradual closure of Head Post Offices and amalgamation of the network had by the end of the 1970s eliminated the two smallest classes, E and F, leaving Class D with the large market towns.

happen at all, in accord with many informal understandings which in effect comprised the Custom of the Office (though this ancient term had itself been abandoned long ago). The understandings were policed – no other word will do – by the unions, and above all the UPW.

The big city sorting depot was not an environment that lent itself to any straightforward business-school analysis, as droves of consultants had discovered. Like so much else in the Post Office, it relied at all times on effective relationships between individuals, which in many cases had to straddle the old Official/Staff divide. Where these broke down, the result was easily derided by outsiders as a real-life enactment of the 1959 British film comedy *I'm Alright, Jack* on a grotesque scale. Manual sorting was a process horribly prone to mishaps. Where it ran smoothly, as it did across most of the country for most of the time, managers could enjoy an orderly existence from one month to the next. But nowhere had this profoundly introverted and insular culture yet been remotely reconciled with a serious quest for higher productivity. While senior managers were preoccupied with catching spanners before they could drop into the works ('the mail must get through'), the unions were devoted to a defence of their members' earnings – which entailed, even for those without darker political motives, flipping spanners into the air on a more or less daily basis. Basic wages were generally towards the bottom end of the national range for unskilled workers. Overtime rates allowed postmen and sorters to double or even treble the basic wage in their weekly take-home pay, but access to a steady flow of overtime opportunities depended on the preservation of more restrictive practices and incidental job protection schemes than any *Head Postmasters' Manual* could ever have recorded. (Postmen and Postmen Higher Grade, for example, commonly worked alongside each other in the sorting process; but no Postman was allowed by the Union to do work formally assigned to PHGs, and no PHG could step into a Postman's role, however briefly and whatever the demands of the mail. Again, overtime was generally interpreted as a pay supplement required for performing almost any non-compulsory task: how many hours of overtime would be payable for a given task was open to negotiation, but seldom had much to do with the length of time actually taken to do it.) Any pursuit of higher productivity by management was always likely to pose a threat of fewer overtime hours or lower rates or both – especially when letter and parcel volumes were stalling or dipping lower, as in the 1970s. Constant vigilance was needed, and a majority in the workforce looked to the UPW to provide it. Those individuals prepared to give up their evenings and weekend afternoons for the grinding procedural tedium of trade union business took up the cudgels and the spanners on their behalf.

Views on the permissibility of this or that union tactic had changed, too. While the great majority of individual postmen remained as loyal and conscientious as ever in their daily routines, general attitudes towards pay and conditions reflected by the 1970s a quasi-industrial culture in the workplace that had less and less in common with the public-service ethos that was still central to the general image of the Royal Mail. Much of the resulting strain fell upon the UPW itself, with its dozen or so salaried officers and many hundreds of officials attending to Union business on part- or full-time release from their postal duties (while still paid by the Royal Mail). Tensions existed at every level of the Union between the dictates of political expediency within a huge organization and the unrestrained demands of local activists in London and some other cities – notably Oxford and Liverpool – who were often, to put it mildly, less inclined to compromise. Branch secretaries, district organizers, Executive Council officers – all could find themselves under intense pressure from below to be the scourge of those above them. Inevitably, the pressures were greatest at the top, where the demands of the rank and file had ultimately to be reconciled with what the Post Office was prepared to offer.

The pressures on Jackson had become well-nigh intolerable even before Margaret Thatcher arrived in Downing Street. He did not share a widespread aversion to talk of higher productivity. While the Union had to assert its sense of co-ownership – 'we have as much right in saying how this business is managed as any manager', he proclaimed at the 1978 Annual Conference, by way of welcoming Barlow to the chairmanship – it also had to acknowledge a shared responsibility for modernizing the postal business.[27] Hence Jackson's outspoken support for mechanization and his readiness to work with Ken Young towards a better regulation of the workplace. He was scornful, now, of those who claimed a right to share power in the Post Office but walked away from any blame for its financial predicament. He was determined to see the Union play its part in ensuring the health of the service, even (or especially) in the face of declining traffic volumes. When he and Bill Ryland issued a joint statement in *The Post* in January 1976 urging cooperation between management and unions – 'to restore the Postal Business to the performance level of 1972–3 and to establish a stronger position for 1976–7' – it was not hard to see them as twin gamekeepers for the one troubled estate.[28] There were many at lower levels of the Union who resented this double-act deeply and were viscerally committed to a much more adversarial stance. Events in the years up to 1980 conspired to ensure an acrimonious parting of the ways.

The process began with the Grunwick affair, a notorious trade union dispute in north-west London that erupted in October 1976 and commanded media headlines for almost twelve months.[29] Local officials of the UPW were determined to support the embattled workers of a privately owned film-processing firm, Grunwick, whose employer objected to union representation on his premises. At first, sorters in the company's local post office at Cricklewood were deterred by the courts from persisting with secondary action against the firm, which was heavily reliant on the Royal Mail. London officials from LDC3 tried hard to win backing for renewed industrial action at the Annual Conference in May 1977, but were out-voted by a large majority.* Many London branches of the Union nonetheless went ahead and blacked Grunwick's mail, and Jackson had to expend much precious goodwill retrieving the situation to avoid the possibility of heavy fines against the UPW. When postmen in the local branch went on cancelling deliveries, they were temporarily suspended from the Union. Compounding the ugly fall-out from Cricklewood was a row in the spring of 1977 over an intended boycott of mails to South Africa, in protest against its apartheid regime. The courts took a more equivocal stance on this, but again the action was abandoned – leaving in its wake an unfounded but festering resentment in many parts of the Union that postmen, unlike other workers, seemed to have no right to strike. The Carter Report, published in July that year, added to Jackson's woes by endorsing the Split. He insisted the Union would bitterly oppose it, but such official support for a policy always vehemently rejected by the UPW was undeniably a personal setback, and it hardly served to persuade his critics that his moderate political stance was winning prizes for the workforce – the Split, after

* Reports on the 1977 Conference included mention of a first speech from the rostrum by a young postman from Slough, venting his anger over the injustice of incremental pay scales that depressed the earnings of young employees doing the same work as their elders. Alan Johnson told delegates that during the strike of 1971, 'as a man of twenty with a wife and three children, he drew £1 a week more for his wife and kids from the Social Security than he earned for a 43 hour week working for the Post Office'. (*The Post*, Vol. 80, No. 6, 30 June 1977, p. 17.) The eventual scrapping of incremental scales by the end of 1979 was one of the achievements in which Tom Jackson later took most pride.

all, threatened perhaps a 40 per cent reduction in the UPW's membership. It was a measure of the General Secretary's beleaguered position by 1978 that one of the individuals suspended over the Grunwick affair, a District Organizer for the London Region and LDC3 committee man called Derek Walsh, came close to having a motion of censure against him passed at the Annual Conference. Delegates rejected it by just 9,694 votes to 9,033.

By this date, the General Secretary had all but given up pleading with a string of Special and Annual Conferences to see that a cooperative approach by the Union might serve the membership better than constant hostilities. The effort had worn him down, to little avail: delegates increasingly came to Conference to pitch their own views of the world, not to listen to their leader's recommendations. But Jackson had a keener appreciation than his members that time was not on the Union's side – and in the autumn of 1978 he had a conversation with Keith Joseph that opened his eyes to the scale of the changes that might follow a Conservative win at the polls. Over the next six months – despite a serious crisis in his personal life, with the failure of his marriage and the need for an operation to remove an eye that kept him out of the office for ten weeks after Christmas – Jackson made one last bid to push his union into a new stance on productivity. In negotiations with Young during January, sometimes conducted at his home, he took the risk of leading the Executive Council into a provisional deal with the Personnel Director. It promised a 9 per cent increase in wages – and a consolidation of various pay supplements into the basic hourly rate, which the Union had sought for years – in exchange for a set of 'efficiency agreements'. But for tactical reasons in the face of an intensely difficult political environment – this was Labour's Winter of Discontent – Jackson opted to keep the negotiations secret for several weeks. When the terms were finally revealed – and were seen to include an acceptance of some long-resisted innovations, including traffic measurements in the workplace and more use of part-timers – they prompted unofficial strikes in London. They were rejected in a ballot of UPW members late in March by a 6-to-1 majority.

The vote was preceded by vicious recriminations, which appear to have pushed Jackson very close to resigning. Certainly he was wounded by the response – or as he characterized it in a passionate speech to the 1979 Annual Conference two months later, 'all the lies, all the disgusting things which were written about us [and] circulated to Branches throughout the country. I have never been in a worse situation in my life . . .'[30] The gulf between Jackson and his critics at the May Conference was painfully apparent. He warned of the storm about to break over them all, telling delegates about his meeting six months before with the man who was now Industry Secretary in the newly elected Thatcher government, and the threat hanging over the postal monopoly itself.[31] Three votes of no confidence were nonetheless moved against him and the Executive Council over the deal rejected in March. None was carried, but this did not avert a motion of censure, 'for bringing the UPW into disrepute'. It was moved by the LDC3's Walsh (again) and a well-known branch secretary from London's Western District Office called Frank Osei-Tutu. Jackson fought back passionately:

> I tell you we did the best we could, and now we are to be censured for it . . .
> There is no need for a public execution, no need for this conference to go
> on record against the EC . . . It is important, colleagues, that you should
> realize that what is happening now is the desire of some of our people to
> have another go at us. To want to do it again, and again, and again, and
> again.

His opponents insisted on a vote. 'We ourselves have been in disrepute with our memberships', declared Walsh, 'because . . . we trusted you to bring back the goods – And you didn't, Tom.'[32] In a show of hands, the censure motion was approved.

Jackson's influence, and his interest in remaining at his post, waned rapidly thereafter. If the rank-and-file activists apparently had little interest in what he had to say, the new Conservative government had even less. Jackson was appalled at the Labour Party's response to its 1979 defeat at the autumn party conference, deriding it in a fierce column in *The Post* of October 1980 – 'The muddling on the platform . . . The gross intolerance of many of the delegates who booed and jeered . . . The hypocrisy of Anthony Wedgwood Benn . . .' – and he made no attempt to hide his view that it was being led astray by the hypocritical antics of the Left.[33] He tried to find common cause with the Post Office Board in refuting ministers' arguments in favour of diluting the postal monopoly, without success. He laboured hard over a package of reforms for the UPW in 1980, which attracted 126 amendments and was then voted down. (One of the few adopted proposals was that the UPW should henceforth be known as the Union of Communications Workers, or the UCW, to remind employees of British Telecom that membership was not restricted to those in the postal service.*) He went on exhorting the membership to see that change had to come, while appealing to the Government to give the Post Office more time to adjust. But neither side was listening.

Jackson was convinced – especially after the leak in September 1980 of the letter referring to the possibility of privatization – that the Split would lead to the ruin of the Post Office and its traditional values: 'That which has stood the test of time since 1840 is at risk', as he told a Westminster rally against the British Telecommunications Bill in April 1981. He also firmly believed that BT's management and the POEU alike would come to rue their support for the Bill. While proclaiming the Union's formal rejection of it, though, he made no real effort to mobilize opposition and accepted that the workforce was broadly resigned to it.[34] In October 1981, within weeks of the Split finally happening, and having completed fifteen years as General Secretary, he announced his early retirement to the Executive Council. A column in *The Post* a few days later was the first of several in which he set down his profound disappointment at the way the past decade had unfolded. Why, he asked, could the Post Office not have been efficiently managed as a unified whole?

> The answer is two fold. First the old Civil Service atmosphere was never dispelled from the Post Office after 1969. The new dawn, the new adventure, the excitement never came. Management limped on as before, did not take advantage of new opportunities, neglected the future while carefully cultivating the past. Timid, unadventurous and slow to change. Secondly, there were those who saw a bright future for telecommunications and a poor future for posts. . . . All they have got [by taking through the Split] is a lot of hard work beating competition for services they should have developed years ago.[35]

Stepping down at the Annual Conference in 1982, he confessed he had always aspired to be the longest-serving holder of the post. But the first General Secretary, Bill Bowen, had served sixteen years – and Jackson had no need to spell out why another two years were beyond him. Like other leaders before him, he believed power in the Union had seeped disastrously away from the centre and out into district and branch com-

---

* The house newspaper of the Union remained *The Post*, but incorporated an old-fashioned telephone into the design of its name on the masthead, by way of a nod to its British Telecom readership.

mittees where too many were prepared to wield it irresponsibly. But it was not an occasion for taking his critics to task. Instead, he used his last opening speech to heed what many in the Union now sensed acutely: his departure was coinciding with a profound change in the Post Office's stance on industrial relations.[36] Jackson noted a marked reluctance by the Board to consult on many topics previously open to joint discussion, and a refusal to contemplate arbitration. His successor, Alan Tuffin, took up the same theme, writing his first column for *The Post* as General Secretary three months later: 'All the time the Union is being tested as to its willingness and, in turn, its ability to combat what appears to be a new style . . . of management. All of a sudden Post Office management seem to want to manage without any help from the Union and its activists'.[37] Management's style had indeed changed, under the leadership of a Chairman determined not to waste the leeway he had won for the Post Office at the end of 1980.

3 . OF MARKETS AND MARKETING

The son of a docks clerk in Hull, the fifty-year-old Dearing had been a career civil servant almost since leaving school at the age of sixteen. He had been a highly effective Deputy Secretary since 1974, handling one of the trickiest briefs in Whitehall: it had fallen to him to package Tony Benn's radical ideas for the regeneration of British industry, and to present them to a broadly incredulous array of the country's largest private-sector employers. By 1980 he was a short step away from becoming a Permanent Secretary with his own department. To have risen so far from a humble social background marked out Dearing as the kind of able official that had always prospered in the relatively classless, meritocratic environment of the Post Office. Slim and always immaculately dressed, with hawkish features and an air of intense enthusiasm for the job in hand, Dearing carried about him an air of brisk efficiency that won his colleagues' respect. He also had something of General Montgomery about him. There was a striking physical resemblance, the same emphasis on keeping fit – he would invariably shun lifts in favour of bounding up the nearest flight of stairs – and the same streak of asceticism. At grand Post Office dinners, the Chairman was always likely to be found passing on the main course in favour of a plate of scrambled eggs. Among his head office staff, it was well-known that he would customarily drive his own chauffeur home on Friday evenings and pick him up again the following Monday morning. (The chauffeur lived closer to London.) And while he was far too shy and self-effacing for any display of Monty-like personal eccentricity, Dearing was always just as passionate as the hero of Alamein about the importance of visiting the men in the front line. From the earliest days of his chairmanship, he took one day a week to call on local branches of the postal network.

Through his first months Dearing saw an urgent need to boost the depleted morale of local managers that might suggest all kinds of fanciful comparisons with a famous desert turnaround. He took charge of a Post Office that felt as though it had been in retreat for an awfully long time. Barlow may have called a temporary halt and begun a successful regrouping, but the future telecoms-less Post Office – with a workforce of 204,000 – was still widely reckoned to be a slowly shrinking business.* This outlook Dearing rejected from his very first day. He gave a series of speeches soon after his arrival that proclaimed the Post Office a growth business. Privately, he doubted his own ability to manage 'that most difficult thing, the successful fighting retreat': as he recalled, it was 'much easier to manage an advance . . .'[38] In public, he could talk about market segments and pricing curves with complete conviction. (His training in the civil service had included a year as one of the inaugural students on the London Business School's Sloan Programme.) Now he was intent on launching a textbook business turnaround. If it could be pursued with discipline and flair, insisted Dearing, the Post Office stood on the brink of a new era. For the better part of two decades – since the arrival of Tony Benn as Postmaster General in 1964, perhaps – the Post Office had been on the receiving end of countless critiques, in some instances facile and ill-informed but many of them constructive and backed up, like the Carter Report, with thousands of pages of diligent analysis. Dearing would provide his new colleagues with the leadership they needed to turn commentary and analysis into practical reforms. He formed a small Chairman's Executive Committee (CEC) to meet two or three times a month as the primary engine of change. Its original members were Young, Wainwright and the Finance Director, Charles Beauchamp;

* The workforce total comprised 155,000 rank-and-file postal workers in the UCW, 21,000 counter staff and clerical workers in the NFSP, 14,000 supervisory and managerial staff in the POMSA, 7,000 engineering and technical staff in the POEU, 5,000 clerical staff in the CPSA and a miscellaneous 2,000 others (PO (80)39, BT Archives, TCC 55/12/34). As ever, this excluded the postmasters and postmistresses running more than 20,000 post offices on a commissions basis, and all those who worked for them.

they were soon joined by the three ablest senior managers – Cockburn, Walmsley and Alan Clinton, known inevitably as the Young Turks – together with John Roberts as its Secretary. The CEC generated a stream of Action agendas that pushed forward a genuine reappraisal of Post Office operations on many fronts.

For a start, the physical business of shifting the mails each night was significantly improved. The contraction of the national rail network after the Beeching Report of 1963 had prompted a steady increase in the use of road transport in the 1970s, but a more sophisticated integration of road, rail and air was needed. More use had been made of inland air services since the introduction in July 1979 of postal flights in and out of Liverpool's Speke Airport. From 1982, the 'Spokes at Speke' were fitted into a national air network that also incorporated the East Midlands Airport, where flights could be integrated with a new road and rail hub centred on the nearby city of Derby. This did nothing to slow the trend away from dependence on the railways, aggravated by poor time-keeping on the trains and a series of damaging strikes by the rail unions: in the ten years to 1982, the proportion of the letter post carried by rail had dropped from 90 per cent to 55 per cent.[39] Though any financial benefits from mechanization remained as elusive as ever, at least the work of installing the eighty or so MLOs planned in the early 1970s was no longer crawling along to a seemingly geological time-table. The programme had virtually ground to a halt by 1980, with just thirty-three MLOs up and running. The next few years saw its impetus renewed, with completion scheduled for 1985, and seldom a month went by without another major conversion plan being approved (often at great expense).

Many of the country's biggest sorting offices were still in buildings that dated from the nineteenth century. Some, like Paddington, were lavishly refurbished; others, like Glasgow's George Square, had to be relocated to new sites altogether.[40] Inside these new MLOs, the working environment was changing out of all recognition. Since the dawn of photography, large sorting depots had presented much the same image – of rows of postmen standing in front of sorting frames or surrounded by sacks hanging from 'drop-bag fittings', with great quantities of mail stacked all around them. Now this traditional, semi-industrial scene was giving way to a cleaner, sparser interior more redolent of the control room in a giant utility company. Keyboard operators were seated at long lines of Easy View Coding Desks, focused intently on the letters passing silently in front of them while giant box-like machines hummed and whirred around them. It was an increasingly computerized environment, as the technology devised over the course of more than three decades began to be fully applied at last.

So what fresh applications might still be round the corner? A couple of years before his retirement as Managing Director in December 1980, Denis Roberts had gone to Japan to find out. The answer, as Currall had foreseen seven years earlier, was Optical Character Recognition, which replaced the coding operator with a beam of light that automatically scanned printed codes (and even scribbled addresses) on passing envelopes and sent instructions accordingly to the dot-printers. Here was the breakthrough that made every step since the birth of the Transorma in 1927 into a half-way house. Roberts discovered that the Japanese were already giving 26 per cent of their mail the OCR treatment, a figure which looked likely to rise steadily. (He could not help observing that whereas the Post Office had been top dog in the world of postal technology at the start of the 1970s, 'in certain respects we now lag behind other postal administrations, both in innovation and in levels of achievement'. Currall had warned in 1973 that other countries' postal services might steal a march on the Post Office: urgent remedies were needed to avert this dire possibility.[41]) Plans were made in 1981 for a rapid start on OCR trials, to be overseen by Dearing's 'Board Member for Mails Network and Development', Alan Clinton.[42] The snag was that everything still depended on the public's voluntary adoption of postcodes. After ten years of intense marketing in Japan, 96 per cent of the country's mail carried codes. After twenty years of half-hearted marketing in Britain, scarcely 50 per cent had been achieved. Belatedly, the publicity budget for post-coding was now acknowledged as a properly heavy expense: by 1984–5 it was up to £1.6m. As this might suggest, the Post Office in the early 1980s was finally being cajoled into abandoning its inhibitions over marketing.

The cajoler-in-chief was Nigel Walmsley, the youthful head of marketing backed by Barlow in 1977. Walmsley was always warmly supported by Dearing – it was perhaps no coincidence that he had worked briefly for Dearing as a secondee to the Department of Industry in the mid-1970s – and he was appointed by him to the first fully fledged Post Office Board of the post-Split era in October 1981. Walmsley pioneered a campaign to sell tailored wares to separate kinds of 'customer' (a novel concept in itself). It had taken a while to work out the details, given the paucity of marketing data available in 1977. But in 1978 Barlow had launched a huge research project – known as the Mail Classification

Scheme – aimed at discovering who posted what to whom. Primarily
designed to identify operational improvements, it provided plenty of
grist for the marketing mill, too. Walmsley and his team were able to
identify the biggest-spending customer groups – utility companies, banks,
direct mail advertisers and so on – and set out to offer them attractive
discounts for higher volumes, in return for bulk-mailing arrangements
that could reduce costs for the Post Office. Those who pre-sorted their
mails by destination, for example, could expect a lower postage rate.
'Industrial pricing' of this kind sparked a series of lively discussions with
the Treasury and the Department of Industry. The postal monopoly had
always been understood in Whitehall to imply a 'one-size-fits-all'
approach to pricing. Dearing backed the marketing men against his former colleagues, and by the end of 1981 the new business model had been
ushered in. At the same time, the Chairman authorized a substantial
boost to Walmsley's budget for the promotion of mail services – lifting it
to almost £50m a year – and the Post Office became one of the top ten
advertisers by spend in the country.[43]

This fundamental change of outlook within the Post Office (as we
can see clearly enough in retrospect) was nicely timed, for it coincided
with a broader development in society at large. Postal traffic volumes
had hitherto always closely tracked the general performance of the
economy, but in the sharp recession of 1980–81, GDP dropped 3.5 per
cent – and mail traffic sailed on without a blip. By the autumn of 1982
it was growing in absolute terms. Within the space of just a few years,
all those bleak traffic forecasts of the 1970s were looking almost comi-
cally wide of the mark. (See Appendix A, Chart 11.) The impact of
personal computers, ink-jet printers and high-speed copier machines on
office processes transformed postal volumes in a way that almost no
one had predicted five years earlier. Computers were also facilitating
bulk-mailings from head offices in place of scattered mailings across
office networks. The implications of all this were far from obvious to
the general public. For most people, the post still meant primarily social
mail – 'letters for the rich, letters for the poor' – but by the mid-1980s
the reality was that letters from banks had long since overwhelmed letters of thanks: social mail in the UK accounted for only around 15 per
cent of the whole inland letters market and the other 85 per cent was
business correspondence. Of this, financial mail accounted for almost
50 per cent (of the total), with commercial mail about 25 per cent and
direct mail 10 per cent.[44] The lion's share of all business mail came from
about 100,000 customers, with the 1,000 largest customers accounting

for perhaps two thirds of the total revenues. Herein lay the real key to the economics of the postal business, as Walmsley had been among the first to grasp.

Had mechanization been abandoned, as some had urged in the past, the postal service might have been overwhelmed. But the installation of the MLOs promised a future service efficient enough to ensure that the Post Office would be a match for the transformation of its marketplace. Hence the time had come, as Walmsley pointed out to colleagues in a series of innocuously titled but truly radical papers, for them to ditch the assumptions about a 'managed decline' that had prevailed since the 1960s. Inland letter volumes could be set an annual growth target of 1 per cent for 1982–7, with an overall growth of roughly 5 per cent for the period, but this in his view looked 'somewhat conservative'.[45] (The actual figure would turn out to be just over 26 per cent.) Various policy initiatives duly began to reflect a novel optimism. A corporate advertising campaign early in 1982 was the first of its kind in peacetime since the days of Stephen Tallents in the 1930s. Additional investment was approved for a string of new product ideas, many of them launched in the 1970s but so far of limited impact. Most offered customers faster and more secure deliveries in one way or another and were marketed with names like Expresspost, Intelpost (for facsimile messages), Direct Mail and Admail. The most successful was Datapost, an overnight delivery service originally created in 1970, which now expanded domestically and took off into overseas deliveries too, with a fleet of smartly liveried red Datapost aeroplanes handling courier business between Britain and twenty-eight other countries.

Another business line that prospered as a result of the marketing renaissance – and that had in fact been thriving for some years already – was the promotion of new stamps as must-have items for the collector's album. Ever since Tony Benn's success with his Stamps Seminar in the summer of 1966, the Post Office had been much less abstemious about 'special issues', generally producing half a dozen sets or more each year with a keen eye to the philatelic market. In a sense, it had caught up with the commercial opportunity offered by cleverer technology. Printing had been restricted in the first century after 1840 to the use of 'recess-engraved' plates and 'letterpress' methods (generally used for higher- and lower-value stamps respectively, and usually involving just a single colour). These were skilled and expensive, labour-intensive operations, unsuited to the mass production of modern stamp designs. A far cheaper methodology had arrived in the 1930s: 'photogravure' technology etched a design onto the surface of cylinders that could be used in sequence for the high-speed rotary printing of complex, multi-coloured stamps. It was a process that the Post Office had in fact first used in 1934, but it had only been extended very gradually across a range of (mostly lower-valued) definitive stamps for thirty years thereafter. Things changed in the late 1960s. By 1970 the use of recess-engraved plates had been all but abandoned – the Machin £1 stamp of 1969 had been among the last set of designs to use them. Photogravure printing had since then been made available for stamps of all kinds. The result was a stream of special issues – by no means all 'commemoratives' linked to specific events – and they could be mass-produced to almost any design, however elaborate. They featured many higher-value stamps, too, which made no difference to the printing costs but handily obliged dealers and collectors to dig deeper into their pockets. The proceeds were substantial and represented almost a pure profit. Disclosure of the actual figures might indeed have embarrassed the Post Office in the mid-1970s, when philatelic profits of £10m–15m a year had been submerged under mounting deficits on the combined mail services that peaked at £117m in 1974–5.[46]

The appointment in 1980 of a chairman with a stamp collection of his own coincided happily with a new enthusiasm for British stamps.* A special issue, bearing a portrait of the Queen Mother, even appeared on the front cover of *Time* magazine in August 1980 to mark her eightieth birthday. Responsibility for the marketing of new issues fell to the Post Office's Philatelic Bureau, now located in Edinburgh, but as chairman of the Stamp Advisory Committee, Walmsley took a lively interest in its affairs – and no wonder: in a paper of 1982 reviewing plans for eight commemorative sets in 1984, he predicted a net contribution from philatelic sales in 1982–3 of almost £33m.[47] (The Treasury had set £56m as the cash dividend expected of the Post Office for that same year.) Much of the buying interest came from foreign dealers – based especially in France, Germany, Italy and the United States – with whom the Post Office kept in close contact through a network of overseas sales

---

* Days after arriving at the Post Office, Dearing asked the Director of Philately, John Mackay, to show him round the National Postal Museum, which was still housed over the road from St Martin's in King Edward Building. Dearing was shaken to see a box containing, like some saint's relics, the charred remains of the first sheets of stamps printed with a portrait of George V, which had been caught in the conflagration on the night the CTO was destroyed, in December 1940. The Director had to parry a searching interrogation from his Chairman about future fire precautions. (John Mackay, interview with author, 15 September 2009.)

agents. Many in UK philatelic circles voiced concern over the abundance of new issues, which they saw as a threat to the integrity of stamp-collecting. This was no longer just a matter of aesthetics; they believed the Post Office, in diluting the scarcity value of special stamps, risked killing the golden goose. Their unease, though, did nothing to diminish the appetite of foreign wholesale dealers – and it went on growing.

Consistently remunerative as the stamp sales were, the Post Office by the 1980s had far more important issues to manage in the international marketplace. The 1970s had seen a steady decline in the conveyance of overseas mail by sea – the surface:air ratio moved from 85:15 in 1970–71 to 57:43 in 1985–6.[48] Fast passenger ships had all but disappeared; container fleets had proved horribly unreliable; tariff charges (set by the Union Postale Universelle (UPU)) had risen alarmingly; and many foreign postal authorities had shown scant interest in upholding traditional service standards. Airmail volumes over the period had grown accordingly. (See again Appendix A, Chart 6.) In addition to its 'All-Up' services for the European market, the Post Office had introduced an array of other, reduced-rate services on a worldwide basis, including an Air Parcels operation. The decline of sea mails and the rise of airmails had largely coincided, offsetting each other in the aggregate overseas traffic numbers. But the shift from one to the other was plain to many inside the Post Office – not least Walmsley himself, who had spent five years in the 1970s working on international freight contracts for both sea- and airmails. In 1981, he and Alan Clinton proposed a drastic reappraisal of the future of the airmail business. The Post Office had to do more than increase its investment in marketing and sales, research and product development, vital as all these would be in effecting a recovery from the harsh 1979–81 recession. It needed, they suggested, to undertake 'a fundamental redefinition of the business we are in'.[49] This would mean engaging 'in the provision of international services required by potential customers . . . through whatever means are most effective' – or to put it less obliquely, offering a comprehensive service in other countries as well as Britain, with or without the agreement of their national postal administrations. This would involve defying UPU regulations, but the commercial logic was compelling.

A new subsidiary (the Overseas Freighting Service (OFS), which would be renamed 'Argonaut' in 1982) had already been approved in principle by the Board some months earlier – and the Clinton/Walmsley proposal set out its aims unequivocally:

Hitherto, we have rigorously followed the UPU regulations, but several postal administrations, notably the Dutch, have not. In consequence, we have lost large quantities [of business] . . . [We need] a radical new approach for sending large volumes of traffic to other countries without using the formal services of the distant postal administration as our agent, thereby avoiding the payment of [UPU-dictated] imbalance charges and circumventing slow and inefficient postal services that unfortunately exist in many developing countries. OFS has enormous potential . . . [and] would also provide the key for us to gain entry into handling the direct exportation of manufactured goods . . . Although we shall not be telling other postal administrations about OFS, news of it is bound to reach them eventually. Most will dislike it . . .[50]

The potential scope for international carriers to operate unilaterally across borders was already on show within the Post Office's own back yard. An Australian logistics company called Thomas Nationwide Transport (TNT) was offering British customers a parcel post that surpassed anything available from the railways, by using computers to document the movement by road of packages from door to door. (A private-sector American logistics company founded in 1973, Federal Express, had been using computers to track its parcel-post operations in a similar way across the US since 1979.) Arguing to his Post Office colleagues that they would have to follow suit, Walmsley warned the Board in May 1982: 'the threat posed by TNT was a new dimension in that the business now faced a well-financed and expert competitor who was moving into home delivery, an area in which the Post Office had hitherto enjoyed a monopoly position . . .'[51] (He meant a de facto rather than a legal monopoly, of course – the Post Office's letters monopoly had never applied to parcels.) Over the next few months, the Post Office fought back aggressively in defence of its domestic market. Reviewing the outcome at the end of September, Walmsley and Clinton were able to note with some satisfaction 'the recent decision by TNT to pull out of the home delivery market, a decision which reflected much credit on the competitive energies of [Post Office] staff at local, regional and Headquarters level throughout the Business'.[52] It was a coup that pleased Dearing enormously.

There was no doubt that the driving force behind this, and much else besides, was Walmsley – so his announcement a few weeks later that he was leaving the Post Office for an offer he couldn't refuse in the media industry came as a blow. (He went off to become Managing Director of Capital Radio, one of the first commercial broadcasting stations, set up in 1973.) Dearing did not disguise his personal disappointment; nor did he really succeed after 1982 in finding a successor to Walmsley who could offer the Post Office's marketeers the same calibre of leadership. Dearing always set great store by having people at the top with a vision of what they wanted to achieve, and this mattered to him. There was, however, another individual whose marketing achievements had been making a notable difference to the Post Office for a few years, as Dearing had acknowledged in making him Deputy Chairman in October 1981 – an appointment that also signalled very usefully the importance of the (relatively small) business that he ran. Sam Wainwright was the Managing Director of the Giro and Remittance Services, which since 1977 he had rejuvenated as the 'National Girobank'. His leadership had more or less single-handedly transformed a lacklustre money remittance network with a doubtful future into a fully fledged banking business, with possibly profound implications for the role of the Post Office in local communities across the country.

Wainwright had been hired by Ryland and had joined the Post Office several months before Barlow's arrival in 1977. A Whitehall committee had for some months been looking into the feasibility of merging the Giro operation into the Treasury-controlled National Savings Bank. Unaware of its existence until after he had accepted the position of Managing Director, Wainwright was confronted with a report from this committee recommending an amalgamation. He opposed this vehemently and made clear he was ready to quit immediately unless allowed to expand the Giro as a self-standing business.[53] A 52-year-old former financial journalist and successful City banker, he had accepted a halving of his City salary in order to pursue his own vision of a 'National Giro' as a popular 'bank for the unbanked'. This made him a forceful protagonist on its behalf, and the Treasury's report was shelved.* Dearing, who may have had a hand in his appointment in 1977, backed Wainwright's plans enthusiastically. The two men became close friends, and Dearing spent much of every Friday at Wainwright's head office in the City's Milk Street, a short walk from St Martin's. With the Chairman behind him, Wainwright proceeded to assemble – in the face of constant objections from the Treasury and a series of political rows triggered by vested interests in the financial services industry – all the moving parts required for a viable commercial bank.

---

* The committee behind it was chaired by a senior Treasury official, Rosalind Gilmore. A year after leaving the civil service in 1982 she joined Wainwright's management team herself and was National Girobank's Marketing Director from 1983 to 1986.

The organization was re-christened, and better agency terms were negotiated with the Post Office's Counters Department. Retail deposit accounts were inaugurated, followed by the issuance of certificates of deposit, corporate deposit-taking and a full range of funding activities in the money markets. Overdraft and personal-loan facilities were developed, along with personal-insurance products sold by National Girobank as the agent for third-party suppliers. When the Thatcher government imposed a windfall banking tax in 1981, to recoup some of the profits made on the back of abnormally high interest rates, Dearing joined with Wainwright to try to persuade the Government that National Girobank was subtly different from the clearers. Their point was taken, and ministers agreed to an injection of public funds to compensate for the windfall tax surrendered. Nonetheless, by the early 1980s National Girobank was a fully subscribed member of the clearing banks' club, with access to all the standard arrangements for cheque-clearing and inter-bank payments. It had computerized back offices to match any in the industry, and was one of the pioneers of free banking, for customers in credit, of credit cards and of ATM machines. (It collaborated with the Co-Op Bank and two building societies to establish an ATM network called 'Link'.) By 1984–5 what had been a loss-making operation in the 1970s was making almost £20m a year and a highly respectable return on net assets. Its profits were small in the context of the Post Office's finances as a whole, but that was not the point. National Girobank was ubiquitous and open at convenient hours, including Saturday mornings. It provided Post Office customers, especially in rural areas, with a banking service equal to most of their needs, and it was as trusted as the Post Office itself. By 1985, it had 1.8 million customer accounts.

4. LESS PEACE, MORE EFFICIENCY

In 1977, when Wainwright had arrived at the office on his first day as Managing Director, he had almost brought the entire operation to a halt. He vividly recalled stepping out of the lift that morning and noticing immediately that the hall clock outside his office door was an hour slow.[54] To the considerable surprise of his new office staff, Wainwright pulled across a chair, stood up to reach the clock and was about to adjust it when he felt a hand on his shoulder. One of his new colleagues, better versed in the workplace conventions of the day, warned him in all seriousness that touching the hands of the clock would be regarded by the POEU as a cause for unofficial industrial action: no manager could usurp the job of a union member, and adjusting clocks would unquestionably fall into that category. Word of the clock adjustment would travel fast, and the Managing Director might have an engineers' strike on his hands before lunchtime. Utterly bemused, Wainwright ceded the point – and in retirement, could reflect that his colleague had been absolutely right. Throughout his time as Managing Director, Wainwright had to struggle with industrial relations crises that more than once seemed to him – justly or otherwise (and he was an inveterate worrier) – capable of closing down his business altogether. They were especially bad at Bootle, where the lower grades of the CPSA and SCPS unions were heavily infiltrated with supporters of the Labour Party's Militant Tendency faction, based in nearby Liverpool. For the Chairman of the Post Office, however, Wainwright's difficulties were just a small part of the wider problem.

Dearing did not begin his chairmanship resolving to confront the unions, but he very soon decided some abrupt change of tack was urgently required. He had watched over Post Office affairs as a civil servant since 1975, but the power of the Union branch network and its influence on daily operations had still come as a shock in 1980: 'I hadn't realized the depth, pervasiveness and strength of it.'[55] The Monopolies and Mergers Commission's report on postal operations in Inner London, commissioned in the summer of 1979, was published just in time for Dearing's move to the Post Office, and it provided a crash course on a key dimension of the problem.* The central question addressed by the MMC was simple: why, given a 30 per cent fall in Inner London's mail volumes over the previous ten years, had its postal workforce shrunk by only 10 per cent? The gist of the answer was that 28,000 postmen were manning a regime tantamount to 'a state within a state', where the Post Office's writ scarcely ran at all. Local UPW representatives called the shots, despite the fact that Inner London comprised the hub of the national postal service. And branch committees had stymied most attempts to reduce the size of the workforce. Part-timers were still

---

* In a long report that was short on light relief, the authors may have enjoyed their review of the postal depots at London's railway stations, where 'the provision of additional BRUTES for Post Office use only would permit an early improvement in the efficiency of operations' (Monopolies and Mergers Commission, *The Inner London Letter Post: A Report on the Letter Post Service in the Area Comprising the Numbered London Postal Districts*, HC515, HMSO, 1980, para. 7.23). This was not a call for drastic measures in the personnel department, but a reference to 'British Rail Universal Trolley Equipment', which was reckoned to be too thin on the ground. BRUTES were large cages on wheels for shifting the mail, not to be confused with smaller wheeled trolleys, called YORKs after the station that invented them.

completely excluded. As for work-measure tools, a boycott at the national level even extended in London to a total ban on time-clocks. But if local representatives enjoyed such power, what was the position of the UPW and its Executive Council? Strikingly, the report thought they shared the same objectives as the Post Office's management. Unfortunately, given the paramount importance of the Union's Annual Conference and the constitutional right of branch officials to second-guess every policy at the point of implementation, the Union had no ability to deliver its side of any significant agreement. In the Post Office itself, the report identified many individual failings – including a failure to pursue mechanization with sufficient vigour – but one general comment summarized them: 'management is in danger of losing its will to take management decisions, and forgetting that it has a duty to do so'.[56]

By the time the MMC report appeared, the London Region had just seen a promising new start made in a highly unusual fashion. Late in 1979, a new London Postal Region director had been appointed: this was Bill Cockburn, still only thirty-six but promoted on the strength of some impressive contributions to corporate planning and postal finance since his days juggling the fund-raising calendar with the Bank of England. If the UPW's London leaders expected to find him a callow youth, they were soon disillusioned. No less striking than his age was the young Scotsman's novel approach to the Union's representatives. Feisty and clearly ready for a bare-knuckle fight if they wanted one, Cockburn was also far more accessible than his predecessors. A series of private discussions led, just before Christmas, to managers and London District Council leaders convening in a hotel for the weekend to thrash out a genuinely innovative deal on productivity. Cockburn returned to St Martin's with a deal that would secure grassroots cooperation in pursuit of productivity savings, in exchange for the payment of bonuses to local UPW branches worth 70 per cent of any gains. The exact terms owed much to Cockburn's counterpart on the LDC, John Taylor, a gifted and charismatic figure whom others – managers and Union officers alike – had often found intimidating. Taylor insisted that no mention should be made in any agreement of the word 'productivity'. So 'Improved Working Methods', or IWM, was the title cooked up for the bargain.* It was generous to those involved, but promised net sav-

* At this point the commanding figure within the London District Council, Taylor seemed to many people, including Tom Jackson, to be a future General Secretary of the Union. He chaired it in 1982–3 – but alcoholism and a tempestuous private life tragically wrecked his career a few years later.

ings for the Post Office that might nonetheless prove significant. By the time Dearing took over, IWM had been embraced by the Board – Barlow had endorsed it on the spot, with Young's support, after hearing the details from Cockburn – and plans were being made to extend IWM across the capital by the end of 1980 and then well beyond London. (It was only briefly noted by the authors of the MMC report: they wished it well but decided against commenting on the details.[57])

While he welcomed the boldness behind IWM, Dearing was in no doubt by 1981 that it could only ever comprise one of many initiatives that would be required if attitudes in the workplace were to be altered as he intended. He took a tough line himself – for instance, by asserting that the Post Office would completely ignore terms and conditions inside British Telecom when dealing with unions whose memberships straddled both businesses – and he exhorted colleagues to follow his example. Essential measures opposed by the unions would have to be imposed by executive action. Inveterate troublemakers would have to be confronted and removed: the UPW branch secretary at the strike-prone Western District Office, Frank Osei-Tutu, was dismissed; so, eventually, was the Chairman of the branch, Bill Willoughby, though action against him seemed likely at one point to provoke a national stoppage. (This was allayed by Jackson's intervention in November 1981, and by allowing Willoughby to return to work for a while, a temporary compromise much resented among Post Office managers.) 'Ron gave the lead that enabled the rest of us to pull off things in our own field', recalled Ken Young of Dearing's role. 'We were given our head and encouraged to do the difficult things, whereas in the previous climate of the 1970s there had always been reasons why they couldn't be done.'[58] Young's own particular triumph, in keeping with the Job-like patience that characterized all of his endeavours, was a protracted affair. It began with his submission to the Board of a report in November 1981, 'Manpower Resourcing and Utilisation in the Postal Business', based on a close study of staffing practices by Martin Fish, director of the Post Office's own internal management college.[59] (The latter was generally known as Coton House, the name of a fine Georgian manor in Warwickshire acquired and refurbished by the Post Office in 1970–71 to provide the facilities hitherto based at Bletchley Park.) The content of the 62-page report was a lot more compelling than its title; in fact it was nothing less than an invitation to disavow the approach to industrial relations taken by the Post Office since the early 1950s. The postal unions enjoyed a degree of 'involvement' in the business that was uncommon even in the nationalized industry sector, and far in excess of anything in the private sector. True, this had contributed to a generally harmonious environment that compared favourably with the levels of militancy and disruption evident across much of British industry. But had that harmony been bought at too high a price, in terms of business efficiency? By the time the report got around to spelling out this question in its conclusion, it had already documented the answer in some style. There needed to be less peace, more efficiency. One chapter listed fifty-four recommendations. 'The unions can be expected to resist the recommended changes and their resistance will not be easily over-come ... There will therefore be the need for a carefully developed implementation strategy.'[60] The Board agreed.

Less peace duly followed. Young and his colleagues had their strategy and stuck to it, not least by working to spread the adoption of IWM. Cockburn was promoted in June 1982 from his LPR post to a national role as Board Member for Finance, Counters and Planning, and he championed the scheme wherever he could. By April 1983, it had been extended to cover more than half the workforce. In the process, one large sorting depot after another was alerted to the notion that the measurement of savings had to involve the application of some kind of standard measure of manual postal work – something the Post Office had tried and failed to do for half a century. As management set about trying to claw back the initiative, unofficial stoppages multiplied and UCW opposition to postal mechanization flared again. (Cooperation was withdrawn early in 1983 on any increased use of coded sorting for inward mails.) Attending the Annual Conferences of the UCW and POEU in 1983, Young found among the delegates 'a greater mood of frustration ... and there had been at both conferences an unfortunate theme of betrayal by the Executive Councils'.[61] This weighed on events in the second half of 1984, when the Post Office moved to adopt IWM nationally as one of a formal list of reforms including big concessions by the Union on the use of part-timers and casual labour. The resulting package was a sort of upside-down version of the Magna Carta, with the UCW's barons required to sign as a guarantee of the kingdom's future prosperity. Increasingly wary of the jibe of betrayal, the barons insisted on taking orders from their local and regional retinues: they were pre-pared to sign only if authorized to do so by a Special Conference.

This prompted an unprecedented foray into 'internal communications' by the Post Office (communicating, that is, with local managers – direct communications with the workforce, as part of the unwritten rules of the workplace, had been exclusively the preserve of Union officers since the early 1950s). A briefing booklet was produced in November 1984, *Safeguarding the Future of the Mails Business*, sent to all local managers and supervisors, which laid out new guidelines to be adopted on everything from mechanization and duty rosters to overtime and a greater reliance on part-timers ('associate grades'). It gave a detailed summary of all the negotiations through recent months, along with instructions on how managers should prepare their local UCW counterparts for the weighty decisions facing them at their Special Conference. The results were disappointing. When the three-day UCW Conference assembled at Bournemouth in March 1985, its delegates accepted many aspects of IWM in principle, but they rejected any move towards making it compulsory for all sorting offices – local officers would still be left with the right to veto its adoption – and they refused to license the Union to engage in any talk about more use of part-timers. Against the background of recent radical reforms to trade union law, the delegates' attitude looked well short of the wholehearted endorsement of a fresh approach that the Board had hoped for.* Appearing on the front page of *Courier* a few weeks later, Dearing's response was unequivocal. The Post Office had waited patiently for many months, but would now act in defiance of the Bournemouth votes – 'and I have to tell you that we shall be pressing ahead quickly. These issues have been on the table for at least a decade: time has run out. Management has instructions to proceed.' Weeks later, at its Annual Conference, the UCW climbed down: *Safeguarding the Mails* was ratified and the Executive Council was empowered by delegates, in effect, to settle the final negotiations at its discretion. By the end of the summer, a series of Business Efficiency Agreements had been signed that finally addressed most of the key issues to the Board's satisfaction. Union objections to the introduction

* The delegates at Bournemouth seemed almost oblivious to the magnitude of the changes wrought in the legal environment for trade unions by the Thatcher government's reforms. Its 1980 and 1982 Employment Acts had sharply curtailed the scope for lawful picketing of a workplace and almost entirely removed the blanket immunity from tort enjoyed by trade unions since 1906: injunctions could now be sought from the courts to halt strikes, and unions that flouted the law could be sued for damages, which might extend to a sequestration of their assets. Legal immunity could still be claimed for industrial action – but in the wake of the Trade Union Act of 1984 immunity was now conditional on the support of a simple majority in a secret pre-strike ballot. For those attending the UCW Conference who might have failed to note how dramatically the political environment was changing, the newspapers on the first morning carried official confirmation of the capitulation of the National Union of Miners after their year-long battle with the Government.

of mechanization were lifted; plans for a centrally coordinated parcel service 'replicating the culture of competitors' were accepted; limits on the day-to-day authority of union officers in the workplace were acknowledged.[62] This was heralded as a watershed for the Post Office. In fact more time was needed, as even the optimists conceded, for it to be clear whether or not a new era of industrial relations had really begun. In the meantime, at least the many confrontations since Jackson's departure in 1982 had been weathered – and Dearing's colleagues had successfully signalled a new readiness to act in defiance of UCW strictures.

One of the sharpest disagreements over the period had concerned a decision by the Post Office, indignantly rejected by the Union, to drop special bonuses for Post Office staff in Northern Ireland. These had survived against the odds for many years. On a visit to the Province in 1971, Bill Ryland had been shocked to hear at first hand of the dangers faced by postal staff as a consequence of the Troubles since 1969. More or less on impulse, Ryland had awarded them two extra days of Christmas leave. This had been replaced in 1974 with annual cheques for £50. It was a clumsy arrangement, producing awkward anomalies in practice, and several attempts were made at Belfast's own behest to shelve it, all firmly rebutted by the Union. Dearing and Young finally overrode the objections in 1982 and the payments were scrapped. It was a sensible move – allowing additional cash to be awarded instead to postal staff in need of special help or deserving recognition for their work in especially dangerous locations – but entailed an obvious risk of appearing callous. For no one in 1982 with any knowledge of Northern Ireland could doubt that its postal staff were still working under considerable duress.

5. BEYOND THE CALL OF DUTY

As had been the case in Dublin prior to 1922, the Post Office in Belfast had for almost sixty years been headed by senior men appointed from London, most of them English and all of them – and their wives, too – guaranteed Protestants. (This was a prerequisite that Ulster's political establishment confidentially drew to London's attention more than once in the 1960s. The single exception was a Catholic Dubliner who had chaired the Northern Ireland Post Office Board since 1968; but Paddy Manson had served with the British Army in the war and been

awarded the Military Cross in the Italian campaign, which sealed his
credentials in all quarters.) Stripped of its historical infrastructure in the
Republic, the Post Office had retained just over a dozen head offices in
the Province, supported by thirty branch offices and almost 700 sub-
offices. With just over 3,000 postal staff, its Lilliputian scale allowed
it to function almost like a family business. (The same was true of the
NI telecoms operation, which was roughly the same size.) Individuals
across the Six Counties were well-known to each other and to their
senior managers in Belfast. They were generally well-known in their
own communities, too, especially in the rural areas, where most postmen stayed long in the same job. It could hardly have been otherwise
prior to the 1960s, for it was historically a countryside with few formal
addresses. The Province was divided, like the rest of Ireland, into many
thousands of 'townland' districts and only an experienced postman
could handle the difficulties posed almost everywhere by having a few
dozen families of the same name in one scattered neighbourhood. When
mechanization and postcodes loomed – and the spreading ownership of
private telephones made directories essential – townlands were superseded by postal districts. The Post Office was obliged to mount a
'Naming and Numbering' project, which it began in 1964. Tying even
the remotest farmsteads to a named road on a map for the first time was
a prodigious undertaking, and was inevitably opposed by some as a
gimcrack idea, alien to the very history of Ulster.* Responsibility for the
work was handed in 1966 to a young APCII travelling officer, Danny
Carty, who had just returned home to the Province after a three-year
stint in Scotland. Carty was a man who knew about maps – fortuitously,
he had worked for Ordnance Survey in Northern Ireland for four years
before joining the Post Office in 1958 – and in wrapping up the project
successfully by 1969 he made his mark.

The neat inclusiveness of the completed postal map was sadly at odds
by then with the deepening sectarian divide across the Province. After
street riots in 1969 prompted the deployment of British troops and the

---

* A campaign against the project attracted lively support from groups such as the Ulster
Place-Name Society and the Federation of Ulster Local Studies, as well as the Celtic Studies
Department at Queen's University, Belfast. With their support, some isolated district coun-
cils across Northern Ireland went on resisting the imposition of modern addresses for years.
All succumbed in the end, with the exception of County Fermanagh, which has retained its
townlands to this day. In having no address map, Fermanagh is thus unique in the United
Kingdom – but at one with most rural areas of the Irish Republic (which copes by having
more post offices per head than any other country in Europe, by a wide margin).

start of a concerted campaign by Republican gunmen, the Post Office had to contend with bigger and far uglier problems than backwoodsmen opposed to postcodes. It was soon given a taste of what the new-born Irish Post Office had had to contend with in the Civil War of 1922–3. As then, the IRA turned very quickly to robbing post offices. But now, as agents of a welfare state, post offices offered incomparably richer pickings than in the 1920s. Each morning, all of the Head Post Offices in the Province needed to distribute cash to their local network. It generally went out in 'remittance vans', and the sums involved could be substantial. By early 1970, the IRA had perfected its gathering of instant intelligence on the despatch of these vehicles within Belfast itself and a long string of sub-offices had been raided in the wake of receiving their funds. The city's Head Postmaster, Bob Gaston, called a meeting of his managers to review tactics. It was decided that Royal Mail van deliveries would be abandoned. Instead, two non-uniformed managers would carry remittances to the sub-offices in their own unmarked car, posing as ordinary members of the public. The assignment was taken on, apparently without the slightest regard for personal safety, by the two Chief Inspectors of the head office in Belfast's Royal Avenue. One of them, Alex Bell, recalled this singular duty in his ninetieth year:

> We would drive up to a post office and I would walk in, wearing my big Dexter coat with a big pocket and my shopping bag in it. I'd have my pass card at the ready, with my rank and so on. I would show this to the sub-postmaster, and I'd say: 'That's my card, I'm from the Head Office, and I've some business to concern all of you. Could I speak to you in your own office behind the counter?' Yes, they says, right-oh. So I would go round into the office and then I would produce my shopping bag with their remittance in it. I'd say: 'That's your remittance there, sign here for it.' I don't think the IRA ever really realized how the money was getting out to the network. We were never molested in any one way or another.[63]

This was one brand of courage, and there were to be many others displayed in the Northern Ireland Post Office over the years that followed. Indeed, resisting the urge simply to put up the shutters for good was in itself a gutsy decision for many individuals, running vulnerable Crown branches and sub-offices that were repeatedly attacked by both Republican and Loyalist gangs. The Post Office worked closely with the National Federation of Sub-Postmasters (NFSP) to give the sub-office network as much protection as possible. (Its top officer in Northern Ireland, Israel Abernethy, served on the NFSP's national council and ensured the full engagement of his members.) There ensued a grim kind of arms race. Extra protection was first provided for counter staff by the installation of sheets of reinforced glass. After this led to assaults with sledgehammers, metal grilles were built over the glass. When more raiders then began turning up with guns, special entrances had to be built with one-way mirrors that could allow the gunmen to be seen before they got inside the building: this provided staff with just enough time to hit the alarm bell and retreat to safety. Even this offered no protection against crazed attacks of a more outlandish kind. One sub-office at Twinbrook in West Belfast, notoriously attacked more than two dozen times in all, once had an external wall demolished by a gang that rammed it with a JCB digger. Its sub-postmistress, Rita Fahey, never once surrendered any of the cash locked away in a heavy safe. Most offices were fitted with one of these, and there were many terrible stories of staff having family members kidnapped and held hostage until the safe was opened. Sometimes whole families were held captive within a sub-office, while gunmen waited for access to a time-locked safe. In an extraordinary number of cases, individuals put up a level of resistance on the Post Office's behalf that entailed great personal bravery. Inevitably, lives were lost. A sub-postmaster shot during a raid on his office in June 1979 was the twenty-first member of the Post Office's Northern Ireland staff to die in the first ten years.*

Trying to protect its counter staff was just one dimension of a broader challenge posed for the Post Office by the Troubles. The morning postman on his rounds had been a part of the social fabric for generations, in Ireland as in mainland Britain. But once the community in Ulster was sufficiently divided against itself to trigger the indiscriminate killing of strangers on a street, where did that leave your friendly postman? What was his allegiance to be, on those streets of Belfast or along those lanes of South Armagh where sectarian loyalties had become a lethal matter? The response by the Post Office was unequivocal from the start. It would constitute neutral territory, aligned with neither side of the sectarian divide. Expressions of Republican or Loyalist allegiance in the workplace were banned. The boycotting of mail for political parties on either side was forbidden. Individuals with any police record of involvement in the Troubles were ruthlessly excluded. Well-meaning envoys

---

* This does not include the first postal worker to die in the Troubles. A London postman, Zbigniew Uglik, travelled to the Province as a freelance photographer in July 1970. He was shot dead by the British army as he climbed over a wall in a curfew area.

from one side or the other, offering to provide escorts for postmen in especially dangerous neighbourhoods, were firmly rebuffed. And it was rare indeed for established routines to be surrendered in the face of danger. Two postmen who for years walked the streets of the Bone – a strictly Catholic, Republican area of West Belfast – were ex-Irish Guardsmen, as conspicuously non-Republican as their uniforms were unfailingly immaculate. (Chief Inspector Bell offered both men the chance to be moved to different walks, but it was firmly declined. '"No way, Mr Bell", they says. 'These people all know us well!"'[64]) For historical reasons, the Post Office was well-suited to this approach. It had always been open to young Catholics, which was certainly not true of other major employers in the Province such as the shipyards. (Harland & Wolff's yards had fewer than 100 Catholics out of more than 20,000 workers at the end of the 1970s.) The male workforce of the Post Office – 90 per cent of the total – was divided more or less equally between Catholics and Protestants, at a time when the working population of the Six Counties was hardly more than one third Catholic.[65] Of course, the higher one looked in the organization, the less balanced was the picture – but even this underwent a notable correction in 1980. In readiness for the Split, Chairman Paddy Manson gave way to separate directors for telecoms and for the postal service. The first man appointed as the Postal Director was a Catholic, who had originally come to Belfast as a seventeen-year-old with all his worldly possessions in a shoulder bag – Danny Carty.

Small as a jockey and sharp as a pin, Carty brought to the job an unrivalled knowledge of the Post Office in the Province and a shrewd understanding of its social importance. His career since his mapping days of the 1960s had encompassed responsibility for overseeing the construction of a brand new Head Office and sorting depot for Belfast, on Tomb Street facing the Donegall Quay of the city's docks; and he had worked as Financial Controller of the Telecoms business for four years prior to his appointment in 1980. As the first Postal Director, he moved into a headquarters in Belfast's Queen Street, a few blocks from the Royal Avenue site of the old Head Office. His staff occupied three floors of a building that fortuitously housed the US Consulate on the first floor and sat opposite the city's central police station. The road outside was therefore barricaded with gates and concrete roadblocks, an appropriate physical expression of the siege environment in which the whole of the NI Post Office had to operate. A few years later, as part of his homework for the regular speeches that were required of him, Carty drew up a summary of the security crises it had encountered in a single year.[66] The inventory for the twelve months from January to December 1983 ran as follows:

Staff:	KILLED		2
	INJURED	Physically	9
		Severe shock	66
	HOSTAGE SITUATIONS		12
Attacks with violence on:	POST OFFICES		50
	VEHICLES		31
	BUILDINGS		11
Bomb incidents:			25
Vehicles damaged or destroyed:			36

Shocking as are these numbers for a single year – and a total of twenty-nine postal workers were killed in the course of the Troubles – they mostly reflect the continuing vulnerability of individual offices to armed robbery, or the murder of postmen targeted by the IRA as part-time members of the Ulster Defence Regiment. The violence might have been far worse if Republicans had chosen to see the institution of the Post Office as a proxy for the Crown and therefore in itself a legitimate political target. In general, they did not. Of course, the Post Office like many other large businesses suffered extensive physical damage to its premises. When that occurred, its staff invariably took pains to minimize the disruption to postal services. This was heeded by grateful local communities, if only for the simple reason that life in many areas could not continue without the neighbourhood post office. Northern Ireland included some of the poorest, most deprived areas of modern Europe, where whole communities relied on welfare payments. It was the postmen who delivered the Giro cheques for unemployment benefit; and it was post office counters that handed over cash on presentation of the cheques, just as they also paid out pensions and family allowances. This was well understood on all sides. One of Carty's abiding memories in retirement would be the sight of a postman walking unharmed between two warring factions during a riot: both sides stopped hurling bricks just long enough to let him pass. Carty saw it happen more than once – 'like Moses parting the Red Sea, the postman would just walk through them and then the rioters would start again'.[67] By the same token, while nothing could stop sporadic robberies, the role of postal counters as welfare-cash dispensers at least gave the Post Office some leverage against persistent attacks on the largest branches. Carty was not afraid to use it. In 1984, he closed the sub-office that served the huge Creggan estate adjacent to the Bogside area of Derry. His decision followed a series of violent assaults against the staff there, but was nonetheless bitterly opposed by local councillors and community spokesmen. The closure was undoubtedly a great inconvenience to those they represented. After a lengthy stand-off, a City Council deputation travelled to London to protest in person to the Post Office Chairman. Dearing summoned Carty for a three-way meeting. Each side had to present its case in front of the other, then both had to withdraw while the Chairman considered the position. Two minutes later (or so Carty recalled) Dearing asked them back in and made the tersest possible announcement. 'Any decision that Mr Carty makes in terms of Northern Ireland, I will support him. Thank you, gentlemen.'[68] The Creggan sub-office remained closed for the next four years.

Had the Derry delegates appreciated beforehand the rapport between Carty and his Chairman, they could have saved themselves the trouble of a journey. Dearing made a first visit to Belfast in Carty's early months, and the two men – so similar to each other in a host of ways – hit it off immediately. Carty was delighted to find in his Chairman someone genuinely concerned over the plight of Northern Ireland's staff. Two or three times a year, formal ceremonies were held in Belfast for the presentation of awards – with cheques attached and sometimes an all-expenses-paid weekend break in London – to honour individuals like Rita Fahey who had shown conspicuous bravery in the course of their work for the Post Office. About 150 people were so honoured each year. Dearing agreed to attend at least one of these ceremonies a year, sometimes two, though all publicity was studiously avoided. He unfailingly showed up – not for him, the last-minute apology pleading the pressure of Board business – and he always made a huge impression, speaking from the heart on each occasion and taking the time to talk to everyone he met there. Dearing was highly regarded in the Province as no Chairman before or since. He greatly admired Carty, too, partly out of respect for Carty's dedication to the Post Office in the face of considerable risk to himself and his family (his car had to be fitted with a special bomb-detecting device) and partly because he rated him highly as a manager. In 1983–4, following up on its 1980 report, another MMC committee (under the same chairman) conducted a second investigation into the letter post service. The efficiency of the London postal districts was this time reviewed alongside appraisals of the Belfast,

Glasgow and Cardiff Head Post Offices. By almost every measure, Belfast came out top: the report's authors commended its performance since 1979, noting that significant annual savings could be made in the other three cities if they 'were brought up to the present level of efficiency of Belfast . . .'[69] Dearing was later fond of quoting Carty's response at the MMC's hearings in Belfast, when asked by the chairman of the investigation why his city was out-performing the rest of the country: 'We do the ordinary things extraordinarily well'. One of the not-so-ordinary things done for the visiting MMC party was certainly done well, but without their knowledge. Led by their chairman, Sir Godfray Le Quesne QC, they asked one morning if a lunchtime walk around the city centre could be arranged. Alert to the security risk posed by a senior London silk walking the pavements of Belfast, Carty had fortunately made plans for this in advance. He put in a hasty call to the police and the walk went ahead – chaperoned by half a dozen Special Branch men posing as street cleaners 'with brushes and little vans parked in Donegall Place'.[70]

Carty had necessarily forged close links with the police over the years, and these were formalized in 1987 when he was appointed a member of the Northern Ireland Police Authority. From about this time onwards, he accumulated a long list of Board positions in the Province. While this suited the needs of the service rather well, putting the head of the local Post Office at the very heart of Northern Ireland's public life, it was in some ways a surprising way for Carty's career to have developed. But in 1986 he had lost direct executive responsibility for operations in Northern Ireland, and been consigned until his retirement in 1997 to the role, in effect, of an influential non-executive chairman. This came about as an unintended consequence of a profound and far-reaching reorganization of the Post Office at a national level, from which Northern Ireland could hardly be excluded.

6. DEARING'S DARING DESIGN

That second report by the MMC was strikingly different from the first, submitted in 1980. The first one could scarcely have been more damning. The 1984 verdict was more encouraging by far. There were copious references to the progress made since 1979; and where the first report had frequently expressed surprise at management's neglect of this or that issue – from excessive overtime and the complete absence of part-timers to the poor handling of foreign mails and lack of attention to marketing – its successor repeatedly deferred to the enlightened views of management. It was a momentous change of tone, evident throughout a prodigiously detailed analysis of postal operations. Indeed, given the scale of the many changes recorded, the second report's cautious conclusion – Was the Post Office 'pursuing a course of conduct which operates against the public interest'? Answer: too early to say – now seems more than a little churlish. Its authors had complimentary things to say about an extensive range of topics, from marketing and mechanization to industrial relations and computerization. What they had drawn up was in fact a catalogue of the many ways in which Dearing's leadership had begun to transform the Post Office. Here was a Corporation at long last registering the kind of operational improvements that the keenest advocates of the Split had envisaged in the sixties. Board members in 1969–70 had had to cope with dozens of ambitious papers exploring the scope for a fresh start, but nothing much had come of them. Dearing had set out brave objectives – to restore managers' morale, to promote the marketing function, to modernize the road–rail links, to revive the mechanization process – and had achieved them. Productivity was rising (even in London), and real unit costs were falling, at rates not seen since the 1940s. One outcome was a dramatically improved financial performance. In his first month as formal Chairman of the reconstituted Post Office in October 1981, Dearing had asked his Finance Director, Charles Beauchamp, for a forecast of operating profits in 1982–3. Beauchamp had come back warning of a £45m loss. By far the biggest earner would be the Philatelic Bureau, selling stamps that no one would ever use. (Philately profits were forecast at £26m; inland letters and overseas mails were projected to lose £65m and £22m respectively.)[71] In the event, by the middle of the decade the Post Office had left this gloomy outlook far behind. The growth in business mail by 1984–5 had underpinned a 24 per cent jump in the volume of 1st class letters since 1979–80; adjusted for inflation, Group turnover over the same five years had climbed by 17 per cent. With its dependence on a giant infrastructure of essentially fixed costs, rising sales put a wholly different complexion on the Post Office's performance and its profits moved into a different league. Pre-tax profits in 1984–5, at £144m, were more triple those recorded for 1979–80.[72]

This was all in line with the bold predictions that Dearing had been making from the start. 'Too many people underestimate the potential of the Royal Mail', he wrote in a front-page article for *The Post* early in 1982. 'I think the postal business could actually expand throughout the

1980s and I think it will be a vast business in twenty years' time.'[73] In the early days, Dearing had had no solid grounds for this brave public optimism. And in private, he was far less sanguine. It was not just the unions' control of the workplace that worried him. Dearing admired the esprit de corps that existed across its senior echelons, but was surprised to find how profoundly the Post Office's centuries-old enjoyment of a state monopoly had cut it off from the outside world. 'This was its weakness – that it was an island culture, and didn't realize how very different it really was.'[74] Within his first three months, in a note to his Executive Committee, Dearing floated the idea of a radically different kind of Post Office. 'As you will know, I am strongly attracted by organization of the Postal Business into a number of profit centres.'[75] He had to admit that the current mix of line management (from Head Postmasters to Regional Directors to the Managing Director, Posts) seemed to rub along with the essentially functional divisions of the centre. 'These lines are well understood and work.' But the mix was much less suited to a rapidly changing environment, in which products and services were increasingly seen as a better basis for organization. 'There is no postal business as such; there are several businesses, each behaving differently in the marketplace.' Hence the case for profit centres. Denis Roberts agreed, at least in principle.[76] Perhaps surprisingly, the Young Turks did not. They sent back a candid thumbs-down for the whole idea, via a memo to Roberts. 'Our main and fundamental finding [after long discussion] is that there is nothing seriously wrong with the organisation of PHQ [Postal Headquarters] as it is now constituted ... nor do we believe that it would be sensible to introduce a product-based organization for letters, parcels and counters ... and none of us favour a root and branch approach.'[77] But Dearing did. Determined to prevail over the more cautious instincts of even his closest colleagues, he turned like others before him to outside consultants for help. Several different firms were taken on in various contexts. Above all, Dearing worked closely with an outside consultant called Leslie Deighton, whose Corporate Consulting Group (CCG) was commissioned in March 1983 to review the whole organization of the Post Office.

Less than eight months later, and with the benefit of some forthright guidance from the Chairman on what he was expecting, CCG handed over a report as punchy as it was blessedly brief.[78] The gist of a succinctly documented fifty-page analysis was that a Board comprised chiefly of functional heads (operations, marketing, personnel and so on) no longer looked appropriate. At the same time, the regional organization set up

in 1935–40 was on its last legs. The Regional Directors and Head Postmasters were all generalists, bound together in 'constructive tension'
and struggling to deliver increasingly specialized services on the basis of
'a high level of goodwill and pragmatic adjustment'. CCG offered three
possible solutions, but the first two were almost academic. The third,
which it called its 'Class of Market' option and acknowledged was a far
more formidable challenge than either of the two alternatives, bore a
close resemblance to the future postulated by Dearing at the outset. It
proposed that there should be a set of 'fully dedicated product management structures': the Post Office would be transformed into a cluster of
businesses, each answerable to its own Board executive and reliant
upon a separate organization in the field with its own marketing, finance
and personnel departments. In short, hard on the heels of the Split that
had taken half a century to get off the mark, there was now a case being
made for the Break-Up. CCG suggested this would have a compelling
logic. The Post Office had already embarked on several commercial
initiatives that demanded skills and a market-oriented ethos sharply
at odds with the 1930s organization installed by Thomas Gardiner.
Along with much more ambitious strategies for Counters and Parcels,
newly commercial units had been launched such as Argonaut in freight-
forwarding or Datapost International in premium delivery services.
Such developments, ventured CCG, seemed bound to force the pace:
'[they] potentially position the Post Office for a radically different future
and introduce the conditions which could make alternative structures
for managing the business both necessary and desirable'. On the very
last page of a thick volume of appendices, CCG laid out their summary
blueprint ('Attachment M') for the 'Class of Market' Post Office. Alongside the familiar Board-level box for a National Girobank Managing
Director sat three new boxes – one each for Counters, Letters and Parcels, all with their own field organizations reporting up through district
managers to three Managing Directors. The traditional all-purpose
Head Postmasters would disappear, as would the Regional Directors.

   Dearing unsurprisingly found all this immensely appealing, but had
no illusions about how shocking it would seem to many. 'Intellectually
it is an attractive organisational structure', he noted in a Board paper
responding to the Report, 'but to achieve it would mean great organisational upheaval as well as resistance.'[79] Yet by the end of 1983, the
Board had enthusiastically embraced the idea of a multi-business structure in principle and had committed itself to making a first move in that
direction. Dearing's resolution was the key, but there were other factors

that also helped his colleagues set aside their reservations. Projections of traffic volume and revenues, which for so many decades had erred on the side of optimism, were now being regularly eclipsed by the actual outturn. So much for the mails being in long-term decline. Prospects for the letter and parcel businesses of the Royal Mail had never in recent times looked so bullish, and the idea of giving them their own separate management teams seemed timely. It looked particularly enticing to Bill Cockburn, who was now emerging as the most effective of Dearing's younger lieutenants. Cockburn had abandoned his 1980 reservations and become a robust advocate of the Royal Mail as an autonomous arm of the Post Office that would run the Letters and Parcels businesses. There was one other factor also well articulated by Cockburn, in his role as the Finance, Counters and Planning Director. There had been a sharp fall in the volume of Government-related transactions handled by the Counters division in 1982–3. A month before the CCG report was presented to the Board, Cockburn submitted a plan to prune the net-work by 5 per cent over the next two and a half years. It sparked an anguished debate round the Board table, as the minutes recorded. 'Public reaction to this [closure plan] could damage other Post Office businesses, notably mails and parcels. There was therefore a strong argument in terms of the Corporation's performance and profitability as a whole for not going down this road of faster closures until Counters was clearly established as a separate business . . .'[80] The CCG report, in this respect as many others, fell on fertile ground.

In January 1984, a first step was taken towards the Break-Up with a rejigging of the Board. The Counters business was separated from Finance and given its own MD, Alan Clinton; and the Royal Mail emerged as a self-standing entity for the first time, to handle letters and parcels under Bill Cockburn's leadership. In the field, where the number of Head Post Offices was reduced again, a new managerial cadre of 'Controllers' was introduced for the Counters operation; and additional Assistant Head Postmasters were appointed in many cities to speed along the evolution of separate product services. The changes of 1984 involved, in the words of the 1984–5 Strategic Plan, 'a big programme of reorganisation and development which will extend throughout the business'.[81] It was mirrored at the centre by a relocation of the Postal Headquarters from the old GPO North in St Martin's to a building just off Buckingham Palace Road: Dearing grabbed an opportunity to take over the lease of the old British Steel head office at 33 Grosvenor Place, and 800 or so Post Office managers began arriving there in November.

The basic shape of the Post Office remained unchanged in 1984 – but a palpable sense of unfinished business now hung over the entire organization, and those at the centre knew their Chairman was contemplating far grander designs. Probably even Dearing was less than certain at this stage how far to go down the road so elegantly marked out by CCG. To finalize his thinking, and to take a measure of reactions to it across the country, he kicked off a consultation exercise which (as in 1934–5) had a strong flavour of turkeys being asked for their views on Christmas. Half a century before, a Committee on Metropolitan and Regional Organization had taken on the task of inviting the Surveyors and their assistants to express a view on a putative future that would involve their demise. In 1984–5, Dearing assigned much of the canvassing work to Deighton and his CCG colleagues, and it was the Regional Directors whose turn had come to discuss their own non-future. The process lasted over twelve months: as Dearing recalled, 'it was a long run up to the wicket'.[82] This was a gentlemanly way of describing what was often a deeply uncomfortable year. Many of those accustomed to speaking on behalf of the whole Post Office kicked back hard against the idea of fragmenting it into four separate businesses (counting Girobank as the fourth). There were endless arguments over dinners and at weekend retreats. How would the public react to being told by a Counters person that they were not responsible for a problem encountered over a parcel? How could it be right to duplicate so many supporting services? Who would vouch for the integrity of intra-group trading? The young Personal Assistant in Dearing's office at the time, Jonathan Evans, watched the Chairman's progress at close quarters. 'He came up against a lot of internal opposition. I can hear him saying: "These Regional Directors, individually they're all wonderful people. But put them all together, and it's just impossible!" Anyway, he saw them off. He just railroaded it through . . .'[83] He had taken soundings over many months from those he trusted. By the early months of 1985, Dearing was ready to forge ahead. The Post Office would be divided into four businesses with their own national organizations – and the transition to this new world would be accompanied by a significant devolution of responsibilities away from the centre.[84]

There is no evidence that Dearing consciously set about his reform of the Post Office as anything other than a fulfilment of the undertaking he had given, late in 1980, that it could put its own house in order. He never spoke of reorganization as a prelude to privatization. On the contrary: he insisted in November 1983 that a huge effort would have to go into an internal-communications exercise, 'to overcome the natural resistance to change and to dispel possible fears, linked to experience of British Telecom, that the changes were being made to prepare the way for privatisation'.[85] Thinking on this score within the Government was quite another matter. Postal privatization may have been shelved in 1980, but there had never been a decision to rule it out – and the powers to alter the legal shape of the Post Office were there in the 1981 Telecom Act. By 1983, the sale of many large but essentially peripheral publicly owned assets – including companies such as the British Sugar Corporation, Amersham International and the British Technology Group – had been achieved with surprising ease. This encouraged the Government to promote the privatization of core nationalized industries as a central plank of its economic policy (and of its political ideology, too) after Thatcher's election victory of June 1983. 'No state monopoly is sacrosanct', as her Financial Secretary, John Moore, announced a few months later.[86] Until this point, the growing evidence of a simultaneous turnaround in the Post Office's fortunes had merely prompted the Treasury to lift the level of the quasi-dividend (or 'negative external financing limit' usually referred to as just 'the negative EFL' or even plain 'EFL') it required of the Corporation. Now, the apparently revitalized Post Office appeared in a new light altogether. Writing in October 1983 to the Trade and Industry Secretary, Cecil Parkinson, to argue against the Treasury's latest demands, Dearing insisted 'a very profitable business like ours' deserved more respect. Its achievements since 1980 had marked it out as 'a service which is unique among the significant postal administrations throughout the world in its return on capital, and which has been entirely self-financing for a number of years'.[87] This had already been well noted. An article published in *Lloyds Bank Review* in July 1983 by two influential academic economists, Michael Beesley and Stephen Littlechild, had proposed a list of privatization targets that included the Post Office.[88] When the Cabinet sub-committee in charge of privatization policy drew up a list of its twenty-three main candidates in January 1984, it included (as one item) the Post Office and the National Girobank.[89]

Not much consideration seems to have been given to the Post Office's candidacy during 1984. All available hands were turned to the business of assuring a successful sale of 50.2 per cent of British Telecom that November. But after Dearing began talking to DTI officials early in 1985 about his plans for the Break-Up – and after the triumph of British Telecom's flotation in November 1984 attracting over 2 million investors – the privatization of the Post Office was suddenly a very live prospect. It had the enthusiastic backing of Parkinson's successor at the

DTI, Norman Tebbit. His intentions were plain from the moment he responded to the Break-Up plans by instructing the Post Office to begin work on separate audited accounts for Counters and for the Royal Mail. A little ominously, Dearing was told in February 1985 that the MMC's refusal to give the Post Office an absolutely clean bill of health in its 1984 Report had gone down badly with the Cabinet.[90] By August 1985, Tebbit was writing to the Chairman to endorse plans for a separation of the parcels business from Royal Mail, and to urge ahead the establishment of the Post Office's four businesses as independent legal entities. Enclosed with the letter was a draft of 'Post Office Objectives', a document now required of the DTI by statute. Tebbit's third objective would have amazed any of Dearing's predecessors, not least William Barlow:

> To ensure the most responsive and efficient use of resources, I shall want continually to consider the possibilities for introducing private capital into Post Office activities and I would welcome your positive and regular recommendations in this area.[91]

Dearing had little time to comply with Tebbit's request until the end of 1986. Detailed planning of the Break-Up consumed him for several months and culminated in a masterly paper that he wrote for the Board in November 1985. In eight pages it provided all his senior colleagues with the instructions they needed to implement the biggest upheaval since the regionalization of the thirties.[92] Gardiner's project had taken seven years to implement. Dearing oversaw the completion of the Break-Up over the course of just ten months of 1986 – even though, as the Board acknowledged in authorizing it, 'the scale of the [implicit] personnel problems ... was immense and unparalleled in the Post Office ...'[93] The minutes of Dearing's Executive Committee through 1986 present a record of corporate transformation that any large company in the private sector might have been proud to pull off.[94] For the Letters business and for Counters, four new Territories (slightly differently mapped out in each case) replaced the old Regions – though Scotland, Wales and Northern Ireland retained their nominal status with country Boards under non-executive heads (one of them, Danny Carty) – and the Regional Directors were retired or reassigned.* Across the four Territo-

---

* The four Territories for Letters were Royal Mail London, Royal Mail West, Royal Mail East and Royal Mail North. The latter was based in Edinburgh but included the north-east of England and Northern Ireland as well as Scotland, and two years later was extended to

ries, Head Office buildings were established, management structures and union pay arrangements overhauled, staffing resources realigned, intra-group trading rules fixed and financial budgets struck – all separately, for the two operations. Parcels went through a similar but less radical upheaval, establishing its traditional business as 'Network 1', with special services and Datapost in separate networks of their own. Roberts, Cockburn and Tony Garrett became the first Managing Directors of Counters, Letters and Parcels respectively in April 1986 while Ken Young was made Vice-Chairman. All were soon busy on Five Year Plans, a prominent feature of Post Office planning from this point onwards, and the first of these needed to provide for yet another layer of reorganization within each business. This saw the creation of sixty-three new districts for Letters, thirty-two for Counters and twelve for Parcels. All had their own District Managers (finally replacing the last of the Head Postmasters, of whom there had still remained about 200 across the country in 1985). The whole process triggered a relocation of hundreds of managers, including some who had only just settled into new jobs created in 1984. For not a few of his critics, Dearing's boldly imposed designs brought the culture of the traditional Post Office to a much lamented end. But, as Tilling had predicted, most quickly adapted to the new era. One of the Regional Directors most opposed to the Break-Up was the Chairman of the Midlands Postal Board based in Birmingham, Ian Cameron, who as a young APCII in Norwich had helped to map out the very first postcodes in 1958. Dearing bore no grudges, and happily acceded to Cameron's request for family reasons to be able to stay in Birmingham as the General Manager for a Counters Area that covered the Midlands, Wales and the South-West.

The trade unions also adapted to the reorganization without serious disruptions on the ground. It inevitably posed a head-on challenge to their own structures, which had always been geared to the needs of pay bargaining with a single Post Office (and which in due course would need to be fundamentally revised to keep the Unions abreast of the Post Office). But by the time the new districts went operational, in October 1986, many agreements had been struck with the new managers at a local level. At a national level, the UCW consistently asserted its opposition to the Break-Up. Alan Tuffin led a UCW delegation to the Commons

---

include some of Lancashire and Yorkshire too, in the interests of achieving a broad parity of business volumes between the zones. (Initial plans to base it in Manchester were perhaps fortunately headed off by Cockburn's colleagues north of the border.)

in July 1986 to present the Union's views to the Select Committee for Trade and Industry. The whole reorganization, he said, was 'an insult to the vast number of Managers, Head Postmasters and their staffs who, through their general knowledge of all parts of the Post Office, have served the public well . . .'[95] The Board was repeatedly accused of acting entirely at the behest of the Government, in readiness for the privatization of the Post Office. This was to misconstrue the genesis of Dearing's initiative – and the Chairman himself regularly stressed to colleagues how important it was to try countering any impression they were simply puppets of the Government. It was hard for Dearing or anyone else, though, to argue that the Union's fears were baseless, because ministers had conspicuously declined to rule privatization out.[96] By the autumn, press reports of the work being done in Whitehall left little doubt that a sell-off of the Post Office indeed loomed in one form or another.

Dearing's response was straightforward. He would not be drawn on either the likelihood of privatization or its desirability, even within closed meetings at the Post Office. In public, he insisted through most of 1986 that ownership was a matter for ministers, not the Board. This studied neutrality had eventually to be refined, and in December he approved the preparation of publicity materials which, while sticking to a fastidious neutrality, put far more emphasis on the importance of keeping the existing Post Office together as a corporate whole.[97] This line was prompted by the imminent appearance of a discussion paper from the think-tank that had been set up by Keith Joseph in 1974, the Centre for Policy Studies (CPS).[98] Entitled *Privatise the Post*, it advocated a dismemberment of the Post Office and the sale of all four of its businesses at the rate of one a year through 1987–90. Dearing was disconcerted to see the rationale behind his Break-Up carried through to this conclusion. He was as firmly opposed to dismemberment now as he had been in 1980, and had never seen the Break-Up as a prelude to privatization, which would entail, in his view, intra-group trading on a mind-numbing scale. It also flew in the face of preserving an institutional culture that he had come to prize highly and still believed was compatible with a mix of four commercial businesses. Dearing declined the invitation to attend a CPS-sponsored debate in January, but could plainly see the lines of a wider public debate that had now begun. A leader in *The Times* gave the CPS paper a cautious welcome. 'It is indeed arguable that of all the various state-owned bodies, the Post Office's unwieldy bulk is in most need of slimming. The question is not so much whether as when – and how?'[99] Early in the New Year, as part of the forward planning for 1987–8, Dearing accordingly commissioned a study into the feasibility of privatization. The predictable findings were embraced by the Board as broadly compatible with its existing position: privatization could bring huge benefits but would have to apply to the Post Office as a whole. On this basis, for many of Dearing's Board colleagues, neutrality soon gave way in private to a measured enthusiasm.

Dearing himself decided, a few months later, to step down from the chairmanship. If he was privately torn over the prospect of privatization, he never acknowledged as much. His own explanation for leaving was characteristically modest: he was too hands-on by temperament, he told colleagues. Delegation had never been his strength. The Break-Up implied a level of autonomy for the separated businesses that made it inappropriate for the Post Office to go on with an Executive Chairman like himself. (Few colleagues agreed.) Meanwhile, a review of the reorganization process by some outside consultants suggested that, in most important respects, it had been a resounding success and that it had also been carried through without denting the unique profitability of the Post Office, to which Dearing had so proudly drawn attention in 1983. The Post Office was still, apparently, without peer in the European industry for which broadly comparable data were available (and none elsewhere in the world matched the standards achieved in Europe). It was almost alone in delivering a twice-daily service: only Eire and Belgium offered anything comparable. Its tariff schedule was by most measures the lowest in Europe: only Denmark's postal service could claim to rival its prices. And its profitability contrasted with loss-making services in all other countries of Europe except Luxembourg. This cheering assessment offered a stark contrast with all the many bleak appraisals of the Post Office that had littered the 1970s. No doubt it would have appealed to Dearing that he could leave on the back of a job well done. As he himself recorded in a paper with his own reflections on the events of 1986–7: 'We have managed to achieve a very major organisational change in a very short time . . . something [of] which one of the commentators to the [independent] enquiry group said, "it happened so fast, it took your breath away". A great opportunity has been created.'[100] At the age of fifty-seven, he had time to make an impact in another walk of public life and was keen to do so. And he went out of his way, in announcing his departure in July, to insist there had been no disagreements between himself and the Government over any privatization plans.[101]

He could say this without fear of contradiction, for throughout his final months in the chair he kept his distance from the DTI officials busy on the sell-off plans. Only on one occasion, by his own recollection, did he ever presume to give the Prime Minister any advice on the subject. During the campaigning ahead of the June 1987 general election, he suggested to her that speculation about a forthcoming privatization was actually quite helpful as a catalyst for those pushing through cultural changes at the Post Office. Indeed, he specifically asked her to refrain from ruling out a sell-off for Royal Mail, if she ever did conclude for any reason that it was not a feasible policy.[102] Thatcher had long since formed a high regard for Dearing – he was one of her very best appointments, she told a Cabinet colleague around the time of his resignation – but on this score she let him down. A few days later, on 2 June, Thatcher and her senior ministers hosted a morning press conference at which they were quizzed, not for the first time, about forthcoming privatization plans. The Chancellor suggested the next Conservative administration would want to start with the British Airports Authority, moving on as quickly as possible thereafter to the water authorities and the nation's electricity industry. At this moment, according to the next day's report in *The Times*, the Prime Minister leaned forward with an interjection. 'Mrs Thatcher suddenly volunteered to general surprise: "I have indicated that the GPO – the Royal Mail – would not be privatized. People feel very strongly about it and so do I".'[103]

While the reporters were surprised, Dearing was exasperated, several of his colleagues were deeply disappointed, and ministers and civil servants at the DTI were amazed. All had come to believe – unsurprisingly, given the way that Thatcher had pressed Joseph to explore the possibility of dismembering the Post Office in the autumn of 1980, and in light of how much effort had gone into a detailed study of sale options in the intervening years, let alone the progress of the privatization policy in general – that a sell-off was the goal. Some press commentators asserted accordingly that the Prime Minister's veto had been a rush of blood to the head; others suggested alternatively that she had carefully decided to take this line on the basis of an uncharacteristically sentimental attachment to the Royal Mail. (It was even suggested that her father, while running a grocer's shop in Grantham in the 1930s, might have been a sub-postmaster – though there is no record of his having been so.) Both views were mistaken. Thatcher had given serious thought to the possibility of privatizing the Post Office and had concluded – against the Treasury's advice – that it was too fraught with political difficulties. 'I'm not prepared to have the Queen's head privatized', as she had reportedly put it in a conversation with Nigel Lawson some months earlier, in rejecting a Treasury brief that plans be prepared for a sale . 'It was against our advice, because we thought that it could be privatized', recalled Gerry Grimstone, who led the Treasury's privatization unit at this time, 'so we were surprised. But it was a deeply held belief of hers, that the public wouldn't stand for it.'[104] It was perhaps unfortunate that her firm view had been overlooked until this late hour – but postal privatization was now off the agenda for the foreseeable future. Still, if Dearing had restored the Post Office to its status as the best in the world, as many thought, perhaps the time had come for the Corporation nonetheless to assert itself as a successful operator that deserved a new kind of independence.

13

Thwarted ambitions,
1987–2002

At the village post office, Mrs Goggins was outside, looking out
for Pat, and trying to get cool.

'Morning Pat!' she called. 'Isn't it hot! *And* we're going to be
without water today.'

... He began his round with the village letters. Along the
winding streets, through narrow passageways, in and out of cot-
tage gardens he went, and everyone was pleased to see him.

From *Postman Pat's Thirsty Day* (1985)
by John Cunliffe and Celia Berridge

1. FALLING OUT OF STEP

Best in the world or not, the British Post Office was openly admired by
its foreign counterparts in the late 1980s. Its senior managers got top
billing at international postal conferences. Their foreign counterparts
paid regular visits to London for briefing sessions on the British approach
to postal modernization and the more arcane intricacies of postal productivity agreements. Officials from New Zealand came three times in
the run-up to their own postal reform of April 1987, which turned a
government department into a trio of state-owned enterprises with a
gradually shrinking antipodean postal monopoly. Born and raised in the
Welsh valleys, Ken Young found an invitation to visit Wellington some
weeks later for the launch of New Zealand Post irresistible. (The inaugural Rugby World Cup fell in May and June, hosted by New Zealand
and Australia.) It proved to be the first of many such ambassadorial
missions for Young, whose Board responsibilities multiplied over the
next few years and encompassed being Deputy Chairman from March
1990. On one occasion, he was invited to visit the Japanese Post Office
and found himself shown into the Tokyo boardroom, where local officials

were lining the walls three-deep to take notes on what he had to tell them about how the Royal Mail ran its business.[1] Even in Britain, where the extent of its international reputation was rarely appreciated, the Post Office enjoyed an elevated status in the public sector. An editorial in *The Times* referred to it early in 1987 as 'that jewel in the crown' of the nationalized industries.[2]

All this was matched by a palpable new mood within the Post Office itself. Perhaps for the first time in its history since Rowland Hill's hey-day, it had acquired the self-confidence and sufficient belief in its own potential to think it could prosper as a genuinely autonomous body. Gone was the residual timidity with which many senior figures had ini-tially responded to Dearing's radical proposals at the beginning of the decade. Fading at last was the restraining civil service culture of the pre-1969 era, so woefully prolonged through the 1970s. Revitalized and reorganized by Barlow and Dearing, the four separate businesses set up by the end of 1986 were being run by managers with a novel sense of ambition. There were those who feared still that the scale and diversity of the Corporation might render it unmanageable, whether as a quasi-commercial enterprise in the public sector or indeed as a privatized entity. Most top executives of the Post Office had no such reservations. They took huge encouragement from soaring traffic volumes. They also had, from October 1987, a new Executive Chairman who brought to the Post Office a managerial creed and set of business instincts well honed in the private sector. Bryan Nicholson had just served for three years as Chairman of the Manpower Services Commission, a non-departmental product of the corporatist Heath government charged with coordinating education, training and anti-unemployment meas-ures. (It was gradually wound up after his departure.) But his background was otherwise entirely commercial: he had worked for twenty years in the computer and electronics sector, first with Sperry Rand of the US and then with Rank Xerox, whose UK and German operations he headed for five years. Offered the chairmanship in the spring of 1987 – after an informal interview lasting all of ten minutes – Nicholson had initially assumed that preparing the Post Office for privatization would be an important part of his brief.[3] He was surprised and disappointed by the Thatcher veto. Indeed, in his first few weeks in the job he even asked City advisers to look into the feasibility of a giant management buy-out, just in case the Prime Minister might have second thoughts on privatization. But once it was clear she was not for turning, he decided that building on Dearing's achievements would still leave him with a challenging and worthwhile agenda.*

If Dearing had sometimes struck colleagues as self-effacing almost to a fault, the same could not be said of Nicholson. Days before quitting his office in Grosvenor Place, it occurred to Dearing that his own very modest taste in office furnishings might strike his successor as a little shabby. Considerate as ever, he had a huge rug brought into the office from his own home and laid across the floor to lift the general ambience. On his arrival, Nicholson took one look at the decor and ordered a refurbishing of the Chairman's office from top to bottom.[4] Dearing's frugality was to be a thing of the past. But in adopting a grander style by far, which was not always popular, the new man asserted an essential message. Nicholson wanted to imbue the Post Office with a finer appreciation of its own worth, not to say importance: he insisted in a thousand ways that it behave like the aspiring, market-oriented competitor its Corporation status had always supposedly implied. His approach matched the greater willingness to experiment and keener appetite for risk that were striking features of the Dearing legacy.

Unfortunately, they were not reciprocated by any new readiness in Whitehall to let the Post Office have more control over its own affairs. On the contrary, ministers and officials began to take an unprecedented interest in the Post Office. This was a paradoxical outcome of the 1987 election. Thatcher had killed off the privatization project. Yet now, like Banquo's ghost, privatization was part of the background to every discussion of future objectives. Freshly appointed as Minister at the Department of Trade and Industry and Chancellor of the Duchy of Lancaster, Ken Clarke summed up the position for the Board Members at their first meeting: 'His own preference would have been for privatising all the Post Office. But he and his colleagues were governed by the emphatic statements made by the Prime Minister during the election period and this certainly excluded Royal Mail. He would hope that the Royal Mail could be interpreted as being limited to Letters and the sale of stamps, but . . . he did not think it a realistic probability that privatisation would be on the agenda. He did not however wholly exclude the possibility'.[5] It went on being 'not wholly excluded' until early in 1989, when a DTI Strategy

---

* It was not a job he ever really considered abandoning. Like Dearing and Barlow before him, Nicholson was at least partly motivated by a sense of public service – not to mention the personal satisfaction of running an organization that his own father had joined as a thirteen-year-old telegram boy in 1906.

Review informed the Board of a decision to rule out privatization 'of any part of the Post Office' within the lifetime of the current Parliament – and even then, no public announcement was to be made to this effect.[6] The studied ambiguities of these years were in a sense a compliment to the Post Office. Its strong resurgence since 1979–80 had made it an obvious privatization target, until the Thatcher veto. Privatization had had a tremendous political run in the meantime. Since the flotation of half of British Telecom in November 1984, the Government had completed the sale of British Aerospace, Britoil and Cable & Wireless. In the first five months of 1987 alone, it sold off first British Airways, then Rolls-Royce, in two huge sales that grossed almost £2bn for the Treasury. The possibility that the Post Office might one day go the same way could hardly be ignored, especially not by DTI officials who had been researching the prospect almost since 1984. Keeping open this option required that the Department and its ministers should monitor developments at the Post Office extremely carefully – hence their heightened interest.

The result was a tension that was rarely creative. Political and commercial schedules ran to different timescales and often clashed. Ministers continued, as vigorously as ever, to second-guess Board and executive decisions on every major topic from pay and pricing to corporate plans and capital spending. They also set targets for its individual component businesses as well as for the Post Office as a whole, a striking encroachment on its internal affairs that was rebuffed initially, but not for long. Worse, ministers were even more generally inclined than in the past to veto any initiatives aimed at longer-term objectives – launching into new sectors of the postal market, for example, or investing in joint ventures with foreign partners – which might heighten the Corporation's exposure to financial risk in the near term. Official exchanges took on an adversarial tone, even as the Post Office appeared to flourish as never before. Its operational performance over the next several years was to be impressive on many levels. By 1992–3, the volume of letters carried by the Royal Mail would be a staggering 50 per cent higher than in 1983–4. (Dearing had been right.) It would cope with this expansion, while hugely improving its quality of service as defined by letter delivery times. General surveys of customer opinion would rate the Post Office consistently superior to the services delivered by the gas, water and electricity utility companies, and its post-tax profits would shortly begin to rise steeply. Nonetheless, the Government and the Post Office were to find themselves frequently out of step, with damaging consequences.

2. GOODBYE TO GIROBANK

There was another reason why the Post Office in these years could not quite put the possibility of privatization behind it: Thatcher's veto did not apply to Girobank. Six months before the June 1987 election, Dearing wrote to Sam Wainwright's successor as the head of Girobank, Malcolm Williamson, asking him to prepare for a possible change of government. Pondering a Labour win, Dearing harked back intriguingly to the idea promoted by Tony Benn in the 1960s:

> For a Labour Government, I know that [your fellow director] Mr Simpson is already looking into all the aspects of a merger with the National Savings Bank, to form a People's Bank. I would like him to regard his objective as being the most practical possibility against the criterion that Girobank in the form of a new people's bank, should remain a full Bank within the banking community. . . . [He should] address his mind to the case in which over a period of, say, three years, Girobank, with strong Government support, could develop into a bank with a high level of retail deposits, mortgage business and other features that would be relevant to the average working man and woman.[7]

Instead, as Dearing and Williamson had both thoroughly anticipated, the re-election of the Thatcher government brought an early decision to cut Girobank out of the Post Office and sell it off as a separate enterprise. The Chancellor, Nigel Lawson, had always insisted there could be no case for maintaining any kind of a commercial bank in the public sector, and formal tenders for a sale were announced in June 1988. This came as a crushing disappointment to many in the Corporation.

The Treasury, scouring the ground for its next privatization targets, had started pressing for a sale of Girobank early in 1985. Wainwright himself was sympathetic to the notion: worn down by his travails with the public-sector unions, he believed in his retirement that only in the private sector would the bank fulfil its potential. Dearing and most of his other Board colleagues believed a separate sale of the bank would be damaging, not just to the finances of Counters but also to the industrial relations climate of the Post Office as a whole. There was no mistaking the Board's antipathy to the idea. A measure of its disaffection can be taken from the response of the Finance Director to a report prepared by Hambros Bank, late in 1985, on the all-important relationship between Girobank and Counters that would follow any sale. It urged that the bank should be allowed to retain or dispense with its link with Counters, at its own discretion – while Counters should be barred from offering any banking services in competition. 'The philosophy of the Report is to require the Post Office, and in particular the Counters business, to quickly bleed itself to death for the greater glory of privatizing Girobank . . .', wrote an indignant Philip Sellers to his Chairman that December. '[It's clear that] if this sort of view prevails, then John Roberts [as the head of Counters] can pack his bags and go home. There is absolutely nothing in this report that's of any benefit to the Post Office Board.'[8] As he noted acerbically, the Post Office would not even be entitled to the proceeds of the sale.

The least bad option in the Board's view would be to try to keep the bank within the Post Office family by accepting a management buy-out (MBO) by its own staff – and Williamson as Girobank's Managing Director decided in the course of 1986 that he was ready to take a run at it. Given Dearing's go-ahead, in that pre-election memo of December 1986, Williamson assembled a buy-out team through 1987. It included the bank's Walter Simpson – which added an interesting twist. Simpson was married to Morag Macdonald, who as Secretary to the Post Office was one of the three-member vendor team set up to deal with the buy-out. (As a qualified barrister, she needed no alerting to the legal niceties of this situation, but it must have required some delicate rules at the kitchen table.) Work on the MBO went ahead for several months following the 1987 election. The Board under its new Chairman agreed in April 1988 that it would be sympathetically considered. Shortly afterwards, Williamson paid a visit to Kenneth Clarke at the DTI to apprise him of the MBO plans, accompanied by Macdonald to represent the Post Office. Clarke had just returned to his Department from a good lunch. Puffing on a cigar with his feet up on the desk, he was characteristically candid with his guests, as Macdonald recalled. 'He said to Malcolm at the outset: "Well, politically it would be quite impossible, so now persuade me why I should do it." Malcolm went ahead with his pitch: he was very keen. Clarke listened politely. Then he just shook his head and said: "Can't be done. If it failed after the sale, I'd be crucified." And that, more or less, was the end of the discussion.'[9] At its monthly meeting in May, the Post Office Board duly (and perhaps a little supinely) agreed that an MBO would not be such a good idea after all. But the Board's City advisers had already made it clear in January that the timetable decreed by the Government effectively ruled out a stock market flotation. There was therefore no privatization option left but to invite

sealed bids from other banks. Expressions of interest were soon flooding in.

Thus began a sale process that dragged on for more than two years.
Some doubted that any purchaser would be found, given the nature of
the bank's umbilical connections with the Post Office. When ninety indi-
cations of interest had finally been sifted down to seven indicative bids
and these were opened in September 1988, there was consternation all
round: the highest offer by far was from a state-owned French bank,
Crédit Lyonnais. Passing Girobank from one state owner to another was
not what the proponents of a sale had had in mind. Its rejection led to
the withdrawal of all the bidders and six months of confusion ensued. A
second round of bidding followed from January to April 1989 which
produced a completely different short-list, the highest bid this time
coming from a building society, Alliance & Leicester (owned today by a
Spanish bank, Santander).[10] This was deemed acceptable; but a bank had
never before been acquired by a building society, and ensuring the sale
complied with all the technicalities of building society law only
compounded the huge complications flowing from the Girobank's
dependence on the Counters business. A Post Office team led by Roberts
and Sellers' successor as Finance Director, Richard Close, had to crawl
through a succession of seemingly endless negotiating tunnels to arrive
at not one but two contracts – one for the sale and the other (of nightmarish complexity) to govern the subsequent relationship between the
Post Office and the purchaser.*

The process did nothing for the performance of the bank in the meantime and was accompanied by much tut-tutting across the Post Office.
Girobank's success since Wainwright's arrival had been a matter of
considerable pride among the postal staff; it was part of the fabric of the
business. (New graduate recruits, for years past, had been more or less
obliged to open a Girobank account on their first day: as a future
director recalled of his own experience in 1972, 'no doubt it wasn't true,
but I was told I wouldn't get paid until this was done'.[11]) Several of

---

* When the Alliance & Leicester decided in 1996 to go for a stock market flotation, it was
Roberts who wrote a paper for the Board proposing that the Post Office seize the opportunity to improve the terms of its trading contract with Girobank. This had continued to generate about 30 per cent of the Counters network's revenues. But Roberts noted the Counters
management had rated the relationship 'unexciting'. In particular, Counters had been
'excluded from growth through relationships with other banks in the personal banking sector and [disadvantaged by] an inequitable sharing of profits generated in the bill payment
and cash markets'. (BP 44(96), 'Commercial Relationship with Girobank', July 1996, Post
69/Red Books.)

Roberts's own management team in the Counters business came close to resigning. His Operations Director, Richard Dykes, was that rare creature in the organization, a manager appointed at a senior level from the outside world, and had joined the Counters business just three years earlier. The sale stripped away an asset he had thought was going to be an important part of the business's future. Dykes recalled: 'It seemed to be knocking a prop away from under the business. My colleagues running marketing and personnel [Dick Wheelhouse and Bob Peaple] agreed. We were all opposed to the sale and felt strongly about it.'[12] And among Nicholson's senior executives, the Government's commitment to the sale was wryly contrasted with the enthusiastic support of most other European governments – especially the French – for the fostering of Giro systems in their post offices. Accident-prone to the end, the sale negotiations were topped off by a colourful row over the future leadership of Girobank. The purchaser was promised the services of Williamson; but he himself had other ideas once the senior line-up became clear, and he baled out for a top banking job elsewhere. The sale to Alliance & Leicester, completed in July 1990, was closed for £112m, which included £39m for the repayment of debts owed to the Post Office. This was hardly a princely multiple of operating profits that reached £30.2m for 1989–90 – reflecting the perceived level of risk inherent in the bank's continuing relationship with the Post Office's network – and it marked a net loss, after tax and expenses, of £63m against the £170m book value of Girobank prior to the sale. But it was a far better outcome than had seemed likely to many sceptical observers two years earlier.

A notable sequel to the sale featured what must surely rank as one of the more expensive typing errors ever made, subsequently detailed in an official report on the sale and the role of the DTI in the process.[13] Girobank had a leasing business, the eighth-largest of its kind in the country, which Alliance & Leicester was legally precluded from buying and therefore had to be sold off separately. It essentially comprised a collection of high-quality financial assets, promising a future stream of payments which the Post Office's City advisers, Schroders, estimated to be worth between £310m and £320m. When four final bids were received, one of them exceeded this valuation by a very wide margin: Norwich Union Life Insurance had offered £378m. To prepare for confirmation later of the final audited balance sheet prior to sale on 31 January 1990, accountants to the process were given a chance to review the NU's calculations. They discovered, on 30 January, that someone had added £27.5m where they should have subtracted it, resulting in a

£55m overstatement of the price that NU had put on the table. In conveying this embarrassing news to NU's Chairman, however, Schroders thoughtfully pointed out how very much the Prime Minister appreciated hearing of the auction's result and how very much indeed she was looking forward to inviting the Chairman to Downing Street quite shortly, in order to thank and congratulate him in person. The final outcome was loosely attributed in the official report to the existence of another potential bid, and went unremarked at the time: 'Schroders spoke on several occasions to The Norwich Union during this period ... and succeeded in persuading The Norwich Union to increase their offer to £342m on 5 February'.

3 . THE DRAS DISPUTE AND A RADICAL PROPOSAL

Dominant as Dearing had been in the Chairman's role, to those working in the Royal Mail there was another individual who by the late 1980s had come to encapsulate the new sense of purpose in the postal service like no one else: Bill Cockburn, who had been Managing Director of the Letters business since 1986. Far more visible to most of the workforce than either Dearing or Nicholson, Cockburn was an uncompromising figure with an impressive ability to set clear goals and to hound those around him until they were achieved. He was a former civil servant who had joined the Post Office in 1961 but had now emerged as a forceful businessman – a rarer accomplishment in the higher ranks of the Post Office than it was usually convenient to acknowledge. A Board non-executive in the 1990s nicely described him as a one-man proxy for the market forces kept at bay by the letters monopoly. He also had the energy and charisma needed for the day-to-day leadership of the organization. At management conferences, he could thrash out policy differences in the bar until well into the small hours and still surface for an early breakfast with twice as much gusto as anyone else on the team. (As one interviewer noted at the end of a shrewd profile many years later, 'You get the impression that Cockburn could happily chat about business all day and all night'.[14]) His toughness and determination could occasionally make him an abrasive colleague. As head of Letters, he ran the dominant service within the Royal Mail but formally ranked no higher in the organization than the head of the Parcels business – conceptually a discrete business after 1986, in the interests of making its managers more accountable and its accounts more transparent, but in practice still largely inseparable from the Letters operation. Cockburn had no time for this parity of status, and there were Parcels managers who retired bruised from the fray. But the same controlled aggression made Cockburn a formidable and respected negotiator with men like LDC3's John Taylor in the UCW. Hence his career-boosting 'breakthrough' with the introduction of London's IWM in 1979 and its replication across the country.

Assisted by a de facto deputy who handled most of the paperwork, Jerry Cope, Cockburn had spent much of the 1980s to date struggling with working-practice reforms and a stream of local union agreements. These complemented the work being done by Ken Young on national issues including pay and efficiency agreements in the separate businesses. Unfortunately, it was becoming apparent by the early months of 1988 that neither Cockburn's IWM agreements nor indeed Young's *Safeguarding the Mails* agreement of 1985 had had anything like the lasting impact once hoped for. Seen initially as harbingers of a fundamentally altered climate of industrial relations, they were turning out to have marked just more milestones on a long and wearying road. The impact of IWM arrangements had boosted productivity usefully in many large sorting offices. (The bonus gains, awkwardly, had been largest where the inefficiencies had been most egregious – but that was in the nature of the deal.) No one, though, really believed the authority of the UCW's leadership had been much strengthened, nor the stranglehold of local branch officials much weakened, by the new regime. Indeed, since IWM deals were all local by nature, it was increasingly branch officials who were dictating decisions within the UCW. And a fixation with bonuses did nothing to make sorting offices more easily manageable. The frequency of unofficial stoppages, especially in London, was fast rising again by the time of Dearing's exit. The departing architect of the new Post Office himself had no illusions that anything had fundamentally changed in this respect.[15] Within a few months, Cockburn was sitting down with Cope to plan a more combative assault on the problem.

Their immediate concern was to address a dire shortage of postmen across the Outer London region. As the MMC Report of 1980 had pointed out, the manning inefficiencies of the capital had long since saddled the Post Office with far too many employees in the largest sorting offices of the inner city, and far too few postmen in the suburbs where it needed them.[16] Or to put it another way, the stranglehold of the UCW over all working practices in the inner city ensured a generous level of overtime earnings that made postal jobs attractive (just as the printers' unions made jobs in Fleet Street highly desirable). But the population of the Inner London boroughs had dropped by more than 50 per cent since 1900 – and a rapidly declining urban workforce meant far fewer applicants for postal jobs across the wider London region, where the UCW's writ was less powerful. Low wages, anti-social hours, high travel costs and little or no special financial assistance left Outer London postmen even worse off than the semi-skilled employees of other large organizations – the railways, local authorities and the NHS – that were similarly strapped for new recruits. IWM arrangements were by 1987 winding down in many parts of the country. Cockburn proposed that advantage be taken of this to offer extra money to recruits in the south-east. He and Cope – who was now the London Postal Region's Director – conceived the idea of paying what were called 'Difficult Recruitment Area Supplements' (DRAS). There was never much doubt that this would prompt a 'DRAS dispute' with the UCW. The idea of differential pay terms according to location struck at the heart of national pay bargaining, which was one of the few sources of real authority left for the union's Executive Council. The prospect of a serious clash, far from deterring Cockburn and his colleagues, added to the appeal of pressing forward. Cockburn was convinced of the need to take a more robust line in the workplace, and a conflict over DRAS would involve the UCW opposing management's proposal to put more money on the table. At least from a PR point of view, this looked to Cockburn a more promising issue than the usual working-practices minutiae that glazed the eyes of every outsider. Cockburn had in mind another break with the standard choreography of past postal disputes, too, by which to signal a fresh approach.

Serious industrial action at the Royal Mail generally ran through a familiar routine. Management would begin with a statement of historical intent. The postal service would be suspended in pursuit of a fundamental long-term goal. But the critical difference between a sorting office and a factory took only a day or two to become apparent. Any factory wracked by a dispute could be shut down: machines could be switched off, gates closed and suppliers turned away. The mails, by contrast, just kept on coming. Unless they could be diverted to other regions – 'out-of-area postings' that were impossible in a major dispute – mountains of unsorted mail were soon shockingly on display to the general public. Management then found itself under intense pressure from the politicians to compromise over its initial objective. Days later, the workforce would return with few real concessions made and the compensatory prospect of extensive overtime to clear the postal backlog. This left local executives out of pocket as well as burdened with a tense atmosphere in the workplace for months to follow. It was a pattern of events recalled by Cockburn himself as akin to Snakes and Ladders – 'with the snakes way longer than the ladders, so you could never make as much ground on the way up as you'd lose on the way down'.[17]

He and Cope spent much of the first half of 1988 preparing for a different outcome to the DRAS confrontation. Events moved inexorably towards a strike after the UCW's Annual Conference had censured its own Executive Council for taking an excessively open-minded attitude to the problem. A one-day national stoppage was called for 31 August, and attracted almost unanimous support. (Belfast was the only major sorting office to ignore it.) But the real action began when staff turned up for work the next day. Cockburn decreed that not a penny of additional overtime would be paid for tackling the backlog. At London's Western District Office in Rathbone Place, just off Oxford Street, fifteen part-timers were instead hired to clear it – and 2,000 regular staff promptly walked out in protest.[18] The same pattern of events unfolded across most of south-east England and the East Midlands. UCW leaders appealed for calm, were ignored by local officials and gave the walkouts their belated approval. At the end of the first week in September, more than 100,000 staff remained on strike. It was suddenly apparent that a huge well of disaffection had been tapped. The Break-Up of the Corporation into four businesses, the mooted sale of Girobank, the talk of closures for the Counters network, anxiety over privatization rumours and (not least) a dip since 1986 in postmen's earnings relative to general wage trends – all had contributed to a widespread dissatisfaction that produced a climactic month for industrial relations across the whole Post Office. It took another fortnight for the DRAS strike to subside, by which time Cockburn, Cope and their colleagues found themselves at the bottom of an even longer snake than usual.

With a newly appointed Minister, Tony Newton, anxious to curtail any further risk to the postal service – and the Board itself genuinely alarmed that a tough stand might risk a total breakdown of industrial relations – a compromise had to be accepted over the clearing of the backlog: Cockburn had to abandon his stand against overtime bonuses and the Union gave way on the employment of temporary workers to help with the work. To resolve the original cause of the dispute, a variant of DRAS had eventually to be agreed which flooded the whole of

The fall-out from the DRAS dispute of 1988 in the *Courier* and *The Post*

south-east England with supplements.[19] (There were to be 'no ponds or islands', in the Union's own colourful phrase.) The Letters business actually recovered surprisingly quickly. By mid-1989, Ken Young – as Acting Chairman in the absence of Nicholson, who had been hospitalized for a heart by-pass operation – was able to assure the media that the Post Office was back on track.[20] But in the months immediately after the

THE OFFICIAL JOURNAL OF THE
UNION OF COMMUNICATION WORKERS
VOLUME 91 NO 11, NOVEMBER 1988

the *POST*

WHAT AN INSULT!

The General Secretary replies to Bill Cockburn's article in last month's *Courier*

DID YOU see the front page of the October *Courier*? It had an article by Mr Bill Cockburn, Managing Director Letters with the screaming headline WE MUST WIN BACK OUR REPUTATION. There have been many letters and telephone calls to UCW Headquarters expressing anger at the arrogance in the article.

It is not we that have to win back our reputation, it is Mr Cockburn. It is not postmen and postwomen, with other grades, that have rocked the customers' confidence, it is Senior Management.

If Mr Cockburn believes it was a "totally unnecessary strike"

then he should have paid attention to the warnings I and my colleagues gave him in July. Had he paid attention to our members' anger and frustration, then the strike may have been avoided. Instead he chose to ignore the warnings as he has chosen to do in the past. Yes, he is correct, we have

had, in the space of just one year, three confrontations – all as a result of Post Office decisions.

But Mr Cockburn, on each occasion, was warned that unless he responded positively and constructively, those bust-ups would be inevitable, not by choice but because of Post Office intransigence.

A year ago the Post Office were warned about the Shorter Working Week: that a one hour reduction paid for out of new productivity savings was no solution to our 20 year old claim. They dismissed the warnings as a bluff. And we came to the knife-edge of a pre-Christmas strike.

They were warned that team briefings would fail if local managers abused the arrangements – which of course they promptly did, leading to its failure. It should have been withdrawn, but, no, Mr Cockburn, by going to the High Court, imposed it on the workforce. That in itself is an admission of defeat, for team briefings are now a laughing

Continued on page 2 ●

STRIKE

Members of the North London C&CS branch picket the Whitechapel Crown Office during the 24 hour strike on 28 October in protest over Post Office plans to downgrade crown offices to sub-Post Offices.
Full story on page 3. Photo: Laurie Sparham/Network.

MERGER PLANS IN TROUBLE

Merger plans between the UCW and the NCU have run into trouble after differences between the two unions surfaced during the Labour conference. See page 3 for the full story.

GCHQ DAY 7 FOR FREEDOM'S SAKE

Thousands of trade unionists protest at the Government's attack on basic liberties. Page 3.

Don't go P&O

The TUC is calling on trade unionists not to use P&O Ferries. Page 4.

SA support

3,000 South African post and telecoms workers are still sacked after their strike, but the union's president still found time to send a message of support to this Union in its struggles with the Post Office. Page 5.

Italian jobs

Jane Woddis talks to Italian trade unionists about how to prepare for the 1990s. Page 6.

Equal pay for women

A new Lords' decision may make it easier for women to fight for equal pay, says Jo Richardson, Labour's shadow Minister for Women, on page 7.

Five day week

In two offices where a five day week has been introduced it has proved very popular. Read all about it on page 12.

dispute, its outcome seemed much more damaging. Profits had been badly dented, to no avail. And the battle over overtime payments had left much acrimony in its wake. A typically feisty review of events by Cockburn in October's *Courier* ('We Must Win Back Our Reputation!') drew a bitter response from the UCW's Alan Tuffin in November's *Post* ('What an Insult!'), followed by a series of unusually personal attacks by Tuffin aimed at the whole Board. By December, the General Secretary was warning of 'massive discontent' that might portend further trouble.[21] When the Post Office set up an internal inquiry into the debacle, the Union refused to participate.

Informal inquests began immediately. The elimination of unofficial strikes had been envisaged earlier in the year as part of a 'New Deal' for the Letters business, due for a public launch in November 1988. Instead, Nicholson and his Executive Committee gathered for a weekend retreat that month at which they anguished over their failure to identify and articulate any compelling strategy on industrial relations. There was frustration, too, over the lack of any clear lead from the Government about its long-term intentions for the Post Office: their lack of progress 'reflected the general difficulty in defining strategy in the current vacuum and uncertainty (particularly over privatisation) caused by the Minister's policy review'.[22] But whatever the explanation, their predicament called for an urgent response. As the marketing men in the Letters business were insisting, future growth depended on having a reputation for reliable service. Constant unofficial stoppages would be immensely damaging. By the end of 1988, Cockburn and Cope had together decided that the existing framework of industrial relationships could not endure much longer. Neither side carried the authority needed to implement lasting reforms: the Post Office Board had no choice but to kowtow to ministers; and the UCW's leaders were constantly second-guessed by their local representatives. The question facing the Royal Mail was whether to go on trying to reconcile reform initiatives with the existing framework – or alternatively, to think about replacing it altogether. Cockburn and Cope were already puzzling over this when the results of a Ministerial Strategic Review landed in January 1989. They seized on its findings to make a radical proposal.

Dearing had foreseen in one of his final papers in 1987 that any decision not to go ahead with privatization 'makes action to reduce the monopoly highly probable'.[23] Sure enough, the Government now disclosed it had 'decided in principle' to restrict the Post Office's letters monopoly to items posted for 50p or less in place of the existing £1 threshold. 'It had been judged politically unacceptable to leave the monopoly untouched, but there was no enthusiasm in Government for removing it completely . . .'[24] This acknowledged a steadily mounting campaign by several private companies which had invested in fledgling courier businesses they were anxious to legitimize. Cockburn's priority since early 1987 had been to suggest counter-measures, short of court action, that would see off the couriers.* Now a different and more thoughtful response was needed. Cockburn saw the Ministerial Review as a chance for nothing less than a redrawing of the parameters of the postal service. Armed with a coherent plan of its own, the Board could begin lobbying MPs to win support for a package that would be offered to Government in straight exchange for public endorsement of a curtailment of the monopoly. Reporting back to it on a series of meetings with DTI officials over the next few months, Cockburn confirmed that ministers appeared ready to contemplate a definite break with the past. Late in February he gave the Board an oral report of a meeting that he appears to have attended alone, at which the total abolition of the monopoly had been discussed:

> It would be likely to provoke national strikes in the short term although it might well lead over a period to more realistic attitudes in the much smaller Letters Business which would remain . . . While a change to 50 pence would not improve the operating environment, complete abolition of the monopoly could do so, but only after a period of significant upheaval . . . [The Post Office had listed the substantial financial and industrial relations risks this might pose.] The Ministers believed however that these risks, including possible industrial action, might well be worth taking in order to increase choice for customers.[25]

Tony Newton, and his Secretary of State, David Young, were evidently not inclined to regard the Thatcher veto on privatization as a bar to other fundamental reforms. In May, Cockburn told his colleagues: 'it was clear that Government was looking for radical action, and was anxious in particular to see disaggregation of the Letters Business and contracting out of services'.[26] How far some of these reports back from Whitehall were really Cockburn's way of moving things along, as opposed to fair summaries of ministerial thinking, is not always clear. But by the spring, anyway, Cope had been set to work on the requisite plan needed to let the Post Office regain the initiative.

---

* In the autumn of 1987, Coventry City Council announced its decision to post 200,000 letters a year to local ratepayers via Coventry Courier Services (CCS), a tiny business that guaranteed a cheap next-day delivery anywhere within the Coventry area. Always looking for 'well-judged pressure short of legal action', Cockburn noted that the City Council was Labour-controlled. (CEC 66(87), 'Implications for the Letter Monopoly', November 1987, Post 69/389.) Its councillors soon found themselves on the receiving end of some stiff warnings from UCW officials. Shades here, surely, of Thomas Witherings alerting the burghers of Hull to the existence of the new monopoly and their need to abide by it.

This was good timing. In July 1989, the DTI received a new Secretary of State. As an ardent Thatcherite and one of the earliest champions of privatization – he had chaired a Tory policy group to work on the idea as far back as 1969, and had overseen some of the crucial first flotations – Nicholas Ridley made a famous start at the Department. He told journalists on his first day that the Government had no proper role to play in industry; so he had nothing to do, and 12,000 civil servants to help him do it. This left him room, though, to explore reforms of the public sector, and he was seen airing typically radical thoughts. As one of his DTI officials recalled: 'he had taken a look through all the boring papers he wasn't going to touch and had decided there were two things which were actually quite interesting – and one of them was the Post Office.'[27] There followed a curious few months, in which Ridley and some of his many civil servants set about developing one set of reform ideas for the Royal Mail, while Cockburn and his team were finalizing another. Ridley was intrigued by his predecessor's support for a lower monopoly threshold, and characteristically asked his officials to explore the scope for a much bolder reduction. The City accountants Ernst & Young were commissioned to investigate the costs of 1st and 2nd class letters, with a view to identifying two sensible prices. One possibility was that a new monopoly threshold might be set to split the difference, giving private competitors a run at 1st class mail. This prompted a marathon number-crunching session, without yielding any clear answers.

In the meantime, Cockburn and Cope finalized their own plans for a shake-up of the Letters business, and on 24 October 1989 they presented them to the Board.[28] Just three years after the inauguration of Dearing's restructuring, their proposals envisaged another huge advance towards a fully commercial operation and went well beyond anything being contemplated by DTI officials. In a bold rethinking of the 1968 two-tier post, the 'Letters Business Strategic Review' talked about creating a 'standard service' for the mails which would be tied to a single delivery each day (usually coded as 'Once Over the Ground', or OOG) but not necessarily to next-day delivery. This service would continue to enjoy a state monopoly. Other, faster delivery services would be managed with an innovative use of private contractors, perhaps for delivery work as well as broader support services. This latter sector of the postal market would be opened up to competitors, who might be granted access to the Royal Mail's own network. An enormous amount of detailed work would be required on the 'mechanics of change', but the Royal Mail would be amenable to a wide range of possibilities: 'the intention would be to move to a radically different Letters Business than that which had operated in the past, with a number of independent profit centres, some operating within the monopoly and some outside it . . .' Nicholson and his colleagues had their reservations about some of this. The OOG proposal had been examined and rejected more than once since 1980. They were in no doubt that ministers would have to be warned at the outset of the 'enormous industrial relations problems as well as public relations and political issues involved . . .' But they endorsed the basic concept of the standard service as 'a sensible mixture of the natural monopoly . . . and free market forces' – and they relished the idea of taking a strategic initiative to the Government rather than being constantly dictated to by ministers. Nicholson, Cockburn and Cope went off to present the new thinking to Ridley in December.

By this time, Ridley and the Post Office had had their differences. He had rejected the Board's Corporate Five Year Plan for 1990–95, which he thought insufficiently tough on costs. The Board had responded with a terse letter making clear to DTI officials that, given the intended significance of the Plan, 'a difference of view now existed between the Post Office and the Government'.[29] Ridley had also reiterated his predecessor's opposition to higher tariffs, which seemed certain to mean a big drop in pre-tax profits for 1989–90. (These were eventually to settle at £116m, the lowest level recorded since 1981–2.) But Ridley the arch-Thatcherite was still looking for radical solutions, and these seemed unlikely to come from the accountants.* He was impressed by what the Post Office was now proposing. Indeed, according to a very detailed account in the Board's own minutes, Ridley's response could hardly

---

* Their investigation into delivery costs produced a wide range of answers that depended on the starting assumptions. If it was assumed, for example, that the postal network already existed in order to provide next-day delivery for 1st class letters, then marginal extra costs could be attributed to 2nd class letters; and the difference between 1st and 2nd class costs would be huge. Alternatively, the costs of the network could be divided equally between all letters passing through it. This would leave 2nd class letters cheaper only to the extent that less urgent delivery schedules meant less overtime and lower labour costs; and the resulting difference between 1st and 2nd class costs would be tiny. The most sensible answer, as Ernst & Young concluded (and as the Post Office had pointed out at an early stage), was to base stamp prices not on costs derived from accounting at all, but on calculations of the impact of different prices on consumer behaviour. First prize in such calculations would go to the price differential that resulted in a mix of 1st and 2nd class letters allowing the Post Office to minimize the number of peak traffic hours imposed on the network. In the event, neither the accountants nor the economists made much of an impression on the process: prices through the 1990s were generally set, subject to Treasury approval, to maximize revenues within what were deemed to be politically acceptable limits.

have been more positive.[30] He backed almost every main aspect of the presentation, only demurring at intervals to suggest a still more radical approach. This applied, inter alia, to the timing: 'the Secretary of State appeared to be so enthusiastic for the strategies under consideration that his own preference might be to press for their more rapid development than would otherwise be the case'. Ridley urged his guests to press ahead with research into the details while he tested out reactions among his colleagues and among prospective private competitors.

By February 1990, however, it was already clear that Ridley was running into difficulties. Preliminary talks between the Post Office and the UCW had not been encouraging – Tuffin 'had seen no way of gaining his members' support' – and had led to press speculation about changes to the monopoly.[31] Against the background of an increasingly politicized debate over the Royal Mail's future, Ridley had been advised by his officials that altering the monopoly would require legislation. 'This was apparently unattractive to him', noted the minute of another Board discussion, 'and he would want the initiative for any such [monopoly] change to come from the Post Office.' Cockburn's team was happy to oblige and put plenty of effort into further preparatory papers.[32] But time was running out. As so often in the past, Westminster's political timetable was not easily reconciled with the complexity of postal reform. When Nicholson and Cockburn returned to the DTI for another meeting in June 1990, Ridley had to tell them that insufficient time remained for the present Parliament to contemplate any statutory changes of the kind implied by their proposals. The reform package would have to be put on hold until after the next election. A few weeks later, Ridley's career was brought to a sudden end by some intemperate remarks about Germany and the EU after a press interview – leading, as he put it in his memoirs the next year, to '[a] disgraceful piece of sensational journalism' – for which he was hounded into resignation.[33] The Post Office had lost the attentions of one of the cleverer and more genuinely interested ministers to have come its way.

It was not to be the last unexpected resignation of 1990. Riots in central London in March over the hugely unpopular poll tax had left the Conservatives at Westminster deeply anxious over their consistently poor rating in opinion polls. The sudden resignation in November of the Deputy Prime Minister, Geoffrey Howe, emboldened Margaret Thatcher's opponents within the party to mount a challenge to her leadership. The key divisive issues included her personal style and her implacable objection to joining the European single currency – prompting

Howe in his resignation speech to the Commons to deliver a lethal attack on her whole attitude to Europe – but the list of grievances against Thatcherism, driving her out of office at the end of November 1990, did not extend to privatization. Its progress had been one of the more acclaimed achievements of her eleven years in Downing Street. Her successor, John Major, had been a keen advocate of the policy while Chief Secretary to the Treasury in 1987–9 – and once he had been installed at the head of a new Cabinet, the DTI's files on Post Office privatization were soon being dusted off. This effectively scotched Cockburn's Strategic Review and Ridley's successor, Peter Lilley, spiked it in February 1991. Lilley informed the Post Office Chairman: 'his current preferences were for further efficiency measures, and for exploring the scope for deregulation and privatisation'.[34] This sudden rehabilitation of the policy banished in 1987 was not the cue for any sweeping reappraisal of the Post Office's future but piecemeal privatization was an evident possibility.[35] A small Post Office business selling TV licences, Subscription Services Ltd (SSL), was desperate at this time to find ways of diversifying away from its overwhelming dependence on an administrative contract with the BBC. It was barred from doing so in March, to the Board's dismay, by a Government intent on pushing ahead with sale plans – even after a confidential report from City advisers that SSL was 'not an obvious candidate for privatisation' and might not attract a single serious bidder.[36] Attention then turned to each of the Post Office's three main businesses.

4. TAKING STOCK OF COUNTERS

There was one obvious (if rarely remarked) rationale for trying to push the Counters business into the private sector: most of it was there already. The expansion of the postal network in the Victorian era had relied heavily on the recruitment of local shopkeepers to run its sub-offices, under the watchful eye of the nearest Head Postmaster. The Post Office provided the stock and cash balance for daily counter operations, and a wage based on a sliding scale of fees per transaction. The sub-postmaster provided just about everything else. Modern guidelines for this business model were laid down by the Hobhouse Committee in 1908, when the private operators accounted for about 23,000 outlets compared with just over a thousand Crown offices. It was not an arrangement that appealed much to the early trade unionists. Some championed the idea of bringing all the self-employed sub-postmasters and sub-postmistresses onto the establishment as Crown employees, as was noted in Chapter 7, but the resulting wage-bill would have sunk the Post Office.* The hybrid structure had generally functioned to most people's satisfaction, as intermittent official reviews confirmed across the ensuing decades.[37] The network remained fundamentally unchanged as it entered the 1980s, by which time it had picked up its 'Counters' moniker and comprised just over 20,000 sub-offices operating alongside about 1,500 Crown offices. At this point, like every other aspect of the post-Split Corporation of 1981, it was subjected to a series of lively reassessments.

These came to two main conclusions. On the one hand, Counters could look forward to a transformation of its prospects, if it adopted a more businesslike stance. Counters controlled by far the largest retail chain in the country (defining 'retail' rather loosely) and might thrive anew, given more of an overtly commercial culture. This eventually prompted a drive to lift the commissions paid by central and local government bodies, which for years had been fixed at 'cost-plus' with a tiny profit margin. Counters moved in the late 1980s to a market-based pricing regime, which was none too popular in Whitehall but marked a big step towards turning it from a bureaucracy into a genuine business. Various other initiatives were financially trivial by comparison, but made a useful contribution to the changing image of post offices. A few hundred Crown offices, for example, opened 'Post Shops' in 1984. New retail offerings included a set of children's stationery products that drew on the startling success since 1981 of a BBC children's television series, *Postman Pat*. Based on the adventures of a postman driving his little red delivery van round the hills of a fictionalized Cumbrian landscape, it created a cast of plasticine characters that attracted a national following. It was not quite as elevated as *Night Mail*; but Postman Pat, his black and white cat, Jess, and his local postmistress, Mrs Goggins, did more for the image of the Post Office than any fictional characters since Miss Lane and her customers in *Lark Rise to Candleford*.

On the other hand, and less encouragingly, the reappraisal of Counters exposed the fact that its entire business model could be left

---

* Great care had always been taken over defining the status of those who worked in the sub-office network. Loose references to sub-postmasters and their assistants as postal employees could sometimes slip through – and there were occasional legal battles over the issue – but the Post Office was always adamant that they fell outside the formal workforce, even while supervising (as many did) postmen who belonged to it.

looking frail unless action were taken to prune the network of some conspicuously redundant outlets. One review, early in 1983, assessed the commercial viability of all town sub-offices using a set of benchmarks laid down in 1945 (and largely ignored in the meantime). It reckoned about 20 per cent of the total were surplus to network requirements, suggesting a need to close about 1,600 of them. The review's author also questioned the rationale for retaining almost a third of Crown offices, judging many to be of marginal economic value and around 170 to be financially non-viable.[38] Even the vaguest possibility of privatization greatly heightened the sensitivity of any closures debate. Financial viability was plainly only one of several considerations bearing on the future of any location. Many a local post office, sitting within a village shop, was essential to its community's sense of identity, however nugatory its weekly takings. And the way that a children's character like Postman Pat could become a household brand name was a fair reflection of how highly many people valued the idea of the rural post office, even if they rarely set foot inside one. Nor did it take a degree in economics to see that the individual components of a network could never, by definition, be properly evaluated as stand-alone entities. Certainly there were sub-offices where the cost of the minimum scale payment and the provision of a basic cash balance exceeded the revenues to the Post Office. But who could put a figure on the value to the network of having postal services – and welfare payment channels – so universally available? Deliberations over the appropriate, and acceptable, level of closures soaked up a huge amount of management time through the 1980s. In reality, closures were scarcely a bone of contention between the Post Office and the Government. It was repeatedly acknowledged by both that the rural network was effectively untouchable. Meanwhile, the finer arguments over the valuation methodology to be used for town sub-offices – which can be traced back for decades – were now increasingly eclipsed by market forces. Existing sub-postmasters in dodgy locations were steadily disappearing as their real incomes wilted and replacements could not be found.

Under the day-to-day direction of John Roberts, and with the explicit approval of the Treasury, several hundred sub-offices had to be closed by 1987. By then, Dearing's reorganization had set up Counters as an independent business. Roberts and his colleagues were poring over cost-reduction targets, marketing plans and financial goals just as diligently as their counterparts in the Royal Mail (and with a similarly prodigious appetite for paperwork).* In November 1987, yet another Post Office study was commissioned from the MMC, this time with a brief to look at the work of the Crown offices. Reporting in June 1988, it complimented the management team on 'a creditable performance' since 1986 – while noting that 'there appears to have been little management or development' of counter services for many years previously – and it proffered the customary list of specific 'Ways to Do Better', of which there were eighty, for the future.[39] It was No. 61 that drew most attention, and fierce opposition from the UCW that would last for many years: 'We . . . commend Counters' plans to merge or regrade 750 Crown offices, but recommend that Counters should consider regrading a much larger number. Those managing sub-offices and franchises [i.e. post offices being run by high-street retail chains on a franchise basis] should be given the widest opportunity to use [sic] their entrepreneurial activities . . .'

This struck some as a veiled way of saying that Counters belonged in the private sector. The truth is that the business was never remotely eligible for sale as a commercial concern. This is not to say it was poorly run. On the contrary: having asserted in July 1988 that his team would turn its back on the option of a managed decline and go for a strategy of constant if gradual improvement, Roberts led them accordingly. Morale was high, among a group of managers determined to show that Counters could at last flourish as a business in charge of its own destiny. It notched up some substantial achievements over the next few years. The unions were persuaded to accept a significant increase in the use of part-time staff. Contracts were struck with major national retailers such as Asda and Sainsbury's for them to accommodate post offices as paying franchisees. Cash-wholesaling activities were expanded and improved. Jonathan Evans, head of employment relations for Counters around this time, recalled the sense of exhilaration felt by colleagues: 'It had been a neglected area for years, and we were given our heads to go after whatever opportunities we could find. We all shared a real sense that we were going to transform the business.'[40] In 1991–2, Evans led a team

---

* The level of paperwork within the Post Office was rising alarmingly in the late 1980s. This had been anticipated by Dearing's Executive Council as a dangerous side-effect of having four separate businesses. A 1986 paper on the problem was aptly titled 'Suffocation by Bumf' (Minute 86/89, CEC 22 October 1986, Post 69/262). It offered no easy answers. 'It had to be recognized however that the constant request for unnecessary information . . . was a reflection of an underlying management attitude and style which would need to change. But such change would inevitably be slow.' This turned out to be an epic understatement.

that reorganized the management of the entire network. Its 1986 Territories (since then shrunk from four to three) were abolished in favour of seven regions with their own General Managers. Revenues climbed steadily. From less than £800m a year in the late 1980s, they had risen to just over £1bn by 1992–3. The fact remained, however, that Counters judged as a normal retail business was far from a marketable enterprise. Post-tax profits never rose above 1–2 per cent of revenues. Most of its customers called at post offices for postal services or for government-related benefits and licences that reflected no genuine retail proposition. The one dimension of its activities that had seemed by the mid-1980s to offer scope for expansion had been its ownership of Girobank.[41] Now the bank had new owners, with different priorities of their own and a half-share (at least) of whatever margins the bank could make.

Furthermore, the outlook for the business was still clouded, in 1991 as for years past, by two related areas of financial uncertainty. First, who would bear the cost in future years of maintaining the rural portion of the Counters network? Rural letter delivery costs were modestly subsidized by urban delivery profits, and no one was challenging the good sense of this (though any curtailment of the letters monopoly might prompt second thoughts about this, if new entrants were to begin picking off the most lucrative urban walks). Nor was a similar cross-subsidization of the rural Counters network a huge problem so long as the Post Office was regarded as a public service. But in the financial environment that had prevailed since the mid-1980s, with the imposition of strict financial targets, this long-standing question had taken on a sharper edge. How far was the rural network properly a postal cost at all, and how far a public good for which taxpayers should expect to pay?[42] One proposal made by the Group Finance Director in 1986 was that the fixed cost of the rural network should be shouldered by the government bodies that used it most. Several million men and women visited post offices every week to collect their pensions and other welfare state allowances. Why not dispense with commissions to the Post Office and have the state pay directly for the infrastructure? Indeed, Sellers wondered whether the very largest of them, the Department of Health and Social Security (DHSS), ought not to be levied with a fixed annual fee that by itself would plug any deficit.[43]

Roberts and his colleagues on the executive of the Counters business reacted with alarm at the very idea, and were still extremely shy of it in 1991. They lived in constant fear of the DHSS switching its welfare payments from the Post Office channel to an exclusive reliance on automated credit transfer (ACT) through the banking system, and believed that even hinting at the Sellers proposal in Whitehall might tip the DHSS against them. Here lay the second unresolved issue hanging over Counters: how solid a commitment was the Government prepared to make to the role of the Post Office as the access point for government services – or the 'Government Gateway', as it came to be called? As Roberts had pointed out regularly through the 1980s, Counters relied for well over half its income on agency commissions from Whitehall. About 30 per cent came from the DHSS, and the same again from other departments and British Telecom. All of these contractors were intermittently prone to hinting that a decisive shift to ACT would one day make everything simpler and cheaper. They were surely right – but such a shift might also fatally undermine the Counters business – unless, of course, Counters could in the meantime build up new activities that would need to go a long way beyond selling Postman Pat stationery. Yet by the early 1990s, the business had been several times frustrated in its attempt to develop new lines of service, for which the requisite legal powers were denied it by a succession of DTI ministers. Plans to introduce a range of over-the-counter insurance products bearing the Post Office brand had had to be abandoned at the last moment, for example, after ministers gave way to protests from the insurance brokers' lobby. (Post Office policies would be unfair competition for other insurers, it was argued, because they would be seen as carrying an implicit government guarantee.) Ministers were ready to contemplate undermining the role of the Counters business in the public sector, but had little interest – at least until the mid-1990s – in underwriting any new role for it in the private sector, with all the political risks which that might entail. The result was ever more sub-office closures, steadily eroding the size of the network despite all the effort expended on improving its efficiency. (See Appendix A, Chart 12.)

5. LAUNCHING PARCELFORCE, AND SALVAGING IT

Rather like the Telegraph, Parcels had got off to a poor financial start as a Post Office business in the nineteenth century and had been struggling ever since to put things right. Those ill-advised early contracts with the railway companies had been costly indeed. The great difference between the two consistently loss-making services in modern times was that

Parcels, unlike the Telegraph, had not run out of customers. The demand for inland telegrams had almost fizzled out entirely by the time the 1977 Carter Report pointed out that the residual fixed costs of the Telegraph were indefensible. Parcels by contrast had always offered a genuinely popular service. Any item up to 22 lb in weight could be collected at any post office and would be conveyed to any address in the country at a postage rate geared to weight but not distance. The business had never been granted a legal monopoly, but its ubiquity had in practice guaranteed it a niche market, whatever the competition in other respects from the railways and a handful of road haulage companies. In 1975, the business carried 200 million parcels, only about 25 per cent fewer than in its peak traffic years in the late 1950s.

Unfortunately, buoyant demand had historically never translated into profits. By the time that Nigel Walmsley came to take an interest in the business after 1977, Parcels had lost money every year but one since 1953 (when it first began reporting its results separately). The Post Office was fixated on the problem that parcel postage rates were much too low but could not be raised without a severe risk that trade customers would then find it cheaper to set up their own distribution systems. The fear was understandable: bulk users of the parcel post such as mail order companies and large publishers accounted in the 1970s for half the traffic.[44] There had been so much despondency about this in the darker days of the Ryland era that a case was even made for quitting the business altogether. When bolder counsels prevailed, in 1975–6, prices were driven up sharply – and demand plummeted, as if to confirm the depth of the dilemma facing the business: in 1976–7 losses reached £18m, on total revenues of £108m. The way out of the dilemma, as Walmsley and his marketing men finally showed, was to peg higher prices to a much wider range of services – including express and courier services, both domestic and international – and to promote them with flair and imagination. When this approach was coupled in the 1980s to a concerted attack on costs – with more mechanized sorting and fewer distribution centres, 'Parcels Concentration Offices' paralleling the role of the MLOs for letters – the result was a dramatic recovery to breakeven and then an unprecedented run of rising profits. In its first year as a separate business, 1986–7, Parcels doubled its pre-tax profits to £31m and they jumped again to £40m in 1987–8.

This encouraged the Post Office to take a more ambitious view of the business – as it certainly needed to do. For it was obvious by 1987 that – just as was also happening in the telecoms market around this time – a new kind of competitor from outside the traditional Postal, Telegraph and Telephone ('PTT') industry was surfacing in the European postal market, handling parcels and express mail deliveries. Private courier businesses were sprouting up everywhere, and some were substantial companies. Two giant US corporations, Federal Express and United Parcel Service (UPS), both looked poised for a significant expansion of their European networks based on fleets of road vans and use of their own aircraft. Neither they nor their Australian-owned rival, TNT, yet had any significant foothold in the UK market, but Dearing and Cockburn were concerned over their potential impact and determined to forestall it.* In November 1987, the Post Office hired a senior executive from the European courier industry as the new head of Parcels. Nick Nelson was a former British Airways cargo manager who had latterly been running the operations of DHL Express Delivery Group out of Brussels. Within months, he was injecting a new urgency into various initiatives and drawing up plans to accelerate some hitherto undemanding investment schedules.[45] He also pushed the Post Office into a slightly belated recognition that the use of computers and handheld devices to keep track *en route* of individual posted items ('track and trace') was to be an essential aspect of the industry in future.[46] Parcels began to pick up the kind of impetus envisaged when it had first been given its own formal (but unpublished) accounts at the start of the 1950s. Its status, though, remained as ambiguous as ever: in what sense was it genuinely a separate business at all? True, it had its own management structure – organized round those three networks set up in 1986 – and by 1988 it was also preparing to move its headquarters from 33 Grosvenor Place to a new site in Milton Keynes, far from the other postal business centres. (This was part of a huge decentralization exercise. Counters had moved its head office to just south of Blackfriars Bridge at the end of Dearing's tenure; the Letters head office was to be relocated to Old Street on the edge of the City; and a new head office with fewer than

---

* In March 1987, Dearing agreed with his Executive Committee that he 'would write to the Director General of the Dutch Post Office identifying the threat, as the British Post Office saw it, from the encroachment of the private sector and posing the question of how the postal administrations might defend themselves against it. That letter would be copied to all European administrations and might suggest a meeting in London in the summer to consider the issues' (Minute 87/25, CEC 4 March 1987, Post 69/263). Perhaps concerted action might indeed have made their markets much harder to penetrate, but it was never achieved. Instead, some of those European administrations – led by the Dutch – were eventually to forge alliances with the private sector in ways that did not occur to Dearing in 1987.

thirty staff was to be set up in a grand building on the south side of St James's Square, overlooking Pall Mall.) Yet parcels still jostled with letters in the postman's pouch, in the back of every mail van and along the corridors of every TPO. At an operational level, the two streams of the morning post remained inseparable. Their managers agreed it was inconceivable that either should have to surrender use of the inviolable Royal Mail brand.[47] And the UCW, though it had distinct letter and parcel branches at a local level, refused to contemplate having separate national officers for the two businesses. Here was the rub: Union edicts applied equally to Letters and Parcels without distinction – and in the autumn of 1988 this brought Parcels close to disaster.

The DRAS dispute damaged the Parcels business severely. Its trade customers had good reason to prefer using the Royal Mail – which offered a much more convenient channel for returned goods – but they also had plenty of alternative couriers, using non-unionized labour, with sharper prices and (relatively speaking) total reliability. Many contracts were lost. A quarter of the business's revenues came from nine major accounts. All agreed their confidence in the Royal Mail had been badly shaken by the September strikes.[48] Prospective new customers were lost, too. A planned tie-up with Littlewoods, a mail order firm despatching about 50 million items a year, would have expanded the business by a fifth and involved the integration of almost thirty new delivery depots. Littlewoods turned instead to Federal Express. The financial impact of it all was horribly apparent in the results for 1988–9: profits slumped to just £8m. By the time this figure was published, Nelson had at least made progress in winning Board support for a brave set of measures to rescue the business. First and foremost, as its biggest customers all insisted, it needed to be distanced from the Letters business as quickly and completely as possible. This would be reflected in the adoption of fully audited accounts of its own, starting in 1990–91. (Until now, it had produced only headline revenue and profit numbers.) If the Board insisted on further battles over the DRAS issue before this separation was achieved, warned Nelson, 'the Parcels Business would be unlikely to survive . . .'[49] In addition to a substantial investment in new plant and vehicles, it had then to establish itself as a European competitor. This would necessarily entail in-house access to a substantial fleet of aircraft. Building one from scratch within a reasonably short timescale was totally impractical for the Royal Mail – given the capital costs involved and the lead times on aircraft acquisition – so a joint venture with a private partner in the aviation sector would be essential.[50]

It was a realistic and resourceful response to the debacle of 1988 – but was soon waylaid by the DTI. In a 180-degree reversal of the stance taken by Norman Tebbit in 1985 – and while at the same time pressing Cockburn for 'radical action' on other fronts – Tony Newton objected to the use of public capital to part-fund any joint venture with a private-sector partner, and the Post Office was instructed to avoid even preliminary discussions with interested parties. Nelson's verdict on this, minuted at a March 1989 Board meeting, was a fair summary of the position:

> [The] future of the Parcels Business was at risk unless it was able to move decisively into the international sector. It was, however, impossible to proceed further without talking to potential partners . . . [and] by denying the Parcels Business the opportunity to enter into a joint venture, Government was exposing it to long term strategic risks in a market in which competitors were amalgamating at an accelerating rate . . .[51]

Appropriately turning a blind eye on Nelson's behalf to the Department's veto, the Board sanctioned the start of talks with a promising partner. By May 1989, negotiations were well under way with Walker Aviation, the parent company of Jersey European Airways. A deal was struck over the summer by which Royal Mail bags would be carried at night, with the costs substantially defrayed by revenues from day-time passenger flights. Alas, it came to a messy end. Legal documents had been all but completed by November and the press release to announce the partnership was just being finalized, when the DTI grounded the whole project. Some officials actually expressed support for it, as did one of the Prime Minister's political advisers. But Ridley, however enthusiastic about Cockburn's plans for the Letters business, was opposed to the new strategy for Parcels. This was partly because he doubted the logic of the move: 'He found it hard to accept that it was necessary for the Post Office to own 49 per cent of an air transport business in order to achieve its air transport needs.'[52] He was also opposed in principle to any public–private joint venture.

Ideological objections to Nelson's rescue package were supplemented by a series of government interventions in the business throughout 1989–90. Officials insisted on being given access to all working papers behind the new plan – much to the Board's chagrin – and decisions on pricing were endlessly delayed. Meanwhile the business was running into serious difficulties in the marketplace. Some elaborate efforts to rebuild its image after the DRAS episode prompted a sizeable jump in costs. This coincided with a sudden downturn in demand, reflecting the onset of the 1989–91 recession. A new brand name, 'Parcelforce', was launched in February 1990, but its appearance coincided with an almost total collapse in the profitability of the underlying business. It just squeaked into the black for 1989–90, only then to be hit by a nasty surprise from the accountants. They announced in the summer of 1990 that auditing Parcels separately from Letters had revealed an anomalous cross-subsidy from past years, correcting which would lop £60m off Parcelforce's net income in 1990–91.[53] After also taking aboard its share of a huge Exceptional Loss for 'restructuring and development', the business was plainly in deep trouble: it would eventually report a loss for 1990–91 of £131m. Its predicament was overshadowing all other policy matters. There ensued a tense and often scarcely coherent debate over its future that set the Post Office, the Treasury and the DTI at loggerheads for much of the next two years.

With the monthly losses mounting around him, Nelson prepared a second recovery plan, which was reviewed by the Board in October 1990.[54] Perhaps he drew for inspiration on the current estimates of growth in the general market for parcels and express deliveries: Nelson cited projections for the next six-year period of almost 40 per cent for the inland market and almost 45 per cent for the international market. If Brussels managed to trim the franchise of regulated monopolies in Europe, as promised, the whole industry seemed likely to become a lot more competitive. Private-sector firms 'were responding energetically' and Parcelforce had to do the same. Nelson had a list of fifty-seven separate projects, virtually a do-or-die agenda for the business. The Treasury scanned the list and decided by early 1991 that it would just mean throwing good money after bad. The accounting embarrassment was an additional headache, since it might lead to charges of unfair competition. Since bona fide competitors were now climbing over each other to build networks, said the Treasury, the best solution for Parcelforce was obvious: it needed to be transferred 'as soon as possible to the private sector through a trade sale offer'. Ministers were urged not to be too squeamish about accepting a knockdown price, to bring the whole unhappy episode to a quick close.[55]

The Post Office appointed McKinsey to look at ways of fundamentally repositioning the business. The consultants were already at work on Herculean interview schedules by March 1991, when Peter Lilley asked for a privatization study to be prepared within eight weeks to clarify 'the extent to which it might be feasible to advance substantially the timetable for a sale'.[56] It was all too much for Nelson, who departed over the summer for a career in school-teaching. It was also soon clear that the problems of privatizing Parcelforce as an autonomous business had been badly underestimated. The head of the usual advisory team from Schroders, Gerry Grimstone, warned the Board that a sale might not be achievable.* So it proved. By the summer of 1992, no progress had been made with the sale and little headway either with plans for a turnaround of the business, which remained conspicuously un-turned round. The structure of the traditional business was altered, yet again, with a halving of the number of districts in Network 1 – but internal reorganization was now looking increasingly like a substitute for any serious reappraisal of the business's position in the marketplace. Parcelforce managers were allowed no scope to explore genuinely radical options: they were obliged, for example, to steer clear of joint-venture possibilities. This left the business as a detached observer of events that were starting (as we shall see) to reshape the European industry.[57] Work on different schemes for Parcels privatization itself – known as 'Project Daniel' – went slowly round in circles. By July 1992, the best and perhaps the only solution appeared to be a sale to the management. The chairmanship of an MBO committee was handed, inevitably, to John Roberts (who was about to move from Counters into a broader planning and strategy position as 'MD Group Services', which he became in January 1993). It was noted that if this MBO failed, 'the Business would have to be run down, leaving a residual service to be reabsorbed in Royal Mail . . . [which] would be a difficult and costly task . . .'[58] Just three months later, Roberts had to report back that the prospect of failure was all too real.

Fortunately, another option had opened up in the meantime. A new boss at the DTI, Michael Heseltine, styling himself as 'President of the Board of Trade', had launched a comprehensive review of the structure and organization of the whole Post Office – in effect, the preparatory work for its full privatization. This was codenamed 'Project Lion'. None of the biblical scholars at the DTI had any idea how Project Daniel

---

* 'Schroders had not been asked to express a view on whether a sale [of Parcelforce] would be sensible at all financially, but in Mr Grimstone's own view it did not appear to be so, and the balance of advantage lay with retaining the Business within the Post Office . . .' (Minute 91/45, POBM 21 May 1991, E12421/Board minutes). Grimstone, a director of Schroders and formerly head of privatization matters at the Treasury, was the doyen of City advisers on all matters pertaining to privatization. No doubt his view was also well known to the DTI.

would fare from being assimilated into Project Lion, but at least Parcelforce could now cease to be the centre of attention. A bigger drama beckoned.

6. 'THE ONE THAT GOT AWAY'

Politically astute and the kind of Board chairman who loved to work as a Mr Fix-It in support of his executive colleagues, Nicholson was well suited to the highly politicized environment that marked the years after the Thatcher veto. Within the limits set by the veto itself and by the scrutiny of the Post Office by DTI officials who believed the veto might one day be lifted, he worked hard to engineer the change of culture he thought essential to the future success of the Corporation, whatever its statutory position. The need for it seemed blatantly apparent to him, as to all those who arrived at the Post Office in mid- or late career. Though it was almost twenty years since the Post Office had left the civil service, the prevailing in-house culture remained essentially as it had been in 1969. Managers did not move in and out of the organization, as though it was a commercial company. Most saw themselves in lifetime careers, which they pursued within the framework of carefully structured managerial hierarchies where fewer rules were made explicit than in the business world. Those newcomers who adjusted to this successfully (there were many who did not) were either former civil servants – like Richard Dykes – with an instinctive understanding of the culture, or individuals unusually adept at building office relationships. There were very few in either category – and almost none of them were women. (One who joined around this time but soon moved on was Kate Jenkins, who had spent much of the 1980s in the Cabinet Office reporting directly to Margaret Thatcher on a restructuring of the management of the civil service. As Director of Industrial Relations and Organization Development, she found a difficult job made no easier by an almost complete dearth of women in the upper ranks.[59]) An outsider whom Nicholson was particularly pleased to discover within his first few days in October 1987 was Ian Raisbeck, a former colleague. Raisbeck had been recruited by Bill Cockburn as Director of Quality and was promoting a managerial philosophy, 'Total Quality Management' (TQM), with which he had engineered a significant shift in staff attitudes at Rank Xerox. Nicholson had seen it work there and now gave Raisbeck his active support again. Against the odds, Raisbeck flourished and

Nicholson helped him to build a partnership with Cockburn that eventually made TQM into one of the more effective campaigns aimed at modernizing the Post Office culture.

In essence the TQM approach set aside the usual kind of management directives based on financial data for the organization as a whole, in order to focus instead on the details of employee behaviour which had a direct bearing on how the organization was perceived by its customers. By encouraging constant incremental changes in the workplace, often minor in themselves, it was believed that TQM would gradually improve the overall quality of the Post Office's services in ways that traditional policy-making decisions could never do. Many in the management ranks took some persuading of this, but in many large offices it was embraced by the workforce with an enthusiasm that took managers by surprise. Since TQM relied heavily on individual postal workers using their own initiative, it was welcomed as empowering those in the front line of operations with little formal authority but years of experience – a concept reminiscent of the philosophy espoused by the post-war advocates of joint control for the unions. Nicholson and Cockburn saw it rather differently, as a way of strengthening relations between individual employees and team leaders, who represented management within the local workplace. Too much power had been ceded in the past, it was argued, to the stronger counterpart relationship between employees and union reps in the workplace. A better balance would be a core objective of TQM. But the greater emphasis on engaging with employees was anyway redolent for a while of the early 1950s. Ultimately, the need for managers to coordinate the process led to a proliferation of instruction papers and manuals for team leaders that produced a box-ticking culture with which the Post Office was only too comfortable. But for a few years from 1988 contemporaries were in no doubt TQM made a significant contribution to impressive gains in operating efficiency.

Its particular appeal for Nicholson was its emphasis on the quality of the Post Office's performance, which always interested him far more than bare profit margins. Merely turning a profit was scarcely much of an achievement, in his view, given the scale of its monopoly privileges. ('My mantra to the managers and the District Head Postmasters was "Don't talk to me about how well you're doing financially: you've got a bloody monopoly, so if you can't produce a surplus, you ought to be shot . . ."'[60]) Nicholson sent his colleagues a paper in December 1988 entitled 'Post Office Mission, Values and Conduct'. It was full of sentiments 'intended as guiding principles to underpin the process of culture change within the Corporation. ... The adoption of these statements signals the start of a long and gradual change in the way our organisation behaves'.[61] Missions and values would follow for all the individual businesses. It would be easy, decades later, to dismiss much of this as fashionable guff signifying nothing of lasting importance. (Mission statements, charters and quality targets were being adopted all across the public sector: this was the rising tide that floated John Major's Citizen's Charter of 1992.) But as a way of signalling the significance of Raisbeck's TQM programme, it served its purpose – and helped draw attention to the importance of non-financial measures. Nicholson used to insist to his senior managers that the public would gauge the Post Office's efficiency by two simple measures above all else: the length of the (often notorious) queues in their local post office and the reliability of next-day delivery for 1st class letters. He was appalled to discover, early in his tenure, that claims of a 90 per cent (or so) next-day delivery for 1st class letters were based on an incomplete analysis: they focused on the time that elapsed from the collection of a letter to its despatch from the delivery office – which was very different from its arriving on the customer's doormat. (It was, he recalled, 'neither more nor less than a legal fake'.[62]) Once the statistics were gathered on an end-to-end basis acceptable to Nicholson, the next-day 1st class delivery quotient dropped to nearer 70 per cent. So it may be a fair measure of TQM's impact that by 1992–3, of 1st class letters posted in the UK, almost 92 per cent were delivered the next day – by the Chairman's own yardstick. Of 2nd class letters, over 98 per cent were delivered within three days.

This kind of progress helps explain why many managers took a jaundiced view of privatization when talk of the possibility revived in 1991. Even on the Board, where a majority had been disappointed by Thatcher's veto of 1987, there were some members for whom the Post Office was far from broke and so needed no fixing. Ken Young, the Deputy Chairman, now approaching retirement, was openly opposed to a change he thought quite unnecessary.[63] Among senior managers in their early fifties, many of whom had joined as civil servants in the early 1960s, there was a scarcely disguised hostility to the idea. No doubt some had understandable misgivings about their own personal prospects, as they surveyed the upheavals that had followed privatization within British Telecom and other giant utilities since 1984. Another factor was the strong sense of loyalty felt by many to the Post Office as an institution with several business dimensions but just one history and one binding culture – and it seemed most unlikely that this unity would survive any process of privatization, given the (as most thought) impossibility of running the Counters network as a private business.

Cockburn and the strategy team under Cope were aware of the deep reservations held at all levels of the organization, and had substantially shared them in years past. Nonetheless, the Government's rebuttal of their Letters strategy and their mounting frustration over ministerial interference pushed them, over the course of 1991, to a firm conviction that change was needed. They decided that a degree of independence tantamount to autonomy – or 'Commercial Freedom', as this came to be coded – was the only possible destination for the Post Office if it was going to retain, let alone build upon, its post-Dearing vigour. There were only two logical ways to proceed at this point: they could seek to establish Commercial Freedom within the public sector; or alternatively strike out into the private sector. Across Europe, others were facing the same choice. The French seemed to have decided that La Poste would take the public road. The Dutch and the Germans, having both incorporated their national posts and telecoms operations as publicly owned enterprises in 1989, seemed to be heading for the private-sector alternative. Either option, in theory, seemed workable. Both could, in theory, leave managers with freedom to adopt not dissimilar business strategies. (As if to illustrate the point, in 1991 the French, Dutch and German post offices all joined their counterparts from Canada and Sweden in taking up 50 per cent of a joint-venture European courier business ('GD-Net'), set up for customers wanting packages to be 'tracked' in transit. The other half of the business would be owned by one of the most successful private courier companies, TNT.) In the end, ministers would have to choose which way was best for Britain's Post Office.

In the wake of Thatcher's departure, policy discussions inside the DTI had quickly identified this as a key decision – and officials within the Department, asked by ministers to explore the commercialization options, had no difficulty setting down the rationale for a complete end to state ownership. It seemed most unlikely that Commercial Freedom would be accessible within the British public sector; precedents, after all, were hard to spot. In addition to the improbability of politicians disciplining themselves to respect any arm's-length arrangement, European competition laws would pose a massive problem for any genuinely competitive Post Office funded by the state. By the end of 1991 it was probably already true to say that shifting the Post Office into the private sector, in one guise or another, had become one of the Department's foremost policy objectives. This was not yet apparent to the Post Office itself: what the Board perceived instead was a steady rejection by the Government of all innovative ideas. One such initiative was a plan to join the GD-Net venture, which the Board thought a critical departure for the state PTTs of the European industry.* The DTI blocked the plan, on the grounds that its lawyers had decided participation in the venture would be illegal.[64] But the story was much the same, whether the context was European joint ventures, operational reforms or possible asset sales. Fresh thinking was vetoed. Or as Nicholson would put it, recalling the apparent sense of drift around this time, 'we were forced into going ex-strategy'.[65] He announced to ministers late in 1991 that he would be leaving at the end of his term, nine months later, to take up a chairmanship elsewhere. He saw no prospect of a serious move towards privatization, and anyway seems to have had his doubts by this stage that it would ever be politically achievable. In fact, DTI officials had just been instructed by the Major government to avoid any significant new ventures that might complicate a full-scale privatization. If the Conservatives were to win the forthcoming 1992 election – admittedly, as most people thought, a decidedly big If – selling the Post Office would be high on the policy agenda. Cockburn inadvertently discovered this, early in 1992, by intimating to Nicholson that he would soon be leaving as well. Frustrated by the constant battling with Whitehall, he had decided to accept a lucrative job outside the Post Office. No sooner had he notified the Chairman of his decision than Cockburn found himself whisked across town to see the Permanent Secretary at the DTI, who offered to double his salary immediately if he would agree to stay.[66] As Cockburn himself was quick to appreciate, he had been identified as the man to lead the Post Office through privatization if Major triumphed at the polls.

And so it transpired. Cockburn stayed, John Major pulled off a surprise victory in April 1992 – and by July Michael Heseltine was announcing the setting-up of Project Lion. It was confirmed shortly afterwards that the roles of Chairman and Chief Executive were to be divided. Cockburn became the Chief Executive in October, and Nicholson on his

---

* 'Failure to provide tracked services would inevitably lead to the loss of this valuable business for postal administrations, and if the British Post Office were excluded from the [GD-Net] arrangement it would inevitably lose its market share of international express business. In addition, its domestic market could be put at risk as successful international couriers exploited their position in this country . . .' (Minute 91/69, POBM 30 July 1991, Post 69/Red Books). GD-Net proved less of a watershed than expected, but the Board's analysis was prescient enough.

retirement would be succeeded in January by a non-executive Chairman –
Mike Heron, appointed to the Post Office after thirty-four years as an
executive manager at Unilever, culminating in four years on the Anglo-
Dutch group's main Board as Personnel Director.* By the end of October,
Cockburn had already moved the Corporation's HQ from St James's to
the head office of the Letters business at 148 Old Street. Assembling there
for its regular monthly meeting on 27 October 1992, the Board agreed on
a memorandum to the Government in which Members finally brought
themselves formally to recommend privatization – though they came to it
almost as a last resort and not without noting in the process the dissent
of Ken Young, set to retire two months later:

> [I]n the view of some Members, the fact that the Post Office had performed
> very creditably for many years within existing public sector constraints
> should not be lightly dismissed, and a full analysis of the status quo option
> ought therefore to be included in the memorandum to Government. It was
> however well recognised that the maintenance of the status quo could not
> provide the same assurance for the future, and that some change was neces-
> sary. The merits of the commercialisation case ought therefore to be fully
> presented, and its advantages, both operational and financial, clearly
> explained. The memorandum might then however go on to make the point
> that because the Board recognized that Government views made commer-
> cialisation an impractical option, the Post Office had also considered, and
> recommended privatisation . . .[67]

It was agreed in the same Board discussion that, 'while the Board had
always in the past refused to comment on privatisation issues, taking
the line that ownership was a matter for Government, that was no
longer sustainable' – and a more forthright support for the policy would
have to be adopted in due course.

From this point on, a privatization team under Jerry Cope worked in
tandem with the Project Lion team at the DTI on a steady stream of
papers and analyses to pave the way for the necessary legislation. The

---

* Heron had also taken a prominent role in the business world's involvement with education and training, and in October 1993 became Chairman of the National Council for
Vocational Qualifications. It was an interest he shared with Bryan Nicholson, who after
chairing the Manpower Services Commission in 1984–7 had become Chairman of the
Council for National Academic Awards in 1988. Ron Dearing had since then taken on this
position, as the first of many assignments in the education sector which became the former
Chairman's principal interest in the 1990s – leading to his Dearing Report on Higher Education in 1997.

difficulties they faced were daunting. The Post Office had been converted into four businesses in 1986, of which three remained. How these would relate to each other commercially in the aftermath of privatization was an exceedingly complex problem to which Cope's team and the officials in Whitehall alike devoted huge amounts of time. Within a few months, however, it was uncomfortably apparent to both sides that the contents of the privatization package were far from agreed. The final objective kept changing, and each version posed questions with no obvious answers. Initially, Parcelforce was to be sold on its own. But how would it then relate to Royal Mail Letters? Next the whole of the Post Office was to be put on the block – but on what contractual foundations was a privatized Counters network to be built? At a very late stage in the work, the network was excluded. But then how was it going to co-exist with a privatized Royal Mail? The Counters issue was especially critical. Cockburn was strongly opposed to breaking up the Post Office. As chairman of an informal group of national post offices called Unipost, he had heard his European counterparts extolling the commercial potential of the British Post Office: 'They were looking to us as a kind of benchmark.'[68] Cutting the Corporation in half did not strike him as a logical first step to realizing that potential. Others working on the mechanical details of the privatization saw things differently. Indeed, those on Cope's own Project Lion team thought it self-evident that Counters could not possibly be included in the sale – and so gave the issue far less attention than it deserved. As Cope recalled: 'We all knew the Government was taking a different view [at first] and wanted to include Counters. But we just assumed that sooner or later they would abandon the idea as too complicated'.[69] The inclusion of Counters in the sale was indeed eventually abandoned, but only after the Government's opponents had been given ample time to present privatization as a mortal threat to every village post office in the land. Addressing the Conservative Party Conference in 1992, Heseltine had held up a copy of the *Exchange & Mart* newspaper, observing that sub-office franchises were advertised for sale every week. It was a dramatic way of pointing out to the Tory faithful that the Counters business was part of the private sector already. But it probably alerted a wider audience to the less palatable truth that, if sub-offices could be bought and sold like second-hand cars, they could also end up in the scrap yard.

The odd such flourish aside, Heseltine brought to the cause little of the vim and dash he had shown a decade earlier over, say, the sale of council houses. By his own account, he needed persuading by one of his junior ministers, the arch-Thatcherite Edward Leigh, that it was a good idea in the first place.[70] And it was never his priority. Through much of 1992–3, as the Minister responsible for energy as well as trade and industry, Heseltine was engulfed in a long-running crisis over the supply contracts between the recently privatized electricity industry and the British coal industry that was itself slated for privatization in 1994. Privatization lost its most outspoken champion when Leigh was sacked in May 1993 for his vehement opposition to the Maastricht Treaty. Then Heseltine himself was temporarily removed from the fray. He had a heart attack in June 1993, which was just about the time that his officials were struggling to deal with detailed studies of the Post Office by the City accountants to the sale project, KMPG. Their views were not encouraging, and Heseltine's absence for some months resulted in a slackening of the pace. No one else in Major's Cabinet showed much interest in sustaining it. The Board did its best to keep up the momentum. Heron wrote to the DTI in October 1993 to reiterate the unanimous view of his colleagues 'that the present system under which we operate is uncommercial, unduly restrictive and is fast becoming an untenable basis for maintaining a highly successful leading edge subsidy-free postal business', but ministers took little notice.[71] Perhaps that 'subsidy-free' status was half the problem: there was no sense whatever of a financial crisis that could only be resolved by privatization. Things looked different at British Rail, where the privatization timetable ran almost exactly in parallel with the Post Office's. There, the financial background and the pressures from Brussels ruled out any possibility of a retreat. Perhaps the attitude of the Prime Minister himself also played its part: Major confided in more than one colleague that no proposal to sell off rural post offices would ever have his support. Those of a Machiavellian bent suspected Major of playing along with the idea of a Post Office privatization as a useful way of keeping a potential rival busy. (It was in July 1993 that Major, famously beset by the 'bastards' in the Cabinet, was forced by the level of dissent in his party into putting himself up for re-election as the party's leader.)

With most Tory politicians keeping their distance, the promotion of the sale fell principally to Bill Cockburn himself, assisted by Roberts and Cope. He set about it with his customary energy, passionately entreating MPs to heed the startling transformation that the German version of Commercial Freedom had made of Deutsche Post since 1989. But the Post Office was statutorily precluded from spending any money on a PR campaign, and he could not call on professional advisers for assistance.

This was hugely problematic, since neither the Post Office nor the DTI had given much thought to how the interrelationship between the different parts of the post-privatization postal service could be explained in simple terms to the general public. Nor, with public audiences, could Cockburn even express open support for privatization: he had to code his message in terms of a neutral support for Commercial Freedom. Some of his external PR advisers urged that the Post Office should break with this constraint and express open support for privatization, but it never happened.[72] Cockburn's personal enthusiasm for the measure was scarcely concealed, but this, too, was a mixed blessing for the cause.* Cockburn plainly stood to gain financially from any sale – perhaps handsomely so, to judge from the salary scales and enormous bonuses being enjoyed by the bosses of other de-nationalized entities – as his opponents were ever ready to point out. And on top of all these impediments, Cockburn faced an opposition campaign that was led in Westminster by one of Labour's most formidable debaters, Robin Cook.

Perhaps there was only one way that the pro-privatization camp was ever going to prevail: a series of postal strikes, backed by massed ranks of angry banner-waving UCW members, might conceivably have turned the battle to Cockburn's advantage. But the Post Office now chanced to find itself confronted with a UCW led by one of the shrewder politicians in the history of the Union. In 1980, three years after making his debut at the 1977 Annual Conference as a 27-year-old postman from Slough, Alan Johnson had made his mark by championing the IWM initiative outside London. Tom Jackson, who always prided himself on being able to spot a talented newcomer, had then personally backed his candidacy for the Executive Council, to which he was duly elected in 1981. Despite only being in his early thirties, Johnson orchestrated the UCW's national response to IWM brilliantly over the next few years, effectively acting as the Union counterpart to Jerry Cope. In 1987 he became a national officer, stepping into John Taylor's shoes as an Assistant Secretary, and he succeeded Alan Tuffin as the General Secretary in 1992.† Once Heseltine had announced his plans for postal privatization

*It occasionally drew fire from Westminster. Forty-four Labour MPs, including Tony Benn, supported an Early Day Motion in March 1993 complaining that Cockburn had 'abandoned the normal neutrality of a senior public official' and calling for his resignation. It was tabled by Peter Hain, a former head of the UCW's research department elected to Parliament in 1991 who would go on to serve in the Cabinet under both Tony Blair and Gordon Brown.

† He was elected as General Secretary Designate in January 1992, understudying Tuffin for

in July that year, there was never any doubt the UCW would be fiercely opposed to it. On top of the ideological objections which had been aired so many times since the late 1920s, there was a keener awareness by this date of what privatization might entail for jobs: British Telecom had shed 100,000 workers since 1984. Feelings in the Union were therefore running high. But Johnson saw immediately how vitally important it would be for the anti-privatization camp to present itself as defending the Post Office as a whole, rather than the interests of the Union.

He was fortunate insofar as the preceding couple of years had been a period of unusual calm and stability in the workplace. Now he would run a campaign dressed up as a popular appeal. Nothing would be allowed to intrude upon it that might even vaguely smack of union militancy. Johnson would have no truck with UCW rallies; nor was he interested in a campaign that preached to the converted of the Labour Party and the TUC. Instead, he would focus all the Union's efforts on persuading Tory MPs that support for the measure would stir a hornets' nest in every constituency. This meant, above all, mobilizing the public's latent affection for Mrs Goggins and the local postie. ('Postman Pat Event Days' were indeed organized for children – and the media – wanting to learn more about the Post Office.) With three close associates, Johnson formed a campaign committee that took over all the decision-making – not just for the UCW but for the sub-postmasters' NFSP as well. They managed to defeat a series of motions in favour of strike action at the 1993 Annual Conference, aligning the Union instead with a broader public protest under the inspired banner, 'Stand by Your Post'.

It worked. Afficionados of the Westminster lobbying scene were amazed at the ingenuity and persuasiveness of Johnson and his fellow campaigners. Playing hard on the inevitability of widespread network closures and truncated local delivery services in the event of any successful privatization, they raised awkward questions across the country. Then they met privately with dozens of seriously unsettled Conservative backbenchers, to explain why it was all so terribly unnecessary. A Cabinet meeting reviewed the prospects in March 1994. Shortly afterwards, officials at the DTI received a call from Heseltine. One of them, David Sibbick, recalled: 'We had been drafting a White Paper for the legislation. Suddenly we were told, keep going but now write it on green

---

twelve months before properly taking over from him. But Tuffin spent the intervening year as General Secretary of the TUC, leaving Johnson effectively in sole charge of the UCW from the start of 1992.

paper.'[73] This altered the whole mood of the contest. Green Papers are a basis for soliciting people's views, and ministers moved smartly to distance themselves from any 'premature conclusions'. It was clear, at least in Whitehall, that the retreat had begun. The Counters business was dropped from the putative sale shortly after the publication of the Green Paper in June.[74] (Ironically, it did relatively well out of the privatization episode because the Green Paper laid out guidelines for allowing the network to engage in future in a range of more commercial activities.) But the damage had been done. Over the summer recess, Johnson's campaign hired Lowe Bell, erstwhile PR advisers to Margaret Thatcher. Their Chairman, Tim Bell, had originally offered his company's services to the Post Office. There had been some preliminary discussion of what a PR campaign on behalf of privatization might achieve – but in the end Cockburn, mindful of the legal constraints on Post Office spending, had had no option but to bin Bell's proposal.[75] Now Lowe Bell helped hammer home the opposition's arguments in a final burst of campaigning across the country and at the party conferences in October. They concentrated on the constituencies of the known Tory waverers, and on Northern Ireland – where no Unionist MP could afford to run foul of a strong local pride in the Post Office as it existed.

In mobilizing support for the status quo in areas remote from Westminster, the PR men were also drawing attention to the fact that – as most politicians were uncomfortably aware – there was no great enthusiasm for privatization among postal workers themselves. In London and the other major conurbations, there was always strong support for the UCW's official stance. Beyond the heavily politicized sorting depots of the big cities, meanwhile, privatization was quietly but revealingly ignored. In country areas remote from the clash of principles and policy debates were tens of thousands of people – postmen and Crown office counter staff as well as those working on commission as self-employed sub-postmasters and sub-postmistresses in tiny offices and village shops – for whom working in the Post Office essentially meant delivering a public service to the local community. It did not appear to them an obvious candidate for private ownership and the prospect of privatization, to the extent that it registered at all, was probably at best vaguely disconcerting.

Nowhere in Britain was more remote than the Scottish Highlands and Islands. The Scotland and Northern Ireland division of the Post Office set up in 1991 had almost 17,000 employees, of whom around 3,000 worked in Scottish rural areas far from the conurbations of Glasgow, Edinburgh and Aberdeen. Among their responsibilities was

the delivery of a daily postal service to about fifty inhabited islands off
the west coast and far to the north, from Mull and Tiree to Skye and the
Outer Hebrides, Orkney and the distant Shetlands. Across these islands,
and great expanses of the Highlands too, were dotted hundreds of post
offices – many of them run by the kind of sub-postmistresses who might
well stay at the same location for a half-century or more (a clutch of
them could be found, in a good year, in the list of recipients of British
Empire Medals in the Queen's Honours Lists).* Each of their premises
still boasted a plaque on the outside wall, put up in the 1930s: 'Post
Office for Money Orders, Savings Bank, Parcel Post, Telegraph, Insurance and Annuity Business'. Not a few had 'Post Office and Royal Mail'
in Gaelic, as well ('Oific A' Phuist, Post Rioghial'). The postmen here
rose earlier in the morning than most, covered greater distances each
day and often had to make light of the worst winter weather in Britain.
Above all, their daily routines were as valued by local people as those of
any postmen anywhere, and perhaps rather more so. The services they
offered were as crucial to their communities as the (government-owned)
ferries of Caledonian MacBrayne that linked all of the larger Western
Isles to the mainland – and that brought the mails regularly each day to
red Post Office vans awaiting their arrival at the quaysides.

Over the two decades since the 1969 incorporation, those working in
the Highlands had had no reason to feel the Post Office was in urgent
need of a new owner. Their conditions of service had been greatly
improved, leaving behind the old days that had often begun before
6 a.m. and finished late in the evening. The postman's kit had been modernized, replacing some quasi-military uniforms with woollen sweaters,
soft hats, better outdoor protective clothing and what the designers
liked to call smart casual wear. The mail service they provided had
improved, too: the number of daily flights from the south of England
had risen since the middle of the 1980s – landing in places like Lerwick,
Kirkwall and Stornoway as well as Inverness and Aberdeen – so that,
with 10–15 per cent of the incoming mails now arriving by air, many
island post offices could deliver letters from London on the day after
posting. If the Royal Mail generally enjoyed a high standing in the
region, though, any recent improvement in its delivery schedules had
only added to the reserves of goodwill patiently cultivated for many

---

* The 'North of Scotland District', comprising the region north of a line drawn roughly
west to east through Fort William, contained 700 post offices out of a total of more than
2,000 for Scotland as a whole.

years from Edinburgh. The 1969 Act had established a Scottish Postal Board. Through most of the 1970s it had been chaired by a Welshman, Trevor Carpenter, who had earned a reputation for his rendition of Gaelic folk songs. He had been succeeded in 1980 by Henry Tilling, whose solicitous attention to the needs of the Highlands through his four-year chairmanship entailed regular excursions to the west coast. After the reorganization of 1986, the non-executive Postal Board's Chairman, Ian Barr, worked hard on community relations, just like Danny Carty in Northern Ireland. Barr had a generous budget for the role, and there were many local causes – most notably, perhaps, the St Magnus Mid-Summer Arts Festival in Orkney – that were substantially backed by the Royal Mail.

Probably no other feature of the Royal Mail did as much for its image as a public service in Scotland – and indeed far beyond – as the postbus network (the first operation, it could be said, combining mail deliveries and passenger transport by road since the era of the Royal Mail coaches). Gathering in Glasgow in 1993 for the twenty-fifth anniversary of its inauguration, the instigators and champions of the network could celebrate an initiative that had truly made a contribution to everyday life in the region. After a faltering first few years, the idea had been championed strongly from 1972 by Carpenter and his Operations Controller, Jim Hall. The two of them had insisted that, by providing vehicles with passenger facilities in place of standard Royal Mail vans, they could enable postmen on their rounds in the Highlands and Islands to offer a valuable transport service.* In the wake of the 1969 Act, the Royal Mail had acquired a nationalized-industry status which had made it eligible for government subsidies, and these allowed the postbus service to be developed at no net cost to Edinburgh, though profits were generally pretty meagre. Some of the vehicles – mostly adapted mini-buses but also smaller vans and even plain estate cars – were put on Lowland routes, in East Lothian and the Borders, but the great majority of them worked the quiet roads of the Western Isles and

---

* The postbus concept had originally been mooted by a government paper, the Jack Report, in 1961. Tony Benn had backed the idea in 1964–6, and the first postbuses were established in 1967 in Wales, a few parts of rural England and later Northern Ireland, which is where Jim Hall first encountered them. Their potential value to rural communities greatly appealed to the UPW: in its evidence to the Hardman Enquiry in 1971, the Union urged more use of postbuses 'to include items for local delivery by local tradesmen. . . . Using marginal costing techniques, [the concept] should prove both profitable and socially useful' ('The Postal Service', 17 March 1971, EC 106/71, UCW/2/4/28).

the Highlands. Over the course of twenty years, the network had come to comprise about 140 routes, and by 1993 it was carrying about 80,000 passengers a year.* Some were foreign visitors, alerted to the postbus network's existence by tourist boards in their own countries. Most were local people, especially the elderly in many remote locations who had come over the years to rely on this singular Royal Mail service:

> They were passing their days and the end of their lives in places where almost every building, from church to library to school to shop and station, had been transformed into something else, and seldom something beneficial to them – a hotel, a holiday home, a new business, a restaurant, a ruin. All the former certainties had largely dissolved around them, which was why they cherished anything which remained. Like their particular postbus, about which many felt proprietorial, as if it was their very own.[76]

The publicity attracted by the postbuses was out of all proportion to their modest financial significance, but was a measure of the social importance attached to postmen in the Highlands. Inevitably, when privatization began to appear a real possibility, its opponents in Scotland were quick to cite the postbus network as the kind of public service that would face extinction. The General Manager for Scotland and Northern Ireland, John Mackay, tried hard to counter this assumption. Opening a new head office in Inverness in 1993, he installed a centralized administration for the postbuses under a District Postmaster – 'and that was not an initiative we'd have taken, as I constantly reminded people, if the network was about to be scrapped'.[77] He himself was convinced that a privatized Post Office would flourish as a business ('just like British Telecom had already done'), and he told many audiences this was his preferred outcome. Few responded with much warmth. As a sympathetic columnist noted in the *Glasgow Herald* after watching him speak at a conference at Gleneagles in April 1994: 'John Mackay's speech was not universally acclaimed; the hankering for state control of every village Post Office still lives and breathes in suspicious Scotland'.[78] The Scottish media were in general opposed to privatization, and it was viewed with deep misgivings by many of Mackay's own managers – who in this respect were probably not much different from staff across the rest of Britain.

---

* The postbus network is still running in 2011, but was cut back significantly in 2009. The Royal Mail Group estimates the current number of postbus passengers to be around 50,000 a year.

By the autumn of 1994, the sell-off proposal was clearly running foul of the public mood – a failure that many were quick to see as a vindication of Margaret Thatcher's deep conviction that, as a candidate for privatization, the Post Office would be different from all the rest. In reversing past nationalizations, the Government had been dealing with commercial entities: a change of ownership entailed no great reassessment of their purpose in life. A proposed move for the Post Office from the public to the private sector was now being seen, by contrast, as endorsing a fundamental break, by substituting a commercial view of its activities in preference to the late-Victorian model built around public service. This surely required a groundswell of popular support, which the Government had done almost nothing to encourage. It was still conspicuously absent. Work on the preparations for privatization by November 1994 had lasted a little over two years, and the Government's commitment to a future Bill was scheduled for inclusion in the Queen's Speech. When supporters and opponents of the prospective legislation sat down in Parliament to hear plans for the Bill formally announced, Her Majesty had nothing whatever to say, and the Speech made no reference to it at all. It had been abandoned, consigning vast quantities of preparatory reports, accountancy homework and draft legislation to the waste bin. No other big privatization project ever came to such an ignominious end. As Heseltine recalled, 'It's the one that got away'.[79] Major's Cabinet, with a steadily dwindling Commons majority through these years, had decided the Bill was all too likely to be defeated in the House. Nine Tory MPs had insisted they would vote against it, which threatened to wipe out the Government's majority, and perhaps its ailing credibility too.

7. RECORD PROFITS BUT A DEARTH OF INVESTMENT

The fundamental premise of the successful 'Stand by Your Post' campaign had been that the postal status quo was robust, and a sensible basis on which to plan for future growth. This turned out over the next few years to be an unduly optimistic assessment. Cockburn quickly decided his own future lay elsewhere (wryly telling friends: 'I can't privatize the Post Office, so I'll privatize myself'), which represented a setback for the leadership of the whole organization.[80] He was succeeded in October 1995 by John Roberts, a man with no enemies who was universally respected for his knowledge of the Post Office and all its ways. Like most members of the management team he was to lead, however, Roberts was essentially a gifted and hard-working civil servant. With each passing year, the lack of people at the top with business skills and attitudes was becoming more conspicuous and more costly to the Post Office. Policy guidance from the DTI, meanwhile, slipped into abeyance. Still convinced that only a privatized Post Office would be sustainable in the long run, many in the Department felt frustrated – far more so than at the time of the Thatcher veto, having on this occasion come so much closer to the finish line. They had no interest in exploring the possibilities of a French-style state enterprise. But with at most two years left before the next general election, there was too little time to rebuild any momentum for a second sale campaign. The mood at the Treasury, as ever, was more pragmatic. It had favoured a lucrative sale while this appeared practical. Failing that, the Treasury turned to ensuring that the taxpayer could reap the maximum possible benefit from the Post Office in the existing circumstances. This was working out, from its viewpoint, rather well.

The remarkable growth in the volume of the mails since the early 1980s was continuing. First- and second-class letters together had reached 16 billion in 1993–4 – a jump of one third since Dearing's 1986 reorganization – and would rise through 17 billion in 1995–6 and 18 billion in 1997–8. The benefits of higher traffic for the business were as potent as ever. Operating profits at the Royal Mail had been £126m in 1990–91, the first year for which its accounts were published (in the 1991–2 Report) separately from those of the Parcels business. In 1994–5 they were more than three times higher, at £430m. The Government then pushed through a 1p rise in the price of 1st and 2nd class stamps in July 1996, which was hardly needed on commercial grounds but was a lucrative exploitation of the monopoly, helping to lift Royal Mail operating profits to just short of £500m in 1997–8. Net profits for the Post Office Group as a whole, having surmounted the Parcelforce crisis, rose through the mid-1990s to unprecedented levels: they more than doubled over four years, from £195m in 1993–4 to £447m in 1997–8. The impact on the Corporation itself, however, was not quite the blessing that all these numbers might suggest. Instead of easing back on its cash demands of the Post Office in the shape of negative EFL targets – which were in effect a proxy for dividends – the Treasury more than doubled them. The Post Office had to hand over a sum equivalent to 93 per cent of its post-tax profits for 1993–4, compared with 43 per cent

in 1992–3 and an average of just under 60 per cent through the 1980s.*
(The privatized utilities in the mid-1990s were meanwhile paying out
around 40 per cent of their profits in dividends to shareholders, as was
noted by the Post Office.[81]) The Treasury extracted around 75 per cent
over the years that followed – though the target was set not as a percentage, but in absolute cash terms – and swept aside an attempt by
Heseltine to establish a new EFL regime that might have afforded the
Post Office some limited respite from its demands.[82] As profits soared,
the Post Office faced negative EFL demands far beyond any normal
'pay-out ratio' in the corporate sector and equivalent to more than
twice the size of its tax bills. (See Appendix A, Chart 13.) Reviewing this
development in the 1995–6 Annual Report, Michael Heron talked of
'the biggest cash demand in the history of the Post Office'; and he was
not exaggerating. The Treasury was asking for almost as much, over the
next three years, as it had received over the previous ten. (Higher stamp
prices had just been approved, so perhaps higher payments back to the
Treasury were simply seen in the Government as a function of the Post
Office's revenue-raising powers.) Since the negative EFL targets were
set in absolute cash terms rather than as a percentage of post-tax profits, ensuring that they could be met over the 1990s undeniably put a
squeeze on current spending. Some of the consequences were bizarre.
Cockburn noted as early as April 1994 that 'staff numbers had been
kept unnecessarily high because there was insufficient money to fund
the early retirement of surplus staff'.[83]

   One feature of the impressive financial performance of the 1990s was
rather curious. Beginning in 1990–91, the Corporation suspended its
cash contributions into the main Post Office pension pot. Since this
proved a boon for reported profits over the next decade or so (and an
embarrassment thereafter) it might easily be supposed, given the pressure on the Board to keep profits rising in the 1990s, that trousering a
pension contribution of about £125m a year was a financial stratagem
with a dubious motive. This would be to underestimate the clout of the
actuaries. The Corporation's main pension fund was the PO Staff Super-
annuation Scheme (POSSS). It had in fact been closed to new entrants
in April 1987, and replaced with a new PO Pension Scheme (POPS).

---

* Technically, ownership of the negative EFL payments remained with the Post Office,
insofar as they stayed on its balance sheet. Since the Post Office was obliged to invest them
in gilt securities, however, the cash ended up with the Government. (When the Government
turned to investing in the Royal Mail during the post-Millennium decade, redemption of the
gilts was to be used as a convenient way of providing the cash.)

But the Post Office had to go on ensuring the POSSS had sufficient assets to match its future liabilities, which in 1987 amounted to a little over £7bn. At the time of the scheme's closure, its invested assets closely matched this sum and the actuaries deemed it 'fully funded'.[84] Over the next four years, rising stock markets lifted the current value of the assets substantially higher. By early 1991, the assets were valued at more than 120 per cent of liabilities. To continue adding to the pot in these circumstances, said the actuaries, would expose the Group to tax penalties. (The Inland Revenue had rules to prevent companies siphoning excessive pre-tax profits off into pension plans.) The Board was therefore advised to initiate a 'contributions holiday', suspending its annual payments into POSSS. So it was not a simple case of boosting the bottom line – and meeting the Treasury's EFL demands – at the pension pot's expense. Given that the Corporation's after-tax profits in 1990 had been cut to £3m, though, the clear recommendations from the actuaries were welcome indeed – and the Board went to some trouble to ensure the holiday could be applied retrospectively to the first half of the 1990–91 financial year.[85] And once the holiday had been instituted, the Board was understandably reluctant to abandon it. The actuaries suggested in October 1994 that contributions might need to be resumed again, starting either in 1995–6 or 1997–8.[86] The Board, increasingly exercised about its negative EFL payments, opted for the later date. It was noted that market conditions would inevitably be different by then, 'and that "best estimate" views were that recommencement . . . on 1 April 1997 was unlikely', and so it was to prove. The actuaries in September 1996 were happy to stand by their justification of the contributions holiday. A Board minute that month carried an ominous caveat, however. The liabilities burdening the POSSS were steadily climbing, as the scheme's membership grew older and better paid. They had now topped the £10bn mark, and the estimated value of the scheme's assets had slipped from 122 per cent of liabilities, five years earlier, to around 110 per cent. More to the point, asset values for the POSSS relied on the buoyancy of an historically long-lived bull market – 'and it was fully recognized that a 10–15 per cent drop in the value of unit trusts could in effect bankrupt the Post Office'.[87] The Group Finance Director, Richard Close, nicely compared the situation to sitting with an elephant in a rowing boat. If the elephant moved an inch, they might all capsize.

The most conspicuous and troubling aspect of the Treasury's general attitude to the Post Office after 1994 was the constraint it placed on investment. Treasury rules dictated that each year's capital spending be funded, in effect, out of that year's net profits, struck after settlement of the negative EFL requirement as well as the payment of corporation tax. So the bigger the negative EFL demand, the smaller the remnant available for the capital budget. (All significant capital-spending projects still remained subject to Treasury approval in the usual way.) The result, despite record profits, was a dearth of funding for the longer-term modernization needs of the Post Office. 'Stand by Your Post' had been a happy slogan for the anti-privatization campaigners. It would have been a poor description of the Treasury's stance once the campaign was over. Some projects had to be abandoned altogether, despite the Board's fears of a hostile public reaction. Plans were cancelled, for example, for a $3\frac{1}{2}$-mile extension to the Mail Rail under the streets of London, which would have connected Paddington station to the Royal Mail's hub depot at Willesden.[88] The Mail Rail's days were numbered. Even more important was the strain placed on the Royal Mail's efforts to keep its sorting operations at the forefront of postal technology.

The long-standing mechanization agenda had, in a sense, been fulfilled by the late 1980s. The public's neglect of postcodes had finally been overcome; and the last Mechanized Letter Offices (MLOs) had been activated by July 1986, more or less on schedule.[89] Hence, in large part, the success with which rapidly rising letter volumes had been managed. But now 'mechanization' had given way to 'automation'. Those OCR devices encountered by Denis Roberts on his 1980 trip to Tokyo had been adopted and refined through a series of prototypes by Royal Mail engineers.* (The first, used at Mount Pleasant in 1983, was unfortunately christened the V1 – duly followed in 1987 by the V2.) A new Royal Mail Technology Centre was opened at Swindon in 1985, replacing the research station at Martlesham Heath in Suffolk that had itself replaced Dollis Hill in the early 1970s. (Martlesham Heath was ceded to British Telecom.) Swindon's boffins coordinated work not just on the OCR scanners that could replace individual coding operators but also on fancy ink-jet printers to work with them. These printers could shoot codes onto ten passing envelopes a second, which was five times faster than the old machines that used hot pins pressing on phosphor tape to

---

* The computer brain of the OCR scanner needed to be equipped with the equivalent of a dictionary, which could allow it to recognize not just typescript but written scrawls as well. Since each letter of the alphabet and each numerical digit can be written in such a wide variety of ways, many thousands of different permutations needed to be accommodated. The number '9', for instance, had approximately 600 entries. (Tom Norgate, interview with author, 10 June 2010.)

impress codes on the mail.[90] A string of other clever innovations followed – transferring video pictures of code data around the network, for example, to allow the deciphering of problem addresses in remote locations. By 1992, the Royal Mail was ready to start replacing every MLO with an APC – an Automated Processing Centre. And four years later, it began to install the huge all-in-one machines that brought together the various innovations of the past decade or so. The so-called Integrated Mail Processor (IMP), which made its debut at Watford APC in August 1996, could receive unsorted mail at one end of the depot and churn out sorted and postmarked mail ready for despatch at the other end. Notwithstanding its acronym, it was also capacious and extremely heavy. IMPs needed a ground-floor berth. Many, perhaps most, of the MLOs in the country were old, two- or three-storey buildings that could not accommodate them. Even where new machines could be squeezed into old buildings, too many of their premises were positioned in city centre locations now increasingly ill-suited to the task. The sum required to upgrade the Royal Mail estate was enormous – and in the shadow of those huge EFL payments, the budget never came close to matching it. Cope, appointed to the Board as Managing Director of Strategy and Personnel in April 1996, recalled: 'Without doubt, the rationalization of the estate went ahead far too slowly'.[91]

Whatever the inadequacy of the buildings programme, at least the money was there for the machines. The purchase of the IMPs from AEG of Germany represented the Post Office's largest ever single investment, with an initial advance payment to the manufacturer of £52m. This far exceeded anything available for international joint ventures. Heseltine wrote to Heron in December 1996 to say he would look on such ventures favourably – 'though no project could exceed £10m, and total investments for one year could not exceed £20m'.[92] While this may have been intended as a sop to the Post Office, there was scope for concern that the Royal Mail might be left behind by trends in the international market. True, it enjoyed roughly a 20 per cent share of the £2.5bn a year market for international mail regulated in traditional ways by the UPU. But there was now a nascent market for unregulated international mail – courier packages carrying generally far higher rates, for express delivery – as yet worth perhaps half as much. The Royal Mail's share of this was negligible. More significantly, there was also a growing postal market in the deregulated portion of domestic mail inside many European countries. Current estimates put this market's value at almost £11bn a year – and the Royal Mail as yet had no presence in it at all.[93]

The Board's concern was hardly allayed by the speed with which some of its counterparts had overtaken the Post Office in the privatization stakes. The Dutch floated their state entity as 'KPN' in 1995, and the Germans were openly positioning their Deutsche Post to follow in its wake. A corporate plan submitted to the DTI three years earlier had anticipated these developments – and alluded to parallel developments in countries such as Sweden, New Zealand and Singapore – as a way of making the case for UK privatization. Under a 'Shareholder Control' heading, it had noted: 'The reputation of the British Post Office as a commercial and organisational pace-setter is being threatened by developments in other administrations.'[94] Late in 1996, the Dutch KPN announced it was merging with easily the most aggressive of the private courier companies, TNT. This sent a shock wave round the European postal industry. Suddenly it was more than just the Post Office's reputation as a pace-setter that seemed under threat. The Board observed in October that a combined KPN–TNT 'would provide the Dutch with an important first opportunity to provide a global service'. This might even involve a challenge to the postal services within the UK. The Board minutes recorded a little wistfully that the Royal Mail, just like its Dutch counterpart, had spent a lot of time looking at prospective partners. 'However, given Government's rejection of previous initiatives, the Post Office had indicated to the DTI that further time and money would not be spent [on such work].'[95]

While no doubt intended to sound an admonishing note, this message for the DTI had another significance. Events in the international market – which appear menacing in retrospect – still seemed of secondary importance at the time. Management had other pressing problems. None weighed more heavily in 1996–7 than a further serious deterioration in industrial relations. Ken Young's retirement in 1992 had left a conspicuous gap at Board level. It was made worse by the retirement of Derek Gladwin as a non-executive in 1994. (Not until ten years later would another senior figure from the trade union world, Margaret Prosser of the Transport and General Workers' Union, join the Board – making a similarly important contribution, much in line with Gladwin's over the years.) A new Personnel Director, Brian Thomson, was appointed in 1996. An engaging Geordie who had spent three years as Director and General Manager in London, Thomson already enjoyed a close personal rapport with many senior union figures. He was one of those few who had come into the Post Office from outside the civil service and managed to adapt to its ways successfully – probably helped by

an earlier career in the shipbuilding industry, which many observers
thought in some ways comparable with the postal service.* He nonetheless found himself confronted with a level of local antagonism – especially
in London – that left little room for rational discussion. The defeat of
the privatization policy had not greatly depressed morale across the
broad body of postal managers – whose views were mixed, as we have
noted – but it had done wonders for the self-confidence of rank-and-file
officials in the Union.

Having seen off the great bugbear feared since 1979, local reps began
to feel their de facto control over the workplace in many locations could
now extend to a greater influence over the policies of the Post Office as a
whole. They were in no mood to put up with any compromise over management initiatives they disliked. And one such soon emerged. Christened
'Employee Agenda', it was designed to introduce a new emphasis on
team-work, to help sorting offices take full advantage of the staffing efficiencies made possible by automation.[96] But preparing for it involved
substituting regular duties for overtime across the network – a measure
that was firmly rebuffed in many large offices. Thomson recalled: 'We
stumbled because we couldn't explain team-working with sufficient
exactness. The worst possible interpretations were put on it.'[97] Unofficial
strikes began to multiply, against the wishes of the Union's own leadership.[98] Even a 1½-hour reduction in the working week towards the end of
1995 brought little relief. A recent restructuring of the MLO network in
London aggravated the situation there. It was soon apparent that a crisis
of unusual gravity loomed. Royal Mail managers began to give consideration, not for the first time, to the possibility of withdrawing the financial
support given to the Union 'for services such as Check Off [i.e. the deduc-
tion of union subs from wage slips], facilities time [i.e. paid absence from
work on union business], and its annual conference. The removal of this
support had the potential to damage the union financially and, as had
been seen in other industries, could reduce membership by up to 20 per
cent'.[99] Word of this did nothing to improve the atmosphere – and it culminated, at the end of August 1996, in a four-day national strike. It was
a breakdown in industrial relations that many compared with 1988.

---

* De facto control by the unions was a feature of daily life in most of the shipyards of the
1960s and 1970s, generally leaving companies dependent on local managers who built up
fiefdoms by accommodating themselves to union power. Thomson had worked for Swan
Hunter on Tyneside before joining British Shipbuilders – recruited by Richard Dykes, who
spent three years on secondment there in 1977–80. The two of them worked together in the
late seventies, before joining the Post Office separately in 1985–6.

In a signal respect, it was actually even worse. The decision to strike over the Employee Agenda followed sixty hours of negotiation with the Union's General Secretary, Alan Johnson, and his senior colleagues at ACAS. It included the longest continuous ACAS session on record. A deal had eventually been reached – but Johnson, to his considerable embarrassment, failed to carry it inside the Union. His recommendation of the terms was rejected, confirming what had been increasingly apparent even before the defeat of the privatization plan, that the national officers of the Union had lost much of their traditional authority. This was no reflection on the individuals concerned, but the consequence of a sweeping reorganization of the Union four years earlier, aimed at matching it more closely to the shape of the Royal Mail itself. At one level, this was simply about modernizing the branch structure. An official who would eventually succeed Johnson, Derek Hodgson, had presided over a reduction in the number of branches from not far short of a thousand to fewer than a hundred. This had greatly improved communications within the Union, and it later helped to facilitate a smooth merger between the UCW and the National Communications Union in 1995, to form the Communication Workers Union (CWU). But the reorganization had also involved a second and rather more potent change.

Cockburn had carried through a 'Business Development' Plan for Royal Mail Letters in 1991: the four Territories and sixty-three districts of the 1986 Dearing design had been consolidated into just nine large geographical divisions.* (Parcels and Counters, as we have seen, had taken through their own parallel reorganizations to much the same effect.) To match the Royal Mail's move, the Union had adopted an 'Industrial Relations Framework', setting up nine divisions of its own. Johnson had signed off on this as a sensible consolidation of the Union's negotiating channels: branch secretaries effectively lost their local negotiating powers to new and more powerful 'Area reps' and 'Divisional reps'. But the rank and file of the Union had then demanded a further twist to the divisional format that was much less to Johnson's liking. Conference approved the setting up of decentralized committees across the divisions, blandly coded as 'coordinating machinery'. In practice these provided a platform for the emergence of younger officials intent, as they saw it, on making the Union more democratic. Every General

---

* The nine divisions were London, South-East, South-Central, South-West (including South Wales), East, Midlands, North-West (including North Wales), North-East, and Scotland & Northern Ireland.

Secretary since the war had had to contend with a London District Council proud of its semi-independence. Now that the LDC had become the London Divisional Committee, Johnson was faced with eight replicas of the old LDC around the rest of the country. It did not take their leaders long to work out that any alliance of five or more Divisional Committees could hold sway over the National Executive. When they began flexing this power, it brought a whole era of UPW/UCW politics to a sudden end. Johnson's forebears had relied on the central importance of each year's Annual Conference in the decision-making process. By managing the delegates skilfully, with the right mix of platform oratory and back-room skulduggery, they had (usually) managed in the end to swing Conference decisions and settle the Union's key policies for another year. Johnson had all the old skills in spades, but they were no longer sufficient. Local activists at the divisional level – including future leaders like Billy Hayes from Liverpool and Dave Ward from London – saw policy-making as a more continuous process that needed national leaders to be in constant engagement with those in the regions. When they took a stand against team-working in 1996, Johnson was powerless to change their minds. By the start of 1997, in fact, he was losing control over the Union across a wide range of issues. An invitation from Tony Blair to take up the nomination for a safe Labour seat in Parliament before the 1997 general election was warmly received. He made it, with just three weeks to spare, and was duly elected as MP for Hull West.

8. DEATH BY A THOUSAND PLANS

With the election of the Blair government on 1 May, it was time to discover whether the second option instead of straight public ownership – Commercial Freedom within the public sector – might after all be achievable, despite all the discouraging signs since 1995. Labour's election manifesto had reminded voters of the party's past opposition to the Tories' privatization scheme. It had otherwise done no more than restate a vague enthusiasm for giving the Post Office 'greater commercial freedom to make the most of new opportunities'. Now this state of grace needed to be defined. Three months before quitting as its General Secretary, Johnson had arranged for the CWU to present its own version as a mock Green Paper. There would be a redefined legal status, allowing total freedom to borrow commercially – outside the PSBR – and to take on joint ventures and acquisitions. Dividends would be paid in place of negative EFL targets, and would be set not by the Treasury but by the Board itself. Services enjoying monopoly status would be subject to price controls, and there would be 'a small regulatory panel' to oversee the gradual liberalization of the postal sector. Roberts was given a preview of the Paper and told the Board 'in many ways it mirrored the Post Office's own views'.[100] Mild-mannered and far more attuned – after thirty years of diligent service – to the art of the possible than to blitzkrieg assaults on the status quo, Roberts nonetheless shared the conviction of all his senior executive colleagues that a radically different framework was urgently needed for the postal services. On its sixteenth day in office, the Labour government launched a formal Review of the Post Office. Roberts quipped to the press: 'We've had more reviews than the West End'. Reactions to the announcement were generally upbeat. Now the General Secretary of the CWU, Derek Hodgson told the press it was 'marvellous news'. Media comment was overwhelmingly supportive. 'The Post Office is considered a British success story', reported *The Times*, 'but it has felt hampered in its efforts to compete.' Heron, Roberts and Cope came away from their first formal presentation to their new Minister at the DTI, Ian McCartney, bucked by his intimation 'that he would welcome an increase in the Post Office's commercial freedoms'.[101] With such a consensus for reform, what could possibly go wrong?

Twelve months later, the Review was still proceeding and the DTI seemed to be locked in a struggle with Gordon Brown's Treasury over the future level of negative EFL payments. Net profits at the Post Office for 1997–8 marked another steep rise over the previous year – up 22 per cent to £447m – and the payments to the Treasury again creamed off almost three quarters of the total. A virtually unchanged target sum (£310m) had been set for 1998–9 and the sums targeted for the next three-year period exceeded those of the past six years. With the Review in limbo, some familiar problems were surfacing. Contemplating basic changes that might slacken their reins on the Post Office, DTI ministers appeared intent first on tightening their grip just in case of surprises, as had happened from the start of 1991. McCartney had called a halt to the conversion of Crown offices into sub-offices – a programme opposed by the unions because of its impact on jobs – with almost the first swipe of his ministerial pen. (He reversed his position eighteen months later.) By 1998, few indeed were the decisions that did not merit a detailed review by his officials. Regional issues with an impact on local economies could prompt intense debate – especially, as over a reorganization

of the North-West postal infrastructure, where Labour city councillors
had an interest in protecting local jobs. Major corporate plans from the
Post Office were received by ministers not as statements of commercial
intent but as a basis for negotiation, which the Board found increasingly
exasperating. One set of de facto negotiations that never failed to prove
especially irritating for the Board concerned salaries at the most senior
levels of the Post Office. Tense exchanges on this delicate topic had
recurred almost since 1969. (Bill Ryland had signed off his final Chairman's Statement in the Annual Report of 1976–7 with a fierce rebuke to
the Government for allowing two seats on his Board to remain unfilled
for months – a situation he blamed squarely on a collapse in Post Office
directors' real salaries.[102]) The Board still felt in the late 1990s that
senior executive salaries were simply inadequate, and far below those
paid for comparable jobs in the private sector. The Government turned
a deaf ear to repeated appeals from the Board for a less parsimonious
stance, and it prompted a row in March 1998. McCartney's response
two months later was to suggest that he wanted to appoint some new
Members, 'although this was no reflection on the contribution of the
present Members'.[103] This strengthened a long-standing perception at
the Post Office that ministers, while underrating the importance of
executive pay, also set little store by the contributions of non-executive
directors on the Board. Two of them, including the head of the Board's
Remuneration Committee, Sir Christopher Harding, felt so affronted
that they immediately indicated their intention of resigning, which they
did in June.[104]

Behind the interminable delays, an impasse had been reached. The
DTI's officials were still as keen as ever to proceed with privatization,
and to clarify the options for ministers had produced yet another Review
in April 1998.[105] In deference to Labour's election manifesto, the policy
would now have to be configured as a sale of 49 per cent of the equity
but this scarcely diluted its potency. By July 1998, the Department's
City advisers were lined up behind this approach: it would be the best
way, they had concluded, to ensure the genuine independence of an
'Independent Post Office Corporation' (IPOC).[106] Despite festering
arguments on other scores, the Treasury backed the sale option, too.
Michael Heron's successor as Chairman of the Post Office, Neville Bain,
had hardly been in his new job more than a few weeks when he was
taken aside by a Treasury Minister in April 1998 and told the Government was 'pretty convinced' that a sale was now the right way forward.[107]
International investors were intrigued by what was happening to the

25. Five General Secretaries of the postal workers' union. *Top left*: Charles Geddes (1897–1983), whose elegant cigarette-holder belied his toughness. He dominated every aspect of the UPW during his tenure from 1944 to 1956 and sought to build on the wartime spirit of cooperation between Staff and Officials; (*top right*) Ron Smith (1915–99), built like a heavyweight boxer, who inherited a fractious union and struggled to uphold the Executive Council's waning authority for some years before stepping down in 1966; (*below left*) Tom Jackson (1925–2003), an ebullient and hugely popular figure with the rank and file, who gave the UPW a novel prominence in national politics but found his brave attempts to modernize it thwarted from the left and right alike; (*below right*) Alan Tuffin (b.1933) being congratulated on his retirement in 1993 by his successor, Alan Johnson (b.1950), both of whom had to contend with a string of reorganizations in the Post Office that raised questions over the structure of the union.

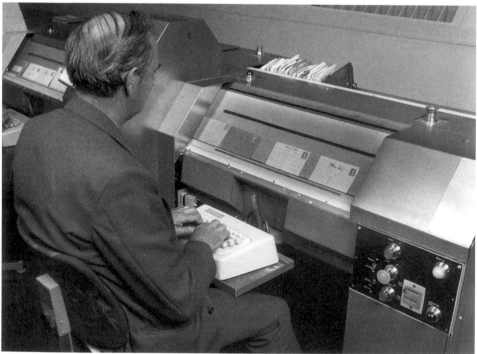

26. Mechanization before automation. *Above*: The Transorma (1936–68), manufactured in the Netherlands and known to postal workers for good reason as 'The Rattler', linked keyboard operators to a giant box weighing more than ten tons and full of levers, chutes and buckets designed to sort letters by their final destination. *Below*: The Easy View Coding Desk, introduced in 1975, marked the culmination of more than fifteen years' work on the concept of using a keyboard/printer unit to impress letters with postcode data.

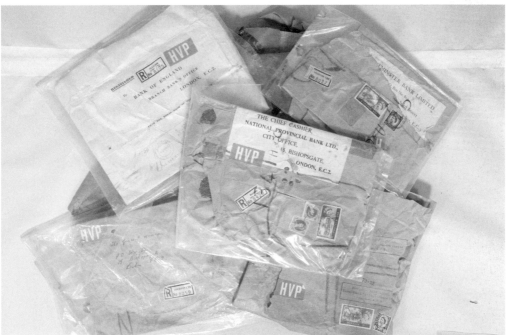

27. The TPO network and the Great Train Robbery. *Above*: Preparing the Down Special to Aberdeen (W. H. Auden's *Night Mail* train) at London's Euston station in the early 1960s. Mailbags with potentially valuable contents carried an 'HVP' ('High Value Package') label and were generally on view in separate piles along the platform before being loaded aboard the train. *Below*: Some of the stolen HVP packets, emptied of their cash, which were found strewn around the Buckinghamshire farmhouse used briefly by the Great Train Robbers as a hideaway after the crime in August 1963.

28. Two of the last Postmasters General. *Above*: Tony Benn (b.1925), who took a more executive stance than any of his predecessors, showered officials with novel ideas and proposals from his very first day in 1964 and pushed hard for a more commercial approach. *Below*: John Stonehouse (1925–88), watching the Prime Minister, Harold Wilson, being given a demonstration of new technology at the National Giro Centre late in 1968.

29. Behind the scenes in the UPW's 1971 national strike. *Above*: Tom Jackson works the telephone at his desk, surrounded by members of the union's Executive Council. *Below*: No postal strike ever deterred the public from continuing to post letters, and the completeness of the 1971 action soon resulted in silent sorting depots piled high with mail, collected by non-union staff. It was media coverage of the mounting back-post that usually prompted politicians to press Post Office managers into a settlement of any serious strike within a few days – but not in 1971.

30. From civil servants to business leaders. *Top left*: Ronald German (1905–83), the Director General in Tony Benn's day, who was wont to 'come in after an ample lunch, sink into an armchair … and ask "What has that young man been up to today?"'; (*top right*) William (Bill) Ryland (1913–88), Chairman 1971–7 with a seemingly inexhaustible appetite for work; (*below left*) William Barlow (b.1924), who as Chairman in 1977–80 finally accomplished a separation of the postal and telephone services; (*below right*) Ron (later Lord) Dearing (1930–2009), who led a radical reorganization in 1986.

31. Banners and slogans of 1992–4. *Above*: The UCW General Secretary, Alan Johnson, protesting with leaders of the UCW's Manchester Branch in front of Manchester Town Hall. *Below*: While the UCW's leadership was careful to avoid identifying anti-privatization with familiar images of labour unrest, many individual postal workers were not slow to express their angry rejection of the policy.

32. Managers with a brief, and a minister with a problem. *Left*: After a year as a non-executive director, Allan Leighton (b.1953) took over as Executive Chairman in March 2002, invited by Tony Blair to manage the Royal Mail with strictly no interference from ministers. *Right*: Adam Crozier (b.1964), Chief Executive 2003–10, shouldered much of the burden of transforming the Royal Mail into a modern commercial business, and devoted huge amounts of time to oppressive regulatory issues. *Below*: A *Sun* cartoon lampooning Labour's Business Secretary, Peter Mandelson, in July 2009 for abandoning his Bill aimed at privatization of the Royal Mail, which had provoked opposition from more than a hundred government backbenchers as well as the postal workers' union.

European postal industry. In the Netherlands, KPN demerged its postal subsidiary as 'TPG', with its own stock market listing in June 1998. The chances of a lucrative sale of half of the Royal Mail looked bright. Officials at the DTI tried to force the pace. It was announced publicly in April that the 49 per cent option was being considered as part of the Government's Review process. The Prime Minister was said to be personally supportive of the idea. This added to a growing sense of optimism within the Post Office. Profits were running at a record level. The sale of various assets had also raised unprecedented levels of cash. (Property disposals included the sale of King Edward Building to an American bank. The GPO North building had already been sold in 1984, to a Japanese bank, so this marked the final severance of the Post Office's historical identification since 1829 with St Martin's-le-Grand.)* Submitting their annual Five Year Plan, Roberts and Cope pitched it as 'the last . . . based on Government requirements rather than a commercially driven Plan . . .'[108]

There was just one problem: government ministers could not bring themselves to take a final decision. They were caught in a political dilemma, which the April announcement only made more acute. Coming just four years after the triumphant anti-privatization campaign, the prospect of any sale appalled the CWU's leaders. In a Board paper reviewing the situation in May, Roberts noted 'a minority share sale is clearly opposed by DTI Ministers and is being actively campaigned against by [the] CWU . . .'[109] He and Neville Bain had a meeting in July with McCartney and his Department head (still styled 'President of the Board of Trade'), Margaret Beckett, but they came away no wiser. The Government's commitment to change was firm, the Board was told. It was just the Government's objective that remained obscure: 'there was still no settled view on the scope of the change'.[110]

Peter Mandelson arrived as Secretary of State at the end of the month.

---

* The sale of KEB meant a new home was needed for the National Postal Museum, which the Board hoped to rehouse with generous amenities for the public: 'research had indicated that a central London site was the ideal location for a museum [of this scope] and was in fact essential . . .' (Minute 97/131, POBM 9 December 1997, Post 69/Red Books). In the meantime, most of its contents were added to the archives at the BPMA, with large items put into storage at a business park in Essex. The lack of a proper postal history museum in the land of the Royal Mail is a curious anomaly that many have tried and failed to address over recent decades. Plans were even mooted in 1979–80 to convert St Botolph's Aldersgate Church near St Martin's-le-Grand ('the postmen's church') into a museum, but they came to nothing (see PO Management Board Minute M79/38, 6 March 1979, BT Archives, TCC 15/23). Perhaps the 2011 Postal Services Act will prompt a fresh initiative.

He made an immediate impact, apparently quickly accepting the proposition that a complete transformation of the Post Office was urgently needed. Above all, he was ready to make a decision. But what would this entail? A biography of Mandelson by a seasoned political commentator, Donald Macintyre, was published in 1999.[111] It drew on extensive access to his private papers and Mandelson's own recollections of his career to that point – and it included a detailed review of what had happened the previous autumn. By this account, Mandelson used his very first meeting with Gordon Brown at the Treasury to broach the critical topic – and came to a quick conclusion. 'Mandelson understood the Chancellor to take the viewpoint that the politics were not right for privatisation; it was best to leave it alone.' Mandelson concurred with this. The two men then separately persuaded Blair that privatization was 'a non-starter given our manifesto commitment', as Mandelson put it in his own memoirs a decade later.[112] The CWU, unaware of this decision, continued campaigning. At the 1998 Labour Party Conference, Mandelson had to sit through an angry speech by Alan Johnson's successor, Derek Hodgson, in which the CWU General Secretary openly appealed to Labour MPs to 'save our Post Office'. But in fact the real drama lay elsewhere, in a fierce stand-off between Mandelson and Brown over what kind of Commercial Freedom, short of privatization, might be ceded to the Post Office. As little as possible, seemed to be the Treasury's preference. Mandelson's proposal to grant wider and more flexible borrowing powers was stonewalled for two months by the Chancellor.[113] At an eventual meeting of the full DTI and Treasury teams in Brown's office, the personal animosity between Mandelson and Brown (a problem of long standing) caused officials some embarrassment. After a personal intervention by Blair, a compromise was reached and the conclusions of the Government Review launched in May 1997 were at last unveiled by Mandelson in December. Largely at Blair's behest, part-privatization was retained as a possibility for the future, but this was not much noted at the time. The media generally saw the outcome as a damp squib. Modest changes to the financial rules for the Post Office were not of much interest, and most journalists treated the absence of a commitment to a 49 per cent sale as a personal setback for Mandelson. This may have owed something to off-the-record briefings from Mandelson's detractors within the Government to the effect that the DTI Secretary had lost his nerve over privatization. (An alternative briefing for the unions' consumption was that the Chancellor had indeed saved the Post Office, just as Hodgson had urged at the autumn conference.) It was an unedifying episode, more revealing in retrospect about the conduct of the Labour government than was apparent at the time. It also meant, for the second time in little more than four years, that the prospect of a Royal Mail company in the private sector had been dangled and withdrawn.

In the meantime, Mandelson had already begun handing the Post Office more discretion over its own affairs where he was able to do so. This facilitated a momentous development in the international arena. Earlier in 1998, Deutsche Post had begun buying shares in DHL, the only non-American international courier business with any claim to being a proper rival for TNT. Here was further evidence that, in the battle for supremacy in a future global marketplace, its Dutch and German counterparts were threatening to snatch a lead on the Post Office that might prove decisive. It was also confirmation, if anyone still needed it, that the couriers and the great behemoths of the traditional mail industry would not inhabit separate marketplaces for much longer. The convergence timetable was already a lively topic in Brussels. Since issuing a Green Paper on postal liberalization in 1991, the European Commission had been building support for a phased removal of national postal monopolies: a 1997 Directive had proposed the future introduction of limits to the franchise of 'reserved' postal services within EU member states. The Post Office, with its international status plainly threatened, needed to respond to these developments – and by 1998 was also keen to do so, by way of raising internal morale. But now DHL and TNT were spoken for, and neither FedEx nor UPS were truly eligible for partnerships (though the Post Office explored possible deals with both of them over many months). Two tiny joint-venture agreements were struck in July with partners in Sweden and the Netherlands by Royal Mail International, the small Group unit responsible for overseas activities. RMI seemed most unlikely, though, to come up with a deal commensurate with the size of the Post Office. Its expertise over the years had lain in the negotiation of arcane UPU contracts and the organization of goodwill visits and educational tours. Even within the Post Office, RMI was regarded as a kind of cross between the Foreign Office and the British Council. If a game-changing transaction was to be found, it would have to involve the mainstream mails.

It was Parcelforce that now provided what was needed. Its senior managers spotted the potential of a European network for the reliable ('time-certain' in the industry's jargon) delivery of parcels on a two- to three-day schedule. The domestic PTTs were offering a much inferior service. The couriers were focused on expensive fast-delivery services. A fully commercial, pan-European time-certain parcel post might win a valuable niche in the market. And the Parcelforce team had identified a way of starting to build it, too – in the shape of German Parcel, the fourth-largest postal operator in Germany and a leading constituent of a private franchise network called General Parcel. Its owner-manager, Rico Back, had a passionate vision of how this new time-certain business might look, but he lacked the capital to pursue it on his own. As a subsidiary of the Post Office, his business could provide the basis of a new international strategy. Jerry Cope took up the project and was soon persuaded of its potential. He pushed hard to complete the acquisition, establishing a rapport with Back, whose obvious management skills were essential to its success. But it carried a price tag of around £320m, an unprecedented sum for an initiative of this kind, and it was scornfully dismissed by some in Whitehall. Without Mandelson's resolute support, it would surely have been blocked. Mandelson made a special effort to approve it, and the purchase of German Parcel was announced in the middle of January 1999. It would be the keystone, in years to come, of a semi-autonomous business (re-christened GLS), one day to represent the single most profitable part of the entire Post Office.

Wretchedly for all concerned, Mandelson himself had by then been swept from office, in the wake of a furore just before Christmas over his personal finances. As with Ridley in July 1990, and Leigh and Heseltine (albeit temporarily) in 1993 – and, indeed, Tony Benn in July 1966 – a supportive Minister at the centre of critical events for the Post Office had made an untimely exit. Mandelson was succeeded at the DTI by Stephen Byers, a Blairite with close links to Number Ten. Byers soon agreed with his officials that it made sense to look again at the possibilities for postal reform, and the publication of the Post Office White Paper was postponed. There followed six months of intense debate over how to instil some of the disciplines of privatization in the absence of the real thing. When the White Paper finally emerged in July 1999, however, it was profoundly different in spirit from Mandelson's Review. Ministers and officials had by then had time to take a longer and harder look at what was happening inside the Post Office. This appears to have heightened their appreciation of the political risks inherent in the liberalization policy – perhaps understandably so, for it was apparent by early 1999 that the Post Office was grappling with an astonishing number of critical initiatives. Under Bain, appointed at the end of a protracted selection process that had straddled the June 1997 election, it seemed to be intent on proving that it could move ahead with or without the benefit of a coherent government policy. The new Chairman himself was a New Zealander by birth, with an accomplished career behind him in the international confectionery and consumer goods markets. He had a strong belief in management's capacity to galvanize the performance of large organizations: on his appointment, he was acclaimed rather waspishly by *The Times* as 'an accountant's accountant and a self-confessed expert on self-governance', about which he had written extensively.[114] Shocked at first by the dearth of any of the normal business processes he had expected to find in place at the Post Office – 'there was no strategy, no real budgeting as such, no planning beyond trying to finish the year on a pinhead as far as borrowings were concerned' – he set out to chivvy the organization into adopting more of a commercial culture.[115] He rallied the Board's support for an ambitious programme of change to tackle the twin challenges of market liberalization and electronic technology. The threat from private-sector couriers was still far easier to apprehend than the menacing implication of e-mails and the internet, but there were droves of consultants on hand to confirm that both phenomena presaged a fundamental break with the past.

Roberts and his senior colleagues responded bravely with a welter of initiatives. Internationally, the German Parcel deal was to be followed over the next two years by eight further acquisitions of parcel-post companies, plus the purchase of local express-mail operators in the US and Singapore as well as Sweden and Germany. Postal liberalization was coming, and the Post Office would be ready for it, as 'a complete distribution company with global reach'.[116] On the domestic front, every single business faced upheaval. There were to be new distribution centres for Parcelforce, new letter delivery systems for Royal Mail (accompanied by a rebuilding of Mount Pleasant, no less), new agreements with the CWU (in pursuit of another fresh start, this time christened 'The Way Forward'), new visions for the Counters business and new geographical boundaries across the country for parcels, mails and Counters. A hugely expensive sorting depot for international mails was to be built near Heathrow with a state-of-the-art computer system (the project's name was 'WAND', for Worldwide Advanced Network Distribution). And for the top-level management structure presiding over all this activity, there was to be the most radical overhaul since Dearing's shake-up of 1986. Between April and October 1999, the Post Office was broken up into ten new business units, each engaging directly with a significant sector of the marketplace. Supporting services were available from a further eleven new units via commercial contracts that allowed these, too, to function as profit centres. All this applied the very latest thinking on optimal corporate structures – evident around this time in many other large organizations, including the BBC and the NHS – and was designed to turn the Post Office into an 'internal marketplace'. It was called 'Shaping for Competitive Success'.[117] This was not to be confused with the 'Competitive Overhead Strategic Structure Programme', the 'Harnessing Technology Project' or the 'Finance Excellence Programme' which ran alongside it, not to mention the installation of an entirely new Group-wide computer system. Topping everything off was a thoughtful re-examination of branding issues. Reflecting on the importance of 'The Post Office' as a brand name for Counters, to set beside the Royal Mail and Parcelforce, it struck the senior team not unreasonably that the time had come to acknowledge the successful evolution of the 1986 Break-Up by restricting the use of 'Post Office' to Counters exclusively. Alongside all their other concerns, they launched a study group to come up with a new umbrella name for the group as a whole.

Mastering an overview of this agenda must have been a formidable undertaking. As the Board Member responsible for strategy, Jerry Cope produced a series of annual corporate plans, each a tour de force of factual compilation and shrewd, wide-ranging analysis.[118] Within the plans and the many papers that went with them to the DTI, both Cope and Roberts stressed repeatedly that success depended not just on the Post Office's own efforts but on the willingness of the Government to be a sympathetic and supportive partner. This does not seem to have been the principal message drawn from their scrutiny of the Corporation by Labour ministers after Mandelson's departure. Instead (to judge from their reaction) they perceived a highly volatile situation, fraught with politically explosive issues. This was compounded by a poor relationship between ministers and the Board: Bain knew that some of Byers' own civil servants were sceptical of their Minister's willingness to take any unpopular decisions, which did nothing to bolster Bain's own confidence in the Government's approach.[119] He himself, meanwhile, failed to inspire much confidence at the DTI that he was sensitive to the politics of postal reform. This can hardly have come as a surprise to officials: Bain had had no previous experience of the UK public sector when they appointed him, and started out as a complete stranger to the ways of Whitehall. These were now telling weaknesses.

One aspect in particular of the Post Office's affairs cast a pall over preparations for the publication of a supposedly seminal White Paper –

the long-gestated automation of the Counters network. When initiated late in 1995, plans to link every post office to a national computer system had envisaged a launch date before the end of 1996. The main contractor was ICL, a UK company that was now part of the Japanese Fujitsu group. The first client was also a partner in the project: the Benefits Agency (BA) acting on behalf of the Department of Social Security (DSS, now stripped of Health). Commissions paid by the BA of about £350m a year comprised by far the largest source of income for the Counters business, and substantial shared savings were eagerly anticipated.[120] The 'Horizon' project involved the installation of computers at 40,000 work-stations across 18,000 post offices, so delays were only to be expected. But it was evident by the autumn of 1997 that software development problems at ICL were going to stretch the timetable to breaking point and perhaps beyond. By then – as an independent report from PA Consultants grimly concluded – all three major parties to the project seemed so firmly committed as to have no practical choice but to persevere with it.

This underestimated the additional strain on the DSS of funding pressures applied by the Treasury. Having ruled that fraud savings could not be treated as cash gains in doing the financial arithmetic, the Treasury set investment parameters that were incompatible with the constant stream of delays from ICL. The Permanent Secretary of the DSS, Ann Bowtell, took the Horizon file home with her for Christmas 1997 and returned in the New Year with a recommendation that the DSS should pull out of the project. Benefit payments through the Counters network should instead be replaced as soon as possible by automated credit transfer through the banking system. Here was the outcome dreaded by Roberts and his Counters team throughout the 1980s, threatening eventually to deprive the business of a third of its revenues. Hand-wringing discussions in search of a workable compromise lasted through the whole of 1998. As costs soared and software bugs went on breeding, the Post Office found itself edged by the Treasury to the sidelines of a dispute with obvious implications for the future of the entire Counters business. Finally, in May 1999, the Government imposed a settlement (of sorts) by which the DSS bowed out as an investment partner but agreed to postpone the first transfer of benefits to ACT until 2003.

This left the Post Office with the unenviable task of deciding whether or not to proceed with the launch, just three months later, of a project on which it was now guaranteed to lose substantial sums of money. Some frantic number-crunching allowed only one conclusion: the losses from a cancellation would be even higher than the losses from going ahead without a DSS contract.[121] The deal was done, and installation of the computers began in September. (Benefits would eventually be paid into personal 'Post Office Card Accounts', which account holders with a POCA card could access via a card machine on the counter of their local post office.) Astonishingly, it was noted by the Board that even at this stage, after four years of development, 'serious doubts over the reliability of the software remained'.[122] The Board had taken some comfort earlier in the crisis from the Post Office's supposedly modest financial exposure in the event of disaster striking. Now that it had struck, the auditors changed their minds. They insisted that the ICL contract was in accounting terms a defunct asset and a massive write-off was needed. An exceptional charge of £571m hit the half-year income statement in November – landing the Post Office with a post-tax loss of £415m for 1999–2000, in shocking contrast with the handsome profits of the 1990s. (See Appendix A, Chart 14.)

Against this toxic background, it is not surprising that ministers and officials at the DTI began to attach a great deal more importance to the future regulation of any Post Office armed with Commercial Freedom. The outcome was a signal shift from the line taken by Mandelson. Publication in July 1999 of the White Paper *Post Office Reform: A World Class Service for the 21st Century* by his successor, Stephen Byers, appeared to be less concerned with Commercial Freedom for the Post Office than with political freedom for ministers – freedom, that is, to distance themselves from the fall-out of any serious mishaps as the Post Office repositioned itself in the marketplace. Of the 188 paragraphs contained in *Post Office Reform*, the great majority were devoted to the future workings of a new Regulator to be called the Postal Services Commission ('Postcomm'), the augmented role of the Post Office Users' National Council – now to be called the Consumer Council for Postal Services, or 'Postwatch' as it was to be universally known – and the relations between the two of them and Whitehall. In designing a new vehicle for the future of the UK's postal services, the Government appeared to have lavished so much attention on the installation of a powerful braking system that it had scarcely bothered at all with the spluttering state of the engine.

What exactly was envisaged as the final status for the Post Office remained tantalizingly unclear. In proposing that it become a public limited company, it could be supposed – as the CWU angrily protested – that privatization still lay around the corner. Parliamentary clearance would not be required for the disposal of shares as part of a joint venture, which also riled the Union. Yet in stipulating that any sale of shares by the Government would be subject to primary legislation in Parliament, the White Paper seemed intent at the same time on impeding the road to privatization. The critical political decisions over how far, and how quickly, liberalization of the postal industry should be allowed to proceed in the UK market were still to be settled. The full implication of this emerged a few months later. One of the few specific liberalization measures in the White Paper was a commitment to cut the price threshold for the letters monopoly from £1 to 50 pence. When ministers gathered at Bournemouth for Labour's 1999 Annual Conference in September, they ran into a fierce campaign against the cut by the CWU. It was only a year since the Union's attack on part-privatization at the last Conference. To avert a full-blown public row, and probably a platform defeat for the Government, Byers had to abandon his monopoly reduction. (It was dropped in October.) This was precisely the kind of clash that the Government hoped to avoid in future, as Byers now pointed out. Issues such as the scope of the postal monopoly, he announced, were no longer to be the Government's responsibility, but would be meticulously determined by the Regulator. Moreover, this would be not a single individual, as for utilities privatized in the past, but a full-blown Commission with a Board of half a dozen members. (Its first Chairman would be Graham Corbett, who had had a crash course on the kind of disasters that could befall the Post Office: he had chaired the interdepartmental committee eventually charged with sorting out the Horizon debacle.) Above all, Postcomm would be wholly independent, at least in theory. And here was the rub. For if it proved to be so in practice – though this went unsaid – the Government would in effect be ceding control over the country's postal system to an untouchable third party. In the process, it would be replacing a monopoly enshrined in law with a licensing system subject to periodic amendment. It would be the end of the regime established in 1635.

It was to be some time before the implications of the Government's bold approach came to be generally appreciated by the public – or, indeed, by the politicians who had themselves masterminded it. But for Roberts and his executive colleagues, the potential threat was immediately apparent. And the prospect of an intrusive regulator – curbing tariff rises and driving down revenues by curtailing (or even abolishing) the barriers against private competition in the postal market – could not have surfaced at a worse moment. With a ghastly suddenness, and more or less coinciding with the passage of the Postal Services Act in July 2000 that enacted most of the White Paper's provisions and set up Post-comm, it became apparent that the run of hugely profitable years through the 1990s had come to an end. In fact, the profitability of the Post Office was on the brink of collapsing. The 1999–2000 financial year ended with an embarrassing net loss – the first since 1975–6 – but this was easily blamed on Horizon. Pre-tax profits before accounting for exceptional items were still a healthy £474m. More pertinent were the emerging forecasts for the outcome of 2000–2001: pre-tax profits looked unlikely to reach much more than £100m. This was less than the £170m or so boost to the P & L statement provided by the continuing holiday on pension contributions to the POSSS, still being renewed annually. In other words, the underlying profitability of the postal services had evaporated.* How could this have happened?

Inland mail volumes, which had grown year after year since 1982, had begun to falter ominously for reasons none could doubt were at least partly linked to the steep rise of e-mail traffic.[123] But this was hardly an abrupt event – and some residual growth was anyway still being achieved. The explanation rather lay in what was happening to costs. Non-staff expenses by the middle of 2000 were running 20 per cent above levels a year earlier. The anticipated savings on several major schemes, including the installation of IMPs in sorting offices, had gone missing. Net wage costs under 'The Way Forward' were proving a cruel disappointment for local managers (though not for the Union). And on top of all the operational setbacks, the P & L was having to foot the bill for all those special projects that could promise only a gradual pay-back. (The one-off costs of 'Shaping for Competitive Success', for example, were estimated at £64m.[124]) Even more important than the cost squeeze that could be itemized by the accountants was a deeper and less palatable truth. Managers at all levels were spending so much time

---

* The actuaries had earlier advised that the holiday might need to be ended in 1997–8 and this looked to be unavoidable in the summer of 1997, when Gordon Brown's first budget abolished the 20 per cent tax relief on dividend payments received by occupational pension funds. The impact on POSSS reduced its funding level from 110 per cent in March 1997 to a notional 99 per cent. But the actuaries allowed the final decision over whether or not to resume contributions to be postponed until September 1998 – by which time a strong investment performance had lifted the funding level back to almost 107 per cent and the holiday was extended until March 2003. (POB (97)59x and POB (98)65x, Post 69/Red Books.) The POSSS and the new PO Pension Scheme funds were merged in 2000–2001, having won several pension industry awards in their final two years apart. The resulting combination was the Royal Mail Pension Plan, or RMPP.

on the myriad reorganizations under way that they had too little time left to focus on controlling basic costs in a rapidly changing environment. The Post Office was facing death by a thousand plans.

Its initial confidence that it could handle several massive changes all at once now began to look more like a disastrous complacency. Had the run of record profits since 1994 bred a hubristic belief that no objectives were too stretching for the Post Office? (Indeed, had the volume growth of the 1990s actually distracted the Post Office from the need to chase mundane cost reforms and basic changes to working practices – both of which might prove far harder to implement in the future, if that volume growth should one day start to sag?) Now the multiple goals it had set for itself proved simply bewildering. Many projects were ailing badly. The WAND project for a Heathrow Worldwide Distribution Centre was starting to look like a magic trick that had gone horribly wrong: its computer systems could not meet the demands made of them, and costs were running far out of control. Just as alarming for the top management, it was impossible for those at the centre of the business to pin down the true scale of the financial reversal. Underlying many of the initiatives since 1997 was a commitment to the decentralization of decision-making. That was the essence of the internal-market philosophy. But 'Shaping for Competitive Success' had left the Post Office looking dangerously beyond anyone's control: the internal contracts simply proved unworkable. For months, no one really knew what was happening to the business at all. Roberts and his immediate lieutenants were in no position to identify all the cost problems, let alone remedy them. As a Financial Overview reported back to the Board in October 2000: 'To date, no mandatory top-down cost reduction action had been instituted, as the Executive Board was preferring to work through the process of the new management model in placing the onus on business units to invoke recovery plans'.[125] In more ways than one, the Post Office's costs were out of control.

9. DATING THE DUTCH

Another interpretation of the mounting crisis was that the Post Office lacked enough entrepreneurial souls to handle the ambitions it had set for itself. Or as Cope frankly acknowledged, in presenting his 2000–2005 Strategic Plan to the Board in March 2000: 'Managerial skills for the envisaged environment were in short supply'. Cope told his

colleagues that the Plan 'highlighted a number of tensions created by the
pace of change in the Post Office's markets on the one hand and the
essentially public sector culture and high fixed costs [of the organiza-
tion] on the other ... [The Post Office retained] a prevailing public
sector ethos to customer service and product development rather than a
commercial, entrepreneurial culture.'[126] Coming more than a decade
after Dearing's observation in 1987 that 'a great opportunity has been
created', this was disappointing to say the least – but the accelerating
liberalization of the world's postal industry had opened up the prospect
of an apocalyptic solution. Perhaps the Post Office could pull off a merger not merely with one of the new couriers, but with one of Europe's
other leading state entities?

It was a notion that had been vaguely aired a few times in recent
years. In May 1997, a Board paper on the Parcels business mooted the
idea of joining forces with the recently formed KPN–TNT of the Netherlands 'probably as part of a wider collaboration involving letters and
even UK operations'.[127] The Dutch were by far the most appealing prospective partner. The German post office was too large; the Scandinavian
offices were too small; and the French had their own ideas on state-
owned businesses. The Dutch operation, on the other hand, looked
ideally complementary. It had a good record of cost-cutting in its small
domestic market. Its profit margins were the best in the industry and its
managers had proved themselves adept in exploiting international
opportunities. The Post Office – running more than 100,000 delivery
rounds a day to 26 million addresses, with a daily letter post of around
75 million items – need have no fear of being overwhelmed by a company based in the Netherlands (pop. 16 million); but it could dream of
being half of the world's leading postal operator outside the US. In
1998, KPN–TNT had spun off its postal business as TPG, still 45 per
cent owned by the Dutch government but now a majority-owned public
company with its own stock exchange listing. This ownership profile
might once have posed a ticklish problem for a Labour government, but
over the course of 1999 it occurred to senior officials at the Treasury
that TPG's status might open up an intriguing way forward. Privatization of the Post Office was out of the question. (As if to confirm as
much, the former CWU leader Alan Johnson was appointed successor
to Ian McCartney as the Post Office's Minister at the DTI in July 1999.
He was adamant in public about the Government's commitment to 100
per cent public ownership.[128]) But perhaps TPG's private-sector status
might offer the UK government another way of arriving at very much

the same destination. True, new regulatory machinery could potentially offer ministers extra protection against postal misadventures. But would it not be so much safer to have the Post Office securely lodged in the private sector via a full-blown merger with a foreign partner already thriving there? The same thought seems to have occurred to some of the brightest merger merchants in the City around this time. Bankers keen to pitch the idea to the Post Office needed first to be sure of the Treasury's support. There was a meeting of minds over the summer.

The bankers, from UBS Warburg, turned up at the Post Office with their slightly breathtaking idea in the autumn of 1999. The Post Office would hive off the Counters network as a separate business that would remain in state ownership. Royal Mail, Parcelforce and German Parcel would then be merged with TPG into a company that would be 50 per cent owned by its UK shareholder(s). Roberts and his Finance Director liked it enough to award the bank an immediate mandate to explore it in detail.* Bankers, lawyers and accountants began the painstaking preparations for a formal approach to be made. By the middle of 2000, though, 'Project Beta' was effectively on hold. The impact of Horizon on the Post Office's finances was one problem. An added twist was that the UBS Warburg team and its leader, David Freud, had meanwhile taken on a mandate to handle the stock market flotation in November 2000 of Deutsche Post. (Roberts was furious over this and came close to firing them, but relented in the end.) For the next few months, other concerns crowded the Post Office's diary. The future of the Counters network was again under intense scrutiny, with the possibility that the Government might back the funding of a 'universal banking' model. Also, and rather more awkwardly, a long-running stand-off between the Post Office and the fledgling Postcomm now came to a head.

By the start of 2001 it had been apparent for months that the two parties had scarcely reconcilable notions of how liberalization of the postal sector ought to unfold. Bain, immensely frustrated over the lack of any real commercial freedom at the Post Office, had found his chairmanship a long and unrewarding slog. Neither he nor anyone else on the Board could see Postcomm's plans as anything but a disaster for the postal service. In January, Members aired among themselves the fantastical notion that they might turn their back on the whole process and actually abandon the process of applying for a postal licence. As the

---

* The Board Member for Finance since 1989 was Richard Close, who sadly died in office in April 2000.

minutes recorded without undue hyperbole, this 'could cause some major constitutional problems ... which would be politically and presentationally difficult for the Government'.[129] The impasse dragged on for another two months, with Postcomm refusing to make any significant changes to the draft licence. By the time the Board Members met again on 13 March, they had steeled themselves for a desperate act of brinkmanship.

They resolved to stop short of announcing a withdrawal from the licensing process, but only just. In accord with a Board decision, Neville Bain later that day sent the Secretary of State one of the more remarkable letters ever to pass between the Post Office and the Government in modern times. The Board, it said, had accepted an analysis showing 'that the Licence [which Postcomm is offering the Post Office] is incompatible with the commercial objectives which have been agreed with the Government as shareholder, including the desirability of taking part in the likely consolidation of the global postal industry in a way that secures value for the UK'.[130] Bain listed a string of conditions that he and his colleagues thought completely unacceptable. These ranged from a lack of any appeal process and an excessive control over the Group's competitive strategy, to the extension of price controls to cover services falling beyond the limits historically defined by the postal monopoly ('in direct contradiction to Government's expressed intentions'). Then came a virtual ultimatum – 'I am therefore writing to inform you that the Board is intending to write to Postcomm on Monday 19th March, withdrawing our Licence application' – followed by a few helpful suggestions as to how this might be averted. Ministers were not impressed. Six days of intense discussion followed, at the end of which the Government made various essentially cosmetic concessions without yielding an inch on the most radical aspects of the licence. Before March was out, the new regulatory regime promised in the 2000 Act was in place, and Postcomm was driving it. The Board had had to give way on most points of substance, and Bain's chairmanship was effectively over (though he remained in post until the end of his contract in December).

Sweeping aside warnings about the negative implications of all this for the Dutch merger idea, the Government turned back to it with renewed enthusiasm. It was now 'Project Olympus', given added potency by the success of the Deutsche Post flotation. (The sale of a 25 per cent stake in DP had been eight times oversubscribed by eager investors.) In the meantime, good relations with the Dutch had been further improved by the successful launch of a small joint venture with them and Singa-

pore Post in international mails. On 1 April 2001, the Post Office
Corporation gave way to a new entity with a fresh name: Consignia plc.
Three weeks later, postal executives and the UBS Warburg team were
sitting down with the Treasury to work out how to push Olympus forward. In early exchanges with TPG in 2000, the Dutch company had
responded positively, but had insisted that no deal would be possible
unless the UK government first reduced its stake in the Post Office to a
minority holding comparable with the Dutch government's stake in
TPG. Word was passed from Number Ten via the Dutch Prime Minister
that this condition would be met:

> [The UK government] fully recognizes that it will need to reduce signifi-
> cantly its shareholding, over a given period, if the joint venture is to succeed.
> And if satisfactory terms on all the other outstanding issues can be agreed
> between the two companies . . . [it] will not let the shareholding issue get
> in the way of a deal. It will be able to make the specific commitments neces-
> sary at the time the deal is announced.[131]

By the time the June 2001 general election was safely past and the Government was ready for formal talks to begin, it was apparent to all
involved that the terms of any prospective deal had already moved significantly in favour of the Dutch. The Post Office's 2000–2001 profits
had ended up at a meagre £64m – despite the ample assistance of the
continuing holiday on pension contributions – and the latest valuation
of Consignia (minus the post offices network) suggested it would be
exchanged for at most a 40 per cent slice of the merged venture. Moreover, the Dutch government had reduced its shareholding in TPG to 35
per cent (and set 10 per cent as its eventual goal). In keeping with the
Prime Minister's word, the Treasury was facing the need to arrange for a
substantial flotation of Post Office shares. Nonetheless, the City professionals were left in no doubt of the Government's desire to press ahead.
The outcome might be sugared in all kinds of ways. The headquarters of
the merged company could be in London. Whatever the complex arithmetic of the equity allocation, it would be presented as a marriage of
equals. Shares sold by the UK government could pass to various trusts –
including, perhaps, a trust holding stock for distribution to employees.
The bankers, anyway, were to leave the PR challenge to Whitehall. Their
main task was to come up with a suitable structure. And if it involved
some complicated agreements – along the lines of existing Anglo-Dutch
giants like Royal Dutch/Shell, say, or Unilever – that might usefully give
past opponents of naked privatization pause for thought.

TPG's management was excited at the prospect of the merger. One of the keenest advocates was its Finance Director, Peter Bakker, who in November 2001 took over the reins in Amsterdam as Chief Executive. The Post Office's negotiating team was led by Roberts, Cope and the newly appointed Finance Director, Marisa Cassoni. Bain took no part in the process, and his departure was widely anticipated. But no permanent successor had yet been identified, and the chairmanship was assigned on an interim basis to another non-executive, Allan Leighton, who had been recruited to the Board only in April 2001, primarily to help improve the retail performance of the Counters network. He took no more of a direct role in the talks than had Bain. The two management teams exchanged reams of data through the last three months of 2001. 'Apollo' (Consignia) and 'Hesperus' (TPG) then convened in London on 10 January 2002 for a first formal planning session, with a view to announcing 'Helios' (their merged company) in mid-March. It was a heady prospect.

Then the talks ran into a problem. Its repeated reorganizations had left the Post Office embarrassingly short of consistently presented data on its past performance. Pro forma historical statements for the current businesses were simply beyond the wit of any accountant to devise, and the Dutch were dismayed to find they therefore had no way of verifying the soundness of the financial projections they had been given. The bankers to TPG, Goldman Sachs, wrote to UBS Warburg late in January with a thirty-page questionnaire, intended as the basis of a searing audit.[132] But the accountants commissioned for the work came away empty-handed. There followed a desperate recalibration of the deal by both parties. The Treasury was so alarmed at the speed with which Consignia's finances were unravelling that it was ready to make huge concessions to keep the deal alive. The Dutch were prepared to continue, but strictly on their own, revised terms – and these left the word 'merger' in place only as a politeness. The Amsterdam-based executives took an uncompromisingly commercial line, as they were obliged to do for the sake of their own shareholders. A formal proposal was tabled by Goldman Sachs on TPG's behalf in the middle of February. It ran tersely through the weaknesses of the target company, for which explicit remedies had to be agreed at the outset. It amounted to a devastating indictment – coming more than three decades after the incorporation of 1969 and twenty years after the Split with British Telecom – of the state of the Post Office as a commercial business. At the core was a brutal rejection of the plausibility of its accounts:

Meaningful historical financial information on [Consignia] is difficult to
obtain. . . . The process of delivery of the financial projections and restructuring plans to [TPG] has demonstrated that [Consignia's] management
does not have the necessary management reporting systems to provide
historic, current and projected financial information.[133]

Heavy injections of cash by the UK government could perhaps compensate for the frailty of the figures. They might even provide some
protection against the unnerving vulnerability of the pension fund.
(After ten years of no corporate contributions to the POSSS, the overall
pension assets were now down to less than 102 per cent of liabilities
and the Dutch were alarmed to find that over 80 per cent of the assets
were held as equities. Stock markets around the world had been dropping steadily since May 2000. Any significant further fall in the value of
Consignia's portfolio might land it with a deficit running into billions of
pounds.)[134] But the dowry demanded by TPG went well beyond the
scope of any cheques from the Treasury.

The Dutch wanted legally binding agreements with the two parties
who were capable of undoing the best-laid plans. The first was Postcomm. The new Regulator had privately expressed support for the deal
in principle, but in January 2002 was not prepared to postpone for more
than a few days the publication of proposals for a sweeping liberalization of the UK market.[135] TPG executives wanted to see a package that
would at least assure them of no surprises for the next five years. The
second potential wrecker was the CWU. In the twelve months to March
2001, Consignia had lost 66,000 employee days to strikes. A further
42,000 had been lost in a single stoppage in May 2001. Half of all the
UK's official strikes were happening at the Royal Mail. An independent
review of the problem had been published in July 2001, acknowledging
'the frankly dire state of industrial relations which has developed in
many of its workplaces'.[136] Bakker and his colleagues ran a postal business that had seen not one single strike since 1983. They demanded a
five-year collective labour agreement with the CWU, backed by financial
arrangements that would inflict a penalty on employees for any breach
of contract. No doubt they were right to believe the success of any merger would be dependent on the goodwill of the Union at all levels. Yet, as
of February 2002, no attempt had yet been made to alert the Union's
membership to what was afoot, presumably because the risks of premature disclosure were judged too great. (Even a mild reference in Labour's

June 2001 election manifesto to 'alliances and joint ventures' for the Post Office had drawn some hostile fire.) This left government ministers and Consignia managers scarcely any time at all to pull off an unprecedented breakthrough with Union leaders, if the latter were to be persuaded of the merger's merits in time for an agreement within days. DTI officials prepared speaking notes for some lavishly choreographed briefing sessions. These would appeal to the CWU to see the historic importance of the proposed transaction. It would mark the formal demise of the centuries-old Post Office, but would open up a far more secure future for its customers and employees alike.

The sessions never happened. At some point around the end of February, Peter Bakker and his colleagues decided that Olympus was after all a mountain they could not climb. The rebuff, with only weeks to go before the planned announcement of the deal, came as a rude shock to government ministers. Tony Blair summoned the Interim Chairman to Downing Street and asked him to make a candid assessment of the transaction. Leighton was a businessman renowned for his part in the turnaround of Asda, once an ailing supermarket chain and now a leader in its industry. He also had a reputation for blunt speaking. He returned to Downing Street just days later and told the Prime Minister that Olympus was a deal that could not be done.[137] Consignia was losing millions of pounds a week, and had no cash reserves, no reliable accounts and no credible forecasts. In the most unlikely event that the Dutch were to buy it and launch a rescue programme, Leighton then added for good measure, the result would surely be a complete stoppage by the workforce and a halt to the mails – just in time to coincide in June 2002 with the celebration of the Queen's Golden Jubilee. Blair had no interest in testing the truth of this bleak prediction. Yet he and his ministers were now faced with a Post Office in total financial disarray. Five years of frenetic reorganizations had reduced it to a state of virtual collapse. Blair had no choice but to order a complete rethink of the Government's approach. This would entail putting Consignia under fresh management. In the circumstances, there was really only one man to whom the Government could turn.

14

No end of a crisis,

2002–10

Dear Sir, I am sending to you my voice . . .
so that postmen, seven hours all weekday dawns, can walk the shortcuts
    of small towns
carrying these fly-wing weights, the dried leavings of my nights.
Whistling spirits of the written world,
who set out when the road has nothing to be seen by but a streetlight's
    glass eye,
but their feet can write the route with eyes shut.
Think what they glimpse of us, still in slippers, in warm furred interiors –
illegible creatures, as we exist, if we exist at all between letters.

                  Alice Oswald, *In Praise of Postmen* (2002)

I. BACK FROM THE BRINK

Any attempt to set the events of recent years in a historical perspective
may seem foolhardy; but so much has happened since 2002 that even
after ranging over more than five centuries this history would be incomplete if it stopped at the outset of the last decade. There have been
endless echoes of the past. One of Allan Leighton's first acts as Chairman was to turn for help to McKinsey, the consultancy that had delved
so deeply into the operations of the Post Office in the 1960s. Summarizing the strategic implications of its initial study, presented as 'Project
Acorn' in July 2002, McKinsey might almost have quoted verbatim
from its report of August 1965. The message was equally terse. 'Royal
Mail . . . presently makes no money in aggregate and is about to be
threatened right across its business system . . . The Royal Mail's current
organization, structure and style are major impediments to taking
decisive action and [to] an integrated approach to resolving these

issues . . .'[1] The line of wise men chairing investigative committees stretching back through Carter and Priestley to Bridgeman and his Edwardian precursors acquired a fresh name with the submission in 2008 of yet another independent review, presided over by a former Deputy Chairman of the communications regulator Ofcom, Richard Hooper. Like the Carter Report, the Hooper Review bristled with do-or-die prescriptions, and was refreshed with a formal Update in September 2010. And throughout the period – usually in private but occasionally in public, too – politicians wafted the prospect of privatization as their final goal. Not that this could be inferred from their parties' election manifestoes, which in general stuck to the party line taken on the Post Office in earlier decades. The Tories remained discreetly silent; Labour went on enthusing over the potential for a People's Bank within the Post Office while retaining the Royal Mail 'in public ownership'; and the Liberal Democrats – like the Liberals under Lloyd George in 1929 – called for a reshaping of the ownership structure. It seemed appropriate that the 2010 coalition government's bid to reopen the route to privatization should be led by its Liberal Democrat ministers.

Plus ça change, however, has not been the hallmark of the recent past. Events since 2002 have diminished the status of the old monopoly-based Royal Mail founded by Charles I and have threatened its survival as the kind of national postal service inherited from the twentieth century. Its finances have been battered and desperately stretched, its UK monopoly has been superseded and its business volumes have fallen into a steep and continuing decline: the average daily mailbag – comprising all letters, packets and parcels – peaked in 2005 at just over 80 million items and has since then contracted in six years by more than a fifth, to 62 million, as a consequence of the digital revolution and the dramatic migration of social and 'transactional' letters to websites, e-mails and text messaging. Even at the start of 2002, the gravity of the impending crisis – though not, perhaps, the full scale of it – was already well apparent to Leighton. He could recall being shown elaborate management papers in his short time as a non-executive, presenting a 'Traffic Lights' analysis of the business. Each operation had its own appropriate signal. Leighton knew he was expected to admire the sophistication of it all. What struck him far more forcibly was that almost all the lights were on 'red'.[2] Once the collapse of Project Olympus had alerted the Prime Minister to this, Leighton was in a position to lay down his own terms for the chairmanship that the Government pressed him to accept. He demanded an unequivocal promise that he would have a free hand to do whatever he thought necessary to rescue the situation. He would be issuing orders from a burning deck. There would be no scope for debate, let alone direct interference by ministers or their officials. He would also be running the business as a fully commercial entity, with the management rather than Government to be held publicly responsible for all the consequences. Blair and his Secretary of State at the DTI, Patricia Hewitt, assured Leighton these terms were understood and accepted. Here was the kind of contract that had been denied to William Barlow by Thatcher's Cabinet in 1979, precipitating his sudden exit. And as if to confirm a sense of the present catching up with the past, the man who had followed Barlow was soon paying the first of many visits to the new Chairman's office. 'Ron Dearing used to come and see me regularly', recalled Leighton. 'He was always extremely supportive: we were kindred spirits. I think Ron saw that I was going to try to execute what he had proposed doing after 1986.'[3] When it came to making a personal impact, though, Leighton was in a class of his own, as the rank and file of the Royal Mail quickly discovered.

'Beauty' Blackwood once appeared early in the morning at the Mount Pleasant sorting centre: as Secretary to the Post Office, it might be recalled, he turned up there in July 1890 to forestall the threat of a walk-out by London's postmen. Dawn visits by the head of the service had assuredly not been a regular feature of life at Mount Pleasant in the twentieth century. So when the doorman at the security gate of that huge depot found himself stirred just after five o'clock one morning in April 2002 by an unshaven figure in an overcoat claiming to be the Chairman, the immediate response naturally entailed a profane reference to Napoleon Bonaparte. After a series of telephone calls and a disbelieving reappraisal of the situation, Leighton was eventually admitted. It was the first of many unannounced visits that he regularly made to the workplace through the next seven years.* His determination to engage personally with employees at every level was partly aimed at reviving the morale of the workforce, badly dented by media coverage of the collapse in profits. It also reflected his lifetime conviction, buoyed up by an extremely successful business career to date, that those at the coalface in any business knew the most about it. He set out to ask

---

* Word of this disconcerting habit spread quickly. After his first few months, Leighton was rarely challenged again to prove his identity. Instead, he was invariably greeted with exactly the same five words wherever he appeared. 'It was always the same. I'd say: "Hi, how are you doing?" and they'd say: "Oh shit, it's the Chairman!"' (Allan Leighton, interview with author, 27 May 2010.)

ordinary postmen and their supervisors what was going on – and they were not slow to respond. This led to some surprising revelations. It turned out, for example, that the calibre of shoes purchased for postmen had been downgraded in 2001 as part of a cost-cutting exercise. Many individuals had found the inferior style uncomfortable and had switched to trainers. This had prompted a spate of disciplinary actions, since trainers were disallowed under the uniform rules. Worse was to follow, when Leighton took a closer interest in the footwear. 'They told me there were 18,000 pairs of size 8 shoes in a Swindon warehouse, purchased because that was the average size and a very good discount had been available. But that was the shoe budget gone – so for months only size 8s had been available.'[4] Other embarrassing disclosures included news (or so it was said) of 20,000 new bicycles in the same warehouse, which had reportedly been there for ten years. As the anecdotal evidence mounted of a business struggling to cope, the consultants from McKinsey were sleuthing their way to the same conclusion. The twenty or so business units launched by 'Shaping for Competitive Success' were, perforce, all flying blind. Supposedly set up as independent profit centres, their finances depended overwhelmingly on costs allocated to them by others, over which they themselves had no control whatever. Far more serious than surplus stashes of shoes and cycles was the disclosure that the Royal Mail had no idea where it was making or losing money. A painstaking reconstruction of its economics by McKinsey calculated the net profit on revenues of £5.7bn to be more or less zero. Leighton managed to identify an operating loss of £67m for 2001–2, deducted a £250m benefit to the income statement from the still continuing pension-contributions holiday and came up with a figure transmutable, for PR purposes, into the phrase 'losing a million a day'. He never doubted that a wholly fresh start was required.

It duly followed. The Consignia name was dumped in favour of the Royal Mail Group. Permission for this had to be obtained from Buckingham Palace. Leighton managed this within weeks, usefully embellishing his reputation as a man who could get things done. (The Queen, it was said, had pointedly remarked of the second name change in two years that it was nice to be asked.) 'Shaping for Competitive Success' was slammed hard into reverse, as the Group was consolidated once again into Letters, Parcelforce, GLS (formerly German Parcel) and the Counters network of Post Office Ltd. An outsider with forty years' experience of retail banking with the Midland Bank and HSBC, David Mills, was immediately hired as the new Managing Director of Post

Office Ltd. At Leighton's first meeting with 150 or so of the top managers, he announced that a third of them would be gone within twelve
months. Plans were laid to cut by half the fourteen existing management layers between the Chairman and the humblest postman. By the
time the Annual Report for 2001–2 was published, Leighton had already
launched a 'Three Year Renewal Plan'. The auditors had been enjoined
to bless exceptional charges of £1.1bn against the financial year just
ended. This produced a post-tax loss of £945m – leaving the loss of
1999–2000 far behind – but it provided some essential reserves to cope
with the heavy costs to come. These would have to provide, inter alia,
for 30,000 redundancies. To no one's surprise, one of the first to go was
John Roberts, who had served as Chief Executive since October 1995,
though his departure was amicable enough. It was reported that one
prominent MP had described Roberts as 'just too nice to do the job',
which the *Guardian* opined was 'known to be a common view in Whitehall'.[5] Most of his former colleagues would follow him over the next
two years, including (to the Royal Mail's detriment, as many thought)
Jerry Cope. As the core of his new management team, Leighton picked
one seasoned professional from the industry and one surprising newcomer. The first was Elmar Toime, who had just completed almost a
decade at the helm of New Zealand Post and was familiar with best
practice in the industry – although, as the wags pointed out, NZ Post
handled roughly the same volumes as the sorting depot at Reading. (He
nonetheless collected an annual salary of £500,000, which in his first full
year was accompanied by a bonus of £150,000; John Roberts in 2001–2
had received a salary of £212,000 and no bonus at all.) The second
new hire was Adam Crozier, an executive with an impeccable if eclectic
consumer marketing background. Originally trained (like Leighton) at
Mars, Crozier was a former Saatchi & Saatchi advertising executive
and the ex-CEO of the Football Association. He was a soft-spoken
Scot, and his calm demeanour contrasted from the start with the Chairman's own ebullience. He and Toime joined Leighton, as Group Chief
Executive and Executive Deputy Chairman respectively, early in 2003.

Together they rescued the Group from certain collapse. The Board
was advised by the auditors in May 2002 that unless letters of assurance
with promises of additional funding could be obtained from the Government, the 2001–2 accounts could not be signed off for the business
as a going concern. Disconcerting talks with auditors and lawyers were
a feature of the next twelve months. Thereafter, the retreat from the
brink began. It was not apparent for some time: indeed, ailing measures

of performance attracted public hostility and savage media criticism throughout 2004. But the Government held its nerve and Leighton's team was left to its own agenda. Initiatives that had been postponed, reconsidered and shelved again for years – finally closing down the remaining, shrunken TPO operations, for example – were at long last pushed through. Conversely, all those castles in the air erected in the late 1990s – notably the internal marketplace, with its twenty-one profit centres – were unceremoniously demolished. Non-executive but always a forceful presence, Leighton led a return to basic commercial goals, to be simply stated and then pursued single-mindedly. The Group's entire transport network was rationalized, with the romance of the TPO trains abandoned in favour of a much heavier reliance on more efficient airline services. The mainstay of the Royal Mail, its Letters business, was transformed with new sorting routines and delivery patterns: the 'Once Over the Ground' plans formulated in the early eighties – and first mooted by Benn in 1965 – were at last enacted in 2003–4 as 'Single Day Delivery'.[6] The Post Office network was reduced with the elimination of 3,500 sub-offices, but closures were planned with an awareness of basic retailing skills that left the network as a whole far less impaired than might have been expected on the evidence of earlier, much more modest closure programmes. The workforce at Parcelforce, faced with a blunt choice between a radical reconstruction of the operation's finances or liquidation, adjusted to fierce cost reductions that had been ducked in the early nineties. GLS, encouraged to expand in the pan-European market, began to emerge as the most profitable parcels business in the entire postal industry.

After the kitchen sink loss of 2001–2, the Group began to claw its way back to operational profitability. This was now to be defined, moreover, without the benefit of the pension contributions holiday, which was finally discontinued in 2003–4. Even setting aside the pension complications, disentangling the profit numbers for the years of the Renewal Plan and its aftermath was still no task for the faint-hearted. A welter of exceptional items and the adoption of a new basis of accounting – switching to 'IFRS' rules in place of 'UK GAAP' – made it impossible at the time to quantify the Group's progress with much confidence.* But

---

* During the financial year 2005–6, the Group adopted the International Financial Reporting Standards (IFRS) finally endorsed by the European Union in 2004. Its conventions, each known by a numbered International Accounting Standard (IAS), replaced the Generally Accepted Accounting Principles used previously. IAS 19 on Employee Benefits entailed some modest changes to accounting for the pension deficit – and the adoption in future of

at least there was every appearance of a restored financial viability, and this was a vital tonic for the confidence of the Group in general. It suggested encouragingly that a qualitative transformation had at last been begun. A postal business still seen five years earlier as essentially a legacy of the civil service even by its own leading lights – nowhere more eloquently than in Cope's strategy papers of 2000 – had started to think of itself as a genuinely commercial organization. It was a process of change impressively orchestrated away from the limelight by Crozier as Chief Executive – Toime struggled with his role and left in November 2004 – with extensive support from McKinsey: the consultants produced a string of trenchant reports under a project leader, Michael Mire, who in many ways picked up roughly where his erstwhile colleague Roger Morrison had left off in 1967. Presiding over it all was a Board with several forceful non-executives who were not afraid of lively debates over the future direction of the Group.

Progress in industrial relations was in some ways no less opaque than in the Post Office's finances, but here too a new era seemed about to begin. The independent review of 2001, chaired by Lord Sawyer, had spoken of the need for 'a fundamental change in the industrial relations climate'.[7] The Dutch in 2002 had wasted no time deciding this represented, for them, too great a challenge. Leighton's confidence that he and Crozier could meet it was central to his chairmanship. In keeping with his instinctive belief in the importance for any business of winning the commitment of its rank-and-file employees, Leighton put a premium on achieving a direct rapport between management and the workforce. This meant taking an imaginative approach to all personnel matters – with constant briefings, financial incentives and easy access to those at the top. ('Tell Allan' and 'Tell Adam' campaigns promised e-mailed replies from them once they had been told.) It emphatically did not mean relying on the branch channels of the CWU, which Leighton and Crozier were prepared to step around if they thought the Union was being obstructive. But direct communication with the workforce had been the Union's exclusive preserve for generations. A clash was inevitable, and did not take long to arrive. In June 2003, the CWU held a ballot to give the leadership a mandate for a national strike, the first since 1996, in support of a rejected wage claim. The Union was startled by Leighton's response. He proceeded to write a weekly letter to every

---

an item known, appropriately enough, as SORIE (a Statement of Recognized Income and Expenditure) noting actuarial gains and losses on invested pension funds.

postal worker, sent to their home and setting out in blunt, colloquial fashion ('this was *Sun*-speak, not a corporate letter') why they should vote against the Executive's recommendation.[8] This continued for three weeks, and was accompanied by a barrage of video presentations in every sorting depot in the country. The CWU was outraged at the tactic – and totally nonplussed. It ended in a famous, some would say notorious, defeat for the Union. Strikes followed, but they were 'unofficial' and collapsed a few weeks later. It was a notable coup for the management. The Government discreetly appealed to Leighton not to rub in the implications too ruthlessly. (In his time at the Asda supermarket chain, Leighton had taken a combative line towards the retail workers' union, USDAW, encouraging a sharp fall in union membership among Asda employees.) Heeding the request, he drew back from seizing the moment to curb all practical and financial assistance for the Union. The CWU was allowed to go on relying on the Royal Mail, for example, to deduct members' subscriptions via the payroll system. Local officials went on being released from postal duties on full or part pay, as for decades past, so that they could attend to Union business.

The result, for a while, was promising. Unofficial strikes dropped off sharply. Managers and Union reps at a local level began working together more effectively than for many years, exchanging tales of Leighton's latest bold foray as they went along.* The Union's Executive under the General Secretary, Billy Hayes, elected as Hodgson's successor in 2001, had been put on notice that Leighton would take every opportunity to win over the workforce by breaking its loyalty to the CWU. When the Renewal Plan was successfully concluded in 2005, Leighton was able to show there was more to this new approach than just his personal charisma. Under a bonus scheme called 'Share in Success', set up in 2002, the return to operational profitability produced a payment of around £1,500 for every employee. (It was in fact much the kind of arrangement that Viscount Wolmer had pressed on the Bridgeman Committee back in 1932, to no avail. The long-forgotten Wolmer's

---

* A typical tale recounted the time Leighton was travelling to the Midlands by car with his Human Resources Director, when he heard by telephone that postmen at a large sorting depot near their route had taken unofficial action. A picket line had been set up there. Leighton cancelled his schedule and drove straight to the depot. After those on the picket line had explained their case to him, Leighton stood on a box and told them: 'If I'd been treated like that, I'd have gone on strike too.' The story was often repeated within the Union; and the unit's manager was reportedly sacked shortly afterwards. (Billy Hayes, interview with author, 31 August 2010.)

enthusiasm for profit-sharing had at last found an effective champion.) The CWU had little option but to go along with the new mood. Its warnings that any lay-off programme would be fought to the last ditch had left it looking badly wrong-footed: in reducing the workforce by 30,000 to around 193,000, redundancy packages were made so generous that postmen queued up for them, just as Leighton had predicted. Nor could the Union turn to Labour ministers for help. True to his word in 2002, Blair ensured there was none of the notorious back-door collusion that had seen Tom Jackson making regular visits to Number Ten in the Wilson/Callaghan era.

However, Labour's readiness to stand behind Leighton and his colleagues in defiance of union pressure was not without its limits. This became abruptly apparent in 2005. Leighton and Crozier had stressed to ministers since 2003 that in their view there was only one sustainable business model for the Royal Mail: it would need to be privatized. They had pressed the Government repeatedly for a commitment to this policy, and repeatedly they had been promised that it would be formally adopted as soon as circumstances allowed. So the relevant wording of Labour's manifesto for the May 2005 general election came as a nasty jolt: 'we have given the Royal Mail greater commercial freedom and have no plans to privatise it. Our ambition is to see a publicly owned Royal Mail fully restored to good health . . .'[9] The postal workers' union had signed up to the so-called Warwick Agreement the previous July, by which Labour had secured union funding for its 2005 campaign. The wording in the prospectus about the Royal Mail was the price of the CWU's support.[10] Labour policy advisers privately assured Leighton and Crozier that the phrasing was loose enough to leave plenty of room for a future sale of a minority equity stake.

Leighton set out in 2006 to build on his 'Share in Success' scheme by offering shares in Royal Mail to all its employees. He proposed to the DTI that a fifth of the equity be distributed, under a plan resembling the ownership scheme run for its employees by the John Lewis retail chain. This brought his relations with the CWU to a new low. The Union was flatly opposed to the idea, fearing it would be a precursor to full privatization, and soon found common cause with the Treasury in resisting it. Much to his disappointment, Leighton had to settle in February 2007 for a 'phantom' arrangement, the 'ColleagueShare Plan', offering an equivalent bonus prospect with no distribution of real equity. This time it was the Union bosses to whom the Government made a discreet appeal for magnanimity. But Union members – and in particular the branch officials within the London region, where the commitment to hallowed working practices was strongest – were in no mood now to compromise over long-standing objections to other emerging management goals. When these were spelt out in the early summer of 2007, the Union responded with a second ballot for national strike action. Leighton believed the 'ColleagueShares', though second best to real ones, would weigh heavily against a positive vote: employees, after all, still stood to gain over £5,000 each by 2012 if management's plans were allowed to progress smoothly. But he had underestimated the resilience of the Union and its deep roots in the workplace. To Leighton's great disappointment, the vote produced a 77.5 per cent majority for action. A series of national strikes followed between June and October. He and Crozier responded combatively, warning that no overtime would be paid for clearing post-strike backlogs. (And this time, unlike in 1988, the ban was comprehensively enforced.) The crisis was brought to a close only after intervention by the new Labour Prime Minister, Gordon Brown. It left behind a residue of bitterness on both sides, with Leighton openly rueing his earlier decision not to mount a full-blown offensive against the Union after the ballot of 2003. Meanwhile the non-intervention pact struck between Leighton and Blair in 2002 was a thing of the past: the Brown government opted for a different stance.

Taken in the round, and despite the setbacks to the Chairman's own hopes of privatization, the accord reached between Leighton and Blair in 2002 had paid off handsomely for Royal Mail over the past five years. Virtually insolvent at the outset, the Group reported operating profits of more than £300m in 2004–5 and the same again in 2005–6. Reported net profits for the two years were £151m and £395m respectively. It could plausibly be argued that all of its main businesses were at least making a positive contribution to the bottom line, and no Royal Mail Board had been able to make that claim for years. The flames on the deck had been dowsed. Briefly, there was a danger of this being mistaken for the end of the crisis. As Crozier recalled: 'We made a mistake describing the Three Year Plan as a Renewal when it should have been called a Rescue.'[11] In reality, the task of modernizing the Group had hardly yet begun. With Leighton now taking more of a back-seat role – and increasingly preoccupied with other business interests in Canada – Crozier prepared for the next stage. This would involve many more redundancies again and an assault on the more egregious restrictive practices in the workplace, to prepare for a basic reappraisal of the

Royal Mail's future. He and his colleagues had to begin reassessing the products and services with which the Group was planning to respond to the impact of the digital revolution – in a marketplace where the fulfilment of home-shopping orders over the internet seemed set eventually to become as important to Royal Mail as the traditional bulk-mail business of letters from banks and utilities. Most pressing of all in 2005–7, management had to persuade the Government of the case for making a substantial investment in new machinery and facilities. The need for it was not hard to illustrate. In comparison with its leading European counterparts, Royal Mail was still a long way off the pace of change in the industry. Automation in its seventy or so Mail Centres, for example, now allowed about 70 per cent of letters to be sorted for individual postmen's walks, but best practice with 'walk-sorting' in Germany was more like 90 per cent. Even more glaring was a far bigger discrepancy at the local level. British postmen were still sorting their own mail by hand at the start of the day, much as they had always done. 'Delivery prep' took up many hours a week, well over a third of the total, and the associated labour costs were still as core to the economics of the Royal Mail as ever. But thanks to the postcode, machines existed to handle this work too. In the best European operations, local 'walk-sequencing' machines were almost as entrenched as walk-sorting machinery. Royal Mail had yet to install a single one. There were many other dispiriting contrasts to be confronted – and Whitehall now acknowledged them. There was broad backing for Crozier's modernization plans. Up to £1.2bn would be made available as a loan to the Group on commercial terms, and there was formal agreement that the Government would not be seeking to receive a dividend.[12] In fact, at this point midway through the decade, the Group just needed a fair wind behind it, as it set out on a modernization course already well charted by the Germans, the Dutch and several others.

2. POCA, PENSIONS AND POSTCOMM

Alas for Crozier and his colleagues, the wind now dropped alarmingly, with a sudden and dramatic downturn in the volume of addressed letters within the UK, as across most of the Western world. It slid down by over 3 per cent in 2006–7, which immediately looked like the start of the terminal decline in the basic demand for postal services that some business strategists within the Post Office had predicted in the earliest days of e-mails.[13] Changes in the annual volume of letters had historically tracked changes in the general economic growth rate quite closely. Coinciding almost exactly with the turn of the Millennium, the two rates of change had parted company: by early 2007 they were far apart and heading ominously in opposite directions. (See Appendix A, Chart 15.) This was much more serious than the flattening out of letter volumes in the late 1970s, which had looked at the time like the start of a long, slow decline. Industry analysts across Europe began predicting seismic falls over the next five years. Payment transactions via the internet threatened huge swathes of business mail. Social mail, some warned, was destined for virtual extinction. The volume of text messages sent in the UK in 2007 jumped 36 per cent higher than the previous year's total, up to an extraordinary 59 billion texts.[14] As telephones had once overtaken the demand for telegrams, so e-mails and the internet were, it seemed, finally catching up with letters. Volume again dropped by over 3 per cent in 2007–8, even before the onset of recession in 2008 and the international banking crisis. At this juncture, faced with 'structural decline' on the one hand and the worsening business environment on the other, the Royal Mail Group found its predicament made immeasurably more difficult in ways that make a pointed nautical metaphor hard to avoid: if the sails of the Group were starting to flap for a lack of wind, there was soon water rushing in through some gaping shot-holes below the waterline.

Early in 2006 the Government informed the Post Office of its intention from 2008 to encourage a faster move away from the payment of state benefits via Post Office products – primarily the Post Office Card Account (POCA) – and towards more reliance on the banking system. It was the long-awaited sequel to the Horizon debacle of 1999. The decision presaged a reduction over time in the number of POCA cardholders from about 4 million to just a small rump of customers with no other means of accessing their benefit and pension payments. Given the importance of POCA-payment commissions to most sub-postmasters, this was obviously a policy initiative with serious consequences for the Post Office. The full impact of the proposal was really grasped only after its managers calculated that the current network of about 14,500 sub-offices – already down from about 18,000 at the turn of the century – might have to shrink to about 4,000 if it was to remain financially viable without a direct government subsidy. Nothing in the postal arena ever concentrated politicians' minds better than the prospect of post office closures in their own constituencies.* Long discussions ensued. The search for a mutually acceptable trade-off between a closure programme and a future subsidies budget dragged on for most of 2006. Literally dozens of permutations were examined. The Trade and Industry Secretary, Alistair Darling, finally announced in December 2006 that £1.7bn would be set aside for five annual subsidies and for compensation payments to the dispossessed sub-postmasters of 2,500 sub-offices that would face closure in 2007–8. The POCA system did indeed see a gradual decline in its customer numbers in the years that followed – but by stepping back from a sudden closure of the system, and staging a more gradual migration of benefit payments to the banks, the Government had at least managed to avert disaster for the Post Office. In the meantime, another potentially crippling blow had hit the Group as a whole.

Just as the occasional Cassandra had warned in the 1990s, the main pension fund (now aggregated as the RMPP) had taken a series of knocks in declining financial markets, with results that now threatened to overwhelm the Group's P & L statement. For thirteen years until 2003, substantial surpluses on the fund had prompted the Corporation – at the actuaries' behest – to suspend its cash contributions to the pension pot. But an actuarial valuation of the fund in the autumn of 2003 recorded assets worth only 91 per cent of liabilities, implying a deficit of £2.5bn.[15] As already noted, the 'holiday' was declared over. Regular contributions were resumed in 2003–4, with a payment of £243m. In addition, the Group now felt it necessary to make a 'deficit adjustment' which added £132m to that year's bill. The net effect was an abrupt swing into heavy pension expenses, exacerbated by the cost of the redundancies negotiated during the Renewal Plan. The total bill went on climbing slowly for a couple of years. Then, in the autumn of 2006, the actuaries produced another valuation for the fund as of March 2006. Its assets were now short of meeting liabilities by £3.4bn. This triggered a sobering reappraisal of the situation, which left the long holiday of 1990–2003 feeling like a distant memory. It was decided that the deficit repair payments should be set at £260m a year for the next seventeen years, index-linked to keep up with inflation. In addition, the

---

* It would need another whole chapter to take account properly of the social importance of sub-post offices. With the decline of public transportation in many rural areas and the growing complexity of state bureaucracy, especially for older people left behind by on-line applications, the attentive figure behind the post office counter in many a village shop provided a help and comfort to local customers that went far beyond the sale of stamps – as no constituency MP in the land could afford to ignore.

actuaries advised that – faced with a much lower discount rate, raising the present value of future payments, as well as the rising longevity of the average employee – the regular yearly contributions should now equate to 20 per cent of total pensionable pay, rather than just over 12 per cent as previously. The combined impact was a steep jump in the annual cost of servicing the pension plans, to more than £700m. The defined-benefits scheme was closed to new entrants from January 2008 and replaced by a defined-contributions scheme. Even so, Royal Mail was to be burdened with an annual bill of around £800m for the fore-seeable future. And if asset values in the markets were to sink again, this figure might still fall short of what was needed.

Even this financial calamity paled during 2007 by comparison with a third source of trouble. Postcomm's firepower seems to have come as a surprise to Labour ministers.[16] In 1999 and 2000, they had judged tough regulation to be a sound policy for the long term – a sort of proxy for the benefits of privatization – but had given too little thought to what it might entail in the nearer term. (Just like the Whigs and uniform penny postage in 1840, to draw a charitable comparison.) In the event, the initial tensions between the regulator and Royal Mail after 2002 soon led to acrimony and eventually to a state of daggers-drawn confrontation. Blair's assurance to Leighton in the spring of 2002 that he would be completely free of interference from Westminster turned out not to have been quite the ticket that Leighton had supposed at the time. There was little real difficulty over Postcomm's strictures aimed at ensuring the continuation of the universal-service obligation, but regulatory control over pricing was a much more inflammatory issue. Above 80 per cent of Royal Mail's revenues came from operations made subject to price controls. Regulation applied not just to its 'monopoly services' but also to many services faced with unregulated competitors. (People still spoke of the Royal Mail's monopoly, though the powers it now enjoyed courtesy of its Postcomm licence were, as noted, very different in law from the statutory powers it had enjoyed before the Act of 2000.) And tariff pricing was to be governed by a formula, familiar in the regulatory world, which involved Postcomm passing judgement on the efficiency of Royal Mail's operations.* This in time guaranteed plenty of friction: many oddities of the postal service that had been more or less ignored during

---

* Prices would be allowed to rise at the rate of the Retail Price Index (RPI) less a percentage rate (x) reflecting the assessed efficiency of the underlying operation. The greater its efficiency, the lower the 'x' factor and the higher the permissible price rise.

the era of rapid growth since the early 1980s, not least its bizarre over-time rituals and rigid manning practices, were by 2006 starting to look like crazy inefficiencies. Above all, however, it was the statutory power of the Regulator actively to promote competition at the incumbent's expense that really poisoned the atmosphere. To many people's sur-prise, this objective came to weigh as heavily with the Regulator as the protection of the universal-service obligation. Postwatch, the con-sumer protection body, took a different view that was often far more sympathetic to Royal Mail's predicament. Postcomm brusquely elbowed Postwatch aside, insisting that policies to force open the marketplace for new entrants were no more than a fulfilment of the obligation laid on EU member states by a 'Third Directive' of 2002. All were called upon stead-ily to curb the franchise of their remaining state postal monopolies. Elsewhere in Europe, though, moves in this direction – where they happened at all – were invariably implemented by mutual consent after detailed commercial negotiation. Given a deadline of 2010, later extended, there was no need for haste. Royal Mail's counterparts across the Continent therefore watched in amazement as its domestic business began to be dismantled by Postcomm, supposedly in deference to the Brussels ruling. Few politicians at Westminster took much notice. Most, indeed, seemed intent on staring in the opposite direction.

Competitors delighted at this turn of events included TNT and DHL, subsidiaries respectively of the Dutch and German post offices. Other aspiring rivals were home-grown companies such as UK Mail, the larg-est independent postal operator, which had hired Bill Cockburn as a non-executive director in 2002. (Retired Royal Mail employees and Whitehall officials with postal expertise found themselves greatly in demand as the market began to open up.) None of these businesses had any local network, and they could not (as yet, anyway) challenge the 'last mile' delivery business of the Royal Mail. But Royal Mail's other core activity, which could be regarded as separate, was its 'consolida-tion' business – collecting, sorting and transporting mails. If it were obliged to make its own 'last mile' network available to others, at an attractive 'wholesale access price', then efficient competitors might be able to make a decent living in large sectors of this 'consolidation' mar-ketplace. This, in 2004, was precisely what Postcomm ordained should happen. It opened a gateway into the wholesale market for specialized operators, with no delivery capabilities of their own but high-tech sort-ing services attuned to the needs of the all-important business customer. This had been the approach taken by the telecoms Regulator, Ofcom, to

British Telecom, which had been forced after 1984 to provide access to its local telephone network. Despite the successes of the Three Year Renewal Plan, however, Royal Mail was still far less robust than had been the newly privatized telecoms business. The result, for Royal Mail, was a disaster – much, in fact, as Neville Bain had warned in his letter to Byers of March 2001. About a third of its total revenues in 2006 came from consolidation activities on behalf of bulk-mail customers, who until that year were more or less totally dependent on its de facto monopoly service. Postcomm predicted a slow erosion of this dominance, against a background of rising aggregate demand. Its expectations were confounded on both counts. Aggregate volume began declining. And once the new competitors began to sell their services aggressively, in 2007, Royal Mail's share of the market plunged. Over the next four years, it was to drop from 100 per cent to below 40 per cent.

Nor was the damage restricted simply to loss of revenues. When Royal Mail lost a bulk-mail contract with a large corporate account, it generally lost all contact with that customer. It was losing relationships with hundreds of its largest accounts. Given their disproportionate importance to Royal Mail, the 'access ruling' by Postcomm struck at the sustainability of its whole business. The burden on managers' time was another heavy cost. From 2006, Crozier and some of his immediate colleagues were spending at least a third of their time locked in bitter wrangling over 'upstream-access headroom', 'downstream-access prices' and other such thorny issues that had suddenly become matters of the gravest consequence. Most astounding of all, it had little option but to provide access to the 'last mile' network at rock-bottom prices that failed properly to cover all of Royal Mail's associated costs. In effect, a state-owned company struggling with a marketplace in the throes of a profound transition was being obliged to hand large subsidies to private-sector rivals. The Royal Mail itself reckoned these subsidies were worth about £100m a year, an estimate contested by competitors but never by Postcomm. In theory, it could curb them by raising its wholesale prices – which were open to negotiation with the private sector – but this would risk inviting an even bigger disaster. Virtually all postal services were opened up to unrestricted competition from January 2006. (This move by Postcomm, rather than the legislative landmark of 2000, was widely and understandably seen as the real termination of Royal Mail's historical monopoly.) Postcomm thus cleared the way for new entrants to break into the local delivery business, without being subject to the universal-service obligations imposed on Royal Mail. This remarkable concession in principle allowed competitors to launch networks – just like William Dockwra's in the seventeenth century – within selected, highly profitable areas such as the City of London. Fortunately for Royal Mail, Dockwra's potential successors hung back, but the threat of 'bypass networks' springing up in city centres was nonetheless an acute concern for its management.

Postcomm's assault undeniably brought significant benefits for many corporate customers – and perhaps for the general public as well, though this was more arguable, given that Royal Mail's predicament soon led to a curtailment of services for ordinary users of the post. Express courier vans, anyway, became almost as familiar on the roads of British towns and villages as the red vans of Royal Mail. (More than forty companies were soon competing in the parcels sector, where Postcomm had deliberately skewed the market in their favour through pricing and new-product constraints on Royal Mail after January 2006.) But the speed and longer-term implications of the liberalization campaign troubled many observers. Leighton and Crozier always insisted that the threat of future competition could be seen as a valuable catalyst for what they were trying to do, just as Dearing had once suggested that talk of privatization would be helpful. Timing, though, was all. The two men at its head argued passionately that Royal Mail needed more time to recover, and rejected Postcomm's liberalization as premature.* It needled Crozier in particular that the liberalization process adopted for other big utilities in earlier decades was now being applied to Royal Mail in reverse order. Instead of a successful investment programme and modernization leading to gradual deregulation and then open competition – as had happened not just in telecoms but in many other sectors, including the gas and electricity industries – 'everything happened backwards'.[17] The open competition was arriving way ahead of the modernization.

This had one especially damaging consequence, aggravating a long-standing problem for the postal services in their entirety: there was no agreed destination. There had been no proper debate in 1999 or in the

---

* One of their presentational difficulties was that any allusion by them to Royal Mail's continuing frailty cut across their efforts to keep up the morale of the workforce with a stress on the progress that was being made. Leighton was genuinely proud of what had already been achieved. When Postcomm's Chairman, Nigel Stapleton, sniffed on one occasion in June 2005 at claims of a turnaround, Leighton responded angrily in the media: 'What does he think, we've all been at Skegness for three years?' This was a rare outburst. Leighton was fond of talking in his first year or two about 'wreckulation' as the new regulation – but great care was taken after 2004 to avoid fuelling a public row with Postcomm.

years since about what kind of universal mail system and post office network the country needed to have. The Government in 1999 had handed over to an independent regulatory body not only the implementation of postal policy but its formulation as well. Yet beyond espousing the desirability of greater efficiency and open competition in the marketplace, Postcomm itself had never been required to set out any detailed strategic objectives. The establishment of the Shareholder Executive in 2003, to manage the Government's role as shareholder in public corporations, made little apparent difference (though it certainly had an impact on the conduct of the Royal Mail Group's dealings with Government, and made them no simpler). How Postcomm proposed to reconcile Royal Mail's universal-service obligation with a much reduced commercial franchise was still a mystery in 2007, when that franchise began its sudden contraction. There had been no political debate, and surprisingly little discussion of the issues in the media. Those questions raised by the *Economist*, after the 1957 Priestley Commission, about the natural limitations of universal service in a modern industrial society (noted on p.414) had never been addressed. They raised, for all politicians, extremely awkward issues. Carrying private mail up 26 million garden paths every day entailed a massively expensive fixed infrastructure. New ways of ensuring the postal service's maximum efficiency had, in theory, been opened up by the advent of privatization as a workable concept in the 1980s. But what sort of compromise would be desirable, between fostering open competition and treating mail delivery as a natural monopoly? Neither Conservative nor Labour governments had shown much appetite for tackling the subject, and the debate over the Post Office network's future had been grudging: Labour had faced up to the difficulties of funding the network in the digital era only when forced to do so by the crisis over the POCA system. Even then, the debate had been restricted to the arithmetic of closures and subsidies. Little time had been spent on the underlying conundrum: how were socially desirable financial services to be channelled through the Post Office, if government departments had cheaper alternatives to hand and the Treasury refused to countenance capitalizing the Post Office as a proper bank?

3. A LONG AND LOADED PAUSE

The arrival of Gordon Brown and a new administration in June 2007 brought a valuable if belated opportunity to have that critical debate. It was also apparent by the closing months of 2007 that Royal Mail was saddled with its own equivalent of the Post Office network's POCA crisis. Concerned over the deterioration in industrial relations evidenced by the summer's national postal strikes and disturbed by the mounting pension deficit – not to mention a sharp downturn in operating profits, as lower mail volumes began to corrode Group margins, and the cooling of relations with Leighton – the Brown government in December 2007 announced yet another independent review. It would have a wide brief, to explore all the options for retaining Royal Mail with its universal-service obligation (USO). The chairman would be Richard Hooper. He was a businessman with almost thirty years' experience of telecoms, an industry in which those with too much reverence for the past could easily end up with no future. Invited to propose the solution to a multilayered problem dissected and documented by dozens before him, often to little avail, he set off with a chirpy disregard for the odds – and within five months had produced an Interim Report with a magisterial diagnosis of the ailing patient's problems. Hooper's summary, cannily produced well ahead of any recommendations, was accorded almost universal consent. All could agree, including the CWU's leaders, that the postal marketplace might soon be altered out of all recognition; that Royal Mail had to speed up its modernization or risk finding itself no longer equal to the demands of the USO; and that the existing regulatory regime was no longer suited to the broader demands being made of it. None could deny the pension deficit was now a matter for serious alarm. The case for a break with the past on every score could not have been starker.

Then, just as Hooper and his team were completing their work on linking diagnosis to prescription, events took an unexpected turn. To general astonishment at Westminster, Gordon Brown reshuffled his Cabinet in October 2008 and appointed Baron Mandelson of Foy and Hartlepool – his erstwhile Blairite adversary, newly ennobled for the job – as Secretary of State at the DTI, or the Department for Business, Enterprise and Regulatory Reform as it had now become. This would turn out to be a mixed blessing. The happy aspect of the appointment was almost immediately obvious. The new Minister, recalling his ill-fated December 1998 Review, had a genuine interest in postal reform. His arrival more or less coincided with the submission of the finished Hooper Report.[18] Mandelson seized on it as a chance to complete some unfinished business, and the Report handed him a formidable agenda. Its authors could do little about the contraction of the letters market – now expected to shrink at a scary 5–10 per cent annually for the next few years – but they had recommendations for fixing everything else. Regulation of the postal sector (they argued) should pass from Postcomm to Ofcom, which could handle it in the wider context of other communications media like e-mails and the internet, and would bring the experience of regulating BT in broadly comparable circumstances. This transfer (which was backed by Postcomm's own Chairman, Nigel Stapleton) would create an opportunity to reassess some key assumptions behind the current regulatory approach. Ownership of the pension fund should pass to the Government, a transfer accepted by the Treasury (where the funding of future liabilities could be treated as an academic issue, leaving the Exchequer to reap the instant benefit of assets recently valued at almost £24bn). And in support of an accelerated modernization drive, a large chunk of equity in the Royal Mail should pass from state ownership to one or more of its private-sector peers who, in partnership with it, might help to transform its performance. (The Post Office network would be run separately and would remain wholly publicly owned.) This last recommendation was welcomed by the management, who gave the Report their strong endorsement in all its essentials.

Less encouraging, at least for Royal Mail itself, was the single-mindedness with which Mandelson and his government colleagues latched on to the idea of an equity sale as the solution to the many problems described so succinctly by Hooper. Crozier and his executive team attached more urgency to a clarification of their operating environment, and in particular a discussion about regulatory goals. Hooper himself was at pains in his Report to stress that its main recommendations were to be taken as inseparable parts of a multifaceted response. But the Government seized on the notion of swallowing the pension fund and passing the Royal Mail into the embrace of a 'strategic partner' as the gist of the challenge. Still flushed with the confidence that marked the early months of his premiership, Brown was greatly attracted by the prospect of a clean break with the past – and the boldness of it certainly appealed to Mandelson. Of course, they could anticipate fierce opposition from the CWU – but the Government would insist that no more than 49 per cent of the equity would be for sale and therefore Royal Mail would technically be remaining in public ownership. It was a sophistry, shunned by the Hooper Report itself, that supposedly would square the sale proposal with the 2005 manifesto's privatization disclaimer. In practice, as the Union fully appreciated, it would make little difference from a managerial viewpoint whether private interests held

49 or 99 per cent of the equity. Any partner investing billions in Royal Mail would be governed by company law, not Whitehall. Who that partner might be was still uncertain when Mandelson unveiled the Report in the House of Lords nine days before Christmas 2008. But he was able to wave a piece of paper at their Lordships which, he said, indicated a definite interest from at least one third party – a case, perhaps, not of 'peace in our time' but privatization just in time.

A Postal Services Bill enabling the sale and providing for the transfer of the pension fund was introduced into the Lords in February 2009. Mandelson was determined that his second run at postal reform would end in triumph by the summer. There were three snags. The first caused the Government little apparent concern, but stirred much resentment around Royal Mail's headquarters (shortly to be relocated from Old Street to Unilever House on the corner of London's Blackfriars Bridge). Arguing the case for involving a strategic partner, ministers scarcely concealed their readiness to accept the implication that Royal Mail managers on their own were simply not up to the job. This seemed an odd way to capitalize on all that Leighton and Crozier had achieved. It was also damaging to morale and irritating to senior executives, and it misrepresented the Hooper Report, which set store by a private-sector partner only partly with a view to their augmenting the pool of available corporate experience. Just as important was the fact that a measure of private ownership would open up access to capital sources unfettered by Treasury approval procedures – and would be mightily helpful, too, at 'removing the spectre of political intervention, enabling management to make decisions about modernization on a commercial basis ...'[19] This spectre went largely unmentioned by Labour ministers through the early months of 2009. The second problem was much more serious. In flagging their objective of a part-privatization, the Government had landed itself in a Catch-22 predicament. It was publicly asserting that only the introduction of a 'strategic partner' for Royal Mail could allow the postal sector to be overhauled for a brighter future. But as it very soon discovered in private talks with the most eligible of those strategic partners, they had no interest in taking any stake in that sector until *after* it had been overhauled to make it fit for commercial investment. This would involve not just a resolution of the pension crisis but a scrapping of the regulatory regime designed to boost Royal Mail's competitors. When they realized this was not on offer, both Deutsche Post and the Dutch TPG – now renamed the TNT Group – turned their backs on any deal at all. (The passing of seven years had done little, it seemed, to resolve the impasse reached over Project Olympus.) This left the Government in negotiation with a leading private equity company, CVC Capital Partners, as the sole prospective purchaser – bidding for only 30 per cent of the company and not prepared to pay anything like the minimum £3bn that it had been hoped a 49 per cent stake might be worth.

Even this might not have finished off the initiative, but there was a third obstacle to progress which was to prove as insuperable as ever. The CWU remained unconvinced by any justification for an equity sale, of whatever size. Crozier and his team were by now well embarked on a modernization programme seeking to achieve within five years what had taken ten to fifteen years at Deutsche Post and TNT. It was to involve profound changes to the work culture. Several hundred walk-sequencing machines had finally been purchased. Once these were installed, postmen would no longer need to start their daily rota hours ahead of the normal working day, as they had done for centuries. This would mean an altered way of life for all, disrupting family routines and prompting fears of another heavy round of redundancies. (A rash of unofficial strikes would follow in the autumn, as both sides wrestled with the implications.) Against this background, the Union's member-ship eyed the prospect of private ownership with real apprehension. Its leaders campaigned hard against the Bill and publicly threatened to withdraw financial support for the Labour Party. Most of Mandelson's Cabinet colleagues, meanwhile, were privately in favour of any policy that could be relied upon to keep Royal Mail out of the headlines.* In the Commons, over a hundred Labour backbenchers sided with the Union and signed an Early Day Motion opposing any part-privatization. The Tories backed the Bill. This left an increasingly beleaguered Prime Minister contemplating the possibility of a humiliating alliance with the Opposition against his own left-wing MPs and a powerful trade union, with less than a year to go before the next general election. Brown anguished for months over the risk of proceeding, while Mandelson pleaded the case for pressing ahead. 'Gordon was fed up with the CWU', as Mandelson recorded in his political memoir barely more than twelve

---

* This priority was acknowledged by one senior government minister with disarming frank-ness during a discussion with one of the candidates to succeed Leighton as Chairman in 2009. The candidate asked what might be regarded by the Government as a fundamental objective for the Group under his chairmanship. 'What we want', came the reply, 'is for it not to be a problem.' As a shared vision for the future, this understandably failed to inspire and the candidate withdrew. (Jonathan Evans, interview with author, 3 December 2010.)

months later. 'Privately, he did not hide his anger. He was convinced that Hooper was right, but the more we talked about it, the more nervous he seemed about the prospect of a political scrap to get the Bill through.'[20] The outcome, as Mandelson later candidly admitted, was the adoption in July of a preprepared 'exit strategy'. The Bill was abandoned, with the blame laid on unpropitious market conditions (though these had unquestionably improved since December). Hooper, to his dismay, found his report dropped overnight, and the political caravan moved on. Any wider debate over the future of the postal service had, yet again, been aborted.

The Government's failure to find a strategic partner did not pass unnoticed in the capital markets. Financial analysts had long since lowered their expectations of the 'snail-mail' postal sector. This latest setback confirmed many in their assessment that Royal Mail might have left it too late to proceed with any successful privatization. The prospect of making a decent return out of the belated modernization of the traditional industry, still evident at the time of Deutsche Post's flotation in 2000, had faded. When the TNT Group unveiled its 2010–15 strategy to market analysts in December 2009, its domestic Dutch postal business was conspicuously relegated to also-ran status. TNT had decided to settle (at best) for 'actively maintaining a sustainable Dutch Mail business' where annual revenues were expected to slide by 4–6 per cent over the period. The future unmistakably lay with its international networks – with revenue growth objectives set between 7 and 18 per cent a year – handling European parcels, intercontinental freight and a wide range of specialized services for business customers.[21] Four months later, in April 2010, TNT announced plans to spin off its domestic Dutch mail operations. Shares in the group rose 5 per cent on the news.[22]

Thrust back on its own resources, the Royal Mail would have to grasp the different opportunities offered by the UK domestic sector, with its immeasurably greater scale and scope, to prove the markets wrong. It would do so under fresh management. Leighton had stepped down in March 2009, the proud owner of a bright red pillar box outside his home, bearing an inscription 'to the longest serving chairman in the history of the Royal Mail'. Almost as impressive, if less snappy, he had been the second-longest-serving permanent head of the Post Office since 'Beauty' Blackwood in the nineteenth century. (Only Thomas Gardiner had served longer, with his tenure as Director General extended by the war.) Crozier announced nine months later that he would be leaving in May 2010, to run commercial television's ITV, another erstwhile industry leader facing an urgent need to reinvent itself. A few months before leaving, he succeeded in securing a crucial agreement with the CWU on the modernization plans – no mean feat, given the sweeping changes they portended and the jobs already eliminated. (Since 2005–6, another 25,000 jobs had gone in addition to the initial round of 30,000 redundancies under Leighton's Three Year Renewal Plan: the workforce was now down to 168,000.) Crozier and Leighton together were widely and justifiably credited with having salvaged the Group from the traumas of 2001–2. But with 2008–9 having ended in a post-tax loss of £229m and with a rapidly worsening negative cash flow, the business still posed a massive challenge for their successors. The steep profits revival of the years 2003–6 had now been mirrored rather alarmingly by an equally steep drop back into losses. (See again Appendix A, Chart 14.) The new Chairman, Donald Brydon, was a prominent City figure with a string of other chairmanships to his name. A Scot trained in the mathematical sciences, he had had a distinguished career in the world of fund management – which seemed grimly ironic, given the announcement within months of his arrival that the actuarial deficit on the pension fund had ballooned to £10.3bn. And appointed in May 2010 as Chief Executive was Moya Greene, a Newfoundlander – and the fulfilment, after a mere ninety-seven years, of Miss Cale the Clerk's dream in 1913 that the Post Office might one day be run, yes, by a woman.

One of Canada's most prominent business figures, Greene arrived straight from running Canada Post since 2005. While her successful record there was widely noted in the press, her role as a civil servant in overseeing the 1995 privatization of Canadian National Railway attracted even more comment. For the general election three weeks prior to her appointment had ushered in the 2010 coalition government. The Business Department had been handed to Liberal Democrat ministers, whose party was committed to a policy of part-privatization for the Royal Mail. And among the twenty-two bills listed in the Queen's Speech of 25 May was a Postal Services Bill that would essentially resurrect the legislation ditched by Labour in July 2009, allowing privatization, in whole or in part, of the Royal Mail while leaving the Post Office network in public ownership. After the flopped auction of 2009, however, there appeared to be a shrewder appreciation now that privatization was not an end in itself to be pursued at the expense of the wider debate. The coalition government, unlike Labour, seemed intent on leaving any sale decisions until well after all the necessary legal and statutory preparations had been made in Westminster and Brussels. This left plenty of time for tough decisions on the fundamental structure of the postal business – and of the regulatory regime within which it would have to operate.

There had been a long and loaded pause since the end of 2007. While ministers had weighed their options, not many decisions had been taken. The new Chief Executive observed as much, giving the Board her first impressions at the start of September 2010.[23] The business seemed to be caught in a state of suspended animation, said Greene. She left her colleagues in no doubt that she was going to move quickly to reanimate it. Her objective would be to secure the viability of the Group as a self-standing business – Rowland Hill would have applauded that – and this would entail senior managers spending far more time listening to customers, and far less time talking to regulators. An Update to the Hooper Review was published ten days later. It broadly endorsed all the recommendations of 2008, but with some notable shifts of emphasis. In particular, finding a 'strategic partner' was no longer seen as an integral part of the drive to attract private capital. A 'reduced need for corporate experience' as part of the deal was at least partly justified on the basis of Greene's recruitment, although she had hardly yet begun her tenure.[24] Perhaps her first impressions had made a forceful impact. Was the new stance also, though, a tacit acknowledgement that strategic partners interested in buying into Royal Mail might be less readily found than had once been hoped? As for the regulatory climate, it seemed at least possible that a transfer of Postcomm's responsibilities to Ofcom might be accompanied by some reining back of the threat to Royal Mail's primacy. Greene soon appeared to be winning allies. The CWU, so conspicuously silent in 1999–2000, seemed ready to back her demands for regulatory reform. And the Hooper Update suggested a future regime might be well-advised to draw back from allowing competitors to offer delivery services without facing the same universal obligations as applied to Royal Mail.[25] Optimists noted this could effectively restore the inviolability of the Royal Mail's 'last mile' delivery network, which in 2010 was still essentially unchallenged and might yet be the key to restoring its profitability.

The Postal Services Bill was introduced into the House of Commons in October 2010. By the time it reached the statute books on 13 June 2011, some significant amendments had been made. One addition provided for the continued use of the Queen's head on British stamps, even in the event of the Royal Mail passing into foreign ownership. Other changes addressed issues of rather more immediate concern. As a result, and in line with Hooper's reflections on the regulatory regime, the 2011 Act went some way towards countering the disastrous impact of the Postal Services Act of 2000 by handing the future Regulator a clear brief. As Postcomm's successor, Ofcom would now be required to ensure that the provision of a universal postal service was 'financially sustainable' and this would include 'the need for a reasonable commercial rate of return. . .'; and the Act effectively ruled out any challenge to the Royal Mail's role as the universal-service provider for the next ten years.[26] Ministers had also given up trying to make a Treasury takeover of the pension fund (and its deficit) firmly conditional on a (still putative) restructuring of the ownership. The cash requirements of the pension fund in 2011–12, coming on top of the cash demands of the continuing modernization, were so far beyond the Group's resources that scope had to be left in the end for a more urgent government appropriation of the fund. After all the tense political confrontations sparked by legislative proposals for the Post Office since the 1980s, the final emergence of the 2011 Act went almost wholly unremarked in the media – and unopposed by the CWU, which had little interest in campaigning against a measure potentially vital to the future of its members' pensions. It was a slightly eerie anti-climax to so many years of bitter argument, but this of course reflected the fact that it was in many ways a curious statute – and scarcely a landmark of postal legislation to set beside the Acts of 1981 and 1969, let alone 1840, 1711 or 1635. In most respects, it was concerned not with implementing bold measures but with enabling future changes to follow – as and when possible, assuming the approval of the EU authorities in Brussels, and subject to events in the commercial marketplace over which the Government itself would have limited, if any, control. The Post Office network would now be a candidate for mutualization, if enough sub-postmasters and interested parties showed sufficient enthusiasm for the idea. The network itself would be open to all sorts of new ideas and services, if others came forward to champion them. Local post offices and Royal Mail would henceforth enjoy a close and entirely beneficial relationship, if ways could be found to develop it successfully (though the Act took every opportunity to underscore the fact that Royal Mail and Post Office Ltd would in future exist as quite distinct operational entities). Above all, there would be 'innovative business strategies' for Royal Mail, shares for its employees and additional sources of capital to spend on modernization – if one or more investors could be found in the private sector to warrant proceeding with a privatization of the business. No shortage, then, of consummations devoutly to be wish'd – but if others should fail to live up to the Government's aspirations, it was easy to imagine how the Act might in the end fall short of instigating any real action at all.

The various conditions were not of course presented as providential outcomes, more or less immune to government influence. They were put forward – much like the fresh starts envisaged in the Green Paper of 1994 and the White Paper of 1999 – as future developments that ministers looked forward to promoting with energy and imaginative leadership. Any bystander confidently expecting this to happen, however, would surely draw little encouragement from the events of the past half-century. British governments since the departure of Tony Benn in 1966 have repeatedly demonstrated the truth that, for politicians, grappling with any serious reform of the postal service is to be regarded, in that most alarming of Sir Humphrey Appleby's phrases, as very brave indeed. The prospective rewards have always lain too far into the future; the penalties of failure have looked unnerving and only too immediate. Hence the rejection of the Split option by Wilson's government in the 1960s, the jettisoning of privatization by the Major government in the early 1990s, the equivocation of Blair's government after 2004 and the open retreat by Brown's in 2009. Only Margaret Thatcher's government had the courage to embark on a reform agenda – and even she drew back from the uproar she thought might greet plans to sell off the business behind the Queen's head. There has been almost half a century of procrastination that it would be overly charitable to describe as benign neglect. The incorporation of 1969 made no difference to the reality that Britain's postal service existed within a framework determined by the Government. The safety-first approach of most ministers thereafter meant that policy questions of steadily increasing urgency were too often left unresolved, or shuffled off in ways that contributed directly, after the turn of the Millennium, to the demise of the service as a viable business.

Reform of the Post Office in modern times has simply not struck MPs of either party at Westminster as an important enough issue on which to risk precious electoral (or trade union) goodwill. In part, this has probably reflected a deep-lying assumption shared by many politicians that, as Adam Smith observed in *The Wealth of Nations*, a Post Office is essentially a straightforward enterprise, requiring no great imagination to run: 'It is, perhaps, the only mercantile project which has been successfully managed by, I believe, every sort of Government. The capital advanced is not very considerable. There is no mystery in the business.

The returns are not only certain, but immediate'.[27] This acquiescence in the status quo has also represented an oblique plaudit of sorts for the Post Office, which by the 1960s had weathered so many storms as to seem indestructible to most outsiders. Even when the case for reform was eloquently argued by radical ministers like Tony Benn, Keith Joseph and (all too briefly) Nicholas Ridley – who all shared, if nothing else, a willingness to break abruptly with the past – it was hard for most of their colleagues to imagine that much was really at stake. It was surely a feature of British society, and always had been, that the public grumbled about the postal service from time to time. To take the complaints too seriously would be to ignore the remarkable ability of those in charge of the service to go on adapting it, as they had done for centuries. And indeed, for much of the twentieth century this implicit compliment was surely deserved. In many respects, the close-knit body of men who comprised the Official Side of the Post Office – almost as anonymous when corporate managers after the Break of 1969 as they had been when civil servants before it – exhibited all the familiar virtues of the British civil service. The descendants of James Hickes and Thomas Hasker, Anthony Trollope and F. H. Williamson were (in general at least) as hard-working, loyal and conscientious as their forebears. They ran a postal service that other nations sought to emulate for decades. In the process, they also managed to build a modern telephone service; they adapted – with the assistance of thousands of tireless Whitley Committee members and dedicated trade union officials – to coexistence with the only big industrial labour force in Britain that, for generations, made formal control of the workplace a political objective and effective day-to-day control a de facto reality; and they doggedly pursued a fiendishly difficult mechanization of the mails that triumphed just in time for the Post Office to cope with a wholly unexpected boom in postal traffic and generated, in the 1990s, massive cash dividends for the taxpayer.

But changes in technology and the marketplace transformed the nature and the context of the operations under the Post Office's control. These changes happened first and most obviously to the telephone business; they caught up with the postal service in the 1980s. International competitors, alternative products and services, new working practices for the labour force and higher expectations among customers – the 'global postal industry', as the altered environment was suddenly being described, made huge demands of the Post Office many years before e-mails and the internet triggered the sharp contraction of letter mails.

Different skills and attitudes were required of those who managed the service. It is hard not to conclude, as many did at the time within White-hall and inside the Post Office itself, that privatization could and should have facilitated this massive adjustment – for the posts in the 1990s, as for telephones in the 1980s. The parallel with the telephone industry's experience was relevant enough, but it needed to be explained. Only the political will was missing.

Perhaps, despite all the discouraging precedents, the 2011 Act will after all prompt this long-delayed outcome. Its passage through Parliament stirred surprisingly little opposition – though the fact that, in most respects, it paved the way for changes rather than giving effect to them left open the possibility of battles to come – and the rapidly declining importance of social and transactional mails meant the political stakes, in a sense, might now be considerably less daunting than in earlier times. The scale of the postal environment's transformation is so apparent to all – employees and union leaders, customers and the wider public – that building a consensus in favour of a restructured postal service may be significantly easier than it proved to be in the 1990s. Retaining the status quo, after all, is scarcely an option: today's Royal Mail, left to its own devices, is not about to generate massive dividends for the Treasury. By the same token, of course, it may not have quite the same appeal for potential corporate acquirers as it would assuredly have had twenty years ago. So privatization may come, willy-nilly, to mean a sale of shares to the public. Given regulatory safeguards for the long-term health of the business and a compelling reminder of its still essential role – no one, after all, has yet discovered a way to digitalize the delivery of physical objects to the doorstep – it is not hard to imagine a flotation that might attract widespread support. At least it would have a certain historical resonance. It would lead the Royal Mail down the road taken by British Telecom in 1984. It might make available a sizeable slice of the equity for the workforce, engaging employees with the governance of the mails in line with aspirations aired by the postal unions since 1919 and offering a share of the ownership to the sub-postmasters and sub-postmistresses who have been a mainstay of the organization since its creation. Above all, a flotation might allow the Government to reconcile the potentially bruising business of privatization itself with a preservation of that abundant goodwill towards the Royal Mail among the general public which yet remains one of the great legacies of its extraordinary past.

Appendix A: Charting the growth

Subject to some re-working to take account of inflation, the following charts are based on unadjusted figures produced by the Post Office since 1840 – though few if any categories of these have been immune to occasional and sometimes puzzling gaps, and all harbour marginal inconsistencies (some less marginal than others) over time. With this important proviso, the charts offer a broad overview of the timing and magnitude of the postal service's growth since the start of the Victorian era, and of its recent sharp contraction. The data on which the charts are based, and a note on sources, can be found at this BPMA website: www.postalheritage.org.uk/mastersofthepost.

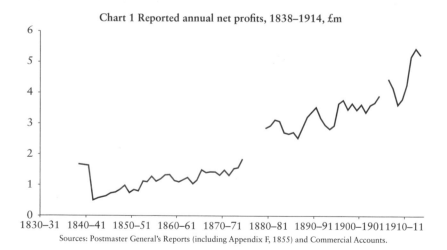

Chart 1 Reported annual net profits, 1838–1914, £m

Sources: Postmaster General's Reports (including Appendix F, 1855) and Commercial Accounts.

Chart 2 The growth of the mails, 1840–1920

a) Volume of postal packets of all kinds, billions   b) Volume per head of population

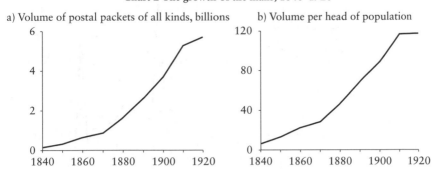

Note: 'Postal packets' comprised all items in footnote on p. 285 except parcels
Source: *Post and Postal Services* by F. H. Williamson, Post 72/211

Chart 3 Total number of employees since 1854, thousands

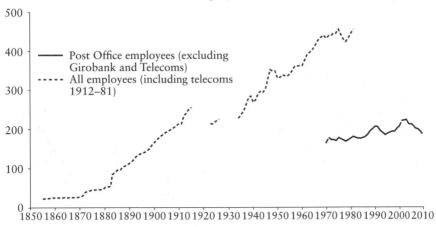

Post Office employees (excluding Girobank and Telecoms)
All employees (including telecoms 1912–81)

Sources: Postmaster General's Reports, Headquarters' Summaries, Post Office Board
Papers and Royal Mail Annual Reports

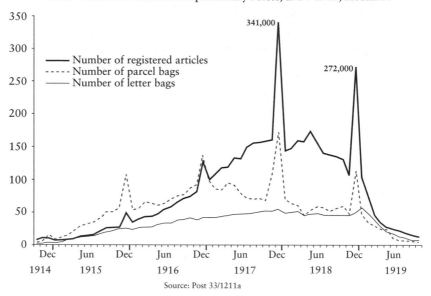

Chart 4 Mails for the British Expeditionary Forces, 1914–1919, thousands

Source: Post 33/1211a

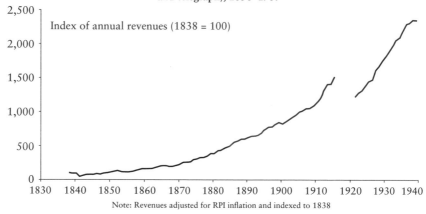

Chart 5 Real (inflation-adjusted) revenues (including telephones and telegraph), 1838–1939

Index of annual revenues (1838 = 100)

Note: Revenues adjusted for RPI inflation and indexed to 1838

Sources: Postmaster General's Reports; Alan Clinton, *Post Officer Workers*, Appendix 28

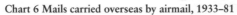

Chart 6 Mails carried overseas by airmail, 1933–81

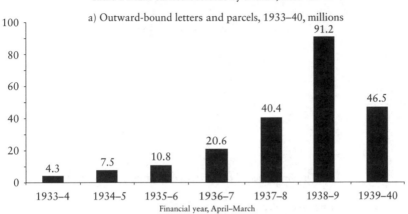

a) Outward-bound letters and parcels, 1933–40, millions

Financial year, April–March

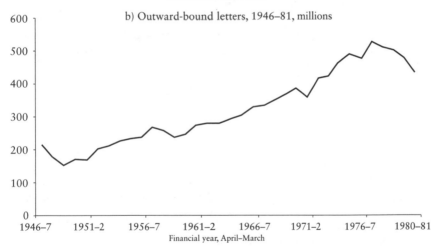

b) Outward-bound letters, 1946–81, millions

Financial year, April–March

Sources: Commercial Accounts (Post 92/14) and Royal Mail Annual Accounts

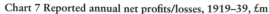

Chart 7 Reported annual net profits/losses, 1919–39, £m

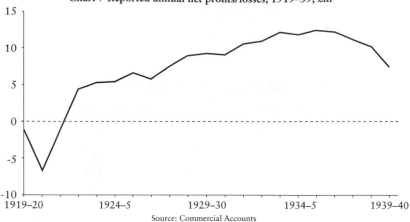

Source: Commercial Accounts

Chart 8 The divergence of postal/telecoms profits, 1939–81

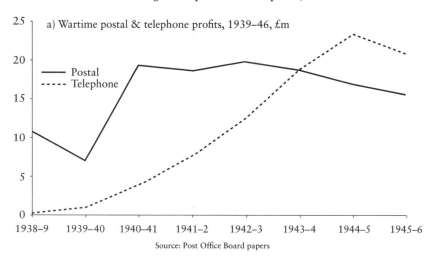

a) Wartime postal & telephone profits, 1939–46, £m

Source: Post Office Board papers

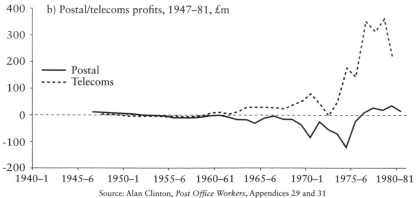

b) Postal/telecoms profits, 1947–81, £m

Source: Alan Clinton, *Post Office Workers*, Appendices 29 and 31

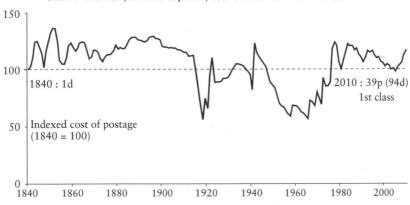

Chart 9 The real (inflation-adjusted) cost of a standard letter since 1840

Note: Index based on cost of ½ oz letter postage, adjusted for inflation

Sources: Historic prices and Office of National Statistics

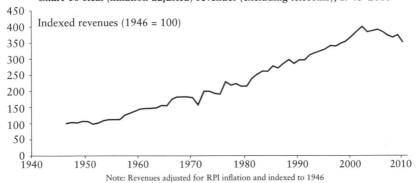

Chart 10 Real (inflation adjusted) revenues (excluding telecoms), 1946–2010

Note: Revenues adjusted for RPI inflation and indexed to 1946

Sources: Commercial Accounts, Royal Mail Annual Reports, Royal Mail Group Annual Reviews

Chart 11 Letters delivered by Royal Mail, 1920–2010, billions

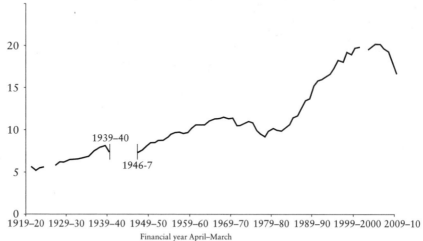

Financial year April–March
Note: 'Letters' defined as postal packets; see Chart 2
Sources: Headquarters Summaries, Commercial Accounts and Annual Reports

Chart 12 Total number of post offices since 1854, thousands

Note: Data unavailable for period from 1915 to 1950
Sources: Postmaster General's Reports, Commercial Accounts, Royal Mail Annual Reports and Post Office Ltd Accounts

Chart 13 The returns to the Exchequer from the Post Office Corporation, 1976–2001, £m

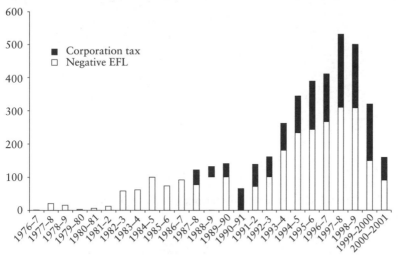

Note: No returns recorded prior to 1976–7
Sources: Hansard, Royal Mail Annual Reports, Royal Mail Group Records

Chart 14 – Reported Post Office net profits/losses, 1981–2010, £m

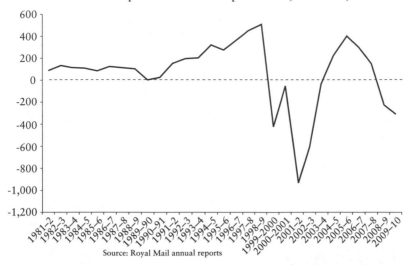

Source: Royal Mail annual reports

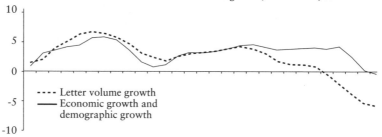

Chart 15 Letter volumes and economic growth, 1983–2010, %

Note: Data refer to three-year moving average annual growth rates

Source: *Modernise or Decline: Policies to Maintain the Universal Postal Service in the United Kingdom*, Hooper Report, 2008 (updated).

Appendix B: Masters of the Post

(A) MASTERS/COMPTROLLERS-GENERAL OF THE POSTS AND OTHER EARLY TITLE-HOLDERS

Sir Brian Tuke	*c.*1512–45
John Mason	1545–66
Sir Thomas Randolph	1567–90
John Stanhope	1590–1607
Charles Stanhope	1607–35
Mathew de Quester ('Postmaster for Foreign Parts')	1628–32
Sir John Coke	1635–40
Sir Francis Windebank	1635–40 (?)
Thomas Witherings ('Master of Foreign Posts'/ Deputy to Sir John Coke)	1632–40
Philip Burlamachi/Earl of Warwick/Sir Edmond Prideaux and others	1640–45
Sir Edmond Prideaux	1645–53
John Manley	1653–5

(B) POSTMASTERS GENERAL

John Thurloe	1655–60
Henry Bishop (with John Wildman)	1660–63
Daniel O'Neale	1663–4
Catherine O'Neale	1664–7
Henry Bennet, Lord Arlington	1667–77
James, Duke of York	1677–85
Lawrence Hyde, Earl of Rochester	1685–9
John Wildman	1689–91

(C) JOINT POSTMASTERS GENERAL

Sir Robert Cotton	1691–1708
Sir Thomas Frankland	1691–1715
Sir John Evelyn	1708–15
Lord Cornwallis	1715–20
James Craggs	1715–20
Edward Carteret	1720–39
Galfridus Walpole	1720–25
Edward Harrison	1725–32
Lord Lovel, Earl of Leicester	1733–59
Sir John Eyles	1739–44
Sir Everard Fawkener	1745–58
Earl of Bessborough	1759–62
Robert Hampden	1759–65
Earl of Egmont	1762–3
Lord Hyde	1763–5
Lord Grantham	1765–6
Earl of Bessborough (2nd term)	1765–6
Earl of Hillborough	1766–8
Francis, Lord le Despencer	1766–81
Earl of Sandwich	1768–71
Henry Thynne (later Lord Carteret)	1771–89
Viscount Barrington	1782
Earl of Tankerville	1782–3
Lord Foley	1783–4
Earl of Tankerville (2nd term)	1784–6
Earl of Clarendon	1786
Lord Walsingham	1787–94
Earl of Westmorland	1789–90
Earl of Chesterfield	1790–98
Earl of Leicester	1794–9
Lord Auckland	1798–1804
Earl Gower	1799–1801
Lord Charles Spencer	1801–6
Duke of Montrose	1804–6
Earl of Buckinghamshire	1806–7
Earl of Carysfort	1806–7

Earl of Sandwich	1807–14
Earl of Chichester	1807–23
Earl of Clancarty	1814–16
Marquess of Salisbury	1816–23

(D) POSTMASTERS GENERAL

	Date of appointment
Earl of Chichester (continuing from 1807)	? September 1823
Lord Frederick Montagu	4 July 1826
Duke of Manchester	17 September 1827
Duke of Richmond	14 December 1830
Marquess of Conyngham	5 July 1834
Lord Maryborough	31 December 1834
Marquess of Conyngham (2nd term)	8 May 1835
Earl of Lichfield	30 May 1835
Lord Lowther, Earl of Lonsdale	15 September 1841
Earl of St German's	2 January 1846
Marquess of Clanricarde	14 July 1846
Earl of Hardwicke	6 May 1852
Viscount (later Lord) Canning	8 January 1853
Duke of Argyle	30 November 1855
Lord Colchester	13 March 1858
Earl of Elgin and Kincardine	24 June 1859
Duke of Argyle	11 May 1860
Lord Stanley of Alderley	28 August 1860
Duke of Montrose	19 July 1866
Marquess of Hartington (later Duke of Devonshire)	30 December 1868
William Monsell (later Lord Emley)	24 January 1871
Lord Lyon Playfair	13 November 1873
Lord John Manners	3 March 1874
Henry Fawcett	14 May 1880
George John Shaw-Lefevre (later Lord Eversley)	7 November 1884
Lord John Manners (2nd term)	29 June 1885
Lord Wolverton	10 February 1886
Henry Cecil Raikes	5 August 1886
Sir James Fergusson	21 September 1891
Arnold Morley	19 August 1892

Duke of Norfolk	5 July 1895
Marquess of Londonderry	10 April 1900
J. Austen Chamberlain	15 August 1902
Edward George Villiers, Lord Stanley	9 October 1903
Sidney Buxton	11 December 1905
Herbert Samuel	19 February 1910
Charles E. H. Hobhouse	10 February 1914
Herbert Samuel (2nd term)	28 May 1915
J. A. Pease (later Lord Gainford)	21 January 1916
Albert H. Illingworth (later Lord Illingworth)	13 December 1916
Frederick G. Kellaway	4 April 1921
A. Neville Chamberlain	2 November 1922
Sir William Joynson-Hicks	12 March 1923
Sir Laming Worthington-Evans	29 May 1923
Vernon Hartshorn	23 January 1924
Sir William Mitchell-Thomson (later Lord Selsdon)	13 November 1924
H. B. Lees-Smith	10 June 1929
C. R. Atlee	4 March 1931
W. G. A. Ormsby-Gore (later Lord Harlech)	4 September 1931
Sir Kingsley Wood	12 November 1931
George Tryon (later Lord Tryon)	7 June 1935
W. S. Morrison	5 April 1940
Harry Crookshank	6 February 1943
Earl of Listowel	4 August 1945
Wilfred Paling	23 April 1947
Ness Edwards	2 March 1950
Earl De La Warr	6 November 1951
Charles Hill	8 April 1955
Ernest Marples	17 January 1957
Reginald Bevins	21 October 1959
Tony Benn	19 October 1964
Edward Short	4 July 1966
Roy Mason	5 April 1968
John Stonehouse	1 July 1968–
	30 September 1969

(E) SECRETARIES TO THE POST OFFICE

	Date of appointment
John Avent	20 June 1694
Benjamin Waterhouse	(?) 1700
Henry Weston	(?) 1714
Joseph Godman	(?) 1720
[Ralph Allen: Effectively the controller of the by- and cross-posts]	1719–64
W. Rouse	(?) 1730
Thomas Robinson (also Solicitor to the Post Office)	(?) 1737
John D. Barbutt	15 September 1738
George Shelvocke	22 July 1742
Henry Potts	19 March 1760
Anthony Todd	1 December 1762
Henry Potts (2nd term)	19 July 1765
Anthony Todd (2nd term)	6 January 1768
[John Palmer: Surveyor & Comptroller General]	1786–92
Sir Francis Freeling	7 June 1798
Colonel W. L. Maberly	29 September 1836
[Rowland Hill: Adviser to Her Majesty's Treasury]	1839–42
[Rowland Hill: Secretary to the Postmaster General]	1846–54
Rowland Hill	22 April 1854
John Tilley	15 March 1864
Stevenson A. Blackwood (later Sir S. Arthur Blackwood)	1 May 1880
Sir Spencer Walpole	10 November 1893
Sir George H. Murray	10 February 1899
Sir H. Babington Smith	1 October 1903
Sir Matthew Nathan	17 January 1910
Sir Alexander F. King	1 October 1911
Sir Evelyn Murray	24 August 1914

(F) DIRECTORS GENERAL

	Date of appointment
Sir Donald Banks	14 April 1934
Sir Thomas Gardiner	9 August 1936

Sir Raymond Birchall	1 January 1946
R. A. (later Sir Alexander) Little	1 October 1949
Sir Gordon Radley	1 October 1955
Sir Ronald German	1 June 1960
J. (later Sir John) Wall (as 'Deputy Chairman')	1 November 1966

(G) CHAIRMEN OF THE BOARD

Viscount Hall of Cynon Valley	1969–70
A. W. C. (later Sir William) Ryland	1971–7
Sir William Barlow	1977–80
Sir Henry Chilver *	1980–81
Ron (later Lord) Dearing	1981–7
Sir Bryan Nicholson	1987–92
M. (later Sir Michael) Heron *	1993–8
Dr Neville Bain *	1998–2001
Allan Leighton *	2002–9
Donald Brydon *	2009–

* Non-Executive Chairmen

(H) CHIEF EXECUTIVES

Bill Cockburn	1993–5
John Roberts	1995–2002
Adam Crozier	2003–10
Moya Greene	2010–

(I) RESPONSIBLE GOVERNMENT MINISTERS

	Date of appointment
Ministers of Posts and Telecommunications, 1969–74	
John Stonehouse (Con)	1 October 1969
Christopher Chataway (Con)	24 June 1970
Sir John Eden (Con)	7 April 1972
Secretaries of State for Industry, 1974–83	
Tony Benn (Lab)	5 March 1974
Eric Varley (Lab)	10 June 1975

Sir Keith Joseph (Con)	4 May 1979
Patrick (later Lord) Jenkin (Con)	14 September 1981

Secretaries of State for Trade and Industry, 1983–2007

Cecil Parkinson (Con)	12 June 1983
Norman (later Lord) Tebbit (Con)	16 October 1983
Leon (later Lord) Brittan (Con)	2 September 1985
Paul Channon (later Lord Kelvedon) (Con)	24 January 1986
Lord Young (Con)	13 June 1987
Sir Nicholas (later Lord) Ridley (Con)	24 July 1989
Peter Lilley (Con)	14 July 1990
Michael (later Lord) Heseltine (Con)	10 April 1992
Ian (later Lord) Lang (Con)	5 July 1995
Margaret Beckett (Lab)	2 May 1997
Peter Mandelson (Lab)	27 July 1998
Stephen Byers (Lab)	23 December 1998
Patricia Hewitt (Lab)	8 June 2001
Alan Johnson (Lab)	6 May 2005
Alistair Darling (Lab)	5 May 2006

Secretaries of State for Business, Enterprise and Regulatory Reform,
   2007–9

John Hutton (Lab)	28 June 2007
Lord Mandelson (Lab)	3 October 2008

Secretaries of State for Business, Innovation and Skills, 2009–

Lord Mandelson (Lab)	5 June 2009
Vince Cable (Lib Dem)	12 May 2010

(J) GENERAL SECRETARIES OF THE UPW/UCW/CWU (SINCE 1920)

William (Bill) Bowen	1920–36
T. J. (Tom) Hodgson	1936–49
Charles Geddes	1949–57
Ron Smith	1957–67
Tom Jackson	1967–82
Alan Tuffin	1982–93
Alan Johnson	1993–7
Derek Hodgson	1997–2001
Billy Hayes	2001–

Appendix C: Thomas Witherings' letter to the Mayor of Hull

Right worshopfull

Whereas his Ma[jes]tie by his proclamacon dated at Bagshot the last of July 1635 hath beene pleased to comannd me his servant to settle a runing post to runn day and night betwixt the Cittie of London and Edenbrough and diverse other by parts upon this Road as perticularly to your Towne of Hull and for the better Maintinance of the said service his Ma[jes]tie hath therein provided that noe post or posts whatsoever shall take up receive or deliver any letter or letters whatsoever other then the posts or Messengers appointed by me which proclamaçon you have received and for the better performance of the same, his Ma[jes]tie in his said proclamacon hath charged and Comaunded all iustices of peace Maiors Sheriffs Bayliffs Constables headboroughs and all others his officers and Ministers whatsoever to be aiding and assisting to me in the due accomplissmente of his Ma[jes]ties pleasure therein of w[hi]ch I have perticularly adviced you intreating you thereby to punish s[u]ch delinquents instead of w[hi]ch punishment I find you that are Magistrats w[hi]ch are comannded to obey his Ma[jes]t[i]es proclamacon hath in your owne perticulars continually sent and received letters by ordinary posts Contrary to his Ma[jes]t[i]es proclamacon and instead of punishing the same have supported them as may appeare plainely by your owne actions in receiveing and delivering letters to the said posts w[hi]ch weekly continue to goe and come betwixt your towne and the Cittie of London neglecting his Ma[jes]ties Comannd therein not withstanding it being a record of w[hi]ch I am bound perticularly to informe the Lord[es] of his Ma[jes]t[i]es most [honourable] previe Counsell of the same except by this bearer my honoured friend I shall receive a satissaciall answere not by words but in deeds according to his Ma[jes]ties said proclamacon all w[hi]ch at the instance of this gentleman the bearer hereof I have thought fit to advice you before my Complaint he haveing undertooke that from you I shall have all iustice and right soe with my kind respect I take leave and rest

Your most affectionate
[ff]riend and servant
to Command

January this 28th 1636
[January 31 received]

Thomas With[rin]gs

Notes and references

INTRODUCTION

1. Ivor Halstead, *Post Haste: The Story of the Post Office in Peace and War*, Lindsay Drummond, 1944, p. 62.
2. Post 94/11. Entitled 'Roades, Salarys, Stages &c', the book itself bears no date but sets out a revision of postmasters' salaries linked to the arrival in 1667 of a new head of the service, the first to be described as the 'Postmaster General'.
3. The description, attributed to W. E. Clery, is quoted in Alan Clinton, *Post Office Workers: A Trade Union and Social History*, Allen & Unwin, 1984, p. 49.
4. Ron Dearing, interview with author, 14 October 2008.
5. It is catalogued as Post 23/220 ('To be viewed with 1:1 supervision <u>only</u>'). Details of the London Unaffordable Arts Fair were carried in the *Evening Standard* of 25 June 2010. Copies of *Ulysses* went on being confiscated until 1934, when exceptions began to be made. The publisher Allen Lane posted a copy to his London address from Paris, with the contents roundly advertised on the outside of the package, and the Post Office delivered it. But it was only after the title's publication in England in 1936 that the Home Office formally rescinded the confiscation orders. Papers relating to this history are in Post 23/9.

PART ONE: ARM OF THE STATE
1. 'A thing above all things', 1512–1659

1. H. S. Bennett, *The Pastons and Their England: Studies in an Age of Transition*, Cambridge University Press, reprinted 1975, p. xvi.
2. Scholars have pored over the Paston Letters since their first publication as five volumes in 1787–94. It did nothing to diminish their fascination when all of the originals disappeared without trace in the immediate aftermath of their publication. They were rediscovered several decades later, just in time to stymie a gathering suspicion that the letters were perhaps just a little too good to be true. For the full story of their rediscovery, see James Gairdner, *The Paston*

Letters: Introduction and Supplement, Westminster, Archibald Constable and Co., 1901, pp. i–xxx. It was clearly a painful saga for Gairdner to set down. In preparing a complete edition of the letters in 1872–5 he had several times been frustrated in his attempts to find those original letters that were still missing. Half of them finally surfaced just as he was completing his 1872–5 edition, and were found just where he had expected them to be. ('It was mortifying, I confess, not to have received earlier intelligence of a fact that I had suspected all along.') The other half turned up in 1889, prompting Gairdner to work on a revised six-volume edition, which was published in 1904. A modern edition, *The Paston Letters and Papers of the Fifteenth Century,* edited by Norman Davis, was published by Oxford University Press in 1971.

3. Bennett, *The Pastons and Their England,* p. 121.

4. Margaret Paston to Sir John, 5 March 1475, Gairdner Letter No. 866, Davis, *Paston Letters and Papers,* p. 374.

5. Sir John to John Paston III 'or to Mistress Margaret his mother', 28 September 1471, Gairdner Letter No. 782, ibid., p. 442.

6. J. A. Chartres, *Internal Trade in England, 1500–1700,* Studies in Economic and Social History, Macmillan, 1977, p. 40.

7. Sir John to Margaret Paston, 7 August 1465, Gairdner Letter No. 600, Davis, *Paston Letters and Papers,* p. 138.

8. An extensive collection of Gresham's surviving letters was published in J. W. Burgon, *The life and times of Sir Thomas Gresham compiled chiefly from his correspondence preserved in her majesty's state-paper office: including notices of many of his contemporaries,* 2 vols., London, 1839.

9. Quoted in Chartres, *Internal Trade in England,* p. 40.

10. Philip Beale, *A History of the Post in England from the Romans to the Stuarts,* Ashgate, 1998, pp. 156–7.

11. James Shapiro, *1599: A Year in the Life of William Shakespeare,* Faber & Faber, 2005, p. 260.

12. Stanley Wells, *Shakespeare for All Time,* Macmillan, 2002, p. 29. A photograph of the inventory of assets accompanying Greenway's will is printed on p. 42. Wells notes elsewhere: 'It is quite possible that, if letters written by Shakespeare ever turn up, they will be in Latin' (p. 14).

13. For an interesting sample of them, see Beale, *History of the Post,* pp. 87–92.

14. George Cavendish, *The Life and Death of Cardinal Wolsey,* first published 1641 (ed. Richard S. Sylvester), Oxford University Press, 1959, pp. 7–10. Scholars have quibbled over some of the details in the story, written at an unknown date in the reign of Henry VIII. But the key point is Cavendish's belief in the anecdote – which he claimed to have heard from Wolsey's own mouth.

15. The main source is *The King's Book of Payments,* supplemented by the papers of the Privy Council under Henry VIII. Almost fifty items from his reign are cited in an invaluable guide to the original records of early postal history, *The Inland Post (1392–1672): A Calendar of Historical Documents,* ed. J. W. M. Stone, Christie's-Robson Lowe, 1987, pp. 2–7.

16. Quoted in full by Beale, *History of the Post,* Appendix Two, pp. 234–5.

17. Beale, *History of the Post*, pp. 178–9. In an excellent general account of the Tudor Posts, pp. 137–89, Beale suggests the North Road was not made a permanent route until 1557.

18. See F. George Kay, *Royal Mail: The Story of the Posts in England from the Time of Edward IVth to the Present Day*, Rockliff, 1951, pp. 14–15. For a narrative of 1588 drawing extensively on the letters of the admirals, see John Sugden, *Sir Francis Drake*, Barrie & Jenkins, 1990, pp. 218–62.

19. The actual sum was £1,485. See Kay, *Royal Mail*, p. 7.

20. Peter Edwards, *The Horse Trade in Tudor and Stuart England*, Cambridge University Press, 1988, p. 4.

21. Quoted in Beale, *History of the Post*, p. 138.

22. For a more detailed account of this far from transparent arrangement, see John E. Crofts, *Packhorse, Waggon and Post: Land Carriage and Communications under the Tudors and Stuarts*, Routledge and Kegan Paul/University of Toronto Press, 1967, pp. 68–9. 'The matter was never, I believe, put in terms of a bargain; but a bargain was implicit . . .'

23. Quoted in Howard Robinson, *The British Post Office: A History*, Princeton University Press, 1948, p. 14.

24. The 1583 Orders in Council were republished in 1618 in *Proclamations in the reign of Elizabeth, collected by the Industry of Humphrey Dyson, of the City, Public Notary*. A lengthy extract from Dyson's republication is quoted in George Walker, *Haste, Post, Haste! Postmen and Post-Roads through the Ages*, George Harrap, 1938, pp. 98–100.

25. Walker suggested in *Haste, Post, Haste!* that the King's Posts of Tuke's time had evolved by 1600 into a substantially commercial postal service. 'That which began as part of the machinery of State had already become a convenience for ordinary villagers' (p. 135). Walker was a Congregational preacher from Croydon who had spent much of his life as a journalist and schools administrator in South Africa. Perhaps a more conventional academic background might have brought more attention to his generally neglected assessment of the sixteenth-century records. He appears to have read widely and carefully among the State and Privy Council papers of the Tudor century. He quotes from them liberally (though without citing chapter and verse) in support of the proposition that the Posts were being extensively used by commoners by the 1590s. Indeed, he suggests popular access to the Posts may have been a commonplace even within Tuke's own lifetime. Whatever the original objectives of the Crown, in his contention, 'the letters in the bag [from the mid-century onwards] were not all filled with the grave matters discussed in the presence of the King and dealing with weighty matters of State; some of them had no more serious burden than how many pounds of sugar were needed to make damson jam' (p. 123). Kay, *Royal Mail*, takes an equally sanguine view: 'Merchants and farmers, constables and innkeepers, soldiers and sailors were using the [Elizabethan] Posts, almost in spite of the declared restrictive policy of the Government as regards their public use . . .' (p. 16). Other postal historians have taken a

more cautious line, including Robinson (*British Post Office*), an American academic who still rates as one of the foremost authorities on the Post Office. 'By 1600 posting was, as yet, largely a service for the court, though some use was made of the facilities by persons on private business' (p. 21). It would seem hard to make sense of many contemporary references, or indeed of much that happened later, unless we accept that a much broader convergence was under way by 1600 than Robinson allowed for.

26. Quoted in Stone (ed.), *Inland Post*, p. 22.

27. Ibid., p. 24.

28. J. W. M. Stone, 'An Early Postmaster's Book', *The Philatelist*, November/ December 1984, p. 257. An abridged version of the Book is included in Stone (ed.), *Inland Post*, Appendix 7.

29. Quoted in Walker, *Haste, Post, Haste!*, p. 135.

30. See Beale, *History of the Post*, pp. 211–17.

31. Quoted in R. H. Coase 'The Postal Monopoly in Great Britain: An Historical Survey', in J. K. Eastham (ed.), *Economic Essays in Commemoration of the Dundee School of Economics, 1931–55*, privately publ. 1955, p. 26.

32. The Privy Council reviewed the operations of the Post in some detail in 1628, noting that 'till the 15th of September 1625 there was paid to all the posts of the Roads of England but £3,404 3s 4d per annum. Then . . . there were new Stages settled the several fees whereof does amount to £720 17s 0½d [per] annum which was so settled . . . [and] hath continued till this present time to the great prejudice of his Majesty not now useful' (quoted in Beale, *History of the Post*, p. 217). The cost of Henrietta Maria's passage is taken from N. A. M. Rodger, *The Safeguard of the Sea: A Naval History of Britain*, Vol. 1, HarperCollins, 1997, p. 370.

33. Quoted in Robinson, *British Post Office*, p. 35.

34. Quoted in Beale, *History of the Post*, p. 219.

35. Cited in Charles R. Clear, *The Birth of the Postal Service*, PO Green Paper xv, 1935, p. 3. He gives no reference for the contemporary source.

36. The letters of Henrietta Maria, starting with her first letters to Charles in 1624 and continuing until within a few months of her death in 1669, were first collected and edited by M. A. E. Green for publication in 1857. For the importance of her correspondence in the story of her marriage to Charles, see Katie Whitaker, *A Royal Passion: The Turbulent Marriage of Charles I and Henrietta Maria*, Weidenfeld & Nicolson, 2010.

37. Kevin Sharpe, 'Thomas Witherings and the Reform of the Foreign Posts, 1632–40', *Bulletin of the Institute of Historical Research*, 1984, Vol. 57, Issue 136, p. 154. See also C. R. Clear, *Thomas Witherings and the Birth of the Postal Service*, Post Office Green Papers, xv, 1935, and Brian Austen, *English Provincial Posts*, Phillimore, 1978, pp. 2–7.

38. Robinson, *British Post Office*, p. 33

39. Ibid., p. 29n.

40. Ibid., p. 29.

41. Quoted in ibid., p. 30, in a useful summary of the 1633–5 reforms.

42. Robinson, ibid., notes that the document is in Coke's handwriting, and points out that the editor of the state-papers volume for 1635, John Bruce, also clearly believed it to be by Coke (pp. 32–3). Beale, *History of the Post*, suggests the paper may be dated to 1620–22, since it is now to be found in the state papers for these dates, and puts forward the rather startling proposition that it may have been penned at that time by John Stanhope (pp. 212–13). Since the paper cites the putative cost of the Posts to be £4,125 – which is the precise sum of the two costs quoted in the 1628 Privy Council minutes – this must surely be mistaken. It also seems inherently unlikely that Stanhope, at the venerable age of seventy-five, could have authored such a radical set of proposals. On no other occasion in forty-five years did either he or his son display any recorded enthusiasm for serious reforms of any kind. Coke's authorship seems altogether more plausible, and wholly consistent with the unfolding of events in 1632–5. In all likelihood, it was written by Coke after discussions with Witherings in 1635, and somehow misplaced in the 1620 papers at a later date.

43. For the full text of the Proclamation, see Beale, *History of the Post*, pp. 228–9.

44. Quoted in J. W. Hyde, *The Post in Grant and Farm*, A. & C. Black, 1894, p. 86. Hyde had worked in the Post Office for twenty-five years before turning to postal history, and had been a senior official in Edinburgh.

45. Ibid., p. 93.

46. Sharpe, 'Thomas Witherings', p. 160.

47. The document is quoted at length in Hyde, *Post in Grant and Farm*, pp. 108–19.

48. Post 23/1. The letter survives today as the oldest document held in the British Postal Museum and Archive (BPMA) and is the only pre-1660 document in the archives. (See Appendix C.)

49. See, for example, R. M. Willcocks, *England's Postal History to 1840*, privately published, 1975: 'Of many hundreds of letters of this [early] period examined by the author, not one bearing an indication that it was carried in the post between August 1642 and 1648 has been seen ...' Willcocks was satisfied that a public postal service during the Civil War 'was quite out of the question for a dozen reasons. ... From 1642 to 1648 or 1649 it is practically certain that no public post (as we understand it) existed'. He believed that a surviving 'broadside' advertisement bearing a list of receiving postmasters in London, published in 1652, was in effect 'a notice announcing that after a break of nine to eleven years, the post was now carrying the public letters again' (pp. 12–15).

50. Hyde, *Post in Grant and Farm*, p. 193.

51. A settling of old scores followed the 1660 Restoration, and was amply documented in state papers. Several examples are cited by Robinson, *British Post Office*, p. 51.

52. Peter Gaunt, 'Interregnum Governments and the Reform of the Post Office, 1649–59', *Bulletin of the Institute of Historical Research*, October 1987,

Vol. 60, Issue 143, p. 298. Gaunt states elsewhere: 'there seems [in 1650] to have been little real progress towards change or reorganization and no concrete proposals reached council or parliament . . . Presumably, therefore, the system of inland and foreign posts run by Prideaux and Witherings respectively was functioning reasonably well' (p. 284). This refers to the second year after the end of the war, but is nonetheless hardly compatible with the view that there had been a substantial breakdown of the Posts since 1642.

53. Hyde, *Post in Grant and Farm*, p. 208.

54. The omission was righted in the *Missing Persons* volume of 1993.

55. See his entry in the *Oxford DNB*. Prideaux was appointed Attorney General in 1649 and retained that office, earning a handsome income from the law, until his death in 1659.

56. Quoted in Robinson, *British Post Office*, p. 45.

57. C. H. Firth and R. S. Rait (eds.), *Acts and Ordinances of the Interregnum, 1642–1660*, HMSO, 1911, pp. 1110–13.

58. Gaunt, 'Interregnum Governments', p. 298.

59. See C. H. Firth, 'Thurloe and the Post Office', *English Historical Review*, xiii (1898).

60. Quoted in ibid., p. 528.

2. A network for the nation, 1660–1764

1. Maurice Ashley, *John Wildman, Plotter and Postmaster*, Jonathan Cape, 1947, pp. 66–7. I have drawn heavily on Ashley's book, and an essay that he contributed nearly twenty years later to a *festschrift* in honour of another authority on the seventeenth century, 'John Wildman and the Post Office', in Richard Ollard and Pamela Tudor-Craig (eds.), *For Veronica Wedgwood These: Studies in Seventeenth-Century History*, Collins, 1986. The *Oxford DNB* has an extensive entry on Wildman by Richard L. Greaves.

2. In his *Oxford DNB* entry published in 2004, Richard L.Greaves is dismissive about the scaffold story but includes many new details about Wildman's extraordinary career.

3. C. H. Firth, 'Thurloe and the Post Office', *English Historical Review*, xiii (1898), p. 530.

4. Ashley, *John Wildman*, p. 171. Howard Robinson, in *The British Post Office: A History*, Princeton University Press, 1948, makes only a fleeting reference to Wildman and appears not to have been aware of Ashley's biography, published just as Robinson's work was completed.

5. Quoted in Robinson, *British Post Office*, p. 49.

6. Ibid., p. 52.

7. For the details and contemporary quotes, see Ashley, *John Wildman*, pp. 167–71 and 175–85.

8. The volume entitled 'Roades, Salarys, Stages &c' is a record of past and future wage rates for the postmasters. (Post 94/11.) The book itself carries

no date, but research into the tenure of the postmasters in it has suggested it was written in 1667. An anonymous modern note on the frontispiece reads: 'This must refer to a revision of salaries in 1667 when Lord Arlington took the Farm'. The Book of Annual Payments (Post 94/9) and the other nine volumes for the finances of 1672–7 (Post 94/1-8 and Post 94/10) are included – together with thirteen volumes of correspondence – in the papers of Arlington's Deputy Postmaster General, Colonel Roger Whitley. These are known as the Peover Papers because they were kept for over two centuries at Peover Hall near Knutsford, the country seat in Cheshire of Whitley's descendants, the Mainwaring family. They were passed to the Post Office archives for safe keeping in 1902. (See Post 94/25 for correspondence relating to the history of the Papers.) The collection begins with the first extant cash book, for 1672 (Post 94/1). Cash books went on being compiled annually after Whitley's departure, starting in 1677–8 (Post 2/1).

9. See Robinson, *British Post Office*, p. 80.

10. Mark Kishlansky, *A Monarchy Transformed: Britain 1603–1714*, Allen Lane, 1996, p. 319.

11. See John Brewer, *The Sinews of Power: War, Money and the English State, 1688–1783*, Harvard University Press, 1989.

12. A map of the City prepared immediately after the Great Fire of London placed the Letter Office, which it identified as the 'Post House', in Threadneedle Street. Research in the 1970s suggested it had been on a site there since as early as 1653. See R. M. Willcocks, *England's Postal History to 1840*, privately published, 1975, p. 23, and the same author's 'The Letter Office in the Fire of London', *The British Mail Coach*, No. 1, Spring 1974. (This was a short-lived periodical of the Great Britain Postal History Group of the Postal History Society, and merged with the *Journal of Postal History* after Issue No. 29 in June 1981.)

13. For an account of Joseph Williamson's interest in the Post Office and his relationship with James Hickes, see Susan E. Whyman, 'Postal Censorship in England 1635–1844', a paper presented to the Oxford–Princeton Partnership Conference on the History of Censorship, September 2003. English diplomats overseas who sent secret intelligence back to London relied, for example, on the services of the Chester Road Clerk: 'They addressed their letters to fictitious names, known by Hickes, who took them out of the post and gave them to Williamson' (p. 8). See also the same author's *The Pen and the People: English Letter Writers 1660–1800*, OUP, 2009, pp. 48–53.

14. Calendar of State Papers 1666–7, p. 95. Hickes dated his letter 3 September, which may have been a simple mistake: Threadneedle Street burned down on the night of Monday/Tuesday, 3/4 September. Or possibly he and his family fled early on the Monday, thinking the fire would reach the Office sooner than it did. Hickes wrote a second letter on 4 September, addressed to his postmasters on the Chester Road, telling them he and his family were safe and had taken refuge in Barnet. See Willcocks, *England's Postal History*, p. 23.

15. Quoted in Robinson, *British Post Office*, p. 57.

16. This and the following two, longer quotations from Hickes's correspondence are taken from J. W. Hyde, *The Post in Grant and Farm*, A. & C. Black, 1894, pp. 297–9.

17. The original documents are held in Post 94/12, 14, 16, 18, 20 and 22. The typed transcriptions are in Post 94/13, 15, 17, 19, 21 and 23. An index of names survives as Post/24.

18. Post 94/13.

19. Post 94/12.

20. Whitley to Captain Lullman, 13 March 1673, Post 94/12.

21. Whitley appears to have gone to Cheshire to be with his daughter, who was to marry in October 1677. (The Mayor of Chester in 1693 was a Whitley, perhaps the Colonel or possibly his son.) See Report by J. G. Hendy, Curator of the Historical Manuscripts Commission, Post 94/25, where Whitley's letters of 1677 are quoted.

22. See entry by G. E. Aylmer in the *Oxford DNB*. The Post Office Notice of March 1678 announcing the move 'to Sir Robert Viner's house' can be found in M. M. Raguin (ed.), *British Post Office Notices: 1666–1899*, Vol. 1, privately published, 1991, p. 8. Raguin collected many Notices now lost but reprinted in contemporary newspapers. His volumes are kept at the BPMA.

23. The numbers are quoted in the entry for 'Post and Postal Service' in *Encylopaedia Britannica*, 11th edn, 1911, pp. 176–92.

24. Robinson, *British Post Office*, p. 65.

25. See Raguin (ed.), *British Post Office Notices*, and also D. G. Haslam and C. Moreton, *Post Office Notices Extracted from the London Gazette 1660–1800*, Postal History Society of Lancashire and Cheshire, 1988.

26. Comments from *The Gentleman's Magazine*, 1815, quoted in 'Post and Postal Service', *Encylopaedia Britannica*, pp. 176–92.

27. Quoted in Robinson, *British Post Office*, p. 67.

28. Thomas Gardiner, *A General Survey of the Post Office, 1677–82*, ed. Foster W. Bond, Special Series No. 5, Postal History Society, 1958. The tree-chart for the Chester Road is printed on p. 71. Its five main branches show routes extending as far as Sheffield, Manchester and Kendal to the east, and Worcester, Ludlow and Aberdovy to the west. A photocopy of the *Survey* is available on the open shelves of the BPMA, complete with its front cover, on which is written: 'This book did belong to King James, I had it from coll Graham'.

29. Brian Austen, *English Provincial Posts*, Phillimore, 1978, p. 36.

30. David Ogg, *England in the Reign of Charles II*, Oxford University Press, 1967, p. 525.

31. See the entry for 13 June 1667, Robert Latham (ed.), *The Shorter Pepys*, Bell & Hyman, 1985, p. 789.

32. Daniel Defoe, *A Tour Thro' the Whole Island of Great Britain*, quoted in Robinson, *British Post Office*, pp. 85–6.

33. Herbert Joyce, *The History of the Post Office*, Richard Bentley & Son, 1893, p. 55.

34. The evidence for this continuity of nomenclature is set out by Ashley, 'John Wildman', in Ollard and Tudor-Craig (eds.), *For Veronica Wedgwood These*, pp. 211–12.

35. Ibid., p. 298

36. The authority of the Postmasters General was limited in some surprising ways. They had no control, for example, over the 'private office', which went on handling intercepted inland letters illicitly in Lombard Street under an independent government appointee until 1742. The last such head of the office was rather curiously a clergyman, the Dean of Lincoln. After his nocturnal services were dispensed with, he was made the Bishop of Bath and Wells in 1743. See R. E. M. Peach, *The Life and Times of Ralph Allen*, D. Nutt, 1895, p. 124.

37. Joyce, *History of the Post Office*, p. 70.

38. Wryly noting a conspicuous lack of revenues from his postmaster in Chichester, for example, Whitley wrote to him demanding 'a just acco'nt for the future, or if you would rather bee att a Certeinty, & avoid ye trouble of accompting, I will farme ye By-letters of yo'r Stage (as I doe in severall others) if you like this way make a faire proposeall ...' (Whitley to Robert Tayer, December 1673). The letter is quoted in Willcocks, *England's Postal History*, p. 33.

39. A good account of the by-post farms can be found in Willcocks, *England's Postal History*, pp. 32–9. Willcocks brings to bear his very detailed knowledge as an authoritative collector and philatelist.

40. The account that follows, of Quash's relationship with Ralph Allen and the origins of the latter's career, is based on an excellent biography by Benjamin Boyce, *The Benevolent Man: A Life of Ralph Allen of Bath*, Harvard University Press, 1967, and the further research by Willcocks, *England's Postal History*. I have presented the story shorn of the scholarly caveats which accompany their treatment of facts that in some places are no more than strong suppositions or probabilities.

41. Adrian E. Hopkins (ed.), *Ralph Allen's Own Narrative, 1720–61*, Special Series No. 8, Postal History Society, 1960, p. 18.

42. Ibid., p. 16.

43. Ibid., pp. 17–18.

44. Ibid., p. 29.

45. Ibid., p. 17.

46. By contrast with Allen's reticence, late-Victorian writers loved to dwell on the iniquities of Georgian times as a reminder of the Olympian standards of their own Post Office. One Victorian biographer of Allen observed that 'in this arduous work [of building the cross-post network] he had to encounter, not simply the ordinary difficulties and complications of postal business in itself, but the perverse, obstructive, and reactionary tactics of the Government, out of which had sprung the evasion, the dishonesty, the delays, the trickery, and the rapacity of the officials employed, from the post-boys to the postmasters and the higher officials. . . . [The government] had one aim and one alone, that was, to get as large a revenue as they could, without

regard to increasing population, advancing civilization, or political necessity.' (Peach, *Life and Times*.)

47. Boyce, *Benevolent Man*, p. 28.

48. Willcocks, *England's Postal History*, p. 45. Quash's signature accompanies
Allen's on two bonds guaranteeing his honest administration of his recently
deceased parents' wills. The author notes that, 'when Ralph Allen could
have asked anyone of a hundred people to sign them with his brother, he
asked Quash, eighteen years after he had dropped into oblivion'. He is
strongly inclined to see this as the clue to the slight mystery over the younger
man's extraordinary success. 'Here is the perfect answer, for Quash knew
much more about cross-posts than Allen, he had trained Allen, and would
seem to have been his right-hand man throughout.'

49. Hopkins, *Ralph Allen's Own Narrative*, p. 24.

50. A Parliamentary Committee of 1797 looking into the appointment of one of
Allen's successors, John Palmer, was assured by Palmer himself that £12,000
a year would be a reasonable estimate of Allen's profits. (*Report of the
Committee on Palmer's Agreement*, quoted in Robinson, *British Post Office*,
p. 109.) Palmer, born in Bath in 1742 and still living there when Allen died
in 1764, may have heard stories about the great man's wealth, but there is
no evidence that the two of them ever met.

51. Ibid., p. 102.

52. Quoted in Boyce, *Benevolent Man*, p. 217.

53. William Maitland, *Survey of London* (1756), quoted in Whyman, *Pen and
the People*, p. 56.

54. The 1797 *Report of the Committee on Palmer's Appointment* listed the
'Gross Product', Expenses and Net Product from 1724. The figures are
quoted in J. C. Hemmeon, *The History of the British Post Office*, Harvard
University Press, 1912, as part of an appendix with seven tables that sets out
a summary of the Post Office's finances from 1724 to 1907.

55. Whyman, *Pen and the People*, p. 58. On the growing importance of letters
in the eighteenth century, see also Clare Brant, *Eighteenth-Century Letters
and British Culture*, Palgrave Macmillan, 2006.

56. Whyman, *Pen and the People*, p. 5.

57. See for example Neil McKendrick, John Brewer and J. H. Plumb, *The Birth
of a Consumer Society: The Commercialization of Eighteenth-Century England*, Europa Publications, 1982. Neither Allen nor the Post Office warrant
a mention.

3. Coaches and communications, 1764–1829

1. Herbert Joyce, *The History of the Post Office*, Richard Bentley & Son,
1893, p. 46

2. In a celebrated feud between the Postmasters General in 1784–6, one
refused to sign a bill for furniture purchased by the other, deploring it as

'gross impropriety'. The Secretary advised signing to bring matters to a close, 'though upon the whole some of the things were rather too good'. See Kenneth Ellis, *The Post Office in the Eighteenth Century: A Study in Administrative History*, OUP, 1958, p. 107.

3. Earl of Clarendon to Lord Grantham, 12 July 1765, quoted in Ellis, *Post Office in the Eighteenth Century*, p. 14.

4. Several colourful references to the Post Office clerks' prying eyes in the eighteenth century are quoted in Howard Robinson, *The British Post Office: A History*, Princeton University Press, 1948, pp. 120–25. One of the most famous came in a letter home from Benjamin Franklin, while he was living in London. As well as being the colonial agent for several of the American colonies, Franklin was also one of the Deputy Postmasters General of the New York Post Office. This seemingly high status gave his letters no protection whatever. 'The letters I have received from my friends in Boston have lately come to hand, badly sealed, with no distinct Impression, appearing as if they had been opened.'

5. Ellis, *Post Office in the Eighteenth Century*, p. 76.

6. Robinson, *British Post Office*, p. 76. See pp. 60–77 for a detailed account of the Georgian Post Office's intelligence activities, on which my summary has drawn heavily.

7. See Henry Parris, *Constitutional Bureaucracy: The Development of British Central Administration since the Eighteenth Century*, Allen & Unwin, 1969. 'Probably the War Office was the first department to have an official corresponding in function with the modern Permanent Secretary . . . [But] the Post Office was not far behind' (p. 42).

8. Ellis, *Post Office in the Eighteenth Century*, p. 40. Willcocks, in *England's Postal History*, states that 'the weight [of franked mail] was estimated to equal that of all charged letters'. He adds that franks 'were said to be five-sixths of the total Irish mail' (p. 56).

9. Cited in Robinson, *British Post Office*, p. 118.

10. Ibid., p. 53.

11. This, 'the first remittance ever made of its kind', was noted in a memorandum to the Treasury, unsigned but probably from Todd (Post 1/9, TLB, pp. 95–105, 28 January 1764). He also noted there, cautiously and correctly, that 'the Postage [revenues from New York] cannot for a long while be expected to exceed the charges of management, because in the Colonies, settled in part only, where the Towns are situated at a great distance from each other, there is a continual necessity of erecting new offices . . .' A much quoted claim by Benjamin Franklin in 1774, that the American Office was yielding three times as much as the Irish Post Office, can be dismissed as wishful thinking. New York's average yearly profits over the 1761–74 period were no more than £600. The Irish Post Office was earning £4,000 a year as its share of the packet-boat services across the Irish Sea alone.

12. Post 1/10, TLB, p. 129, 22 December 1775.

13. Quoted in Joyce, *History of the Post Office*, p. 208.

14. See D. G. Haslam and C. Moreton, *Post Office Notices Extracted from the London Gazette 1660–1800*, Postal History Society of Lancashire and Cheshire, 1988.

15. Post 1/10, TLB, p. 166, 4 November 1776.

16. Extracted from Book IV, 'The Winter Evening', from *The Task*, by William Cowper.

17. I'am grateful to Professor Rick Trainor for drawing Parson Woodforde's forbearance to my attention.

18. See Charles R. Clear, *John Palmer: Mail Coach Pioneer*, Blandford Press, 1955, p. 15.

19. Some striking examples are cited in Robinson, *British Post Office*, pp. 129–30, drawing on nineteenth-century estimates by, among others, Samuel Smiles, author of *The Life of Thomas Telford, with an Introductory History of Roads and Travelling in Great Britain*, 1867. London to York was scheduled to take four days in 1750 and three in 1780. London to Sheffield over the same period was reduced from four days to a little over one, and London to Bristol was cut from two days to about sixteen hours.

20. A handwritten though incomplete copy of the Plan, included in the BPMA as Post 96/20, Part 2, comprised twenty-two separate proposals. They are printed in full in Frederick Wilkinson, *Royal Mail Coaches: An Illustrated History*, Tempus, 2007, along with a summary of the subsequent objections from the Post Office and Palmer's rebuttal of them, pp. 28–37.

21. Wilkinson, *Royal Mail Coaches*, p. 31.

22. See Edmund Vale, *The Mail-Coach Men of the Late Eighteenth Century*, Cassell, 1960, p. 28.

23. *Observations on Mr Palmer's Plan for Reform and Improvement in the management of the business of the General Post Office*, Post 96/20.

24. Ibid.

25. Ellis, *Post Office in the Eighteenth Century*, p. 101.

26. For the story of the early ballooning craze, see Richard Holmes, *The Age of Wonder*, Harper Press, 2008, pp. 137–62.

27. Ellis, *Post Office in the Eighteenth Century*, p. 103. Ellis gives a graphic and well-documented account of the vicious campaign waged by Todd and his associates (pp. 101–3). It contrasts strikingly with Herbert Joyce's 1893 version of events: 'Palmer maintained to the end of his life that . . . he was thwarted and opposed by the Post Office. This charge, so far as it refers to those by whom the Post Office was managed and controlled, we believe to be groundless. . . . Anthony Todd, the secretary, was eminently a man of peace' (Joyce, *History of the Post Office*, pp. 217–18).

28. Post 1/13, TLB, p. 36, 5 August 1786. Palmer had asked to have a new position, reporting directly to the Treasury – and Pitt was ready to accede to this, until the lawyers reminded him of the 1711 Act's provisions restricting any involvement in postal matters to employees of the Post Office. For Palmer to have run the Post without being an employee would have needed

Parliamentary legislation. Pitt baulked at this, though Palmer pressed him on several occasions to reconsider.

29. I am grateful to Martin Daunton for this intriguing point.

30. Cited in Wilkinson, *Royal Mail Coaches*, p. 38.

31. Quoted in Stanley Harris, *The Coaching Age*, London, 1885, p. 279.

32. The description of Palmer was by the Earl of Chesterfield, appointed Postmaster General in 1790, and is quoted in Vale, *Mail-Coach Men*, p. 28.

33. See Robinson, *British Post Office*, p. 151.

34. *Report of the Commissioners of 1788 on the Post Office*, quoted in ibid., pp. 151–2.

35. J. C. Hemmeon, *The History of the British Post Office*, Harvard University Press, 1912, p. 244.

36. See Ellis, *Post Office in the Eighteenth Century*, p. 118.

37. Clear, *John Palmer*, p. 26.

38. A good account of abuses in the packet-boat services can be found in Howard Robinson, *Carrying British Mails Overseas*, George Allen & Unwin, 1964, pp. 60–65. Several senior officials owned shares in the packet boats whose operations and expenses they were supposed to be monitoring. The 1788 Commissioners put a stop to this, with one exception. Nine years later, Francis Freeling confirmed to another parliamentary inquiry that no officials owned any shares in boats 'excepting Mr Todd, who has a fourth share of the Grantham on the Falmouth station, and whose Failure of Memory alone will account for his having said [to the inquiry] that he had none when he was asked the question' (p. 64).

39. Quoted in Vale, *Mail-Coach Men*, p. 27.

40. The six letters are reprinted in full in Clear, *John Palmer*, pp. 55–63, in a book largely devoted to a blow-by-blow account of the extraordinary story.

41. Two volumes of personal letters written between April 1794 and November 1796 survive in the Royal Mail archive, along with two volumes of printed papers and instructions for those running the coach network between 1792 and 1817. (Post 10/24-27.) Joyce quotes from them quite liberally (*History of the Post Office*, pp. 284–90), but it is Edmund Vale's 1960 book on the mail coaches (*Mail-Coach Men*) that uses the letters to suggest the importance of Hasker's work, unjustly neglected in Vale's view. His attention was drawn to them in the 1950s by the archivist at St Martin's-le-Grand. Their survival, he noted, 'was really quite miraculous in view of the fearful and indiscriminate depradations which had been made by pulp-hunters during the paper shortages of the last two wars' (p. 7).

42. Vale, *Mail-Coach Men*, p. 59.

43. Madeleine Elsas (ed.), *Iron in the Making: The Dowlais Iron Company Letters, 1782–1860*, Glamorgan County Records Committee, 1960.

44. Peter Mathias, *The First Industrial Nation: An Economical History of Britain 1700–1914*, Methuen, 1969, p. 198.

45. See Stanley Harris, *The Coaching Age*, London, 1885, pp. 275–94, for a useful collection of Time Bills showing the duration of Royal Mail journeys by the 1830s. Coach times from London included Oxford in 6 hours 38 minutes, Portsmouth in 8 hours 17 minutes, Dover in 17 hours (including dinner in Canterbury), Newcastle in 29 hours 50 minutes, Holyhead in 26 hours 55 minutes – and Edinburgh in 42 hours 23 minutes. The precision of the journey times was a measure of the obsessive regard for time-keeping that distinguished the Royal Mail from the start.

46. For examples of this practice, see Joyce, *History of the Post Office*, pp. 401–2.

47. Frederic Hill, the brother of Rowland, gave an account of the coach's arrival in his *Autobiography*. 'Every one was aware that a great battle must be taking place, and while the result was yet unknown, we were all on the tiptoe of eager expectation.' Quoted in Robinson, *Carrying British Mails Overseas*, p. 240.

48. Charles G. Harper, *Stage Coach and Mail in Days of Yore*, 2 vols., London, 1903, Vol. 1, p. 250.

49. The full story is told in Charles G. Harper, *The Exeter Road: The Story of the West of England Highway*, London, 1899, pp. 162–4. Harper (1863–1943) was one of the most prolific writers about the mail coach era, writing more than a dozen books on the great Post Roads.

50. Ellis, *Post Office in the Eighteenth Century*, comments on Todd's last years that 'his memory meant time immemorial and his prestige was immense'. He makes no attempt to reconcile this with the outspoken attack by the 1797 Committee of the House of Commons on Todd's retention of office (p. 122). Ellis's account of the eighteenth-century Post Office takes a surprisingly charitable view of Todd's whole career.

51. Hemmeon, *History of the British Post Office*, pp. 245 and 247.

52. See Joyce, *History of the Post Office*, p. 405. From his vantage point in the 1890s, Joyce enjoyed reminding his readers of the shockingly mercenary ways of an earlier era: 'A service that was not self-supporting was, at the beginning of the century, regarded by the Post Office authorities as an abomination . . .' (p. 350).

53. See Holmes, *Age of Wonder*, p. 207.

54. A summary of Johnson's reforms to the London Penny Post can be found in Willcocks, *England's Postal History*, pp. 73–4.

55. Statistics on their growth were collected by a Parliamentary Select Committee on Postage, which delivered three reports in 1838. The penny posts are described in the Appendix to the 3rd Report.

56. Joyce, *History of the Post Office*, states that 275 towns had no free delivery, 'and – what proves a constant source of contention between the Post Office and the inhabitants – even in those towns in which the letters are delivered free, the limits of the free delivery are not defined' (p. 410).

57. Quoted in Robinson, *British Post Office*, p. 220.

58. For a summary of the dilemma posed for the Post Office by ship letters between 1780 and 1830, see Robinson, *Carrying British Mails Overseas*, pp. 111–13.

59. Robinson, *British Post Office*, p. 254. The author provides his own map of the packet stations of the early nineteenth century on p. 162.

60. Hyphens come and go in various forms of the street's name. Even the signs on either side of today's street carry two different versions, one with a single hyphen and one with none.

61. Joyce, *History of the Post Office*, p. 420.

4. Rowland Hill and postal reform, 1830–64

1. Anthony Trollope, *An Autobiography* (first publ. 1883), Penguin Books, 1993, pp. 45–6. He was less than certain where this dignitary hailed from – 'I think Saxony, but I am sure it was a Queen . . .'

2. Rowland Hill made the point in his autobiography: 'I applied for permission to see the working of the London office, but was met by a polite refusal': R. Hill and G. B. Hill, *The Life of Sir Rowland Hill and the History of Penny Postage*, 2 vols., De La Rue, 1880, Vol. 1, p. 246n.

3. Quoted in Martin Daunton, *Royal Mail: The Post Office since 1840*, The Athlone Press, 1985, p. 17.

4. Secretary Maberly to the 1837–38 Parliamentary Select Committee, quoted in Daunton, *Royal Mail*, p. 22.

5. See G. M. Young, *Victorian England: Portrait of an Age*, OUP, 1960. 'In 1830, except for the collection and management of the revenue, for defence, and the transmission of letters, there was hardly anything which a Frenchman or a Prussian would have recognized as an administration' (p. 39).

6. Howard Robinson sets out the figures cited by the Commissioners in his *Carrying British Mails Overseas*, George Allen & Unwin, 1964, p. 122n, and observes that the annual expenses of the continuing services doubled between 1817 and 1827.

7. Quoted in Howard Robinson, *The British Post Office: A History*, Princeton University Press, 1948, p. 285.

8. J. C. Hemmeon, *The History of the British Post Office*, Harvard University Press, 1912, p. 246.

9. The description, by Lord Lowther, is quoted in Robinson, *British Post Office*, p. 250.

10. Quoted in Daunton, *Royal Mail*, p. 17.

11. Quoted in Robinson, *British Post Office*, p. 251.

12. Ibid., p. 255.

13. Herbert Joyce, *The History of the Post Office*, Richard Bentley & Son, 1893, p. 427.

14. *Public Education: Plans for the Government and Liberal Instruction of Boys in Large Numbers. Drawn from Experience* was published anonymously in 1822, and then again in a revised edition under the brothers' names in 1825.

15. Quoted in Daunton, *Royal Mail*, p. 13. The diary entry was recorded in 1821, when Hill was twenty-six.

16. Gavin Fryer and Clive Akerman (eds.), *The Reform of the Post Office in the Victorian Era and Its Impact on Economic and Social Activity*, 2 vols., The Royal Philatelic Society, 2000, Vol. 1, p. 17.

17. Ibid., p. 20.

18. See ibid., p. 46.

19. Outspoken critics included J. R. McCulloch, the leading Ricardian economist and the first professor of political economy at University College London, and J. W. Croker, the Tory politician and writer who famously quit the Commons after 1832 rather than sit in a post-Reform Parliament.

20. Wallace's Parliamentary Select Committee could only bring itself in 1838 to back a uniform twopenny postage.

21. Quoted in Robinson, *British Post Office*, p. 290.

22. Quoted in ibid., p. 292.

23. Ibid., p. 293.

24. An alternative construction on events, favoured by Willcocks, is that the 4d trial was so successful that Hill and the Chancellor were happy to bring the penny post's launch forward. (*England's Postal History*, p. 131.) But there is no evidence this was the case, and it seems inherently unlikely given the unfinished state of preparations.

25. For a history of the Stamp Office, see Harry Dagnall, *Creating a Good Impression: Three Hundred Years of the Stamp Office and Stamp Duties*, HMSO, 1994.

26. For a good brief history of stamps through the reign of Queen Victoria, see Chapter 9 of Asa Briggs, *Victorian Things*, B. T. Batsford, 1988, pp. 327–68. The Penny Black's catalogue price at Stanley Gibbons early in 2009 was £8,500 for a specimen in pristine mint condition.

27. Entry in *Oxford DNB* by G. E. Dixon.

28. Obituary in *The Times*, 25 February 1913.

29. *Pall Mall Gazette*, 9 August 1879. For the full article, see p. 19 of a cuttings book filed in Post 111/17.

30. See 'The Story of Stanley Gibbons' by Michael Briggs, published in a special anniversary edition of *Gibbons Stamp Monthly* magazine in 2005. I am grateful to Michael Briggs for drawing it to my attention. My account of Gibbons' life draws heavily on articles in the magazine by him and by John Holman.

31. Covering Gibbons' travels between 1891 and 1907, the scrapbook now exists in two parts. One is in private ownership and the other is held in the company archives of Stanley Gibbons Ltd.

32. 'I am so pestered in consequence of the deluge of letters and small pamphlets in prose and verse,' wrote Wordsworth in March 1841, 'that if I were

to attend to one half of them I should really have no time for myself' (quoted in Robinson, *British Post Office*, p. 301). It seems worth remarking that Wordsworth had himself earned a modest salary since 1813 as 'Distributor of Stamps' for Westmorland – but this job entailed providing papers for official usage that had already been embossed by the Stamp Office in London, and of course had nothing to do with postage stamps.

33. The letter of dismissal is quoted in full in Hill's autobiography, Hill and Hill, *Life of Sir Rowland Hill*, Vol. 1, p. 466. The subsequent correspondence follows on pp. 466–72.

34. Ibid., p. 479.

35. Joyce, *History of the Post Office*, p. 400.

36. The quotation is from C. P. Snow, *Trollope*, Macmillan, 1975, p. 58, which has many lively passages, and some good illustrations, depicting the novelist's day job throughout his career with the Post Office.

37. His appointment back to England followed directly upon a recommendation from Rowland Hill, who wrote to the Postmaster General, the Marquess of Clanricarde, in July 1851: 'The prompt and satisfactory completion of the revision of the Rural Posts in Mr Kendrick's district [of Ireland] is very creditable to Mr Trollope to whom the duty was entrusted, . . . and I beg to recommend that the advantage of his assistance be afforded to one of the English Surveyors in the performance of the similar duties'. Quoted in R. H. Super, *The Chronicler of Barsetshire: A Life of Anthony Trollope*, University of Michigan Press, 1988, p. 63. See also the same author's *Trollope in the Post Office*, University of Michigan Press, 1981.

38. Quoted in Victoria Glendinning, *Trollope*, Hutchinson, 1992, p. 196. A moving biography of the man, this contains the best guide to his use of his postal experience in his novels, and the author herself brings a novelist's insight to the impact of the penny post: '[it] speeded up business transactions, friendships and love affairs. It opened up new possibilities of intensity and a whole new field of anguish' (p. 193).

39. On Trollope's reputation as a novelist during his own lifetime, and later, see Philip Waller, *Writers, Readers and Reputations: Literary Life in Britain, 1870–1918*, OUP, 2006, pp. 199–201.

40. The Secret Inquiry produced a revealing public report on letter-opening practices since 1712. Howard Robinson drew upon it to include a colourful chapter, 'The Sanctity of Correspondence', in his 1948 history (*British Post Office*).

41. Clanricarde to Russell, 26 November 1846, quoted in Henry Parris, *Constitutional Bureaucracy: The Development of British Central Administration since the Eighteenth Century*, Allen & Unwin, 1969, p. 144.

42. Edmund Yates, *Recollections and Experiences*, 2 vols., Richard Bentley & Son, 1884. Rather like Trollope, if at a less elevated level, he managed to juggle his Post Office and writing careers for many years. His gossip journalism caused him to be ejected from the Garrick Club in 1858 for writing a scurrilous sketch about Thackeray, a fellow member. Dickens, one of

Yates's closest friends, was also a Garrick member and refused to back Yates's expulsion. It was this that caused the celebrated estrangement between Thackeray and Dickens. On this and Yates's career in magazine journalism, see Waller, *Writers, Readers and Reputations*, pp. 418 and 497.

43. Yates, *Recollections and Experiences*, Vol. 1, Chapter 3, especially pp. 90–99.

44. Colin G. Hey, *Rowland Hill: Genius and Benefactor 1795–1879*, Quiller Press, 1989, p. 81. Hey provides a useful reminder of the sheer cussedness of many of the officials with whom Hill had to contend.

45. Quoted in Daunton, *Royal Mail*, p. 5.

46. See Robinson, *British Post Office*, p. 355. As the author, an American, suggests, it is possible that the Hills got the idea from Washington: the Postmaster General of the United States had been filing annual reports since 1823.

47. See G. M. Trevelyan, *English Social History*, Longmans, Green, 1944, Chapter XVII.

48. Robinson, *British Post Office*, p. 287.

49. Yates, *Recollections and Experiences*, Vol. 1, p. 103.

50. C. R. Perry, *The Victorian Post Office: The Growth of a Bureaucracy*, Royal Historical Society/Boydell Press, 1992, p. 8.

51. See Fryer and Akerman (eds.), *Reform of the Post Office*, Vol. 1, pp. 521–3.

52. Hill's *Post Office Journal*, 5 June 1863. See Fryer and Akerman (eds.), *Reform of the Post Office*, Vol. 1, p. 581.

53. Palmerston to Gladstone, 21 May 1863, quoted in Perry, *Victorian Post Office*, p. 9.

54. The speech appeared in *The Times* of 11 June 1864, a cutting of which Hill duly added to his *Journal*.

55. Yates, *Recollections and Experiences*, Vol. 2, p. 225.

56. Ibid., pp. 96–9.

57. Perry, *Victorian Post Office*, p. 60. In Perry's view, Gladstone's admiration for the management at St Martin's was 'undoubtedly excessively great'.

58. See Hey, *Rowland Hill: Genius and Benefactor*, p. 83.

59. See Super, *Trollope in the Post Office*, pp. 54–5.

60. Fryer and Akerman (eds.), *Reform of the Post Office*, Vol 1, Introduction, p. xx.

61. Snow, *Trollope*, p. 130. He points out that the March 1864 letter was sent a fortnight before Hill's retirement. 'The thought occurs, though it may be over-suspicious, was Trollope, just for once, being disingenuous or diplomatic? . . . He couldn't avoid realizing that the succession in the top places at the Post Office was about to be decided.' If so, it did Trollope no good. He was passed over for promotion in the subsequent reshuffling of jobs, and his disappointment contributed to his decision in 1867 to retire to his novel-writing – though he took on some freelance assignments, including a visit to Washington in 1868 on the Post Office's behalf to negotiate with the US government on the handling of transatlantic mails.

62. Daunton, *Royal Mail*, p. 35. The harshness of Daunton's judgement may have been partly responsible for the impassioned defence of Hill in Colin Hey's 1989 biography (*Rowland Hill: Genius and Benefactor*).

63. Daunton, *Royal Mail*, p. 130. Daunton gives a succinct summary of the protracted battles over rail-contract pricing in the 1840s and 1850s. A crucial question after 1853 was whether prices should represent only a contribution to the operating cost of the trains being used, or a contribution also towards the capital cost of the tracks beneath the trains. Characteristically, Hill fought to uphold the 'marginal pricing' approach, but had in the end to accept contracts far more favourable to the railway companies.

64. *The Economist*, 23 August 1851.

65. See Boyd Cable, *A Hundred Year History of the P&O, 1837–1937*, London, 1937, p. 150.

66. Quoted in Daunton, *Royal Mail*, p. 159.

67. He was giving evidence to a Select Committee on Packet and Telegraphic Contracts in 1860. Quoted in ibid., p. 162.

68. *The Times*, 16 February 1856, p. 6.

69. Quoted in Robinson, *British Post Office*, p. 359.

70. Quoted in Daunton, *Royal Mail*, p. 164.

71. Ibid., p. 170. Daunton provides a detailed account of the renegotiation of the contracts with both Cunard and P&O, pp. 161–71.

72. In fact, it was part of that infinitely complex process by which nineteenth-century government in Britain passed from the era of *laissez-faire* individualism to the more collectivist culture of the three pre-1914 decades. The chronology of the process and, indeed, how far it really happened in a linear fashion were subjects of scholarly dispute for generations. For a summary, see Harold Perkin, 'Individualism versus Collectivism in Nineteenth Century Britain: A False Antithesis', *Journal of British Studies*, Vol. XVII, 1977, pp. 105–18.

5. In a league of its own, 1864–1914

1. Three other officials would follow in his footsteps over the next forty years: J. W. Hyde (in 1885), Herbert Joyce (1893) and R. C. Tombs (1905). Autobiographical accounts of careers with the Post Office include, over the same period, those of Edmund Yates (1884) and F. E. Baines (1895) – as well, of course, as those of Rowland Hill (1880), Anthony Trollope (1883) and Frederic Hill (1893). William Lewins himself also wrote a *History of Savings Banks*, which appeared in 1866.

2. William Lewins, *Her Majesty's Mails*, Sampson Low, Son, and Marston, 2nd edn, 1865, p. 278.

3. C. R. Perry, *The Victorian Post Office: The Growth of a Bureaucracy*, Royal Historical Society/Boydell Press, 1992, p. 206.

4. Ibid., p. 297.

5. F. E. Baines, *Forty Years at the Post Office: A Personal Narrative*, 2 vols., R. Bentley & Son, 1895, Vol. 1, p. 261. The other ten cities were Bath, Bournemouth (another of the author's home towns), Bristol, Exeter, Hull, Leeds, Newcastle, Southampton, Glasgow and Belfast. Inevitably, as Baines acknowledged, he was comparing numbers that were not strictly like for like: the earlier costs were drawn on a slightly narrower basis. But this scarcely weakened his point.

6. The proceedings at the anniversary dinner are covered in some detail by Robinson, *British Post Office*, pp. 417–20.

7. Martin Daunton, *Royal Mail: The Post Office since 1840*, The Athlone Press, 1985, p. 205.

8. See Christian Wolmar, *Fire & Steam, A New History of the Railways in Britain*, Atlantic Books, 2007, pp. 153–6. 'Locomotive men, for example, started as cleaners then became "passed" cleaners, who were able to fire locomotives, then firemen and "passed" firemen ... Then, at last, they became drivers but at first were confined to shunting engines around the yard or the occasional short goods run. It was only in their fifties that they would get the freedom of the rails and become one of the elite, driving passenger expresses around the country.'

9. Daunton, *Royal Mail*, p. 199.

10. Ibid., p. 193.

11. Perry, *Victorian Post Office*, p. 19.

12. Baines, *Forty Years at the Post Office*, Vol. 1, p. 253.

13. Jeffrey Kieve, *The Electric Telegraph: A Social and Economic History*, David & Charles, 1973, p. 67.

14. See Martin Daunton, *State and Market in Victorian Britain: War, Welfare and Capitalism*, Boydell Press, 2008.

15. Baines, *Forty Years at the Post Office*, Vol. 1, pp. 299–306. He drew up a formal plan for his proposed Post Office telegraph department in 1856, and submitted it to the Treasury the following year, copied both to the Prime Minister, the Earl of Derby, and to Lord Stanley of Alderley, who would later, as Postmaster General from 1860, lock horns with Rowland Hill. (It is intriguing that Baines makes no mention in his memoir of writing directly to Hill himself.) The young clerk got no response from the Treasury, but Stanley wrote back to say he was sympathetic to his approach, '[which] has long been the view which I have taken of the subject'. The Prime Minister also replied, acknowledging that Baines's scheme was 'certainly large, original and recommended by the analogy of the Post-Office'. Derby said he would keep the plan 'and consult others upon it'. It was finally published as a Parliamentary Paper in April 1868. Baines looked back with understandable satisfaction in 1894, noting that 'every part of the scheme of 1856 ... is now in full operation'.

16. Daunton considered it 'perhaps the most important' of all (*Royal Mail*, p. 311).

17. Edmund Yates, *Recollections and Experiences*, 2 vols., Richard Bentley & Son, 1884, Vol. 1, p. 306.

18. Quoted in Perry, *Victorian Post Office*, p. 95.

19. The provincial press had become so frustrated by the end of 1865 that it had supported the establishment of a cooperative news agency to find some alternative arrangement. The new body was called the Press Association. See C. R. Perry, 'The Rise and Fall of Government Telegraphy in Britain', *Business and Economic History*, Vol. 26, no. 2, 1997, p. 418. My account of the telegraph and telephone stories draws heavily on this author's scholarship, here and in *The Victorian Post Office*.

20. Arthur Hill, *Government Telegraphs*, Edinburgh Review, January 1869, pp. 154–69. Rowland Hill recorded in his diary for 15 January 1869: 'an excellent article on "Government Telegraphs", written by Alfred on my suggestion. The object is two-fold, first, to show the very extravagant bargains which have been made, and for which Scudamore and the Tory Government are mainly responsible, and thus indirectly to assist Frederic and Pearson; and, second, to aid the Liberal cause ...' (Gavin Fryer and Clive Akerman (eds.), *The Reform of the Post Office in the Victorian Era and Its Impact on Economic and Social Activity*, 2 vols., The Royal Philatelic Society, 2000, Vol. 2, p. 705). The Hill dynasty remained a potent force long after Rowland Hill's resignation in 1864.

21. Quoted in Perry, 'Rise and Fall of Government Telegraphy', p. 421.

22. For details of the department's early financial performance, see Kieve, *Electric Telegraph*, pp. 176–85.

23. Perry, 'Rise and Fall of Government Telegraphy', p. 419.

24. Yates, *Recollections and Experiences*, Vol. 2, pp. 199–200.

25. Quoted in Perry, *Victorian Post Office*, p. 128.

26. Before 1870, the provincial press was receiving 6,000 words a day by telegraph from London while Parliament was sitting. By 1900, this had risen to 110 million words a day, effectively at no extra charge to the press. As C. R. Perry observes (*Victorian Post Office*, p. 139), this was estimated to be costing the Post Office £375,000 a year by the turn of the century, which might be compared with a net loss for the Telegraph Department in 1900–1901 of £364,810.

27. Frank Scudamore (Junior), *A Sheaf of Memories*, T. Fisher Unwin, 1925, p. 17.

28. His son recalled the family's exodus to Istanbul in the opening chapter of his autobiography.

29. *Daily News*, 25 July 1876, quoted in Perry, 'Rise and Fall of Government Telegraphy', p. 142.

30. Perry, *Victorian Post Office*, p. 37.

31. Ibid., pp. 40 and 150.

32. Quoted in ibid., p. 33.

33. Lawrence Goldman (ed.), *The Blind Victorian: Henry Fawcett and British Liberalism*, CUP, 1989, p. 34.

34. Leslie Stephen, *Life of Henry Fawcett*, Smith, Elder & Co., 1885, pp. 414–15.

35. Fawcett to his father, 7 April 1883, quoted in Stephen, *Life of Henry Fawcett*, p. 416.

36. The growth statistics, taken from *Annual Reports of the Postmaster General*, are quoted in Daunton, *Royal Mail*, p. 92.

37. Stephen, *Life of Henry Fawcett*, p. 420.

38. Ibid., p. 443.

39. Minute on Report of the Committee upon the Circulation Department of the GPO, Post 14/232, quoted in Daunton, *Royal Mail*, p. 224.

40. H. G. Swift, *A History of Postal Agitation*, rev. edn, Percy Bros., 1929, p. 115.

41. Ibid., p. 117.

42. *Oxford DNB* entry by L. W. Chubb and Graham Murphy.

43. See Daunton, *Royal Mail*, p. 328, for a compelling chart of this decline. Adopting the Post Office's own terminology, he describes net income as 'net revenue'.

44. Stephen, *Life of Henry Fawcett*, p. 446.

45. Goldman (ed.), *Blind Victorian*, p. 50.

46. Perry, *Victorian Post Office*, p. 163.

47. Ibid.

48. Ibid., p. 189. The Post Office negotiators were led by its solicitor, Robert Hunter, who was generally credited with the brilliant drafting of a contract that substantially survived the arbitration process.

49. Quoted in Perry, *Victorian Post Office*, p. 163.

50. Quoted in Perry, *Victorian Post Office*, pp. 163 and 172.

51. Quoted in Daunton, *Royal Mail*, p. 114.

52. Ibid., p. 111.

53. Alan Clinton, *Post Office Workers: A Trade Union and Social History*, Allen & Unwin, 1984, p. 49.

54. H. D. S. M. Blackwood (ed.), *Some Records of the Life of Stevenson Arthur Blackwood KCB*, Hodder & Stoughton, 1896, p. 492.

55. Report of the Interdepartmental Committee on Post Office Establishments, 15 December 1896, Post 71/124.

56. Evidence presented to the Tweedmouth Committee on 25 July 1895, P.P. Vol. 90, 1897, pp. 158–62. (Post 71/124.) I am grateful to Hilary McKendrick for drawing the significance of TB in the Post Office to my attention.

57. Murray to Chamberlain, 11 May 1904, quoted in Perry, *Victorian Post Office*, p. 281.

58. Wilkins memorandum, 13 June 1914, ibid., p. 281.

59. Quoted in Daunton, *Royal Mail*, p. 293.

60. Post 30/2385B. The *Saturday Review* of 23 November 1912 published a long lament for the destruction of Smirke's building. Several years later, in May 1919, a later Postmaster General would be reported as agreeing that its demolition was 'unfortunately and foolishly done' (Post 30/2918, File XXVII).

PART TWO: WAR AND PEACE
6. 'Men to trenches, women to benches', 1914–21

1. Quoted in Lyn Macdonald, *1914–18: Voices & Images of the Great War*, Michael Joseph, 1988.
2. Charles Messenger, *Terriers in the Trenches: The History of the Post Office Rifles*, Picton Publishing, 1982, pp. 7–8.
3. Quoted in Niall Ferguson, *The Pity of War*, Allen Lane The Penguin Press, 1998, p. 176.
4. Post 33/307, File IV. The postal orders remained legal tender until 4 February 1915.
5. Post 56/85, *History of the POR 8th Battalion City of London Regiment 1914–1918*, London, 1919, pp. 5–7.
6. Christopher Andrew, *The Defence of the Realm: The Authorized History of MI5*, Allen Lane, 2009, p. 45. For the story of the Royal Navy deserter, and of several other, rather more successful spies who were arrested in the three years before the war on the basis of intercepted letters, see pp. 37–50. The HOW system, and the arrangements made to organize the data derived from it, 'laid the foundations for MI5's future development' (p. 52).
7. Ibid., p. 37. One of the German Admiralty's postmen, and perhaps the most important, was a certain Karl Gustav Ernst, who ran a barber's shop in North London's Caledonian Road and used to cut the hair of prison officers at Pentonville Prison. By one account, he was unearthed in 1907 when visited by a senior German naval intelligence officer: the latter was in London accompanying the Kaiser on a state visit and was trailed by the Special Branch of the Metropolitan Police as he made his way to Ernst's shop. (Graham Mark, *British Censorship of Civil Mails during World War I*, Stuart Rossiter Trust Fund, 2000, p. 10.) This engaging and often repeated story, worthy of a John Buchan novel, sadly has no basis in any of the intelligence records from 1907–9. 'Not a single case [of German espionage] was reported to the War Office by the police' during these years. One way or another, however, Ernst's activities were certainly known to the Security Service by 1911 and were kept under surveillance with the Post Office's help from then until the outbreak of the war. '[Ernst] was well integrated into British life and was discovered after his arrest in August 1914 to have British nationality.' (Andrew, *Defence of the Realm*, pp. 10 and 81.)
8. Edward Wells, *Mailshot: A History of the Forces Postal Service*, Defence, Postal and Courier Services Directorate of the Royal Engineers, 1987, p. 22.
9. Ibid., p. 35.
10. Ibid., p. 46.
11. Ibid., p. 49.
12. In addition to Edward Wells' *Mailshot*, my account of how REPS and the Army Postal Service evolved over the 1902–14 period draws on the work of two other, privately published studies – Edward B. Proud's *History of British*

Army Postal Service, Vol. 2: *1903–1927*, publ. 1982, and Alistair Kennedy and George Crabb, *The Postal History of the British Army in World War I: Before and After, 1903–1929*, publ. 1977. A fascination with the postmarks and other technical paraphernalia of the APS in the Great War has helped over the years to produce a rich haul of detailed papers on the REPS record.

13. Post 47/12, *Army Postal Services: Review of a Year's Work, August 1914–1915*.

14. From the diary of Gerald Burgoyne, quoted in Charles Messenger, *Call-to-Arms: The British Army 1914–18*, Cassell, 2006, p. 438.

15. James E. Edmonds, *Official History of the Great War: Military Operations, France and Belgium, 1916*, Vol. 1, Macmillan, 1932, p. 72.

16. Ibid., p. 129. The *Official History* lists just fourteen losses for the whole war.

17. Post 47/3.

18. It covered 150,000 square feet and was put up within two months, to prepare for the Christmas post of 1915. The 1919 REPS report thought it 'probably as good a piece of work as [was] ever carried out by HM Office of Works'. Another 50,000 square feet were added in the autumn of 1916. (Post 33/5506, File VIII, *Home Depot: Report on Organization and Development*.)

19. Archives Account No. 8402-28 (File E-2) at the National Army Museum.

20. For a comprehensively annotated list of all APO and FPO dated postmarks, see Proud, *History of British Army Postal Service*, pp. 60–311. When military intelligence officers realized in mid-1916 that captured mailbags might help the enemy to locate individual units, it was decided to move the numbered postmarks around between different locations from time to time. Collecting all the numbers used by any single unit is just one of the challenges taken on by modern aficionados of military postal history.

21. Post 33/5506, Part 1, *The German Field Postal Service during the Great War*, prepared by the General Headquarters of the British Army on the Rhine, May 1923. In the report's view, the German army had acknowledged the importance of military training in theory – but in practice, and in contrast to the British approach, 'the Postal Ministry was undoubtedly the predominant partner, while the War Department looked upon the service as something outside its province and "not to be worried about"', pp. 201–2.

22. Post 33/58A, *Summary of Evidence by the Secretary, Evelyn Murray, to the Royal Commission of Enquiry into the Gallipoli Campaign*, Section 1, para. 3, February 1917.

23. Herbert Samuel, *Memoirs*, Cresset Press, 1945, p. 109n.

24. Post 33/1211A, *Statistics of APS Work for Expeditionary Forces 1914–19*.

25. Post 33/307, File III, *Explosive and Dangerous Substances*.

26. As Director of the APS, William Price in 1919 organized the compilation of a series of reports on the historical record of the REPS unit, which he intended should be included in a general history of the wartime work of the Royal Engineers. Thirteen files were collected. (Post 33/5506.) File V, *A Memorandum on Army Postal Service in Various Theatres of War, 1914–*

1919, comprised an overview. Others looked in more detail at operations in the Mediterranean and the Middle East (File II), Salonika (File VI), Northern Russia (Files IX and X) and France (File XIII). The operations of the Home Depot were the subject of File VIII. Quotations in this paragraph have been taken from the respective files.

27. The story has recently been reconstructed by a local historian. See Margaret Flaws, *Spy Fever: The Post Office Affair*, The Shetland Times Ltd, 2009.

28. Post 30/4261, *Mails for HM Ships*, File III.

29. Edmonds, *Official History*, p. 127.

30. Post 56/57, *Report on Postal Censorship during the Great War*, by A. S. L. Farquharson, 1920, p. 293. His section on relations with the Post Office concluded: 'Communications on all matters affecting the mails was made with the Secretary's Office . . . and a very close and cordial liaison grew up, the Post Office clerks rendering very great help in all matters, especially of technical detail'. What Farquharson did not know was that the Censorship Department apparently harboured a German spy for the duration of the war. His name was Julius Silber – and it was perhaps fortunate that he took a job in censorship rather than Home Depot, where the availability of information on the location of British ships and regiments might have made him a genuine menace. See Ronald Seth, *The Spy Who wasn't Caught: The Story of Julius Silber*, Robert Hale, 1966.

31. The Postmaster General preferred it that way, as the officer in charge of the Postal Censorship Department explained in a report after the war, 'giving as his reason the inadequacy of his staff'. Lt. Col. A. S. L. Farquharson added that the Post Office was 'by its whole tradition and principles, an inappropriate department to delay and ransack the mails, which it is its duty to protect and expedite'. So much for the history of the Secret Office. (Post 56/57, *Report on Postal Censorship during the Great War*, by A. S. L. Farquharson, 1920, p. 293.)

32. Wells, *Mailshot*, p. 62.

33. Murray's circular was dated 1 May 1919. (Post 33/1884A.) It is possible he was largely responding to pressure from his colleagues: William Price in January had just begun the work cited above in note 26. The reports collected on the home record were stored in seven separate files, Post 33/307.

34. Post 33/5506, Files XIV, XV and XVI. F. H. Williamson was given the task of sounding out his REPS colleagues. Price was initially keen on the idea: 'I am certain we could put together a very interesting collection from the various theatres of war, eg the sleigh team from Archangel!!!' But others were not so sure. Williamson eventually wrote back to the Museum in November: 'I fear that it would not be practicable . . .'

35. Post 33/5506, File XVII.

36. Post 56/85, *History of the POR*.

37. Messenger, *Call-to-Arms*, records that 'some 300 only of the 900 who had entered the trenches sixteen days before were relieved and went into reserve' (p. 26).

38. Post 56/85, *History of the POR*, p. 12.

39. Ibid., p. 25.

40. Post 33/695, File I, Report of the Post Office Whitley Council Special Committee on Temporary Workers, May 1920. The aggregate figures given in the report imply a total of well over 75,000 serving men. The discrepancy probably arises from the report's inclusion of men who served in territorial units at home.

41. Post 30/3381A, File I.

42. Samuel, *Memoirs*, p. 109.

43. Post 30/3721, File III.

44. Post 30/3381A, Files II and IV.

45. Post 56/103, Letter from Engineer-in-Chief to all Supervising Engineers, 6 November 1915.

46. Post 30/3721, File III.

47. Martin Daunton, *Royal Mail: The Post Office since 1840*, The Athlone Press, 1985, p. 49.

48. Post 33/307, File I.

49. Ibid., File VII.

50. F. E. Baines, *Forty Years at the Post Office: A Personal Narrative*, 2 vols., R. Bentley & Son, 1895, Vol. 2, p. 77.

51. Post 33/329, File XVIII

52. See Meta Zimmeck, 'Marry in Haste, Repent at Leisure: Women, Bureaucracy and the Post Office, 1870–1920', in Mike Savage and Anne Witz (eds.), *Gender and Bureaucracy*, Blackwell, 1992, p. 77. On Victorian society's need for an employer like the Post Office, see also Meta Zimmeck, 'Jobs for the Girls: The Expansion of Clerical Work for Women, 1850–1914', in Angela V. John (ed.), *Unequal Opportunities: Women's Employment in England 1800–1918*, Basil Blackwell, 1986.

53. From Scudamore's evidence in the *Report on the Re-organisation of the Telegraph System, 1871*, quoted in Hilda Martindale, *Women Servants of the State, 1870–1938*, Allen and Unwin, 1938, pp. 17–18.

54. Martindale, *Women Servants of the State*, p. 177.

55. Samuel Cohn, *The Process of Occupational Sex-Typing: The Feminization of Clerical Labour in Great Britain*, Temple University Press, 1985, p. 124.

56. A. L. Matthison, *The Sun Shines on Woolverton*, University of Birmingham, 1957, p. 96. The author joined the Post Office as a boy sorter in 1884 and worked as a telegraphy clerk at Cannon Street from 1886 to 1895. There were 253 clerks at the station. In 1957, when the author was eighty-eight, he was still attending an annual reunion at which twenty of his contemporaries gathered together for tea.

57. Meta Zimmeck, 'Marry in Haste', pp. 80–81.

58. Quoted in Sarah Boston, *Women Workers and the Trade Union Movement*, Davis-Poynter, 1980, p. 79.

59. Martindale, *Women Servants of the State*, p. 179.

60. Post 30/3889C, quoted in Helen Glew, *Women's Employment in the General Post Office, 1914–1939*, University of London, Institute of Historical Research, Ph.D. thesis, 2010.

61. Annual Report 1913–14, p. 25, Post 92/10.

62. F. G. C. Baldwin, *The History of the Telephone in the United Kingdom*, Chapman & Hall, 1925, p. 270.

63. Post 33/695, File IV. The figure, from an official report in May 1920, excludes women in the Engineering and Stores Division but their numbers were modest.

64. Ibid.

65. Quoted in Martin Pugh, *Women and the Women's Movement in Britain, 1914–1959*, Macmillan, 1992, p. 26.

66. The percentage figures for all female civil servants are those reported by the Ministry of Reconstruction's 1919 Sub-Committee on the Employment of Women in the Civil Service, quoted in Meta Zimmeck, '"Get Out and Get Under": The Impact of Demobilization on the Civil Service, 1918–32', in Gregory Anderson (ed.), *The White Blouse Revolution: Female Office Workers since 1870*, Manchester University Press, 1988, p. 91.

67. Quoted in ibid., p. 90.

68. Post 30/3577B. This sentence is actually crossed out, but catches the flavour of the correspondence.

69. Quoted in Gail Braybon, *Women Workers in the First World War: The British Experience*, Croom Helm, 1981, p. 204.

70. Ibid., p. 157.

71. Irene Clephane, *Towards Sex Freedom*, John Lane, 1935, quoted in Braybon, *Women Workers*, p. 185.

72. Post 33/695, File I, Report of the Whitley Special Committee on Temporary Workers in the Post Office, October 1920.

73. Post 33/695, File IV, Report of the National Whitley Council Sub-Committee on Temporary Staffs, May 1920.

74. Post 33/331, File I, Memorandum by E. Raven, *Provision for Ex-Servicemen in the Post Office*, December 1920.

75. Post 33/331, File IV.

76. Post 33/331, File VII, Gardiner to Peel, 14 January 1921.

77. Post 33/314, File I, Memorandum of 18 August 1921. Curiously, a statistical table attached to the memorandum gives the total of servicemen recruited since the Armistice as 22,172. This figure had been amended for the body of the memorandum, and went on being amended in a stream of subsequent papers.

78. Post 30/3404, File VIII

79. Post 33/695, File I.

80. Report of the Sub-Committee of the National Council, May 1920, p. 93. (Post 33/695, File 4.)

81. Post 122/2991, Minutes of 2 September 1919 meeting. The same file contains transcripts of subsequent meetings on 22 October and 17 December to approve the constitution of the Departmental Council.

82. Constitution of the Whitley Council for the Post Office, Post 122/2991.

83. Michael Moran, *The Union of Post Office Workers: A Study in Political Sociology*, Macmillan, 1974, p. 28.

84. Post 115/427, *The Post*, 3 January 1920.

85. Alan Clinton, *Post Office Workers: A Trade Union and Social History*, Allen & Unwin, 1984, p. 460.

7. From *ancien régime* to modern age, 1921–39

1. Stephen Ferguson, *GPO Staff in 1916*, An Post, 2005, pp. 16–22. See also Ferguson's *At the Heart of Events: Dublin's General Post Office*, An Post 2008.

2. Norway's refreshingly candid account, detailing the frustrations of official life before the events of Easter 1916 as well as the story of the Rising itself, was written some time in the late 1920s and entitled *Irish Experiences in War*. It has been published – along with many other primary documents relating to the GPO's experience of the Rising – in Keith Jeffery, *The GPO and the Easter Rising*, Irish Academic Press, 2006.

3. Jeffery, *GPO and the Easter Rising*, p. 46.

4. Ibid., pp. 49–50.

5. The Minutes Volumes are classified as Post 36/1-216 and the Minuted Papers as Post 31/1-109.

6. Quoted in C. I. Dulin, *Ireland's Transition: The Postal History of the Transitional Period, 1922–25*, MacDonnell Whyte, 1992, p. 14.

7. Ibid., p. 9.

8. Report of the House of Commons Select Committee on Telephones, 9 August 1898, p. xiii. See also Douglas C. Pitt, *The Telecommunications Function in the British Post Office: A Case Study of Bureaucratic Adaptation*, Saxon House, 1980, p. 52.

9. Post 33/5529.

10. The phrase, coined by the American scholar Robert Merton, is quoted in a review of modern academic research into the workings of bureaucratic organizations in Chapter 1 of Pitt, *Telecommunications Function*.

11. *The Times*, 18 November 1920. The earlier articles were dated 15–22 July.

12. Report of the Coates Committee on Telephone Charges; P.P. 1920 [247] viii 551, paras. 21 and 32.

13. Report of the Cecil Committee on the Telephone Service; P.P. 1922 [54] vi 197, para. 2.

14. Ibid., para. 8.

15. J. T. Foxell and A. O. Spafford, *Monarchs of All They Surveyed: The Story of the Post Office Surveyors*, HMSO, 1952, p. 43.

16. Alan Woodland, *HPOs & SSOs: Survey of Matters Warranting Classification*, privately published, 1964. I am indebted to Ian Cameron for his analysis of the figures.

17. Pitt, *Telecommunications Function*, p. 64.
18. C. R. Perry, *The Victorian Post Office: The Growth of a Bureaucracy*, Royal Historical Society/Boydell Press, 1992, p. 11. He attributes this view to Sir Edward Hamilton, who served in conjunction with Murray's own father as Joint Permanent Secretary of the Treasury, 1902–7.
19. D. O. Lumley, *The Last Secretary to the Post Office*, p. 5, Post 33/5529.
20. Ibid., pp. 10 and 2. The difficulties posed for officials in the 1920s are reflected in the archives of the Post Office today. With no executive body at its head through these years, no regular minutes were taken as a record of policy-making.
21. W. K. Mackenzie, 'Postal Circulation', *Bulletin of the Postal History Society*, No. 197, p. 16. A second instalment of the paper was published in *Bulletin* No. 199.
22. Evelyn Murray, *The Post Office*, G. P. Putnam's, 1927, p. 41.
23. See Martin Daunton, *Royal Mail: The Post Office since 1840*, The Athlone Press, 1985, pp. 143–5.
24. For the story of the installation of Strowger exchanges across London in the interwar years, see J. H. Robertson, *The Story of the Telephone: A History of the Telecommunications Industry of Britain*, Pitman, 1947, pp. 148–76.
25. Jeffrey Kieve, *The Electric Telegraph: A Social and Economic History*, David & Charles, 1973, p. 249.
26. This was Sir Samuel Hoare, the Secretary of State for Air from 1922 to 1929, writing in the *Daily Telegraph* on 19 September 1930, and quoted in Daunton, *Royal Mail*, p. 184.
27. Post 33/191A.
28. Quoted in Henry Parris, *Staff Relations in the Civil Service: Fifty Years of Whitleyism*, Allen & Unwin, 1973, p. 163.
29. October 1926 Report, para. 9, Post 47/374.
30. Helen Glew, *Women's Employment in the General Post Office, 1914–1939*, University of London, IHR, Ph.D. thesis, 2010, p. 66.
31. *Opportunity*, March 1921, Post 115/86. Quoted in Glew, *Women's Employment*, p. 67.
32. Open letter by J. Bowen to UPW members, 1 May 1926, Post 65/190.
33. Murray, *Post Office*. It was one of several titles on Whitehall departments, edited by Sir James Marchant and all written by their respective department heads.
34. Ibid., pp. 175, 177, 187–8 and 189.
35. Thus, Robertson, *Story of the Telephone*, concluded in 1947: 'the remarkable revolution effected in telecommunications between 1919 and 1939 has been helped by close cooperation between the [Post Office] administration and the industry' (p. 177).
36. Ibid., p. 231.
37. Ibid., p. 196.
38. Murray to the Postmaster General, Post 122/5951.

39. Lumley, *Last Secretary*, p. 8.
40. *Daily Express*, 14 January 1928.
41. See Robertson, *Story of the Telephone*, pp. 234–45 for an account of the lobbying at this time.
42. Report of the Hardman Lever Committee on the Inland Telegraph Services; P.P. 1928 Cmd 3058 xii 441.
43. Alan Clinton, *Post Office Workers: A Trade Union and Social History*, Allen & Unwin, 1984, p. 284.
44. The Simon Report, handed to the Postmaster General in February 1929, made forty-five detailed recommendations. Its general conclusion was that 'the hitherto accepted policy of acquiescence in the adverse trend of telegraphy traffic should be modified'. File POE 8A, Post 72/234.
45. *The Times*, 13 July 1928.
46. *The Times*, 25 August 1928.
47. File POE 11, Post 72/234.
48. *The Times*, 30 September and 1/2 October 1929.
49. *The Times*, 9 October 1929. Lees-Smith's speech dismissing Wolmer's articles had been reported in the previous day's paper.
50. Viscount Wolmer, *Post Office Reform, Its Importance and Practicality*, London, 1932, p. 21.
51. Report of the Tomlin Commission on the Civil Service; P.P. 1930–1 Cmd 3909 x 517. Murray and Raven gave their evidence on 12–13 December 1929. Bromley's criticism of postal pay is at paras. 3669–99.
52. Ibid., paras. 230–32, Chapter VIII.
53. G. C. Peden in the *Oxford DNB*.
54. John C. W. Reith, *Into the Wind*, Hodder & Stoughton, 1949, p. 158.
55. File POE 2, Post 72/234.
56. *The Times*, 4 January 1932.
57. 13 January 1932, File POE 7, Post 72/234.
58. File POE 3, Post 72/234.
59. Philip Williamson (ed.), *The Modernisation of Conservative Politics: The Diaries and Letters of William Bridgeman 1904–35*, The Historians' Press, 1989, p. 254. The author is quoting from a memorandum written by MacDonald on 19 February 1932.
60. File POE 1, Post 72/234.
61. Summaries of the evidence given by witnesses are held in Post 73/64. The voluminous papers relating to the Enquiry are contained within Files POE 1-50, held in Post 72/234-237.
62. *The Times*, 23 August 1932.
63. Files POE 10 and 29, Post 72/234. It was subsequently claimed by some that Attlee had espoused a public corporation, but he stopped just short of this in his evidence, as too in an article he wrote later (see *New Statesman and Nation*, 7 November 1931, pp. 565–6). In effect, though, his 'agency' would have been little different from a public corporation.

64. File POE 41, Post 72/237. Reith had given his January 1930 paper to the Winter Conference of the Institute of Public Administration.

65. File POE 23, Post 72/236.

66. Post 73/64.

67. *The Times*, 3 September 1932.

68. Para. 6, Strohmenger Report, Post 33/4451.

69. Raven to Murray, 23 March 1933, Post 33/5529.

70. Murray to Wood, 18 January 1933, Post 33/5529.

71. Murray to Raven, 7 June 1933, Post 33/5529.

72. Murray to Wood, 10 August 1933, Post 33/5529.

73. *The Times*, 15 November 1933.

74. The principal reports included those of the sub-committees on the Postal Services (Post 72/267–68), the Personnel Department (Post 72/269 and 272) and the Engineering Department (Post 72/270–71).

75. Tony Benn, *Out of the Wilderness: Diaries 1963–67*, Arrow Books, 1988, p. 411.

76. From 'A Review of Work since October 1933', memorandum by Stephen Tallents, p. 4, 24 January 1935, File I, Post 33/5699.

77. POBM 2 April 1935, Post 69/3.

78. POBM 3 July 1934, Post 69/1.

79. Richard F. Robinow, *Peter in the Post Office*, John Lane The Bodley Head, 1934.

80. Quoted in Forsyth Hardy, *The GPO Film Unit, 1933–40*, a reminiscence of the Unit written in 1990, Post 108/91. The author quotes from a letter he received from Grierson himself in February 1936: 'The shadows of Hollywood are large, and naturally [so]. See documentary as a fight for just ten minutes' time in the average theatre programme. It is not by any means a prairie fire, nor was it intended to be, but the damn thing is positively ablaze for all that'.

81. Scott Anthony, *Night Mail*, British Film Institute, 2007, p. 79.

82. The reaction was recalled by Basil Wright, quoted in Elizabeth Sussex, *The Rise and Fall of British Documentary: The Story of the Film Movement Founded by John Grierson*, University of California Press, 1975, pp. 70–71.

83. Sussex, *Rise and Fall of British Documentary*, p. 71.

84. POBM 14 January 1936, Post 69/5.

85. J. G. Hines, *The British Long-Distance Network*, Post Office Green Papers No. 43, 1938, p. 16.

86. *The Times*, 18 December 1934.

87. *The Observer*, 4 December 1938. Quoted in Clinton, *Post Office Workers*, p. 294.

88. For a photograph of the Penarth post office, see Julian Osley, *Built for Service*, BPMA Publications, 2010, p. 64.

89. E. T. Crutchley, *GPO*, Cambridge University Press, 1938.

90. Quoted in Anthony, *Night Mail*, p. 79. The dismantling of the Tallents legacy took a few years. The distinguished members of the Postal Commit-

tee followed Grierson out of the door within a few months: 'In general, the
designs favoured by the [Poster] Group did not meet with the approval of
the Postmaster General and, as the outside members resented criticism of
their taste, the Postmaster General dissolved the Group early in 1938'
(memorandum by C. J. Miles, February 1944, File VI, Post 33/5699).
91. Charles Stuart (ed.), *The Reith Diaries*, Collins, 1975, p. 110.
92. Reith, *Into the Wind*, p. 176.
93. Ibid., p. 221.
94. Ibid., p. 252.
95. Daunton, *Royal Mail*, p. 181.
96. Wolmer, *Post Office Reform*, p. 83. The campaigner for postal reform was
less than wholly consistent in criticizing the Post Office for declining to sub-
sidize airmails. It was, after all, adhering to the business principles asserted
by Wolmer's hero, Rowland Hill. No doubt Wolmer would have rejected
this by forecasting a profitable future for airmails, if only the Post Office
could have taken a more entrepreneurial approach.
97. File POE 23, para. 5, Post 72/236.
98. Frederick Williamson, *The Air Mail Service*, Post Office Green Papers No. 1,
1933, p. 14.
99. D. O. Lumley, the former private secretary to Evelyn Murray, played a leading part in the development of the airmail service in the 1930s and authored
two Green Papers (Nos. 23 and 45) about it. The second, published in 1939,
contains useful summaries of volume growth, especially on pp. 8–9 and
16–20.
100. Lumley, Green Paper No. 23, p. 14.
101. Crutchley, *GPO*, p. 96.
102. See Howard Robinson, *Carrying British Mails Overseas*, George Allen &
Unwin, 1964, pp. 290–94.
103. G. C. Peden in the *Oxford DNB*.
104. Reith, *Into the Wind*, p. 309.

8. Pillar of the nation, 1939–49

1. *The Times*, 16 August 1928.
2. See, for example, A. J. Gill, the Deputy Engineer-in-Chief, 'The Work of the
Engineering Department during the Present War', November 1944 (Post
56/115); Sir Thomas Gardiner, Director General 1936–45, 'An Account of
the Work of the Post Office during the Second World War', 1946 (Post
56/22); H. R. Harbottle, Senior Engineering Director, 'The Provision of Line
Communications for the Fighting Services during the War', Institution of
Post Office Electrical Engineers, 1946 (Post 56/121, held at the BT Archive).
3. Gill, 'Work of the Engineering Department', p. 2. 'The basic schemes [for
telegraph services to be used by the armed services] were foreshadowed in
1938 and the provision then made enabled the demands from the Services

to be met without serious difficulty, although the equipments installed in some cases exceeded in size any previously in existence' (p. 9).

4. Gardiner, 'Account of the Work', p. 23.

5. POBM, 8 November 1938, Post 69/9. Reductions in the waiting list for telephone installation would have been more impressive, the Board was told, 'had it not been for the extent to which the Department has been occupied since May and particularly during the crisis' on work for the defence services.

6. BP 55(38) 26 October 1938, Post 69/9. The paper itself is missing, replaced with a short note: 'The attached copy ... is forwarded for your personal information. Owing to its very confidential nature, you are asked to return the report unless you definitely wish to retain it'. Twelve copies were sent out, and six were apparently returned.

7. Gill memorandum, Post 56/115.

8. Engineering Department War Diaries, September 1939–August 1940, Post 56/136.

9. BP 40(38), 'Football Pool Traffic', Post 69/8.

10. Gardiner, 'Account of the Work', p. 49.

11. Engineering Diaries, Post 56/136.

12. BP 23(40), 'Franco-British Stamp Issue', 11 April 1940, Post 69/12.

13. POBM, 4 July 1940, Post 69/12.

14. BP 31(40), 'Home Defence – Army Postal Services', 25 June 1940, Post 69/12.

15. War Diary of W. R. Roberts, Post 47/409.

16. Ian Hay, *The Post Office Went to War*, HMSO, 1946, p. 61.

17. Gill memorandum, p. 11, Post 56/115.

18. BP 35(40), 'Postal Services under War Conditions', Post 69/12.

19. Hay, *Post Office Went to War*, p. 11.

20. 'In the case of Invasion, arrangements have been made for mails for enemy-occupied territory to be held at appropriate "backward" offices until such time as they can be disposed of. For example, if Great Yarmouth was cut off, mails for that area would be held, firstly at Peterborough or, if Peterborough was in difficulties, at Nottingham' (BP 14(41), 'Report by Director of Postal Services on Some Current Problems', 6 June 1941, Post 69/13).

21. BP 37(39), 'Financial Position: Review of Economies', 18 July 1939, Post 69/11. The financial position had been laid out in BP 35(39), Post 69/11. The possible service reductions were discussed at the Board meeting of 25 July 1939.

22. BP 23(45), 25 September 1945, Post 69/26.

23. W. S. Morrison to Herbert Morrison, 31 December 1942, attached to BP 7(43), Post 69/18.

24. The UPW told the Board in May 1941, for example, that it was 'much perturbed at the prospective withdrawal of staff' (POBM 8 May 1941, Post 69/13). The union in February 1944 admonished D. J. Lidbury, now the Assistant Director General responsible for personnel matters, for doing far

too little to resist government pressure. It proposed the following month to make its own representations to the Recruitment Committee chaired by Herbert Morrison (POBM 3 March 1944, Post 69/23).

25. POBM 6 June 1940, Post 69/12.

26. At the UPW's Annual Conference in 1935, the growing presence of women in many offices was virulently attacked in terms that even Alan Clinton, understandably inclined to take a charitable view of most Union activities, admits 'can only be described as ugly and unpleasant' (*Post Office Workers: A Trade Union and Social History*, Allen & Unwin, 1984, p. 428).

27. Post 33/4185, Files I–VI.

28. POBM 1 August 1940, Post 69/12.

29. POBM 12 December 1940, Post 69/12.

30. POBM 11 July 1941, Post 69/13.

31. Gardiner, 'Account of the Work', p. 48.

32. POBM 6 February 1942, Post 69/15.

33. POBM 13 October 1944, Post 69/23.

34. The possibility of developing a wire broadcasting service after the war was reviewed again by the Board early in the summer of 1943, and rejected. The issues were summarized in BP 15(43), Post 69/18. The Deputy Director General, Raymond Birchall, probably spoke for many when he warned: '. . . there was a risk of the Post Office being dragged into controversies about programmes, which could hardly fail in the long run to have a damaging effect on its general prestige' (POBM 7 May 1943, Post 69/18).

35. The Scottish UPW leader, George Douglas, told the Executive Council in July 1948: 'He regretted it had not been possible to make known to the British public and to the Union in general that during the war, when the Americans . . . came to Great Britain with every intention of carrying American methods into every communications system, . . . it had been found that the PO engineers were miles ahead of them in technical development . . . [The Americans] had, therefore, scrapped their system and technical build-up and had asked the British Government to let them have British Telephonists to handle their communications . . .' But American senior officers, obviously unfamiliar with British labour traditions, had apparently refused to relinquish control over their borrowed staff. 'The upshot of that was that an ultimatum was put to the Americans to scrap their American system, otherwise the British Telephonists would walk out of their exchanges. The Commanding Officer of the American Communications had been compelled to climb down and the British Girls and British Engineers did their job under British conditions.' (UPW Executive Council Minutes 1948–9, pp. 512–15, UCW/2/1/32.) Douglas was speaking in favour of a post-war motion to block an invitation 'to bring in American industrialists with a view to [introducing] alleged efficiencies in British industry'. Many union officials still felt genuinely aggrieved over the Simon Report of 1929, and its 'lessons from America'. The Council's debate in 1948 proved a storm in a teacup: the proposed invitation was actually being extended to an official delegation of US trade unionists. The

General Secretary, Charles Geddes, expressed some concern over 'the anti-Americanism which was creeping into the debate' – though he then explained that an official delegation was infinitely preferable to having unofficial US visitors, who just went home 'and talked a good deal of American tripe'.

36. Gordon Radley in the *Oxford DNB*.
37. Gardiner, 'Account of the Work', p. 42, Post 56/22.
38. Gill memorandum, p. 16, Post 56/115.
39. Paul Gannon, *Colossus: Bletchley Park's Greatest Secret*, Atlantic Books, 2007, pp. 131–3. My account of the Colossus story draws heavily on this comprehensive modern study.
40. Ken Dalton, 'The Tunny Machine', in F. H. Hinsley and A. Stripp (eds.), *Code-breakers: The Inside Story of Bletchley Park*, Oxford University Press, 1993, p. 171. Publication of this book, a compilation of essays by almost thirty of the men and women who served at Bletchley, illuminated many aspects of a story that until the 1990s had only been poorly explained, if at all.
41. Report by Gordon Welchman, quoted in Gannon, *Colossus*, p. 253.
42. Quoted in Gannon, *Colossus*, p. 246.
43. Imperial War Museum audio tape No.18332, quoted in ibid., p. 256.
44. BP 8(46), 'Memo on Post Office Research' by A. S. Angwin, 27 March 1946, Post 69/27. He recalled that wartime research projects had included 'Top Secret work in connection with the Intelligence Service which employed almost 50% of our Research facilities'.
45. Few of their personal papers have survived. The BT Archive contains a box of Chandler's papers (Accession 96/0065) which includes his brief correspondence in 1976 with Professor Brian Randell, who presented a first paper on the achievements of the Colossus team to an academic conference on the history of computing in New Mexico in June 1976. Chandler recalled for Randell the night before the Mark 2 Colossus went into service on 1 June 1944, when he sat up into the small hours to correct one last design fault while '[b]y way of diversion, at about 3am, a nearby radiator started leaking, sending a pool of warm water towards the equipment ...' A paper written by Gordon Radley in 1948, 'The Post Office Research Station at Dollis Hill', mentioned neither Colossus nor Tommy Flowers (BT Archive, TCB 451, Box 2).
46. Quoted in Gannon, *Colossus*, pp. 266–7.
47. Hinsley and Stripp, *Codebreakers*, p. 12. F. H. Hinsley concludes that 'the invasion of Normandy was carried out on such tight margins in 1944 that it would have been impractical – or would have failed – without the precise and reliable intelligence provided by Ultra [i.e., from Enigma and Fish decrypts] about German strengths and order of battle'.
48. BP 13(44), 'Closing of Country Sub-Offices', 25 March 1944, Post 69/21.
49. K. S. Holmes, *Operation Overlord: A History of the Work of the Army Postal Service in Relation to Overlord*, Special Series No. 38, The Postal History Society, 1984, p. 87.
50. *The Times*, 21 May 1941.

51. The statistics are set out by Howard Robinson, *Carrying British Mails Overseas*, George Allen & Unwin, 1964, pp. 299–300. The detailed story is told in an unpublished account by a former archivist of the Post Office, E. C. Baker, 'The Airgraph Service, 1941–4', Post 50/19.

52. Holmes, *Operation Overlord*, p. 89.

53. Ibid., p. 86.

54. Ibid., pp. 17 and 83–6.

55. Ibid., p. 43.

56. Ibid., p. 33.

57. Ibid., p. 66.

58. Ibid., p. 80.

59. UCW/2/13/27/1-2.

60. Quoted in Clinton, *Post Office Workers*, p. 418.

61. BP 20(46), 'Staff Consultation in the Post Office' by J. S. Scholes, 20 September 1946, Post 69/27. The paper provided the Board with a brief history of recent industrial relations in the Department.

62. Clinton, *Post Office Workers*, p. 327.

63. Henry Parris, *Staff Relations in the Civil Service: Fifty Years of Whitleyism*, Allen & Unwin, 1973, p. 191. The author was commissioned by way of commemorating the fiftieth anniversary of the National Whitley Council in 1969, and his book draws upon many revealing interviews, including several with Charles Geddes (1897–1983).

64. UPW Executive Council Minutes 1945–46, p. 395, UCW/2/1/29. The wages quoted are those applicable in April 1946, after the consolidation of wartime bonuses.

65. UCW/2/13/27/1.

66. BP 5(46) and BP 30(46), Post 69/27; BP 35(47), Post 69/31; and POB 76(48), Post 69/37.

67. The Public Relations Director told the Board he had talked to a group of about a hundred women members of the Auxiliary Territorial Service, soon due for demobilization. He had asked them to consider joining the Post Office, 'but the great majority had said "No" . . . Their main objections were that the hours were too long and the commencing wages too low'. POBM 8 March 1946, Post 69/29.

68. Birchall complained to his colleagues about the poor success rate of women in the P&TO admission tests: 'It seemed ridiculous that women who had shown in practice [during the war] that they could do the work satisfactorily should be rejected on such a large scale, and it suggested that something might be wrong with the tests' (POBM 8 July 1949, Post 69/43).

69. BP 20(47), 'Recruitment to the Manipulative Grades; Discharge of Temporary Staff' by J. Scholes, 29 May 1947, Post 69/31.

70. POBM 11 April 1947, Post 69/33.

71. BP 34(47), POSB Annual Report 1946, Post 69/31 and POB 74(48), POSB Annual Report 1947, Post 69/37. The staffing crisis prompted the setting up in November 1947 of an 'Organization and Methods Working Party' to

look at ways of reshaping the bank to cope with the hugely expanded volume of its business.

72. POBM 7 October 1947, Post 69/33.

73. BP 29(45), 'Post Office Revenues and Expenditure: Forecasts of the General Position up to 1948–49', Post 69/26.

74. POBM 8 November 1945, Post 69/26.

75. POBM 7 February 1947, Post 69/33.

76. POBM 6 May 1949, Post 69/43.

77. A year into his tenure as Postmaster General, Wilfred Paling reported back to the Board on a visit he had just made to the South-West Region. 'His impression was that the staff in general were contented and in high spirits. He had been unhappy to see what really bad working conditions existed in many offices, mainly owing to the work having outgrown accommodation' (POBM 7 May 1948, Post 69/37).

78. POBM 7 November 1947, Post 69/33.

79. POBM 5 November 1948, Post 69/37.

80. UPW Executive Council Minutes 1945–46, pp. 8–14, UCW/2/1/29. The intrepid challenger was a senior officer of the union, John Moohan, dismissed a few years later for cheating on his union expenses.

81. *The Times*, 12 June 1947.

82. Clinton, *Post Office Workers*, p. 491.

83. POBM 5 October 1945, Post 69/26.

84. POBM 9 May 1947, Post 69/33.

85. POBM 8 October 1948, Post 69/37.

86. POBM 6 May 1949, Post 69/43.

87. UPW Executive Council Minutes 1949–50, p. 197, UCW/2/1/33. More background to the December outcome can be found at pp. 81–3 and 109–14.

88. *The Times*, 20–22 January 1947. The single reference to the Post Office came by way of explaining that it was 'certainly not impossible for an undertaking directly managed by a Government department . . . to combine these qualities [of commercial and technical enterprise, responsiveness to consumers' preferences and efficiency in operation]'. But it was 'not usual', and finding an appropriate status for Labour's nationalized industries was therefore going to need careful thought. Predictably, perhaps, the Special Correspondent writing the series concluded that the Labour government was seriously adrift and had 'no policy whatever for the control of public or private monopolies'.

89. Douglas C. Pitt, *The Telecommunications Function in the British Post Office: A Case Study of Bureaucratic Adaptation*, Saxon House, 1980, p. 106.

90. Attlee evidence to the Post Office Enquiry, March 1932, File POE 10, Post 72/234.

91. Memorandum dated 12 October 1949, quoted in UPW Executive Council Minutes 1949–50, p. 113–14, UCW/2/1/33.

92. Quoted in Parris, *Staff Relations*, op.cit., p. 176.

PART THREE: NO ORDINARY BUSINESS
9. Bright hopes blighted, 1949–64

1. UPW Executive Council Minutes 1949–50, UCW/2/1/33, pp. 237–9.
2. See Chapter 8, note 35.
3. For an account of the 1947–8 struggle, see Frank Bealey, *The Post Office Engineering Union: The History of the Post Office Engineers, 1870–1970,* Bachman & Turner, 1976, pp. 264–7. The author concludes (p. 292): 'The Communist Party ... made converts in every grade, at every level. But not all those they convinced became Communists: many merely supported the dissident faction because it was organising and mobilising opposition to the leadership. Thus the extent of the actual Communist Party penetration can be exaggerated. Although in 1947 the Executive was split eight to eight ... there were only five paid-up members of the Communist Party among the eight opponents of the leadership.'
4. UPW Executive Council Minutes 1948–49, UCW/2/1/31, pp. 325–7.
5. All the quotations in this paragraph are taken from UPW Executive Council Minutes 1949–50, UCW/2/1/33, pp. 291–3.
6. UPW Executive Council Minutes 1950–51, UCW/2/1/34, p. 212. No record has been found of the 1950 trip, which presumably went ahead without the UPW's participation. There were certainly numerous missions to the US by TUC representatives at this time, 'who under Marshall Plan auspices had the opportunity of examining the best American practice, [and] came back advocating union co-operation in the introduction of "scientific management" – an idea which would have aroused bitter hostility as recently at the nineteen-thirties' (Henry Pelling, *A History of British Trade Unionism*, Macmillan, 3rd edition, 1976, p. 236).
7. Pelling, *History of British Trade Unionism*, p. 19.
8. Ibid., p. 187.
9. UPW Executive Council Minutes 1948–49, UCW/2/1/32, pp. 690–96.
10. UPW Executive Council Minutes 1951–52, UCW/2/1/35, pp. 82–3.
11. POBM, 7 June 1951, Post 69/52.
12. POBM, 14 February 1952, Post 69/54.
13. See, in relation to these examples, UCW/2/1/35, p. 235; UCW/2/1/36, p. 212; UCW/2/1/36, pp. 68–9; and UCW/2/1/36, pp. 317–18.
14. UPW Executive Council Minutes 1953–54, UCW/2/1/37, pp. 64–5.
15. POB (53)64, 'The Turn of the Screw: Staff Economies and Morale' by D. O. Lumley, 23 November 1953, Post 69/55.
16. POBM 12 May 1955, Post 69/58.
17. Sargent's views were set down in the minutes, POBM 8 February 1951, Post 69/52. He elaborated on them in a later memorandum, BP 41(51), 'Staff Relations in the Post Office', 25 May 1951, Post 69/51. He was broadly optimistic, declaring of the Joint Production Councils: 'their potentiality for good is very great indeed'. But he offered a cautionary conclusion. 'It is only

necessary to mention such factors as the inflamed feelings on the subject of recognition of Staff Associations . . . and the recent outbreak of "working to rule" in a number of offices, to dispel any sort of complacency.'

18. UPW Executive Council Minutes 1953–54, UCW/2/1/37, pp. 235–6.
19. POB (52)32, 'The Post Office and the Industrial Charter' by S. D. Sargent, 21 April 1952, Post 69/53. The paper was written in response to the Conservative government's publication of its guide to best practice in industrial management. This was the Charter that prompted Churchill's private comment, 'I do not agree with a word of this' (quoted in Peter Clarke, *Hope and Glory: Britain 1900–1990*, Allen Lane, 1996, p. 243).
20. Keith Middlemas, *Politics in Industrial Society: The Experience of the British System since 1911*, André Deutsch, 1980, p. 407. See also Alan Campbell, Nina Fishman and John McIlroy (eds.), *British Trade Unions and Industrial Politics*, 2 vols., Ashgate, 1999: 'At the mid-point of Churchill's administration, it appeared that the Conservatives had consolidated the wartime intimacy between governments and unions and that this partnership would continue indefinitely' (Vol. 1, p. 78).
21. POBM 11 November 1954, Post 69/56.
22. *The Times*, 4 May 1951. See also Alan Clinton, *Post Office Workers: A Trade Union and Social History*, Allen & Unwin, 1984, p. 517.
23. UPW Executive Council Minutes 1950–51, UCW/2/1/34, p. 187. Geddes made the same point to De La Warr in private discussions that they had together on more than one occasion.
24. POBM 3 December 1953, Post 69/55.
25. For thorough summaries of all the wage negotiations from 1947 to 1955, see Clinton, *Post Office Workers*, pp. 511–20.
26. POB (52)30, 'Forecast of Commercial Accounts 1951–2 to 1954–5', Post 69/53.
27. Denis Roberts, interview with author, 12 October 2008.
28. The oral memoirs of postal workers collected by the British Library Sound Archive (BLSA), in association with Royal Mail Group, include many observations like Denis Roberts's about the 1950s. More than 100 interviews recorded in 2001–3 for *An Oral History of the Post Office* are part of BLSA's National Life Story Collection. A selection of forty-seven interviews can be heard on a CD, *Speeding the Mail*, produced by the BLSA and the British Postal Museum & Archive in 2005. Tracks 1, 4, 6, 12, 15, 21, 28 and 37 are all memories of the 1950s that attest to the continuity of long-cherished traditions – and Track 12 records a former Head Postmaster of Edinburgh recalling: 'sorting offices in the 1950s . . . were the same, by and large, as they must have been a hundred years before . . .'
29. The motorization story, with many excellent illustrations, is recounted in detail in Julian Stray, *Moving The Mail . . . by Road*, BPMA Publications, 2006.
30. POBM 2 March 1950, Post 69/49.

31. W. K. Mackenzie, 'Postal Circulation', *Bulletin of the Postal History Society*, No. 199, 1976, p. 7.
32. POB (50)32, 'Post Office Man Power, April 1950', Post 69/48.
33. J. J. M. L. Marchand, *Modernization of Postal Services*, De Boekerij of the Netherlands, 1946, pp. 65, 70 and 123. See also Douglas N. Muir, *The Transorma at Brighton*, published privately in 2006 by the Postal Mechanisation Study Circle, Monograph No. 1, under the auspices of the BPMA.
34. BP 8(46), 'Research' by Stanley Angwin, 27 March 1946, Post 69/28.
35. MAC (Letter-Sorting Machine) Paper No. 1, 'Mechanisation of Letter Sorting' by W. T. Gemmell, 27 November 1946, Post 17/460.
36. MAC (Letter-Sorting Machine) Paper No. 1A, 'Some Speculations of Future Developments' by R. O. Carter, 20 December 1946, Post 17/460.
37. BP 25(46), 'Postal Mechanisation' by Alexander Little, 15 October 1946, Post 69/27.
38. Minutes of MAC meeting, 7 January 1947, Post 17/459.
39. MAC minutes, 31st meeting, 14 April 1964, Post 17/454.
40. MAC's 4th Progress Report, March 1949, Post 17/461 Part 1.
41. MAC's 9th Progress Report, October 1952, Post 17/461 Part 1.
42. Memorandum No. 27, unsigned, March 1953, Post 17/460.
43. POBM 2 February 1956, Post 69/60.
44. MAC minutes, 4th meeting, 22 March 1956, Post 17/454.
45. MAC minutes, 5th meeting, 26 April 1956, Post 17/454.
46. MAC minutes, 9th meeting, 16 January 1957, Post 17/454.
47. MAC minutes, 10th meeting, 4 April 1957, Post 17/454. The consultants urged 'the development of high speed electronic sorting of letters pre-coded by the public' and thought this might be achievable within a few years. The MAC minutes noted they had 'underestimated the costs of the high speed machines and the mechanical difficulties in the way of developing them. As a result the timetable they had set was unrealistic.'
48. MAC Paper No. 58, 'An Appreciation of Electronic Sorting/Coding' by K. S. Holmes, January 1958, Post 17/455 Part 2.
49. G. P. Copping and H. J. Langton, *Sorting Letters by Machine*, Institution of Post Office Electrical Engineers, 1958, p. 14, Post 17/172.
50. MAC minutes, 23rd meeting, 24 April 1959, Post 17/454.
51. The example is taken from H. Dagnall, *The Mechanised Sorting of Mail*, privately published, 1976, held in the library of the BPMA. It provides one of very few useful overviews of the subject.
52. Copping and Langton, *Sorting Letters by Machine*, p. 25.
53. The first public demonstration of phosphorescent dots being used as a postcode is generally identified with a visit to Luton in July 1960 by the delegates attending a CCEP conference in Eastbourne. It is certainly the case that Luton was the principal location for experimental work with coding materials. Most of the SPLSMs at Norwich, moreover, continued to be basic operator-controlled machines until 1961. (See MAC Papers Nos. 85, 92 and

100, Post 17/455 Parts 2 and 6.) But the use of phosphorescent dots at Norwich in July 1959 was described for me in detail by one of the two APCs involved on the day, Ian Cameron. I am indebted to him for the story of the Marples visit.

54. POBM 11 June 1959, Post 69/66.
55. *The Times*, 29 July 1959, p. 3.
56. MAC minutes, 24th meeting, 6 November 1959, Post 17/454.
57. MAC Paper No. 115, presenting the minutes of a meeting held at Headquarters on 29 September 1964, Post 17/455 Part 6.
58. POBM 30 April 1959, Post 69/66.
59. MAC Papers Nos. 1 to 127, dated between January 1956 and July 1968, are contained in Post 17/455 Parts 1–6.
60. R. O. Bonnet, 'Report of a Fact-Finding Mission to France', April 1964, MAC Paper No. 109, Post 17/455 Part 6.
61. UPW Executive Council Minutes 1952–3, UCW/2/1/36, p. 318.
62. J. Keith Horsfield, 'Post Office Finance', *Lloyds Bank Review*, April 1956. Horsfield was the Director of Finance & Accounts under the Comptroller General, Sir Kenneth Anderson. Details of the 1955 reform were set out in a White Paper, *Report on Post Office Development and Finance*, Cmd 9576.
63. *The Status of the Post Office*, March 1960, Cmnd 989, and *Memorandum on the Post Office Bill*, December 1960, Cmnd 1247.
64. MAC minutes, 1st meeting, 16 November 1955, Post 17/454.
65. MAC minutes, 6th meeting, 31 May 1956, Post 17/454.
66. *Report of the Working Party on the Regional Organisation of the Post Office*, HMSO, 1951.
67. On their response to Lumley's report, see Douglas C. Pitt, *The Telecommunications Function in the British Post Office: A Case Study of Bureaucratic Adaptation*, Saxon House, 1980, pp. 113–14. Of course, the Telecommunications business had difficulties of its own in dealing with the Treasury, as Pitt notes: 'Periods of capital restriction, alternating with periods of relative easement, occasionally spelt chaos' (p. 107).
68. POBM 2 February 1956, Post 69/60.
69. POB (56)8, 'Engineering Developments' by Brigadier L. H. Harris, Post 69/60.
70. POBM 13 November 1964, Post 69/73.
71. Clinton, *Post Office Workers*, p. 523.
72. UPW Executive Council Papers, 10 October 1958, UCW/2/4/2, pp. 914–16.
73. Pitt, *Telecommunications Function*, p. 122.
74. R. A. (Dick) Hayward, the UPW's Deputy General Secretary who stood in for Geddes in 1954–5, had voiced his fears about this in 1954: 'Mr Hayward ... expressed his concern with regard to the trend he had sensed in discussions with the Post Office not only to downgrade the work of the staff represented by the Union, but the job as a whole. He visualized, not many years hence, [a day when] promotion to Head Postmasterships would be taken away from the manipulative grades and given to the clerical and executive people' (UPW Executive Council Minutes 1953–4, UCW/2/1/37, p. 83).

75. POBM 7 June 1951, Post 69/52. It remained a feature of the London Post Office for many years that its workforce included many who switched between postal jobs and working for London Transport.
76. Middlemas, *Politics in Industrial Society*, p. 429.
77. It is recounted in UPW Executive Council Papers, June–September 1958, UCW/2/4/1, pp. 96–9, 200 and 340.
78. UPW Executive Council Minutes 1947–48, UCW/2/1/31, pp. 168–9.
79. 'My committee will endeavour to get things moving over the whole field where mechanisation, or experimental work to that end, appears useful. . . . The committee will not undertake detailed work. It is intended to shape policy and to see that it is implemented.' Radley to Geddes, 5 November 1955. The Executive approved a motion on 8 November accepting membership, and a first UPW delegate was appointed, D. L. Brown. (UPW Executive Council Minutes 1955–6, UCW/2/1/39, p. 213.) Brown's first report back to the Executive, in January 1956, laid the basis for Conference's decision to pursue shorter hours as the main adjunct to mechanization (ibid., p. 261).
80. MAC minutes, 10th meeting, 4 April 1957, Post 17/454.
81. A. W. C. Ryland told UPW officers: 'he had never heard it argued before that the benefits of productivity should be shared before they had been realised' (UPW Executive Council Papers, June–September 1959, UCW/2/4/4, p. 715).
82. Minutes of Post Office/UPW meeting at Headquarters, 21 May 1959, UPW Executive Council Papers, June–September 1959, UCW/2/4/4, pp. 709–16. Ryland's letter is set out in UPW Executive Council Papers, February–May 1959, UCW/2/4/3, pp. 217–19.
83. Reginald Bevins, *The Greasy Pole*, Hodder & Stoughton, 1965, pp. 77–8.
84. Tony Benn, *Out of the Wilderness: Diaries 1963–67*, Arrow Books, 1988, p. 245.
85. Profiles of several top officials were printed in the *Observer*, 8 March 1964, filed in Post 111/89.
86. This side of him was evident at a meeting in the autumn of 1956 with representatives of a small independent trade union, the Government Overseas Cable & Wireless Operators' Association, founded in 1924. They were there to ask for a less abrasive attitude to their union by the UPW. Smith bullied and berated them for the best part of an afternoon, with a brusqueness that plainly took them aback. (Verbatim record, UCW/2/1/40, pp. 278–93.)
87. See Clinton, *Post Office Workers*, pp. 525–6.
88. See ibid., p. 527. The motion proposed by the LDC at the rally 'on behalf of the Executive Council' was a frontal challenge to the UPW's senior hierarchy: 'We believe that the Executive Council has shown a marked lack of real leadership in this instance [i.e., over the shorter working week] . . . We charge the Executive Council with procrastination and call upon it to bestir itself . . . it might well be the time for testing the feeling of the members towards taking industrial action' (UPW Executive Council Papers, October 1959–January 1960, UCW/2/4/5, pp. 1182–4).
89. See Clinton, *Post Office Workers*, pp. 546–50.

90. As the UPW's own historian puts it, in a delicate understatement of the profound shift of sentiment within the workplace dating from about this time, 'the Union was becoming something different from what it had been' (ibid., p. 526).

91. Bevins, *Greasy Pole*, p. 132. He died in 1996, but there remains as yet no entry for him in the *Oxford DNB*.

92. A letter to the Departmental Whitley Council of 5 May 1959 warned: '. . . it is at least possible that longer-term influences are now at work, that we have reached the end of a long period of continuous expansion of postal traffic and that in the future it will be increasingly difficult to maintain the present traffic levels against the competition of the telephone, the telex service and unaddressed circulars to say nothing of the possibility of advertising by post being replaced by the use of other media' (UPW Executive Council Papers, June–September 1959, UCW/2/4/4, pp. 123–4).

93. Bevins to D. C. Balaam, 28 March 1961, Post 122/1132.

94. See *The Times*, 18 October 1881, in Post Office press cuttings, p. 383, Post 111/18.

95. BP 37(47), 'Work of the Investigation Branch', 25 November 1947, Post 69/31.

96. See *The Illustrated London News*, 31 May 1952, p. 913.

97. Bruce Reynolds, *The Autobiography of a Thief*, Bantam Press, 1995, pp. 60–61. Reynolds gives a strikingly detailed account of how the robbery was carried out – but makes a point of stressing that he only returned home in 1954 from a three-year gaol sentence in Wandsworth Prison. He describes how, six months after his release aged twenty-two, he began robbing houses with a man called Harry: 'He had been involved in the Eastcastle mailbag job . . . [after which] despite intense police activity for over a year there were no charges. I was in awe of Harry'.

98. POB (52)43, 'Working Party on Security of Mails', 30 May 1952, Post 69/53.

99. POBM 12 June 1952, Post 69/54.

100. POB (56)49, 'The Investigation Branch', 23 June 1956, Post 69/60.

101. POBM 12 May 1955, Post 69/58.

102. POBM 17 July 1958, Post 69/64.

103. Post 122/10002.

104. *Evening News*, 10 April 1959.

105. POBM 12 November 1959, Post 69/66.

106. Osmond to the Postal Services Director, 21 September 1960, Post 120/95.

107. Bevins disclosed the figure in his autobiography in 1965 (*Greasy Pole*, p. 125) – to the horror of Post Office officials.

108. POBM 3 November 1960, Post 69/68.

109. Notes of a Discussion at KEB, 6 October 1960, Post 120/134.

110. POB (56)49, 'The Investigation Branch', 23 June 1956, Post 69/60. The IB's device was attached to the keyhole on the outside of the safe. 'If it is moved more than six thousandths of an inch it sounds an alarm.'

111. G. H. Young to L. P. Palmer, 26 September 1961, Post 120/134.

112. IB memorandum to PSD/HMB, 10 April 1962, Post 120/134.

113. *Daily Express*, 27 January 1962. Most papers covered the story, but the *Express* made more of it than any of its Fleet Street rivals: 'A Jesse James-style mail train robbery by moonlight on a lonely stretch of track in Essex failed, it is believed, only because a delayed freight train came along first.'

114. E. G. Hucker to G. R. Downes, 8 November 1962, Post 120/134. Scribbled at the head of the letter are the words 'Letter sent at IB request'.

115. 'Notes of a meeting on 5[?]th February 1963 to discuss security matters', Post 120/134.

116. R. J. Mitchell to Postal Services Department, 30 January 1963, Post 120/134.

117. Annotation to IB papers of 15 February 1963, Post 120/134.

118. Circular letter by Chief Superintendent of Postal Services, 19 February 1963, Post 120/134.

119. 'A Message From the TPO Whitley Committee about Security on TPOs and SCs', 26 July 1963, Post 120/134.

120. The Clerk-in-Waiting was Henry Tilling, who recounted the story in an interview with the author, 15 September 2009.

121. See in particular John Gosling and Dennis Craig, *The Great Train Robbery*, W. H. Allen, 1964; Peta Fordham, *The Robbers' Tale*, Hodder & Stoughton, 1965; Piers Paul Read, *Train Robbers*, W. H. Allen, 1978; and Peter Guttridge, *The Great Train Robbery*, The National Archives, 2008.

122. Chief Constable Brigadier Cheney to the Controller of the Postal Services Department, 8 May 1964, Post 120/95.

123. C. G. Osmond to D. Wesil, 20 August 1963, Post 120/134. Wesil was at this time the Deputy Chief Inspector of Postal Services, a post he held from September 1961 until the autumn of 1963. He was a man with an uncanny knack of turning up at the centre of one critical issue after another.

124. Read, *Train Robbers*, pp. 66–7. Members of the gang found an HVP carriage at the Stonebridge Park yards near Wembley, according to this account. 'There were no bars on the windows: indeed the coach which carried millions of pounds up and down the country every night seemed to have no special defences at all.' Read's version of events, based on what the robbers told him, contains much pure fiction – as he came to appreciate in the course of writing it – but this part of his story rings true. He refers at one point to the robbers having possession of an official Post Office list of HVPs for an Up Special, and suggests 'this proved that their informant was in touch with someone on the train itself' (p. 63). But his book presents no other evidence in support of the robbery being in any way an 'inside job'.

125. R. F. Yates, 'Report on the Great Train Robbery', 12 May 1964, pp. 32–4, Post 120/147.

126. Fordham immersed herself in the story as thoroughly as did her barrister husband who acted for four of the defendants. (One of them was Bruce Reynolds' brother-in-law, John Daly, who was the only defendant in the 1964 trial to be acquitted.) She wrote in *The Robbers' Tale*: 'Having started the inquiry with the impression that [the sidelining of three HVP carriages] was not sabotage, I found that I ended with a nasty feeling that it was. . . .

Yet the fact remains that a senior engineer, of great experience, maintains, after examination of these vans that there was no sabotage' (pp. 48–9).

10. Getting out of the civil service, 1964–9

1. 'Friday 4 October . . . I came home [to London from the 1963 Labour Party Conference in Scarborough] in the train with Peter Shore . . . We talked about a number of things, including the tremendous challenge that the Post Office would offer a Labour Minister.' Tony Benn, *Out of the Wilderness: Diaries 1963–67*, Arrow Books, 1988, p. 67. After writing the diary for a few years, he dictated daily entries onto a Dictaphone from 1966.
2. Ibid., '30 October 1963', p. 72.
3. *Guardian*, 19 June 1964, reprinted in Tony Benn, *The Regeneration of Britain*, Victor Gollancz, 1965. Of the ten new business ideas in the article, five related to Posts and five to Telecommunications. They included standard envelope sizes (to promote faster mechanization), a GIRO credit transfer system, rural postal bus services – and 'telephone interpreter units' which might offer callers a simultaneous translation service.
4. Henry Tilling interview with author, 15 September 2009.
5. Benn, *Out of the Wilderness*, '4 November 1964', p. 178.
6. Ibid., '27 November 1964', p. 194.
7. The six quotations in this paragraph are taken from the entries in the 1964 diary for 21 and 23 October, 7 December, 31 October, 17 November and 20 July respectively.
8. Ibid., '19 October 1964', p. 160.
9. Ibid., '13 January 1965', p. 203.
10. Ibid.
11. Ibid., '26 July 1965', p. 298.
12. Ibid., '22 October 1964', p. 170.
13. Interview with Donald Wratten, 16 August 1990, quoted in Jad Adams, *Tony Benn*, Macmillan, 1992, p. 230.
14. Benn, *Out of the Wilderness*, '21 October 1964', p. 167.
15. Quoted in Adams, *Tony Benn*, p. 234.
16. Benn, *Out of the Wilderness*, '5 August 1965', p. 306. Benn noted that German had fretted over 'the tendency towards commercialising everything'. He himself had no such doubts. 'But of course it isn't commercialising in the ordinary sense of private enterprise. It is trying to introduce some sane and sensible economic criteria into public enterprise in place of the awful old muddle and confusion that went on before.'
17. Adams, *Tony Benn*, p. 266.
18. Benn was ready to acknowledge this himself by April 1965. He asked his personal secretary, Miss Goose, what she thought about the obvious tension in the air. 'She said that I was good for the department but that the department did feel that I ought to be more appreciative of the good points and

not appear to be so critical. There may be strength in this argument ...'
(Ibid., '8 April 1965', p. 243).

19. Ibid., '28 May 1965', p. 265.
20. Ibid., '3 May 1963', p. 14.
21. Harold Nicolson's comment is quoted in Miranda Carter, *The Three Emperors*, Fig Tree, 2009.
22. For a detailed study of the King's reign from a philatelist's viewpoint, see Douglas N. Muir's *George V and the G.P.O.: Stamps, Conflict & Creativity*, BPMA Publications, 2010.
23. Benn, *Out of the Wilderness*, '24 March 1965', p. 238.
24. Eric Gill to the Controller of the PO Supplies Department in 1937, quoted in Stuart Rose, *Royal Mail Stamps: The History of Their Design*, Phaidon Press, 1980, p. 24. Rose was Typographical Adviser to the PMG in 1965 and later became the first Design Director of the Post Office.
25. BP 62(57), 'Post Office Philatelic Services and Post Office Museum', by Alan Wolstencroft, 3 October 1957, Post 69/62. The project team's report had suggested a Bureau could be set up for about £20,000 a year, while the profits from regular new issues might reach at least £300,000 a year. Wolstencroft endorsed the idea of having two issues a year and urged that planning should begin for a 'Postal and Stamp Museum'.
26. 'The Committee has shown remarkably little interest in the possibility that its taste in design might differ from that of the people who use the stamps or collect them.' Memo to the PMG, 1965, quoted in Douglas N. Muir, *A Timeless Classic: The Evolution of Machin's Icon*, BPMA Publications, 2007, p. 64. My account of the tussles over stamp design and the Queen's head in 1964–6 draws heavily on Chapter 5 of Muir's book, pp. 55–106.
27. POB (57)62, 'Post Office Philatelic Services and Post Office Museum', by Alan Wolstencroft, 3 October 1957. The Board opted to set aside the idea of a special philatelic department 'until further evidence was available of the results of the liberalisation which had recently been taking place' (POBM 17 October 1957, Post 69/62).
28. Joe Slater 'was absolutely shocked by the idea. He said it was dynamite and that it would cause a major storm and the women in Britain would hate it and the Cabinet would not agree to it and that people on our side of the House would be opposed to it'. Benn, *Out of the Wilderness*, '5 November 1964', p. 179.
29. The SAC minutes recorded only that 'the new ideas mooted at this meeting would be tried out [later in 1965] so far as practicable' (quoted in Muir, *Timeless Classic*, p. 58).
30. Benn, *Out of the Wilderness*, '11 February 1965', p. 218.
31. Gentleman's own account of the episode, given to him directly, is quoted in Muir, *Timeless Classic*, pp. 58–60.
32. Benn, *Out of the Wilderness*, '15 February 1965', p. 219.
33. Muir, *Timeless Classic*, p. 66.
34. Benn, *Out of the Wilderness*, '10 March 1965', p. 231.

35. Both views are quoted in Muir, *Timeless Classic*, p. 75.

36. Derek Mitchell to D. P. Wratton (private secretary to the PMG), 12 October 1965, Post 122/9851.

37. Benn, *Out of the Wilderness*, '14 October 1965', p. 335.

38. Ibid., '2 November 1965', p. 344.

39. Quoted in Muir, *Timeless Classic*, p. 81.

40. Ibid., p. 87.

41. Ibid., p. 100.

42. Ibid., p. 102.

43. Benn, *Out of the Wilderness*, 16 July 1964, p. 131.

44. Ibid., '18 December 1964', p. 197.

45. Benn minute to the Prime Minister, 2 March 1965, Post 122/11322.

46. Benn, *Out of the Wilderness*, '8 March 1965', p. 229.

47. 'Report on a Visit to the Bell System, May 1963', para. 54, Post RY0002/03. The main report stretched to 133 pages, and made fifty-seven separate recommendations to help address 'the reasons why [the Bell system] is able to give better service than the Post Office with relatively fewer staff . . .'

48. Paper attached to submission by John Ricks to the Treasury/Post Office Working Party, 25 May 1965, Post 122/11322.

49. Callaghan had been a full-time official of the Inland Revenue Staff Federation from 1936 to 1947, with a break for wartime service in the Royal Navy. In a Fabian research paper that he published in 1953, he wrote admiringly of the successes achieved by the Post Office's Departmental Whitley Council – and of the well-deserved status of the leading unions within the Post Office, warranted 'by virtue of the fact that they are stable, efficient, and democratically run, and give good service to their members'. Callaghan took the opportunity to remind his Fabian readers that the UPW was the only union after 1946 whose members voted for it to join the Labour Party. 'It consistently and strongly supports the policy of the Party.' (*Whitleyism: A Study of Joint Consultation in the Civil Service*, Fabian Research Series No. 159, 1953, p. 34.)

50. Callaghan to Wilson, 10 March 1965, Post 122/11322.

51. 'The Case for Change', sent by Shepherd to H. A. Daniels, 13 May 1965, Post 122/11322. Shepherd's initial draft expounded on the management problems caused by civil service grading of Post Office jobs, but these paragraphs had to be cut from the final paper. Daniels, the EOD Director and also a member of the joint working party with the Treasury, told Shepherd in a margin note that he had 'very serious misgivings . . . which I have shared with the DG and which he shares'. Caution was their byword.

52. Benn, *Out of the Wilderness*, '3 June 1965', p. 269.

53. Ibid., '21 June 1965', p. 277.

54. Shepherd to Daniels, 23 June 1965, Post 122/11322.

55. *Final Report of the Treasury/Post Office Working Party on the Organisation of the Post Office*, 16 July 1965, Post 122/11322.

56. Callaghan to Wilson, 20 July 1965, Post 122/11322.

57. Benn minute to the Prime Minister, 9 August 1965, Post 122/11322.

58. Benn, *Out of the Wilderness*, '14 September 1965', p. 319.

59. Roger Morrison, interview with author, 6 October 2009.

60. Benn, *Out of the Wilderness*, '28 July 1965', p. 302.

61. McKinsey Memorandum of Proposal, 24 February 1965, Post 122/10228.

62. London Postal Region files on McKinsey project, Post 73/282.

63. Christopher D. McKenna, *The World's Newest Profession: Management Consulting in the Twentieth Century*, CUP, 2006, p. 170.

64. McKinsey Progress Review, 29 October 1965, Post 122/10228.

65. McKinsey Memorandum, 'Overall GPO Organization', 23 February 1966, Post 122/12108.

66. German told his colleagues: 'I find the arguments ... very confused ... I cannot help feeling that McKinsey's idea is to play down the role of the engineer ... The setting up of separate Posts and Telecoms Regions is not something to be decided as a result of this sort of memo. ... I do not envy the Chief Executive his role when there is the degree of separation visualised by Mr Roger Morrison.' His DDG-Posts was even more forthright: 'I agree with you that much of this memorandum is half-baked ... [and] based on inadequate knowledge if not preconceived ideas. ... I really wonder whether they have fully approached [i.e. appreciated?] the realities of Ministerial responsibility.' (German memorandum to the Directorate, 24 February 1966, and Wolstencroft to German, 25 February 1966, Post 122/12108.)

67. *The Post*, 13 November 1965. Benn had perhaps been a little unwise to compare his efficiency goals at the Post Office with the better value offered to consumers by the new supermarkets. 'The Post Office is not to be likened to a supermarket', wrote Smith. '... We do not need a supermarket mentality to make the Post Office more efficient.'

68. Minutes of the Regional Directors' Conference, 2–3 November 1965, Post 122/11324.

69. Benn, *Out of the Wilderness*, '23 November 1965', p. 354.

70. Many of them can be found in Posts 122/12107, 122/12108 and 122/12109.

71. A detailed paper on the proposed split of HCR provides a dramatic picture, in particular, of the telephone service's growth in the south-east of England. In 1945, there had been 6,643 staff employed in telephone managers' offices (TMOs) in HCR and capital expenditure on telephones had been £2.3m. In 1965, there were 17,897 staff in the TMOs and the capital expenditure was £31.6m. Over the same period, the number of Head Post Offices in the region grew just 15 per cent, from 19,760 to 22,812. (See annexes to Paper for the PMG on reorganization of the Home Counties Region, Post 122/12110.)

72. Benn to German, 14 February 1966, Post 122/12108.

73. Benn, *Out of the Wilderness*, '12 January 1966', p. 374.

74. Anderson was one of the directors whose status at Headquarters was immediately threatened by the prospective Semi-Split. He complained to German that he would be forced, in effect, into taking a half-time job on full pay.

'The alternative would be to resign forthwith in disgust, which however would cost me £5,000. Having still some satisfaction in what we all achieved as a result of Marples, Hill and De La Warr, I see no reason to mince words with the present Minister.' (Anderson to German minute, 3 February 1966, Post 122/12107.)

75. Benn to Callaghan, 9 March 1966; Treasury official to Benn, 21 March 1966; Post 122/12108.

76. Benn, *Out of the Wilderness*, '4 April 1966', p. 401.

77. Ibid., '11 May 1966', p. 411.

78. German to Benn, 3 June 1966, Post 122/12109.

79. McKinsey Memorandum, 'Regional Organization', 13 June 1966, Post 122/12109.

80. Tilling, interview with author, 15 September 2009.

81. Benn, *Out of the Wilderness*, '4 July 1966', p. 443.

82. Benn, ibid., '8 July 1966', p. 449.

83. Edward Short, *Whip to Wilson*, Macdonald, 1989, p. 283.

84. *Reorganisation of the Post Office*, Cmnd 3233, March 1967.

85. Post 122/11342.

86. German to Morrison, 10 March 1966, Post 122/10230.

87. Wolstencroft to Short, 18 July 1966, Post 122/10230.

88. Most of the relevant papers for the work done between September 1965 and May 1966 are filed in Post 73/282, Post 122/10228–10230, Post 122/10284, Post 122/10375 and Post 122/12302–12304.

89. *Notes*, Vol. 42, No. 6, February 1966.

90. Report to the Select Committee on Nationalised Industries, February 1966, Post 122/10230.

91. McKinsey Memorandum of Proposal, 'Study of GPO Organization', 13 September 1966, Post 122/12600.

92. Wall to Tinniswood, 28 November 1966; Tinniswood to Wall, 8 December 1966; Post 122/12600.

93. 'Notes of a Presentation by the Regional Directors to McKinsey's on 23rd November, 1966', File Three, Post 73/282.

94. McKinsey Memorandum, 'Progress Review on Organization', 12 December 1966, Post 122/12600.

95. *Reorganisation of the Post Office*, paragraphs 33 and 34.

96. Yet another McKinsey report, 'Changing Working Practices', accompanied the final organizational report in March 1967 and specified the approximate staff numbers at each level of responsibility. Senior, middle and junior management ranks together would employ 684 in Posts and 425 in Telecommunications. Rank-and-file workers, with their supervisors, would number 169,700 and 211,800 respectively. (Post 122/12600.)

97. 'Notes of a Presentation', p. 6.

98. Wolstencroft to Ryland, 22 November 1966, Post 73/464.

99. Even in London, the gains were as yet far from secure. 'As you may know, our efforts to recover all the "lost time" highlighted by the Project Team at

North West District Office have met with strenuous resistance from the
UPW, both at local and national levels . . . We need now to move quickly at
NWDO if we are to make a go of this and I would be most grateful for
your help in ensuring that the latest [cost-saving] proposal gets a fair wind'
(Holmes to Wolstencroft, 23 May 1967, File Three, Post 73/282).

100. This report, 'Organizing for Corporation Status', took on a curious life of
its own. Maurice Tinniswood wrote a summary of it in April 1967 which he
intended to circulate to the unions, but this was blocked by the Postmaster
General. There were requests for the report itself to be disclosed, notably from
the POEU's General Secretary, Charles Smith. 'The McKinsey investigation,
as the first inquiry into internal Post Office organization as a whole ever
made by an independent body of consultants, naturally has aroused great
interest among our members' (Smith to Maurice Tinniswood, 17 May 1967,
Post 122/11446). Repeated refusals to disclose its contents angered many
on the Staff Side and led to rumours that the Wilson Cabinet had scotched
it at the last moment – either because it had urged the breakup of the Post
Office in strident terms, or because it had called for the sale of the Telecoms
business into the private sector. Neither speculation seems justified. On the
other hand, it is odd that Ted Short went out of his way, in the annual parliamentary debate on Post Office Prospects on 15 March 1967, to deny that
there was any such thing as a Final Report from McKinsey – which at best
was splitting hairs. And it is even odder that no copy of the report has
survived in the archives. When the Post Office Review ('Carter') Committee
of 1976–7 looked into McKinsey's 1966–7 organizational study, it had to
conclude: 'There is no document that records the findings of this study as
such' (PON 12, Post 122/12087). Probably the March report simply urged
the Semi-Split with a clarity that, if disclosed, might have exposed the White
Paper's guarded stance.

101. Wall to Short, 1 October 1967, Post 122/12600. On a copy of Morrison's
memorandum 'Review of Draft Booklet', 5 July 1967, Wolstencroft scribbled
a margin note: 'This is too naïve for words . . .' Wall and Wolstencroft had
another reason for distancing themselves from McKinsey: both men were
deeply uneasy about how much the Post Office had spent on the firm's
services. That autumn, the Exchequer and Audit Department looked hard at
McKinsey's contract. 'In the end they decided not to make any reference to
the subject in their report on the [1966–7] Accounts – which would have
meant that it would have been taken to the Public Accounts Committee – but
it was a close thing' (Wall to Wolstencroft, 24 October 1967, Post 122/12600).

102. Nancy Martin, *The Post Office: From Carrier Pigeon to Confravision*, J. M.
Dent, 1969. The author was given extensive assistance by the Post Office to
produce an attractive overview of all its contemporary activities, complete
with diagrams of automated sorting machines. 'Confravision' was a briefly
topical name for what later came to be known as video-conferencing.

103. The resulting proposals were known as the Wells Schemes (1923 and later),
the Gould–Smith Schemes (1937 and 1947), the Wolstencroft Committee

Report (1958) and the Report of the Study Group on the Long Term Planning of the Postal Services (1964). They are summarized in a Note for the Carter Review of 1976–7, Post 23/131.

104. Benn, *Out of the Wilderness*, '18 October 1965', p. 337.

105. Post 122/10278. The Director General told the RDs: 'There are at present acute shortages of postmen in London and in many provincial centres. These are seriously affecting the quality of service and giving rise to excessive and expensive overtime . . . [Assuming] the present pattern of service is maintained, we shall need about 8,000 more men for the mail service by 1970–1 and ten years from now the additional number required will be about 17,000.'

106. A. B. Harnden (on behalf of all RDs) to Wolstencroft, February 1967. The letter followed a private meeting of all the RDs on 18 October 1966 and the circulation of a confidential paper by Ken Holmes, setting out a devastating critique of the Two-Tier Mail. (Post 122/10278.)

107. The committee Wolstencroft had chaired in 1957–8 could hardly have been more explicit in this regard. 'We can see some quite serious difficulties [in introducing a two-tier system], but no fatal weakness in it . . .', as it concluded in its report. 'In saying this, we feel that we ought to add that in our view the introduction of a two-tier letter scheme in any form would call for a fundamental review of the whole of the national mail circulation system. We should not like it to be thought that such a scheme could be simply grafted on to the existing structure.' (First Report of the Study Group on Two-Tier Letter Service, October 1958, Post 122/6012.) This was the last of twenty-eight files in Post 122 recording the Study Group's work.

108. Wolstencroft to Short, 23 May 1967, Post 122/10278. With Head Postmasters under huge pressure to revise all their duty schedules, 'we cannot hope simultaneously to make much progress with the productivity measures which we have in hand following McKinsey'.

109. 'Two-Tier Letter Service', Memorandum to Regional Directors by Dennis Wesil, March 1967, Post 122/10278.

110. 'To call the proposed higher paid service by such a name [i.e. 1st class] holds out every possibility of justified criticism . . .': para. 1, 'First and Second Class Letter Service', Report by the Study Group on Long Term Planning, Post 23/87.

111. 'We have a difficult job to persuade a very conservative body of men that this rather drastic change is not only necessary but that it should be welcomed enthusiastically': Tom Jackson to Wolstencroft, 25 March 1968, Post 23/92.

112. *The Times*, 23 August 1968, and the *Daily Mail*, 28 August 1968. Many press cuttings on the episode are to be found in Post 122/14237a and Post 122/14237b.

113. Parliamentary Clerk to Wolstencroft, 14 October 1968, Post 23/119.

114. From paras. 8, 10 and 11 of 'A Survey of the New Inland Letter Service', April 1969, Post 114/29.

11. A dismal decade, 1969–79

1. Armstrong to Stonehouse, 5 March 1969. The reference came from a director of the Bank of England and had been passed to Armstrong by its Governor, Sir Leslie O'Brien. The top mandarin naturally stopped short of slamming the door completely – 'This may well not be an unanswerable comment but it makes me feel that we need further reports before we can regard him as a strong candidate' – but his message could hardly have been clearer. (TNA, FV 66/19.)

2. *The Times*, 23 May 1969, p. 29.

3. *The Times*, 1 October 1969, p. 3.

4. *The Times*, 3 October 1969, p. 11.

5. Stonehouse to the Prime Minister, 9 April 1969, TNA FV 66/19.

6. POBM 13 October 1969, Post 69/266.

7. 'Notes of a Board Discussion', appended to POBM 5 October 1970, Post 69/179.

8. PO (70)53, 'Relations between the Post Office and the Government', March 1970, Post 69/85.

9. POBM 2 February 1970, Post 69/179.

10. Its title and contents have been lost – but it was later agreed by the Board that its 'comments . . . about the postal business were wholly unacceptable' (POBM 23 November 1970, Post 69/179).

11. PO (70)68, Post 69/85. This paper, signed off by Vieler, actually set out an acute analysis of future trends in postal traffic which still reads well today. It concluded by putting its money on a forecast of future letter volumes that saw little or no increase in the first half of the 1970s, followed by a steadily accelerating growth through the 1980s.

12. PO (70)130, 'Postal Tariff Proposals', May 1970, Post 69/86. The paper noted that *The Times* had gone up by 500 per cent, a standard loaf of bread by 366 per cent, the minimum London bus fare by 300 per cent and a pint of milk by 120 per cent.

13. POBM 1 June and 8 June 1970, Post 69/179.

14. *The Times*, 24 July 1970, p. 6.

15. Wood to Chataway, 4 November 1970, TNA FV 66/20.

16. Christopher Chataway, interview with author, 10 March 2010.

17. The Board's statement ran in part: 'We note the intended announcement with considerable regret and great personal sympathy for the Chairman. . . . We place on record with gratitude his unceasing efforts and courageous actions in shaping the course of the Corporation in its first and particularly difficult year, the achievements of which bear testimony to his leadership' (POBM 24 November 1970, Post 69/179). Hall telephoned Ryland two days later to urge that the Board issue a statement saying it was considering its position. Ryland dutifully passed this on to the Board, but it was then agreed that no policies had been affected by the Chairman's departure 'and

that therefore no question of Members reconsidering their position arose . . .' (POBM 27 November 1970, Post 69/179).

18. Quoted in Alan Clinton, *Post Office Workers: A Trade Union and Social History*, Allen & Unwin, 1984, p. 550.
19. Ibid.
20. Tony Benn, *Out of the Wilderness: Diaries 1963–67*, Arrow Books, 1988, '22 October 1964', p. 170.
21. He was adamant that McKinsey reforms should not be introduced piece-meal. 'We do not consider that a McKinsey examination [of any individual branch] is sufficient evidence upon which to base revision proposals . . . [until] the findings have had national discussions and even then only follow-ing normal consultation and inspection procedures' (Jackson to G. R. Downes, Director of Postal Services, 29 December 1966, Post 122/304). But Jackson was far from opposed to McKinsey's ideas, and invited the consult-ants to make a presentation to the Executive Council at UPW headquarters in Clapham in February 1967. It was generally well received, though it took ten weeks for the minutes of the event to be agreed.
22. *The Times*, 13 January 1971.
23. Paper submitted to the EC by Jackson, 15 January 1971, EC 41/71, UCW/2/4/28.
24. The Department of Employment funded a study by two academics, John Gennard and Roger Lasko, that was published in 1975 under the title 'The Impact of the 1971 Postal Strike on Those Involved'. It analysed events in UPW branches in Bristol and Liverpool. Half the UPW telephonists in Bris-tol resigned from the union, a slightly smaller proportion in Liverpool.
25. *The Times*, 10 February 1971.
26. Paper submitted to the EC by Jackson, 24 February 1971, EC 84/71, UCW/2/4/28.
27. Alan Tuffin, interview with author, 18 February 2010. The Associated Doc-uments in the Executive Council archive of the Union contain no record of any meeting held during the 1971 strike.
28. Chataway, interview with author, 10 March 2010.
29. Hardman Report, HMSO, May 1971, para. 20, Post 65/279.
30. *Conference Chronicle*, 16 May 1974, UCW/2/13/67. The 1974 Conference was unusual in keeping this convenient four-page record of each day's pro-ceedings. Most others left only long, impenetrable summaries of motions, amendments and votes, together with a verbatim typescript of all speeches, unedited and with no index. Most of my accounts of Conference events rely heavily on the report subsequently published in *The Post*.
31. Ibid., para. 4.2.
32. Ibid., para. 6.20.
33. Howard Brabrook, interview with author, 15 February 2010. Brabrook was a 23-year-old Personal Assistant to Ryland and was charged with keeping the minutes of all the emergency executive's meetings.

34. Hardman Report, paras. 7.9 and 7.10.

35. Ken Young, interview with author, 23 February 2010.

36. Chataway, interview with author, 10 March 2010.

37. A. W. C. Ryland, 'The Post Office as a Business', based on a lecture to the IEE on 4 March 1971, *Electronics and Power: The Journal of the Institution of Electrical Engineers*, Vol. 17, 1971, pp. 274–6.

38. Malcolm Argent, interview with author, 16 October 2009. 'On the other hand, to be fair to Ryland, at the end he said I could have any job I wanted – and I knew after Howland Street that there was nothing that could scare me in future.'

39. Benn, *Out of the Wilderness*, '26 October 1964', p. 174.

40. Ibid., '23 November 1965', p. 354.

41. *The Post*, Vol. 80, No. 8, 17 August 1977. The UPW, which had originally backed the Girobank idea strongly in 1920, tried in vain to persuade Labour's National Executive to develop it as a 'State Bank', set up within the framework of the Post Office and run by postal employees.

42. Young, interview with author, 23 February 2010.

43. Figures taken from a 1976 report by NEDO, 'A Study of the UK Nationalized Industries, Background Paper 3', quoted in Michael Corby, *The Postal Business 1969–79: A Study in Public Sector Management*, Kogan Page, 1979, p. 96.

44. Corby, *Postal Business*, pp. 83–5.

45. Ibid., p. 88.

46. Ibid., p. 95.

47. John Mackay, interview with author, 15 September 2009. He joined as an APCII in 1963, progressed through various jobs in management services, personnel and finance in the 1970s and became Territorial General Manager for Royal Mail North in 1986.

48. Corby, *Postal Business*, p. 210.

49. POB (69)83, 'The Letter Post Plan'. The response was noted in the minutes with what looks like faint praise but may just have been a stiff formality: 'The Board welcomed the enterprise and foresight of Mr Vieler's paper on the Letter Post Plan, which had been received with encouragement' (POBM 19 December 1969, Post 69/266).

50. Board presentation of 19 December 1969, Post 17/283.

51. N. C. C. de Jong, 'Introductory Paper', at the International Conference on Postal Mechanization, May 1970, *Proceedings of the Institution of Mechanical Engineers*, Vol. 184, 1969–70.

52. *The Post*, Vol. 76, No. 7, 29 July 1972. It was largely Jackson's personal advocacy of mechanization, in a special report for the 1975 Conference, that finally overcame the Union's ban on cooperation: 'Without mechanisation, a real decline in the level of services, jobs and earnings is a certainty' (*The Post*, Vol. 79, Special Conference Issue, July 1975).

53. PO (73)201, 'Review of Mechanization', pp. 14–15 and 19, Post 69/99 (Part 1 of 9).

54. Report of Post Office Review Committee ('Carter Report'), July 1977, HMSO, Cmnd 6850, p. 24.

55. Statistics attached to Notes of the Informal Joint Group on Postal Productivity, 15 December 1970, Associated Documents of the Executive Council, UCW/2/4/28. Correspondence linked to the football pools had accounted for 281 million posted letters in 1969–70, down from 561 million in 1965–6.

56. The wording adopted for the Chairman's Statement in the 1973–4 Annual Report, with minor revisions, was used on many occasions: 'Because of inflation, the liabilities of the Fund have gone up and the cash value of the Consols has gone down, so that the funding mechanism for pre-Corporation liabilities is now seen to be hopelessly inadequate. The Post Office is seeking talks with the Government with the object of achieving a more equitable and realistic arrangement.'

57. 'Now that the Post Office was entering negotiations against Government advice, with the stated aim of preparing proposals jointly with the unions to be put to Government, it could be regarded as inappropriate to consult the Department of Industry about the line to be taken in negotiations . . .' (Minute 74/157, POBM 13 May 1974, Post 69/183).

58. 'The Post Office's Letter Post Services', 2nd Report of Select Committee on Nationalised Industries, December 1975; P.P. 1975–6, xxxiv, pp. 295–513. The Post Office's evidence is at pp. 345–52.

59. 6th Annual Report of POUNC, 1974–5; P.P. 1975–76, xl, para. 137.

60. 'The Post Office's Letter Post Services', 2nd SCNI Report, para. 8.

61. POBM 19 May 1975, Post 69/184.

62. Wilson had told the 1974 Conference in Bournemouth: 'We entirely reject the idea, put forward in some quarters, of separating the Postal side of the Post Office from the Telecommunications side'. The Post, Vol. 78, No. 8, Special Conference Issue, 1974.

63. Appendix to PO (70)71, Post 69/86.

64. Carter Report, para. 1.

65. POBM 6 October 1975, Post 69/184.

66. See R. J. S. Baker, 'The Postal Service: A Problem of Identity', Political Quarterly, January 1976, p. 69. Baker was a former Assistant Secretary turned academic. Perhaps this article itself owed something to Ryland's decision to mount a lively campaign. Baker reviewed the disparate businesses of his old employer and concluded that 'such a conglomerate of strange bedfellows cannot continue much longer'.

67. POBM 26 January 1976, File 2 of 12, Post 69/185.

68. STC Communications Lecture, 17 May 1976, Ryland Papers RY0004/08, Post 123.

69. 'The Post Office's Letter Post Services', 2nd SCNI Report, para. 130.

70. Carter Report, para. 9.2.

71. Ibid., Summary of Recommendations, para. 80.

72. Ibid., para. 9.7.

73. 'Ball-bearing chief to be head of Post Office', The Times, 6 May 1977.

74. William Barlow, interview with author, 21 September 2009.

75. See Clinton, *Post Office Workers*, pp. 395ff.

76. Robert Jenkins, *Tony Benn: A Political Biography*, Writers and Readers Cooperative, 1980, p. 215.

77. Minute 75/312, POBM 6 October 1975, Post 69/184.

78. Ibid.

79. Minute 76/170, POBM 22 March 1976, Post 69/185.

80. PO (76)204, 'Industrial Democracy' by Ken Young; POBM 20 September 1976, Post 69/185.

81. Minutes of meeting chaired by Kaufman, 4 May 1977, Barlow Papers WB3.

82. November Speech, Barlow Papers, File 1, WB5.

83. Barlow itemized his priorities for the Board itself at the end of November. He reiterated the gist of his speech to the managers, but was a little less guarded than he had been in public on one issue: 'the unions expected wide-ranging consultation, but instead of this leading to amicable progress, changes were only slowly achieved ... [and] with industrial action at various levels because of pay disputes, numerous possibilities for improvement were being held up indefinitely'. (Minute 77/335, POBM 29 November 1977, Post 69/186.) In his speech to the managers, Barlow had noted 'the postal manning pattern is a key issue', to which he would be attaching special importance. But he had also urged his listeners 'to be extremely careful when talking to employees about productivity ... The word [productivity] conjures up opposition'.

84. *The Post*, Vol. 80, No. 5, 21 May 1977. (It might be noted in passing that copies of *The Post* for 1977 were bound as Vol. 80 even though Vol. 79 had contained 1975's issues. This is explained by a mix-up in 1976 which had seen copies filed as Vol. 79 (first half-year) and Vol. 78 (second half-year), both incorrect.)

85. Barlow, interview with author, 21 September 2009.

86. Carter Report, paras. 9.15 and 9.16.

87. Minutes of the Industrial Development Board, Barlow Papers, WB2.

88. Ibid., minutes for 27 March 1979.

89. Barlow Papers, File 5, WB6.

90. Ibid.

91. Ibid. The man was a Communist Party member, but Barlow's protests were in vain. 'Varley told me that the matter had been taken up to the highest level and discussions had taken place with the Prime Minister.' Barlow explained that the man's own union, the POEU, had found him a constant source of discord. 'I therefore said that I felt that the appointment was an unsatisfactory one.' Record of Conversation with Eric Varley, 12 December 1978.

92. Carter Report, para. 1.14.

93. *The Post*, Vol. 80, No. 5, 21 May 1977.

94. PO (78)18, 'Postal Business Medium Term Plan 1978–83' by Denis Roberts, March 1978, Part 6 of 10, Post 69/128.

95. John Lloyd, 'Post Office entering uncharted territory', *Financial Times*, 9 May 1978.
96. Barlow, interview with author, 21 September 2009.
97. Carter Report, para. 6.1.
98. Nigel Walmsley, interview with author, 19 November 2009.
99. Barlow, interview with author, 21 September 2009.
100. Paras. 12 and 16 of White Paper, *The Post Office*, July 1978, Cmnd 7292.
101. PO (79)16, 'Future Structure of the Post Office', March 1979, Post 69/130.
102. PO (79)19, 'The Personnel Interface', March 1979, Post 69/130.
103. POBM 24 April 1979, Minute 79/87, Post 69/188.
104. Barlow, interview with author, 21 September 2009.

12. Once more unique, 1979–87

1. Monopolies and Mergers Commission, *The Inner London Letter Post: A Report on the Letter Post Service in the Area Comprising the Numbered London Postal Districts*, HC515, HMSO, 1980, para. 1.1. Joseph's remarks about a possible need to abolish the postal monopoly were made in the House of Commons on 2 July 1979.
2. William Barlow, interview with author, 21 September 2009.
3. Ron Dearing, interview with author, 14 October 2008.
4. Ibid.
5. Ibid.
6. 'Report to the Secretary of State by the Five Full-Time Members', Barlow Papers, File 1, WB6. Barlow also wrote another extended review of the experiment, which ran to many pages and can be found in WB4. It is not clear whether this second paper was shown to DTI officials or used by Barlow only for his own private briefings, but it included a section on each of a dozen reasons why Industrial Democracy had, in his view, been an unmitigated disaster.
7. Thatcher looked back on this early episode of her premiership, in a forthright passage of her memoirs that lambasted those in the post-war Conservative Party guilty of defeatism in the face of the Left's advance. 'They have all the outward show of a John Bull – ruddy face, white hair, bluff manner – but inwardly they are political calculators who see the task of Conservatives as retreating gracefully . . . Jim Prior was infected by it too, and it made him timid and overcautious in his trade union policy.' (Margaret Thatcher, *The Downing Street Years*, HarperCollins, 1993, pp. 104–5.)
8. Barlow to Butler, 26 October 1979, Barlow Papers, File 1, WB6.
9. The report was compiled, from extensive interviews and observation of the Board's meetings, by the Industrial Relations Research Unit at the University of Warwick. For a copy of the report and a record of the Board's responses, see PO (79)14, 'Minutes of Discussion of SSRC Report', 6 November 1979, Barlow Papers, File 3, WB6.

10. Barlow, interview with author, 21 September 2009.

11. Minute 80/6, POBM 8 January 1980, Post 69/189.

12. John Roberts, interview with author, 16 October 2008.

13. 'Of thirty-two candidates interviewed, twenty-five turned down the job of heading the new post and Giro authority' (*Guardian*, 17 April 1980).

14. Jonathan Evans, interview with author, 3 December 2010.

15. Barlow, interview with author, 21 September 2009.

16. Ibid. On the day that the Split decision was officially announced, Barlow took Ken Young out for lunch to talk about how they could work together as colleagues at British Telecom. 'He was taken aback when I intimated my wish to stay in the Post Office. The challenge of a labour-intensive business was more appealing to me than the [prospect of] inexorable technological growth at BT.' (Young, interview with author, 23 February 2010.)

17. Minute 80/66, POBM 9 September 1980, Post 69/189.

18. David Parker, *The Official History of Privatisation*, Vol. 1, Routledge, 2009, p. 86.

19. Dearing, interview with author, 14 October 2008.

20. Minute 80/26, POBM 15 April 1980, Post 69/189. In the subsequent Board discussion, Joseph's letter was castigated as 'vague and imprecise' but it was acknowledged that postal competition might have to be confronted. The Post Office would not oppose it *per se*, but it would have to be introduced on a fair basis: 'the Post Office would certainly wish to avoid the odium of being the licensing authority for its own competitors … In particular, it would be necessary to ensure that the control machinery was adequate to prevent much wider competition than the Government had in mind …'

21. Minute 80/71, POBM 23 October 1980, Post 69/189.

22. Minute EC80/34 of the Chairman P & G's Executive Committee, 'Privatisation of Counters: Premature Disclosure of Government Proposals', 26 September 1980, Post 69/255.

23. Minute EC80/35, 'Privatisation of Counters: Policy Considerations', 26 September 1980, Post 69/255.

24. Minute 80/99, POBM 16 December 1980, Post 69/189.

25. Minute 80/71, POBM 23 October 1980, Post 69/189.

26. Dearing, interview with author, 14 October 2008.

27. *The Post*, Vol. 81, No. 7, 30 June 1978.

28. *The Post*, Vol. 79, No. 1, 31 January 1976.

29. For the UPW's historian, writing in the early 1980s, the Grunwick affair had cast a huge shadow over the recent past – see Alan Clinton, *Post Office Workers: A Trade Union and Social History*, Allen & Unwin, 1984, pp. 585–94.

30. Annual Conference proceedings, 24 May 1979, UCW/2/13/73/8.

31. 'I spoke to Sir Keith Joseph some six months ago', announced Jackson in a speech on the Monday of the Conference. 'He talked of dividing the Post Office, of giving over part of the Post Office telecoms to private industry and he even soliloquised on the ending of the letter monopoly. This man is now in charge of Post Office affairs and his prejudices could affect us all. …

Unless his worst excesses are curbed by his Cabinet colleagues, the Postal monopoly is under real threat.' (*The Post*, Vol. 82, No. 8, 31 May 1979.)

32. The debate over the 1979 pay negotiation is recorded in the verbatim account of the 1979 Annual Conference proceedings. (UCW/2/13/73/8.) Osei-Tutu told delegates he had met privately with Jackson on 29 March. 'Tom said to me, Frank, what is going [on] outside – I am thinking of resigning, retiring. And my answer to him is, "No, Tom, don't resign". And that is true.' Jackson made no effort to deny it. A summary of the pay debate can be found in *The Post*, Vol. 82, No. 11, 31 July 1979, but it conveys little of the emotional intensity of the verbatim account.

33. *The Post*, Vol. 83, No. 12, 31 October 1980.

34. Ken Young noted the workforce's attitude in a paper to the Posts and Girobank Board. 'As a general point, and despite the declared opposition of [the] UCW and MSA [the Management Staffs Association] to the principle of separation, there has been little adverse reaction by the workforce to the forthcoming changes, although this could change markedly if Government proceeds with its latest proposals [for a reduction in postal and telecom monopoly privileges].' ('Post Office Reorganisation: An Appreciation of Industrial Relations Implications', November 1980, PO (80)39, BT Archives, TCC 55/12/34.)

35. *The Post*, Vol. 84, No. 10, 31 October 1981.

36. *The Post*, Vol. 85, No. 6, June 1982.

37. *The Post*, Vol. 85, No. 8, August 1982.

38. Dearing, interview with author, 14 October 2008.

39. Minute 82/78, POBM 25 May 1982, Post 69/192.

40. The plans for Paddington and Glasgow can be found in POB (81)36 and POB (81)34.

41. *The Post*, Vol. 82, No. 5, 28 April 1979. The Post Office handed over Roberts's report for full publication in the paper over two issues. His views on the less inspiring progress being made in Canada and the US appeared the following week.

42. POB (81)18, Post 69/133. The Board Member should not be confused with the UPW's historian of the same name. They were not related.

43. Walmsley, interview with author, 19 November 2009.

44. POB (86)24, 'Royal Mail Marketing Plans and Objectives, 1986–7' by A. D. Garrett, February 1986, Post 69/155. The overall increase in inland letters since 1980, at around 20 per cent, was 'without parallel in the post-war period'.

45. Minute 82/139, POBM 28 September 1982, Post 69/192. Walmsley's papers included titles like 'Pricing Prospects and Commercial Initiatives in 1983–4', POB (82)99, and 'Inland Letter and Packet Product Review', POB (82)115.

46. The deficits on mails services were £32m in 1972–3, £58m in 1973–4, £117m in 1974–5 and £14m in 1975–6. (Report of Post Office Review Committee ('Carter Report'), July 1977, HMSO, Cmnd 6850, p. 23.)

47. POB (82)102, 'Special Stamp Programmes', Post 69/192. Walmsley explained to the Board in September 1982 that the issues proposed for 1984 'had sought to both preserve the integrity of stamp collecting as a serious hobby and maintain revenue by balancing potentially popular high revenue-earning issues ... with those of a more serious theme such as urban renewal which provided scope for display of good design skills' (Minute 82/129, POBM 28 September 1982, Post 69/192).

48. POB (87)4, Post 69/162.

49. POB (81)50, 'Overseas Mails Services: A Marketing Strategy for Recovery', December 1981, Post 69/133.

50. Ibid., Annex 4.

51. Minute 82/79, POBM 25 May 1982, Post 69/192.

52. Minute 82/123, POBM 28 September 1982, Post 69/192.

53. Sam Wainwright, interview with author, 18 February 2010.

54. Ibid.

55. Dearing, interview with author, 14 October 2008.

56. *Inner London Letter Post*, para. 11.47.

57. Ibid., para. 9.27.

58. Young, interview with author, 23 February 2010.

59. 'Manpower Resourcing and Utilisation in the Postal Business', report attached to POB (81)29, November 1981, Post 69/133.

60. Ibid., p. 47.

61. Minute 83/108, POBM 21 June 1983, Post 69/193.

62. Minutes 85/138 and 140, POBM 23 July 1985, Post 69/195.

63. Alex Bell, interview with author, 4 May 2010.

64. Ibid.

65. The breakdown of the workforce by religion was painstakingly investigated by the Fair Employment Commission for Northern Ireland, which presented its final report in 1989. While its statistics noted that the Catholic representation within management grades of the Letters business was only 24 per cent, the report's own conclusions preferred to focus on the unusually high proportion of Catholics in the workforce as a whole. 'The Commission found that there were areas of significant under-representation of Protestants in the Post Office ... [It] should implement necessary affirmative action measures to ensure fair participation in employment in the Post Office to members of the Protestant community' (para. 12.1).

66. Carty private papers, in his possession.

67. Danny Carty, interview with author, 4–5 May 2010.

68. Ibid.

69. Monopolies and Mergers Commission, *The Post Office Letter Post Service*, Cmnd 9332, HMSO, 1984, para. 1.29.

70. Carty, interview with author, 4–5 May 2010.

71. POB (81)8 and POB (81)22, Post 69/133.

72. Post Office Report and Accounts 1988–9, pp. 46–8.

73. 'Would you advise your own child to join the Post Office?', *The Post*, Vol. 85, No. 2, February 1982.

74. Dearing, interview with author, 14 October 2008.

75. Unnumbered CEC Paper, 'Possible Long Term Organisation in Posts' and 'Note by Ron Dearing', 30 July 1980, Post 69/245. (CEC papers were unnumbered throughout 1980.)

76. Minute 80/18, CEC 6 August 1980, Post 69/255.

77. Ibid. The memo to Roberts was signed by Walmsley, Cockburn and C. H. Briscoe, the Finance Director for Posts. Given subsequent events, its uncompromising rejection of profit centres provides a measure of Dearing's personal impact in the 1980s: 'We all believe that it is dangerous to look to organisational changes in themselves to smooth away the difficulties of the business. Moreover, changes of any magnitude of themselves would put the Business into disarray at a very critical time.'

78. Corporate Consulting Group, 'Report on the Structure of the Post Office', November 1983, Post 72.

79. POB (83)151, 'Organisational Review' by R. Dearing, November 1983, Post 69/143.

80. Minute 83/170, POBM 25 October 1983, Post 69/193.

81. POB (83)28, Post 69/145.

82. Dearing, interview with author, 14 October 2008.

83. Evans, interview with author, 3 December 2010.

84. A paper delivered to the Regional Directors' Conference in November 1984 by C. H. Briscoe had argued strongly for this devolution. 'At the moment we are running two Post Offices. The first is the theoretical one in which there is maximum devolution, increased personal accountability, and the pushing of decision-taking to the lowest practicable level. . . . The second Post Office, the actual one, remains a highly centralized, highly bureaucratic machine, and [is] becoming more so by the hour.' (CEC 10(85), Post 69/254.)

85 . Minute 83/189, POBM 22 November 1983, Post 69/193.

86. Quoted in Parker, *Official History of Privatisation*, p. 172.

87. Dearing to Parkinson, 6 October 1983, attached to POBM 6 October 1983, Post 69/193. Parkinson resigned suddenly just a few days later after the disclosure of an extramarital affair.

88. M. Beesley and S. Littlechild, 'Privatisation: Principles, Problems and Priorities', *Lloyds Bank Review*, July 1983, pp. 1–20.

89. Parker, *Official History of Privatisation*, p. 176.

90. Tebbit to Dearing, 26 February 1985, quoted in Minute 85/165, POBM 24 September 1985, Post 69/195.

91. Draft of 'Post Office Objectives', Tebbit to Dearing 7 August 1985, Annex A to POB (85)151, Post 69/154.

92. POB (85)148, 'Post Office Organisation', November 1985, Post 69/154.

93. Minute 85/203, POBM 26 November 1985, Post 69/195.

94. See the minutes for 1986 and 1987 in Post 69/262 and Post 69/263.

95. *The Post*, Vol. 89, No. 7, July 1986.

96. In a guarded response to a parliamentary question in February, the DTI's Minister of State, Geoffrey Pattie, told the Commons: 'We have not decided whether the [Post Office] Corporation might be privatised and we therefore have no plans at present to prepare it for privatisation' (*The Post*, Vol. 89, No. 6, June 1986).
97. Minute 86/213, POBM 16 December 1986, Post 69/196.
98. Robert Albon, *Privatise the Post*, Centre for Policy Studies, January 1987.
99. *The Times*, 5 January 1987.
100. POB (87)67, Post 69/164. Dearing's paper fronted a series of written responses to the independent review by his colleagues.
101. *The Times*, 23 July 1987. 'Sir Ron . . . insisted he had not been pushed out because of potential disagreements with the Government over piecemeal privatisation of Post Office businesses. Ministers have made strenuous efforts in the past year to persuade Sir Ron to stay, particularly as he was the architect of its dramatic turnaround in recent years. . . . He said, "If the Post Office had been in trouble, I would have stayed".'
102. Dearing, interview with author, 14 October 2008.
103. *The Times*, 3 June 1987.
104. Lawson recounted the conversation immediately afterwards to his senior officials at the Treasury (Gerry Grimstone, interview with author, 2 September 2010).

13. Thwarted ambitions, 1987–2002

1. Young, interview with author, 23 February 2010.
2. *The Times*, 5 January 1987.
3. Bryan Nicholson, interview with author, 17 November 2010.
4. Morag macdonald Simpson, interview with author, 11 March 2010.
5. Dearing memo to Board Members, 30 July 1987, E12421. A briefing paper for Dearing ahead of the meeting, attached to the memo, observed that privatization had effectively been cancelled, 'to the personal disappointment of very many Board Members'.
6. Minute 89/5, POBM 24 January 1989, E12421/Board Minutes. The media's continuing preoccupation with the prospects for privatization was apparent at the time of Young's appointment as Deputy Chairman. It was reported in *The Times* that this would 'inevitably be interpreted as part of a process towards eventual partial privatisation' (1 March 1990).
7. Dearing to Williamson memo, 1 December 1986, E12421/Girobank file.
8. Sellers to Dearing memo, 16 December 1985, E12421/Girobank file.
9. Morag Macdonald Simpson, interview with author, 11 March 2010.
10. The September 1988 short-list comprised Crédit Lyonnais, Westpac, the Bank of Scotland and a consortium that included another state-owned French bank, Crédit Agricole. The February 1989 short-list comprised Alliance and Leicester, the Co-op, the Bank of Ireland and Singer & Friedlander.

11. Jerry Cope, interview with author, 1 July 2010.

12. Richard Dykes, interview with author, 30 March 2011.

13. All figures in this paragraph have been taken from 'The Sale of Girobank plc', National Audit Office Report, February 1993, HC 456, pp. 1–13.

14. Andrew Davidson, *Management Today*, 1 December 1996.

15. 'Believe me, the union didn't change during my time, or my successor's time ... The leadership had its hands tied by the democratic nature of the union's decision-taking; [and the postmen thought] because they worked in a monopoly, and because they were publicly owned, that [they] weren't subject to the disciplines of the market ... So really the business was stuck.' (Dearing, interview with author, 14 October 2008.)

16. Monopolies and Mergers Commission, *The Inner London Letter Post: A Report on the Letter Post Service in the Area Comprising the Numbered London Postal Districts*, HC515, HMSO, 1980, para. 8.6. 'Although ... we believe that present establishments are excessive, we accept that there are and have been difficulties in recruiting postmen of the calibre and in the numbers required.'

17. Bill Cockburn, interview with author, 2 December 2009.

18. Minute 88/141, POBM 2 September 1988, Post 69/198.

19. Minute 89/4, POBM 24 January 1989, E12421/Board minutes. Nicholson thought that, in the event they were to persevere with DRAS, the Board 'must assume that there would be sufficient support within Letters for industrial action to destroy the network'.

20. *Financial Times*, 18 July 1989. The 1988–9 results, said Young, 'showed a well-managed recovery from the dispute'. Pre-tax trading profits ended up at £170m, which was thought to reflect a £40m reduction due to DRAS. An initial Board estimate had put the cost at £80m. (Minute 88/151, POBM 16 September 1988, Post 69/198.)

21. *The Post* of December 1988 featured an open letter from Tuffin to his membership. 'In the Post Office we have seen all the consequences of the original decision to break the industry up into separate self-contained units. That fundamental error has led to massive discontent: The Post Office now has the worst industrial relations record of any major industry in Great Britain ... [and] I am fearful that the industry is heading for more trouble ...'

22. Minutes of CEC meeting, 30 November 1988, Post 69/264.

23. POB (87)77, 'Key Strategic Planning Issues', June 1987, Post 69/164.

24. Minute 89/5, POBM 24 January 1989, E12421/Board minutes.

25. Minute 89/30, POBM 28 February 1989, Post 69/199.

26. Minute 89/118, POBM 23 May 1989, Post 69/199.

27. David Sibbick, interview with author, 15 October 2008. The erstwhile secretary of the Carter Committee in the 1970s had been brought back to postal duties at the DTI as a temporary adviser to Ridley on his plans to revise the monopoly. (The other topic that interested Ridley was, rather oddly, the work being done by British Chambers of Commerce.)

28. Minute 89/259, POBM 24 October 1989, E12421/Board minutes.

29. Minute 90/24, POBM 27 February 1990, Post 69/Red Books. The Five-Year Plan for 1990–95 had 'set out an agenda for . . . drawing together the link between monopoly changes and greater commercial freedom'.

30. Minute 89/304, POBM 19 December 1989, E12421/Board minutes. One of Ridley's advisers, it should be said, had a clearer memory of the disagreements. Sibbick recalled some very lively opposition from the Post Office to Ridley's own preliminary ideas on market liberalization – and a good deal of ministerial irritation with the Post Office's thinking, especially its suggested revision to delivery patterns. 'I think Ridley very much lost patience with the Post Office in the end.' (Sibbick, interview with author, 15 October 2008.) After Ridley's resignation, Sibbick was appointed Director of Posts at the DTI, a position he held until 2000.

31. Minute 90/18, POBM 27 February 1990, E12421/Board minutes.

32. Minute 90/41, POBM 27 March 1990 and Minute 90/68, POBM 22 May 1990, E12421/Board minutes.

33. Nicholas Ridley, *My Style of Government*, Hutchinson, 1991, p. 224.

34. Minute 91/15, POBM 26 February 1991, E12421/Board minutes.

35. The DTI's Permanent Secretary told the Post Office's Chairman: 'nothing had emerged that suggested Government was any nearer developing a coherent policy for the future of the Post Office and its businesses . . .' (Minute 91/25, POBM 26 March 1991, E12421/Board minutes).

36. Minute 91/25, POBM 26 March 1991, E12421/Board minutes.

37. See, for example, two seminal reports written by J. E. Yates in 1949–50: POB (49)40, 'Scale Payment Sub Post Offices', Post 69/41, and POB (50)20, 'Sub Post Offices – Standards of Accommodation', Post 69/48.

38. John Fletcher, 'Review of the Counter Network', February 1983, Post 112/57.

39. Monopolies and Mergers Commission, *Post Office Counters Services*, Cm. 398, HMSO, 1988, Post 71/434.

40. Jonathan Evans, interview with author, 3 December 2010. A wide-ranging improvement strategy was laid out in 'Business Plan for Counters', noted in Minute 88/124, POBM 26 July 1988, Post 69/198. The successful implementation of all but four of the MMC recommendations was reviewed three years later, and noted in Minute 91/49, POBM 21 May 1991, Post 69/Red Books.

41. 'Girobank is crucial to Counters . . . and we have to look to it to provide the means of Counters getting into such areas as cheque encashment, credit cards and other more general banking activities which could open up substantial new markets as older ones decline' (A. J. Roberts, 'Presentation on the Future of Counters', January 1983, Post 69/504).

42. At one of his Executive Committee meetings in 1986, Dearing had spelt this out explicitly: 'rural services were social in character and it was therefore debatable whether the costs of these services should be borne by society as a whole or by postal customers. This was not to say that the Post Office was now seeking a subsidy for such services, but it was right, in the Chairman's

view, that Government should at least be made aware of the issue of social cost at a time when profit targets were being set so that there was a basis for pursuing the issue at some later date' (Minute 86/12, CEC 5 February 1986, Post 69/262). The Committee was discussing a paper on the topic, CEC 9(86), 'Profit Target: Services Provided on Social Grounds'.

43. Minute 86/12, CEC 5 February 1986, Post 69/262.

44. Carter Report, para. 10.39.

45. Minute 88/104, POBM 28 June 1988, Post 69/198.

46. Ibid. The new ventures included such thorny acronyms as HAL-CON (Heavy-and-Large, on Consignment) and DITAT (Datapost Inland Tracking and Tracing).

47. Minute 88/18, CEC 9 March 1988, Post 69/264.

48. Minute 88/222, POBM 13 December 1988, Post 69/198.

49. Minute 89/4, POBM 24 January 1989, E12421/Board minutes.

50. POB (89)6, 'Parcels Strategy for 1992' by N. Nelson, Post 69/174.

51. Minute 89/26, POBM 21 March 1989, Post 69/199.

52. Minute 89/300, POBM 19 December 1989, Post 69/199.

53. Post Office Report and Accounts 1990–91, Note 2, p. 69.

54. POB (90)72, 'Parcelforce Recovery Plan' by N. Nelson, October 1990, E12421/Board papers. The Board's review of it is in Minute 90/118, POBM 30 October 1990, E12421/Board minutes.

55. Minute 91/29, POBM 26 March 1991, E12421/Board minutes.

56. Minute 91/37, POBM 23 April 1991, E12421/Board minutes.

57. 'In the interim period [i.e. until after privatization] it is also clear that no significant decisions can be made on Parcelforce International Strategy . . . since that [sic] might have implications for potential purchasers' (POB (92)46, 'Privatisation of Parcelforce' by Richard Close, July 1992, E12421/ Board papers).

58. Minute 92/65, POBM 28 July 1992, E12421/Board minutes.

59. Kate Jenkins, interview with author, 22 March 2011.

60. Bryan Nicholson, interview with author, 17 November 2010.

61. POB (88)108, 'Mission, Values and Conduct' by Bryan Nicholson, December 1988, Post 69/172.

62. Nicholson, interview with author, 17 November 2010.

63. Young, interview with author, 23 February 2010. 'I really thought that the Post Office was now a successful organization providing a good service, making a reasonable profit and [sitting on] a far better pricing record than other overseas Post Offices.'

64. 'Failure to provide tracked services would inevitably lead to the loss of this valuable business for postal administrations, and if the British Post Office were excluded from the [GD-Net] arrangement it would inevitably lose its market share of international express business. In addition, its domestic market could be put at risk as successful international couriers exploited their position in this country . . .' (Minute 91/69, POBM 30 July 1991, Post 69/Red Books). In the event, GD-Net proved less of a watershed than

expected, but the Board's analysis was prescient enough. The launch of GD-Net marked a crisis for the UPU, where the decision of some members to join forces with a private-sector competitor against domestic state administrations caused outrage. Whitehall and its own lawyers advised the Post Office in January that it had no legal authority to join the renegades. A paper prepared for the Board by Parcelforce's new head, Peter Howarth, warned of the possible outcome: 'Royal Mail International expect the JVC [i.e. the joint venture with TNT] to compete keenly in the UK, where it has a relatively large delivery force ...' (POB (92)5, 'International Express Delivery and the Joint Venture: Update', January 1992, Post 69/Red Books).

65. Nicholson, interview with author, 17 November 2010.

66. Cockburn, interview with author, 2 December 2009.

67. Minute 92/93, POBM 27 October 1992, E12421/Board minutes. Setting up the management arrangements for the work on privatization early in the New Year, Cockburn noted they would take effect immediately – 'assuming that the Secretary of State announces a decision [on privatization] in line with the Board's recommendation' (POB (93)5, 'Management of Possible Privatisation', January 1993, Post 69/Red Books).

68. Cockburn, interview with author, 2 December 2009.

69. Cope, interview with author, 1 July 2010.

70. 'My junior Minister, Edward Leigh, raised the issue of privatizing the Post Office. I was immediately sceptical because I thought, as everybody does, that everyone's favourite is the postman and I just thought it would be politically extremely difficult. . . . I don't remember the arguments [among the ministerial team at the DTI], I just remember them taking place – and I just found that I wasn't being persuasive. I wasn't persuading myself in arguing with Edward Leigh. His arguments were better than mine and so I became persuaded' (Heseltine, interview with author, 24 November 2009).

71. Heron to Paul Salvidge, 21 October 1993, Royal Mail records. Heron was careful as ever to avoid ruling out a Plan B completely: if privatization were to be judged impractical, 'the case for commercial freedom would still stand and we would earnestly press for this to be provided in another way (eg a PLC model similar to the Dutch Post Office and many others around the world)'. But the Board was intensely sceptical of any alternatives to privatization. As Heron had put it six months earlier in a letter to Edward Leigh: 'That is not to say that there are no other options but we are not aware of any proven alternatives within our governmental system' (Heron to Leigh, 25 March, 1993, Royal Mail records).

72. One agency, the Public Policy Unit, urged a bold pro-privatization campaign to force the hand of the Major government, '[which] seems to be in a state of hovering indecision' (memo to Bill Cockburn, 6 July 1993, Royal Mail records).

73. Sibbick, interview with author, 15 October 2008.

74. *The Future of Postal Services: A Consultative Document*, June 1994, Cm. 2614.

75. Cockburn, interview with author, 2 December 2009.

76. Joan Burnie and Douglas Corrance, *Postbus Country: Glimpses of Rural Scotland*, Canongate Press, 1994, p. 90. The authors provide a comprehensive list of the routes set up in Scotland between 1968 and 1994. For a brief historical account, see Jim Hall, 'Getting Going with Postbuses', in *Cross Post: The Journal of the Association of Friends of the National Postal Museum*, Vol. 6, No. 3, Autumn 1996.

77. Mackay, interview with author, 15 September 2009.

78. Brian Meek, *Glasgow Herald*, 11 April 1994.

79. Michael Heseltine, interview with author, 24 November 2009.

80. 'I think we had created a great platform for privatization. Having worked since 1995 with a number of large private-sector companies, I realize today that the potential was actually far greater than I imagined at the time' (Cockburn, interview with author, 2 December 2009).

81. Minute 94/48, POBM 10 May 1994, Post 69/Red Books.

82. Minute 95/117, POBM 7 November 1995, Post 69/Red Books. Heseltine argued for a 50 per cent cap on the negative EFL payment. He appeared to have won agreement on this, but the Treasury subsequently overrode it.

83. Minute 94/39, POBM 12 April 1994, Post 69/Red Books.

84. POB (88)2, 'Pension Fund Deficiency', January 1988, Post 69/168.

85. Minutes 91/3 and 91/16, POBM 29 January and 26 February 1991, Post 69/Red Books. The contributions holiday was at first authorized to start only from 1 April 1991. Once this decision had been made, however, the Trustees were persuaded to accept a 'retrospective holiday' allowing the contributions made in the second half of 1990–91 to be recouped by the Post Office. Ken Young was assigned the sensitive task of explaining all this to the unions.

86. Minute 94/93, POBM 4 October 1994, E12421/Board minutes.

87. Minute 96/91, POBM 26 September 1996, Post 69/Red Books.

88. Minute 94/19, POBM 1 February 1994, E12421/Board minutes.

89. Minute 86/133, POBM 22 July 1986, Post 69/196.

90. I am indebted to Tom Norgate of the Post Office Mechanisation Study Circle for his guidance on this and many other aspects of the mechanization story.

91. Cope, interview with author, 1 July 2010.

92. Quoted in Minute 96/123, POBM 10 December 1996, Post 69/Red Books.

93. These market-share estimates are taken from Minute 94/118, POBM 6 December 1994 and Minute 95/19, POBM 7 February 1995, Post 69/Red Books. See also POB (94)29, 'International Pipeline Project' by Peter Howarth, 27 April 1994, Post 69/Red Books.

94. POB (92)22, 'Corporate Plan & Investment and Financing Review 1992–3', Post 69/Red Books.

95. Minute 96/98, POBM 8 October 1996, Post 69/Red Books.

96. POB (95)11, 'Royal Mail's Employee Agenda', was discussed by the Board on 7 March 1995. Neither the paper nor the minutes have been traceable – they are among the substantial number of privately circulated Board papers from these years that appear to have gone missing.

97. Brian Thomson, interview with author, 29 June 2010.

98. 'Close contact was being maintained with the Union's leadership, who were also deeply concerned by the current situation, and were disowning illegal industrial action. Despite this, local activists were persisting . . .' (Chief Executive's Monthly Report, Minute 95/44, POBM 9 May 1995, Post 69/ Red Books).

99. Minute 96/42, POBM 2 April 1996, Post 69/Red Books.

100. Minute 97/17, POBM 11 February 1997, Post 69/Red Books.

101. Minute 97/67, POBM 10 June 1997, Post 69/Red Books.

102. Ryland wrote: '. . . that there should be such uncertainty [over the composition of the Board] at this difficult time is most unsatisfactory. It is hardly surprising however when, uniquely, the salaries of Board Members of nationalised industries have been virtually frozen for over five years. Their pay today is worth only half of what it was some five years ago' (Annual Report, 1976–7).

103. Minute 98/52, POBM 12 May 1998, Post 69/Red Books.

104. Peter Allen and Sir Christopher Harding were disinclined, like many before them, to risk having an unseemly public row over Board salaries, but on stepping down both formally 'expressed their disappointment at leaving' (Minute 98/66, POBM 9 June 1998, Post 69/Red Books).

105. Minute 98/38, POBM 14 April 1998, Post 69/Red Books.

106. Minute 98/81, POBM 14 July 1998, Post 69/Red Books. The Government's advisers were bankers Dresdner Kleinwort Benson and accountants KMPG. Roberts told the Board, in presenting his monthly Report, that they 'had concluded that commercial freedom would be easier under the 49 per cent share sale option'.

107. 'Geoffrey Robinson [the Paymaster General] called me in within my first month and said: "We are pretty convinced we want to sell this on. How do you feel about that?" . . . He was very keen to go' (Neville Bain, interview with author, 17 November 2010). Bain responded just as he had during final interviews for the chairmanship the previous autumn: he was carefully non-committal, while saying that his natural instinct as a businessman would be to see private enterprise as a sensible way of instilling more useful disciplines.

108. POB (98)43, 'Post Office Corporate Plan 1998–2003', June 1998, Post 69/ Red Books. 'Given full, unambiguous and sustainable commercial freedoms, there is no reason in principle why the Post Office should not emulate the success of the privatised utilities . . .'

109. POB (98)34, 'The Post Office Review' by John Roberts, May 1998, Post 69/ Red Books.

110. Minute 98/80, POBM 14 July 1998, Post 69/Red Books.

111. Donald Macintyre, *Mandelson and the Making of New Labour*, Harper-Collins, 1999. Mandelson's handling of the Post Office brief in 1998 is recounted at pp. 474–8 of the paperback edition, published in 2000.

112. Peter Mandelson, *The Third Man: Life at the Heart of New Labour*, Harper-Press, 2010, pp. 263–5. He records finding three clear priorities on his desk

in July 1998, one of which 'was to decide what to do with the Royal Mail, a great national institution ... which clearly needed transforming if it was to survive in the modern telecommunications market'.

113. Discussing Brown's opposition to subsequent plans for a reform of the NHS, Mandelson notes in his memoir that the Chancellor 'used much the same argument [as] he had made against my plan to allow the Royal Mail to borrow, invest and expand' (ibid., p. 364).

114. *The Times*, 4 March 1998. His books included *Successful Management* (Macmillan, 1995) and, co-authored with David Band, *Winning Ways through Corporate Governance* (Macmillan, 1996).

115. Neville Bain, interview with author, 17 November 2010.

116. POB (00)94, 'Performance of Overseas Subsidiaries' by Jerry Cope and Heather Buttersworth, December 2000, Post 69/Red Books. At the outset, in April 1999, Roberts set down a summary of the strategy to be followed, see POB (99)26, 'Deployment of European Parcels Strategy', Post 69/Red Books.

117. POB (98)57, 'Shaping for Competitive Success' by Jerry Cope and others, September 1998, Post 69/Red Books. The paper captured perfectly the compounding complexity of the postal industry.

118. The 1997, 1998 1999 and 2000 corporate plans can be found in Post 69/Red Books as POB (97)44, POB (98)43, POB (99)35 (see Min 99/58, 7–8 June) and POB (00)28 respectively.

119. One of the DTI's civil servants had told the Chairman: '[Byers] thinks that people in his position at the DTI will be there for no longer than eighteen months, [and meanwhile] every decision he has to make on the Post Office is down[side], so he's going to procrastinate for as long as he can' (Bain, interview with author, 17 November 2010).

120. Minute 96/53, POBM 2 April 1996, Post 69/Red Books. The sharing of savings had the attraction of locking the BA into a long-term contract. But it also left the Post Office having to negotiate not only with suppliers over the future cost of the system, but also with the BA and the Treasury over the definition of savings. This proved problematic.

121. See in particular POB (99)47, 'Implication on the Post Office of the 24 May 1999 Horizon Agreement', and POB (99)48, 'Accounting, Funding and Tax Implication of the 24 May 1999 Horizon Agreement', Post 69/Red Books.

122. Minute 99/90, POBM 14 September 1999, Post 69/Red Books.

123. 'The Board expressed concern at the potentially fragile loyalty of [1st class letter] customers in this new [communications] model. Should there be a protracted period of service disruption (industrial action) to postal services, a change in habit could be observed which could result in large scale abandonment of physical mail in favour of the electronic channel' (Minute 00/118, POBM 10 November 2000, Post 69/Red Books). The Board went on to discuss an investment proposal for the Post Office to build its own e-commerce strategy. 'There is no history to guide decision-making and levels of uncertainty are high', explained a background Board paper,

acknowledging the current spate of dotcom failures in the business world. It nonetheless advised the Post Office to assume e-commerce would become 'mainstream reality for almost all businesses and consumers' within two to five years, 'taking the pessimistic to optimistic range' (POB (oo)86x, November 2000, Post 69/Red Books).

124. Minute 99/114, POBM 26 October 1999, Post 69/Red Books.
125. Minute oo/99, POBM 10 October 2000, Post 69/Red Books.
126. Minute oo/34, POBM 14 March 2000, Post 69/Red Books.
127. POB (97)34, 'Packages, Express and International Markets' by Jerry Cope, May 1997, Post 69/Red Books. The paper was based on a study of the Parcelforce business by consultants LEK.
128. 'We are committed to the Post Office being 100 per cent publicly owned ...' *The Times*, 28 March 2000.
129. Minute 01/06, POBM 9 January 2001, Post 69/Red Books.
130. Neville Bain to Stephen Byers, 13 March 2001, Royal Mail Group records.
131. 'Project Olympus, Board briefing note', prepared by UBS Warburg, September 2001. Blair's message, conveyed via the Dutch Prime Minister, is cited on p. 17 of a 48-page document. (Royal Mail Group records.)
132. David Livingstone of Goldman Sachs to David Freud of UBS Warburg, 25 January 2002. (Royal Mail Group records.)
133. 'Transaction Proposal to [Consignia]', p. 9. Goldman Sachs used Maxima and Tango as its codenames for Consignia and TPG. (Royal Mail Group records.)
134. 'Roadmap to Efficient Asset Reallocation', paper prepared for the Royal Mail Group and Consignia Pension Plan, November 2002. (Royal Mail Group records.)
135. 'Both the Secretary of State and Consignia attempted to delay the announcement due to the sensitivities around the Olympus negotiations. Postcomm did delay one week while they met with [TPG] and then they went ahead with the announcement' (Consignia Chief Executive's Report, February 2002 (Royal Mail Group records)).
136. The Sawyer Review was chaired by Tom Sawyer, a former General Secretary of the Labour Party, and was published in July 2001.
137. Allan Leighton, interview with author, 27 May 2010.

14. No end of a crisis, 2002–10

1. McKinsey, *Preliminary Findings from Project Acorn*, p. 58. (Royal Mail Group records.)
2. Allan Leighton, interview with author, 27 May 2010.
3. Ibid.
4. Ibid.
5. *Guardian*, 4 May 2002. His departure was not officially confirmed until some months later.

6. See, for example, Tony Benn, *Out of the Wilderness: Diaries 1963–67*, Arrow Books, 1988, '19 September 1965', p. 321: 'We need to alert the postal staff casually to the likelihood of a feasible one-delivery-a-day service . . .'

7. Sawyer Review, July 2001, para. 155.

8. Leighton, interview with author, 27 May 2010.

9. *Britain Forward Not Back*, Labour Party Manifesto 2005, pp. 21–2.

10. The CWU had at first been surprised at Warwick to hear from the Secretary of State, Patricia Hewitt, that any wording would have to be cleared with Leighton. In the end, it was worked out between the Union and one of the Special Advisers at Number Ten, Geoffrey Norris. The CWU's General Secretary, Billy Hayes, ran into Leighton at Labour's party conference in the autumn. 'He mentioned the party policy [on privatization] that was being discussed and said: "No one discussed it with me." ' (Billy Hayes, interview with author, 31 August 2010.)

11. Adam Crozier, interview with author, 4 October 2010.

12. Royal Mail Group press release, 8 February 2007.

13. Morag Macdonald Simpson recalled attending a Board meeting in 1994, towards the end of her career as Company Secretary, at which an IT boffin made a presentation on the impact of the internet and e-mail traffic that reduced her colleagues to a thoughtful silence. 'We knew then there were very difficult times ahead.' (Interview with author, 11 March 2010.)

14. *Modernise or Decline: Policies to Maintain the Universal Postal Service in the United Kingdom*, Hooper Review, Cm. 7529, December 2008, p. 41.

15. This triennial actuarial valuation is not to be confused with the accounting valuation, drawn up under an accounting rule (initially SSAP24 and subsequently FRS 17) which required assets to be valued each year at current market prices. The latter valuation had to be used by the Group in its published financial statements, in ways that can be left to the accounting cognoscenti. But it produced even more alarming deficits, starting with £4.6bn in 2003–4 and rising to £5.6bn in 2005–6 (when FRS 17 was superseded by IAS 19, in accordance with the Group's adoption of international accounting rules).

16. The DTI Minister during the preparation of the Postal Services Bill was the former postman Alan Johnson, and he never concealed his disappointment at the outcome. 'I would say, that [i.e. the regulatory structure] was the biggest failure of the lot . . . It wasn't a bad idea to say why not have a team of regulators, rather than one individual, which had been the approach in other sectors. It sounded like a good idea. In actual fact it was a disaster.' (Johnson, interview with author, 20 July 2010.)

17. Crozier, interview with author, 4 October 2010.

18. *Modernise or Decline: Policies to Maintain the Universal Postal Service in the United Kingdom*, Hooper Review, Cm. 7529, December 2008.

19. Ibid., pp. 73–4.

20. Peter Mandelson, *The Third Man: Life at the Heart of New Labour*, HarperPress, 2010, p. 479.

21. TNT Group Press Release, *Vision 2015*, 3 December 2009. Its summary of the position within the Netherlands might almost have been describing the UK market: 'The Mail business in the Netherlands will be subject to accelerated further volume declines due to substitution and competition, burdened by relatively high labour costs and an uncertain regulatory environment, putting pressure on profits and cash flows going forward. The negotiations with labour unions so far have not delivered a path forward towards structurally closing the wage gap with competition [sic]. If that were to remain the case, a deep restructuring will be unavoidable given the sharp decline in volumes and revenues.'

22. *Business Week*, 8 April 2010.

23. Donald Brydon, interview with author, 25 October 2010.

24. *Saving the Royal Mail's Universal Postal Service in the Digital Age*, Update of the Hooper Review, Cm. 7937, September 2010, p. 32.

25. Ibid., p. 36. 'To protect against the dangers of cherry-picking, the regulator would ensure as level a playing field as possible by not allowing competitors a free run in the more lucrative areas of the market whilst Royal Mail's hands are tied by the demands of the universal postal service obligation.'

26. Postal Services Act 2011, paras. 29 (4) and 45 (14).

27. Adam Smith, *The Wealth of Nations*, 1776, Book 5, Chapter 2, Part I.

Sources and bibliography

UNPUBLISHED SOURCES

The Royal Mail Archive is managed by the British Postal Museum & Archive (BPMA) and is currently held at Freeling House, adjoining the Royal Mail's main central London sorting office at Mount Pleasant. The collection is organized into more than 150 'Post' series. Where individual items are cited in this book and given a source note, the latter generally provides the relevant Post number along with a reference number and a brief description, where appropriate.

The Royal Mail kindly granted me access to the entire archive, which would otherwise have been subject in the normal way to the Thirty Year Rule (now giving way to a Twenty Year Rule) limiting access to all recent public records in the UK. The second half of the book draws in particular on the records created by the Post Office Board, which was set up in 1934. Bound volumes for each year from 1934 until 1969, and boxed files from 1970 to 1992, contain copies of papers presented to the Board and copies of the minutes of its meetings. All are catalogued within Post 69. The abbreviation used for Board papers changed from time to time, moving from BP to POB, then to PO and finally back to POB. Board minutes are referred to throughout as POBM. Once they started to be numbered, minutes were given with the year first, e.g. 80/41 for 1980's Minute No. 41. Records referred to as Post 69/Red Books contain Board papers and minutes for the years from 1990 to 2002, which have yet to be added to the published catalogue.

After 1981, both Board papers and POBM that dealt with especially sensitive issues were increasingly excluded from the general circulation of Board materials and were 'issued to Members on a personal basis'. Most were subsequently omitted from the collected Board papers and POBM, and from the Red Books too. Some (but by no means all) have since been located and filed temporarily under the reference number E12421. They include Board materials and also papers relating to Girobank.

Below the main Board, a Post Office Management Board existed from 1970 to January 1980. It was replaced by a Chairman's Executive Committee (CEC), which ran from 1980 to 1992. Minutes of CEC meetings are cited with year first and minute number second, as for Board minutes, and CEC papers are similarly cited in the same way as Board papers. The CEC was replaced by a Post Office Executive Board in 1992.

In principle, all Board papers of the Post Office prior to 1981 were retained within the Post Office archive, whether they related to postal or telecommunications issues. But after the newly demerged British Telecommunications had established its own archive in 1981, it took in many papers held by the telecommunications side of the business since 1969, and various other pre-1981 materials have since then been transferred into it from the Royal Mail Archive. The BT Archive is located in High Holborn in London. It has one catalogue citation for volumes of Board minutes (TCC 15) and another for collected Board papers (TCC 55). Few references have been made here to the BT Archive, but it will be valuable to postal historians in the future and has material that can fill some gaps in the Royal Mail Archive (e.g. TCC 55/12 contains almost forty otherwise missing Board papers for 1980). It also holds, of course, a wealth of material relating to the earlier history of the telephone business.

Also held at the BPMA are the collected private papers of several leading figures in the Post Office's history. They notably include papers belonging to four chairmen in the modern era: William Ryland (1971–7), William Barlow (1977–80), Ron Dearing (1981–7) and Bryan Nicholson (1987–92). The Royal Mail Group meanwhile retains many documents from recent years that have not yet been transferred to the Royal Mail Archive. These are sourced here as 'Royal Mail Group records'.

The archived papers of the Union of Post Office Workers are held in the Modern Records Centre at the University of Warwick. The UPW became the Union of Communications Workers in 1980, and after merging with the National Communications Union it emerged in 1995 as the Communications Workers Union. The archive is catalogued at MSS.148 and references to it are cited as e.g. UCW/2/13/27/1. It includes Executive Council (EC) minutes (which are very detailed and helpfully indexed until 1960), and papers/associated documents submitted to the EC. These are quoted by their date and the contemporary reference which – in contrast to the order adopted by the POBM – puts the number first and year second, e.g. EC 84/71 for Paper 84 in 1971.

Records held in The National Archives at Kew, formerly the Public Record Office, are cited as TNA with the appropriate file number.

Finally, oral interviews were an important source for the third section of the book. A list of those interviewed is included in the Acknowledgements. Material drawn from the interviews is cited with the interviewee's name and the date of the interview.

MAIN PRIMARY PRINTED SOURCES

Rowland Hill, *Post Office Reform: Its Importance and Practicability*, 1837, and *Post Office Journal, 1839–69*, both reprinted in Gavin Fryer and Clive Akerman (eds.), *The Reform of the Post Office in the Victorian Era and Its Impact on Economic and Social Activity*, 2 vols., The Royal Philatelic Society, 2000

Coates Committee Report on Telephone Charges; P.P. 1920 [247] viii 551

Cecil Committee Report on the Telephone Service; P.P. 1922 [54] vi 197

Hardman Lever Committee Report on the Inland Telegraph Services; P.P. 1928 Cmd 3058 xii 441

Tomlin Commission Report on the Civil Service; P.P. 1930–31 Cmd 3909 x 517

Report of the Working Party on the Regional Organisation of the Post Office, HMSO, 1951

Report on Post Office Development and Finance, White Paper, Cmd 9576, October 1955

The Status of the Post Office, White Paper, Cmnd 989, March 1960

Memorandum on the Post Office Bill, White Paper, Cmnd 1247, December 1960

Reorganisation of the Post Office, White Paper, Cmnd 3233, March 1967

Select Committee on Nationalised Industries, 1st Report, 'The Post Office'; P.P. 1966–7, xvii, pp. 34–7

Select Committee on Nationalised Industries, 2nd Report, 'The Post Office's Letter Post Services'; P.P. 1975–6, xxxiv, pp. 295–513

Carter Committee Report, Cmnd 6850, HMSO, July 1977

Carter Committee Report Appendix, Cmnd 6954, HMSO, November 1977

The Post Office, Cmnd 7292, July 1978

The Inner London Letter Post: A Report on the Letter Post Service in the Area Comprising the Numbered London Postal Districts, Monopolies and Mergers Commission, HC515, HMSO, 1980

The Post Office Letter Post Service, Monopolies and Mergers Commission, Cmnd 9332, HMSO, 1984

Post Office Counters Services, Monopolies and Mergers Commission, Cm. 398, HMSO, 1988

The Future of Postal Services: A Consultative Document, Cm. 2614, June 1994

Post Office Reform: A World Class Service for the 21st Century, Cm. 4340, July 1999

Independent Review of Industrial Relations between Royal Mail and the Communication Workers Union ('Sawyer Report'), July 2001

Modernise or Decline: Policies to Maintain the Universal Postal Service in the United Kingdom, Hooper Review, Cm. 7529, December 2008

Saving the Royal Mail's Universal Postal Service in the Digital Age, update of the Hooper Review, Cm. 7937, September 2010

CONTEMPORARY ACCOUNTS, ARTICLES AND MEMOIRS

Albon, Robert, *Privatise the Post*, Centre for Policy Studies, January 1987

Baines, F. E., *Forty Years at the Post Office: A Personal Narrative*, 2 vols., R. Bentley & Son, 1895

Baker, R. J. S., 'The Postal Service: A Problem of Identity', *Political Quarterly*, January 1976

Benn, Tony, *The Regeneration of Britain*, Victor Gollancz, 1965

—, *Out of the Wilderness: Diaries 1963–67*, Arrow Books, 1988

—, *Against the Tide*, Hutchinson, 1989

Bevins, Reginald, *The Greasy Pole*, Hodder & Stoughton, 1965

Blackwood, H. D. S. M. (ed.), *Some Records of the Life of Stevenson Arthur Blackwood KCB*, Hodder & Stoughton, 1896

Callaghan, James, *Whitleyism: A Study of Joint Consultation in the Civil Service*, Fabian Research Series No. 159, 1953

Cavendish, George, *The Life and Death of Cardinal Wolsey* (ed. Richard S. Sylvester), OUP, 1959

Coase, R. H., 'The Postal Monopoly in Great Britain: An Historical Survey', in *Economic Essays in Commemoration of the Dundee School of Economics, 1931–55*, ed. J. K. Eastham, privately publ. 1955

Copping, G. P. and H. J. Langton, *Sorting Letters by Machine*, Institution of Post Office Electrical Engineers, 1958

Crutchley, E. T., *GPO*, Cambridge University Press, 1938

Dagnall, H., *The Mechanised Sorting of Mail*, privately publ., 1976

Davis, Norman (ed.), *The Paston Letters and Papers of the Fifteenth Century*, Oxford University Press, 1971

Defoe, Daniel, *A Tour Thro' the Whole Island of Great Britain*, with an introduction by G. D. H. Cole, 2 vols., London, 1927

Derviche-Jones, A. D., *History of the Post Office Rifles: 8th Battalion City of London Regiment 1914–1918*, Gale and Polden, 1919

Firth, C. H., 'Thurloe and the Post Office', *English Historical Review*, Vol. 13, No. 51 (July 1898), pp. 527–33

Foxell, J. T. and A. O. Spafford, *Monarchs of All They Surveyed: The Story of the Post Office Surveyors*, HMSO, 1952

Green, M. A. E., *Letters of Queen Henrietta Maria*, R. Bentley, 1857

Hay, Ian, *The Post Office Went to War*, HMSO, 1946

Hill, Arthur, 'Government Telegraphs', *Edinburgh Review*, January 1869

Hill, Rowland, *Post Office Reform; Its Importance and Practicability*, Charles Knight & Co., 1837

— and George Birkbeck Hill, *The Life of Sir Rowland Hill and the History of Penny Postage*, 2 vols., De La Rue, 1880

Holmes, K. S., *Operation Overlord: A History of the Work of the Army Postal Service in Relation to Overlord*, Special Series No. 38, The Postal History Society, 1984

Hopkins, Adrian E. (ed.), *Ralph Allen's Own Narrative 1720–61*, The Postal History Society, Special Series No. 8, 1960

Horsfield, J. Keith, 'Post Office Finance', *Lloyds Bank Review*, April 1956

Lewins, William, *Her Majesty's Mails*, Sampson Low, Son, and Marston, 2nd edition, 1865

Lumley, D. O., *Air Mail Operation*, Post Office Green Paper Number 23, 1935, and *Air Mail*, Post Office Green Paper Number 45, 1939

Mackenzie, W. K., 'Postal Circulation', *Bulletin of the Postal History Society*, Nos. 197 and 199, 1976

Mandelson, Peter, *The Third Man: Life at the Heart of New Labour*, HarperPress, 2010

Marchand, J. J. M. L., *Modernization of Postal Services*, De Boekerij of the Netherlands, 1946

Matthison, A. L., *The Sun Shines on Woolverton*, University of Birmingham, 1957

Murray, Evelyn, *The Post Office*, G. P. Putnam's, 1927

Rawlings, R. W., *The Civil Service and the People*, Lawrence and Wishart, 1945

Raikes, Henry St John, *The Life and Letters of Henry Cecil Raikes*, Macmillan, 1898

Reith, John C. W., *Into the Wind*, Hodder & Stoughton, 1949

Ridley, Nicholas, *My Style of Government*, Hutchinson, 1991

Robinow, Richard F., *Peter in the Post Office*, John Lane The Bodley Head, 1934

Samuel, Herbert, *Memoirs*, London, 1945

Scudamore, Frank Ives, *The Day Dreams of a Sleepless Man*, London, 1875

—, *A Sheaf of Memories*, London, 1925

Short, Edward, *Whip to Wilson*, Macdonald, 1989

Stephen, Leslie, *Life of Henry Fawcett*, London, 1885

Swift, H. G., *A History of Postal Agitation: From Eighty Years Ago to the Present Day*, C. Arthur Pearson, 1900; rev. edn, Percy Bros., 1929

Thatcher, Margaret, *The Downing Street Years*, HarperCollins, 1993

Trollope, Anthony, *An Autobiography*, Penguin Books, 1993

Williamson, F. H., *The Air Mail Service*, Post Office Green Paper Number 1, 1933

Wolmer, Viscount, *Post Office Reform: Its Importance and Practicality*, London 1932.

Yates, Edmund, *Recollections and Experiences*, 2 vols., London, 1884

SECONDARY SOURCES

(i) Academic articles and other papers

Boon, Barry, *A Short History of the Post Office Rifles*, privately publ., available at the National Army Museum (Archives Account 8402–28, File A)

Clear, C. R., *Thomas Witherings and the Birth of the Postal Service*, Post Office Green Papers, Number 15, 1935

'Post and Postal Service', in *Encylopaedia Britannica*, 11th edn, 1911, pp. 176–92

Gaunt, Peter, 'Interregnum Governments and the Reform of the Post Office, 1649–59', *Bulletin of the Institute of Historical Research*, October 1987, Vol. 60, Issue 143

Glew, Helen, *Women's Employment in the General Post Office, 1914–1939*, University of London, Institute of Historical Research, Ph.D. thesis, 2010

MacDonagh, Oliver, 'The Nineteenth-Century Revolution in Government: A Reappraisal', *The Historical Journal*, Vol. 1 (1958), pp. 52–67

Muir, Douglas, *The Transorma at Brighton*, Postal Mechanisation Study Circle Monograph No. 1, privately publ., 2006

Perkin, Harold, 'Individualism versus Collectivism in Nineteenth Century Britain: A False Antithesis', *Journal of British Studies*, Vol. X V I I, 1977, pp. 105–18

Perry, C. R., 'The Rise and Fall of Government Telegraphy in Britain', *Business and Economic History*, Vol. 26, No. 2, 1997

Sharpe, Kevin, 'Thomas Witherings and the Reform of the Foreign Posts, 1632–40', *Bulletin of the Institute of Historical Research*, Vol. 57, Issue 136 (November 1984)

Sternberg, Giora, 'Epistolary Ceremonial: Corresponding Status at the Time of Louis XIV', *Past & Present*, No. 204 (August 2009), pp. 33–88

Whyman, Susan E., 'Postal Censorship in England 1635–1844', paper presented to the Oxford–Princeton Partnership Conference on the History of Censorship, September 2003

Woodland, Alan, *HPOs & SSOs: Survey of Matters Warranting Classification*, privately publ., 1964

Zimmeck, Meta, 'Marry in Haste, Repent at Leisure: Women, Bureaucracy and the Post Office, 1870–1920', in Mike Savage and Anne Witz (eds.), *Gender and Bureaucracy*, Blackwell, 1992

—, 'Jobs for the Girls: The Expansion of Clerical Work for Women, 1850–1914', in Angela V. John (ed.), *Unequal Opportunities: Women's Employment in England 1800–1918*, Basil Blackwell, 1986

—, '"Get Out and Get Under": The Impact of Demobilization on the Civil Service, 1918–32', in Gregory Anderson (ed.), *The White Blouse Revolution: Female Office Workers since 1870*, Manchester University Press, 1988

(ii) Books

Adams, Jad, *Tony Benn*, Macmillan, 1992

Anderson, Gregory (ed.), *The White Blouse Revolution: Female Office Workers since 1870*, Manchester University Press, 1988

Andrew, Christopher, *The Defence of the Realm: The Authorized History of MI5*, Allen Lane, 2009

Anthony, Scott, *Night Mail*, British Film Institute, 2007

Ashley, Maurice, *John Wildman: Plotter and Postmaster*, Jonathan Cape, 1947

—, 'John Wildman and the Post Office', in *For Veronica Wedgwood These: Studies in Seventeenth-Century History*, eds. Richard Ollard and Pamela Tudor-Craig, Collins, 1986

Austen, Brian, *English Provincial Posts*, Phillimore, 1978

Baldwin, F. G. C., *The History of the Telephone in the United Kingdom*, Chapman & Hall, 1925

Barnett, Correlli, *The Audit of War: The Illusion & Reality of Britain as a Great Nation*, Macmillan, 1986

Beale, Philip, *A History of the Post in England from the Romans to the Stuarts*, Ashgate, 1998. Revised and expanded as *England's Mail: Two Millennia of Letter Writing*, Tempus, 2005

Bealey, Frank, *The Post Office Engineering Union: The History of the Post Office Engineers, 1870–1970*, Bachman & Turner, 1976

Bennett, H. S., *The Pastons and Their England: Studies in an Age of Transition*, Cambridge University Press, reprinted 1975

Boston, Sarah, *Women Workers and the Trade Union Movement*, Davis-Poynter, 1980

Bowie, A. G., *The Romance of the British Post Office*, S. W. Partridge & Co., 1897

Boyce, Benjamin, *The Benevolent Man: A Life of Ralph Allen of Bath*, Harvard University Press, 1967

Brant, Clare, *Eighteenth-Century Letters and British Culture*, Palgrave Macmillan, 2006

Braybon, Gail, *Women Workers in the First World War: The British Experience*, Croom Helm, 1981

Briggs, Asa, *Victorian Things*, B. T. Batsford, 1988

Burnie, Joan and Douglas Corrance, *Postbus Country: Glimpses of Rural Scotland*, Canongate Press, 1994

Bushell, T. A., *Royal Mail: A Centenary History of the Royal Mail Line, 1839–1939*, Trade & Travel Publications, 1939

Cable, Boyd, *A Hundred Year History of the P&O, 1837–1937*, Ivor Nicholson and Watson, 1937

Campbell, Alan, Nina Fishman and John McIlroy (eds.), *British Trade Unions and Industrial Politics*, 2 vols., Ashgate, 1999

Carter, Miranda, *The Three Emperors*, Fig Tree, 2009

Chartres, J. A., *Internal Trade in England, 1500–1700*, Studies in Economic and Social History, Macmillan, 1977

Clarke, Peter, *Hope and Glory: Britain 1900–1990*, Allen Lane, 1996

Clear, Charles R., *John Palmer: Mail Coach Pioneer*, Blandford Press, 1955

Clinton, Alan, *Post Office Workers: A Trade Union and Social History*, George Allen & Unwin, 1984

Cohn, Samuel, *The Process of Occupational Sex-Typing: The Feminization of Clerical Labour in Great Britain*, Temple University Press, 1985

Corby, Michael, *The Postal Business 1969–79: A Study in Public Sector Management*, Kogan Page, 1979

Crofts, John E., *Packhorse, Waggon and Post: Land Carriage and Communications under the Tudors and Stuarts*, Routledge and Kegan Paul/University of Toronto Press, 1967

Dagnall, Harry, *Creating a Good Impression: Three Hundred Years of The Stamp Office and Stamp Duties*, H M S O, 1994

Daunton, Martin, *Royal Mail: The Post Office since 1840*, The Athlone Press, 1985

Dulin, C. I., *Ireland's Transition: The Postal History of the Transitional Period 1922–25*, McDonnell Whyte, 1992

Edmonds, James E., *Official History of the Great War: Military Operations, France and Belgium, 1916*, Vol. 1, Macmillan, 1932

Ellis, Kenneth, *The Post Office in the Eighteenth Century: A Study in Administrative History*, Oxford University Press, 1958

Ferguson, Stephen, *GPO Staff in 1916*, An Post, 2005

—, *At the Heart of Events: Dublin's General Post Office*, An Post, 2008

Flaws, Margaret, *Spy Fever: The Post Office Affair*, The Shetland Times Ltd, 2009

Fordham, Peta, *The Robbers' Tale*, Hodder & Stoughton, 1965

Freud, David, *Freud in the City*, Bene Factum Publishing, 2008

Gairdner, James, *The Paston Letters: Introduction and Supplement*, Westminster Archibald Constable and Co., 1901

Gall, Gregor, *The Meaning of Militancy? Postal Workers and Industrial Relations*, Ashgate, 2003

Gannon, Paul, *Colossus: Bletchley Park's Greatest Secret*, Atlantic Books, 2007

Glendinning, Victoria, *Trollope*, Hutchinson, 1992

Goldman, Lawrence (ed.), *The Blind Victorian: Henry Fawcett and British Liberalism*, Cambridge University Press, 1989

Gosling, John and Dennis Craig, *The Great Train Robbery*, W. H. Allen, 1964

Guttridge, Peter, *The Great Train Robbery*, The National Archives, 2008

Halstead, Ivor, *Post Haste: The Story of the Post Office in Peace and War*, London, 1944

Harper, Charles G., *The Exeter Road: The Story of the West of England Highway*, Chapman & Hall, 1899

—, *Stage Coach and Mail in Days of Yore*, 2 vols., Chapman & Hall, 1903

Hemmeon, J. C., *The History of the British Post Office*, Harvard University Press, 1912

Hey, Colin G., *Rowland Hill: Genius and Benefactor 1795–1879*, Quiller Press, 1989

Hinsley, F. H. and A. Stripp (eds.), *Codebreakers: The Inside Story of Bletchley Park*, Oxford University Press, 1993

Holmes, Richard, *The Age of Wonder*, HarperPress, 2008

Hyde, J. W., *The Post in Grant and Farm*, A. & C. Black, 1894

Jackson, G. Gibbard, *From Post Boy to Air Mail: The Story of the British Post Office*, Sampson Low, Marston, 1930

Jeffery, Keith, *The GPO and the Easter Rising*, Irish Academic Press, 2006

Jenkins, Robert, *Tony Benn: A Political Biography*, Writers and Readers Publishing Cooperative, 1980

John, Angela V. (ed), *Unequal Opportunities: Women's Employment in England 1800–1918*, Basil Blackwell, 1986

Joyce, Herbert, *The History of the Post Office*, Richard Bentley & Son, 1893

Kay, F. George, *Royal Mail: The Story of the Posts in England from the Time of Edward IVth to the Present Day*, Rockliff, 1951

Kennedy, Alistair and George Crabb, *The Postal History of the British Army in World War I: Before and After, 1903–1929*, publ. privately, 1977

Kieve, Jeffrey, *The Electric Telegraph: A Social and Economic History*, David & Charles, 1973

Kishlansky, Mark, *A Monarchy Transformed, Britain 1603–1714*, Allen Lane, 1996

McKenna, Christopher D., *The World's Newest Profession: Management Consulting in the Twentieth Century*, Cambridge University Press, 2006

Mark, Graham, *British Censorship of Civil Mails During World War I*, The Stuart Rossiter Fund, 2000

Martin, Nancy, *The Post Office: From Carrier Pigeon to Confravision*, J. M. Dent, 1969

Martindale, Hilda, *Women Servants of the State, 1870–1938*, Allen and Unwin, 1938

Messenger, Charles, *Terriers in the Trenches: The History of the Post Office Rifles*, Picton Publishing, 1982

—, *Call-to-Arms: The British Army 1914–18*, Cassell Military Paperbacks, 2006

Middlemas, Keith, *Politics in Industrial Society: The Experience of the British System since 1911*, André Deutsch, 1979

Moran, Michael, *The Union of Post Office Workers: A Study in Political Sociology*, Macmillan, 1974

Muir, Douglas N., *Postal Reform & The Penny Black: A New Appreciation*, National Postal Museum, 1990

—, *A Timeless Classic: The Evolution of Machin's Icon*, BPMA Publications, 2007

—, *Stamps, Conflict & Creativity*, BPMA Publications, 2010

Norway, Arthur H., *History of the Post Office Packet Service between the Years 1793–1815*, Macmillan, 1895, reprinted in paperback by Kessinger Publishing, 2010

Ogg, David, *England in the Reign of Charles II*, Oxford University Press, 1967

Osley, Julian, *Built for Service*, BPMA, 2010

Parker, David, *The Official History of Privatisation*, Vol. 1, Routledge, 2009

Parris, Henry, *Constitutional Bureaucracy: The Development of British Central Administration since the Eighteenth Century*, Allen & Unwin, 1969

—, *Staff Relations in the Civil Service: Fifty Years of Whitleyism*, Allen & Unwin, 1973

Peach, R. E. M., *The Life and Times of Ralph Allen*, D. Nutt, 1895

Pelling, Henry, *A History of British Trade Unionism*, Macmillan, 3rd edn, 1976

Perry, C. R., *The Victorian Post Office: The Growth of a Bureaucracy*, Royal Historical Society/Boydell Press, 1992

Pitt, Douglas, *The Telecommunications Function in the British Post Office: A Case Study of Bureaucratic Adaptation*, Saxon House, 1980

Proud, E. B., *History of British Army Postal Service*, 2 vols., publ. privately, 1982

Pugh, Martin, *Women and the Women's Movement in Britain, 1914–1959*, Macmillan, 1992

Read, Piers Paul, *Train Robbers*, W. H. Allen, 1978

Reynolds, Mairead, *A History of the Irish Post Office*, MacDonnell Whyte, 1983

Robertson, J. H., *The Story of the Telephone: A History of the Telecommunications Industry of Britain*, Pitman, 1947

Robinson, Howard, *The British Post Office: A History*, Princeton University Press, 1948

—, *Carrying British Mails Overseas*, George Allen & Unwin, 1964

Savage, Mike and Anne Witz (ed.), *Gender and Bureaucracy*, Blackwell, 1992

Seth, Ronald, *The Spy Who wasn't Caught: The Story of Julius Silber*, Robert Hale, 1966

Shapiro, James, *1599: A Year in the Life of William Shakespeare*, Faber & Faber, 2005

Smith, William, *The History of the Post Office in British North America, 1638–1870*, Cambridge University Press, 1920

Snow, C. P., *Trollope*, Macmillan, 1975

Sugden, John, *Sir Francis Drake*, Barrie & Jenkins, 1990

Standage, Tom, *The Victorian Internet*, Phoenix, 1999

Stone, J. W. M. (ed.), *The Inland Post (1392–1672): A Calendar of Historical Documents*, Christie's–Robson Lowe, 1987

Stray, Julian, *Moving the Mail . . . by Road*, BPMA Publications, 2006

Stuart, Charles (ed.), *The Reith Diaries*, Collins, 1975

Super, R. H., *Trollope in the Post Office*, University of Michigan Press, 1981

—, *The Chronicler of Barsetshire: A Life of Anthony Trollope*, University of Michigan Press, 1988

Sussex, Elizabeth, *The Rise and Fall of British Documentary: The Story of the Film Movement Founded by John Grierson*, University of California Press, 1975

Tombs, R. C., *The King's Post*, Bristol, 1905

Vale, Edmund, *The Mail-Coach Men of the Late Eighteenth Century*, Cassell, 1960

Walker, George, *Haste, Post, Haste*, Harrap, 1938

Waller, Philip, *Writers, Readers and Reputations: Literary Life in Britain, 1870–1918*, Oxford University Press, 2008

Wells, Edward, *Mailshot: A History of the Forces Postal Service*, Defence, Postal and Courier Services Directorate of the Royal Engineers, 1987

Wells, Stanley, *Shakespeare for All Time*, Macmillan, 2002

Whitaker, Katie, *A Royal Passion: The Turbulent Marriage of Charles I and Henrietta Maria*, Weidenfeld & Nicolson, 2010

Whyman, Susan E., *The Pen and the People: English Letter Writers 1660–1800*, Oxford University Press, 2009

Wilkinson, Frederick, *Royal Mail Coaches: An Illustrated History*, Tempus, 2007

Willcocks, R. M., *England's Postal History to 1840*, privately publ., 1975

Williams, L. N. and M., *Stamps of Fame*, Blandford Press, 1949

Williamson, Philip (ed.), *The Modernisation of Conservative Politics: The Diaries and Letters of William Bridgeman 1904–35*, The Historians' Press, 1989

Wolmar, Christian, *Fire and Steam: A New History of the Railways in Britain*, Atlantic Books, 2007

Woodward, C. Douglas, *The Vanished Coaching Inns of the City of London*, Historical Publications Ltd, 2009

Young, G. M., *Victorian England: Portrait of an Age*, Oxford University Press, 1960

Credits and Permissions

Archive images and materials from the British Postal Museum & Archive (BPMA) are copyright © Royal Mail Group Ltd, 2011, and are reproduced courtesy of the BPMA. The author would like to thank the BPMA for its permission to use the following:

Plates from the BPMA
Plate 1: *top left* – Brian Tuke (Post 118/2010); *top right* – Ralph Allen (Post 118/1880); *bottom left* – John Palmer (Post 118/2102); *bottom right* – Francis Freeling (Post 118/949). Plate 2: *above* – Lombard Street GPO (Post 118/1839); *below* – Prior Park, Bath (Post 118/1882). Plate 3: *top left* – Post-boy (P7396); *top right* – Newcastle postman (Post 118/1018); *bottom left* – Windsor postman (H6640); *bottom right* – late-Victorian postman (P9251). Plate 4: *above* – Inland Letter Office at Lombard Street (Post 118/1003); *below* – inside St Martin's-le-Grand GPO (Post 118/1334). Plate 5: *above* – the Bath–London Royal Mail coach (Ob. 2011-0014); *below* – the Louth–London Royal Mail coach and train (H1396c). Plate 6: *above* – staff team of Victorian TPO (P9414); *below* – loading mails bound for India (H6705). Plate 7: *above* – Rowland Hill (Post 118); *below* – Henry Fawcett (P5420). Plate 9: *top left* – Anthony Trollope (Post 118); *bottom right* – Arthur Stevenson Blackwood (H4602); *bottom left* – Frank Scudamore (Post 118). Plate 10: *top* – Aldeburgh sub-post office (H1245); *middle* – Wangford sub-post office (P9546); *bottom* – Woodbridge Crown post office (P9550). Plate 11: *above* – King Edward Building postmen (Post 118/5083); *below* – indoor staff at South-East District Office (Post 118/5384). Plate 12: *above* – women telephone operators, *c.*1914 (C298); *below* – women of the Post Office Savings Bank (H11221). Plate 13: *above* – mail bags inside Home Depot, 1916 (Post 56/6); *below* – Home Depot on Armistice Day, 1918 (Post 56/6). Plate 14: *above* – wartime postwomen of Barnet (P6020); *below* – horse-drawn

van with a woman driver (H3960). Plate 15: *above* – Field Post Office on the Western Front (Post 56/6); *below* – letters from home on the Western Front (Post 56/6). Plate 16: *above* – loading mail aboard RAF biplane in 1920–21 (H6647); *below* – Imperial Airways launch ceremony, 1934 (Post 118/198). Plate 17: *top left* – Daimler van (P11075); *top right* – Maudsley van (P17676); *middle left* – Ford van (P9714); *middle right* – Morris Minor prototype (H6798); *bottom left* – 'Z' type Morris van (P13447); *bottom right* – Morris diesel van (P24658). Plate 18: *above* – sorting aboard a TPO in the 1930s (H11060); *below* – loading the Mail Rail (Post 118/381). Plate 19: *top left* – Evelyn Murray (Post 118); *bottom left* – Kingsley Wood (H4780). Plate 20: *above* – postmen emptying mailbags onto conveyor (Post 118); *below* – one of the sorting halls at Mount Pleasant (Post 118/142). Plate 21: *above* – postwoman during the London Blitz (Post 118/1359). Plate 22: *below* – devastation at Mount Pleasant in 1943 (Post 118/1457). Plate 23: *above* – printed airmail stationery for POWs (Post 118/1598); *below* – airgraph technician reviewing print-out (Post 118/1428). Plate 24: *left* – Thomas Gardiner (H4800). Plate 26: *above* – Transorma in Brighton (Post 118/5152); *below* – operator seated at Easy View Coding Desk (Post 118/5689). Plate 27: *above* – loading the Down Special at Euston (Post 118/2245); *below* – HVP packets exhibited at Great Train Robbers' trial (E1956b). Plate 28: *above* – Tony Benn (P9183); *below* – John Stonehouse with Harold Wilson (Post 118/5372). Plate 30: *top left* – Ronald German (Post 118/2537); *top right* – William Ryland (P10039); *bottom right* Ron Dearing (Post 118).

Text Illustrations from the BPMA
p. 29 – Witherings' letter of 1636 (Post 23/1); p. 33 – front page of Cromwell's 1657 Act (Post 118/5750); pp. 40–41 – double-page spread from 'Roads, Salarys, Stages' (Post 94/11); p. 42 – first page of 'Book of Payments' (Post 94/9); p. 49 – Colonel Whitley letter to Postmaster Watts (Post 94/12); p. 86 – notice of prepayment for letters to New York (Post 107); p. 102 – Hasker's instruction to his guards (P8913); p. 104 – advertisement for Ballard's Beasts (P8167); p. 110 – notice re delivery of express letters (Post 107); p. 131 – notice of 1839 rally for penny postage (Post 107); p. 134 – notice re cancellation of stamps (Post 107); p. 143 – Time Bill used on early TPO (Post 118/5729); p. 152 – *Punch* cartoon of 'Sir Rowland Le Grand' (Post 118); p. 172 – notice of Medical Department regulations (Post 107); p. 189 – *Punch* cartoon of Fawcett as 'The Man For The Post' (Post 118/5097); p. 218 –

notice re interrupted service to Boer Republics (Post 107); p. 225 – notice prohibiting matches in mails to the armed forces (Post 107); p. 232 – announcement of losses at Festubert (Post Office Circular, 15 June 1915); p. 316 – notice of 1911 Aerial Post (P8911); p. 317 – notice of collection times for first airmail to India (Post 118/1059); p. 351 – Queen Elizabeth's 1941 airgraph to Auchinleck (Post 118/1430); p. 614 – front page of the *Courier*, October 1988 (Post 92/930); and p. 615 – front page of *The Post*, November 1988 (Post 115/532).

Thanks are also due to the BPMA for its permission to reproduce Grace Golden's two watercolours, *A London Loading Platform*, 1948 (Post 109/374) and *Euston Station, Loading the TPO*, 1948 (Post 109/508) inside the front and back covers of the book.

The author would in addition like to thank:

Plate 8 – The City of London, London Metropolitan Archives, for permission to reproduce *above* – St Martin's-le-Grand by moonlight, 1830 (Collage 27838) and *below* – Smirke's GPO closed for demolition, 1911 (Collage 48916).

Plate 9 – Stanley Gibbons Ltd for permission to reproduce *top right* – portrait of Stanley Gibbons.

Plate 19 – National Portrait Gallery London for permission to reproduce *top right* – Viscount Wolmer (x32880) and *bottom right* – Stephen Tallents (x164609).

Plate 21 – BT Heritage for permission to reproduce *below* – wartime telephone operators wearing helmets (TCE 361/ARC278).

Plate 22 – BT Heritage for permission to reproduce *left* – front of the bomb-damaged Central Telegraph Office in 1940 (TCB417/E11766) and *right* – back of same (TCB417/E11770).

Plate 24 – BT Heritage for permission to reproduce *right* – Tommy Flowers (TCB417/E79932) and *below* – the Colossus computer of 1944 (TCB417/E79925).

Plate 25 – Communication Workers Union for permission to reproduce *top left* – Charles Geddes; *top right* – Ron Smith; *bottom left* – Tom Jackson; *bottom right* – Alan Tuffin and Alan Johnson.

Plate 29: Communication Workers Union for permission to reproduce *above* – Tom Jackson and colleagues during the 1971 strike; *below* – abandoned sorting office during the 1971 strike.

Plate 31: Communication Workers Union for permission to reproduce *above* – Alan Johnson and the 'Don't KO the PO' campaign poster; *below* – UCW members protesting against privatization, 1994.

Plate 32 – Royal Mail Group Photo Library for permission to reproduce the portraits of *left* Allan Leighton and *right* Adam Crozier (Refs. 4714426 and 4714587 respectively).

Plate 32: News International Syndication for permission to reproduce *below* – the cartoon by Andrew Davey from the *Sun* of 30 June 2009.

Thanks are also due to:

– News International Syndication for permission to reproduce as the text illustration on p.434 the cutting from *The Times* of 9 August 1963 with a staff story on the Great Train Robbery.

– Communication Workers Union for permission to reproduce as the text illustration on p.615 the front page of the *Courier* newspaper of November 1988.

– Royal Mail Group for permission to reproduce the stamp images on the back cover. (Stamp designs © Royal Mail Group Ltd. All rights reserved. The Penny Black is a registered trade mark of Royal Mail Group Ltd. © Royal Mail Group Ltd. All rights reserved.)

– The Royal Philatelic Society London, for making available digital copies of the following stamps for reproduction on the cover: the 1½d brown British Empire Exhibition – first commemorative issue (1924); the 1d red King George V 'Silver Jubilee' issue (1935); the ½d green King Edward VIII (1936); 1d red King George VI Centenary of First Adhesive Postage Stamps (1940); the 1s 6d grey-blue Queen Elizabeth II 'Coronation' issue (1953); the 1s 6d multicoloured 'Shakespeare Festival' designed by David Gentleman (1964); the 4d multicoloured '25th Anniversary of the Battle of Britain' designed by David Gentleman (1965); and the £1 black 'Machin head' designed by Arnold Machin – last of recess printed high values (1969).

– Andrew Claridge of Grosvenor Auctions for making available digital copies of the following stamps for reproduction on the cover: the Penny Black (1840), the 4d blue Cape of Good Hope 'triangular' (1853), the £5 orange Queen Victoria (1880s), the 4½d Queen Victoria 'Jubilee' issue – first bicoloured series (1887–92), the £1 green King George V 'Sea Horses' design (1913) and the £1 black Postal Union Congress issue (1929).

– Tim Hirsch of Spink for making available the digital copy for reproduction on the back cover of the 2d blue 'Post Office' Mauritius (1847).

The maps accompanying the text have been specially drawn for this book, but have relied heavily on original art work by the following:

– Howard Robinson, who for his book *The British Post Office*, 1948, Princeton University Press, compiled versions of Maps A ('The Elizabethan Roads'), E ('The Great Roads and principal Cross Roads, 1756') and F ('Royal Mail coach routes, 1835').

– Alan W. Robertson, who drew up versions of Maps B, C and D based on Thomas Gardiner's Survey of 1677, for a study privately published in 1961, *Great Britain: Post Roads, Post Towns and Postal Rates, 1635–1839* (available at the BPMA, ref. 1 ROB).

–Andrew Perry , whose 1998 booklet for the National Postal Museum, *The Post Office and King Edward Building*, included a version of Map G ('Headquarters buildings in and around St Martin's-le-Grand').

– An unknown artist who compiled a version of Map H ('Central London's District Offices and Mail Rail') catalogued at the BPMA (Post 118/5665).

– J.G. Hines, who compiled Map J ('Underground Cables in the Long-Distance Telephone network 1914–38') as part of his Post Office Green Paper No.43, *The British Long-Distance Network*, pub. 1938.

Finally, the author gratefully acknowledges permission to quote from the following:

– 'Night Mail', *Collected Works*, Copyright © 1976, 1991, The Estate of W.H. Auden, granted by permission of The Wylie Agency (UK) Ltd.

– *The Lion and the Unicorn: Socialism and the English Genius*, by permission of Bill Hamilton, literary executor of the George Orwell Estate.

– *A Child's Christmas in Wales*, by Dylan Thomas, published by Orion Publishing Group, by permission of David Higham Associates.

– *Out of the Wilderness, Diaries 1963–67*, published by Hutchinson, by kind permission of Tony Benn.

– 'Aubade', *Collected Poems* by Philip Larkin, published by The Marvell Press and Faber & Faber, copyright © the Estate of Philip Larkin, 1988, by permission of Faber & Faber.

– 'The Postman' from *Rounding the Horn: Collected Poems* by Jon Stallworthy, published by The Carcanet Press Limited, by kind permission of the author.

– *Postman Pat's Thirsty Day* by John Cunliffe and Celia Berridge, published by Scholastic Books, by permission of David Higham Associates.

– *In Praise of Postmen* by Alice Oswald, reprinted by kind permission of United Agents on behalf of the author.

Index

plates, maps, charts, illustrations etc are given in italics